WITHDRAWN

DATE DUE

10-25-12	

BRODART, CO.   Cat. No. 23-221

FEDERAL PUBLIC LAND AND RESOURCES LAW

SIXTH EDITION

by

GEORGE CAMERON COGGINS
Frank Edwards Tyler Professor of Law
University of Kansas

CHARLES F. WILKINSON
Moses Lasky Professor of Law
University of Colorado

JOHN D. LESHY
Harry D. Sunderland Distinguished Professor of Law
University of California
Hastings College of the Law

ROBERT L. FISCHMAN
Professor of Law and Harry T. Ice Faculty Fellow
Indiana University—Bloomington

FOUNDATION PRESS

2007

This publication was created to provide you with accurate and authoritative information concerning the subject matter covered; however, this publication was not necessarily prepared by persons licensed to practice law in a particular jurisdiction. The publisher is not engaged in rendering legal or other professional advice and this publication is not a substitute for the advice of an attorney. If you require legal or other expert advice, you should seek the services of a competent attorney or other professional.

Nothing contained herein is intended or written to be used for the purposes of 1) avoiding penalties imposed under the federal Internal Revenue Code, or 2) promoting, marketing or recommending to another party any transaction or matter addressed herein.

© 1981, 1987, 1993, 2001, 2002 FOUNDATION PRESS
© 2007 By FOUNDATION PRESS
       395 Hudson Street
       New York, NY 10014
       Phone Toll Free 1–877–888–1330
       Fax (212) 367–6799
       foundation–press.com
Printed in the United States of America

ISBN 978–1–59941–163–7

 TEXT IS PRINTED ON 10% POST CONSUMER RECYCLED PAPER

PREFACE TO THE SIXTH EDITION

When George Coggins and Charles Wilkinson first introduced these materials in 1980, their preface justified the departure from the private-law orientation of prior natural resources casebooks, especially the seminal one by Clyde Martz. The rise of the public interest as the central principle animating judicial opinions, legislation, and extensive regulation is no longer breaking news. It has now withstood decades of challenge, and continues to serve as the foundation for this book.

This edition of FEDERAL PUBLIC LAND AND RESOURCES LAW seeks to re-emphasize the smooth pace and lively context of the book. While expanding the scope of coverage and revising materials to focus attention on more recent cases, we have resisted the temptation to make the notes in this casebook encyclopedic. Professor Coggins and Glicksman already succeed as thorough compilers in their treatise on PUBLIC NATURAL RESOURCES LAW.

Instead of burdening the casebook with more excerpts and ancillary materials (especially maps), we have established a web site on which we post a rich assortment of supplemental materials. Please visit it at: www.law.indiana.edu/publicland

This updated edition reflects some substantial reorganization. In general, our aim is to allow classes to cover the material in chapters 1-5 more efficiently before getting to the resource-specific chapters. Chapter 1 now contains the primer on the federal lands as they are organized today. A new selection of perspectives has notes and questions. Chapter 2 is more concise and focused more narrowly on the old cases and doctrines that continue to exert influence on current conflicts. All of the trust materials are now consolidated in chapter 2. Courses may now cover the historical materials more briefly, and with less repetition later in the term. However, sufficient case materials remain in the chapter to provide fodder for class discussion and analysis.

Chapter 3 addresses the ubiquitous concern of state-federal relations, with special emphasis on constitutional law. Chapter 4 consolidates four overarching legal issues that pervade natural resources law along with many other subjects of public administration. Chapter 5 closes in on other cross-cutting issues peculiar to federal land management, including access.

Chapters 6–12 address the law resource-by-resource. While we expect all courses to cover at least parts of each of the first five chapters, we have designed the book so that teachers may pick and choose which resources to cover. This book works equally well as a survey to touch upon many resource issues, or as an in-depth exploration of three or four resources.

The Sixth Edition Statutory Supplement is a useful accompaniment to this casebook for courses that seek to stress the skills of statutory interpretation. It collects relatively complete versions of just about all of the laws discussed in the principal cases and notes.

Overall, we strive to provide teaching materials that challenge students while conveying the sense of human drama and place that attracted each of us to this legal specialty.

A word about the editing form and style used throughout. We have sought to be rigorous in eliminating irrelevant or tangential matters. Discussions of repetitive procedural defenses, common statements of law (particularly boilerplate recitations on the scope of judicial review), and string citations are generally excluded. Thus, any case or article reproduced below is not necessarily complete—it probably is not—and we advise the researching student to consult the original.

Most original footnotes have also been omitted. Where footnotes are retained, they still bear the court's or author's original number. Footnotes inserted by the editors are preceded by an asterisk instead of a number. Textual deletions are indicated by "* * *," but omissions of authorities have not been signaled.

We of course accept full responsibility for the inevitable errors and omissions commonly associated with these ventures.

Thanks in the preparation of this edition go to Brad Daniels, Ryan Murray, Angela King, and Mark Rohr, law students who provided superb research assistance, and to Lara Gose for excellent secretarial support. As with prior editions, a number of colleagues and friends made helpful suggestions and provided vital information: Deb Donahue, John Echeverria, Daniel Feller, Joe Feller, Eleanor Huffines, Bob Keiter, Karin Sheldon, Deborah Williams, and Ted Zukoski. They join the ranks of helpful reviewers and commenters on prior editions: Gail L. Achterman, Harrison C. Dunning, Kent Frizzell, David H. Getches, Arthur D. Smith, Sally K. Fairfax, H. Michael Anderson, Maryanne Chambers, Cameron LaFollette, Darius M. Adams, Kaid Benfield, Grove Burnett, Larry McBride, Zygmunt Plater, Deborah Reames, Johanna Wald, Molly McUsic, Federico Cheever, David Watts, Bruce Kramer, Henry Smith, Patty Beneke, Ken Weiner, Armin Rosencranz, Amy Kelley, Peter Appel, Bob Anderson, and Jamie Grodsky.

Errors of course are ours (especially Fischman's). As always we welcome feedback from users (send to rfischma@indiana.edu).

GEORGE CAMERON COGGINS
CHARLES F. WILKINSON
JOHN D. LESHY
ROBERT L. FISCHMAN

February, 2007

ACKNOWLEDGEMENTS

The following copyrighted material has been reprinted with permission of the copyright holder:

Coggins, George C. and Robert Glicksman. 1 PUBLIC NATURAL RESOURCES LAW § 1.9. Reprinted from Public Natural Resources Law, George C. Coggins and Robert Glicksman, with permission of Thomson West.

Conklin, Charles. PLLRC Revisited—A Potpourri of Memories, 54 Denver L.J. 445, 446–47 (1977). Reprinted with permission of the Denver University Law Review.

DURBIN, KATHIE. TREE HUGGERS: VICTORY, DEFEAT & RENEWAL IN THE NORTHWEST ANCIENT FOREST CAMPAIGN 201–06 (1996) (Mountaineers Press, Seattle, WA). Reprinted with permission of the author.

Feller, Joseph. Grazing Management on the Public Lands: Opening the Process to Public Participation, 26 Land & Water L.Rev. 569, 575–76 (1991). Reprinted with permission of the author.

Fischman, Robert L. What is Natural Resources Law?, 78 U. Colo. L. Rev. 721 (2007). Reprinted with permission of the University of Colorado Law Review.

Fischman, Robert L. *Cooperative Federalism and Natural Resources Law*, 14 N.Y.U. Envtl. L.J. 179 (2005). Reprinted with permission of the New York University Environmental Law Journal.

Fischman, Robert L. THE NATIONAL WILDLIFE REFUGES: COORDINATING A CONSERVATION SYSTEM THROUGH LAW (2003). Reprinted with permission from "The National Wildlife Refuges" by Robert L. Fischman. Copyright (c) 2003 by the author. Reproduced by permission of Island Press, Washington, D.C.

Foss, Phillip. POLITICS AND GRASS 3–4, 74, 77 (Univ. of Washington Press 1960). Reprinted with permission of the University of Washington Press.

Hardin, Garrett. The Tragedy of the Commons, 162 Science 1243 (1968). Reprinted with permission of *Science* magazine and the American Association for the Advancement of Science.

Keele, Denise M., Robert W. Malmsheimer, Donald W. Floyd, and Jerome E. Perez. 2006. Forest Service Land Management Litigation 1989–2002. Journal of Forestry 104(4):196–202. Copyrighted by and reprinted with permission of the Society of American Foresters.

Keiter, Robert B. The Law of Fire: Reshaping Public Land Policy in an Era of Ecology and Litigation, 36 Envtl. L. 301, 344–48 (2006). Reprinted with permission of Environmental Law, Lewis and Clark College.

Keiter, Robert B. Ecology and the Public Domain, KEEPING FAITH WITH NATURE: ECOSYSTEMS, DEMOCRACY, AND AMERICA'S PUBLIC LANDS 71–79 (2003). Reprinted with permission of Yale University Press.

Laitos, Jan G. and Thomas A. Carr, The Transformation on Public Lands, 26 Ecology Law Q. 140, 178–84 (1999). Reprinted from Ecology Law Quarterly, vol. 26 No. 2, pp. 140, 178–84 by permission of the Regents of the University of California. Copyright (c) 1999 by the Regents of the University of California.

Lazarus, Richard J. Changing Conceptions of Property and Sovereignty in Natural Resources: Questioning the Public Trust Doctrine, 71 Iowa L. Rev. 631, 633, 710, 715–16 (1986). Reprinted with permission of the Iowa Law Review.

Leopold, Aldo. The Land Ethic, A SAND COUNTY ALMANAC (1949, 1977). Reprinted with permission of Oxford University Press.

Paul, Rodman W. CALIFORNIA GOLD 20–25 (1947). Reprinted by permission of the publisher from CALIFORNIA GOLD: THE BEGINNING OF MINING IN THE FAR WEST by Rodman W. Paul, pp. 20–25, Cambridge, Mass.: Harvard University Press, Copyright (c)1947 by the President and Fellows of Harvard College.

Peffer, E.L. THE CLOSING OF THE PUBLIC DOMAIN 214–224 (1951). Reprinted with permission from Peffer, Louise The Closing of the Public Domain Copyright (c) 1951 by the Board of Trustees of the Leland Stanford Jr. University, renewed by David Peffer.

Rasker, Ray, et al. Prosperity in the 21st Century West: The Role of Protected Public Lands (Sonoran Institute July 2004) pp. 2–10. Reprinted with permission of the Sonoran Institute.

Rule, Lauren M. Enforcing Ecosystem Management Under the Northwest Forest Plan: The Judicial Role, 12 Fordham Envtl, L. J. 211, 222–27 (2000). Reprinted with permission of Fordham Environmental Law Review.

Sax, Joseph L. *Mountains Without Handrails: Reflections on National Parks*, University of Michigan Press, copyright (c) 1980. Reprinted with permission of the University of Michigan Press.

Sax, Joseph L. "Fashioning a Recreation Policy for Our National Parklands: The Philosophy of Choice and the Choice of Philosophy" 12 *Creighton Law Review* 973, reprinted with permission. Copyright (c) 1979 by Creighton University.

Society of American Foresters. 1975. Impact of the Monongahela Decision of August 21, 1975: Position of the Society of American Foresters. Journal of Forestry 73(12):758. Copyrighted by and reprinted with permission of the Society of American Foresters.

Stroup, Richard L. and John A. Baden, Natural Resources: Bureaucratic Myths and Environmental Management 118–27 (1983). Reprinted with permission of Pacific Research Institute.

Wilkinson, Charles F. The Public Trust Doctrine in Public Land Law, 14 U.C. Davis L. Rev. 269 (1980). This work, copyright 1980 by Charles F. Wilkinson, was originally published in the *UC Davis Law Review*, vol. 14, p. 269, copyright 1980 by The Regents of the University of California. All rights reserved. Reprinted with permission.

Wood, Harold W., Jr. Pinchot and Mather: How the Forest Service and Park Service Got That Way, Not Man Apart, December 1976. Reprinted with permission of Friends of the Earth.

Yaffee, Steven Lewis. THE WISDOM OF THE SPOTTED OWL: POLICY LESSONS OF A NEW CENTURY 141–143 (Island Press 1994). From *The Wisdom of the Spotted Owl* by Steven Lewis Yaffee. Copyright (c) 1994 by the author. Reproduced by permission of Island Press, Washington, D.C.

*

SUMMARY OF CONTENTS

TABLE OF CONTENTS

TABLE OF CASES

Principal cases are in bold type. Non-principal cases are in roman type. References are to Pages.

Federal Public Land and Resources Law

*

CHAPTER 1

Public Land Law: An Introduction

A. The Field of Public Land Law

Many people are unaware of the full extent to which the United States government owns or controls land. Many are generally familiar with the flagship national parks, the "crown jewels" of the federal land holdings. Those who have gazed into the Grand Canyon, marveled at the natural wonders of Yellowstone, or found incomparable beauty in Yosemite Valley may have breathed a prayer of thanksgiving that some of our predecessors had the wisdom to protect those unique areas for the awe of generations then unborn. But the national parks are merely the tip of the federal iceberg: they account for only a part of the lands managed by the National Park Service, which in turn are only about 12 percent of the nation's total federal land. Many people may have visited national forests without realizing that they are in a management system separate from the national parks, in the charge of a different agency (the U.S. Forest Service) in a different cabinet department (Agriculture rather than Interior).

Only in the West and in Alaska are the existence and activities of the Bureau of Land Management (BLM) common knowledge, but this little-publicized agency controls more federal land than any other, nearly one-tenth of the total national land surface. Most citizens also are at least vaguely aware that a variety of federal agencies own land for some purpose, from post offices to reservoirs, from military forts to wildlife refuges, and from atomic reactor sites to office buildings. In all, the United States owns in fee about 650 million acres, or about 28 percent of all land in the country. The United States owns an additional 60 million acres of subsurface mineral rights underlying state and private lands.

Public land law is at the core of the history of national economic development, but it encompasses far more than mundane legalities. Federal land policy impelled homesteaders to seek new lives, validated gold rush mining claims, brought about the range wars, and helped justify construction of massive water projects in the West. Even today the livelihoods of pipeline roughnecks, subsistence hunters, loggers, cattle barons, mineral prospectors, and other latter-day rugged individualists remain intertwined with public land law. Contemporary concern over the uses and abuses of the public lands and natural resources goes much deeper than interest in romantic exploits. Lord Macaulay long ago noted that the true test of American institutions would come when the free public domain was exhausted and an increased population competed for ownership of the land

and its depleted resources. That time has long since arrived, and the competition is intense. The controversies, large and small, that contribute to the growth and direction of federal land and resources law provide some of the most entertaining and informative studies in all of legal literature.

This book is organized around the concepts that certain lands and the resources they contain are, indeed, public, and that public natural resources law is an expression of and is guided by the public interest. Through its elected representatives, society professes to see virtue in many things; for example, it wishes to have both energy production and wilderness preservation. Decisions as to how individual tracts of public land will be managed must be determined through such competing impulses. Of course as the country and its economy have changed radically over the years, the issues and forums of public land disputes have likewise changed, as has the nature of public land law. However, the one enduring element is the argument over what course of action will best serve the public interest.

It took the United States a long time to fully embrace the notion that large tracts of federal lands should be retained in federal ownership and managed by federal agencies for the general public interest. For a century and a half, public land law existed basically to facilitate the disposal of federal lands and resources into state and private hands, and several thousand separate statutes were adopted over the years concerned with disposition of the federal lands. These were, in turn, interpreted and applied in thousands of court cases and administrative rulings. It is not, then, difficult to see that the practice of public natural resources law for a long time approached the arcane. Moreover, it was common to ignore or evade public land laws in the Nation's restless expansion across the continent.

Starting a little more than a century ago, the nature of public land law began to change as the United States began reserving ever-increasing tracts of land for permanent retention in federal ownership. From a single-minded emphasis on disposal, public land law grew to mean those statutes, rules, practices, and common law doctrines which define who has a right to own or use a parcel of federal land or its tangible resources. Over the course of the following decades, public considerations began to overshadow the central place of private rights, private disputes, and private law as components of overall public land law. Whether viewed as a new direction in traditional public land management, or as an instance of counterproductive federal overregulation, modern federal land and resources law encompasses far more than questions of property rights. Today's natural resources lawyer now must be conversant with such subjects as federal land planning, environmental impact statements, competing recreational, preservation, wildlife and cultural values, and other limitations on economic activity. Professors Coggins and Glicksman argue that the phrase "public land law"—traditionally referring to laws relating to public domain disposition—is outmoded. To reflect more accurately the modern focus, they suggest the term "public natural resources law."

The search for the public interest in managing public resources presents huge challenges. A modern public land dispute may arise in many forms, such as:

— should cattle or wild horses or elk be removed from an overgrazed tract of public land?

— what considerations govern whether to sell timber from a national forest?

— does a hunter have a right of access over an unpatented mining claim?

— should off-road vehicles be banned from certain areas?

— how can an agency balance oil drilling and wildlife protection?

— should creation of a wilderness area impliedly override state water laws?

— should a road to a potentially valuable mineral deposit be cut through an area used by grizzly bears for denning?

But, in every such case, the initial inquiries are the same: Where lies the public interest? Who decides where it lies in particular situations? What are the legal and practical consequences of the choice?

Preconceptions of the public interest are hazardous to mental health. To ardent wilderness advocates, wilderness preservation is one of the highest endeavors of organized society. But potential wilderness areas may have supplied the lumber that built wilderness advocates' houses, the materials with which their vehicles are built, and the fuel that makes them go. Few who complain of pollution from the local utility generating plant would readily give up air conditioning altogether. On the other hand, those who espouse production over all else have an equally narrow perspective. There are points of diminishing returns: the oil burned or old growth timber cut now will not be available ten or twenty years from now to fuel even more expansion for us and for our descendants. Further, as society grows richer, it values more than ever things that cannot be readily measured in the marketplace. Many more people now prefer to watch birds than to hunt them. Legislation has gradually come to reflect these public preferences. More and more preservation and recreation land systems have been created in the past three decades, and more and more lands have been set aside for special, non-economic purposes.

Compared to times past, there are fewer heroes or villains in modern public land controversies, only people with differing conceptions of the public interest. Most state and local politicians now concede that not all federal environmental regulation or public interest litigation is necessarily bad. There is wide consensus that development of some federal natural resources is appropriate if done in an environmentally sound manner. Natural resource extraction industries are generally accepting of (or at least resigned to) the new fabric of legal constraint; increasingly, they seek accommodation.

Even though the conservation movement won some notable victories in the late 19th century, it is fair to say that non-commodity-oriented interests did not achieve an equal, or even significant, voice until the 1970s. But now they have, and the principal modern controversies examined in this book tend to subordinate private rights to an initial determination of public rights in the decisional process. No longer is the question of whether a ski resort should be developed on public land one solely between the developer and the federal agency. No longer is the condition of BLM grazing lands of concern to ranchers alone. In these and many other disputes over use of public lands, a new class of disputants successfully challenged all of the old assumptions and ushered in a new era.

This new class is not just the self-styled "public interest" organization. For example, in some cases, private landowners have risen up in litigation against new mines or logging operations, partly reflecting "not in my backyard" attitudes. Allied to new landowner attitudes is a new aggressiveness on the part of non-consumptive economic users of public lands. Resorts, guides, river outfitters, and backpacking equipment manufacturers, to name a few, have resisted development of a resource valuable to them as primitive real estate. Growing numbers of economists and political conservatives are calling into question the many federal subsidies afforded to developers of public lands and resources.

Still, many of the largest changes have come about through institutional strategies and actions by environmental organizations. Among the most active and effective organizations are groups like the Sierra Club whose names adorn many of the cases in this book. Other organizations, such as the Pacific Legal Foundation and the Mountain States Legal Foundation (where conservative Interior Secretaries James Watt and Gale Norton earned their spurs), are financed by industries and libertarian foundations to present a more limited view of the public interest in resource litigation. Some powerful economic interests have large stakes in the direction of public land policy. Oil companies have paid billions of dollars for the privilege of drilling on offshore and other federal lands. Other energy companies have leased federal coal and coalbed methane. Public utilities rely upon federal fossil fuels, federal dams for hydroelectric power, and federal land for siting generation and transmission facilities. Timber companies still harvest hundreds of millions of board feet of timber from national forests annually, and many small communities are dependent on such harvesting. Coalitions among otherwise divergent entities are common. In the 1980's, for instance, when a large coal slurry pipeline was proposed to send Wyoming coal to Louisiana, common cause was joined by environmentalists, ranchers (fearing the shipment of scarce western water), and railroads (fearing the loss of lucrative shipping contracts).

Federal land management agencies are frequently caught in the middle. Historical missions and practices have been severely eroded by new statutes, and new missions have been charted, but congressional directives have often held out little concrete guidance in concrete situations, and procedural requisites have proliferated. Diverse stakeholders argue that their conception of the public interest should prevail in the circumstances, and all sides are willing to resort to litigation or political processes if dissatisfied with agency decisions. In most public resource disputes, agencies decide who wins and where the public interest lies. Effective advocates know how to influence agency behavior, first and foremost.

We believe that the student should know how legal rules are fashioned as well as what they are. In fact, the law in this area is an ever-changing complex of rules derived from and altered by different sources. Although the final determination usually resides in Congress, each of the three branches of government has the power to alter or upset the result reached in another branch. Throughout this volume are scattered "non-legal" or "quasi-legal" materials affording a glimpse into the interactive and inter-disciplinary nature of public land law.

From about 1964 to 1980 a veritable revolution was worked in federal public land law. Hundreds of old United States Code sections were swept away at a stroke. Courts opened their doors to new kinds of public interest law suits challenging public resource administration. Congress applied planning and environmental mandates to all federal land management agencies. Land and water preservation earned greater protection through new laws. The oldest federal land agency, the Forest Service, received thoroughgoing reform legislation, and the Bureau of Land Management secured a statutory mission in the sweeping Federal Land Policy and Management Act. The Alaska National Interest Lands Conservation Act of 1980 capped off the era by allocating more than 100 million federal acres to various conservation systems.

This wave of developments led to a predictable backlash, manifested first in the "Sagebrush Rebellion" of the late 1970s and early 1980s, and later in the short-lived "County Supremacy" movement of the 1990s. In the meantime, the federal agencies plodded on, moving forward to implement these sweeping new mandates and, not surprisingly, finding themselves buffeted both from those who thought the pace was too slow and those who thought it too fast.

In the twenty-first century, the public lands are seeing more than ever controversies growing out of competition among different kinds of recreationists (e.g., off-road vehicles versus hikers), and conflicts between recreationists and preservationists. Still, there are throwbacks to earlier eras; a new concern with energy development is putting more pressure on federal lands in Alaska and the Rocky Mountains. There is a massive boom in coalbed methane production in Wyoming and a few other parts of the West. Much of the western livestock industry is under siege from economic conditions and environmental restraints. The enormously rich history of public land law and policy leads to only two safe predictions: There will be more change, and it will be interesting.

Robert L. Fischman, What is Natural Resources Law?

78 U. Colo. L. Rev. 721 (2007).

Natural resources law is a field with divided loyalties. It has one foot in statutory, administrative law and the other in common law property. Within the ambit of environmental concerns, management of natural resources looms large. It can justifiably claim an important role in any course of study in environmental law. Similarly, any advanced property curriculum ought to consider the myriad forms of rights and allocative schemes in natural resources law. Yet, many practitioners and professors identify themselves as specialists in the field of natural resources, rather than in a natural resources sub-specialty of environmental or property law. * * *

* * *

[There are] * * * four attributes that justify separate pedagogical treatment of natural resources law as an independent course in law schools. First, the *in-situ* character of extractive activities that dominate natural resources law raises special problems and generates place-based approaches to governance. Second, the deeper roots of natural resources law present particularly vexing interpretive issues for applying the old statutes, deeds, and doctrines to contemporary conflicts. Third, ecosystem management is central to natural resources law problems. Fourth, despite the now-paramount importance of administrative tools, natural resources law still displays a broader array of property interests that go beyond the variations studied in the first-year property class.

* * *

In his 1981 introduction to a symposium on trends in natural resources law, Professor David Getches described four rationales for offering a natural resources law course. First, the subject brings together doctrines from diverse fields, such as constitutional law, administrative law, property, regulated industries, and federal courts. Second, it applies fundamental legal skills, such as statutory interpretation and analytical reasoning. Third, it embraces a wide range of social and ethical concerns. And, fourth, it requires students to understand the relevance of non-legal disciplines such as economics and geoscience.

While Getches' justifications for a natural resources law course remain compelling today, they fail to differentiate natural resources law from many other subjects, especially environmental law. * * *

* * *

A.   EXTRACTION VS. PROCESSING AND DISPOSAL

Perhaps the most obvious difference between a natural resources law class and an environmental law class concerns the subjects of the disputes. Natural resources law focuses mostly on extraction and primary production of goods and services. It is about the stuff of consumption. In contrast, environmental law focuses on secondary processing, transportation, manufacturing, and disposal. It is more about the unwanted side effects of consumption.

* * *

Two attributes are important in understanding why extraction generally highlights different issues from the processing/disposal concerns at the heart of the conventional environmental law class. First, natural resources are largely fodder for transformation, and their value is principally utilitarian in what they will serve in their next incarnation. The renowned musician and labor activist, Utah Phillips, tells a story that captures the natural resources value-in-use perspective. He attended a public school assembly of over two thousand students:

> [A]long the side of the stage was the suit-and-tie crowd sitting there from the school district and the principals, teachers, and the main speaker following me from the Chamber of Commerce. Something inside of me snapped. And I got to the microphone, I looked out on the sea of faces, and I said something to the effect of: "You're about to be told one more time that you're America's most valuable natural resource. Have you seen what they do to valuable natural resources? . . . Don't ever let them call you a valuable natural resource. They're going to strip mine your soul. They're going to clear-cut your best thoughts for the sake of profit, unless you learn to resist . . . !
>
> Well, I was picked up bodily and carried to the door hurling epithets over my shoulder, something to the effect of "Make a break for it kids! Flee to the wilderness!"*

Phillips' story is based on the widespread understanding that we treat resources in a purely utilitarian (and often wasteful) manner. There is some interesting theory but little resource management law based on the type of intrinsic valuation we assign to humans in other areas of law. We may ask of an endangered fly, "what is it good for?" in natural resources policy, but we don't accept the same question as a basis for justifying the value of people ("what good are you?").

Natural resources law is dominated by this "resource-ist," utilitarian approach rather than by a naturalist intrinsic value approach. Indeed, the "natural" in "natural resources" law may be optional. * * * When the Republican Party took control of the U.S. House of Representatives in 1995, the first act of the newly installed chairman of the House Committee on Natural Resources was to remove the word "Natural" from the title of his committee, in an attempt to remove any taint of intrinsic valuation from the committee's business. For Committee Chair Don Young, "natural" connoted the "nonsense upon stilts" of natural law and the preservationist strain of conservation personified by John Muir.

The second significant attribute of the extractive character of natural resources disputes is that they generally involve problems *in situ*. Unlike factories, roads, or even landfills, there is little choice about where to locate a mine, a scenic trail, or a fishery. As mining companies are wont to say about minerals, natural resources are where we find them. In that respect, natural resources law gets at land use much more directly than does environmental law. Control of soil disturbance, management of habitat, and conservation of traditional patterns of land use are among the most difficult problems the law faces. Because private land use control is the last

---

* UTAH PHILLIPS, THE MOSCOW HOLD (Red
House Records 1999).

outpost of near-exclusive state/local control, there are a host of special federalism issues and approaches that arise as a result.

Though federalism is a staple of environmental law, its manifestation in natural resources law offers a different, broader approach to the inducements that spur states to align their activities with federal goals. In environmental law, cooperative federalism is narrowly circumscribed around state permitting and standard setting overseen by the federal government to assure compliance with national minimum criteria. Natural resources law employs a wider array of cooperative tools, including place-based collaboration, state favoritism in federal process, and federal deference to state process.

* * *

B.   INTERPRETIVE TECHNIQUES

Professor Dan Tarlock has observed that environmental law possesses a lush canopy but shallow roots. In contrast, old statutes deeply influence contemporary natural resources law. Important examples include the R.S. 2477 law of 1866 authorizing the disposition of rights-of-way, the 1885 Unlawful Inclosures Act limiting obstructions to public land access, and the 1872 general mining law. In Charles Wilkinson's phrase, these "lords of yesterday" present peculiar problems of statutory interpretation.

For instance, natural resources law emphasizes how courts interpret old statutes in light of new circumstances. Some decisions, exemplified by *Union Oil v. Smith,* interpreting the 1872 General Mining Law, employ great flexibility in modifying seemingly strict statutory language to fit social policy or longstanding practice. *Union Oil* recognized that, as a practical matter, exploration precedes discovery of a valuable mineral deposit, and that some physical occupation is necessary and protected for exploration. Therefore, the Court recognized that some rights of exclusive possession may be asserted against private claim-jumpers notwithstanding the literal terms of the 1872 statute, which prohibit location of a mining claim until discovery. Other decisions, exemplified by the *Monongahela* ruling interpreting the 1897 organic act for the Forest Service, hold fast to strict textualism, despite its harsh consequences. The *Monongahela* decision suspended a substantial part of the Forest Service's longstanding logging program because it accommodated modern clear-cutting practices, such as marking boundaries of sale areas rather than each individual tree, at odds with the literal terms of the 1897 organic act. The juxtaposition of two interpretive approaches to statutes based on antiquated resource management methods is a much better fit for natural resources law than environmental law.

The problem of modernizing old statutes is seldom at the center of environmental law disputes. Therefore, it provides a justification for a separate natural resources course. In addition, the natural resources curriculum offers students a range of materials other than statutes and regulations that present their own special interpretive problems. Old patents, or deeds, present similar problems for determining how resources that were not valued at the time of the transfer should be treated today. * * *

* * *

Another interpretive tool, economic analysis, seeks to understand law in terms of incentives for behavior and efficiency of results. However, natural resources economics differs significantly from environmental economics in the way it treats changes in resource value over time, or "path-dependence." Path-dependence relates the way decisions made in earlier time periods shape the options for later time periods. Most environmental economics examines a snapshot of values in a single time period, such as the costs and benefits of lowering an ambient air quality standard. While environmental economics discounts future costs/benefits, it does not typically evaluate how a decision made today will affect the range of opportunities in the future. Determining "optimal" pollution levels is not sensitive to information about the future. In contrast, natural resource economic analysis models the abundance of a resource as a function of abundance during earlier time periods. Deciding on a production schedule for minerals, fish, timber, or water requires an evaluation of the optimal time for extracting a particular quantity of resources. It requires information about future prices and available amounts of the resource. Particularly with water and biological resources that may grow over time, "optimal" extraction requires serious projection of future trends.

* * *

C. THE ASYMMETRIC CONVERGENCE TOWARD ECOSYSTEM MANAGEMENT

Over the past thirty-five years, both environmental law and natural resources law have struggled to broaden their scopes to encompass ecological concerns. This parallel effort has narrowed the gap between the fields as they converge, albeit at different rates, toward an ecosystem management perspective. Ecosystem management has legal as well as social and natural scientific dimensions. It is a framework both for understanding the biology of what makes ecosystems function in a healthy fashion and for crafting socio-economic incentives. Key elements of ecosystem management include the maintenance of ecological integrity, collaborative and cooperative decision-making, and adaptive management to continually adjust to the unexpected.

* * *

* * * [Compared to environmental law,] natural resources law has more deeply engaged with ecosystem management. Its experience suggests different approaches from those employed by environmental law. Natural resources law has a closer relationship with ecology than does pollution control law. Because it has been far more involved in managing living systems, natural resources law also has a much firmer grounding in the social dimension of ecosystem management.

Natural resources law has grappled with the science side of ecosystem management, particularly in administering public property. The best example of this is the Forest Service's struggle to implement the diversity provision of the NFMA. The litigation over the viability of northern spotted owl populations in the Pacific Northwest forests led the Forest Service to conduct several seminal iterations of landscape-level planning that helped lay the foundation for ecosystem management.

* * *

Finally, natural resources law's obsession with comprehensive, land-use planning has pushed it further into experimentation with the adaptive management element of ecosystem management. It is principally the organic legislation for the federal public land systems that promotes natural resources planning. These organic acts offer a different model of lawmaking from the media-based statutes that shape most of (the ossified rules of) environmental law. Organic law provides a charter to orchestrate individual units into a system of lands/waters in order to achieve a coordinated goal. For instance, though each national wildlife refuge was established for a particular reason, organic legislation seeks to align all refuges "to sustain and, where appropriate, restore and enhance, healthy populations" of animals and plants using "modern scientific resource programs." One of the five hallmarks of organic legislation is comprehensive planning for each unit of a public land system. The planning process is particularly important because it translates broad requirements (e.g. system mission, uses and criteria) into site-specific measures and prescriptions through public participation. Students taking natural resources law, even if they study only one of the public land organic statutes, get a firm grounding in the issues of planning, including the pitfalls of comprehensive rationality and the need for perpetual readjustment. This is the heart of adaptive management. For instance, the planning process for the national wildlife refuges does not end when a plan is adopted. It continues into a phase of implementation and evaluation. Each step of plan implementation, under adaptive management, is an experiment requiring review and adjustment.

D.   THE PROPERTY PALETTE

* * * [Despite the rise in importance of administrative law, the natural resources] field retained a dazzling array of property interests that go beyond the variations on the fee simple absolute that are the heart of a property law class. This is the property law foundation of natural resources law that continues to provide an important contrast with environmental law.

Natural resource law's coverage of the property interests incident to mining under the 1872 General Mining Law neatly illustrates peculiar forms of property that delight and enlighten students. The formula for the state-created and federally recognized *pedis possessio* right to prospect is as close to a true sweat equity as anything in American property law. The *pedis possessio* limitation of being enforceable against a fellow prospector but not against the federal government also illustrates nicely the conventional legal view of property as not the thing itself but the ability to assert a claim against someone else. The unpatented mineral right perfected under the general mining law is a fifth-amendment-protected form of property notwithstanding the absence of a deed. It is the apogee of the

Lockean vision of property in federal law, and provides concrete examples of both the strengths and weaknesses of this social vision. It also illustrates the importance of myth (both of Locke's un-propertied, pre-colonial America, and of the American rugged individualist miner) in sustaining the rights of ownership.

B. THE FEDERAL LANDS AND RESOURCES

Except for the area of the original thirteen colonies, Texas, and Hawaii, the United States government once owned nearly all of the land within its present borders. The real estate comprising this original "public domain" is probably the richest in the variety and extent of its natural resources of all comparable areas in the world. The forests, farmlands, rivers, mineral wealth, and scenic wonders are of literally inestimable economic, social, and aesthetic value. Though the federal government owns and manages Indian reservations, these lands are generally excluded from the laws, statistics, and courses pertaining to federal public lands.

Most of the original national legacy passed out of federal ownership as the public lands were opened for settlement and development. Easy availability of land was the primary incentive for pioneers, then settlers, to move west and populate the Nation. Each wave of settlers chose the available lands that were then thought to be the most economically valuable. New cities grew up around the ports and many of the strategic river junctions. The heart of public land policy was to promote the small family farm: After the best agricultural lands in the Midwest were settled, the homesteaders moved to the Willamette Valley in Oregon, the Central Valley in California, and other verdant lowlands. Prospectors and mining firms claimed the land over the fabulous gold, silver, iron, and copper deposits in areas such as the California Mother Lode country, the Comstock Lode in Nevada, the Mesabi Range in Minnesota, and Butte in Montana. The timber industry obtained prime timber lands throughout the country; their relatively low-lying lands in the Pacific Northwest remain especially valuable. In this century, reclamation projects were built to irrigate otherwise arid homesteads in the Great Plains, the Great Basin between the Sierra Nevada and Rocky Mountains, and elsewhere.

In the mid–19th century, Congresses and presidents withdrew a few public land parcels from the various programs for disposition into private hands and dedicated—or "reserved"—them for some specific purpose. Reservation for other than military or Indian purposes began haltingly with the establishment of Yellowstone National Park in 1872, and "conservation" momentum has grown ever since. Homesteading largely ended in 1934, and eventually retention supplanted disposition as official federal public land policy. In the modern era, however, land selection by the State of Alaska and Alaska Natives removed nearly 150 million acres from federal ownership. Furthermore, some minor sales or exchanges of lands especially suited for certain forms of non-federal ownership are still authorized, and in recent years some significant proposals for disposal of thousands of acres of federal land have been packaged with wilderness designations or other conservation measures in particular places. Conversely, some acquisitions of private lands by the federal government will continue for such purposes as creating new national wildlife refuges or expanding parks. On balance, however, today the outlines of the federal land estate seem reasonably stable, despite periodic proposals for renewed large-scale disposition.

The United States owns about 28 percent of the nation's land area, or 650 million acres. Although federal public lands are located in all states, the highest proportion is found in eleven western states (Arizona, California, Colorado, Idaho, Montana, Nevada, New Mexico, Oregon, Utah, Washington, and Wyoming) and especially in Alaska, which still has about 250 million federal acres, or about 38 percent of all federal lands. All told, federal lands constitute nearly half of the land in the eleven western states in the lower 48 and about two-thirds of the land in Alaska. (Because nearly all of these states have relatively small populations, they still have more non-federal land per capita than states in the East and Midwest.) While federal lands are a smaller proportion of total land area in states outside the West, a number of non-western states have sizeable chunks of federal lands; e.g., 4 million acres of Michigan, 3 million acres each in Arkansas, Florida, and Minnesota, almost that number in North Carolina and Texas, and more than 2 million in Virginia. Eleven other non-western states have more than one million acres of federal land. Federal land and resources law is increasingly national, as the principal cases in this new edition attest, being drawn from all regions of the country.

The federal government also owns major less-than-fee interests. In addition to such holdings as acquired waterfowl easements, the United States retains subsurface mineral interests under some 60 million acres of private and state land in the West. The federal government asserts sovereignty over the resources of the outer continental shelf, an area of over half a billion acres extending from 3 miles offshore (3 marine leagues off the Florida and Texas coasts) seaward to the edge of the continental shelf. These mineral rights include immensely valuable deposits of fossil fuels.

Because of the historical pattern of national disposition, the federal lands tend to be relatively more arid and infertile, higher in elevation, and remote from major transportation systems. Nevertheless, such generalizations may prove too much: in fact, vast riches of many kinds remain in federal ownership. The last of several blue-ribbon commissions to study federal land policy, the congressionally created Public Land Law Review Commission, had this to say in its 1970 Report, One Third of the Nation's Land, p. 22:

> One of the most important characteristics of the public lands is their great diversity. Because of their great range—they are found from the northern tip of Alaska to the southern end of Florida—all kinds of climate conditions are found on them. Arctic cold, rain forest torrents, desert heat, mountain snows, and semi-tropical littoral conditions are all characteristic of public lands in one area or another.
>
> Great differences in terrain are also typical. The tallest mountain in North America, Mount McKinley in Alaska, is on public

lands, as is the tallest mountain in the 48 contiguous states, Mount Whitney in California. But the lowest point in the United States, Death Valley, is also on public lands, as are most of the highest peaks in the White Mountains of New Hampshire and the Appalachians of the southeastern states.

Not all of these lands are mountains and valleys, however. Vast areas of tundra and river deltas in Alaska are flat, marked only with an incredible number of small lakes. Other vast areas in the Great Basin area of Nevada and Oregon are not marked with lakes, but with desert shrubs. Still other areas of rolling timber-covered mountains extend for mile after mile, both in the Pacific Northwest and the Inland Empire of Idaho, eastern Washington, and western Montana, and in the Allegheny, Green, and Ouachita Mountains of Pennsylvania, Vermont, and Arkansas. And still other vast areas are rangelands used for grazing domestic livestock.

However, not all of these public lands can be characterized as vast wild or semi-developed expanses. In many instances, Federal ownership is scattered in relatively small tracts among largely privately owned lands. The condition of the land may still be undeveloped, but our consideration of how the land should be used is necessarily influenced by the scattered nature of the Federal ownership. In some cases, public lands are found almost in the midst of urban areas and here again we must view the use of the lands in relation to the surrounding lands.

The great diversity of these lands is a resource in itself. As needs of the Nation have changed, the public lands have been able to play a changing role in meeting these needs. Whether the demand is for minerals, crop production, timber, or recreation, and whether it is national or regional, the public lands are able to play a role in meeting them.

A brief introductory note on terminology [from George C. Coggins & Robert Glicksman, 1 PUBLIC NATURAL RESOURCES LAW § 1.9]:

"Public domain" has had two traditional meanings. It referred, first, to lands acquired by the United States from other sovereigns, including Indian tribes, and still federally-owned. This meaning contrasts with "acquired lands," which were once in private or state ownership. "Public domain" also took on the connotation of "lands open to entry and settlement." This meaning is the opposite of "reserved" and "withdrawn" lands. As virtually all federal lands are now off-limits to traditional entry and settlement, this [term is an artifact]. * * *

"Acquired lands" are lands the United States acquired from private or state owners by gift, purchase, exchange, or condemnation. In most but not all cases, such lands actually have been "reacquired," because the United States previously had purchased or won them from foreign and Indian sovereigns. Distinguishing between lands because of ownership origins that go back over a century is a policy with little to recommend it, but some statutes and judicial opinions maintain the distinction. * * *

The meaning of the term "public lands" has varied greatly. In common parlance, the term simply means all lands owned by the United States. Matters are not that simple, however. At some times, the term was synonymous with both meanings of "public domain" described * * * above. Its common law definition came to be "unreserved and unappropriated public domain lands open to entry, settlement, and appropriation." But the common law meaning, never precise, has been superseded to a considerable extent by statutory definitions. In 1920, for instance, Congress defined "public lands" for purposes of federal power development to mean unreserved lands "subject to private appropriation and disposal." Congress in 1976 complicated the matter further by defining public lands as "any land and interest in land owned by the United States * * * and administered by the Bureau of Land Management, without regard to how the United States acquired ownership," except Indian and offshore lands. A 1979 statute defines public lands as all federally-owned lands for limited purposes.

The terms "public lands" and "federal lands" may also include less than full fee interests, such as severed mineral estates. They usually do not, however, refer to submerged lands off the seacoasts (over which the United States asserts jurisdiction but not title), or lands held in trust for Indians. Like so much of public land law, in other words, consistency is not a hallmark and generalization is hazardous.

Comparison of Federal Land With Total Acreage By State
(In Thousands of Acres)

State	Acreage owned by the Federal Government	Acreage of state[1]	Percent owned by Federal Government[2]
Alabama	1,234	32,678	3.8
Alaska	250,281	365,482	62.4
Arizona	32,389	72,688	44.6
Arkansas	3,238	33,599	9.6
California	43,713	100,207	43.6
Colorado	24,239	66,486	36.5
Connecticut	14	3,135	0.5
Delaware	8	1,266	0.6
Dist. of Columbia	9	39	22.7
Florida	3,066	34,721	8.8
Georgia	1,864	37,295	5.0
Hawaii	618	4,105	15.1
Idaho	33,079	52,933	62.5
Illinois	574	35,795	1.6
Indiana	501	23,158	2.2
Iowa	195	35,860	0.5
Kansas	673	52,511	1.3
Kentucky	1,234	25,512	4.8
Louisiana	1,159	28,868	4.0
Maine	168	19,848	0.8
Maryland	167	6,319	2.6
Massachusetts	72	5,035	1.4
Michigan	4,079	36,492	11.2
Minnesota	4,206	51,206	8.2
Mississippi	1,647	30,223	5.5

State	Acreage owned by the Federal Government	Acreage of state[1]	Percent owned by Federal Government[2]
Missouri	2,095	44,248	4.7
Montana	25,783	93,271	27.6
Nebraska	647	49,032	1.3
Nevada	58,226	70,264	82.9
New Hampshire	759	5,769	13.2
New Jersey	119	4,813	2.5
New Mexico	26,626	77,766	34.2
New York	106	30,681	0.3
North Carolina	2,356	31,403	7.5
North Dakota	1,771	44,452	4.0
Ohio	392	26,222	1.5
Oklahoma	1,323	44,088	3.0
Oregon	32,315	61,599	52.5
Pennsylvania	670	28,804	2.3
Rhode Island	4	677	0.6
South Carolina	1,107	19,374	5.7
South Dakota	2,662	48,882	5.4
Tennessee	1,658	26,728	6.2
Texas	2,568	168,218	1.5
Utah	34,005	52,697	64.5
Vermont	372	5,937	6.3
Virginia	2,284	25,496	9.0
Washington	12,152	42,694	28.5
West Virginia	1,178	15,411	7.6
Wisconsin	1,182	35,011	5.3
Wyoming	31,071	62,343	49.8
Total	652,550	2,271,343	27.7

1. Excludes inland water.
2. Excludes trust properties.
SOURCE: PUBLIC LAND STATISTICS 2000, TABLE 1–3, P. 7

The federal lands contain a wide array of valuable resources. In some instances, use of a parcel for development of one resource can be entirely compatible with a different use: timber harvesting can benefit some wildlife and recreation resources by creating meadows beneficial for deer habitat; a wilderness area can provide watershed protection for downstream development; a reclamation project for irrigation purposes can also produce electrical energy and recreation. But sometimes management for one type of use is fundamentally inconsistent with other uses. The designation of a tract of federal land as wilderness generally eliminates timber harvesting and mineral development. Developing the mineral resources of another tract may be inconsistent with recreation, timber harvesting, or grazing. Logging may impair wildlife and destroy cultural resources. Avoiding or resolving such resource conflicts is the overriding problem of modern land law. This book identifies and treats somewhat distinctly seven major resources of the federal lands—water, minerals, timber, range, wildlife, recreation, and preservation. Each deserves its own introduction.

WATER

Water tends to be in the middle of many tough resource use choices. Availability of water has always been a limiting factor for development in many Trans–Mississippi regions. Wallace Stegner, one of the most respected modern commentators on the American West, observed that the region's aridity and large concentration of public lands are the two most distinctive features of western society. See W. Stegner, THE SOUND OF MOUNTAIN WATER 33 (1969). Justice Rehnquist, who was one of the most prolific public land law opinion writers, along with Justices Field, Van Devanter, and McKenna, commented in California v. United States, 438 U.S. 645, 648–50 (1978):

* * * The final expansion of our Nation in the 19th century into the arid lands beyond the hundredth meridian of longitude, which had been shown on early maps as the "Great American Desert," brought the participants in that expansion face to face with the necessity for irrigation in a way that no previous territorial expansion had.

* * * [During the last half of the nineteenth century] irrigation expanded throughout the arid States of the West, supported usually by private enterprise or the local community. By the turn of the century, however, most of the land which could be profitably irrigated by such small scale projects had been put to use. Pressure mounted on the Federal Government to provide the funding for the massive projects that would be needed to complete the reclamation, culminating in the Reclamation Act of 1902.

The arid lands were not all susceptible of the same sort of reclamation. The climate and topography of the lands that constituted the "Great American Desert" were quite different than the climate and topography of the Pacific Coast States. * * * [T]he latter States not only had a more pronounced seasonal variation and precipitation than the intermountain States, but the interior portions of California had climatic advantages which many of the intermountain States did not.

Almost two-thirds of the run-off in the eleven western states, and all the great western rivers, originate on federal lands. These lands comprise most of the Continental Divide, the Sierra Nevada, the Cascade Range, and other mountainous areas in the West. Moreover, much of the federal lands in the east were purchased into federal ownership in the early twentieth century because of their value as watersheds. Although water is a renewable (as well as reusable, and storable) resource, there has never been enough in the right places at the right times to fulfill human desires, especially in arid regions. In the twentieth century, the United States, through at least eight separate agencies, developed water resources in an engineering effort unparalleled in history. These projects have provided irrigation water, municipal drinking supplies, electricity, and recreational opportunities, but they have also taken a heavy toll on wildlife and the amenities of free-flowing rivers. Problems of federal ownership and development of water—and particularly those concerning state-federal relationships—are examined in Chapter 6.

MINERALS

Minerals found on the public lands have played a signal role in the economic and social history of the Nation. The discovery of gold in the California foothills in 1848 prompted the true opening of the west, and later bonanzas would lead miners and then settlers to many other western states. Mining has long been subject to "boom and bust" cycles, but in spite of virtually unlimited prospecting for over a century, the federal lands are still thought to hold large deposits of minerals. Fossil fuels like coal, oil, and gas, and fertilizer minerals like phosphate and sodium compounds, exist in large quantities on federal land. Federal coal production rose from 285 million tons annually in 1991 to nearly 400 million tons annually today, and the proportion of national coal production coming from federal lands rose from about one-quarter to over one-third over the same period. Today, federal lands onshore and offshore account for about 35 percent of total domestic production of oil and gas, up from 16 percent in 1989. Much of the nation's output of precious metals and other "hardrock" minerals (gold, silver, nickel, lead, copper, zinc, molybdenum, etc.) also come from deposits found wholly or partially on federal lands. The value of cumulative federal production over the years is many billions of dollars. The legal regimes governing mineral extraction and the problems they create vis-à-vis other resources are taken up in Chapter 7.

TIMBER

The federal government owns about 18 percent of the nearly 500 million acres of commercial timber lands in the United States. Six-sevenths of federal commercial timber is in national forests. Before World War II, federal timber holdings managed by the Forest Service and the Bureau of Land Management were managed conservatively, producing only about five percent of the national total timber harvest. One result of that former conservatism is that the federal lands still hold a comparatively large amount of old-growth, virgin timber of great economic value, especially in the Pacific Northwest. About half of the national softwood timber inventory is located on national forests, roughly three times the amount owned by the forest industry, with small private owners and other public entities controlling the rest. Many of the lands containing timber, particularly the extraordinary stands of old-growth Douglas fir, redwood, and pine, also contain unique scenic and aesthetic values. The timber resource is explored in Chapter 8.

GRAZING

More acres of federal lands are used for domestic livestock grazing than for any other single use except recreation. The number of animals on the federal range has declined substantially, but ranchers still graze cattle and sheep on about 159 million acres of BLM lands and 85 million acres within the national forests. Federal land forage is, however, only a tiny fraction of the total grass consumed by livestock in the country. Historically, the public domain was a "commons" where grazing was allowed with no federal regulation whatsoever, a situation that took a great toll on the forage resource.

Today millions of domestic animals spend part of their lives on federal rangeland, sharing the forage with thousands of wild horses and burros and millions of antelope, deer, moose, and mountain sheep. In spite of federal regulation since the 1930's (and earlier, in the case of national forests), the public range is largely in "fair" or "poor" condition and overgrazing by modern standards is still widespread in some areas. Regulation to reconcile competing uses of the range and to increase the productivity of grazing lands is the dominant theme of Chapter 9.

WILDLIFE

The federal lands contain some of the most valuable wildlife habitat in the world. Maintenance of animal and plant populations in the wild is important to hunters, to industries that depend upon wildlife products or that support recreational pursuits, and to people who only watch wildlife. Everyone benefits from the essential services, such as pollination and pollution assimilation, that healthy ecosystems provide.

The native ranges of certain species, such as wild turkey, moose, elk, and mountain sheep, correspond closely to public land holdings. Even in many eastern states, big game species depend heavily on habitat found on federal lands. In some instances, the public lands offer the last refuge for species in danger. The 96 million acre National Wildlife Refuge System's primary mission is to maintain healthy populations of plants and animals. The national debate over drilling in the Arctic National Wildlife Refuge, one of some 550 units of the system, illustrates the passion that wildlife disputes can engender. Conflict over resource uses involving wildlife impacts cuts across all federal land systems; and all of the systems include some kind of wildlife resource protection mandate in their charters. Management and protection of the wildlife resource on federal lands is the subject of Chapter 10.

RECREATION

Minerals, timber, water, forage, and even wildlife are commonly considered the conventional resources on the public lands. Nothing better symbolizes the evolution of federal land policy in the last half-century than the emergence of recreation and preservation as co-equal and competing resources. As an economic matter, the recreation resource swamps all of the commodity resources combined. American leisure time, affluence, and ease of transportation continue to spur increases in demand for recreational opportunities on the federal lands. Every major federal land system offers something of a recreational nature to somebody, from hiking to power-boating to resorts. One can tour a national park by car, shoot the rapids on a wild river, fish, swim, and boat in federal reservoirs, ride jeeps through grazing districts, hunt game in wildlife refuges, and collect rocks in national forests. These opportunities have been considered "givens," unchallenged rights available to all citizens. But, as in the case of all resources, the underlying productivity of the recreation resource can be threatened by human overuse. The legal questions arising from conflicts among different kinds of recreational uses, and between recreation and other resources, are addressed in Chapter 11.

PRESERVATION

American society is indelibly marked by Henry David Thoreau's declaration that "in wildness is the preservation of the world." In 1868 John Muir adopted that directive, stepped on the wharf in San Francisco, and said, "take me anywhere that is wild." Muir found what he was looking for in the public lands of the Sierra Nevada. Because of the work of Muir and others, Congress was moved to set aside numerous national parks in the late 19th and early 20th centuries. National parks were and are an important part of the preservation resource, but government officials came to recognize the need to preserve truly wild areas without roads, lodges, or restaurants. From obscure philosophical beginnings, the movement to preserve wild areas succeeded in persuading Congress to create a new system of federal lands, the dominant purpose of which is preservation. One of the most articulate wilderness advocates, the late Justice William O. Douglas, made the following observations on the place of preservation in national resource priorities:

> * * * The islands of wilderness, even if they never shrink in acreage, shrink *per capita*. For the pressure of population is ever and ever greater; and the year is drawing near when one who wants to backpack or travel by pack train into the High Sierras, the Northern Cascades, the Wind River Range, or the Tetons must get a permit—just as he does today for picnicking along Rock Creek Park, Washington, D.C. * * *

William O. Douglas, A Wilderness Bill of Rights 61–70 (1965).

The preservation resource also includes archeological, historical, and cultural artifacts, structures, and settings. The public lands are rich in sites that are part of the nations' cultural as well as natural heritage. Increasingly, even wilderness is viewed through a cultural lens that examines the human influences on natural landscapes. The legal underpinnings of the preservation movement, and its implications for other federal land uses, are explored in the concluding Chapter 12.

These, then, are the primary resources of the public lands. For every proposed use there are phalanxes of disparate advocates and opponents. Some claim that if the United States were to "lock up" for preservation many of these resources, catastrophic social and economic consequences would follow. On the other hand, opening all federal lands for wholesale, unregulated development would irreparably wound a special part of the national spirit and many local economies. Because compromise pervades our political, legal, and administrative mechanisms, resource decisions mostly fall in the middle of the two extremes. It is within this diverse and emotional context that legislators, land management officials, and judges must operate in making and reviewing decisions affecting the national resources.

It is difficult to locate a common legal denominator among the many diverse instances of present federal ownership. The federal purposes behind construction of a post office and creation of a wilderness area are so different that comparison in legal terms is nearly impossible. Several decades ago one writer divided all federal holdings into three broad classifications: resource preservation lands; multiple resource use lands; and lands used for specific non-resource-oriented purposes. Jerome Muys, The Federal Lands, in Federal Environmental Law 495 (1974). The "resource preservation" lands include the National Park System (which includes monuments, preserves, recreation areas, seashores, lakeshores, trails, and rivers), wilderness areas, and the National Wildlife Refuge System. The "multiple use" category includes national forests (including the national grasslands), the BLM lands (the traditional "public domain"), outer continental shelf lands, and the lands administered for power, irrigation, or flood control purposes by the Federal Energy Regulatory Commission, the Army Corps of Engineers, and the Bureau of Reclamation. The final "non-resource-oriented" category is a catchall for all other forms of federal land ownership. That category is not necessarily negligible—the Department of Defense administers millions of acres—but the focus of this volume is on the vast bulk of the federal lands in the two "resource" categories.

Professors George C. Coggins and Robert Glicksman's three volume treatise, PUBLIC NATURAL RESOURCES LAW (updated regularly) is a useful complement to this casebook, covering all the topics addressed here in comprehensive fashion. Robert Glicksman & George C. Coggins, MODERN PUBLIC LAND LAW IN A NUTSHELL, is based on and keyed to this casebook. Jan C. Laitos, NATURAL RESOURCES LAW (2002), is a hornbook summarizing the law and offering an introduction to natural resource economics. Professor Fischman maintains a web site that supplements and updates the material in this casebook: www.law.indiana.edu/publicland.

C. MANAGEMENT OF FEDERAL LANDS

The federal government owns retained and acquired lands for many diverse purposes, but the focus of this volume is on the federal lands classified as national forests, BLM or public lands, national parks and monuments, national wildlife refuges, and wilderness and other protected areas. Public land management systems are usually classified according to what uses are allowed in them. With the "use" of disposition by sale or grant now mostly a memory, the primary or dominant public land uses are for mining, grazing, logging, recreation, wildlife (including the services of biodiversity), and preservation. The national forests and the BLM lands are commonly described as "multiple use" lands in which all of the above uses are permitted, although in practice some uses tend to predominate on some lands. Furthermore, although national park system lands and national wildlife refuges tend to have dominant uses (recreation, preservation, and wildlife), other uses may be permitted on some of these lands. All of this is by way of saying that federal land classification is not an exact science. No classification of public lands is exclusive or immutable (even classifications chosen expressly by Congress), and overlapping functions and common problems are more of a rule than an exception. The distribution of federal lands to agencies with delegated management powers is as much a function of historical contingency as it is rational deliberation.

This section briefly describes the four principal federal land management agencies. It also discusses preservation lands—such as wilderness areas and wild and scenic rivers—some of which are managed by each of those four agencies. It introduces major federal legal entities, other than courts, which contribute to public land law development. Finally, the section concludes with a discussion of the special status and history of federal lands in Alaska.

1. THE NATIONAL FOREST SYSTEM

The withdrawals of the "forest reserves" from the public domain beginning in 1891, the creation of Gifford Pinchot's Forest Service in the Department of Agriculture, and the transfer of the Forest Reserves to Agriculture in 1905, combined to create the present National Forest System. Some of the original reservations were later returned to the public domain, and other national forest land has been transferred to the Department of the Interior, but national forests still contain about 193 million acres, the second largest system by acreage. (Proposals to transfer management of the national forests back to Interior have surfaced every decade or two, but none has yet succeeded.)

The National Forest System was also the prime beneficiary of the first major program to reacquire into federal ownership, primarily for conservation purposes, lands from private owners. Between 1912 and World War II, the Forest Service purchased several million acres of agriculturally depressed or abandoned land east of the Mississippi under the so-called Weeks Act. It also acquired what came to be known as the National Grasslands by purchase from bankrupt dirt farmers in the western Great Plains during the drought-ridden years of The Great Depression. These 24 million acres of acquisitions plus the forest reservations from the public domain has given the Forest Service landholdings in nearly every state.

The forest reserves that became the national forests were established "to improve and protect the forest * * * [and] for the purpose of securing favorable conditions of water flows, and to furnish a continuous supply of timber." 16 U.S.C. § 475. For decades, the management of the forests was primarily custodial: before World War II they supplied less than five percent of the annual timber harvests. It was not until 1940 that the annual harvest from the national forests exceeded 2 billion board feet; that figure doubled by 1951; doubled again by 1959; and reached 12 billion board feet in 1966. With the post-war housing boom and the relative depletion of privately-owned commercial forests, pressure on the national forests to produce more saw timber led first to a refinement of Pinchot's utilitarian philosophy and then to the enactment of the multiple use mandate into law. Multiple–Use, Sustained–Yield Act of 1960, 16 U.S.C. §§ 528–531. Environmental restrictions and other factors have reduced the average annual cut today to a fraction of what it was. The management of the timber resource on the national forests is now controlled in large part by the National Forest Management Act of 1976 (NFMA), 16 U.S.C. § 1601 et seq., discussed in detail in Chapter 8.

2. THE BLM PUBLIC LANDS

The unreserved, public domain lands were administered by the Department of the Interior's Grazing Service until 1946, when it was merged with the General Land Office to form the Bureau of Land Management. These were the "lands nobody wanted" when the era of resource disposal came to an end. In the lower 48 states, the BLM is responsible for the management of nearly 180 million acres of mostly arid and semi-arid land, nearly all of it in the eleven western states and Alaska. In Alaska, the BLM retains jurisdiction over about 86 million acres, a sharp reduction from three decades ago owing to statehood grants, grants to Alaskan Natives under the Native Claims Settlement Act of 1971, and transfers to other agencies under the Alaska National Interest Lands Conservation Act of 1980.

BLM stewardship has not, for the most part, undone the damage wrought before the agency existed. Like the Forest Service, the BLM evolved internally a multiple use philosophy over the years, but with emphasis on grazing and mining instead of logging (leading some wags to call it the "Bureau of Livestock and Mining"). BLM's "organic" management act is the Federal Land Policy and Management Act of 1976 (FLPMA), 43 U.S.C. §§ 1701–1784.* Although late to the game of managing federal lands for conservation purposes, BLM has in the last couple of decades come to administer a "National Landscape Conservation System," which encompasses a hodgepodge of units including wilderness areas, national monuments, and "areas of critical environmental concern." In addition to administering its system of surface lands, the BLM is also responsible for managing all 700 million acres of subsurface mineral rights owned by the United States. BLM has traditionally been given challenging management tasks with little funding compared to other federal agencies. The BLM's transition from a custodial agency dominated by ranching and mining interests to a modern, conservation-oriented land management agency is one of the more interesting stories of public land policy and is dealt with especially in Chapters 7 (mining) and 9 (grazing).

3. THE NATIONAL WILDLIFE REFUGE SYSTEM

The National Wildlife Refuge System's origins date to President Theodore Roosevelt's reservation of Pelican Island, Florida, for the benefit of wildlife in 1903. The President and the Congress reserved federal lands and purchased nonfederal lands piecemeal over the years under various authorities. In 1966, as part of a legislative package for protecting endangered species, Congress established the Refuge System with broad-reaching management authority. The refuges languished for another thirty-one years before receiving a modern organic statute setting forth a clear mission of maintaining a healthy network of habitats for plants and animals. *See* National Wildlife Refuge Administration Act, as amended by the National Wildlife Refuge System Improvement Act of 1997, 16 U.S.C. §§ 668dd–ee. The U.S. Fish and Wildlife Service (FWS) in the Department of the Interior administers the System. The System comprises about 92 million acres in

---

* FLPMA continued Congress's longstanding lack of consistency in semantics by defining BLM lands as "public lands." 43 U.S.C. § 1702(e). In some other contexts, Congress has defined "public lands" to include the national forests; e.g., 16 U.S.C. § 1332 (Wild, Free–Roaming Horses and Burros Act of 1971). In its 1970 Report, the Public Land Law Review Commission used "public lands" to describe *all* federally-owned areas, which is also a common, if confusing, usage.

fee ownership (75 million of which are in Alaska), together with lesser interests such as waterfowl easements on another 4 million acres. Currently, the agency operates approximately 550 national wildlife refuges and thousands of waterfowl production areas.

The National Wildlife Refuge System is the only category of federal lands administered primarily for the conservation of wildlife, although states have wildlife areas and wildlife management is a concern on practically all federal lands. Additions to the System are funded through special segregated tax revenues derived from such sources as sale of duck stamps, but the refuges have suffered from under-funding, political neglect, and popular overuse. Although wildlife conservation is the main criterion in refuge management under the relevant statutes, almost every other common use is allowed to some extent on some refuges. Typical legal issues growing out of FWS management are dealt with in Chapter 10.

4. THE NATIONAL PARK SYSTEM

Among the uses allowed and encouraged on the foregoing three systems are forms of recreation such as bird watching, camping, and hunting; to that extent they can be considered "recreational lands." The various categories of lands within the National Park System are, however, devoted primarily to recreation and preservation. The System now encompasses nearly 84 million acres (which includes 4 million acres of private land) located in almost every state. An orientation toward preservation has characterized the Park Service since its inception in 1916, but its mission has been broadened substantially by assignment of responsibility for recreation areas, urban parks, cultural areas, and the like. The approximately 60 national parks, the most famous units in the System, are still managed for the "enjoyment of future generations," but more intensive recreation is typical on other land designations within the System.

The recreation opportunities created by the Hoover Dam inspired Congress in 1936 to designate the lake and surrounding shoreline as the Lake Mead National Recreation Area. The concept was followed at Lake Powell, Flaming Gorge, Ross Lake, and some other impoundments. Congress also experimented with national parkways such as Blue Ridge in the 1930's. Concern about the incongruence of parks and roads, however, led to the formation of the Wilderness Society in protest, and the parkway system has not been expanded. Recreation continued to grow as an important facet of public land policy. Congressional desires to satisfy demand for outdoor recreation resulted in an explosion of new land categories, many under NPS jurisdiction. There are now national seashores (e.g., Point Reyes in California), national lakeshores (e.g., Sleeping Bear in Michigan), national rivers (e.g., the Buffalo in Arkansas), the Boundary Water Canoe Area in Minnesota, national wild and scenic rivers (e.g. the Allagash in Maine), national trails (e.g., the Pacific Crest), national gateway parks (e.g. Golden Gate in and near San Francisco), and the fourteen national preserves. The Park Service also manages historical memorials, battlefield monuments, and many of the Washington, D.C. area parks and memorials. The ever increasing number of national park units and the diversity of categories has led to criticism of "park barrel" politics that designate areas, such as Steamtown National Historical Site, that dilute the focus of the System. Chapter 11 addresses a variety of issues growing out of the popularity of recreation on federal land.

5.   THE PRESERVATION LANDS AND OTHER GENERIC CATEGORIES

The national park lands are to be managed for preservation as well as recreation, but many felt that park resources alone were too few and too vulnerable for national needs. In 1964 Congress created yet another lands category by passage of the Wilderness Act, 16 U.S.C. § 1131–1136, under which lands so designated are to be devoted primarily to preservation. Some nine million acres, in roadless areas of over 5,000 acres "untrammeled by man," were set aside initially, and the National Wilderness Preservation System has continued to grow. Additions to the System, now encompassing over 100 million acres (60 percent of it in Alaska), have been and are being carved out of other federal lands by a lengthy process of selection, inventory, presidential recommendation, and congressional designation. A wilderness area is managed by the agency under whose jurisdiction the area fell before designation.

Another federal lands category is that of national monuments, usually created by Presidential proclamation under authority of the 1906 Antiquities Act, 16 U.S.C. § 431–433. This statute authorizes the President to reserve federal lands to protect "historic landmarks, historic and prehistoric structures, and other objects of historic or scientific interest." Although only the "smallest area compatible with the proper care and management of" the object(s) protected is to be so reserved, large areas such as Grand Canyon, Death Valley, and Glacier Bay National Parks were first protected by Presidential proclamation under this statute. President Clinton revived the statute from nearly two decades of disuse, and employed it to protect more acres of federal land than any chief executive other than Jimmy Carter, who designated more than 56 million acres of national monuments in Alaska in 1978. Many of President Clinton's monuments were designated on BLM land, and BLM remains the manager. Congress has sometimes legislated national monuments, and has usually confirmed Presidential monuments. For example, Congress confirmed nearly all the acreage in President Carter's monuments in the Alaska National Interest Lands Conservation Act of 1980.

In the last few decades Congress has added to the categories of land that are managed primarily for preservation purposes. The Wild and Scenic Rivers Act of 1968 and the Alaska National Interest Lands Conservation Act of 1980 were landmarks; the latter created such new designations as "park preserve." More recently, designating tracts of federal land as "national conservation areas" or "national recreation areas" (the latter expanding upon the designations given earlier to such areas as Lake Mead) has gained popularity in Congress. While neither is generally as strictly preservationist as wilderness, both are considerably less resource-exploitive than traditional multiple use designations. These and other related legal developments have led commentators to label (as a trend rather than a general truth) the era since 1964 as the "Age of Preservation."

6. THE LEGAL OFFICES

An agency with special pertinence to public land law is the Office of the Solicitor in the Department of the Interior. The Solicitor is general counsel to the Secretary. The Solicitor's Office houses all the lawyers who give legal advice to the Department's disparate land management agencies. Lawyers in the Solicitor's Office write opinions, draft regulations, and render legal advice to the land management agencies. The Solicitor's Office does not, however, represent the Department in court; that task is left to the Department of Justice. Although the General Counsel in the Department of Agriculture serves a similar function for the Forest Service, the concentration of resource issues in Interior and the wealth of Solicitor's Opinions (collected in Interior Decisions) mean that the Interior Solicitor's Office is a primary source of law on the public lands.*

Another important entity for lawyers involved in public land law is the Interior Board of Land Appeals (IBLA), the major organ of the Interior Department's Office of Hearings and Appeals. Since 1970, several kinds of decisions of land management agencies (especially BLM) may be appealed to the IBLA, which possesses broad authority delegated by the Secretary to decide such appeals. Many of the roughly 1000 appeals filed each year with the IBLA involve mineral resources (including royalty disputes), but the agency's jurisdiction also encompasses a wide variety of subjects including grazing, special use permits, wilderness review, and wild horses and burros. The IBLA usually sits in panels of three judges each (although en banc decisions are possible). Judges are appointed by the Secretary, and IBLA jurisdiction and processes are set out in 43 C.F.R. Part 4. The Forest Service also has quite an elaborate internal administrative appeal process, but it is not lodged in a separate division. Rather, the appellate chain leads from the Supervisors of individual forests through the Regional Foresters to the Chief of the Forest Service, and ultimately to the Secretary of Agriculture.

7. THE UNITED STATES CONGRESS

Since the nation's founding, Congress has played a critical role in public land law and policy making. Through much of the nineteenth century, the importance of the federal lands—as a source of revenue, for military strategy, and as an element in the nation's "Manifest Destiny" to spread from sea to sea—ensured close legislative scrutiny. Influential congressional representatives were active on public lands issues, not only in the halls of Congress, but in the courts (representing private citizens in public lands disputes) and (ethical standards being somewhat more lax than they are today) as private investors and speculators. Daniel Webster, Thomas Hart Benton, Henry Clay and other legislative giants left their mark on public land policy in many ways. In the latter part of the century,

---

* Coauthor John Leshy was Solicitor of the Interior Department from 1993 to 2001.

Senator William Stewart of Nevada (the principal drafter of the Mining Law, who made a fortune in various mining ventures and as a lawyer representing claimants) and Congressman George Julian of Indiana were perhaps the most influential, although a number of others, such as Senator (and later Secretary of the Interior) Henry Teller of Colorado, were also prominent.

Following completion of the task of admitting the first 48 states in 1912, the priority of public lands issues on the congressional agenda was somewhat reduced. The closing of this frontier coincided with the emergence of the United States as a world power, and other competing responsibilities captured more congressional attention. Throughout the past hundred years, in fact, public lands issues have been viewed on Capitol Hill as something of a sideshow, with representatives from the remainder of the nation often tending to defer to members from the western states.

The committee structure in Congress plays a crucial role in all legislation, and public land policy is no exception. Under various names and with varied jurisdictions, there were almost from the beginning specific committees in both houses of Congress with primary responsibility over public land legislation. For most of the nation's existence (from 1805 to 1951 in the House, and from 1816 to 1948 in the Senate) these were called committees on Public Lands or Public Lands & Surveys. Separate committees on mines and mining existed in each house from 1865 until 1947. Thereafter, the Public Lands and Mining Committees in each house were collapsed (in 1948 in the Senate, and in 1951 in the House) into committees on "Interior and Insular Affairs." The House Interior Committee became the House Natural Resources Committee in 1992. Its counterpart in the Senate became the Committee on Energy and Natural Resources in 1977. These committees (usually referred to as "resource committees" for convenience) generally are "stacked" with westerners for good reason: Westerners actively seek such committee assignments to enhance their influence over issues of concern back home, and non-westerners tended to avoid the assignments. As a result, the chairs of these committees, commonly the two most influential legislators on public lands issues in the entire Congress, were usually (though not always) from the West. Some have had great impact, such as Senator Henry M. "Scoop" Jackson of Washington (chair of the Senate Committee from 1963 until 1981), and Congressmen Wayne Aspinall of Colorado and Morris Udall of Arizona (chairs of the House Committee from 1959 to 1973 and from 1977 to 1991, respectively).

Like the public land policy universe in general, however, the congressional committee jurisdictional allocation is quite untidy. Legislation dealing with most aspects of the Forest Service is primarily the responsibility of the agriculture committees in both houses, although jurisdiction on some issues, such as wilderness designation in the national forests, is shared with the resources committees. Wildlife issues on federal lands are partly the responsibility of committees other than the resources committees. Of course, the appropriations committees of both houses can have great say in public land policy, both through their power over the purse-strings, and through the increasingly common technique of attaching substantive legislative "riders" to appropriations bills. Significant legislative struggles in recent years—over such issues as whether to prohibit land patenting under the Mining Law, whether to increase grazing fees on public lands, whether to drill for oil in the Arctic National Wildlife Refuge, and how much road-building and timber harvesting should take place in the national forests—have taken place primarily in the appropriations process.

Some public land legislation is generic, applicable to all lands in a particular management system (such as the Federal Land Policy and Management Act or the National Forest Management Act). But some, such as legislation creating a particular national park, is specific to a particular state. In recent years, something of a trend has emerged to package certain kinds of legislation (such as that designating lands of a particular agency as wilderness, or designating a cluster of wild and scenic rivers) on a state-wide basis. Congress traditionally will not enact public land legislation that primarily affects a single state without the support (or at least the acquiescence) of most, if not all, of the state's congressional delegation. The 1980 Alaska legislation recounted immediately below was a rare exception; the Alaska congressional delegation stoutly resisted it but in the end was defeated by a broad national coalition spearheaded by environmental groups.

8. THE SPECIAL CASE OF ALASKA

The public land law eras that played themselves out over the course of two centuries in the Lower 48 States were recreated, compressed, and intensified in Alaska. The high-stakes events in the largest public lands state—"The Last Pork Chop," as one writer dubbed it—can only be briefly summarized here.

The word Alaska means "Great Land," but the territory was long known as "Seward's Folly" after the Secretary of State who engineered its purchase from Russia in 1867. Because of Alaska's daunting remoteness and clime, the new sovereign did little with it for many decades. Alaska became a federal judicial district in 1884 and a territory in 1912. Alaskans, like other territorial residents before them, chafed under rule from Washington, D.C. but their cries of "colonialism" were perhaps even stronger. When statehood came to Alaska in 1959, its 375 million acres (well over twice the size of Texas) remained almost completely in federal ownership because only a relatively negligible amount of land was suitable for home-steading or other disposition under the public land laws then existing. Meanwhile, over the years since Alaska was purchased, Congress had given almost no attention to Alaska Natives. No treaties with them had been negotiated and almost no reservations had been established by statute or executive order.

Alaskans drove the most successful statehood bargain of all. Under the Alaska Enabling Act, the new state government won the right to select 104 million acres of federal land. State officials promptly ordered surveys to determine the choicest parcels. At about the same time, rumors of extensive oil and gas deposits were bruited about as mineral companies conducted exploration programs. In the mid–1960's, Alaska Natives began to protest in earnest, taking the position that their aboriginal title had never been disturbed and that any administrative transfers of title to the state or the mining industry would violate Native property rights. Interior Secretary Stewart Udall listened and, in 1966, acted. In a bold stroke he suspended the issuance of almost all patents and mineral leases. The pressure heightened in 1968 when the discovery of massive oil deposits on state-selected lands at Prudhoe Bay on Alaska's north slope was confirmed. Udall then withdrew all unreserved lands in Alaska from all forms of entry (Public Land Order 4582, the 1968 "Superfreeze") until Congress had resolved the Native claims.

It took three more years before the Alaska Native Claims Settlement Act of 1971 (ANCSA), 43 U.S.C. § 1601–1624, became law. Paving the way for the Alaska Pipeline, ANCSA extinguished all Native title, granted Alaska Natives the right to select 44 million acres of federal land in the state, provided Natives nearly $1 billion in federal funds, and allowed state selections to resume. The 1971 Act also reflected the emerging power of the modern environmental movement. ANCSA's so-called "d(2)" provision, 43 U.S.C. § 1616(d)(2), authorized the Secretary of the Interior to withdraw up to 80 million acres of land that might merit inclusion in four "national interest" systems (national parks, forests, wildlife refuges, and wild rivers). Thus, after ANCSA, four major potential sets of landowners—the state, Alaska Native corporations, the mineral companies, and the United States—were undergoing overlapping and conflicting selection processes involving hundreds of millions of acres. The d(2) "national interest" withdrawals were frustrating to those Alaskans who wanted no impediments to mineral development.

By the terms of ANCSA, the d(2) withdrawals expired on December 16, 1978. Although Congress had labored hard, it had failed to complete work on conservation legislation that would have protected the lands permanently. Faced with the prospect of these lands being opened back up to exploitation, President Jimmy Carter and Secretary of the Interior Cecil Andrus executed massive, overlapping withdrawals and Antiquities Act reservations that effectively extended the d(2) withdrawals and staved off mineral development and state selections of these federal lands. Congress finally finished the legislation in a lame-duck session after the 1980 elections and on December 2, 1980, President Carter signed the Alaska National Interest Lands Conservation Act (ANILCA) into law. This major and complex legislation (it encompasses 181 pages in statutes-at-large) is found at 16 U.S.C. § 3101–3233 and in scattered sections of titles 16 and 43.

Superseding (but confirming the effectiveness of) the Carter withdrawals, ANILCA allocated more than 103 million acres, mostly former BLM lands, to the federal conservation systems. It added 43.5 million acres to the National Park System, 53.7 million acres to the National Wildlife Refuge System, and 56.4 million acres to the National Wilderness Preservation System. Thirteen rivers were added to the National Wild and Scenic Rivers System. Congress made two special designations for BLM lands, the 1.2 million acre Steese Conservation Area, and the 1 million acre White

Mountains National Recreation Area. The acres allocated to specific preservation systems far exceeded the 103 million acres actually affected because of some double classifications; for example, large amounts of the new national parks and wildlife refuges were also simultaneously designated as wilderness.

ANILCA multiplied the size of the major preservation systems several times over. In one fell swoop it doubled the size of the national park system; tripled the size of the national wildlife refuge system, and quadrupled the size of the national wilderness preservation system. Similarly, ANILCA made significant alterations in the amount of lands administered by federal agencies nationally. The following changes in total agency land holdings, according to the most recent available figures, have been wrought primarily by ANILCA and by state and Native selections of BLM lands in Alaska:

Federal Agency Land Holdings (by millions of acres)

Agency	1978	2005
Bureau of Land Management	481	262
Forest Service	189	193
Fish and Wildlife Service	31	96
National Park Service	27	79
All other agencies	48	23
TOTAL PUBLIC LANDS	775.9	653

ANILCA also includes many provisions dealing with Alaska public lands generally, not just lands added to the preservation systems. It implements a preference for rural residents to engage in subsistence hunting and fishing, including traditional uses of snowmobiles and motorboats, on federal lands in Alaska. It allows many existing uses in the new wilderness areas, including cabins and access by airplanes and motorboats, to continue. Detailed provisions govern mineral development on ANILCA lands and timber harvesting in Alaska's national forests.

D. Perspectives on Public Land and Resources Law

The following excerpts offer a taste of the secondary literature that synthesizes many of the legal and policy issues discussed in the chapters to follow. It may be helpful to read through this commentary now to get a sense of the broader issues that cut across many resource disputes. However, a closer examination of the ideas expressed in this section may wait for encounters with particular cases that raise the concerns discussed. The casebook will refer back to these excerpts in opportune places. Most of the notes following cases in later chapters suggest consideration of incremental law reform. The readings below are intended to be more provocative in their prescriptions.

Aldo Leopold was an early ranger in the U.S. Forest Service, an avid hunter and angler, the father of wildlife management science, co-founder of The Wilderness Society, and an inspiration to countless through his collection of essays in the posthumously published book excerpted below. His ideas continue to shape law, the goals of conservation organizations, and many public land administrators.

Aldo Leopold, The Land Ethic

A SAND COUNTY ALMANAC (1949, 1977).

When God-like Odysseus returned from the wars in Troy, he hanged all on one rope a dozen slave-girls of his household whom he suspected of misbehavior during his absence.

This hanging involved no question of propriety. The girls were property. The disposal of property was then, as now, a matter of expediency, not of right and wrong.

Concepts of right and wrong were not lacking from Odysseus' Greece: witness the fidelity of his wife through the long years before at last his black-prowed galleys clove the wine-dark seas for home. The ethical structure of that day covered wives, but had not yet been extended to human chattels. During the three thousand years which have since elapsed, ethical criteria have been extended to many fields of conduct, with corresponding shrinkages in those judged by expediency only.

The Ethical Sequence

This extension of ethics, so far studied only by philosophers, is actually a process in ecological evolution. Its sequences may be described in ecological as well as in philosophical terms. An ethic, ecologically, is a limitation on freedom of action in the struggle for existence. An ethic, philosophically, is a differentiation of social from anti-social conduct. These are two definitions of one thing. The thing has its origin in the tendency of interdependent individuals or groups to evolve modes of co-operation. The ecologist calls these symbioses. Politics and economics are advanced symbioses in which the original free-for-all competition has been replaced, in part, by co-operative mechanisms with an ethical content.

The complexity of co-operative mechanisms has increased with population density, and with the efficiency of tools. It was simpler, for example, to define the anti-social uses of sticks and stones in the days of the mastodons than of bullets and billboards in the age of motors.

The first ethics dealt with the relation between individuals; the Mosaic Decalogue is an example. Later accretions dealt with the relation between the individual and society. The golden rule tries to integrate the individual to society; democracy to integrate social organization to the individual.

There is as yet no ethic dealing with man's relation to land and to the animals and plants which grow upon it. Land, like Odysseus' slave-girls, is still property. The land-relation is still strictly economic, entailing privileges but not obligations.

The extension of ethics to this third element in human environment is, if I read the evidence correctly, an evolutionary possibility and an ecological necessity. It is the third step in a sequence. The first two have already been taken. Individual thinkers since the days of Ezekiel and Isaiah have asserted that the despoliation of land is not only inexpedient but wrong. Society, however, has not yet affirmed their belief. I regard the present conservation movement as the embryo of such an affirmation.

An ethic may be regarded as a mode of guidance for meeting ecological situations so new or intricate, or involving such deferred reactions, that the path of social expediency is not discernible to the average individual. Animal instincts are modes of guidance for the individual in meeting such situations. Ethics are possibly a kind of community instinct in-the-making.

The Community Concept

All ethics so far evolved rest upon a single premise; that the individual is a member of a community of interdependent parts. His instincts prompt him to compete for his place in the community, but his ethics prompt him also to co-operate (perhaps in order that there may be a place to compete for).

The land ethic simply enlarges the boundaries of the community to include soils, waters, plants, and animals, or collectively: the land.

This sounds simple: do we not already sing our love for and obligation to the land of the free and the home of the brave? Yes, but just what and whom do we love? Certainly not the soil, which we are sending helter-skelter downriver. Certainly not the waters, which we assume have no function except to turn turbines, float barges, and carry off sewage. Certainly not the plants, of which we exterminate whole communities without batting an eye. Certainly not the animals, of which we have already extirpated many of the largest and most beautiful species. A land ethic of course cannot prevent the alteration, management, and use of the "resources," but it does affirm their right to continued existence, and, at least in spots, their continued existence in a natural state.

In short, a land ethic changes the role of Homo sapiens from conqueror of the land-community to plain member and citizen of it. It implies respect for his fellow-members, and also respect for the community as such.

In human history, we have learned (I hope) that the conqueror role is eventually self-defeating. Why? Because it is implicit in such a role that the conqueror knows, ex cathedra, just what makes the community clock tick, and just what and who is valuable, and what and who is worthless, in community life. It always turns out that he knows neither, and this is why his conquests eventually defeat themselves.

In the biotic community, a parallel situation exists. Abraham knew exactly what the land was for: it was to drip milk and honey into Abraham's mouth. At the present moment, the assurance with which we regard this assumption is inverse to the degree of our education.

* * *

To sum up: a system of conservation based solely on economic self-interest is hopelessly lopsided. It tends to ignore, and thus eventually to eliminate, many elements in the land community that lack commercial value, but that are (so far as we know) essential to its healthy functioning.

It assumes, falsely, I think, that the economic parts of the biotic clock will function without the uneconomic parts. It tends to relegate to government many functions eventually too large, too complex, or too widely dispersed to be performed by government.

An ethical obligation on the part of the private owner is the only visible remedy for these situations.

The Land Pyramid

An ethic to supplement and guide the economic relation to land presupposes the existence of some mental image of land as a biotic mechanism. We can be ethical only in relation to something we can see, feel, understand, love, or otherwise have faith in.

The image commonly employed in conservation education is "the balance of nature." For reasons too lengthy to detail here, this figure of speech fails to describe accurately what little we know about the land mechanism. A much truer image is the one employed in ecology: the biotic pyramid. I shall first sketch the pyramid as a symbol of land, and later develop some of its implications in terms of land-use.

Plants absorb energy from the sun. This energy flows through a circuit called the biota, which may be represented by a pyramid consisting of layers. The bottom layer is the soil. A plant layer rests on the soil, an insect layer on the plants, a bird and rodent layer on the insects, and so on up through various animal groups to the apex layer, which consists of the larger carnivores.

The species of a layer are alike not in where they came from, or in what they look like, but rather in what they eat. Each successive layer depends on those below it for food and often for other services, and each in turn furnishes food and services to those above. Proceeding upward, each successive layer decreases in numerical abundance. Thus, for every carnivore there are hundreds of his prey, thousands of their prey, millions of insects, uncountable plants. The pyramidal form of the system reflects this numerical progression from apex to base. Man shares an intermediate layer with the bears, raccoons, and squirrels which eat both meat and vegetables.

* * *

Land, then, is not merely soil; it is a fountain of energy flowing through a circuit of soils, plants, and animals. Food chains are the living channels which conduct energy upward; death and decay return it to the soil. The circuit is not closed; some energy is dissipated in decay, some is added by absorption from the air, some is stored in soils, peats, and long-lived forests; but it is a sustained circuit, like a slowly augmented revolving fund of life. There is always a net loss by downhill wash, but this is normally small and offset by the decay of rocks. It is deposited in the ocean and, in the course of geological time, raised to form new lands and new pyramids.

* * *

The process of altering the pyramid for human occupation releases stored energy, and this often gives rise, during the pioneering period, to a deceptive exuberance of plant and animal life, both wild and tame. These releases of biotic capital tend to becloud or postpone the penalties of violence.

* * *

The Outlook

It is inconceivable to me that an ethical relation to land can exist without love, respect, and admiration for land, and a high regard for its value. By value, I of course mean something far broader than mere economic value; I mean value in the philosophical sense.

Perhaps the most serious obstacle impeding the evolution of a land ethic is the fact that our educational and economic system is headed away from, rather than toward, an intense consciousness of land. Your true modern is separated from the land by many middlemen, and by innumerable physical gadgets. He has no vital relation to it; to him it is the space between cities on which crops grow. Turn him loose for a day on the land, and if the spot does not happen to be a golf links or a "scenic" area, he is bored stiff. If crops could be raised by hydroponics instead of farming, it would suit him very well. Synthetic substitutes for wood, leather, wool, and other natural land products suit him better than the originals. In short, land is something he has "outgrown."

* * *

The case for a land ethic would appear hopeless but for the minority which is in obvious revolt against these "modern" trends.

The "key-log" which must be moved to release the evolutionary process for an ethic is simply this: quit thinking about decent land-use as solely an economic problem. Examine each question in terms of what is ethically and esthetically right, as well as what is economically expedient. A thing is right when it tends to preserve the integrity, stability, and beauty of the biotic community. It is wrong when it tends otherwise.

* * *

The mechanism of operation is the same for any ethic: social approbation for right actions: social disapproval for wrong actions.

By and large, our present problem is one of attitudes and implements. We are remodeling the Alhambra with a steam-shovel, and we are proud of our yardage. We shall hardly relinquish the shovel, which after all has many good points, but we are in need of gentler and more objective criteria for its successful use.

NOTES AND QUESTIONS

1. Does Leopold's "land ethic" provide a realistic touchstone for modern lawmaking? What evidence would you expect to see in a society's laws that indicates progress toward Leopold's ethic? Is it possible to measure integrity, stability, and beauty?

2.   Is the Leopold land ethic the same as allegiance to a particular place, or "homeland"? Many disputes discussed in this book involve local residents pitted against others with competing visions for the future of an area. Is an ethic of place necessarily a "land ethic"?

3.   Roderick Nash, an influential historian of the American environmental movement, argues that:

> environmental ethics [is] a logical extrapolation of powerful liberal traditions as old as the republic. The American past contains a highly visible liberation movement with interesting similarities to contemporary environmentalism. If the abolition of slavery marked the limits of American liberalism in the mid-nineteenth century, perhaps biocentrism and environmental ethics are at the cutting edge of liberal thought in the late twentieth.

Roderick Nash, THE RIGHTS OF NATURE 200 (1989). How apt is the liberation analogy for a movement concerned less with the sanctity of individual parts of an ecosystem than with the healthy functioning of the whole?

4.   Leopold suggests that the root of our ecological problems lies in our view of land use "as solely an economic problem." As you work through the materials in this casebook, consider whether modern public land and resources law views disputes in purely economic terms. To the extent that the law now considers a wider range of concerns, does that represent progress toward the "land ethic"?

Although Garrett Hardin was not trained as an economist, his famous article, excerpted below, offers an economic framework for understanding many resource management conflicts. It has had a profound influence on American law. Many of the disputes examined in this casebook can be categorized as a tragedy of the commons. As you read Hardin's description, and then one potential solution by Stroup and Baden, consider what conditions set the stage for the tragedy.

Garrett Hardin, The Tragedy of the Commons
162 SCIENCE 1243 (1968).

The tragedy of the commons develops in this way. Picture a pasture open to all. It is to be expected that each herdsman will try to keep as many cattle as possible on the commons. Such an arrangement may work reasonably satisfactorily for centuries because tribal wars, poaching, and disease keep the numbers of both man and beast well below the carrying capacity of the land. Finally, however, comes the day of reckoning, that is, the day when the long-desired goal of social stability becomes a reality. At this point, the inherent logic of the commons remorselessly generates tragedy.

As a rational being, each herdsman seeks to maximize his gain. Explicitly or implicitly, more or less consciously, he asks. "What is the utility to me of adding one more animal to my herd?" This utility has one negative and one positive component.

1) The positive component is a function of the increment of one animal. Since the herdsman receives all the proceeds from the sale of the additional animal, the positive utility is nearly +1.

2) The negative component is a function of the additional overgrazing, created by one more animal. Since, however, the effects of overgrazing are shared by all the herdsmen, the negative utility for any particular decision-making herdsman is only a fraction of –1.

Adding together the component partial utilities, the rational herdsman concludes that the only sensible course for him to pursue is to add another animal to his herd. And another; and another. * * * But this is the conclusion reached by each and every rational herdsman sharing a commons. Therein is the tragedy. Each man is locked into a system that compels him to increase his herd without limit—in a world that is limited. Ruin is the destination toward which all men rush, each pursuing his own best interest in a society that believes in the freedom of the commons. Freedom in a commons brings ruin to all. * * *

In an approximate way, the logic of the commons has been understood for a long time, perhaps since the discovery of agriculture or the invention of private property in real estate. But it is understood mostly only in special cases which are not sufficiently generalized. Even at this late date, cattle-men leasing national land on the western ranges demonstrate no more than an ambivalent understanding, in constantly pressuring federal authorities to increase the head count to the point where overgrazing produces erosion and weed-dominance. * * *

The National Parks present another instance of the working out of the tragedy of the commons. At present, they are open to all, without limit. The parks themselves are limited in extent—there is only one Yosemite Valley—whereas population seems to grow without limit. The values that visitors seek in the parks are steadily eroded. Plainly, we must soon cease to treat the parks as commons or they will be of no value to anyone.

What shall we do? We have several options. We might sell them off as private property. We might keep them as public property, but allocate the right to enter them. The allocation might be on the basis of wealth, by the use of an auction system. It might be on the basis of merit, as defined by some agreed upon standards. It might be by lottery. Or it might be on a first-come, first-served basis, administered to long queues. These, I think, are all the reasonable possibilities. They are all objectionable. But we must choose—or acquiesce in the destruction of the commons that we call our National Parks.

Richard L. Stroup & John A. Baden
Natural Resources: Bureaucratic Myths and Environmental Management 118–19, 123–27 (1983).

When well-trained economists look at the [Forest Service] planning process, they see many problems in the way values are assigned, in the way criteria are set, and in the lack of distinction between the two. These problems can be easily explained. They are caused by the lack of good data inherent in a failure to price outputs as well as inputs, in a failure to recognize the opportunity cost of capital, and to the pressures that must come to bear when decision makers are held accountable only through the political system. The wonder is that the national forests have been managed as well as they have.

Privatizing the national forests should end many of the obstacles to good management. Not only would decision makers be given larger amounts of validated and continuously updated information, but political obstacles to efficient management would largely disappear. Perhaps just as important, environmentalists, timber producers, miners, recreationists, and others who make demands on the Forest Service would quickly move away from their carping and faultfinding toward positive and constructive accommodation.

Whenever someone owns a piece of land, everyone with a potential interest in it begins to act *as if* they cared about everyone else. Each party's goals can best be reached by close, constructive, and even imaginative cooperation with all other parties. This results whenever trade occurs by the rule of willing consent, for such trade must be mutually beneficial. This process contrasts sharply with debates over public land, where the name of the game is discrediting the other side's views and rejecting compromises unless defeat appears imminent. When the price is zero, each side naturally wants it all.

* * *

* * * We believe that it does not matter very much who owns a resource when it comes to determining how that resource will be used. Any owner, whatever his goals, will find those goals frequently met more fully by cooperation with others through trade. Since dollars, additional wilderness lands, buffer zones for existing wilderness, and other items attainable through trade are desired by any potential owner, it follows that even a zealot who owns the land can gain by listening carefully and discussing constructively the alternatives proposed by nonowners who desire wilderness, mineral, or other values from the landowner. Until all rights are (for the moment) optimally allocated among competing and compatible uses and users, further trade can make all parties to the trade better off in the pursuit of their various goals.

* * *

The point is that if a mining company bought an entire forest, it would have every incentive to maximize the value of the 98 percent that it didn't really want by carefully considering the amenity effects of its exploration and mining operations. Similarly, if the Audubon Society submitted the high bid on ecologically critical portions of all the resold part of the forest, it would carefully consider its information and preferences. Demanding more only increases the required bid. The major reason we expect improvement in forest management is that a market system holds every private owner accountable to the rest of society by having to outbid everyone else—

or reject others' bids—for every alternative forgone (or destroyed) on the land.

* * * But what about the individual who does not want to buy a part of the national forest but still wants access? Consider what people from Montana do when they want to use facilities in New York City but do not want to purchase real estate there. Just as some of the living space in New York is rented by the day or by the month, some of the private land in our country is leased by the hour, the week, or the year. Some people will pay a higher price for vacations filled with amenities, and many owners of the world's resources are happy to accommodate such vacationers. Access to a unique ecological site may be compared with access to a Rembrandt painting. In both cases, the admission fee can make it worthwhile for the owner to share the asset and, indeed, take elaborate precautions against its depreciation.

A key feature of our proposal is that the immense forest wealth of our nation would be more broadly shared among all citizens. Instead of a few favored firms and individuals enjoying the benefits of the forest, everyone would benefit from the revenues. Those revenues would capture the high bidder's estimate of the present capitalized value of all future benefits that could be derived from the land.

How large would the revenues from the sale of the national forests be? No one really knows. But it is not the *average* person's value that would determine the sale price of any tract. It is, rather, the most optimistic view, shared by the minimum number of people necessary to win the auction for a piece of land. * * *

* * * With the constructive attitudes and imaginative entrepreneurship unleashed by implementation of our proposal, the national forests could be sold for several hundred billion dollars.

* * *

Our proposal would help the American productivity problem * * *. [I]t would make better use of the mineral, timber, recreation, and amenity values found in the public forests. * * * Perhaps as important to the future of the nation would be a fundamental change in attitude. From the fierce and never-ending battles of lobbyist pressures and alarmist rhetoric would emerge a positive sum game. Rewards would be given for imaginative and constructive solutions to resource conflicts rather than for carefully articulated pleas and raw political clout. The formidable power of American entrepreneurs would be shifted from the negative sum political arena to the positive sum private arena, where every change must be mutually beneficial.

NOTES AND QUESTIONS

1.   Stroup and Baden offer one possible response to the tragedy of the commons that Hardin describes: create a better system of private property rights to eliminate the open commons. Would it work as well for allocating the scarce recreational resources of the national parks as it would to

allocate range on grazing land? What about for resources that yield no direct revenue, such as biodiversity? As we shall see, privatization through property disposition has been an important response to the problems of commons management on the public lands. Can markets capture the value of environmental amenities currently enjoyed diffusely by millions of people? Consider also the issues of equity that arise from private solutions to public commons management.

2.   How would the privatization solution initially assign property interests in the environment? Should custom and history play a role? Or, is auction to highest bidder the best approach? If nobody bids for a particular resource, does that mean that it lacks value? Is Leopold's land ethic completely at odds with privatization?

3.   Hardin goes on to suggest that "mutual coercion, mutually agreed upon" is the solution to the commons problem. Do the legal tools of legislation, administrative rulemaking, and judicial determination each represent forms of "mutual coercion, mutually agreed upon"?

4.   Elinor Ostrom is a leading scholar documenting the various ways in which people sharing a resource self-organize to avoid tragic outcomes. Self-initiated development of norms and local, self-organized institutions can protect common resources from over-exploitation. As you read the cases in this book, consider how the law honors (or runs roughshod over) local customs and non-governmental organizations that do not carry the official imprimatur of government. *See* Elinor Ostrom, GOVERNING THE COMMONS (1990).

5.   C.S. Lewis wrote that "what we call Man's power over Nature turns out to be a power exercised by some men over other men with Nature as its instrument." THE ABOLITION OF MAN (1947). Consider this dimension of property disposition and coercive regulation in public land and resources law: "Conquest basically involved the drawing of lines on a map, the definition and allocation of ownership * * *, and the evolution of land from matter to property. The process had two stages: the initial drawing of the lines * * * and the subsequent giving of meaning and power to those lines." Patricia Nelson Limerick, THE LEGACY OF CONQUEST (1987).

The next excerpt describes ecosystem management, a fuzzy term that categorizes many of the new approaches to resource management considered in the chapters that follow. As you read, consider the value judgments inherent in the components of ecosystem management considered by legal institutions. Also, consider how global warming complicates all of the following approaches to managing public resources.

Robert B. Keiter, Ecology and the Public Domain
KEEPING FAITH WITH NATURE: ECOSYSTEMS, DEMOCRACY, AND AMERICA'S PUBLIC LANDS 71–79 (2003).

On Definitions, Principles, And Law

Ecosystem management is still a young and evolving concept—one that has not yet been captured in a succinct and tidy sound bite. Most commentators agree, however, on several key propositions that go to the core of emerging ecosystem management policies. With an extinction crisis looming, biodiversity conservation and ecosystem restoration are major ecosystem management concerns. But the human presence on the landscape cannot be ignored, which means that economic, social, and political concerns must be factored into any ecological management policy. To address these interrelated concerns, ecosystem management has embraced sustainability as a paramount policy goal. Sustainability is defined broadly: it includes both ecological and economic sustainability as measured by the needs of both current and future generations. To achieve these sustainability objectives, planning and management decisions must be framed in ecologically relevant geographical and temporal terms, unconstrained by conventional boundary lines, jurisdictional jealousies, or short-term political, economic, or social considerations. Management on this enlarged scale requires collaborative, cross-jurisdictional planning protocols as well as adaptive management approaches. In combination, these propositions represent a dramatic departure from traditional natural resource management institutions and policies, and introduce controversial new complexities into the public land policy equation.

Numerous general definitions of ecosystem management have been proffered, but none has yet been universally accepted or endorsed. According to the Ecological Society of America, ecosystem management is "management driven by explicit goals, executed by policies, protocols, and practices, and made adaptable by monitoring and research based on our best understanding of the ecological interactions and processes necessary to sustain ecosystem composition, structure, and function." Another comprehensive definition posits that "ecosystem management integrates scientific knowledge of ecological relationships within a complex sociopolitical values framework towards the general goal of protecting native ecosystem integrity over the long term." Yet another definition emphasizes ecological goals: "Ecosystem management focuses on the condition of the [ecosystem] with goals of maintaining soil productivity, gene conservation, biodiversity, landscape patterns, and the array of ecological processes." Another definition, however, downplays the concept's scientific origins and goals: "the application of ecological and social information, options, and constraints to achieve desired social benefits within a defined geographic area over a specified period." Other suggested definitions have tended to emphasize either the biological or social-political aspects of the concept depending largely on the proponent's professional affiliation or disciplinary background.

Not surprisingly, a less striking diversity in views can be found in the original federal agency definitions of ecosystem management. According to the Interagency Ecosystem Management Task Force, the ecosystem approach was "a method for sustaining or restoring natural systems and their functions and values. It is goal driven, and it is based on a collaboratively developed vision of desired future conditions that integrates ecological economic and social factors. It is applied within a geographic framework defined primarily by ecological boundaries." * * * [Professor Keiter then surveys the different ecosystem management definitions of the public land agencies and concludes that while they] generally agreed on the goal of maintaining sustainable ecosystem, they did not all place the same emphasis on related economic concerns—a clear reflection of the divergent statutory mandates governing each agency.

Because these proffered definitions are so general, the ecosystem management concept has also been defined in terms of governing principles. First, to ensure healthy natural resource systems and to address pressing species extinction concerns, a primary goal (objective) of ecosystem management is to maintain and restore biodiversity and sustainable ecosystems. Second, because people are a part of nature and human values inform any natural resource policy, ecosystem management goals must be socially defined—ordinarily through broad public participation—to incorporate ecological, economic, and social concerns into workable sustainability strategies. Third, because species and ecological processes transcend jurisdictional boundaries, ecosystem management requires coordination among federal agencies and collaboration with state, local, and tribal governments as well as opportunities for public involvement in planning and decision processes. Fourth, given the dynamic, nonequilibrium nature of ecosystems and the unpredictability of related disturbance processes, ecosystem management requires management on broad spatial and temporal scales in order to accommodate ecological change and to address multiple rather than single resources. Fifth, given the important role science plays in understanding natural systems, ecosystem management is based on integrated, interdisciplinary, and current scientific information that can be used to address risk and uncertainty. Sixth, because ecosystem management and accompanying science are still experimental, ecosystem management requires an adaptive management approach that includes establishing baseline conditions, monitoring, reevaluation, and adjustment to reflect changes in scientific knowledge as well as evolving human concerns.

In each instance, these governing ecosystem management principles represent a stark departure from traditional resource management has emphasized the production of commodities and services. Whereas ecosystem management contemplates broad public involvement in defining sustainability goals, traditional resource management has generally relied on the technical expertise of agency officials to establish priorities and strategies. Whereas ecosystem management disregards administrative boundaries and promotes institutional coordination, traditional resource management has been highly deferential to jurisdictional boundaries and agency officials have jealously guarded their own managerial prerogatives. Whereas ecosystem management acknowledges that resource systems are dynamic and nonequilibrium in character, traditional management has taken a more static and deterministic view of the landscape. Whereas ecosystem management views natural resources in a holistic, interrelated, and systematic context, the traditional management approach has focused on individual resources and short-range time frames. Whereas ecosystem management employs an adaptive approach to establishing resource policies and priorities, traditional management has usually established firm production targets and resisted subsequent modifications in order to promote predictability. While not exhaustive, this comparison between the two policies demonstrates how an ecological perspective alters the narrow and rigid management approaches that have dominated natural resource policy.

* * *

The concept of ecosystem management offers land managers an opportunity to break down the humanity-nature or utilitarian-preservation dichotomy that has characterized natural resource policy for the past century. Even the words *ecosystem management* imply a merging of the natural and human: *ecosystem* suggests a natural setting shaped primarily by ecological processes, while *management* contemplates a human presence and involvement in shaping the natural world. Utilitarianism or multiple-use management, with its strong commitment to efficiency and scientific planning, has gradually acknowledged that human interests in natural resources cannot be defined solely in economic terms but must also include biological, aesthetic, and other considerations. The preservationist movement, despite its long-standing commitment to aesthetics, has been influenced profoundly by recent scientific developments; it is now using the ecological sciences to protect biodiversity, natural processes, and linkage corridors in a dynamic landscape setting. Both philosophical schools have generally accepted the cogent scientific and philosophical arguments supporting the need to safeguard all species—not just charismatic megafauna—against extinction. And managers from the public land agencies—whether multiple-use or preservationist in orientation—are all well aware that resource decisions inevitably trigger repercussions beyond their immediate boundaries, which can also affect their own management options and strategies. In short, ecosystem management concepts are being embraced by both the utilitarian and preservation schools of conservation thought. Whether this new ecological perspective can finally fuse these two divergent philosophies together will depend on related political developments and how these new principles are applied on the ground.

Criticisms And Challenges

The emerging doctrine of ecosystem management cuts profoundly against many of the long-standing assumptions undergirding natural resource law and policy. Property rights and most natural resource laws are based upon the notion of fixed boundaries, which have rarely been defined in ecological terms. The very concept of legal ownership implies certainty and stability, but the nature of ecosystems is instability and disequilibrium, requiring flexible management strategies based on adaptive experimentation. The existing legal order is generally designed to ensure prompt and tangible financial returns, while ecological management gives priority to biodiversity conservation and often requires managerial forbearance. Critics have seized upon these and other problems in an effort to discredit new ecosystem management concepts.

One key point of contention is whether ecosystem management has any substantive content or whether it is merely a process. Noting that many ecosystem management definitions give priority to biodiversity conservation and ecosystem integrity goals, critics assert that ecosystem management is really just a poorly disguised effort to elevate environmental protection goals above commodity production on the public domain. They reject this transparent shift in management priorities, arguing that it violates existing legal standards governing public lands, has not been endorsed by the general public, and ignores important countervailing economic and social considerations. Other analysts, taking a more circumspect view, suggest that neither ecosystem protection nor biodiversity conservation can properly be regarded as a process that enables natural resource managers to identify specific production, protection, and restoration goals. These goals, however, are not inherent in ecosystem management but reflect "desired social benefits" that should be "defined by society, not scientists." Under this approach, biodiversity conservation and ecological preservation may (or may not) be a desired social benefit that emerges from ecosystem management processes.

A second major point of contention focuses on the inherent difficulty in defining and using ecosystem boundaries for management purposes. Because the ecosystem concept originally was conceived as a theoretical construct for research purposes to establish experimental boundaries, critics contend that ecosystems are ill-suited for land management purposes. They note that the ecosystem concept is inherently malleable and can be defined on multiple scales and in diverse settings. If ecosystem management is applied on a large scale (which is what most proponents envisage), then critics fear that regulatory chaos will ensue. On the public lands, managers confronting transboundary issues will face an unsolvable dilemma in determining whose legal mandate should prevail in the event of a conflict over resource priorities. Private landowners, on the other hand, will face the prospect of an expanding federal regulatory presence that could limit their land use and development options. Others, also concerned about potential boundary problems, believe ecosystem management requires clearly defined, place-based boundaries, which will enable managers to address concrete resource problems.

A third potential problem is the inherent vagueness and uncertainty of the ecosystem management concept and related terms. Ecosystem management definitions that do not establish definitive priorities among environmental protection and related socioeconomic concerns provide managers with little clear guidance on how the policy should be implemented on the ground. In the event of a conflict between ecological and economic objectives, should the manager authorize a timber sale or mining project on undeveloped land, or does ecosystem management dictate a negative decision in this instance? From an economist's perspective, the vague ecosystem management concept provides no evident basis for making a cost-benefit analysis or for determining appropriate trade-offs. Even if the protection of ecosystem integrity or biodiversity conservation is the highest priority, critics ask how these concepts are to be defined and measured. They similarly question whether the amorphous concept of sustainability provides any clearer guidance. Relatedly, they observe that uncertainty pervades ecological science, and that scientists frequently disagree among themselves over basic concepts and the proper interpretation of experimental results. They note that the inherent instability and unpredictability of ecological processes make it difficult to define a clear management target or goal. Given these definitional problems, critics believe, it is virtually impossible to set meaningful ecosystem management standards, which means there is no bases for measuring management performance or for holding managers accountable. From a commercial perspective, these definition problems can create intolerable uncertainty, deter financial planning, and increase transaction costs. From the government's perspective, an expanded planning regime could prove exceedingly costly and bureaucratically unwieldy.

Fourth, critics have questioned whether ecosystem management can be reconciled with basic democratic principles. Several critics have charged that an ecosystem management policy based on protecting ecosystem integrity is so technical that it essentially vests scientists with ultimate management authority and effectively excludes affected parties and the general public from any meaningful role in management decisions. From this perspective, ecosystem management recalls an earlier and thoroughly discredited era when claims of scientific expertise were allowed to dictate natural resource policy without regard to competing social value preferences. One particularly harsh critic, noting that a widely cited ecosystem management proponent has advocated "avoid[ing] the democratic trap of giving equal weight to all interest groups [because] many would destroy biodiversity for economic gain," asks who would be entitled to serve as nature's proxy in determining appropriate management objectives. An unduly vague ecosystem management policy that lacks clearly articulated and enforceable standards would also violate fundamental democratic principles of government accountability. Moreover, because ecosystem management contemplates interagency coordination to achieve shared ecological objectives, any ambiguity in the basic policy could undermine coordination efforts and leave participants without any clear sense of direction or accomplishment. Coordination merely for coordination's sake is the antithesis of an efficient and accountable bureaucracy.

Fifth, noting that several ecosystem management models contemplate local collaborative processes to set the resource policy agenda, environmental critics fear these processes will inevitably promote commodity production over countervailing ecological goals. If ecosystem management is merely a process to establish natural resource priorities, they fear, industry and its allies in resource-dependent communities will dominate that process, as they have in the past. They note that the environmental constituency tends to be concentrated in urban areas and is thus logistically unable to participate effectively in locally based collaborative processes where the critical decisions would be made. They also are concerned that locally based collaborative processes will tend to ignore or discount important scientific evidence documenting ecological conditions in order to promote local economic interest. Eschewing local partnership arrangements, they would rather place their faith in national regulatory standards, which are designed to protect environmental values and are enforceable in courts. In fact, * * * environmental critics are concerned that ecosystem management is simply a subterfuge to return maximum discretion to the land manager or to local partnerships. Unless ecosystem management policy contains legally enforceable standards promoting clearly defined ecological preservation goals, they reject it as merely another effort to decrease environmental protection of the public lands.

Finally, critics have asserted that there simply is no legal basis for ecosystem management on public lands, which makes it an entirely illegitimate policy. Not only does existing law contain no explicit ecosystem management provisions, but congress has failed to adopt proposed ecosystem management legislation when presented with the opportunity to do so. Granted, one might stitch together legal authority supporting ecological management policies from the diverse environmental and other statutes governing public lands, but critics believe these laws do not displace the governing organic mandates, which clearly mandate commodity production and other tangible outputs as primary policy goals. As a practical matter, in the aftermath of the 1994 elections and the Republican recapture of Congress, the term *ecosystem management* itself was called into question and deleted from the working vocabulary of many Washington-based policy makers otherwise committed to instituting new ecological policies on public lands. (The term has not, however, disappeared from the policies and practices of land managers outside the nation's capital, though the George W. Bush administration is no proponent of it either.) Thus, convinced that ecosystem management lacks a strong legal or political foundation; critics argue that any administrative policies promoting ecological objectives must first meet existing multiple-use and other statutory standards governing the public domain.

Nonetheless, ecosystem management has plainly taken hold on the public domain, and it is proving resilient enough to surmount these criticisms and problems. Indeed, within the federal bureaucracy, the halls of Congress, and elsewhere, an overt struggle is under way between the proponents and opponents of ecosystem management to shape the concept to fit their particular agendas and predispositions. While acknowledging that both definitional and technical problems must still be resolved, public land agencies are nevertheless engaged in myriad ecosystem-based experiments, employing new scientific insights and cooperative decision making models to reshape natural resource policy on the ground. Related ecological reforms are also evident in several recent legislative and administrative initiatives. Whether the term of art is ecosystem management, an ecosystem approach, integrated resource management, or collaborative stewardship, there is general agreement on the underlying rationale and direction for new ecological approaches to public land management. How these experimental endeavors fare and whether any universal lessons emerge from them will help further shape ecosystem management strategies and determine whether they represent a viable long-term natural resource policy. In the meantime, with the spotted owl controversy as a catalyst, federal ecosystem management policy has already gained a measure of legitimacy from the courts and developed a momentum of its own across the federal landscape.

NOTES AND QUESTIONS

1. Does ecosystem management help define the public interest for balancing competing demands on federal lands? If ecosystem management

is "goal-driven," who determines the goal and how? Is it whatever comes out of a neutral, fair process?

2.   How does ecosystem management compare to cost-benefit analysis? Is it an alternative method of optimizing public benefits that avoids the challenges of monetization?

3.   One of American property law's great successes is the clarity with which boundaries are defined. Ecosystem management challenges that fundamental goal of property law. Does ecosystem management represent a final step away from the property roots of natural resources law? What would shifting boundaries mean for the investment and liberty interests that rely on stable expectations? How would Stroup and Baden react to Keiter's excerpt?

4.   What role should science plan in ecosystem management? Generally, the ecological sciences are not able to provide a detailed list of prescriptions for restoring or maintaining sustainable ecosystems. Sustainable ecosystems may not even be possible in areas adapted to periodic disturbances, such as disease outbreaks and fire. Should scientists make the policy calls related to public land management? The case study of the northern spotted owl dispute in the Pacific Northwest at the end of the timber chapter provides a factual setting for answering these questions.

Professor Holly Doremus observes that environmental advocates "may once have thought that emphasizing the scientific aspects of natural resource decisions would systematically work to their advantage, but the [George W.] Bush administration has shown that is not the case." Holly Doremus, *The Purposes, Effects, and Future of the Endangered Species Act's Best Available Science Mandate*, 34 ENVTL. L. 397, 253 (2004). The Administration took its lead from Justice Scalia's characterization of the Endangered Species Act's requirement that the government "use the best scientific and commercial data available" in his opinion for the majority in Bennett v. Spear, 520 U.S. 154, 176–77 (1997). With typical certitude, Scalia said the "obvious purpose" of this requirement was:

> to ensure that the ESA not be implemented haphazardly, on the basis of speculation or surmise. While this no doubt serves to advance the ESA's overall goal of species preservation, we think it readily apparent that another objective (if not indeed the primary one) is to avoid needless economic dislocation produced by agency officials zealously but unintelligently pursuing their environmental objectives.

Free-market skeptics of regulation and other opponents of regulation in natural resource management, drawing on popular critiques of "junk science" (e.g. Peter Huber, GALILEO'S REVENGE, 1991), demand that environmental management decisions be "affirmatively supported by data that * * * [satisfies] the stringent burden of proof applied in research science." *Id.* at 263. What kind of certainty or level of scientific peer review ought we demand of public land managers in reviewing their decisions? Should the burden of precaution be borne by those who have an economic stake in commercial use of public resources?

Professor Doremus offers an alternative approach that she claims:grapples openly with the limits of scientific data, and the values that necessarily inform interpretation and application of limited data. * * * Over the long run, learning over time is likely to be essential to actually achieving the goals of conservation. Resource management decisions are frequently iterative. The information supporting them should become stronger, and the political discretion permitted the decision maker correspondingly narrower, over time. Learning has too often been impeded by the unwillingness of environmentalists to concede the limits of the currently available scientific information. Letting go of spurious claims of scientific certainty would allow them to press far more strongly for increasing the information available to support management decisions, through targeted research funding, baseline data collection efforts, and regulatory incentives for information production.

Doremus at 305. Her remedies include more frank acknowledgment of the limits of science, and more money and effort directed to scientific research. What proportion of their austere budgets should resource management agencies dedicate to the research component of adaptive management? Does ecosystem management fit her bill, or is it an example of environmentalists using the cloak of science to disguise their policy preferences?

Ecosystem management is an approach to public land and resource disputes rooted in the natural and social sciences. Professor Sax identifies the moral and aesthetic elements of conservation values. Consider which approach comes closest to realizing Leopold's vision. Is there an important expressive function of collectively owned land managed to achieve goals representing the aspirations of society?

Joseph L. Sax, Mountains Without Handrails: Reflections on the National Parks

Pp. 103–09 (1980).

* * * [M]ost conflict over national park policy does not really turn on whether we ought to have nature reserves (for that is widely agreed), but on the uses that people will make of those places—which is neither a subject of general agreement nor capable of resolution by reference to ecological principles. The preservationists are really moralists at heart, and people are very much at the center of their concerns. They encourage people to immerse themselves in natural settings and to behave there in certain ways, because they believe such behavior is redeeming.

Moreover, the preservationists do not merely aspire to persuade individuals how to conduct their personal lives. With the exception of Thoreau, who predated the national park era, they have directed their prescriptions to government. The parks are, after all, public institutions which belong to everyone, not just to wilderness hikers. The weight of the preservationist view, therefore, turns not only on its persuasiveness for the individual as such, but also on its ability to garner the support—or at least the toler-ance—of citizens in a democratic society to bring the preservationist vision into operation as official policy. It is not enough to accept the preservation-ists simply as a minority, speaking for a minority, however impressive. For that reason I have described them as secular prophets, preaching a message of secular salvation. I have attempted to articulate their views as a public philosophy, rather than treating them merely as spokesmen for an avoca-tion of nature appreciation, because the claims they make on government oblige them to bear the weightier burden.

This is not to say that what they preach cannot be rejected as merely a matter of taste, of elitist sentiment or as yet another reworking of pastoral sentimentalism. It is, however, to admit that their desire to dominate a public policy for public parks cannot prevail if their message is taken in so limited a compass. If they cannot persuade a majority that the country needs national parks of the kind they propose, much as it needs public schools and libraries, then the role they have long sought to play in the governmental process cannot be sustained. The claim is bold, and it has often been concealed in a pastiche of argument for scientific protection of nature, minority rights, and sentimental rhetoric. I have tried to isolate and make explicit the political claim, as it relates to the fashioning of public policy, and leave it to sail or sink on that basis.

It may also seem curious that I have put the preservationists into the foreground, rather than the Congress or the National Park Service. Of course Congress has the power to be paternalistic if it wishes, and it often is. It thinks a lot of things are good for us, from free trade and a nuclear defense system to public statuary and space exploration. But no unkindness is intended by the observation that Congress doesn't really think at all. At best it responds to the ideas that thinkers put before it, considers the merits of those thoughts, tests them against its sense of the larger themes that give American society coherence, and asks whether the majority will find them attractive or tolerable. The fundamental question then—and the question I have tried to address here—is whether the ideas of nature preservationists meet these tests. If they do, Congress will ultimately reflect them.

The National Park Service, and other bureaucracies that manage nature reserves, are also basically reflective institutions. Strictly speaking, they enforce the rules Congress makes, doing what they are told. But no administrative agency is in fact so mechanical in its operation. It has its own sense of mission, an internal conception of what it ought to be doing, and that sense of mission also harks back to what thinkers have persuaded it, institutionally, to believe. If the Park Service is basically dominated by the ideology of the preservationists, it will act in certain ways, given the opportunity. If, on the other hand, it has come to believe in the commodity-view of the parks, it will behave quite differently. Thus, again, the capacity of the preservationist view to persuade is the essential issue.

At the same time, no bureaucracy behaves simply according to its own sense of mission. It lives in a political milieu, with constituencies of users and neighbors who impose strong, and at times irresistible, pressures on it.

What the general public believes about the appropriate mission of the national parks is also essential. If the preservationist is to prevail, he must gain at least the passive support of the public, which will indirectly be felt by the Park Service in the decisions it makes in day to day management. * * *

[T]o the preservationists themselves, in whose ranks I include myself, the message is that the parks are not self-justifying. Your vision is not necessarily one that will commend itself to the majority. It rests on a set of moral and aesthetic attitudes whose force is not strengthened either by contemptuous disdain of those who question your conception of what a national park should be, or by taking refuge in claims of ecological necessity. Tolerance is required on all sides, along with a certain modesty.

NOTES AND QUESTIONS

1. How does the preservation agenda differ from ecosystem management?

2. Are preservationists like the prohibitionists who prompted the Eighteenth Amendment to the U.S. Constitution? Is there always a moral or ethical dimension to resource allocation disputes in public natural resources law? Does the answer depend on whether the issue involves a "crown jewel" national park or a run-of-the-mill BLM grazing district? Are preservationists any more moralistic than other groups with competing visions for public land use, such as cattle-grazers? Are there alternative foundations on which to argue for preservation?

3. Because parks and other federal land programs are not self-justifying, agencies seek to build strong constituencies to support budget requests and management initiatives. The strong public support for the national parks is the envy of every federal land program. How should an agency resolve the tension between increasing the number of visitors to maximize public exposure (and, hopefully, support), and limiting public use in order to enhance the quality of the visitor experience?

This final excerpt returns us to economics, which is a key component of the debate over environmental management. This study challenges some common assumptions about what kinds of resource use are best for local economies.

Prosperity in the 21st Century West: The Role of Protected Public Lands

Ray Rasker et al., pp. 2–10 (Sonoran Institute 2004).

The vast expanses of open space are the defining characteristic of the West. More than half the region's land is in public ownership and managed by the Bureau of Land Management, U.S. Forest Service, National Park

Service, and U.S. Fish and Wildlife Service. In mountainous regions, some counties are 80 percent publicly owned and in states like Arizona and Nevada, that number is as high as 90 percent.

It is no surprise then that another distinguishing characteristic of the West is the heated debate over how these lands should be managed. Some people prefer that public lands be set aside and protected for their scenic and recreational values. Others prefer they be used for resource extraction, in the form of oil and gas development, mining, and logging. These debates—between preservation or extractive uses of public lands—are most passionate in the rural West, where jobs are few and space is plentiful.

A typical example is playing itself out in Utah. When the Grand Staircase–Escalante National Monument was established in 1996, local reaction was negative, even hostile. President Bill Clinton and Interior Secretary Bruce Babbitt were hung in effigy in the town of Escalante, and residents in Kanab released black balloons in symbolic mourning. Over time, some have grudgingly accepted the new Monument. Others have embraced it as their economic salvation, hoping hordes of tourists, and eventually new businesses and residents, will flock to some of the most economically depressed towns in rural Utah.

Today, a proposed new Wilderness Area in central Idaho—the Boulder White Clouds Wilderness—is being heralded by some as critical to the well-being of the economy. Early this year more than 130 business leaders in Idaho sent letters to Congressman Mike Simpson in support of the wilderness proposal. Others in the West see just the opposite; that "increased federal intervention" will stifle an economy dependent on public lands for natural resources like timber and minerals. Pat Davison, an accountant, business adviser, and candidate for governor of Montana, said, at a recent forum for gubernatorial candidates, that Montanans must "take back their state" from environmental extremists blocking development of Montana's coal, oil and gas, timber and precious metals.

* * *

In the past decade, a widening body of research has shown that amenities, such as environmental quality, a slower pace of life, low crime rates, scenery, recreational opportunities, or "quality of life" for short, are influencing peoples' decision to live and to do business in rural areas. * * * [T]elecommunications technology has allowed businesses to operate far from urban centers, in scenic rural areas with a high quality of life. Power (1991) demonstrated that these "footloose entrepreneurs" bring their businesses with them when they locate to areas like the Greater Yellowstone region.

A new theory of economic development has emerged, shifting from "jobs first, then migration," to "migration first, then jobs". As the theory goes, people first decide where they want to live, and then create jobs for themselves in their new location. In turn, the in-migration of people seeking a higher quality of life stimulates the local economy. For example, the construction industry benefits as the demand grows for new homes. Local retailers learn to cater to the tastes of these new arrivals, selling everything from espresso and mountain bikes to new homes. When retirees with nest eggs—both seniors and early retirees—move to a rural town, they in turn fuel other sectors, such as the health industry (both health care and health clubs). In sum, the influx of new people with ideas, experience, and investment income into high-amenity areas stimulates new growth that goes beyond lower-wage, economically vulnerable tourism jobs.

* * *

Shumway and Otterson (2001) found that the greatest number of new migrants to the West are in what they call "New West" counties, characterized by their recreational nature, scenic amenities, proximity to national parks or other federal lands, and a preponderance of service-based economies. They concluded that in the New West, the importance of mineral, cattle, and lumber production is dwarfed by an economy that is now based on "a new paradigm of the amenity region, which creates increased demands for amenity space, residential and recreational property, second homes, and environmental protection."

However, the importance of amenities is not limited to newcomers. * * * [A] survey of business owners in the northern portion of the Greater Yellowstone area, found that amenities were more important as a magnet to keep locals from leaving than as a lure for newcomers. These amenities included recreation opportunities such as ski areas and wildlife viewing, social amenities such as low crime rates and the friendliness of the town, and environmental amenities such as scenery.

* * *

An important finding of previous research has been a differentiation between the growth in low-wage service industries, like lodging and recreational services, and high-wage services such as engineering, real estate, finance and business services. This latter category is also known as the "producer services"—those closely tied to the production of goods. For example, engineering services are used in manufacturing, while architectural, financial and real estate services are used for construction. While many areas in the West are scenic, with abundant wildlife and free-flowing rivers, researchers have found that areas that also have an educated workforce and ready access to larger markets via air travel and highways are poised to have growth in the high-wage producer services.

* * *

When federal agencies set aside public land for conservation, the local response is often negative, even hostile. Much of the concern is driven by a commonly held view that the West still depends on public lands for timber, minerals, oil and gas resources. From this point of view, public lands and resource development is the lifeblood of rural communities, and curtailing resource extraction hurts the well-being of rural people.

* * *

* * * However, today these industries provide few jobs. They have not been a significant source of new jobs or personal income in the last three decades.

This doesn't mean that resource industries should disappear. They can be an important part of an increasingly diverse economy. In some communities, and for some families, resource extraction will continue to be important. But these are the exceptions. * * *

Most of the concern over the economic impacts of conservation of public lands comes from rural areas. But while it is commonly believed that these areas depend on resource industries, personal income from employment in mining, oil and gas development, logging, and the lumber and wood products, these industries represent less than 5 percent of total personal income in 2000. Along with farming and ranching, the traditional resource staples of the rural West represent 8 percent of total personal income. This is down from 20 percent in 1970.

Meanwhile, the biggest source of real income growth, accounting for half of net growth since 1970, has been "non-labor income." This is also referred to as money earned from investments and transfer payments like retirement benefits, health care and disability insurance payments, Medicare and Medicaid and welfare.

The second biggest source of growth in the rural West has been service-related industries, accounting for more than one in three new dollars of net growth. Jobs in these industries are a mix that includes high-wage occupations in health, engineering, and business services, but also relatively low-wage occupations such as those found in restaurants and hotels.

Since most of the growth in the rural West is in services, the success of rural communities depends in large part on their ability to go beyond lower-paid tourism jobs and attract higher wage services. Public lands draw people employed in business services, engineering, finance, real estate, and other high-wage service sectors. But such workers also need ready access to larger population centers, as too much isolation, even when surrounded by spectacular scenery, can be a detriment to economic growth.

* * *

It turns out there is an inverse relationship between resource dependence and economic growth; the more dependent a state's economy is on personal income earned from people who work in the resource extractive industries, the slower the growth rate of the economy as a whole.

NOTES AND QUESTIONS

1. Suppose, over the next decade, scarcity reverses the relationship between resource dependence and economic growth. Should federal policy shift as a result? Should public land management be closely tied to decisions that maximize local economic benefits?

2. Should public land policy be a follower or a leader of demographic changes in local communities?

CHAPTER 2

History of Public Land Law: Ownership Rights and Obligations

The policy of the United States toward the lands it owns has changed drastically since the Revolutionary War ended. The treaty with Britain established the western boundary of the new nation at the Mississippi River, but seven of the thirteen original states claimed land under their colonial charters to large portions of this Western wilderness. Disputes over these claims among the former colonies and with the national government occupied much time and attention in the nation's early years.

Once these were resolved, and as the Native Americans were subdued in the nation's relentless march to the west, the national policy for the next century or more was to sell or give away the public lands to individuals, corporations, and states in order that the nation would be tamed, farmed, and developed. Individuals were granted land by credit or cash sale and later by the process of establishing farms, or homesteading. Newly admitted states were granted land outright for education, transportation, and other purposes. A vast amount of land was given to railroads in return for construction of the rails that opened up the West. Other laws allowed the private acquisition of timber and mineral resources essentially for free. These means cumulatively disposed of well over one billion acres of federal land.

These various granting mechanisms were often tainted by maladministration and chicanery, even while achieving the larger purpose of sustaining the westward expansion. Gradually, in reaction to a growing concern about fraud and waste, national policy began a shift toward the end of the 19th century. Sometimes with and sometimes without the official imprimatur of Congress, the Executive Branch began to "withdraw" specific tracts of land from the operation of the disposition laws and to "reserve" some of them for specific national purposes. A classification process evolved by which certain federal lands were deemed chiefly valuable for one or more specific uses. Active management of the retained lands gradually replaced custodial management, and professional bureaucracies grew up to meet that need. Continuing public concern about depletion of mineral, timber, and forage resources in the early 20th century led to further restrictions on federal largess, and accelerated the trend toward national retention of ownership. Indeed, in the early 20th century the United States embarked on a major program of land acquisition for conservation purposes, which created a system of national forests in the eastern part of the country (and often involved the reacquisition of land previously sold or given away). Large scale disposition ended in 1934. Since then, the special case of Alaska aside, the national land base has remained relatively stable.

Occasionally a movement arises seeking to change that basic configuration. Some free market and private property advocates are discomfited by the national government's ownership of nearly a third of the Nation's land, and states occasionally attempt to assert title or more control over the federal lands within their borders. Nevertheless, the tradition of national ownership and control has endured and indeed been strengthened over the last century. The prospect is for continued retention of a large federal land base, and even its expansion through acquisitions primarily for purposes of environmental protection, restoration, and recreation.

Most contemporary federal land controversies cannot be fully comprehended without an understanding of public land law history. Standard terms still in current use, such as "withdrawal," "entry," "location," "patent," or "in lieu selection," are foreign to those not versed in historical developments. As will be apparent in the materials that follow, modern public land litigation often hinges on interpretation of century-old statutes or cases. While public land law history is a complicated and intricate mosaic, some themes constantly recur, and furnish a rich context for contemporary management challenges and legal applications.

Public land law history is important for more than just general background. Two centuries of legal development cannot be ignored, even as change accelerates. The rights, interests, and liabilities created over the past two hundred years are established, and modern systems must recognize them. Century-old cases still are persuasive precedent. And some century-old statutes, enacted with a view of the future that did not always prove out, continue to pose legal problems in modern public land management. In addition to recounting the stories of the development of public land law, this chapter will also consider some of the critical legal issues that arise directly from that history: the rights attached to private land title derived from the United States as a prior owner; federal and state trust doctrines for resource management; and the extent of administrative authority over public lands.

This chapter begins by sketching out how the United States first asserted ownership over public lands, resolved the controversies with the colonies, established a legal basis for wresting title from Native Americans, and embarked on a program of acquisition from foreign governments. Part B then proceeds to the ways in which the Nation disposed of two-thirds of its conquests and purchases. The trust doctrines that grew out of acquisition and disposal are best understood in their historical context and are discussed here. Then the chapter concludes in part C with the rise of the conservation movement and the change in policy from disposition to retention, with an emphasis on the legal foundations of active agency management of public resources.

This chapter was compiled from many sources. The primary authorities include Paul Gates, HISTORY OF PUBLIC LAND LAW DEVELOPMENT (1968); Louise Peffer, THE CLOSING OF THE PUBLIC DOMAIN (1951); Benjamin H.

Hibbard, A HISTORY OF PUBLIC LAND POLICIES (1924, U. Wis. ed., 1965); Roy Robbins, OUR LANDED HERITAGE (1942) (2d ed., 1976). Basic non-legal sources are collected in Charles Wilkinson, *The Law of the American West: A Critical Bibliography of the Nonlegal Sources*, 85 MICH. L.REV. 953 (1987).

A.   ACQUISITION OF THE PUBLIC DOMAIN

All of the land the United States has acquired on the North American continent was previously "owned" both by foreign nations and by Indian tribes, and some of it was subject to claims under the charters of some of the original colonies. Federal acquisition came about by a combination of cession, purchase, and conquest.

1.   FROM THE ORIGINAL COLONIES

Upon ratification of the 1783 Treaty of Paris ending the Revolutionary War, the infant United States gained dominion over lands between the Alleghenies and the Mississippi. But "western land claims" of seven of the thirteen original colonies complicated efforts to establish a national policy for these lands. Virginia's claim, the largest, stretched across what later became six states in the Midwest. The claims were grounded in sweeping interpretations of colonial charters from the British Crown. Some of the colonial charters contained a final phrase extending their width "to the South Sea" (the Pacific Ocean) whereas others, like Maryland and Pennsylvania, had western boundaries fixed in reference to meridians of longitude. Before the American Revolution, Britain had acted to limit the scope of these grants, and in fact such limitations were among the grievances against the Crown cited by Thomas Jefferson in the Declaration of Independence.

As the Revolutionary War was brought to its successful conclusion, one of the most pressing issues was how to repay the tremendous debt owed to soldiers and other war supporters. The most attractive option relied on public land sales to generate the necessary revenue. Ultimately, the founders agreed on a deal under which the states would cede western land claims to the national government to help fund these and other expenses. States without western land claims, which tended to be smaller and less populous anyway, staunchly opposed the claims, fearing the larger states would become even richer and more populous through sales and settlement of the western lands. The issue (and the closely linked question of whether and how new states might be created) was a major and divisive one in the deliberations over the Articles of Confederation and eventually the Constitution.

New York led the way in 1780, ceding its western land claims to the national government. Virginia followed in 1783, and all of the other states with western claims except Georgia ceded their rights in the next few years. Georgia, the youngest and poorest of the states, had western land claims which included much of present-day Alabama and Mississippi, and it was eager to sell this land. In 1795 its legislature (all but one of whose members had an interest in the matter either in shares or bribes) approved a deal that sold 40 million acres for just $500,000. The sale was later overturned, but in the meantime the purchasers had resold the land for triple the price (the secondary purchasers included a member of Congress and Judge James Wilson of the U.S. Supreme Court). It took until 1802 for national pressure to force Georgia to cede its western claims to the federal government. Some years after that, in the celebrated case of Fletcher v. Peck, 10 U.S. (6 Cranch.) 87 (1810), the Court, per John Marshall, awarded the secondary purchasers compensation on the basis of breach of the sales contract, despite the fraud in the background.

The Articles of Confederation adopted during the Revolutionary War did not expressly authorize the Confederation Congress to govern the western lands. This did not stop it from enacting major laws—especially the Land Ordinance of 1785 and the Northwest Ordinance of 1787—that set a pattern for federal land policy which has in some respects endured to the present. Most important for present purposes, in these laws the national government 1) assumed the major responsibility of owning large tracts of land and managing them to serve the ends of national policy; and 2) prohibited states and local governments from interfering with U.S. policy. Doubts about the congressional authority here played out in the Constitutional Convention of 1787. The significance of the 1785 survey system is evident to anyone observing the ground from the window of an airplane. Part B of this chapter describes how this early legislation created a disposal system along with legal issues that remain important today.

2. FROM FOREIGN NATIONS

It had taken more than 170 years from the establishment of Jamestown in 1607 for settlement to begin in earnest in this New West (across the Appalachians to the Mississippi—the area outside the thirteen original colonies once the western land claims were ceded), an area larger than the original thirteen colonies. Such a huge area might have been expected to satisfy even the most voracious land hunger of the 3 million citizens of the new United States for many years. In fact, however, opportunity and opportunism so coincided that, over the next ninety years, national land ownership quadrupled.

Besides the Indians, only England, Spain, and Russia had, at the time of the Revolution, claims to land in North America. Dutch and Swedish claims had long been extinguished and the French government had more recently been defeated and ejected from the continent. The British settlements in Canada attracted the continuing but unsuccessful attention of American expansionists. Other lands claimed by the English and the Spanish (and later the Mexicans) gradually succumbed to Manifest Destiny. Acquisition of the tenuous Russian claims was last and easiest.

In the 1790's, the population of the United States expanded 35 percent, three new states were admitted, and national economic policies brought about stability, prosperity, and new settlement. Beyond the Alleghenies, trade flowed through New Orleans and other Spanish-held ports on the

Mississippi. When Spain ceded its Louisiana lands to France in 1800, the new Republic saw a menace.

LOUISIANA PURCHASE

The negotiations that Jefferson began with Napoleon for the purchase of New Orleans were greatly aided by the decimation of a French expeditionary force in Santo Domingo, now in the Dominican Republic. Although doubtful that he could accept without constitutional amendment, Jefferson decided he could not refuse Napoleon's unexpected, unparalleled offer to sell the entire Louisiana Territory. A grave danger was turned into a great political victory, and 523 million acres were added to the public domain in 1803 for three cents an acre, doubling the territory of the United States.

New England Federalists were unhappy with Western prospects, fearing the growing influence of the Democratic–Republican representatives from the frontiers. Lewis and Clark promptly penetrated the new territory and beyond, but settlement proceeded mostly east of the Mississippi. Louisiana attained statehood in 1812, but admission of Missouri did not occur until 1821, as the slavery question began to loom larger.

FLORIDA ACQUISITION AND SETTLING THE NORTHERN BORDER

Irritations on remaining borders with Spanish territory continued. Indians raided Georgia from the Spanish holdings and slaves sought freedom in them. In 1817–19, Indian conflicts became acute in Florida, whereupon Andrew Jackson crossed into Florida, defeated the Creeks, and summarily executed their leaders and two accused British instigators, all of which Spanish officials were powerless to prevent. Spain accepted the inevitable and agreed to surrender East and West Florida and its claims to the Oregon Territory in exchange for only a guarantee of its Texas border and payment of claims by the United States. In 1818, Great Britain agreed to extend the Canadian border along the 49th parallel from Minnesota to the Rocky Mountains. A similar dispute over the boundary of Maine was not settled until 1842.

TEXAS, THE TREATY OF GUADALUPE HIDALGO, AND THE GADSDEN PURCHASE

Hundreds of millions of acres of productive federal land remained unsettled in the first half of the 19th century, but the insatiable American land hunger led explorers and settlers further afield. The storied Mountain Men, with the indomitable Jedediah Smith in the vanguard, explored most of the unmapped West while decimating the beaver in the Rockies. Stephen Austin established colonies in Texas, Marcus Whitman led settlers to Oregon, and Brigham Young took the Mormon Saints to the "place" that became Utah. Between 1845 and 1853, the United States acquired another 781 million acres, of which 613 million acres were added to the public domain.

After Mexico gained its independence from Spain, it made the mistake of contracting with promoters such as Austin to bring in American settlers. The generous grant terms offered to Texas immigrants were taken by

20,000 Americans and their one thousand slaves by 1830. The Mexican officials quickly regretted their invitation, however, as the Americans resented Mexican efforts to outlaw slavery and to require Catholicism. The Alamo and Texas independence followed, in 1835–36.

But the newly independent "nation" was unexpectedly refused admission into the United States for another nine years because of the slavery question. Under the Missouri Compromise of 1820, northern legislators had anticipated only two more slave states; they were now unwilling to admit an area (46 times the size of Massachusetts) in which five or six additional "slavocracies" could be created. Manifest Destiny eventually won out: the 1844 election of James K. Polk was a victory for expansion. The United States first annexed and then admitted Texas the following year.

Admission, however, was on different terms from those worked out with other new states. During its independence, Texas had granted away some 30 million acres but still had a huge debt, fueled by many questionable tricks of finance. The United States left the remaining lands in the possession of the new State to avoid investigating prior practices and assuming the debt. After annexation, Texas sold 79 million acres of its western lands (now parts of New Mexico, Oklahoma, Wyoming, Colorado, and Kansas) to the federal government, the only Texas acreage to enter the national "public domain."

Boundary and other disputes with Mexico continued, and negotiations failed while feeling ran high. A Mexican incursion into the disputed territory gave President Polk a pretext for declaring war, and the Mexicans were soundly defeated. In the 1848 Treaty of Guadalupe Hidalgo, Mexico ceded most of the Southwest, including California, to the United States for $15 million. For a pittance, the Nation gained title to spectacular scenic resources, including the Grand Canyon and other wonderlands of the Colorado Plateau, the Sierra Nevada, and San Francisco Bay. This territory contained vast mineral wealth, although Congress did not learn of the January 1848 discovery of gold in the California foothills until after it ratified the Treaty. Shortly thereafter, with railroads being projected or promoted in all directions, it was seen that a New Orleans to San Diego line would require additional land for a favorable route. In 1853, James Gadsden negotiated the purchase of Arizona below the Gila River from Mexico for $10 million.

THE OREGON COMPROMISE

In the meantime, the United States had agreed with Great Britain on the northwest boundary. The area around the Columbia had long been used by the Hudson's Bay Company in its trapping operations. But the British were overwhelmed by the influx of American settlers in the 1840's, and the beaver had virtually disappeared. Recognizing the inevitable, England agreed to a boundary fixed at the 49th parallel, except that Vancouver Island below that line was retained for Canada. The settlement of the Oregon question added 180 million acres north of California to the public domain.

THE ALASKA PURCHASE

The surprising acquisition of Alaska had not been preceded by public demand or even public discussion. The Russians were anxious to sell, however, and Secretary of State Seward wanted to buy, so the transaction happened quickly in 1867. For $7.2 million, the United States purchased an enormous unsurveyed area only lightly touched by human habitation.

Alaska was the last significant addition to the federal public domain. Later acquisitions of Hawaii, Puerto Rico, the Philippines, Guam, Samoa, the Virgin Islands, and smaller Pacific islands made few additions to the public lands.

3.   FROM INDIAN TRIBES

Of course the lands ceded from the colonies and acquired from foreign nations between 1789 and 1867 were also subject to the claims of their inhabitants, the American Indians. The Native Americans fiercely resisted white intrusions into their ancestral tribal lands. They were eventually subdued, decimated by European diseases, defeated in conflicts, and removed to "reservations" or assimilated. In the process, however, legal questions of land ownership and title had to be resolved.

The following opinion by Chief Justice John Marshall is a landmark in public land law. It reconciled the property rights of the United States, American Indian tribes, foreign nations, and the settlers anxious to obtain title to real estate on the frontier. In doing so, the Court laid the legal predicates for the federal disposition program and the westward expansion.

Johnson v. M'Intosh

Supreme Court of the United States, 1823.
21 U.S. (8 Wheat.) 543.

■ CHIEF JUSTICE MARSHALL delivered the opinion of the Court.

[The litigation involved title to land within what is now the State of Illinois. Johnson claimed title based on grants in 1773 and 1775 from chiefs of the Illinois and Piankeshaw tribes. In 1795, these tribes entered into treaties with the United States, retaining certain lands as reservations but ceding to the federal government other land, including that earlier transferred to Johnson's predecessors. In 1818, the United States granted to defendant M'Intosh a patent to the parcels in question. Johnson then brought this quiet title action.] * * * [The inquiry] is, in a great measure, confined to the power of Indians to give, and of private individuals to receive, a title, which can be sustained in the courts of this country. * * *

On the discovery of this immense continent, the great nations of Europe were eager to appropriate to themselves so much of it as they could respectively acquire. Its vast extent offered an ample field to the ambition and enterprise of all; and the character and religion of its inhabitants afforded an apology for considering them as a people over whom the superior genius of Europe might claim an ascendancy. The potentates of the old world found no difficulty in convincing themselves that they made ample compensation to the inhabitants of the new, by bestowing on them civilization and Christianity, in exchange for unlimited independence. But as they were all in pursuit of nearly the same object, it was necessary, in order to avoid conflicting settlements, and consequent war with each other, to establish a principle, which all should acknowledge as the law by which the right of acquisition, which they all asserted, should be regulated, as between themselves. This principle was, that discovery gave title to the government by whose subjects, or by whose authority, it was made, against all other European governments, which title might be consummated by possession.

The exclusion of all other Europeans, necessarily gave to the nation making the discovery the sole right of acquiring the soil from the natives, and establishing settlements upon it. It was a right with which no Europeans could interfere. It was a right which all asserted for themselves, and to the assertion of which, by others, all assented. * * *

In the establishment of these relations, the rights of the original inhabitants were, in no instance, entirely disregarded; but were, necessarily, to a considerable extent, impaired. They were admitted to be the rightful occupants of the soil, with a legal as well as just claim to retain possession of it, and to use it according to their own discretion; but their rights to complete sovereignty, as independent nations, were necessarily diminished, and their power to dispose of the soil, at their own will, to whomsoever they pleased, was denied by the original fundamental principle, that discovery gave exclusive title to those who made it.

While the different nations of Europe respected the right of the natives, as occupants, they asserted the ultimate dominion to be in themselves; and claimed and exercised, as a consequence of this ultimate dominion, a power to grant the soil, while yet in possession of the natives. These grants have been understood by all, to convey a title to the grantees, subject only to the Indian right of occupancy.

The history of America, from its discovery to the present day, proves, we think, the universal recognition of these principles. * * *

[The opinion then discussed various competing claims to the New World, many dating to the 15th and 16th centuries, made by Spain, Great Britain, Portugal, France, and Holland. It described the French and Indian War between France and Great Britain, at the end of which, by treaty of 1763, France ceded Canada to Great Britain and fixed the western boundary of the British colonies at the Mississippi.] This treaty expressly cedes, and has always been understood to cede, the whole country, on the English side of the dividing line, between the two nations, although a great and valuable part of it was occupied by the Indians. Great Britain, on her part, surrendered to France all her pretensions to the country west of the Mississippi. It has never been supposed that she surrendered nothing, although she was not in actual possession of a foot of land. She surrendered all right to acquire the country; and any after attempt to purchase it from the Indians, would have been considered and treated as an invasion of the territories of France.

By the 20th article of the same treaty, Spain ceded Florida, with its dependencies, and all the country she claimed east or southeast of the Mississippi, to Great Britain. Great part of this territory also was in possession of the Indians.

By a secret treaty, which was executed about the same time, France ceded Louisiana to Spain; and Spain has since retroceded the same country to France. At the time both of its cession and retrocession, it was occupied chiefly by the Indians.

Thus, all the nations of Europe, who have acquired territory on this continent, have asserted in themselves, and have recognized in others, the exclusive right of the discoverer to appropriate the lands occupied by the Indians. Have the American States rejected or adopted this principle?

By the treaty which concluded the war of our revolution, Great Britain relinquished all claim, not only to the government, but to the "propriety and territorial rights of the United States," whose boundaries were fixed in the second article. By this treaty, the powers of government, and the right to soil, which had previously been in Great Britain, passed definitively to these States. * * *

The States, having within their chartered limits different portions of territory covered by Indians, ceded that territory, generally, to the United States, on conditions expressed in their deeds of cession, which demonstrate the opinion, that they ceded soil as well as jurisdiction, and that in doing so, they granted a productive fund to the government of the Union. The lands in controversy lay within the chartered limits of Virginia, and were ceded with the whole country northwest of the river Ohio. * * * The ceded territory was occupied by numerous and warlike tribes of Indians; but the exclusive right of the United States to extinguish their title, and to grant the soil, has never, we believe, been doubted.

After these States became independent, a controversy subsisted between them and Spain respecting boundary [sic]. By the treaty of 1795, this controversy was adjusted, and Spain ceded to the United States the territory in question. This territory, though claimed by both nations, was chiefly in the actual occupation of Indians.

The magnificent purchase of Louisiana, was the purchase from France of a country almost entirely occupied by numerous tribes of Indians, who are in fact independent. Yet, any attempt of others to intrude into that country, would be considered as an aggression which would justify war.

Our late acquisitions from Spain [of Florida] are of the same character; and the negotiations which preceded those acquisitions, recognize and elucidate the principle which has been received as the foundation of all European title in America.

The United States, then, have unequivocally acceded to that great and broad rule by which its civilized inhabitants now hold this country. They hold, and assert in themselves, the title by which it was acquired. They maintain, as all others have maintained, that discovery gave an exclusive right to extinguish the Indian title of occupancy, either by purchase or by conquest; and gave also a right to such a degree of sovereignty, as the circumstances of the people would allow them to exercise.

* * * Conquest gives a title which the courts of the conqueror cannot deny, whatever the private and speculative opinions of individuals may be, respecting the original justice of the claim which has been successfully asserted. The British government, which was then our government, and whose rights have passed to the United States, asserted a title to all the lands occupied by Indians, within the chartered limits of the British colonies. It asserted also a limited sovereignty over them, and the exclusive right of extinguishing the titles which occupancy gave to them. These claims have been maintained and established as far west as the river Mississippi, by the sword. The title to a vast portion of the lands we now hold, originates in them. It is not for the courts of this country to question the validity of this title, or to sustain one which is incompatible with it. * * *

[T]he tribes of Indians inhabiting this country were fierce savages, whose occupation was war, and whose subsistence was drawn chiefly from the forest. To leave them in possession of their country, was to leave the country a wilderness; to govern them as a distinct people, was impossible, because they were as brave and as high-spirited as they were fierce, and were ready to repel by arms every attempt on their independence. * * *

Frequent and bloody wars, in which the whites were not always the aggressors, unavoidably ensued. European policy, numbers and skill prevailed. As the white population advanced, that of the Indians necessarily receded. The country in the immediate neighborhood of agriculturists became unfit for them. The game fled into thicker and more unbroken forests, and the Indians followed. The soil, to which the crown originally claimed title, being no longer occupied by its ancient inhabitants, was parcelled out according to the will of the sovereign power, and taken possession of by persons who claimed immediately from the crown, or mediately, through its grantees or deputies. * * *

However extravagant the pretension of converting the discovery of an inhabited country into conquest may appear; if the principle has been asserted in the first instance, and afterwards sustained; if a country has been acquired and held under it; if the property of the great mass of the community originates in it, it becomes the law of the land, and cannot be questioned. So too, with respect to the concomitant principle, that the Indian inhabitants are to be considered merely as occupants, to be protected, indeed, while in peace, in the possession of their lands, but to be deemed incapable of transferring the absolute title to others. However this restriction may be opposed to natural right, and to the usages of civilized nations, yet, if it be indispensable to that system under which the country has been settled, and be adapted to the actual condition of the two people, it may, perhaps, be supported by reason, and certainly cannot be rejected by courts of justice. * * *

[The Court affirmed the judgment of the District Court of Illinois in favor of defendant M'Intosh.]

NOTES AND QUESTIONS

1.   What kind of title to real estate did the European nations obtain by claiming lands in the New World? What kind of title did the United States receive from these European nations when it executed treaties with them? What interest did the Indians have? What steps did the United States need to take in order to "clear" title obtained from foreign nations so that the United States could dispose of land for settlement? What, in short, is the chain of title to the public domain?

2.   Indian title (also called aboriginal title or Indian right of occupancy) is a unique property interest. It allowed Indian tribes to reside, hunt, and fish upon their aboriginal lands and to sue trespassing parties for damages. It also allowed tribes to transfer title, but only to or with the consent of the United States, a limitation that has had modern implications, explored in note 5, below. But Indian title can be taken by the United States without payment of just compensation. Tee–Hit–Ton Indians v. United States, 348 U.S. 272 (1955). Absent U.S. consent, Indian title cannot be affected by the actions of states or private parties. On Indian title, see F. Cohen, Handbook of Federal Indian Law (2005 ed.).

3.   Johnson v. M'Intosh acknowledged the right of the United States to obtain Indian title by "conquest" as well as by "purchase." In actual practice, the federal government usually went through the formal process of purchase, although bargaining power was hardly equal. As the Secretary of the Interior dryly noted in his 1862 Annual Report: "Although the consent of the Indians [to yield their territory to advancing settlement] has been obtained in the form of treaties, it is well known that they have yielded to a necessity which they could not resist." John O'Sullivan, editor of a widely circulated magazine, nicely captured the national sentiment—and gave expression to the whole westward movement—when he criticized foreign interference with the U.S. annexation of Texas in 1845:

> Away, away with all these cobweb tissues of rights of discovery, exploration, settlement, contiguity, etc. * * * The American claim is by the right of our manifest destiny to overspread and to possess the whole of the continent which Providence has given us for the development of the great experiment of liberty and federative self-government entrusted to us. It is a right such as that of the tree to the space of air and earth suitable for the full expansion of its principle and destiny of growth.

Quoted in Richard White, It's Your Misfortune and None of My Own: A History of the American West 73 (1991). Arrangements with Indians were usually embodied in treaties until 1871, when the House of Representatives rebelled at being cut out of the process (treaties being subject to confirmation only by the Senate). After that date, the United States continued the process of clearing Indian title and establishing reservations by other means, primarily statutes and executive orders. A leading authority in Indian law estimated that the clearing of Indian title resulted, by the end of World War II, in the payment to tribes of between 500 million and one billion dollars. Felix Cohen, *Original Indian Title*, 32 Minn. L.Rev. 28

(1947). In 1946, Congress passed the Indian Claims Commission Act, which created a process for tribes to try to recover payments for past dealings where the U.S. had engaged in "dishonorable dealings" with tribes. 25 U.S.C. §§ 70–70v–1.

4.   Most tribes, by treaty or otherwise, transferred the majority of their aboriginal lands to the United States and reserved some of the remaining lands to themselves. These transactions had the effect of resolving Indian title, and converted the lands and resources the tribes reserved into "recognized" property interests which are compensable property interests protected by the Fifth Amendment. Legal title to these lands are generally held in trust by the United States, with beneficial interest in the tribes. Lands ceded by the tribes in these transactions were cleared of Indian claims. This left the United States free to open them for homesteading or other disposition, or to retain them for other purposes.

5.   Indian title has continuing importance. As Johnson v. M'Intosh held, Indian land transactions are valid only if approved by the United States. This rule, codified in the Indian Trade and Intercourse Act of 1790, now found, as amended, at 25 U.S.C. § 177, regularized frontier property dealings and allowed reasonably orderly disposition of the lands by the United States through various land grants, homesteading, and other devices. But there were many transactions like those to Johnson, where tribes purported to convey title to non-federal parties but which were never sanctioned by the United States. In modern times considerable litigation has sought to declare such transactions void. In 1985, the Supreme Court held invalid a 1795 land transfer from the Oneida Nation to the State of New York, never approved by Congress, and ruled that the tribe's suit for possession was not barred by the statute of limitations or other defenses based on the passage of time. Oneida County v. Oneida Indian Nation, 470 U.S. 226 (1985). But, in a claim of tribal immunity from state taxes, City of Sherrill v. Oneida Indian Nation, 544 U.S. 197 (2005), the court held that the tribe's long delays "in seeking equitable relief against New York" or the city of Sherrill "spanning several generations, evoke the doctrines of laches, acquiescence, and impossibility, and render inequitable the piecemeal shift in governance this suit seeks unilaterally to initiate". A number of such claims have been settled, with the tribes receiving title to part of their aboriginal lands. See, e.g., Maine Claims Settlement Act of 1980, 25 U.S.C. §§ 1721–1735.

6.   This principle has also limited the ability of federal land agencies to dispose of or manage federal lands that have remained subject to Indian title which has not been extinguished. See, e.g., Cramer v. United States, 261 U.S. 219 (1923) (voiding a federal patent to lands to which Indian title had not been cleared). In United States v. Dann, 470 U.S. 39 (1985), the Court rejected the claim of Western Shoshone Indians that grazing leases issued on federal lands were unauthorized, holding that Indian title to 13 million acres in western Nevada had been extinguished because the tribe had been compensated in a money damages case brought pursuant to the Indian Claims Commissions Act of 1946.

7. Today, some 56 million acres of Indian lands are held in trust by the United States. Even though bare legal title is in the United States, they are not properly public lands, because they are held in trust for Indian beneficiaries. Nevertheless, Indian lands are not unaffected by modern policies regarding publicly owned resources. The Bureau of Indian Affairs, which oversees the federal government's trust management responsibility for these lands, is located in the Department of the Interior, and the laws and processes governing development of Indian resources in some cases resemble those applicable to public lands. See Del–Rio Drilling Programs, Inc. v. United States, 146 F.3d 1358 (Fed. Cir. 1998). See generally Michael Blumm & Judith Royster, NATIVE AMERICAN NATURAL RESOURCES LAW: CASES AND MATERIALS (2002).

8. Indian treaty or other rights may limit or otherwise influence how non-Indian federal resources are managed. The most obvious example is where federal reserved water rights for Indians can have a major effect on management of other public resources, as discussed in Chapter 6. Sometimes Indians reserved hunting and fishing rights on lands ceded to the United States, and these have been recognized in modern times, and may run with the land when the United States disposes of it. The most prominent example concerns the rights of Northwest Indian tribes under the so-called "Stevens treaties" (negotiated by federal representative Isaac Stevens in the mid-nineteenth century) of "taking fish, at usual and accustomed grounds and stations [including off-reservation sites] * * * in common with all citizens of the Territory." See Washington v. Washington State Commercial Passenger Fishing Vessel Assn., 443 U.S. 658 (1979). See also Minnesota v. Mille Lacs Band of Chippewa Indians, 526 U.S. 172 (1999) (Tribe's treaty right to hunt and fish on lands it ceded to the United States was not abrogated by subsequent events, including the admission of Minnesota to the Union). Other decisions have rejected such claims. See, e.g., South Dakota v. Bourland, 508 U.S. 679 (1993) (Tribe's reservation of right to hunt and fish on land ceded to the federal government did not give tribe the right to apply its game laws to non-Indians using these lands); United States v. Peterson, 121 F.Supp.2d 1309 (D. Mont. 2000) (Congress abrogated the treaty right to hunt on a tract of federal land when it reserved the land as part of Glacier National Park).

B. DISPOSITION OF THE PUBLIC DOMAIN

1. THE DISPOSITION SYSTEM

The vast public domain had many suitors: states, entrepreneurs and other developers, speculators, military veterans, and settlers. Even before the Revolution, speculation in the unsettled western lands and squatting upon them before they were formally opened to settlement or surveyed were common habits of the colonists. Other colonial practices, such as rewarding war veterans with a grant of lands, also became entrenched in public policy or tradition. Prominent from the beginning was a conflict between those who sought to use the public domain to advance the social ideal of an agrarian society dominated by small, independent farmers and those to whom land was a source of federal revenue to be maximized.

a.   THE SURVEY AND EARLY LAND LAWS

The Confederation Congress enacted some important public land laws. The enduring contribution of the Land Ordinance of 1785 was the rectangular survey system by which the lands were divided into square townships of 36 identically-numbered sections, each section containing 640 acres (which equals one square mile). This is the foundation of U.S. property recordation, which is unsurpassed in its precision and abstraction. Most of Alaska and parts of the intermountain West are still unsurveyed, but elsewhere the surveysystem was mostly completed by the 1930s.

METHOD OF NUMBERING
TOWNSHIPS.
North and South from Base Line and East and West from Meridian.

The regularity of the survey system allowed land to be treated as a "commodity defined by numbers." Arno Linklater, MEASURING AMERICA 174 (2002). This had a profound influence on the American landscape, economy, and culture. "A uniform, invariable shape that took no account of springs or hills or swamps was an obstacle to efficient agriculture, but to a financier tracking the rise and fall in land values, it was a great convenience." *Id.* Moreover, "[f]ree enterprise was born out of land dealing, and long before the first business corporation existed, land companies issued shares and created many of the financial and legal structures that the nineteenth-century stockdealing, capitalist economy used to finance the railroads and industrialization of the United States." *Id.* at 149.

THEORETICAL
TOWNSHIP DIAGRAM
SHOWING
METHOD OF NUMBERING SECTIONS
WITH ADJOINING SECTIONS

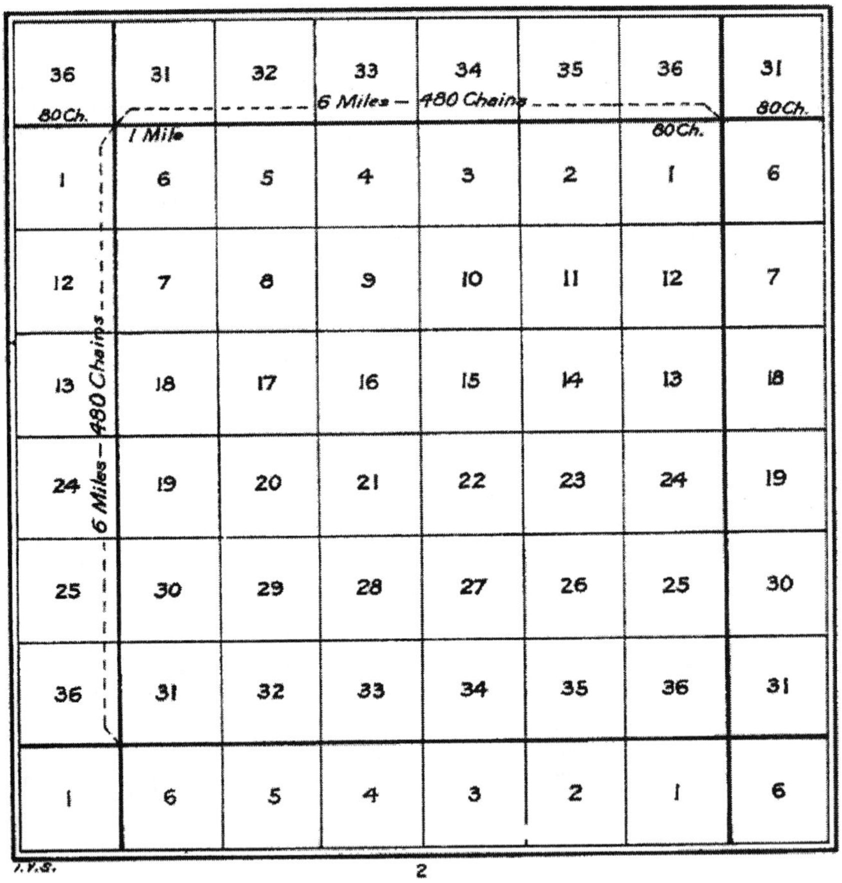
36 31 32 33 34 35 36 31
80 Ch.
6 Miles — 480 Chains
80 Ch.
1 Mile
80 Ch.
1 6 5 4 3 2 1 6
12 7 8 9 10 11 12 7
13 18 17 16 15 14 13 18
24 19 20 21 22 23 24 19
25 30 29 28 27 26 25 30
36 31 32 33 34 35 36 31
1 6 5 4 3 2 1 6
6 Miles — 480 Chains
2

Under the Land Ordinance of 1785, once surveyed, lands were to be offered at auction for a minimum price of one dollar an acre, and section 16 in each township was reserved for public education. No limitations on speculation were imposed, and no provisions for the protection of squatters, already numerous, were made. Little settlement was accomplished under the Act, for surveying proceeded slowly, Indian resistance in the Ohio

Territory was strong, and large scale speculators were attempting to make private deals with the Confederation Congress. That body viewed land sales as an important revenue source and it discharged debts to Revolutionary War veterans and refugees with scrip, a kind of coupon, entitling them to select lands from the Military Reserves in Ohio.

The Confederation Congress also enacted the Northwest Ordinance of 1787, which created a system of government for the territory north of the Ohio River to which Virginia had ceded its colonial claim. Among other things, it called for three to five states to be formed from the territory, to be admitted to the Union "on an equal footing with the original States, in all respects whatever," upon reaching a target population of 60,000. The Ordinance also prohibited slavery in these new states (except that escaped slaves from other states would be returned to their owners). Also significant was its provision that the territorial government and "new States, shall never interfere with the primary disposal of the Soil by the United States * * *, nor with any regulations Congress may find necessary for securing the title in such soil to the bona fide purchasers." 32 JOURNALS OF THE CONTINENTAL CONGRESS 334–43 (Roscoe Hill ed., 1936).

A number of provisions in the Northwest Ordinance influenced the framers of the U.S. Constitution. But doubts about the authority of the central government under the Articles of Confederation to legislate with respect to territorial matters were a consideration when they met in Philadelphia that same year. The framers responded by including three clauses of relevance. Article IV, section 3, clause 1, provides for the admission of new states. Article I, section 8, clause 17 (the "Enclave" Clause), gives Congress exclusive authority over the seat of government and other places purchased for the erection of "needful Buildings." The third, Article IV, section 3, clause 2 (the Property Clause), is most important for our purposes, and reads, in relevant part: "The Congress shall have Power to dispose of and make all needful Rules and Regulations respecting the Territory or other Property belonging to the United States."

The drafting of the language that would become the "Property Clause" of Article IV, section 3, did not generate much excitement. But federal lands remained an abiding concern of the national government. One of the first acts of Congress under the new Constitution was to reconfirm and extend the provisions of the Northwest Ordinance of 1787. See Act of August 7, 1789, ch. VIII, 1 Stat. 50. About a quarter of all legislation enacted by Congress up to the Civil War related to public lands and land settlement. Roy Robbins, OUR LANDED HERITAGE 236.

b. DISPOSITION BY FOREIGN GOVERNMENTS

One of the first tasks of the new national government was to determine just what lands were "Property belonging to the United States." Predecessor governments had made various grants of land over which the American government eventually gained sovereignty. In the Jay Treaty of 1794, the young Nation agreed to recognize pre-existing grants, and this practice was followed in all subsequent acquisitions. Translating this simple principle into reality proved an immense task. Language difficulties, political patronage appointments of land officials, incomplete foreign records, abandonment of grants, and similar factors complicated the process.

One legacy of this policy is the long, narrow boundary pattern visible in plat maps and aerial photographs of areas in former French colonial outposts such as Detroit, Vincennes, Fort Wayne, St. Louis, and New Orleans. One reporter noted how the distinctive culture of New Orleans grew out of its origins as a French colony with land distribution designed to maximize the number of plots with river frontage:

> The original plantations in the Mississippi River oxbow that later cradled New Orleans were long, thin strips, starting at the river and running north, toward the lake. "People grow accustomed to the geometry in which they live," English said. "When it came to laying out lots in New Orleans, they naturally laid them out long and narrow. That led to the long and narrow shotguns [shotgun-style houses]." The shotguns, in turn, helped develop the close-knit neighborhoods that New Orleanians love. A shotgun's salient feature is its lack of privacy. Getting from the front room to the kitchen, which is usually in the back, means walking through everybody else's room or around the outside. On the narrow lots, shotguns sit close together, so neighbors are also on top of each other. "That communal culture everybody talks about in New Orleans, that warmth, all that life on the street, you could say that originates with the need for every plantation to have a little piece of riverfront," English said.

Dan Baum, *Letter from New Orleans: The Lost Year*, THE NEW YORKER, Aug. 21, 2006, at 44, 56 (quoting Professor Elizabeth English of Louisiana State University).

It took generations for the courts and Congress to decide the validity and extent of prior grants made by the governments of Great Britain, Spain, France, and Mexico. The claims ranged from the size of town lots in Detroit to a 1.5 million acre grant in Florida. The disputes were widespread and long-lasting; 126 such cases were decided by the Supreme Court before 1860, and many more thereafter. In addition to the poor fit between the U.S. survey system and the (mostly unsurveyed) foreign land grants, many foreign grants were conditioned upon the performance of some task such as building mills, distilling alcohol, or constructing roads. "[I]ncredible forgeries, fraud, subornation, and perjuries" were all too common. Territorial administrators participated in the purchase and fabrication of prior land grants. Corruption was so common that one historian felt compelled to protest that "[n]ot all public officials participated in the grab and by no means all of the claims acquired by officers were improperly obtained or tainted with fraud." Paul Gates, HISTORY OF PUBLIC LAND LAW DEVELOPMENT 228. *See also id*. at 87–119.

The claimants of large tracts generally prevailed in the end because of their persistence, congressional sympathy, and superior representation before Congress, courts, and commissioners. (Daniel Webster and Thomas Hart Benton represented claimants while serving in the U.S. Senate.) But not always. In one of the most celebrated disputes, most of the claims of Swiss immigrant Johann Sutter, whose mill was the site of the discovery that triggered the California Gold Rush, to vast acreage in California pursuant to grants from Mexico in the early 1840s were in the end rejected by the courts. See, e.g., United States v. Sutter, 62 U.S. (21 How.) 170 (1858); In re Sutter, 69 U.S. (2 Wall.) 562 (1864). Ultimately, 34 million acres in nineteen states were confirmed to grantees of former governments, and these lands were usually the most desirable acreage that otherwise would have been available to settlers. Contemporary public land disputes may still turn on the difficult interpretive issues of foreign land grants. See e.g. United States v. Beggerly, 524 U.S. 38 (1998) (quiet title dispute in Gulf Islands National Seashore involving a 1781 Spanish land grant).

2.   STATE LANDS AND TRUST DOCTRINES

The thirteen original states, along with early admittees Vermont, Maine, Tennessee and Kentucky (and, later, Texas and Hawaii), have never been considered "public land" states, because the federal government never had appreciable ownership of lands within their borders. Whether or not a state is considered a public land state has no legal significance, but a practical problem arose as subsequent states entered the union. From the admission of Ohio in 1803 to that of Alaska in 1959, the state-making procedure involved Congress and the people of the territories in complicated political disputes. Generally, territories became states well before the federal government had disposed of public lands. Territorial interests seeking statehood were brought, sometimes with great reluctance, to give up plans some entertained for either acquiring or controlling the federal lands found within their borders.

By a curious legal quirk, however, new states did automatically receive some land at statehood; namely, the lands underlying navigable waters within their boundaries. The starting point for this implied grant was the Supreme Court's decision that title to lands underlying navigable waters in the original thirteen states had passed from the British Crown to their colonies, before the establishment of the United States. Martin v. Waddell's Lessee, 41 U.S. (16 Pet.) 367 (1842). In that case, Chief Justice Taney wrote that "when the people of New Jersey took * * * into their own hands the powers of sovereignty, the prerogatives and regalities which before belonged either to the crown or the parliament, became immediately and rightfully vested in the state." Upon the establishment of the national government, the states held "the absolute right to all their navigable waters and the soils under them for their own common use, subject only to the rights since surrendered by the Constitution to the general government." This state right, however, is encumbered with a historic limitation that it be exercised for the common good.

This section explores two important doctrines that grew out of the key role that navigable waters have always played in the life and economy of nations. How these old doctrines ought to be extended or constrained in modern times is a continuing question for public land law. A third subsection examines other trust responsibilities that states must meet in order to fulfill the terms of statehood grants. The peculiar constitutional arrangements of federalism in the United States give rise to these related but distinct trust doctrines. Application of trust principles remains an important theme in federal public and law today.

a.   THE EQUAL FOOTING DOCTRINE

Alabama was admitted to the Union in 1819, having been carved out of territory formerly claimed by Georgia, and ceded to the United States in 1802. The Georgia deed of cession to the United States was substantially the same as the one made by Virginia when it ceded its Western land claims in the 1780s. In particular, they both stipulated that the ceded land "should be considered a common fund for the use and benefit of all the United States, to be faithfully and bona fide disposed of for that purpose, and for no other use or purpose whatever."

The following dispute involved title to submerged land covered by tidal waters. (During this era, the terms navigable and tidal were interchangeable.) The plaintiff claimed title under a patent from the United States, confirmed by an 1836 Act of Congress. Defendants claimed title under a prior Spanish land grant recognized by Georgia in 1795. The trial court ruled for defendants, holding that, because the land was below tidal waters when Alabama became a state in 1819, the United States had no authority later to grant title to plaintiffs. The Supreme Court affirmed, and Mr. Justice McKinley's majority opinion contained the following comments about state admission on an equal footing and the corresponding powers and duties of the United States.

Pollard v. Hagan

Supreme Court of the United States, 1845.
44 U.S. (3 How.) 212.

We think a proper examination of this subject will show, that the United States never held any municipal sovereignty, jurisdiction, or right of soil in and to the territory, of which Alabama or any of the new states were formed; except for temporary purposes, and to execute the trusts created by the acts of the Virginia and Georgia legislatures, and the deeds of cession executed by them to the United States, and the trust created by the treaty with the French republic, of the 30th of April, 1803, ceding Louisiana.
* * *

* * * Taking the legislative acts of the United States, and the states of Virginia and Georgia, and their deeds of cession to the United States, and giving to each, separately, and to all jointly, a fair interpretation, we must come to the conclusion that it was the intention of the parties to invest the United States with the eminent domain of the country ceded, both national and municipal, for the purposes of temporary government, and to hold it in trust for the performance of the stipulations and conditions expressed in the deeds of cession and the legislative acts connected with them. To a correct understanding of the rights, powers, and duties of the parties to these contracts, it is necessary to enter into a more minute examination of the rights of eminent domain, and the right to the public lands. When the United States accepted the cession of the territory, they took upon them-

selves the trust to hold the municipal eminent domain for the new states, and to invest them with it, to the same extent, in all respects, that it was held by the states ceding the territories. * * *

When Alabama was admitted into the union, on an equal footing with the original states, she succeeded to all the rights of sovereignty, jurisdiction, and eminent domain which Georgia possessed at the date of the cession, except so far as this right was diminished by the public lands remaining in the possession and under the control of the United States, for the temporary purposes provided for in the deed of cession and the legislative acts connected with it. Nothing remained to the United States, according to the terms of the agreement, but the public lands. And, if an express stipulation had been inserted in the agreement, granting the municipal right of sovereignty and eminent domain to the United States, such stipulation would have been void and inoperative; because the United States have no constitutional capacity to exercise municipal jurisdiction, sovereignty, or eminent domain, within the limits of a state or elsewhere, except in the cases in which it is expressly granted.

By the 16th clause of the 8th section of the 1st article of the Constitution, power is given to Congress "to exercise exclusive legislation in all cases whatsoever, over such district (not exceeding ten miles square) as may by cession of particular states, and the acceptance of Congress, become the seat of government of the United States, and to exercise like authority over all places purchased, by the consent of the legislature of the state in which the same may be, for the erection of forts, magazines, arsenals, dockyards, and other needful buildings." Within the District of Columbia, and the other places purchased and used for the purposes above mentioned, the national and municipal powers of government, of every description, are united in the government of the union. And these are the only cases, within the United States, in which all the powers of government are united in a single government, except in the cases already mentioned of the temporary territorial governments, and there a local government exists. The right of Alabama and every other new state to exercise all the powers of government, which belong to and may be exercised by the original states of the union, must be admitted, and remain unquestioned, except so far as they are, temporarily, deprived of control over the public lands.

We will now inquire into the nature and extent of the right of the United States to these lands, and whether that right can in any manner affect or control the decision of the case before us. This right originated in voluntary surrenders, made by several of the old states, of their waste and unappropriated lands, to the United States, under a resolution of the old Congress, of the 6th of September, 1780, recommending such surrender and cession, to aid in paying the public debt, incurred by the war of the Revolution. The object of all the parties to these contracts of cession, was to convert the land into money for the payment of the debt, and to erect new states over the territory thus ceded; and as soon as these purposes could be accomplished, the power of the United States over these lands, as property, was to cease.

Whenever the United States shall have fully executed these trusts, the municipal sovereignty of the new states will be complete, throughout their respective borders, and they, and the original states, will be upon an equal footing, in all respects whatever.

* * *

* * * This right of eminent domain over the shores and the soils under the navigable waters, for all municipal purposes, belongs exclusively to the states within their respective territorial jurisdictions, and they, and they only, have the constitutional power to exercise it. To give to the United States the right to transfer to a citizen the title to the shores and the soils under the navigable waters, would be placing in their hands a weapon which might be wielded greatly to the injury of state sovereignty, and deprive the states of the power to exercise a numerous and important class of police powers. But in the hands of the states this power can never be used so as to affect the exercise of any national right of eminent domain or jurisdiction with which the United States have been invested by the Constitution. For, although the territorial limits of Alabama have extended all her sovereign power into the sea, it is there, as on the shore, but municipal power, subject to the Constitution of the United States, "and the laws which shall be made in pursuance thereof."

By the preceding course of reasoning we have arrived at these general conclusions: First. The shores of navigable waters, and the soils under them, were not granted by the Constitution to the United States, but were reserved to the states respectively. Second. The new states have the same rights, sovereignty, and jurisdiction over this subject as the original states. Third. The right of the United States to the public lands, and the power of Congress to make all needful rules and regulations for the sale and disposition thereof, conferred no power to grant to the plaintiffs the land in controversy in this case.

The judgment of the Supreme Court of the state of Alabama is therefore affirmed.

■ MR. JUSTICE CATRON dissented. * * *

NOTES AND QUESTIONS

1. Article IV, section 3, clause 1 of the Constitution provides, in pertinent part, simply that "New States may be admitted by the Congress into this Union." As explained in Coyle v. Smith, 221 U.S. 559, 566–67 (1911), the "equal footing doctrine" assures those new states that they will possess governmental authority equal to all other states. *Coyle* struck down a provision in Oklahoma's statehood admission act that prevented the new state from moving the location of its state capitol for a brief period of time.

2. Although Justice McKinley used some sweeping language characterizing the expectation that the U.S. would not retain and manage lands in new states, only *Pollard's* narrow holding has survived the test of time. More than a century after *Pollard*, the U.S. Supreme Court put it this way:

> Arizona's contention that the Federal Government had no power, after
> Arizona became a State, to reserve waters for the use and benefit of
> federally reserved lands rests largely upon statements in Pollard's
> Lessee v. Hagan, 3 How. 212 (1845), and Shively v. Bowlby, 152 U.S. 1
> (1894). Those cases and others that followed them gave rise to the
> doctrine that lands underlying navigable waters within territory ac-
> quired by the Government are held in trust for future States and that
> title to such lands is automatically vested in the States upon admission
> to the Union. But those cases involved only the shores of and lands
> beneath navigable waters. They do not determine the problem before
> us and cannot be accepted as limiting the broad powers of the United
> States to regulate navigable waters under the Commerce Clause and to
> regulate government lands under Art. IV, § 3, of the Constitution.

Arizona v. California, 373 U.S. 546, 596–97 (1963). Such statements did not
prevent many in the West from insisting on the invalidity of federal land
ownership in the course of the 1970s Sagebrush Rebellion and the 1990s
County Supremacy Movement. Nonetheless, federal courts remain steadfast
in their refusal to extend the *Pollard* doctrine to anything beyond submerged lands.

3. The rule in *Pollard* has broadened in some respects over time. It
might have been limited only to those new states like Alabama which were
carved out of the land claims of the original thirteen colonies. It has,
however, long been read as applying to all new states. A water law treatise
once nicely summarized the current doctrine this way:

> On the public domain within states created out of territories, the states
> acquired title to the beds and banks up to high-water mark of that
> water which was navigable under the federal test on the date of
> admission of each such state. In these states, the federal government
> continued to hold nearly all of the remaining land as public domain,
> the newly admitted states acquiring only thin ribbons of land compris-
> ing the beds and banks of navigable waters. That may sound ridicu-
> lous, but it is true.

R. Clark, 1 WATERS AND WATER RIGHTS 250–51 (1967).

Remarkably, it was not until 1988 that the Supreme Court decided
that under the equal footing doctrine the states took title at statehood also
to submerged lands lying under waters that were influenced by the tide,
but were not navigable in fact. Phillips Petroleum Co. v. Mississippi, 484
U.S. 469 (1988). The Court found that the "ebb and flow of the tide"
standard has the benefit of history, uniformity, certainty, and ease of
application. Justice O'Connor and two others dissented on the ground that
"[n]avigability, not tidal influence, ought to be acknowledged as the universal hallmark of the public trust."

4. The states' title is not "granted" by the federal government, but
rather passes automatically to the state at statehood. A uniform federal test
is used to determine navigability:

> [S]treams or lakes which are navigable in fact must be regarded as
> navigable in law; that they are navigable in fact when they are used, or

are susceptible of being used, in their natural and ordinary condition, as highways for commerce, over which trade and travel are or may be conducted in the customary modes of trade and travel on water; and further that navigability does not depend on the particular mode in which such use is or may be had—whether by streamboats, sailing vessels or flatboats—nor on an absence of occasional difficulties in navigation, but on the fact, if it be a fact, that the stream in its ordinary condition affords a channel for useful commerce.

United States v. Holt State Bank, 270 U.S. 49, 56 (1926). This seemingly simple principle—in which the key question is navigability determined at a precise moment in time; namely, statehood—can create enormous uncertainty in the real world. It may be many years before a determination of navigability-at-statehood, and therefore title, is made. In the meantime, the states hold inchoate claims to the beds of water bodies that may have been navigable when the states were admitted to the Union. In 1971 the Supreme Court decided that Utah and not the United States owned the bed of the Great Salt Lake. That case turned on slim factual findings about the extent to which ranchers used boats to haul livestock from the mainland to islands in the lake for grazing in 1896, when Utah became a state. Utah v. United States, 403 U.S. 9 (1971). The difficulties in proving historical, commercial use of waters remain embedded in all applications of the *Pollard* doctrine.

5. Is recreation commerce? When Alaska became a state in 1959, "guided fishing and sightseeing trips began to be conducted [on the Gulkana River] with watercraft customary for that time period. A substantial industry of such transportation for profit emerged." Who owns the bed of the Gulkana? The Ninth Circuit held for the state in Alaska v. Ahtna, Inc., 891 F.2d 1401, 1405 (9th Cir. 1989), cert. denied, 495 U.S. 919 (1990).

6. "Navigability" is a confusing concept, partly because it serves federal purposes other than determining title to the beds of water bodies. For example, "navigability" helps determine the extent of federal admiralty jurisdiction, and it was frequently used in the country's early legal history as a shorthand for "commerce" in defining the extent of Congress's power to regulate. See, e.g., Gibbons v. Ogden, 22 U.S. 1 (1824). Congress has in modern times sometimes continued the practice of using "navigable waters" as the touchstone for federal regulatory power, even when it defines those waters as "waters of the United States." See, e.g., Rapanos v. United States, 126 S. Ct. 2208 (2006). Adding to the difficulty, states may apply their own definitions of navigability for determining public rights to use the surface of waters overlying private land. See, e.g., Arkansas v. McIlroy, 595 S.W.2d 659 (Ark. 1980).

7. Navigability-for-title disputes still find their way to the courts whenever there is a reason to determine ownership of beds of water bodies; e.g., for mineral development. Considerable litigation has occurred in Alaska to sort out ownership of riverbeds. See, e.g., Alaska v. United States, 201 F.3d 1154 (9th Cir. 2000). Given the abundance of water and federal land in Alaska, and its history of state-federal animosities, it is easy to foresee many problems if the state is vested with title to threads or ribbons

of submerged lands throughout the many national parks, wildlife refuges, and other federal reservations found within its borders.

8. Even if the state succeeds to ownership of the beds of waters navigable at statehood, the United States is not without legal authority to regulate the waters or the resources they contain. In Alaska v. Babbitt, 72 F.3d 698 (9th Cir. 1995), the court determined the scope of "public lands," as defined in the Alaska National Interest Lands Act (ANILCA) for purposes of applying that statute's preference for subsistence hunting and fishing by rural residents. The court held that the statutory definition includes navigable waters (overlying state lands) in which the United States has reserved water rights. The Ninth Circuit later reaffirmed this holding after the Alaska Supreme Court came to a contrary conclusion. Katie John v. United States, 247 F.3d 1032 (9th Cir. 2001).

9. The Court in Pollard v. Hagan did not resolve questions of title to submerged lands off the coasts of the United States. Many of these lands hold rich oil and gas deposits. In United States v. California, 332 U.S. 19 (1947), the Supreme Court held that the United States, and not the coastal states, owned these submerged lands. The coastal states then sought a political remedy, and the issue became a hot one in the 1952 Presidential election. When Dwight Eisenhower won that election and helped sweep the Republicans into control of Congress, the United States gave the states title to lands underneath coastal waters up to three miles offshore (or three marine leagues, along the Gulf of Mexico) in the Submerged Lands Act of 1953, 43 U.S.C. §§ 1301–1315. The United States retained ownership and jurisdiction of lands further out. Many of these submerged lands off the coast contain enormously valuable petroleum deposits.

10. The *Pollard* principle is subject to a very important exception; namely, the Court has held that the United States may reserve the beds of navigable waters for federal purposes prior to statehood and this prevents title from passing to the new state. The Court has, however, adopted the interpretive principle that such reservations must be clearly expressed in order to be effective. See, e.g., Utah Div. of State Lands v. United States, 482 U.S. 193 (1987). Where such clarity is not found, the *Pollard* rule recognizes that states have inholdings in the submerged lands underlying water bodies that were navigable at statehood in federal reservations such as national parks, even if they were created prior to statehood. In its most recent decision on this issue, the Court split 5–4, the slim majority holding that the U.S. had reserved part of the bed of Lake Coeur d'Alene and part of the St. Joe River to bar transfer of title to Idaho at statehood. Idaho v. United States, 533 U.S. 262 (2001).

11. Sometimes the application of these rules can have large fiscal and environmental consequences. In 1957 the Secretary of the Interior formally proposed a withdrawal of lands (including submerged lands under navigable waters) in northeast Alaska in order to create the Arctic National Wildlife Refuge. The withdrawal was not formally completed, however, until after Alaska gained statehood in 1959. The state later sued to quiet title to the submerged lands to advance its desire to exploit possible oil and gas resources in the area, which is to the east of the giant Prudhoe Bay oil

field that supplies Alaska with the bulk of its state revenue. The Supreme Court ruled that the 1957 proposal effectively segregated the submerged lands and prevented them from passing to the State at statehood. United States v. Alaska, 521 U.S. 1 (1997). Justice O'Connor, writing for the majority, reasoned that (1) the 1957 proposal "reflected a clear intent to reserve submerged lands as well as uplands;" (2) the Interior Department's position, expressed in a regulation promulgated in 1952, was that a proposal for a withdrawal temporarily segregated the lands in the proposal pending final action by the Secretary; and (3) the Statehood Act contained a specific provision that the State would not take title to "lands withdrawn *or otherwise set apart* as refuges or reservations for the protection of wildlife," 72 Stat. 340–41 (emphasis added), and the temporary segregation in 1957 fell within the italicized language of the Statehood Act. Therefore, federal ownership of the submerged lands in the Refuge survived statehood and the *Pollard* principle. Justice Thomas, joined by Chief Justice Rehnquist and Justice Scalia, dissented.

The "Great Land" of Alaska continues to spawn litigation in this area. In Alaska v. United States, 545 U.S. 75 (2005), the U.S. Supreme Court held that the United States reserved title to the bed of Glacier Bay National Monument (whose eponymous glaciers have retreated 55 miles inward in the past two centuries) so that it did not pass to the State at statehood. The majority noted, among other things, that efforts to protect the brown bear (and its food supply in estuarine waters) had been influential in the movement to protect the area. Dissenting Justice Scalia, with characteristic acerbity, scorned the majority's "Ursine Rhapsody" and would have found the strong presumption in favor of title passing to the state not rebutted.

NOTE: THE SAGEBRUSH REBELLION AND COUNTY SUPREMACY MOVEMENTS

Federal ownership of large tracts of lands within the borders of western states has always been a politically attractive whipping boy for western politicians. Some defenders of "states' rights" were outraged when Congress in 1976 made explicit what had long been implicit: the United States was going to retain most BLM-managed public lands in federal ownership. Their bitterness was not assuaged by the fact that primary shapers of this legislation, the Federal Land Policy and Management Act, were westerners in Congress.

Growing environmental restrictions on the use of these federal lands combined with a disaffection with national government in the late 1970s to create a movement to claim ownership of federal lands in the western states. Called the "Sagebrush Rebellion" by its supporters, and the "Great Terrain Robbery" by opponents, the movement was led by disgruntled ranchers whose grazing privileges on public lands were threatened with reduction. Utah Senator Orrin Hatch, succumbing to oratorical excess in his support for the rebellion, saw the local federal land manager as akin to the Sheriff of Nottingham. The Sagebrush Rebels asserted that their claim of ownership had a constitutional basis, putting forward primarily a tenth amendment and an equal footing argument (relying on *dicta* in Pollard v. Hagan). Several Western states, led by Nevada, passed laws claiming ownership of BLM-managed public land and, in a couple of cases, national forest land as well. (Shortly after the Nevada legislature enacted this statute into law, state officials hurried to Washington to make sure that their claim of ownership would not result in interruption of federal payments to the state which were based on continuing federal land ownership. The various programs authorizing these payments are described at *infra* p. 159.)

The Rebellion gained considerable publicity in 1980; Ronald Reagan declared himself a Sagebrush Rebel during his successful campaign for the Presidency, but his Administration defended federal ownership against state claims to the contrary. Litigation sought to test these claims, but the courts never reached the merits in any final judgment. See Nevada ex rel. Nevada State Bd. of Agric. v. United States, 512 F. Supp. 166 (D. Nev. 1981), aff'd, 699 F.2d 486 (9th Cir. 1983).

In the 1990s, conservation restrictions on the use of federal land led to another outbreak of anti-federal sentiment, again led by ranchers in the rural Rocky Mountain west. Once again continuing federal ownership and management of federal lands was claimed to be unconstitutional. This time around, however, two things were different. First, no state joined the movement, although a few counties did. Second, the courts did get to the merits of the claim, and soundly rejected it.

United States v. Gardner

United States Court of Appeals, Ninth Circuit, 1997.
107 F.3d 1314, cert. denied, 522 U.S. 907 (1997).

■ CHOY, CIRCUIT JUDGE

[The Gardners owned a ranch near the Humboldt National Forest in Nevada, and had a permit to graze some cattle on a portion of the forest. A fire burned a portion of their allotment in 1992, and the Forest Service and the State of Nevada reseeded the burned area and closed it to grazing for two years to allow it to recover. The Gardners disobeyed the closure order and were fined for trespassing. They refused to pay, and the U.S. brought a lawsuit seeking damages and an injunction.]

I.   The United States' Title to Federal Land in Nevada[1]

Gardners argue that grazing their livestock in the Humboldt National Forest without a permit does not constitute trespass because the federal government does not have title to the land on which the grazing took place.

---

1. An Amicus Brief was filed on behalf of the states of New Mexico, Alaska, Maine, Montana, Oregon, Vermont, and, significantly, Nevada supporting the position of the United States in this case. Additionally, a federal district court in Nevada has held that title to the public lands within Nevada's boundaries rests in the United States. *United States v. Nye County*, 920 F. Supp. 1108 (D. Nev. 1996).

Gardners contend that, while the United States may have received the land in question from Mexico in the Treaty of Guadalupe Hidalgo in 1848, the United States was entitled only to hold the land in trust for the creation of future states, and was not authorized to retain the land for its own purposes. After Nevada became a state, Gardners argue, all of the public lands within the state boundaries reverted to the state of Nevada.[2] * * *

The claim by Gardners that it is the duty of the United States to hold public lands in trust for the formation of future states is founded on a case dealing with land acquired by the United States from the thirteen original states. In that case, *Pollard's Lessee v. Hagan,* 44 U.S. (3 How.) 212, the Supreme Court discussed the extent of the United States' authority over lands ceded to it from Virginia and Georgia to discharge debt incurred by those states during the Revolutionary War. The Court stated that the United States held this land in trust for the establishment of future states. Once those new states were established, the United States' authority over the land would cease. This decision was based on the terms of the cessions of the land from Virginia and Georgia to the United States. Before becoming a state, however, Nevada had no independent claim to sovereignty, unlike the original thirteen states. Therefore, the same reasoning is not applicable to this case, in which the federal government was the initial owner of the land from which the state of Nevada was later carved.

* * *

The United States, then, was not required to hold the public lands in Nevada in trust for the establishment of future states. Rather, under the Property Clause, the United States can administer its federal lands any way it chooses, including the establishment of a national forest reserve.

II. The Equal Footing Doctrine

Gardners argue that, under the Equal Footing Doctrine, a new state must possess the same powers of sovereignty and jurisdiction as did the original thirteen states upon admission to the Union. Because the federal government owns over eighty percent of the land in the state of Nevada, Gardners argue, Nevada is not on an equal footing with the original thirteen states.[3] Gardners claim that Nevada must have "paramount title and eminent domain of *all* lands within its boundaries" to satisfy the Equal Footing Doctrine. * * *

---

2. Gardners point out that [in 1979 Nevada] * * * passed a statute claiming ownership over all public lands within its boundaries, Nev. Rev. Stat. 321.5973. Gardners claim that the passage of this law further demonstrates that title to the public lands in Nevada properly rests in the state, not the federal, government. Gardners fail to note, however, that the Nevada statute by its own terms excludes national forest lands from the public lands claimed by Nevada. *See* Nev. Rev. Stat. § 321.5963.

3. For example, in New Hampshire the federal government owns just under thirteen percent of the land. The federal government owns between two and seven percent of the land within the borders of nine of the other original thirteen states. In Connecticut, New York and Rhode Island, less than one percent of the land is owned by the federal government. Bureau of Land Management, U.S. Department of the Interior, Public Land Statistics 1993, at 5, Table 3 (September 1994).

[T]he Supreme Court has declined to extend the Equal Footing Doctrine to lands other than those underneath navigable waters or waters affected by the ebb and flow of the tides. * * * [Here the Court cited and discussed *Scott v. Lattig,* 227 U.S. 229, 244 (1913) and *Texas v. Louisiana,* 410 U.S. 702, 713 (1973), for the proposition that the Equal Footing Doctrine] does not operate to reserve title to fast dry lands to individual states.

Moreover, the Supreme Court has long held that the Equal Footing Doctrine refers to "those attributes essential to [a state's] equality in dignity and power with other States." *Coyle v. Smith,* 221 U.S. 559, 568 (1911). The Court has noted that a new state enters the Union "in full equality with all the others," and that this equality may forbid a compact between a new state and the United States "limiting or qualifying political rights and obligations." *Stearns v. Minnesota,* 179 U.S. 223, 245 (1900). However, "a mere agreement in reference to property involves no question of equality of status." *Id.* The Court has observed that "[s]ome States when they entered the Union had within their boundaries tracts of land belonging to the Federal Government; others were sovereigns of their soil." *United States v. Texas,* 339 U.S. 707, 716 (1950). While these disparities may cause economic differences between the states, the purpose of the Equal Footing Doctrine is not to eradicate all diversity among states but rather to establish equality among the states with regards to political standing and sovereignty.

The Equal Footing Doctrine, then, applies to political rights and sovereignty, not to economic or physical characteristics of the states. Moreover, the Equal Footing Doctrine applies primarily to the shores of and lands beneath navigable waters, not to fast dry lands. Therefore, the Equal Footing Doctrine would not operate, as Gardners argue, to give Nevada title to the public lands within its boundaries.

III. The Validity of Nevada's "Disclaimer Clause"

When Congress invited Nevada to join the Union in 1864, it mandated that the Nevada constitutional convention pass an act promising that Nevada would "forever disclaim all right and title to the unappropriated public lands lying within said territory, and that the same shall be and remain at the sole and entire disposition of the United States...." Nevada Statehood Act of March 21, 1864, 13 Stat. 30, 31 § 4. The state constitutional convention did so. Ordinance of the Nevada Constitution.

* * *

Gardners are correct in their argument that the disclaimer is declaratory. However, the United States did not need the disclaimer clause to gain title to the public lands in Nevada. The United States already had title to those lands through the Treaty of Guadalupe Hidalgo, and the disclaimer clause was merely a recognition of the preexisting United States title, as opposed to a grant of title from Nevada to the United States.

IV. The Tenth Amendment

Gardners argue that federal ownership of the public lands in Nevada is unconstitutional under the Tenth Amendment. Such ownership, they argue, invades "core state powers reserved to Nevada," such as the police power.

Federal ownership of the public lands within a state does not completely divest the state from the ability to exercise its own sovereignty over that land. The state government and the federal government exercise concurrent jurisdiction over the land. * * * *Kleppe v. New Mexico* * * * The state of Nevada, then, is not being unconstitutionally deprived of the ability to govern the land within its borders. The state may exercise its civil and criminal jurisdiction over federal lands within its borders as long as it exercises its power in a manner that does not conflict with federal law. * * *

NOTES AND QUESTIONS

1. Does Nevada own the beds of waters within its borders, including those within forest reserves, which were navigable at statehood, under the doctrine of Pollard v. Hagan? If it does, does the court adequately explain why the equal footing doctrine draws a line between the beds of navigable waters and uplands? Is there a principled basis for that line other than that the Supreme Court applied the doctrine to the beds of navigable waters in Pollard v. Hagan because at that time the Court viewed the relationship between the national government and the states differently from how it viewed the relationship in later cases? Is that explanation satisfactory?

2. Why do you suppose Nevada and other states filed an *amicus* brief in support of the United States? At this time, Nevada still had on its books the 1979 statute it had passed claiming ownership of BLM public lands.

3. Why don't opponents of federal land management, and particularly of the restrictions on use that come with this management, take their case to Congress rather than to the courts? Why, in other words, do they often choose to couch their opposition in arguments that it is unconstitutional for the federal government to own these lands?

b.   THE PUBLIC TRUST DOCTRINE

The public trust doctrine is another principle relevant to submerged lands. While the equal footing doctrine focuses on the intent of the United States in transferring title to lands under navigable waters, the public trust doctrine concentrates on the duties of the state in managing and disposing those lands. The two doctrines are linked historically as well. James R. Rasband, *The Disregarded Common Parentage of the Equal Footing and Public Trust Doctrines*, 32 LAND & WATER L.REV. 1 (1997). An opinion by the Supreme Court in 1892 is the key precedent endorsing a fiduciary duty that the new states implicitly acquired along with ownership of submerged beds.

Illinois Central Railroad Co. v. Illinois

Supreme Court of the United States, 1892.
146 U.S. 387.

■ JUSTICE FIELD delivered the opinion of the court.

[The State of Illinois granted to the Illinois Central Railroad—an entity which, Justice Field noted, was already the recipient of a large federal railroad land grant—a significant chunk of downtown Chicago's waterfront on Lake Michigan, including the submerged lands in Chicago's harbor. The grant was made under dubious circumstances, passing over the Governor's veto after a surreptitious change in the recipient from the City of Chicago to the railroad. The grant provided for royalty payments to Chicago, but its city council refused to accept them. Four years later, the Illinois Legislature passed legislation purporting to revoke the grant, and the Illinois Attorney General brought suit to quiet title in the state to the submerged harbor lands. The district court held for the State. Reciting the Pollard v. Hagan rule that the State succeeded to ownership of lands beneath navigable waters, Justice Field wrote that Illinois had acquired title to the lands in dispute at statehood.]

The question, therefore, to be considered is whether the legislature was competent to thus deprive the State of its ownership of the submerged lands in the harbor of Chicago, and of the consequent control of its waters; or, in other words, whether the railroad corporation can hold the lands and control the waters by the grant, against any future exercise of power over them by the State.

* * * [T]he State holds the title to the lands under the navigable waters of Lake Michigan, within its limits, in the same manner that the State holds title to soils under tide water, by the common law, * * * and that title necessarily carries with it control over the waters above them whenever the lands are subjected to use. But it is a title different in character from that which the State holds in lands intended for sale. It is different from the title which the United States hold in the public lands which are open to preemption and sale. It is a title held in trust for the people of the State that they may enjoy the navigation of the waters, carry on commerce over them, and have liberty of fishing therein freed from the obstruction or interference of private parties. The interest of the people in the navigation of the waters and in commerce over them may be improved in many instances by the erection of wharves, docks and piers therein, for which purpose the State may grant parcels of the submerged lands; and, so long as their disposition is made for such purpose, no valid objections can be made to the grants. [Such] grants * * * do not substantially impair the public interest in the lands and waters remaining * * *. But that is a very different doctrine from the one which would sanction the abdication of the general control of the State over lands under the navigable waters of an entire harbor or bay, or of a sea or lake. Such abdication is not consistent with the exercise of that trust which requires the government of the State to preserve such waters for the use of the public. The trust devolving upon the State for the public, and which can only be discharged by the management and control of property in which the public has an interest, cannot be relinquished by a transfer of the property. The control of the State for the purposes of the trust can never be lost, except as to such parcels as are used in promoting the interests of the public therein, or can be disposed of without any substantial impairment of the public interest in the lands and waters remaining. * * * [T]he distinction [must be maintained] between a

grant of such parcels for the improvement of the public interest, or which when occupied do not substantially impair the public interest in the lands and waters remaining, and a grant of the whole property in which the public is interested * * *. General language sometimes found in opinions of the courts, expressive of absolute ownership and control by the State of lands under navigable waters, irrespective of any trust as to their use and disposition, must be read and construed with reference to the special facts of the particular cases. A grant of all the lands under the navigable waters of a State has never been adjudged to be within the legislative power; and any attempted grant of the kind would be held, if not absolutely void on its face, as subject to revocation. The State can no more abdicate its trust over property in which the whole people are interested, like navigable waters and soils under them, so as to leave them entirely under the use and control of private parties, except in the instance of parcels mentioned for the improvement of the navigation and use of the waters, or when parcels can be disposed of without impairment of the public interest in what remains, than it can abdicate its police powers in the administration of government and the preservation of the peace. In the administration of government the use of such powers may for a limited period be delegated to a municipality or other body, but there always remains with the State the right to revoke those powers and exercise them in a more direct manner, and one more conformable to its wishes. So with trusts connected with public property, or property of a special character, like lands under navigable waters, they cannot be placed entirely beyond the direction and control of the State.

The harbor of Chicago is of immense value to the people of the State of Illinois in the facilities it affords to its vast and constantly increasing commerce; and the idea that its legislature can deprive the State of control over its bed and waters and place the same in the hands of a private corporation created for a different purpose, one limited to transportation of passengers and freight between distant points and the city, is a proposition that cannot be defended. * * *

Any grant of the kind is necessarily revocable, and the exercise of the trust by which the property was held by the State can be resumed at any time. Undoubtedly there may be expenses incurred in improvements made under such a grant which the State ought to pay; but, be that as it may, the power to resume the trust whenever the State judges best is, we think, incontrovertible. The position advanced by the railroad company in support of its claim to the ownership of the submerged lands and the right to the erection of wharves, piers and docks at its pleasure, or for its business in the harbor of Chicago, would place every harbor in the country at the mercy of a majority of the legislature of the State in which the harbor is situated.

We cannot, it is true, cite any authority where a grant of this kind has been held invalid, for we believe that no instance exists where the harbor of a great city and its commerce have been allowed to pass into the control of any private corporation. But the decisions are numerous which declare that such property is held by the State, by virtue of its sovereignty, in trust for the public. The ownership of the navigable waters of the harbor and of the lands under them is a subject of public concern to the whole people of the State. The trust with which they are held, therefore, is governmental and cannot be alienated, except in those instances mentioned of parcels used in the improvement of the interest thus held, or when parcels can be disposed of without detriment to the public interest in the lands and waters remaining. * * *

NOTES AND QUESTIONS

1.   Is the Court saying that certain kinds of government-owned property are different from other kinds, and justifies a continuing servitude or limitation on their title? What kinds? What makes these lands different from other government lands?

2.   Is this just a special form of eminent domain? Is that what Justice Field meant when he said grants of such land are "necessarily revocable"? Did he mean that the State can choose to take the land back at any time (in effect, exercising a right of eminent domain), not by paying the grantee fair market value, but rather simply compensating the grantee for its "expenses incurred in improvements made under such a grant"?

Or is the idea simply one of police power regulation; namely, that the state does not, by granting this land, "abdicate general control" over it? Is Justice Field saying that property like a harbor has such high public values that the state does not relinquish, by mere transfer of title, strong regulatory control over how such lands are used, in order to protect the public interest. (Today, of course, the notion of regulatory police power has evolved so that it is generally understood to apply to the use of practically all kinds of property.)

3.   What is the source of this public trust limitation? The federal constitution? Federal common law? State law? Can it be overturned by statute?

4.   In 1990, history seemed to repeat itself when a federal district court applied it to void the conveyance by Illinois of submerged lands under Lake Michigan to a university for expansion of its campus. Lake Michigan Fed'n v. U.S. Army Corps of Engineers, 742 F. Supp. 441 (N.D. Ill. 1990). Illinois Central continues to spawn re-examination. Douglas L. Grant, *Underpinnings of the Public Trust Doctrine: Lessons from Illinois Central Railroad*, 33 ARIZ. ST. L.J. 849 (2001); Joseph D. Kearney & Thomas W. Merrill, *The Origins of the American Public Trust Doctrine: What Really Happened in Illinois Central*, 71 U. CHICAGO L.REV. 799 (2004). On the role of public land policies, railroads, and shipping in the rise of Chicago, see William Cronon, NATURE'S METROPOLIS (1991).

5.   State courts have used the public trust doctrine to uphold public access to dry sand beaches (Matthews v. Bay Head Improvement Ass'n, 471 A.2d 355 (N.J. 1984)); to require strict judicial review when state parklands are leased for private use (Gould v. Greylock Reservation Comm'n, 215 N.E.2d 114 (Mass. 1966)); to demand payment of full market value when

state lands are leased (Jerke v. State Dept. of Lands, 597 P.2d 49 (Mont. 1979)); to prevent a state from relinquishing its claims to ownership of beds of water bodies that were possibly navigable at statehood (Defenders of Wildlife v. Governor Jane Dee Hull, 18 P.3d 722 (Ariz. Ct. App. 2001)); to confer standing on an environmental group to challenge a timber sale on state forest lands because of its allegation that harm to a stream and its fish will result (Selkirk–Priest Basin Ass'n v. Idaho ex rel. Andrus, 899 P.2d 949, 953–55 (Idaho 1995)); and to guide water management in Hawaii (In re Water Use Permit Applications (Waiahole Ditch), 9 P.3d 409 (Haw. 2000)). For a review of the doctrine at the state level, see Arnold L. Lum, *How Goes the Public Trust Doctrine: Is the Common Law Shaping Environmental Policy?*, 18 NAT. RES. & ENV'T 73 (Fall 2003).

California has taken it the furthest. In 1940 the City of Los Angeles had established appropriative rights under state law to the waters of four non-navigable tributaries to Mono Lake below the eastern escarpment of the Sierra Nevada range. Over time the City's diversions lowered the lake level with serious environmental effects. In National Audubon Society v. Superior Court, 658 P.2d 709 (Cal. 1983), the Court held that the City's vested water rights were subject to reexamination by the State Water Board in order to protect the public trust: "The human and environmental uses of Mono Lake—uses protected by the public trust doctrine—deserve to be taken into account. Such uses should not be destroyed because the state mistakenly thought itself powerless to protect them." 658 P.2d at 732.

––––––––––––

At the dawn of modern environmental era, Professor Sax revived Illinois Central, identifying it as a taproot of resource protection law. Joseph L. Sax, *The Public Trust Doctrine in Natural Resources Law: Effective Judicial Intervention*, 68 MICH. L.REV. 471 (1970). Sax emphasized the trust's utility as a mechanism for the courts to limit the discretion of executive branch agencies. The considerable scholarly debate about whether and how the doctrine should apply to federal land and natural resource management is captured in the following two excerpts.

Charles F. Wilkinson, The Public Trust Doctrine in Public Land Law

14 U.C. DAVIS L. REV. 269 (1980).

* * * The federal public lands are at the outer reaches of the public trust doctrine. * * * [I]nland federal lands are not "trust resources" according to the classic formulation of the doctrine. * * * In addition to the lack of direct support in either common law or Indian law, there are a number of compelling policy reasons supporting the conclusion that the public trust doctrine, at least in its classic form, does not apply to the public lands. First, the history of public land policy denies the existence of any prohibition against disposition of federal lands. * * * No serious suggestion could be made that private title to some 1.4 billion acres is

clouded due to the United States' inability to convey clear title. Second, public land law is a heavily statutory field. The legislative matrix is sufficiently comprehensive that doubts can fairly be raised as to whether there is room for a broad, common law doctrine to operate.

Another basis for objection arises from the diversity of the public lands. * * * For example, it is one thing to refer to the dominant-use National Park Service as a trustee; it is a far different matter to place traditional trust obligations on the BLM, which must reconcile the congressionally sanctioned multiple-use tug and pull among economic and noneconomic uses. This range of geographic and legal diversity makes it difficult to apply a single, unitary doctrine to all of the public lands.

Finally, while there may be majesty aplenty on the public lands, there are many, even in these land-appreciative days, who would say that most of the public land holdings are common, even mundane. * * *

[Wilkinson then argued that many modern court decisions have, implicitly or explicitly, applied public trust notions, and he advocates reading them more explicitly into the interpretation and application of statutes.] * * * The modern [public lands and natural resources] statutes are premised on the high station that today's society accords to the economic and environmental values of the federal lands and resources. They are rigorous laws designed to protect the public's interest in the public's resources. The legislation requires that public lands and resources not be sold, except in limited and exceptional circumstances; that the public resources are to be nurtured and preserved; that the public is to play a measured but significant role in decision-making; and that the lands and resources are to be managed on a sustained-yield basis for future generations.

The whole of these laws is greater than the sum of its parts. The modern statutes set a tone, a context, a milieu. When read together they require a trustee's care. Thus we can expect courts today, like courts in earlier eras, to characterize Congress' modern legislative scheme as imposing a public trust on the public resources. * * * The trust concept has been properly invoked as the best available formulation of the central doctrinal forces in public land law—that increasingly tough strictures are required, and have been imposed, on land management officials; that land management is not a private business; that ultimate accountability is to the public; and that over time the public and Congress have come to place ever greater importance on the nation's public natural resources.

The trust notion, as a generic concept, is an appropriate description of the federal role in public land law. It is a common-sense description that has evolved in regard to the inland public lands just as it has developed in closely related subject areas. The more difficult issue * * * is determining the scope and content of the trust. [After concluding that it cannot be enforced against the Congress, he sketches out some possible applications.]

[It could] operate as a limitation on the discretion of administrative agencies. First, it might be used, as it has been in several states, to require express legislative authority when public resources are being unreasonably used by administrative agencies to promote private gain. Second, it would provide the basis for an ultimate "hard look" doctrine for reviewing administrative action. As such, it would be a doctrine advanced by environmentalists and by industry and would have no ideological content. The doctrine could be invoked by industry, for example, to emphasize the high standard of care incumbent on the Forest Service if it mishandled a timber sale, or on the BLM if it unreasonably delayed the processing of competitive bidding on a mineral lease.

* * * [It could] affect the interpretation of a number of statutes. For example, the question of impliedly reserved water rights has been largely resolved on National Forest lands, but the extent of protection afforded to wildlife and public recreational and aesthetic opportunities by other land-management systems has not been determined. * * * The answers to all of these questions would be affected if the courts construed the acts to effectuate Congress' intent to act as a trustee charged with the duty of protecting and preserving the public resources.

* * * Another use of the public trust doctrine in regard to public lands is what might be called the action-forcing cases. * * * The questions arise whether public land managers can be compelled to take affirmative action, including litigation, to protect federal lands, and whether the public trust doctrine can play a part in such determinations.

Richard J. Lazarus, Changing Conceptions of Property and Sovereignty in Natural Resources: Questioning the Public Trust Doctrine

71 Iowa L. Rev. 631, 633, 710, 715–16 (1986).

* * * [T]he historical function of the public trust doctrine has been to provide a public property basis for resisting the exercise of private property rights in natural resources deemed contrary to the public interest. In recent decades, however, especially during the last ten years, modern trends in natural resources law increasingly have eroded traditional concepts of private property rights in natural resources and substituted new notions of sovereign power over those resources. These trends, reflected in a wide variety of legal contexts ranging from federal environmental protection statutes and new state resource allocation laws to evolving common-law principles of tort law, are currently weaving a new fabric for natural resources law that is more responsive to current social values and the physical characteristics of the resources. By continuing to resist a legal system that is otherwise being abandoned, the public trust doctrine obscures analysis and renders more difficult the important process of reworking natural resources law. Of even broader concern, the doctrine threatens to fuel a developing clash in liberal ideology between furthering individual rights of security and dignity, bound up in notions of private property protection, and supporting environmental protection and resource preservation goals, inevitably dependent on intrusive governmental programs designed to achieve longer-term collectivist goals.

* * *

* * * [A]part from its failure to provide needed candor, and its inflexibility in the face of changing values and knowledge, reliance on the doctrine should be abandoned because it offers too tenuous a basis for protecting important environmental protection and resource conservation objectives. Three separate factors * * * favor such a strategic retreat. First, trust values will never adequately reflect modern environmental concerns. Second, the doctrine unjustifiably relies on the judiciary to further its environmental goals and, consequently, ultimately depends on a proenvironment judicial bias that is not enduring. Third, recent judicial decisions, in particular those of the Supreme Court, make it clear that any special legal status the trust rationale has enjoyed in the past is waning.

* * *

Simply put, the public trust doctrine, even if aimed at promoting needed resource conservation and environmental protection goals, is a step in the wrong direction. The doctrine amounts to a romantic step backward toward a bygone era at a time when we face modern problems that demand candid and honest debate on the merits, including consideration of current social values and the latest scientific information. The complex and pressing resource allocation and environmental protection issues we currently face will continue to tax severely the most concerted societal efforts and the best legal and scientific minds. Dramatic shifts in legal rules, primarily in traditional notions of private property, will continue to be necessary, challenging the patience and understanding of the public, to whom the law must ultimately justify its legitimacy. Although perhaps unfortunate, short of a major redirection of this nation's social and economic infrastructure, little, if any, room is left in these tasks ahead for the mythopoeism of the public trust doctrine.

NOTES AND QUESTIONS

1. Professor Huffman has been a persistent critic of the expansion of the public trust doctrine to include modern environmental concerns. He argues that the public trust doctrine is simply a run-of-the-mill easement under state property law to accommodate navigation and fishing. James L. Huffman, *A Fish Out of Water: The Public Trust Doctrine in a Constitutional Democracy*, 19 ENVTL. L. 527 (1989). Professor Pearson is skeptical that the public trust doctrine will ever be a viable part of federal public land litigation. He argues that the courts will not second-guess Congress's implementation of its trust responsibility for federal lands, and concludes that the public trust notion "empowers the political branches of government to implement substantive choices despite objections in the judicial branch." He contrasts this with the doctrine's operation in state law, where it "empowers the judicial branch to overturn substantive choices made by the political branches. * * * Night, meet day." Eric Pearson, *The Public Trust Doctrine in Federal Law*, 24 J. LAND, RESOURCES & ENVTL. L. 173, 176–77 (2004).

2. In connection with Professor Wilkinson's suggestion that there is room for the courts to apply the public trust doctrine in this heavily

statutory field, consider the following 1978 amendment to the National Park Organic Act (16 U.S.C. § 1):

> Congress further reaffirms, declares and directs that the protection, management and administration of [the various areas of the National Park System] shall be conducted in light of the high public value and integrity of the National Park System and shall not be exercised in derogation of the values and purposes for which these areas have been established, except as may have been or shall be directly and specifically provided by Congress.

Around the same time that Congress revisited the Park System charter, environmentalists argued that non-statutory trust duties of the National Park Service and the BLM required those agencies to take affirmative steps to protect water resources on the lands under their management from depletion. A federal district court disagreed:

> To the extent that plaintiff's argument advances the proposition that defendants are charged with "trust" duties distinguishable from their statutory duties, the Court disagrees. Rather, the Court views the statutory duties previously discussed as comprising all the responsibilities which defendants must faithfully discharge.
>
> The legislative history of the 1978 amendment to 16 U.S.C. § 1a–1 makes clear that any distinction between "trust" and "statutory" responsibilities in the management of the National Park System is unfounded. Moreover, Congress specifically addressed the authority upon which plaintiff relies to support its "trust theory":
>
>> The committee has been concerned that * * * [a federal court] may have blurred the responsibilities articulated by the 1916 Act creating the National Park Service * * *.
>>
>> [T]he committee strongly endorses the Administration's proposed amendment to the Act of August 18, 1970, concerning the management of the National Park System to refocus and insure the basis for decisionmaking concerning the system continues to be the criteria provided by 16 U.S.C.A. § 1 * * *. This restatement of these highest principles of management is also intended to serve as the basis for any judicial resolution of competing private and public values and interest in * * * areas of the National Park System.
>
> Senate Report 95–528, supra, at 14, 7–8 (emphasis added). By asserting an explicit statutory standard "as the basis of any judicial resolution" of Park management issues, Congress eliminated "trust" notions in National Park System management. The Court also concludes that §§ 1701 and 1782(c) of title 43 United States Code embody the entire duty and responsibility to manage and protect Bureau of Land Management lands generally with which the Secretary is charged.

Sierra Club v. Andrus, 487 F. Supp. 443, 449 (D.D.C. 1980), *aff'd on other grounds sub nom*. Sierra Club v. Watt, 659 F.2d 203 (D.C. Cir. 1981).

Did the Court err in giving conclusive weight to what a congressional committee in 1976 thought was the proper interpretation of the 1916 National Park Service organic act? In fact, the same Senate Committee Report contained the following statement (at p. 9): "The Secretary has an absolute duty, which is not to be compromised, to fulfill the mandate of the 1916 Act to take whatever actions and seek whatever relief as will safeguard the units of the National Park System." Should courts look beyond statutes to find management principles for public lands?

3.   If the public trust doctrine is a rationale for exercising closer judicial review of actions by federal land management agencies, does or should it apply to all such actions, or only certain kinds? For example, suppose Congress authorizes the BLM to lease federal lands for grazing at an "appropriate" fee, and fair market value is one dollar per acre. May the BLM set the fee at a nickel per acre without violating the public trust?

4.   Another way to think about the doctrine is this: If it bears some analogy to private trust principles, who are the beneficiaries of the trust? The general public? Taxpayers? Do the beneficiaries include extractors of resources of the federal lands (miners, grazers, loggers)? Those who consume those extracted resources? Future generations? Suppose Congress has authorized the Secretary of the Interior to lease federal lands for energy development upon a determination that it would "serve the public interest." If foreign supplies of oil are cut off, and an energy shortage grips the country, could a court use the public trust doctrine to order the Secretary to lease certain lands for oil development?

5.   Even the doctrine's strongest modern advocates do not think it applies to the Congress. Given Congress's broad power over federal lands under the Property Clause, can one make a serious argument that the public trust doctrine may be judicially enforced to prevent Congress from, say, selling Yosemite Valley to private parties, or authorizing it to be leased and strip-mined?

c.   GRANTS TO STATES AND MORE TRUST OBLIGATIONS

States were primary beneficiaries of federal land disposition policy, especially through land grants made as part of the statehood process. The creation of new states on an "equal footing" with other states was first and foremost a political process, worked through the Congress. The admission of Ohio in 1803 created the basic model for later federal land grants to new states. Congress agreed to grant the Buckeye State one section per township (four percent of its land area) for the benefit of its common schools, five percent of the net proceeds of federal land sales within the state for road-building funds, and other incidental interests in land.

The grants to the states took two basic forms. The first, and more important, were "in-place" grants of specified numbered sections of land. These were usually for the purpose of supporting the new state's "common schools." The actual location of these lands could not be determined until the land was surveyed and section lines established. The survey might not be completed for many decades after statehood; indeed, there is still some federal land that has never been surveyed. If, before survey, the federal government had disposed of or made other uses of these land sections by formal reservation or withdrawal, the states were given the right to make "in lieu" selections of other available federal lands as "indemnity" for the unsatisfied "in-place" school grants. Andrus v. Utah, below, involved this type of grant. The second form was "quantity" grants of a specified amount of acreage, not identified on the ground by survey, but rather to be selected by the state from available federal land, to support various public purposes, such as highways, jails, or other public purposes. Under both forms, the granted lands were not expected to be used as actual sites for schools, highways, jails, and so forth (although they could be used for such purposes). Instead, they were supposed to be sold or leased or otherwise managed to produce income to be devoted to these purposes. Several states retained a significant portion of granted lands and manage them as "school trust" systems. There is a growing body of state law governing the management of these state trust lands, discussed in the notes following the case below.

As more and more states were admitted, the purposes of the grants were modified, and the quantities of the grants were gradually liberalized. Some new states were given federal lands for higher education, for jails and other public buildings, and for internal improvements other than roads. Utah (admitted in 1896) was the first to be given four sections of federal land in every township, or about 11 percent of the acreage in the state, for common schools. Arizona and New Mexico (admitted in 1912) each received that amount of common school lands, plus over 2 million acres of other federal lands for various public purposes. As the following case shows, the terms and effect of statehood grants still provoke litigation.

Andrus v. Utah

Supreme Court of the United States, 1980.
446 U.S. 500.

■ Justice Stevens delivered the opinion of the Court.

The State of Utah claims the right to select extremely valuable oil shale lands located within federal grazing districts in lieu of and as indemnification for original school land grants of significantly lesser value that were frustrated by federal preemption, or private entry, prior to survey. The question presented is whether the Secretary of the Interior is obliged to accept Utah's selections of substitute tracts of the same size as the originally designated sections even though there is a gross disparity between the value of the original grants and the selected substitutes. We hold that the Secretary's "grossly disparate value" policy is a lawful exercise of the broad discretion vested in him by § 7 of the Taylor Grazing Act of 1934, as amended in 1936, 43 U.S.C. § 315f, and is a valid ground for refusing to accept Utah's selections.

Utah became a State in 1896. In the Utah Enabling Act of 1894, Congress granted Utah, upon admission, four numbered sections in each township for the support of public schools. [Eds. note: The Act awarded

Utah numbered sections 2, 16, 32 and 36 in each township] The statute provided that if the designated sections had already "been sold or otherwise disposed of" pursuant to another act of Congress, "other lands equivalent thereto * * * are hereby granted." The substitute grants, denominated "indemnity lands" were "to be selected within [the] State in such manner as [its] legislature may provide with the approval of the Secretary of the Interior."

Because much of the State was not surveyed until long after its admission to the Union, its indemnity or "in lieu" selections were not made promptly. On September 10, 1965, Utah filed the first of 194 selection lists with the Bureau of Land Management of the Department of the Interior covering the land in dispute in this litigation. The 194 indemnity selections include 157,255.90 acres in Uintah County, Utah, all of which are located within federal grazing districts created pursuant to the Taylor Grazing Act.

In January 1974, before Utah's selection lists had been approved or disapproved, the Governor of Utah agreed that the Secretary of the Interior could include two tracts comprising 10,240 acres of selected indemnity lands in an oil shale leasing program, on the understanding that the rental proceeds would ultimately be paid to the State if its selections were approved. The proceeds of the leases are of substantial value.

In February 1974, the Secretary advised the Governor that he would not approve any indemnity applications that involved "grossly disparate values."[4] He wrote:

> * * * In January 1967, the then Secretary of the Interior [Stewart Udall] adopted the policy that in the exercise of his discretion under, inter alia, Section 7 of the Taylor Grazing Act, he would refuse to approve indemnity applications that involve grossly disparate values. That policy remains in effect.

> In the present case, although the land values are not precisely determined, it appears that the selections involve lands of grossly disparate values, within the meaning of the Department's policy. While the Department is not yet prepared to adjudicate the State's applications, I feel it is appropriate at this time to advise you that we will apply the above-mentioned policy in that adjudication.

[The State promptly challenged this policy in federal court. The lower courts ruled for Utah, and the Supreme Court granted certiorari, noting that seven western states still had unsatisfied indemnity selection rights to nearly 700,000 acres.]

I

The Enabling Act of each of the public land States admitted into the Union since 1802 has included grants of designated sections of federal lands

---

4. Suggested guidelines of the Department of the Interior provide that the policy will not be applied unless the estimated value of the selected lands exceeds that of the base lands by more than $100 per acre or 25% whichever is greater. If the values are grossly disparate using those criteria, the case will be submitted to the Washington office for evaluation of all the circumstances.

for the purpose of supporting public schools. Whether the Enabling Act contained words of present or future grant, title to the numbered sections did not vest in the State until completion of an official survey. Prior to survey, the Federal Government remained free to dispose of the designated lands "in any manner and for any purpose consistent with applicable federal statutes." In recognition of the fact that the essentially random grants in place might therefore be unavailable at the time of survey for a variety of reasons, Congress authorized grants of indemnity or "lieu" lands of equal acreage.

As Utah correctly emphasizes, the school land grant was a "solemn agreement" which in some ways may be analogized to a contract between private parties. The United States agreed to cede some of its land to the State in exchange for a commitment by the State to use the revenues derived from the land to educate the citizenry.

The State's right to select indemnity lands may be viewed as the remedy stipulated by the parties for the Federal Government's failure to perform entirely its promise to grant the specific numbered sections. The fact that the Utah Enabling Act used the phrase "lands equivalent thereto" and described the substituted land as "indemnity lands" implies that the purpose of the substitute selections was to provide the State with roughly the same resources with which to support its schools as it would have had had it actually received all of the granted sections in place. Thus, as is typical of private contract remedies, the purpose of the right to make indemnity selections was to give the State the benefit of the bargain.

The history of the general statutes relating to land grants for school purposes confirms this view. Thus, for example, in 1859, when confronted with the fact that many settlers had occupied unsurveyed lands that had been included in school grants, Congress confirmed the settlers' claims and granted to the States "other lands of like quantity." 11 Stat. 385. The substitution of an equal quantity of land provided the States a rough measure of equal value.

The school land grants gave the States a random selection of public lands subject, however, to one important exception. The original school land grants in general, and Utah's in particular, did not include any numbered sections known to be mineral in character by the time of survey. United States v. Sweet, 245 U.S. 563. This Court so held even though the Utah Enabling Act "neither expressly includes mineral lands nor expressly excludes them." The Court's opinion stressed "the practice of Congress to make a distinction between mineral lands and other lands, to deal with them along different lines, and to withhold mineral lands from disposal save under laws specially including them." Mineral lands were thus excluded not only from the original grants in place but also from the indemnity selections.[11] Since mineral resources provide both the most significant potential source of value and the greatest potential for variation in value in

11. Under the 1891 general indemnity selection statute then in effect, selections were limited to "unappropriated, surveyed public lands, not mineral in character." 26 Stat. 796–797.

the generally arid western lands, the total exclusion of mineral lands from the school land grants is consistent with an intent that the States' indemnity selections of equal acreage approximate the value of the numbered sections lost.

In 1927, some nine years after the decision in United States v. Sweet, Congress changed its policy to allow grants of school lands to embrace numbered sections that were mineral in character. But the 1927 statute did not expand the kinds of land available for indemnity selections. Thus, after 1927 even if the lost school lands were mineral in character, a State was prohibited from selecting mineral lands as indemnity. It was not until 1958 that Congress gave the States the right to select mineral lands to replace lost school lands, and that right was expressly conditioned on a determination that the lost lands were also mineral in character. 43 U.S.C. § 852. For 30 years, then, States were not even permitted to select lands roughly equivalent in value to replace lost mineral lands. The condition in the 1958 statute, that the lost lands be mineral in character before mineral lands could be selected as indemnity, rather clearly reflects an intention to restore the character of the indemnity selection as a substitute of roughly equal value.

Throughout the history of congressional consideration of school land grants and related subjects—a history discussed at great length in the voluminous briefs submitted to us—we find no evidence whatever of any congressional desire to have the right to select indemnity lands do anything more than make the States whole for the loss of value resulting from the unavailability of the originally designated cross section of lands within the State. There is certainly no suggestion of a purpose at any time, including 1958, to allow the States to obtain substantially greater values through the process of selecting indemnity land.

Thus, viewing the program in this broad historical perspective, it is difficult to identify any sensible justification for Utah's position that it is entitled to select any mineral lands it chooses regardless of the value of the school sections lost. Nevertheless, Utah is quite correct in arguing that the Secretary has no power to reject its selections unless Congress has given it to him. We have no doubt that it has.

II

Prior to the 1930's, cases in this Court had made it perfectly clear that the Federal Government retained the power to appropriate public lands embraced within school grants for other purposes if it acted in a timely fashion. On the other hand, it was equally clear that the States' title to unappropriated land in designated sections could not be defeated after survey, and that their right to indemnity selections could not be rejected if they satisfied the statutory criteria when made, and if the selections were filed before the lands were appropriated for other purposes. The authority of the Secretary of the Interior was limited to determining whether the States' indemnity selections met the relevant statutory criteria.

In the 1930's, however, dissatisfaction with the rather loose regime governing use and disposition of unappropriated federal lands, prompted mostly by the waste caused by unregulated stock grazing, led to a series of congressional and executive actions that are critical to this case. By means of these actions, all unappropriated federal lands were withdrawn from every form of entry or selection. The withdrawal did not affect the original school land grants in place, whether or not surveyed, but did include all lands then available for school indemnity selections. The lands thus withdrawn were thereafter available for indemnity selections only as permitted by the Secretary of the Interior in the exercise of his discretion.

The sequence of events was as follows. In 1934, Congress enacted the Taylor Grazing Act "[t]o stop injury to the public grazing lands by preventing overgrazing and soil deterioration, to provide for their orderly use, improvement, and development, to stabilize the livestock industry dependent upon the public range, and for other purposes." Section 1 authorized the Secretary of the Interior to establish grazing districts in up to 80 million acres of unappropriated federal lands; the establishment of such a district had the effect of withdrawing all lands within its boundaries "from all forms of entry of settlement." That section also expressly provided that "Nothing in this Act shall be construed in any way * * * to affect any land heretofore or hereafter surveyed which, except for the provisions of this Act, would be a part of any grant to any State * * *." Thus, § 1 preserved the original school land grants, whether or not the designated sections had already been identified by survey, but the statute made no provision for school indemnity selections.

Because the Taylor Grazing Act as originally passed in 1934 applied to less than half of the federal lands in need of more orderly regulation, President Roosevelt promptly issued Executive Order 6910 withdrawing all of the unappropriated and unreserved public lands in 12 western States, including Utah, from "settlement, location, sale or entry" pending a determination of the best use of the land. The withdrawal affected the land covered by the Taylor Grazing Act as well as land not covered by the statute. The President's authority to issue Executive Order 6910 was expressly conferred by the Pickett Act.

Congress responded to Executive Order No. 6910 by amending the Taylor Grazing Act in 1936 in two respects that are relevant to this case. First, it expanded the acreage subject to the Act. Second, it revised § 7 of the Act, to give the Secretary the authority, in his discretion, to classify both lands within grazing districts and lands withdrawn by the recent Executive order as proper not only for homesteading, but also, for the first time, for satisfaction of any outstanding "lieu" rights, and to open such lands to "selection." The section [43 U.S.C. § 315f], thus amended, provided in pertinent part:

"The Secretary of the Interior is authorized, in his discretion, to examine and classify any lands withdrawn or reserved by Executive order * * * or within a grazing district, which are * * * proper for acquisition in satisfaction of any outstanding lieu, exchange or script rights or land grant, and to open such lands to entry, selection or location for disposal in accordance with * * * applicable public-land laws. * * * *Such lands shall not be subject to disposition * * * until after the same have been classified * * *.*" (Emphasis added.)

The changes in this section were apparently prompted in part by the fact that while the Taylor Grazing Act withdrawal preserved the States' school grants in place, no provision had been made in the 1934 version for the States' indemnity selections from land within grazing districts even though the States had expressed the concern that "the establishment of a grazing district would restrict the State in its indemnity selections." While this omission may not have been critical in 1934 when the Act was passed—since only about half of the unappropriated federal land was then affected—by 1936, as a consequence of Executive Order No. 6910, no land at all was available in the public domain for indemnity selections. It is therefore reasonable to infer that the amendments to § 7 were at least in part a response to the complaint expressed in congressional hearings in 1935, that there was no land available under current law for indemnity selections.

The 1936 amendment to § 7 rectified that problem, but did not give the States a completely free choice in making indemnity selections. Rather, Congress decided to route the States' selections through § 7, and thereby to condition their acceptance on the Secretary's discretion. That decision was consistent with the dominant purpose of both the Act and Executive Order No. 6910, to exert firm control over the Nation's land resources through the Department of the Interior. In sum, the Taylor Grazing Act, coupled with the withdrawals by Executive order, "locked up" all of the federal lands in the western States pending further action by Congress or the President, except as otherwise permitted in the discretion of the Secretary of the Interior for the limited purposes specified in § 7.

This was Congress' understanding of the Taylor Grazing Act in 1958 when it amended the school land indemnity selection statute to permit selection of mineral lands. * * * Since Congress was specifically dealing with school indemnity selections, the reports make it perfectly clear that Congress deemed school indemnity selections to be subject to § 7 of the Taylor Grazing Act. And since the congressional decision in 1958 to allow school land indemnity selections to embrace mineral lands was expressly conditioned on a determination that the lost school lands were also mineral in character, it is manifest that Congress did not intend to grant the States any windfall. It only intended to restore to the States a rough approximation of what was lost.

We therefore hold that the 1936 amendment to the Taylor Grazing Act conferred on the Secretary the authority in his discretion to classify lands within a federal grazing district as proper for school indemnity selection. And we find no merit in the argument that the Secretary's "grossly disparate value" policy constitutes an abuse of the broad discretion thus conferred. On the contrary, that policy is wholly faithful to Congress' consistent purpose in providing for indemnity selections, to give the States a rough equivalent of the school land grants in place that were lost through pre-emption or private entry prior to survey. Accordingly, the judgment of the Court of Appeals is reversed.

■ JUSTICE POWELL, with whom THE CHIEF JUSTICE, JUSTICE BLACKMUN, and JUSTICE REHNQUIST join, dissenting.

Since the early days of the Republic, the Federal Government's compact with each new State has granted the State land for the support of education and allowed the State to select land of equal acreage as indemnity for deficiencies in the original grant. Today, the Court holds that the Taylor Grazing Act abrogated those compacts by approving selection requirements completely at odds with the equal acreage principle. Nothing in the Court's opinion persuades me that Congress meant so lightly to breach compacts that it has respected and enforced throughout our Nation's history. * * *

Utah has selected land in satisfaction of grants made to support the public education of its citizens. Those grants are part of the bilateral compact under which Utah was admitted to the Union. They guarantee the State a specific quantity of the public lands within its borders. * * * Nothing in the Taylor Grazing Act empowers the Secretary to review Utah's selections under a comparative value standard explicitly at odds with principles consistently respected since the early days of our Republic.

NOTES AND QUESTIONS

1. This case illustrates a number of prominent features of federal land disposal and management policy over time. For example, what was the rationale behind the "in-place" grants, giving the states isolated sections of land scattered across the entire state? What kind of federal preemption would frustrate Utah from getting its in-place grants? How could settlers enter federal lands prior to surveying in a way that would frustrate the in-place grants?

2. How does the majority read the word "equivalent" in the statute giving the state indemnity rights? How does the dissent read it? Does the majority opinion leave it open to a future Secretary to repeal Secretary Udall's "grossly disparate value" policy? Is, in other words, the Secretary's power to reject an unequal value selection the same as a duty to reject it? (This question of executive discretion recurs throughout public natural resource law.) Does the majority opinion provide any clues to resolving it?

3. What was the rationale behind Congress's long-standing practice of not disposing of lands that were deemed "mineral in character" at the time of survey under the land disposal laws? This practice was so entrenched that the Supreme Court had no difficulty deciding, in United States v. Sweet, 245 U.S. 563 (1918) (discussed in the principal case), that the statehood common school grant to Utah excluded federal lands "mineral in character," even though Congress had not deemed it necessary to say so specifically in the statehood enabling act. This policy of "withhold[ing] mineral lands from disposal save under laws specially including them" (*Sweet*, at 567) was followed until the second decade of the twentieth century, when Congress began to authorize federal land grants that simply reserved minerals in federal ownership. Federal mineral policy is dealt with in more detail in Chapter 7.

4. While Utah might be said to have been looking for a windfall here, consider the flip side of the problem: California never got the opportunity to take title to several sections of "in-place" common school grants in its Central Valley because the federal government, prior to their being surveyed, included the area in the Elk Hills Naval Petroleum Reserve. Oil was later discovered on the land, and the "lost" sections are worth many millions of dollars. No federal land in California is available for indemnity selection that comes close to the value of these "lost" sections. Does California have a remedy? Does the federal government satisfy the "solemn [statehood] agreement" by offering as indemnity lands of equal acreage, but worth much less in value? Illustrating the political nature of the process, California began with litigation but then took its grievance to the Congress. Congress responded by giving California a share of the proceeds of Elk Hills reserve when it was auctioned off in 1996. See 104 Pub. L. No. 106, 110 Stat. 186.

5. Notice also the Court's discussion of the Taylor Grazing Act, President Franklin Roosevelt's withdrawal of essentially all the public domain lands in 1934 and 1935, and Congress's responsive amendment of the Taylor Grazing Act in 1936. Should those events affect the outcome of this case? Didn't the Secretary have to interpret "equal value" in the statehood act in deciding whether to patent indemnity lands to the state, whether or not the land had been withdrawn by FDR and the Congress? Apart from their effect on state school indemnity selections, this sequence of actions effectively closed the public domain to widespread disposition.

6. Litigation over in lieu land selection was not quelled by the principal case. See, e.g., Oregon v. Bureau of Land Mgmt., 876 F.2d 1419 (9th Cir. 1989). There is a great deal of money at stake for states. Utah earned almost $94 million in 2005 from school trust land revenue.

NOTE: STATE MANAGEMENT OF FEDERALLY GRANTED LANDS

Early statehood grants tended to be rather loosely worded in expressing the purposes of the grants, and the states exploited this by using the proceeds derived from federally granted lands for purposes other than those sought to be served. Over time, the Congress responded to these abuses by progressively tightening the language in the grants. Grants to later admitted states such as Oklahoma, New Mexico, and Arizona have quite detailed terms. These states may dispose of the granted land only for "full value," and Congress also sometimes required procedural safeguards such as public notice and an auction. These various restrictions on management and disposition of federal land grants to states are often referred to as creating a "trust" to be administered for the designated beneficiaries; e.g., common schools. Federally granted lands to serve common schools are usually called "school trust lands." This "trust"—concerned primarily with the raising and expenditure of money derived from these lands—is distinct from the "public trust doctrine" applied in the *Illinois Central Railroad* decision, *supra* p. 80.

The U.S. Supreme Court has issued a number of decisions strictly enforcing the restrictions placed on federal land grants. In Ervien v. United States, 251 U.S. 41 (1919), for example, the Court rejected the New Mexico legislature's attempt to devote 3 percent of the proceeds of sales and leases of federally granted lands to advertising the virtues of living and investing in New Mexico. The Enabling Act was, in the Court's view, "special and exact," and "in prophetic realization" Congress had anticipated "that the state might be tempted to do that which it has done, lured * * * to speculative advertising in the hope of a speedy prosperity." 251 U.S. at 47–48. The Court traced the history of statehood land grants, and enforced the "full value" requirement for common school land grants, in Lassen v. Arizona, 385 U.S. 458 (1967). Other Supreme Court decisions enforcing the restrictions are Alamo Land & Cattle Co. v. Arizona, 424 U.S. 295 (1976), and ASARCO, Inc. v. Kadish, 490 U.S. 605 (1989).

One lower federal court took strict enforcement to a very high level. In United States v. New Mexico, 536 F.2d 1324 (10th Cir. 1976), the Court held that New Mexico could not use income from a federal land grant made for the purpose of supporting "miners' hospitals for disabled miners" to help underwrite a consolidation of state hospitals, which changed its Miners' Hospital into a more limited facility, with disabled miners eligible to receive care at other institutions. The court explained (536 F.2d at 1326–27):

> While the underlying motivation for the trust may have been a desire on the part of Congress generally to provide for the health care of miners, the specific purpose of the trust was the establishment and maintenance of a "miners' hospital." The wording of the Enabling Act evidences a determination by Congress that the health needs of New Mexico miners could best be provided by a separate hospital for miners. To imply a more expansive purpose for the trust than that stated in the Enabling Act is to indulge in a license of construction which Congress intended to prevent.

What happens to the proceeds from this federal land grant when there are no more miners in New Mexico? Is this statutory interpretation too wooden? Should the courts be more flexible? If not, what is New Mexico's remedy?

Some statehood enabling acts not only set out detailed restrictions, but went further to require the new state to put identical restrictions in its state constitution. For an illustration of the politics behind this process, see John Leshy, *The Making of the Arizona Constitution*, 20 ARIZ. ST. L.J. 1, 7–27 (1988). See also Eric Biber, *The Price of Admission: Causes, Effects, and Patterns of Conditions Imposed on States Entering the Union*, 46 AM. J. LEGAL HIST. 119 (2004). This has led to a series of state Supreme Court decisions also strictly enforcing the terms of the federal land grants, as a matter of federal law (the enabling acts) or of state law (similar restrictions expressed in the state constitution or statutes). See, e.g., Oklahoma Educ. Ass'n, Inc. v. Nigh, 642 P.2d 230 (Okl. 1982).

Some interesting issues are raised in this litigation. In many states, state school trust land has long been leased for livestock grazing for small sums of money. Often, in fact, state lands are interspersed with federal lands that are likewise leased for grazing. In some modern cases (especially in Idaho and New Mexico) environmental interests have sought to bid against ranchers for renewal of their grazing leases, not to graze the land but to retire it from grazing. If the environmentalists outbid the ranchers, must the state lease them the land? This can raise severe political problems for state land boards which have traditionally been friendly to ranching interests. To the extent the school trust is designed to produce income, and not cows, it would seem ranchers have an uphill argument. See, e.g., Idaho Watersheds Project v. State Bd. of Land Comm'ns, 982 P.2d 367 (Idaho 1999) (state law administered to exclude conservation interests from bidding on grazing leases on state land violated state constitution by removing potential bidders who might provide "maximum long term financial return" to the schools); Forest Guardians v. Wells, 34 P.3d 364 (Ariz. 2001) (state may not reject application of high bidder for state land grazing lease just because bidder's object is restoration or preservation of grazing land); Montanans for the Responsible Use of the School Trust v. State ex rel. Bd. of Land Comm'rs, 989 P.2d 800 (Mont. 1999) (state statutes that fail in certain respects to recover full market value for school trust lands are inconsistent with the state constitution). But see Forest Guardians v. Powell, 24 P.3d 803 (N.M. Ct. App. 2001) (neither environmentalists nor parents of school children have standing to sue to challenge state administration of school trust land, including leasing the land without advertisement or public auction; among other things, plaintiffs cannot show that increased competition would result in more funds actually going to schools because the legislature could choose to offset any increase from trust lands by reducing appropriations from the state general fund).

There also may be a question whether state school trust land can be exchanged for federal or private land elsewhere. Such exchanges are usually negotiated on an equal value basis as determined by appraisal. Where the statehood enabling act (and/or state law) requires a public auction before disposition, are such exchanges legal? The Arizona Supreme Court said no in Deer Valley Unified School District v. Superior Court, 760 P.2d 537 (1988). As will be explored in Chapter 5, land exchanges allow for reconfiguration of ownerships to better serve public and private management goals. Environmental and other interests in Arizona have tried twice to persuade Arizona voters to amend the state constitution to overrule this decision, but lost both times by very narrow margins.

A second, related issue is to what extent does the trust emphasis on income production prevent the state from managing some of its federally granted lands for such purposes as recreation, wildlife, and wilderness? Does the trust require income maximization over the short run, without considering the long run? Or may a state choose not to lease some of its granted land for mineral production or livestock grazing now, in the expectation that it might be more valuable for other purposes, even though those other purposes cannot, at least in the short run, produce as much income? May the grant purpose of promoting the common schools be served by setting aside a tract of state school trust land as an environmental "classroom" or laboratory where schoolchildren can observe biodiversity?

See, e.g., Branson School Dist. RE–82 v. Romer, 161 F.3d 619 (10th Cir. 1998) (rejecting a facial challenge to a rewrite of the management principles underlying the state school land trust that shifted "away from its prior focus on short-term profit maximization toward a more sustainable approach focusing on the long-term yields of the trust lands"). For a comprehensive view of the history, policy issues, and a state-by-state view of state trust lands, see Peter W. Culp et al., Trust Lands in the American West: A Legal Overview and Policy Assessment (Lincoln Institute of Land Policy and Sonoran Institute, 2005). See generally Jon A. Souder and Sally K. Fairfax, STATE TRUST LANDS: HISTORY, MANAGEMENT, AND SUSTAINABLE USE (1996).

TRUST PROBLEMS

Consider the following two problems to contrast and review the various trust doctrines discussed in this chapter.

1. Tall Grass Prairie State Park in central Indiana contains the only remaining remnant of a native tall prairie grass ecosystem in the state. The park is only one square mile—the state acquired ownership of the parkland as an original school land section in 1816.

Late last year, a visiting South African tourist discovered diamonds in the park. Apparently, the glacial deposit of diamonds is a rare but not unheard-of geological legacy. Now the state legislature is considering selling the parkland to Trump Diamond, Ltd. for a substantial sum of money which will be deposited in a trust fund for public education. Trump plans to mine the diamonds. Unfortunately, mining will destroy the prairie ecosystem.

You represent Friends of the Grassland, a prairie preservation group. How will you argue against the sale? What are the strengths and weaknesses of an argument based on the public trust?

2. Gary, Indiana was founded by the U.S. Steel Corporation in 1906 because of its favorable location on the shore of Lake Michigan. In the decades that followed, the giant steel mills spurred numerous industrial uses of the lakeshore. You also represent Citizens for a Clean Gary (CCG). CCG is outraged over the State of Indiana's pitiful efforts to clean up the Lake Michigan shoreline, which has been contaminated by a century of industrial activity. Your aim is to force the state to clean up the area so that residents can use it for fishing and swimming again. What are the strengths and weaknesses of a trust argument?

NOTE: OTHER GRANTS TO STATES

Congress made many other grants to the states outside the statehood enabling act process. Some of these were influenced by the lively debate over much of the Nation's first century regarding whether the national government could constitutionally play a role in financing or otherwise promoting public works projects in the states—so-called "internal improvements." At one time or another, for example, such luminaries as Thomas

Jefferson, James Madison, and James Monroe thought the Constitution needed to be amended in order to give the national government such authority. Federal land grants offered those with a narrow view of federal authority a way to justify federal involvement, and Congress "[c]heerfully [began] exploiting this constitutional loophole" early on. Daniel Feller, THE PUBLIC LANDS IN JACKSONIAN POLITICS 49 (1984). Six million acres of federal land grants to western states went to support canal building and river navigation improvements, and another 3 million acres for roads, in the first half of the nineteenth century. The canal grants started the practice of parceling out alternate sections of land along the canal right-of-way. This practice reached stupendous proportions with the railroad land grants, discussed further below.

In an 1841 statute, Congress gave every public land state an outright grant of 500,000 acres for internal improvements (minus acreage that had already been received for those purposes). Diversion of these funds to other purposes by recipient states helped influence Congress to abandon this general grant approach in 1889 in favor of specific trust grants such as that in United States v. New Mexico, *supra* p. 98. Meanwhile, Congress had also decided to give states the unclaimed, seemingly useless swampland within their borders. After an experimental grant to Louisiana, the General Swamp Land Act of 1850 allowed states to select and acquire such lands under certain criteria. Administrative implementation was so lacking, however, that erroneous and fraudulent selections were common. Congress intended that 5 or 6 million acres would pass by this method, but states ultimately selected over 80 million acres of purported swamplands, though not all selections were approved for fee title. According to historian Paul Gates, one agent for the state of Mississippi reportedly "judged as swampland all tracts over which a boat could pass [so he] drove a work animal 'hitched to a canoe across thousands of acres' of pinelands at fairly high elevations, listed his selections and, though contested by the Federal government, they were finally patented to the state." HISTORY OF PUBLIC LAND LAW DEVELOPMENT 328.

By the famous Morrill Act of 1862, each state (including the original, "non-public land" states) received the rights to 30,000 acres of federal lands for each of its senators and representatives, to be used for support of an agricultural and mechanical college. These grants differed from the norm in that states could not select federal lands within their boundaries, but rather were given "scrip" for the acreage, entitling them to sell public lands located anywhere, even outside their boundaries, if the lands were available for disposal. There was inevitably some evasion of the conditions, and great landed estates grew out of speculation in scrip, but Morrill's purpose of providing low-cost, practical higher education has been realized in some measure by the establishment of what have become known as "land grant colleges," a number of which have evolved into major universities such as Cornell, Michigan State, and Purdue.

The Morrill Act was one of the few disposition laws that allowed the non-public land states to share directly in the proceeds from sale of public domain land. The controversy between East and West had raged for decades with inconclusive results. "Distribution," "deposit," and similar revenue sharing schemes from which eastern states would benefit either never passed or were short-lived due to economic exigencies. While mostly losing its battle for a direct cut in the proceeds from western lands, eastern interests have had much more success, starting shortly after the Civil War, in pressuring the national government to withdraw and reserve millions of acres of public lands in the west for conservation and preservation purposes, often in the face of western opposition.

3. GRANTS TO PRIVATE PARTIES

The complexities of federal law governing the transfer of lands into state ownership, and the related trust doctrines, continue to generate many legal controversies. However, the federal government disposed of far more land to private parties in order to spur economic and social development of the nation. The legacy of these private grants is evident in many disputes over the extent of private rights conveyed. In particular, disputes over access to lands and ownership of roads are a consequence of the development patterns that emerged from private grants. The law governing access rights is considered in Chapter 5A.

Individuals serving the armed forces in time of war were given special rights to public lands. Grants of public land to military veterans have ancient origins; they conveniently reward military adventurers while moving a restive population to the frontiers. The practice was followed by the United States after the Revolution, and for as long thereafter as the Nation was land rich and cash poor. In all, the United States conveyed approximately 70 million acres as bounty for military service. Because the grants were commonly made in assignable scrip, ownership concentration became common, and absentee ownership generated disputes with squatters and others. The practice ended after the Spanish–American War, but scrip continued to dribble into government land offices in the mid–20th century. By a 1955 statute, scrip of all descriptions had to be recorded within two years, and any unsatisfied existing rights were to be extinguished by purchase thereafter. Hibbard at 138–39; Jerry A. O'Callaghan, *The War Veteran And The Public Lands, in* THE PUBLIC LANDS 109–119 (V. Carstensen ed. 1968).

a. GRANTS TO FARMERS AND RANCHERS

For 150 years official national public land policy was directed primarily at getting the lands into the hands of the pioneer, the individual farmer seeking a new life on the frontier. The official policy was undercut from many directions, and it sometimes resulted in heartbreak instead of prosperity. It did succeed in that millions were able to build new lives on cheap or free land, upon which they developed communities, commerce, and other attributes of civilization. The country was developed and unified; the lands and resources nurtured and sustained the characteristic American ingenuity and industry; and the Nation rapidly rose to pinnacles of wealth and power. But the national policy also failed in many respects. Disdain for legal requirements bred widespread lawlessness. The development of individual and corporate monopoly ownerships operated to exclude the small farmer, and many could not make a go of it.

CREDIT AND CASH SALES

The young nation had a legacy of debt and only two sources of revenue: tariffs and land sales. After some years of inconclusive debate over whether revenue-raising or settlement was the more important objective, whether sales should be for cash of on credit, and whether landholdings should be limited, Congress passed the Land Act of 1796. It continued the 36–section–per–township rectangular system of survey first adopted by the Congress of the Confederation in 1785. It also authorized land auctions at minimum prices of $2.00 per acre (Hamilton had advocated 20 cents), but with only five percent of the purchase price down, the balance due in a year. To administer this system, the General Land Office was created in 1812. It remained in business until it was absorbed into the BLM in 1946.

The 1796 Act did not produce the revenue anticipated. Thereafter Congress progressively liberalized the credit terms and other conditions. Sales greatly increased (giving rise to the enduring phrase "doing a Land Office business"), but speculation became common and many settlers could not make payments. That led to a series of relief acts by which delinquents were relieved of prospect of forfeiture. Relief only increased speculation and indebtedness; by the end of 1819, the federal government was holding many millions of dollars of delinquent debt from purchasers. In 1820 Congress ended its experiment with credit sales, although it continued its liberality toward hard-pressed settlers for decades.

The 1820 Act required cash at the time of purchase at auction but reduced the price to $1.25 per acre. Public lands offered but unsold at auction were opened to private entry at a lower price. Settlers detested auction sales and urged their postponement year after year to thwart cash-rich speculators. In the great rush westward, vast acreage considered undesirable remained unsold in the older public land states. In 1854 the Graduation Act was passed, providing that the price for land long unclaimed would be reduced in proportion to the time unsold, down to $1.00 per acre after 10 years, and down to 12.5 cents after 30 years ("one-bit" land). The Graduation Act triggered another land rush. Coupled with sales under other statutes, an unprecedented amount of land passed out of the public domain in the 1850's, causing endless confusion and antagonism. States, railroads, miners, speculators, and settlers all disputed with the federal government and each other. Ferment for land reform grew side by side with political ferment over slavery.

PREEMPTION

Since before the Revolution, the common practice—as epitomized in the exploits of Daniel Boone—was to stake out a claim on the edge of the frontier and later, perhaps, pay whomever turned out to be the owner. Squatting had a long, if less than honorable, history; in the early days of the Republic, troops were called out on several occasions to remove squatters from land owned by the government or speculators. As Jefferson noted in 1776, "they will settle the lands in spite of everybody." The United States struggled with the problem for a century. While the right of "preemption" usually prevailed, the dilemma between the desire to accommodate the actual settlers and protection of actual or potential purchasers was never finally resolved.

Preemption was the preferential right of settler-squatters to buy their claims at modest prices without competitive bidding or, alternatively, to be paid compensation for any improvements they had made before eviction. A uniform policy was hard to come by: eastern congressmen criticized the Westerners for being greedy, lawless, disloyal land-grabbers who had no respect for order, absentee owners, or Indian rights. Western representatives, however, presented the squatters as loyal people who had exhausted their resources in reaching the West and who had defended the frontier against the marauding Indians.

Prior to 1841, Congress passed over two dozen statutes which created a process for validating *pre-existing* claims of squatters. Several million acres were patented in this way. Then, the General Preemption Act of 1841, 5 Stat. 453, finally authorized *prospective* preemption as part of a package of provisions engineered by Henry Clay. The Act abandoned the view that all settlement on unoffered public land was illegal, but it sanctioned further settlement only on public land that had been surveyed. Occupying settlers could obtain a maximum of 160 acres for $1.25 per acre, if they met a number of eligibility conditions. The Act was abused by the common sports of the day, speculation and fraud, which included the practice of squatting on timberland, stripping it bare, and then abandoning the claim for another. It was estimated in 1849 that "not three of a hundred" preemption declarations actually went to patent (documentary fee title). Prior to the Civil War, preemption tended to achieve its goals of settlement and title security in spite of its many problems, but abuses so mounted after the War that eventually, in 1891, it was repealed. In one notable case, the Supreme Court voided a preemption claim in the Yosemite Valley, finding that a narrow interpretation "is the only construction which preserves a wise control in the government over the public lands, and prevents a general spoliation of them under the pretence of intended settlement and preemption." The Yosemite Valley Case (Hutchings v. Low), 82 U.S. (15 Wall.) 77, 88 (1872).

HOMESTEADING

"By 1862, the government had made such great progress in disposing of the public domain that only about one billion acres still remained the property of the United States. Perhaps two thirds of this remaining domain, however, was not arable land, and could not be parceled out so easily." Roy Robbins, OUR LANDED HERITAGE 236. The proportion of the total federal revenue that derived from land sales had declined drastically. The cash requirement favored speculators and was thought to retard settlement. The government had resorted to "donation" acts, essentially giving away to actual settlers lands it wished quickly settled, such as Oregon.

The South had previously opposed liberalizing public land grants, correctly fearing that new antislavery states would be created. But the secession of the slaveholding states opened the way for the northern legislators to push through a program of distribution for farming that would, in various permutations, remain on the books for more than a century. The great Homestead Act of May 20, 1862 authorized entry onto 160 acres of any public land subject to preemption. To those who met the requirements, the land was free, except for filing fees. A settler was allowed six months to establish actual residence after application. Thereafter, actual settlement and cultivation were required for five years, to be supported by affidavit, at which point fee simple title would be conveyed in a document called a patent. (In practice, however, many homesteaders chose not to wait the five years, but instead "commuted" their claim by payment.)

Other forms of disposition (preemption, cash sales, state and railroad grants) remained in effect. More specialized land grant acts, summarized below, complicated the overall picture. Indian reservations were broken up both by treaty and, starting with the Dawes Act in 1884, by allotment to individual tribal members. In either case, many of the lands soon passed into white hands. As the Nation rebuilt after the Civil War, this somewhat incongruous congregation of public land disposal laws of the United States combined to produce what Vernon Parrington described as the "Great Barbecue," a generation's unparalleled exploitation of public natural resources.

As homesteading became a national preoccupation (by the 1880's, homesteads constituted a majority of new farms), difficulties in its administration multiplied. A fundamental problem with the original Homestead Act was that the semi-arid federal lands beyond the 100th meridian were, for the most part, simply not sufficiently productive to support farming units of 160 acres or less. Surveying was limited, fragmented, incomplete, and sometimes downright fraudulent. Like preemption claims, homestead claims were sometimes used as a pretense to strip public lands of timber without any payment. The tide toward disposition at any cost flowed strongly; federal officials who tried to hew to the strict letter of the law or decried abuses put their jobs in jeopardy. Lands that remained in public ownership were considered to be a grazing commons for livestock owners, and this gave rise to a generation of "range wars" among settlers, sheepherders, and cattle ranchers. Notwithstanding the many difficulties and fraud, much of the less arid part of the West was settled under the Homestead and cognate acts. From 1868 to 1904, nearly 100 million acres were homesteaded, many if not most by the yeoman tillers of the soil that the expressed national policy was intended to benefit.

DESERT LANDS

Although lands east of the 100th meridian were settled quickly, arid public lands to the west often went begging because they were unsuitable to conventional farming without irrigation, which usually demanded larger blocs of land and access to substantial capital for water storage and delivery facilities. By 1877, much of the remaining unclaimed land was in the arid and semi-arid regions of the West. Although circumvention of the acreage limitations of the Homestead Act was scarcely unknown, pressure built for more specialized disposition laws under which larger tracts could pass legally. One solution, large grants to corporations, was in bad odor in the wake of the railroad land grant abuses recounted further below. Instead, Congress enacted the Desert Land Act of 1877. It authorized entry of up to 640 acres of public land at only 25 cents an acre, with patent to follow upon proof that the land had been irrigated. (This Act also made state laws the primary engine for allocating rights to water on federal and formerly federal land, a policy which has endured and is addressed in Chapter 6.) Although over 33 million acres would eventually be entered, and over 10 million acres patented (*see* Paul Gates, HISTORY OF PUBLIC LAND LAW DEVELOPMENT 643), the Desert Land Act did not accomplish its purposes. Large corporations snatched the bulk of the available lands through dummies. Some people received patents after hauling a can of water to the claim and swearing that irrigation had been achieved. Very little land ever became irrigated; most claims were used for stock grazing. Eventually, failure of private irrigation efforts led to the Reclamation Act of 1902.

STOCK–RAISING HOMESTEADS

With the repeal of preemption and historian Frederick Jackson Turner's famous pronouncement of the closing of the frontier by 1890, it might seem that entry for homesteading and other purposes would have declined if not ceased by 1900. That was not to be the case. Congress was still determined to create settlement opportunities through federal land disposal. In spite of a growing sentiment for a leasing system, even among cattlemen, the Stock–Raising Homestead Act of 1916, 43 U.S.C. §§ 291–301 (repealed 1976), authorized entry on 640 acres of land "designated" as chiefly valuable for grazing, on minimal conditions. In a few years over 50 million acres had been entered and more than 30 million acres patented. The 1916 Act not only caused the usual settler heartbreak, speculation, and aggrandizement, but also, in breaking up the great public domain grazing areas, contributed to the deterioration of the range. It had one feature that set it apart from practically all other disposition laws: Instead of passing fee simple title, it reserved the minerals in the United States, creating "split-estate" lands that give rise to contemporary disputes and litigation, recounted in Chapter 7, section D.

The sponsor of the Stock–Raising Homestead Act was Edward Taylor of Colorado. Interestingly, he was also the sponsor of the Taylor Grazing Act of 1934, 43 U.S.C. § 315 et seq., which reversed the policies of the 1916 Act. The 1934 Act ushered in the end of the homesteading era, as recounted in Andrus v. Utah, *supra* p. 90. While Franklin Roosevelt's executive withdrawals in the wake of the Act effectively closed most of the public domain to disposition, homesteading remained possible, if barely so, until it was officially ended with repeal of the Homestead Act and other surviving disposition statutes in the Federal Land Policy and Management Act of 1976 (FLPMA), 43 U.S.C. §§ 1701–1784. Although FLPMA repealed nearly all the laws relating to homesteading and other disposals of the federal lands, it allowed them to continue to apply in Alaska until 1986. See 43 U.S.C. § 1701 note.

b. GRANTS FOR RECLAMATION

The beginnings of fundamental changes in the national policy of disposition came in the federal treatment of renewable resources, notably water and timber. The Desert Land Act of 1877 opened the arid lands and allowed state water laws to be the primary source of authority over most water allocation, but the laws did nothing to solve the physical problem of water scarcity. Many lands were still available for homesteading, but they would go unclaimed until large-scale water diversion and storage capacity was developed. Neither the states nor private entrepreneurs were able to meet this widely perceived need.

In 1878 John Wesley Powell, a Civil War veteran (who lost an arm in the battle of Shiloh) and leader of the path-breaking trip down the Colorado River through the Grand Canyon in 1869, issued his landmark Report on the Land of the Arid Regions of the United States. Bernard DeVoto called it "[o]ne of the most remarkable books ever written by an American." This report, widely admired as a landmark step in characterizing the reality of western lands and settlement possibilities, was a warning of the need to adapt the public land disposition and settlement laws and policies to the realities of the arid West. It did not fall on particularly receptive ears. As DeVoto put it, "[i]t is a scientific prophecy and it has been fulfilled—experimentally proved. Unhappily the experimental proof has consisted of human and social failure and the destruction of land." Wallace Stegner, Beyond the Hundredth Meridian xxii (1954).

As it became apparent that the Desert Land Act had failed to achieve its sponsors' aim of increased productivity through private irrigation efforts,

> Congress took action by dusting off one of Powell's core ideas. In 1888 it authorized an irrigation survey * * * to identify the reservoir sites and canal rights-of-way necessary to develop irrigation in the arid lands. These lands were to be withdrawn from the public domain and reserved for the construction of an appropriate infrastructure.

> Speculators, however, kept a close eye on the [results]. It took no great intelligence to divine which lands the new surveys would propose to irrigate, and with water the value of those lands would rapidly appreciate. So speculators * * * hastened to file on land before it could be withdrawn. [In response the Interior Department in August 1889] invoked an obscure amendment to the Irrigation Survey's first appropriation bill, authorizing it to withdraw from entry "all lands made susceptible of irrigation." * * * The Department determined to apply [the withdrawal] to the entirety of the public domain and to close all public land to entry. Moreover it made the closure retroactive to * * * the previous year, throwing nearly a year's worth of claims into administrative limbo. * * *

The resulting furor doomed the Irrigation Survey. Land filings in the late 1880s and early 1890s averaged 25 million acres a year. Dryland farming may have faltered on the prairies, but Americans were still hungry for land * * *. Nothing since the Civil War and Reconstruction had made so many Americans so mad.

William deBuys, SEEING THINGS WHOLE: THE ESSENTIAL JOHN WESLEY POWELL 213–14 (2001). Congress stepped in and rescinded the Department's power to reserve land, gutted Powell's budget, and greatly diminished his influence.

The need for irrigation remained, however, and Congress finally responded with the Reclamation Act of 1902, 43 U.S.C. § 371 et seq., called the Newlands Act after its sponsor, the aptly named Senator Francis Newlands of Nevada. The act authorized the federal government to embark on a major program to irrigate western lands. The Reclamation Act led to federal construction and operation of many major water projects in the West, irrigating mostly private lands. Water rights for the projects are generally perfected under state, not federal law, but reclamation law also assumes some continuing federal control over the use of the water. The original contemplation was that, while the United States would make the capital investments out of federal funds, the projects would be financed by the proceeds from federal land sales, and the water users would repay the costs of project construction and maintenance. It did not work out that way. Congress soon began to amend the law to extend repayment terms and forgive debts. The end result has been rather heavy subsidies for western agriculture. The reclamation program is critically examined in the late Marc Reisner's now-classic work, CADILLAC DESERT (1993).

The reclamation program eventually grew beyond the wildest hopes of its sponsors. By 1906 the Reclamation Service had commenced projects in fifteen states for the irrigation of 2.5 million acres. Still to come were such huge undertakings as Hoover Dam, which marked a transition in reclamation from primarily serving agriculture to multiple aims including flood control and municipal and industrial water. The course of diverted water under the Reclamation Act never did run smooth; many technical and economic problems were encountered, and the program sometimes fell short of living up to its original promise of carrying out the Jeffersonian vision of peopling the West with small family farms. The 1902 Act limited reclamation project water deliveries to a maximum of 160 acres per "any one landowner," and required the landowner to be "an actual bona fide resident on such land." Even though the Supreme Court unanimously upheld the acreage limitation with a ringing declaration that reclamation projects were "designed to benefit people, not land," and to distribute benefits "in accordance with the greatest good to the greatest number of individuals," enforcement of this restriction was, to put it charitably, spotty. Ivanhoe Irrigation Dist. v. McCracken, 357 U.S. 275, 297 (1958). The federal government, the states, and the project beneficiaries were more interested in building and operating projects than in social engineering.

After the Carter Administration proposed to get tougher about enforcement, Congress enacted legislation in 1982 which significantly liberalized the acreage limitation (and repealed the residency requirement). Reclamation Reform Act of 1982, 43 U.S.C. §§ 390aa to 390zz–1. A significant part of this legislative overhaul was to require larger landowners who exceeded the new 960 acre limitation to pay "full cost" for federally-delivered water.

c.   GRANTS OF TIMBER

Another fundamental shift in public land policy can be traced through successive congressional treatments of lands chiefly valuable for timber. For centuries, of course, the forest was the enemy, the wilderness standing between the pioneer and agrarian productivity. Timber was cleared from public lands to make way for agriculture. It has been conservatively estimated that by 1900, trees containing 600 billion board feet of lumber had been cut down to clear the land. On the other hand, some of the earliest examples of federal reservations and protection of lands for public purposes grew out of the national need for timber for construction of naval vessels in the early nineteenth century. See Paul Gates, HISTORY OF PUBLIC LAND LAW DEVELOPMENT 532–34 (1970).

Demand for lumber from growing Midwestern cities created vast logging industries in Michigan, Wisconsin, and other forested states. Wood-burning steamboats and railroad engines added to demand. The public lands supplied most of this seemingly insatiable market, usually by fraudulent means, including outright theft. By the use of their own "claim clubs," lumbermen seldom paid more than the minimum $1.25 per acre price, if they paid at all. Sawmills operated on federal land in Minnesota for eleven years before an acre of public land was sold. When reformer Secretary of the Interior Carl Schurz initiated timber trespass prosecutions in the 1870's, Congress responded by refusing to appropriate funds for protecting the federal forests.

In 1872 Congress enacted the Timber Culture Act, which gave settlers forty acres of public lands if they would plant and cultivate trees. A few groves planted under this Act have survived on the Great Plains, but the main use of the Act was preemptive, for a settler could control the Timber Culture land claimed for thirteen years without payment. Ten million acres went to patent under this Act. In spite of the known abuses, Congress followed up with the Timber and Stone Act of 1878, which allowed persons to appropriate public lands "chiefly valuable for timber (or stone)" in several western states for $2.50 an acre. Abuses under this Act were also common. Occasionally the executive branch tried to protect federal timber lands from wholesale exploitation and privatization. The lonely efforts of General Land Commissioner W.A.J. Sparks to this end between 1885–87 was noteworthy, but had little lasting effect except to stir up western antagonism. The long history of exploitation of federal forest land eventually led to the rise of the first conservation movement (and forest reserves) toward the end of the nineteenth century.

d.   GRANTS TO MINERS

Old public land laws like preemption, homesteading, and railroad grants have passed into the mists of history, but mining is a somewhat different story: it is still governed to a large extent by a statute that was anachronistic even before the frontier was closed. Full treatment of the Mining Law of 1872 and more modern statutes is found in Chapter 7; only a few historical developments will be touched on here.

Although the Land Act of 1785 had reserved to the Nation one-third of the precious metals on public lands, that measure died with ratification of the Constitution. Twenty years later, Congress authorized leasing of public lands in Indiana, Illinois, and Missouri for lead mining purposes, to raise revenue and to insure federal supplies of a strategic metal. This experiment lasted from 1807 until 1846, when it was abandoned. It did result in two important cases in early public land law; namely, United States v. Gratiot, *infra* p. 118, United States v. Gear, 44 U.S. (3 How.) 120 (1845) (holding that unauthorized mining on the public domain is an actionable trespass).

As discussed in Andrus v. Utah, *supra* p. 90, federal land disposal policy had traditionally distinguished between public lands that were "mineral in character" and other lands; only the latter were generally subject to disposal under the homestead and other non-mineral disposal laws. Between the repeal of the early experiment with mineral leasing in 1846 and the adoption of the federal Mining Act of 1866, no federal law authorized entry onto or disposition of mineral lands. Nevertheless, from 1847 on, most of the mineral land east of the Mississippi, including the immensely valuable iron and copper ore in Michigan and Minnesota, went for $1.25 an acre via preemption, cash purchase, or homestead. The government was unable or unwilling to check this seeming perversion of the public land acts, and the local people found nothing strange in homestead entries on claims virtually worthless for agriculture.

The great California Gold Rush initiated by James Marshall's discovery in early 1848 took place almost entirely on federal lands. Yet the only law governing the mining activity was the "law of the mining camps." The customary mining camp law was conceived out of necessity, it was simple, it followed a general common-sense principle of first in time, first in right, and it was sometimes enforced at the end of a rope. It contained useful specifics such as requirements for the marking of mining claims, limits on their acreage and the number that could be held, requirements to diligently develop them, and so forth. Similar customary "laws" governed mining camps that mushroomed and died all over the West in the years that followed the Gold Rush, because Congress took no action until 1866.

THE CALIFORNIA GOLD RUSH

Rodman W. Paul, CALIFORNIA GOLD

Pp. 20–25 (1947).

In the history of almost any of the American states one can find a few events and trends that in significance stand out from the purely local as sharply as a single tree upon a desert plain. The Gold Rush is an instance. Within California the Gold Rush was a revolution that changed forever the character of the state. Beyond California's boundaries it was a magnetic force that sent its lines of attraction into every nation.

Within two years of Marshall's discovery every civilized country knew the name "California," although at that time few persons in Europe, or Asia, or Latin America could have identified Illinois, or Massachusetts, or Georgia. In all parts of the world men made ready to seek the Golden Fleece, or to venture their money in the expeditions organized by those more daring than themselves, or to invest in the expansion of trade and shipping to which the Gold Rush was giving rise.

Even if cautious men decided to remain at home and keep their capital with them, still they could not escape entirely the effects of the train of events set in motion [by Marshall's discovery.] * * * In the United States alone, gold production multiplied seventy-three times during the six years that began in 1848, and from a position of insignificance among the gold producing nations, the United States climbed upward so rapidly that during the period from 1851 to 1855 it contributed nearly 45 per cent of the world's total output. The result was an inflation that affected all the countries on the earth's surface.

More dramatic and more immediately obvious was the functioning of the Gold Rush as a population movement. * * *

* * *

How many joined in the rush of "forty-eight," "forty-nine," and the early fifties will never be known with any degree of accuracy, but it is clear that the influx of 1848 was comparatively so small that it was no more than a prelude to the stampede of 1849 and the subsequent years. * * * California's population jumped from 14,000 in 1848 to something less than 100,000 at the close of 1849, and that it then advanced to 223,000 by the latter part of 1852.

California's state law provided that "in actions respecting 'mining claims' proof shall be admitted of the customs, usages or regulations established and in force at the bar or diggings embracing such claims; and such customs, usages or regulations, when not in conflict with the Constitution and laws of this State, shall govern the decision of the action." Congressional silence until 1866 meant that California mining law involved a dynamic (that is, ongoing) incorporation into its own law of the mining camp customs:

> [The customary mining law] prescribed the acts by which the right to mine a particular piece of ground could be secured and its use and enjoyment continued and preserved and by what non-action on the part of the appropriator such right should become forfeited or lost and the ground become, as at first, publici juris and open to the appropriation of the next comer. They were few, plain and simple, and well understood by those with whom they originated. They were well adapted to secure the end designed to be accomplished, and were adequate to the judicial determination of all controversies touching mining rights.

Morton v. Solambo Copper Mining Co., 26 Cal. 527 (1864).

The miners were technically trespassing on federal land. When Colonel Mason of the U.S. Army outpost at Monterey, California toured the Sierra gold fields in the summer of 1848, he engaged in "serious reflection" about how the government ought to extract a fee from the miners, but prudence won out: "[U]pon considering the large extent of country, the character of the people engaged, and the small scattered force at my command [many of his soldiers had deserted to look for gold], I resolved not to interfere." His warning proved prophetic: "[S]till the Government is entitled to rents for this land, and immediate steps should be devised to collect them, for the longer it is delayed the more difficult it will become." Mason's report is reprinted in Thomas Donaldson, The Public Domain: Its History with Statistics 312–17 (1884).

In the late 1850s, the United States had attempted to oust miners by asserting (after intervening in private litigation involving the validity of title to certain mineral land in California) that the land was owned by the national government. A circuit court endorsed the idea and issued an injunction against continued mining, United States v. Parrott, 1 McCall. (C.C.) 271, Fed. Cas. No. 15,998 (1858), and President Lincoln authorized the military to remove the miners. As civil war clouds were gathering, one California Senator reportedly said this would lead California to join the South in rebellion. Shortly thereafter, Chief Justice Stephen Field of the California Supreme Court (and later a U.S. Supreme Court Justice), a leader of Union loyalists, wrote in Biddle Boggs v. Merced Mining Co., 14 Cal. 279, 374 (1859) (on rehearing), aff'd on other grounds sub nom. Mining Co. v. Boggs, 70 U.S. 304 (1865), that the federal government owned the lands being mined because the miners had "no license in the legal meaning of that term."

> The most which can be said is that the [national] government has forborne to exercise its rights [as landowner], but this forbearance confers no positive right upon the miner, which would avail as a protection against the assertion of its claims to the mineral. The supposed license from the general government, then, to work the mines in the public lands, consists in its simple forbearance. Any other license rests in mere assertion, and is untrue in fact, and unwarranted in law.

Id. at 374–75. This was not a popular decision in California.

THE GENERAL MINING LAW OF 1872

Between 1850 and 1866, various bills to regulate mining activities were introduced in Congress, particularly when conflicts between miners and other settlers became acute, but discussion bogged down over such questions as how to exclude the Chinese from the harvest of metals. After much legislative maneuvering by Senator William Stewart of Nevada (who made a fortune representing miners) to get around the opposition of Congressman George Julian of Indiana (who wanted the United States to reap some direct financial benefit from the minerals it owned), Congress finally produced the Mining Law of 1866 under the quaint title: "An Act granting the Right of Way to Ditch and Canal Owners over the Public Lands," with which it was scarcely concerned.

The 1866 Act legalized the miners' trespasses by declaring that "mineral lands are free and open to exploration and occupation" under local usage and custom. Lode claims, which are veins of ore, could be patented—fee title obtained—if the miner expended $500 in labor or improvements and filed a description with the local land office. The law retroactively validated existing claims. The area of the claim was limited to a maximum of 20 acres, and the cost for a patent was $5 per acre. Surface rights and extralateral rights were flexible, depending upon where the vein went. Four years later, Congress corrected an oversight in the earlier law by allowing the location of so-called "placer claims," which encompasses deposits in unconsolidated beds like gravel, defined as "all forms of deposit, excepting veins of quartz, or other rock in place." Placer locations were limited to 160 acres, and could be purchased for $2.50 an acre.

The Mining Law of 1872, 30 U.S.C. §§ 22–39, still the main statutory provision for hardrock mining, and sometimes called the "miners' Magna Carta," consolidated and modified the 1866 and 1870 laws. It qualified coverage by referring to "valuable" minerals, it required $100 worth of annual development work for either type of claim, and made other adjustments.

The Supreme Court described the principal interest granted by the 1872 Act—the unpatented mining claim—this way in Belk v. Meagher, 104 U.S. 279, 283–84 (1881):

> A mining claim perfected under the law is property in the highest sense of that term, which may be bought, sold, and conveyed, and will pass by descent. There is nothing in the act of Congress which makes actual possession any more necessary for the protection of the title acquired to such a claim by a valid location, than it is for any other grant from the United States. Congress has seen fit to make the possession of that part of the public lands which is valuable for minerals separable from the fee, and to provide for the existence of an exclusive right to the possession, while the paramount title to the land remains in the United States. * * *

The reach of the 1872 Act has been progressively limited by various subsequent statutes. Fossil fuels, along with other non-metallic minerals like potash and sodium ores, were put into a leasing system in 1920. Common varieties of widely occurring minerals were put under a discretionary sales system in the mid-twentieth century. A growing number of environmental and other regulatory restrictions now apply to activities under the miners' Magna Carta. These are discussed in Chapter 7.

e. GRANTS TO RAILROADS

By the mid–19th century, the West wanted railroads. Congress had been granting railroads rights-of-way up to 100 feet wide through the public lands since 1835. (In 1852 it adopted a general law to that effect which also authorized the use of earth, stone, and timber from adjacent public lands.) In 1850, a statute granted Illinois, Mississippi, and Alabama even-numbered sections of non-mineral public land within six miles of the proposed Chicago to Mobile rail line. The states assigned the land to the builder, and the rush was on. (Thereafter, odd-numbered rather than even-numbered sections of non-mineral public land were given to the railroads, to avoid interfering with the practice of granting even-numbered sections 16 and 36 to new states to support common schools.)

The transcontinental rail lines received the largest grants. Justice Rehnquist reviewed the history in an important modern case dealing with the nature of the property rights patented:

> The idea of a transcontinental railroad predated the California gold rush. * * * [A]nimating it all was the desire of the Federal Government that the West be settled. This desire was intensified by the need to provide a logistical link with California in the heat of the Civil War. That the venture was much too risky and much too expensive for private capital alone was evident in the years of fruitless exhortation; private investors would not move without tangible governmental inducement.
>
> In the mid–19th Century there was serious disagreement as to the forms that inducement could take. Justice Story, in his Commentaries on the Constitution, described one extant school of thought which argued that "internal improvements," such as railroads, were not within the enumerated constitutional powers of Congress. Under such a theory, the direct subsidy of a transcontinental railroad was constitutionally suspect—an uneasiness aggravated by President Andrew Jackson's 1830 veto of a bill appropriating funds to construct a road from Maysville to Lexington within the State of Kentucky.
>
> The response to this constitutional "gray" area, and source of political controversy, was the "checkerboard" land grant scheme. The Union Pacific Act of 1862 granted public land to the Union Pacific Railroad for each mile of track that it laid. Land surrounding the railway right of way was divided into "checkerboard" blocks. Odd numbered lots were granted to the Union Pacific; even numbered lots were reserved by the Government. As a result, Union Pacific land in the area of the right of way was usually surrounded by public land, and vice versa. The historical explanation for this peculiar disposition is that it was apparently an attempt to disarm the "internal improvement" opponents by establishing a grant scheme with "demonstrable" benefits. * * * As one historian noted: * * * "In later donations the price of the reserved sections was doubled so that it could be argued, as the Congressional Globe shows ad infinitum, that by giving half the land away and thereby making possible construction of the road, canal, or railroad, the government would recover from the reserved sections as much as it would have received from the whole." [Gates at 345–46 (1968).]

* * *

The "internal improvements" theory was not the only obstacle to a transcontinental railroad. In 1853 Congress had appropriated monies and authorized Secretary of War Jefferson Davis to undertake surveys of various proposed routes for a transcontinental railroad. Congress was badly split along sectional lines on the appropriate location of the route—so badly split that Stephen A. Douglas, now a Senator from Illinois, in 1854 suggested the construction of a northern, central, and southern route, each with connecting branches in the East. That proposal, however, did not break the impasse.

The necessary impetus was provided by the Civil War. Senators and Representatives from those States which seceded from the Union were no longer present in Congress, and therefore the sectional overtones of the dispute as to routes largely disappeared. * * *

* * * As is often the case, war spurs technological development, and Congress enacted the Union Pacific Act in May 1862. Perhaps not coincidentally, the Homestead Act was passed the same month.

Leo Sheep Co. v. United States, 440 U.S. 668 (1979) (the legal issues in this case are discussed in Chapter 5A).

Eventually over 90 million acres of public lands were granted to the railroads directly. Another 35 to 40 million acres were granted to states to be used by the railroads. This was all in addition to another 200 million acres of public lands disposed of to support general "internal improvements," some of which were also granted to railroads.

This massive disposition program, like the others, was not always carried out smoothly. The first transcontinental line is the best known story, and illustrates some of the problems. The 1862 Act provided the railroads construction loans and a 400 foot right of way, together with their choice of ten odd-numbered sections of public land within a 20–mile belt for every mile built. Just two years later Congress doubled the size of the grant to twenty sections and expanded the belt to a width of 40 miles. To promote a northern route from Minnesota to the Pacific, Congress granted the Northern Pacific Railroad Company forty sections per mile, selected within a strip of land 80 miles wide in existing states and 120 miles wide in the territories. The United States withdrew most lands within the belt from other forms of disposal.

In furtherance of homesteading, the Act required the railroads to dispose of their lands within three years at $1.25 per acre. The Supreme Court eventually upheld the device of "disposing" of the lands by mortgaging them to affiliates, Platt v. Union Pacific R.R. Co., 99 U.S. (9 Otto) 48 (1878), and watered down a provision for reversion to federal ownership if conditions were not met. Schulenberg v. Harriman, 88 U.S. (21 Wall.) 44

FEDERAL LAND GRANTS FOR RAILROADS

LAND GRANT LIMITS
The shading shows the approximate limits
of the areas in which the railroads received
their land grants

ACREAGE GRANTED
The shaded areas are in proportion to the
acreage received by the railroads. They do
not show the exact location of the granted lands
which in general formed a checkerboard pattern

Bureau of Land Management

(1874).* While the railroads were being built, enormous quantities of land
were withdrawn from settlement, and the railroads frequently delayed
selection to avoid taxes. The West, which had pressed hard for railroad land
grants, became hostile to the railroads as the supply of free land dried up.

* Only a few isolated forfeitures, declared
by Congress, ever resulted from the widespread failures to comply. The timber-rich "O
& C" lands in western Oregon (originally
granted to underwrite construction of the
Oregon and California Railroad) were returned to the public domain in that fashion.

From 1871 on, most efforts were directed at redressing real and imagined grievances stemming from railroad ownership and practices, but few effective remedies were ever instituted. Gates at 341–86.

The Gilded Age was one of the low points of public morality in the United States, but the changes wrought by the railroad land grants had some positive effects. Railroads encouraged and directed immigration, and were also among the first promoters of tourism centered on the wonders of the West. The Northern Pacific, for example, was one of the prime movers behind the creation of the world's first national park at Yellowstone. The West was developed, and many towns sprang up in the railroads' wake. Socially and economically, the railroad enterprise was instrumental in ending the frontier.

Prior and subsequent federal reservations of land within railroads' grant areas raised "in lieu" selection problems analogous to those faced by Utah in Andrus v. Utah, *supra* at p. 90. The Forest Lieu Exchange Act of 1897 allowed the railroads to exchange their inholdings in reserved lands for other lands outside the federal reservations; the Transportation Act of 1940, 49 U.S.C. § 65(b), released railroads from rate limitations in exchange for their relinquishment of in lieu rights.

The railroad land grants have had one enduring legacy for modern public land management law and policy: the "checkerboard" problem. Well over 100 million acres, in alternate odd-numbered sections, were granted to the railroads, directly and indirectly, between 1850 and 1871. When the even-numbered sections the national government retained did not pass out of federal ownership by homesteading or other means, and the era of disposition faded, the checkerboard remained. The use of federal lands as a grazing commons exacerbated the awkward landownership pattern. As a leading public land historian put it:

> The methods adopted by users of the range are well known to readers of Western fiction. Great blocks of the public domain were fenced in by established ranchers for their exclusive use. * * * By 1885, illegal fencing had become so general that Congress passed a law prohibiting [enclosures of the public domain]. In 1886, President Cleveland, by proclamation, ordered removal of all fences. Secretary Lamar immediately threatened prosecution if the removals were not carried out without delay. Unfortunately, he did not have a staff in the field large enough or always willing to enforce the President's order and the new law.

Louise Peffer, THE CLOSING OF THE PUBLIC DOMAIN 80–81 (1951). The legacy of "checkerboarded" ownership is manifest in the large number of disputes over access to and across federal lands, discussed in Chapter 5A.

C. RESERVATION, WITHDRAWAL, AND REACQUISITION

Throughout the 19th century, unprecedented population and economic growth and territorial expansion had taken place. In 1893, historian

Frederick Jackson Turner called attention to the fact that the 1890 census had declared the end of the frontier with these words: "Up to and including 1880 the country had a frontier of settlement, but at present the unsettled area has been so broken into by isolated bodies of settlement that there can hardly be said to be a frontier line." For Turner, the end of the frontier "closed the first period of American history," for up to then "American history has been in a large degree the history of the colonization of the Great West. The existence of an area of free land, its continuous recession, and the advance of American settlement westward, explain American development." This demographic change, along with a growing recognition of the shortcomings of public land disposal policy (and growing perception of the abuse of the public land laws), contributed to the rise of a national movement that would first significantly limit, and eventually replace, that into federal ownership). Conservation would become a critical national concern.

Federal land policy in the first century of the Nation's existence had not been exclusively one of disposal. There were occasions when federal lands were held for the common good to serve interests of national importance. Withdrawals by the executive for military purposes and, beginning around mid-century, for Indian reservations, were common. Nonetheless, the assumption was widespread that most federal lands would eventually pass out of national ownership. The Property Clause made clear that the national government, not the states, would supervise the disposal process, but it did so in terms which seemed to recognize that the United States might retain and manage some property interests for national purposes. Early on, in fact, the U.S. created a system for leasing rather than selling certain federal lands with mineral values in the Midwest. Eventually, the constitutionality of this practice came before the U.S. Supreme Court.

United States v. Gratiot

Supreme Court of the United States, 1840.
39 U.S. (14 Peters) 526.

■ THOMPSON, J.

[The U.S. brought an action on a debt, alleging that the defendants, who had a federal license to smelt lead ore obtained from U.S. mines in Illinois had not paid the U.S. the royalty in kind provided in the license, of six pounds of lead for every 100 pounds smelted. The defendants responded by challenging the constitutionality of the 1807 federal statute which authorized the President to contract for the development of lead on the public lands. Senator Thomas Hart Benton argued for the defendants that the only authority the Property Clause gave Congress over the public lands was "to dispose of them, and to make rules and regulations respecting the preparation of them for sale; for their preservation, and their sale." "The power to make rules and regulations, applies to the power to dispose of the lands. The rules are to carry the disposal into effect; to protect them; to explore them; to survey them." If the Property Clause were understood to have authorized federal retention and management, Benton went on, the states would have stoutly resisted, and those with western land claims policy. The consequence was the emergence of a policy to retain many tracts of land in federal ownership (and acquire or reacquire other tracts would have never ceded them. The Court's unanimous response was curt:]

The term territory, as here used [in the Property Clause] is merely descriptive of one kind of property; and is equivalent to the word lands. And Congress has the same power over it as over any other property belonging to the United States; and this power is vested in Congress without limitation; and has been considered the foundation upon which the territorial governments rest. * * * [T]he words "dispose of," cannot receive the construction contended for at the bar; that they vest in Congress the power only to sell, and not to lease such lands. The disposal must be left to the discretion of Congress. And there can be no apprehensions of any encroachments upon state rights, by the creation of a numerous tenantry within their borders; as has been so strenuously urged in the argument. The law of 1807, authorizing the leasing of the lead mines, was passed before Illinois was organized as a state; and she cannot now complain of any disposition or regulation of the lead mines previously made by Congress. She surely cannot claim a right to the public lands within her limits. It has been the policy of the government, at all times in disposing of the public lands, to reserve the mines for the use of the United States. And their real value cannot be ascertained, without causing them to be explored and worked, under proper regulations. The authority given to the President to lease the lead mines, is limited * * * to a short period, so as not to interfere with the power of Congress to make other disposition of the mines, should they think proper to do so.

NOTES AND QUESTIONS

1. Does *Gratiot* resolve whether the admission of Illinois as a state in 1818 might affect Congress's power over this property? The statute authorizing lead mine development under federal control had been enacted in 1807, but the license to *Gratiot* was not issued until September 1834, after statehood. Does that make any difference?

2. The last sentence of the excerpt of the Court's opinion in *Gratiot* seems to suggest that if Congress had authorized the President to issue long-term rather than short-term leases of lead mines, then the outcome might have been different. Is there any basis for reading the Property Clause as saying Congress may retain the lands in national ownership and control for some time, but must eventually dispose of them?

3. Should the Court's reference to a power "without limitation" really be taken literally? Could Congress enact a law prohibiting political speech on federal land? Many of the early exceptions to the general policy of disposing fee-simple rights in the early era related to national security concerns. Federal war powers authority strengthened the legal basis for withdrawal of timber suitable for the navy's ship masts, and lead deposits for the production of ordnance.

4. The most limiting (and tragic) interpretation of the Property Clause ever put forward by the U.S. Supreme Court came in its most infamous decision. In Dred Scott v. Sandford, 60 U.S. (19 How.) 393, 432–52 (1856), Chief Justice Taney took the view that the "territory" referred to in the Property Clause referred only to the territory that some of the

original states had ceded to the United States. He also narrowly read Congress's power to make "needful rules and regulations" under the Property Clause. The Court's conclusion that Congress could not prohibit slavery in territories and new states made the Civil War inevitable. The Court had never before, and has never after, taken such a view of the Property Clause.

With the legal foundation provided by *Gratiot*, Congress dramatically accelerated the pace of reservation as the nineteenth century drew to a close. Also, the purposes for which lands were reserved broadened substantially. The following case illustrates the emerging impulse to permanently hold some land in federal ownership to serve such broader cultural purposes. Here, the legal question concerned acquisition through condemnation in order to complete a reservation.

United States v. Gettysburg Elec. R. Co.

Supreme Court of the United States, 1896.
160 U.S. 668.

■ JUSTICE PECKMAN delivered the opinion of the court.

[The United States sought to condemn the Railroad's land for inclusion in what was to be Gettysburg National Military Park.] The really important question to be determined in these proceedings is, whether the use to which the petitioner desires to put the land described in the petitions is of that kind of public use for which the government of the United States is authorized to condemn land.

It has authority to do so whenever it is necessary or appropriate to use the land in the execution of any of the powers granted to it by the Constitution.

* * * In [the relevant acts] of Congress * * * the intended use of this land is plainly set forth. * * * [W]hen the legislature has declared the use or purpose to be a public one, its judgment will be respected by the courts, unless the use be palpably without reasonable foundation. Many authorities are cited in the note, and, indeed, the rule commends itself as a rational and proper one.

* * * Upon the question whether the proposed use of this land is a public one, we think there can be no well founded doubt. And also, in our judgment, the government has the constitutional power to condemn the land for the proposed use. It is, of course, not necessary that the power of condemnation for such purpose be expressly given by the Constitution. The right to condemn at all is not so given. It results from the powers that are given, and it is implied because of its necessity, or because it is appropriate in exercising those powers. Congress has power to declare war and to create and equip armies and navies. It has the great power of taxation to be exercised for the common defence and general welfare. Having such powers, it has such other and implied ones as are necessary and appropriate for the purpose of carrying the powers expressly given into effect. Any act of Congress which plainly and directly tends to enhance the respect and love

of the citizen for the institutions of his country and to quicken and strengthen his motives to defend them, and which is germane to and intimately connected with and appropriate to the exercise of some one or all of the powers granted by Congress must be valid. This proposed use comes within such description. * * *

The end to be attained by this proposed use, as provided for by the act of Congress, is legitimate, and lies within the scope of the Constitution. The battle of Gettysburg was one of the great battles of the world. The numbers contained in the opposing armies were great; the sacrifice of life was dreadful; while the bravery and, indeed, heroism displayed by both the contending forces rank with the highest exhibition of those qualities ever made by man. The importance of the issue involved in the contest of which this great battle was a part cannot be overestimated. The existence of the government itself and the perpetuity of our institutions depended upon the result. Valuable lessons in the art of war can now be learned from an examination of this great battlefield in connection with the history of the events which there took place. Can it be that the government is without power to preserve the land, and properly mark out the various sites upon which this struggle took place? Can it not erect the monuments provided for by these acts of Congress, or even take possession of the field of battle in the name and for the benefit of all the citizens of the country for the present and for the future? Such a use seems necessarily not only a public use, but one so closely connected with the welfare of the republic itself as to be within the powers granted Congress by the Constitution for the purpose of protecting and preserving the whole country. * * *

No narrow view of the character of this proposed use should be taken. Its national character and importance, we think, are plain. The power to condemn for this purpose need not be plainly and unmistakably deduced from any one of the particularly specified powers. Any number of those powers may be grouped together, and an inference from them all may be drawn that the power claimed has been conferred.

* * * This, we think, completes the review of the material questions presented by the record. The first and important question in regard to whether the proposed use is public or not, having been determined in favor of the United States, we are not disposed to take any very technical view of the other questions which might be subject to amendment or to further proof upon the hearing below.

NOTES AND QUESTIONS

1. Exactly which provision of the Constitution provides the basis for federal authority to condemn or acquire a historic battlefield site? Is it the same basis for the constitutionality of the Louisiana Purchase? Can the same rationale be used to support condemnation for nature preservation and recreational uses? Does the fifth amendment's requirement that the United States pay just compensation for taking property imply a federal power of eminent domain? What in the Constitution determines whether acquisition of a historic battlefield site is a historical purpose?

How about acquisition of the Louisiana Purchase? Condemnation for nature preservation and recreational uses?

In Buffalo River Conservation & Recreation Council v. National Park Service, 558 F.2d 1342 (8th Cir. 1977), cert. denied, 435 U.S. 924 (1978), the court curtly rejected a challenge to federal condemnation of land for the Buffalo National River in Arkansas, noting that "[f]or at least eighty years the power of the United States to create parklands has been a recognized and popular function of the national government."

Consider the following description of the role that national parks played in the dawn of the era of reservation:

> Nature was a vital cohesive force in a country that lacked the glue of ethnic, religious and racial homogeneity. Reinforcing the shared commitment to republicanism, democracy and free enterprise, a literal sense of common ground could mitigate the centrifugal tendencies of heterogeneity. The fabled frontier thesis of Frederick Jackson Turner (1893), which rooted American culture, character and intellect firmly in the unmodified nature that colonists encountered on the frontier, represented the culmination of a way of thinking about nature as a moral quality imbued with a redemptive virtue that rubbed off almost magically on those who came into contact with it, metamorphosing Europeans into Americans.
>
> In settler nations whose white citizens are increasingly cut off from their pioneer pasts in suburban environments, the national park enshrines nature's recruitment for patriotic purposes.

Peter Coates, Nature 108 (1998). Does this help justify application of the Gettysburg Electric R.R. Co. holding to acquisition of national parks? Of course, Native Americans and others outside of the dominant political culture of the time would attach a very different meaning to nature in the national parks.

2. In 2005, the U.S. Supreme Court set off a fire storm of controversy in narrowly (5–4) deciding that a private development plan served a public purpose, and thus did not run afoul of the fifth amendment when eminent domain was used to acquire property for the developer. Kelo v. City of New London, 545 U.S. 469 (2005). As in *Gettysburg Electric R.R. Co.*, the majority in *Kelo* accorded great deference to the legislative determination that the development would be for a public purpose. Should the Court examine more critically the judgment of a local body than it does congressional findings? Before *Kelo*, the Court had never regarded the issue of whether a use is public for purposes of the fifth amendment condemnation as raising a significant judicial question. See Hawaii Housing Auth. v. Midkiff, 467 U.S. 229 (1984) (the government must show only a rational relationship to a conceivable public purpose); Berman v. Parker, 348 U.S. 26 (1954) (slum clearance for redevelopment an acceptable public use). The Court's sharp split in *Kelo* might portend an eventual judicial narrowing of the scope of public purposes in eminent domain law. This conceivably could have implications for federal land; for example, by limiting the government's ability to acquire land by condemnation and then lease it to private parties for such purposes as mineral development.

3. The General Condemnation Act of 1888, 40 U.S.C. § 3113, permits federal officers authorized to acquire real estate for "public uses" to employ condemnation whenever they "believe[] that it is necessary or advantageous to the Government to do so." A number of federal statutes authorize the government to acquire lands for particular purposes specifically by "donation," "exchange," or "purchase with donated or appropriated funds." See, e.g., 16 U.S.C. § 460w–2 (Apostle Islands National Lakeshore Act). But such statutes do not limit the application of generic authority such as the General Condemnation Act. See United States v. 16.92 Acres of Land, 670 F.2d 1369 (7th Cir. 1982) ("unless it desires to exclude condemnation, there is no need for Congress to specifically include 'condemnation' as a permissible method of property acquisition in a statute").

The Weeks Act, which authorized the purchase of "such forested, cut-over, or denuded lands within the watersheds of navigable streams as in [the Secretary of Agriculture's] judgment may be necessary to the regulation for the flow of navigable streams or for the production of timber," prohibited such acquisition "until the legislature of the State in which the land lies shall have consented to the acquisition of such land by the United States for the purpose of preserving the navigability of navigable streams." 16 U.S.C. § 515. The Migratory Bird Conservation Act contains a somewhat similar requirement that the Secretary of the Interior obtain the consent of the state before acquiring migratory bird habitat, 16 U.S.C. § 715f. After North Dakota, piqued at the federal government's refusal to complete the Garrison Diversion (a federal water project the state thought it had been promised), sought to revoke its consent to acquire wetlands easements, the Supreme Court held that consent could not be revoked with regard to already completed acquisitions and new ones made within the terms of the original consent, at least so long as the United States did not unreasonably delay in carrying out its acquisitions. North Dakota v. United States, 460 U.S. 300, 314–15 (1983).

4. Sometimes Congress authorizes a federal agency to condemn private land within the boundaries of a conservation unit only when development inconsistent with the conservation purpose is proposed. Sometimes Congress has given the federal land manager direct zoning authority over the private inholding where local regulation is non-existent. See, e.g., 16 U.S.C. § 460aa–3 (Sawtooth National Recreation Area). Other federal statutes limit the purposes for which eminent domain authority may be exercised. For example, the Federal Land Policy and Management Act gives the BLM condemnation authority only to provide access to federal lands. 43 U.S.C. § 1715(a).

5. Federal condemnation procedures are summarized in Kirby Forest Industries, Inc. v. United States, 467 U.S. 1 (1984), involving a Park Service acquisition to expand Big Thicket National Park in Texas.

1. The Emergence of Withdrawal and Reservation: Forests and Scenery

Congress reserved four sections of land in Arkansas as early as 1832 because it contained hot springs thought to be of medicinal value (4 Stat.

405). The conservation-oriented writings of George Perkins Marsh supplied a rationale for action by federal reformers such as Interior Secretary Carl Schurz (1877–81), who argued that federal retention of timberlands was necessary to prevent fraud and soil/water degradation. Before the national movement to conserve forests took off, there were other precedents for resource protection reservations outside of Indian and military reservations. Congress took a faltering step toward conservation when it gave Yosemite Valley to California in 1864 on the "express conditions that the premises shall be held for public use, resort and recreation [and] shall be inalienable for all time." See 13 Stat. 325 (1864). But it was the creation of Yellowstone National Park as a "pleasuring ground" on a large and remote tract of federal lands in northwest Wyoming in 1872 which may rightly be regarded as the beginning of the modern federal lands systems.

In sheer acreage terms, however, a more significant milestone was enactment of what Charles Wilkinson called a "little-noticed, seemingly innocuous" single sentence buried deep in an 1891 law blandly entitled the General Revision Act, which repealed the Preemption and Timber Culture Acts, among other things. That sentence, added in conference committee with no comment in the Senate and a meager discussion in the House, authorized the President to "set apart and reserve * * * any part of the public lands wholly or in part covered with timber or undergrowth, whether of commercial value or not, as public reservations." 16 U.S.C. § 471.

Examine the language of the General Revision Act. Does it authorize the President to set aside desert or alpine land with few or no trees or other vegetation? Over the next sixteen years, a succession of Presidents (mostly Republican, as it turned out) used the General Revision authority to reserve nearly 80 percent of the lands today embraced in the national forest system. Many areas reserved under this statute contained substantial tracts of unforested land, and a number of them were eventually made into "crown jewel" national parks; e.g., Grand Canyon, Bryce Canyon, Lassen, King's Canyon, and Rocky Mountain. The seeds of some early national wildlife refuges were also sown by presidential reservations under the Act. Samuel P. Hays, CONSERVATION AND THE GOSPEL OF EFFICIENCY 47 (1959).

Theodore Roosevelt best embodies the presidential impulse to promote conservation through reservation. His bold assertions of executive authority to reserve federal land for various purposes (such as wildlife habitat) were left almost completely undisturbed by Congress and the courts. They were not without controversy, however, and the signal they sent of a possible end of the disposition era caused some backlash in the west.

In 1907 an Oregon Senator, Charles Fulton, attached a rider to a vital Agriculture appropriations bill that repealed the President's authority to make new forest reserves in six northwestern states (Oregon, Washington, Idaho, Montana, Colorado, and Wyoming). See 34 Stat. 1269–71. When the bill reached the White House, Roosevelt responded in typical fashion. Over the next few days, a "forced draft of Administration clerks—some of them working forty-eight hour shifts—completed all the paperwork necessary for the President to proclaim twenty four new forest reserves, and eleven enlarged ones, in the six states specified." Edmund Morris, Theodore Rex 487 (2001). As the ink was drying on these new orders, Roosevelt signed the appropriations bill into law. The statute (rather casually) announced that the forest reserves shall be known hereafter as national forests. Great controversies raged over Theodore Roosevelt's actions, but a new age in public land law had dawned.

U.S. Forest Service. Gray Towers NHS

In 1897 Congress enacted, also through a rider to an appropriation bill, what came to be known as the "organic act" for what would become the national forests. It gave the Secretary of the Interior general authority to manage the Forest Reserves and to issue rules and regulations regarding their occupancy and use. The statute began by announcing that no national forest should be established "except to improve and protect the forest within the boundaries, or for the purpose of securing favorable conditions of water flows, and to furnish a continuous supply of timber for the use and necessities of citizens of the United States." It disclaimed any intent to "prohibit any person from entering upon such forest reservations for all proper and lawful purposes" so long as such persons "comply with the rules and regulations covering such forest reservations." It also authorized the Secretary to "make such rules and regulations * * * as will insure the objects of such reservations; namely, to regulate their occupancy and use, and to preserve the forests thereon from destruction." The statute also set out criminal penalties for violations. These provisions are now found in 16 U.S.C. §§ 475, 478, 551.

Congress transferred management authority over the Forest Reserves to the Secretary of Agriculture in 1905, except for functions relating to surveys and patenting and, importantly, prospecting for minerals and locating mining claims. See 16 U.S.C. § 472. Forest Service Chief Gifford Pinchot immediately began using the legislative delegation of management authority to limit a wide range of uses, especially grazing, that had long been informally tolerated on federal lands. Pinchot deployed an active corps of rangers to regulate activities in the national forests. But, there remained genuine questions as to the constitutionality of the entire enterprise. The following two classic public land law opinions, issued the same day, crushed the hopes of opponents and laid the conservationists' fears to rest.

United States v. Grimaud

Supreme Court of the United States, 1911.
220 U.S. 506.

■ JUSTICE LAMAR:

The defendants were indicted for grazing sheep on the Sierra Forest Reserve without having obtained the permission required by the regulations adopted by the Secretary of Agriculture. They demurred on the ground that the forest reserve act of 1897 was unconstitutional, in so far as it delegated to the Secretary of Agriculture power to make rules and regulations, and made a violation thereof a penal offense. [The lower court dismissed the federal prosecutions, and the government appealed.] * * *

Under these acts, therefore, any use of the reservation for grazing or other lawful purpose was required to be subject to the rules and regulations established by the Secretary of Agriculture. To pasture sheep and cattle on the reservation, at will and without restraint, might interfere seriously with the accomplishment of the purposes for which they were established. But a limited and regulated use for pasturage might not be inconsistent with the object sought to be attained by the statute. The determination of such questions, however, was a matter of administrative detail. What might be harmless in one forest might be harmful to another. What might be injurious at one stage of timber growth, or at one season of the year, might not be so at another.

In the nature of things it was impracticable for Congress to provide general regulations for these various and varying details of management. Each reservation had its peculiar and special features; and in authorizing the Secretary of Agriculture to meet these local conditions, Congress was merely conferring administrative functions upon an agent, and not delegating to him legislative power. The authority actually given was much less than what has been granted to municipalities by virtue of which they make by-laws, ordinances, and regulations for the government of towns and cities. Such ordinances do not declare general rules with reference to rights of persons and property, nor do they create or regulate obligations and liabilities, nor declare what shall be crimes, nor fix penalties therefor. * * *

It must be admitted that it is difficult to define the line which separates legislative power to make laws, from administrative authority to make regulations. This difficulty has often been recognized, and was referred to by Chief Justice Marshall in Wayman v. Southard, [23 U.S. 1

(1825)], where he was considering the authority of courts to make rules. He there said: "It will not be contended that Congress can delegate to the courts, or to any other tribunals, powers which are strictly and exclusively legislative. But Congress may certainly delegate to others powers which the legislature may rightfully exercise itself." What were these nonlegislative powers which Congress could exercise, but which might also be delegated to others, was not determined, for he said: "The line has not been exactly drawn which separates those important subjects which must be entirely regulated by the legislature itself, from those of less interest, in which a general provision may be made, and power given to those who are to act under such general provisions to fill up the details."

* * * [W]hen Congress had legislated and indicated its will, it could give to those who were to act under such general provisions "power to fill up the details" by the establishment of administrative rules and regulations, the violation of which could be punished by fine or imprisonment fixed by Congress, or by penalties fixed by Congress, or measured by the injury done. * * *

[T]he authority to make administrative rules is not a delegation of legislative power, nor are such rules raised from an administrative to a legislative character because the violation thereof is punished as a public offense.

It is true that there is no act of Congress which, in express terms, declares that it shall be unlawful to graze sheep on a forest reserve. But the statutes from which we have quoted declare that the privilege of using reserves for "all proper and lawful purposes" is subject to the proviso that the person so using them shall comply "with the rules and regulations covering said forest reservation." The same act makes it an offense to violate those regulations; that is, to use them otherwise than in accordance with the rules established by the Secretary. Thus the implied license under which the United States has suffered its public domain to be used as a pasture for sheep and cattle, mentioned in Buford v. Houtz, 133 U.S. 320, was curtailed and qualified by Congress, to the extent that such privilege should not be exercised in contravention of the rules and regulations.

If, after the passage of the act and the promulgation of the rule, the defendants drove and grazed their sheep upon the reserve, in violation of the regulations, they were making an unlawful use of the government's property. In doing so they thereby made themselves liable to the penalty imposed by Congress.

It was argued that, even if the Secretary could establish regulations under which a permit was required, there was nothing in the act to indicate that Congress had intended or authorized him to charge for the privilege of grazing sheep on the reserve. These fees were fixed to prevent excessive grazing, and thereby protect the young growth and native grasses from destruction, and to make a slight income with which to meet the expenses of management. In addition to the general power in the act of 1897, already quoted, the act of February 1st, 1905 [33 Stat. 628] clearly indicates that the Secretary was authorized to make charges out of which a revenue from forest resources was expected to arise. * * *

The Secretary of Agriculture could not make rules and regulations for any and every purpose. Williamson v. United States, 207 U.S. 462 [1908]. As to those here involved, they all relate to matters clearly indicated and authorized by Congress. The subjects as to which the Secretary can regulate are defined. The lands are set apart as a forest reserve. He is required to make provision to protect them from depredations and from harmful uses. He is authorized "to regulate the occupancy and use and to preserve the forests from destruction." A violation of reasonable rules regulating the use and occupancy of the property is made a crime, not by the Secretary, but by Congress. The statute, not the Secretary, fixes the penalty. * * *

NOTES AND QUESTIONS

1. *Grimaud* was a remarkable case. When it first came before the Court, the lower court opinion dismissing the prosecution was affirmed when the Justices split 4–4. A little more than a month later, however, the Court granted the government's motion for rehearing, and more than a year after that reversed the lower court without a single dissent. In the meantime, Justices Hughes, Van Devanter, and Lamar had joined the Court. The author of the opinion is Joseph R. Lamar, not to be confused with the earlier Justice Lucius Quintus Cincinnatus Lamar, who holds the distinction of being the only former Interior Secretary to serve on the Supreme Court (1888–1893).

2. *Grimaud* was a federal criminal prosecution. Did that aspect make the delegation issue harder or easier? Is the Court correct in characterizing this statute as not delegating legislative power, but merely giving the administering agency "power to fill up the details"? How much substantive guidance did Congress give the Secretary in this legislation?

3. Consider the Court's "impracticability" argument. At issue in *Grimaud* was the Forest Service's general regulation requiring a permit before grazing livestock in a Forest Reserve. Was it impracticable for Congress to make the decision that a permit ought to be required? Had Congress made such a decision?

4. In Whitman v. American Trucking Ass'n, 531 U.S. 457 (2001), the Supreme Court unanimously upheld the Clean Air Act's broad delegation of authority to the Environmental Protection Agency to set ambient air quality standards, and applied the test of whether the Congress had laid down an "intelligible principle" for the agency to conform to in exercising the authority granted. Justice Scalia's opinion pointed out that in its entire history the Court had struck down only two statutes on nondelegation grounds, "one of which provided literally no guidance for the exercise of discretion, and the other of which conferred authority to regulate the entire economy on the basis of no more precise a standard than stimulating the economy by assuring 'fair competition'." 531 U.S. at 474. Did the 1897 Act supply such an "intelligible principle"? What was it?

Light v. United States

Supreme Court of the United States, 1911.
220 U.S. 523.

■ Justice Lamar:

The defendant was enjoined from pasturing his cattle on the Holy Cross Forest Reserve, because he had refused to comply with the regulations adopted by the Secretary of Agriculture, under the authority conferred by the act of June 4, 1897, (30 Stat. 35), to make rules and regulations as to the use, occupancy and preservation of forests. * * *

The bill alleged, and there was evidence to support the finding, that the defendant, with the expectation and intention that they would do so, turned his cattle out at a time and place which made it certain that they would leave the open public lands and go at once to the Reserve, where there was good water and fine pasturage. When notified to remove the cattle, he declined to do so and threatened to resist if they should be driven off by a forest officer. He justified this position on the ground that the statute of Colorado provided that a landowner could not recover damages for trespass by animals unless the property was enclosed with a fence of designated size and material. Regardless of any conflict in the testimony, the defendant claims that unless the Government put a fence around the Reserve it had no remedy, either at law or in equity, nor could he be required to prevent his cattle straying upon the Reserve from the open public land on which he had a right to turn them loose.

At common law the owner was required to confine his live stock, or else was held liable for any damage done by them upon the land of third persons. That law was not adapted to the situation of those States where there were great plains and vast tracts of unenclosed land, suitable for pasture. And so, without passing a statute, or taking any affirmative action on the subject, the United States suffered its public domain to be used for such purposes. There thus grew up a sort of implied license that these lands, thus left open, might be used so long as the Government did not cancel its tacit consent. Buford v. Houtz, 133 U.S. 326 [1890]. Its failure to object, however, did not confer any vested right on the complainant, nor did it deprive the United States of the power of recalling any implied license under which the land had been used for private purposes.

It is contended, however, that Congress cannot constitutionally withdraw large bodies of land from settlement without the consent of the State where it is located; and it is then argued that the act of 1891 providing for the establishment of reservations was void, so that what is nominally a Reserve is, in law, to be treated as open and unenclosed land, as to which there still exists the implied license that it may be used for grazing purposes. * * *

The United States can prohibit absolutely or fix the terms on which its property may be used. As it can withhold or reserve the land it can do so indefinitely, Stearns v. Minnesota, 179 U.S. 243 [1900]. It is true that the "United States do not and cannot hold property as a monarch may for private or personal purposes." * * *

"All the public lands of the nation are held in trust for the people of the whole country." United States v. Trinidad Coal Co., 137 U.S. 160 [1890]. And it is not for the courts to say how that trust shall be administered. That is for Congress to determine. The courts cannot compel it to set aside the lands for settlement; or to suffer them to be used for agricultural or grazing purposes; nor interfere when, in the exercise of its discretion, Congress establishes a forest reserve for what it decides to be national and public purposes. In the same way and in the exercise of the same trust it may disestablish a reserve, and devote the property to some other national and public purpose. These are rights incident to proprietorship, to say nothing of the power of the United States as a sovereign over the property belonging to it. Even a private owner would be entitled to protection against willful trespasses, and statutes providing that damage done by animals cannot be recovered, unless the land had been enclosed with a fence of the size and material required, do not give permission to the owner of cattle to use his neighbor's land as a pasture. They are intended to condone trespasses by straying cattle; they have no application to cases where they are driven upon unfenced land in order that they may feed there.

Fence laws do not authorize wanton and willful trespass, nor do they afford immunity to those who, in disregard of property rights, turn loose their cattle under circumstances showing that they were intended to graze upon the lands of another. * * *

NOTES AND QUESTIONS

1. The forest reserves transferred to the Agriculture Department's Forest Service encompassed almost 100 million acres of land susceptible to grazing. Pinchot's 1906 grazing regulations were "incendiary to the cattle industry," with several western legislatures passing memorials denouncing it, labeling Pinchot as a dictator and carpetbagger. Fred Light, a longtime rancher in the Roaring Fork River valley in Colorado, was a widely respected figure, and his fight became a cause celebre in Colorado and in ranching circles nationally, with stock associations and the Colorado legislature contributing to the payment of his attorneys' fees. Once he lost, he "acceded graciously and obtained federal permits for his animals [and o]ther ranchers grudgingly followed." Wilkinson, CROSSING THE NEXT MERIDIAN 91–92.

2. How does Light's complaint differ from Grimaud's?

3. How does the Court characterize the powers of the federal government over the public lands? As a sovereign? As a proprietor (ordinary landowner)? Compare Pollard v. Hagan, *supra* p. 70. Can the difference between the formulations in the two cases be explained by the evolution in congressional policy between 1845 and 1911? Does the Colorado law governing liability for cattle trespass apply to some (all?) (any?) federal lands?

4. Are there intimations of a "public trust" doctrine in this decision? Is the view expressed here of the enforceability of the trust in the courts consistent with Illinois Central Railroad, *supra* p. 80? Does *Light* support

Wilkinson's views about the trust inferred from federal public land statutes? See *supra* p. 84.

———

As the twentieth century approached, the public land policies of the nineteenth century had served their intended goals, albeit crudely. But altered circumstances and opinions began to bring about fundamental changes. Most land that could be productively farmed without irrigation had already passed out of federal ownership; private irrigation was but a drop in the bucket; western grazing lands were in poor condition; wildlife resources were at historical lows; and timber resources were severely depleted. Scandal was common, reforms had been repeatedly thwarted, and the trend toward large holdings and monopoly grew. Clear thinkers like John Wesley Powell had forcefully urged new methods of dealing with the public domain in relation to western settlement, but his career had been cut short by a hostile congressional reaction to the blanket withdrawals for the irrigation survey in 1889. A few years later, Gifford Pinchot emerged as the strongest advocate for fundamental revision in public land policy.

> By any standards, Gifford Pinchot was a magnificent bureaucrat. In his time the Forest Service was the most exciting organization in Washington. It was more a family than a bureau. In the field, around campfires, and in his home GP discussed the next moves and gave his associates the feeling that they served on the general staff in a national crusade. A natural leader, he chose his men well, gave them authority, aroused an esprit de corps and sent them forth to save the forests. * * * In a matter of months his new "forest rangers" were winning over the West. * * *

> What was needed now was a word, a name—to sum up the concept. A conversation with forester Overton Price brought up the fact that government forests in India were called "conservancies." Pinchot and Price liked the ring of the word, and thus a concept that had originated in the seminal thinking of such men as Thoreau and Marsh now had an expressive name—conservation. * * *

> The conservation movement was a river of many tributaries, and if GP was not, as he liked to believe in his later years, its fountainhead, he was nevertheless one of its vital sources. He was a key man of a key decade, and his leadership was crucial in persuading the American people to turn from flagrant waste of resources to programs of wise stewardship.

Stewart L. Udall, THE QUIET CRISIS 97–108 (1963)

While the Forest Reserves were the first great system of public lands that had been withdrawn from the public domain, the national park system was close behind. After the withdrawal and reservation of Yellowstone 1872, Congress had created a handful of other national parks, among them Mackinac Island in Michigan in 1875, Sequoia and Yosemite in 1890, Mount Rainier in 1899, and Crater Lake in 1902. It was not until 1916, however, that Congress created the National Park Service (NPS), with organic authority to administer this young National Park System. The quietly revolutionary statute directed NPS to "conserve the scenery and the natural and historic objects and the wild life [in national parks] and to provide for the enjoyment of the same in such manner and by such means as will leave them unimpaired for the enjoyment of future generations." 16 U.S.C. § 1. Udall characterizes scenic preservation as something other than conservation-for-use. Is scenic, ecological, or historical preservation a resource use?

Harold W. Wood, Jr., Pinchot and Mather: How the Forest Service and Park Service Got That Way

NOT MAN APART, December 1976.

Gifford Pinchot was the person most responsible for establishing the US Forest Service and dedicating it to utilitarian uses of natural resources. Stephen Mather was the person most responsible for organizing the National Park Service, dedicated to the preservation of natural features in the undisturbed state. The conflicts epitomized by these agencies have continued into the present day, so an understanding of the contrasting viewpoints of these two architects of policy may help us understand some of the land-use conflicts we still have to deal with. * * *

Pinchot's fundamental attitude toward the environment was utilitarian. He consistently favored resource development over mere preservation, as illustrated by two controversies of his day—issues we are still struggling with. One contest was over the Adirondack Forest Preserve in New York, where voters had passed an amendment to the state constitution that prohibited any timber from the area being sold, removed, or destroyed. Pinchot felt that the prohibition was tremendous waste and said forestry had nothing to do with decoration of public places, "that scenery is altogether outside its province." * * *

But by far the most famous episode in the utilitarian/aesthetic battle was the controversy over Hetch Hetchy Valley in Yosemite National Park. The preservationists, led by John Muir and the Sierra Club, believed that the park should not be violated. San Francisco, however, wanted to build a dam to provide a water supply for the city. Pinchot sided with the city and used his influence in Washington on its behalf.

Pinchot was adamant in his position: "I am fully persuaded that * * * the injury * * * by substituting a lake for the present swampy floor of the [Hetch Hetchy] valley. * * * is altogether unimportant compared with the benefits to be derived from its use as a reservoir." * * * Pinchot, like others, ignored the fact that alternative sites were available, if at a higher cost of construction.

John Muir's view on Hetch Hetchy was just as succinctly put: "Dam Hetch Hetchy! As well dam for water-tanks the people's cathedrals and churches, for no holier temple has ever been consecrated by the heart of man."

The Sierra Club and its allies lost Hetch Hetchy to the dam-builders in 1913. It is probable that the controversy, with all its publicity, helped generate public support in 1916 for the National Park Service Act, which would better protect National Parks from such encroachment.

Pinchot expanded his philosophy of forestry into a full-scale political ideology in 1905 when he became Chief Forester of the newly established US Forest Service, which had jurisdiction over the forest reserves. In his instructions from Agriculture Secretary James Wilson in 1905 (which Pinchot wrote himself), he was told: "All the resources of forest reserves are for use * * * where conflicting interests must be reconciled, the question will always be decided from the standpoint of the greatest good for the greatest number in the long run." With this last phrase, Pinchot thought he had found an unbeatable formula for success. * * *

His utilitarian attitude led him to believe that national parks, and not just national forests, should be open to such development as grazing and lumbering. As early as 1904 he recommended to Congress that the national parks be transferred to the Forest Service for administration. He opposed bills to create a separate National Park Service by saying it was "no more needed than two tails to a cat."

The Forest Service consistently opposed bills to create new parks and reliably suggested national forest status instead. When the bill to establish Glacier National Park appeared in Congress, Pinchot objected because the only commercial use to be allowed was removal of dead, down, or decaying timber by settlers. He prepared a rival measure to permit timber cutting, water power development, and railroad construction within the park.

Stephen Mather was every bit as energetic as Pinchot and just as dedicated to his own cause. * * *

Some of Mather's biggest struggles in protecting the parks came during World War I, at the beginning of his administration. Secretary Lane was a "hawk" on the President's cabinet and favored using all resources in the war effort. It is reported that after Mather had failed to keep cattle out of Yosemite legally, he had some of the cows caught and staked near trails, hoping to incite hikers into denouncing the business to their Representatives. (Mather always denied this; he said it was too good an idea to be his own.) * * *

While the National Park Service is usually considered preservationist, Mather was not a complete purist. He believed that the national parks should be opened up to development to provide visitors' accommodations. Much of his effort went into having roads constructed and improved, having inns and hotels built, and encouraging railroads to bring people to the parks.

He did all of this, however, within certain limits. For example, he refused to allow railroad lines within Yellowstone Park, although he had gone out of his way to encourage railroad lines to the Park.

While he believed in providing inns and hotels, he wouldn't allow such concessions unwarranted power. When the Great Northern Railroad set up a sawmill to construct a hotel in Glacier National Park, Mather watched the progress carefully. When the hotel was finished, he reminded the company that the sawmill and its sawdust must go. The company asked for a little more lumber, which Mather reluctantly let it have. The stay expired on August 10, 1925, and the railroad company again asked for more time, although the hotel was already taking in tourists. Mather was in the park on business at the time, so that afternoon he rounded up the Park Service trail crews and had the sawmill blown up. * * *

It might seem that Mather's attitude was ambivalent. The parks were dedicated to preservation, but also to the people's enjoyment. Translating this dualistic approach into workable policies is much more difficult than interpreting a simple utilitarianism such as Pinchot's. Nevertheless, Stephen Mather had criteria and sound reasoning with which to provide suitable development compatible with preservation. Considering the enormous pressure to commercialize the parks, Mather did an admirable job of keeping preservation foremost.

It cannot be said that Mather objected to sustained-yield forestry, and he did not think that national park standards and management practices should be applied to national forests. In contrast, Pinchot implacably felt that national parks should be managed just as the national forests were. * * *

It is ironic that Pinchot had such a comprehensive view of managing natural resources, even speaking of conserving human resources, and yet entirely neglected aesthetic values. Mather certainly did not attempt to enlarge his ideas on preservation into a political philosophy, as Pinchot did, but he still accepted the need for both preservation and utilitarian conservation—as long as the utilization wasn't in the national parks.

If it were not for Pinchot's recalcitrant opposition to the preservationists, the utilitarian and aesthetic schools of conservation probably would not have become so split. For many years, agency rivalry between the Forest Service and the National Park Service created ugly moods. The squabbling was often as much over jurisdiction as philosophy. But, partly in response to the Park Service's carving new parks and monuments out of national forests, the Forest Service began its own program of recreational development and safeguards for scenic resources. With the help of men such as Arthur Carhart, Robert Marshall, and Aldo Leopold of the Forest Service, a system of wilderness areas began developing in the 1930's. Without the competition, it is likely that this would not have been done for a long time.

The conventional division of early "reservationists" into the two competing schools of utilitarian conservation and aesthetic preservation is an oversimplification. Even John Muir, the avatar of transcendentalist preservationism, employed utilitarian arguments to support protecting Hetch Hetchy and other wild areas. See Stephen Fox, THE AMERICAN CONSERVATION MOVEMENT: JOHN MUIR AND HIS LEGACY (1981) (arguing, in part, that the more significant split in reservation advocates was between

professionals and amateurs); Bryan G. Norton, TOWARD UNITY AMONG ENVI-
RONMENTALISTS (1991) (arguing, in part, that philosophical differences
among advocates for conservation/preservation are only slightly manifest in
actual policy prescriptions).

Pinchot and Mather were men of affairs, personally wealthy, influential, and highly placed in the national government. Their names will long
live in public land annals. But John Muir's legacy eclipses their fame. Muir
never held an important position except, perhaps, President of the young
Sierra Club, which he helped found in 1892. He was a philosopher, a
traveler, a nature lover, and a writer. He lived in and for the mountains.
His contribution to public land and resources law was spiritual, a lasting
legacy of love for the land and its creatures. He was the archetypal
preservationist whose ironbound, indomitable will more than matched
those of the "timber barons" and other large-scale users of the land whom
he so despised.

Muir inspired a new ethic that has been absorbed into the American
consciousness, an ethic that is not less real for its lack of precise definition.
Its most important manifestation has been the formation of groups composed of private citizens who, like Muir, are willing to devote their time and
money to environmental causes. Muir's contribution to public land policy is
incapable of measurement. But the esteem that he has inspired in later
generations is reflected in the fact that more things in California, from
Muir Woods to the John Muir Trail (not to mention the USS John Muir),
are named after him than any other individual.

The national park system today, though now larded with some "park-
barrel" units of questionable distinction, comes as close to sacrosanct as
any federal program. The Gettysburg battlefield, along with other military
sites, were transferred to the park system in 1933 when they began to be
regarded as historical and archeological, rather than strategic defense,
resources. Since that time, the system has grown both through reservation
and acquisition. With the modernizing 1978 amendments, the 1916 organic
act remains the touchstone for park protection. National park management
is considered in detail in Chapters 11 and 12.

One other important enactment of the reservation era was the Weeks
Act of 1911, 36 Stat. 961, 16 U.S.C. § 513, which authorized the purchase
of timber lands in the East and added them to the national forest system.
Historian Roy Robbins said this "marked the extension of the conservation
movement from the Western regional focus to the nation at large." OUR
LANDED HERITAGE 370. Western Senators supported the Weeks Act, leading
Robbins to speculate they hoped the east would get sick of the forest
reserves and help them abolish the reserves across the country. It didn't
happen.

The roots of the Weeks Act were planted in 1900 when Congress
directed the Secretary of Agriculture to "investigate the forest conditions in
the Southern Appalachian Mountain region." The next year Secretary
James Wilson recommended the establishment of a forest reserve there, but
Congress did nothing. Eventually, support for the concept of forest reserves
spread to New England and then to the Ozarks, the Mississippi headwa-

ters, and Texas. Then, as Gifford Pinchot wrote in his autobiography, the "combined pressure finally overcame the [congressional] resistance [which was led by] that famous idealist, Joe Cannon, Speaker of the House, whose position was 'Not one cent for scenery.' " BREAKING NEW GROUND 240 (1947). With disastrous floods fresh in congressional minds, the Weeks Act of 1911, 36 Stat. 961, authorized the purchase of "forested, cut-over or denuded lands within the watershed on navigable streams" (the limitation to navigable streams reflecting a constitutional sensitivity about the reach of national power). In 1924, the Clarke–McNary Act added "the production of timber" as a purpose for forest acquisition. 43 Stat. 564.

By 1930, sufficient land had been acquired to establish ten national forests in the Appalachians. Then, in the New Deal, President Franklin Roosevelt, who often gave his profession as a "forester," pushed for a large expansion of the program, and more than two dozen national forests were established on his watch from Texas and Florida to Wisconsin and Missouri. The system grew more slowly after that (and one national forest in Florida was converted into an Air Force base during World War II). In its 1970 report, the Public Land Law Review Commission opined that a "major enlargement of national forests ... through acquisition of private land would not ... further any contemporary national purpose."

Today there are about fifty eastern national forests in twenty three states, but many of them are in a patchwork of fragmented ownership, with only about half the land inside the forest boundaries federally owned. Rather than expanding their boundaries, most current enlargements to the acquired national forests occur when the United States purchases or exchanges land for inholdings. Also complicating eastern national forest management is the widespread private ownership of subsurface mineral rights underneath federal land. The federal government purchased mineral rights with only about one-third of the 24 million acres. In the Allegheny National Forest in Pennsylvania, for example, the government owns about two-thirds of the land surface but less than 2 percent of the mineral rights. Eastern national forests comprise about 13 percent of the total national forest acreage, but only about 6 percent of the total forested land in the east. About 15 percent of the eastern national forests are grazed by livestock. Amendments to the 1897 organic act in 1960, 1974, and 1976 comprehensively rewrote the charter for the national forests, while retaining the utilitarian purpose. Acquired and reserved national forest lands are largely treated the same under these authorities. Chapters 5E and 8 treat the current law of national forest management.

2. MINERAL RESERVES

Forests and monumental scenery led the shift in federal policy from disposal to retention, but mineral resources also played an important role. The Mining Act of 1872 was as subject to abuse as the other disposal laws, but it survived because of inertia and the belief that the law was vital to national development. By the turn of the 20th century, however, it was becoming apparent that the Mining Law did not serve the nation's needs for fossil fuels and fertilizer minerals. Legislation for disposition of federal coal lands was first passed in 1864, and by 1873 had evolved into a system which provided for entry and patent in a fashion similar to agricultural entry, but at a higher price. This was in sharp contrast to the free mining policy for metals. The usual abuses led President Roosevelt in 1906 to withdraw from all forms of entry 66 million acres where "workable coal is known to occur," and to call for a leasing system. Much of the land withdrawn was later returned to the public domain, but the attention created helped pass several statutes in ensuing years that severed the rights to underlying coal from the surface estate, reserving the former for the United States. The 30–odd million acres patented under the Stock–Raising Homestead Act, for instance, are said to overlay more energy in the form of coal than Saudi Arabia has as oil. (These "split-estate" lands are considered in Chapter 7D.)

In the meantime, petroleum had gone from a curiosity to a highly valuable resource. Oil strikes all over the country caused fevers reminiscent of the Gold Rush. The legal status of petroleum on federal lands was somewhat unclear until Congress, in the Oil Placer Act of 1897, confirmed that petroleum locations were to be governed by the General Mining Law of 1872. This opened the door for the industry to enter and locate mining claims on the public lands without obtaining government approval, to explore for and obtain a vested property right to any petroleum deposits they discovered, to develop the resource without paying the United States any rental or royalty payments, and to acquire fee simple title to the land and all the minerals it might contain for a mere $2.50 per acre.

Fearing that all oil lands would soon pass into private ownership, forcing the Navy (which was converting from coal to oil) to buy back the oil that was being given away, President William Howard Taft in 1909 asked Congress to put petroleum under a leasing system so the United States would have more control over the development of this strategic resource on the public lands. Then, following in Theodore Roosevelt's footsteps, without advance warning, he went further and issued an order that "withdrew" from the Mining Law and other disposition acts 3 million acres of federal land in Wyoming and California thought to be valuable for oil. Uncertain of the constitutional basis for his action, Taft requested congressional validation, which Congress promptly supplied in the Pickett Act of 1910. The Pickett Act also stipulated that lands subsequently withdrawn would still be open to "metalliferous" mineral entry. While the Act granted the executive broad power to make "temporary" withdrawals for all "public purposes," it was prospective only, and expressly refused to say whether Taft's 1909 withdrawals were valid. In 1915, the Supreme Court upheld the validity of Taft's prior withdrawals in the landmark case of United States v. Midwest Oil, 236 U.S. 459 (1915), considered in detail *infra* p. 418. *Midwest Oil* endorsed broad executive authority to reserve public lands. The Court held that a longstanding pattern of congressional acquiescence to executive withdrawals amounted to an implied delegation of authority under the Property Clause.

It took five more years of struggle after *Midwest Oil*, but finally, in 1920, Congress enacted the minerals legislation that reformers like

Roosevelt and Taft wanted. The Mineral Leasing Act, 30 U.S.C. § 181 et seq., remains a cornerstone of natural resources law. It withdrew from location all fossil fuels (coal, oil, gas, and oil shale) and other specified, non-metallic minerals (potash, potassium, sodium, and sulfur). Thus ended the governmental policy of outright sale or grant of these particular mineral resources. It required competitive bidding for leases of lands thought to contain minerals, and authorized the issuance of exploration or prospecting permits for other lands, which could ripen into leases if valuable deposits were discovered. The leases require royalties, with the money going to states, the Reclamation Fund, and the federal treasury. The leasing system was later extended to the offshore lands and to geothermal resources.

The most important thing about the Mineral Leasing Act, however, was how it addressed the issue of public versus private control over the development of these fossil fuel and fertilizer minerals found on federal land. Section 13 of the Act authorized the Secretary of the Interior "under such necessary and proper rules and regulations as he may prescribe," to issue prospecting permits and leases under certain terms and conditions.

In United States ex rel. McLennan v. Wilbur, 283 U.S. 414 (1931), the Court relied on *Grimaud* to uphold secretarial rejections of applications for permits to explore for oil and gas. The Court, finding that the Act did not expressly preclude the Interior Secretary's decision to deny the permits on conservation grounds, upheld the exercise of "reasonable discretion" to "promote the public welfare." A refusal to lease is closely related to a decision to withdraw particular areas of federal lands from mineral leasing. The relationship between these two ways to say no to development of federal minerals is explored in more detail at *infra* p. 435.

Fundamental reform of the 1872 General Mining Law's system of disposal is a perennial public policy debate and Congress frequently attempts to enact bills overhauling the old act. But, despite great interest in sustaining domestic supplies of oil, gas, and coal, the leasing system of reserved minerals is widely supported. Legislative reforms to the mineral leasing law tinker at the margins, focusing on environmental protection and the pace of development.

3.   RANGE RESOURCES

The tragedy of the commons is nowhere more evident than in the history of grazing on the public domain. After the lands chiefly valuable for farming, timbering, mining, townsites, etc. had been claimed by successive waves of settlers and entrepreneurs, most of the public lands remaining were useful principally for grazing. By 1930, the federal government still owned 340 million acres of federal land in the arid and semi-arid West. About 140 million acres was reserved parks, refuges, and forests (some 90 percent of this in national forests, and much of it open to livestock grazing); about 12 million acres was reserved mineral lands, and the remaining 190 million acres were unreserved and unappropriated. Naturally, it was in the economic self-interest of ranchers to take for their own herds and flocks all of the free forage available. Late in the nineteenth century, the number of livestock on the public lands exploded, particularly in the arid lands of the southwest. Then a combination of drought and harsh winters decimated herds, but not before millions of acres of marginal, semi-arid lands were turned into wastelands by the resulting overgrazing. Disputes among homesteaders, ranchers, and sheepherders over these commons sometimes flared into violent range wars, and have ascended into the mists of legend in Western history, immortalized in such classic stories (and films) as Shane. As the following case shows, until 1934, state law— that is, almost no law—applied on the public domain because the federal government failed to regulate grazing.

Omaechevarria v. Idaho

Supreme Court of the United States, 1918.
246 U.S. 343.

■ Justice Brandeis delivered the opinion of the Court.

For more than forty years the raising of cattle and sheep have been important industries in Idaho. The stock feeds in part by grazing on the public domain of the United States. This is done with the Government's acquiescence, without the payment of compensation, and without federal regulation. Buford v. Houtz, 133 U.S. 320, 326 [1890]. Experience has demonstrated, says the state court, that in arid and semi-arid regions cattle will not graze, nor can they thrive, on ranges where sheep are allowed to graze extensively; that the encroachment of sheep upon ranges previously occupied by cattle results in driving out the cattle and destroying or greatly impairing the industry; and that this conflict of interests led to frequent and serious breaches of the peace and the loss of many lives. Efficient policing of the ranges is impossible; for the State is sparsely settled and the public domain is extensive, comprising still more than one-fourth of the land surface. To avert clashes between sheep herdsmen and the farmers who customarily allowed their few cattle to graze on the public domain near their dwellings, the territorial legislature passed in 1875 the so-called "Two Mile Limit Law." It was enacted first as a local statute applicable to three counties, but was extended in 1879 and again in 1883 to additional counties, and was made a general law in 1887. * * * To avert clashes between the sheep herdsmen and the cattle rangers, further legislation was found necessary; and in 1883 * * * [a state statute] was enacted which prohibits any person having charge of sheep from allowing them to graze on a range previously occupied by cattle. For violating this statute the plaintiff in error, a sheep herdsman, was convicted in the local police court and sentenced to pay a fine. The judgment was affirmed by * * * the Supreme Court of Idaho. On writ of error from this court the validity of the statute is assailed on the ground that the statute is inconsistent both with the Fourteenth Amendment and with the Act of Congress of February 25, 1885, c. 149, 23 Stat. 321, entitled, "An act to prevent unlawful occupancy of the public lands."

* * * The police power of the State extends over the federal public domain, at least when there is no legislation by Congress on the subject. We cannot say that the measure adopted by the State is unreasonable or

arbitrary. It was found that conflicts between cattle rangers and sheep herders on the public domain could be reconciled only by segregation. In national forests, where the use of land is regulated by the Federal Government, the plan of segregation is widely adopted. And it is not an arbitrary discrimination to give preference to cattle owners in prior occupancy without providing for a like preference to sheep owners in prior occupancy. For experience shows that sheep do not require protection against encroachment by cattle, and that cattle rangers are not likely to encroach upon ranges previously occupied by sheep herders. The propriety of treating sheep differently than cattle has been generally recognized. That the interest of the sheep owners of Idaho received due consideration is indicated by the fact that in 1902 they opposed the abolition by the Government of the free ranges. * * *

It is further contended that the statute is in direct conflict with the Act of Congress of February 25, 1885 [the Unlawful Inclosures Act, considered *infra* p. 369]. That statute which was designed to prevent the illegal fencing of public lands, contains at the close of § 1 the following clause with which the Idaho statute is said to conflict: "and the assertion of a right to the exclusive use and occupancy of any part of the public lands of the United States in any State or any of the Territories of the United States, without claim, color of title, or asserted right as above specified as to inclosure, is likewise declared unlawful, and hereby prohibited."

An examination of the federal act in its entirety makes it clear that what the clause quoted from § 1 sought to prohibit was merely the assertion of an exclusive right to use or occupation by force or intimidation or by what would be equivalent in effect to an enclosure. That this was the intent of Congress is confirmed by the history of the act. The reports of the Secretary of the Interior upon whose recommendation the act was introduced, the reports of the committees of Congress, and the debates thereon indicate that this alone was the evil sought to be remedied, and to such action only does its prohibition appear to have been applied in practice. * * *

The Idaho statute makes no attempt to grant a right to use public lands. * * * The State, acting in the exercise of its police power, merely excludes sheep from certain ranges under certain circumstances. Like the forcible entry and detainer act of Washington, which was held in Denee v. Ankeny [246 U.S. 208 (1918)] not to conflict with the homestead laws, the Idaho statute was enacted primarily to prevent breaches of the peace. The incidental protection which it thereby affords to cattle owners does not purport to secure to any of them, or to cattle owners collectively, "the exclusive use and occupancy of any part of the public lands." For every range from which sheep are excluded remains open not only to all cattle, but also to horses, of which there are many in Idaho. This exclusion of sheep owners under certain circumstances does not interfere with any rights of a citizen of the United States. Congress has not conferred upon citizens the right to graze stock upon the public lands. The Government has merely suffered the lands to be so used. Buford v. Houtz. It is because the citizen possesses no such right that it was held by this court that the

Secretary of Agriculture might, in the exercise of his general power to regulate forest reserves, exclude sheep and cattle therefrom. *Grimaud*; *Light*.

All the objections urged against the validity of the statute are unsound. The judgment of the Supreme Court of Idaho is

Affirmed.

■ JUSTICE VAN DEVANTER and JUSTICE MCREYNOLDS dissent.

NOTES AND QUESTIONS

1. Why does the state open range law not apply in *Light*, *supra* p. 129, yet does apply here? Omaecheverria's sheep were mixing with cows on "public domain" lands then under the supervision of the General Land Office (GLO), the predecessor of today's Bureau of Land Management. The GLO had no management policy; it was custodial. Would the result have been different if the GLO had formally adopted a policy of allowing cattle and sheep to mix on its lands, and licensed Omaechevarria to occupy federal rangeland with cows? Or if the land was reserved as a national forest, and the U.S. Forest Service permitted a sheepherder to put sheep within two miles of cows?

2. Is the effect of state law here to enclose the public lands and give certain kinds of livestock preference (specifically, cattle over sheep) for their use? If so, why doesn't this violate the Unlawful Inclosures Act?

3. Does the Idaho law give cattle ranchers a property right to graze on federal lands? Could the state do that if it wished?

4. What principle emerges from this case about when a state may enforce its own laws on federal lands? May a state enforce its criminal and civil laws, including taxing and regulatory statutes, on such lands only where Congress has specifically allowed it, or can it do so where Congress has not specifically forbidden it? Does it depend upon the character of the state laws?

5. Omaechevarria is a Basque name pronounced OH-mah EH-cheh ba-RRIH-ah, with the primary accent on the RRIH. Does his ethnic identity provide any clue about what cultural conflicts may have been behind the Idaho legislation to help cattle ranchers?

———————

By the early 1930s, overgrazing and drought had reduced the public grazing lands, never very productive, to a state of crisis. Neither free access nor enlarged homesteads contributed to betterment of range conditions. In 1930, President Hoover revived a plan originally broached a century earlier, and suggested that the United States convey all the remaining public domain to the states to be used to support public education. But the proposal never gained traction in Congress.

Public lands ranchers, and one of their longstanding champions in Congress, Edward Taylor of Colorado, eventually came around to the view that something had to be done because of conflicts among livestock owners and deteriorating rangelands. Shortly after FDR's inauguration in March 1933, new Secretary of the Interior Harold Ickes wrote to ask for FDR's support for pending legislation giving the Secretary "broad powers to limit and regulate the use of the public domain for grazing purposes with the view to preventing partial or total destruction of a natural resource which is essential for our future well being." FDR wrote in longhand at the bottom, "Yes, but there will be a howl," and sent it back to Ickes. The reaction Roosevelt predicted was not strong enough to kill the idea; the next year, he signed the Taylor Grazing Act into law. 43 U.S.C. § 315 et seq.

E.L. Peffer, The Closing of the Public Domain

Pp. 214–224 (1951).

The Taylor Grazing Act passed the House of Representatives on April 11, 1934 and the Senate on June 12. Between these dates occurred what was later considered the most devastating of conceivable condemnations of past land policy. The dust storms of May 11 carried sands from Western deserts to the sidewalks of New York and sifted them down around the dome of the Capitol in Washington. They provided what Senator Gore of Oklahoma later called "the most tragic, the most impressive lobbyist, that have ever come to this Capital." * * *

PROVISIONS OF THE TAYLOR GRAZING ACT

The Taylor Grazing Act vests in the Secretary of the Interior authority to create grazing districts in areas "which in his opinion are chiefly valuable for grazing and raising forage crops," but not until local reactions, gained through public hearings, had been ascertained. The Secretary is empowered to make all necessary regulations to carry out the purposes of the act and to grant grazing permits for periods up to ten years, with preference to settlers and landowners within or near the respective districts. He is instructed to enter into co-operative agreements with other departments of the government, with state land officials, and users of the districts. He may accept gifts of land or make exchanges of public land outside of grazing districts for private or state-owned lands within their limits. * * * Section 15 of the bill provides that isolated or disconnected tracts or parcels of 640 acres or more of grazing land, not capable of being included within grazing districts, may be leased to owners of contiguous property. (These have come to be known as Section 15 lands.) * * *

The amendment to the Taylor Grazing Act passed Congress on June 20, 1936, and was approved by the President on June 26. It increased the area to which the law applies to 142,000,000 acres and created the post of Director of Grazing, which appointment was to be made by the Secretary of the Interior and approved by the Senate. * * * Western interests were considered in the further stipulation that "No Director of Grazing, Assistant Director, or grazier shall be appointed who at the time of appointment or selection has not been for one year a bona-fide citizen or resident of the State or of one of the States in which such Director, Assistant Director, or grazier is to serve." * * *

SUBSEQUENT WITHDRAWALS

At long last the government was able to care for its grazing lands. The Taylor Grazing Act did not itself do, however, what has been claimed for it—"close the public domain to further entry by homesteaders and [bury] a policy which had been slowly dying." That was accomplished, in effect, but with no express intention of permanence, by two executive orders of the President, those of November 26, 1934 and February 5, 1935. In November, acting under the authority of the Taylor Grazing Act, he withdrew for classification all public land in the twelve Western states. Then, in February, he withdrew all remaining parcels in all other states for use in connection with Federal Emergency Relief Administration.

The President by these withdrawals implemented the classification feature of the Taylor Grazing Act and made certain that it would apply to all remaining Western public lands. Thus it was that the classification which for more than fifty years had been urgently recommended by the land specialists of the country was finally authorized. It was not done until the results of nature's own classification had become disastrously apparent.

If the Taylor Grazing Act and supporting measures did not completely close the public domain, they at least were a signpost pointing to a radical change in direction of public land policy. They represented official admission of the exhaustion of the values which had made the public domain a dynamic force in the building of the country. There was still land in plenty, but such opportunity as it might have represented had literally "gone with the wind." Overgrazed, wind-eroded expanses, interspersed with rocky peaks and barren slopes, were all that remained of the public domain in 1934. The days of its greatness * * * had long since passed. The open public domain of the future was to be more a sentimental and political issue than an active factor in American life.

The Taylor Act put livestock grazing on the "public domain" under government regulation and control for the first time, through a permit system where fees could be charged. Recall that this shift from custody to management happened on national forests three decades earlier. The Taylor Act also authorized adjustments like land exchanges, and a classification scheme for continued disposition of land. In short, just as the forest reservation provision in the 1891 legislation had flowered into the national forest system, the Taylor Act brought into being a new federal land system. The lands under its aegis were usually simply called the "public lands" or, since the Bureau of Land Management was created in 1946 to manage them, the "BLM lands." The BLM did not receive comprehensive organic legislation for its system of lands until Congress enacted FLPMA in 1976.

However, FLPMA continued to authorize grazing permits and fees. Chapter 9 considers the current legal issues surrounding grazing on public lands.

The Taylor Grazing Act did not bring immediate improvement to range conditions; indeed, perhaps half of BLM's rangeland acreage and riparian-wetlands areas today remain, by BLM's own estimates, impaired. The grazing lands before 1934 had not been "managed" in the modern sense, and the changeover to a new system embodying a new philosophy was not without difficulty. The following reminiscences made in 1974 by Ferry Carpenter, a Harvard-trained lawyer who was the first director of the Grazing Service, illustrate some of the practical difficulties of implementation.

> [In Grand Junction I conducted] the first meeting ever held under the recently passed Taylor Grazing Act to see whether they could put the show on the road or not. I got my appointment on September 7 and on the 12th I was here, with no instructions what to do, and this is what I found: Grand Junction was packed with stockmen. The cattle boys had the LaCourt Hotel and the woolgrowers had the LaHarpe Hotel, and neither would speak to the other. There were so many of them and the next morning when we looked around for a hall, we couldn't begin to get them in any hall. We adjourned and went out on the city park here and took over the exhibition building. The cowboys sat on one side * * * and the sheepherders on the other * * * and we got ready for business like a peace talk between two nations that had been fighting—and they had been fighting and I knew they had been fighting. What were they there to talk about? Why did Congress wake up and say they should have to drag grass into the conservation program? They put water in under the Reclamation Act; put trees under the Forest Act; put minerals and oils under the Mineral Reserve Act. But not the grass. Everybody could get the grass if you knew how to get it. All of a sudden they passed the Taylor Grazing Act. The boys out here didn't know the Act existed but they were there to see that they got their share of the grass. There were two factions and they were ready to continue the war they had been having for fifty years to fight over it. That's the woolgrowers and the cowboys.
>
> I didn't get any help from Washington on what to do. There wasn't anybody in the whole Department that knew which end of the cow got up first. I went to the Land Office. I said "You want me to straighten out this land—give me a map of it." "Oh! We haven't got any map. There is filing on it day and night all over 27 local land offices, but we haven't got any map." "Well, how in the hell can I find the land if I haven't got a map!" "That's for you." That was for me. So, when I came here, I said I'm supposed to set up grazing districts. I don't know whether you want them or not and I wouldn't know where they go and Washington doesn't know where they would go and nobody knows where they would go. But you fellows have been fighting over this thing, you know every blessed acre there is and the poorer the acre, the harder you fight for it. I found that out, too. But I had one little piece of advice that I followed—and I am going to follow it until the end of

my days—and it was a little saying by Justice Cardozo on the Supreme Court. "When the task is to clean house, it is sensible and usual to first consult with the inhabitants." There I was and there were the inhabitants—cowboys ready to jump and sheepherders ready to jump—everybody at each other's throat. But they were the inhabitants.

Well, they read a message from President Roosevelt. He said it was a great day for the West. Read a message from Secretary Ickes; he said he was the Lord's anointed! And now we got down to business and they began asking me questions about the Act, like how near was near. I didn't know how near was near. I didn't know the answer to them but I did know what to do with them. So, I said, all right; you woolgrowers go out there and caucus and pick five men to speak for you. You cowboys do the same.

Quoted in Charles Conklin, *PLLRC Revisited—A Potpourri of Memories*, 54 Denv. U. L.Rev. 445, 446–47 (1977).

In theory, the Taylor Act was an interim measure: the range management it authorized was to control "pending final disposition." In fact, the creation of grazing districts and Franklin Roosevelt's withdrawal orders marked the "closing of the public domain," even though a few small tracts were claimed as homesteads thereafter. By the time Congress enacted FLPMA in 1976, officially declaring the federal policy of retention, the age of wholesale disposition was over; the age of retention and management was middle-aged; and the age of conservation and recreation was well underway. Preserving that old enemy of the settler, wilderness, had become a prominent goal of national policy.

The chapters that follow build on the history of private interests in public resources to illustrate the various ways that developments after the 1930s transformed the field. From the Taylor Act forward, no public land law could fail to grapple with the overarching theme of finding the public interest in resource management. The history of the era of intensive management for the public interest is still being written, and the current disputes are the focus of the rest of this casebook.

CHAPTER 3

FEDERALISM ON THE PUBLIC LANDS

Many contemporary as well as historical natural resource disputes involve the allocation of jurisdictional power. Many of these struggles play out between federal and state governments. Tensions among governmental divisions are inherent in our federal system, and are bound to continue. While the federal government's ownership of federal lands and resources is seldom questioned, the issue of which sovereign's law controls their management is raised every day. The answer is usually context-specific, requiring case-by-case analysis.

The starting point for considering the federal law of public land and resource management is, of course, the constitutional power of Congress. The commerce, treaty, and spending clauses of the U.S. Constitution have all had some relevance to the public lands. For the most part, federal-state conflicts over federal lands are governed by three constitutional principles stemming from the Enclave Clause (Article I, § 8, cl. 17), the Supremacy Clause (Article VI, cl. 2), and the Property Clause, (Article IV, § 3, cl. 2).

In general, state law applies on federal land except under three circumstances. First, in areas where states have formally ceded some or all jurisdiction, commonly deemed enclaves, state law applies only to the extent reserved by the state or provided by federal law. Second, intergovernmental immunities bar some types of state regulation, especially taxation of federal property, on all public lands. Third, and most importantly, state law does not apply where Congress has preempted it through valid legislation. Though the federal statutes we study in this class rely heavily on the Property Clause authority of the Constitution, Congress can preempt state laws under any of its constitutionally enumerated powers.

Congress has responded to concerns of states in waiving aspects of federal immunity, sharing revenue from public lands, and incorporating state concerns into land management decisions. This chapter covers the constitutional, statutory, and regulatory settings under which the federal-state tension plays out.

A. JURISDICTION WITHIN FEDERAL ENCLAVES

Article I, § 8, cl. 17 of the U.S. Constitution provides (emphasis added):

> Congress shall have power to exercise *exclusive Legislation* in all Cases whatsoever over such District (not exceeding ten Miles square) as may, by Cession of particular States, and the Acceptance of Congress, become the Seat of the Government of the United States, and *to*

exercise like Authority over all Places *purchased* by the *Consent* of the Legislature of the State in which the Same shall be, for the Erection of Forts, Magazines, Arsenals, dock-Yards, and *other needful Buildings.*

This Clause's reference to "exclusive legislation" has always been interpreted as meaning "exclusive jurisdiction." The lands to which this clause applies are commonly called "federal enclaves," and the clause has come to be known as the Enclave Clause. As described more fully in the notes following the next case, enclaves can be found sprinkled among practically all categories of federal land including some but not all military bases, post offices, and national parks. However, only about 6 percent of the federal lands fall wholly or partially in this category. There is, unfortunately, no systematic, unified, up-to-date catalogue of such lands readily available.

Fort Leavenworth R. Co. v. Lowe

Supreme Court of the United States, 1885.
114 U.S. 525.

■ JUSTICE FIELD delivered the opinion of the court.

[Plaintiff railroad has, since 1880, owned a railroad within the federal Fort Leavenworth Military Reservation. The state levied a property tax on the railroad, which the railroad paid under protest. The railroad then brought suit, arguing that the property, being entirely within the Reservation, was exempt from state taxation.]

The land constituting the Reservation was part of the territory acquired in 1803 by cession from France, and, until the formation of the State of Kansas, and her admission into the Union, the United States possessed the rights of a proprietor, and had political dominion and sovereignty over it. For many years before that admission it had been reserved from sale by the proper authorities of the United States for military purposes, and occupied by them as a military post. The jurisdiction of the United States over it during this time was necessarily paramount. But in 1861 Kansas was admitted into the Union upon an equal footing with the original States, that is, with the same rights of political dominion and sovereignty, subject like them only to the Constitution of the United States. Congress might undoubtedly, upon such admission, have stipulated for retention of the political authority, dominion and legislative power of the United States over the Reservation, so long as it should be used for military purposes by the government; that is, it could have excepted the place from the jurisdiction of Kansas, as one needed for the uses of the general government. But from some cause, inadvertence perhaps, or overconfidence that a recession of such jurisdiction could be had whenever desired, no such stipulation or exception was made. The United States, therefore, retained, after the admission of the State, only the rights of an ordinary proprietor; except as an instrument for the execution of the powers of the general government, that part of the tract, which was actually used for a fort or military post, was beyond such control of the State, by taxation or otherwise, as would defeat its use for those purposes.

So far as the land constituting the Reservation was not used for military purposes, the possession of the United States was only that of an individual proprietor. The State could have exercised, with reference to it, the same authority and jurisdiction which she could have exercised over similar property held by private parties. This defect in the jurisdiction of the United States was called to the attention of the government in 1872. * * * The Attorney General replied * * * that to restore the federal jurisdiction over the land included in the Reservation, it would be necessary to obtain from the State of Kansas a cession of jurisdiction, which he had no doubt would upon application be readily granted by the State Legislature. It does not appear from the record before us that such application was ever made; but, on the 22d of February, 1875, the Legislature of the State passed an act entitled "An Act to cede jurisdiction to the United States over the territory of the Fort Leavenworth Military Reservation," the first section of which is as follows:

"That exclusive jurisdiction be, and the same is hereby ceded to the United States over and within all the territory owned by the United States, and included within the limits of the United States military reservation known as the Fort Leavenworth Reservation in said State, as declared from time to time by the President of the United States, saving, however, to the said State the right to serve civil or criminal process within said Reservation, in suits or prosecutions for or on account of rights acquired, obligations incurred, or crimes committed in said State, but outside of said cession and Reservation; and saving further to said State the right to tax railroad, bridge, and other corporations, their franchises and property, on said Reservation." Laws of Kansas, 1875, p. 95.

The question as to the right of the plaintiff to recover back the taxes paid depends upon the validity and effect of the last saving clause in this act. As we have said, there is no evidence before us that any application was made by the United States for this legislation, but, as it conferred a benefit, the acceptance of the act is to be presumed in the absence of any dissent on their part. The contention of the plaintiff is that the act of cession operated under the Constitution to vest in the United States exclusive jurisdiction over the Reservation, and that the last saving clause, being inconsistent with that result, is to be rejected. [The opinion then quoted Art. 1, § 8, cl. 17.]

The necessity of complete jurisdiction over the place which should be selected as the seat of government was obvious to the framers of the Constitution. * * *

Upon the second part of the clause in question, giving power to "exercise like authority," that is, of exclusive legislation "over all places purchased by the consent of the Legislature of the State in which the same shall be, for the erection of forts, magazines, arsenals, dock-yards, and other needful buildings," the Federalist [No. 43] observes that the necessity of this authority is not less evident. "The public money expended on such places," it adds, "and the public property deposited in them, require that they should be exempt from the authority of the particular State. Nor would it be proper for the places on which the security of the entire Union may depend to be in any degree dependent on a particular member of it. All objections and scruples are here also obviated by requiring the concurrence of the States concerned in every such establishment." "The power," says Mr. Justice Story, repeating the substance of Mr. Madison's language, "is wholly unexceptionable, since it can only be exercised at the will of the State, and therefore it is placed beyond all reasonable scruple." [quoting Story's Constitutional Commentaries, vol. 2, § 1219] This power of exclusive legislation is to be exercised, as thus seen, over places purchased, by consent of the Legislatures of the States in which they are situated, for the specific purposes enumerated. It would seem to have been the opinion of the framers of the Constitution that, without the consent of the States, the new government would not be able to acquire lands within them. * * *

But not only by direct purchase have the United States been able to acquire lands they needed without the consent of the States, but it has been held [in Kohl v. United States, 91 U.S. 367 (1875)] that they possess the right of eminent domain within the States, using those terms, not as expressing the ultimate dominion or title to property, but as indicating the right to take private property for public uses when needed to execute the powers conferred by the Constitution; and that the general government is not dependent upon the caprice of individuals or the will of State Legislatures in the acquisition of such lands as may be required for the full and effective exercise of its powers. * * *

Besides these modes of acquisition, the United States possessed, on the adoption of the Constitution, an immense domain lying north and west of the Ohio River, acquired as the result of the Revolutionary War from Great Britain, or by cessions from Virginia, Massachusetts and Connecticut; and, since the adoption of the Constitution, they have by cession from foreign countries, come into the ownership of a territory still larger, lying between the Mississippi River and the Pacific Ocean, and out of these territories several States have been formed and admitted into the Union. The proprietorship of the United States in large tracts of land within these States has remained after their admission. There has been, therefore, no necessity for them to purchase or to condemn lands within those States, for forts, arsenals, and other public buildings, unless they had disposed of what they afterwards needed. Having the title, they have usually reserved certain portions of their lands from sale or other disposition, for the uses of the government.

This brief statement as to the different modes in which the United States have acquired title to lands upon which public buildings have been erected will serve to explain the nature of their jurisdiction over such places * * *. When the title is acquired by purchase by consent of the Legislatures of the States, the federal jurisdiction is exclusive of all State authority. This follows from the declaration of the Constitution that Congress shall have "like authority" over such places as it has over the district which is the seat of government; that is, the power of "exclusive legislation in all cases whatsoever." Broader or clearer language could not be used to exclude all other authority than that of Congress; and that no other authority can be exercised over them has been the uniform opinion of Federal and State tribunals, and of the Attorneys General. The reservation which has usually accompanied the consent of the States that civil and criminal process of the State courts may be served in the places purchased, is not considered as interfering in any respect with the supremacy of the United States over them; but is admitted to prevent them from becoming an asylum for fugitives from justice. * * *

* * * These authorities are sufficient to support the proposition which follows naturally from the language of the Constitution, that no other legislative power than that of Congress can be exercised over lands within a State purchased by the United States with her consent for one of the purposes designated; and that such consent under the Constitution operates to exclude all other legislative authority.

* * *

Where, therefore, lands are acquired in any other way by the United States within the limits of a State than by purchase with her consent, they will hold the lands subject to this qualification: that if upon them forts, arsenals, or other public buildings are erected for the uses of the general government, such buildings, with their appurtenances, as instrumentalities for the execution of its powers, will be free from any such interference and jurisdiction of the State as would destroy or impair their effective use for the purposes designed. Such is the law with reference to all instrumentalities created by the general government. Their exemption from State control is essential to the independence and sovereign authority of the United States within the sphere of their delegated powers. But, when not used as such instrumentalities, the legislative power of the State over the places acquired will be as full and complete as over any other places within her limits.

As already stated, the land constituting the Fort Leavenworth Military Reservation was not purchased, but was owned by the United States by cession from France many years before Kansas became a State; and whatever political sovereignty and dominion the United States had over the place comes from the cession of the State since her admission into the Union. It not being a case where exclusive legislative authority is vested by the Constitution of the United States, that cession could be accompanied with such conditions as the State might see fit to annex not inconsistent with the free and effective use of the fort as a military post. * * *

The Military Reservation of Fort Leavenworth was not, as already said, acquired by purchase with the consent of Kansas. And her cession of jurisdiction is not of exclusive legislative authority over the land, except so far as that may be necessary for its use as a military post; and it is not contended that the saving clause in the act of cession interferes with such use. There is, therefore, no constitutional prohibition against the enforcement of that clause. The right of the State to subject the railroad property to taxation exists as before the cession. The invalidity of the tax levied not being asserted on any other ground than the supposed exclusive jurisdiction of the United States over the reservation notwithstanding the saving clause, the judgment of the court below must be

Affirmed.

NOTES AND QUESTIONS

1. Was the Fort Leavenworth land "purchased?" If so, was it purchased with the "consent" of the state, under the terms of the Enclave Clause? Did Kansas cede "exclusive" jurisdiction over Fort Leavenworth to the United States?

2. To the extent any of the answers in the first paragraph is no, is Kansas's cession governed by the Enclave Clause, or something else? What else? Put another way, if the Enclave Clause were the sole basis for the adjustment of jurisdiction on public lands, would the State's cession of jurisdiction have been void?

3. By its terms, the Enclave Clause is very limited. *Fort Leavenworth's* flexible interpretation has been the norm and it has prevented abrupt walls and gaps in jurisdiction from forming at federal land boundaries. The Court has upheld a wide variety of jurisdictional arrangements not within the literal terms of the Clause. What do you suppose was the intent behind the Enclave Clause? Did the Court construe the clause strictly in accordance with its intent? If the Clause were strictly or literally construed, would it prevent the United States from condemning state or private land in a state for use for federal purposes (e.g., a military base) without state consent? In fact, it has long been held that Congress possesses an inherent power of eminent domain, acknowledged in the fifth amendment, as an attribute of its sovereignty, and it has long been assumed that this power can be exercised in a state without its consent. *See, e.g.*, United States v. Gettysburg Elec. R. Co., 160 U.S. 668 (1896), *supra* p. 120.

4. In Collins v. Yosemite Park & Curry Co., 304 U.S. 518 (1938), the Court reviewed the complex series of statutes creating Yosemite National Park. The Park comprised both federal public domain land and acquired land (the United States had conveyed Yosemite Valley and the Mariposa Big Tree Grove of giant sequoias to California in 1864 and reacquired it in 1906). California had ceded jurisdiction to the U.S. in 1919, but had reserved the right to tax specified transactions. Noting that the Enclave Clause "has never been strictly construed," the Court upheld the arrangement and made it clear that the states and the federal government were free to adjust jurisdiction wholly outside of the strictures of the Enclave Clause:

> The United States has large bodies of public lands. These properties are used for forests, parks, ranges, wild life sanctuaries, flood control, and other purposes which are not covered by [the enclave clause]. In Silas Mason Co. v. Tax Commission of Washington, 302 U.S. 186 [1937] we upheld in accordance with the arrangements of the State and National Governments the right of the United States to acquire private property for use in "the reclamation of arid and semiarid lands" and to hold its purchases subject to state jurisdiction. In other instances, it may be deemed important or desirable by the National Government and the State Government in which the particular proper-

ty is located that exclusive jurisdiction be vested in the United States by cession or consent. No question is raised as to the authority to acquire land or provide for national parks. As the National Government may, "by virtue of its sovereignty" acquire lands within the borders of states by eminent domain and without their consent, the respective sovereignties should be in a position to adjust their jurisdictions. There is no constitutional objection to such an adjustment of rights.

304 U.S at 529–30.

5.   If it is not found in the Enclave Clause, what is the authority for the United States to enter into these consensual arrangements with states which allocate jurisdiction over federal lands? The Property Clause (considered further below)? The inherent power of the U.S. as a sovereign? Is the Court in these cases essentially saying that consensual jurisdictional arrangements over federal land which are reached through the political processes of the state and federal governments will be enforced by the courts without serious scrutiny, because the political processes of both governments provide a sensible check on their content? Is there anything objectionable about that?

6.   Why would a state ever want to voluntarily relinquish a piece of its sovereignty, by ceding to the U.S. partial or exclusive jurisdiction over an area of land within its borders?

7.   In fact, states have often attached conditions or retained some jurisdictional powers in ceding jurisdiction over particular tracts of federal land to the federal government. The result is that jurisdictional arrangements on enclaves may be quite complex. The obscurity as well as complexity of these cessions of jurisdiction can lay traps for the unwary. For example, in United States v. 319.88 Acres of Land, 498 F. Supp. 763 (D. Nev. 1980), the United States condemned a private inholding in the Nevada portion of the Lake Mead National Recreation Area, part of the National Park System and managed by the National Park Service. At issue was the fair market value of the land. The property owner claimed the value was $880,000, calculated on the assumption its highest use was for a gambling casino. The U.S. discovered just before trial that Nevada had in 1974 ceded to the U.S. jurisdiction over all land within the boundaries of the Lake Mead National Recreation Area, including this private inholding. The state cession had reserved only the right to serve process on the land. Therefore, relying on a Park Service regulation prohibiting gambling "on privately owned lands within park areas under the legislative jurisdiction of the United States," the U.S. argued the value was only $240,000, because the highest non-gambling use of the property was for recreational home sites. The U.S. prevailed.

8.   Must a cession of jurisdiction be express? In United States v. Brown, 552 F.2d 817, 819 (8th Cir. 1977), the court of appeals held that the state of Minnesota had effectively ceded jurisdiction over the waters of Voyageurs National Park (VNP). The cession was not express. The state had participated in and supported the creation of the VNP. A few months before federal legislation creating the park was signed into law in late 1971,

the state had enacted legislation donating to the United States 25,000 acres of state-owned land within the boundaries of the 219,000 acre VNP. While the state did not transfer its claim of ownership (based on the assumption that the waters were navigable at statehood) of the beds of 80,000 acres of lakes within the park to the federal government, the court of appeals held in *Brown* that the state had effectively ceded jurisdiction over the waters. United States v. Armstrong, 186 F.3d 1055, 1060 (8th Cir. 1999) reaffirmed this holding "without reservation" even though the state had enacted another statute in 1995 providing that "[o]wnership of and jurisdiction over these waters and their beds has not been ceded by the state, either expressly or implicitly, to the United States." The court said this was ineffective based on prior Supreme Court decisions holding that once a state cedes jurisdiction under the Enclave Clause, it cannot unilaterally reassert it.

NOTE: ASSIMILATION OF STATE LAW IN FEDERAL ENCLAVES

Even where states have ceded jurisdiction over federal land and the U.S. has accepted the cession, the Congress can give some jurisdiction back to the states, by specific or generic legislation. In fact, several federal statutes address matters of state and federal jurisdiction within enclaves. The Buck Act, enacted in 1947, 4 U.S.C. §§ 104–110, allows states to collect uniform income, gasoline, sales, and use taxes within enclaves, although direct taxation of the United States and federal instrumentalities (such as officers' clubs, United States v. State Tax Comm'n, 412 U.S. 363 (1973)), is barred. Other statutes allow state unemployment and workers' compensation laws to apply to persons who live and work on federal lands, including federal enclaves. 26 U.S.C. § 3305(d); 40 U.S.C. § 290. State property taxes do not reach federal property, but federal Impact Aid payments are made to local school districts serving children of federal employees living on federal property, whether or not they are within federal enclaves. 20 U.S.C. §§ 236–244, 631–647. In the area of civil liberties, the Supreme Court, in Evans v. Cornman, 398 U.S. 419 (1970), held that the Fourteenth Amendment requires states to allow residents of federal enclaves to vote in state elections.

In 1825 Congress passed the first Assimilative Crimes Act to provide a body of criminal laws for federal enclaves. The Act, now codified at 18 U.S.C. § 13, "assimilates" criminal laws of the host state when no federal law applies, and provides for prosecution in federal court under the "borrowed" state substantive law:

> Whoever within or upon any of the places now existing or hereafter reserved or acquired as provided in section 7 of this title, is guilty of any act or omission which, although not made punishable by any enactment of Congress, would be punishable if committed or omitted within the jurisdiction of the State, Territory, Possession, or District in which such place is situated, by the laws thereof in force at the time of such act or omission, shall be guilty of a like offense and subject to a like punishment.

18 U.S.C. § 7, referred to in the Assimilative Crimes Act, defines lands covered by the Act as follows:

> Any lands reserved or acquired for the use of the United States, and under the exclusive or concurrent jurisdiction thereof, or any place purchased or otherwise acquired by the United States by consent of the legislature of the State in which the same shall be, for the erection of a fort, magazine, arsenal, dockyard, or other needful building.

The Assimilative Crimes Act has survived challenges that it is beyond Congress's power to incorporate state laws enacted after the Act's effective date. In United States v. Sharpnack, 355 U.S. 286 (1958), for example, the prosecution was based upon sex crimes as defined in a 1950 Texas statute, but the most recent reenactment of the Assimilative Crimes Act had been in 1948. The Court rejected the challenge, upholding dynamic, ongoing incorporation of state laws.

There is no comprehensive, ongoing incorporation of state *civil* as opposed to criminal laws in federal enclaves. This can lead to anomalous results. In Arlington Hotel Co. v. Fant, 278 U.S. 439 (1929), plaintiff hotel guests sued to recover the value of their property lost when the hotel in Hot Springs National Park burned down. In 1832, Congress had reserved four sections of federal land, including where the hotel was located, for medicinal purposes. In 1903 Arkansas ceded, and the United States in 1904 accepted, "sole and exclusive jurisdiction" over the resort. At that time Arkansas common law made the innkeeper an insurer of guests' property, but in 1913 the Arkansas law was changed to make the innkeeper liable only for negligence. There concededly being no contrary federal law, plaintiffs claimed, and the Arkansas courts held, that the cession effectively "froze" the law applicable to Hot Springs as of 1904, making the innkeeper strictly liable without proof of negligence, even though the hotel fire occurred in 1920. The Supreme Court, without discussion, agreed. The rationale is a principle borrowed from international law; namely, that "whenever political jurisdiction and legislative power over any territory are transferred from one nation or sovereign to another," those laws "intended for the protection of private rights" of the country losing jurisdiction "continue in force until abrogated or changed by the new government or sovereign." Chicago, Rock Island & Pac. R.R. Co. v. McGlinn, 114 U.S. 542, 546 (1885). Interestingly, the *Arlington Hotel* litigation originated in state court, even though the state had ceded "sole and exclusive jurisdiction" over the area to the federal government. Although the Supreme Court did not directly address the matter in that case, it seems that state courts may, if they choose to do so, exercise jurisdiction over causes of action arising under federal law in enclaves, even when the state does not expressly reserve such authority.

In 1928, Congress had provided a measure of assimilation of civil law by incorporating on an ongoing basis state wrongful death and personal injury laws. 16 U.S.C. § 457. But under *Arlington Hotel*, other state civil laws in effect at the time the state cedes and the U.S. accepts jurisdiction are effectively frozen until altered by Congress. In a few instances, federal land management agencies have assimilated state civil laws selectively by administrative action. A notable example is the Park Service's incorporation of state fishing laws that do not conflict with federal laws or regulations. 36 C.F.R. § 2.3(a). Violators of the incorporated state laws are prosecuted before federal magistrates.

NOTES AND QUESTIONS

1. Does borrowing this principle from international law make sense in this context, where the "new" sovereign, the United States, does not normally pass laws implementing the full range of police powers? Assuming no federal law exists on the subject today, what law applies to an innkeeper's liability for property loss that occurs in 2007 in Hot Springs National Park?

2. Should Congress pass a comprehensive "Assimilative Civil Law Act" to eliminate the problem raised by Arlington Hotel v. Fant? Congress took a preliminary step in 1976 by granting the Interior Department authority to cede back to states all or part of federal jurisdiction within units of the National Park System, 16 U.S.C. § 1a–3, but it appears the authority has been employed sparingly.

B. Intergovernmental Immunities & Revenue Sharing

The Court generally described the effect of the doctrine of intergovernmental immunities in *Fort Leavenworth*: federal property must be "free . . . from such interference . . . as would destroy or impair their effective use." The doctrine, derived from the Supremacy Clause (Article VI, cl. 2) is also the basis for the immunity of federal property from state tax laws.

As new states were created, other questions arose. The first was one of title: did the state obtain title to all or part of federal lands found within their borders at statehood? Pollard v. Hagan, 44 U.S. (3 How.) 212 (1845), *supra* p. 70, held that the states did, under the equal footing doctrine, come into title of lands underlying navigable waters. But the United States retained title to large amounts of other land, not under navigable waters, in new states. Except for the relatively few situations in which a state formally ceded some or all jurisdiction over these lands to the U.S., the question remained: Did the federal government have only the proprietary powers of an ordinary private owner of these lands, or could it assert the far more expansive power of a sovereign? Some early cases contained suggestions that federal power was limited to that of a proprietor. But after the disastrous and wholly anomalous view of the property clause embraced by the Supreme Court in the *Dred Scott* decision, the Court began again to speak broadly of congressional power under the Property Clause. In Gibson v. Chouteau, 80 U.S. (13 Wall.) 92, 99 (1872), for example, the Court upheld the claim of the holder of a federal patent to land in the State of Missouri against a competing claim by another who was relying on state law. The Court repeated that Congress's power under the Property Clause "is subject to no limitations;" that Congress has an "absolute right" to decide upon the disposition of federal land; and that "[n]o State legislation can interfere with this right or embarrass its exercise." *Gibson* was followed by decisions in which the Supreme Court moved toward an explicit recognition of federal sovereign as well as proprietary power over federal lands.

In 1917 a unanimous Supreme Court, speaking through a Justice from Wyoming, Willis Van Devanter, seemed to definitively resolve the matter. Utah Power & Light Co. v. United States, 243 U.S. 389 (1917). The utility had built electric generation works on national forests in Utah without federal permission, and argued Utah law should apply, because there had been no cession of jurisdiction by the state under the Enclave Clause. The Court replied:

> To this we cannot assent. Not only does the Constitution (Art. IV, § 3, cl. 2) commit to Congress the power "to dispose of and make all needful rules and regulations respecting" the lands of the United States, but the settled course of legislation, congressional and state, and repeated decisions of this court have gone upon the theory that the power of Congress is exclusive and that only through its exercise in some form can rights in lands belonging to the United States be acquired. True, for many purposes a State has civil and criminal jurisdiction over lands within its limits belonging to the United States, but this jurisdiction does not extend to any matter that is not consistent with full power in the United States to protect its lands, to control their use and to prescribe in what manner others may acquire rights in them. Thus while the State may punish public offenses, such as murder or larceny, committed on such lands, and may tax private property, such as live stock, located thereon, it may not tax the lands themselves or invest others with any right whatever in them. * * * From the earliest times Congress by its legislation, applicable alike in the States and Territories, has regulated in many particulars the use by others of the lands of the United States, has prohibited and made punishable various acts calculated to be injurious to them or to prevent their use in the way intended, and has provided for and controlled the acquisition of rights of way over them for highways, railroads, canals, ditches, telegraph lines and the like. The States and the public have almost uniformly accepted this legislation as controlling, and in the instances where it has been questioned in this court its validity has been upheld and its supremacy over state enactments sustained. And so we are of opinion that the inclusion within a State of lands of the United States does not take from Congress the power to control their occupancy and use, to protect them from trespass and injury and to prescribe the conditions upon which others may obtain rights in them, even though this may involve the exercise in some measure of what commonly is known as the police power. "A different rule," as was said in Camfield v. United States, "would place the public domain of the United States completely at the mercy of state legislation."

It results that state laws, including those relating to the exercise of the power of eminent domain, have no bearing upon a controversy such as is here presented, save as they may have been adopted or made applicable by Congress.

Absent a rather clear expression by Congress, states are generally prohibited from regulating the federal government itself. Outside the public lands context, for example, the Supreme Court has used Supremacy Clause-based notions of federal immunity to construe ambiguous statutes as not subjecting federal agencies to state permit processes, even if they did subject federal agencies to substantive state environmental regulation. *See* Hancock v. Train, 426 U.S. 167 (1976) (Clean Air Act); EPA v. California ex rel. State Water Resources Control Bd., 426 U.S. 200 (1976) (Clean Water Act). Like other immunities, this regulatory immunity can be waived. In fact, Congress swiftly reversed the results in those cases by amending the statutes in question to make clear that federal agencies needed state permits. *See* 91 Stat. 711 (1977) (Clean Air Act); 91 Stat. 1597, 1598 (1977) (Clean Water Act).

A similar notion of federal regulatory immunity has been applied in the federal lands context. For example, BLM issued a right-of-way permit to a unit of the federal Department of Energy to construct a power line across BLM lands. The permit was issued under the Federal Land Policy and Management Act, which requires such permits to "contain * * * terms and conditions which will * * * require compliance with State standards for [inter alia] environmental protection * * * if those standards are more stringent than applicable Federal standards." 43 U.S.C. § 1765(a)(iv). In Columbia Basin Land Protection Association v. Schlesinger, 643 F.2d 585, 602–06 (9th Cir. 1981) and Citizens and Landowners Against the Miles City/New Underwood Powerline v. Secretary, U.S. Dept. of Energy, 683 F.2d 1171 (8th Cir. 1982), the courts held that the Department of Energy had to conform to state power line siting standards, but did not need to obtain a state permit.

Another important aspect of federal immunity blocks plaintiffs from invoking estoppel doctrines to bind the federal government by "acts of its officers or agents in entering into an arrangement or agreement to do or cause to be done what the law does not sanction or permit." Utah Power & Light Co. v. United States, 243 U.S. 389 (1917) addressed this issue and its formulation continues to be the law on the application of estoppel based on the conduct of federal employees. The utility had built electric generation works on national forests in Utah without explicit permission from the Forest Service. One of the utility's defenses was that:

> when the forest reservations were created an understanding and agreement was had between the defendants, or their predecessors, and some unmentioned officers or agents of the United States to the effect that the reservations would not be an obstacle to the construction or operation of the works in question; that all rights essential thereto would be allowed and granted under the [relevant statute]; that consistently with this understanding and agreement and relying thereon the defendants, or their predecessors, completed the works and proceeded with the generation and distribution of electric energy, and that in consequence the United States is estopped to question the right

of the defendants to maintain and operate the works. Of this it is enough to say that the United States is neither bound nor estopped by acts of its officers or agents in entering into an arrangement or agreement to do or cause to be done what the law does not sanction or permit.

* * * And, if it be assumed that the rule is subject to exceptions, we find nothing in the cases in hand which fairly can be said to take them out of it as heretofore understood and applied in this court. A suit by the United States to enforce and maintain its policy respecting lands which it holds in trust for all the people stands upon a different plane in this and some other respects from the ordinary private suit to regain the title to real property or to remove a cloud from it.

In modern times, the Supreme Court has continued to reject arguments that the government should be estopped in particular circumstances, although it has said it is "hesitant * * * to say that there are *no cases* in which the public interest in insuring that the Government can enforce the law free from estoppel might be outweighed by the countervailing interest of citizens in some minimum standard of decency, honor and reliability in their dealings with their Government." Heckler v. Community Health Servs. of Crawford County, 467 U.S. 51, 58 (1984) (emphasis in original). Some lower courts have allowed estoppel against the United States in extreme cases. For example, in United States v. Wharton, 514 F.2d 406 (9th Cir. 1975), the Ninth Circuit held that the BLM was estopped by its conduct from ejecting a family that had resided on a federal parcel since 1919.

Congress has enacted some limited waivers of its sovereign immunity. The Color of Title Act, 43 U.S.C. §§ 1068–1068b, allows adverse possession claims against the United States, but only where the claimant has (a) good faith adverse possession for more than 20 years, and either cultivation or erection of valuable improvements, or (b) continuous good faith possession since January 1, 1901. Knowledge of federal ownership is a bar. *See, e.g.,* Day v. Hickel, 481 F.2d 473 (9th Cir. 1973). The Quiet Title Act of 1972, 28 U.S.C. §§ 2409a, 1346(f), 1402(d), waives immunity, on specified terms, as to those who claim title based on a valid conveyance rather than on adverse possession, but many private claims are barred by its 12–year statute of limitations, which generally begins to run on the date a plaintiff knew or should have known of the opposing claim to title by the United States. *See* Block v. North Dakota, 461 U.S. 273 (1983).

Federal sovereignty and the Supremacy Clause immunize federal property from state tax laws. But the federal tax immunity does *not* generally extend to situations where the state imposes taxes not on the federal government directly, but rather on federal employees or private contractors doing business with the federal government on federal lands. Such decisions go back a long way; in Forbes v. Gracey, 94 U.S. 762 (1876), the Supreme Court held that a state has the power to tax a miner's interest in a mining claim on federal land, even though the United States retained legal title to the land and the mineral. In United States v. County of Fresno, 429 U.S. 452 (1977), the Court upheld a county tax on the possessory interest of Forest Service employees in housing on federal land provided by the federal government. Noting that the legal incidence of the tax fell directly on private citizens (the federal employees), the Court was not moved by the fact that it might indirectly impose an economic burden on the Forest Service (by requiring it to pay its employees more). Instead, it said the tax can be invalidated "only if it discriminates against the Forest Service or other federal employees, which it does not do."

Of course, such judicial decisions narrowly construing federal tax immunity do not negate the power of Congress to broaden the immunity by statute. But here the "political safeguards of federalism"—the powerful influence state governments have on national government policymaking—frequently come into play. Perhaps the most vivid illustration of this influence is in the various ways that Congress has sought to compensate for the tax exempt status of federal lands. While Congress has not waived its immunity from taxation, it has adopted many programs to provide payments in lieu of taxes so that state and local governments will realize an income stream from federal lands.

Historically, a common way to do this is to pay the states (or local governments) a percentage of proceeds from resource development. For example, counties receive 25 percent of cash receipts the federal government realizes from timber harvesting on national forests, 16 U.S.C. § 500, and 50 percent of such receipts on the timber-rich "Oregon & California" (O & C) lands administered by the BLM. 43 U.S.C. § 1181f. The Wildlife Refuge Revenue Sharing Act provides that 25 percent of the revenues realized from the development of refuge resources are paid to the local counties. 16 U.S.C. § 715s. The state of origin receives 50 percent of revenues from all onshore oil and gas leases under the provisions of the Mineral Leasing Act—except Alaska, which receives 90 percent of such revenues. 30 U.S.C. § 191.

Not all federal-land-based payments to state and local governments are tied to federal resource development. The Payment In Lieu of Taxes Act (PILOT), 31 U.S.C. § 6901 et seq., provides a minimum federal payment of 75 cents per acre of land managed by the BLM, Forest Service and Park Service to local governments regardless of development revenues, and provides other forms of compensation. Adopted in 1976, PILOT follows on a similar program, dating back to 1935, which reimburses local governments for revenues lost because of the tax-exempt status of national wildlife refuges. *See* 16 U.S.C. § 715s. The PILOT formula is complicated; among other things, its payments are reduced depending on money received through timber revenue sharing. In Lawrence County v. Lead–Deadwood School Dist., 469 U.S. 256 (1985), the Court held that counties are free to spend PILOT funds for any governmental purposes, and that the states cannot place restrictions on such county expenditures. The Court reviewed the legislative history showing concern for "the local governments that bore the brunt of the expenses associated with federal lands, such as law enforcement, road maintenance, and the provision of public health services."

Other forms of federal-lands-based aid to state and local governments are somewhat more obscure. The Federal Highway Act has traditionally increased the federal contributing share for construction of interstate and other federal highways in any state where the percentage of federal and Indian landholdings in that state (other than national forests, parks, and monuments) exceeded 5 percent of the state's total land area. 23 U.S.C. § 120.

On the whole, there is much evidence that the states with significant amounts of public lands receive far more economic benefits from federal land ownership than detriments, and there seems to be a "pork-barrel" element in such federal revenue sharing programs. For example, Gallatin County, Montana, received $1.13 in federal PILOT money in fiscal year 2001 for every acre of federal land, whereas private forest and grazing land was taxed between 44 and 70 cents per acre. On top of this, besides federal payments in lieu of taxes, Montana receives substantial direct revenues by taxing private development activities on federal lands. *See, e.g.,* Commonwealth Edison Co. v. Montana, 453 U.S. 609 (1981) (upholding the application of Montana's 30 percent severance tax to lessees of federal coal). It also receives 50 percent of the federal revenues from the coal leasing. And it receives substantial revenues from the state's large tourist industry, which is attracted by the resources located on federal lands.

While the various formulae for these state and local payments set the amounts that are to be paid, the funds must, in almost all cases, be appropriated out of the U.S. Treasury each year by Congress. (The congressional appropriations committees abhor true "revolving" funds where the payments are automatic, because it diminishes their power over the purse strings.) Sometimes a temptation exists to cut the payments in favor of some other competing priority for federal funds, but in practice these appropriations are very popular, and payments are almost never interrupted or significantly cut.

When the amount of federal aid is tied directly to resource development (as in the timber stumpage and mineral leasing payments), the effect is to make state and local governments advocates of more federal timber sales and mineral leasing. This effect has been criticized by environmental advocates, who have long tried to persuade Congress to "uncouple" payments to state and local governments from resource development. In 2000, Congress guaranteed counties reliant upon national forest timber sale revenues a stable level of payment for the next several years, regardless of the amount of federal timber sold. However, the impermanence of annual budget deals deciding how much the federal government will mitigate for reductions in logging have made local planning extremely difficult. The George W. Bush Administration has repeatedly proposed selling public land to generate the revenue sufficient to cover a stable contribution to county school systems. Congress, though, has resisted such a deal.

The financial incentive sometimes leads state or local governments to bring lawsuits against federal land managers when they restrict resource development, or to intervene as defendants in cases seeking to apply environmental laws to reduce timber harvesting. Resource developers sometimes try to "partner" with the states in order to lessen their opposition to federal resource development. For example, federal law currently puts 100 percent of the federal revenue from the lucrative oil and gas development on the outer continental shelf in the federal treasury. 43 U.S.C. § 1338. Many, indeed nearly all, coastal states have been opposed to federal oil and gas leasing on the outer continental shelves off their shores, driven mostly by local environmental concerns. In response, the oil and gas industry and its supporters in Congress have favored giving the coastal states a share of federal offshore oil and gas lease revenues, such as happens onshore, in the hopes of inducing states to back off their opposition. In 2006 Congress approved legislation that for the first time gives some coastal states in the Gulf of Mexico a share of federal royalties.

While state and local governments tend to support federal resource development to increase their revenue sharing payments, Alaska took its self-interest to new heights when, in 1993, it sued the United States for $29 billion, claiming it had lost this amount in foregone revenue sharing payments because the federal government had withdrawn some areas of federal land in the state from mineral leasing. Finding "two hundred years of law recognizing in the Federal Government a virtually unfettered discretion as to the management of its own lands," and also finding it undisputed that the United States had "made no promise to make federal mineral lands productive of royalty revenues for the State," the court dismissed the suit. State of Alaska v. United States, 35 Fed. Cl. 685 (1996), *aff'd without opinion*, 119 F.3d 16 (Fed. Cir. 1997).

Alaska's revenue sharing has been an issue in the long-running national debate over whether to open the coastal plain of the federal Arctic National Wildlife Refuge to oil and gas development. As noted earlier, Alaska receives 90 percent rather than the usual state share of 50 percent of federal onshore mineral leasing revenues. Proponents of drilling the Arctic Refuge have argued that revenue from oil and gas lease sales and development would help balance the federal budget, but the argument is not very effective so long as the federal share is only 10 percent. In early 1996 Congress sent the President legislation that would have opened the Refuge to drilling, but cut Alaska's share from 90 percent to 50 percent. President Clinton vetoed the legislation (part of a massive "budget reconciliation" bill) on environmental grounds in January 1996. Alaska has argued that Congress has no power to change the revenue sharing formula because it was first included in the Alaska Statehood Act (72 Stat. 339 (1958)) which, Alaska maintains, is a solemn contract between sovereigns that cannot be breached.

The Congressional Research Service prepares useful reports describing various federal revenue sharing programs of land management agencies. The National Library for the Environment indexes them at http://www.ncseonline.org/NLE/CRS/.

C. The Property Clause

For most practical purposes relating to federal land management, the Enclave Clause and intergovernmental immunities doctrine are now overshadowed by the Property Clause. That Clause, Article IV, § 3, cl. 2, provides, in pertinent part, that "[t]he Congress shall have Power to dispose of and make all needful Rules and Regulations respecting the Territory or other Property belonging to the United States." The earliest Property Clause cases dealt with Congress's power to put in place the governmental machinery, such as a judicial system, to govern territories. They read the Clause broadly; indeed, they seemed to assume that Congress would have the power even if the Property Clause did not exist. See, e.g., The American Insurance Co. v. 356 Bales of Cotton, 26 U.S. (1 Pet.) 511, (1828) (Marshall, J.) Then, in 1840, the Court decided United States v. Gratiot, *supra* p. 118. *Gratiot* boldly declared Congress' power to be "without limitation"

Only a handful of cases raising Property Clause issues were decided over the succeeding years. In McKelvey v. United States, 260 U.S. 353 (1922), three sheepherders were denied passage over public lands by defendant cattle ranchers who, after warning and threatening them, "shot and seriously injured one of [them], threatened to finish him, and did other things calculated to put all three in terror." The ranchers were convicted of violating that part of the Unlawful Inclosures Act which prohibits any person, "by force, threats, [or] intimidation" from preventing or obstructing anyone "from peaceably entering upon * * * any tract of public land." 43 U.S.C. § 1063. On appeal, defendants claimed Congress's prescription of criminal penalties was beyond its power and an encroachment on the state police power. Writing for the Court, Justice Van Devanter (from Wyoming and formerly Assistant Attorney General for public lands) would have none of it: "It is firmly settled that Congress may prescribe rules respecting the use of the public lands. It may sanction some uses and prohibit others, and may forbid interference with such as are sanctioned." In Hunt v. United States, 278 U.S. 96, 100 (1928), the Court summarily brushed aside Arizona's argument that the U.S. could not kill large numbers of deer on federal lands in northern Arizona without conforming to state law. The program was conducted after elimination of the deer's chief predators—mountain lions, coyotes, wolves, bobcats and eagles—to protect local ranching operations caused the deer population to explode more than twenty-fold in fewer than two decades. The Court said simply that "the power of the United States to * * * protect its lands and property does not admit of doubt, * * * the game laws or any other statute of the state to the contrary notwithstanding."

The cascade of new environmental and natural resource legislation in the 1960s and 70s reignited property clause conflicts by giving federal agencies new, farther-reaching powers. Ironically, the following landmark case on the extent of Congressional power grew out of a law that mainstream environmental groups played almost no role in enacting or monitoring. Wild horses and burros are feral, which means that they are "in between" domesticated animals and true wildlife. They descend from livestock first introduced by Spaniards and other settlers. Ranchers and others have long considered them pests that should be killed for dog food. This attitude resulted in a drop in the wild horse population from perhaps 2 million in the early 1900s to about 17,000 in 1971, when Congress passed the Wild Free–Roaming Horses and Burros Act. Congressman Walter Baring of Nevada, in whose state many wild horses and burros roam, co-sponsored the Act. He credited a constituent, Velma Johnston (widely known as "Wild Horse Annie"), with awakening Americans to the drastic decline of these animals on federal lands.

Kleppe v. New Mexico
Supreme Court of the United States, 1976.
426 U.S. 529.

■ JUSTICE MARSHALL delivered the opinion of the Court.

At issue in this case is whether Congress exceeded its powers under the Constitution in enacting the Wild Free–Roaming Horses and Burros Act.

[The Act], 16 U.S.C. §§ 1331–1340, was enacted in 1971 to protect "all unbranded and unclaimed horses and burros on public lands of the United States," § 2(b) of the Act, 16 U.S.C. § 1332(b), from "capture, branding, harassment, or death." § 1 of the Act, 16 U.S.C. § 1331. The Act provides that all such horses and burros on the public lands administered by the Secretary of the Interior through the Bureau of Land Management (BLM) or by the Secretary of Agriculture through the Forest Service are commit-ted to the jurisdiction of the respective Secretaries, who are "directed to protect and manage [the animals] as components of the public lands * * * in a manner that is designed to achieve and maintain a thriving natural ecological balance on the public lands." § 3(a) of the Act, 16 U.S.C. § 1333(a).* If protected horses or burros "stray from public lands onto privately owned land, the owners of such land may inform the nearest Federal marshal or agent of the Secretary, who shall arrange to have the animals removed."[1] § 4 of the Act, 16 U.S.C. § 1334.

Section 6 of the Act, 16 U.S.C. § 1336, authorizes the Secretaries to promulgate regulations, see 36 CFR § 231.11 (1975) (Agriculture); 43 CFR pt. 4710 (1975) (Interior), and to enter into cooperative agreements with other landowners and with state and local governmental agencies in fur-therance of the Act's purposes. On August 7, 1973, the Secretaries executed such an agreement with the New Mexico Livestock Board (the Livestock Board), the agency charged with enforcing the New Mexico Estray Law, N.M. Stat. Ann. § 47–14–1 et seq. (1953).[2] The agreement acknowledged

* [Eds. note: The Act defines the "public lands" to include national forests as well as BLM-managed lands.]

1. The landowner may elect to allow straying wild free-roaming horses and burros to remain on his property, in which case he must so notify the relevant Secretary. He may not destroy any such animals, however. § 4 of the Act, 16 U.S.C. § 1334.

2. Under the New Mexico law, an es-tray is defined as:

"Any bovine animal, horse, mule or ass, found running at large upon public or private

lands, either fenced or unfenced, in the state of New Mexico, whose owner is unknown in the section where found, or which shall be fifty [50] miles or more from the limits of its usual range or pasture, or that is branded with a brand which is not on record in the office of the cattle sanitary board of New Mexico * * *." N.M. Stat. Ann. § 47–14–1 (1966).

It is not disputed that the animals regu-lated by the Wild Free–Roaming Horses and Burros Act are estrays within the meaning of this law.

the authority of the Secretaries to manage and protect the wild free-roaming horses and burros on the public lands of the United States within the State and established a procedure for evaluating the claims of private parties to ownership of such animals.

The Livestock Board terminated the agreement three months later. Asserting that the Federal Government lacked power to control wild horses and burros on the public lands of the United States unless the animals were moving in interstate commerce or damaging the public lands and that neither of these bases of regulation was available here, the Board notified the Secretaries of its intent

> "to exercise all regulatory impoundment and sale powers which it derives from the New Mexico Estray Law, over all estray horses, mules or asses found running at large upon public or private lands within New Mexico * * *. This includes the right to go upon Federal or State lands to take possession of said horses or burros, should the Livestock Board so desire." App. 67, 72.

The differences between the Livestock Board and the Secretaries came to a head in February 1974. On February 1, 1974, a New Mexico rancher, Kelley Stephenson, was informed by BLM that several unbranded burros had been seen near Taylor Well, where Stephenson watered his cattle. Taylor Well is on federal property, and Stephenson had access to it and some 8,000 surrounding acres only through a grazing permit issued pursuant to the Taylor Grazing Act. After BLM made it clear to Stephenson that it would not remove the burros and after he personally inspected the Taylor Well area, Stephenson complained to the Livestock Board that the burros were interfering with his livestock operation by molesting his cattle and eating their feed.

Thereupon the Board rounded up and removed 19 unbranded and unclaimed burros pursuant to the New Mexico Estray Law. Each burro was seized on the public lands of the United States and, as the director of the Board conceded, each burro fit the definition of a wild free-roaming burro under § 2(b) of the Act. App. 43. On February 18, 1974, the Livestock Board, pursuant to its usual practice, sold the burros at a public auction. After the sale, BLM asserted jurisdiction under the Act and demanded that the Board recover the animals and return them to the public lands.

[New Mexico promptly sued the U.S. in federal district court, claiming the Wild Free–Roaming Horses and Burros Act was unconstitutional. The district court found the act unconstitutional because it] "conflicts with * * * the traditional doctrines concerning wild animals," 406 F. Supp. 1237, 1238 (1975), and is in excess of Congress' power under the Property Clause of the Constitution, Art. IV, § 3, cl. 2. That Clause, the court found, enables Congress to regulate wild animals found on the public land only for the "*protection* of the public lands from damage of some kind." 406 F. Supp., at 1239 (emphasis in original). Accordingly, this power was exceeded in this case because "[t]he statute is aimed at protecting the wild horses and burros, not at protecting the land they live on." Ibid. We noted probable jurisdiction, 423 U.S. 818 (1975), and we now reverse.

* * * In passing the Wild Free–Roaming Horses and Burros Act, Congress deemed the regulated animals "an integral part of the natural system of the public lands" of the United States, § 1 of the Act, 16 U.S.C. § 1331, and found that their management was necessary "for achievement of an ecological balance on the public lands." According to Congress, these animals, if preserved in their native habitats, "contribute to the diversity of life forms within the Nation and enrich the lives of the American people." § 1 of the Act, 16 U.S.C. § 1331. Indeed, Congress concluded, the wild free-roaming horses and burros "are living symbols of the historic and pioneer spirit of the West." § 1 of the Act, 16 U.S.C. § 1331. Despite their importance, the Senate Committee found:

> "[these animals] have been cruelly captured and slain and their carcasses used in the production of pet food and fertilizer. They have been used for target practice and harassed for 'sport' and profit. In spite of public outrage, this bloody traffic continues unabated, and it is the firm belief of the committee that this senseless slaughter must be brought to an end." S.Rep. No. 92–242, 92d Cong., 1st Sess., 2 (1971), U.S. Code Cong. & Admin.News 1971, p. 2149.

For these reasons, Congress determined to preserve and protect the wild free-roaming horses and burros on the public lands of the United States. The question under the Property Clause is whether this determination can be sustained as a "needful" regulation "respecting" the public lands. In answering this question, we must remain mindful that, while courts must eventually pass upon them, determinations under the Property Clause are entrusted primarily to the judgment of Congress. Light v. United States, 220 U.S. 523, 537 (1911); United States v. Gratiot, 14 Pet. 526, 537–538 (1840).

Appellees [New Mexico] argue that the Act cannot be supported by the Property Clause. They contend that the Clause grants Congress essentially two kinds of power: (1) the power to dispose of and make incidental rules regarding the use of federal property; and (2) the power to protect federal property. According to appellees, the first power is not broad enough to support legislation protecting wild animals that live on federal property; and the second power is not implicated since the Act is designed to protect the animals, which are not themselves federal property, and not the public lands. As an initial matter, it is far from clear that the Act was not passed in part to protect the public lands of the United States or that Congress cannot assert a property interest in the regulated horses and burros superior to that of the State.[8] But we need not consider whether the Act can be upheld on either of these grounds, for we reject appellees' narrow reading of the Property Clause.

Appellees ground their argument on a number of cases that, upon analysis, provide no support for their position. Like the District Court,

8. The Secretary makes no claim here, however, that the United States owns the wild free-roaming horses and burros found on public land.

appellees cite Hunt v. United States, 278 U.S. 96 (1928), for the proposition that the Property Clause gives Congress only the limited power to regulate wild animals in order to protect the public lands from damage. But *Hunt,* which upheld the Government's right to kill deer that were damaging foliage in the national forests, only holds that damage to the land is a sufficient basis for regulation; it contains no suggestion that it is a necessary one.

Next appellees refer to Kansas v. Colorado, 206 U.S. 46, 89 (1907). The referenced passage in that case states that the Property Clause "clearly * * * does not grant to Congress any legislative control over the states, and must, so far as they are concerned, be limited to authority over the property belonging to the United States within their limits." But this does no more than articulate the obvious: that the Property Clause is a grant of power only over federal property. It gives no indication of the kind of "authority" the Clause gives Congress over its property.

* * *

Lastly, appellees point to dicta in two cases to the effect that, unless the State has agreed to the exercise of federal jurisdiction, Congress' rights in its land are "only the rights of an ordinary proprietor * * *." Fort Leavenworth R. Co. v. Lowe, 114 U.S. 525, 527 (1885). See also Paul v. United States, 371 U.S. 245 (1963). In neither case was the power of Congress under the Property Clause at issue or considered and, as we shall see, these dicta fail to account for the raft of cases in which the Clause has been given a broader construction.[9]

In brief, beyond the *Fort Leavenworth* and *Paul* dicta, appellees have presented no support for their position that the Clause grants Congress only the power to dispose of, to make incidental rules regarding the use of, and to protect federal property. This failure is hardly surprising, for the Clause, in broad terms, gives Congress the power to determine what are "needful" rules "respecting" the public lands. And while the furthest reaches of the power granted by the Property Clause have not yet been definitively resolved, we have repeatedly observed that "[t]he power over the public land thus entrusted to Congress is without limitations." United States v. San Francisco, 310 U.S., at 29.

* * *

The decided cases have supported this expansive reading. It is the Property Clause, for instance, that provides the basis for governing the territories of the United States. And even over public land within the States, "[t]he general government doubtless has a power over its own property analogous to the police power of the several states, and the extent to which it may go in the exercise of such power is measured by the

9. Indeed, Hunt v. United States, 278 U.S. 96 (1928), and Camfield v. United States, 167 U.S. 518 (1897), both relied upon by appellees, are inconsistent with the notion that the United States has only the rights of an ordinary proprietor with respect to its land. An ordinary proprietor may not, contrary to state law, kill game that is damaging his land, as the Government did in *Hunt;* nor may he prohibit the fencing in of his property without the assistance of state law, as the Government was able to do in *Camfield.*

exigencies of the particular case." Camfield v. United States, 167 U.S. 518, 525 (1897). We have noted, for example, that the Property Clause gives Congress the power over the public lands "to control their occupancy and use, to protect them from trespass and injury, and to prescribe the conditions upon which others may obtain rights in them * * *." Utah Power & Light Co. v. United States, 243 U.S. 389, 405 (1917). And we have approved legislation respecting the public lands "[i]f it be found to be necessary, for the protection of the public or of intending settlers [on the public lands]." Camfield v. United States, 167 U.S., at 525. In short, Congress exercises the powers both of a proprietor and of a legislature over the public domain. Although the Property Clause does not authorize "an exercise of a general control over public policy in a State," it does permit "an exercise of the complete power which Congress has over particular public property entrusted to it." United States v. San Francisco, 310 U.S., at 30 (footnote omitted). In our view, the "complete power" that Congress has over public lands necessarily includes the power to regulate and protect the wildlife living there.[10]

Appellees argue that if we approve the Wild Free–Roaming Horses and Burros Act as a valid exercise of Congress' power under the Property Clause, then we have sanctioned an impermissible intrusion on the sovereignty, legislative authority and police power of the State and have wrongly infringed upon the State's traditional trustee powers over wild animals. The argument appears to be that Congress could obtain exclusive legislative jurisdiction over the public lands in the State only by state consent, and that in the absence of such consent Congress lacks the power to act contrary to state law. This argument is without merit.

Appellees' claim confuses Congress' derivative legislative powers, which are not involved in this case, with its powers under the Property Clause. Congress may acquire derivative legislative power from a state pursuant to Art. I, § 8, cl. 17, of the Constitution by consensual acquisition of land, or by nonconsensual acquisition followed by the State's subsequent cession of legislative authority over the land. Paul v. United States, 371 U.S. 245, 264 (1963); Fort Leavenworth R. Co. v. Lowe, 114 U.S. 525, 541–542 (1885).[11] In either case, the legislative jurisdiction acquired may range from exclusive federal jurisdiction with no residual state police power, to concurrent, or partial, federal legislative jurisdiction, which may allow the State to exercise certain authority.

---

10.   Appellees ask us to declare that the Act is unconstitutional because the animals are not, as Congress found, "fast disappearing from the American scene." § 1 of the Act, 16 U.S.C. § 1331. At the outset, no reason suggests itself why Congress' power under the Property Clause to enact legislation to protect wild free-roaming horses and burros "from capture, branding, harassment, or death," ibid., must depend on a finding that the animals are decreasing in number. But responding directly to appellees' contention, we note that the evidence before Congress on this question was conflicting and that Congress weighed the evidence and made a judgment. What appellees ask is that we reweigh the evidence and substitute our judgment for that of Congress. This we must decline to do.

11.   * * * The Clause has been broadly construed, and the acquisition by consent or cession of exclusive or partial jurisdiction over properties for any legitimate governmental purpose beyond those itemized is permissible. Collins v. Yosemite Park Co., 304 U.S. 518, 528–530 (1938).

But while Congress can acquire exclusive or partial jurisdiction over lands within a State by the State's consent or cession, the presence or absence of such jurisdiction has nothing to do with Congress' powers under the Property Clause. Absent consent or cession a State undoubtedly retains jurisdiction over federal lands within its territory, but Congress equally surely retains the power to enact legislation respecting those lands pursuant to the Property Clause. And when Congress so acts, the federal legislation necessarily overrides conflicting state laws under the Supremacy Clause. U.S. Const., Art. VI, cl. 2. * * * As we said in Camfield v. United States, 167 U.S., at 526, in response to a somewhat different claim: "A different rule would place the public domain of the United States completely at the mercy of state legislation."

Thus, appellees' assertion that "[a]bsent state consent by complete cession of jurisdiction of lands to the United States, exclusive jurisdiction does not accrue to the federal landowner with regard to federal lands within the borders of the state," is completely beside the point; and appellees' fear that the Secretary's position is that "the Property Clause totally exempts federal lands within state borders from state legislative powers, state police powers, and all rights and powers of local sovereignty and jurisdiction of the states," is totally unfounded. The Federal Government does not assert exclusive jurisdiction over the public lands in New Mexico, and the State is free to enforce its criminal and civil laws on those lands. But where those state laws conflict with the Wild Free–Roaming Horses and Burros Act, or with other legislation passed pursuant to the Property Clause, the law is clear: the state laws must recede. * * *

In short, these cases do not support appellees' claim that upholding the Act would sanction an impermissible intrusion upon state sovereignty. The Act does not establish exclusive federal jurisdiction over the public lands in New Mexico; it merely overrides the New Mexico Estray Law insofar as it attempts to regulate federally protected animals. And that is but the necessary consequence of valid legislation under the Property Clause.

Appellees' contention that the Act violates traditional state power over wild animals stands on no different footing. Unquestionably the States have broad trustee and police powers over wild animals within their jurisdictions. But as Geer v. Connecticut cautions, those powers exist only "in so far as [their] exercise may be not incompatible with, or restrained by, the rights conveyed to the federal government by the constitution." [Geer v. Connecticut, 161 U.S. 519, 528 (1896).] "No doubt it is true that as between a State and its inhabitants the State may regulate the killing and sale of [wildlife], but it does not follow that its authority is exclusive of paramount powers." Missouri v. Holland, 252 U.S. 416, 434 (1920). * * * We hold today that the Property Clause also gives Congress the power to protect wildlife on the public lands, state law notwithstanding.

In this case, the New Mexico Livestock Board entered upon the public lands of the United States and removed wild burros. These actions were contrary to the provisions of the Wild Free–Roaming Horses and Burros Act. We find that, as applied to this case, the Act is a constitutional exercise of congressional power under the Property Clause. We need not, and do not, decide whether the Property Clause would sustain the Act in all of its conceivable applications.

Appellees are concerned that the Act's extension of protection to wild free-roaming horses and burros that stray from public land onto private land, § 4 of the Act, 16 U.S.C. § 1334, will be read to provide federal jurisdiction over every wild horse or burro that at any time sets foot upon federal land. While it is clear that regulations under the Property Clause may have some effect on private lands not otherwise under federal control, Camfield v. United States, 167 U.S. 518 (1897), we do not think it appropriate in this declaratory judgment proceeding to determine the extent, if any, to which the Property Clause empowers Congress to protect animals on private lands or the extent to which such regulation is attempted by the Act. * * *

NOTES AND QUESTIONS

1. In 2005 the BLM estimated that its lands contained about 27,000 wild horses and 4000 burros. Nevada hosts nearly half of these animals. New Mexico's population of wild horses is down to just 82 animals and no wild burros remain on federal lands in the state. Since Congress enacted the Wild Free–Roaming Horses and Burros Act, a little over 200,000 wild horses and burros rounded up as excess have been "adopted" into private ownership.

2. Congress' mandate for the Secretary to maintain a "thriving ecological balance" through a horse and burro conservation program is a classic case of misconceiving science. Ecologists generally reject the existence of a "balance" in ecology, instead relying on probabilistic descriptions of disturbance reaction. More to the point, though, horses and burros do serious damage to native ecosystems. As an expert on ungulate species memorably put it, "legal status does not equate with ecological legitimacy." He went on to note that:

> By passage of [the Wild Horses and Burros Act], Congress declared that it felt it had the power to override the results of 500,000 years of separate evolution of New World and Old World equid lineages, and furthermore invalidated the extinction of North American equids near the end of the Pleistocene. Congress may have given legal status to these noxious herbivores, but Congress sees the natural world through a different visual filter than serious ecologists.

Bruce E. Coblentz, Letter to the Editor, 13 Natural Areas J. 3 (1993).

Was the Court too hasty in dismissing New Mexico's challenge to Congress' scientific findings? There may have been counterpart large ungulate animals in prehistoric times, perhaps driven to extinction by ancestors of Indians. The Act rests on firmer ground in concluding that the horses and burros "are living symbols of the historic and pioneer spirit of the West." 16 U.S.C. § 1331.

3. Who owns the wild burros at issue in *Kleppe*? Is ownership relevant? Geer v. Connecticut, 161 U.S. 519 (1896), cited in Justice Marshall's

opinion, held that a state could forbid the export of game taken within its borders without contravening the so-called "dormant" commerce clause of the U.S. Constitution. The decision rested in part on the concept that the states "owned" the wildlife within their borders in trust for the people. The idea of state "ownership" eroded over time, and *Geer* was overruled two years after *Kleppe*, in Hughes v. Oklahoma, 441 U.S. 322 (1979). The Court explained that abandoning the "19th century legal fiction of state ownership" left the states with "ample allowance for preserving, in ways not inconsistent with the commerce clause, the legitimate state concerns for conservation and protection of wild animals." 441 U.S. at 335–36.

4.   Justice Marshall's opinion says that New Mexico's "fear" of losing all authority over federal lands with a broad reading of the Property Clause "is totally unfounded." Is it? In this connection, can New Mexico regulate hunting (other than for wild horses and burros) on federal lands after *Kleppe*?

5.   Although *Kleppe* was unanimous, new information has come to light that suggests the Court's unanimity was in doubt for a time. When the papers of former Supreme Court Justice Thurgood Marshall were made public after his death, they were found to contain a cryptic note from Chief Justice Burger regarding *Kleppe*, dated a few days before the Court issued its judgment:

> The enthusiasm that the rancher-water Justices exhibited for my scholarly analysis of the grazing problems leads me to abandon the idea of separate writing. I assumed ranchers would want to be free to shoot trespassing burros but if Byron [White] and Bill Rehnquist want to put wild burros on a new form of "welfare" I will submit. In short, I join you.

6.   If the Property Clause gives Congress plenary preemptive power over federal lands, where does that leave the limitations in the Enclave Clause? Does *Kleppe*'s reading of the Property Clause make the Enclave Clause superfluous? Could, for example, Congress adopt legislation abrogating the right of Kansas to tax railroad property within military reservations (and thus undo the state's reservation of jurisdiction upheld in *Fort Leavenworth*)? Or consider this: Suppose New Mexico had in 1960 ceded exclusive jurisdiction to the U.S. over a tract of land in a national forest within its borders, except that the state expressly reserved the power to regulate wild horses and burros on the tract. Can the U.S. nevertheless enforce the Wild Horse and Burro Act on this tract under *Kleppe*?

7.   Could Congress unilaterally (without state consent) oust all state laws and establish exclusive federal jurisdiction on all federal lands under the Property Clause? In Commonwealth of Virginia v. Reno, 955 F. Supp. 571 (E.D. Va. 1997), Virginia argued that the operation of a federal correctional facility on federal land within its borders exceeded the jurisdiction over some of the property involved that Virginia had previously ceded to the national government under the Enclave Clause, and therefore the facility had to be closed. Judge Ellis, providing the most comprehensive exploration of the relationship between the two constitutional clauses in modern times, rejected the claim. He observed that judicial construction of

the Enclave Clause "is both broader and narrower than its wording and history suggest," that the Property Clause provides a "separate mechanism[] by which the federal government may obtain, hold, and regulate its property," and that the Enclave Clause "in no way diminishes the government's power over federal property held pursuant to the Property Clause." Therefore any limitations in Virginia's cession of jurisdiction could not defeat Congress's power to regulate and control the correctional facility. While his decision was on appeal, Virginia's pursuit of a political remedy succeeded, with Congress enacting legislation closing the facility, mooting the issue. *See* 122 F.3d 1060 (4th Cir. 1997).

8. For an argument that the decline of the Enclave Clause and the ascent of the Property Clause in the Supreme Court has moved generally in parallel with the evolution of congressional policy over federal lands from a vendor to a custodian to an active manager, see Eugene R. Gaetke, *Refuting the "Classic" Property Clause Theory*, 63 N.C. L.Rev. 617 (1985). For a recent comprehensive history and ringing endorsement of a broad interpretation of the Property Clause, see Peter Appel, *The Power of Congress "Without Limitation": The Property Clause and Federal Regulation of Private Property*, 86 Minn. L.Rev. 1 (2001). For an argument that the Property Clause frames an attitude through which the Supreme Court has fashioned a kind of constitutional common law that favors retention of federal land in national ownership, national over state and local authority, and environmental conservation, see John D. Leshy, *A Property Clause for the Twenty–First Century*, 75 U. Colo. L.Rev. 1101–25 (2004).

NOTE: NUCLEAR WASTE DISPOSAL

Although it has been almost fifty years since the federal government embarked on a program of promoting the use of nuclear energy for peaceful purposes, a final decision on a permanent repository for the resulting long-lived radioactive wastes has not yet been made. In 1982, Congress enacted the Nuclear Waste Policy Act, directing the Department of Energy to undertake a wide-ranging review of possible sites around the country. This effort bogged down, and in 1987 Congress amended the Act to narrow the appraisal of possible repository sites to just one: Yucca Mountain on federal land in the Nellis Air Force Range and Nuclear Testing Site northwest of Las Vegas. The state government went ballistic, as it were—filing lawsuits, enacting obstructive legislation, and otherwise attempting to assert a veto to the federal plan. One of the lawsuits raised questions about whether Congress's constitutional power over federal lands supported the 1987 amendments. State of Nevada v. Watkins, 914 F.2d 1545 (9th Cir. 1990). The court, relying principally on Kleppe v. New Mexico, found that the Property Clause left the matter to Congress, and the Enclave Clause does not limit that power by requiring the consent of the State. The court went on to hold that the equal footing doctrine and Pollard v. Hagan did not restrict Congress's power over federal property, and rejected several other constitutional arguments.

Litigation and legislative maneuvering continued; see State of Nevada v. U.S. Dep't of Energy, 993 F.2d 1442 (9th Cir. 1993). In February 2002, President Bush endorsed the Yucca Mountain site. In Nuclear Energy Inst. v. EPA, 373 F.3d 1251 (D.C. Cir. 2004), the court resolved a number of additional challenges to the Nuclear Waste Policy Act brought by Nevada. One was a variation on its earlier argument that it exceeded Congress's power under the Property Clause. The court rejected the challenge, finding its role "extends, at most, to determining whether there is a rational relationship between Congress's stated end and its chosen means," and then finding that Congress's action "easily passes this test." 373 F.3d at 1303–14. Another Nevada argument was that various constitutional doctrines contain an implicit "equal treatment for states" standard (echoing the "equal footing doctrine") that requires Congress to use "facially neutral, generally applicable criteria" to select federal land as the site for a national nuclear waste repository. The court rejected this as well, finding "no basis in the Constitution for Nevada's proposed 'equal treatment' requirement." Among other things, the court said that "Congress's decision to designate Yucca Mountain for development as a repository does not in any way regulate Nevada's activities; it merely prescribes the use of a particular piece of *federal* property." (Emphasis in original) It concluded this part of its opinion as follows:

> We fail to see * * * how the constraints demanded by Nevada's claim would be consistent with the plenary nature of Congress's Property Clause authority or the considerable deference that we accord to Congress's judgment in exercising that authority. Under Nevada's proposed requirement, every time Congress decides to use federal property in a manner that incidentally burdens a State—for example by designating such property for use as a military installation, a prison, a dam, a storage or disposal site, or a conservation area—it must formulate neutral selection criteria and apply those criteria to every piece of federal property in the Nation before selecting a site. Courts presumably would be required to scrutinize the substantive basis of the legislation in question to ensure that the criteria were genuinely neutral and generally applied. This is far more intrusive than any requirement that there be a rational basis for Congress's judgment that a particular regulation respecting a particular property is "needful." The substantive constraint on legislation and the judicial role implicit in Nevada's "equal treatment" requirement are, in our view, totally at odds with the broad interpretation given to Congress's Property Clause powers.

373 F.3d at 1308.

Congress also authorized construction of a Waste Isolation Pilot Project (WIPP) on federal land in New Mexico for disposal of military radioactive waste. Like Nevada, New Mexico opposed the project in and out of court, with but limited success. See New Mexico v. EPA, 114 F.3d 290 (D.C. Cir. 1997). The facility is now in operation. Do these examples of federal imposition of wastes on unwilling public land states rise to the level of an equal footing problem? If you represented Nevada, what legal strategy would you suggest in the light of these cases?

THE PROPERTY CLAUSE AND NON–FEDERAL LAND

The Court in *Kleppe v. New Mexico* did not expressly address Congress's power, under the Property Clause, to regulate wild horses and burros when they wander off federal property. A substantial line of cases affirms that the Property Clause does give Congress authority to regulate activities occurring *off* federal lands if their effects can be felt on federal lands. The first case was Camfield v. United States, *infra* p. 370. It upheld the application of the Unlawful Inclosures Act to prohibit certain kinds of exclusionary fencing on private lands surrounding federal property. *Camfield* was followed by United States v. Alford, 274 U.S. 264 (1927), where the Court, speaking through Justice Holmes, rejected Alford's contention that a 1910 federal statute which prohibited leaving unextinguished a fire "in or near" any public forest could not be enforced on private lands. "The danger depends upon the nearness of the fire, not upon the ownership of the land where it is built. * * * The statute is constitutional. Congress may prohibit the doing of acts upon privately owned lands that imperil the publicly owned forests." These cases did not indicate how far the Congress could go in regulating activities on nonfederal land, especially in the modern environmentally conscious age.

Minnesota v. Block

United States Court of Appeals, Eighth Circuit, 1981.
660 F.2d 1240, *cert. denied*, 455 U.S. 1007 (1982).

■ JUDGE BRIGHT

These appeals arise from three consolidated cases involving multiple challenges to provisions of the Boundary Waters Canoe Area Wilderness Act of 1978 (BWCAW Act or the Act). * * * [Plaintiff-appellants State of Minnesota, the National Association of Property Owners (NAPO) and numerous individuals, businesses, and organizations] allege that Congress unconstitutionally applied federal controls on the use of motorboats and snowmobiles to land and waters not owned by the United States. * * *

The BWCAW, a part of the Superior National Forest, consists of approximately 1,075,000 acres of land and waterways along the Minnesota–Canadian border. * * * [The Court recounted the long efforts by the national government, starting with the first reservation of forest land in 1902, to protect the boundary waters area, including its "primitive character." This culminated in enactment of the BWCAW]. At issue here are portions of section 4 of the Act, the provision barring the use of motorized craft in all but designated portions of the wilderness. Section 4(c) limits motorboat use to designated lakes and rivers, allowing a maximum of either ten or twenty-five horsepower motors on these waters. Section 4(g) permits certain limited mechanized portages. Section 4(e) restricts the use of snowmobiles to two designated trails. With these exceptions, the Act as construed by the federal government and by the district court, prohibits all other motorized transportation on land and water falling within the external boundaries of the wilderness area.

The boundaries of the BWCAW circumscribe a total surface area of approximately 1,080,300 acres—920,000 acres of land and 160,000 of water. The United States owns approximately 792,000 acres of land surface, while the State of Minnesota owns approximately 121,000 acres of land,[12] in addition to the beds under the 160,000 acres of navigable water. Congress recognized that Minnesota would retain jurisdiction over the waters, but provided that the State could not regulate in a manner less stringent than that mandated by the Act. * * *

On appeal, Minnesota and the intervening plaintiffs [argue, among other things] * * * that Congress acted in excess of its authority under the property clause by curtailing the use of motor-powered boats and other motorized vehicles on lands and waters not owned by the United States * * *.

* * * [W]e must decide the question left open in *Kleppe*—the scope of Congress' property clause power as applied to activity occurring off federal land. Without defining the limits of the power, the Court in *Kleppe,* relying on its decision in Camfield v. United States, 167 U.S. 518 (1897), acknowledged that "it is clear the regulations under the Property Clause may have some effect on private lands not otherwise under federal control." * * *

Under this authority to protect public land, Congress' power must extend to regulation of conduct on or off the public land that would threaten the designated purpose of federal lands. Congress clearly has the power to dedicate federal land for particular purposes. As a necessary incident of that power, Congress must have the ability to insure that these lands be protected against interference with their intended purposes. As the Supreme Court has stated, under the property clause "[Congress] may sanction some uses and prohibit others, and *may forbid interference with such as are sanctioned.*" McKelvey v. United States, 260 U.S. 353, 359 (1922) (emphasis added).

* * *

Having established that Congress may regulate conduct off federal land that interferes with the designated purpose of that land, we must determine whether Congress acted within this power in restricting the use of motorboats and other motor vehicles in the BWCAW. In reviewing the appropriateness of particular regulations, "we must remain mindful that, while courts must eventually pass upon them, determinations under the Property Clause are entrusted primarily to the judgment of Congress." Kleppe v. New Mexico, supra, 426 U.S. at 536. Thus, if Congress enacted the motorized use restrictions to protect the fundamental purpose for which the BWCAW had been reserved, and if the restrictions in section 4 reasonably relate to that end, we must conclude that Congress acted within its constitutional prerogative.

12. Private parties own approximately 7,300 acres of land.

Congress passed the BWCAW Act with the clear intent of insuring that the area would remain as wilderness and could be enjoyed as such. Specifically concerning the motor use regulations, Congressman Fraser, in introducing the 1978 Act, stated:

> The bill has four major thrusts. First, and most important, it seeks to end those activities that threaten the integrity of the BWCA's wilderness character by expressly prohibiting the following uses: * * * Recreational uses of motorized watercraft and snowmobiles * * *.

Congress based its conclusions on certain statutory findings:

> SECTION 1. The Congress finds that it is necessary and desirable to provide for the protection, enhancement, and preservation of the natural values of the lakes, waterways, and associated forested areas known (before the date of enactment of this Act) as the Boundary Waters Canoe Area, and for the orderly management of public use and enjoyment of that area as wilderness, and of certain contiguous lands and waters, while at the same time protecting the special qualities of the area as a natural forest-lakeland wilderness ecosystem of major esthetic, cultural, scientific, recreational and educational value to the Nation. [92 Stat. 1649.]

Hearings and other evidence provided ample support for Congress' finding that use of motorboats and snowmobiles must be limited in order to preserve the area as a wilderness. Testimony established that the sight, smell, and sound of motorized vehicles seriously marred the wilderness experience of canoeists, hikers, and skiers and threatened to destroy the integrity of the wilderness.

As a result of considerable testimony and debate and a series of compromises, Congress enacted section 4 in an attempt to accommodate all interests, determining the extent of motorized use the area might tolerate without serious threat to its wilderness values.

The motor use restrictions form only a small part of an elaborate system of regulations considered necessary to preserve the BWCAW as a wilderness. The United States owns close to ninety percent of the land surrounding the waters at issue. Congress concluded that motorized vehicles significantly interfere with the use of the wilderness by canoeists, hikers, and skiers and that restricted motorized use would enhance and preserve the wilderness values of the area. From the evidence presented, Congress could rationally reach these conclusions. We hold, therefore, that Congress acted within its power under the Constitution to pass needful regulations respecting public lands.

NOTES AND QUESTIONS

1. Refresher question: How did the State of Minnesota come to gain title to the subsurface land (26 percent of the total acreage) it owned in the Boundary Waters Canoe Area?

2. Other modern decisions reach similar results. In Free Enterprise Canoe Renters Association v. Watt, 549 F. Supp. 252 (E.D. Mo. 1982), *aff'd,*

711 F.2d 852 (8th Cir. 1983), the court relied on Minnesota v. Block to hold that the National Park Service could prohibit the use of state roads within the Ozark National Scenic Riverway for canoe pickups by canoe renters who lacked a Park Service permit. United States v. Lindsey, 595 F.2d 5 (9th Cir. 1979) was a repeat of *Alford,* upholding the prosecution of a person who built a campfire without permission on state land within the boundaries of Hells Canyon National Recreation Area, contrary to a Forest Service regulation.

3.   Is Congress's Property Clause power to regulate activities on *state* land any greater or lesser than its power to regulate activities on *private* land? Should it be? The Supreme Court has expressed much concern in recent years with federal commerce clause regulation that directly impacts state government operations. *See* New York v. United States, 505 U.S. 144 (1992); Printz v. United States, 521 U.S. 898 (1997). Does it make any difference that the regulation here is of activities by private persons (recreational boaters and snowmobilers) using state lands? If the state had not ceded jurisdiction to the U.S. over the waters of the Park, would the federal regulation still be valid? Suppose Minnesota decides to relocate its state capital to a site within the BWCAWA. Would that strengthen the state's claim that the federal statutory restrictions cross the constitutional line?

4.   What was the injury to federal lands from the operation of motorboats on waters over state lands? Was it physical or aesthetic? (Is there a clear line between the two?) Does the reach of Congress's power in this context turn on whether there is a physical impact on federal lands?

5.   In this case, a fairly extensive record showed that, in fashioning the BWCAW, Congress considered the need to regulate activities on non-federal land in order to protect federal land. Does Congress need to show, in statutes or legislative history, the connection between activities it regulates on non-federal lands and federal lands? What kind of connection, and how strong must it be? Or is the court here saying that there is no meaningful judicial review of Congress's exercise of its Property Clause power? Compare the Supreme Court's current view of the commerce clause that Congress must draw a "explicit connection" between the subject it is regulating and interstate commerce. *See* United States v. Morrison, 529 U.S. 598, 612 (2000) (holding that extensive congressional findings connecting the statute's goal and interstate commerce are not sufficient to make the statute constitutional).

6.   Should there be a more searching judicial inquiry when the federal land management agency seeks to regulate activities off federal land in order to protect the federal land, but the statute giving the agency generic regulatory authority is silent on whether that authority may be extended to activities off federal land? Sometimes Congress has expressly regulated activities on non-federal inholdings in legislation protecting large tracts of federal land. *See* 16 U.S.C. § 460aa–3 (Sawtooth National Recreation Area, giving federal land manager direct zoning authority over private inholding where there is no local regulation).

7. The cases addressing the reach of Congress's Property Clause power over non-federal lands generally involve regulation of activities on inholdings (tracts of nonfederal land entirely surrounded by federal land). Should a different test be employed if the federal government seeks to regulate conduct on non-federal lands outside the boundaries of a federal reservation? Could Congress regulate signs or billboards on non-federal land leading to national parks, because of their aesthetic impact on the park experience? Could it regulate sources of noise for the same reason? Could it regulate to prevent the filling of isolated wetlands on private land near a national park on the ground that those wetlands are useful to sustain natural systems found in the park? Could Congress use the Property Clause to prohibit all hunting of migrating animals whose habitat is on the public lands only during certain seasons of the year? Some recent Supreme Court decisions suggest that Congress's power under the Commerce Clause to reach as far as these hypotheticals is doubtful. To the extent that is true, can the Property Clause be used to fill the gap?

8. Consider the following problem: Chaco Culture National Historic Park seeks to provide visitors with the experience of how the ancient cliff and canyon dwellers lived hundreds of years ago in the Southwest. As part of protecting the historic and educational qualities of the park, the Park Service seeks to keep the nighttime sky dark and the dazzling star show visible. The Service regards unlighted night skies as key to protecting the attributes for which Congress protected the area: a place that retains ancient qualities. Recent suburban and exurban development around Albuquerque has created light pollution. That is, residential and street lighting is creating a glow in Chaco that extinguishes many of the dimmer stars and detracts from the remote and timeless qualities of the park. Unlike the air pollution that reduces daytime visibility at national parks, Congress has never regulated the source of light pollution under the Commerce Clause. May Congress respond to this concern by enacting legislation under the property clause that places restrictions on the design, placement and operation of lighting in the counties near the park? What findings would you put in such legislation, if you were drafting it for Congress?

D. OTHER CONSTITUTIONAL AUTHORITIES OVER FEDERAL LANDS AND NATURAL RESOURCES

Although the Property Clause would appear to provide an ample basis for a vast array of legislation relating to lands and natural resources owned by the United States, federal authority to regulate activities on or off federal lands may also be found in the Commerce, Spending, and Treaty Clauses. Sometimes the courts address these constitutional powers in contexts relevant to federal natural resources. For example, Congress's authority over interstate commerce includes federal control of navigation, which has been held sufficient to support federal hydropower licenses issued in contravention of state law. First Iowa Hydro–Elec. Co–op. v. FPC, 328 U.S. 152 (1946). The spending power has been used to justify such things as federal water projects to promote the general welfare, especially in the West. United States v. Gerlach Live Stock Co., 339 U.S. 725 (1950).

The treaty power supports a general exercise of federal power off as well as on public lands, and has been repeatedly exercised in connection with wildlife and water resources. In the landmark case of Missouri v. Holland, 252 U.S. 416 (1920), the Court upheld the 1918 Migratory Bird Treaty Act, which had been adopted to implement a 1916 treaty with Great Britain (on behalf of Canada). Missouri challenged the legislation as an interference with state authority and beyond the power of Congress to enact. Justice Holmes's characteristically terse opinion explained:

> The State * * * founds its claim of exclusive authority upon an assertion of title to migratory birds, an assertion that is embodied in [state] statute. No doubt it is true that as between a State and its inhabitants the State may regulate the killing and sale of such birds, but it does not follow that its authority is exclusive of paramount powers. To put the claim of the State upon title is to lean upon a slender reed. Wild birds are not in the possession of anyone; and possession is the beginning of ownership. The whole foundation of the State's rights is the presence within their jurisdiction of birds that yesterday had not arrived, tomorrow may be in another State and in a week a thousand miles away. * * *
>
> Here a national interest of very nearly the first magnitude is involved. It can be protected only by national action in concert with that of another power. The subject matter is only transitorily within the State and has no permanent habitat therein. But for the treaty and the statute there soon might be no birds for any powers to deal with. We see nothing in the Constitution that compels the Government to sit by while a food supply is cut off and the protectors of our forests and our crops are destroyed. It is not sufficient to rely upon the States. The reliance is vain, and were it otherwise, the question is whether the United States is forbidden to act.

Only eight years before *Holland*, the Court had struck down federal wildlife regulation on the ground that it interfered with the rights of states because they were then regarded as owning the wildlife within their borders. The Abby Dodge, 223 U.S. 166 (1912). Although *Holland* upheld Congress's power to regulate wildlife under the treaty power, since 1937 the Supreme Court's broad reading of the Commerce Clause as a source of congressional power has led to more reliance upon it to uphold federal regulation of wildlife. *See* Andrus v. Allard, 444 U.S. 51 (1979) (Migratory Bird Treaty Act also justified under the commerce clause).

In recent years the Supreme Court has fashioned limits on the Commerce Clause to overturn federal statutes. See United States v. Lopez, 514 U.S. 549 (1995) (Congress's Commerce Clause power exceeded when it made it a federal crime to possess a firearm within 500 feet of a school); United States v. Morrison, 529 U.S. 598 (2000) (same result when Congress provided a federal cause of action for damages to women harmed by acts of violence directed against them because of their gender). These decisions require that a regulated activity "substantially affect" interstate commerce before the activity is within Congress's power to regulate under the Commerce Clause.

To date these decisions have not had demonstrable impact in the wildlife context, albeit they have produced lower court decisions where judges have rather bitterly split on the question. *See* National Assoc. of Home Builders v. Babbitt, 130 F.3d 1041 (D.C. Cir. 1997) (Endangered Species Act's application to protect a species of fly with a small, wholly intrastate habitat was within Congress's constitutional power to regulate interstate commerce); Gibbs v. Babbitt, 214 F.3d 483 (4th Cir. 2000) (same result with respect to prohibition of taking endangered red wolf on private land, with Judge Luttig explicitly acknowledging in a dissent that Congress "could plainly regulate" in the area of endangered species under the Property Clause, at 509); Rancho Viejo v. Norton, 323 F.3d 1062 (D.C. Cir. 2003), *reh'g en banc denied*, 334 F.3d 1158, 1160 (D.C. Cir. 2003) (Roberts, J.'s dissent from the denial of rehearing en banc, referring to the "hapless toad"—the species involved—became an issue in his confirmation hearings for Chief Justice of the United States); GDF Realty Investments, Ltd. v. Norton, 326 F.3D 622 (5th Cir. 2003), *reh'g en banc denied*, 362 F.3d 286 (5th Cir. 2004) (six judges dissenting). The Supreme Court's more recent decision in Gonzales v. Raich, 545 U.S. 1 (2005), seems to open the way to ending the argument because it reaffirms the expansive New Deal decision, Wickard v. Filburn, 317 U.S. 111 (1942), and holds that Congress may regulate small isolated instances relatively unconnected with interstate commerce as part of a large, comprehensive regulatory scheme. *See* Michael C. Blumm and George Kimbrell, *Gonzalez v. Raich, the Comprehensive Scheme Principle, and the Constitutionality of the Endangered Species Act*, 35 ENVTL. L. 491 (2005).

In a related development, the Court has invoked constitutional concerns about federalism to construe federal environmental regulatory statutes narrowly. *See* Rapanos v. United States, 126 S. Ct. 2208 (2006) (Justice Kennedy's concurrence providing a plurality for remand requiring site-specific evaluation of wetlands to determine whether they have a "significant nexus" to navigable waters); Solid Waste Agency of Northern Cook County v. U.S. Army Corps of Engineers, 531 U.S. 159 (2001) (rejecting a broad interpretation of Clean Water Act where it "would result in a significant impingement of the State's traditional and primary power over land and water use"). Whether this approach to statutory construction will have impact in the field of federal land and natural resources law remains to be seen.

NOTES AND QUESTIONS

1.   Could Congress's power to "regulate Commerce * * * among the several States," U.S. Const., Art. I, § 8, justify the Wild Horse and Burro Act? Is it easier or harder to justify it under the Commerce as opposed to the Property Clause? *Cf.* Columbia River Gorge United—Protecting People and Property v. Yeutter, 960 F.2d 110, 113–14 (9th Cir. 1992) (federal legislation authorizing the establishment of a bi-state commission to regu-

late land use along the scenic Columbia River Gorge, which includes federal, state, and private lands along the river, was upheld under the Commerce Clause, the court noting that the Property Clause might also have been used, although it did not decide that question).

2.   As the Supreme Court narrows Congress's power under the Commerce Clause in decisions such as *Lopez* and *Morrison*, might the Property Clause emerge as a useful source of authority for regulatory schemes that are connected in some way to federal lands, that might be beyond Congress's authority under the Commerce Clause? *See* Peter Appel, *The Power of Congress "Without Limitation": The Property Clause and Federal Regulation of Private Property*, 86 MINN. L.REV. 1, 122 (2001) ("Congress could prohibit individuals from harming endangered and threatened species off federal property if members of those species sometimes occupy federal lands and if Congress reasonably concludes that extraterritorial preservation of such species preserves the overall value of federal lands"); Holly Doremus, *Patching the Ark: Improving Legal Protection of Biological Diversity*, 18 ECOLOGY L.Q. 265, 292 (1991) (*Kleppe*'s reasoning "could justify federal protection of virtually any biological resource"). Could the Congress simply declare that listed endangered species are the property of the United States, and invoke the Property Clause to justify protecting them? What about using the Property Clause to prohibit the destruction of wetlands on private lands on which migratory birds rely, if those birds also use federal lands? How strong a showing would Congress have to make of the value of the migratory birds to the federal lands and resources, and of the value of the wetlands sought to be protected to the migratory birds, in order to use the Property Clause?

3.   Suppose the United States entered into a treaty with other countries in which mutual commitments were made to protect endangered species within each signatory nation's borders. Would that support enactment of the domestic Endangered Species Act to protect species that might not be protected under the Commerce Clause? Even if those species don't cross international boundaries? Is it sufficient that the treaty be aimed at the preservation of all species as a common heritage of mankind?

E.   FEDERAL PREEMPTION

The Constitution's Supremacy Clause, Article VI, clause 2, protects federal action authorized by the Constitution from interference by state law. Generally, in this context, local law is regarded as standing on the same footing as state law, although Congress may choose to preempt one and not the other. Sometimes Congress specifically and unequivocally addresses the extent to which state law is preempted in any given circumstance. When that happens, the result is foregone; if Congress says that state law is preempted, that ends the matter.

Much more often, however, a congressional intent regarding preemption of state law is simply not clear on the face of federal statutes or in their legislative history. In these situations, preemption depends on determining whether, under the circumstances of the particular case, the state law "stands as an obstacle to the accomplishment and execution of the full purposes and objectives of Congress." Hines v. Davidowitz, 312 U.S. 52 (1941). Courts tend to use one of two modes of inquiry in determining whether state laws are preempted. One is to examine whether Congress has occupied the regulatory field, leaving no room for state law to operate. This may be found where the federal regulation is "so pervasive as to make reasonable the inference that Congress left no room for the States to supplement it. Or the Act of Congress may touch a field in which the federal interest is so dominant that the federal system will be assumed to preclude enforcement of state laws on the same subject." Rice v. Santa Fe Elevator Corp., 331 U.S. 218 (1947). In most traditionally federal areas or areas where uniform national regulation is important, such as aliens, navigation, Indian affairs, labor, and civil rights, the Supreme Court has been quick to find preemption. *See generally* Laurence Tribe, American Constitutional Law 1174–79, 1204–1212 (3d ed. 2000). Federal lands have never been regarded as such an area. Indeed, state law has always played an important role, applying to much private activity on federal lands.

Therefore, in public land and resources law, the dominant mode of inquiry is the other mode: whether Congress intended to preempt state law in a particular context. In Kleppe v. New Mexico, the conflict between state and federal law was irreconcilable: New Mexico law provided that the burros could be rounded up, sold, and killed, while federal law prohibited harassment, sale, or killing. Seldom is the incompatibility so clear-cut. In most cases, Congress has been at least somewhat solicitous of state sensibilities when enacting laws governing federal lands. Sometimes, in fact, Congress cannot reach a consensus on the extent to which state law should be preempted. In such circumstances, it often resorts to a favorite device of negotiators and drafters; namely, papering over the lack of agreement by either silence or ambiguity. This leaves the question of preemption for the courts to resolve. Moreover, as a practical matter, it is difficult for Congress to anticipate and provide clear answers on the role of state law in individual settings, particularly in complex, generic legislation. In these instances, which are probably at least as numerous as those in which Congress provides clear answers, the compatibility of federal and state law becomes more difficult to determine.

As *Kleppe* shows, there is no doubt Congress can preempt state authority on the public lands. The more frequent and vexing question is whether, in particular contexts, Congress intended to do so. The following cases explore that question.

Ventura County v. Gulf Oil Corp.

United States Court of Appeals, Ninth Circuit, 1979
601 F.2d 1080, *affirmed without opinion*, 445 U.S. 947 (1980)

■ Judge Hufstedler

The question on appeal is whether the County of Ventura ("Ventura") can require the federal Government's lessee, Gulf Oil Corporation ("Gulf"), to obtain a permit from Ventura in compliance with Ventura's zoning ordinances governing oil exploration and extraction activities before Gulf can exercise its rights under the lease and drilling permits acquired from the Government. The district court denied Ventura's motion for a preliminary injunction, and dismissed Ventura's second amended complaint. Ventura appeals. * * *

On January 1, 1974, the Department of the Interior, Bureau of Land Management, pursuant to the Mineral Lands Leasing Act of 1920 (30 U.S.C. §§ 181 et seq.), leased 120 acres located within the Los Padres National Forest in Ventura for purposes of oil exploration and development. * * * [Gulf's proposal to drill an oil well on the lease had been approved by the Geological Survey, Department of the Interior; the Forest Service; and the Oil & Gas Division of the State of California Resources Agency. D]rilling operations were commenced on April 28, 1976 * * *.

Throughout this period the leased property has been zoned Open Space ("O–S") by Ventura. Under its zoning ordinance, oil exploration and extraction activities are prohibited on O–S property unless an Open Space Use Permit is obtained from the Ventura County Planning Commission in accordance with Articles 25 and 43 of the Ventura County Ordinance Code. The O–S Use Permits are granted for such time and upon such conditions as the Planning Commission considers in the public interest. The permits contain 11 mandatory conditions and additional conditions are committed to the Planning Board's discretion.

On May 5, 1976, Ventura advised Gulf that it must obtain an O–S Use Permit if it wished to continue its drilling operations. Gulf refused to comply, and on May 20, 1976, Ventura brought suit * * *.

Although Ventura and amicus argue extensively that congressional enactments under the Property Clause generally possess no preemptive capability, we believe that Kleppe v. New Mexico (1976) 426 U.S. 529, is dispositive. * * * In light of *Kleppe,* the renewed attempt to restrict the scope of congressional power under the Property Clause in the present case is legally frivolous.

Ventura next contends that even if Congress had the power to enact overriding legislation, there is no evidence of either a congressional intent to preempt local regulation or a conflict between local and federal law that can be resolved only by exclusion of local jurisdiction. We need not consider the extent to which local regulation of any aspect of oil exploration and extraction upon federal lands is precluded by federal legislation; the local ordinances impermissibly conflict with the Mineral Lands Leasing Act of 1920 and on this basis alone they cannot be applied to Gulf.

The extensive regulation of oil exploration and drilling under the Mineral Leasing Act is evident from the present record. The basic lease assigned to Gulf in 1974 contains approximately 45 paragraphs including requirements of diligence and protection of the environment as well as reservation of a one-eighth royalty interest in the United States. Because the lands lie within a National Forest, the lease requires Gulf's acceptance of additional Department of Agriculture conditions designed to combat the environmental hazards normally incident to mining operations. Specific drilling permits were also required from the Department of the Interior, Geological Survey, and the Department of Agriculture, Forest Service. The Geological Survey * * * approved the proposed drilling on February 25, 1976, subject to 10 conditions which assure continued and detailed supervision of Gulf's activities. And on March 8, and April 15, 1976, the Forest Service issued a drilling permit subject to conditions focusing upon protection of the National Forest. Finally, Gulf is subject to the extensive regulations governing oil and gas leasing (43 C.F.R., Part 3100) and both sub-surface and surface operations (30 C.F.R., Part 221) promulgated by the Secretary of the Interior under his authority "to prescribe necessary and proper rules and regulations to do any and all things necessary to carry out and accomplish the purposes" of the act. (30 U.S.C. § 189.) And since the lease concerns lands within a National Forest, Secretary of Agriculture regulations governing oil and gas development are also applicable. (36 C.F.R., Part 252.)

Despite this extensive federal scheme reflecting concern for the local environment as well as development of the nation's resources, Ventura demands a right of final approval. Ventura seeks to prohibit further activity by Gulf until it secures an Open Space Use Permit which may be issued on whatever conditions Ventura determines appropriate, or which may never be issued at all. The federal Government has authorized a specific use of federal lands, and Ventura cannot prohibit that use, either temporarily or permanently, in an attempt to substitute its judgment for that of Congress.

The present conflict is no less direct than that in Kleppe v. New Mexico, supra. Like *Kleppe,* our case involves a power struggle between local and federal governments concerning appropriate use of the public lands. That the New Mexico authorities wished to engage in activity that Congress prohibited, while the Ventura authorities wish to regulate conduct which Congress has authorized is a distinction without a legal difference. * * *

Ventura * * * [relies on] reservations of local jurisdiction contained in sections 30 and 32 of the Mineral Lands Leasing Act (30 U.S.C. §§ 187, 189).[4] It contends that * * * [a finding of preemption] is unwarranted

---

4. Before its 1978 amendment, section 30 provided in pertinent part:

"Each lease shall contain provisions for the purpose of insuring the exercise of reasonable diligence, skill, and care in the operation of said property; * * * [provisions for worker safety and welfare, for the prevention of 'undue waste' and several other subjects] * * * and such other provisions as he may deem necessary to insure the sale of the production of such leased lands to the United States and to the public at reasonable prices, for the protection of the interests of the United States, for the prevention of monopoly, and for the safeguarding of the public welfare. None of such provisions shall be in conflict with the laws of the states in which the leased property is situated."

Section 32 provides:

"The Secretary of the Interior is authorized to prescribe necessary and proper rules and regulations and to do any and all things necessary to carry out and accomplish the purposes of this chapter * * *. Nothing in this chapter shall be construed or held to affect the rights of the States or other local authority to exercise any rights which they may have, including the right to levy and collect taxes upon improvements, output of mines, or other rights, property, or assets of any lessee of the United States."

given the broad savings provisions contained in the Mineral Lands Leasing Act.

The proviso in § 187 [section 30] provides that "[n]one of *such provisions* shall be in conflict with the laws of the states in which the leased property is situated." (30 U.S.C. § 187.) But, as Gulf points out, by the use of the language "such provisions," the proviso relates only to the provisions of the preceding sentence. These provisions relate to employment practices, prevention of undue waste and monopoly, and diligence requirements. There is no mention of land use planning controls. Moreover, the proviso assures only that the Secretary of the Interior shall observe state standards in drafting the lease's terms. It is not a recognition of concurrent state jurisdiction.

Nor is the savings clause in § 189 [section 32] of any avail. * * * The proviso preserves to the states only "any rights which they may have." While this is an express recognition of the right of the states to tax activities of the Government's lessee pursuant to its lease and has been relied upon in part to uphold forced pooling and well spacing of federal mineral lessee operations, the proviso cannot give authority to the state which it does not already possess. Although state law may apply where it presents "no significant threat to any identifiable federal policy or interest," the states and their subdivisions have no right to apply local regulations impermissibly conflicting with achievement of a congressionally approved use of federal lands and the proviso of § 189 does not alter this principle.

Finally, we are reassured in the correctness of our decision by policy considerations implicitly reflected in the structure and operation of the Mineral Lands Leasing Act of 1920 and the National Environmental Policy Act of 1969 (42 U.S.C. §§ 4321 et seq.). As Ventura recognized in filing its second amended complaint, the National Environmental Protection [sic] Act ("NEPA") and the guidelines, regulations, and Executive Orders issued in pursuance of that act, mandate extensive federal consideration and federal-local cooperation concerning the local, environmental impact of federal action under the Mineral Lands Leasing Act. If federal officials fail to comply with these requirements, Ventura has a remedy against those officials.

Our decision does not mean that local interests will be unheard or unprotected. In rejecting a local veto power while simultaneously guarding local concerns under NEPA, local interests can be represented, the integrity of the federal leases and drilling permits reconciling national energy needs and local environmental interests can be protected, and the ultimate lessee will be responsible to a single master rather than conflicting authority.

Although we recognize that federal incursions upon the historic police power of the states are not to be found without good cause * * * we must affirm because "under the circumstances of this particular case, [the local ordinances] stand as an obstacle to the accomplishment and execution of the full purposes and objectives of Congress." (Hines v. Davidowitz (1941) 312 U.S. 52, 67 * * *). "[W]here those state laws conflict * * * with other legislation passed pursuant to the Property Clause, the law is clear: The state laws must recede." (Kleppe v. New Mexico. * * *)

AFFIRMED.

NOTES AND QUESTIONS

1.   Does the Ninth Circuit here correctly construe section 30 of the Mineral Leasing Act (quoted in footnote 4 of its opinion)? Shouldn't state or local land use laws be regarded as intended to promote "safeguarding of the public welfare"? If so, does the last sentence of section 30 preserve the applicability of such laws to federal mineral leases?

2.   Does section 30 authorize the Secretary to include in a mineral lease a clause expressly requiring the lessee to comply with state and local laws? Could the Secretary, in other words, reverse the outcome of this case by her choice of lease terms? Can the Secretary do this even if it makes the lessee responsible to possibly "conflicting authority" rather than a "single master," in the words of the *Ventura County* opinion?

3.   Conversely, if the Mineral Leasing Act had been construed as ambiguous on the preemption issue, could the Secretary have preempted state law by including a provision in the lease that said the lessee did *not* have to comply with state or local land use laws? While federal preemption is often, as here, found in statutes themselves, the Supreme Court has recognized that "agency regulations implementing federal statutes have been held to pre-empt state law under the Supremacy Clause," Chrysler Corp. v. Brown, 441 U.S. 281, 295–96 (1979), if the agency is acting within the scope of authority delegated to it by the Congress. Should the courts give stricter scrutiny to preemption claims arising from an agency regulation rather than from a statute?

4.   In Gulf Oil Corp. v. Wyoming Oil & Gas Conservation Comm'n, 693 P.2d 227 (Wyo. 1985), decided after *Ventura County*, the Wyoming Supreme Court held that a decision by the state regulatory commission to issue Gulf a permit to drill a well on national forest land Gulf had leased from the federal government, subject to the condition that Gulf refrain from using its preferred access route to the well site, was not preempted by federal law. The Commission had rejected the route—which would have extended an existing county road for about 3.8 miles over national forest land and private land—in part because of its aesthetic impacts and lack of reclaimability. Relying on the same two sections of the Mineral Leasing Act as involved in *Ventura County*, the Wyoming court distinguished the Ninth Circuit's reasoning this way:

> In contrast to the zoning ordinance[] at issue in *Ventura County*, [state] mining permit requirements designed to safeguard the environment * * * constitute legitimate means of guiding mineral development [on federal lands] without prohibiting it. * * * [W]e find no intent by Congress to exclude states from regulating mining activities

on federal land so as to safeguard environmental values. Neither do we find a direct conflict between [the Commission order] and federal laws or objectives.

5.   Section 32 of the Mineral Leasing Act was before the U.S. Supreme Court in Commonwealth Edison Co. v. Montana, 453 U.S. 609 (1981). At issue was whether Montana's sizeable severance tax on coal production could be applied to federal coal production within the state. After rejecting the argument of the coal producers and their out-of-state utility customers that the tax placed an impermissible burden on interstate commerce, the majority held that section 32 "expressly authorized the States to impose severance taxes on federal lessees without imposing any limits on the amount of such taxes." It found "nothing in language or legislative history" of the Act to support the assertion that Congress "intended to maximize and capture *all* 'economic rents' from the mining of federal coal * * *. By definition, any state taxation of federal lessees reduces the 'economic rents' accruing to the Federal Government, and appellants' argument would preclude any such taxes despite the explicit grant of taxing authority to the States by § 32." Justice Blackmun, joined by Justices Powell and Stevens, dissented, but only on commerce clause grounds. Does section 32's specific reservation of any rights the state "may have" to tax the "output of mines" leased under the Act provide a stronger basis for finding no preemption of state taxes than section 30 provides for state environmental regulation? If so, could Ventura Co. achieve its objectives by charging a "user tax" pegged to the degree of environmental adverse impact?

6.   Determining whether federal statutes preempt sometimes requires very close reading. Does Section 32, for example, answer the question what rights the states have to tax the output of federal mines, or does it just preserve whatever rights the states had before enactment of the Mineral Leasing Act (which may be none)?

7.   Even where Congress seems to address preemption head-on in a statute, the results may be debatable. Remember that Congress will often have a political motive not to resolve the question clearly. Members of Congress may be split on whether preemption is a good idea. Or Congress may simply be unable or unwilling to examine all the different state laws that might be applied, and decide the extent to which they should apply. The result might be a studied effort to leave, as Yogi Berra allegedly said, the status quo right where it is. Consider, for example: "Nothing in this Act shall be construed as limiting or restricting the power and authority of the United States or * * * as expanding or diminishing Federal or State jurisdiction, responsibility, interests, or rights in water resources development or control." FLPMA, § 701(g), 43 U.S.C. § 1702 Note. Or the following, which appears in several federal laws: "Nothing in this Act shall constitute an express or implied claim or denial on the part of the Federal Government as to exemption from State water laws." *See, e.g.,* 16 U.S.C. § 668dd(j). What does such language say about the application of state law to water found on federal lands? In United States v. Vesterso, 828 F.2d 1234, 1240 (8th Cir. 1987), the court concluded that the phrase "or denial"

in this disclaimer allows a finding that state water law is preempted in a particular situation. Taken as a whole, then, the disclaimer "is not to be interpreted as changing the body of law which interprets the interaction of federal and state interests in water." *Id.*, at note 5. (The general issue of the applicability of state water law to federal lands is explored in Chapter 6.)

8. Ventura County continued in its attempts to influence oil and gas leasing on federal lands, but to little avail. Most recently, the Ventura County Board of Supervisors voted in 2005 to oppose more oil and gas leasing in the Los Padres National Forest. This time around it had the support of the state attorney general, who joined several environmental groups in filing an administrative appeal to the leasing decision. The leases covered several roadless areas and were close to recovery sites for the endangered California condor. The Forest Service rejected the appeal in 2006.

The following preemption case also involved mineral activity on national forest land in California, but this time under a different statutory scheme, and with a different result.

California Coastal Commission v. Granite Rock Co.

Supreme Court of the United States, 1987.
480 U.S. 572.

■ JUSTICE O'CONNOR delivered the opinion of the Court.

This case presents the question whether Forest Service regulations, federal land use statutes and regulations, or the Coastal Zone Management Act of 1972 (CZMA), 16 U.S.C. § 1451 et seq. pre-empt the California Coastal Commission's imposition of a permit requirement on operation of an unpatented mining claim in a national forest.

Granite Rock Company is a privately owned firm that mines chemical and pharmaceutical grade white limestone. Under the Mining Act of 1872, 17 Stat. 91, as amended, 30 U.S.C. § 22 et seq., a private citizen may enter federal lands to explore for mineral deposits. If a person locates a valuable mineral deposit on federal land, and perfects the claim by properly staking it and complying with other statutory requirements, the claimant "shall have the exclusive right of possession and enjoyment of all the surface included within the lines of their locations," 30 U.S.C. § 26, although the United States retains title to the land. The holder of a perfected mining claim may secure a patent to the land by complying with the requirements of the Mining Act and regulations promulgated thereunder, see 43 CFR § 3861.1 et seq.(1986), and, upon issuance of the patent, legal title to the land passes to the patent holder. Granite Rock holds unpatented mining claims on federally owned lands on and around Mount Pico Blanco in the Big Sur region of Los Padres National Forest.

From 1959 to 1980, Granite Rock removed small samples of limestone from this area for mineral analysis. In 1980, in accordance with federal regulations, see 36 CFR § 228.1 et seq. (1986), Granite Rock submitted to the Forest Service a 5–year plan of operations for the removal of substantial amounts of limestone. The plan discussed the location and appearance of the mining operation, including the size and shape of excavations, the location of all access roads, and the storage of any overburden. The Forest Service prepared an Environmental Assessment of the plan. The Assessment recommended modifications of the plan, and the responsible Forest Service Acting District Ranger approved the plan with the recommended modifications in 1981. Shortly after Forest Service approval of the modified plan of operations, Granite Rock began to mine.

Under the California Coastal Act (CCA), Cal. Pub. Res. Code Ann. § 30000 et seq. (West 1986), any person undertaking any development, including mining, in the State's coastal zone must secure a permit from the California Coastal Commission. §§ 30106, 30600. According to the CCA, the Coastal Commission exercises the State's police power and constitutes the State's coastal zone management program for purposes of the federal CZMA. In 1983 the Coastal Commission instructed Granite Rock to apply for a coastal development permit for any mining undertaken after the date of the Commission's letter.

Granite Rock immediately filed an action in the United States District Court for the Northern District of California seeking to enjoin officials of the Coastal Commission from compelling Granite Rock to comply with the Coastal Commission permit requirement * * *.

Granite Rock does not argue that the Coastal Commission has placed any particular conditions on the issuance of a permit that conflict with federal statutes or regulations. Indeed, the record does not disclose what conditions the Coastal Commission will place on the issuance of a permit. Rather, Granite Rock argues, as it must given the posture of the case, that there is no possible set of conditions the Coastal Commission could place on its permit that would not conflict with federal law—that any state permit requirement is *per se* pre-empted. The only issue in this case is this purely facial challenge to the Coastal Commission permit requirement. * * *

Granite Rock and the Solicitor General as amicus [on behalf of the United States] have made basically three arguments in support of a finding that any possible state permit requirement would be pre-empted. First, Granite Rock alleges that the Federal Government's environmental regulation of unpatented mining claims in national forests demonstrates an intent to pre-empt any state regulation. Second, Granite Rock and the Solicitor General assert that indications that state land use planning over unpatented mining claims in national forests is pre-empted should lead to the conclusion that the Coastal Commission permit requirement is pre-empted. Finally, Granite Rock and the Solicitor General assert that the CZMA, by excluding federal lands from its definition of the coastal zone, declared a legislative intent that federal lands be excluded from all state coastal zone regulation. We conclude that these federal statutes and regulations do not, either independently or in combination, justify a facial challenge to the Coastal Commission permit requirement.

Granite Rock concedes that the Mining Act of 1872, as originally passed, expressed no legislative intent on the as yet rarely contemplated subject of environmental regulation. * * * [In an 1897 statute] Congress has delegated to the Secretary of Agriculture the authority to make "rules and regulations" to "regulate [the] occupancy and use" of national forests. 16 U.S.C. § 551. Through this delegation of authority, the Department of Agriculture's Forest Service has promulgated regulations so that "use of the surface of National Forest System lands" by those such as Granite Rock, who have unpatented mining claims authorized by the Mining Act of 1872, "shall be conducted so as to minimize adverse environmental impacts on National Forest System surface resources." 36 CFR §§ 228.1, 228.3(d) (1986). It was pursuant to these regulations that the Forest Service approved the Plan of Operations submitted by Granite Rock. If, as Granite Rock claims, it is the federal intent that Granite Rock conduct its mining unhindered by any state environmental regulation, one would expect to find the expression of this intent in these Forest Service regulations. * * *

Upon examination, however, the Forest Service regulations that Granite Rock alleges pre-empt any state permit requirement not only are devoid of any expression of intent to pre-empt state law, but rather appear to assume that those submitting plans of operations will comply with state laws. The regulations explicitly require all operators within the national forests to comply with state air quality standards, 36 CFR § 228.8(a) (1986), state water quality standards, § 228.8(b), and state standards for the disposal and treatment of solid wastes, § 228.8(c). The regulations also provide that, pending final approval of the plan of operations, the Forest Service officer with authority to approve plans of operation "will approve such operations as may be necessary for timely compliance with the requirements of Federal and *State laws* * * *." § 228.5(b) (emphasis added). Finally, the final subsection of § 228.8, "[r]equirements for environmental protection," provides:

> "(h) Certification or other approval issued by *State agencies* or other Federal agencies of compliance with laws and regulations relation to mining operations will be accepted as compliance with similar or parallel requirements of these regulations" (emphasis supplied).

It is impossible to divine from these regulations, which expressly contemplate coincident compliance with state law as well as with federal law, an intention to pre-empt all state regulation of unpatented mining claims in national forests. Neither Granite Rock nor the Solicitor General contends that these Forest Service regulations are inconsistent with their authorizing statutes.

Given these Forest Service regulations, it is unsurprising that the Forest Service team that prepared the Environmental Assessment of Granite Rock's plan of operation, as well as the Forest Service officer that approved the plan of operation, expected compliance with state as well as federal law. The Los Padres National Forest Environmental Assessment of the Granite Rock plan stated that "Granite Rock is responsible for obtaining any necessary permits which may be required by the California Coastal Commission." The Decision Notice and Finding of No Significant Impact issued by the Acting District Ranger accepted Granite Rock's plan of operation with modifications, [and stated that] * * * "[t]he claimant is further responsible for obtaining any necessary permits required by State and/or county laws, regulations and/or ordinance."

The second argument proposed by Granite Rock is that federal land management statutes demonstrate a legislative intent to limit States to a purely advisory role in federal land management decisions, and that the Coastal Commission permit requirement is therefore pre-empted as an impermissible state land use regulation.

In 1976 two pieces of legislation were passed that called for the development of federal land use management plans affecting unpatented mining claims in national forests. Under the Federal Land Policy and Management Act of 1976 (FLPMA), 43 U.S.C. § 1701 et seq., the Department of the Interior's Bureau of Land Management is responsible for managing the mineral resources on federal forest lands; under the National Forest Management Act (NFMA), 16 U.S.C. §§ 1600–1614, the Forest Service under the Secretary of Agriculture is responsible for the management of the surface impacts of mining on federal forest lands. Granite Rock, as well as the Solicitor General, point to aspects of these statutes indicating a legislative intent to limit States to an advisory role in federal land management decisions. For example, the NFMA directs the Secretary of Agriculture to "develop, maintain, and, as appropriate, revise land and resource management plans for units of the National Forest System, coordinated with the land and resource management planning processes of State and local governments and other Federal agencies," 16 U.S.C. § 1604(a). The FLPMA directs that land use plans developed by the Secretary of the Interior "shall be consistent with State and local plans to the maximum extent [the Secretary] finds consistent with Federal law," and calls for the Secretary, "to the extent he finds practical," to keep apprised of state land use plans, and to "assist in resolving, to the extent practical, inconsistencies between Federal and non-Federal Government plans." 43 U.S.C. § 1712(c)(9).

For purposes of this discussion and without deciding this issue, we may assume that the combination of the NFMA and the FLPMA pre-empts the extension of state land use plans onto unpatented mining claims in national forest lands. The Coastal Commission asserts that it will use permit conditions to impose environmental regulation. See Cal. Pub. Res. Code Ann. § 30233 (West 1986) (quality of coastal waters); § 30253(2) (erosion); § 30253(3) (air pollution); § 30240(b) (impact on environmentally sensitive habitat areas).

While the CCA gives land use as well as environmental regulatory authority to the Coastal Commission, the state statute also gives the Coastal Commission the ability to limit the requirements it will place on the permit. The CCA declares that the Coastal Commission will "provide maximum state involvement in federal activities allowable under federal law or regulations * * *." Cal. Pub. Res. Code Ann. § 30004 (West 1986).

Since the state statute does not detail exactly what state standards will and will not apply in connection with various federal activities, the statute must be understood to allow the Coastal Commission to limit the regulations it will impose in those circumstances. In the present case, the Coastal Commission has consistently maintained that it does not seek to prohibit mining of the unpatented claim on national forest land. See 590 F. Supp. at 1373 ("The [Commission] seeks not to prohibit or 'veto,' but to regulate [Granite Rock's] mining activity in accordance with the detailed requirements of the CCA * * *. There is no reason to find that the [Commission] will apply the CCA's regulations so as to deprive [Granite Rock] of its rights under the Mining Act"); "[T]he question presented is merely whether the state can *regulate* uses rather than *prohibit* them. Put another way, the state is not seeking to *determine* basic uses of federal land: rather it is seeking to *regulate* a given mining use so that it is carried out in a more environmentally sensitive and resource-protective fashion".

The line between environmental regulation and land use planning will not always be bright; for example, one may hypothesize a state environmental regulation so severe that a particular land use would become commercially impracticable. However, the core activity described by each phrase is undoubtedly different. Land use planning in essence chooses particular uses for the land; environmental regulation, at its core, does not mandate particular uses of the land but requires only that, however the land is used, damage to the environment is kept within prescribed limits. Congress has indicated its understanding of land use planning and environmental regulation as distinct activities. As noted above, 43 U.S.C. § 1712(c)(9) requires that the Secretary of the Interior's land use plans be consistent with state plans only "to the extent he finds practical." The immediately preceding subsection, however, requires that the Secretary's land use plans "provide for compliance with applicable pollution control laws, including State and Federal air, water, noise, or other pollution standards or implementation plans." § 1712(c)(8). Congress has also illustrated its understanding of land use planning and environmental regulation as distinct activities by delegating the authority to regulate these activities to different agencies. The stated purpose of part 228, subpart A of the Forest Service regulations, 36 CFR § 228.1 (1986), is to "set forth rules and procedures" through which mining on unpatented claims in national forests "shall be conducted so as to minimize adverse environmental impacts on National Forest System surface resources." The next sentence of the subsection, however, declares that "[i]t is not the purpose of these regulations to provide for the management of mineral resources; the responsibility for managing such resources is in the Secretary of the Interior." Congress clearly envisioned that although environmental regulation and land use planning may hypothetically overlap in some instances, these two types of activity would in most cases be capable of differentiation. Considering the legislative understanding of environmental regulation and land use planning as distinct activities, it would be anomalous to maintain that Congress intended any state environmental regulation of unpatented mining claims in national forests to be *per se* pre-empted as an impermissible exercise of state land use planning. Congress' treatment of environmental regulation and land use planning as generally distinguishable calls for this Court to treat them as distinct, until an actual overlap between the two is demonstrated in a particular case.

Granite Rock suggests that the Coastal Commission's true purpose in enforcing a permit requirement is to prohibit Granite Rock's mining entirely. By choosing to seek injunctive and declaratory relief against the permit requirement before discovering what conditions the Coastal Commission would have placed on the permit, Granite Rock has lost the possibility of making this argument in this litigation. Granite Rock's case must stand or fall on the question whether *any possible* set of conditions attached to the Coastal Commission's permit requirement would be pre-empted. As noted in the previous section, the Forest Service regulations do not indicate a federal intent to pre-empt all state environmental regulation of unpatented mining claims in national forests. Whether or not state land use planning over unpatented mining claims in national forests is pre-empted, the Coastal Commission insists that its permit requirement is an exercise of environmental regulation rather than land use planning. In the present posture of this litigation, the Coastal Commission's identification of a possible set of permit conditions not pre-empted by federal law is sufficient to rebuff Granite Rock's facial challenge to the permit requirement. This analysis is not altered by the fact that the Coastal Commission chooses to impose its environmental regulation by means of a permit requirement. If the Federal Government occupied the field of environmental regulation of unpatented mining claims in national forests—concededly not the case—then state environmental regulation of Granite Rock's mining activity would be pre-empted, whether or not the regulation was implemented through a permit requirement. Conversely, if reasonable state environmental regulation is not pre-empted, then the use of a permit requirement to impose the state regulation does not create a conflict with federal law where none previously existed. The permit requirement itself is not talismanic.

* * *

Granite Rock's challenge to the California Coastal Commission's permit requirement was broad and absolute; our rejection of that challenge is correspondingly narrow. Granite Rock argued that any state permit requirement, whatever its conditions, was *per se* pre-empted by federal law. To defeat Granite Rock's facial challenge, the Coastal Commission needed merely to identify a possible set of permit conditions not in conflict with federal law. The Coastal Commission alleges that it will use its permit requirement to impose reasonable environmental regulation. Rather than evidencing an intent to pre-empt such state regulation, the Forest Service regulations appear to assume compliance with state laws. Federal land use statutes and regulations, while arguably expressing an intent to pre-empt state land use planning, distinguish environmental regulation from land use planning. Finally, the language and legislative history of the CZMA expressly disclaim an intent to pre-empt state regulation.

Following an examination of the "almost impenetrable maze of arguably relevant legislation," Justice Powell concludes that "[i]n view of the

Property Clause * * *, as well as common sense, federal authority must control * * *." As noted above, the Property Clause gives Congress plenary power over the federal land at issue; however, even within the sphere of the Property Clause, state law is pre-empted only when it conflicts with the operation or objectives of federal law, or when Congress "evidences an intent to occupy a given field," Silkwood v. Kerr–McGee Corp., 464 U.S., at 248. The suggestion that traditional pre-emption analysis is inapt in this context can be justified, if at all, only by the assertion that the state regulation in this case would be "duplicative." The description of the regulation as duplicative, of course, is based on Justice Powell's conclusions that land use regulation and environmental regulation are indistinguishable, and that any state permit requirement, by virtue of being a permit requirement rather than some other form of regulation, would duplicate federal permit requirements. Because we disagree with these assertions, we apply the traditional pre-emption analysis which requires an actual conflict between state and federal law, or a congressional expression of intent to pre-empt, before we will conclude that state regulation is pre-empted.

Contrary to the assertion of Justice Powell that the Court today gives States power to impose regulations that "conflict with the views of the Forest Service," we hold only that the barren record of this facial challenge has not demonstrated any conflict. We do not, of course, approve any future application of the Coastal Commission permit requirement that in fact conflicts with federal law. Neither do we take the course of condemning the permit requirement on the basis of as yet unidentifiable conflicts with the federal scheme. * * *

■ JUSTICE POWELL, with whom JUSTICE STEVENS joins, concurring in part and dissenting in part.

* * * The most troubling feature of the Court's analysis is that it is divorced from the realities of its holding. The Court cautions that its decision allows only "reasonable" environmental regulation and that it does not give the Coastal Commission a veto over Granite Rock's mining activities. But if the Coastal Commission can require Granite Rock to secure a permit before allowing mining operations to proceed, it necessarily can forbid Granite Rock from conducting these operations. It may be that reasonable environmental regulations would not force Granite Rock to close its mine. This misses the point. The troubling fact is that the Court has given a state authority—here the Coastal Commission—the power to prohibit Granite Rock from exercising the rights granted by its Forest Service permit. This abdication of federal control over the use of federal land is unprecedented. * * *

The dangers of duplicative permit requirements are evident in this case. The federal permit system reflects a careful balance between two important federal interests: the interest in developing mineral resources on federal land, and the interest in protecting our national forests from environmental harm. The Forest Service's issuance of a permit to Granite Rock reflects its conclusion that environmental concerns associated with Granite Rock's mine do not justify restricting mineral development on this portion of a federal forest. Allowing the Coastal Commission to strike a different balance necessarily conflicts with the federal system. * * *

In summary, it is fair to say that, commencing in 1872, Congress has created an almost impenetrable maze of arguably relevant legislation in no less than a half-dozen statutes, augmented by the regulations of two Departments of the Executive. There is little cause for wonder that the language of these statutes and regulations has generated considerable confusion. There is an evident need for Congress to enact a single, comprehensive statute for the regulation of federal lands.

Having said this, it is at least clear that duplicative federal and state permit requirements create an intolerable conflict in decisionmaking. In view of the Property Clause of the Constitution, as well as common sense, federal authority must control with respect to land "belonging to the United States." Yet, the Court's opinion today approves a system of twofold authority with respect to environmental matters. The result of this holding is that state regulators, whose views on environmental and mineral policy may conflict with the views of the Forest Service, have the power, with respect to federal lands, to forbid activity expressly authorized by the Forest Service. I dissent.

■ JUSTICE SCALIA, with whom JUSTICE WHITE joins, dissenting.

* * * It seems to me ultimately irrelevant whether state environmental regulation has been pre-empted with respect to federal lands, since the exercise of state power at issue here is not environmental regulation but land use control. * * * [The California Coastal Act] is plainly a land use statute, and the permit that statute requires Granite Rock to obtain is a land use control device. Its character as such is not altered by the fact that the State may now be agreeable to issuing it as long as environmental concerns are satisfied. Since, as the Court's opinion quite correctly assumes, state exercise of land use authority over federal lands is pre-empted by federal law, California's permit requirement must be invalid. * * *

Any competent lawyer, faced with a demand from the California Coastal Commission that Granite Rock obtain a * * * coastal development permit for its Pico Blanco operations, would have responded precisely as Granite Rock's lawyers essentially did: Our use of federal land has been approved by the Federal Government, thank you, and does not require the approval of the State. We should not allow California to claim, in the teeth of the plain language of its legislation, * * * that it would use the permitting requirement to achieve, not land use management, but only environmental controls. We should particularly not give ear to that claim since it was not the representation made to Granite Rock when application for the permit was demanded. If environmental control is, as California now assures us, its limited objective in this case, then it must simply achieve that objective by means other than a land use control scheme. If and when it does so, we may have occasion to decide (as we need not today) whether state environmental controls are also pre-empted. More likely, however, the question will not arise in the future, as it has not arisen in the past, because of the Federal Government's voluntary accommodation of state environmental concerns—an accommodation that could not occur

here only because California neglected to participate in the proceedings.
* * *

NOTES AND QUESTIONS

1.   *Ventura County* was summarily affirmed (without opinion) by the
Supreme Court eight years before it decided *Granite Rock*. Can the two
cases be reconciled? Surprisingly, in *Granite Rock* only Justice Scalia's
dissenting opinion even cited *Ventura County*, and that only in passing.
Preemption cases are tied to the facts and particular laws involved, but
should the Court in *Granite Rock* have addressed its recent decision in a
closely related context?

2.   Justice O'Connor suggests that if a state regulation is "environmental" rather than "land use" in character, it will not be preempted. Is
the difference between the two clear? Suppose, for example, that on remand
the state Coastal Commission issues Granite Rock a permit to mine, but
requires the mined land to be restored to its approximate original contour
and revegetated to preserve the aesthetics of the coastline. The company
objects, arguing that restoration is so expensive that to require it makes
mining uneconomic, and therefore the condition effectively prohibits mining. Is the condition an "environmental" or a "land use" regulation? Could
California, for example, argue that its public trust doctrine restricts the
Granite Rock Company's plans to open the mine? In other words, is the
state public trust doctrine environmental or land use regulation? Or, is it
an entirely different category of property right?

3.   Could a state interpret its common law of public nuisance to
prohibit this mining operation, on a suit by the state or local government?
(Or on behalf of an environmental group that could show "special injury"?)
In Geier v. American Honda Motor Co., 529 U.S. 861 (2000), the Supreme
Court held that a federal statute that mandated phase-in of auto air bags
preempted state common law negligence claims against auto manufacturers
who failed to install air bags earlier than mandated by the federal standards. The federal statute prohibited states from adopting their own
"safety standard" with respect to the "same aspect of performance" as the
federal standard, but also contained a savings clause providing that compliance with a federal safety standard did not "exempt any person from any
liability under common law."

5.   Note that the majority here only *assumes without deciding* that
FLPMA and the NFMA "preempts the extension of state land use plans
onto unpatented mining claims in national forest lands." On the basis of
the pertinent excerpts from these laws, is that assumption correct? Notice,
as Justice O'Connor's opinion reflects, FLPMA requires that the Secretary
of the Interior's land use plans be consistent with state land use plans "to
the extent he finds practical." 43 U.S.C. § 1712(c)(8). What kind of rea-
son(s) must a federal land manager have in order to defend a decision that
compliance with state land use plans is not "practical"? Modern federal
resource management laws often contain this notion of what has been
called "cooperative federalism," requiring federal land management agen-

cies to comply with state and local law to the maximum extent practicable in various contexts. *See* FLPMA, 43 U.S.C. §§ 1720, 1721(c), 1733(d), 1747, 1765(a); National Forest Management Act, 16 U.S.C. § 1612; Fish and Wildlife Coordination Act, 16 U.S.C. § 661.

6.   The Forest Service here said that Granite Rock is "responsible for obtaining any necessary permits which may be required by the California Coastal Commission." Is the Forest Service saying that it doesn't regard state law as being preempted? Is that what "necessary" means? Or is it saying Granite Rock must get a permit if (and only if) it is legally necessary? Another example of studied ambiguity on the preemption question is provided by 43 U.S.C. § 1712(c)(8), discussed in the majority opinion, which requires the Secretary's land use plans to "provide for compliance with *applicable*" state pollution standards and plans (emphasis added). What does this indicate, if anything, about which state standards and plans are "applicable"? All of them? If not all, which ones?

7.   In a sense, *Granite Rock* was a narrow decision; it decided only that the miner on federal land had to apply for a state permit. As a result, the Court did not address how far the state could go in regulating the mining activity through conditions or limitations placed on the permit. Nevertheless, by giving states the opportunity to apply their permit processes (and by burdening miners with that obligation), the decision significantly shifts regulatory leverage toward the states. Suppose, after this decision, Granite Rock applies to the Commission for a permit. Two years go by and the state is still sitting on the permit application. State law says no mining without a permit. Does the company have any recourse? What? (In fact, after the decision Granite Rock abandoned its plan to open the mine.)

8.   Could the Forest Service here have changed the outcome in the case by providing in its regulations for explicit preemption of state law? Or could it have explicitly preempted state law in either its land use plan for this area of the forest, or its decision approving the company's plan of operations under the regulations? United States v. Brown, 552 F.2d 817, 821 (8th Cir. 1977), *cert. denied*, 431 U.S. 949 (1977), upheld the conviction of a duck hunter for carrying firearms in a national park even though his conduct was lawful under state law. Congress had not spoken directly to the question of hunting in this national park, but Park Service regulations prohibited possession of firearms:

> The National Park Service Act allows the Secretary of the Interior to promulgate "such rules and regulations as he may deem necessary or proper for the use and management of the parks." 16 U.S.C. § 3. The regulations prohibiting hunting and possession of a loaded firearm were promulgated pursuant to that authority, 36 C.F.R. §§ 2.11 and 2.32, and are valid prescriptions designed to promote the purposes of the federal lands within the national park. Under the Supremacy Clause the federal law overrides the conflicting state law allowing hunting within the park.

9.   Would, in Justice Scalia's phrase, "[a]ny competent lawyer" have responded precisely as Granite Rock's lawyers did here, by bringing a facial

challenge to the Coastal Commission's attempt to exercise jurisdiction? Were there any alternative strategies that would, at least in hindsight, have been better? In the years since *Granite Rock*, the Court has repeatedly stressed the heavy burden faced by plaintiffs making facial challenges. *See e.g.*, Rust v. Sullivan, 500 U.S. 173 (1991). More so today than when *Ventura County* was decided, courts are hesitant to engage in the speculative steps of facial challenges, which lie outside of the traditional judicial function to apply law to specific facts.

10. Surprisingly, the Supreme Court did not cite in *Granite Rock* a number of state appellate court decisions that had found state environmental laws applicable to hardrock mining operations on the federal lands. *See* State ex rel. Andrus v. Click, 554 P.2d 969 (Idaho 1976). *But see* Brubaker v. Board of County Commissioners, El Paso County, 652 P.2d 1050 (Colo. 1982) (finding preemption of a county's denial of a zoning permit to conduct exploratory drilling on mining claims on federal land). A federal court later relied primarily on *Brubaker* to preempt a county ordinance that prohibited the issuance of all new surface mining permits in the scenic Spearfish Canyon area of the Black Hills National Forest. South Dakota Mining Ass'n. v. Lawrence County, 977 F. Supp. 1396 (D.S.D. 1997), *aff'd* 155 F.3d 1005 (8th Cir. 1998).

In 1998 Montana voters approved a state initiative which banned cyanide heap-leach gold mining operations throughout the state, including on federal lands, because of water quality concerns. The mining industry promptly challenged it in state and federal courts on a variety of grounds, including preemption. *See* Montana Chamber of Commerce v. Argenbright, 226 F.3d 1049 (9th Cir. 2000) (upholding the initiative election). The Montana Supreme Court held that the proposition did not constitute an unconstitutional regulatory taking. Seven Up Pete Venture v. Montana, 114 P.3d 1009 (Mont. 2005). The mining industry put a repeal of the 1998 initiative on the Montana ballot in the 2004 elections, but it lost decisively.

11. The federal government did not participate at all in *Ventura County*, and it participated only as *amicus* in *Granite Rock*. Why is the federal government frequently *not* a party to these preemption cases, even though management of its lands is directly affected? Further, in *Granite Rock*, why do you think the Reagan Administration argued in favor of preemption, given its strong rhetorical support for states' rights in many contexts?

12. Suppose that the mineral developers in both *Ventura County* and *Granite Rock* needed to locate certain processing and transportation facilities on *non-federal* land; e.g., a pipeline for oil and gas in the former, and a shipping facility for the limestone in the latter. Can the mineral developers rely on preemption of state or local law governing facility siting? If not, does this give state or local governments an effective, if somewhat more indirect, veto over the production of oil from federal lands?

13. Should Congress respond to Justice Powell's plea for a "single, comprehensive statute for the regulation of federal lands"? Why do you suppose it never has? Or should Congress or the courts establish general rules for the proper role for state and local governments on federal lands,

which would presumably vary with the subject-matter? For example, is the national interest in timber or minerals or energy stronger or weaker than the national interest in wildlife or recreation or livestock? Or should preemption turn on the character and strength of the states' interest? Is the state (or local) interest in environmental or consumer protection stronger or weaker than its interest in taxation or health and safety or law enforcement? Should the courts *presume* preemption when the pertinent statutes are unclear, or do the opposite? Because Congress has the ultimate power to draw lines here, should there be a bright-line judicial rule that in effect instructs Congress: "Be clear one way or we'll conclude the other"?

14.   Consider the following fact situations.

A.   The state of Oregon has just enacted a statute which includes a finding that over-grazing of cattle on arid lands can cause soil erosion and water pollution. The statute limits all grazing activities in the state to one cow per five acres per month. Hundreds of ranchers currently hold permits from the federal Bureau of Land Management (BLM) allowing the ranchers to graze their cattle on federal lands in excess of the limits set by the new state law. The federal statute authorizing the BLM to issue grazing permits states that it "neither diminishes nor enlarges" state authority on public lands. Other than that statement, the statute is silent on the issue of the application of state law. Does the new Oregon statutory limit on grazing apply to ranchers with federal permits?

B.   Clark County, Montana's comprehensive county land use plan prohibits oil/gas drilling within 500 feet of a church or school without a county-issued, special-use permit. Does this restriction apply to holders of federal permits allowing them to drill for federally owned oil/gas?

NOTE: A "DORMANT PROPERTY CLAUSE"?

Where title to land is concerned, a federal "common law" may override state property law in some instances, even when the U.S. acquires property whose characteristics of title had, until then, been fully controlled by state property law. In United States v. Little Lake Misere Land Co., 412 U.S. 580 (1973), the United States had acquired private land in Louisiana for a bird refuge, with the seller reserving the mineral rights. Louisiana law provided that, where the federal government was the purchaser, the seller's mineral rights would never lapse, even though they would lapse from nonuse if they had been located under private lands. Noting, among other things, this discrimination against the United States, the Court held that federal common law, not state law, controlled the property right the federal government acquired. The Court did not cite the Property Clause, but Professor Peter Appel has suggested that the Court was really applying a "dormant emanation" from that Clause, analogous to the dormant commerce clause used by the Supreme Court to strike down state legislation in situations where Congress has not acted. Appel, 86 MINN. L.REV. at 125–27 (2001).

United States v. Albrecht, 496 F.2d 906 (8th Cir. 1974) extended *Little Lake Misere*. This case involved a federal program to protect the principal

waterfowl breeding grounds in the continental United States, the northern
Great Plains, and especially North Dakota. A 1958 amendment to the
Migratory Bird Hunting Stamp Act provided that funds raised from the
sale of federal hunting stamps could be used to acquire "waterfowl production areas." 16 U.S.C. § 718d(c). The focus of federal acquisition under this
authority has been on so-called "prairie potholes," which were described by
the court this way: "Each square mile * * * is dotted by approximately 70
to 80 potholes of three to four feet deep. * * * [On certain types of land]
the potholes usually retain water through July or August, and therefore,
provide an excellent environment for the production of aquatic inverte-
brates and aquatic plants, the basic foods for breeding adult ducks and
their offspring. Essential to the maintenance of the land as a waterfowl
production area is the availability of shallow water in these numerous
potholes during the usually drier summer months."* In *Albrecht*, the
defendants' assignors had sold a "waterfowl easement" to the United
States, which prohibited the seller from draining potholes on the land. A
"stealthy ditchdigger" caused the area to be drained, and the United States
brought suit to force defendants to fill in the ditches. Defendants argued
that the easement was invalid because North Dakota law did not recognize
a "waterfowl easement" property interest. The court replied:

> [U]nder the context of this case, while the determination of North
> Dakota law in regard to the validity of the property right conveyed to
> the United States would be useful, it is not controlling, particularly if
> viewed as aberrant or hostile to federal property rights. Assuming
> *arguendo* that North Dakota law would not permit the conveyance of
> the right to the United States in this case, the specific federal govern-
> mental interest in acquiring rights to property for waterfowl produc-
> tion areas is stronger than any possible "aberrant" or "hostile" North
> Dakota law that would preclude the conveyance granted in this case.
> *Little Lake,* [412 U.S.] at 595, 596. We fully recognize that laws of real
> property are usually governed by the particular states; yet the reason-
> able property right conveyed to the United States in this case effectu-
> ates an important national concern, the acquisition of necessary land
> for waterfowl production areas, and should not be defeated by any
> possible North Dakota law barring the conveyance of this property
> right. To hold otherwise would be to permit the possibility that states
> could rely on local property laws to defeat the acquisition of reasonable
> rights to their citizens' property pursuant to 16 U.S.C. § 718(c) and to
> destroy a national program of acquiring property to aid in the breeding
> of migratory birds. We, therefore, specifically hold that the property
> right conveyed to the United States in this case, whether or not
> deemed a valid easement or other property right under North Dakota

---

* The "Prairie Pothole" region of the northern Great Plains in the U.S. and Canada has been described as "one of the most extensive and valuable freshwater resources in the world," although little appreciated. More than two-thirds of North American ducks depend upon the potholes, which is "threatened with a process of destruction by incremental acts of land drainage." See John H. Davidson and Philip P. Chandler, *The Minimal Effects Exemption and the Regulation of Headwater Wetlands under Swampbuster, with a Coda on the Theme of SWANCC,* 31 Envtl. L. Rptr. 11417 (2001).

law, was a valid conveyance under federal law and vested in the United States the rights as stated therein. Section 718d(c) specifically allows the United States to acquire wetland and pothole areas and the "interests therein."

In North Dakota v. United States, 460 U.S. 300, 317–21 (1983), the Supreme Court applied the *Little Lake Misere Land Co.* principle in the context of the same waterfowl easement acquisition program involved in *Albrecht*. The typical easement acquired by the federal government contained a legal description of a parcel of land, and imposed restrictions on all wetland areas within the parcel, including not only those already in existence or subject to recurrence but also "any enlargements of said wetlands areas resulting from normal or abnormal increased water." North Dakota enacted a state law that authorized landowners to drain any after-expanded wetland or water area, contrary to the terms of easements the U.S. had already acquired, and also limited easements to a maximum term of 99 years. The Court found the state law "hostile to federal interests" and said it could not be applied. "To respond to the inherently fluctuating nature of wetlands, the Secretary has chosen to negotiate easement agreements imposing restrictions on after-expanded wetlands as well as those described in the easement itself. As long as North Dakota landowners are willing to negotiate such agreements, the agreements may not be abrogated by state law." The same analysis was followed with regard to the state attempt to impose a term limit on the federally acquired easements.

Little Lake Misere Land Co. and *North Dakota v. United States* are discussed in John D. Leshy, *A Property Clause for the Twenty–First Century*, 75 U. COLO. L.REV. 1101, 1117–23 (2004), as examples of the Court developing a kind of "constitutional common law" that calls close questions in favor of national rather than state or local control over national lands (an idea contrary to the general notion that most property law in the country is state law), and calls close questions in favor of conservation rather than development of those lands.

Another situation where a federal law of property may come into play is in the area of water rights. In some circumstances, the United States may appropriate available water through state legal processes for purposes that are not recognized as "beneficial" under state water law, but which are necessary to carry out federal land programs. For a recent example of how this may work, see the Great Sand Dunes legislation enacted in 2000, 16 U.S.C. § 410hhh–7, and John D. Leshy, *Water Rights for Federal Land Conservation Programs: A Turn-of-the-Century Evaluation*, 4 WATER L.REV. 273 (2001).

COOPERATIVE FEDERALISM

As the preemption material illustrates, Congress rarely exercises all of its enumerated powers under the Constitution. Instead, practical and political circumstances dictate power sharing in natural resources law. This sharing is commonly called "cooperative federalism."

Robert L. Fischman, Cooperative Federalism and Natural Resources Law

14 N.Y.U. ENVTL. L.J. 179 (2005).

The broad conception of cooperative federalism includes all programs with incentives for state, tribal, and local jurisdictions to help advance federal law. Natural resources law provides important additional tools to extend cooperative federalism beyond pollution control. Compared to commerce clause regulation of pollution, the property clause of the constitution provides a stronger basis for exclusive federal control of federally owned natural resources. Nonetheless, a strong tradition of decentralized management exists in domestic resource management law.

* * *

While pollution control law began employing cooperative federalism in the early 1970s, federal resource management remained largely independent of state implementation until the "Sagebrush Rebellion" of the late 1970s and early 1980s. Though the Sagebrush Rebellion failed to transfer federal public land management authority to states or commodity users, it did prompt more state cooperative involvement in federal land administration. A heightened willingness of the federal government to work with states as well as an increased capacity of the states to offer substantive expertise and clearly articulated policies supported the rise of this informal, administrative federalism. The informal, ad-hoc, complex arrangements facilitating greater state leverage over federal lands decisions remain intact today.

For instance, states often accept statutory invitations to participate in resource planning for federal multiple use lands. The planning process encourages federal agencies to manage consistently with state objectives and, in some cases, provides formal mechanisms for states to assert their interests. In other situations, states may secure seats at the table to collaborate in reviewing proposed federal projects and seeking ways to mitigate the effects of federal decisions. Finally, as the *Granite Rock* case illustrated, states may assert police powers to regulate environmental impacts from federal resource management decisions, such as mining.

* * *

The disparate forms of cooperative federalism arrangements revealed by natural resources law can be organized into three categorical approaches: place-based collaboration, state favoritism in federal process, and federal deference to state process.

a. PLACE–BASED COLLABORATION

One tool that has emerged under the broad conception of cooperative federalism is place-based collaboration. A place-based collaboration is a system of decision-making about the environment that is unique to a particular site or region. Rather than impose a uniform model for interaction, place-based collaborations grow from the particular circumstances of the locus and nature of a dispute. The chief strength of this approach is that it brings a wide range of stakeholders and regulatory jurisdictions, state and federal, together to engage in holistic management. Place-based collaborations are one of the most popular current approaches to cooperative federalism in natural resources law. They soften the command-and-control requirements that typically bind parties in environmental law; instead, they employ more flexibility to create a region-specific approach. Place-based collaboration also helps satisfy many of the criteria for ecosystem management.

* * *

The ESA explicitly authorizes [a] tool of place-based collaboration, the incidental take permit. This permit waives the otherwise strict prohibition on harm to listed species' habitat. In order to secure such a permit, a party must complete a habitat conservation plan ("HCP"). Many placed-based collaborations originate with the need to combine enough mitigation habitat to qualify for an incidental take permit. Examples include the land use plans for San Diego and the lower Colorado River. In those cases, the federal government participates in negotiations with landowners, state agencies, and land use regulators in order to tailor a plan that both meets the needs of the permitees and ensures protection of the imperiled species.

Some collaborative bodies, such as the Valles Caldera Trust and the Columbia River Gorge Commission, have actual decision-making authority. The Valles Caldera board, composed of seven presidential appointees and two neighboring federal land managers, has proprietary control over a large parcel of land purchased by the federal government. The cooperative aspect of the board is reflected in the legislative requirement that the presidential appointees represent particular governmental entities (or organizations) or possess specific expertise. Similarly, the Columbia River Gorge Commission, composed of representatives appointed by affected counties and the Washington and Oregon governors, has land use planning oversight authority over a zone on either side of the gorge. The federal government has a non-voting chair on the Commission, but influences behavior through legislation and grants.

Sometimes place-based management results not from multi-party collaboration, but rather from bilateral negotiation between the federal government and a state or tribe. For instance, FWS recently signed an agreement ceding to the Confederated Salish and Kootenai Tribal Governments a wide range of management and maintenance programs on the National Bison Range. Spurred by legislation promoting delegation of some refuge administration activities to tribes, the FWS specifically contracted with the tribes to conduct wildlife management, fire protection, visitor services, and maintenance in the Bison Range. The tribes have special historic and cultural claims on the Bison Range resources. But broad delegations of management authority on refuge system lands to states have been common for some time as "coordination areas." While states and tribes generally gain power and funding through the place-based refuge management agreements, the federal government may also seek some control it might not otherwise have. For instance, the FWS recently entered into an agreement with the Nisqually Tribe to share tribal land within the boundaries of the Nisqually National Wildlife Refuge and work together on ecological restoration and recreation.

b. STATE FAVORITISM IN FEDERAL PROCESS

Another approach found in a broad conception of cooperative federalism is state favoritism in the federal process ("procedural favoritism"), which is well entrenched in natural resources law. This coordinating tool reserves a special role for states in the process by which the federal government makes environmental decisions. Though it does not guarantee that the state view will prevail, federal agency decision-makers have a responsibility at least to document their consideration of the state's view and to explain why it did not prevail. The state's direct avenue to assert its interests often is not open to other stakeholders in the federal decision.

The federal land planning provisions are excellent examples of procedural favoritism. States and counties may engage in their own planning exercises in order to receive the special consideration afforded by the foundational laws governing federal multiple use land management. For instance, the legislation guiding management of Bureau of Land Management ("BLM") lands, the Federal Land Policy Management Act ("FLPMA"), requires the BLM to coordinate with state and local governments in the development of land use plans "to the extent consistent with the laws governing the administration of the public lands," and to consider input concerning land use decisions from states (and other non-federal entities). Likewise, the National Forest Management Act ("NFMA") requires the Secretary of Agriculture to coordinate with the natural resource "planning processes of State and local governments." * * * Federal statutory preference for consistency with a state or local plan is an incentive for states to be more organized than they otherwise might be in developing their own objectives.

The George W. Bush administration has used procedural favoritism to give special voice to elected state, local, and tribal officials in federal resource management. Though this may be a way to avoid listening to national environmental groups without forsaking public participation entirely, it certainly has given procedural favoritism a shot in the arm.

* * *

[An] example of the Bush administration's use of procedural favoritism is the 2005 National Forest Roadless Rule. This rule reversed a 2001 regulation that prohibited logging and other development activities in nearly 60 million acres of roadless areas in the national forests. In place of the national prohibition, the [2005] rule invites state governors to petition the Forest Service to promulgate special rules establishing management requirements for roadless areas within the state. The rule binds the Forest Service to act on the state petition within a definite time-frame but reserves federal national forest management authority. The roadless rule's version of procedural favoritism is similar to the Wild and Scenic Rivers Act, which provides an alternative to congressional river designation where a governor applies to the Secretary of the Interior for administrative designation of rivers protected under state law.

The state petition provision of the roadless rule has received a great deal of attention from governors of Western states, where most of the national forest roadless areas occur. It offers an additional avenue for state influence over national forest management that goes beyond participation in individual forest plans. The petition must contain seven categories of information, including how recommended management actions would affect animals and how the petitioned actions compare to existing state policies, which makes the petition an arduous requirement for the states. [In 2006 a federal magistrate overturned the 2005 Roadless Rule for failure to comply with the ESA and NEPA.] * * *

c. FEDERAL DEFERENCE TO STATE PROCESS

Federal deference to state process is created when legislation specifies that a state policy, standard, or plan, if adopted in accordance with certain procedures, will be employed by the federal government in its own national decisions. While procedural favoritism gives states an advantage over other stakeholders in asserting their interests in federal decision-making, the third category, federal deference, provides greater assurance that the federal government will actually comply with the state position.

The best example of this approach to cooperative federalism is the Coastal Zone Management Act's ("CZMA") consistency criterion. The CZMA provides funding and guidelines for states to use in developing coastal zone management plans. Once the National Oceanic and Atmospheric Administration approves a state's plan, all activities authorized or carried out by federal agencies that affect the coastal zone must be consistent (to the maximum extent practicable) with the state's plan. Federal licenses, leases, and permits are covered by the consistency criterion, which gives the state a great deal of leverage to condition proposed projects by insisting on modifications necessary to achieve consistency with state specifications.

* * *

C. The Lessons of Inducement in Cooperative Federalism

The great value of examining natural resources law in a review of cooperative federalism is to broaden our conceptual understanding. Natural resources programs enrich the discourse of cooperative federalism by illustrating coordination approaches overlooked in pollution control, even if those approaches are seldom recognized as belonging to a common category. Also, a review of the full spectrum indicates a critical predictor of success: effective inducement. The elements of inducement are the tools creating both positive and negative incentives that promote coordination. Challenges to coordination exist where federal and state interests diverge. In those cases, inducements must prompt the governments into cooperative federalism.

Usually, the federal government has ultimate authority to make a preemptive determination. Also, the federal government generally shapes the playing field by defining the tools of inducement. However, situations do occasionally arise where states induce the federal government to cooperate, sometimes after adopting a variety of regimes, which regulated industries seek to preempt with uniform federal legislation.

Though the approaches to cooperative federalism may emphasize such administrative practices as standard-setting, planning, certifying, and permitting, there is a monetary incentive lurking in the background. Money, especially federal grants, almost always sweetens a cooperative deal. The sad truth about the implementation of environmental law is that it is largely limited by what agencies (and sometimes third parties, such as private attorneys general) can afford to do. While the legal structure of cooperative federalism is very important, it is the funding for it that most controls the extent of participation by states. The strength of the inducement in cooperative federal relationships will depend on the significance of the funds at stake. * * *

Other inducements to cooperative federalism similarly come in gradations of strength. Participation in cooperative federalism is most attractive when the federal government is largely bound by the state determination, as in CZMA consistency. A less powerful, but still attractive, lure for state participation in federal procedure is the relatively formal consideration given to state and local resource plans found in FLMPA general management planning. On the weak end of the spectrum, the roadless rule's invitation for states to submit proposals comes with little in the way of procedural or substantive assurance that state efforts will yield significant influence on the federal decision-makers. This spectrum of federal deference to state preference through procedure mirrors the tailoring component of the standard pollution control model, where states are more likely to participate where the EPA has relatively weak abilities to override their choices.

Place-based collaborations suggest another form of inducement as they offer attractive political rewards and are supported by the literature addressing ecosystem management. Though aspects of the Superfund remediation process resemble place-based collaboration, pollution control law lags behind in this aspect of cooperative federalism.

CHAPTER 4

Overarching Legal Issues

In modern public land and resources law, certain statutes and judicial doctrines repeatedly arise in administration and litigation. This chapter examines the key issues that guide federal management and serve often as a backdrop to the resource-specific laws. All of these issues involve some form of limitation on the federal agencies that manage natural resources.

Section A deals with the framework of the Administrative Procedure Act (APA), which establishes the ground rules under which all federal agencies operate. Of particular importance to federal land law is judicial review of agency actions under this statute. Section A also explores the judicial doctrines that relate to litigation. Section B examines the National Environmental Policy Act, or "NEPA" as it is universally known, a pervasive influence in this field since it was enacted nearly four decades ago. It shapes agency procedure by requiring analysis and public participation before an agency commits to a particular course of action. Section C takes up the Endangered Species Act (ESA). It establishes important procedures that guide agency behavior, and has also emerged as a much-used litigation lever. The vast majority of litigation in public natural resources law involves some combination of these three statutes. They are the vehicles for plaintiffs seeking injunctive relief from agency action (or inaction).

Section D concludes this chapter with a discussion of private rights in public resources. It reviews the circumstances under which agency action is limited by property expectations and contractual promises. Unlike the administrative limitations enforceable by injunction under the APA, NEPA, and the ESA, these private rights prompt courts to order compensation for interference that goes beyond what the law permits.

A. The APA and Judicial Review

Written in response to the massive increase in the scale of the administrative state during the New Deal, the APA established the basic framework for both internal agency procedure and judicial review of agency actions. We will focus on judicial review because that is the lens through which this casebook examines most of the law in this area. Also, litigation is an exceedingly important tool shaping management of land and natural resources. This subchapter begins by addressing the administrative and constitutional law doctrines that establish the thresholds for judicial review. Before litigation gets to the merits of a question, it must surmount

206

certain barriers to the courts. Then, the subchapter addresses the scope of judicial review for those cases that are decided on their merits.

Intensive judicial review of federal land and resource decision-making did not really become routine until the last quarter of the twentieth century. The Forest Service appeared in the Supreme Court as early as 1911 (in *Grimaud* and *Light, supra* p. 126), but those were constitutional challenges to federal power; nothing approaching a major national forest management issue made it to the courts until around 1970. The BLM historically has had a reasonably large litigation load, but its cases almost always arose out of essentially private disputes involving such things as mining claims, mineral leases, and homestead applications. The National Park Service and the U.S. Fish & Wildlife Service were rarely in court until the 1970s.

Several things gave rise to the boom in public policy litigation involving federal lands and resources litigation beginning in 1970. First, the courts became more aggressive in reviewing administrative actions of all kinds. A confluence of court decision and statutory reform lowered many barriers to judicial review, especially standing and sovereign immunity. In that respect, federal land law has joined the mainstream of administrative law. The so-called "hard look" doctrine of judicial review fashioned in Citizens to Preserve Overton Park, Inc. v. Volpe, 401 U.S. 402 (1971), licensed the courts to scrutinize both the substance of federal agency decisions and the processes by which they were reached. Although the Court thereafter cautioned the lower courts to stick to "their appointed function" and not to substitute their judgments for those of the agencies, *see* Vermont Yankee Nuclear Power Corp. v. NRDC, 435 U.S. 519 (1978), this has still left much room for the courts to play a significant role in federal land management.

Second, Congress in the modern era has enacted much more hard statutory law to govern these federal land decisions. These laws govern both the process by which agencies make decisions, (principally, NEPA, enacted in 1969), and the substance of those decisions. It is far easier to sue over violations of specific statutory commands, such as those in the ESA (1973) and, to a lesser extent, in the National Forest Management Act (1976) (NFMA), and the Federal Land Policy and Management Act (1976) (FLPMA), than it is to challenge an action taken pursuant to vague, discretionary mandates that were characteristic of earlier eras. Administrative regulations implementing the management statutes have also become much more detailed. The result is that plaintiffs are increasingly able to challenge land agencies for alleged violations of the law where the facts are not at issue.

Third, judicial review burgeoned in part simply because many new classes of plaintiffs and lawyers arose. Recreational and environmentally-concerned members of the public organized themselves to pursue judicial remedies when aggrieved by agency action. With the help of private foundations, several "public interest law firms" on both the left and right sides of the political spectrum became active litigators on public lands issues.

Most federal land law litigation involves principles of administrative law, because the typical lawsuit is brought by a private party against a federal agency. Some aspects and doctrines of administrative law figure prominently in the context of litigation over federal lands and resources questions. Before a litigant can obtain a ruling on the merits of a suit against the agency, it must run a procedural obstacle course.

1.   Barriers to Judicial Review: The Procedural Obstacle Course

a.   STANDING

Most cases involving federal lands and natural resources are filed pursuant to the APA, which authorizes suit by any person "adversely affected or aggrieved by agency action within the meaning of a relevant statute." 5 U.S.C. § 702. The groundbreaking case construing that statute in the context of federal lands is Sierra Club v. Morton, 405 U.S. 727 (1972). The Sierra Club sought to enjoin a huge ski resort development by private interests in the Mineral King Valley, basing its standing upon an allegation that it had "a special interest in the conservation and sound maintenance of the national parks, game refuges and forests of the country." The Court held that this allegation was insufficient to establish standing, but in the process expanded traditional standing doctrine so as to turn nominal defeat into a long-term victory for environmental plaintiffs. Specifically, the Court noted that the Club's complaint "alleged that the development 'would destroy or otherwise adversely affect the scenery, natural and historic objects and wildlife of the park and would impair the enjoyment of the park for future generations.' " The Court said it did not "question that this type of harm may amount to an 'injury in fact' sufficient to lay the basis for standing" under the Administrative Procedure Act, because "[a]esthetic and environmental well-being, like economic well-being, are important ingredients of the quality of life in our society, and the fact that particular environmental interests are shared by the many rather than the few does not make them less deserving of legal protection through the judicial process." 405 U.S. at 734. But the Club had inadequately pleaded standing, because it failed to allege that "its members would be affected in any of their activities or pastimes by the Disney development. Nowhere in the pleadings or affidavits did the Club state that its members use Mineral King for any purpose * * *." The Court also validated the representation by an organization of its members ("associational standing"), and held that once standing is found, the substantive challenge to agency action is not confined to the grounds for standing. On remand, the Sierra Club amended its complaint to allege such use by its members, and the lawsuit continued to the merits.

Sierra Club v. Morton marked the end of the era when administrative decision-making and litigation were matters limited to the agency itself and the permit applicant, affected property holder, or prosecuted violator. After opening standing to interest groups, the courts embraced a more pluralistic model of participation, which resulted in changes to agency procedures as well. The ability to appeal an agency decision to a court is a powerful bargaining chip for an interest group to gain access to officials making decisions.

In United States v. Students Challenging Regulatory Agency Procedures, 412 U.S. 669 (1973), the Court liberalized the doctrine even further. It found plaintiff law students' allegations that they could be injured by a proposed 2.5 percent surcharge on railroad freight rates (because a possible result could be less recycling and increases of litter on recreational trails they used) sufficient to withstand a motion to dismiss their claim that the Interstate Commerce Commission should have prepared an environmental impact statement under NEPA in deciding whether to object to the proposed rate increase. That was the high-water mark, for the Supreme Court has since taken a more conservative view of standing.

Today, the court divides the taking analysis into two parts. The first part is the "prudential component" served by the "zone of interests" test, which assures that the court hears only from plaintiffs representing the concerns that Congress sought to address in its legislation. This part of the takings test is judicial policy, not court law. The "zone of interests" test typically raises few issues for environmental groups because modern natural resources statutes almost always seek to ensure some level of environmental protection or conservation in their operation. The "zone of interests" test might be a barrier to economic development interests or commodity producers suing under environmental laws, although the Supreme Court deftly narrowed that possibility in Bennett v. Spear, 520 U.S. 154 (1997). The Court there held that ranchers and irrigation districts which might lose water as a result of an ESA biological opinion had standing to challenge that opinion, concluding that the ESA was intended to serve not only the purpose of protecting species, but also of avoiding "needless economic dislocation produced by agency officials zealously but unintelligently pursuing their environmental objectives." 520 U.S. at 176–77.

The second part of the takings analysis is a constitutional component derived from the doctrine of separation of powers. Its aim is to limit the judicial role to relatively narrow cases with a plaintiff that has "such a personal stake in the outcome ... as to assure the concrete adverseness which sharpens the presentation of the issues." Baker v. Carr, 369 U.S. 186, 204 (1962). Over time, the Court has expanded on the constitutional component, which now contains three elements. Plaintiffs must show that 1) they have suffered an injury-in-fact; 2) the injury is fairly traceable to the challenged action (causation); and 3) a favorable decision from the court will be likely to redress that injury. Unlike prudential standing, Congress may not waive or loosen the requirements of the constitutional component, though it may help define what kinds of injuries are cognizable by courts.

The following case illustrates how the constitutional component of standing may close the courthouse doors to plaintiffs who would otherwise have associational standing.

Lujan v. National Wildlife Federation

Supreme Court of the United States, 1990.
497 U.S. 871.

■ JUSTICE SCALIA delivered the opinion of the Court.

[The National Wildlife Federation (hereinafter respondent) brought suit against the Interior Department in 1985, alleging violations of several federal statutes in the administration of what the complaint styled as the BLM's "land withdrawal review program." In the first part of its opinion, the Court recounted the history of such withdrawals, and of related "classifications" of federal land for retention or disposal, which had together created a "chaotic" situation for federal land managers and private users.]

[As a result, in the Federal Land Policy and Management Act of 1976 (FLPMA), Congress had authorized review of existing classifications of public lands in the land use planning process FLPMA created. The statute also said that] the Secretary could "modify or terminate any such classification consistent with such land use plans." [43 U.S.C.] § 1712(d). It also authorized the Secretary to "make, modify, extend or revoke" withdrawals. § 1714(a). Finally it directed the Secretary, within 15 years, to review withdrawals in existence in 1976 in 11 western States, § 1714(*l*)(1), and to "determine whether, and for how long, the continuation of the existing withdrawal of the lands would be, in his judgment, consistent with the statutory objectives of the programs for which the lands were dedicated and of the other relevant programs," § 1714(*l*)(2). The activities undertaken by the BLM to comply with these various provisions [to review and possibly revoke existing withdrawals and to reclassify public lands for disposal or various uses] constitute what respondent's amended complaint styles the BLM's "land withdrawal review program," which is the subject of the current litigation.

In its complaint, respondent averred generally that the reclassification of some withdrawn lands and the return of others to the public domain would open the lands up to mining activities, thereby destroying their natural beauty. * * * [The complaint alleged that in carrying out this program, the Department had violated FLPMA and the National Environmental Policy Act (NEPA).]

We first address respondent's claim that the Peterson and Erman affidavits alone suffice to establish respondent's right to judicial review of petitioners' actions. Respondent * * * claims a right to judicial review under § 10(a) of the [Administrative Procedure Act], which provides: "A person suffering legal wrong because of agency action, or adversely affected or aggrieved by agency action within the meaning of a relevant statute, is entitled to judicial review thereof." 5 U.S.C. § 702. * * *

We assume, since it has been uncontested, that the allegedly affected interests set forth in the affidavits—"recreational use and aesthetic enjoyment"—are sufficiently related to the purposes of respondent association that respondent meets the requirements of § 702 if any of its members do.

As for the "agency action" requirement, we think that each of the affidavits can be read, as the Court of Appeals believed, to complain of a particular "agency action" as that term is defined in § 551. The parties agree that the Peterson affidavit, judging from the geographic area it describes, must refer to * * * [a BLM order] terminating the withdrawal classification of some 4500 acres of land in that area. * * *

We also think that whatever "adverse effect" or "aggrievement" is established by the affidavits was "within the meaning of the relevant statute"—i.e., met the "zone of interests" test. The relevant statute, of course, is the statute whose violation is the gravamen of the complaint—both the FLPMA and NEPA. We have no doubt that "recreational use and aesthetic enjoyment" are among the sorts of interests those statutes were specifically designed to protect. The only issue, then, is whether the facts alleged in the affidavits showed that those interests of Peterson and Erman were actually affected.

The Peterson affidavit averred:

"My recreational use and aesthetic enjoyment of federal lands, particularly those in the vicinity of South Pass–Green Mountain, Wyoming have been and continue to be adversely affected in fact by the unlawful actions of the Bureau and the Department. In particular, the South Pass–Green Mountain area of Wyoming has been opened to the staking of mining claims and oil and gas leasing, an action which threatens the aesthetic beauty and wildlife habitat potential of these lands." App. to Pet. for Cert. 191a.

Erman's affidavit was substantially the same as Peterson's, with respect to all except the area involved.

* * * In ruling upon a Rule 56 motion, "a District Court must resolve any factual issues of controversy in favor of the non-moving party" only in the sense that, where the facts specifically averred by that party contradict facts specifically averred by the movant, the motion must be denied. That is a world apart from "assuming" that general averments embrace the "specific facts" needed to sustain the complaint. As set forth above, Rule 56(e) provides that judgment "shall be entered" against the nonmoving party unless affidavits or other evidence "set forth specific facts showing that there is a genuine issue for trial." * * *

At the margins there is some room for debate as to how "specific" must be the "specific facts" that Rule 56(e) requires in a particular case. But where the fact in question is the one put in issue by the § 702 challenge here—whether one of the respondent's members has been, or is threatened to be, "adversely affected or aggrieved" by Government action—Rule 56(e) is assuredly not satisfied by averments which state only that one of the respondent's members uses unspecified portions of an immense tract of territory, on some portions of which mining activity has occurred or probably will occur by virtue of the governmental action. It will not do to "presume" the missing facts because without them the affidavits would not establish the injury that they generally allege.

* * *

■ [JUSTICE BLACKMUN, joined by JUSTICES BRENNAN, MARSHALL, and STEVENS, dissented, arguing that the two affidavits were sufficient to establish standing, and that the district court abused its discretion by refusing to consider the four supplemental affidavits. The dissenters pointed out that the government's summary judgment motion did not require the plaintiffs to prove standing, but just to show a genuine factual issue as to their alleged injury. The two affidavits "doubtless could have been more artfully drafted, but they definitely were sufficient to withstand the Government's summary judgment motion."]

NOTES AND QUESTIONS

1. How big a setback is this for environmental protection advocates? Was the failure here simply one of inadequate homework in making detailed showings of injury; that is, is it simply an insistence that the plaintiffs' lawyers carefully dot their "i"s and cross their "t"s? Or is the conservative majority signaling a broader effort to close the doors of the federal courts to broad-based challenges to sweeping federal programs? Could the Wildlife Federation ever show injury sufficient to satisfy the Court's majority that it had the right to challenge the BLM's withdrawal review program?

Suppose Congress adopts legislation acknowledging that "all Americans have [a] property right—a tenancy in common" in federal lands, or in the continued existence of endangered species anywhere in the world. Could Congress go on to say that violation of those rights constitutes injury to all holders of those rights, and thereby accord standing to all Americans? *See* Cass Sunstein, *What's Standing After Lujan? Of Citizen Suits, Injuries, and Article III*, 91 MICH. L.REV. 163, 234 (1992). Prof. Richard J. Pierce, Jr. has stated that "[m]odern standing law is closer to a part of the political system than to a part of the legal system. It is characterized by numerous malleable doctrines and numerous inconsistent precedents. Judges regularly manipulate the doctrines and rely on selective citation of precedents to further their own political preferences." *Is Standing Law or Politics?*, 77 N.C. L.REV. 1741, 1786 (1999).

2. The Court further tightened its approach to standing in Lujan v. Defenders of Wildlife, 504 U.S. 555 (1992) (*Lujan II*), by holding that environmental organizations had no standing to challenge a Department of the Interior regulation implementing the Endangered Species Act (ESA) requirement that federal agencies consult with the Department to ensure that their actions will not jeopardize protected species. The regulation exempted agency actions occurring outside of the territory of the United States from the consultation obligation and the jeopardy standard. In response to the government's motion for summary judgment on the standing issue, the plaintiffs introduced affidavits from their members. For instance,

> Ms. Skilbred averred that she traveled to Sri Lanka in 1981 and "observed th[e] habitat" of "endangered species such as the Asian elephant and the leopard" at what is now the site of the Mahaweli

project funded by the Agency for International Development (AID) [a federal agency], although she "was unable to see any of the endangered species"; "this development project," she continued, "will seriously reduce endangered, threatened, and endemic species habitat including areas that I visited . . . [, which] may severely shorten the future of these species"; that threat, she concluded, harmed her because she "intend[s] to return to Sri Lanka in the future and hope[s] to be more fortunate in spotting at least the endangered elephant and leopard." When Ms. Skilbred was asked at a subsequent deposition if and when she had any plans to return to Sri Lanka, she reiterated that "I intend to go back to Sri Lanka," but confessed that she had no current plans: "I don't know [when]. There is a civil war going on right now. I don't know. Not next year, I will say. In the future."

Id. at 563–564.

The majority, speaking through Justice Scalia, conceded that "the desire to use or observe an animal species, even for purely aesthetic purposes, is undeniably a cognizable interest for purpose of standing," but held that the affidavits did not show the kind of "imminent injury" required for standing. Past visits to the area "prove[] nothing" and Skilbred's vague future plans did not meet the standing test. "Such 'some day' intentions—without any description of concrete plans, or indeed even any specification of when the some day will be—do not support a finding of the 'actual or imminent' injury that our cases require." *Id.* at 564. Could the standing problem in *Lujan II* be overcome through better crafting of affidavits? Suppose Skilbred had purchased a plane ticket for a return trip to Sri Lanka? Would that establish sufficient injury?

Do you agree with the following observation?

[The Lujan cases] promoted a view of standing requirements that systematically disadvantaged citizen suits. The inherent temporal and spatial uncertainties associated with ecological cause and effected coupled with the fragmentation of decision-making authority . . . seemed poised to render the Court's heightened standing requirements of injury, causation, and redressability virtually insurmountable.

Richard Lazarus, *Environmental Law and the Supreme Court: Three Years Later*, 19 Pace Envtl. L.Rev. 658 (2002). As the following notes explain, the Court subsequently pulled back from its more extreme analysis in the *Lujan* cases.

3.   Informational standing. NEPA's pervasive, essentially procedural, tool of environmental protection through environmental impact analysis allows plaintiffs who have concrete interests to attain standing without the need for a strong showing of directly caused, redressable harm outside of the informational deficiencies from a NEPA violation. Justice Scalia's *Lujan II* opinion acknowledged in a footnote that " 'procedural rights' are special: The person who has been accorded a procedural right to protect his concrete interests can assert that right without meeting all the normal standards for redressability and immediacy." But this could not confer standing on "persons who have no concrete interests affected" by the

214CHAPTER 4 OVERARCHING LEGAL ISSUES

procedural noncompliance. 504 U.S. at 573 n. 6. Procedural standing remains an important basis for suits in many public natural resources disputes, and became easier to establish following Federal Election Commission v. Akins, 524 U.S. 11 (1998), where plaintiffs obtained standing to challenge an agency failure to make certain records public pursuant to election law. The Court held that the plaintiffs' "injury in fact" was their "inability to obtain information" required by statute. 524 U.S. at 21.

4. A looser test for injury. In Friends of the Earth v. Laidlaw Environmental Services, 528 U.S. 167 (2000), the Court distinguished *Lujan II* in determining that private plaintiffs had standing to seek civil penalties payable to the government under the Clean Water Act, even though the district court found that the defendant's actions, while out of compliance with the Act, had not resulted in "any health risk or environmental harm." Justice Ginsburg's majority opinion decided that the relevant injury "is not injury to the environment but injury to the plaintiff," and plaintiffs' "reasonable concerns" that defendant's pollution may have damaged land they otherwise would have used is sufficient injury for standing. Their affidavits and testimony sufficiently asserted that defendants' activities "directly affected [their] recreational, aesthetic, and economic interests."

5. Redressability. A plaintiff must also show a "substantial likelihood" that the relief the plaintiff seeks will "redress the injury" it claims to suffer. Several cases from the Tenth Circuit have held that plaintiffs who have objected to various governmental actions have failed to meet this requirement. For example, a coal company had no standing object to an exchange of land and coal between the United States and a private entity. The court reasoned that the alleged injury—the opportunity to bid on the coal should it be retained in federal ownership and put up for bid—could not be redressed by the court. Instead, the decision to offer the coal for competitive leasing—even on federal land not closed to the leasing program—was entirely within the discretion of the executive branch. Ash Creek Mining Co. v. Lujan, 969 F.2d 868 (10th Cir.1992). The companion case of Wyoming ex rel. Sullivan v. Lujan, 969 F.2d 877 (10th Cir.1992) rejected standing of the state of Wyoming, which receives a share of coal lease proceeds, for the same reason. *See also* Baca v. King, 92 F.3d 1031 (10th Cir.1996) (rancher with permits to graze cattle on BLM land denied standing to object to a BLM land exchange that privatized some of the public land where his cattle grazed, resulting in cancellation of his grazing permits, because court could not order the Secretary to allow the public lands to be grazed if the exchange were voided, since that was "completely within the Secretary of the Interior's discretion").

b. SOVEREIGN IMMUNITY

The doctrine of sovereign immunity shields governmental wrongs from judicial review. In an earlier era, the doctrine was employed with some frequency in public lands cases. *See generally* Antonin Scalia, (yes, that Scalia), *Sovereign Immunity and Nonstatutory Review of Federal Administrative Action: Some Conclusions from the Public Lands Cases*, 68 MICH. L.REV. 867 (1970). In litigation challenging agency action and seeking equitable relief rather than damages (which is the vast bulk of litigation in the federal lands context), the sovereign immunity rule had long been largely swallowed by its exceptions before Congress applied the coup de grace in 1976. An amendment to the APA, 5 U.S.C. § 702, abolished sovereign immunity for most purposes:

> An action in a court of the United States seeking relief other than money damages and stating a claim that an agency or an officer or employee thereof acted or failed to act in an official capacity or under color of legal authority shall not be dismissed or relief therein be denied on the ground that it is against the United States or that the United States is an indispensable party.

Because the amendment applies only to suits for "other than money damages," compensation suits continue to be governed by the Federal Tort Claims Act, 28 U.S.C. § 1346(b), 2671 et seq., see Chapter 11, and the Tucker Act, 28 U.S.C. § 1346(a), 1391. Specific statutes limiting the waiver of sovereign immunity prevail over the more general waiver in 5 U.S.C. § 702. The most important examples of specific limited waiver in the federal lands context are the Color of Title Act and the Quiet Title Act, which apply when persons seek to establish property rights on public lands.

A general six year statute of limitations applies to civil actions commenced against the United States. 28 U.S.C. § 2401(a). Though seemingly straightforward, it is not always easy to apply. *See* Ayers v. Espy, 873 F.Supp. 455, 462 (D.Colo.1994) (party challenging a recent application of a regulation adopted more than six years earlier, and not the regulation itself, not barred); *see also* United States v. Beggerly, 524 U.S. 38 (1998) (no equitable tolling of the Quiet Title Act).

c. EXHAUSTION OF REMEDIES AND THE FORECLOSURE RULE

A variety of doctrines operate to further the policy of requiring litigants to seek relief in the agencies before resorting to the courts. The federal land management agencies all have some form of internal administrative appeal process, although they vary widely. There are two basic forms. One kind of process employs disinterested administrative law judges to adjudicate disputes. The best example of this quasi-judicial body is the Interior Board of Land Appeals, to which many BLM and some FWS decisions can be appealed. The other kind of administrative appeal process employs agency officials in regional and headquarters offices to review the decisions of land units and regions, respectively. These reviewers are not disinterested. In fact, many of these appeal decision-makers are also in the position of implementing agency policy and evaluating the performance of the very officials whose decisions are being appealed. The best example of this kind of system is the Forest Service appeals process for agency projects and plans. For a comparison and summary, see Bradley C. Bobertz and Robert L. Fischman, *Administrative Appeal Reform: The Case of the Forest Service*, 64 U. COLO. L.REV. 372 (1993). Forest Service administrative appeals were reformed by legislation in 1994 (106 Stat. 1419) and substantially modified in 2003. *See* Healthy Forests Restoration Act, 117 Stat. 1887 (codified at 16 U.S.C. § 6501 et seq.); 68 Fed. Reg. 33581 (2003). However, some of the restrictions of the appeals have since been overturned by courts. *See* Earth Island Institute v. Ruthenbeck, 459 F.3d 954 (9th Cir.2006).

Exhaustion requires plaintiffs to have availed themselves of administrative remedies and review before mounting a court challenge. The exhaustion doctrine is flexible, involving balancing tests in which a wide variety of equities can be considered. An adjunct to the exhaustion doctrine is the requirement that a plaintiff must normally raise all factual and legal issues during agency review: otherwise, the plaintiff may be "foreclosed" from raising those issues on review. The foreclosure doctrine is also flexible and is not rigidly applied if extenuating circumstances are shown.

In Kleissler v. United States Forest Service, 183 F.3d 196 (3d Cir. 1999), the court, relying on the 1994 Forest Service appeals reform legislation, held that plaintiffs had failed to exhaust administrative remedies by neglecting to bring to the attention of the Forest Service specific concerns it had with two proposed timber cutting projects. The court observed: "The policy underlying [this reform] is simple: objects and issues should first be reviewed by those with expertise in the contested subject area." It rejected plaintiffs' entreaty to take a "flexible and liberal view" of the exhaustion requirement. Among other things, the court noted that while the plaintiff was unrepresented by counsel during the administrative process, he was "not a neophyte" in these matters, being a founding member of an environmental group whose website described its "Paper Monkeywrench" methods of encouraging writing letters and filing appeals with the Forest Service so that the agency "has more work to do." *See also* Shenandoah Ecosystems Defense Group v. U.S. Forest Service, 144 F.Supp.2d 542 (W.D.Va.2001); *but see* Sierra Club v. Dombeck, 161 F.Supp.2d 1052, 1066 (D.Ariz.2001) (exhaustion not required where it would be futile). The reference to "monkeywrench" methods is from Edward Abbey's cult novel, THE MONKEYWRENCH GANG (1975), whose protagonist engages in a variety of disruptive and illegal tactics to protect the environment in southern Utah from various kinds of development projects.

d. RIPENESS AND AGENCY ACTION

Ripeness is another administrative law defense that has become more important in federal land and resources law as a result of recent Supreme Court decisions. Also, courts only review those agency decisions that constitute "final agency action[s]" under the APA.

All federal agencies prepare resource management plans for areas under their jurisdiction. The following case concerns a Forest Service plan. At the time, the Forest Service prepared more detailed, elaborate plans than any other agency. (This case also provides a useful introduction to federal land and resources planning, a subject treated in more detail in Chapter 5E.)

Ohio Forestry Association, Inc. v. Sierra Club

Supreme Court of the United States, 1998.
523 U.S. 726.

■ JUSTICE BREYER delivered the opinion of the Court.

The Sierra Club challenges the lawfulness of a federal land and resource management plan adopted by the United States Forest Service for

Ohio's Wayne National Forest on the ground that the plan permits too much logging and too much clearcutting. We conclude that the controversy is not yet ripe for judicial review.

The National Forest Management Act of 1976 (NFMA) requires the Secretary of Agriculture to "develop, maintain, and, as appropriate, revise land and resource management plans for units of the National Forest System." 16 U.S.C. § 1604(a). * * * The National Forest Service, which manages the System, develops land and resource management plans pursuant to NFMA, and uses these forest plans to "guide all natural resource management activities," 36 CFR § 219.1(b) (1997), including use of the land for "outdoor recreation, range, timber, watershed, wildlife and fish, and wilderness." 16 U.S.C. § 1604(e)(1). In developing the plans, the Service must take both environmental and commercial goals into account. See, e.g., § 1604(g); 36 CFR § 219.1(a) (1997).

This case focuses upon a plan that the Forest Service has developed for the Wayne National Forest located in southern Ohio. When the Service wrote the plan, the forest consisted of 178,000 federally owned acres (278 sq. mi.) in three forest units that are interspersed among privately owned lands, some of which the Forest Service plans to acquire over time. The Plan permits logging to take place on 126,000 (197 sq. mi.) of the federally owned acres. At the same time, it sets a ceiling on the total amount of wood that can be cut—a ceiling that amounts to about 75 million board feet over 10 years, and which, the Plan projects, would lead to logging on about 8,000 acres (12.5 sq. mi.) during that decade. According to the Plan, logging on about 5,000 (7.8 sq. mi.) of those 8,000 acres would involve clearcutting, or other forms of what the Forest Service calls "even-aged" tree harvesting.

Although the Plan sets logging goals, selects the areas of the forest that are suited to timber production, and determines which "probable methods of timber harvest," are appropriate, it does not itself authorize the cutting of any trees. Before the Forest Service can permit the logging, it must: (a) propose a specific area in which logging will take place and the harvesting methods to be used; (b) ensure that the project is consistent with the Plan; (c) provide those affected by proposed logging notice and an opportunity to be heard; (d) conduct an environmental analysis pursuant to the National Environmental Policy Act of 1969 (NEPA); to evaluate the effects of the specific project and to contemplate alternatives; and (e) subsequently take a final decision to permit logging, which decision affected persons may challenge in an administrative appeals process and in court. Furthermore, the statute requires the Forest Service to "revise" the Plan "as appropriate" 16 U.S.C. § 1604(a). Despite the considerable legal distance between the adoption of the Plan and the moment when a tree is cut, the Plan's promulgation nonetheless makes logging more likely in that it is a logging precondition; in its absence logging could not take place.

[The Sierra Club challenged the plan, alleging that the logging it countenanced violated several federal laws. The district court ruled in favor of the Forest Service on the merits. The court of appeals found that the matter was ripe and then ruled for the plaintiff, finding that the Plan improperly favored clearcutting and therefore violated NFMA.]

* * * We find that the dispute is not justiciable, because it is not ripe for court review.

As this Court has previously pointed out, the ripeness requirement is designed

> "to prevent the courts, through avoidance of premature adjudication, from entangling themselves in abstract disagreements over administrative policies, and also to protect the agencies from judicial interference until an administrative decision has been formalized and its effects felt in a concrete way by the challenging parties." Abbott Laboratories v. Gardner, 387 U.S. 136, 148–149 (1967).

In deciding whether an agency's decision is, or is not, ripe for judicial review, the Court has examined both the "fitness of the issues for judicial decision" and the "hardship to the parties of withholding court consideration." Id., at 149. To do so in this case, we must consider: (1) whether delayed review would cause hardship to the plaintiffs; (2) whether judicial intervention would inappropriately interfere with further administrative action; and (3) whether the courts would benefit from further factual development of the issues presented. These considerations, taken together, foreclose review in the present case.

First, to "withhol[d] court consideration" at present will not cause the parties significant "hardship" as this Court has come to use that term. Ibid. For one thing, the provisions of the Plan that the Sierra Club challenges do not create adverse effects of a strictly legal kind, that is, effects of a sort that traditionally would have qualified as harm. [T]hey do not command anyone to do anything or to refrain from doing anything; they do not grant, withhold, or modify any formal legal license, power or authority; they do not subject anyone to any civil or criminal liability; they create no legal rights or obligations. Thus, for example, the Plan does not give anyone a legal right to cut trees, nor does it abolish anyone's legal authority to object to trees' being cut.

Nor have we found that the Plan now inflicts significant practical harm upon the interests that the Sierra Club advances—an important consideration in light of this Court's modern ripeness cases. As we have pointed out, before the Forest Service can permit logging, it must focus upon a particular site, propose a specific harvesting method, prepare an environmental review, permit the public an opportunity to be heard, and (if challenged) justify the proposal in court. The Sierra Club thus will have ample opportunity later to bring its legal challenge at a time when harm is more imminent and more certain. Any such later challenge might also include a challenge to the lawfulness of the present Plan if (but only if) the present Plan then matters, i.e., if the Plan plays a causal role with respect to the future, then-imminent, harm from logging. Hence we do not find a strong reason why the Sierra Club must bring its challenge now in order to get relief.

* * *

The Sierra Club does say that it will be easier, and certainly cheaper, to mount one legal challenge against the Plan now, than to pursue many challenges to each site-specific logging decision to which the Plan might eventually lead. It does not explain, however, why one initial site-specific victory (if based on the Plan's unlawfulness) could not, through preclusion principles, effectively carry the day. And, in any event, the Court has not considered this kind of litigation cost-saving sufficient by itself to justify review in a case that would otherwise be unripe. The ripeness doctrine reflects a judgment that the disadvantages of a premature review that may prove too abstract or unnecessary ordinarily outweigh the additional costs of—even repetitive—post-implementation litigation.

Second, from the agency's perspective, immediate judicial review directed at the lawfulness of logging and clearcutting could hinder agency efforts to refine its policies: (a) through revision of the Plan, e.g., in response to an appropriate proposed site-specific action that is inconsistent with the Plan, or (b) through application of the Plan in practice, e.g., in the form of site-specific proposals, which proposals are subject to review by a court applying purely legal criteria. Hearing the Sierra Club's challenge now could thus interfere with the system that Congress specified for the agency to reach forest logging decisions.

Third, from the courts' perspective, review of the Sierra Club's claims regarding logging and clearcutting now would require time-consuming judicial consideration of the details of an elaborate, technically based plan, which predicts consequences that may affect many different parcels of land in a variety of ways, and which effects themselves may change over time. That review would have to take place without benefit of the focus that a particular logging proposal could provide. Thus, for example, the court below in evaluating the Sierra Club's claims had to focus upon whether the Plan as a whole was "improperly skewed," rather than focus upon whether the decision to allow clearcutting on a particular site was improper, say, because the site was better suited to another use or logging there would cumulatively result in too many trees' being cut. And, of course, depending upon the agency's future actions to revise the Plan or modify the expected methods of implementation, review now may turn out to have been unnecessary.

This type of review threatens the kind of "abstract disagreements over administrative policies," Abbott Laboratories, 387 U.S., at 148, that the ripeness doctrine seeks to avoid. In this case, for example, the Court of Appeals panel disagreed about whether or not the Forest Service suffered from a kind of general "bias" in favor of timber production and clearcutting. Review where the consequences had been "reduced to more manageable proportions," and where the "factual components [were] fleshed out, by some concrete action" might have led the panel majority either to demonstrate that bias and its consequences through record citation (which it did not do) or to abandon the claim. * * *

Finally, Congress has not provided for pre-implementation judicial review of forest plans. Those plans are tools for agency planning and management. The Plan is consequently unlike agency rules that Congress has specifically instructed the courts to review "pre-enforcement." Nor does the Plan, which through standards guides future use of forests, resemble an environmental impact statement prepared pursuant to NEPA. That is because in this respect NEPA, unlike the NFMA, simply guarantees a particular procedure, not a particular result. Compare, 16 U.S.C. § 1604(e) (requiring that forest plans provide for multiple coordinated use of forests, including timber and wilderness) with 42 U.S.C. § 4332 (requiring that agencies prepare environmental impact statements where major agency action would significantly affect the environment). Hence a person with standing who is injured by a failure to comply with the NEPA procedure may complain of that failure at the time the failure takes place, for the claim can never get riper.

The Sierra Club makes one further important contrary argument. It says that the Plan will hurt it in many ways that we have not yet mentioned. Specifically, the Sierra Club says that the Plan will permit "many intrusive activities, such as opening trails to motorcycles or using heavy machinery," which activities "will go forward without any additional consideration of their impact on wilderness recreation." At the same time, in areas designated for logging, "affirmative measures to promote undisturbed backcountry recreation, such as closing roads and building additional hiking trails" will not take place. These are harms, says the Sierra Club, that will not take place at a distant future time. Rather, they will take place now.

This argument suffers from the legally fatal problem that it makes its first appearance here in this Court in the briefs on the merits. The Complaint, fairly read, does not include such claims. Instead, it focuses on the amount and method of timber harvesting. The Sierra Club has not referred us to any other court documents in which it protests the Plan's approval of motorcycles or machinery, the Plan's failure to close roads or to provide for the building of trails, or other disruptions that the Plan might cause those who use the forest for hiking. As far as we can tell, prior to the argument on the merits here, the harm to which the Sierra Club objected consisted of too much, and the wrong kind of, logging.

The matter is significant because the Government concedes that if the Sierra Club had previously raised these other kinds of harm, the ripeness analysis in this case with respect to those provisions of the Plan that produce the harm would be significantly different. The Government's brief in the Court of Appeals said

> "If, for example, a plan incorporated a final decision to close a specific area to off-road vehicles, the plan itself could result in imminent concrete injury to a party with an interest in the use of off-road vehicles in that area."

And, at oral argument, the Solicitor General agreed that if the Sierra Club's claim was "that [the] plan was allowing motorcycles into a bird-watching area or something that like, that would be immediately justiciable." Thus, we believe these other claims that the Sierra Club now raises are not fairly presented here, and we cannot consider them.

For these reasons, we find the respondents' suit not ripe for review. We vacate the decision of the Court of Appeals, and we remand this case with instructions to dismiss.

NOTES AND QUESTIONS

1. The decision was unanimous. The lawyers for the Forestry Association have interpreted the decision as exemplifying "the theme expressed in Lujan v. NWF that many programmatic issues should not be heard by courts, and that judicial review is more manageable in site-specific controversies." Steven P. Quarles & Thomas Lundquist, *The Supreme Court Restricts the Availability of Forest–Wide Judicial Review in Ohio Forestry Ass'n v. Sierra Club*, 28 Envtl. L. Rptr. 10621 (1998). Is this a decision about the availability of review of broad issues addressed in land use plans, or is it merely about the timing of such review? More specifically, when the Forest Service gets around to conducting a timber sale under this plan, may the Sierra Club challenge not only the specific sale, but also the terms of the plan which authorizes it? *See, e.g.,* Wilderness Society v. Bosworth, 118 F.Supp.2d 1082 (D.Mont.2000) (plaintiffs may challenge "forest-wide standards" adopted in a land use plan in the context of site-specific final agency actions). Suppose a plan authorizing timber harvesting in a particular area was adopted in 1996, and in 2003 the sale was proposed and an environmental group sued, challenging the plan. Generally speaking, a challenge to federal agency action must be brought within six years from the time the cause of action accrues. 28 U.S.C. § 2401. Is there a statute of limitations problem here?

2. Generally speaking, the U.S. Forest Service, like other federal land management agencies, formerly integrated NEPA compliance into its planning process, with plans either accompanied by or taking the form of environmental impact statements. (But the 2005 Forest Service planning rules divorces the planning process from NEPA entirely. *See infra* p. 474.) Justice Breyer acknowledges that review of NEPA compliance in connection with the preparation of land use plans is immediately available. This sets up the possibility of bifurcated review of generic agency decisions reached in the planning process—NEPA review immediately upon promulgation of the plan, with review of the plan itself awaiting some later implementing action. In City of Williams v. Dombeck, 151 F.Supp.2d 9 (D.D.C.2001) the court held that challenges to the merits of a Forest Service land exchange (whether the appraisal of land value was improper, and whether the agency had properly concluded the public interest would be served) were not ripe because, after the agency approved the exchange, the local county had voted down a zoning ordinance which was necessary to allow the exchange to go forward. The court went on, however, to hold ripe a challenge to the adequacy of the Forest Service's NEPA compliance on the exchange. *See also* Kern v. Bureau of Land Management, 284 F.3d 1062 (9th Cir.2002).

3. In Park Lake Resources Ltd. Liab. Co. v. U.S. Dept. of Agriculture, 197 F.3d 448 (10th Cir.1999), a mining company challenged a Forest

Service decision to designate as a Research Natural Area an area of national forest that contained a unique alpine ecosystem including ten rare plant species. Applicable regulations did not forbid mining activities on the land, and the plaintiff had not made a concrete proposal to conduct operations on mining claims it had located in the area. Finding that it would be "speculative gymnastics" to foresee what the Forest Service might do if a specific proposal were submitted to it, the court held the challenge was not ripe. Does this conclusion follow from *Ohio Forestry?*

4.   Were the questions presented in *Ohio Forestry* legal or factual or both? Is it relevant that the APA never uses the words "standing," "ripeness," "exhaustion," "primary jurisdiction," and so forth, but simply says that "the reviewing court shall decide all relevant questions of law"? 5 U.S.C. § 706.

5.   It is sometimes said that the flip side of ripeness (challenging action too early) is mootness (challenging action too late). In Fund for Animals v. Babbitt, 89 F.3d 128 (2d Cir.1996), animal rights groups challenged a U.S. Fish & Wildlife Service decision to fund a "moose investigation project" being carried out by the state of Vermont. Plaintiffs claimed the funding was being used by the state to carry out a moose hunt, and that the federal agency should have complied with NEPA before deciding whether to fund it. The district court held that the state was no longer receiving federal funds directly related to the hunt, and dismissed the case as moot. Vacating and remanding, the court of appeals found this conclusion premature, because the state was continuing to receive federal funds that could be used to facilitate future moose hunts.

Reviewable Actions

Closely related to the question of ripeness is the issue of whether the agency has taken any reviewable "action" at all. Eight years before *Ohio Forestry*, Justice Scalia, in Lujan v. National Wildlife Federation, went on to say—after finding that the plaintiff had made an insufficient showing of standing—that the environmental group's challenge to Interior's alleged "land withdrawal review program" was not proper because there was no

"agency action" within the meaning of the APA § 702, much less a "final agency action" within the meaning of § 704. The term "land withdrawal review program" * * * is simply the name by which [the Department has] occasionally referred to the continuing (and thus constantly changing) operations of the BLM in reviewing withdrawal revocation applications and the classifications of public lands and developing land use plans as required by the FLPMA. It is no more an identifiable "agency action"—much less a "final agency action"—than a "weapons procurement program" of the Department of Defense or a "drug interdiction program" of the Drug Enforcement Administration. As the District Court explained, the "land withdrawal review program" extends to, currently at least, "1250 or so individual classification terminations and withdrawal revocations." 699 F.Supp., at 332.[2]

2. Contrary to the apparent understanding of the dissent, we do not contend that no "land withdrawal review program" exists, any more than we would contend that

NOTES AND QUESTIONS

1. Does the majority in *Lujan (I)* allow the government to avoid effective judicial review of general policy decisions altogether? Suppose a Secretary of the Interior quietly decides, upon taking office, never to reject any proposed mineral development anywhere on the federal lands, and she approves fifty different leases and mineral developments early in her tenure, rejecting none. In a challenge to the Secretary's decision to approve the fifty-first development, the Wilderness Society argues not only that the individual leasing decision is illegal, but also that the Secretary's knee-jerk pro-mining stance is arbitrary and capricious and inconsistent with the Secretary's statutory responsibility to make individual decisions in individual cases whether mineral development is in the public interest. The plaintiff also seeks to depose the Secretary and her staff to establish that such a policy exists. What should the court do?

2. It could work the other way too. Suppose the Secretary quietly resolves never to do anything to promote coal development on federal lands because of her concern about greenhouse gas emissions. Suppose an energy company applies to the Secretary for six different federal coal leases in six western states, and she rejects each one for the stated reason that, in each individual case, no more coal leasing is needed to satisfy market demand. May the applicant challenge these decisions in one lawsuit and argue (and seek discovery to try to prove) that the Secretary has a general policy that is inconsistent with her duty to make individual decisions in individual circumstances?

Enacted in 1976, the Federal Land Policy and Management Act (FLPMA) directs the Interior Secretary, in § 603 (43 U.S.C. § 1782), to inventory all BLM lands and identify roadless areas with "wilderness characteristics." Such inventoried areas became so-called "wilderness study areas" (WSAs). To protect Congress's own jealously-guarded prerogative that it—and not BLM or the Interior Secretary—have the final say on whether any such lands ought to be added to the National Wilderness Preservation System, FLPMA specifically instructed the Secretary to manage WSAs "in a manner so as not to impair the suitability of such areas for preservation as wilderness." § 1782(c). (Wilderness issues are taken up in detail in Chapter 12.) At issue in Norton v. SUWA is whether the federal courts can review whether BLM is living up to the "non-impairment" standard in its regulation of off-road vehicles (ORVs) in WSAs. We examine ORV regulation in greater detail in Chapter 11.

Damage from ORV traffic has emerged in the last quarter-century as perhaps the biggest single threat to protecting roadless areas on federal lands. One reason is that the sheer numbers of ORV riders have boomed. In

no weapons procurement program exists. We merely assert that it is not an identifiable "final agency action" for purposes of the APA. * * *

Utah, where this case arose, the number of registered ORVs has gone up 1000 percent since BLM did its initial wilderness inventory in 1991. SUWA's complaint which began this lawsuit alleged that BLM had simply not regulated ORV use in several specific roadless tracts, allowing roads to be created de facto in roadless areas, and converting trails and tracks into ORV raceways. The effect, SUWA alleged, was effectively to disqualify such areas from congressional designation as wilderness. In SUWA's view, BLM's regulatory failure violated, among other things, Congress's mandate that BLM manage WSAs according to a strict "non-impairment" standard.

Norton v. Southern Utah Wilderness Alliance

Supreme Court of the United States, 2004.
542 U.S. 55.

■ JUSTICE SCALIA delivered the opinion of the Court.

In this case, we must decide whether the authority of a federal court under the Administrative Procedure Act (APA) to "compel agency action unlawfully withheld or unreasonably delayed," 5 U.S.C. § 706(1), extends to the review of the United States Bureau of Land Management's steward-ship of public lands under certain statutory provisions and its own planning documents.

II

* * * [Plaintiffs' assert] that BLM failed to take action with respect to ORV use that it was required to take. Failures to act are sometimes remediable under the APA, but not always. We begin by considering what limits the APA places upon judicial review of agency inaction.

The APA authorizes suit by "[a] person suffering legal wrong because of agency action, or adversely affected or aggrieved by agency action within the meaning of a relevant statute." 5 U.S.C. § 702. Where no other statute provides a private right of action, the "agency action" complained of must be *"final* agency action." § 704 (emphasis added). "Agency action" is defined in § 551(13) to include "the whole or a part of an agency rule, order, license, sanction, relief, or the equivalent or denial thereof, *or failure to act."* (Emphasis added.) The APA provides relief for a failure to act in § 706(1): "The reviewing court shall ... compel agency action unlawfully withheld or unreasonably delayed."

Sections 702, 704, and 706(1) all insist upon an "agency action," either as the action complained of (in §§ 702 and 704) or as the action to be compelled (in § 706(1)). The definition of that term begins with a list of five categories of decisions made or outcomes implemented by an agency—"agency rule, order, license, sanction [or] relief." § 551(13). All of those categories involve circumscribed, discrete agency actions * * *.

The terms following those five categories of agency action are not defined in the APA: "or the equivalent or denial thereof, or failure to act." § 551(13). But an "equivalent ... thereof" must also be discrete (or it would not be equivalent), and a "denial thereof" must be the denial of a discrete listed action (and perhaps denial of a discrete equivalent).

The final term in the definition, "failure to act," is in our view properly understood as a failure to take an *agency action*—that is, a failure to take one of the agency actions (including their equivalents) earlier defined in § 551(13). * * * The important point is that a "failure to act" is properly understood to be limited, as are the other items in § 551(13), to a discrete action.

A second point central to the analysis of the present case is that the only agency action that can be compelled under the APA is action legally *required*. This limitation appears in § 706(1)'s authorization for courts to "compel agency action *unlawfully* withheld." * * * As described in the Attorney General's Manual on the APA, a document whose reasoning we have often found persuasive, empowers a court only to compel an agency "to perform a ministerial or non-discretionary act," or "to take action upon a matter, without directing *how* it shall act." Attorney General's Manual on the Administrative Procedure Act 108 (1947) (emphasis added).

Thus, a claim under § 706(1) can proceed only where a plaintiff asserts that an agency failed to take a *discrete* agency action that it is *required to take*. These limitations rule out several kinds of challenges. The limitation to discrete agency action precludes the kind of broad programmatic attack we rejected in Lujan v. National Wildlife Federation, 497 U.S. 871 (1990).

* * *

The limitation to *required* agency action rules out judicial direction of even discrete agency action that is not demanded by law (which includes, of course, agency regulations that have the force of law). Thus, when an agency is compelled by law to act within a certain time period, but the manner of its action is left to the agency's discretion, a court can compel the agency to act, but has no power to specify what the action must be.

* * *

III

A

With these principles in mind, we turn to SUWA's * * * claim, that by permitting ORV use in certain WSAs, BLM violated its mandate to "continue to manage [WSAs] ... in a manner so as not to impair the suitability of such areas for preservation as wilderness," 43 U.S.C. § 1782(c). SUWA relies not only upon § 1782(c) but also upon a provision of BLM's Interim Management Policy for Lands Under Wilderness Review, which interprets the nonimpairment mandate to require BLM to manage WSAs so as to prevent them from being "degraded so far, compared with the area's values for other purposes, as to significantly constrain the Congress's prerogative to either designate [it] as wilderness or release it for other uses."

Section 1782(c) is mandatory as to the object to be achieved, but it leaves BLM a great deal of discretion in deciding how to achieve it. It assuredly does not mandate, with the clarity necessary to support judicial action under § 706(1), the total exclusion of ORV use.

SUWA argues that § 1782 *does* contain a categorical imperative, namely the command to comply with the nonimpairment mandate. It contends that a federal court could simply enter a general order compelling compliance with that mandate, without suggesting any particular manner of compliance. * * * [But g]eneral deficiencies in compliance * * * lack the specificity requisite for agency action.

The principal purpose of the APA limitations we have discussed—and of the traditional limitations upon mandamus from which they were derived—is to protect agencies from undue judicial interference with their lawful discretion, and to avoid judicial entanglement in abstract policy disagreements which courts lack both expertise and information to resolve. If courts were empowered to enter general orders compelling compliance with broad statutory mandates, they would necessarily be empowered, as well, to determine whether compliance was achieved–which would mean that it would ultimately become the task of the supervising court, rather than the agency, to work out compliance with the broad statutory mandate, injecting the judge into day-to-day agency management. To take just a few examples from federal resources management, a plaintiff might allege that the Secretary had failed to "manage wild free-roaming horses and burros in a manner that is designed to achieve and maintain a thriving natural ecological balance," or to "manage the [New Orleans Jazz National] [H]istorical [P]ark in such a manner as will preserve and perpetuate knowledge and understanding of the history of jazz," or to "manage the [Steens Mountain] Cooperative Management and Protection Area for the benefit of present and future generations." 16 U.S.C. §§ 1333(a), 410bbb–2(a)(1), 460nnn–12(b). The prospect of pervasive oversight by federal courts over the manner and pace of agency compliance with such congressional directives is not contemplated by the APA.

NOTES AND QUESTIONS

1. Did the United States contest the fact that ORV use may be impairing the roadless areas in question? What was its defense? The majority of the Tenth Circuit panel below had said the government's argument seeks to carve out a "no-man's land" where agencies could behave unlawfully yet be permanently sheltered from judicial review. Is that right? Is the Supreme Court here saying the federal courts have no jurisdiction to stop agency inaction even if it causes irreversible destruction of some of the nation's few remaining wildlands, in apparent violation of a congressional mandate?

2. Is the Court saying the courts may never review a BLM decision to dawdle and disregard its duty not to impair WSAs, so long as the BLM avoids taking "final agency action"? That it can review BLM "inaction" in this context only if BLM announces to the world that it has made a final decision to do nothing about ORVs in WSAs? If the federal land manager wants to avoid judicial meddling, should it simply say it is "monitoring"

the ORV problem and will consider taking action if it looks like "impairment" is occurring, and then just do nothing? That is, not ever admit that it had made a final decision not to take action?

3.   What if wilderness advocates petition the BLM to adopt a rule closing certain WSAs to ORVs because "impairment" of their wilderness values is occurring, and the BLM rejects the petition. Is the rejection agency action subject to judicial review? (The Administrative Procedure Act requires agencies to "give an interested person the right to petition for the issuance * * * of a rule," and requires the agency to respond promptly and give a "brief statement of the grounds" if it decides to deny the petition. 5 U.S.C. §§ 553(b) and (e). *See generally* Telecommunications Research and Action Center v. FCC, 750 F. 2d 70 (D.C.Cir.1984) (setting out standards for agency handling of petitions for rulemaking, known as TRAC standards).)

4.   Does Congress's desire to keep for itself the decision whether a particular tract of federal land will be designated as wilderness distinguish this case from the wild horses, New Orleans Jazz, and Steens Mountain examples Justice Scalia cites in the last paragraph of the opinion, above? Does the Court here in effect authorize BLM to take that decision out of Congress's hands, by allowing ORVs to create a spider's web of roads throughout a "roadless" area? Could this be what Congress had in mind in FLPMA? Does Congress have a remedy?

5.   Did the congressional mandate of "no impairment" prohibit ORVs in wilderness study areas? Is it clear that Congress intended to give BLM a "great deal of discretion" to determine how to achieve the "non-impairment" standard? Suppose BLM says that it will allow, but carefully monitor, ORV use in wilderness study areas, but it does not require a permit for such uses. A motorcycle club announces that it is going to hold a massive off-road rally through the heart of a WSA. Thousands of motorcyclists are planning to participate. Wilderness advocates allege the rally will devastate the wilderness values in the area, permanently (or at least for a generation or two) rendering the area incapable of qualifying for congressional protection as wilderness. Can a federal court hear the case?

6.   If BLM decides to exclude ORV users from WSAs, can they seek relief in federal courts? Does Justice Scalia's approach unbalance the playing field, closing the federal courthouse doors to wilderness protection advocates, when they are open to ORV users?

7.   Suppose Congress has required the Secretary to promulgate regulations to implement the "non-wilderness-impairment" standard of FLPMA by a date certain, and the Secretary has failed to do so? Are the courts open to enforce that deadline? If so, what if the Secretary responds with a one-sentence regulation that says: "BLM will monitor off-road vehicle use in wilderness study areas and will take any action necessary to carry out the 'non-impairment' mandate?" Does Norton v. SUWA leave any room for the courts to strike down such a regulation?

8.   Is it true that by Scalia's "reckoning, the discretion how to achieve the object * * * becomes discretion not to achieve it—at least, so far as a

court is concerned"? Bret C. Birdsong, *Justice Scalia's Footprints on the Public Lands,* 83 DENV. U. L.REV. 259 (2005). Professor Birdsong notes that Justice Scalia wrote extensively on public lands issues as a young professor. Professor Birdsong explores the apparent paradox that Professor Scalia seemed to favor judicial review of public lands matters, while Justice Scalia seems to abhor it. Or as Birdsong put it: "Justice Scalia's footprints on the public lands led in 1970 to the door of the federal courthouse. Today they lead away from it." Professor Birdsong argues Professor Scalia was defending the right of public lands users with property-like claims to seek judicial review of agency action; Justice Scalia has tried to limit the scope of judicial review when sought by representatives of the broader public interest— private attorneys general without property claims. More broadly, Justice Scalia has used the public lands context to mount a counter-reformation to the celebrated "reformation" of administrative law—a reform that opened it to broader judicial review—fashioned by courts and commentators in the 1970s.

e.   COMMITTED TO AGENCY DISCRETION BY LAW

Closely related to the issues decided in Norton v. SUWA is the realm of actions committed to agency discretion by law, and therefore not fit for judicial review. The Administrative Procedure Act, 5 U.S.C. § 701(a), contains two exceptions to the general availability of judicial review: where "(1) statutes preclude judicial review; or (2) agency action is committed to agency discretion by law." The first exception has little or no application in federal land and resources law as statutes expressly precluding judicial review are rare.

The applicability of the second exception is very limited, but it occasionally operates in federal land and resources law. Citizens to Preserve Overton Park, Inc. v. Volpe, 401 U.S. 402 (1971) described this as a "very narrow exception," applicable only in "those rare instances" where the statute controlling the decision was framed so broadly as to give the agency "no law to apply." There was, in other words, a "basic presumption in favor of judicial review."

Since *Overton Park,* it is a rare case where agency discretion is so broad as to block judicial review in the public natural resources law. One important exception to the general presumption of reviewability is, however, when a plaintiff seeks to require an agency to bring an action to enforce federal law. The Supreme Court has analogized this to prosecutorial discretion in criminal cases, and reversed the presumption of reviewability. Heckler v. Chaney, 470 U.S. 821 (1985). Heckler did not say such prosecutorial decisions regarding civil law enforcement were unreviewable, only that they were "presumptively unreviewable," 470 U.S. at 832.

Suppose the statute establishing Petrified Forest National Park provides that the "Secretary of the Interior shall protect against the theft and destruction of the petrified wood found in the park." Suppose evidence clearly shows looting and theft is widespread and enforcement practically non-existent, so that, if nothing is done, within a few years a large portion of the petrified wood in the park will have been carried off by looters and tourists. Can persons who visit the park, and who are allegedly harmed by the loss, bring a federal court action against the Park Service requiring it to take steps to safeguard park resources?

2. THE SCOPE OF JUDICIAL REVIEW

Agency administration dominates modern public land law; therefore, litigation typically centers on the records constructed by the agencies to support a decision. It is the exceptional case that retains the pre-modern, property attribute of having a district court conduct a trial to determine facts. In other words, with the exception of rights-of-way and other title or takings actions, primary jurisdiction over dispute resolution rests with the agency. The courts accept agency fact findings unless they are unsupported in the record.

Agency records are the outcome of either formal or informal procedures. When agencies employ formal, quasi-judicial procedures, which generally involve impartial decision-makers that are shielded from ex parte communications, courts employ an appellate-style review standard: the administrative findings must be supported by substantial evidence. Far more common in public land law are informal procedures, where line officers gather studies, expert staff recommendations, and public opinion to make a judgment. Review of these informal decisions employs the "arbitrary and capricious" scope of review discussed below. Quasi-legislative agency action, namely rulemaking, is subject to special procedures of "notice and comment" through publication in the Federal Register. 5 U.S.C. § 554. Notwithstanding the special procedures, courts review rulemaking in this field of law under the same "arbitrary and capricious standard."

Generally speaking, review of an administrative agency action under the APA is confined to the agency's own administrative record. Camp v. Pitts, 411 U.S. 138, 142 (1973). If the agency record is inadequate for some reason, the "proper course, except in rare circumstances, is to remand to the agency for additional investigation." Florida Power & Light Co. v. Lorion, 470 U.S. 729, 744 (1985). Judge Richard Posner summarized the approach this way in a case challenging a Forest Service timber sale:

> In such a suit the district court is a reviewing court * * * it does not take evidence. * * * Not often, anyway. An evidentiary hearing in district court may be necessary to reconstruct the agency's action or the grounds thereof, if the action and its ground were not set forth in written decision, though an even better response might be to stay the judicial review proceeding until the agency completed the record. * * * [O]nly in an emergency should a reviewing court * * * conduct its own evidentiary hearing.

> Confining the district court to the record compiled by the administrative agency rests on practical considerations that deserve respect. Administrative agencies deal with technical questions, and it is imprudent for the generalist judges of the [federal bench] to consider testimonial and documentary evidence bearing on those questions

unless the evidence has first been presented to and considered by the agency. Trees may seem far removed from the arcana of administrative determination, but one has only to glance at the documents submitted in this case to realize that "silviculture" is in fact a technical field, and not just one with a dry and forbidding vocabulary.

Therefore only if there is no record and no feasible method of requiring the agency to compile one in time to protect the objector's rights—in short, only (to repeat) if there is an emergency—should an objector be allowed to present evidence in court showing why the agency acted unlawfully.

Cronin v. U.S. Dept. of Agriculture, 919 F.2d 439, 444–45 (7th Cir.1990). These days agency decisions of any moment are usually explained in some sort of written record of decision, making review strictly confined to the administrative record almost universal.

It is sometimes said that the core of administrative law is encapsulated in the slogan: "Factual questions are for the agency and legal questions are for the court." That describes the basic positions typically taken by advocates in public land litigation. Government lawyers argue that the case turns on factual determinations with which management officials have expertise. Lawyers attacking management decisions contend that the case depends on legal analysis of statutes, regulations, or the Constitution—matters more within the special qualifications of courts. Normally the APA defines the scope of review in public lands cases. 5 U.S.C. § 706:

To the extent necessary to decision and when presented, the reviewing court shall decide all relevant questions of law, interpret constitutional and statutory provisions, and determine the meaning or applicability of the terms of an agency action. The reviewing court shall—

(1) compel agency action unlawfully withheld or unreasonably delayed; and

(2) hold unlawful and set aside agency action, findings, and conclusions found to be—

(A) arbitrary, capricious, an abuse of discretion, or otherwise not in accordance with law;

(B) contrary to constitutional right, power, privilege, or immunity;

(C) in excess of statutory jurisdiction, authority, or limitations, or short of statutory right;

(D) without observance of procedure required by law.

In the argot of administrative law, the circumstances described by 5 U.S.C. § 706(2)(A) through (D) are bundled together under term "arbitrary and capricious." The courts, as well as the commentators, seldom fully agree as to the appropriate scope and depth of judicial review in any set of circumstances. In *Overton Park*, for example, the Court held that the Secretary's decision was arbitrary because the record showed that the Secretary had not thoroughly considered all relevant factors surrounding the availability of alternative routes for a highway. The Court said that though the "arbitrary, capricious, abuse of discretion" standard of review was narrow, the reviewing court's inquiry "is to be searching and careful." That has scarcely ended the matter. In a subsequent decision not involving federal lands, Motor Vehicle Mfrs. Ass'n v. State Farm Mut. Auto. Ins. Co., 463 U.S. 29, 43 (1983), the Court said that an agency's decision may be arbitrary and capricious if it

> has relied on factors which Congress had not intended it to consider, entirely failed to consider an important aspect of the problem, offered an explanation for its decision that runs counter to the evidence before the agency, or is so implausible that it could not be ascribed to a difference in view or the product of agency expertise.

Professor William Rodgers has developed an inventive typology that he terms "the central premise of judicial review." When there is a "vague mandate" from Congress, the substantive decision will often be left to the agency but the courts will scrutinize the procedures followed by the agencies, and may determine whether the agency considered all relevant factors and whether it based its decision on irrelevant factors. When the controlling legislation provides a "specific mandate," the courts will also analyze the substance of the decision by determining whether it conformed to the statutory intent. William Rodgers, Energy and Natural Resources Law 190–240 (2d ed.1983).

Most decisions in this and succeeding chapters discuss and apply many of the principles of judicial review identified in this brief summary. The following opinions frame some of the general issues of judicial review.

Udall v. Tallman

Supreme Court of the United States, 1965.
380 U.S. 1.

■ Chief Justice Warren delivered the opinion of the court.

[The facts were rather bewildering; in a nutshell: In 1941, the President by Executive Order No. 8979 created the Kenai National Moose Range in Alaska, and withdrew most of it from "settlement, location, sale, or entry or other disposition * * * under any of the public-land laws applicable to Alaska." In 1948, the Secretary of the Interior issued an order (No. 487) withdrawing lands in Alaska, including most of the Moose Range, from "settlement, location, sale or entry * * *." In 1951, the Secretary issued still other orders (Nos. 751, 778) withdrawing a small part of the lands previously withdrawn from "all forms of appropriation under the public-land laws, including the mining laws and the mineral-leasing laws."

In 1953 the BLM announced that, pending a possible revision in the general policy regarding oil and gas leasing in federal wildlife reserves like the Moose Range, action on pending oil and gas lease offers in such refuges would be "suspended." In 1954 and 1955, the Griffin group applied for oil and gas leases in the northern part of the Moose Range. Action on them was suspended in accordance with the 1953 directive. Finally, in 1958, the Secretary issued an order closing the southern half of the Moose Range to oil and gas leasing in order to protect wildlife, but making lands in the northern half available for leasing. 23 Fed.Reg. 5883 (1958). This order also said that (1) "pending" offers to lease upon which action had been suspended "will now be acted upon;" and (2) offers to lease land now open to leasing will be "accepted for filing" beginning August 14, 1958.

On August 14, the Tallman group filed applications to lease the same lands that were the subject of the earlier-filed Griffin applications. The applicable statute at the time gave preference to the "person first making application for the lease." The Secretary issued the leases to the Griffin group, and the Tallman group sued. The district court held for the Griffin group. The court of appeals reversed, holding that, because of the various orders described above, the lands had been withdrawn from mineral leasing at the time of the Griffin applications. Therefore they were "nullities," and the Tallman group was thus the first applicant to lease these lands.] * * *

When faced with a problem of statutory construction, this Court shows great deference to the interpretation given the statute by the officers or agency charged with its administration. "To sustain the Commission's application of this statutory term, we need not find that its construction is the only reasonable one, or even that it is the result we would have reached had the question arisen in the first instance in judicial proceedings." Unemployment Comm'n v. Aragon, 329 U.S. 143, 153. * * * "Particularly is this respect due when the administrative practice at stake 'involves a contemporaneous construction of a statute by the men charged with the responsibility of setting its machinery in motion, of making the parts work efficiently and smoothly while they are yet untried and new.'" Power Reactor Dev. Co. v. Electricians, 367 U.S. 396, 408. When the construction of an administrative regulation rather than a statute is in issue, deference is even more clearly in order.

> "Since this involves an interpretation of an administrative regulation a court must necessarily look to the administrative construction of the regulation if the meaning of the words used is in doubt. * * * [T]he ultimate criterion is the administrative interpretation, which becomes of controlling weight unless it is plainly erroneous or inconsistent with the regulation." Bowles v. Seminole Rock Co., 325 U.S. 410, 413–414.

In the instant case, there is no statutory limitation involved. While Executive Order No. 8979 was issued by the President, he soon delegated to the Secretary full power to withdraw lands or to modify or revoke any existing withdrawals. * * * Public Land Order No. 487 was issued by the Secretary himself.

Moreover, as the discussion in Section I of this opinion demonstrates, the Secretary has consistently construed Executive Order No. 8979 and Public Land Order No. 487 not to bar oil and gas leases. * * * The Secretary's interpretation had, long prior to respondents' applications, been a matter of public record and discussion. * * * [A]lmost the entire area covered by the orders in issue has been developed, at very great expense, in reliance upon the Secretary's interpretation. In McLaren v. Fleischer, 256 U.S. 477, 480–481, it was held:

"In the practical administration of the act the officers of the land
department have adopted and given effect to the latter view. They
adopted it before the present controversy arose or was thought of, and,
except for a departure soon reconsidered and corrected, they have
adhered to and followed it ever since. Many outstanding titles are
based upon it and much can be said in support of it. If not the only
reasonable construction of the act, it is at least an admissible one. It
therefore comes within the rule that the practical construction given to
an act of Congress, fairly susceptible of different constructions, by
those charged with the duty of executing it is entitled to great respect
and, if acted upon for a number of years, will not be disturbed except
for cogent reasons."

If, therefore, the Secretary's interpretation is not unreasonable, if the
language of the orders bears his construction, we must reverse the decision
of the Court of Appeals.

Executive Order No. 8979, 6 Fed.Reg. 6471, provided:

None of the above-described lands excepting [a described area] shall be
subject to settlement, location, sale, or entry, or other disposition
(except for fish trap sites) under any of the public-land laws applicable
to Alaska, or to classification and lease * * *.

"Settlement," "location," "sale" and "entry" are all terms contemplating
transfer of title to the lands in question. It was therefore reasonable for the
Secretary to construe "or other disposition" to encompass only dispositions
which, like the four enumerated, convey or lead to the conveyance of the
title of the United States—for example, "grants" and "allotments." An oil
and gas lease does not vest title to the lands in the lessee. Moreover, the
term "public-land laws" is ordinarily used to refer to statutes governing
the alienation of public land, and generally is distinguished from both
"mining laws," referring to statutes governing the mining of hard minerals
on public lands, and "mineral leasing laws," a term used to designate that
group of statutes governing the leasing of public lands for gas and oil. * * *

* * *

The placement of the fish trap exception—"(except for fish trap
sites)"—a phrase admittedly not relating to alienation of title to land, does
tend to cut against the Secretary's interpretation of Executive Order No.
8979. However, it appears that the exception was designed to assure the
Alaskans, whose livelihood is largely dependent on the salmon catch, that
they could continue—despite the order—to use fish traps. * * * Since it
was a reassurance not technically necessary and therefore not functionally
related to any part of the regulation, it is no surprise to find it carelessly
placed. * * * We do not think the position of the fish trap exception is
sufficient to justify a court's overturning the Secretary's construction as
unreasonable.

Public Land Order No. 487 withdrew the lands it covered from "settlement, location, sale or entry," but contained no reference to "other
disposition." Nor did it contain anything analogous to the fish trap exception. The reasonableness of the Secretary's interpretation of Public Land

Order No. 487 therefore follows a fortiori from the reasonableness of his construction of Executive Order No. 8979.

NOTES AND QUESTIONS

1. The Court found that no "disposition" was involved and that the mining laws were not "public land laws." Does the Court draw a clear roadmap through this mess of terms and phrases? Does a land order that withdraws lands "from settlement and entry, or other form of appropriation" remove the lands from the operation of the hardrock mining laws? In *Mason v. United States*, 260 U.S. 545 (1923), a miner argued that "other form of appropriation" meant forms akin to "settlement" (at a time when homesteading was still active), and that mining claims were acquired by "location." The Supreme Court held against the mining claimant:

> Here the supposed specific words are sufficiently comprehensive to exhaust the genus and leave nothing essentially similar upon which the general words may operate. If the appropriation of mineral lands by location and development be not akin to settlement and entry, what other form of appropriation can be so characterized? None has been suggested, and we can think of none.

Mason was not cited in Udall v. Tallman. On whether mineral leases are "dispositions," is it relevant that the first section in the Mineral Leasing Act, 30 U.S.C. § 181, states that "deposits of * * * oil * * * shall be subject to disposition in the form and manner provided by this chapter"? Is the Mineral Leasing Act a "public land law"? The general subject of withdrawals is treated in more detail in Chapter 5.

2. Udall v. Tallman is often cited for the general proposition that courts should defer to administrative interpretations of regulations and statutes. Why should such administrative interpretations receive deference? Can't courts interpret statutes at least as well as agency lawyers can?

3. Here, in fact, the issue was not statutory interpretation, but rather how prior agency orders should be interpreted. Should the agency be given more, the same, or less deference in that context? Hadn't the executive branch here created the problem by its welter of confusing, seemingly inconsistent, and somewhat overlapping orders of withdrawal? Does the general idea that ambiguities in a contract or other document are ordinary construed against the drafter come into play here? (Is the contest here essentially between the government and a private party, or between two private parties?) Should private contract notions be applied in the context of federal lands where the government is the sovereign as well as the landowner? *See Mobil Oil* and discussion, *infra* p. 347.

The key question in many cases of judicial review is not whether an agency has discretion, but how far that discretion should go. Courts accord deference to agency judgment, but how much deference is appropriate under the APA? The "deference" issue is frequently raised in federal lands litigation because of the large number of administrative interpretations of statutes and orders, found especially in agency regulations and written opinions of agency lawyers. The next case addressed the issue in the context of one of the largest construction projects in history. Prudhoe Bay is the biggest oilfield ever discovered in North America. At the time of this litigation, geologists estimated its size to be 9.6 billion barrels, but as of the end of 2006 it has produced nearly 12 billion barrels, with at least another two billion to go.

Wilderness Society v. Morton (the TAPS case)

United States Court of Appeals, District of Columbia Circuit, 1973 (en banc). 479 F.2d 842, *cert. denied*, 411 U.S. 917 (1973).

■ JUDGE WRIGHT

The question before us in these cases is whether a permanent injunction should issue barring appellee Secretary of the Interior from carrying out his stated intention of granting rights-of-way and special land use permits [SLUPs] necessary for construction by appellee Alyeska Pipeline Service Company (Alyeska), across lands owned by the United States, of a 48–inch-wide oil pipeline which would stretch some 789 miles from Prudhoe Bay on the North Slope of the State of Alaska to the Port of Valdez on the southern Pacific coast of Alaska. * * *

[The district court issued a preliminary injunction against the project in April 1970 for failure to comply with the National Environmental Policy Act (NEPA) on the proposal. In August 1972, following preparation of an environmental impact statement, the district court dissolved the injunction and dismissed the case.]

While the parties to this action have managed to produce a record and a set of briefs commensurate with the multi-billion-dollar project at stake, the basic contentions of the parties, and our views with respect thereto, may be summarized quite briefly. Appellants contend that issuance of certain rights-of-way and special land use permits by the Secretary of the Interior to Alyeska and to the State of Alaska would violate Section 28 of the Mineral Leasing Act of 1920, 30 U.S.C. § 185, by exceeding the width limitation of that section.*

[The oil companies, through their agent TAPS (Trans–Alaska Pipeline System), acknowledged a need for a 54–foot "primary" right-of-way (the pipe itself was 48 inches in diameter), an additional parallel 46–foot "secondary" right-of-way for construction purposes, another 100–foot right-of-way for a haul road alongside the pipeline, and temporary use of an additional 200–500 feet on each side of all river and stream crossings and for construction camps at some other locations. The Interior Department was prepared to issue SLUPs for the area of the right-of-way outside the 50–foot statutory limitation.]

In brief, it is our view that the legislative history clearly indicates that when Congress enacted Section 28 it intended that all construction work take place within the confines of the width limitation of the section—that is, within the area covered by the pipe itself (4 feet) and 25 feet on either side. In addition, the relevant regulations require that all special land use permits be revocable, and we hold that the permit in this case does not meet the requirement as it has previously been construed. Since all parties agree that construction of the proposed 48–inch diameter pipeline is impossible if all construction work must take place within the width limitation of Section 28, we must enjoin issuance of this special land use permit until Congress changes the applicable law, either by amending Section 28's width limitation or by exempting this project from its provisions. * * *

* * * [W]hile our maxims of statutory construction might have led us to conclude that Congress "must have intended" that those building pipelines could make use of land outside the statutory right-of-way for construction purposes, the legislative history [of the Mineral Leasing Act] simply indicates otherwise. One might have expected the Congress of the United States to exercise foresight in a situation in which it was expressly warned that the statute it was enacting was then, or might in the future become, ineffective. But such foresight was notably lacking. Foresight no doubt would have been the wisest choice in this instance, since after the passage of the Mineral Leasing Act pipeline technology developed to permit construction of larger pipelines needing greater amounts of construction space. It might fairly be said that Congress overreacted to the prior excesses of railroad rights-of-way. But it is not our function, when we pass on either the constitutionality of statutes or their interpretation, to substi-

* [Eds.: At the time, Section 28 authorized the Secretary of the Interior to issue rights of way across public lands and national forests for oil and gas pipelines "to the extent of the ground occupied by said pipeline and twenty-five feet on each side of the same under such regulations and conditions * * * as may be prescribed by the Secretary * * * Provided further, that no right-of-way shall hereafter be granted over said lands for the transportation of oil or natural gas except under and subject to the provisions, limitations, and conditions of this section."]

tute our opinion as to what is wise for that of Congress. Congress chose not to be foresightful; it chose to retain control of the width of pipeline rights-of-way over public land itself, and that decision and its consequences must stand until Congress chooses otherwise.

Appellees have placed their primary reliance on the administrative practice with respect to SLUPs. While we find it unnecessary to review the administrative history in great detail, looking at that history in the light most favorable to appellees it indicates (1) that ever since the Mineral Leasing Act was passed the informal policy of the Bureau of Land Management has been to permit those constructing pipelines to use land for construction purposes outside the statutory right-of-way; (2) that since 1960 this informal practice has begun to become formalized through the procedure of granting SLUPs for construction space to supplement the statutory right-of-way; and (3) that the Department of the Interior and other agencies have granted SLUPs for a multitude of purposes other than pipeline purposes for the last 100 years, oftentimes in situations where the SLUP "supplemented" a limited statutory right-of-way. Appellees argue that this administrative practice should be accorded great weight and deference in the interpretation of the effect of Section 28 on SLUPs for construction purposes, and should lead us to conclude that Section 28 does not affect the Secretary's authority to issue SLUPs.

* * * We do not question the settled principle that administrative interpretations of statutes are entitled to great weight. Udall v. Tallman, 380 U.S. 1 (1965). But it is our firm belief that a line must be drawn between according administrative interpretations deference and the proposition that administrative agencies are entitled to violate the law if they do it often enough. Not to draw this line is to make a mockery of the judicial function. "[T]he courts are the final authorities on issues of statutory construction * * * and 'are not obliged to stand aside and rubber-stamp their affirmance of administrative decisions that they deem inconsistent with a statutory mandate or that frustrate the congressional policy underlying a statute.' * * * " Volkswagenwerk Aktiengesellschaft v. F.M.C., 390 U.S. at 272. * * * An administrative practice which is plainly contrary to the legislative will may be overturned no matter how well settled and how long standing.

Balancing the maxim of deference to administrative interpretations with the principle that the courts remain the final arbiter of the meaning of the law is unquestionably a difficult process. [We must] analyze the rationales behind the doctrine of deference and * * * ask if they apply in this case. * * * [I]f they do not, the maxim of deference must inevitably bow before the principle of judicial supremacy in matters of statutory construction. Application of that methodology to the instant case leads us to conclude that "[t]hose props that serve to support a disputable administrative construction are absent here." Zuber v. Allen, supra, 396 U.S. at 193.

Perhaps the primary rationale behind the doctrine of deference is the idea of administrative expertise. * * * "Administrative construction is less potent than it otherwise would be where it does not rest upon matters peculiarly within the administrator's field of expertise." Thompson v. Clifford, 408 F.2d 154, 167 (D.C.Cir.1968).

There * * * is no need for administrative expertise in resolving the question of the meaning of Section 28. Expertise might be needed to decide what is a reasonable pipeline construction area, but it is not needed to decide whether Section 28 precludes construction outside the statutory right-of-way. * * *

The second basic rationale for the doctrine of deference is the concept of congressional acquiescence in the administrative interpretation. "Under some circumstances, Congress' failure to repeal or revise [a statute] in the face of such administrative interpretation has been held to constitute persuasive evidence that that interpretation is the one intended by Congress." Zemel v. Rusk, 381 U.S. 1, 11 (1965). Thus in actual cases courts have to analyze whether there is any reason to believe that the particular administrative interpretation in question came to the attention of Congress so that it might reasonably be said that Congress, by failing to take any action with respect thereto, approved the interpretation. As we have had occasion to note, "Legislative silence cannot mean ratification unless, as a minimum, the existence of the administrative practice is brought home to the legislature." Thompson v. Clifford, supra, 408 F.2d at 164.

Applying the rationale to the present case, there is absolutely no indication that the practice of granting SLUPs for pipeline construction purposes has ever been brought to the attention of Congress, either through testimony at a congressional hearing or by any other means. Nor is the practice of granting SLUPs for pipeline construction purposes of such public knowledge that it is reasonable to assume that congressmen, as members of the general public, knew of the practice. * * *

* * *

CONCLUSION

"[G]reat cases are called great," Mr. Justice Holmes said 70 years ago, "not by reason of their real importance in shaping the law of the future, but because of some accident of immediate overwhelming interest * * *." Northern Securities Co. v. United States, 193 U.S. 197, 400 (1904) (dissenting opinion). The same may be said about the present litigation over the Alaska pipeline. These cases are indeed "great" because of the obvious magnitude and current importance of the interest at stake: billions of gallons of oil at a time when the nation faces an energy crisis of serious proportions; hundreds of millions of dollars in revenue for the State of Alaska at a time when financial support for important social programs is badly needed; industrial development and pollution of one of the last major unblemished wilderness areas in the world, at a time when we are all becoming increasingly aware of the delicate balance between man and his natural environment.

But despite these elements of greatness, the principles of law controlling these cases are neither complex nor revolutionary. Although the first part of this opinion went to great lengths to demonstrate that special land use permits for construction purposes were illegal under the Mineral Leasing Act, at the heart of that discussion is the following very simple point. Congress, by enacting Section 28, allowed pipeline companies to use a certain amount of land to construct their pipelines. These companies have now come into court, accompanied by the executive agency authorized to administer the statute, and have said, "This is not enough land; give us more." We have no more power to grant their request, of course, than we have the power to increase congressional appropriations to needy recipients. * * *

In the last analysis, it is an abiding function of the courts, in the course of decision of cases and controversies, to require the Executive to abide by the limitations prescribed by the Legislature. The scrupulous vindication of that basic principle of law, implicit in our form of government, its three branches and its checks and balances, looms more important in the abiding public interest than the embarkation on any immediate or specific project, however desirable in and of itself, in contravention of that principle. We think it plain that the Executive Branch, when confronted with the legal problems attendant upon the Alaska pipeline, should have taken note of the limitations that had been prescribed by Congress, and should have presented to Congress the case for revision of the basic statute.

NOTES AND QUESTIONS

1. What was Alyeska's argument that the statutory limitation to fifty feet did not control? Is the statute clear?

2. Would the result have been the same in the *TAPS* case if the Department of the Interior had published a formal regulation in the Federal Register interpreting the right-of-way grant to apply only to the ground actually occupied by the pipeline, and reciting that a special land use permit (SLUP) would be issued for any additional land needed? The U.S. Supreme Court has generally followed the rule that an agency is bound by its own formal regulations. In the federal lands area, as elsewhere, the usual (although not wholly consistent) practice is for federal agencies to flesh out statutory provisions with (or create new processes through) detailed regulations. These are typically adopted after notice and opportunity for comment through the Federal Register, and compiled in the Code of Federal Regulations (CFR).

3. Suppose that, instead of a statutory standard, the fifty-foot limitation came from an longstanding rule promulgated by the Interior Department implementing general language of mineral leasing legislation. Could the Secretary issue the right-of-way permit under the rule? Do agencies have more discretion in interpreting their own rules than in interpreting statutes? How would the Udall v. Tallman court answer these questions?

4. How much knowledge is required in the Congress in order for a court to find that Congress has acquiesced in an interpretation of a statute made by an administrative agency? The knowledge of one member of Congress? Of one committee, in one house of Congress? Does it make any

difference that the membership in Congress whose awareness of agency interpretation is in question will usually not be the same membership as that of the Congress which enacted the statute the agency is interpreting?

5.   Suppose that the Mineral Leasing Act specifically provides that oil lessees shall pay "a maximum rental of five cents per acre leased." Assume that figure, never changed by Congress, has been rendered trivial by inflation. Can the Secretary of the Interior promulgate a regulation raising the rental to $5 per acre? Would oil industry arguments against that increase be any different from the environmentalist plaintiffs' argument in the *TAPS* case?

6.   The district court had found the Department's compliance with NEPA adequate. Environmentalists asked the court of appeals to overturn this ruling, but the court thought it unnecessary to address the merits of the NEPA issue once it had found the permit unlawful. This left the oil companies facing the possibility of further delay through renewed NEPA litigation if Congress merely amended the Mineral Leasing Act to authorize a wider right-of-way. Seven months after the Supreme Court denied certiorari in the *TAPS* case, Congress overhauled the right-of-way portion of the Mineral Leasing Act. It authorized rights-of-way in excess of the fifty-foot limitation in certain cases, added substantial regulatory controls aimed at protecting the environment, and made other changes. 30 U.S.C. § 185. The same legislation, by a narrow margin (Vice–President Agnew casting the tie-breaking vote in the Senate) exempted the TAPS from further environmental review.

The ultimate goals of the plaintiffs in the *TAPS* case were primarily to strengthen environmental regulation of the construction and operation of the TAPS, and to force the Department to give more serious consideration to an alternative route for the pipeline, from the North Slope across Canada to the U.S. Midwest. Environmentalists preferred this route for two basic reasons. First, the all-land route would avoid the need to ship oil by tanker through hazardous waters south of the pipeline's terminus in Valdez, Alaska, and would connect with existing pipelines for shipment to the areas of greatest demand for imported oil in the eastern United States. Second, it was widely expected that a second pipeline, to transport natural gas off the North Slope, would also be necessary, and would likely involve a route through Canada to the Midwest. The environmentalists thought a single corridor for both pipelines was preferable.

The litigation and subsequent legislation substantially achieved the goal of tighter environmental regulation of the pipeline; practically all observers have conceded that the result was a better, environmentally safer pipeline, which currently delivers about 15 percent of the country's domestically produced oil. At its peak, the pipeline added two million barrels per day to the U.S. domestic oil supplies (about what improved auto efficiency standards would supply). Questions still arise whether all the safeguards are being observed. Previously undetected leaks and corrosion discovered in 2006 shut down the pipeline for a time, disrupting production. The right-of-way had a thirty year term. In 2004 Interior Secretary Gale Norton renewed the right-of-way for an additional thirty years.

Congress's 1973 decision to short-cut further environmental review foreclosed a closer look at the Canadian alternative. That meant oil tanker traffic from the pipeline's southern terminus would remain a hazard, and the rest, as they say, is history: the Exxon Valdez struck Bligh Reef south of Valdez in March 1989, causing a massive oil spill that fouled waters, beaches, and wildlife across Prince William Sound and beyond. *See* In re the Exxon Valdez v. Hazelwood, 270 F.3d 1215 (9th Cir.2001). Meanwhile, despite various proposals over the years, a second pipeline for natural gas has not yet been built, and the gas produced with the North Slope oil is being reinjected in the ground, awaiting a way to transport it to market.

NOTE: THE CHEVRON DOCTRINE AND DEFERENCE TO SPECIAL FORMS OF AGENCY INTERPRETATIONS

In Chevron, USA, Inc. v. Natural Resources Defense Council, 467 U.S. 837, 842–45 (1984), reversing a lower court decision, the Supreme Court upheld an Environmental Protection Agency rule interpreting the Clean Air Act. In doing so, the Court announced a new category of deference:

> When a court reviews an agency's construction of the statute which it administers, it is confronted with two questions. First, always, is the question whether Congress has directly spoken to the precise question at issue. If the intent of Congress is clear, that is the end of the matter; for the court, as well as the agency, must give effect to the unambiguously expressed intent of Congress. If, however, the court determines Congress has not directly addressed the precise question at issue, the court does not simply impose its own construction on the statute, as would be necessary in the absence of an administrative interpretation. Rather, if the statute is silent or ambiguous with respect to the specific issue, the question for the court is whether the agency's answer is based on a permissible construction of the statute.

> "The power of an administrative agency to administer a congressionally created * * * program necessarily requires the formulation of policy and the making of rules to fill any gap left, implicitly and explicitly, by Congress." Morton v. Ruiz, 415 U.S. 199, 231 (1974). If Congress has explicitly left a gap for the agency to fill, there is an express delegation of authority to the agency to elucidate a specific provision of the statute by regulation. Such legislative regulations are given controlling weight unless they are arbitrary, capricious, or manifestly contrary to the statute. Sometimes the legislative delegation to an agency on a particular question is implicit rather than explicit. In such a case, a court may not substitute its own construction of a statutory provision for a reasonable interpretation made by the administrator of an agency.

> We have long recognized that considerable weight should be accorded to an executive department's construction of a statutory scheme it is entrusted to administer, and the principle of deference to administrative interpretations "has been consistently followed by this Court whenever decision as to the meaning or reach of a statute has involved

reconciling conflicting policies, and a full understanding of the force of the statutory policy in the given situation has depended upon more than ordinary knowledge respecting the matters subjected to agency regulations.''

* * * If this choice represents a reasonable accommodation of conflicting policies that were committed to the agency's care by the statute, we should not disturb it unless it appears from the statute or its legislative history that the accommodation is not one that Congress would have sanctioned.

How does this special formulation of deference to matters of statutory interpretation square with APA § 706, which states that "the reviewing court shall decide all relevant questions of law" and interpret "statutory provisions"? If *Chevron* had been decided before Udall v. Tallman or the *TAPS* case, would the results have been different?

Why should the courts defer to agencies in statutory interpretation? Judge Wright in *TAPS* suggests that "administrative expertise" and the fact that Congress may be said to have ratified an agency's interpretation are two reasons to defer. It might also be said, however, that courts and the agencies operate differently, have different traditions and cultural imperatives, and respond to different pressures. For example, federal courts with life tenure don't have political accountability. The mission of the courts is to determine and get the law right. To do that, the courts look at the general legal landscape.

Agencies, on the other hand, have some continuing political accountability to the Congress and through the President. This, it can be argued, merits deference from the courts. Agencies want to get it politically right—what the times and political context demand. Agencies will examine the issue in a specific context—here public land law—and the historic relationship between Congress and land management agencies. Like many agencies, the federal land management agencies have relatively direct and continuous relationships with the Congress, especially their relevant authorizing committees and appropriations subcommittees. As a result they are likely to have better insight into legislative purposes and meaning, and to be more sure-footed in these matters than the courts, who get involved only episodically. Furthermore, unlike courts, agencies are not as bound by notions of stare decisis. In short, agencies' interpretive methods are more of a joint venture with Congress than the arms' length review the courts provide. But, what the current Congress would like to see happen may not be the same as what the enacting Congress may have wanted.

Chevron deference typically applies to agency interpretations made through notice and comment rulemaking. Does it apply in other circumstances? In recent years the Supreme Court has more precisely defined where the Chevron doctrine applies. For instance, in United States v. Mead Corp., 533 U.S. 218, 226–27 (2001), the Court stated: "We hold that administrative implementation of a particular statutory provision qualifies for Chevron deference when it appears that Congress delegated authority to the agency generally to make rules carrying the force of law, and that the agency interpretation claiming deference was promulgated in the exercise of that authority." *See also* Christensen v. Harris County, 529 U.S. 576 (2000) (no *Chevron* deference for interpretations contained in an agency opinion letter).

In Southern Ute Tribe v. Amoco, 119 F.3d 816 (10th Cir.1997), *aff'd en banc*, 151 F.3d 1251 (10th Cir.1998), *rev'd on other grounds*, 526 U.S. 865 (1999), the question was whether to construe early twentieth century statutes reserving "coal" to the United States as including a reservation of coalbed methane gas. The Solicitor of the Interior Department in a 1981 Opinion had concluded that the gas was not reserved with the coal. In rejecting this conclusion, the court of appeals concluded that the opinion did not deserve *Chevron* deference because it was not promulgated either through notice-and-comment rulemaking, nor through an adjudication. It observed in a footnote:

> A Solicitor's opinion is issued at the personal discretion of the Solicitor, without notice and comment, and can be overruled or modified at any time. The opinion at issue here, although presented as authoritative statutory construction, is nothing more than a public pronouncement that Interior will not assert the federal government's right to CBM under its reservation of coal; in that context, the opinion is a valid and useful document. As a simple policy statement, however, the Solicitor's opinion fails to provide the procedural protections required for Chevron deference to attach.

It concluded: "Agencies can make law only in two formats, legislative rules and adjudications; the Solicitor's opinion was not promulgated with the procedural protections attendant to either format. Accordingly, *Chevron* does not mandate that we give deference to the 1981 Solicitor's opinion."

In cases like these where *Chevron* is inapplicable, the courts employ the so-called *Skidmore* doctrine, after Skidmore v. Swift & Co., 323 U.S. 134, 140 (1944), where the Supreme Court said:

> We consider that the rulings, interpretations and opinions of the [agency], * * * while not controlling upon the courts by reason of their authority, do constitute a body of experience and informed judgment to which courts and litigants may properly resort for guidance. The weight of such a judgment in a particular case will depend upon the thoroughness evident in its consideration, the validity of its reasoning, its consistency with earlier and later pronouncements, and all those factors which give it power to persuade, if lacking power to control.

While Solicitors can and do overrule prior decisions at any time, agency rules are not so easily cast aside. In Motor Vehicle Mfrs. Ass'n v. State Farm Mut. Auto. Ins. Co., 463 U.S. 29, 42 (1983), the Court said "an agency changing its course by rescinding a rule is obligated to supply a reasoned analysis for the change beyond that which may be required when an agency does not act in the first instance."

See generally Jerry L. Mashaw, *Between Facts and Norms: Agency Statutory Interpretation as an Autonomous Enterprise*, 55 U. TORONTO L.J. 497 (2005); Peter Strauss, *When the Judge is Not the Primary Official With Responsibility to Read: Agency Interpretation and the Problem of Legislative*

History, 66 CHI.-KENT L.REV. 321 (1990). For other interesting observations about agency expertise, congressional delegation, and *Chevron* deference, see Elena Kagan, *Presidential Administration*, 114 HARV. L.REV. 2245, 2372–84 (2001).

The federal land management agencies all have internal manuals that contain detailed guidelines for the conduct of agency business and various miscellaneous matters. These manuals often include key interpretations of Congress' substantive management mandates. Unfortunately, no clear line, legal or otherwise, separates what is set forth in an agency manual and what is published as a formal regulation. Some manual provisions have been published for comment in the Federal Register or otherwise promulgated in accordance with the APA's standards for regulations, but most have not.

For those manual provisions that were not subject to the rigors of notice and comment rulemaking, there is likely no *Chevron* deference. But there is also a question whether they are legally binding on the agency, so that they may be enforced by courts. The federal courts have not reached entirely consistent results on the issue. The most thorough recent analysis is Wilderness Soc'y v. Norton, 434 F.3d 584, 596 (D.C. Cir.2006) (holding that National Park Service manual of policies, which were not promulgated using notice-and-comment procedures, are not binding on the agency). *See also* Rhodes v. Johnson, 153 F.3d 785, 788 (7th Cir. 1998) (notice-and-comment publication in the Federal Register makes a Forest Service environmental handbook binding).

Courts deciding whether manuals are binding look at both substantive and procedural aspects of the administrative material. The substantive dimension is the content of the manual policy. It is concerned with whether the policy encodes, through particular standards, methods, and binding language, duties an agency must meet. The procedural dimension is the manner in which the agency promulgates the manual provision. Robert L. Fischman, *From Words to Action: The Impact and Legal Status of the 2006 National Wildlife Refuge System Management Policies*, 26 STAN. ENVTL. L.J. 77 (2007).

B.   THE NATIONAL ENVIRONMENTAL POLICY ACT (NEPA)

A procedural element common to almost all federal land and resource management decision-making is the National Environmental Policy Act of 1969 (NEPA), 42 U.S.C. § 4321 et seq. While all federal land management agencies now engage in land use planning under specific statutes (a subject explored in Chapter 5E), the land management agencies must observe NEPA procedures while promulgating plans. But NEPA is not limited to formal planning (nor is it limited to decisions about federally owned lands and resources). It comes into play whenever agencies contemplate "major Federal actions significantly affecting the quality of the human environment." 42 U.S.C. § 4332(2)(c). It forces every federal agency to put its reasoning and conclusions regarding such actions into writing and make them subject to public scrutiny and judicial review.

Some claim that NEPA is merely another layer of bureaucratic red tape or a mechanism allowing willful zealots to delay worthy developments. Some ardent environmentalists express disappointment with NEPA's limitations and lack of substantive impact. All agree, however, that the statute has played a major role in modernizing the management of the federal lands.

NEPA's legislative history does little to illuminate its intended meaning and effect. Few legislators (other than Senator Henry Jackson, its principal sponsor) appreciated the potential sweep of the statute. President Nixon proclaimed the statute the herald of a new environmental era while believing it to be little more than an innocuous statement of policy. It turned out to be a good deal more; the federal courts (particularly the lower courts) quickly began developing a "common law" surrounding the statute's application, and applied it vigorously across a wide range of actions. Although the Supreme Court has not shown the same enthusiasm for the statute, NEPA has been ingrained into the fabric of administrative decision-making and the culture of bureaucracy.

The Supreme Court explained the relationship between the two key sections of NEPA in Robertson v. Methow Valley Citizens Council, 490 U.S. 332 (1989):

> Section 101 of NEPA declares a broad national commitment to protecting and promoting environmental quality. 42 U.S.C. § 4331. To ensure that this commitment is "infused into the ongoing programs and actions of the Federal Government, the act also establishes some important 'action-forcing' procedures." * * *

> The [section 102] statutory requirement that a federal agency contemplating a major action prepare such an environmental impact statement serves NEPA's "action-forcing" purpose in two important respects. It ensures that the agency, in reaching its decision, will have available and will carefully consider detailed information concerning significant environmental impacts; it also guarantees that the relevant information will be made available to the larger audience that may also play a role in both the decisionmaking process and the implementation of that decision.

> * * *

> The sweeping policy goals announced in § 101 of NEPA are thus realized through a set of "action-forcing" procedures that require that agencies take a " 'hard look' at environmental consequences," and that provide for broad dissemination of relevant environmental information. Although these procedures are almost certain to affect the agency's substantive decision, it is now well settled that NEPA itself does not mandate particular results, but simply prescribes the necessary process. If the adverse environmental effects of the proposed action are adequately identified and evaluated, the agency is not constrained by NEPA from deciding that other values outweigh the environmental

costs. In this case, for example, it would not have violated NEPA if the Forest Service, complying with the Act's procedural prerequisites, had decided that the benefits to be derived from downhill skiing at Sandy Butte justified the issuance of a special use permit, notwithstanding the loss of 15 percent, 50 percent, or even 100 percent of the mule deer herd. Other statutes may impose substantive environmental obligations on federal agencies, but NEPA merely prohibits uninformed— rather than unwise—agency action.

What does it mean to say that NEPA is purely procedural, and "merely prohibits uninformed—rather than unwise—agency action"? Does it mean that even if an environmental analysis reveals that the proposed action could be disastrous environmentally, the statute imposes no obligation on the agency to act differently—or at least no obligation that a court will enforce? Can this be all Congress had in mind in enacting the statute? Or does its ventilation function ensure that no agency would go forward with an environmentally disastrous decision, knowing the consequences?

Section 102 provides, in pertinent part:

The Congress authorizes and directs that, to the fullest extent possible: (1) the policies, regulations, and public laws of the United State shall be interpreted and administered in accordance with the policies set forth in this chapter, and (2) all agencies of the Federal Government shall—

(A) utilize a systematic, interdisciplinary approach which will insure the integrated use of the natural and social sciences and the environmental design arts in planning and in decisionmaking which may have an impact on man's environment;

(B) identify and develop methods and procedures, in consultation with the Council on Environmental Quality established by subchapter II of this chapter, which will insure that presently unqualified environmental amenities and values may be given appropriate consideration in decisionmaking along with economic and technical considerations;

(C) include in every recommendation or report on proposals for legislation and other major Federal actions significantly affecting the quality of the human environment, a detailed statement by the responsible official on—

(i) the environmental impact of the proposed action,

(ii) any adverse environmental effects which cannot be avoided should the proposal be implemented,

(iii) alternatives to the proposed action,

(iv) the relationship between local short-term uses of man's environment and the maintenance and enhancement of long-term productivity, and

(v) any irreversible and irretrievable commitments of resources which would be involved in the proposed action should it be implemented.

* * *

(E) study, develop, and describe appropriate alternatives to recommended courses of action in any proposal which involves unresolved conflicts concerning alternative uses of available resources; * * *.

The "detailed statement" referred to in section 102(2)(c) has come to be known as an environmental impact statement, or EIS.

NEPA creates the President's Council on Environmental Quality (CEQ) which was originally envisioned as a counterpart to the Council of Economic Advisors. In the early 1970s, the CEQ prepared "guidelines" for the environmental impact statement process. These guidelines functioned somewhat like Restatements of the Law, in that they attempted to capture the best of the agency experience and judicial guidance concerning NEPA's implementation. During the Carter Administration, the CEQ rewrote the guidelines and published them as binding regulations. The CEQ's NEPA regulations (found at 40 C.F.R. Part 1500) have proved so useful to the agencies and the courts that they have not been seriously tinkered with, and remain valuable sources of insight into NEPA processes and requirements. In addition, nearly every federal land management agency has its own counterpart NEPA regulations.

NEPA litigation traditionally raised one of two questions: (1) Must the agency prepare a full EIS on some action that is before it? (2) If an EIS is prepared, is it adequate? Answering the first question involves determining whether an agency is proposing a "major Federal action significantly affecting the quality of the human environment" (MFASAQHE, unpronounceable in polite company). To determine whether the action will have a significant environmental effect, the CEQ regulations usually require the agency to prepare an environmental assessment (EA). 40 C.F.R. § 1501.4. If the conclusion is negative, the agency makes a finding of no significant impact (FONSI). Judge Richard Posner has described the EA as a "rough-cut, low-budget environmental impact statement designed to show whether a full-fledged environmental impact statement—which is very costly and time-consuming to prepare and has been the kiss of death to many a federal project—is necessary." He went on to say that " 'rough-cut' and 'low-budget' are relative terms" for in that case the EA on a timber sale to harvest trees on 26 acres was 112 pages long, or 4.3 pages per acre. Cronin v. U.S. Department of Agriculture, 919 F.2d 439, 443 (7th Cir.1990).

If the agency has promulgated an EIS, the adequacy issues frequently litigated include the following: Were the likely environmental impacts sufficiently identified and discussed? Were reasonable alternatives to the proposed action (and their environmental impacts) identified and addressed? Were adverse opinions and comments included and discussed? Was the statement sufficiently detailed? As agencies have incorporated NEPA processes into their routine decision-making, the focus of litigation has inevitably shifted from the failure to prepare an EIS to the adequacy of the EIS.

As NEPA matured, the EA increasingly came to be seen as a "mini-EIS" rather than a distinct category of evaluation answering the question of whether a contemplated action would significantly affect the environment. In the 1970s, agencies prepared over a thousand final EISs almost every year. The numbers of EISs began to drop off in the early 1980s. For the past twenty years, EIS production has held steady at about 400 to 600 each year. In contrast, agencies produce approximately 50,000 EAs each year. Agencies will mitigate the impacts of a proposed action to lower them below the significance threshold. This results in a "mitigated FONSI." As the size and number of EAs grew, so did the litigation over the adequacy, scope, and timing of an EA. Many agencies now have guidelines guaranteeing that EAs provide public participation opportunities. *See, e.g.*, Forest Service Handbook 1909.15.

The Forest Service consistently leads other federal agencies in the number of EISs prepared every year. But, the Interior Department agencies also make a strong showing. The reported NEPA decisions and commentary on them are voluminous. For general reference, see Daniel Mandelker, NEPA LAW AND LITIGATION (periodic updates). A growing number of states have adopted "little NEPAs," patterned after the federal law. Such SEPAs (state environmental policy acts) can come into play in federal land management to the extent state law applies on federal lands.

Agencies, especially those operating under the direct control of the President (this would include just about all agencies in public land law), have strong preferences about whether and how they should proceed to implement projects or permits. The following case deals with NEPA's role in shaping agency choice.

Metcalf v. Daley

United States Court of Appeals, 9th Circuit, 2000.
214 F.3d 1135.

■ JUDGE TROTT

FACTUAL BACKGROUND

The Makah, who reside in Washington state on the northwestern Olympic Peninsula, have a 1500 year tradition of hunting whales. In particular, the Makah target the California gray whale ("gray whale"), which annually migrates between the North Pacific and the coast of Mexico. During their yearly journey, the migratory gray whale population travels through the Olympic Coast National Marine Sanctuary ("Sanctuary"), which Congress established in 1993 in order to protect the marine environment in a pristine ocean and coastal area. A small sub-population of gray whales, commonly referred to as "summer residents," live in the Sanctuary throughout the entire year.

In 1855, the United States and the Makah entered into the Treaty of Neah Bay, whereby the Makah ceded most of their land on the Olympic Peninsula to the United States in exchange for "[t]he right of taking fish and of whaling or sealing at usual and accustomed grounds and stations...." Despite their long history of whaling and the Treaty of Neah Bay, however, the Makah ceased whaling in the 1920s because widespread commercial whaling had devastated the population of gray whales almost to extinction. * * *

[In 1946 the U.S. signed the International Convention for the Regulation of Whaling. The Convention regulates whaling through the International Whaling Commission ("IWC"). In 1946, the IWC banned the taking or killing of gray whales. The 1949 Whaling Convention Act implements domestically the Convention through the National Oceanic and Atmospheric Administration ("NOAA") and the National Marine Fisheries Service ("NMFS").]

[In 1994 gray whales had sufficiently recovered from over-hunting that they were removed from the federal endangered species list. In response to this recovery, the Makah decided to resume the hunting of whales migrating through the Sanctuary. The Makah asked NOAA and NMFS to represent it in seeking approval from the IWC for an annual quota of up to five gray whales. In 1995 the NMFS agreed to "work with" the Makah to obtain an aboriginal subsistence quota from the IWC. The United States acted accordingly at the 1995 IWC meeting, in a 1996 formal written agreement with the tribe, and at the 1996 IWC meeting. In August 1997, NOAA prepared a draft EA, which it distributed for public comment. On Oct. 13, 1997, NOAA and the Makah signed a new written agreement preparing for the resumption of whale hunting. On Oct. 17, 1997, NOAA issued a final EA and FONSI.]

[In 1997 the IWC approved a quota of whales to be taken, which included an average annual harvest of four whales by the Makah. In 1998, NOAA set the domestic subsistence whaling quotas for 1998 and allowed the Makah to engage in whaling pursuant to the IWC-approved quota and Whaling Convention Act regulations.]

* * *

A.

* * * [W]e have observed in connection with the preparation of an EA that "[p]roper timing is one of NEPA's central themes. An assessment must be 'prepared early enough so that it can serve practically as an important contribution to the decisionmaking process and will not be used to rationalize or justify decisions already made.' "

* * *

In this case, the Federal Defendants did (1) prepare an EA, (2) decide that the Makah whaling proposal would not significantly affect the environment, and (3) issue a FONSI, but they did so after already having signed two agreements binding them to support the Tribe's proposal. * * * According to appellants, "by making a commitment to authorize and fund the Makah whaling plan, and then drafting a NEPA document which simply rubber-stamped the decision . . ., defendants eliminated the opportunity to choose among alternatives, . . . and seriously imped[ed] the degree to which their planning and decisions could reflect environmental values."
* * *

B.

We begin by considering appellants' argument that the Federal Defendants failed timely and in the proper sequence to comply with NEPA. As provided in the regulations promulgated to implement NEPA, "[a]gencies shall integrate the NEPA process with other planning *at the earliest possible time* to insure that planning and decisions reflect environmental values, to avoid delays later in the process, and to head off potential conflicts." 40 C.F.R. § 1501.2 (emphasis added); see also id. § 1502.5 ("An agency shall commence preparation of an [EIS] as close as possible to the time the agency is developing or is presented with a proposal. . . ."). * * * Thus, the issue we must decide here is whether the Federal Defendants prepared the EA too late in the decision-making process, i.e., after making an irreversible and irretrievable commitment of resources. We conclude that they did.

The purpose of an EA is to provide the agency with sufficient evidence and analysis for determining whether to prepare an EIS or to issue a FONSI. 40 C.F.R. § 1508.9. Because the very important decision whether to prepare an EIS is based solely on the EA, the EA is fundamental to the decision-making process. In terms of timing and importance to the goals of NEPA, we see no difference between an EA and an EIS in connection with when an EA must be integrated into the calculus. In the case at bar, the Makah first asked the Federal Defendants to help them secure IWC approval for a gray whale quota in 1995; however, NOAA/NMFS did not prepare an EA until 1997. During these two years, the United States and the Makah worked together toward obtaining a gray whale quota from the IWC. In January 1996, an NOAA representative informed his colleagues that "we now have interagency agreement to support the Makah's application in IWC for a whaling quota of 5 grey whales." More importantly, in March 1996, more than a year before the EA was prepared, NOAA entered into a contract with the Makah pursuant to which it committed to (1) making a formal proposal to the IWC for a quota of gray whales for subsistence and ceremonial use by the Makah and (2) participating in the management of the harvest. * * *

The Federal Defendants did not engage the NEPA process "at the earliest possible time." Instead, the record makes clear that the Federal Defendants did not even consider the potential environmental effects of the proposed action until long after they had already committed in writing to support the Makah whaling proposal. The "point of commitment" in this case came when NOAA signed the contract with the Makah in March 1996 and then worked to effectuate the agreement. It was at this juncture that it made an "irreversible and irretrievable commitment of resources." * * * Although it could have, NOAA did not make its promise to seek a quota from the IWC and to participate in the harvest conditional upon a NEPA determination that the Makah whaling proposal would not significantly affect the environment.

Had NOAA/NMFS found after signing the Agreement that allowing the Makah to resume whaling would have a significant effect on the environment, the Federal Defendants would have been required to prepare an EIS, and they may not have been able to fulfill their written commitment to the Tribe. As such, NOAA would have been in breach of contract. Although the United States delegates to the 1996 IWC meeting ultimately withdrew their proposal for a Makah aboriginal subsistence whaling quota, they did so with the Tribe's approval and because the proposal did not have adequate support from other IWC delegations, not in order to reconsider environmental concerns. The firmness of the 1996 Agreement became even clearer and more resolute in 1997 when NOAA entered into a new, similar contract with the Tribe to pursue its whaling quota at the 1997 IWC meeting. This Agreement was signed four days before the final EA in this case was issued. In the EA, the agencies referred to this second Agreement as having "renewed the cooperative Agreement" signed in 1996. This is strong evidence that NOAA and other agencies made the decision to support the Tribe's proposal in 1996, before the EA process began and without considering the environmental consequences thereof. By the time the Federal Defendants completed the final EA in 1997, the die already had been cast. The "point of commitment" to this proposal clearly had come and gone. * * *

It is highly likely that because of the Federal Defendants' prior written commitment to the Makah and concrete efforts on their behalf, the EA was slanted in favor of finding that the Makah whaling proposal would not significantly affect the environment. As the court below noted, "the longer the defendants worked with the Tribe toward the end of whaling, the greater the pressure to achieve this end.... [A]n EA prepared under such circumstances might be subject to at least a subtle pro-whaling bias." The EA itself somewhat disingenuously claims in 1997 that the "decision to be made" is "whether to support the Makah Tribe in its effort to continue its whaling tradition," when in point of fact that decision had already been made in contract form. To quote the 1996 Agreement, "after an adequate statement of need is prepared, NOAA ... will make a formal proposal to the IWC for a quota of gray whales...." * * *

NEPA's effectiveness depends entirely on involving environmental considerations in the initial decisionmaking process. Moreover, the Supreme Court has clearly held that treaty rights such as those at stake in this case "may be regulated ... in the interest of conservation ..., provided the regulation ... does not discriminate against the Indians." Puyallup Tribe v. Department of Game of Wash., 391 U.S. 392, 398 (1968). Here, before preparing an EA, the Federal Defendants signed a contract which obligated them both to make a proposal to the IWC for a gray whale quota and to participate in the harvest of those whales. We hold that by making such a firm commitment before preparing an EA, the Federal Defendants failed to take a "hard look" at the environmental consequences of their actions and, therefore, violated NEPA.

* * *

We want to make clear, however, that this case does not stand for the general proposition that an agency cannot begin preliminary consideration of an action without first preparing an EA, or that an agency must always prepare an EA before it can lend support to any proposal. We have discussed this distinction in Association of Pub. Agency Customers, Inc. v. Bonneville Power Admin., 126 F.3d 1158 (9th Cir.1997), where we pointed out that "an agency can formulate a proposal or even identify a preferred course of action before completing an EIS." We noted also that "Council on Environmental Quality ('CEQ') regulations actually encourage identification of a preferred course of action during the NEPA process...." (citing 40 C.F.R. § 1502.14(e)). Rather, our holding here is limited to the unusual facts and circumstances of this case where the defendants already had made an "irreversible and irretrievable commitment of resources"—i.e., by entering into a contract with the Makah before they considered its environmental consequences and prepared the EA.

REVERSED and REMANDED.

■ JUDGE KLEINFELD, dissenting.

I respectfully dissent.

The federal government reconciled two policies, one favoring aboriginal Indian interests and another favoring preservation of sea mammals, by choosing to advance the Indian whale-hunting interests. But before allowing the Indians to hunt whales, the government took the "hard look" at environmental consequences that was required by law. Nothing more was required. The majority opinion errs in three respects: (1) it imposes a novel version of the "objectivity" requirement that cannot be applied in a predictable, consistent manner by other panels in other cases; (2) it misconstrues the regulation that controls the time when an environmental assessment ought to be prepared; (3) it requires that a new environmental assessment be prepared without finding anything wrong with the old one. Obviously the agency did not prepare the environmental assessment until its officials had already decided that they wanted to let the Makah Indians hunt whales. Why else would they have gone to the trouble of preparing an environmental assessment? But without identifying something wrong with the environmental assessment (and we have not), we have no warrant for setting it aside.

First, "objectivity." There is a statutory and regulatory basis for inferring that an environmental assessment must be "objective." But what does "objective" mean? The majority concedes that the agency can "identify a preferred course of action" before preparing the environmental assessment. * * *

But then the majority apparently holds that the environmental assessment in this case fails the objectivity test because "it is highly likely that," because the agency had committed itself to the tribe, "the EA was slanted." This holding cannot be * * * applied in a predictable, consistent manner. The agency's policy choice, to allow the Makah tribe to hunt whales if it could, cannot be said to "slant" the environmental assessment, when we do not identify anything wrong with the environmental assessment, unless the test of objectivity is exactly what we say it is not, "institutional bias within an agency" and subjective partiality. All the majority shows is that the agency knew the answer it wanted before it asked the question. * * * To show that the environmental assessment is not objective, an objector must show that there is something wrong with the assessment, not just that the agency that prepared it wanted a particular result.

The meaning of "objective" is "expressing or involving the use of facts without distortion by personal feelings or prejudices." Thus our inquiry should be focused on the text of the environmental assessment that the agency prepared, not on the motivations that the agency had for slanting it. Of course it had a motive to slant the statement in favor of its preferred policy. Any executive agency can be expected to try to advance its and the president's policy preferences. If we require a record cleansed of any indication of a policy preference, all we will do is push the indicators of agency preference off the written record into the land of winks and nods, and choosing people to prepare the reports who, because of their known policy preferences, can be counted on to reach the conclusions the agency wants. We should read the environmental assessment and decide whether it states the facts without distortion, and fairly sets out the alternatives and the reasons for and against them. The district judge did so, and found nothing wrong with the environmental assessment, and neither have we. That should be the end of the "objectivity" inquiry.

Second, timing. The majority holds that the "at the earliest possible time" requirement in the regulations means before "making an irreversible and irretrievable commitment of resources." I agree with that proposition of law. But then the majority goes on to say that because the agency's commitment to the Makah tribe preceded the environmental assessment, the environmental assessment came too late. I respectfully disagree with the application of law to facts, though the issue is close.

* * *

Promising to support the Makah whaling proposal before the International Whaling Commission was not an "irretrievable commitment of resources," for several reasons. Signing the contract did not entitle the Indians to kill whales. International Whaling Commission approval was sufficiently unlikely * * * so that no one could count on any whale hunts despite the agency's support. There was no point wasting the public's time and money on an environmental assessment until and unless the International Whaling Commission made Makah whale hunting a possibility. Doing the NEPA process before the agency action is even possible, as today's majority requires, is like setting a wedding date, booking the hall, buying the dress, and paying the band before the couple has gotten engaged.

Even after the International Whaling Commission approved a Makah whale quota, the Makah still could not hunt whales * * *. The agency had to decide upon and promulgate regulations. An earlier version of the contract, made when the agency was likely to fail (it did fail) before the International Whaling Commission, said that the agency would adopt regulations within 30 days after the International Whaling Commission approved the quota. But once the Commission looked likely to come around, * * * the agency and the Makah signed a novation replacing the old contract. The new contract obligated the Makah Tribal Council, but not the federal agency, to adopt a management plan and regulations. The agency's hands were not tied. If the agency had changed policy, and decided not to issue regulations permitting Makah whale hunting as a result of the environmental assessment, the political strength of the advocacy groups opposing whale hunting, or anything else, the Makah might reasonably have regarded the policy change as a bad faith betrayal. But government changes policy continually, restrained only by concerns for fairness, public opinion, and that the incentives it offered in the future to induce private action would have to be higher to the extent that people felt they could not rely on the stability of government policies. Specific performance of the contract could not have been compelled and it is hard to imagine a damages remedy.

* * *

It is impractical to suppose that executive agencies will be uncommitted to policies when they prepare environmental assessments and environmental impact statements. It is precisely their determinations to move ahead with one proposal or another that occasions the assessments and impact statements. So long as the agency prepares an objective statement giving the initiative the required "hard look," prior to going ahead with it, it has done its duty, and even if it prepares the statement too late, it is pointless to require another one unless there is something wrong with the one the agency submitted. Environmental assessments and environmental impact statements are unlikely to persuade agency personnel, who initiated a project, to change their minds. Few things in government are as hard to shake as a bureaucratic policy choice.

The value of the environmental assessments and impact statements comes mostly after the agency has settled on a policy choice. The process of preparing them mobilizes groups that may generate political pressure sufficient to defeat the executive initiative. Exploration of the alternatives, and the facts brought out in preparation, may educate the agency, so that the initiative is modified in a useful way. The process may educate the agency about interests and concerns of which it was not aware, so that implementation will be more sensitive. The quality of the statement may persuade Congress or others who must pass on the agency proposal that the agency was wrong in its policy choice. The statement also stands as an archive with which the public may evaluate the correctness of the agency's policy choices after implementation, to decide whether the agency has done what it promised during implementation, and whether to repose more or less confidence in the agency's policy choices in the future. Preparation and publication of the statements eliminate the agency's monopoly of information, thus enabling other participants in the political process to use the information to overcome the agency's policy choice. None of these values were subverted in this case by the agency's commitment to the Makah Tribe. And nothing has been shown to be wrong with the environmental assessment. There is a legitimate clash of values between those who care more about whale hunting from the point of view of the hunter, and those who care more from the viewpoint of the whale. The political organs of government have the authority to choose. We have no warrant in this case to interfere.

NOTES AND QUESTIONS

1.   Does NEPA require an agency to be impartial or unbiased? Would that be consistent with the notion that agencies are created to develop a professional corps of experts to implement laws? What would constitute an objectively "slanted" EA that would provide the evidence of agency bias satisfying the dissent? How would that be different from institutional bias? For an example of an agency seeking to retain a monopoly on information to control debate over an issue, see Western Watersheds Project v. Kraayenbrink, D. Idaho, 2006 WL 2735772, Sept. 25, 2006 (preliminary injunction on the implementation of grazing regulations where the EIS did not disclose a critical analysis of their adverse environmental impacts by a scientific advisory group).

2.   Is the dissent correct that there is no point wasting time and money on an EA until the IWC approved the whale hunting? Or, was there no point in wasting the time and money applying for the IWC exemption until an EA determined whether hunting would have a significant effect on whale and marine conservation? The dissent views the environmental analyses as having value to outside groups that seek to mobilize to defeat an executive action. Often, though, outside groups would prefer to shape the action/policy in the first place through early involvement.

Suppose the president announces in a state-of-the-union address a goal of national energy independence by 2020? At what point should the various departments that would be involved in achieving this goal, such as, Interior, Energy, and Transportation, prepare an EIS? Should it happen the day after the speech, when the agencies are setting their research and regulatory priorities? Or, sometime later when plans are more concrete, such as when a proposed regulation is published or a pilot bio-fuel power plant is proposed? Moreover, what should be the scope of each agency's analysis? Should the agencies pool their resources and produce a single EIS? For two approaches to the NEPA question in the context of broad federal initiatives, see Kleppe v. Sierra Club, 427 U.S. 390 (1976) (upholding the Interior Department's decision not to prepare a single EIS on a collection of separate federal decisions to develop coal resources in he northern Great Plains, as the mining industry was shifting its focus from the Appalachian/Midwest to the western plains); and Scientists' Institute for Public Information, Inc. v. Atomic Energy Commission, 481 F.2d 1079 (D.C.Cir. 1973) (requiring an EIS for the Commission's liquid metal fast breeder reactor program).

3.   Remedy for inadequate EAs. In Metcalf v. Daley, the court ordered the agency to repair its flawed EA by preparing another EA. This is consistent with National Audubon Society v. Hoffman, 132 F.3d 7 (2d Cir.1997), where the court found that the Forest Service violated NEPA in an EA for constructing a road and then logging in a portion of the Green Mountain National Forest in Vermont. In that case, the court ordered another EA, despite its conclusion that the Service failed to consider a number of relevant environmental factors and to include sufficient mitigation to justify the FONSI.

In contrast, Blue Mountains Biodiversity Project v. Blackwood, 161 F.3d 1208 (9th Cir.1998), ordered the Forest Service to prepare an EIS where the EA for a series for timber salvage sales did not adequately support its claim that mitigation would reduce impacts to no significance. Is it ever appropriate for a court to order an agency to prepare an EIS rather than redo an EA with the option of either further mitigation to FONSI or going on to an EIS? An important factor in Blue Mountains Biodiversity Project was the failure of the Service to adequately address cumulative effects of multiple salvage logging projects following a massive fire in the Umatilla National Forest in Oregon. In this case, the EIS remedy was, in part, related to the segmentation of post-fire salvage into discrete salvage sales.

4. Scope of analysis. In Thomas v. Peterson, 753 F.2d 754 (9th Cir.1985), the court required the Forest Service to analyze the impact of subsequent, anticipated timber sales in conjunction with a decision to build a road whose justification depended on the sales. The key CEQ regulation (40 C.F.R. 1508.25) requires agencies to consider in a single analysis actions that are connected, cumulative, or similar. Connected actions include those that cannot or will not proceed unless other actions are taken previously or simultaneously, and those that are interdependent parts of a larger action and depend on the larger action for their justification. In a part of Metcalf v. Daley not excerpted, the majority and dissent disagree over whether *Thomas* is applicable to the Makah whaling case. Is it? What is the connection between the signed agreement with the tribe and the subsequent regulation permitting whale hunting?

Thomas v. Peterson also considered the Forest Service's argument that it was sufficient to consider the cumulative environmental effects in NEPA documentation it would produce in connection with the timber sales, after the road was built. The court would have none of it:

> A central purpose of an EIS is to force the consideration of environmental impacts in the decisionmaking process. That purpose requires that the NEPA process be integrated with agency planning "at the earliest possible time," 40 C.F.R. § 1501.2, and the purpose cannot be fully served if consideration of the cumulative effects of successive, interdependent steps is delayed until the first step has already been taken.

> The location, the timing, or other aspects of the timber sales, or even the decision whether to sell any timber at all affects the location, routing, construction techniques, and other aspects of the road, or even the need for its construction. But the consideration of cumulative impacts will serve little purpose if the road has already been built. Building the road swings the balance decidedly in favor of timber sales even if such sales would have been disfavored had road and sales been considered together before the road was built. Only by selling the timber can the bulk of the expense of building the road be recovered.
> * * *

The Forest Service argues that the sales are too uncertain and too far in the future for their impacts to be analyzed along with that of the road. This comes close to saying that building the road now is itself irrational. We decline to accept that conclusion. Rather, we believe that if the sales are sufficiently certain to justify construction of the road, then they are sufficiently certain for their environmental impacts to be analyzed along with those of the road. * * * Where agency actions are sufficiently related so as to be "connected" within the meaning of the CEQ regulations, the agency may not escape compliance with the regulations by proceeding with one action while characterizing the others as remote or speculative.

More recently, in Fund for Animals v. Hall, 448 F.Supp.2d 127 (D.D.C. 2006), a court overturned a series of regulations opening specific areas of the National Wildlife Refuge System to hunting. The court held that the FWS violated NEPA by failing to consider the cumulative impacts in making a series of FONSIs for each refuge-specific hunting rule. The Court suggested that the FWS needed to consider the cumulative impacts of refuge hunting system-wide.

5. Significance. The CEQ regulations defining the key trigger for an EIS states that an agency should consider both the context and intensity of impacts in deciding whether a proposed action will significantly affect the environment. Included in the ten factors considered under intensity is "the degree to which the effects on the quality of the human environment are likely to be highly controversial." 40 C.F.R. 1508.27(b). Controversial means "a substantial dispute [about] the size, nature, or effect ... of the action rather than the existence of opposition to a use." Greenpeace Action v. Franklin, 14 F.3d 1324, 1335 (9th Cir.1992). Does this reverse the usual burdens of proof of harm in law? Can a project opponent secure a judicial remand simply by raising issues of uncertainty, which are ubiquitous in ecology?

6. Irreversible and irretrievable commitments. Do you agree with the majority or dissent on whether the agreement between the federal government and the tribe was an irreversible and irretrievable commitment? The dissent, in a portion of its opinion not excerpted, analogizes the agreement to the oil/gas leases in Conner v. Burford, 848 F.2d 1441 (9th Cir.1988). In that case, the court did not require an EIS for leases that contained stipulations denying the owner the right of surface occupancy, but did require detailed analyses for other leases lacking such a stipulation. What is the proper application of *Conner* to the *Metcalf* facts? Did the federal government commit itself to promulgating regulations permitting whale hunting if the IWC approved the Makah exception? Does it matter whether the commitment was enforceable against the United States?

In contrast to *Conner*, Park County Resource Council v. U.S. Department of Agriculture, 817 F.2d 609 (10th Cir.1987), held that the federal agency was not required to prepare an EIS prior to issuing oil and gas leases on national forest land. The agency had done an environmental assessment exceeding 100 pages in length which concluded that an EIS was not required. The court summed up this way:

[I]n light of the substantial EA, of the mitigating lease restrictions requiring further environmental appraisal before any surface disturbing activities commence, of the nebulousness of future drilling activity at the time of leasing, and of the continuing supervision of the federal agencies involved over future activities, the agency's decision in this case that the lease issuance itself was not a major federal action significantly affecting the quality of the human environment was not unreasonable. Furthermore, there clearly was a rational basis to defer preparation of an EIS until a more concrete proposal was submitted to BLM.

Subsequent case law applying *Conner* and *Park County* to the complex, multi-step process of oil and gas leasing is covered in Chapter 7.

The next case considers a situation where the Forest Service did prepare an EIS at an early stage in planning. It nonetheless faced a challenge on the grounds that the statement was inadequate.

Robertson v. Methow Valley Citizens Council

Supreme Court of the United States, 1989.
490 U.S. 332.

■ JUSTICE STEVENS delivered the opinion of the Court.

The Forest Service is authorized by statute to manage the national forests for "outdoor recreation, range, timber, watershed, and wildlife and fish purposes." 16 U.S.C. § 528. Pursuant to that authorization, the Forest Service has issued "special use" permits for the operation of approximately 170 alpine and nordic ski areas on federal lands.

The Forest Service permit process involves three separate stages. The Forest Service first examines the general environmental and financial feasibility of a proposed project and decides whether to issue a special use permit. Because that decision is a "major Federal action" within the meaning of NEPA, it must be preceded by the preparation of an Environmental Impact Statement (EIS). If the Service decides to issue a permit, it then proceeds to select a developer, formulate the basic terms of the arrangement with the selected party, and issue the permit. The special use permit does not, however, give the developer the right to begin construction. In a final stage of review, the Service evaluates the permittee's "master plan" for development, construction, and operation of the project. Construction may begin only after an additional environmental analysis (although it is not clear that a second EIS need always be prepared) and final approval of the developer's master plan. This case arises out of the Forest Service's decision to issue a special use permit authorizing the development of a major destination alpine ski resort at Sandy Butte in the North Cascades mountains.

Sandy Butte is a 6,000–foot mountain located in the Okanogan National Forest in Okanogan County, Washington. At present Sandy Butte, like the Methow Valley it overlooks, is an unspoiled, sparsely populated area that the district court characterized as "pristine." In 1968, Congress established the North Cascades National Park and directed the Secretaries of Interior and Agriculture to agree on the designation of areas within and adjacent to the park for public uses, including ski areas. A 1970 study conducted by the Forest Service pursuant to this congressional directive identified Sandy Butte as having the highest potential of any site in the State of Washington for development as a major downhill ski resort.

In 1978, Methow Recreation, Inc. (MRI) applied for a special use permit to develop and operate its proposed "Early Winters Ski Resort" on Sandy Butte and an 1,165 acre parcel of land it had acquired adjacent to the National Forest. The proposed development would make use of approximately 3,900 acres of Sandy Butte; would entice visitors to travel long distances to stay at the resort for several days at a time; and would stimulate extensive commercial and residential growth in the vicinity to accommodate both vacationers and staff.

In response to MRI's application, the Forest Service, in cooperation with state and county officials, prepared an EIS known as the Early Winters Alpine Winter Sports Study (Early Winters Study or Study). The stated purpose of the EIS was "to provide the information required to evaluate the potential for skiing at Early Winters" and "to assist in making a decision whether to issue a Special Use Permit for downhill skiing on all or a portion of approximately 3900 acres of National Forest System land." A draft of the Study was completed and circulated in 1982, but release of the final EIS was delayed as Congress considered including Sandy Butte in a proposed wilderness area. When the Washington State Wilderness Act of 1984 was passed, however, Sandy Butte was excluded from the wilderness designation, and the EIS was released.

The Early Winters Study is a printed document containing almost 150 pages of text and 12 appendices. It evaluated five alternative levels of development of Sandy Butte that might be authorized, the lowest being a "no action" alternative and the highest being development of a 16–lift ski area able to accommodate 10,500 skiers at one time. The Study considered the effect of each level of development on water resources, soil, wildlife, air quality, vegetation and visual quality, as well as land use and transportation in the Methow Valley, probable demographic shifts, the economic market for skiing and other summer and winter recreational activities in the Valley, and the energy requirements for the ski area and related developments. The Study's discussion of possible impacts was not limited to on-site effects, but also, as required by Council on Environmental Quality (CEQ) regulations, see 40 CFR § 1502.16(b) (1987), addressed "off-site impacts that each alternative might have on community facilities, socio-economic and other environmental conditions in the Upper Methow Valley." As to off-site effects, the Study explained that "due to the uncertainty of where other public and private lands may become developed," it is difficult to evaluate off-site impacts, and thus the document's analysis is necessarily "not site-specific." Finally, the Study outlined certain steps that might be taken to mitigate adverse effects, both on Sandy Butte and in the neighboring Methow Valley, but indicated that these proposed steps are merely conceptual and "will be made more specific as part of the design and implementation stages of the planning process."

The effects of the proposed development on air quality and wildlife received particular attention in the Study. [Discussion of the air quality issues is deleted.]

In its discussion of adverse effects on area wildlife, the EIS concluded that no endangered or threatened species would be affected by the proposed development and that the only impact on sensitive species was the probable loss of a pair of spotted owls and their progeny. With regard to other wildlife, the Study considered the impact on 75 different indigenous species and predicted that within a decade after development vegetational change and increased human activity would lead to a decrease in population for 31 species, while causing an increase in population for another 24 species on Sandy Butte. Two species, the pine marten and nesting goshawk, would be eliminated altogether from the area of development.

In a comment in response to the draft EIS, the Washington Department of Game voiced a special concern about potential losses to the State's largest migratory deer herd, which uses the Methow Valley as a critical winter range and as its migration route. The state agency estimated that the total population of mule deer in the area most likely to be affected was "better than 30,000 animals" and that "the ultimate impact on the Methow deer herd could exceed a 50 percent reduction in numbers." The agency asserted that "Okanogan County residents place a great deal of importance on the area's deer herd." In addition, it explained that hunters had "harvested" 3,247 deer in the Methow Valley area in 1981, and that, since in 1980 hunters on average spent $1,980 for each deer killed in Washington, they had contributed over $6 million to the State's economy in 1981. Because the deer harvest is apparently proportional to the size of the herd, the state agency predicted that "Washington business can expect to lose over $3 million annually from reduced recreational opportunity." The Forest Service's own analysis of the impact on the deer herd was more modest. It first concluded that the actual operation of the ski hill would have only a "minor" direct impact on the herd, but then recognized that the off-site effect of the development "would noticeably reduce numbers of deer in the Methow [Valley] with any alternative." Although its estimate indicated a possible 15 percent decrease in the size of the herd, it summarized the State's contrary view in the text of the EIS, and stressed that off-site effects are difficult to estimate due to uncertainty concerning private development.

* * * [T]he EIS also described both on-site and off-site mitigation measures. Among possible on-site mitigation possibilities, the Study recommended locating runs, ski lifts, and roads so as to minimize interference with wildlife, restricting access to selected roads during fawning season and further examination of the effect of the development on mule deer migration routes. Off-site options discussed in the Study included the use of zoning and tax incentives to limit development on deer winter range and migration routes, encouragement of conservation easements, and acquisition and management by local government of critical tracts of land. * * * [T]he proposed options were primarily directed to steps that might be taken by state and local government.

Ultimately, the Early Winters Study recommended the issuance of a permit for development at the second highest level considered—a 16–lift ski area able to accommodate 8,200 skiers at one time. On July 5, 1984, the Regional Forester decided to issue a special use permit as recommended by the Study.[10] In his decision, the Regional Forester found that no major adverse effects would result directly from the federal action, but that secondary effects could include a degradation of existing air quality and a reduction of mule deer winter range. He therefore directed the supervisor of the Okanogan National Forest, both independently and in cooperation with local officials, to identify and implement certain mitigating measures.

[Following exhaustion of administrative remedies, four environmental groups sued to challenge the adequacy of NEPA compliance. They lost in the district court and won in the court of appeals, which found that the Forest Service should have included a "worst-case analysis" in the EIS and also should have developed measures to mitigate the environmental impact of the proposed action.] * * *

* * *

To be sure, one important ingredient of an EIS is the discussion of steps that can be taken to mitigate adverse environmental consequences.[15] The requirement that an EIS contain a detailed discussion of possible mitigation measures flows from both the language of the Act and, more expressly, from CEQ's implementing regulations. Implicit in NEPA's demand that an agency prepare a detailed statement on "any adverse environmental effects which cannot be avoided should the proposal be implemented," 42 U.S.C. § 4332(C)(ii), is an understanding that the EIS will discuss the extent to which adverse effects can be avoided. More generally, omission of a reasonably complete discussion of possible mitigation measures would undermine the "action-forcing" function of NEPA. Without such a discussion, neither the agency nor other interested groups and individuals can properly evaluate the severity of the adverse effects. An adverse effect that can be fully remedied by, for example, an inconsequential public expenditure is certainly not as serious as a similar effect that can only be modestly ameliorated through the commitment of vast public and private resources. Recognizing the importance of such a discussion in

---

10. His decision did not identify a particular developer, but rather simply authorized the taking of competitive bids. It was not until July 21, 1986, almost one month after the District Court affirmed the Forester's decision, that a special use permit was issued to MRI.

15. CEQ regulations define "mitigation" to include:

"(a) Avoiding the impact altogether by not taking a certain action or parts of an action.

"(b) Minimizing impacts by limiting the degree or magnitude of the action and its implementation.

"(c) Rectifying the impact by repairing, rehabilitating, or restoring the affected environment.

"(d) Reducing or eliminating the impact over time by preservation and maintenance operations during the life of the action.

"(e) Compensating for the impact by replacing or providing substitute resources or environments." 40 CFR § 1508.20 (1987).

guaranteeing that the agency has taken a "hard look" at the environmental consequences of proposed federal action, CEQ regulations require that the agency discuss possible mitigation measures in defining the scope of the EIS, 40 CFR § 1508.25(b) (1987), in discussing alternatives to the proposed action, § 1502.14(f), and consequences of that action, § 1502.16(h), and in explaining its ultimate decision, § 1505.2(c).

There is a fundamental distinction, however, between a requirement that mitigation be discussed in sufficient detail to ensure that environmental consequences have been fairly evaluated, on the one hand, and a substantive requirement that a complete mitigation plan be actually formulated and adopted, on the other. In this case, the off-site effects on air quality and on the mule deer herd cannot be mitigated unless nonfederal government agencies take appropriate action. Since it is those state and local governmental bodies that have jurisdiction over the area in which the adverse effects need be addressed and since they have the authority to mitigate them, it would be incongruous to conclude that the Forest Service has no power to act until the local agencies have reached a final conclusion on what mitigating measures they consider necessary. Even more significantly, it would be inconsistent with NEPA's reliance on procedural mechanisms—as opposed to substantive, result-based standards—to demand the presence of a fully developed plan that will mitigate environmental harm before an agency can act.

We thus conclude that the Court of Appeals erred, first, in assuming that "NEPA requires that 'action be taken to mitigate the adverse effects of major federal actions,'" and, second, in finding that this substantive requirement entails the further duty to include in every EIS "a detailed explanation of specific measures which will be employed to mitigate the adverse impacts of a proposed action."

NOTES AND QUESTIONS

1.   The proposed downhill ski resort was never built. A developer pursued a master planned resort without the downhill component, but opponents successfully challenged some of the water rights the developer proposed to use, and subsequently a conservation group acquired most of the property.

2.   What actually was threatening the adverse effects on the deer herd? The ski runs or other activities on federal land? Or the condominiums on private land? Who is responsible for the latter? Does NEPA require the Forest Service to seek to mitigate the adverse environmental effects of the ski area proposal? Did the agency assume a responsibility to mitigate adverse effects? (Notice the possible interplay here of federal law with state and local law on such things as land use planning on nonfederal lands.) What does NEPA require regarding disclosure of those mitigating steps; e.g., must they be described in the EIS?

3.   Notice that the Forest Service decision-making process for ski areas proceeds from the generic to the specific through several layers, from (1) a generic feasibility study through (2) a decision to issue a permit to a

specific developer (and to formulate the terms of the permit) down to (3) the approval of a final master plan. *Methow Valley* involved NEPA compliance on stage 1, but stages 2–3 may also require some form of NEPA documentation. Many federal agency decision-making processes involve such multiple layers. The CEQ regulations characterize the general issue of determining where and how NEPA fits in a staged decision-making process as "tiering." Specifically, "[a]gencies are encouraged to tier their environmental impact statements to eliminate repetitive discussions * * * and to focus on the actual issues ripe for decision at each level of environmental review." 40 C.F.R. § 1502.20; *see also* § 1508.28.

4. A frequent focus of NEPA litigation challenging the adequacy of an EIS (rather than simply a failure to prepare one) turns on the question of "alternatives to the proposed action." Must all alternatives be discussed? What were the alternatives to the ski area proposal here? Alternative designs? Alternative locations (on federal land, and on private land)? Alternative forms of outdoor recreation? Alternative ways to spend discretionary income? Doing nothing? Does NEPA require that each of these, and their environmental impacts, be discussed in the EIS? Does an agency have to discuss alternatives that are beyond its legal authority to implement? Suppose, for example, that the best alternative location for a ski area in the *Methow Valley* case were on nearby private land, over which the Forest Service had no jurisdiction. Must the EIS discuss that alternative?

5. If the Forest Service had said in the EIS that it would require the developer to build an access road according to certain environmentally protective standards, and then later failed to include this requirement in the permit it issued the developer, would the plaintiffs have a cause of action to enforce the promise in the EIS? That is, are agency promises or commitments in the EIS enforceable? Mitigated FONSIs include measures in the actual project description adopted in the administrative record in order to reduce impacts below the level of significance. In this respect, EAs may be more powerful tools of environmental protection than EISs. However, in neither case does NEPA require post-decision monitoring to confirm that mitigation succeeded in moderating or eliminating the project impacts. The following note explores this very important issue.

CAN A FEDERAL AGENCY AVOID AN EIS BY REGULATING THE PROPOSED ACTIVITY TO RESTRICT ITS IMPACT?

In Cabinet Mountains Wilderness v. Peterson, 685 F.2d 678 (D.C.Cir. 1982), environmental advocates challenged a Forest Service decision not to prepare an EIS on a proposal by ASARCO mining company to engage in minerals exploration in a wilderness area in northwestern Montana. Of particular concern were the impacts on the area's high quality grizzly bear habitat. Excerpts from the NEPA discussion follow (the Endangered Species Act issues raised are considered further below).

Both the Forest Service and the FWS concluded that the ASARCO proposal could have an adverse impact upon the grizzly bears, particularly when other concurrent activities in the Cabinet Mountains area were taken into account. Numerous specific recommendations were made to avoid this impact and mitigation measures to protect the grizzly bears were imposed upon the proposal. * * * [T]hese measures were designed to "completely compensate" both the adverse effects of the ASARCO proposal and the cumulative effects of other activities on the bears and their habitat. In light of the imposition of these measures, the Forest Service concluded that implementation of the ASARCO proposal would not result in "any significant effects upon the quality of the human environment." Therefore an EIS was found to be unnecessary.

This court has established four criteria for reviewing an agency's decision to forego preparation of an EIS: (1) whether the agency took a "hard look" at the problem; (2) whether the agency identified the relevant areas of environmental concern; (3) as to the problems studied and identified, whether the agency made a convincing case that the impact was insignificant; and (4) if there was impact of true significance, whether the agency convincingly established that changes in the project sufficiently reduced it to a minimum. The fourth criterion permits consideration of any mitigation measures that the agency imposed on the proposal. As this court noted, "changes in the project are not legally adequate to avoid an impact statement unless they permit a determination that such impact as remains, after the change, is not 'significant.'" Other courts have also permitted the effect of mitigation measures to be considered in determining whether preparation of an EIS is necessary. * * * [If] the proposal is modified prior to implementation by adding specific mitigation measures which completely compensate for any possible adverse environmental impacts stemming from the original proposal, the statutory threshold of significant environmental effects is not crossed and an EIS is not required. To require an EIS in such circumstances would trivialize NEPA. * * *

Because the mitigation measures were properly taken into consideration by the agency, we have no difficulty in concluding that the Forest Service's decision that an EIS was unnecessary was not arbitrary or capricious. The record indicates that the Forest Service carefully considered the ASARCO proposal, was well informed on the problems presented, identified the relevant areas of environmental concern, and weighed the likely impacts. * * *

Finally, we perceive no difficulty in reading the project modifications as requiring compliance by ASARCO. The Forest Service approved the proposal subject to the restrictions and mitigation measures which had been devised during the review process. Failure to abide by the modifications would be contrary to terms of the approval. If necessary, the agency can redress any violations by revoking or suspending its permission to conduct the drilling program.

We conclude that the agency's decision not to prepare an EIS was reasonable and adequately supported. * * * [T]he decision as to whether an EIS should be prepared is left to the agency's informed discretion. * * * For us to overturn it under these circumstances would require an unjustifiable intrusion into the administrative process. We refuse to intrude.

The Ninth Circuit the same year reached the opposite result in another case involving hardrock mining activity on national forest land. In Foundation for North American Wild Sheep v. United States Dept. of Agriculture, 681 F.2d 1172 (9th Cir.1982), the Forest Service had decided not to prepare an EIS on its decision to issue a permit to a mining company allowing the reconstruction of a road to reach its mine. The primary issue was the impact of the mine on a resident Desert Bighorn Sheep herd. Excerpts follow:

> The Service vigorously asserts that the mitigation measures incorporated into the chosen alternative (Alternative B) reduce the potential impact upon the Bighorn to insignificant levels. We cannot agree.
>
> Alternative B * * * provides for the closure of Road 2N06 from April 1 until June 30 in order to avoid undue disturbance of the sheep during the "lambing" season. Second, Alternative B requires the maintenance of a secure, locked gate and a 24–hour guard at the entrance to Road 2N06. Third, a monitoring system is to be undertaken and Road 2N06 is to be closed in the event of a forty percent reduction in the use of the area by the sheep. Finally, the Service contends that the area can be repopulated with Bighorn sheep from other areas if necessary. The efficacy of these mitigation measures was severely attacked by numerous responses to the original draft of the EA. * * *
>
> * * * [I]t appears that the continued use of the lambing area through which Road 2N06 passes is essential to the continued productivity of the herd at issue here. Respondents to the draft EA strongly attacked the Service's assumption that the sheep would return to the area to perform their most sensitive function after that area had been invaded by man for nine months. The Service provided no basis for its assumption in the EA. Evaluation of the reasonableness of this assumption is doubly difficult because of the Service's failure to provide data regarding the quantity of traffic expected to flow through the area. The absence of this crucial information renders a decision regarding the sheep's reaction to the traffic on Road 2N06 necessarily uninformed. Without some sort of informed idea of how the sheep will react to Road 2N06 while it is open, it is impossible to determine whether they will return to the area to "lamb" once the road has been closed. Certainly substantial questions are raised whether the closure of Road 2N06 for three months will serve to mitigate the potential harm to the sheep. Where such substantial questions are raised, an EIS must be prepared.
>
> We also find the provision for a locked gate and a guard at the entrance to Road 2N06 insufficient to reduce the environmental impact of the proposed reopening of the road to less than significant levels. Initially, it is noteworthy that one of the assumptions expressly set forth in the EA is that increased unauthorized traffic on Road 2N06 will result from the reopening of the road regardless of the precautions taken to prevent such traffic. Thus the efficacy of this measure is, under the Service's own assumptions, doubtful. Further this mitigation

provision will only affect the quantum of harm resulting from unauthorized traffic. Consequently, it is manifestly insufficient to mitigate the harm to the sheep emanating from the authorized use of Road 2N06 by ore trucks and is inadequate to remedy the flaws contained in the Service's analysis of that harm.

We also find the monitoring and repopulation provisions contained in Alternative B insufficient to support a reasonable conclusion that the reopening of Road 2N06 will have no significant impact upon the quality of the human environment. NEPA expresses a Congressional determination that procrastination on environmental concerns is no longer acceptable. Yet the provision requiring closure of Road 2N06 in the event of a forty percent reduction in the use of the area by the sheep is just this type of procrastination. It represents an agency decision to act now and deal with the environmental consequences later. Such conduct is plainly inconsistent with the broad mandate of NEPA. Moreover, the provision implicitly treats a forty percent reduction in the sheep's use of the area surrounding Road 2N06 as insignificant. No support for such a conclusion is found in the record.

Reliance on the repopulation scheme * * * [ignores the fact that for repopulation] to be required, there must necessarily be an initial reduction in the population of the herd as well as a corresponding reduction in the sheep population as a whole. This overall population reduction was ignored by the Service. * * * Moreover, the transplant of sheep from another area to the area at issue here would necessarily result in a reduction in sheep population in the area from which the transplanted sheep were removed. This factor was also ignored by the Service. * * *

* * *

In the present case, the Service failed * * * to consider numerous issues obviously relevant to a determination of the likely effect of reopening Road 2N06 on the environment. Under these circumstances, we conclude that the Service's determination that no EIS was required was plainly unreasonable.

NOTES AND QUESTIONS

1.   What explains the difference in result in *Cabinet Mountains* and *Foundation for North American Wild Sheep*? The facts in the record? The degree of deference accorded to the agency? Differences in perception of the importance of the EIS to decision-making?

2.   In National Parks & Conservation Ass'n v. Babbitt, 241 F.3d 722 (9th Cir.2001), the court rejected the National Park Service's FONSI on its adoption of a vessel management plan for Glacier Bay National Park and Preserve which would increase large cruise ship visits to Glacier Bay by up to 72 percent. Among the problems with the EA/FONSI was an inadequate description of proposed mitigating measures and insufficient analysis of the measure's effectiveness.

WHICH FEDERAL ACTIONS REQUIRE NO NEPA ANALYSIS?

Categorical Exclusions

The CEQ regulations authorize federal agencies to adopt "categorical exclusions" ("CEs") of actions that do not individually or cumulatively have a significant effect on the environment. 40 C.F.R. § 1508.4. After an agency promulgates counterpart regulations identifying which of its common actions ordinarily do not require even an EA to confirm no significance, implementation generally requires little notice or documentation.

In the past several years the Forest Service has moved aggressively to expand the use of CEs. In 2005 it attempted to exempt the entire forest planning process from NEPA, as explained further below. And it has used CEs in conducting forest thinning projects that can be characterized as related to fire management policy; e.g., timber harvesting that thins the forest to reduce future fire danger. One change revised the Forest Service Handbook to allow post-fire logging projects up to 250 acres in size, with up to ½ mile of temporary road construction, without the need to prepare an EA or an EIS. 68 Fed. Reg. 44,598 (2003). This is controversial, as environmental groups have charged that this is an end run around NEPA for commercial logging purposes. More recently, the CEQ proposed guidance to clarify and promote the use of categorical exclusions across all of the federal agencies. 71 Fed. Reg. 54816 (Sept. 19, 2006).

Congress has also gotten into the CE act. Section 390 of the Energy Policy Act of 2005 gives federal land managers the benefit of a "rebuttable presumption that the use of a categorical exclusion" under NEPA would apply to several categories of activities involved in developing federal oil and gas leases, including surface disturbances of less than five acres where the total surface disturbance on the lease is not more than 150 acres and a "site-specific analysis" had previously been completed in a NEPA document; and drilling a well in a developed field where previous NEPA documents had "analyzed such drilling as a reasonably foreseeable activity" and had been approved within the last five years.

No Action

Ongoing implementation of plans may not trigger NEPA analysis. In Norton v. Southern Utah Wilderness Alliance, 542 U.S. 55 (2004), *supra* p. 224, the Court also addressed a claim by SUWA that BLM had violated NEPA by failing to prepare a supplemental environmental analysis to the EIS it originally completed on the land use plan, in order to discuss the impact of unexpectedly large ORV traffic in the wilderness study areas in question. The Court noted that:

> in certain circumstances an EIS must be supplemented. A regulation of the Council on Environmental Quality requires supplementation where "[t]here are significant new circumstances or information relevant to environmental concerns and bearing on the proposed action or its impacts." 40 CFR § 1502.9(c)(1)(ii) (2003). In Marsh [v. Oregon Natural Resources Council, 490 U.S. 360 (1989)], we interpreted § 4332 in light of this regulation to require an agency to take a "hard look" at

the new information to assess whether supplementation might be necessary.

SUWA argues that evidence of increased ORV use is "significant new circumstances or information" that requires a "hard look." We disagree. As we noted in Marsh, supplementation is necessary only if "there remains 'major Federal actio[n]' to occur," as that term is used in § 4332(2)(C). 490 U.S., at 374. In Marsh, that condition was met: the dam construction project that gave rise to environmental review was not yet completed. Here, by contrast, although the "*[a]pproval* of a [land use plan]" is a "major federal action" requiring an EIS, 43 CFR § 1601.0–6 (2003) (emphasis added), that action is completed when the plan is approved. The land use plan is the "proposed action" contemplated by the regulation. There is no ongoing "major Federal action" that could require supplementation (though BLM *is* required to perform additional NEPA analyses if a plan is amended or revised).

How might one argue that a land use plan is an ongoing federal action? Does a plan that says a particular area is open to ORV use result in federal "action" with every ORV that travels across a wilderness study area? Because BLM has ongoing authority to revise its plans to restrict activities in appropriate circumstances, is it appropriate to use NEPA to gather the information necessary to determine whether further restrictions are necessary? On the other hand, if plans are deemed ongoing actions, might that require constant supplementation as conditions change over the life of a plan, which may be decades?

Federal inaction or federal acquiescence to state action may fail to trigger NEPA analysis. Consider the following scenario: the State of Tennessee owns Reelfoot Lake, and leases it to the U.S. Fish and Wildlife Service for use as a national wildlife refuge. The lease does not expressly reserve any authority in the State to manipulate the Lake's water level. The State nevertheless proposes to draw down the water level for several months in an attempt to improve sport fishing spawning habitat. No federal funds are involved, and the federal agency stands aside to allow the state agency to operate the spillway to release the water to accomplish the drawdown. Opponents of the drawdown sue to enjoin it, arguing the federal agency should have first prepared an EIS. What result? *See* Bunch v. Hodel, 793 F.2d 129 (6th Cir.1986) (federal agency approval for the state action was necessary under the terms of the lease, and therefore "abdication of the Service's responsibilities under the terms of the lease" does not "transform the drawdown into state action" exempt from NEPA).

No Discretion

A final important category of federal action not requiring NEPA analysis is when the agency has no choice but to act. In South Dakota v. Andrus, 614 F.2d 1190 (8th Cir.1980), the question was whether the Department of the Interior had to prepare an EIS on a decision to issue a mineral patent to Pittsburgh, a mining company, for 240 acres of federal land. The patent conveyed fee simple title to the land, which was covered by a mining claim Pittsburgh had located under the Mining Law of 1872.

The Mining Law entitled Pittsburgh to a patent once it showed the "discovery" of a "valuable mineral deposit" on the claim. The court had this to say:

> We turn first to the question whether the granting of a mineral patent constitutes an "action" within the meaning of NEPA. As the district court noted, it is well established that the issuance of a mineral patent is a ministerial act. * * * Ministerial acts * * * have generally been held outside the ambit of NEPA's EIS requirement. Reasoning that the primary purpose of the impact statement is to aid agency decision making, courts have indicated that nondiscretionary acts should be exempt from the requirement. * * * In light of these decisions, it is at least doubtful that the Secretary's nondiscretionary approval of a mineral patent constitutes an "action" under § 102(2)(C).

> But even if a ministerial act may in some circumstances fall within § 102(2)(C), we still cannot say that the issuance of a mineral patent is a "major" federal action under the statute. * * * [T]he granting of a mineral patent does not enable the private party * * * to do anything. Unlike the case where a lease, permit or license is required before the particular project can begin, the issuance of a mineral patent is not a precondition which enables a party to begin mining operations. 30 U.S.C. § 26. * * * In light of the fact that a mineral patent in actuality is not a federal determination which enables the party to mine, we conclude in present context that the granting of such a patent is not a "major" federal action within the meaning of § 102(2)(C).

> In reaching this conclusion, we do not decide the question whether an EIS should be required at some point after the mineral patent has issued. * * * We note that Pittsburgh's proposed mining project is substantial and that if Pittsburgh decides to build the mine many actions may be necessary. For example, the claims at issue will presumably need permits from the Forest Service for roads, water pipelines and railroad rights of way. 43 U.S.C. § 1761(a)(1) and (a)(6). Moreover, the company may possibly seek to make land exchanges with the Forest Service. We leave to another day the question whether an EIS would be required in connection with any one or more such actions.

Although the court was correct in holding that Pittsburgh did not need a patent in order to extract minerals, the patent did free the company from federal land regulation that would otherwise apply. After getting the patent, Pittsburgh might have been able to put a ski area or condominium development on the land without further federal approval. Does that suggest the court is wrong on the application of NEPA?

In Department of Transportation v. Public Citizen, 541 U.S. 752 (2004), a unanimous decision authored by Justice Thomas, the Court rejected a challenge to the Federal Motor Carrier Safety Administration's regulations addressing cross-border operations of Mexican motor carriers. The Court determined that the agency lacked the discretion under applicable legislation (and under a presidential order lifting a previous moratorium on such traffic) to prevent such cross-border operations, and thus

NEPA's "core focus on improving agency decisionmaking" would not be served by detailed environmental analysis.

THE PLACE OF NEPA IN PUBLIC NATURAL RESOURCES LAW

Preparation of environmental impact statements has become a significant industry in itself, financially benefiting biologists, hydrologists, sociologists, consultants, the paper industry, and many others, including lawyers. The process is time-consuming and can be expensive.

Is it worth it? Is NEPA just an example of proliferating paperwork and red tape that contributes to governmental inefficiency and frustration of citizens' legitimate aims? *See, e.g.,* Joseph L. Sax, *The (Unhappy) Truth About NEPA*, 26 OKLA. L.REV. 239, 239 (1973) ("I know of no solid evidence to support the belief that requiring articulation, detailed findings or reasoned opinions enhances the integrity or propriety of the administrative decisions. I think the emphasis on the redemptive quality of procedural reform is about nine parts myth and one part coconut oil"). Or is NEPA a necessary device to ensure that bureaucrats engage in a minimum of thought before taking irreversible actions that may be very unwise—looking before they leap? Can that question really be answered without knowing what would have occurred without NEPA? Should the federal government be efficient? At least sufficiently efficient so that its trains run on time?

The Supreme Court has taken the narrow view of every NEPA question it has chosen to decide. In spite of the Court's reluctance to allow the tail of environmental evaluation to wag the dog of normal government operations, NEPA remains an important element in federal land and resources management. To some extent it has been merged into more precise organic statutes, such as FLPMA and the National Forest Management Act of 1976. The importance of NEPA as leading to change in federal land and resources law and administration has declined in inverse proportion to the growth of substantive statutory law governing public land management, agencies' increasing familiarity with NEPA requisites, and heightened congressional oversight of public land decisions. But the statute remains a major focus of federal resources litigation. Moreover, there are numerous examples where NEPA prompted the government to think more broadly and deeply about environmental consequences and values. For instance, tenacious litigation in the 1970s challenging the Army Corps of Engineers' 231–mile channelization project on the Cache River in Arkansas saved bottomland hardwood habitat that the federal government would purchase for the Cache River National Wildlife Refuge in the 1980s. It is there that the Ivory–Billed Woodpecker, once thought extinct, is now believed by many scientists to have endured. *See* Environmental Defense Fund v. Froehlke, 473 F.2d 346 (8th Cir.1972); David S. Wilcove, *Rediscovery of the Ivory–Billed Woodpecker*, 308 SCIENCE 1422 (2005).

Reconsider Professor Keiter's explanation of ecosystem management, *supra* p. 38. Both NEPA and the APA focus on a single point in time when an agency makes a decision. Can this deep structural element of administrative law ever accommodate adaptive management? How might NEPA be changed to promote iterative learning without harming its environmental protection function?

Professor Karkkainen proposes to retool NEPA by requiring follow-up monitoring, adaptive mitigation, and an environmental management systems-oriented approach. Shifting from *ex ante* prediction to pragmatic, empirical monitoring would enable systematic error detection and better-informed management over a project's life. Professor Karkkainen also points out that there is little information about how accurate the EIS is in predicting the consequences of decisions. NEPA does not require the agencies nor anyone else "to follow up on [EIS] predictions to determine their accuracy, nor do agencies regularly make it their practice to do so. * * * The little work that has been done to audit the accuracy of such predictions is not encouraging." As he points out, his recommendations for empirically grounded monitoring and adaptive mitigation is broadly congruent with important recent trends in environmental regulation and management generally. Bradley C. Karkkainen, *Toward a Smarter NEPA*, 102 Colum. L.Rev. 903 (2002).

C.   The Endangered Species Act

1.   Introduction and Overview

The federal Endangered Species Act, 16 U.S.C. §§ 1531–1543, sometimes called the "pit bull" of environmental statutes, can be a formidable constraint on a wide variety of federal land uses in certain situations. Helped along by many court decisions, the Act arguably has become the most important national land use law. The act protects only species (and, indirectly, their habitats) that the federal government "lists" through notice and comment rulemaking as threatened or endangered. In general, the Act commands all agencies to "conserve" listed species, and "conservation" is defined as activities necessary to recover species to the point at which they no longer need the protection of the Act. Section 7, 16 U.S.C. § 1536, applies specifically to federal departments and agencies, and is explored immediately below. Section 9, 16 U.S.C. § 1538, prohibits "taking" of a listed species by anyone, whether the government is involved or not. The ESA broadly defines "take" to include indirect harms through habitat modification under certain circumstances. Section 9 is considered further below in this section.

There is no doubt that the ESA is working a substantial revolution in the way we manage federal lands and associated waters. Some say it's because other environmental laws (like the Clean Water Act) and laws calling for "sustained yield" management of federal renewable resources (covered in succeeding chapters) have failed to deliver on their promise. And some say it's because the ESA merely provides the excuse—the final prod or inducement—to move toward more sensible, sustainable management of natural resources that many have long known must come. But the ESA is subject to trenchant criticism on a variety of grounds. For example, its focus on single species in what some have called an "emergency room" atmosphere generally falls short of preserving significant ecosystems.

There is a huge volume of commentary on the Act. Useful discussions can be found in Michael Bean and Melanie Rowland, THE EVOLUTION OF NATIONAL WILDLIFE LAW 192–276 (3d ed. 1997); Oliver A. Houck, *The Endangered Species Act and its Implementation by the U.S. Departments of Interior and Commerce*, 64 U. COLO. L.REV. 278 (1993); ENDANGERED SPECIES ACT: LAW, POLICY, AND PERSPECTIVES (Donald Baur & Robert Irvin, eds. 2002); Symposium, *The Endangered Species Act Turns 30*, 34 ENVTL. LAW 287–744 (2004).

The ESA's substantive bite was forcefully underscored by the U.S. Supreme Court in the following case, one of the leading decisions in natural resources law.

Tennessee Valley Authority v. Hill

Supreme Court of the United States, 1978.
437 U.S. 153.

■ CHIEF JUSTICE BURGER delivered the opinion of the Court.

The questions presented in this case are (a) whether the Endangered Species Act of 1973 requires a court to enjoin the operation of a virtually completed federal dam—which had been authorized prior to 1973—when, pursuant to authority vested in him by Congress, the Secretary of the Interior has determined that operation of the dam would eradicate an endangered species; and (b) whether continued congressional appropriations for the dam after 1973 constituted an implied repeal of the Endangered Species Act, at least as to the particular dam.

[In 1967 the Tennessee Valley Authority, a federal agency, began constructing the Tellico Dam on the Little Tennessee River near Knoxville, after Congress appropriated initial funds for it. The Dam was a multipurpose project designed for flood control, hydroelectric power production, and flatwater recreation. It would inundate 30 miles of the river and some 16,500 acres of land, much of it productive farmland. Shortly after NEPA took effect in 1970, dam construction was enjoined until an EIS was prepared. Following preparation of an EIS and a finding that it complied with NEPA, the district court dissolved the injunction. EDF v. TVA, 371 F.Supp. 1004 (E.D.Tenn.1973), *aff'd*, 492 F.2d 466 (6th Cir.1974).]

[During that litigation] a discovery was made in the waters of the Little Tennessee which would profoundly affect the Tellico Project. * * * [A] University of Tennessee ichthyologist, Dr. David A. Etnier, found a previously unknown species of perch, the snail darter, * * * [a] three-inch, tannish-colored fish, whose numbers are estimated to be in the range of 10,000 to 15,000 * * *.

Until recently the finding of a new species of animal life would hardly generate a cause célèbre. This is particularly so in the case of darters, of which there are approximately 130 known species, 8 to 10 of these having been identified only in the last five years. The moving force behind the snail darter's sudden fame came some four months after its discovery, when the Congress passed the Endangered Species Act of 1973. This legislation, among other things, authorizes the Secretary of the Interior to declare species of animal life "endangered" and to identify the "critical habitat" of these creatures. When a species or its habitat is so listed, [section 7 of the Act] becomes effective:

" * * * All * * * Federal departments and agencies shall, in consultation with and with the assistance of the Secretary [of the Interior], utilize their authorities in furtherance of the purposes of this chapter * * * *by taking such action necessary to insure that actions authorized, funded, or carried out by them do not jeopardize the continued existence of such endangered species and threatened species or result in the destruction or modification of habitat of such species* which is determined by the Secretary, after consultation as appropriate with the affected States, to be critical." 16 U.S.C. § 1536 (emphasis added).

[In 1975, in response to plaintiff's petition, the Interior Secretary listed the snail darter as endangered, declared the area to be inundated as "critical habitat," and announced that impoundment of the river "would result in total destruction of the snail darter's habitat." The TVA insisted that the only remedy was to attempt to transplant the fish to another river.]

[The district court refused relief, calling it "absurd" to think that Congress intended the Act to apply this way, but the court of appeals entered a permanent injunction against closure of the dam until Congress decided otherwise.]

* * *

Following the issuance of the permanent injunction, members of TVA's Board of Directors appeared before Subcommittees of the House and Senate Appropriations Committees to testify in support of continued appropriations for Tellico. The Subcommittees were apprised of all aspects of Tellico's status, including the Court of Appeals' decision. TVA reported that the dam stood "ready for the gates to be closed and the reservoir filled," and requested funds for completion of certain ancillary parts of the project, such as public use areas, roads, and bridges. As to the snail darter itself, TVA commented optimistically on its transplantation efforts, expressing the opinion that the relocated fish were "doing well and ha[d] reproduced."

Both Appropriations Committees subsequently recommended the full amount requested for completion of the Tellico Project. In its June 2, 1977, Report, the House Appropriations Committee stated:

"It is *the Committee's view* that the Endangered Species Act was not intended to halt projects such as these in their advanced stage of completion, and [the Committee] strongly recommends that these projects not be stopped because of misuse of the Act." H.R.Rep. No. 95–379, p. 104. (Emphasis added.)

As a solution to the problem, the House Committee * * * recommended a special appropriation of $2 million to facilitate relocation of the snail darter and other endangered species which threatened to delay or stop TVA projects. Much the same occurred on the Senate side, with its Appropriations Committee recommending both the amount requested to complete Tellico and the special appropriation for transplantation of endangered species. Reporting to the Senate on these measures, the Appropriations Committee took a particularly strong stand on the snail darter issue:

> "This *committee has not viewed* the Endangered Species Act as preventing the completion and use of these projects which were well under way at the time the affected species were listed as endangered. If the act has such an effect, which is contrary to *the Committee's understanding* of the intent of Congress in enacting the Endangered Species Act, funds should be appropriated to allow these projects to be completed and their benefits realized in the public interest, the Endangered Species Act notwithstanding." S.Rep. No. 95–301, p. 99 (1977). (Emphasis added.)

TVA's budget, including funds for completion of Tellico and relocation of the snail darter, passed both Houses of Congress and was signed into law on August 7, 1977. * * *

We begin with the premise that operation of the Tellico Dam will either eradicate the known population of snail darters or destroy their critical habitat. Petitioner does not now seriously dispute this fact. * * *

Starting from the above premise, two questions are presented: (a) would TVA be in violation of the Act if it completed and operated the Tellico Dam as planned? (b) if TVA's actions would offend the Act, is an injunction the appropriate remedy for the violation? For the reasons stated hereinafter, we hold that both questions must be answered in the affirmative.

It may seem curious to some that the survival of a relatively small number of three-inch fish among all the countless millions of species extant would require the permanent halting of a virtually completed dam for which Congress has expended more than $100 million. The paradox is not minimized by the fact that Congress continued to appropriate large sums of public money for the project, even after congressional Appropriations Committees were apprised of its apparent impact upon the survival of the snail darter. We conclude, however, that the explicit provisions of the Endangered Species Act require precisely that result.

One would be hard pressed to find a statutory provision whose terms were any plainer than those in § 7 of the Endangered Species Act. Its very words affirmatively command all federal agencies "to *insure* that actions *authorized, funded,* or *carried out* by them do not *jeopardize* the continued existence" of an endangered species or "*result* in the destruction or modification of habitat of such species * * *." 16 U.S.C. § 1536. (Emphasis added.) This language admits of no exception. Nonetheless, petitioner urges, as do the dissenters, that the Act cannot reasonably be interpreted as applying to a federal project which was well under way when Congress passed the Endangered Species Act of 1973. To sustain that position, however, we would be forced to ignore the ordinary meaning of plain language. It has not been shown, for example, how TVA can close the gates of the Tellico Dam without "carrying out" an action that has been "authorized" and "funded" by a federal agency. Nor can we understand how such action will "insure" that the snail darter's habitat is not disrupted. Accepting the Secretary's determinations, as we must, it is clear that TVA's proposed operation of the dam will have precisely the opposite effect, namely the eradication of an endangered species.

Concededly, this view of the Act will produce results requiring the sacrifice of the anticipated benefits of the project and of many millions of dollars in public funds. But examination of the language, history, and structure of the legislation under review here indicates beyond doubt that Congress intended endangered species to be afforded the highest of priorities.

* * *

In shaping legislation to deal with the problem thus presented, Congress started from the finding that "[t]he two major causes of extinction are hunting and destruction of natural habitat." S.Rep. No. 93, 307, p. 2 (1973). Of these twin threats, Congress was informed that the greatest [sic] was destruction of natural habitats * * *.

As it was finally passed, the Endangered Species Act of 1973 represented the most comprehensive legislation for the preservation of endangered species ever enacted by any nation. Its stated purposes were "to provide a means whereby the ecosystems upon which endangered species and threatened species depend may be conserved," and "to provide a program for the conservation of such * * * species * * *." 16 U.S.C. § 1531(b). In furtherance of these goals, Congress expressly stated in § 2(c) that "all Federal departments and agencies *shall* seek *to conserve endangered species* and threatened species * * *." 16 U.S.C. § 1531(c). (Emphasis added.) Lest there be any ambiguity as to the meaning of this statutory directive, the Act specifically defined "conserve" as meaning "to use and the use of *all methods and procedures which are necessary* to bring *any endangered species* or threatened species to the point at which the measures provided pursuant to this chapter are no longer necessary." § 1532(2). (Emphasis added.) Aside from § 7, other provisions indicated the seriousness with which Congress viewed this issue * * *.

Section 7 of the Act, which of course is relied upon by respondents in this case, provides a particularly good gauge of congressional intent. * * * [T]his provision had its genesis in the Endangered Species Act of 1966, but that legislation qualified the obligation of federal agencies by stating that they should seek to preserve endangered species only "insofar as is practicable and consistent with the[ir] primary purposes * * *." Likewise, every bill introduced in 1973 contained a qualification similar to that found in the earlier statutes. * * *

What is very significant in this sequence is that the final version of the 1973 Act carefully omitted all of the reservations described above. * * *

                                        * * *

* * * [T]he totality of congressional action makes it abundantly clear that the result we reach today is wholly in accord with both the words of the statute and the intent of Congress. The plain intent of Congress in enacting this statute was to halt and reverse the trend toward species extinction, whatever the cost. This is reflected not only in the stated policies of the Act, but in literally every section of the statute. * * * In addition, the legislative history undergirding § 7 reveals an explicit congressional decision to require agencies to afford first priority to the declared national policy of saving endangered species. The pointed omission of the type of qualifying language previously included in endangered species legislation reveals a conscious decision by Congress to give endangered species priority over the "primary missions" of federal agencies. * * *

Furthermore, it is clear Congress foresaw that § 7 would, on occasion, require agencies to alter ongoing projects in order to fulfill the goals of the Act. * * * [An] example is provided by the House Committee Report:

> "Under the authority of [§ 7], the Director of the Park Service would be required *to conform the practices of his agency* to the need for protecting the rapidly dwindling stock of grizzly bears within Yellowstone Park. These bears, which may be endangered, and are undeniably threatened, should at least be protected * * * *by curtailing the destruction of habitat by clearcutting National Forests surrounding the Park*, and by preventing hunting until their numbers have recovered sufficiently to withstand these pressures." H.R.Rep. No. 93–412, p. 14 (1973). (Emphasis added.)

One might dispute the applicability of these examples to the Tellico Dam by saying that in this case the burden on the public through the loss of millions of unrecoverable dollars would greatly outweigh the loss of the snail darter. But neither the Endangered Species Act nor Art. III of the Constitution provides federal courts with authority to make such fine utilitarian calculations. On the contrary, the plain language of the Act, buttressed by its legislative history, shows clearly that Congress viewed the value of endangered species as "incalculable." Quite obviously, it would be difficult for a court to balance the loss of a sum certain—even $100 million—against a congressionally declared "incalculable" value, even assuming we had the power to engage in such a weighing process, which we emphatically do not.

* * * Congress was * * * aware of certain instances in which exceptions to the statute's broad sweep would be necessary. Thus, § 10, 16 U.S.C. § 1539, creates a number of limited "hardship exemptions," none of which would even remotely apply to the Tellico Project. In fact, there are no exemptions in the Endangered Species Act for federal agencies, meaning that under the maxim expressio unius est exclusio alterius we must

presume that these were the only "hardship cases" Congress intended to exempt.[34]

Notwithstanding Congress' expression of intent in 1973, we are urged to find that the continuing appropriations for Tellico Dam constitute an implied repeal of the 1973 Act, at least insofar as it applies to the Tellico Project. * * * TVA points to the statements found in various House and Senate Appropriations Committees' Reports * * * [which] generally reflected the attitude of the Committees either that the Act did not apply to Tellico or that the dam should be completed regardless of the provisions of the Act. * * *

There is nothing in the appropriations measures, as passed, which states that the Tellico Project was to be completed irrespective of the requirements of the Endangered Species Act. These appropriations, in fact, represented relatively minor components of the lump-sum amounts for the entire TVA budget. To find a repeal of the Endangered Species Act under these circumstances would surely do violence to the " 'cardinal rule * * * that repeals by implication are not favored.' " Morton v. Mancari, 417 U.S. 535, 549 (1974) * * *.

The doctrine disfavoring repeals by implication "applies with full vigor when * * * the subsequent legislation is an appropriations measure." * * * We recognize that both substantive enactments and appropriations measures are "Acts of Congress," but the latter have the limited and specific purpose of providing funds for authorized programs. When voting on appropriations measures, legislators are entitled to operate under the assumption that the funds will be devoted to purposes which are lawful and not for any purpose forbidden. Without such an assurance, every appropriations measure would be pregnant with prospects of altering substantive legislation, repealing by implication any prior statute which might prohibit the expenditure. Not only would this lead to the absurd result of requiring Members to review exhaustively the background of every authorization before voting on an appropriation, but it would flout the very rules the Congress carefully adopted to avoid this need. House Rule XXI(2), for instance, specifically provides [that no provision in an appropriations bill]

---

34. Mr. Justice Powell's dissent relies on cases decided under the National Environmental Policy Act to support its position that the 1973 Act should only apply to prospective actions of an agency. The NEPA decisions, however, are completely inapposite. First, the two statutes serve different purposes. NEPA essentially imposes a procedural requirement on agencies, requiring them to engage in an extensive *inquiry* as to the effect of federal actions on the environment; by way of contrast, the [Endangered Species] Act is substantive in effect, designed to *prevent* the loss of any endangered species, regardless of the cost. Thus, it would make sense to hold NEPA inapplicable at some point in the life of a project, because the agency would no longer have a meaningful opportunity to *weigh* the benefits of the project versus the detrimental effects on the environment. Section 7, on the other hand, compels agencies not only to *consider* the effect of their projects on endangered species, but to take such actions as are necessary to *insure* that species are not extirpated as a result of federal activities. Second, even the NEPA cases have generally required agencies to file environmental impact statements when the remaining governmental action would be environmentally "significant." Under § 7, the loss of *any* endangered species has been determined by Congress to be environmentally "significant."

"changing existing law [shall] be in order." (Emphasis added.) See also Standing Rules of the Senate, Rule 16.4. Thus, to sustain petitioner's position, we would be obliged to assume that Congress meant to repeal pro tanto § 7 of the Act by means of a procedure expressly prohibited under the rules of Congress.

* * *

Having determined that there is an irreconcilable conflict between operation of the Tellico Dam and the explicit provisions of § 7 of the Endangered Species Act, we must now consider what remedy, if any, is appropriate. It is correct, of course, that a federal judge sitting as a chancellor is not mechanically obligated to grant an injunction for every violation of law. * * *

But these principles take a court only so far. Our system of government is, after all, a tripartite one, with each branch having certain defined functions delegated to it by the Constitution. While "[i]t is emphatically the province and duty of the judicial department to say what the law is," Marbury v. Madison, 1 Cranch 137, 177 (1803), it is equally—and emphatically—the exclusive province of the Congress not only to formulate legislative policies and mandate programs and projects, but also to establish their relative priority for the Nation. Once Congress, exercising its delegated powers, has decided the order of priorities in a given area, it is for the Executive to administer the laws and for the courts to enforce them when enforcement is sought.

Here we are urged to view the Endangered Species Act "reasonably," and hence shape a remedy "that accords with some modicum of common sense and the public weal." But is that our function? We have no expert knowledge on the subject of endangered species, much less do we have a mandate from the people to strike a balance of equities on the side of the Tellico Dam. Congress has spoken in the plainest of words, making it abundantly clear that the balance has been struck in favor of affording endangered species the highest of priorities, thereby adopting a policy which it described as "institutionalized caution."

Our individual appraisal of the wisdom or unwisdom of a particular course consciously selected by the Congress is to be put aside in the process of interpreting a statute. Once the meaning of an enactment is discerned and its constitutionality determined, the judicial process comes to an end. * * *

We agree with the Court of Appeals that in our constitutional system the commitment to the separation of powers is too fundamental for us to pre-empt congressional action by judicially decreeing what accords with "common sense and the public weal." Our Constitution vests such responsibilities in the political branches.

■ JUSTICE POWELL, with whom JUSTICE BLACKMUN joins, dissenting.

* * * This decision casts a long shadow over the operation of even the most important projects, serving vital needs of society and national defense, whenever it is determined that continued operation would threaten extinction of an endangered species or its habitat.

* * * If it were clear from the language of the Act and its legislative history that Congress intended to authorize this result, this Court would be compelled to enforce it. It is not our province to rectify policy or political judgments by the Legislative Branch, however egregiously they may disserve the public interest. But where the statutory language and legislative history, as in this case, need not be construed to reach such a result, I view it as the duty of this Court to adopt a permissible construction that accords with some modicum of common sense and the public weal.

* * * [The majority's interpretation of section 7] gives it a retroactive effect and disregards 12 years of consistently expressed congressional intent to complete the Tellico Project. With all due respect, I view this result as an extreme example of a literalist construction, not required by the language of the Act and adopted without regard to its manifest purpose.

* * * Under the Court's reasoning, the Act covers every existing federal installation, including great hydroelectric projects and reservoirs, every river and harbor project, and every national defense installation—however essential to the Nation's economic health and safety. The "actions" that an agency would be prohibited from "carrying out" would include the continued operation of such projects or any change necessary to preserve their continued usefulness. The only precondition, according to respondents, to thus destroying the usefulness of even the most important federal project in our country would be a finding by the Secretary of the Interior that a continuation of the project would threaten the survival or critical habitat of a newly discovered species of water spider or amoeba. * * *

I have little doubt that Congress will amend the Endangered Species Act to prevent the grave consequences made possible by today's decision. Few, if any, Members of that body will wish to defend an interpretation of the Act that requires the waste of at least $53 million, and denies the people of the Tennessee Valley area the benefits of the reservoir that Congress intended to confer. There will be little sentiment to leave this dam standing before an empty reservoir, serving no purpose other than a conversation piece for incredulous tourists.

But more far reaching than the adverse effect on the people of this economically depressed area is the continuing threat to the operation of every federal project, no matter how important to the Nation. If Congress acts expeditiously, as may be anticipated, the Court's decision probably will have no lasting adverse consequences. But I had not thought it to be the province of this Court to force Congress into otherwise unnecessary action by interpreting a statute to produce a result no one intended.

NOTES AND QUESTIONS

1. In TVA v. Hill the Department of the Interior (whose Fish & Wildlife Service plays a key role in implementing the Act) was permitted by

the Department of Justice to file an "appendix" to the government's brief on behalf of the TVA, which took precisely the opposite position from TVA. This is very rare; generally the Solicitor General takes the view that the executive has to have a single legal position before the Court. The TVA position was argued to the Court by Attorney General (and former Fifth Circuit Judge) Griffin Bell, who began his argument by brandishing a jar containing a single (dead) snail darter in formaldehyde, to illustrate (to no avail, as it turned out) the ridiculousness of a tiny "worthless" fish stopping a big dam. Professor Zygmunt Plater, attorney for the plaintiffs, later remarked: "It's the only fish story I know where the fish gets smaller and smaller." The plaintiffs' perspective was that the Tellico Dam was an uneconomic boondoggle from the beginning and the snail darter was only one of many ignored costs. The TVA also inflated the dam's benefits. In spite of the scores of millions of dollars already spent to complete 95 percent of the dam, the Chairman of President Carter's Council of Economic advisors stated that "if one takes just the cost of finishing [the remaining 5 percent] against the [total] benefits … it doesn't pay." Marc Reisner, CADILLAC DESERT 327–28 (rev.ed. 1993)

2. Does anything require Congress to protect endangered forms of life? What are the rationales for protecting endangered species? On the utilitarian side, Aldo Leopold once wrote that "[t]o keep every cog and wheel is the first precaution of intelligent tinkering." It has been estimated that perhaps half of all medical prescriptions contain substances first found in a living organism. Or does the ESA rest more on the moral principle of stewardship, evoking Noah and the Flood and the creation myths that all cultures seem to have produced? Leopold develops his ethical principles in greater detail in the essay excerpted *supra* p. 30.

3. *Valuing natural resources.* Chief Justice Burger found that Congress thought the value of endangered species was "incalculable." Is that good policy? Should we value species protection in the abstract, or only insofar as it directly relates to human quality of life? Lately a good deal of attention has been devoted to the idea of putting a value on what has come to be known as "ecosystem services."

> Largely taken for granted, healthy ecosystems provide a variety of critical services. Created by the interactions of living organisms with their environment, these "ecosystem services" provide both the conditions and processes that sustain human life—purifying air and water, detoxifying and decomposing waste, renewing soil fertility, regulating climate, mitigating droughts and floods, controlling pests, and pollinating plants. * * * [R]ecent research has demonstrated the extremely high costs to replace many of these services if they were to fail, on the order of many billions of dollars in the United States for water purification alone. * * * Despite their obvious importance to our well being, ecosystem services have largely been ignored in environmental law and policy.

James Salzman et al., *Protecting Ecosystem Services: Science, Economics, and Law*, 20 STAN. ENVTL. L.J. 309, 310–11 (2001). *See generally* Symposium, 20 STAN. ENVTL. L.J. 309–536 (2001); NATURE'S SERVICES: SOCIETAL

DEPENDENCE ON NATURAL ECOSYSTEMS (Gretchen Daily ed. 1997). As Professor Salzman has noted, "a focus on ecosystem services has the potential to unify disparate parts of environmental law, linking the conservation goals in laws such as the Endangered Species Act and National Forest Management Act more closely with the human health goals in seemingly unconnected laws such as the Clean Air Act and Safe Drinking Water Act." James Salzman, *Valuing Ecosystem Services*, 24 ECOLOGY L.Q. 887, 889 (1997).

In some modern environmental statutes, Congress has effectively required that dollar values be placed upon certain natural resources like wildlife. Most prominently, the Comprehensive Environmental Response, Compensation, and Liability Act of 1980 (CERCLA), makes persons responsible for releases of hazardous substances subject to suits for "damages for injury to, destruction of, or loss of natural resources" resulting from such releases. 42 U.S.C. § 9607(a)(4)(C). The Oil Pollution Act of 1990, enacted in the wake of the Exxon Valdez oil spill in Alaska, created a similar liability for loss of or injury to "natural resources." 33 U.S.C. § 2702(b)(2)(A).

4. *Legislative history as a guide to statutory construction*. Compare the majority opinion and Justice Powell's dissent on the legislative history of the ESA and of the Tellico appropriations bills. How reliable an indicator of congressional intent and statutory construction is legislative history such as committee reports, testimony, and floor debates? In more recent years, the Supreme Court, led by Justice Scalia, has expressed more skepticism about legislative history, and focused more on the statutory text. For a debate on the reliability of legislative history, see Wisconsin Public Intervenor v. Mortier, 501 U.S. 597 (1991), where Justice Scalia stated that Committee reports are not a "genuine indicator of congressional intent;" they do not necessarily indicate "what Congress as a whole thought" because the committee members are a small minority of the membership in each house and most members probably do not read the reports before voting. Justice White, writing for the majority, responded by saying that "common sense" as well as a long practice justifies resort to legislative history materials because they "are not generally so misleading that jurists should never employ them in a good faith effort to discern legislative intent." Who wins this debate? If much of the legislative history of a statute, such as committee reports, are actually written by (unelected) staff members in Congress, is that a sufficient justification for (unelected) judges to ignore it? Would Justice Scalia's position enlarge the power of the judiciary and diminish the power of elected representatives? (Congressional staff are, after all, hired by and subject to the control of members of Congress.) *See generally* Charles Tiefer, *The Reconceptualization of Legislative History in the Supreme Court*, 2000 WIS. L.REV. 205 (2000). For public land law, a special problem of applying legislative history is the anachronistic assumptions and methods considered by Congress in many old statutes still in force.

5. *"Appropriation Riders"—Amending substantive legislation through the appropriations process*. The Supreme Court has on occasion

relied on appropriation acts to reject arguments that federal land management agencies acted unlawfully. In Brooks v. Dewar, 313 U.S. 354, 361 (1941), the Interior Secretary created a system of temporary grazing permits and fees as a transitional phase in implementing the Taylor Grazing Act. The court rejected a rancher's contention that the Secretary lacked authority to do this. The Secretary's system had been disclosed to the Congress, which had appropriated a portion of the money received for range improvements. "The repeated appropriations * * * not only confirms the departmental construction of the statute, but constitutes a ratification of the action of the Secretary as the agent of Congress in the administration of the act." Why didn't that argument work in TVA v. Hill? Would the result in TVA v. Hill have been different if the language in the committee reports quoted in the majority opinion had been in the appropriations statute itself rather than in the reports (substituting "the Congress" for "the Committee" in the quoted excerpts)? In Lincoln v. Vigil, 508 U.S. 182 (1993), the Court expressly reaffirmed that legislative history in appropriations statutes lacks the force of law.

The rules of Congress quoted in the majority opinion in TVA v. Hill do not absolutely forbid substantive legislation in "riders" on appropriations acts. They merely say that such changes shall not be "in order," meaning they are subject to a "point of order." But if no member objects, they may be included. In actual legislative practice, the use of such riders is common. Appropriations acts are one of the few kinds of legislation that Congress must, as a practical matter, enact each year if the government is to continue to function. For that reason, they are convenient vehicles for changing substantive law and can attract riders like honey attracts flies. For a more detailed description of the differences between appropriations acts and authorizing acts, see Andrus v. Sierra Club, 442 U.S. 347, 359–64 (1979) (request for appropriation of funds to operate the National Wildlife Refuge System was not a "proposal for legislation" requiring an EIS under NEPA).

In fact, some landmark pieces of substantive federal natural resources legislation have come in the form of appropriations riders: what came to be known as the first "organic act" for national forests, 30 Stat. 34–36 (1897); the 1907 bill repealing the President's authority to create national forests in six northwestern states, 34 Stat. 1271 (1907); and the "McCarran Amendment," which waived the sovereign immunity of the United States in general stream adjudications in state courts, the 1952 Department of Justice appropriations bill, 43 U.S.C. § 666.

Appropriations acts generally make money available for designated programs for a single fiscal year. It is therefore presumed that an appropriation rider is effective only for that fiscal year, and sometimes the text clearly reflects that fact. In recent years, for example, Congress has included in the annual Interior appropriation bill a rider that says "[n]one of the funds *appropriated or otherwise made available pursuant to this Act* [that is, for a single fiscal year] shall be obligated or expended to accept or process applications for a patent for any mining or mill site claim located under the general mining laws," with certain exceptions. 113 Stat. 1501A–

191 (Interior Department and Related Agencies FY 1998 Appropriation Bill), § 312 (emphasis added). This "patent moratorium" must be renewed each year or it expires. On the other hand, if the Congress writes the rider text clearly to apply beyond the one year life of the bill, it has that effect. Thus, for example, the McCarran Amendment spoke in open-ended terms ("consent is hereby given" to join the U.S. in state court general adjudications of water rights) and it is codified as a permanent law.

6. *Enjoining statutory violations.* Suppose the dam had been completed and the gates closed before the injunction. Would that change the result? In Weinberger v. Romero–Barcelo, 456 U.S. 305 (1982), the Supreme Court distinguished TVA v. Hill and held that federal courts should exercise equitable discretion rather than automatically enjoining a discharge of pollutants into waters in violation of the Clean Water Act's permit requirements. In Water Keeper Alliance v. U.S. Dept. of Defense, 271 F.3d 21, 34 (1st Cir.2001), the court upheld a denial of a preliminary injunction in an ESA case seeking to stop Naval training exercises, finding that TVA v. Hill does not "blindly compel our decision in this case because the harm asserted by the Navy implicates national security and therefore deserves greater weight than * * * economic harm."

7. *The Aftermath of TVA v. Hill—The "God Squad" and Statutory Exemptions.* Despite Justice Powell's confident prediction that Congress would put an end to what he regarded as the foolishness of the Court's construction of the Act, Congress reauthorized the Act in 1978, 1982, and 1988, and each time contented itself with fine-tuning the Act and its processes; weakening or qualifying a few provisions, strengthening others, and adding some new protections. The Act has, in other words, proved to be quite popular and durable.

One of the provisions Congress added in 1978 was what Michael Bean and Melanie Rowland have called an "elaborate and stringent process for exempting federal actions from the section 7 prohibitions * * * [as] a last-resort option, available only after all other avenues for avoiding conflicts have been exhausted." THE EVOLUTION OF NATIONAL WILDLIFE LAW 263 (3d ed. 1997). Ultimately, a seven member cabinet-level committee has responsibility for granting or denying an exemption. Usually known as the "God Squad," it was convened for the first time in connection with the snail darter in 1979. After reviewing all the evidence on the conflict, the committee concluded that the continued existence of the snail darter did outweigh the completion and closing of the Tellico Dam, in substantial part because the dam's alleged benefits were dubious. Nevertheless, thanks to some adroit maneuvering by Tennessee Senator Howard Baker, Congress exempted Tellico from the ESA in a rider on an appropriation bill that the President reluctantly signed, 93 Stat. 437, 449–50 (1979), and TVA closed the dam's gates. As it turned out, however, so many snail darter populations were soon discovered at other locations that the little fish eventually was removed from the list of endangered species.

The exemption process has rarely been initiated and only twice have exemptions been granted. One reason for the disuse of the God Squad is that alternatives to exemption are usually available, the process for getting one is complex and difficult, and potential applicants fear bad publicity. Congress has a few times (besides with the snail darter) passed special legislation to short-circuit the Endangered Species Act's review processes. For example, in 1988 it legislated a go-ahead to construct a telescope on Mt. Graham in the Coronado National Forest in Arizona by deeming § 7 of the Act to be satisfied despite concerns about the impact of the project on the endangered Mt. Graham red squirrel. 102 Stat. 4597 (1988). The statute was not successful. Inartfully drafted, hastily pushed through Congress without the benefit of committee hearings or reports (eventually causing some of its sponsors to seek to reinterpret its effect), it failed to end the controversy. *See* Mount Graham Coalition v. Thomas, 53 F.3d 970 (9th Cir.1995). Another, more effective congressional rider followed, 110 Stat. 1321 (1996). At last report, the red squirrel was surviving despite the telescope. Does the endurance of both the red squirrel and the snail darter suggest that the ESA is overprotective?

2.   SECTION 4: LISTING SPECIES AND DESIGNATING HABITAT

No species, no matter how close to extinction, is protected by the ESA until listed by an agency through notice and comment rulemaking. A quirk complicates the Act's administration: The Secretary of the Interior (through the U.S. Fish & Wildlife Service) has responsibility for terrestrial species, freshwater species, and some marine species (e.g. the sea otter and marine birds), while the Secretary of Commerce (through the Fisheries Service (formerly known as the National Marine Fisheries Service, or NMFS) of the National Oceanic at Atmospheric Administration, or NOAA) has responsibility for most marine species and most anadromous fish. The two agencies share jurisdiction over some species, such as sea turtles and the Atlantic salmon. Hawksbill Sea Turtle v. Federal Emergency Mgt. Agency, 126 F.3d 461, 470 (3d Cir.1997) ("When the turtles are swimming * * * Commerce bears regulatory responsibility, and when the turtles return to the beach, the regulatory baton passes to Interior"). To simplify the text, references to the U.S. Fish & Wildlife Service in connection with administration of the Act should be taken as including the Fisheries Service unless the context indicates otherwise. The listing agency is the same agency that conducts consultations under section 7 of the Act.

The complete ESA list is found at 50 C.F.R. §§ 17.11 (wildlife) and 17.12 (plants). It includes nearly 1200 animals and 750 plants. Some 1300 of these species occur in the United States. Most biologists think these numbers reflect the tip of an iceberg of imperiled organisms. Many of the listed U.S. species are found on federal lands, including mammals (ranging from the grizzly bear to the black-footed ferret); birds (ranging from the California condor to the light-footed clapper rail); reptiles; fish; crustaceans; insects; and assorted plants. New species are being added on a fairly regular basis. Perhaps few have heard of the San Joaquin kit fox, the Attwater's greater prairie chicken, the Santa Cruz long-toed salamander, the Pahranaget bonytail, the Pahrump killifish, or the unarmored three spine stickleback, but the remaining few of those little devils are under Uncle Sam's own wing just as much as the more glamorous species. And these are only the species on the federal list: States are free to make their own lists, and quite a few have done so.

The following case remanding a FWS decision not to list the spotted owl effectively triggered what was to become an important judicial role in the controversy over old-growth timber management in the Pacific Northwest. Efforts to protect the northern spotted owl gave rise to perhaps the most prominent controversy ever to emerge under the ESA. It had the broadest impact on public land management, the most significant regional economic impact, and left a tangled skein of litigation, executive and congressional action. Largely because of its secretive, nocturnal nature, not much was known about the owl before the late 1980s. Something over a thousand breeding pairs occupy several million acres of old growth Douglas fir forests in the Pacific Northwest, about sixty-five percent of which is national forests, another twenty-five percent other federal land, and about ten percent state, tribal, or privately-owned land.

Northern Spotted Owl v. Hodel

United States District Court, Western District of Washington, 1988.
716 F. Supp. 479.

■ JUDGE ZILLY

A number of environmental organizations bring this action against the United States Fish & Wildlife Service ("Service") and others, alleging that the Service's decision not to list the northern spotted owl as endangered or threatened under the [ESA] * * * was arbitrary and capricious or contrary to law.

Since the 1970s the northern spotted owl has received much scientific attention, beginning with comprehensive studies of its natural history by Dr. Eric Forsman, whose most significant discovery was the close association between spotted owls and old-growth forests. This discovery raised concerns because the majority of remaining old-growth owl habitat is on public land available for harvest.

In January 1987, plaintiff Greenworld, pursuant to Sec. 4(b)(3) of the ESA, 16 U.S.C. § 1533(b)(3), petitioned the Service to list the northern spotted owl as endangered. * * *

The ESA directs the Secretary of the Interior to determine whether any species have become endangered or threatened due to habitat destruction, overutilization, disease or predation, or other natural or manmade factors. 16 U.S.C. § 1533(a)(1). The Act was amended in 1982 to ensure that the decision whether to list a species as endangered or threatened was based solely on an evaluation of the biological risks faced by the species, to the exclusion of all other factors. * * *

The Service's role in deciding whether to list the northern spotted owl as endangered or threatened is to assess the technical and scientific data in the administrative record against the relevant listing criteria in section 4(a)(1) and then to exercise its own expert discretion in reaching its decision.

In July 1987, the Service announced that it would initiate a status review of the spotted owl and requested public comment. * * * The Service assembled a group of Service biologists, including Dr. Mark Shaffer, its staff expert on population viability, to conduct the review. The Service charged Dr. Shaffer with analyzing current scientific information on the owl. Dr. Shaffer concluded that:

> the most reasonable interpretation of current data and knowledge indicate [sic] continued old growth harvesting is likely to lead to the extinction of the subspecies in the foreseeable future which argues strongly for listing the subspecies as threatened or endangered at this time. * * *

The Service invited a peer review of Dr. Shaffer's analysis by a number of U.S. experts on population viability, all of whom agreed with Dr. Shaffer's prognosis for the owl, although each had some criticisms of his work.

* * * On December 17 the Service announced that listing the owl as endangered under the Act was not warranted at this time. This suit followed. Both sides now move for summary judgment on the administrative record before the Court.

* * *

The Status Review and the Finding to the listing petition offer little insight into how the Service found that the owl currently has a viable population. Although the Status Review cites extensive empirical data and lists various conclusions, it fails to provide any analysis. The Service asserts that it is entitled to make its own decision, yet it provides no explanation for its finding. An agency must set forth clearly the grounds on which it acted. * * * Judicial deference to agency expertise is proper, but the Court will not do so blindly. The Court finds that the Service has not set forth the grounds for its decision against listing the owl.

The Service's documents also lack any expert analysis supporting its conclusion. Rather, the expert opinion is entirely to the contrary. The only reference in the Status Review to an actual opinion that the owl does not face a significant likelihood of extinction is a mischaracterization of a conclusion of Dr. Mark Boyce: "Boyce (1987) * * * concluded that there is a low probability that the spotted owls will go extinct. He does point out that population fragmentation appears to impose the greatest risks to extinction."

Dr. Boyce responded to the Service: "I did not conclude that the Spotted Owl enjoys a low probability of extinction, and I would be very disappointed if efforts to preserve the Spotted Owl were in any way thwarted by a misinterpretation of something I wrote."

Numerous other experts on population viability contributed to or reviewed drafts of the Status Review, or otherwise assessed spotted owl viability. Some were employed by the Service; others were independent. None concluded that the northern spotted owl is not at risk of extinction.
* * *

The Service invited a peer review of Dr. Shaffer's analysis. Drs. Michael Soule, Bruce Wilcox, and Daniel Goodman, three leading U.S. experts on population viability, reviewed and agreed completely with Dr. Shaffer's prognosis for the owl.

For example, Dr. Soule, the acknowledged founder of the discipline of "conservation biology" (the study of species extinction), concluded:

> I completely concur with your conclusions, and the methods by which you reached them. The more one hears about Strix occidentalis caurina, the more concern one feels. Problems with the data base and in the models notwithstanding, and politics notwithstanding, I just can't see how a responsible biologist could reach any other conclusion than yours.

The Court will reject conclusory assertions of agency "expertise" where the agency spurns unrebutted expert opinions without itself offering a credible alternative explanation. Here, the Service disregarded all the expert opinion on population viability, including that of its own expert, that the owl is facing extinction, and instead merely asserted its expertise in support of its conclusion.

The Service has failed to provide its own or other expert analysis supporting its conclusions. Such analysis is necessary to establish a rational connection between the evidence presented and the Service's decision. Accordingly, the United States Fish and Wildlife Service's decision not to list at this time the northern spotted owl as endangered or threatened under the Endangered Species Act was arbitrary and capricious and contrary to law.

* * *

In deference to the Service's expertise and its role under the Endangered Species Act, the Court remands this matter to the Service, which has 90 days from the date of this order to provide an analysis for its decision that listing the northern spotted owl as threatened or endangered is not currently warranted. Further, the Service is ordered to supplement its Status Review and petition Finding consistent with this Court's ruling.

NOTES AND QUESTIONS

1. If, upon remand, the agency found one acknowledged expert in the field who would testify that the owl was not currently endangered or threatened, would its decision not to list the species be upheld upon judicial review? Even if the plaintiffs produced nineteen experts who were of the contrary opinion, would the agency's decision not to list be arbitrary and capricious? On remand, the agency listed the spotted owl as "threatened." 55 Fed. Reg. 26,114 (1990).

2. The court identifies the plaintiff as an organization called "Greenworld," but the case caption identifies the plaintiff as the owl. Sierra Club v. Morton, 405 U.S. 727 (1972), over Justice Douglas' dissent, rejected the

theory that species other than humans have legal standing. Then, why did the environmental group name the bird as a plaintiff?

3.   Although controversy began before the owl was listed as a result of litigation, the listing gave owl advocates a powerful tool, and they used it. But the ESA was not the sole ground for the several injunctions that followed; a number were based on violations of the National Forest Management Act, the Federal Land Policy & Management Act, and NEPA. The timber industry also initiated some lawsuits of its own. In 1990 Congress stepped in by enacting an appropriations rider that allowed some timber sales to go forward in spite of pending judicial proceedings. The Supreme Court upheld the rider in Robertson v. Seattle Audubon Soc'y, 503 U.S. 429 (1992).

In 1992 new federal court decisions virtually halted timber sales in the region. One enjoined Forest Service timber sales after finding inadequate the agency's EIS on its spotted owl policy. (One of the flaws, ironically, was the EIS's failure to consider the impact on the owl of the BLM timber sales the God Squad had exempted from the Act a few weeks earlier.) Another enjoined BLM timber sales in spotted owl country, not strictly on the basis of the ESA, but because the BLM's resource management plans gave inadequate consideration to the owl.

After a regional "timber summit" conducted by President Clinton in April 1993, the President established a Forest Ecosystem Management Assessment Team to develop a comprehensive new plan for forest management across the region from northern California to the Canadian border. Centerpieces of that plan were a comprehensive approach to forest management throughout the region, regardless of ownership; a focus on maintaining diversity across many species, and not just the owl or other listed endangered species; putting the burden of protection of species on the federal lands where at all possible (to limit restrictions on private, state, and tribal land); using "adaptive management" techniques (adjusting based on experience) where possible; and cushioning impact on displaced timber industry workers through a "jobs in the woods" program. The plan (which drastically reduced timber harvesting from levels most observers thought were unsustainable anyway) and its accompanying EIS were upheld in Seattle Audubon Soc'y v. Moseley, 80 F.3d 1401 (9th Cir.1996), against challenges by both environmentalists and the timber industry. Some controversy still lingers, but the owl and the ESA emerged from the long struggle relatively intact, although the economies of several rural counties in the Northwest changed forever. Chapter 8 considers in detail the way the spotted owl controversy changed timber management in the region.

4.   As the court here noted, Congress amended the ESA in 1982 to require the Secretary to make the listing decision "*solely* on the basis of the best scientific and commercial data available." 16 U.S.C. § 1533(b)(1)(A) (emphasis added). Does this foreclose the U.S. Fish & Wildlife Service from considering the economic hardship that might result from listing a species? A long string of cases, have concluded yes. The government is not required to conduct an actual population count before making a decision about whether to list a species, because the " 'best available data' requirement

makes it clear the Secretary has no obligation to conduct independent studies." Southwest Center for Biological Diversity v. Babbitt, 215 F.3d 58, 60 (D.C.Cir.2000).

5. Does the ESA's mandate to use "best scientific . . . data available" do any more than duplicate the requirement of the APA that federal agencies avoid making arbitrary or capricious decisions? Professor Doremus suggests that the mandate might have been intended to make the courts more aggressive in judicial review, and she cites data that shows the courts have "hardly been a rubber stamp," and in fact have been "far tougher than scientific peer review" on agencies' implementation of the ESA, with agency listing decisions being overturned some 78 percent of the time the courts reached the merits, though few courts have rejected agencies' substantive scientific determinations. Holly Doremus, *The Purposes, Effects, and Future of the Endangered Species Act's Best Available Science Mandate*, 34 Envtl. L. 397 (2004). Are stringent judicial review standards helpful in making judgments about which species ought to receive special protection? Is the listing decision a scientific determination best left to panels of scientists?

Professor Doremus also explains that there are two "dimensions" to the limits of science. *Id.* at 438. "The first is that * * * some decisions under the ESA are inherently not scientific; they require value choices rather than objective interpretation of empirical data." She offers as an example "how much of the historic range of the gray wolf must be occupied before the wolf can be removed from the protected list." Another is how close to extinction a species should be before qualifying for listing. She continues:

> The second dimension is a bit more subtle. Many aspects of ESA decisions are dominated by science, but the existing data is limited and equivocal, leaving a great deal of uncertainty. Choices of how to interpret equivocal data and what to do in the face of uncertainty are not "scientific" as the public understands that term, although they are familiar to scientists and indeed are an unavoidable part of the scientific enterprise.

> Uncertainty is endemic in the ESA context. It can plague our understanding of (among other things): the historic conditions to which the species was exposed and the extent to which those conditions have been altered by human activity; population sizes and trends; life cycles, including the relationship between survival at particular stages and population status; threats to the species and, where there are multiple threats, their relative importance; and the effect of management actions on species.

Id. at 438–39.

In disputes over the use of science in natural resource regulation, both sides tend to "decry the politicization of science," but Professor Doremus turns the equation around, and says the "fundamental problem" is actually what she calls the "scientizing" of politics—the "concealment" of politics "behind a cloak of science."

Who should make listing decisions? Politically appointed officials of the Interior Department, FWS scientists, or outside panels of experts? Should Congress define a particular population level or a particular risk of extinction over a particular span of years as a uniform threshold for listing? What role, if any, should the public play in listing decisions? These questions relate to many issues in natural resources law and are discussed further in the context of ecosystem management, *supra* p. 38.

6.   Notwithstanding Justice Powell's crack about amoeba in the TVA v. Hill dissent, the ESA defines "species" that may be listed as including "any subspecies of fish or wildlife or plants, and any distinct population segment [DPS] of any species of vertebrate fish or wildlife which interbreeds when mature." 16 U.S.C. § 1532(16). Distinct population segments can be especially difficult to define. In Alsea Valley Alliance v. Evans, 161 F.Supp.2d 1154 (D.Or.2001), the court overturned a NMFS decision to list as a DPS the "Oregon Coast Evolutionary Significant Unit (ESU) coho salmon" as threatened under the ESA. Salmon runs are the breeding behavior where fish return from the ocean to reproduce in the same freshwater streams where they were born. Salmon runs are genetically isolated by geography (where the breeding run occurs) and time (when the run occurs). The listing was based partly on a NMFS policy that excluded consideration of coho salmon reared in hatcheries unless they are "considered to be essential for recovery." That policy centers on a concern that the narrow genetic diversity in hatchery populations could lead to more risk of devastating disease or the inability of natural populations to survive relative to hatchery populations. Because hatchery coho interbreed with non-hatchery coho, and thus were part of the same DPS, the court held that it was impermissible for NMFS to make a further distinction and exclude them from consideration in the listing decision. "The NMFS listing decision creates [an arbitrary distinction between] two genetically identical coho salmon swimming side-by-side in the same stream, but only one receives ESA protection." Upon remand, the agency re-listed most of the salmon runs on a slightly different basis that sought to reconcile the conservation concerns with the Act's definition of DPS.

7.   The ESA refers to "inadequacy of existing regulatory mechanism [sic]" as one factor in deciding whether to list. 16 U.S.C. § 1533(a)(1)(D). It also directs the listing agency to take into "account those efforts, if any, being made" by any State or local government "to protect such species." *Id.* § 1533(b)(1)(A). Sometimes efforts are made to avoid listing by securing what are called "candidate conservation agreements," whereby commitments are made to take steps to protect populations. Such an agreement was reached between NMFS and the State of Oregon in an attempt to head off the listing of the Oregon coastal coho, but a reviewing court set aside the agreement because its regulatory commitments were too vague and dependent upon future actions that might not be taken. *See* Oregon Natural Resources Council v. Daley, 6 F.Supp.2d 1139 (D.Or.1998). *See also* Defenders of Wildlife v. Norton, 258 F.3d 1136 (9th Cir.2001). Regulations governing candidate conservation agreements are found at 50 C.F.R.17.22(d) and 17.32(d).

8.   Approximately 85 percent of the species on the ESA list are imperiled by habitat loss. And, the average population of listed species is fewer than one thousand individuals, suggesting that species are not listed until they are at a fairly extreme risk of extinction. It also suggests that for most species to recover and be removed from the list, they must expand into habitat they currently do not occupy. David Wilcove et al., Quantifying Threats to Imperiled Species in the United States, 48 BioScience 607 (1998).

9.   About half of the listed species in the U.S. occur on federal public lands. Does the ESA make habitat recovery the dominant, top-priority use for federal lands that host listed species? The *Northern Spotted Owl* decision is an example of how plaintiffs may use the ESA to achieve broader environmental objectives—in this case, protection of old-growth forests of the Pacific Northwest. Professor Oliver Houck applauds this surrogate role for endangered species:

> Endangered species are useful, though incomplete, indicators of the health of their ecosystems and of the earth we share. While the best indicators may often be mollusks, plants, and lower life forms, the decline of the bald eagle from the effects of chlorinated hydrocarbons is a good indication of the impact of those chemicals on human life. As water quality becomes inadequate to protect the delta smelt, it will also become inadequate for human uses. * * * We accept wildlife indicator thresholds for impacts on water, air, and soil—separate components of the whole. What remains is to test the whole. Endangered species are such a test. The ESA serves in this fashion as an "Earth Pollution Act." It is admittedly an incomplete test whose results need careful interpretation, but the fate of listed species * * * help draw the line.

Why Do We Protect Endangered Species, and What Does That Say About Whether Restrictions on Private Property to Protect Them Constitute "Takings"?, 80 Iowa L.Rev. 297, 327–28 (1995). Is it proper for a plaintiff to use the ESA to advance broader environmental policy goals?

NOTE: CRITICAL HABITAT

The concept of critical habitat is "one of the Act's most contentious, ambiguous, and confusing concepts * * * [with] no clear, consistent, and shared understanding of what it means or what role it is to play." Bean and Rowland, THE EVOLUTION OF NATIONAL WILDLIFE LAW 251. The ESA reinforces this confusion in defining critical habitat as two kinds of areas. First, it is the places where the species currently live which are essential to recovery and "may require special management considerations." Second, it is also the areas outside the places currently occupied by the species but that are essential for recovery. 16 U.S.C. § 1532(5)(A). As with protected species, only habitat designated through notice and comment rulemaking requires protection under the ESA critical habitat provision.

Critical habitat designation guides federal agencies in fulfilling their obligations under Section 7 of the ESA, the provision applied in TVA v. Hill. That is, federal agencies must not take or authorize actions that are either "likely to jeopardize the continued existence of" a listed species, or which would "result in the destruction or adverse modification of [designated critical] habitat * * *." 16 U.S.C. § 1536(a)(2). Many biologists in the U.S. Fish & Wildlife Service believe that, in almost all cases, jeopardy will in fact be found if key habitat is modified, whether or not it is formally designated as "critical." To the extent that is true, formal designation of critical habitat adds little protection to listed species. For that and other reasons discussed in the next paragraph, only about 10 percent of the listed species have designated critical habitat.

The designation of critical habitat can be laborious and expensive, because the designation process is one of the few places where the Secretary must consider the probable economic or other impacts on human activities resulting from the critical habitat designation. *See* 16 U.S.C. § 1533(b)(2) (designation of critical habitat is on the basis of the best available scientific data "and after taking into consideration the economic impact, and any other relevant impact" of such designation, and the Secretary may exclude an area from critical habitat if she determines that the benefits of exclusion outweigh the benefits of inclusion, unless she determines that failure to designate would result in extinction). The judgment and discretion involved led the Tenth Circuit to find that NEPA applied to this determination, see Catron County Board of Commissioners v. U.S. Fish & Wildlife Service, 75 F.3d 1429 (10th Cir.1996), while the Ninth Circuit has held otherwise, see Douglas County v. Babbitt, 48 F.3d 1495 (9th Cir.1995).

The Act requires the Secretary to designate critical habitat at the time the species is listed "to the maximum extent prudent and determinable." 16 U.S.C. § 1533 (a)(3); *see also* § 1533(b)(6)(C). There has been much litigation about the designation of critical habitat. The courts have repeatedly sided with the plaintiffs. *See* Sierra Club v. U.S. Fish & Wildlife Service, 245 F.3d 434 (5th Cir.2001) (rejecting the Service's arguments that critical habitat does not provide much additional protection because critical habitat should focus on "recovery" rather than just "survival" of a species, and the designation "provides informational benefits to the public, state and local governments, and scientific organizations"); New Mexico Cattle Growers Ass'n v. U.S. Fish & Wildlife Service, 248 F.3d 1277 (10th Cir.2001) (same view of critical habitat, although the court, in a suit by livestock operators restricted by the Act, held that the Service's critical habitat determination for the southwestern willow flycatcher did not pay sufficient attention to economic impacts).

Contributing to the Service's lack of enthusiasm for critical habitat designation is the fact that the money for critical habitat designation comes out of the same pot as money for listing. From the Service's perspective, every dollar spent on critical habitat protection is one that cannot be spent on listing, where the protection "bang for the buck" is much greater. Some environmental groups have pushed critical habitat designations hard in litigation, with the belief, or hope, that as court orders to designate critical habitat pile up, Congress will appropriate more money for the task. But experience suggests otherwise. In the meantime, the Service is caught in the middle, being forced to complete more critical habitat designations while undertaking more thorough economic analyses, resulting in the siphoning of resources from the process of determining whether to add candidate species to the list.

A bipartisan group of six Senators asked the nonpartisan Keystone Center to form a committee of experts to review and make recommendation for how the Act's treatment of habitat could be improved. The Keystone Working Group issued a final report in 2006 which concluded that the Act could more effectively protect and conserve habitat needed by listed species, but could not reach consensus on how to do that. Still, the report highlights many salient issues and can be found at the Keystone Center's website, www.keystone.org.

NOTE: RECOVERY PLANS

The 1978 amendments added a provision to § 4 of the ESA requiring the Secretary of the Interior to "develop and implement plans (* * * 'recovery plans') for the conservation and survival of [listed species] * * * unless he finds that such a plan will not promote the conservation of the species." 16 U.S.C. § 1533(f)(1). The Secretary is to give priority to those species "most likely to benefit from such plans." About half of listed species have recovery plans, although only about one-third of the animals do (and only about 15 percent of the mammals).

Recovery plans must, "to the maximum extent practicable," incorporate "a description of such site-specific management actions as may be necessary to achieve the plan's goals for the conservation and survival of the species;" "contain 'objective, measurable criteria' " for determining when the species can be removed from the list; and estimate the time and cost of the measures needed to achieve the goal and intermediate steps for that goal. 16 U.S.C. § 1533(f)(1). But the ESA lacks much specificity of process or standards to measure the sufficiency of plans. As a consequence, what little litigation that has addressed this feature of the Act regards the plans as discretionary. *See, e.g.*, Fund for Animals v. Rice, 85 F.3d 535, 547 (11th Cir.1996) (recovery plans do not have the "force of law" but "are for guidance only," and therefore do not furnish a basis for enjoining construction of a municipal landfill on a wetlands site that is habitat to listed species).

3. Section 7: The Consultation and Conservation Duties

The requirements of section 7 are not limited to federal lands and resources; they have government-wide and national applicability. A good deal of the judicial application of this section has, however, come in the context of integrating section 7 with federal resource management decisions. This part considers the two most important duties for federal agencies created by section 7: consultation (the duty to avoid jeopardy) and conservation (the affirmative duty to aid species recovery).

a. THE CONSULTATION DUTY

We first examined the Thomas v. Peterson challenge in the context of the NEPA (*see supra* p. 256. The court required the Forest Service to prepare an EIS at the time it approves a road that discusses all of the impacts of the road, including the anticipated timber sales facilitated by road access. The following portion of the opinion discusses the Forest Service's responsibilities under ESA § 7(a)(2) for the same road-building decision.

Thomas v. Peterson

United States Court of Appeals, Ninth Circuit, 1985.
753 F.2d 754.

■ JUDGE SNEED

* * * This is another environmental case pitting groups concerned with preserving a specific undeveloped area against an agency of the United States attempting to obey the commands given it by a Congress which is mindful of both environmentalists and those who seek to develop the nation's resources. Our task is to discern as best we can what Congress intended to be done under the facts before us.

Plaintiffs—landowners, ranchers, outfitters, miners, hunters, fishermen, recreational users, and conservation and recreation organizations—challenge actions of the United States Forest Service in planning and approving a timber road in the Jersey Jack area of the Nez Perce National Forest in Idaho. The area is adjacent to the Salmon River, a congressionally-designated Wild and Scenic River, and is bounded on the west by the designated Gospel Hump Wilderness and on the east by the River of No Return Wilderness. The area lies in a "recovery corridor" identified by the U.S. Fish & Wildlife Service for the Rocky Mountain Gray Wolf, an endangered species.

* * *

After [neighboring lands were designated as wilderness by Congress] the Forest Service * * * proceeded to plan timber development in the Jersey Jack area. In November, 1980, the Forest Service solicited public comments and held a public hearing on a proposed gravel road that would provide access to timber to be sold. The Forest Service prepared an environmental assessment (EA), see 40 C.F.R. § 1508.9 (1984), to determine whether an EIS would be required for the road. Based on the EA, the Forest Service concluded that no EIS was required, and issued a Finding of No Significant Impact (FONSI), see 40 C.F.R. § 1508.13. The FONSI and the notice of the Forest Supervisor's decision to go ahead with the road were issued in a single document on February 9, 1981. The decision notice stated that "no known threatened or endangered plant or animal species have been found" within the area, but the EA contained no discussion of endangered species. * * * [The plaintiffs filed this lawsuit after exhausting administrative remedies and one of their principal allegations was that the] road is likely to affect the Rocky Mountain Gray Wolf * * * and the Forest

Service has failed to follow procedures mandated by the Endangered Species Act. * * *

* * *

Once an agency is aware that an endangered species may be present in the area of its proposed action, the ESA requires it to prepare a biological assessment to determine whether the proposed action "is likely to affect" the species and therefore requires formal consultation with the F & WS. The Forest Service did not prepare such an assessment prior to its decision to build the Jersey Jack road. Without a biological assessment, it cannot be determined whether the proposed project will result in a violation of the ESA's substantive provisions. A failure to prepare a biological assessment for a project in an area in which it has been determined that an endangered species may be present cannot be considered a de minimis violation of the ESA.

The district court found that the Forest Service had "undertaken sufficient study and action to further the purposes of the ESA." Its finding was based on affidavits submitted by the Forest Service for the litigation.[7] These do not constitute a substitute for the preparation of the biological assessment required by the ESA.

Given a substantial procedural violation of the ESA in connection with a federal project, the remedy must be an injunction of the project pending compliance with the ESA. The procedural requirements of the ESA are analogous to those of NEPA * * *; under the ESA, agencies are required to assess the effect on endangered species of projects in areas where such species may be present. 16 U.S.C. § 1536(c). A failure to prepare a biological assessment is comparable to a failure to prepare an environmental impact statement.

Our cases repeatedly have held that, absent "unusual circumstances," an injunction is the appropriate remedy for a violation of NEPA's procedural requirements. [citations omitted] Irreparable damage is presumed to flow from a failure properly to evaluate the environmental impact of a major federal action. We see no reason that the same principle should not apply to procedural violations of the ESA.

The Forest Service argues that the procedural requirements of the ESA should be enforced less stringently than those of NEPA because, unlike NEPA, the ESA also contains substantive provisions. We acknowledge that the ESA's substantive provisions distinguish it from NEPA, but the distinction acts the other way. If anything, the strict substantive provisions of the ESA justify more stringent enforcement of its procedural requirements, because the procedural requirements are designed to ensure compliance with the substantive provisions. The ESA's procedural requirements call for a systematic determination of the effects of a federal project

---

7. The district court relied on the Forest Service's assertion that it had worked in "close cooperation" with the F & WS, but that assertion is undermined by letters in the record from the F & WS indicating that the Forest Service had not consulted with the F & WS on the impact of the road and the timber sales on the gray wolf, and that the F & WS felt that the Forest Service was not giving the wolf adequate consideration.

on endangered species. If a project is allowed to proceed without substantial compliance with those procedural requirements, there can be no assurance that a violation of the ESA's substantive provisions will not result. The latter, of course, is impermissible.

The Forest Service would require the district court, absent proof by the plaintiffs to the contrary, to make a finding that the Jersey Jack road is not likely to effect [sic] the Rocky Mountain Gray Wolf, and that therefore any failure to comply with ESA procedures is harmless. This is not a finding appropriate to the district court at the present time. Congress has assigned to the agencies and to the Fish & Wildlife Service the responsibility for evaluation of the impact of agency actions on endangered species, and has prescribed procedures for such evaluation. Only by following the procedures can proper evaluations be made. It is not the responsibility of the plaintiffs to prove, nor the function of the courts to judge, the effect of a proposed action on an endangered species when proper procedures have not been followed.

We therefore hold that the district court erred in declining to enjoin construction of the Jersey Jack road pending compliance with the ESA.
* * *

NOTES AND QUESTIONS

1.   The statute and the joint regulations of the wildlife agencies set up a three-tiered consultation process to ensure that agency actions will not jeopardize the continued existence of a listed species or destroy or adversely modify designated critical habitat. The "no jeopardy" shorthand refers to this obligation. The regulations governing consultation (50 C.F.R. part 402) provide a much clearer picture of the process than the statute. The first step is for the action agency to ask the FWS whether any listed species are found in the action area. If the answer is no, and the action agency determines its action will have no impact on listed species or critical habitat, nothing further is required.

If the action "may affect" a listed species or critical habitat, the second step involves "informal consultation" with the FWS. As part of informal consultation, the action agency often prepares a biological assessment (BA). If, on the basis of the BA, the action agency concludes that the contemplated action is "not likely to adversely affect" a listed species, the FWS may either (1) issue a written concurrence in the determination; or (2) suggest modifications that the action agency could take to avoid the likelihood of adverse effects to the listed species. If no concurrence is reached, or if the BA concludes there will be a "likely affect," then regulations require formal consultation between the two agencies.

The third step is formal consultation between the action agency and the FWS. The outcome of formal consultation is a biological opinion (BO) prepared by the FWS. If the BO shows that jeopardy is likely, it must "include reasonable and prudent alternatives, if any, to avoid these effects." 16 U.S.C. § 1536(b)(3)(A). Thus a BO may have one of three conclusions: no jeopardy; jeopardy with reasonable and prudent alternatives; or jeopardy without such alternatives. Even in a "no jeopardy" BO, the FWS may require measures to minimize the impact of the proposed action. 16 U.S.C. § 1536(b)(4)(ii)–(iii).

Thomas involved the first, "may affect," stage. There was no proof that wolves actually inhabited the Jersey Jack area—only that there "may" have been wolves there. Should sightings of the species in the affected area be required before a court issues an injunction? May the wildlife agency's opinion on the "may be present" determination be questioned by the action agency? Is this opinion reviewable by a court?

2. How does the ESA process compare with the NEPA process? Compare the steps involved in each. For example, is the court correct in stating that the BA requirement of the ESA is comparable to the "environmental impact statement" process of NEPA? The statute expressly provides that the action agency (here, the Forest Service) may use the NEPA process as the vehicle for complying with the BA requirement of the ESA. 16 U.S.C. § 1536(c)(1). The purpose of the BA is to identify any endangered or threatened species "which is likely to be affected by the [proposed] action" and to examine the probable impact of the proposed action.

Do you agree with the court that the substantive aspect of the consultation process (no jeopardy) ought to lead to more stringent enforcement of procedural requirements? How does the court's view compare with Professor Rodger's typology of judicial review, discussed *supra* p. 231?

3. Conner v. Burford, 848 F.2d 1441 (9th Cir.1988), also discussed in Metcalf v. Daley, is another case involving both NEPA and the ESA. In Conner, only those leases lacking "no surface occupancy" (NSO) stipulations required full NEPA analysis at the leasing stage. The NSO leases could defer EISs until post-leasing decisions about drilling. The FWS BOs similarly proposed later consultations on federal actions subsequent to lease issuance that authorized on-the-ground activity on the lease. The court held that all of the leases required BOs that addressed post-leasing activities, even though forecasting what those activities might be was difficult. The U.S. Fish & Wildlife Service must, the court said, determine at the point of leasing whether "post-leasing activities in particular areas were fundamentally incompatible with the continued existence of the species." Compare the analogous situation under NEPA, where federal agencies have been able to postpone full NEPA compliance past the lease issuance stage by including in the lease a stipulation that reserves to the government full authority to prohibit all on-the-ground environmental impacts. Should the approaches to this question of segmenting decisions be identical under NEPA and the ESA? Does the more substantive and protective thrust of the ESA justify a more stringent rule? Or does the "full disclosure" policy of NEPA counsel for a more stringent approach in the NEPA context?

4. The ESA does not define "jeopardy." The FWS regulation defines it to mean "to engage in an action that reasonably would be expected, directly or indirectly, to reduce appreciably the likelihood of *both* the survival *and* recovery of a listed species in the wild by reducing the reproduction, numbers, or distribution of that species." 50 C.F.R. § 402.02

(emphasis added). Thus, appreciably reducing the likelihood of recovery, alone, is not sufficient to trigger jeopardy if survival remains undiminished.

The regulation takes the same approach in defining "adverse modification" of critical habitat for purposes of the consultation to mean changes in critical habitat that "appreciably diminish[] the value of critical habitat for both the survival and recovery of a listed species." 50 C.F.R. § 402.02. Though awkwardly phrased in the affirmative, what this means is a proposed modification of critical habitat which impairs the species' recovery, but does not impair its survival, is not "adverse." In recent years courts of appeals in three circuits have ruled that this regulation is inconsistent with the Act because it is too lenient. For example, in Gifford Pinchot Task Force v. FWS, 378 F.3d 1059, 1070–71 (9th Cir.2004), the court had this to say:

> [T]here is no need to go beyond Chevron's first step in analyzing the permissibility of the regulation; the regulatory definition of "adverse modification" contradicts Congress's express command. As the Fifth and Tenth Circuits have already recognized, the regulatory definition reads the "recovery" goal out of the adverse modification inquiry; a proposed action "adversely modifies" critical habitat if, and only if, the value of the critical habitat for survival is appreciably diminished. See N.M. Cattle Growers Ass'n v. United States Fish and Wildlife Serv., 248 F.3d 1277, 1283 & n. 2 (10th Cir.2001); Sierra Club v. United States Fish and Wildlife Serv., 245 F.3d 434, 441–42 (5th Cir.2001). The FWS could authorize the complete elimination of critical habitat necessary only for recovery, and so long as the smaller amount of critical habitat necessary for survival is not appreciably diminished, then no "destruction or adverse modification," as defined by the regulation, has taken place. This cannot be right. If the FWS follows its own regulation, then it is obligated to be indifferent to, if not to ignore, the recovery goal of critical habitat.

> The agency's controlling regulation on critical habitat thus offends the ESA because the ESA was enacted not merely to forestall the extinction of species (i.e., promote a species survival), but to allow a species to recover to the point where it may be delisted. * * * [I]t is clear that Congress intended that conservation and survival be two different (though complementary) goals of the ESA. Clearly, then, the purpose of establishing "critical habitat" is for the government to carve out territory that is not only necessary for the species' survival but also essential for the species' recovery.

5. In TVA v. Hill, there was no controversy about whether the closing of the dam would jeopardize the snail darter. In more typical situations, there may be a substantial dispute over the action's effect on the species. The BO will give the views of the wildlife consulting agency on the issue. Is the action agency free to ignore the advice? What is a reviewing court to do in the face of such an interagency disagreement? The U.S. Supreme Court has said that biological opinions have a "virtually determinative effect" on the action agency's decision. Bennett v. Spear, 520 U.S. 154 (1997). In that case the question was whether the plaintiff water users had standing to

contest a biological opinion, and one of the issues was whether the threatened reduction in their water diversion (in order to meet the needs of listed species) was, under applicable standing test, "fairly traceable" to the BO, and likely to be redressed if the BO were set aside. The Court explained:

> [W]hile the Service's Biological Opinion theoretically serves an "advisory function," 51 Fed. Reg. 19928 (1986), in reality it has a powerful coercive effect on the action agency. [The government's brief explained that an action agency] "that chooses to deviate from the recommendations contained in a biological opinion bears the burden of 'articulat[ing] in its administrative record its reasons for disagreeing with the conclusions of a biological opinion.' 51 Fed. Reg. 19, 956 (1986). In the government's experience, action agencies very rarely choose to engage in conduct that the Service has concluded is likely to jeopardize the continued existence of a listed species."
>
> [T]he action agency must not only articulate its reasons for disagreement (which ordinarily requires species and habitat investigations that are not within the action agency's expertise), but * * * [it also] runs a substantial risk if its (inexpert) reasons turn out to be wrong. A Biological Opinion * * * alters the legal regime to which the action agency is subject. When it "offers reasonable and prudent alternatives" to the proposed action, a Biological Opinion must include a so-called "Incidental Take Statement"—a written statement specifying, among other things, those "measures that the [Service] considers necessary or appropriate to minimize [the action's impact on the affected species]" and the "terms and conditions ... that must be complied with by the Federal agency ... to implement [such] measures." 16 U.S.C. § 1536(b)(4). Any taking that is in compliance with these terms and conditions "shall not be considered to be a prohibited taking of the species concerned." § 1536(o)(2). Thus, the Biological Opinion's Incidental Take Statement constitutes a permit authorizing the action agency to "take" the endangered or threatened species so long as it respects the Service's "terms and conditions." The action agency is technically free to disregard the Biological Opinion and proceed with its proposed action, but it does so at its own peril (and that of its employees), for "any person" who knowingly "takes" an endangered or threatened species is subject to substantial civil and criminal penalties, including imprisonment. * * *

Early on during ESA implementation, agencies learned not to proceed without a supportive BO. *See* National Wildlife Federation v. Coleman, 529 F.2d 359 (5th Cir.1976) (while section 7 does not give the wildlife agency a "veto" over the action agency, on the facts there, proceeding against its advice was a "clear error of judgment"); Roosevelt Campobello International Park Commission v. EPA, 684 F.2d 1041 (1st Cir.1982) (substantially the same reasoning).

The role of the Incidental Take Statement is explored below, in the Section on the relationship between section 7 and section 9. It has come to play an increasingly important role in the consultation process, but is based on the scope of the section 9 "take" prohibition.

6. Many federal "actions" to which section 7 applies are relatively straightforward—issuing a permit or lease, or constructing a dam or a road. But more abstract actions, such as planning, may also be subject to consultation. This can raise a host of questions, some of them analogous to the "tiering" issues discussed in connection with NEPA. For example, there may be many layers of federal decisions between a broad national, regional, or area plan and an individual, site-specific permit. At what levels is consultation useful and legally required? What can a later consultation on a narrower decision, like issuing a timber sale contract, borrow or assume from an earlier consultation on a broader level, such as issuing a forest plan? Further, especially with respect to decisions that may be implemented over many years (such as a land use plan), what is the consequence of listing a new species while implementation is ongoing? NEPA's requirements in planning conclude once the plan is adopted. *See* Norton v. SUWA *supra* p. 224. However, the consultation duty continues to apply to all actions "authorized, funded, or carried out" by the agency under the plan. 16 U.S.C. § 1536(a)(2). In Pacific Rivers Council v. Thomas, 30 F.3d 1050 (9th Cir. 1994), the court held that the Forest Service needed to reinitiate consultation on an existing forest plan after the NMFS listed Chinook salmon as threatened. Until the Forest Service re-evaluated its plan through formal consultation, it could not go forward with individual timber sales, range activities, or road construction, even if those individual projects consulted on their effects on the salmon.

NOTE: "COUNTERPART" REGULATIONS

Natural resources agencies frequently involved in consultation have begun adopting special rules called "counterpart regulations." Such regulations were contemplated by the original consultation rule adopted to implement the ESA in the 1970s, but were not developed for several decades. Notwithstanding arguments that informal consultation frequently involves interagency negotiations that produce commitments to adopt effective mitigation measures, the Bush Administration's "Healthy Forests" initiative led to 2003 counterpart regulations. The rules relax the general requirement that the wildlife agency provide written concurrence of action agency "not likely to adversely affect" findings for certain land management activities aimed at reducing fire loads on lands managed by the U.S. Forest Service and the BLM. 68 Fed. Reg. 68254 (2003). The ostensible goal is to make consultation more efficient in situations where prompt action is advisable to reduce fire danger, although the generic regulations governing consultation have long had an exception for emergencies. 50 C.F.R. § 402.05 (authorizing informal consultation through "alternative procedures" in "situations involving acts of God, disasters, casualties, national defense or security emergencies, etc." though formal consultation must follow "after the emergency is under control"). The counterpart regulations require the action agency to make the "not likely to adversely affect" decisions by the same standards that would apply to the FWS, and the decision-makers must be scientists who complete a training program approved by the wildlife agencies. Furthermore, their decisions must be documented and the program is supposed to undergo periodic reexamination.

Nonetheless, a district court has overturned a very similar set of rules waiving the concurrence requirement of a "not likely to adversely affect" determination by the EPA in its pesticide regulation program. Washington Toxics Coalition v. U.S. Dept. of the Interior, 457 F.Supp.2d 1158 (W.D.Wash.2006) found the concurrence role of the FWS to be essential to the framework of consultation established by the ESA.

b. THE CONSERVATION DUTY

ESA § 7(a)(2) contains two general directives. The first requires the Secretaries of Commerce and the Interior (supervisors of the wildlife agencies) with major responsibility for implementing the act to "review . . . programs [they administer] and utilize such programs in furtherance of the purposes of [the ESA]." The second is directed at "[a]ll other Federal agencies," and requires them, "in consultation with and with the assistance of the [two Secretaries, to] *utilize their authorities in furtherance of the purposes of [the ESA] by carrying out programs for the conservation of [listed] species. . . .*" 16 U.S.C. § 1536(a)(1) (emphasis added). These affirmative mandates to act are seldom evaluated, compared to the obligation to avoid jeopardy, because there is no consultation-like procedure associated with them to guarantee scrutiny. Nonetheless they may serve to compel agency action under certain, rare circumstances.

Sierra Club v. Glickman

United States Court of Appeals for the Fifth Circuit, 1998.
156 F.3d 606.

■ JUDGE BENAVIDES

This is the latest in a series of cases brought by Sierra Club and others concerned about endangered species that depend on water from the Edwards Aquifer for their survival. * * * The Edwards Aquifer is a 175–mile long underground aquifer that stretches through eight counties in central Texas. The Edwards Aquifer is recharged primarily from surface waters and rainfall seeping through porous earth along its path. Unless removed by human pumping, water in the Edwards Aquifer flows west to east, before turning northeast, where it is discharged through a series of springs on the eastern edge of the aquifer, the two largest of which are the San Marcos Springs in San Marcos and the Comal Springs in New Braunfels. The San Marcos and Comal Springs are the only habitat of five federally endangered and threatened species: the fountain darter, the San Marcos gambusia (which may now be extinct), the San Marcos salamander, the Texas blind salamander, and Texas wild rice (hereinafter collectively referred to as the "Edwards-dependent species"). See 50 C.F.R. §§ 17.11, 17.12.

The Edwards Aquifer is of great economic significance to the State of Texas. Water from the Edwards Aquifer is used by thousands of farmers to irrigate millions of dollars worth of crops, by over two million people as their primary source of water, and by thousands of businesses upon which the entire central Texas economy depends.

Pumping from the Edwards Aquifer, however, can have significant ecological consequences to the Edwards-dependent species. In times of even mild drought, the springflow at both the San Marcos and Comal Springs can decrease enough to threaten the survival of the Edwards-dependent species. Not surprisingly, given these often competing interests, the Edwards Aquifer has been the focus of extensive efforts to conserve its limited water resources. * * *

[In 1995 plaintiffs brought suit against the U.S. Department of Agriculture (USDA), claiming, among other things, that it had violated § 7(a)(1).] * * * [T]he district court held that the USDA "has not utilized its authority to carry out programs for the conservation of previously listed Edwards-dependent species as ESA § 7(a)(1) requires" and that it had not consulted with FWS concerning utilizing its authorities to carry out such programs. The court then ordered the USDA to develop, in consultation with FWS, "an organized program for utilizing USDA's authorities for the conservation of the Edwards-dependent endangered and threatened species as contemplated by the ESA." * * *

[The Court addressed the government's argument that the plaintiffs had no standing to raise the issue because, a]ccording to the USDA, the injury suffered by Sierra Club is caused by the independent actions (i.e., pumping decisions) of third party farmers, over whom the USDA has no coercive control. * * * [T]he relevant inquiry in this case is whether the USDA has the ability through various programs to affect the pumping decisions of those third party farmers to such an extent that the plaintiff's injury could be relieved. In this respect, the USDA argues that "the most [that it] could do vis-à-vis farmers would be to encourage them to use water conservation methods by offering incentives under the discretionary programs described.... However, there is no evidence that, if additional incentives were offered, there is a 'substantial likelihood' that injury at the springs would be relieved." As Sierra Club points out, however, this claim is directly contradicted by the summary judgment evidence.

Three pieces of evidence are significant to a finding of causation in this case. The first document is Cooperative Solutions, a 1995 study (updated in 1996) conducted by the USDA in conjunction with Texas A & M University and the Texas State Soil and Water Conservation Board. One of the programs proposed in that study—providing financial assistance to farmers for the installation of water conservation measures—would save an estimated 38,000 acre-feet of Edwards irrigation water in an average year. The savings would be even greater in a dry year. Not only does the USDA have the authority to carry out such a program, but the USDA itself has described the proposal as cost-effective.

The second key document is the 1996 Biological Evaluation ("BE"), submitted by USDA to FWS during a § 7(a)(2) consultation concerning crop subsidy payments under the 1990 farm bill. According to the USDA's irrigation pumping estimates in that BE, 38,000 acre-feet represent 20% of the total Edwards irrigation pumping in dry years, when the threat to the Edwards-dependent species is greatest, and a much greater percentage in an average year.

The final link in this causal chain is FWS's response to the 1996 BE. In its response, FWS concluded that the springflow effects of a 20% reduction in Edwards irrigation pumping would have a significant impact on the Edwards-dependent species. In fact, FWS "categorically" disagreed with the USDA's statement that a 20% decrease in Edwards irrigation pumping would have no significant effect on the Edwards-dependent species. More-over, the USDA itself acknowledges that "FWS's expertise extends to essentially factual issues regarding how particular actions affect listed species."

Given this evidence, we find the USDA's claim that it has no effect on the irrigation decisions of the farmers to be unpersuasive. To the contrary, the evidence introduced clearly shows that the USDA's failure to adopt any of the above programs is fairly traceable to the injury to the Edwards-dependent species.

* * *

Given the plain language of the statute and its legislative history, we conclude that Congress intended to impose an affirmative duty on each federal agency to conserve each of the species listed pursuant to § 1533. In order to achieve this objective, the agencies must consult with FWS as to each of the listed species, not just undertake a generalized consultation. Consequently, we conclude that the procedures in question were designed to protect Sierra Club's threatened concrete interest in this case. Accord-ingly, we conclude that Sierra Club has standing to pursue this action.

* * *

[The court then turned to the government's argument that no judicial review could be obtained under the ESA citizen suit provision or the APA for various reasons, among them that the USDA's] duties under § 7(a)(1) are not judicially reviewable because there is "no law to apply." In general, there is no law to apply if the statute is drawn in such broad terms that in a given case there would be nothing against which a court could measure agency compliance with the statute. See Citizens to Preserve Overton Park v. Volpe, 401 U.S. 402, 410–11 (1971). The USDA's argument in this respect, however, relies, in large part, on its argument that § 7(a)(1) does not impose a duty on the federal agencies to consult with FWS and develop programs for the conservation of each of the endangered and threatened species. As noted above in our standing discussion, however, we find that § 7(a)(1) contains a clear statutory directive (it uses the word "shall") requiring the federal agencies to consult and develop programs for the conservation of each of the endangered and threatened species listed pursuant to the statute. That Congress has passed a statute that is exceptionally broad in its effect, in the sense that it imposes a tremendous burden on the federal agencies to comply with its mandate, however, does not mean that it is written in such broad terms that in a given case there is no law to apply. On the contrary, given the specific requirements of § 7(a)(1), in any given case there is more than enough law against which a court can measure agency compliance.

The USDA next argues that its duties under § 7(a)(1) are not judicially reviewable because it has a substantial amount of discretion in developing programs for the benefit of the Edwards-dependent species. According to the USDA, because it enjoys a substantial amount of discretion as to ultimate program decisions, it has unreviewable discretion to ignore § 7(a)(1) altogether. This argument is entirely without merit. A mission agency's discretion to make the final substantive decision under its program authorities does not mean that the agency has unlimited, unreviewable discretion. Instead, it means that the court conducting judicial review must require the agency to show that it has considered the relevant factors and followed the required procedures, but that, if the agency has done so, the court may not substitute its judgment on the merits for the agency's judgment. * * *

We turn next to the government's argument that it has complied with the requirements of § 7(a)(1) because the Edwards-dependent species have experienced incidental benefits from national USDA programs designed and carried out for other purposes. As Sierra Club points out, however, the USDA's position directly conflicts with the plain language of § 7(a)(1), which requires each federal agency "in consultation with and with the assistance of [FWS]" to adopt programs "for the conservation of endangered species." The USDA simply cannot read out of existence § 7(a)(1)'s requirement that the USDA's substantive conservation programs for the Edwards-dependent species be carried out "in consultation with and with the assistance of [FWS]." In this case, there is no real dispute that the USDA has never fulfilled its obligations under § 7(a)(1) with respect to the Edwards-dependent species. Accordingly, we find the USDA's argument unavailing.

As a final matter, we note that the USDA has not challenged the scope of the district court's injunction with respect to § 7(a)(1). Thus, we need not address whether the district court properly ordered the USDA to develop, in consultation with FWS, "an organized program for utilizing USDA's authorities for the conservation of the Edwards-dependent endangered and threatened species as contemplated by the ESA." * * *

NOTES AND QUESTIONS

1. How much substance is there in this generally expressed duty to "utilize [the agency's] authorities in furtherance of" the ESA's purposes? If, as here, the species require water conservation by farmers in a drought, must the USDA administer its programs in such a way as to encourage such conservation? Require it? If the statutes under which the USDA furnishes aid to farmers are silent on its authority to administer them to require conservation, does § 7(a)(1) supply such authority?

2. In Pyramid Lake Paiute Tribe of Indians v. U.S. Department of the Navy, 898 F.2d 1410 (9th Cir.1990), the court reviewed the management of Fallon Naval Air Station, which diverts water from the Truckee River feeding Pyramid Lake to a different basin. The Navy leases "buffer zones" of fields surrounding its runways. The irrigated fields replace desert brush and thereby minimize the dangers to aircraft of dust storms and fires. After consultation resulted in no jeopardy opinions, the tribe challenged the leasing based, inter alia, on the conservation duty. The tribe reasoned that less irrigation would result in greater flows in Truckee River, which promotes recovery of endangered fish in the lake. The tribe proposed an alternative to maintaining buffer areas that would use less water. The court, relying on the lower court's fact finding that the tribe's alternative proposal would yield an "insignificant effect" on water availability for the Pyramid Lake fish, rejected the challenge. The court rejected the tribe's theory that the conservation duty requires the navy to employ the "least burdensome alternative" to achieve its objective. Is this an example of national defense actions receiving greater deference from the courts? Would the Sierra Club v. Glickman court have decided this case differently? Does Sierra Club v. Glickman require implementation of agency programs to minimize the burden on species recovery?

3. A respected commentator on the ESA has called this subsection "the monumental underachiever of the ESA family," a "sleeping giant" with the "potential to eclipse all other ESA programs." J.B. Ruhl, *Section 7(a)(1) of the "New" Endangered Species Act: Rediscovering and Redefining the Untapped Power of Federal Agencies' Duty to Conserve Species*, 25 ENVTL. L. 1107 (1995). Professor Ruhl reminds us that the Supreme Court addressed § 7(a)(1) at length in TVA v. Hill, which describes the subsection as containing "stringent, mandatory language" that "reveals an explicit congressional decision to require agencies to afford first priority to the declared national policy of saving endangered species." 437 U.S. at 183, 185. The subsection rather curiously fell into desuetude in both the courts and the agencies; § 7(a)(1) is the only important part of the ESA that is not the subject of implementing regulations.

Professor Ruhl argues that § 7(a)(1) has great promise as "a shield, a sword, or a prod to help federal agencies fulfill [Congress's] vision" in enacting the ESA. He points out, among other things, that § 7(a)(1) applies to "programs" and not just "actions" by federal agencies. Does that mean the wildlife agencies can outline species conservation measures for other agencies to take outside the consultation process of § 7(a)(2)? Does § 7(a)(1) impose a duty on the other agencies to take these measures, even if there is no "action," no "take," and no finding of likelihood of "jeopardy"? How are the wildlife agencies supposed to interact with the other agencies under § 7(a)(1)?

4. From the standpoint of federal land management agencies, is the authority in § 7(a)(1) a blessing by providing flexibility to be proactive in protecting endangered species, without waiting for the formal processes of other parts of the act to kick in? Are its vague promises as susceptible of

judicial enforcement as the more specific commands of sections 7 and 9? Does it support a public trust approach?

5.   The Tenth Circuit recently took a pass on an attempt by logging interests to use § 7(a)(1) as a tool to promote more aggressive timber harvesting practices in the Medicine Bow National Forest in Wyoming's Platte River watershed as a way to produce more water to meet the needs of endangered species downstream. Coalition for Sustainable Resources v. U.S. Forest Service, 259 F.3d 1244 (10th Cir.2001). The court found that judicial review was not warranted at this time because the Forest Service was involved in a large interagency effort to develop a conservation strategy for the Platte River species and was also revising its forest plan.

4.   SECTION 9: THE "TAKE" PROHIBITION

The "take" prohibition applies not only to federal agencies but also to state agencies, corporations, and individuals. Section 9 of the ESA somewhat ambiguously prohibits "take" of "species," but it has always been understood to apply to individual specimens rather than entire populations or the species itself. This is clear from the fact that the same section of the Act also prohibits possessing, selling, or transporting, "species," which only makes sense when applied to individual specimens. Most of the early litigation under the ESA (such as TVA v. Hill) focused on § 7, but gradually § 9 "began to dig its way out of anonymity." Federico Cheever, *An Introduction to the Prohibition Against Takings in Section 9 of the Endangered Species Act of 1973: Learning to Live with a Powerful Species Preservation Law*, 62 U. COLO. L.REV. 109, 143 (1991).

Courts grapple with the meaning of "take," defined by the ESA as "harass, harm, pursue, hunt, shoot, wound, kill, trap, capture, or collect, or to attempt to engage in any such conduct." 16 U.S.C. § 1532(19). The statute does not further clarify the meaning of the terms included in the definition, and the major issue is the extent to which "harm" includes habitat degradation.

The first major decision to apply ESA § 9 was Palila v. Hawaii Dept. of Land and Natural Resources, 471 F.Supp. 985 (D.Haw.1979). In a subsequent series of rulings by the Ninth Circuit and the Hawaii district court extending over two decades, courts held that the state agency violated § 9 by maintaining an exotic game herd in an area where the Palila bird dwelled. Though the game animals did not compete directly with the Palila, they ate shoots and seeds of trees on which the Palila depended. The game's feeding prevented regeneration of the trees on which the Palila absolutely depend, and would therefore doom the viability of the species. This controversial holding led the FWS to rewrite its definition of harm, which came before the Supreme Court in the following case.

Babbitt v. Sweet Home Chapter

Supreme Court of the United States, 1995.
515 U.S. 687.

■ JUSTICE STEVENS delivered the opinion of the Court.

The Interior Department regulations * * * define the statutory term "harm":

"Harm in the definition of 'take' in the Act means an act which actually kills or injures wildlife. Such act may include significant habitat modification or degradation where it actually kills or injures wildlife by significantly impairing essential behavioral patterns, including breeding, feeding, or sheltering." 50 CFR § 17.3 (1994).

This regulation has been in place since 1975.

A limitation on the § 9 "take" prohibition appears in § 10(a)(1)(B) of the Act, which Congress added by amendment in 1982. That section authorizes the Secretary to grant a permit for any taking otherwise prohibited by § 9(a)(1)(B) "if such taking is incidental to, and not the purpose of, the carrying out of an otherwise lawful activity." 16 U.S.C. § 1539(a)(1)(B).

* * *

Respondents in this action are small landowners, logging companies, and families dependent on the forest products industries in the Pacific Northwest and in the Southeast, and organizations that represent their interests. They * * * challenge the statutory validity of the Secretary's regulation defining "harm," particularly the inclusion of habitat modification and degradation in the definition * * * on its face. Their complaint alleged that application of the "harm" regulation to the red-cockaded woodpecker, an endangered species, and the northern spotted owl, a threatened species,[5] had injured them economically.

* * *

Because this case was decided on motions for summary judgment, we may appropriately make certain factual assumptions in order to frame the legal issue. First, we assume respondents have no desire to harm either the red-cockaded woodpecker or the spotted owl; they merely wish to continue logging activities that would be entirely proper if not prohibited by the ESA. On the other hand, we must assume, arguendo, that those activities will have the effect, even though unintended, of detrimentally changing the natural habitat of both listed species and that, as a consequence, members of those species will be killed or injured. Under respondents' view of the law, the Secretary's only means of forestalling that grave result—even when the actor knows it is certain to occur—is to use his § 5 authority to purchase the lands on which the survival of the species depends. The Secretary, on the other hand, submits that the § 9 prohibition on takings, which Congress defined to include "harm," places on respondents a duty to

---

5. Another regulation promulgated by the Secretary extends to threatened species, defined in the ESA as "any species which is likely to become an endangered species within the foreseeable future throughout all or a significant portion of its range," 16 U.S.C. § 1532(20), some but not all of the protections endangered species enjoy. See 50 CFR § 17.31(a) (1994). In the District Court respondents unsuccessfully challenged that regulation's extension of § 9 to threatened species, but they do not press the challenge here.

avoid harm that habitat alteration will cause the birds unless respondents first obtain a permit pursuant to § 10.

The text of the Act provides three reasons for concluding that the Secretary's interpretation is reasonable. First, an ordinary understanding of the word "harm" supports it. The dictionary definition of the verb form of "harm" is "to cause hurt or damage to: injure." Webster's Third New International Dictionary 1034 (1966). In the context of the ESA, that definition naturally encompasses habitat modification that results in actual injury or death to members of an endangered or threatened species.

Respondents argue that the Secretary should have limited the purview of "harm" to direct applications of force against protected species, but the dictionary definition does not include the word "directly" or suggest in any way that only direct or willful action that leads to injury constitutes "harm." Moreover, unless the statutory term "harm" encompasses indirect as well as direct injuries, the word has no meaning that does not duplicate the meaning of other words that § 3 uses to define "take." A reluctance to treat statutory terms as surplusage supports the reasonableness of the Secretary's interpretation.

Second, the broad purpose of the ESA supports the Secretary's decision to extend protection against activities that cause the precise harms Congress enacted the statute to avoid. * * *

Respondents advance strong arguments that activities that cause minimal or unforeseeable harm will not violate the Act as construed in the "harm" regulation. Respondents, however, present a facial challenge to the regulation. Thus, they ask us to invalidate the Secretary's understanding of "harm" in every circumstance, even when an actor knows that an activity, such as draining a pond, would actually result in the extinction of a listed species by destroying its habitat. Given Congress' clear expression of the ESA's broad purpose to protect endangered and threatened wildlife, the Secretary's definition of "harm" is reasonable.[13]

Third, the fact that Congress in 1982 authorized the Secretary to issue permits for takings that § 9(a)(1)(B) would otherwise prohibit, "if such taking is incidental to, and not the purpose of, the carrying out of an otherwise lawful activity," 16 U.S.C. § 1539(a)(1)(B), strongly suggests that Congress understood § 9(a)(1)(B) to prohibit indirect as well as deliberate takings. The permit process requires the applicant to prepare a "conservation plan" that specifies how he intends to "minimize and mitigate" the

---

13. The dissent incorrectly asserts that the Secretary's regulation (1) "dispenses with the foreseeability of harm" and (2) "fail[s] to require injury to particular animals," post, at 19. As to the first assertion, the regulation merely implements the statute, and it is therefore subject to the statute's "knowingly violates" language, see 16 U.S.C. §§ 1540(a)(1), (b)(1), and ordinary requirements of proximate causation and foreseeability. Nothing in the regulation purports to weaken those requirements. To the contrary, the word "actually" in the regulation should be construed to limit the liability about which the dissent appears most concerned, liability under the statute's "otherwise violates" provision. The Secretary did not need to include "actually" to connote "but for" causation, which the other words in the definition obviously require. As to the dissent's second assertion, every term in the regulation's definition of "harm" is subservient to the phrase "an act which actually kills or injures wildlife."

"impact" of his activity on endangered and threatened species, 16 U.S.C. § 1539(a)(2)(A), making clear that Congress had in mind foreseeable rather than merely accidental effects on listed species. No one could seriously request an "incidental" take permit to avert § 9 liability for direct, deliberate action against a member of an endangered or threatened species, but respondents would read "harm" so narrowly that the permit procedure would have little more than that absurd purpose. * * * Congress' addition of the § 10 permit provision supports the Secretary's conclusion that activities not intended to harm an endangered species, such as habitat modification, may constitute unlawful takings under the ESA unless the Secretary permits them.

The Court of Appeals made three errors in asserting that "harm" must refer to a direct application of force because the words around it do. First, the court's premise was flawed. Several of the words that accompany "harm" in the § 3 definition of "take," especially "harass," "pursue," "wound," and "kill," refer to actions or effects that do not require direct applications of force. Second, to the extent the court read a requirement of intent or purpose into the words used to define "take," it ignored § 11's express provision that a "knowing" action is enough to violate the Act. Third, the court employed noscitur a sociis to give "harm" essentially the same function as other words in the definition, thereby denying it independent meaning. The canon, to the contrary, counsels that a word "gathers meaning from the words around it." The statutory context of "harm" suggests that Congress meant that term to serve a particular function in the ESA, consistent with, but distinct from, the functions of the other verbs used to define "take." The Secretary's interpretation of "harm" to include indirectly injuring endangered animals through habitat modification permissibly interprets "harm" to have "a character of its own not to be submerged by its association."

Nor does the Act's inclusion of the § 5 land acquisition authority and the § 7 directive to federal agencies to avoid destruction or adverse modification of critical habitat alter our conclusion. Respondents' argument that the Government lacks any incentive to purchase land under § 5 when it can simply prohibit takings under § 9 ignores the practical considerations that attend enforcement of the ESA. Purchasing habitat lands may well cost the Government less in many circumstances than pursuing civil or criminal penalties. In addition, the § 5 procedure allows for protection of habitat before the seller's activity has harmed any endangered animal, whereas the Government cannot enforce the § 9 prohibition until an animal has actually been killed or injured. The Secretary may also find the § 5 authority useful for preventing modification of land that is not yet but may in the future become habitat for an endangered or threatened species. The § 7 directive applies only to the Federal Government, whereas the § 9 prohibition applies to "any person." Section 7 imposes a broad, affirmative duty to avoid adverse habitat modifications that § 9 does not replicate, and § 7 does not limit its admonition to habitat modification that "actually kills or injures wildlife." Conversely, § 7 contains limitations that § 9 does not, applying only to actions "likely to jeopardize the continued existence of any endangered species or threatened species," 16 U.S.C. § 1536(a)(2), and to modifications of habitat that has been designated "critical" pursuant to § 4, 16 U.S.C. § 1533(b)(2). Any overlap that § 5 or § 7 may have with § 9 in particular cases is unexceptional, see, e.g., Russello v. United States, 464 U.S. 16, and n. 2, 24 (1983), and simply reflects the broad purpose of the Act set out in § 2 and acknowledged in TVA v. Hill.

* * *

When it enacted the ESA, Congress delegated broad administrative and interpretive power to the Secretary. See 16 U.S.C. §§ 1533, 1540(f). The task of defining and listing endangered and threatened species requires an expertise and attention to detail that exceeds the normal province of Congress. Fashioning appropriate standards for issuing permits under § 10 for takings that would otherwise violate § 9 necessarily requires the exercise of broad discretion. The proper interpretation of a term such as "harm" involves a complex policy choice. When Congress has entrusted the Secretary with broad discretion, we are especially reluctant to substitute our views of wise policy for his. See Chevron, 467 U.S. at 865–866. In this case, that reluctance accords with our conclusion, based on the text, structure, and legislative history of the ESA, that the Secretary reasonably construed the intent of Congress when he defined "harm" to include "significant habitat modification or degradation that actually kills or injures wildlife."

In the elaboration and enforcement of the ESA, the Secretary and all persons who must comply with the law will confront difficult questions of proximity and degree; for, as all recognize, the Act encompasses a vast range of economic and social enterprises and endeavors. These questions must be addressed in the usual course of the law, through case-by-case resolution and adjudication.

■ JUSTICE O'CONNOR, concurring.

My agreement with the Court is founded on two understandings. First, the challenged regulation is limited to significant habitat modification that causes actual, as opposed to hypothetical or speculative, death or injury to identifiable protected animals. Second, even setting aside difficult questions of scienter, the regulation's application is limited by ordinary principles of proximate causation, which introduce notions of foreseeability. These limitations, in my view, call into question Palila v. Hawaii Dept. of Land and Natural Resources, 852 F.2d 1106 (C.A.9 1988) (Palila II), and with it, many of the applications derided by the dissent. Because there is no need to strike a regulation on a facial challenge out of concern that it is susceptible of erroneous application, however, and because there are many habitat-related circumstances in which the regulation might validly apply, I join the opinion of the Court.

* * * The regulation has clear application, for example, to significant habitat modification that kills or physically injures animals which, because they are in a vulnerable breeding state, do not or cannot flee or defend themselves, or to environmental pollutants that cause an animal to suffer physical complications during gestation. Breeding, feeding, and sheltering are what animals do. If significant habitat modification, by interfering with these essential behaviors, actually kills or injures an animal protected by the Act, it causes "harm" within the meaning of the regulation. In contrast to Justice Scalia, I do not read the regulation's "breeding" reference to vitiate or somehow to qualify the clear actual death or injury requirement, or to suggest that the regulation contemplates extension to nonexistent animals. * * *

By the dissent's reckoning, the regulation at issue here, in conjunction with 16 U.S.C. § 1540(a)(1), imposes liability for any habitat-modifying conduct that ultimately results in the death of a protected animal, "regardless of whether that result is intended or even foreseeable, and no matter how long the chain of causality between modification and injury." Even if § 1540(a)(1) does create a strict liability regime (a question we need not decide at this juncture), I see no indication that Congress, in enacting that section, intended to dispense with ordinary principles of proximate causation. Strict liability means liability without regard to fault; it does not normally mean liability for every consequence, however remote, of one's conduct. I would not lightly assume that Congress, in enacting a strict liability statute that is silent on the causation question, has dispensed with this well-entrenched principle. In the absence of congressional abrogation of traditional principles of causation, then, private parties should be held liable under § 1540(a)(1) only if their habitat-modifying actions proximately cause death or injury to protected animals. * * * The regulation, of course, does not contradict the presumption or notion that ordinary principles of causation apply here. Indeed, by use of the word "actually," the regulation clearly rejects speculative or conjectural effects, and thus itself invokes principles of proximate causation.

Proximate causation is not a concept susceptible of precise definition. It is easy enough, of course, to identify the extremes. The farmer whose fertilizer is lifted by a tornado from tilled fields and deposited miles away in a wildlife refuge cannot, by any stretch of the term, be considered the proximate cause of death or injury to protected species occasioned thereby. At the same time, the landowner who drains a pond on his property, killing endangered fish in the process, would likely satisfy any formulation of the principle. We have recently said that proximate causation "normally eliminates the bizarre," and have noted its "functionally equivalent" alternative characterizations in terms of foreseeability * * *. Proximate causation depends to a great extent on considerations of the fairness of imposing liability for remote consequences. The task of determining whether proximate causation exists in the limitless fact patterns sure to arise is best left to lower courts. But I note, at the least, that proximate cause principles inject a foreseeability element into the statute, and hence, the regulation, that would appear to alleviate some of the problems noted by the dissent (describing "a farmer who tills his field and causes erosion that makes silt run into a nearby river which depletes oxygen and thereby [injures] protected fish").

In my view, then, the "harm" regulation applies where significant habitat modification, by impairing essential behaviors, proximately (foreseeably) causes actual death or injury to identifiable animals that are protected under the Endangered Species Act. Pursuant to my interpretation, Palila II—under which the Court of Appeals held that a state agency committed a "taking" by permitting mouflon sheep to eat mamane-naio seedlings that, when full grown, might have fed and sheltered endangered palila—was wrongly decided according to the regulation's own terms. Destruction of the seedlings did not proximately cause actual death or injury to identifiable birds; it merely prevented the regeneration of forest land not currently sustaining actual birds.

This case, of course, comes to us as a facial challenge. We are charged with deciding whether the regulation on its face exceeds the agency's statutory mandate. I have identified at least one application of the regulation (Palila II) that is, in my view, inconsistent with the regulation's own limitations. That misapplication does not, however, call into question the validity of the regulation itself. One can doubtless imagine questionable applications of the regulation that test the limits of the agency's authority. However, it seems to me clear that the regulation does not on its terms exceed the agency's mandate, and that the regulation has innumerable valid habitat-related applications. Congress may, of course, see fit to revisit this issue. And nothing the Court says today prevents the agency itself from narrowing the scope of its regulation at a later date.

■ Justice Scalia, with whom The Chief Justice and Justice Thomas join, dissenting.

* * * The Court's holding that the [ESA's] hunting and killing prohibition incidentally preserves habitat on private lands imposes unfairness to the point of financial ruin—not just upon the rich, but upon the simplest farmer who finds his land conscripted to national zoological use. I respectfully dissent. * * *

The regulation has three features which * * * do not comport with the statute. First, it interprets the statute to prohibit habitat modification that is no more than the cause-in-fact of death or injury to wildlife. Any "significant habitat modification" that in fact produces that result by "impairing essential behavioral patterns" is made unlawful, regardless of whether that result is intended or even foreseeable, and no matter how long the chain of causality between modification and injury. See, e.g., Palila v. Hawaii Dept. of Land and Natural Resources, 852 F.2d 1106, 1108–1109 (C.A.9 1988) (Palila II) (sheep grazing constituted "taking" of palila birds, since although sheep do not destroy full-grown mamane trees, they do destroy mamane seedlings, which will not grow to full-grown trees, on which the palila feeds and nests).

Second, the regulation does not require an "act": The Secretary's officially stated position is that an *omission* will do. The previous version of the regulation made this explicit. * * *

The third and most important unlawful feature of the regulation is that it encompasses injury inflicted, not only upon individual animals, but upon populations of the protected species. "Injury" in the regulation includes "significantly impairing essential behavioral patterns, including *breeding*," 50 CFR § 17.3 (1994) (emphasis added). Impairment of breeding does not "injure" living creatures; it prevents them from propagating, thus "injuring" a *population* of animals which would otherwise have maintained or increased its numbers.

None of these three features of the regulation can be found in the statutory provisions supposed to authorize it. * * *

* * * To define "harm" as an act or omission that, however remotely, "actually kills or injures" a population of wildlife through habitat modification is to choose a meaning that makes nonsense of the word that "harm" defines—requiring us to accept that a farmer who tills his field and causes erosion that makes silt run into a nearby river which depletes oxygen and thereby "impairs [the] breeding" of protected fish has "taken" or "attempted to take" the fish. It should take the strongest evidence to make us believe that Congress has defined a term in a manner repugnant to its ordinary and traditional sense.

Here the evidence shows the opposite. "Harm" is merely one of 10 prohibitory words in § 1532(19), and the other 9 fit the ordinary meaning of "take" perfectly. To "harass, pursue, hunt, shoot, wound, kill, trap, capture, or collect" are all affirmative acts (the provision itself describes them as "conduct," see § 1532(19)) which are directed immediately and intentionally against a particular animal—not acts or omissions that indirectly and accidentally cause injury to a population of animals. * * * What the nine other words in § 1532(19) have in common—and share with the narrower meaning of "harm" described above, but not with the Secretary's ruthless dilation of the word—is the sense of affirmative conduct intentionally directed against a particular animal or animals.

The penalty provisions of the Act counsel this interpretation as well. * * * [They produce] a result that no legislature could reasonably be thought to have intended: A large number of routine private activities—for example, farming, ranching, roadbuilding, construction and logging—are subjected to strict-liability penalties when they fortuitously injure protected wildlife, no matter how remote the chain of causation and no matter how difficult to foresee (or to disprove) the "injury" may be (e.g., an "impairment" of breeding). * * * Without the regulation, the routine "habitat modifying" activities that people conduct to make a daily living would not carry exposure to strict penalties; only acts directed at animals, like those described by the other words in § 1532(19), would risk liability.

The Court says that "[to] read a requirement of intent or purpose into the words used to define 'take' ... ignore[s] [§ 1540's] express provision that a 'knowing' action is enough to violate the Act." This presumably means that because the reading of § 1532(19) advanced here ascribes an element of purposeful injury to the prohibited acts, it makes superfluous (or inexplicable) the more severe penalties provided for a "knowing" violation. That conclusion does not follow, for it is quite possible to take protected wildlife purposefully without doing so knowingly. A requirement that a violation be "knowing" means that the defendant must "know the facts that make his conduct illegal." The hunter who shoots an elk in the mistaken belief that it is a mule deer has not knowingly violated § 1538(a)(1)(B)—not because he does not know that elk are legally protected (that would be knowledge of the law, which is not a requirement), but because he does not know what sort of animal he is shooting. The hunter has nonetheless committed a purposeful taking of protected wildlife, and would therefore be subject to the (lower) strict-liability penalties for violation.

The broader structure of the Act confirms the unreasonableness of the regulation. [Justice Scalia then discussed § 7's requirement to avoid "destruction or adverse modification of habitat" determined to be "critical;" that is, "essential to the conservation of the species."] * * * These provisions have a double significance. Even if [§§ 7 and 9] were totally independent prohibitions—the former applying only to federal agencies and their licensees, the latter only to private parties—Congress's explicit prohibition of habitat modification in the one section would bar the inference of an implicit prohibition of habitat modification in the other section. * * * [I]t would be passing strange for Congress carefully to define "critical habitat" as used in § 1536(a)(2), but leave it to the Secretary to evaluate, willy-nilly, impermissible "habitat modification" (under the guise of "harm") in § 1538(a)(1)(B). * * *

NOTES AND QUESTIONS

1. Does the majority say § 9 may be violated even if the actor has no intent to harm a species? What are Justice O'Connor's and Justice Scalia's views on that issue? Is Justice Scalia correct that the various verbs in the "take" definition all require an intentional act against the critter in question?

2. How direct does the connection have to be between habitat destruction and the injury or death of the endangered species, according to the majority opinion? How does Justice O'Connor's view differ? Should the concept of proximate cause and foreseeability in tort law be applied here? Foreseeable to the average person? Or to the trained biologist? As Michael Bean and Melanie Rowland have pointed out, it is common knowledge that draining a pond may kill the fish in it (to use Justice O'Connor's example), but it may not be so obvious that it would kill a turtle in it (to use Justice Scalia's example), because turtles can survive out of water. Yet to a biologist the death of the turtle may be "a highly likely and predictable result," THE EVOLUTION OF NATIONAL WILDLIFE LAW 216. Should a farmer who creates erosion through tilling be liable under § 9 for silt deposition that injures a listed fish?

3. What kind of proof of death or injury must there be to make out a § 9 violation? A dead carcass? Is it enough to show "significant impairment of essential behavioral patterns," without more? How would you analyze the § 9 liability for razing the last remaining breeding ground for the piping plover, making reproduction impossible? How would the following approaches differ?

 a. *Sweet Home* majority opinion

 b. Justice O'Connor's concurrence

c. Justice Scalia's dissent

d. *Palila* opinion

4. Look at the last line quoted in Justice O'Connor's concurring opinion. If the Executive branch took up that invitation and repealed the regulation, would its action be sustained on judicial review?

5. Here and in TVA v. Hill, the U.S. Supreme Court adopted a strong pro-environment interpretation of the ESA. In its NEPA decisions, by contrast, the Court has been much more niggardly in its approach to the statute. What accounts for the difference?

6. Lower court applications of the "take" prohibition reflect intensely fact-specific analyses. *See* Defenders of Wildlife v. Bernal, 204 F.3d 920 (9th Cir.2000) (upholding district court's well-supported factual finding that high school construction in pygmy owl critical habitat would not cause take); Marbled Murrelet v. Babbitt, 83 F.3d 1060 (9th Cir.1996) (upholding injunction against logging project because of reasonable certainty of imminent harm to listed birds who were nesting in the area; among other things, rejecting the timber company's argument that impaired breeding is not a "take" under the ESA because, while it harms the species' population, it does not harm an actual bird); Bensman v. U.S. Forest Serv., 984 F.Supp. 1242 (W.D.Mo.1997) (removal of dead trees used by the Indiana bat for habitat and hibernation may constitute a taking).

7. There are often, of course, multiple causes for a species decline, some traceable to specific actions by individuals or institutions, and some not. A culprit may be, for example, global climate change or the invasion of exotic species, which usually cannot meaningfully be ascribed to discrete individual actions. How should that be accounted for in § 9? Must a specific action be the primary cause, or is a merely contributing cause sufficient to make out a § 9 violation? Are tort notions of causation and allocation of responsibility relevant here? Suppose that previous timber harvesting activities by several different companies have destroyed 95 percent of the habitat of a species and it is now on the endangered list. The ESA may prohibit the owner of the remaining habitat from harvesting anything. The others who contributed to the problem escape liability. Or suppose that half of the natural stream flow of a river has long been diverted by a farmer with a water right valid under state law with a priority date of 1950. Forty percent of the water is being diverted by a city whose water right was perfected in 1980. Native fish in the stream are now listed as endangered, and need 15 percent of the flow in the river to survive. Whose diversion must be cut back in order to keep the fish alive? *See* James R. Rasband, *Priority, Probability, and Proximate Cause: Lessons from Tort Law about Imposing ESA Responsibility for Wildlife Harm on Water Users and Other Joint Habitat Modifiers*, 33 Envtl. L. 595 (2003).

8. Can inaction ever amount to a take in violation of § 9? Suppose a federal land management agency has zoned an area of federal land as suitable for off-road vehicle (ORV) travel, and has declined to impose speed limits or other controls on off-road vehicles, even though endangered species are known to exist there and are susceptible of take by the ORVs.

Individual ORV operators may be liable for a "take" in that circumstance, but prosecuting them may be difficult as a practical matter. A more effective solution would be to persuade the land manager to adopt regulations. May § 9 be used as a hammer to that end? Can a regulatory agency's conscious failure to take protective action that is within its discretion violate § 9?

9.   Other courts have also held that government acting as a regulator can cause takes of protected wildlife. In Strahan v. Coxe, 127 F.3d 155 (1st Cir.1997), *cert. denied*, 525 U.S. 830 (1998), the court held that Massachusetts' commercial fishing regulators had violated § 9 by causing takings of endangered whales when they licensed commercial fishing operations to use gillnets and lobster pots in a manner that was likely to cause whale entanglement, which had been recognized as a major source of human-caused injury or death of whales. The state argued that holding it responsible for take because it licensed fishing gear was the equivalent of holding it responsible for bank robberies because it licensed automobiles that are used in robberies. The court rejected the analogy: A person may operate an automobile licensed by Massachusetts without risking violations of law, but

> it is not possible for a licensed commercial fishing operation to use its gillnets or lobster pots in the manner permitted by the Commonwealth without risk of violating the ESA by exacting a taking. Thus, the state's licensure * * * does not involve the intervening independent actor that is a necessary component of the other licensure schemes which it argues are comparable. * * * In this instance, the state has licensed commercial fishing operations to use gillnets and lobster pots in specifically the manner that is likely to result in a violation of federal law. The causation here, while indirect, is not so removed that it extends outside the realm of causation as it is understood in the common law.

127 F.3d at 164.

NOTE: HABITAT CONSERVATION PLANS (HCPs) AND "NO SURPRISES"

Section 9 takings may be avoided by receiving an "incidental take" permit under § 10, as discussed in *Sweet Home*. This provision was added by Congress in 1982, and has emerged as a major feature of ESA compliance. Michael Bean and Melanie Rowland have noted that while the provision for incidental take permits "seems to ease the Act's restrictions because it permits what was previously prohibited," in fact it "likely increased" the leverage of the wildlife agencies over activities that incidentally take listed species "because it substituted a flexible regulatory authority for a threat of prosecution [under § 9] that few found credible." THE EVOLUTION OF NATIONAL WILDLIFE LAW 234. Incidental take permits are issued upon Secretarial approval of a "conservation plan," which has come to be known as a "habitat conservation plan," or HCP. 16 U.S.C. § 1539(a)(2)(A). Once approved, a plan shields the land embraced within it from some or all § 9 liability. The Secretary must find that the plan includes "steps that the applicant will take to minimize and mitigate the impacts" of the incidental take "to the maximum extent practicable," and that the applicant "will ensure that adequate funding for the plan will be provided." In issuing a permit, the FWS is bound by the § 7 "no jeopardy" standard, and must ensure that the incidental take "will not appreciably reduce the likelihood of the survival and recovery of the species in the wild."

A common situation for an HCP is where a landowner seeks to develop property on which endangered species are found. The landowner will negotiate with the wildlife agency over steps to be taken to protect the species and still allow some development to proceed. The landowner may agree to protect some habitat, and to stage or otherwise carry out the development in a way that provides protection for the species. If the wildlife agency agrees that the measures will meet the terms of the statute, it may approve the plan and issue an incidental take statement. HCPs may cover a few acres, or hundreds of thousands of acres. They may have terms as long as a century. They may cover a single species or several species. Increasingly, they may focus on unlisted as well as listed species, as landowners seek longer term shelter from new regulation, if they agree to take steps to protect against known risks to species from contemplated development.

In the Clinton Administration, under Secretary Babbitt, the USFWS developed a "no surprises" policy to encourage landowners to enter into HCPs. The policy provides that, under certain circumstances, the government would not ask more from the landowner over the term of the plan if unanticipated problems occur. *See* "Habitat Conservation Plans ('No Surprises') Rule", 63 Fed. Reg. 8859 (1998). The policy has engendered some controversy but has led to many millions of acres being brought into HCPs. The only reported decision addressing the policy to date has held a challenge to it unripe. National Wildlife Federation v. Babbitt, 128 F.Supp.2d 1274 (E.D.Cal.2000).

NOTE: REINTRODUCTION OF SPECIES

Full recovery of some listed species may require their reintroduction into areas from which they have been extirpated. One of the most celebrated efforts at reintroduction—to put the gray wolf back into Yellowstone National Park, where it was the only large mammal that had been extinguished from that celebrated ecoregion several decades earlier—became mired in controversy and litigation. Ultimately, however, the effort was successful, some would say fabulously so, from about every perspective.

The ESA authorizes designation of "experimental populations" of a listed species for reintroduction "outside the current range" of the species, if the Secretary determines that the release "will further the conservation of the species." § 10(j); 16 U.S.C. § 1539(j)(2)(A). The Park Service used gray wolves from Canada (where they are abundant) for reintroduction at Yellowstone. The regulation under which the experimental population was reintroduced specifically provided that the reintroduced wolves could be "taken" under certain circumstances (such as when a reintroduced wolf was preying on livestock in the reintroduced area) without violating the Act. But wolves were already naturally migrating into Montana from Canada, and a handful had been seen in the general area of release.

The statute requires that the experimental population must be "wholly separate geographically from nonexperimental populations of the same species." *Id.* § 1539(j)(1). The purpose of this requirement is to maintain protection for indigenous populations while allowing, where separation existed, the FWS some flexibility in setting the terms of reintroduction in order to encourage and provide incentives for acceptance of reintroduction. At Yellowstone, reintroduction opponents (ranchers concerned about wolf depredation on their livestock, and not assuaged by the offer of private nonprofit groups to compensate them for proven losses) were, ironically, joined by some reintroduction supporters (such as the National Audubon Society) in the argument that this separation in populations was lacking. The ranchers argued this made the release illegal. Audubon argued that the lack of separation meant that the rule allowing "take" of reintroduced wolves under certain circumstances was illegal. The USFWS argued that the presence of an occasional outlier wolf in the area (there was no evidence of breeding pairs) did not constitute a separate "population."

A Wyoming district court bought the ranchers' argument and ruled the reintroduction illegal, but was reversed on appeal. Wyoming Farm Bureau Federation v. Babbitt, 987 F.Supp. 1349 (D.Wyo.1997), *rev'd*, 199 F.3d 1224 (10th Cir.2000). The Ninth Circuit in the meantime had upheld the reintroduction and affirmed the conviction on appeal of a person who shot a reintroduced wolf in circumstances unconnected to livestock depredation. United States v. McKittrick, 142 F.3d 1170 (9th Cir.1998). "We must defer to FWS's reasonable interpretation of section 10(j), particularly where the interpretation involves agency expertise." FWS has interpreted the "wholly separate geographically requirement only to apply to populations; this interpretation is reasonable and we decline to disturb it." McKittrick also challenged the Service's decision to make reintroduction and recovery of the gray wolf a priority, because they were so plentiful in Canada and Alaska. The court responded: "The Secretary has broad discretion to determine what methods to use in species conservation, * * * adoption of recovery plans is discretionary, 16 U.S.C. § 1533(f); and the presence of healthy wolf populations in Canada and Alaska does not, in any event, make the recovery of U.S. populations any less crucial." McKittrick's testimony that he did not think he was shooting at a wolf was seemingly undercut by the fact that he was at the time wearing a T-shirt bearing the slogan "Northern Rockies Wolf Reduction Project." An Idahoan recently charged with attempting to poison wolves in a national forest operates an anti-wolf website that provides detailed instructions on how to "successfully poison a wolf," but he maintained his innocence and condemned an "out-of-control federal agency" for conducting a "Gestapo-style raid" on his house. Julie Cart, *Wolves Thrive but Animosity Keeps Pace*, L.A. TIMES, Dec. 27, 2005.

Currently the wolf population in the northern Rockies is one thousand, and Defenders of Wildlife has paid out about $500,000 since 1987 to ranchers who lost cattle and sheep to wolves. Wolves accounted for fewer than 1 percent of the sheep and cattle kills by predators, with domestic dogs, eagles, foxes, and bears accounting for far more. Still, several dozen "problem" wolves have been killed by federal officials. In 2007, the FWS announced that it was ready to de-list the Northern Rockies population of gray wolves due to the success of the reintroduction program.

5. The Relationship between Section 9 and Section 7

HCPs are not used on federal land, but federal agencies may receive an equivalent kind of protection from liability under § 9 through "incidental take statements" included in biological opinions prepared as part of the formal § 7 consultation process. The FWS issues the statements in biological opinions when it concludes that any "taking" of a listed species "incidental to the agency action" is not likely to jeopardize the listed species or result in destruction or adverse modification of critical habitat. *See* 16 U.S.C. § 1536(b)(4)(B), (*o*).

In this connection, notice how the Court in *Sweet Home* interprets § 9 in relation to § 7. Section 9 is considerably more sweeping than § 7, for the latter applies only to federal agency actions, and asks whether the action poses "jeopardy" to the species, rather than focusing on individual "takes." Federal agencies must comply with both, of course, and compliance with § 9 may be achieved through the consultation process called for by § 7. The following case constitutes the most searching analysis to date of how the two sections fit together.

Arizona Cattle Growers' Ass'n v. U.S. Fish & Wildlife Service

United States Court of Appeals for the Ninth Circuit, 2001.
273 F.3d 1229.

■ Judge Wardlaw

At issue in these consolidated cross-appeals is whether the United States Fish and Wildlife Service's provision of Incidental Take Statements pursuant to the Endangered Species Act was arbitrary and capricious under Section 706 of the Administrative Procedure Act. * * *

[The first case involved grazing permits issued by BLM for public land in southeastern Arizona.] The Bureau of Land Management's livestock grazing program for this area affects 288 separate grazing allotments that in total comprise nearly 1.6 million acres of land. The Fish and Wildlife Service's Biological Opinion, issued on September 26, 1997, analyzes twenty species of plants and animals and concludes that the livestock grazing program was not likely to jeopardize the continued existence of the species affected nor was likely to result in destruction or adverse modification of the designated or proposed critical habitat. The Fish and Wildlife Service did, however, issue Incidental Take Statements for various species of fish and wildlife listed or proposed as endangered. * * * ACGA's summary judgment motion focused on two of the ten Incidental Take Statements, those for the razorback sucker and the cactus ferruginous pygmy-owl. * * *

[The second case] challenged Incidental Take Statements set forth in a second Biological Opinion issued by the Fish and Wildlife Service that concerns livestock grazing on public lands administered by the United States Forest Service. * * * The Fish and Wildlife Service examined 962 allotments, determining that grazing would have no effect on listed species for 619 of those allotments and cause no adverse effects for 321 of the remaining allotments, leaving 22 allotments. These allotments were each roughly 30,000 acres, but several of the allotments were significantly larger. In its Biological Opinion, the Fish and Wildlife Service concluded that ongoing grazing activities on 21 out of the 22 allotments at issue would not jeopardize the continued existence of any protected species or result in the destruction or adverse modification of any critical habitat. It determined, however, that ongoing grazing activities would incidentally take members of one or more protected species in each of the 22 allotments, and it issued Incidental Take Statements for each of those allotments. ACGA contested the issuance of Incidental Take Statements for six of the allotments * * *.

* * *

In the district court, the Fish and Wildlife Service argued that the word "taking" as used in ESA Section 7(b)(4) should be interpreted more broadly than in the context of Section 9 of the ESA, relying upon the different purposes, i.e., protective (Section 7) as opposed to punitive (Section 9), served by each Section.

Specifically, it argued that a taking as construed in Section 7 should encompass those situations in which harm to a listed species was "possible" or "likely" in the future due to the proposed action. The district court rejected this contention, and although the Fish and Wildlife Service states that it has abandoned this argument on appeal, it nevertheless maintains that the Section 7 incidental take definition should be interpreted more broadly than the definition of a take under Section 9. * * * We believe that Congress has spoken to the precise question at issue and agree with the district court that the definition of "taking" in Sections 7 and 9 of the ESA are identical in meaning and application.

[The court took up the section 9 take prohibition, starting with the statute, the regulations, and Sweet Home, noting that h]arming a species may be indirect, in that the harm may be caused by habitat modification, but habitat modification does not constitute harm unless it "actually kills or injures wildlife." * * * Defenders of Wildlife v. Bernal, 204 F.3d 920, 924–25 (9th Cir.1999) [quoting *Sweet Home*].

* * *

[The court then described the § 7 consultation process, and noted that the USFWS's biological opinion] must specify whether any "incidental taking" of protected species will occur, specifically "any taking otherwise prohibited, if such taking is incidental to, and not the purpose of, the carrying out of an otherwise lawful activity." 16 U.S.C. § 1536(b)(4); 50 C.F.R. § 17.3. Its determination that an incidental taking will result leads to the publication of the "Incidental Take Statement," identifying areas where members of the particular species are at risk. Contained in the Incidental Take Statement is an advisory opinion which:

(i) specifies the impact of such incidental taking on the species,

(ii) specifies those reasonable and prudent measures that the Secretary considers necessary or appropriate to minimize such impact [and] . . .

(iv) sets forth the terms and conditions . . . that must be complied with by the Federal agency or applicant . . . or both, to implement the measures specified under clause (ii). 16 U.S.C. § 1536(b)(4) (subsection (iii) omitted).

Significantly, the Incidental Take Statement functions as a safe harbor provision immunizing persons from Section 9 liability and penalties for takings committed during activities that are otherwise lawful and in compliance with its terms and conditions. 16 U.S.C. § 1536(o). Any such incidental taking "shall not be considered to be a prohibited taking of the species concerned." Id. Although the action agency is "technically free to disregard the Biological Opinion and proceed with its proposed action . . . it does so at its own peril." Bennett, 520 U.S. at 170.

Consequently, if the terms and conditions of the Incidental Take Statement are disregarded and a taking does occur, the action agency or the applicant may be subject to potentially severe civil and criminal penalties under Section 9.

The structure of the ESA and the legislative history clearly show Congress's intent to enact one standard for "taking" within both Section 7(b)(4), governing the creation of Incidental Take Statements, and Section 9, imposing civil and criminal penalties for violation of the ESA. In 1982, Congress amended the ESA to include Section 7(b)(4) to resolve the conflict between Sections 7 and 9. As noted in the legislative reports, the purpose of Section 7(b)(4) and the amendment to Section 7(o) is to resolve the situation in which a Federal agency or a permit or license applicant has been advised that the proposed action will not violate Section 7(a)(2) of the Act but the proposed action will result in the taking of some species incidental to that action—a clear violation of Section 9 of the Act which prohibits any taking of a species. Absent an actual or prospective taking under Section 9, there is no "situation" that requires a Section 7 safe harbor provision.

We reject the argument that "taking" should be applied differently because the two sections serve different purposes. Interpreting the statutes in the manner urged by the Fish and Wildlife Service could effectively stop the proposed cattle grazing entirely. Such a broad interpretation would allow the Fish and Wildlife Service to engage in widespread land regulation even where no Section 9 liability could be imposed. This interpretation would turn the purpose behind the 1982 Amendment on its head.

This conclusion follows as a practical matter from the statutory scheme. Because of the potential liability imposed on federal agencies whose actions do not comply with conditions in the Incidental Take Statement, agencies regulating land are unlikely to permit nonconforming uses of their land. For this reason, as the Supreme Court has recognized, Biological Opinions exert a "powerful coercive effect" in shaping the policies of the federal agencies whose actions are at issue. Bennett, 520 U.S. at 169 (citations omitted). Here, for example, although ACGA theoretically could choose to disregard the Incidental Take Statements without explanation, the Bureau of Land Management and the Forest Service, as the action agencies, "must not only articulate [their] reasons for disagreement (which ordinarily requires species and habitat investigations that are not within the action agency's expertise), but ... [they run] a substantial risk if [their] (inexpert) reasons turn out to be wrong." Id. As the Bennett Court noted, the action agency rarely, if ever, chooses to disregard the terms and conditions of an Incidental Take Statement. In fact, the Incidental Take Statement challenged in ACGA I began by stating, "[t]he measures described below are non-discretionary, and must be implemented by the agency so that they become binding conditions of any grant or permit issued to the applicant...." As a practical matter, if ACGA's members wish to receive grazing permits, they must comply with the terms and conditions of the Incidental Take Statements. As the district court held in ACGA II, "[i]f Fish and Wildlife Service could issue an Incidental Take Statement even when a taking in violation of Section 9 was not present, those engaging in legal activities would be subjected to the terms and conditions of such statements." The court finds no authority for this result nor do we.

V.   Determining When the Fish and Wildlife Service Must Issue an Incidental Take Statement

[The court then rejected the contention of the USFWS that the ESA requires it to issue an ITS in every section 7 consultation. Instead, it agreed with the district court that] issuing an Incidental Take Statement is "appropriate only when a take has occurred or is reasonably certain to occur." The Fish and Wildlife Service argues that * * * it should be permitted to issue an Incidental Take Statement whenever there is any possibility, no matter how small, that a listed species will be taken. As we believe that Congress has spoken to the precise question at issue, we must reject the agency's interpretation of the ESA as contrary to clear congressional intent. * * * Section 7(b)(4) of the ESA provides:

If after consultation under subsection (a)(2) of this section, the Secretary concludes that—

> (A) the agency action will not violate such subsection, or offers reasonable and prudent alternatives which the Secretary believes would not violate such subsection;
>
> (B) the taking of an endangered species or a threatened species incidental to the agency action will not violate such subsection; and

(C) if an endangered species or threatened species of a marine mammal is involved, the taking is authorized pursuant to section 1371(a)(5) of this title;

the Secretary shall provide the Federal agency and the applicant concerned, if any, with a written statement that—

(i) specifies the impact of such incidental taking on the species, ...

16 U.S.C. § 1536(b)(4). The Fish and Wildlife Service relies on the statutory provision directing the Secretary to provide "a written statement that . . . specifies the impact of such incidental taking on the species." Id. * * *

When read in context, it is clear that the issuance of the Incidental Take Statement is subject to the finding of the factors enumerated in the ESA. The statute explicitly provides that the written statement is subject to the consultation and the Secretary's conclusions. A contrary interpretation would render meaningless the clause stating that the Incidental Take Statement will specify "the impact of such incidental taking." 16 U.S.C. § 1536(b)(4)(i) (emphasis added). We therefore agree with ACGA that the plain language of the ESA does not dictate that the Fish and Wildlife Service must issue an Incidental Take Statement irrespective of whether any incidental takings will occur. * * *

The plain language of the implementing regulations also supports ACGA's argument. * * *

The Fish and Wildlife Service's internal handbook does not alter our conclusion. * * * The Fish and Wildlife Service's handbook instruction to issue an Incidental Take Statement when no take will occur as a result of permitted activity is contrary to the plain meaning of the statute as well as the agency's own regulations. Accordingly, we hold that absent rare circumstances such as those involving migratory species, it is arbitrary and capricious to issue an Incidental Take Statement when the Fish and Wildlife Service has no rational basis to conclude that a take will occur incident to the otherwise lawful activity.

[The court then turned to the individual ITSs.] As a preliminary matter, however, we must address the ACGA II court's application of a "reasonable certainty" standard, about which the Fish and Wildlife Service has made much ado. It argues that "the predicate for issuing an ITS should not be a particular level of certainty that a take will occur, the ITS itself must only not be arbitrary and capricious." This argument misapprehends the ACGA II court's application of the arbitrary and capricious standard to the requirement that the Fish and Wildlife Service must find a take incidental to the otherwise lawful use before it may condition issuance of a permit on enumerated "reasonable and prudent" measures. ACGA II held merely that if the Fish and Wildlife Service cannot satisfy the court to a reasonable certainty that a take will occur, then it is arbitrary and capricious for it to issue an Incidental Take Statement imposing conditions on the use of the land. This is actually a more lenient standard than if the record were required to include evidence of an actual taking incident to the proposed use. Given that the Fish and Wildlife Service must have a reasonable basis to conclude that a take will occur as a result of the anticipated lawful activity, benchmarking such findings against a standard of reasonable certainty puts it to a lesser burden. Moreover, it would be unreasonable for the Fish and Wildlife Service to impose conditions on otherwise lawful land use if a take were not reasonably certain to occur as a result of that activity. * * *

We need not definitively resolve this question, however, because regardless of the dispute over the ACGA II court's application of the arbitrary and capricious standard, we must review de novo the actions of the Fish and Wildlife Service under the arbitrary and capricious standard mandated by the statute. Therefore, pursuant to Section 706 of the APA, we proceed to determine whether the Incidental Take Statements are founded on a rational connection between the facts found and the choices made by the Fish and Wildlife Service and whether it has committed a clear error of judgment. See Motor Vehicle Manuf. Assoc. v. State Farm Mutual Auto., 463 U.S. 29, 43 (1983).

In the Biological Opinion issued in response to ACGA's first request for land use permits, the Fish and Wildlife Service concluded that the direct effects of cattle grazing are infrequent to the razorback sucker, a moderately sized fish listed as endangered in November 1991. Although once abundant in the project area, the Fish and Wildlife Service admitted that there have been no reported sightings of the razorback sucker in the area since 1991 and that "effects of the livestock grazing program on individual fish or fish populations probably occur infrequently." Nevertheless, the Fish and Wildlife Service issued an Incidental Take Statement for the fish, anticipating take as a result of the direct effects of grazing in the project area, the construction of fences, the construction and existence of stock tanks for non-native fish, as well as other "activities in the watershed." Because the Fish and Wildlife Service could not directly quantify the level of incidental take, it determined that authorized take would be exceeded if range conditions in the allotment deteriorated and cattle grazing could not be ruled out as a cause of the deterioration.

Despite the lack of evidence that the razorback sucker exists on the allotment in question, the Fish and Wildlife Service argues that it should be able to issue an Incidental Take Statement based upon prospective harm. While we recognize the importance of a prospective orientation, the regulations mandate a separate procedure for reinitiating consultation if different evidence is later developed:

> Reinitiation of formal consultation is required and shall be requested by the Federal agency or by the Service, where discretionary Federal involvement or control over the action has been retained or is authorized by law and:
>
> (a) If the amount or extent of taking specified in the incidental take statement is exceeded;
>
> (b) If new information reveals effects of the action that may affect listed species or critical habitat in a manner or to an extent not previously considered;

(c) If the identified action is subsequently modified in a manner that causes an effect to the listed species or critical habitat that was not considered in the biological opinion; or

(d) If a new species is listed or critical habitat designated that may be affected by the identified action.

50 C.F.R. § 402.16. * * * Absent this procedure, however, there is no evidence that Congress intended to allow the Fish and Wildlife Service to regulate any parcel of land that is merely capable of supporting a protected species.

The only additional evidence that the Fish and Wildlife Service offers to justify its decision is that "small numbers of the juvenile fish . . . likely survived" in an unsuccessful attempt to repopulate the project area between 1981–1987. This speculative evidence, without more, is woefully insufficient to meet the standards imposed by the governing statute. See 50 C.F.R. § 402.14(g)(8) ("In formulating its biological opinion . . . the Service will use the best scientific and commercial data available. . . ."). Likewise, the Fish and Wildlife Service failed to present evidence that an indirect taking would occur absent the existence of the species on the property. Although habitat modification resulting in actual killing or injury may constitute a taking, the Fish and Wildlife Service has presented only speculative evidence that habitat modification, brought about by livestock grazing, may impact the razorback sucker. The agency has a very low bar to meet, but it must at least attain it. It would be improper to force ACGA to prove that the species does not exist on the permitted area, as the Fish and Wildlife Service urges, both because it would require ACGA to meet the burden statutorily imposed on the agency, and because it would be requiring it to prove a negative.

Based on a careful review of the record, we find that it is arbitrary and capricious to issue an Incidental Take Statement for the razorback sucker when the Fish and Wildlife Service's speculation that the species exists on the property is not supported by the record. We agree with the district court's ruling that the Fish and Wildlife Service failed to establish an incidental taking because it did not have evidence that the razorback sucker even exists anywhere in the area. Where the agency purports to impose conditions on the lawful use of that land without showing that the species exists on it, it acts beyond its authority in violation of 5 U.S.C. § 706.

* * * [The court reached a similar conclusion with respect to several other ITSs, and then turned to an ITS issued on the Cow Flat Allotment, which was considered occupied loach minnow habitat.] Having determined that loach minnow exist on the allotment, Fish and Wildlife Service determined that the loach minnow are vulnerable to direct harms resulting from cattle crossings, such as trampling. Moreover, because the fish use the spaces between large substrates for resting and spawning, sedimentation resulting from grazing in pastures that settles in these spaces can adversely affect loach minnow habitat. The Biological Opinion determines that this indirect effect, along with the direct crushing of loach minnow eggs and the reduction in food availability, will result in take of the loach minnow. The

Incidental Take Statement, however, does not directly quantify the incidental takings of loach minnow and determines that such takings "will be difficult to detect." Defining the incidental take in terms of habitat characteristics, the Fish and Wildlife Service found that take will be exceeded if several conditions are not met. One such condition was if "[e]cological conditions do not improve under the proposed livestock management" plan.

We agree with the district court that the issuance of the Cow Flat Incidental Take Statement was not arbitrary and capricious. Unlike the other allotments in question, the Fish and Wildlife Service provided evidence that the listed species exist on the land in question and that the cattle have access to the endangered species' habitat. Accordingly, the Fish and Wildlife Service could reasonably conclude that the loach minnow could be harmed when the livestock entered the river. Additionally, the Fish and Wildlife Service provided extensive site-specific information that discussed not only the topography of the relevant allotment, but the indirect effects of grazing on the species due to the topography. The specificity of the Service's data, as well as the articulated causal connections between the activity and the "actual killing or injury" of a protected species distinguishes the Fish and Wildlife Service's treatment of this allotment from the other allotments at issue in the two consultations. Thus, we hold that because the Fish and Wildlife Service articulated a rational connection between harm to the species and the land grazing activities at issue, the issuance of the Incidental Take Statements for the Cow Flat Allotment was not arbitrary and capricious.

We now turn to the question whether the Service acted arbitrarily and capriciously by failing to properly specify the amount of anticipated take in the Incidental Take Statement for the Cow Flat Allotment and by failing to provide a clear standard for determining when the authorized level of take has been exceeded.

In general, Incidental Take Statements set forth a "trigger" that, when reached, results in an unacceptable level of incidental take, invalidating the safe harbor provision, and requiring the parties to re-initiate consultation. Ideally, this "trigger" should be a specific number. See, e.g., Mausolf v. Babbitt, 125 F.3d 661 (8th Cir.1997) (snowmobiling activity may take no more than two wolves); Fund for Animals v. Rice, 85 F.3d 535 (11th Cir.1996) (municipal landfill may take fifty-two snakes during construction and an additional two snakes per year thereafter); Mt. Graham Red Squirrel v. Madigan, 954 F.2d 1441 (9th Cir.1992) (telescope construction may take six red squirrels per year); Ctr. for Marine Conservation v. Brown, 917 F.Supp. 1128 (S.D.Tex.1996) (shrimping operation may take four hawksbill turtles, four leatherback turtles, ten Kemp's Ridley turtles, ten green turtles, or 370 loggerhead turtles). Here, however, the "trigger" took the form of several conditions. We must therefore determine whether the linking of the level of permissible take to the conditions set forth in the various Incidental Take Statements was arbitrary and capricious.

ACGA argues that the Incidental Take Statements fail to specify the amount or extent of authorized take with the required degree of exactness. Specifically, ACGA objected to the first condition:

The [S]ervice concludes that incidental take of loach minnow from the proposed action will be considered to be exceeded if any of the following conditions are met:

[Condition 1] Ecological conditions do not improve under the proposed livestock management. Improving conditions can be defined through improvements in watershed, soil condition, trend and condition of rangelands (e.g., vegetative litter, plant vigor, and native species diversity), riparian conditions (e.g., vegetative and geomorphologic: bank, terrace, and flood plain conditions), and stream channel conditions (e.g., channel profile, embeddedness, water temperature, and base flow) within the natural capabilities of the landscape in all pastures on the allotment within the Blue River watershed.

We have never held that a numerical limit is required. Indeed, we have upheld Incidental Take Statements that used a combination of numbers and estimates. See Ramsey v. Kantor, 96 F.3d 434, 441 n. 12 (9th Cir.1996) (utilizing both harvesting rates and estimated numbers of fish to reach a permitted take); Southwest Ctr. for Biological Diversity v. U.S. Bureau of Reclamation, 6 F.Supp.2d 1119 (D.Ariz.1997) (concluding that an Incidental Take Statement that indexes the permissible take to successful completion of the reasonable and prudent measures as well as the terms and conditions is valid); Pac. Northwest Generating Coop. v. Brown, 822 F.Supp.1479, 1510 (D.Or.1993) (ruling that an Incidental Take Statement that defines the allotted take in percentage terms is valid). * * *

We agree with the ACGA II court's conclusion that, "the use of ecological conditions as a surrogate for defining the amount or extent of incidental take is reasonable so long as these conditions are linked to the take of the protected species." * * *

ACGA argues that it is entitled to more certainty than "vague and undetectable criteria such as changes in a 22,000 acre allotment's 'ecological condition.'" In response, the Fish and Wildlife Service argues that "the [Incidental Take Statement] provides for those studies necessary to provide the quantification of impacts which the Cattle Growers claim is lacking."

We disagree with the government's position. The Incidental Take Statements at issue here do not sufficiently discuss the causal connection between Condition 1 and the taking of the species at issue. Based on the Incidental Take Statement, if "[e]cological conditions do not improve," takings will occur. This vague analysis, however, cannot be what Congress contemplated when it anticipated that surrogate indices might be used in place of specific numbers. Moreover, whether there has been compliance with this vague directive is within the unfettered discretion of the Fish and Wildlife Service, leaving no method by which the applicant or the action agency can gauge their performance. Finally, Condition 1 leaves ACGA and the United States Forest Service responsible for the general ecological improvement of the approximately 22,000 acres that comprise the Cow Flat Allotment. * * *

NOTES AND QUESTIONS

1.   How exactly does § 9 fit together with § 7 where, as here, a federal agency is authorizing private action that could modify habitat so as to result in the take of an endangered species? Are certain acts taken by federal agencies forbidden by one of these sections, and not the other? If the action the agency is authorizing would violate § 9, must it also have violated § 7? Here the USFWS found that the federal land managers' authorization of livestock grazing did not cause "jeopardy" and did not adversely modify critical habitat of listed species. Note that the concept of the "incidental take statement" was added to the ESA in 1982 to "resolve the conflict between §§ 7 and 9." How did it do that?

2.   Is the court here sensitive enough to what it calls the "importance of protective orientation"? Here the USFWS uses the ITS process to advocate management of livestock grazing on federal lands that pays close attention to the needs of listed species. While the agency cannot provide details on the number of endangered critters the actions it recommends might save (or the amount of possible "take" such actions would avoid), is the court correct in saying such details are required, given the precautionary approach to ESA enforcement the Supreme Court seemed to approve in TVA v. Hill?

3.   What was the purpose of the conditions the USFWS imposed in the ITSs here? To avoid jeopardy? Or to help the species recover so that they might be taken off the endangered species list? The court seems to say the former is permissible and the latter is not. Why? That is, what's wrong with the USFWS engaging in what the court called "widespread land regulation even where no § 9 liability could be imposed" in these circumstances? If cattle grazing on public land has been a significant factor in the decline of the species that are now on the endangered list, why shouldn't more species-sensitive management be addressed in the § 7 process through the formation of terms and conditions in the ITS?

4.   Is the court of appeals agreeing with the district court that USFWS must find, to a "reasonable certainty," that "take" will occur before it can issue an ITS imposing conditions on the use of the land?

5.   Why was the Cow Flat Allotment different; i.e., what made an ITS appropriate there? But note the court went on to set aside the Cow Flat ITS. Why? Is the court creating an impossible standard for the USFWS to meet by requiring specificity in linkage between management practices and species protection? Or is the court merely saying in this case that the ESA is not a license for the wildlife agencies to use the ITS process of § 7 to roam around requiring promotion of species-sensitive management practices by federal land agencies; and that instead it must pay attention to the facts on the ground?

D.   PRIVATE RIGHTS IN PUBLIC RESOURCES

As Congress constrained resource development through statutes such as NEPA and the ESA, the courts increasingly sought to protect private rights in public resources. Generally, this judicial protection comes in the form of damages. Unlike most of the cases considered in this book, the following decisions are about monetary relief, not injunctions. Some of the rights arise out of federally and state-created property law. Other rights derive from contractual promises made between individuals and the United States. In either case, courts are fundamentally concerned about the imposition of unfair burdens that defeated reasonable expectations.

1. PROPERTY RIGHTS AND "TAKINGS" COMPENSATION

An important constitutional constraint on federal power to regulate natural resource development is the Fifth Amendment to the U.S. Constitution. It bars the federal government from "taking" property for public use without paying just compensation. Most modern takings cases raise issues of so-called "regulatory" takings, first explored in Justice Holmes' opinion in Pennsylvania Coal Co. v. Mahon, 260 U.S. 393 (1922). Although the history of the Fifth Amendment strongly suggests that its framers intended to require compensation only when the government actually took title to private property (as through the exercise of eminent domain authority), the Court ruled that the Constitution required compensation even when the government did not actually take title, but instead regulated the use of the property so severely as to effectively "take" the property. In ruling that a state law* aimed at preventing subsidence of land surface as a result of underground coal mining constituted a taking of the separately-owned mineral estate, Justice Holmes declined to lay down any bright line rules for deciding when a regulation "goes too far" and creates an obligation to compensate. Justice Brandeis registered a strong dissent, arguing that the Pennsylvania subsidence law was a safety measure designed to prevent the public from harm, and should not be regarded as a taking.

Although the Court has attempted over the years to lay down more specific and predictable rules, regulatory takings law remains very fact-specific and the general principles have not advanced very far from where Justice Holmes left them. In Penn Central Transp. Co. v. New York City, 438 U.S. 104 (1978), the Court upheld the application of New York City's landmark preservation law, which offered no monetary compensation to property owners whose rights were limited to prevent the owner of Grand Central Terminal from constructing a new building that would have impaired the Terminal's Beaux Arts facade. Justice Brennan's majority opinion (three Justices dissented) summarized the Court's prior takings cases as identifying several factors of particular significance. One was "[t]he economic impact of the regulation on the claimant and, particularly, the extent to which the regulation has interfered with distinct investment-backed expectations." Another was the "character of the governmental action;" specifically, whether the governmental "interference arises from some public program adjusting the benefits and burdens of economic life to

---

* Most regulatory takings cases involve state law. The fifth amendment compensation requirement applies to states through the fourteenth amendment's due process clause. Chicago, B. & Q. R.R. Co. v. City of Chicago, 166 U.S. 226 (1897).

promote the common good." The majority emphasized that resolution of takings questions involved "essentially ad hoc factual inquiries."

This remains the Court's approach, except for a couple of narrow per se rules. One requires compensation when the government permanently physically occupies private property, no matter how slight. *See* Loretto v. Teleprompter Manhattan CATV Corp. 458 U.S. 419 (1982). The other requires compensation when the government deprives a landowner of *"all* economically beneficial or productive use of land" (emphasis added), sometimes called a "total taking." Lucas v. South Carolina Coastal Council, 505 U.S. 1003 (1992). Even in the "total taking" situation, Justice Scalia, writing for the 5–4 majority in Lucas, recognized an exception to the duty to compensate, because a "property owner necessarily expects the uses of his property to be restricted, from time to time, by various measures newly enacted by the State in legitimate exercise of its police powers." Thus the government has no duty to compensate a landowner, even for a total taking, if its regulation "inhere[s] in the title itself, in the restrictions that background principles of the State's law of property and nuisance already place upon land ownership ... [which could be enforced] by adjacent landowners (or other uniquely affected persons) under the State's law of private nuisance, or by the State under its complementary power to abate nuisances that affect the public generally, or otherwise." *Id.* at 1029.

Regulatory takings lawsuits arising out of federal land management remain quite unusual, especially considering the vast amount of federal land, the large numbers of private persons making use of those lands, and the exercise of federal regulatory authority over those uses. Successful takings claims are very rare. Put a little differently, the great bulk of takings litigation, and the most important Supreme Court decisions, arise out of regulation of private land by state or local governments. Regulatory takings actions (sometimes called inverse condemnation actions) against the United States must be brought in the U.S. Court of Federal Claims under the Tucker Act, 28 U.S.C. § 1491. That court, and the Court of Appeals for the Federal Circuit (to which claims court decisions may be appealed), are on the front lines of addressing these questions.

The materials that follow address takings issues arising in the special context of federal lands and resources. The first case, involving federal protection of wild horses and burros, explores some aspects of basic takings doctrine in deciding whether federal action to protect these creatures as components of federal land may be said to "take" adjacent private property. (Recall the earlier discussion about the reach of the Property Clause to activities on nonfederal land that could affect federal property; e.g., Minnesota v. Block, *supra* p. 173.)

Mountain States Legal Foundation v. Hodel

United States Court of Appeals, Tenth Circuit, 1986.
799 F.2d 1423, *cert. denied*, 480 U.S. 951 (1987).

■ JUDGE MCKAY

The Mountain States Legal Foundation and the Rock Springs Grazing Association (collectively referred to hereinafter as "the Association") brought this action on behalf of their members against the Secretary of the Interior and other government officials to compel them to manage the wild horse herds that roam public and private lands in an area of southwestern Wyoming known locally as the "checkerboard." The checkerboard comprises over one million acres of generally high desert land and has been used by the Association since 1909 for the grazing of cattle. The lands involved in this case are in the Rock Springs District of the checkerboard, an area approximately 40 miles wide and 115 miles long. In this area of the checkerboard, the Association's cattle roam freely on property owned by the Association and on the alternate sections of land owned by the federal government. Thousands of wild horses also roam these lands.

The Association sought a declaratory judgment that the Secretary had mismanaged the wild horses, and that the Secretary's failure to remove wild horses from the Association's land was arbitrary and capricious. On this basis, the Association also sought a writ of mandamus to compel the Secretary to remove the wild horses from its lands and to reduce the size of the wild horse herds on adjacent public lands. The Association also sought damages under the Fifth Amendment for the alleged uncompensated taking of its lands. For this alleged taking, the Association sought to recover $500,000 from the Director of the Bureau of Land Management ("BLM") and ten dollars [sic] from the United States.

The district court granted the Association's petition for mandamus, dismissed the Association's claim against the Director of the BLM, and granted summary judgment for the government on the Association's Fifth Amendment takings claim. The Association appealed the dismissal of the claim against the Director and the grant of summary judgment. The government did not challenge the grant of mandamus on appeal. We affirmed the dismissal, but reversed and remanded the grant of summary judgment, holding that an unresolved factual issue precluded a summary determination of the takings claim. We granted the government's petition for rehearing en banc to consider whether the Secretary's failure to manage the wild horse herds, in accordance with the requirements of the Wild Free–Roaming Horses and Burros Act, 16 U.S.C.A. §§ 1331–1340 (1982), gives rise to a claim for taking of the Association's property under the Fifth Amendment. * * *

Wild horses and burros are the progeny of animals introduced to North America by early Spanish explorers. They once roamed the western rangelands in vast herds. But over time, desirable grazing land was fenced off for private use, while the animals were slaughtered for sport and profit. The herds began to dwindle, and the remaining animals were driven to marginal, inhospitable grazing areas. Alarmed at the decline of these herds, Congress in 1971 enacted the Wild Free–Roaming Horses and Burros Act, 16 U.S.C.A. §§ 1331–1340 (1982), to protect the wild horses and burros from "capture, branding, harassment, or death." * * *

The Association alleges that the Secretary has disregarded its repeated requests to remove wild horses from its lands, that it is prohibited by section 1338 of the Act from removing the wild horses itself, and that the wild horses grazing on its lands have eroded the topsoil and consumed vast quantities of forage and water. In support of its Fifth Amendment claim, the Association argues that "it is the panoply of management responsibilities set forth in the Act and its regulations, including [section 4 of the Act, which provides that, if protected horses or burros 'stray from public lands onto privately owned land, the owners of such land may inform the nearest Federal marshal or agent of the Secretary, who shall arrange to have the animals removed.'], which * * * subject the United States to liability due to its pervasive control over the horses' existence." In our prior opinion in this case, a panel of this court, with one judge dissenting, found that the government's "complete and exclusive control" over wild horses made the Wild Free–Roaming Horses and Burros Act "unique" in the field of wildlife protection legislation. This degree of control, the court said, was potentially "significant" in determining the government's liability under the Fifth Amendment. With the benefit of additional briefing and oral argument, it is now apparent to us that, in the area of wildlife protection legislation, there is nothing novel about the nature and degree of the government's control over wild horses and burros.

At the outset, it is important to note that wild horses and burros are no less "wild" animals than are the grizzly bears that roam our national parks and forests. Indeed, in the definitional section of the Act, Congress has explicitly declared "all unbranded and unclaimed horses and burros on public lands" to be "*wild* horses and burros." 16 U.S.C. § 1332(b) (1982) (emphasis added).

In exercising their powers "to preserve and regulate the exploitation of an important resource," both the state and federal governments have often enacted sweeping and comprehensive measures to control activities that may adversely affect wildlife. [The Court's discussion of such laws, e.g., the Marine Mammal Protection Act, 16 U.S.C. §§ 1361–1407; the Migratory Bird Treaty Act, 16 U.S.C. §§ 703–712; the Bald and Golden Eagle Protection Act, 16 U.S.C. §§ 668–668d; and the Endangered Species Act, 16 U.S.C. §§ 1531–1543, is omitted.]

* * *

With respect to each of these federal wildlife protection statutes, the degree of governmental control over activities affecting the wildlife in question cannot be said to be different in character from that mandated by the Wild and Free–Roaming Horses and Burros Act. Indeed, in some of these examples, the governmental control over the wildlife is more pervasive, more sweeping, and more restrictive than that provided by the Wild Free–Roaming Horses and Burros Act.

Many state wildlife conservation laws provide similar, comprehensive control over activities affecting protected species. Most states, for example, have enacted endangered species laws containing prohibitions that parallel those contained in federal wildlife protection laws.

The foregoing discussion demonstrates the fallacy in the Association's argument that the wild horses are, in effect, instrumentalities of the federal government whose presence constitutes a permanent governmental occupation of the Association's property. In structure and purpose, the Wild Free–Roaming Horses and Burros Act is nothing more than a land-use regulation enacted by Congress to ensure the survival of a particular species of wildlife. It is not unique in its impact on private resource owners.

Of the courts that have considered whether damage to private property by protected wildlife constitutes a "taking," a clear majority have held that it does not and that the government thus does not owe compensation. The Court of Claims rejected such a claim for damage done to crops by geese protected under the Migratory Bird Treaty Act in Bishop v. United States, 126 F.Supp. 449, 452–53 (Ct.Cl.1954), cert. denied, 349 U.S. 955 (1955). * * * Several state courts have also rejected claims for damage to property by wildlife protected under state laws. See, e.g., Jordan v. State, 681 P.2d 346, 350 n. 3 (Alaska App.1984) (defendants were not deprived of their property interest in a moose carcass by regulation prohibiting the killing of a bear that attacked the carcass because "their loss was incidental to the state regulation which was enacted to protect game"). * * *

The majority view that rejects takings claims for damage caused by protected wildlife is consistent with the Supreme Court precedent that controls our decision. * * *

In an unbroken line of cases, the Supreme Court has sustained land-use regulations that are reasonably related to the promotion of the public interest, consistently rejecting the notion that diminution in property value, standing alone, constitutes a taking under the Fifth Amendment. * * * [I]n Kleppe v. New Mexico, 426 U.S. 529 (1976), the Supreme Court recognized the important governmental interest in preserving wild horses and burros in their natural habitat, citing congressional findings that their preservation would " 'contribute to the diversity of life within the Nation and enrich the lives of the American people.' " The provisions of the Wild Free–Roaming Horses and Burros Act advance this important governmental interest.

The Association has not argued, or even suggested that the Act deprives it of the "economically viable use" of its property. Rather, it contends that the consumption of forage by the wild horses, standing alone, requires the government to pay just compensation. In determining whether a particular land-use regulation deprives a property owner of the "economically viable use" of his land, the court must examine the impact of the regulation on the property as a whole. * * *

Considering the economic impact on the Association's property as a whole, the Act does not interfere with the Association's "distinct investment-back expectations" of using its property for grazing cattle. Nor does it impair the Association's right to hold the property for investment purposes. Moreover, the Association has not been deprived of its "right to exclude" the wild horses and burros. Admittedly, the grazing habits of the wild horses have diminished the value of the Association's property. But "a reduction in the value of property is not necessarily equated with a taking." Allard, 444 U.S. at 66. In this case, the reduction in the value of the property pales in comparison to that sustained in Village of Euclid, 272

U.S. at 384 (75% of property value lost) and Hadacheck, 239 U.S. at 405 (92.5% of property value lost).

Whether a particular land-use regulation gives rise to a taking under the Fifth Amendment is essentially on ad hoc inquiry. Although the economic burden imposed on the Association is significant, the Association has not even contended that it has been deprived of the "economically viable use" of its lands. In view of the important governmental interest involved here, we conclude that no taking has occurred and that the district court correctly granted summary judgment for the government.

* * *

■ JUDGE BARRETT, dissenting.

I must respectfully dissent. I continue to adhere to the reasoning of the prior opinion by a panel of this court reversing and remanding the grant of summary judgment on the basis that wild free-roaming horses and burros are not "wild animals." * * * Assuming, however, that the animals protected under the [Wild Horse Act] are "wild animals," I would nonetheless dissent from the majority opinion. [The Association] should not be precluded from litigating its "taking" claim as a matter of law given the Act's unique wildlife protection scheme. Summary judgment is inappropriate and this case should be remanded to the district court to determine whether the facts here, i.e., the amount of damage to [its] property and the cause of that damage, entitle [it] to relief under the Taking Clause of the Fifth Amendment. * * *

■ CHIEF JUDGE HOLLOWAY, joins in the dissents of JUDGES SETH and BARRETT.

NOTES AND QUESTIONS

1. Consider first the federal government's responsibility for the conduct of the wild horses here. Who owns these animals? See note 3 following Kleppe v. New Mexico, *supra* p. 169, discussing the idea of states owning wildlife within their borders. Is ownership relevant to a takings claim like that asserted here? *See generally* Michael C. Blumm and Lucus Ritchie, *The Pioneer Spirit and the Public Trust: The American Rule of Capture and State Ownership of Wildlife*, 35 ENVTL. L. 673, 718–19 (2005). Regardless of technical "ownership," can the horses be considered a federal instrumentality for purposes of takings analysis? Compare the majority and dissenting opinions on this point. How should the concept of ownership affect a takings analysis?

2. Takings cases involving damage caused by governmentally protected wildlife go back many decades, and the majority rule is as described in the majority opinion here—the government is generally immune. For a thorough review of the law in this area, see John Echeverria and Julie Lurman, *"Perfectly Astounding" Public Rights: Wildlife Protection and the Takings Clause*, 16 TULANE ENVTL. L.J. 331 (2003).

3. Is the reason the government protected the horses relevant to the takings question? One of the prongs of the regulatory takings test adopted

by the Supreme Court in Penn Central Transp. Co. v. New York City, 438 U.S. 104 (1978) involved a consideration of the "character of the government action." Would it or should it be easier to find a taking here if the United States was protecting the wild horses' freedom to roam on and off federal land in order eventually to capture and sell them to pet food manufacturers?

4.   Is it fair to impose the costs of feeding the (foraging) wild horses and burros on the adjacent private landowners, when the benefits are much more widely shared? The Rock Springs landowners believed that if the United States wanted to maintain the "noxious herbivores," then it should pay for the forage consumed. Is the constitutional law of takings about fairness? Is it about good governance? Would Congress have considered the statutory program more thoroughly if the United States had to pay for the forage consumed?

Sometimes legislatures offer compensation as a matter of policy even when not compelled by the constitution. For instance, when the Congress decided to expand Redwood National Park by acquiring adjacent property from private landowners, it not only paid for the property, but also established a compensation program for timber industry workers adversely affected. See 92 Stat. 173 (1978). Local sawmills which were adversely affected did not qualify for aid, however, and their claim of a taking was rejected because their loss was merely "an expectancy" that they would continue to receive raw materials from the lands involved. PVM Redwood Co., Inc. v. United States, 686 F.2d 1327 (9th Cir.1982),. If the government chooses to pay private property owners rather than regulate them to serve some public end, does that undermine the regulatory system in the long run, with dire consequences for the public good? For a thorough exploration of the arguments pro and con, see John D. Echeverria, *Regulating Versus Paying Land Owners to Protect the Environment*, 26 J. Land, Resources & Envtl. L. 1 (2005).

If the government often pays property owners to protect the environment instead of regulating them, does that make it easier to find a taking when the government decides to regulate rather than pay? Justice Scalia suggested the answer was yes in Lucas, 505 U.S. at 1018–19 ("[t]he many statutes on the books ... that provide for the use of eminent domain to impose servitudes on private scenic lands preventing developmental uses, or to acquire such lands altogether, suggest the practical equivalence in this setting of negative regulation and appropriation"). Is what the government chooses to do regarding compensation in one circumstance relevant to the courts assessing in another circumstance whether a taking has occurred?

5.   Is it relevant that when the ranchers acquired title to their property in the checkerboard, wild horses were unprotected by federal law? Suppose, in fact, that when they acquired their property, there were no wild horses in the area, because they had been extirpated decades earlier. And suppose the federal government had recently reintroduced wild horses to the federal lands as part of a program to "restore western heritage." In Moerman v. State, 21 Cal.Rptr. 2d 329 (Cal.Ct.App.1993), the court rejected a takings claim brought by a landowner seeking compensation for destruction of fences and loss of forage on his property caused by elk introduced in

the vicinity under a state wildlife restoration program. The court found that the state's general immunity from paying for destruction caused by state-protected wild animals was not affected by the fact that the state wildlife agency captured, tagged, released, and monitored the elk.

6. The majority opinion in the principal case contained a footnote (#8) which pointed out that the federal Endangered Species Act (ESA) allows a person to kill a protected species like a grizzly bear in order to protect people from bodily harm, 16 U.S.C. § 1504(a)(3), (b)(3), but, by implication, not to protect property like sheep. The court went on to say:

> Several state courts have held that, as a matter of state constitutional law, a person may kill wildlife contrary to the state's conservation laws where such action is necessary to protect his property. See, e.g., Cross v. State, 370 P.2d 371 (Wyo. 1962). No case has yet addressed whether a similar right exists under the United States Constitution, though the bodily injury defense contained in the Endangered Species Act suggests a congressional view it does not.

In Christy v. Hodel, 857 F.2d 1324 (9th Cir.1988), *cert. denied*, 490 U.S. 1114 (1989), a rancher was fined for violating the ESA by killing a grizzly bear that apparently had killed his sheep. The court upheld the conviction and rejected the argument that it violated the rancher's constitutional rights:

> The U.S. Constitution does not explicitly recognize a right to kill federally protected wildlife in defense of property. * * * In light of the Supreme Court's admonition [in Bowers v. Hardwick, 478 U.S. 186, 194 (1986)] that we exercise restraint in creating new definitions of substantive due process, we decline plaintiffs' invitation to [so] construe the fifth amendment. * * * [Therefore] we are not required to subject the ESA and the grizzly bear regulation to strict scrutiny. Instead, we must determine whether those enactments rationally further a legitimate governmental objective.

Relying in part on the *Mountain States* case, the court rejected Christy's takings argument, finding that the rancher's loss was "the incidental, and by no means inevitable, result of reasonable regulation in the public interest." As a result of this decision, Mr. Christy has become a poster child for advocates of expanded protections for property rights, as well as for opponents of the ESA.

7. What if domesticated animals, and not wildlife, cause the damage? Alves owned land and had federal grazing permits on intermingled federal land, much like the ranchers in Mountain States. He brought suit for a taking, alleging that the Interior Department failed to keep cattle owned by neighboring Indians from trespassing on and damaging his private land. (The Indians, the Dann sisters, claimed a right to the land under aboriginal title) The court denied relief, holding that the government was not responsible for the trespass:

> [The BLM's] regulatory control over the Danns' livestock does not change the fact that the livestock are properly controlled in the first instance by the Danns, and that Alves' complaint is with the Danns,

not the government. The government is not an insurer that private citizens will act lawfully with respect to property subject to governmental regulation merely because the government has chosen to regulate with respect to grazing on public lands.

Alves v. United Stats, 133 F.3d 1454, 1458 (Fed. Cir. 1998). Is this the correct result? See also Colvin Cattle Co. v. United States, 468 F.3d 803, 809 (Fed.Cir. 2006) (U.S. not liable when grazing permittee's cows allegedly infringe on predecessor rancher's water rights on federal lands).

8. Is the property right at stake here the ranchers' grass, or is it their land as a whole? Suppose, as is almost always the case, the ranchers' land had other economically viable uses; e.g., that the ranchers could have used their grazing land for farming, houses, or businesses? In *Penn Central*, Justice Brennan's majority opinion unequivocally rejected the railroad's claim that the property interest to be considered was its "air rights" to build a skyscraper over Grand Central Station: " 'Taking' jurisprudence does not divide a single parcel into discrete segments and attempt to determine whether rights in a particular segment have been entirely abrogated. In deciding whether a particular governmental action has effected a taking, this Court focuses rather both on the character of the action and on the nature and extent of the interference with rights in the parcel as a whole * * *." 438 U.S. at 131. In *Lucas*, Justice Scalia's majority opinion included a footnote (#7) in which he speculated, in dictum, that the "parcel as a whole" rule might not always obtain, and that it might depend on

> how the owner's reasonable expectations have been shaped by the State's law of property—i.e., whether and to what degree the State's law has accorded legal recognition and protection to the particular interest in land with respect to which the takings claimant alleges a diminution in (or elimination of) value. In any event, we avoid this difficulty in the present case, since the "interest in land" that Lucas has pleaded (a fee simple interest) is an estate with a rich tradition of protection at common law, and since the [trial court found the state regulation] left each of Lucas's beachfront lots without economic value.

More recently, however, the Court reaffirmed the "parcel as a whole" rule by a 6–3 margin, rejecting a landowner's argument that a regional land use agency's temporary (if lengthy) total moratorium on all new construction while it prepared a comprehensive land use plan for the Lake Tahoe basin was a per se taking. The majority said the argument "ignores *Penn Central*'s admonition that in regulatory takings cases we must focus on 'the parcel as a whole.' " Tahoe–Sierra Preservation Council, Inc. v. Tahoe Regional Planning Agency, 535 U.S. 302, 331 (2002). But, how shall the "whole" be determined? Suppose U–Corp has fifty federal mining claims on BLM in Utah, and BLM rejects its plan to develop one claim but approves its plan to develop the others. Has there been a taking? Cf. Naegele Outdoor Advertising v. City of Durham, 803 F. Supp. 1068, 1073–74 (M.D.N.C. 1992) (billboard company's unit of property for purposes of takings analysis is all its billboards in a metropolitan area).

9. Could the ranchers here have argued that the government (through the protected horses) had "permanently physically occupied" their grass, and thus were liable under the per se rule of the *Loretto* case, discussed in the introduction to this section? In 1937 Stearns conveyed land to the United States but reserved the right to coal and some other minerals. The land was included in the Daniel Boone National Forest. The 1977 Surface Mining Control and Reclamation Act (SMCRA, pronounced "smack-ra") forbade most mining in national forests, subject to valid existing rights and certain other exceptions. After the government ruled that Stearns had no valid existing rights (because he did not hold regulatory permits to mine coal as of 1977), and without attempting to qualify under the other exceptions, Stearns brought a takings suit and argued that the 1977 Act had physically occupied the minerals he had reserved. Claims Court Judge Smith, known for his expansive property rights rulings, agreed. The Federal Circuit curtly reversed, quoting numerous precedents for the proposition that a physical taking occurs "when the government itself occupies the property or requires the landowner to submit to physical occupation of its land." Neither happened to Stearns. Thus the argument was "little more than an incredible attempt to transform a regulatory taking claim into a per se physical taking." The court then held that the regulatory taking was not ripe because Stearns had not applied for an exception under the Act. Stearns Co. Ltd. v. United States, 396 F.3d 1354 (Fed.Cir.2005). *See also* Palazzolo v. Rhode Island 533 U.S. 606, 617 (2001) (a physical taking occurs "when the government encroaches upon or occupies private land for its own proposed use"). Despite the narrowness of the "physical occupation" rule, is there an argument here that the Wild, Free–Roaming Horses and Burros Act actually required the rancher/landowner to submit to a physical occupation of its land by the horses? Is the answer that the horses are not a government agent or instrumentality? Is that a sufficient answer?

10. The Wild, Free–Roaming Horses and Burros Act requires the Secretary to remove wild horses and burros that stray from public lands onto privately owned land. The lower court in Mountain States Legal Foundation v. Hodel issued a writ of mandamus requiring the Secretary to effect removal, and the U.S. did not appeal. Is that relevant to the "takings" issue? Does it provide the landowner with a remedy other than compensation? But what about the damage the horses caused to the ranchers' forage before they were removed? A temporary denial of all use might be compensable under some circumstances but not others. *Compare* First English Evangelical Lutheran Church of Glendale v. County of Los Angeles, 482 U.S. 304 (1987), *with* Tahoe–Sierra Preservation Council, Inc. v. Tahoe Regional Planning Agency, 535 U.S. 302 (2002). For a recent discussion of temporary takings, see Bass Enterprises Prod. Co. v. United States, 381 F.3d 1360 (Fed.Cir.2004) (45–month delay in making a decision whether to grant a federal oil and gas lessee a permit to drill the lease was not a temporary taking, but was justified by the circumstances, which involved uncertainty about whether the drilling would cause the release of radioactive materials from an underground nuclear waste storage facility).

11. Another way to think about *Mountain States* is this: Who has the duty to fence—the U.S. or the rancher? In United States ex rel. Bergen v. Lawrence, *infra* p. 383, the Tenth Circuit rejected the rancher's argument that requiring him to remove a fence on his land (or to modify it to allow antelope to pass through to checkerboarded public lands enclosed by the rancher's fence) was a taking requiring compensation. It noted, first, that his antelope-proof fence had effectively been declared a nuisance by the federal Unlawful Inclosures Act to the extent it enclosed federal lands. The Tenth Circuit followed the principal case here in finding that antelope foraging in the checkerboarded area was not a taking. It also noted that the evidentiary record indicated that competition for forage between antelope and cattle was "minimal," and that Lawrence retained the right to exclude antelope from his private land so long as he could do so without "effecting an enclosure of the public lands." *See* 848 F.2d at 1507–08.

12. One useful way for the United States to deal with inholding problems that abound on federal land is to enact a law giving itself a right of first refusal on any private property offered for sale whose use might affect federal lands. The Boundary Waters Canoe Area Wilderness Act gave the United States a right of first refusal at any sale of a nonfederal inholding in the area. The owner of an inholding argued that this provision "took" his property by creating a cloud on his title, deterring potential buyers, and allegedly diminishing its value. In support of the landowner, Minnesota argued that the option on the property created by the statute was itself a property interest "taken" by the United States. The court rejected both arguments:

> In our view, the mere conditioning of the sale of property * * * cannot rise to the level of a taking. Even if some diminution in value results * * * any effect on the landowner's aggregate property rights would be minimal. Section 5(c) does not interfere with the owner's use or enjoyment of his property; it does not compel the surrender of the land or any portion thereof; it does not affect the owner's ability to give his property or to transfer it in any manner to members of his immediate family. Section 5(c) may affect slightly an owner's ability to alienate property, but it has little effect on even that "strand" in the bundle of property rights.

Minnesota v. Block, 660 F.2d 1240, 1255–56 (8th Cir. 1981).

NOTE: PRIVATE PROPERTY INTERESTS IN FEDERAL LANDS

In *Mountain States*, as in most takings litigation, the plaintiff holds private property in fee simple. "Background principles" of property or nuisance law might justify the government's protecting wildlife even with some harm to plaintiff's fee interest. Other than that possibility, however, there is little doubt that plaintiff has a constitutionally protected property interest. Where the plaintiff claims that it has a property interest on federal lands that has been taken by governmental action, by contrast, the analysis is somewhat different: There is often a threshold question as to the existence and character of the property interest alleged to have been taken.

If the alleged property interest in federal lands does not exist, the government has no constitutional duty to provide compensation. Also, the property interest may be in the form of a contract, in which case contract principles rather than constitutional takings principles will usually be applied (a matter dealt with in the next section of this chapter). Finally, even where the plaintiff can legitimately claim a property interest in federal lands, the character of that interest, and of the legitimate investment-backed expectations that underlay it, may be limited. That may frequently tip the balance in the *Penn Central* analysis against finding that a taking has occurred.

Put another way, the law that applies to the federal government's regulation of private property held in fee simple to protect U.S. interests in public lands is a relatively straightforward application of regulatory takings generally. The matter is more complex when the government is regulating a property interest that consists of a less-than-fee interest in federal land. Note that state or federal law may define the contours of such a claimed property interest.

As discussed in more detail in Chapter 9, federal grazing permits are not compensable property rights. On the other hand, in *Mountain States* (as well as in *Penn Central* and most regulatory takings cases) the property interest was defined by state law. In some cases, the property right might be defined by a mixture of federal and state law. For example, in Leo Sheep v. United States, *infra* p. 375, the rancher's private property interest initially came into being through federal law (a grant of federal land to a railroad, subject to some continuing limitations of federal law), but it became a fee interest whose attributes were presumably at least partially controlled by Wyoming law.

In general, the nature and quantum of private rights (if any) in federal lands and resources vary with the mechanisms chosen by Congress to allocate those lands and resources. In United States v. Locke, 471 U.S. 84 (1985) (discussed as a principal case in Chapter 7, *infra* p. 585), the property interest at stake was a federal mining claim. The Court held that the government's power to regulate

> is particularly broad with respect to the "character" of the property rights at issue here. Although owners of unpatented mining claims hold fully recognized possessory interests in their claims, we have recognized that these interests are a "unique form of property." * * * The United States, as owner of the underlying fee title to the public domain, maintains broad powers over the terms and conditions upon which the public lands can be used, leased, and acquired. *See, e.g.,* Kleppe v. New Mexico, 426 U.S. 529, 539 (1976). * * * Claimants thus take their mineral interests with the knowledge that the Government retains substantial regulatory power over those interests. * * *

In Rith Energy v. United States, 247 F.3d 1355, *rehearing denied* 270 F.3d 1347 (Fed.Cir.2001), the court found no categorical taking when federal regulators suspended a company's mining permit upon learning that it was encountering high levels of materials that could pollute the groundwater in the area through what is known as "acid mine drainage."

The court observed that because coal mining is a "highly regulated indus-try, the plaintiff's reasonable investment-backed expectations are an espe-cially important consideration in the takings calculus," and the "likelihood of regulatory restraint is especially high with regard to possible adverse environmental effects, such as potentially harmful runoff from the mining operations, which have long been regarded as proper subjects for the exercise of the state's police power." Should the courts adopt a presump-tion in takings cases that commercial businesses operating on federal lands should have little or no commercial expectation that they will be free from new regulatory burdens, especially those designed to protect the environ-ment?

NOTES AND QUESTIONS

1.   Another section of FLPMA, adopted in 1976, called for BLM to survey its lands and to classify those tracts over 5000 acres with "wilder-ness characteristics" as "wilderness study areas" (WSAs). FLPMA also required that these WSAs generally be managed "so as not to impair [their] suitability for preservation as wilderness" by Congress, subject to some exceptions. 43 U.S.C. § 1982. BLM had interpreted this provision to allow the location of new mining claims in WSAs, but to subject any activities on these claims to a "no impairment" standard. (*See* Chapter 12 12A(3)(b).) A(3)(b).) In 1996 Reeves located forty mining claims in an area of Utah that BLM had sixteen years earlier designated as the Carcass Canyon WSA. Reeves then applied to BLM to conduct mineral activities on the claims. BLM denied the application because the proposal would cause surface disturbance that would violate the "no impairment" standard. Reeves brought a takings claim. In Reeves v. United States, 54 Fed.Cl. 652 (2002), the court found no taking because the plaintiff's property interest in these particular mining claims was very limited; namely, to hold and use the claims in a manner than did not impair wilderness suitability pending congressional decision. Whatever property rights the plaintiff might have had in mining claims located prior to 1976 was irrelevant because FLPMA "superseded" the Mining Law on this point, limiting the rights of holders of mining claims located in WSAs after FLPMA was enacted.

2.   What if, on the facts of *Reeves* (preceding paragraph), Snow had located these mining claims in 1975 (prior to FLPMA), and Reeves had purchased them from Snow in 1996? Could the government argue that Reeves should be held to notice that the claims he was purchasing were encumbered by the FLPMA requirement of "no impairment," and there-fore no taking could occur? In Palazzolo v. Rhode Island, 533 U.S. 606 (2001), a property owner claimed that the state had taken his property by denying his requests to fill and develop wetlands. The lower court held no taking because the plaintiff took title after the state had adopted its wetlands protection law and thus must be deemed to have notice of it. The Supreme Court reversed, holding that the claim was not barred simply by the fact that he acquired title after the state wetlands protection law was enacted. Justice O'Connor, concurring (and the swing vote in the 5–4 decision), noted:

Today's holding does not mean that the timing of the regulation's enactment relative to the acquisition of title is immaterial to the *Penn Central* analysis. Indeed, it would be just as much error to expunge this consideration from the takings inquiry as it would be to accord it exclusive significance. * * * Interference with investment-backed expectations is one of a number of factors that a court must examine. Further, the regulatory regime in place at the time the claimant acquires the property at issue helps to shape the reasonableness of those expectations.

3.   In FLPMA, Congress ordered the Secretary of the Interior to "take any action necessary to prevent unnecessary or undue degradation" of the public lands, including from mining operations. 43 U.S.C. § 1732(b). Suppose the Bureau of Land Management determined that a mine operating on federal mining claims was contaminating water around the mine, or was seriously disrupting the sole habitat for an endangered species, and it ordered the mining claimant to take steps to protect the water quality or the habitat. The claimant determined it could not comply with these restrictions and still make a profit, so it shut the mine down. Does the claimant have an argument that its property interests in its mining claims have been taken by the government, and that compensation is owed? Can it argue a "total taking" of its entire property interest under the *Lucas* per se rule? The Supreme Court has suggested that the *Lucas* "total taking" rule may be limited to the total destruction of value of a full fee interest, not a lesser one. *See* Tahoe–Sierra Preservation Council, Inc. v. Tahoe Regional Planning Agency, 535 U.S. 302, 330 (2002) (referring to Lucas as establishing a rule for cases involving "permanent obliteration of the value of a fee simple estate").

4.   Property rights obtained by private persons in federal lands, where the United States retains the underlying title, are often quite narrow. For example, any property interest involved in a federal mining claim has to do with conducting mining activity. Similarly, whatever property right exists in a timber sale contract has to do with harvesting timber. Neither carries with it a right to engage in alternative uses, such as to build homes or ski areas. Thus, if the government effectively forbids the holder of a mining claim from mining, it is arguably, in Justice Scalia's words, "eliminating the [property interest's] only productive use." If the "total taking" per se rule of *Lucas* applies (see preceding paragraph), may the government still avoid paying compensation?

The answer is yes, if the government can invoke the exception to *Lucas's* per se compensation rule for "background principles" like nuisance law or other limitations found in property law. This raises the question of where and how "background principles" in federal public land law are to be found. Many of the background principles of state property and nuisance law were originally developed in the courts through common law adjudication. In federal public land law, generally speaking, both the private property interests and the government's authority to regulate their exercise are, and have long been, governed almost entirely by statute enacted by Congress. May it be said that federal statutes and administrative regulations implementing them are the "common law" of federal land and resource use for purposes of the *Lucas* analysis? *Cf.* Palazzolo v. Rhode Island, 533 U.S. 606, 629 (2001) ("we have no occasion to consider the precise circumstances when a legislative enactment can be deemed a background principle of state law"). Like the common law, statutes may change over time. Is, for example, the "unnecessary or undue degradation" prohibition in FLPMA a "background principle" that qualifies all mining claims located after it was enacted? On background principles generally, see Michael C. Blumm and Lucus Ritchie, *Lucas's Unlikely Legacy: The Rise of Background Principles as Categorical Takings Defenses*, 29 HARV. ENVTL. L.REV. 321 (2005).

5. Sometimes Congress deflects takings issues with statutory language. Typical is the disclaimer in § 701(h) of FLPMA: "All actions by the Secretary * * * under this Act shall be subject to valid existing rights." This so-called VER language has proved extremely handy and is exceedingly common in federal law. What are "valid existing rights"? Only property rights that are compensable under the Fifth Amendment? Or does the concept encompass an expectancy or other interest that does not rise to the level of compensability under the Constitution? Further, what does "subject to" mean? Does it mean that the Secretary cannot take action under the new regulatory regime that could affect in any way the exercise of such rights? Or does it mean the Secretary may apply new regulations to the exercise of the rights right up to the constitutional limit; i.e., is this a shorthand for saying the Secretary can regulate the exercise of these rights up to the point of burdening their exercise so heavily as to effect a regulatory taking? What is the remedy if the Secretary does not properly respect such "valid existing rights"? An injunction restraining secretarial action? Or compensation? The courts have not provided clear answers to these questions. See, e.g., Stupak–Thrall v. United States, 81 F.3d 651 (6th Cir.), *aff'd by equally divided en banc court*, 89 F.3d 1269 (6th Cir. 1996).

6. The Claims Court has issued sharply inconsistent decisions on whether federal restrictions on water supply to comply with the ESA may constitute a taking. *Compare* Tulare Lake Basin Water District v. United States, 49 Fed. Cl. 313 (2001) (taking found on physical occupation theory), *with* Klamath Irr. Dist. v. United States, 67 Fed. Cl. 504 (2005) (disagreeing). After the Bush Administration decided to pay the takings claimant in *Tulare Lake* rather than appeal, the judge who decided *Tulare Lake* changed his mind, concluding in another water rights takings case that his earlier application of a physical occupation theory could not withstand scrutiny against the Supreme Court's 2002 decision in *Tahoe–Sierra, supra* note 3. Casitas Mun. Water Dist. v. United States, 76 Fed.Cl.100 (Fed. Cl. 2007). *See generally* John D. Leshy, *A Conversation About Takings and Water Rights*, 83 TEXAS L.REV. 1985 (2005).

7. Some businesses disadvantaged by government regulation are pursuing an alternative to constitutional takings liability, by seeking compensation under international trade agreements like NAFTA (the North American Free Trade Agreement). Modern trade agreements typically contain provisions such as, "[n]o party may directly or indirectly take a measure

tantamount to nationalization or expropriation of an investment of an investor of another party without paying just compensation." Foreign companies are increasingly making the argument that an environmental regulation which renders an investment unprofitable is such an indirect nationalization, requiring compensation. One pending case involves federal land. A Canadian company, Glamis Gold Co., is seeking compensation for being thwarted in its plans to develop an open-pit, cyanide, heap-leach goldmine on public lands in the California desert. The U.S. State Department is, so far, resisting the claim for compensation, and further proceedings are pending. In May 2006, Glamis filed a 318 page brief (a "memorial" in NAFTA arbitration lingo) outlining its grounds for complaint.

2. CONTRACT RIGHTS

This section examines contractual limitations on the power of the government to regulate the development of public resources. As a general matter, much of the development of publicly owned resources like oil, gas, and timber is accomplished through contracts between the federal government and the private sector. These contracts can take many forms: leases (e.g., mineral leases governed by the Mineral Leasing Act); contracts of sale (e.g., national forest timber sale contracts); and concession contracts (e.g., National Park Service contracts with companies to run visitor facilities like hotels and restaurants). They are bilateral bargains where a private party undertakes to do something with governmental resources for the benefit of both the government and the other party. They usually involve financial terms. This section is included here because contractual remedies and compensation for contractual breach are closely related to takings issues, and because some constitutional notions are involved. The U.S. Constitution forbids states from enacting laws "impairing the Obligation of Contracts," Art. I, § 10, but it does not by its own terms apply to the federal government; nevertheless, as will be seen below, the courts have in some circumstances provided remedies other than through the takings clause when the national government has acted inconsistent with its contracts.

The Relationship Between Contract Liability and Takings Issues

"Contract rights are a form of property and as such may be taken ... provided that just compensation is paid." United States Trust Co. v. New Jersey, 431 U.S. 1, 19 n.16 (1977). Accordingly, it is well-settled that "[r]ights against the United States arising out of a contract with it are protected by the Fifth Amendment." Lynch v. United States, 292 U.S. 571, 579 (1934). But the broad pronouncement in *Lynch* should not be taken at face value. Although the Supreme Court has not definitively ruled on the matter, the Court of Appeals for the Federal Circuit has generally preferred to decide suits that the U.S. has violated the terms of a contract as contract actions rather than as takings actions. See, e.g., Sun Oil Co. v. United States, 572 F.2d 786, 818 (1978) ("interference with ... contractual rights generally gives rise to a breach claim not a taking claim").

Several reasons are offered for this: First, the United States is acting in its proprietary capacity rather than as a sovereign regulator when it enters into contracts. *See* Hughes Communications Galaxy, Inc. v. United States, 271 F.3d 1060, 1070 (Fed.Cir.2001) ("because the government acts in its commercial or proprietary capacity in entering contracts, rather than in its sovereign capacity ... remedies arise from the contracts themselves, rather than from the constitutional protection of private property rights"). Second, if the ultimate ruling is that the contract has not been breached, then ipso facto any property right it conveys has not been taken. If the U.S. has breached the contract, the contractual remedies, such as rescission and restitution or damages, would presumably be satisfactory compensation for any property right taken. Castle v. United States, 301 F.3d 1328, 1342 (Fed.Cir.2002) ("despite breaching the contract, the government did not take the plaintiffs' property because they retained 'the range of remedies associated with the vindication of a contract' [and] the contract promised either to regulate [plaintiffs] consistently with the contract's terms, or to pay damages for breach"). *See also* United States v. Winstar Corp., 518 U.S. 839, 919 (1996) (Scalia, J., concurring) ("[v]irtually *every* contract operates, not as a guarantee of particular future conduct, but as an assumption of liability in the event of nonperformance: 'The duty to keep a contract at common law means a prediction that you must pay damages if you do not keep it,—and nothing else' ") (emphasis in original).

Contracts Versus Permits

Contracts like mineral leases are often thought to be different from "permits," or governmental exercises of regulatory authority in the form of permission to take certain actions. The line between contracts and permits may, however, be indistinct. Some permits, like contracts, can involve financial terms and other mutual promises. Both permits and contracts are usually governed by a framework of statutes and regulations. Performance under both may be subject to the government's continuing police power. Ski areas on national forests are, for example, developed by private parties under a land use permit issued by the U.S. Forest Service. Then–Circuit Judge Stephen Breyer discussed whether such a "Term Permit" differed from a contract in Meadow Green–Wildcat Corp. v. Hathaway, 936 F.2d 601 (1st Cir.1991), involving a dispute between the federal agency and the permittee over how the permit fee should be calculated:

> This case turns on the meaning of [a provision] in a land use permit that the Forest Service issued to a ski resort owner. It raises a difficult question about the standard of review that a court should apply to the Forest Service's own interpretation of such a document. * * *

> In deciding the meaning of [the document] * * * are we to defer to the agency's interpretation of those words? In other words, are we to treat the Term Permit as if it were an agency regulation, or a statute in which Congress has delegated interpretive power to the administering body? See, e.g., Chevron v. Natural Resources Defense Council, Inc., 467 U.S. 837 (1984) (courts should defer to reasonable agency interpretations of statutes); Udall v. Tallman, 380 U.S. 1, 4 (1965) (courts should give controlling weight to reasonable agency interpretations of regulations). Or, should we treat the Permit like a contract that the

government might make with a private party, giving less weight to the agency's interpretation of the document's language, the meaning of which raises a "question of law?" * * *

We believe that for several reasons we should treat the Term Permit document rather like a contract for reviewing purposes. First, the Permit document itself reads like a contract. It provides long-term authority to use land in return for the permittee's payment of a rental fee. It is twenty-two pages long and contains a highly detailed set of terms and conditions. It uses contract-like language. * * * Both the Forest Supervisor and the permittee have signed the document, the latter placing his signature under the statement that he "accepts and will abide by" the document's "terms and conditions." We think the expectation of a person signing such a document is that its terms would bind both him and the Service. Although the terms of the document give the Service power to change various conditions, such as rental conditions, for the future, or even to revoke the Permit on 30 days notice, nothing in the document, or regulations, or authorizing statute suggests that the Service is to have some special advantage, not shared by the permittee, in interpreting the meaning of the document's terms. Indeed, it would seem surprising and unfair if the terms of this document, without so stating, bind the permittee but leave the other party (the Service) free to interpret those same terms as it wishes (limited only by the bounds of "reasonableness").

Second, the statutes that authorize the Forest Service to issue Term Permits state that their purpose is to allow the construction and operation of "hotels, resort, and other recreational structures," all facilities that "are * * * likely to require long-term financing." These phrases suggest that one function of the permit is to offer a permittee the security needed to raise many millions of dollars in investment. It is difficult to reconcile the Service's desire for "deference" to its interpretation of the Permit with this purpose. We do not see how a document, the terms of which one party remains comparatively free to interpret to its own advantage, can provide the other party (and its financial backers) the security, stability, or assurance a large and long-term investment would seem to require.

Third, the Service's official regulations treat the Term Permit as if it were a kind of contract. * * * [They] state that the Permit is "compensable according to its terms." 36 C.F.R. § 251.51. Moreover, these regulations define a Term Permit very much as they define a "lease," an instrument the terms of which bind the parties. * * * Although the regulations also state that the Government is free to "revoke" or "terminate" the Permit in the manner and for the reasons specified by the Permit, a contract that one party may terminate for specified reasons is no less a contract. * * *

* * * Thus, without holding that the Permit "is" a contract, or that courts should always consider it as such, we shall treat it like a contract for purposes of deciding how much weight to give the inter-

pretation one party (here the agency) offers for one of its nontechnical terms.

Many legal questions can arise as to the extent of the government's authority to regulate activities carried out under its contracts on federal lands without incurring liability. Concern about how the environment will be protected in contracted-for development of federal natural resources is frequently a trigger for such questions being raised. Many years may elapse between the date the contract is formulated and when activities actually take place on the ground. New information about environmental impacts of the action may become available which is different from what the parties assumed when the contract was entered. Because public resources are involved, and because the government's police power is so broad, there is usually no question about the authority of the government to nullify contract terms or require the other party to act or not act, even in ways allegedly inconsistent with the terms of the contract. Questions are often raised, however, about whether the government owes money for doing so. And a kind of feedback loop may operate, because if the government runs the risk of owing money if it regulates more, it may choose to regulate less. The following materials explore these issues.

Mobil Oil Exploration and Producing Southeast, Inc. v. United States

Supreme Court of the United States, 2000.
530 U.S. 604.

■ JUSTICE BREYER delivered the opinion of the Court.

Two oil companies, petitioners here, seek restitution of $156 million they paid the Government in return for lease contracts giving them rights to explore for and develop oil off the North Carolina coast. The rights were not absolute, but were conditioned on the companies' obtaining a set of further governmental permissions. The companies claim that the Government repudiated the contracts when it denied them certain elements of the permission-seeking opportunities that the contracts had promised. We agree that the Government broke its promise; it repudiated the contracts; and it must give the companies their money back.

A description at the outset of the few basic contract law principles applicable to this case will help the reader understand the significance of the complex factual circumstances that follow. "When the United States enters into contract relations, its rights and duties therein are governed generally by the law applicable to contracts between private individuals." United States v. Winstar Corp., 518 U.S. 839, 895 (1996) (plurality opinion). The Restatement of Contracts reflects many of the principles of contract law that are applicable to this case. As set forth in the Restatement of Contracts, the relevant principles specify that, when one party to a contract repudiates that contract, the other party "is entitled to restitution for any benefit that he has conferred on" the repudiating party "by way of part performance or reliance." Restatement (Second) of Contracts § 373 (1979) (hereinafter Restatement). The Restatement explains that "repudiation" is a "statement by the obligor to the obligee indicating that the obligor will commit a breach that would of itself give the obligee a claim for damages for total breach." Id., § 250. And "total breach" is a breach that "so substantially impairs the value of the contract to the injured party at the time of the breach that it is just in the circumstances to allow him to recover damages based on all his remaining rights to performance." Id., § 243.

As applied to this case, these principles amount to the following: If the Government said it would break, or did break, an important contractual promise, thereby "substantially impair[ing] the value of the contract[s]" to the companies, then (unless the companies waived their rights to restitution) the Government must give the companies their money back. And it must do so whether the contracts would, or would not, ultimately have proved financially beneficial to the companies. The Restatement illustrates this point as follows:

> "A contracts to sell a tract of land to B for $100,000. After B has made a part payment of $20,000, A wrongfully refuses to transfer title. B can recover the $20,000 in restitution. The result is the same even if the market price of the land is only $70,000, so that performance would have been disadvantageous to B." Id., § 373.

In 1981, in return for up-front "bonus" payments to the United States of about $158 million [eds: in original, but should be $156 million] (plus annual rental payments), the companies received 10–year renewable lease contracts with the United States. In these contracts, the United States promised the companies, among other things, that they could explore for oil off the North Carolina coast and develop any oil that they found (subject to further royalty payments) provided that the companies received exploration and development permissions in accordance with various statutes and regulations to which the lease contracts were made "subject."

The statutes and regulations, the terms of which in effect were incorporated into the contracts, made clear that obtaining the necessary permissions might not be an easy matter. [The governing statute, the Outer Continental Shelf Lands Act (OCSLA), contained several stages of exploration and development, each requiring government approval. Furthermore, a separate federal law, the Coastal Zone Management Act of 1972 (CZMA), also came into play and gave the pertinent coastal state(s) a near-complete veto over development. The process works like this:

1.   The lessee must obtain Interior approval of its plan of exploration. The statute says that Interior must approve the proposed plan unless it finds that it would "probably cause serious harm or damage" to the environment, among other things. Significantly, the statute requires Interior to make a decision on the proposed plan within 30 days of its submission.

2. The lessee must then obtain an exploratory well drilling permit from Interior, but it must first certify (under CZMA) that its exploration plan is consistent with the affected state's coastal zone management program. The state may object to the lessee's "consistency" assertion, in which case, Interior cannot grant a drilling permit until and unless the Secretary of Commerce overrides the State's objection. (Similarly, if the Clean Water Act requires the lessee to get a National Pollutant Discharge Elimination System (NPDES) permit from the Environmental Protection Agency, once again a state can object on the ground that the plan is inconsistent with the state's CZMA program, unless the Secretary of Commerce overrules the state's objection.)

3. If exploration is successful, the lessee must obtain Interior approval of its plan for developing and producing petroleum, and here too Interior's approval is conditioned upon a "consistency" certification to which States can object, subject to Commerce Department override.

Here, while the lessee was engaged in steps one and two, crafting its exploration plan for submission to Interior and attempting to persuade the state of North Carolina that its plan would be consistent with the state's coastal zone management program, a new federal law, the Outer Banks Protection Act (OBPA), took effect. The OBPA mandated a thirteen-month moratorium on any Interior approvals of actions on OCS leases off the eastern seaboard, to give time for (a) a new Environmental Sciences Review Panel to study and report to Interior on the possible impacts of development and ways to mitigate them, and (b) for Interior to consider them and explain to Congress any differences between Interior's determinations and the Panel's recommendations.

Two days after this Act took effect, Mobil formally submitted its exploration plan to Interior and certified that its plan was consistent with the State's coastal zone management program. Five weeks after that, Interior wrote the North Carolina Governor a letter stating that Mobil's exploration plan would have "only negligible effect on the environment" and "is deemed to be approvable in all respects," but informed the Governor that, because of the OBPA, it was not approving the plan at this time. Shortly after that, in November 1990, North Carolina objected to the companies' CZMA consistency certification on the ground that Mobil had not provided sufficient information about possible environmental impact. Mobil then asked the Secretary of Commerce to override North Carolina's objection.

Before the Secretary of Commerce ruled*, Mobil brought a suit against the United States for breach of contract. The trial judge in the Court of Federal Claims held for the companies, finding the government had repudiated the contracts and thus the companies were entitled to restitution of their "bonus" payments. The Federal Circuit reversed, holding that the State's objection to the companies' CZMA consistency statement would

---

* Eventually, the new review Panel created by the OBPA found a lack of adequate information with respect to certain environmental issues, and the Secretary of Commerce rejected Mobil's request to override North Carolina's objection. In 1996, Congress repealed OBPA.

have prevented the companies from exploring regardless of the government's action. The Supreme Court granted certiorari.]

The record makes clear (1) that OCSLA required Interior to approve "within thirty days" a submitted Exploration Plan that satisfies OCSLA's requirements, (2) that Interior told Mobil the companies' submitted Plan met those requirements, (3) that Interior told Mobil it would not approve the companies' submitted Plan for at least 13 months, and likely longer, and (4) that Interior did not approve (or disapprove) the Plan, ever. The Government does not deny that the contracts, made "pursuant to" and "subject to" OCSLA, incorporated OCSLA provisions as promises. The Government further concedes, as it must, that relevant contract law entitles a contracting party to restitution if the other party "substantially" breached a contract or communicated its intent to do so. See Restatement § 373(1). Yet the Government denies that it must refund the companies' money.

This is because, in the Government's view, it did not breach the contracts or communicate its intent to do so; any breach was not "substantial"; and the companies waived their rights to restitution regardless. We shall consider each of these arguments in turn.

The Government's "no breach" arguments depend upon the contract provisions that "subject" the contracts to various statutes and regulations. Those provisions state that the contracts are "subject to" (1) OCSLA, (2) "Sections 302 and 303 of the Department of Energy Organization Act," (3) "all regulations issued pursuant to such statutes and in existence upon the effective date of" the contracts, (4) "all regulations issued pursuant to such statutes in the future which provide for the prevention of waste and the conservation" of Outer Continental Shelf resources, and (5) "all other applicable statutes and regulations." The Government says that these provisions incorporate into the contracts, not only the OCSLA provisions we have mentioned, but also certain other statutory provisions and regulations that, in the Government's view, granted Interior the legal authority to refuse to approve the submitted Exploration Plan, while suspending the leases instead. * * *

[T]he Government refers to 30 CFR § 250.110(b)(4) (1999), a regulation stating that "[t]he Regional Supervisor may ... direct ... a suspension of any operation or activity ... [when the] suspension is necessary for the implementation of the requirements of the National Environmental Policy Act or to conduct an environmental analysis." The Government says that this regulation permitted the Secretary of the Interior to suspend the companies' leases because that suspension was "necessary ... to conduct an environmental analysis," namely, the analysis demanded by the new statute, OBPA.

The "environmental analysis" referred to, however, is an analysis the need for which was created by OBPA, a later enacted statute. The lease contracts say that they are subject to then-existing regulations and to certain future regulations, those issued pursuant to OCSLA and §§ 302 and 303 of the Department of Energy Organization Act. This explicit reference to future regulations makes it clear that the catchall provision that references "all other applicable . . . regulations," must include only statutes and regulations already existing at the time of the contract, a conclusion not questioned here by the Government. Hence, these provisions mean that the contracts are not subject to future regulations promulgated under other statutes, such as new statutes like OBPA. Without some such contractual provision limiting the Government's power to impose new and different requirements, the companies would have spent $158 million to buy next to nothing. In any event, the Court of Claims so interpreted the lease; the Federal Circuit did not disagree with that interpretation; nor does the Government here dispute it.

Instead, the Government points out that the regulation in question—the regulation authorizing a governmental suspension in order to conduct "an environmental analysis"—was not itself a future regulation. Rather, a similar regulation existed at the time the parties signed the contracts, 30 CFR § 250.12(a)(iv) (1981), and, in any event, it was promulgated under OCSLA, a statute exempted from the contracts' temporal restriction. But that fact, while true, is not sufficient to produce the incorporation of future statutory requirements, which is what the Government needs to prevail. If the pre-existing regulation's words, "an environmental analysis," were to apply to analyses mandated by future statutes, then they would make the companies subject to the same unknown future requirements that the contracts' specific temporal restrictions were intended to avoid. Consequently, whatever the regulation's words might mean in other contexts, we believe the contracts before us must be interpreted as excluding the words "environmental analysis" insofar as those words would incorporate the requirements of future statutes and future regulations excluded by the contracts' provisions. Hence, they would not incorporate into the contracts requirements imposed by a new statute such as OBPA.

* * * [The Government also relies on] OCSLA, 43 U.S.C. § 1334(a)(1), which, after granting Interior rulemaking authority, says that Interior's

> "regulations . . . shall include . . . provisions . . . for the suspension . . . of any operation . . . pursuant to any lease . . . *if there is a threat of serious*, irreparable, or immediate harm or damage to life . . ., to property, to any mineral deposits . . ., or to the marine, coastal, or *human environment*." (Emphasis added.)

The Government points to the OBPA Conference Report, which says that any OBPA-caused delay is "related to . . . environmental protection" and to the need "for the collection and analysis of crucial oceanographic, ecological, and socioeconomic data," to "prevent a public harm." H.R. Conf. Rep. No. 101–653, p. 163 (1990). * * * OBPA mentions "tourism" in North Carolina as a "major industry . . . which is subject to potentially significant disruption by offshore oil or gas development." § 6003(b)(3). From this, the Government infers that the pre-existing OCSLA provision authorized the suspension in light of a "threat of . . . serious harm" to a "human environment."

The fatal flaw in this argument, however, arises out of the Interior Department's own statement—a statement made when citing OBPA to explain its approval delay. Interior then said that the Exploration Plan "fully complies" with current legal requirements. And the OCSLA statutory provision quoted above was the most pertinent of those current requirements. * * * Insofar as the Government means to suggest that the new statute, OBPA, changed the relevant OCSLA standard (or that OBPA language and history somehow constitute findings Interior must incorporate by reference), it must mean that OBPA in effect created a new requirement. For the reasons set out supra, however, any such new requirement would not be incorporated into the contracts. * * *

We conclude, for these reasons, that the Government violated the contracts. Indeed, as Interior pointed out in its letter to North Carolina, the new statute, OBPA, required Interior to impose the contract-violating delay. * * *

* * * OBPA changed pre-existing contract-incorporated requirements in several ways. It delayed approval, not only of an Exploration Plan but also of Development and Production Plans; and it delayed the issuance of drilling permits as well. It created a new type of Interior Department environmental review that had not previously existed, conducted by the newly created Environmental Sciences Review Panel; and, by insisting that the Secretary explain in detail any differences between the Secretary's findings and those of the Panel, it created a kind of presumption in favor of the new Panel's findings.

The dissent argues that only the statements contained in the letter from Interior to the companies may constitute a repudiation because "the enactment of legislation is not typically conceived of as a 'statement' of anything to any one party in particular," and a repudiation requires a "statement by the obligor to the obligee indicating that the obligor will commit a breach." (quoting Restatement § 250). But if legislation passed by Congress and signed by the President is not a "statement by the obligor," it is difficult to imagine what would constitute such a statement. In this case, it was the United States who was the "obligor" to the contract. * * * Although the dissent points out that legislation is "addressed to the public at large," * * * that "public" includes those to whom the United States had contractual obligations. If the dissent means to invoke a special exception such as the "sovereign acts" doctrine, which treats certain laws as if they simply created conditions of impossibility, it cannot do so here. The Court of Federal Claims rejected the application of that doctrine to this case, and the Government has not contested that determination here. Hence, under these circumstances, the fact that Interior's repudiation rested upon the enactment of a new statute makes no significant difference.

We do not say that the changes made by the statute were unjustified. We say only that they were changes of a kind that the contracts did not foresee. They were changes in those approval procedures and standards that the contracts had incorporated through cross-reference. The Government has not convinced us that Interior's actions were authorized by any other contractually cross-referenced provision. Hence, in communicating to the companies its intent to follow OBPA, the United States was communicating its intent to violate the contracts.

The Government next argues that any violation of the contracts' terms was not significant; hence there was no "substantial" or "material" breach that could have amounted to a "repudiation." In particular, it says that OCSLA's 30–day approval period "does not function as the 'essence' of these agreements." The Court of Claims concluded, however, that timely and fair consideration of a submitted Exploration Plan was a "necessary reciprocal obligation," indeed, that any "contrary interpretation would render the bargain illusory." We agree.

We recognize that the lease contracts gave the companies more than rights to obtain approvals. They also gave the companies rights to explore for, and to develop, oil. But the need to obtain Government approvals so qualified the likely future enjoyment of the exploration and development rights that the contract, in practice, amounted primarily to an opportunity to try to obtain exploration and development rights in accordance with the procedures and under the standards specified in the cross-referenced statutes and regulations. Under these circumstances, if the companies did not at least buy a promise that the Government would not deviate significantly from those procedures and standards, then what did they buy?

The Government's modification of the contract-incorporated processes was not technical or insubstantial. It did not announce an (OBPA-required) approval delay of a few days or weeks, but of 13 months minimum, and likely much longer. The delay turned out to be at least four years. And lengthy delays matter, particularly where several successive agency approvals are at stake. Whether an applicant approaches Commerce with an Interior Department approval already in hand can make a difference (as can failure to have obtained that earlier approval). Moreover, as we have pointed out, OBPA changed the contract-referenced procedures in several other ways as well.

The upshot is that, under the contracts, the incorporated procedures and standards amounted to a gateway to the companies' enjoyment of all other rights. To significantly narrow that gateway violated material conditions in the contracts. The breach was "substantia[l]," depriving the companies of the benefit of their bargain. Restatement § 243. And the Government's communication of its intent to commit that breach amounted to a repudiation of the contracts.

The Government argues that the companies waived their rights to restitution. * * * Indeed, acceptance of performance under a once-repudiated contract can constitute a waiver of the right to restitution that repudiation would otherwise create.

The United States points to three events that, in its view, amount to continued performance of the contracts. But it does not persuade us. First, the oil companies submitted their Exploration Plan to Interior two days after OBPA became law. The performance question, however, is not just about what the oil companies did or requested, but also about what they actually received from the Government. And, in respect to the Exploration Plan, the companies received nothing.

Second, the companies subsequently asked the Secretary of Commerce to overturn North Carolina's objection to the companies' CZMA consistency certification. And, although the Secretary's eventual response was negative, the companies did at least receive that reply. The Secretary did not base his reply, however, upon application of the contracts' standards, but instead relied in large part on the findings of the new, OBPA-created, Environmental Sciences Review Panel. Consequently, we cannot say that the companies received from Commerce the kind of consideration for which their contracts called.

Third, the oil companies received suspensions of their leases (suspending annual rents and extending lease terms) pending the OBPA-mandated approval delays. However, a separate contract—the 1989 memorandum of understanding—entitled the companies to receive these suspensions. * * * And the Government has provided no convincing reason why we should consider the suspensions to amount to significant performance of the lease contracts in question.

We conclude that the companies did not receive significant postrepudiation performance. We consequently find that they did not waive their right to restitution.

Finally, the Government argues that repudiation could not have hurt the companies. Since the companies could not have met the CZMA consistency requirements, they could not have explored (or ultimately drilled) for oil in any event. Hence, OBPA caused them no damage. As the Government puts it, the companies have already received "such damages as were actually caused by the [Exploration Plan approval] delay," namely, none. This argument, however, misses the basic legal point. The oil companies do not seek damages for breach of contract. They seek restitution of their initial payments. Because the Government repudiated the lease contracts, the law entitles the companies to that restitution whether the contracts would, or would not, ultimately have produced a financial gain or led them to obtain a definite right to explore. If a lottery operator fails to deliver a purchased ticket, the purchaser can get his money back—whether or not he eventually would have won the lottery. And if one party to a contract, whether oil company or ordinary citizen, advances the other party money, principles of restitution normally require the latter, upon repudiation, to refund that money.

Contract law expresses no view about the wisdom of OBPA. We have examined only that statute's consistency with the promises that the earlier contracts contained. We find that the oil companies gave the United States $158 million [eds: in original, but should be $156 million] in return for a contractual promise to follow the terms of pre-existing statutes and regulations. The new statute prevented the Government from keeping that promise. The breach "substantially impair[ed] the value of the contract[s]." Id., § 243. And therefore the Government must give the companies their money back. * * *

■ JUSTICE STEVENS, dissenting.

Since the 1953 passage of the Outer Continental Shelf Lands Act (OCSLA), 43 U.S.C. § 1331 et seq., the United States Government has conducted more than a hundred lease sales of the type at stake today, and bidders have paid the United States more than $55 billion for the opportunity to develop the mineral resources made available under those leases. [Eds. This is the amount received in bonus bids at lease auction. Over the same time period, Justice Stevens pointed out in a footnote, the U.S. Treasury has received more than $64 billion on royalties from oil and gas production offshore.] The United States, as lessor, and petitioners, as lessees, clearly had a mutual interest in the successful exploration, development, and production of oil in the Manteo Unit pursuant to the leases executed in 1981. If production were achieved, the United States would benefit both from the substantial royalties it would receive and from the significant addition to the Nation's energy supply. Self-interest, as well as its duties under the leases, thus led the Government to expend substantial resources over the course of 19 years in the hope of seeing this project realized.

From the outset, however, it was apparent that the Outer Banks project might not succeed for a variety of reasons. Among those was the risk that the State of North Carolina would exercise its right to object to the completion of the project. That was a risk that the parties knowingly assumed. They did not, however, assume the risk that Congress would enact additional legislation that would delay the completion of what would obviously be a lengthy project in any event. I therefore agree with the Court that the Government did breach its contract with petitioners in failing to approve, within 30 days of its receipt, the plan of exploration petitioners submitted. As the Court describes, the leases incorporate the provisions of the OCSLA into their terms, and the OCSLA, correspondingly, sets down this 30–day requirement in plain language. 43 U.S.C. § 1340(c).

I do not, however, believe that the appropriate remedy for the Government's breach is for petitioners to recover their full initial investment. When the entire relationship between the parties is considered, with particular reference to the impact of North Carolina's foreseeable exercise of its right to object to the project, it is clear that the remedy ordered by the Court is excessive. I would hold that petitioners are entitled at best to damages resulting from the delay caused by the Government's failure to approve the plan within the requisite time.

* * * At the time of the Government's breach, petitioners had no reasonable expectation under the lease contract terms that the venture would come to fruition in the near future. Petitioners had known since 1988 that the State of North Carolina had substantial concerns about petitioners' proposed exploration; North Carolina had already officially objected to petitioners' NPDES submission—a required step itself dependent on the State's CZMA approval. At the same time, the Federal Government's own substantial investments of time and resources, as well as its extensive good-faith efforts both before and after the OBPA was passed to preserve the arrangement, gave petitioners the reasonable expec-

tation that the Government would continue trying to make the contract work. And indeed, both parties continued to behave consistently with that expectation.

While apparently recognizing that the substantiality of the Government's breach is a relevant question, the Court spends almost no time at all concluding that the breach was substantial enough to award petitioners a $156 million refund. * * * In the end, the Court's central reason for finding the breach "not technical or insubstantial" is that "lengthy delays matter." I certainly agree with that statement as a general principle. But in this action, that principle does not justify petitioners' request for restitution. On its face, petitioners' contention that time was "of the essence" in this bargain is difficult to accept; petitioners themselves waited seven years into the renewable 10–year lease term before even floating the Outer Banks proposal, and waited another two years after the OBPA was passed before filing this lawsuit. After then accepting a full 10 years of the Government's above-and-beyond-the-call performance, time is now suddenly of the essence? As with any venture of this magnitude, this undertaking was rife with possibilities for "lengthy delays," indeed "inordinate delays encountered by the lessee in obtaining required permits or consents, including administrative or judicial challenges or appeals," 30 CFR § 250.10(b)(6) (1990). The OBPA was not, to be sure, a cause for delay that petitioners may have anticipated in signing onto the lease. But the State's CZMA and NPDES objections, and the subsequent "inordinate delays" for appeals, certainly were. The Secretary's approval was indeed "a gateway to the companies' enjoyment of all other rights," but the critical word here is "a"; approval was only one gateway of many that the petitioners knew they had to get through in order to reap the benefit of the OCSLA leases, and even that gate was not closed completely, but only "narrow [ed]." Any long-term venture of this complexity and significance is bound to be a gamble. The fact that North Carolina was holding all the aces should not give petitioners the right now to play with an entirely new deck of cards.

The risk that North Carolina would frustrate performance of the leases executed in 1981 was foreseeable from the date the leases were signed. It seems clear to me that the State's objections, rather than the enactment of OBPA, is the primary explanation for petitioners' decision to take steps to avoid suffering the consequences of the bargain they made. As a result of the Court's action today, petitioners will enjoy a windfall reprieve that Congress foolishly provided them in its decision to pass legislation that, while validly responding to a political constituency that opposed the development of the Outer Banks, caused the Government to breach its own contract. Viewed in the context of the entire transaction, petitioners may well be entitled to a modest damages recovery for the two months of delay attributable to the Government's breach. But restitution is not a default remedy; it is available only when a court deems it, in all of the circumstances, just. A breach that itself caused at most a delay of two months in a protracted enterprise of this magnitude does not justify the $156 million draconian remedy that the Court delivers.

NOTES AND QUESTIONS

1.   Justice Breyer acknowledged that the lease did not give Mobil an absolute right to explore for and develop any oil and gas it found on the leased tract. Indeed, the lease merely conveyed the *"opportunity* to try to obtain" the necessary permits and leases under the procedures then in place. (Emphasis in original) The Court has reached the same conclusion with respect to federal mineral leases onshore; that is, a lease issued under the Mineral Leasing Act "does not give the lessee anything approaching the full ownership of a fee patentee, nor does it convey an unencumbered estate in the minerals." Boesche v. Udall, 373 U.S. 472, 477–78 (1963). Breyer used the limited nature of the rights conveyed by the government to justify requiring strict performance by the government. Might the limited nature of the rights be used the opposite way, to allow for enactment of the OBPA without causing a breach?

2.   How broad or narrow are the principles being applied here? Specifically, consider whether the outcome would have been different in the following circumstances:

A.   Suppose Interior, instead of telling Mobil its exploration plan was "approvable in all respects" but for the legislated moratorium in the Outer Banks Protection Act (OBPA), and found that it "will have only negligible effect on the environment," had told Mobil: "We have not finished our review of your exploration plan and have not made any determinations about its environmental effects, and now we must delay a final decision because of the moratorium in the OBPA"? Did Interior's decision to say what it did cost the federal treasury $156 million?

B.   Suppose the OCS Lands Act, the statute governing offshore oil development, had not required Interior to make a decision within 30 days of the company's submission of a proposed exploration plan. 43 U.S.C. § 1340(c)(1). Without a pre-existing statutory time frame, would the more careful scrutiny and delay called for by the OBPA have breached the lease?

3.   How significant is it that the government here took legislative action (the OBPA) that affects its own contracts, when it has a certain self-interest in the matter? The U.S. Constitution contains a provision preventing states (but not the federal government) from "impairing" the obligation of contracts (Art. I, § 10). But, as Professor Tribe has noted, the Court has applied the federal common law of contracts in some circumstances to prevent the national government from repudiating certain contractual obligations with private parties. Laurence H. Tribe, 1 American Constitutional Law 1366 (3d ed. 2000). This matter is explored below in the note on the "sovereign acts" doctrine.

4.   Does Justice Breyer adequately respond to dissenting Justice Stevens' point that because Mobil's ability to go forward with oil and gas exploration and development was so doubtful anyway, the incremental negative effect of the OBPA does not justify complete restitution of the $156 million Mobil paid? As a matter of contract law, is complete restitution automatic once a breach has been found, or is partial restitution

available as a remedy? Should the answer turn on ordinary principles of contract law; that is, whether complete restitution is automatic once a breach is found, or whether instead partial restitution is available as a remedy?

5.   When the OCS Lands Act was overhauled in 1978, a provision (43 U.S.C. § 1334(a)(2)) was added authorizing the Secretary of the Interior to cancel a lease for environmental reasons upon a determination that "(i) continued activity * * * would probably cause serious harm to * * * [the] environment; (ii) the threat of harm or damage will not disappear or decrease to an acceptable extent within a reasonable period of time; and (iii) the advantages of cancellation outweigh the advantages of continuing such lease or permit in force." If a lease issued after 1978 is cancelled under this provision, the lessee is entitled to receive the *lesser* of (1) the fair value of the canceled rights (taking into account all anticipated revenues and all costs, including liabilities for cleanup); or (2) the lessee's out-of-pocket direct expenditures (plus interest) made to acquire and explore and develop the leased tract, minus any revenues (plus interest) the lessee had obtained. (Any lease issued prior to the 1978 amendment cancelled under this provision would be compensated under the first, fair value of the canceled rights.) This cancellation-with-compensation feature has never been exercised and was therefore not at issue in *Mobil Oil*. Does it fairly resolve the tension between investment security and protection of the environment? Why wasn't its existence enough to satisfy those concerned about oil and gas development off North Carolina and persuade them to drop their opposition? If a lease is cancelled under this provision before serious exploration takes place, it may be difficult to appraise what the anticipated revenues would be; therefore, standard #2 would likely govern the measure of compensation.

6.   A somewhat similar situation arose off the left coast, in the Santa Barbara Channel off California. In the early 1980s, the Interior Department issued forty oil and gas leases in the area, taking $1.2 billion in bonus bids. California brought litigation challenging the issuance of the leases without a certification of "consistency" with state coastal zone management plans adopted under the federal Coastal Zone Management Act (CZMA), which had been enacted in 1972. The Supreme Court decided that merely issuing the leases (as compared to later approving exploration and development plans) did not "directly affect" California's coastal zone within the meaning of the CZMA, and thus did not require a consistency determination. Secretary of the Interior v. California, 464 U.S. 312 (1984). Congress responded to this decision in 1990 by amending the CZMA to broaden the circumstances where "consistency" was required. In the meantime, local opposition resulted in the Interior Department issuing a series of orders suspending activities on the forty leases. Eventually California sued the Interior Department to require a CZMA consistency determination on any further suspension orders, and won. California v. Norton, 311 F.3d 1162 (9th Cir. 2002). The oil companies then brought suit in the Claims Court, arguing that the 1990 amendment, as construed by the courts, effectively repudiated their leases, entitling them to rescission and restitution of their bonus bids. The Claims Court agreed in Amber Re-

sources v. United States, 68 Fed.Cl. 535 (Fed.Cl.2005), relying heavily on the Supreme Court's decision in *Mobil Oil*.

7. Outer continental shelf oil and gas development has become a very high-technology, expensive effort as rigs go into deeper water. In the Gulf of Mexico, for example, deepwater rigs may operate more than 200 miles offshore in 10,000 feet of water and drill through more than 20,000 feet of rock, salt and sand. A single well may cost upwards of $100 million. A production platform may cost several billion dollars. That enormous investment may reward richly. In the last several years there have been more than a dozen major commercial discoveries in the deepwater Gulf. The industry's environmental record in the Gulf has been excellent (no major spills because of effective blow-out prevention equipment), although its undersea gathering pipelines and some platforms suffered major damage in recent hurricanes. How should the size and scale and investment required influence the government as regulator and the courts in applying contract principles to these leases?

8. The following is based loosely on a real situation where billions of dollars may be at stake. Suppose that oil and gas leases issued by the Interior Department in deep (2000 feet) water on the outer continental shelf in the Gulf of Mexico have routinely contained a lease term that reduces the royalty the lessee pays to the government, except that if the price of oil rises above $50/barrel, the full royalty is payable. Suppose also that, due to bureaucratic error, leases issued for a period of months omitted the lease term that ends royalty relief when the price of oil exceeds $50/barrel. When apprised of this error, Congress enacts legislation forbidding the Interior Department from issuing any new federal lease to any holder of such a "defective" lease, unless the lessee agreed to amend the lease to provide, prospectively, for the payment of the full royalty when the price of oil is above $50/barrel. Assume the provision is challenged by the holder of a "defective" lease. Is the U.S. effectively breaching the contract embodied in the earlier lease, or is it merely exercising the discretion it has always retained to decide whether and to whom to issue leases? Does it make any difference whether any lessee knew of, or adjusted its bids in light of, this inadvertent omission in the (very lengthy) lease? That at the time the leases were issued without the provision, the price of oil was around $15 barrel?

What Should the Government Put In Its Leases?

Notice how carefully Justice Breyer parsed Mobil's lease to determine just what risks were assumed by the parties. For example, he found that the lease reserved authority for the government to apply some regulations adopted in the future to activities conducted by the lessee, but only regulations adopted under statutes in existence when the lease was issued, and not new statutes like the OBPA. In general, the Secretary of the Interior has broad authority to issue or not issue leases, and to include lease terms to protect the public interest. 30 U.S.C. § 187, discussed in Ventura County v. Gulf Oil Corp., *supra* p. 181. Suppose Mobil's lease included a term which made Mobil's actions under the lease subject to "all statutes, regulations and directives now in force *or hereafter adopted* which seek to protect the environment." *Cf.* Amfac Resorts v. U.S. Dept. of the Interior, 142 F.Supp. 2d 54, 78–80 (D.D.C.2001), *aff'd on other grounds,* 282 F.3d 818 (D.C.Cir.2002) (a provision in the Park Service's standard concession contract requiring the concessioner to comply with all present and future laws and regulations is not impermissibly ambiguous or illusory). Would that have led to a different outcome in this litigation?

An Interior Department regulation which is not a paragon of clarity defines the scope of the rights conveyed by an onshore oil and gas lease. 43 C.F.R. § 3101.1–2. It says the lessee "shall have the right to use so much of the leased lands as is necessary" to develop the minerals leased, subject to three qualifications. The first of these, the specific stipulations in the lease, is straightforward. The second is "restrictions deriving from specific, nondiscretionary statutes." Is the second qualification limited to "specific, nondiscretionary statutes" in place at the time the lease was issued, or does it include subsequently enacted statutes? Does the Supreme Court's decision in *Mobil Oil* offer any guidance on this point? Further, what might be examples of "specific, nondiscretionary statutes"? In Wyoming Outdoor Council v. Bosworth, 284 F.Supp.2d 81, 91–92 (D.D.C.2003), the court concluded that the Endangered Species Act was such a statute within the meaning of the regulation, which made the lessee's claim of right to develop the lease parcel "far from certain." What about the provision in FLPMA that the Secretary of the Interior "shall take *any action necessary* to prevent unnecessary or undue degradation of the [public] lands"? 43 U.S.C. § 1732(b) (emphasis added). It is nondiscretionary, but is it specific?

The third qualification in the Interior Department regulation is "such reasonable measures as may be required by the [supervising federal agency] to minimize adverse impacts to other resource values, land uses or users not addressed in the lease stipulations at the time operations are proposed." The regulation goes on to elaborate on the third qualification this way:

> *To the extent consistent with lease rights granted,* such reasonable measures may include, but are not limited to, modification to siting or design of facilities, timing of operations, and specification of interim and final reclamation measures. At a minimum, measures shall be deemed consistent with lease rights granted provided they do not: require relocation of proposed operations by more than 200 meters; require that operations be sited off the leasehold; or prohibit new surface disturbing operations for a period in excess of 60 days in any lease year.

The italicized phrase is found only in the third qualification. Does this suggest that specific, non-discretionary statutes referred to in the second qualification apply regardless of whether they are "consistent with the lease rights granted"?

Complicating matters a little more, the standard oil and gas lease form used by the Interior Department for a couple of decades contains some roughly similar, but hardly identical, language:

> Rights granted [under this lease] are subject to applicable laws, the terms, conditions, and ... stipulations of the lease, the Secretary of the Interior's regulations and formal orders in effect as of lease issuance, and to regulations and formal orders hereafter promulgated when not inconsistent with lease rights granted or specific provisions of the lease.

These provisions may all be reconciled, but it is not easy. For example, does the phrase "applicable laws" in the standard lease form mean the same thing as "specific, nondiscretionary statutes" in the regulation? We will look at some specific examples of governmental regulation of mineral lessees in Chapter 7B(4) (*Kerr–McGee, Copper Valley*).

––––––––––––––

Now let us examine a similar suite of issues arising from U.S. Forest Service timber sale contracts. In Everett Plywood Corp. v. United States, 651 F.2d 723 (Ct.Cl.1981), the Forest Service partially cancelled a timber sale contract once it discovered that building a road to retrieve the timber would cause unacceptable environmental damage. The timber contractor sued and won damages against the United States. The court noted that the contract contained provisions addressing "various supervening events and the effect such events should have upon the contract," and it "provided for termination in some instances but did not contain any provision for termination in the event that occurred." The contract gave the purchaser the option of terminating if a catastrophic event made performance impracticable, and gave the purchaser a cost adjustment if less-than-catastrophic events occurred, but no provision addressed what would happen if performance of the contract caused unacceptable environmental harm. The court concluded that "the contract as fairly read allocates to defendant the risk of being in breach if it must cancel because of the risk of environmental damage." The court distinguished

> between the power of the government to terminate the contract and the extent of its liability for the exercise of that power. Clearly, the government ought not to have stood idly by and continued with the contract if unacceptable damage to the environment were foreseen. On the other hand, whether the government can terminate the contract and escape making compensation is another issue, the issue we are concerned with. * * *

> * * * Where an event is reasonably foreseeable and a provision is not written into the contract to cover that event, one questions whether that event should be considered supervening, at least where the government is claiming the excuse under a standard contract in which all the provisions are predetermined and accepted on a "take it or leave it" basis by the highest bidder. The government could have promulgated regulations if necessary or inserted a provision to terminate the contract in an event of this type, thereby escaping breach liability. For this court to rewrite the contract and, in effect, insert such a provision might be unfair to the plaintiff, since the appearance of such a

provision initially might have influenced plaintiff's deciding whether to adhere to the contract terms proposed, take it or leave it, or bid a lesser amount. Defendant could have proposed a termination article to cover the case; plaintiff could not have. * * *

Even if the government's knowledge that environmental damage could occur was not dispositive and only probative, given the facts of this case and the decisions of this court in the area of impracticability of performance, the risk of the occurrence of the event is on the government. * * * It was defendant, not plaintiff, who as owner of the tracts to be harvested would be presumed to be the party informed as to soil conditions and geologic structure that might indicate that logging would endanger the environment. * * *

The government designed the logging roads in question. It thus was or should have been in the best position to evaluate the effects of road construction on soil conditions. * * * [T]he fact that the government did design the specified roads is relevant for purposes of allocating the risk of environmental damages caused by the construction of those roads.

651 F.2d 730–31. The court accused the trial judge of

seiz[ing] on a contract doctrine evolved for quite unlike circumstances in order to further the high cause of environmentalism. It is a cause with numerous and devoted adherents, some of whom will not tolerate the balancing of environmental considerations against others perhaps equally high but of a different nature. Here the cause is deemed to override the normal obligations of a government contract, i.e., if the Secretary of Agriculture is acting on behalf of the environment he can make any contract of his Department null and void. The effort of the government which has stepped into the market place and made contracts binding on others, to void them as applied to itself on behalf of some high public policy, is an old phenomenon in the law.

651 F. 2d at 727.

Would you advise the Forest Service to adopt a regulation to provide for cancellation of a timber sales contract upon a determination that the operations would result in serious environmental degradation or resource damage? Could it apply such a regulation to existing contracts as well as new contracts? Could it do so without providing compensation? In fact, a Forest Service regulation provides for cancellation of timber sale contracts when the Chief of the Forest Service determines that "operations thereunder would result in serious environmental degradation or resource damage." The regulation goes on to say that the purchaser is entitled to "reasonable compensation * * * for unrecovered costs incurred under the contract and the difference between the current contract value and the average value of comparable National Forest timber sold during the preceding 6–month period." 36 C.F.R. § 223.116 (2001); *see also* 36 C.F.R. § 223.40 (2001). Is this a fair solution to the problem?

Lease Terms and Bidding Behavior in Competitive Auctions

In many situations the government has something approaching monopoly power to dictate lease terms. But what might be the effect of bidding on a mineral lease or timber sale contract at auction if the government adopts a regulation or a standard contract term that puts the total financial risk of loss on the purchaser, by reserving broad power to cancel a contract any time it determines that unacceptable environmental damage will result? Might the government in effect be trading lower revenues for more protection of the environment? Is there anything unfair (or unconstitutional) about that? Is it good policy? Or is it better to give the bidders some assurance that, if they are ultimately prevented by governmental action from carrying out the venture, they can get some or all of their money back, and therefore presumably attract higher bids? Should the answer be controlled by the government's assessment of how likely it is that unanticipated damage will result? (But how do you measure that, if it's truly unanticipated?) Or is it about more than just monetary risk?

If the government reserves broad power in its contracts to deal with emerging knowledge or changed condition without paying the other party, will it have less incentive to do a good job up front, in assessing what the risks are before it decides to open up an area? On the other hand, if the government does not reserve the power in its contracts, and knows that a decision to restrict activities under the contract may cost the Treasury money, will it have the will to act, or will it be more willing to accept environmental damage rather than take a monetary hit? Keep in mind that the government does not have the same set of incentives as a private party. Among other things, payments for contract damages and constitutional takings do not come out of the responsible agency's budget, but rather out of something called the "claims and judgments fund" administered by the Department of Justice. *See* 31 U.S.C. § 1304. Known in congressional appropriations parlance as a "no year appropriation," it is something akin to a bottomless pit of money. Agency budgets are not, in other words, directly at risk from takings liability arising through their administration of natural resource programs. (Of course, congressional appropriators may take an agency's record on this score into account in doling out funds to it each year as part of the congressional appropriations process.) Should agency budgets be put at risk? If they were, would parochial concerns about their financial well-being make them too cautious to protect the public interest? *See generally* Daryl J. Levinson, *Making Government Pay: Markets, Politics, and the Allocation of Constitutional Costs*, 67 U. CHI. L.REV. 345 (2000).

In Prineville Sawmill Co. v. United States, 859 F.2d 905 (Fed.Cir. 1988), the Court held that a Forest Service decision to reject all bids at a timber sale was an abuse of discretion. Prineville was one of six bidders at the auction. The bidders submitted bids on each of the three species of timber in the sale area, with the total bid determined by multiplying each species bid by the Forest Service's estimate of the volume of timber of that species, and adding the totals together. But the actual price to be paid to the Forest Service would be determined not by what was bid, but by what was actually harvested. Prineville determined the Forest Service had made a serious error in estimating the volume of timber of some species in the sale area. Prineville therefore skewed its bidding by bidding high for the species it thought the Forest Service had overestimated, as it was permitted to do, and this made its overall bid the highest. After the auction, but before the contract was awarded, the Forest Service determined its error and decided to reject all bids. Prineville sued. Although the Forest Service's sales prospectus expressly "reserved the right to reject any and all bids," the court ruled for Prineville, finding the government had an "obligation to treat fairly" the bids it receives in an auction. Here, the government's own error caused the problem, Prineville's bidding behavior was permitted by the Forest Service bidding policies, and for the government to return all the bids "simply to get even more money for its timber" was arbitrary and capricious. But wasn't it rational for the government to correct its error before it signed the contract, and wasn't it fair to Prineville, the government having reserved the authority to reject all bids? Even assuming *Prineville* is correctly decided, should the same degree of judicial scrutiny be applied to acts of a federal land management agency when it is accused of harming the public interest, as opposed to situations where "only money" is at stake, and the agency is accused of dealing unfairly with a private party?

As is often the case with property rights takings claims, the more political branches of government may be quicker and more generous than the courts in responding when governmental contractors encounter problems. Put another way, government contractors often command considerable political power and so, while the government has large power over contract performance, and companies doing business with the government may face some disadvantages, they also enjoy some advantages when times turn sour, because the political process can be more responsive than the marketplace to requests to ease financial distress. During the 1970's, for example, timber companies made lots of money by purchasing timber off the national forests when the market was down and harvesting it when prices were much higher. In the early 1980's, the tables turned. The timber industry in western states went into decline as the housing industry entered a deep recession, and timber sold in federal contracts for $300 per thousand board feet in 1980 brought less than $200 per thousand on the market in 1982. The timber companies took their dilemma to the courts and to Congress. The latter proved more pliable. In North Side Lumber Co. v. Block, 753 F.2d 1482 (9th Cir.1985), *cert. denied*, 474 U.S. 931 (1985), the court refused to void the contracts, finding it had no jurisdiction because the United States had not waived its sovereign immunity for purposes of declaratory relief. In the meantime, however, Congress enacted the Federal Timber Contract Payment Modification Act of 1984, 16 U.S.C. § 618, which relieved timber companies of some contractual obligations.

Important Defenses to Actions Alleging the Government has Breached its Contract: The "Sovereign Acts" and "Unmistakability" Doctrines

Even if the government takes an action that might ordinarily be considered a breach of its contract—by imposing burdens on the other contracting party which are inconsistent with the terms of the contract—two interrelated doctrines can immunize it from liability. The sovereign acts doctrine dates back to Civil War era, when the U.S. Court of Claims recognized that, because the U.S. was a sovereign government as well as a contracting party, its role as sovereign could sometimes outweigh its role as contractor. Jones v. United States, 1 Ct.Cl. 383, 384 (1865) ("Whatever acts the government may do, be they legislative or executive, so long as they be public and general, cannot be deemed specially to [breach] * * * the particular contracts * * * it enters with private persons"). Thus the U.S. cannot be held liable for breach of contract when it takes a "sovereign act" that thwarts performance of its contracts. *See* Horowitz v. United States, 267 U.S. 458, 461 (1925); Edward A. Fitzgerald, *Conoco, Inc. v. United States: Sovereign Authority Undermined by Contractual Obligations on the Outer Continental Shelf*, 27 PUB. CONT. L.J. 755, 777–81 (1998).

The unmistakability doctrine traces back to 19th century cases addressing the application of the "no impairment of contracts" clause in the Constitution. U.S. Const., Art.I, § 10 (which textually applies only to state governments, not the United States). Its essence is that a contract with the government shall not be interpreted as relinquishing the government's power to make "sovereign acts" in the future, even if they can affect rights under its contracts, unless the contract unequivocally says so. That is, "sovereign power, even when unexercised, is an enduring presence that governs all contracts subject to the sovereign's jurisdiction, and will remain intact unless surrendered in unmistakable terms." Merrion v. Jicarilla Apache Tribe, 455 U.S. 130, 148 (1982).

In Biodiversity Associates v. Cables, 357 F.3d 1152 (10th Cir.2004), the court upheld an appropriation act rider that permitted logging on specific parts of the Black Hills National Forest as a means of averting forest fires. The legislation overturned a court settlement previously reached by the U.S. Forest Service and environmental groups. Judge McConnell, writing for the court, made the following comments.

> The legislation specifies forest management techniques for these lands in minute detail, overrides otherwise applicable environmental laws and attendant administrative review procedures, and explicitly supersedes a settlement agreement between the Forest Service and various environmental groups regarding management of these lands.

> * * *

> [The] Rider intrudes on neither executive nor judicial authority. The Rider comports with the current view of executive branch officials regarding management of the national forest. And while the Rider overrides a settlement agreement entered by the district court, that agreement was in fact a private agreement between the parties, in which the Judiciary had little or no independent involvement. To overturn the Rider would thus serve not to vindicate the constitutionally entrusted prerogatives of those two branches, but rather to keep in place a private group's own preferences about forest preservation policy in the face of contrary judgments by the Executive and Con-

gress. True principles of separation of powers prevent settlement agreements negotiated by private parties and officials of the executive branch from encroaching either on the constitutionally vested authority of Congress or on the statutorily vested authority of those officials' successors in office. BCA's claim amounts to the argument that an agreement forged by a private group with a former administration, without serious judicial involvement, can strip both Congress and the Executive of their discretionary powers. The Constitution neither compels nor permits such a result.

The executive branch does not have authority to contract away the enumerated constitutional powers of Congress or its own successors, and certainly neither does a private group. Accordingly, the governance of the Black Hills National Forest must be conducted according to the new rules set by Congress, as Article IV of the Constitution provides.

Even when the Government unmistakably contracts not to exercise its sovereign powers in otherwise permissible ways, that promise cannot be enforced by injunction * * *. At most, such a contract may give rise in certain circumstances to a suit for damages.

Although these doctrines evolved somewhat separately, they are now usually applied in tandem in the U.S. Court of Appeals for the Federal Circuit. A basic inquiry is whether the government action that allegedly breached the contract is aimed at undoing the contract itself and has that effect, or whether instead it is "public and general;" that is, whether it has a broader public purpose and only incidentally affects contract rights. *See* Centex Corp. v. United States, 395 F.3d 1283 (Fed.Cir.2005) (distinguishing between "acts of general legislation and acts that are more particularly directed at relieving the government of its contractual responsibilities"). An act of government is considered public and general so long as the impact on particular contracts is "merely incidental to the accomplishment of a broader governmental objective." United States v. Winstar Corp., 518 U.S. 839, 898 (1996) (Souter, J.) (plurality opinion). This requires "a case-specific inquiry that focuses on the scope of the legislation in an effort to determine whether, on balance, that legislation was designed to target prior governmental contracts." Yankee Atomic Electric Co. v. United States, 112 F.3d 1569, 1575 (Fed.Cir.1997).*

The sovereign acts doctrine was not at issue in the Supreme Court in *Mobil Oil* because the Court of Claims said it did not apply, and the

---

* There is an analogous strand in takings jurisprudence. That is, if a regulation applies to but a few property owners, there is a greater danger that the government is "forcing some people alone to bear public burdens which, in all fairness and justice, should be borne by the public as a whole." Armstrong v. United States, 364 US. 40, 49 (1960). A regulation that applies to many property owners, by contrast, usually secures what Holmes famously called "an average reciproc-ity of advantage," Pennsylvania Coal Co. v. Mahon, 260 U.S. 393, 415 (1922), where the regulatory burden on particular landowners is offset by the benefits of enforcing the regulation against neighboring properties. "The Court has never identified a specific metric for applying this factor, but it is clear that the less comprehensive the regulation the more likely a taking will be found." John D. Echeverria, *Regulating Versus Paying Land Owners to Protect the Environment*, 26 J. LAND, RESOURCES & ENVTL. L. 1, 14 (2005).

Government did not appeal that ruling. To explore how the "sovereign acts" doctrine might have applied in Mobil, suppose that Congress had enacted, not the Outer Banks Protection Act, but a more general OCS Protection Act (OCSPA). Suppose further that the OCSPA (a) was adopted in response to some serious pollution incidents from offshore oil and gas platforms around the world, and required the installation of expensive control equipment; (b) was aimed at toughening environmental review processes and environmental protection standards everywhere on the outer continental shelf (in contrast to the OBPA, which was aimed at this particular geographic area and these particular leases); (c) specifically said its new standards should apply to existing leases; and (d) made it unprofitable for lessees to pursue oil and gas development off North Carolina. Would the OCSPA qualify for the "sovereign acts" defense, and allow the government to avoid a finding that it had breached Mobil's lease? Is there anything in its lease, so far as you can tell from the *Mobil Oil* opinion, that surrendered the government's sovereign power to act in the future in "unmistakable" terms?

Or, suppose the Endangered Species Act (ESA) had not been adopted when the lease to Mobil was issued, but was thereafter enacted. Suppose also there are endangered species in the waters off North Carolina that would be threatened by oil and gas development there, and the ESA effectively prevented Mobil from exploring. Does the sovereign acts doctrine immunize the government from liability for breach of contract?

A number of courts have said yes, in the context of the federal Bureau of Reclamation's contracts to provide federally-subsidized project water to various users. *See, e.g.*, Klamath Water Users Protective Ass'n, 204 F.3d at 1213 ("[i]t is well settled that contractual arrangements can be altered by subsequent Congressional legislation"). A number of decisions of the Ninth Circuit have concluded that the language of the Bureau's contracts reserved authority in the U.S. to reduce water deliveries in order to protect wildlife. *See, e.g.*, O'Neill v. United States, 50 F.3d 677 (9th Cir.1995). The Bureau contracts recite that they are entered into pursuant to the reclamation laws and "all acts amendatory or supplementary thereto." *See* Rio Grande Silvery Minnow v. Keys, 333 F.3d 1109, 1130 (10th Cir.2003). In the *Silvery Minnow* case, the U.S., abandoning a position it had taken in many previous cases, argued that the Bureau of Reclamation contracts left the government with no discretion regarding water delivery. It tried to distinguish the 9th Circuit's decisions (and its own prior position) to the contrary, and asserted that the ESA could not restrict water delivery because the ESA's consultation requirement applies only to federal actions where there is "discretionary Federal involvement or control." *See* 50 C.F.R. § 402.03. Under this view, there was no occasion to consider whether the ESA was a sovereign act. The court avoided the issue when it vacated its earlier opinion on mootness grounds. *See* Rio Grande Silvery Minnow v. Keys, 355 F.3d 1215 (10th Cir.2004).

CHAPTER 5

FEDERAL LAND MANAGEMENT

This chapter concludes the casebook's discussion of cross-cutting doctrine and background principles of federal public land and resources law. Unlike the issues in Chapter 4, which pervade all public administration, the topics of this chapter center on the natural resources agencies and the peculiar circumstances in which they operate today. The controversies discussed below do cut across the resource-specific categories, but they are largely creatures of public land law.

Section A deals with problems of access that are a legacy of the era of disposal. Courts and agencies address both access of the public across private land to reach federal resources as well as access across federal lands for various purposes, including to reach private inholdings. Section B looks generally at delegations of power to make decisions about federal land management to nonfederal decision-makers. Section C examines executive power to withdraw federal lands from the operation of otherwise applicable laws, and to reserve federal lands for particular uses. Section D covers executive power to acquire lands into federal ownership, and to dispose of federal lands by exchange or sale. Finally, Section E examines organic legislation, which provides a charter to guide management of each of the major public land systems.

A. ACCESS TO AND ACROSS FEDERAL LANDS

Problems of access stem largely from the patchwork, haphazard character of federal disposal (and reacquisition) policies, and the sometimes dizzying patterns of land ownership that have resulted. Disputes over access questions involving federal lands result from the collision of past and present law and policy. History can be determinative when the rubber meets the road, as it were, on access. The discussion that follows is divided into two parts: Access across non-federal land to reach federal land, and access across federal land.

1. ACCESS ACROSS NONFEDERAL LAND TO FEDERAL LAND

The disposal era had yet to close before the checkerboard pattern of ownership derived from statehood grants, homestead laws, and, especially, railroad grants created conflicts. The early conflicts grew out of the range wars where competing livestock owners attempted to fence in federal lands for their own, exclusive use. In 1885 Congress enacted the Unlawful Inclosures Act in response to this practice.

Section 1 of the Unlawful Inclosures Act, 43 U.S.C. § 1061, provides: "All inclosures of any public lands * * * constructed by any person * * * to any of which land included within the inclosure the person * * * had no claim or color of title made or acquired in good faith * * * are hereby declared to be unlawful." Section 3, 43 U.S.C. § 1063, prohibits any person"by force, threats, intimidation, or by any fencing or inclosing, or any other unlawful means," from obstructing or preventing "free passage or transit over or through the public lands," or peaceable entries onto the public lands for purposes of establishing a settlement or residence under the public land laws. It also contains the proviso that it does not affect the "right or title of persons, who have gone upon, improved or occupied said lands under the land laws of the United States, claiming title thereto, in good faith." District courts are vested with jurisdiction to order offending fences removed.

The United States brought suit in federal district court in Colorado to compel the removal of a fence built and maintained by the ranchers Camfield and Drury. The following diagram of one township, from the 9th Circuit opinion, illustrates the manner in which the fence was constructed on the privately-owned, odd-numbered sections so as to enclose the even-

6	5	4	3	2	1
7	8	9	10	11	12
18	17	16	15	14	13
19	20	21	22	23	24
30	29	28	27	26	25
31	32	33	34	35	36

numbered sections that remained in federal ownership. The fence is indicated by the dotted lines. Defendants admitted they built the fence, but pointed out that they had installed a swinging gate to afford access to the public domain enclosed, and argued that they were installing irrigation works and developing the land which "was of great importance and utility, and would redound to the great advantage of the United States and its citizens."

Camfield v. United States

Supreme Court of the United States, 1897.
167 U.S. 518.

■ JUSTICE BROWN delivered the opinion of the court.

* * * Defendants are certainly within the letter of this statute. They did enclose public lands of the United States to the amount of 20,000 acres, and there is nothing tending to show that they had any claim or color of title to the same, or any asserted right thereto under a claim made in good faith under the general laws of the United States. The defense is in substance that, if the act be construed so as to apply to fences upon private property, it is unconstitutional.

There is no doubt of the general proposition that a man may do what he will with his own, but this right is subordinate to another, which finds expression in the familiar maxim: Sic utere tuo ut alienum non laedas.* His right to erect what he pleases upon his own land will not justify him in maintaining a nuisance, or in carrying on a business or trade that is offensive to his neighbors. Ever since Aldred's case, it has been the settled law, both of this country and of England, that a man has no right to maintain a structure upon his own land, which, by reason of disgusting smells, loud or unusual noises, thick smoke, noxious vapors, the jarring of machinery or the unwarrantable collection of flies, renders the occupancy of adjoining property dangerous, intolerable or even uncomfortable to its tenants. No person maintaining such a nuisance can shelter himself behind the sanctity of private property.

While the lands in question are all within the State of Colorado, the Government has, with respect to its own lands, the rights of an ordinary proprietor, to maintain its possession and to prosecute trespassers. It may deal with such lands precisely as a private individual may deal with his farming property. It may sell or withhold them from sale. It may grant them in aid of railways or other public enterprises. It may open them to preemption or homestead settlement; but it would be recreant to its duties as trustee for the people of the United States to permit any individual or private corporation to monopolize them for private gain, and thereby practically drive intending settlers from the market. It needs no argument to show that the building of fences upon public lands with intent to enclose them for private use would be a mere trespass, and that such fences might be abated by the officers of the Government or by the ordinary processes of court of justice. To this extent no legislation was necessary to vindicate the rights of the Government as a landed proprietor.

* [Eds. The translation is "so use your own as not to injure another's property" BLACK'S LAW DICTIONARY (1999 ed.).]

But the evil of permitting persons, who owned or controlled the alternate sections, to enclose the entire tract, and thus to exclude or frighten off intending settlers, finally became so great that Congress passed the act of February 25, 1885, forbidding all enclosures of public lands, and authorizing the abatement of the fences. If the act be construed as applying only to fences actually erected upon public lands, it was manifestly unnecessary, since the Government as an ordinary proprietor would have the right to prosecute for such a trespass. It is only by treating it as prohibiting all "enclosures" of public lands, by whatever means, that the act becomes of any avail. The device to which defendants resorted was certainly an ingenious one, but it is too clearly an evasion to permit our regard for the private rights of defendants as landed proprietors to stand in the way of an enforcement of the statute. So far as the fences were erected near the outside line of the odd-numbered sections, there can be no objection to them; but so far as they were erected immediately outside the even-numbered sections, they are manifestly intended to enclose the Government's lands, though, in fact, erected a few inches inside the defendants' line. Considering the obvious purposes of this structure, and the necessities of preventing the enclosure of public lands, we think the fence is clearly a nuisance, and that it is within the constitutional power of Congress to order its abatement, notwithstanding such action may involve an entry upon the lands of a private individual. The general Government doubtless has a power over its own property analogous to the police power of the several States, and the extent to which it may go in the exercise of such power is measured by the exigencies of the particular case. If it be found to be necessary for the protection of the public, or of intending settlers, to forbid all enclosures of public lands, the Government may do so, though the alternate sections of private lands are thereby rendered less available for pasturage. The inconvenience, or even damage, to the individual proprietor does not authorize an act which is in its nature a purpresture of government lands. While we do not undertake to say that Congress has the unlimited power to legislate against nuisances within a State, which it would have within a Territory, we do not think the admission of a Territory as a State deprives it of the power of legislating for the protection of the public lands, though it may thereby involve the exercise of what is ordinarily known as the police power, so long as such power is directed solely to its own protection. A different rule would place the public domain of the United States completely at the mercy of state legislation.

We are not convinced by the argument of counsel for the railway company, who was permitted to file a brief in this case, that the fact that a fence, built in the manner indicated, will operate incidentally or indirectly to enclose public lands, is a necessary result, which Congress must have foreseen when it made the grants, of the policy of granting odd sections and retaining the even ones as public lands; and that if such a result inures to the damage of the United States it must be ascribed to their improvidence and carelessness in so surveying and laying off the public lands, that the portion sold and granted by the Government cannot be enclosed by the purchasers without embracing also in such enclosure the alternate sections reserved by the United States. Carried to its logical conclusion, the inference is that, because Congress chose to aid in the construction of these railroads by donating to them all the odd-numbered sections within certain limits, it thereby intended incidentally to grant them the use for an indefinite time of all the even-numbered sections. It seems but an ill return for the generosity of the Government in granting these roads half its lands to claim that it thereby incidentally granted them the benefit of the whole. * * *

These grants were made in pursuance of the settled policy of the Government to reserve to itself the even-numbered sections for sale at an increased price; and if the defendants in this case chose to assume the risk of purchasing the odd-numbered sections of the railroad company for pasturage purposes, without also purchasing or obtaining the consent of the Government to use the even-numbered sections, and thereby failed to derive a benefit from the odd-numbered ones, they must call upon their own indiscretion to answer for their mistake. The law and practice of the Government were perfectly well settled, and if it had chosen in the past to permit by tacit acquiescence the pasturage of its public lands, it was a policy which it might change at any moment, and which became the subject of such abuses that Congress finally felt itself compelled to pass the act of February 25, 1885, and thereby put an end to them. * * * The defendants were bound to know that the sections they purchased of the railway company could only be used by them in subordination to the right of the Government to dispose of the alternate sections as it seemed best, regardless of any inconvenience or loss to them, and were bound to avoid obstructing or embarrassing it in such disposition. If practices of this kind were tolerated, it would be but a step further to claim that the defendants, by long acquiescence of the Government in their appropriation of public lands, had acquired a title to them as against every one except the Government, and perhaps even against the Government itself.

It is no answer to say that, if such odd-numbered sections were separately fenced in, which the owner would doubtless have the right to do, the result would be the same as in this case, to practically exclude the Government from the even-numbered sections, since this was a contingency which the Government was bound to contemplate in granting away the odd-numbered sections. So long as the individual proprietor confines his enclosure to his own land, the Government has no right to complain, since he is entitled to the complete and exclusive enjoyment of it, regardless of any detriment to his neighbor; but when, under the guise of enclosing his own land, he builds a fence which is useless for that purpose, and can only have been intended to enclose the lands of the Government, he is plainly within the statute, and is guilty of an unwarrantable appropriation of that which belongs to the public at large. It may be added, however, that this is scarcely a practical question, since a separate enclosure of each section would only become desirable when the country had been settled, and roads had been built which would give access to each section. * * *

NOTES AND QUESTIONS

1. Is the Court correct in concluding that Camfield's fence was "within the letter of" the statute? Does the United States even need to rely on the Unlawful Inclosures Act if Camfield's fence constitutes a nuisance?

2. Is the holding here derived more from congressional intent or from "equitable considerations"? In this connection, look closely at the railroad company's argument as amicus curiae. Did Congress intend this result when it created the checkerboards? What do you suppose Congress did intend?

3. The fence here was made possible by an important technological development in the late nineteenth century; namely, the invention and mass production of barbed wire. Where timber for wooden fences was scarce, "[b]arbed wire proved to be the cattle raisers' best friend." Richard White, *Animals and Enterprise*, in OXFORD HISTORY OF THE AMERICAN WEST 264 (1994).

4. Does *Camfield* hold that the United States may regulate private lands that affect the quality of the public lands? Could the United States prohibit, for instance, snowmobiles from operating on private land adjacent to a national wildlife refuge? Or unsightly curio shops or hot dog stands on private land at the entrance to a national park? Or is the United States merely in the same position as any landowner with a "nuisance" next door? (Is a fence a nuisance?) National power to protect the public lands under the Property Clause of the Constitution and the relationship between federal and state law in this context is an important and recurring issue in federal land and resources law; it is addressed in detail in Chapter 3.

5. In Mackay v. Uinta Development Co., 219 Fed. 116 (8th Cir.1914), the question was whether Mackay, a nomadic sheepherder, was liable for trespass damages when he trailed his sheep across open, unfenced checkerboarded private lands while going to and from pastures on public lands. Relying on the Unlawful Inclosures Act as construed in *Camfield*, and on Buford v. Houtz, 133 U.S. 320 (1890), in which the Supreme Court held that congressional acquiescence in their trespasses gave all nomadic herders an implied license to graze their animals on the public lands, the court reversed a judgment for the private landowner, observing:

> This case illustrates the conflict between the rights of private property and the public welfare under exceptional conditions. It is difficult to say that a man may not inclose his own land, regardless of the effect upon others; but the Camfield Case, supra, has been recognized as sustaining the doctrine that "wholesome legislation" may be constitutionally enacted, though it lessens in a moderate degree what are frequently regarded as absolute rights of private property. * * * This large body of land, with the odd-numbered sections of the company and the even-numbered sections of the public domain located alternately like the squares of a checker-board, remains open as nature left it. Its appearance is that of a common, and the company is so using the contained public portions. In such use it makes no distinction between them and its own holdings. It has not attempted physically to separate the latter for exclusive private use. It admits that Mackay had the right in common with the public to pass over the public lands. But the right admitted is a theoretical one, without utility, because practically it is denied except on terms it prescribes. Contrary to the prevailing rule of

construction, it seeks to cast upon the government and its licensees all the disadvantages of the interlocking arrangement of the odd and even numbered sections because the grant in aid of the railroad took that peculiar form. It could have lawfully fenced its own without obstructing access to the public lands. That would have lessened the value of the entire tract as a great grazing pasture, but it cannot secure for itself that value, which includes as an element the exclusive use of the public lands, by warnings and actions in trespass.

A dissenting judge, noting that Mackay's 3500 sheep had stripped 90 percent of the forage off of a 3/4–mile swath of plaintiff's alternating sections of land, would have affirmed the trial court's award of damages for the forage consumed, even assuming Mackay had a right to cross the private lands. *Mackay*, like *Camfield*, addressed in dictum the scenario where a private landowner separately fences in each of his odd-numbered sections. Are the courts correct in concluding that such fences, though they would have the same effect of enclosing public lands, are outside of the Unlawful Inclosures Act?

6. One way to pose the question raised in *Mackay* is to ask, who has the duty where no lands are fenced—the owners of the livestock (to fence them in or otherwise control them to avoid others' lands)? Or the other landowner (to fence her own land or shoo others' livestock away if she wants to avoid trespassing livestock)? The first is the English common law rule, generally followed in the eastern states of the United States. That is, the owner of livestock is liable for trespass if the stock strays on the lands of another. What is the western "common law" answer, according to *Mackay* (and Buford v. Houtz)? Can both answers be "common law"? Writing in an Arizona territorial water law case, Oliver Wendell Holmes once said that an Arizona statute generally adopting the common law of England "is far from meaning that patentees of a ranch on the San Pedro are to have the same rights as owners of an estate on the Thames." Boquillas Land & Cattle Co. v. Curtis, 213 U.S. 339, 345 (1909). For a modern western case holding that while a livestock owner in open range country may have an immunity under state law from trespass damages caused by wandering cows, the owner is not immune from damage claims by motorists injured by collisions with such cows on public highways, see Carrow v. Lusby, 804 P.2d 747 (Ariz.1990).

7. If a landowner has a duty under state law to fence livestock in (the English and eastern states' common law rule), is the United States bound by that rule when it allows livestock to graze on federal land in that state? Some older cases suggest the answer is no; e.g., United States v. Johnston, 38 F.Supp. 4 (S.D.W.Va.1941); Shannon v. United States, 160 Fed. 870 (9th Cir.1908) (arising in Montana). Why not? Note that the United States was not a party in either *Mackay* or Buford v. Houtz, even though federal land was involved. For a case involving livestock and trespass where the federal government was a party, see Light v. United States, *supra* p. 129.

Many current disputes over access concern passage of public land recreationists over surrounding private lands. The map below depicts a portion of Seminoe Reservoir in Wyoming. The Bureau of Reclamation completed Seminoe Dam in 1939 at the confluence of the Medicine Bow and North Platte Rivers, creating a reservoir for irrigation, power production, and recreation. A rare body of water in a remote, dry region, the reservoir attracts recreationists for hunting, fishing, and wildlife observation. Conflicts arose from recreational users accessing the lake across surrounding private land generated the following case.

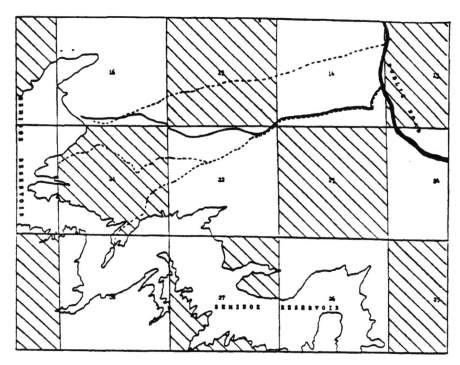

Area Near Seminoe Dam, Carbon County, Wyoming

Odd-numbered sections granted to railroad in 1862 and now owned by plaintiff

Even-numbered sections of public domain

- - - - Pre-existing dirt road

═══ Pre-existing dirt road improved by B.L.M. December 1973

▬▬ Dirt road relocated by B.L.M. December 1973

Leo Sheep Co. v. United States

Supreme Court of the United States, 1979.
440 U.S. 668.

■ Justice Rehnquist delivered the opinion of the Court.

This is one of those rare cases evoking episodes in this country's history that, if not forgotten, are remembered as dry facts and not as adventure. Admittedly the issue is mundane: Whether the Government has an implied easement to build a road across land that was originally granted to the Union Pacific Railroad under the Union Pacific Act of 1862—a grant that was part of a governmental scheme to subsidize the construction of the transcontinental railroad. But that issue is posed against the backdrop of a fascinating chapter in our history. As this Court noted in another case involving the Union Pacific Railroad, "courts, in construing a statute, may with propriety recur to the history of the times when it was passed; and this is frequently necessary, in order to ascertain the reason as well as the meaning of particular provisions in it." United States v. Union Pacific Railroad Co., 91 U.S. 72, 79 (1875). In this spirit we relate the events underlying passage of the Union Pacific Act of 1862. [Justice Rehnquist's recitation of the history of the land grants is excerpted *supra* p. 114.]

* * *

The land grants made by the 1862 Act included all the odd-numbered lots within 10 miles on either side of the track. When the Union Pacific's original subscription drive for private investment proved a failure, the land grant was doubled by extending the checkerboard grants to 20 miles on either side of the track. Private investment was still sluggish, and construction did not begin until July 1865, three months after the cessation of Civil War hostilities.[13] Thus began a race with the Central Pacific Railroad, which was laying track eastward from Sacramento, for the government land grants which went with each mile of track laid. The race culminated in the driving of the golden spike at Promontory Point, Utah, on May 10, 1869.

This case is the modern legacy of these early grants. Petitioners, the Leo Sheep Company and the Palm Livestock Company, are the Union Pacific Railroad's successors in fee to specific odd-numbered sections of land in Carbon County, Wyo. These sections lie to the east and south [should be north, error in original] of the Seminoe Reservoir, an area that is used by the public for fishing and hunting. Because of the checkerboard configuration, it is physically impossible to enter the Seminoe Reservoir

---

13. Construction would not have begun then without the Credit Mobilier, a limited liability company that was essentially owned by the promoters and investors of the Union Pacific. One of these investors, Oakes Ames, a wealthy New England shovel maker, was a substantial investor in Credit Mobilier and also a Member of Congress. Credit Mobilier contracted with the Union Pacific to build portions of the road, and by 1866 several individuals were large investors in both corporations. Allegations of improper use of funds and bribery of Members of the House of Representatives led to the appointment of a special congressional investigatory commit-tee that during 1872 and 1873 looked into the affairs of Credit Mobilier. These investigations revealed improprieties on the part of more than one Member of Congress, and the committee recommended that Ames be expelled from Congress. The investigation also touched on the career of a future President.

In 1872 the House of Representatives enacted a resolution condemning the policy of granting subsidies of public lands to railroads. Of course, the reaction of the public or of Congress a decade after the enactment of the Union Pacific Act to the conduct of those associated with the Union Pacific cannot influence our interpretation of that Act today.

sector from this direction without some minimum physical intrusion upon private land. In the years immediately preceding this litigation, the Government had received complaints that private owners were denying access over their lands to the reservoir area or requiring the payment of access fees. After negotiation with these owners failed, the Government cleared a dirt road extending from a local county road to the Reservoir across both public domain lands and fee lands of the Leo Sheep Company. It also erected signs inviting the public to use the road as a route to the Reservoir.

Petitioners initiated this action pursuant to 28 U.S.C. § 2409a to quiet title against the United States. The District Court granted petitioners' motion for summary judgment, but was reversed on appeal by the Court of Appeals for the Tenth Circuit. The latter court concluded that when Congress granted land to the Union Pacific Railroad, it implicitly reserved an easement to pass over the odd-numbered sections in order to reach the even-numbered sections that were held by the Government. Because this holding affects property rights in 150 million acres of land in the Western United States, we granted certiorari and now reverse.

The Government does not claim that there is any express reservation of an easement in the Union Pacific Act that would authorize the construction of a public road on the Leo Sheep Company's property. Section 3 of the 1862 Act sets out a few specific reservations to the "checkerboard" grant. The grant was not to include land "sold, reserved, or otherwise disposed of by the United States," such as land to which there were homestead claims. 12 Stat., at 492. Mineral lands were also excepted from the operation of the Act. Ibid. Given the existence of such explicit exceptions, this Court has in the past refused to add to this list by divining some "implicit" congressional intent. * * * To overcome the lack of support in the Act itself, the Government here argues that the implicit reservation of the asserted easement is established by "settled principles of property law" and by the Unlawful Inclosures of Public Lands Act of 1885.

Where a private landowner conveys to another individual a portion of his lands in a certain area and retains the rest, it is presumed at common law that the grantor has reserved an easement to pass over the granted property if such passage is necessary to reach the retained property. These rights of way are referred to as "easements by necessity." There are two problems with the Government's reliance on that notion in this case. First of all, whatever right of passage a private landowner might have, it is not at all clear that it would include the right to construct a road for public access to a recreational area.[15] More importantly, the easement is not actually a matter of necessity in this case because the Government has the power of eminent domain. Jurisdictions have generally seen eminent domain and easements by necessity as alternative ways to effect the same result. For example, the State of Wyoming no longer recognizes the common-law easement by necessity in cases involving landlocked estates. It

---

15. It is very unlikely that Congress in 1862 contemplated this type of intrusion, and it could not reasonably be maintained that failure to provide access to the public at large would render the Seminoe Reservoir land useless. Yet these are precisely the considerations that define the scope of easements by necessity. * * *

provides instead for a procedure whereby the landlocked owner can have an access route condemned on his behalf upon payment of the necessary compensation to the owner of the servient estate.[16] For similar reasons other state courts have held that the "easement by necessity" doctrine is not available to the sovereign.

The applicability of the doctrine of easement by necessity in this case is, therefore, somewhat strained, and ultimately of little significance. The pertinent inquiry in this case is the intent of Congress when it granted land to the Union Pacific in 1862. The 1862 Act specifically listed reservations to the grant, and we do not find the tenuous relevance of the common-law doctrine of ways of necessity sufficient to overcome the inference prompted by the omission of any reference to the reserved right asserted by the Government in this case. It is possible that Congress gave the problem of access little thought; but it is at least as likely that the thought which was given focused on negotiation, reciprocity considerations, and the power of eminent domain as obvious devices for ameliorating disputes. So both as matter of common-law doctrine and as a matter of construing congressional intent, we are unwilling to imply rights of way, with the substantial impact that such implication would have on property rights granted over 100 years ago, in the absence of a stronger case for their implication than the Government makes here.

The Government would have us decide this case on the basis of the familiar canon of construction that when grants to federal lands are at issue, any doubts "are resolved for the Government not against it." Andrus v. Charlestone Stone Products Co., 436 U.S. 604, 617 (1978). But this Court long ago declined to apply this canon in its full vigor to grants under the railroad acts. * * *

* * * [I]n United States v. Denver and Rio Grande R. Co., 150 U.S. 1, 14 (1893) [the Court] said:

> It is undoubtedly, as urged by the plaintiffs in error, the well-settled rule of this court that public grants are construed strictly against the grantees, but they are not to be so construed as to defeat the intent of the legislature, or to withhold what is given either expressly or by necessary or fair implication. * * *

> * * * When an act, operating as a general law, and manifesting clearly the intention of Congress to secure public advantages, or to subserve the public interests and welfare by means of benefits more or less valuable, offers individuals or to corporations as an inducement to undertake and accomplish great and expensive enterprises or works of a quasi public character in or through an immense and undeveloped public domain, such legislation stands upon a somewhat different footing from merely a private grant, and should receive at the hands of

---

16. Wyo.Stat.Ann. §§ 24–9–101 to 24–9–104 (1977); see Snell v. Ruppert, 541 P.2d 1042, 1046 (Wyo.1975) (statute "offers complete relief to the shut-in landowner and covers the whole subject matter") * * * In light of the history of public land grants related in Part I of this opinion, it is not surprising that "private" eminent domain statutes like that of Wyoming are most prevalent in the Western United States.

the court a more liberal construction in favor of the purposes for which it was enacted.

Thus invocation of the canon reiterated in Andrus does little to advance the Government's position in this case.

Nor do we find the Unlawful Inclosures of Public Lands Act of 1885 of any significance in this controversy. That Act was a response to the "range wars," the legendary struggle between cattlemen and farmers during the last half of the 19th Century. Cattlemen had entered Kansas, Nebraska, and the Dakota Territory before other settlers, and they grazed their herds freely on public lands with the Federal Government's acquiescence. To maintain their dominion over the ranges, cattlemen used homestead and pre-emption laws to gain control of water sources in the range lands. With monopoly control of such sources, the cattlemen found that ownership over a relatively small area might yield effective control of thousands of acres of grassland. Another exclusionary technique was the illegal fencing of public lands which was often the product of the checkerboard pattern of railroad grants. By placing fences near the borders of their parts of the checkerboard, cattlemen could fence in thousands of acres of public lands. Reports of the Secretary of Interior indicated that vast areas of public grazing land had been preempted by such fencing patterns. In response Congress passed the Unlawful Inclosures Act of 1885.

The Government argues that the prohibitions of this Act should somehow be read to include the Leo Sheep Company's refusal to acquiesce in a public road over its property, and that such a conclusion is supported by this Court's opinion in Camfield v. United States, 167 U.S. 518 (1897). We find, however, that Camfield does not afford the support that the Government seeks. That case involved a fence that was constructed on odd-numbered lots so as to enclose 20,000 acres of public land, thereby appropriating it to the exclusive use of Camfield and his associates. This Court analyzed the fence from the perspective of nuisance law, and concluded that the Unlawful Inclosures Act was an appropriate exercise of the police power.

There is nothing, however, in the Camfield opinion to suggest that the Government has the authority asserted here. In fact, the Court affirmed the grantee's right to fence completely his own land. Obviously if odd-numbered lots are individually fenced, the access to even-numbered lots is obstructed. Yet the Camfield Court found that this was not a violation of the Unlawful Inclosures Act. In that light we cannot see how the Leo Sheep Company's unwillingness to entertain a public road without compensation can be a violation of that Act. It is certainly true that the problem we confront today was not a matter of great concern during the time the 1862 railroad grants were made. The order of the day was the open range—barbed wire had not made its presence felt—and the type of incursions on private property necessary to reach public land was not such an interference that litigation would serve any motive other than spite. Congress obviously believed that when development came, it would occur in a parallel fashion on adjoining public and private lands and that the process of subdivision, organization of a polity and the ordinary pressures of commercial and social intercourse would work itself into a pattern of access roads. The Camfield case expresses similar sentiments. After the passage quoted above conceding the authority of a private landowner to fence the entire perimeter of his odd-numbered lot, the Court opined that such authority was of little practical significance "since a separate enclosure of each section would only become desirable when the country had been settled, and roads had been built which would give access to each section." It is some testament to common sense that the present case is virtually unprecedented, and that in the 117 years since the grants were made, litigation over access questions generally has been rare.

Nonetheless, the present times are litigious ones and the 37th Congress did not anticipate our plight. Generations of land patents have issued without any express reservation of the right now claimed by the Government. Nor has a similar right been asserted before.[24] When the Secretary of Interior has discussed access rights, his discussion has been colored by the assumption that those rights had to be purchased.[25] This Court has traditionally recognized the special need for certainty and predictability where land titles are concerned, and we are unwilling to upset settled expectations to accommodate some ill-defined power to construct public thoroughfares without compensation. The judgment of the Court of Appeals of the Tenth Circuit is accordingly

Reversed.

■ JUSTICE WHITE took no part in the consideration or decision of this case.

NOTES AND QUESTIONS

1. The intent of Congress. Congress created the checkerboard pattern by its grant of alternate sections in an attempt to answer those who argued that the national government lacked the power to carry out "internal improvements" inside states. The lively debates over this issue prior to the Civil War were, like practically everything else in that era, influenced by the institution of slavery, with slaveholders and slave states tending to deny the national government that power. In 1824, John Randolph of

24. This distinguishes the instant case from Buford v. Houtz, 133 U.S. 320 (1890). The appellants there were a group of cattle ranchers seeking, *inter alia,* an injunction against sheep ranchers who moved their herds across odd-numbered lots held by the appellants in order to graze their sheep on even-numbered public lots. This Court denied the requested relief because it was contrary to a century-old grazing custom. The Court also was influenced by the sheep ranchers' lack of any alternative.

"Upon the whole, we see no equity in the relief sought by the appellants in this case, which undertakes to deprive the defendants of this recognized right to permit their cattle to run at large over the lands of the United States and feed upon the grasses found in them, while, under pretence of owning a small proportion of the land which is the subject of controversy, they themselves obtain the monopoly of this valuable privilege." Id., at 332. Here neither custom nor necessity supports the Government.

25. In 1887 the Secretary of Interior recommended that Congress enact legislation providing for a public road around each section of public land to provide access to the various public lots in the checkerboard scheme. The Secretary also recommended that to the extent building these roads required the taking of property that had passed to private individuals, "the bill should provide for necessary compensation."

Virginia said what was on everyone's mind in opposing a bill authorizing federal surveys for roads and canals: "If Congress possesses the power to do * * * [this, it can] emancipate every slave in the United States." 41 Annals of Cong. 1308 (1824). Is this background relevant to the resolution of the question of access posed in *Leo Sheep*? The Circuit Court opinion in *Leo Sheep* had relied upon *Camfield*, *Mackay*, and Buford v. Houtz, cited in the main opinion at note 24, in finding that "Congress, by its 1862 grant to the railroad of the odd-numbered sections, did by implication intend to reserve a right of access to the inter-locking even-numbered sections not conveyed to the railroad." "To hold to the contrary would be to ascribe to Congress a degree of carelessness or lack of foresight which in our view would be unwarranted." 570 F.2d 881, 885 (10th Cir.1977). Clyde Martz, the experienced attorney for plaintiffs, told one of these editors that this passage inspired him to seek certiorari even though only a few square feet of land were involved. For, he said, the U.S. Supreme Court sitting in Washington has a much closer and realistic view of the "carelessness" of which Congress is capable.

2.   Canons of construction of federal grants. In a case decided twenty-three years earlier, and involving this very same railroad land grant, Justice Douglas's majority opinion relied on the "established rule that land grants are construed favorably to the Government, that nothing passes except what is conveyed by clear language, and that if there are doubts they are resolved for the Government, not against it." United States v. Union Pacific R.R. Co., 353 U.S. 112, 116 (1957). The majority concluded that Union Pacific did not own the minerals under the right-of-way over which the railroad passed. *Leo Sheep* does not cite this decision. What policy underlies the idea of construing ambiguities in grants from the United States in favor of the United States? Does it have to do with the generousness of the grants? How does that canon compare to canons of construction in ordinary contract or property law? What justifies interpreting railroad grants differently from other land grants of the same period? See also John D. Leshy, *A Property Clause for the 21st Century*, 75 U. Colo. L.Rev. 1101, 1110–13 (2004).

3.   Purely private disputes (not involving the federal government) can require interpretation of federal land grants. A coal slurry pipeline company and a railroad that it was competing with in the coal transportation business engaged in lengthy litigation over the pipeline company's claim of an access right across the railroad's right of way. *See* Energy Transportation Systems, Inc. v. Union Pacific R.R. Co., 606 F.2d 934 (10th Cir.1979).

4.   How does the Court use subsequent legislative history to understand the respective rights of the federal government and the plaintiff in this case?

5.   Is *Leo Sheep* consistent with *Camfield*? Is what Leo Sheep Company did any different from what the rancher did in *Camfield*?

6.   Is the issue in *Leo Sheep* as simple and straightforward as Justice Rehnquist makes it out to be? The implied reservation of rights later thought to be necessary for the enjoyment of lands retained is not a novel concept in public land jurisprudence. See, e.g., the concept of the implied

federal reserved water right discussed in Chapter 6. Does the Court mean to say that the United States (which made this grant) is in a worse position than the sheepherders in *Mackay* and *Buford*? What relevance does state property law have to the question of asserted federal property rights? Does the "necessity" for an implied easement disappear because the federal government has eminent domain power? Are *Camfield*, *Buford*, and the Unlawful Inclosures Act truly irrelevant or insignificant?

7.   What practical consequences will follow? Obviously, the BLM must condemn and pay for the lands necessary to provide access to the Seminoe Reservoir if the facility is to be used for the purpose intended. Short of condemnation, can the local BLM manager now reach Seminoe Reservoir without paying Leo Sheep Co. an access fee? Does it depend on whether the manager walks or drives a jeep?

8.   Consider the converse of *Leo Sheep*: could the BLM close its lands to plaintiffs, cutting off their access to their property? Sauce for the goose ... ? Does Leo Sheep Co. have an implied right of access across retained U.S. lands? If you were a BLM official, would you recommend such retaliation? Why? Would it work? Is there, ultimately, any "fair" resolution to this controversy available?

9.   If the United States had conveyed the cornering sections it retained to homesteader X, would Leo Sheep Co. have a right of access across X's land? Would X have a right of access across Leo Sheep Co. land? Would state or federal law control the answer to these questions? In Granite Beach Holdings v. State ex rel. Department of Natural Resources, 11 P.3d 847 (Wash.App.2000), the plaintiff, part of a modern breed of land speculator in the West, bought an inholding in an area where the government and conservation groups were actively buying land. Plaintiff argued that it had an implied easement of necessity to cross state land to access and develop the inholding it had purchased, on the theory that the United States was the original grantor and had reserved an easement. Relying on *Leo Sheep*, the Court held that no reservation should be implied in favor of the United States.

———

The next case, like *Leo Sheep*, involves access across non-federal land for federal purposes, and puts a modern twist on the problem litigated in *Camfield*. Rancher Taylor Lawrence constructed a fence twenty-eight miles long in a 20,000 acre area of private, state, and federal land in south central Wyoming that had been "checkerboarded" as a result of the Union Pacific Railroad grant. As in *Camfield*, the fence enclosed federal lands even though it was constructed entirely on his private land. In contrast to *Camfield*, Lawrence had federal permits under the Taylor Grazing Act to graze livestock on the enclosed federal lands. The truly remarkable difference, however, is that the federal government was seeking to open federal land to the passage of wildlife rather than human settlement. Lawrence's fence was antelope-proof, and in the severe winter of 1983 antelope collected against the fence and starved trying to reach their winter range.

The federal government sued Lawrence under the Unlawful Inclosures Act. The district court ordered Lawrence to remove the fence or modify it to allow antelope to go under and over it, and the court of appeals affirmed.

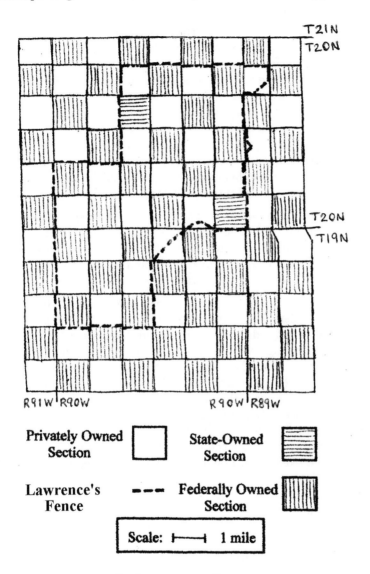

Privately Owned Section	**State-Owned Section**
Lawrence's Fence	**Federally Owned Section**

Scale: ⊢——⊣ 1 mile

United States ex rel. Bergen v. Lawrence

United States Court of Appeals, Tenth Circuit, 1988.
848 F.2d 1502, *cert. denied* 488 U.S. 980 (1988).

■ Judge Anderson

[T]he UIA [Unlawful Inclosures Act] remains federal law, and was amended in 1984 when Congress modified a procedural provision. We refuse to repeal the UIA by implication, and therefore, must give effect to its provisions. The UIA declares enclosures of federal lands to be unlawful and orders that such enclosures be removed. It creates no easements or servitudes. Thus, Lawrence's central argument, that the antelope have no easement across his lands, is not relevant to our decision.[6] We conclude with the district court that "while Leo Sheep has no applicability in this matter, Camfield is dispositive of it."

[The court of appeals then turned to Lawrence's argument that the UIA is "simply inapplicable to antelope" because there was no mention of wildlife in its legislative history. The court observed that section 1 of the UIA is "emphatic and absolute" that "all inclosures of any public lands * * * are * * * declared to be unlawful." 43 U.S.C. § 1061. The court saw no need to look at the history because the statute was clear on its face. It also relied on early cases such as Stoddard v. United States, 214 Fed. 566 (8th Cir.1914), which applied the UIA to fences on private land that obstructed the free range of livestock to public land. Stoddard had concluded that the UIA "was intended to prevent the obstruction of free passage or transit for any and all lawful purposes over public lands."]

Thus, the question becomes whether winter forage by antelope is a lawful purpose of public lands. Any doubt may be resolved by reference to FLPMA, where Congress directed that "the public lands be managed in a manner * * * that will provide food and habitat for fish and wildlife and domestic animals." 43 U.S.C. § 1701(a)(8).

Lawrence objects to the reliance on FLPMA to ascertain the limits of the UIA: "It is absurd to suppose that 1976 declarations of Congress regarding public land administration could be construed to amend by implication the language and purpose of the UIA enacted in 1885." This criticism misses the point of the analysis. Neither this court nor the district court rely on FLPMA to amend the UIA. The UIA proscribes unlawful enclosures; enclosures are unlawful when they deny access to public lands for "lawful purposes"; Congressional guidance in FLPMA is relevant to assist the court in determining what uses of the public lands are lawful, and therefore protected under the UIA. Obviously, lawful uses of the public lands will change over time. For example, as Lawrence notes, the primary purpose of the UIA in the early part of this century was to prevent the exclusion of homesteaders from the public lands. With the repeal of the homesteading laws, that is no longer a "lawful purpose." The district court did not look to FLPMA to determine the intent of Congress in 1885, but rather, to determine what "lawful purposes" were protected by the UIA in 1985. That was both appropriate and necessary. * * *

* * * [T]he UIA preserves access to federal lands for "lawful purposes," including forage by wildlife. Where a fence is constructed so that it does not obstruct other lawful uses of the federal lands, it is not an unlawful enclosure.

---

6. While we do not decide this question, we note in passing that the Wyoming and National Wildlife Federations, as intervenor-appellees, make a strong case for distinguishing the antelope's right of access from the government's case in Leo Sheep. Accordingly, we are not saying that wildlife have no such rights relative to federal lands; we simply do not reach that question in this case. Cf., e.g., Leo Sheep, 440 U.S. at 687 n. 24 (distinguishes Leo Sheep from Buford v. Houtz, 133 U.S. 320 (1890)).

Finally, Lawrence claims that because the fence includes several unlocked gates, there is no unlawful enclosure absent evidence that the fence excludes entry by members of the public with "lawful entitlement to use of the enclosed public lands." * * * We have already held that the UIA applies to wildlife as well as people. It follows that Lawrence's antelope-proof fence is prohibited by the UIA.

NOTES AND QUESTIONS

1. The court also rejected Lawrence's argument that he fit within a defense recognized by the UIA; namely, that he had, in the court's words, a "claim or color of title to the enclosed lands that was acquired in good faith." *See* 43 U.S.C. §§ 1061, 1063. Prior cases had required a color of fee title to assert this defense, and federal grazing permits do not create any title in federal lands. Finally, the court rejected Lawrence's argument that the district court's ruling had unconstitutionally "taken" his property.

2. Do you suppose Congress in 1885 really was interested in safeguarding access by wildlife? Wasn't it more likely to have been interested in protecting homesteaders (such as, perhaps, Lawrence's forebears)? Does the court adequately distinguish *Leo Sheep*?

3. More generally, how should a court construe a century-old statute like this when public values and tastes have changed so dramatically? Probably to most people in 1885, antelope were a source of meat or a nuisance; now they are prized by many in their wild state. Should the interpretation of the statute change to accommodate that shift in public opinion? Justice Rehnquist in *Leo Sheep* noted that the access problem in that case was "certainly * * * not a matter of great concern" when Congress enacted the pertinent statute. But the federal government lost *Leo Sheep* and won *Lawrence*. Why?

4 The Tenth Circuit relied on the words "lawful purposes." But they do not actually appear in the UIA; they are in an earlier court opinion interpreting the UIA. Should that make a difference?

5. In 1991 the state of Wyoming bought Lawrence's private land, declaring it "premier pronghorn winter habitat." Geoffrey O'Gara, *The Last Open Range*, High Country News, Mar. 1, 2004. O'Gara's informative article about fencing and fence removal in the great open spaces of the West describes one of the last places left in the lower forty-eight states where the open range is truly open—the Green Mountain Common Allotment in south-central Wyoming, a tract of land encompassing more than half a million acres managed mostly by the BLM, with some interspersed private parcels. Seventeen different ranching operations run cattle on the land, grazing alongside "wild horse herds and two enormous herds of pronghorn, along with a rich mix of elk, sage grouse, deer and raptors." In 1885 unfenced range was the norm. Today, it is so rare as to merit special note and protection. Should that change in circumstance alter the judicial interpretation of the UIA?

6.   The General Accounting Office ("GAO," now called the Government Accountability Office) surveyed the adequacy of access to BLM and Forest Service lands. The responses of agency officials indicated that permanent, legal public access to more than fifty million acres of these lands (or 14 percent of the total managed by these agencies) was considered inadequate, largely because adjacent private landowners had been increasingly unwilling to provide such access out of a concern about vandalism and potential liability, and their desire for privacy or exclusive personal use of the federal lands in question. The agencies reported that they had been taking steps to acquire legal access, but no follow-up study is yet complete. *Federal Lands: Reasons for and Effects of Inadequate Public Access* (GAO 1992).

2.   ACCESS ACROSS FEDERAL LAND

a.   R.S. 2477 RIGHTS OF WAY

For most of the Nation's first two centuries, it was generally assumed that everyone had the ability to go upon most federal lands as they pleased. In 1866 Congress "acknowledged and confirmed" the right of way "[f]or the construction of ditches and canals" on federal lands to promote irrigation works. The same law issued a broad grant of the right of way "for the construction of highways over public lands." R.S. 2477 (repealed 1976). Nearly two decades later, Congress generally prohibited fencing off the federal lands in the Unlawful Inclosures Act of 1885. More broadly, in decisions like Buford v. Houtz, 133 U.S. 320, 326 (1890), the United States Supreme Court had endorsed the idea of an "implied license, growing out the custom of nearly a hundred years, that the public lands of the United States, especially those in which the native grasses are adapted to the growth and fattening of domestic animals, shall be free to the people who seek to use them, where there are left open and uninclosed, and no act of government forbids this use."

But implied licenses were revocable at will by the United States as landowner. The Forest Service could and did revoke implied grazing licenses by requiring grazing permits, and was upheld in Light v. United States, 220 U.S. 523 (1911), *supra* p. 129. Access to lands in the national park and national wildlife refuge system was always restricted, and the amount of lands in these systems has steadily grown over the years. Finally, in FLPMA, enacted in 1976, Congress culminated a long trend toward ending the historic practice of free and easy access by repealing most of the old statutes authorizing construction of highways, ditches, etc. Instead, FLPMA provided that anyone desiring to cross or use national forests or BLM lands for noncasual purposes must obtain a right-of-way from the relevant agency. 43 U.S.C. §§ 1761–1765. Rights-of-way are discretionary with the federal agency (that is, FLPMA authorizes but does not require the Secretary to issue them). They essentially are permits for limited purposes and limited durations. Holders must pay fair market value for the permits and are subject to potentially extensive regulation by the federal land manager to protect other uses and values of the lands; specifically, the permits must contain terms and conditions to "minimize damage to scenic and aesthetic values in fish and wildlife habitat and otherwise protect the environment." *Id.* § 1765(a). The statute also expresses a preference for right-of-way "corridors" wherever practical, in order to "minimize adverse environmental impacts and the proliferation of separate rights-of-way." 43 U.S.C. § 1763.

However, FLPMA's regime is subject to "valid existing rights," which means that historical origins of access claims remain of more than academic interest today. A rising tide of litigation has centered on whether valid rights exist and, if so, whether and to what extent the agency may regulate the exercise of those rights to further other public purposes. The following case is the most comprehensive effort to grapple with these questions. The opinion covers a lot of ground, provides a textbook example of how history's hand influences management of public lands today. It addresses a number of issues relevant to federal land and resources law, such as statutory construction principles, the relationship between federal public land law and state property law, and judicial versus executive branch land management agency authority over federal lands.

Southern Utah Wilderness Alliance v. BLM

United States Court of Appeals, Tenth Circuit, 2005.
425 F.3d 735.

■ JUDGE McCONNELL

This case involves one of the more contentious land use issues in the West: the legal status of claims by local governments to rights of way for the construction of highways across federal lands managed by the Bureau of Land Management (BLM). In 1866, Congress passed an open-ended grant of "the right of way for the construction of highways over public lands, not reserved for public uses." This statute, commonly called "R.S. 2477," remained in effect for 110 years, and most of the transportation routes of the West were established under its authority. During that time congressional policy promoted the development of the unreserved public lands and their passage into private productive hands; R.S. 2477 rights of way were an integral part of the congressional pro-development lands policy.

In 1976, however, Congress abandoned its prior approach to public lands and instituted a preference for retention of the lands in federal ownership, with an increased emphasis on conservation and preservation. As part of that statutory sea change, Congress repealed R.S. 2477. There could be no new R.S. 2477 rights of way after 1976. But even as Congress repealed R.S. 2477, it specified that any "valid" R.S. 2477 rights of way "existing on the date of approval of this Act" (October 21, 1976) would continue in effect. The statute thus had the effect of "freezing" R.S. 2477 rights as they were in 1976.

The difficulty is in knowing what that means. Unlike any other federal land statute of which we are aware, the establishment of R.S. 2477 rights of way required no administrative formalities: no entry, no application, no license, no patent, and no deed on the federal side; no formal act of public acceptance on the part of the states or localities in whom the right was vested. As the Supreme Court of Utah noted 75 years ago, R.S. 2477 "was a standing offer of a free right of way over the public domain," and the grant may be accepted "without formal action by public authorities." Lindsay Land & Live Stock Co. v. Churnos, 285 P. 646, 648 (1929). [T]he Department of the Interior explained that R.S. 2477 highways "were constructed without any approval from the federal government and with no documentation of the public land records, so there are few official records documenting the right-of-way or indicating that a highway was constructed on federal land under this authority."

To make matters more difficult, parties rarely had an incentive to raise or resolve potential R.S. 2477 issues while the statute was in effect, unless the underlying land had been patented to a private party. If someone wished to traverse unappropriated public land, he could do so, with or without an R.S. 2477 right of way, and given the federal government's pre–1976 policy of opening and developing the public lands, federal land managers generally had no reason to question use of the land for travel. Roads were deemed a good thing. * * * Thus, all pre–1976 litigated cases involving contested R.S. 2477 claims (and there are dozens) were between private landowners who had obtained title to previously-public land and would-be road users who defended the right to cross private land on what they alleged to be R.S. 2477 rights of way.

Now that federal land policy has shifted to retention and conservation, public roads and rights of way in remote areas appear in a different light. Some roads and other rights of way are undoubtedly necessary, but private landowners express the fear that expansive R.S. 2477 definitions will undermine their private property rights by allowing strangers to drive vehicles across their ranches and homesteads. Conservationists and federal land managers worry that vehicle use in inappropriate locations can permanently scar the land, destroy solitude, impair wilderness, endanger archeological and natural features, and generally make it difficult or impossible for land managers to carry out their statutory duties to protect the lands from "unnecessary or undue degradation." 43 U.S.C. § 1732(b). They argue that too loose an interpretation of R.S. 2477 will conjure into existence rights of way where none existed before, turning every path, vehicle track, or dry wash in southern Utah into a potential route for cars, jeeps, or off-road vehicles. For their part, the Counties assert that R.S. 2477 rights of way are "major components of the transportation systems of western states," and express the fear that federal land managers and conservationists are attempting to redefine those rights out of existence, with serious "financial and other impacts" on the people of Utah. Thus, the definition of R.S. 2477 rights of way across federal land, which used to be a non-issue, has become a flash point, and litigants are driven to the historical archives for documentation of matters no one had reason to document at the time.

I. FACTUAL AND PROCEDURAL BACKGROUND

In September and October of 1996, road crews employed by San Juan, Kane, and Garfield Counties entered public lands managed by the BLM and graded sixteen roads (or "primitive trails," as the BLM calls them) located in southern Utah. The Counties did not notify the BLM in advance, or obtain permission to conduct their road grading activities. With a few possible exceptions, none of these roads had previously been graded by the Counties, though some of them showed signs of previous construction or maintenance activity. The roads are claimed by the Counties as rights of way under R.S. 2477; some of them are listed on County maps as Class B or Class D highways. Six of the routes lie within wilderness study areas. Nine are within the Grand Staircase–Escalante National Monument. Six others traverse a mesa overlooking the entrance corridor to the Needles District of Canyonlands National Park. According to the Complaint filed by a consortium of environmental organizations including the Southern Utah Wilderness Alliance (hereinafter collectively referred to as "SUWA"), the areas affected by the Counties' road grading activities "contain stunning red-rock canyon formations, pristine wilderness areas, important cultural and archeological sits [sic], undisturbed wildlife habitat, and significant opportunities for hiking, backpacking and nature study in an area largely undisturbed by road or human . . . development."

SUWA protested to the BLM, but these initial protests resulted in no apparent action against the road grading actions of the Counties. In October of 1996, SUWA filed suit against the BLM, San Juan County, and later Kane and Garfield Counties, alleging that the Counties had engaged in unlawful road construction activities and that the BLM had violated its duties under [various federal laws] by not taking action. The complaint sought declaratory and injunctive relief requiring the BLM to halt the Counties' construction activities and enjoining the Counties from further road construction or maintenance without the BLM's permission. The BLM filed cross-claims against the Counties, alleging that their road construction activities constituted trespass and degradation of federal property in violation of FLPMA. In addition to declaratory and injunctive relief, the BLM sought damages to cover the cost of rehabilitating the affected areas.

The Counties defended on the ground that their road improvement activities were lawful because the activities took place within valid R.S. 2477 rights of way. The district court acknowledged that "the validity and scope of the claimed rights-of-way [were the] key to resolving the trespass claims," Memorandum Decision of May 11, 1998 at 3, but * * * stayed the litigation and referred the issue of the validity and scope of the claimed rights of way to the BLM. * * *

The BLM then conducted a thorough informal adjudication of the Counties' purported rights of way [with public notice, requests to the counties to provide any relevant information, documentary and field investigations, publication of draft determinations, receipt of public comment, and publication of final determinations] * * * concluding that the Counties lacked a valid right of way for fifteen of the sixteen claims, and that Kane County had exceeded the scope of its right of way in the sixteenth claim, the Skutumpah Road.

[The trial court rejected the counties' request for a de novo review of BLM's determinations, and] affirmed the BLM's determinations in their entirety, concluding that the BLM's factual determinations were supported by substantial evidence in the record and that its interpretation of R.S. 2477 was persuasive * * *

III.   TRESPASS CLAIMS AGAINST THE COUNTIES

* * *

The BLM contends, as it did below, that the Counties' actions in grading and realigning the roads in question without prior notice to or authorization from the BLM constituted trespass, whether or not the Counties have a valid R.S. 2477 right of way on those routes. * * * We * * * agree with the BLM, at least in part, and conclude that the holder of an R.S. 2477 right of way across federal land must consult with the appropriate federal land management agency before it undertakes any improvements to an R.S. 2477 right of way beyond routine maintenance. We remand this issue to the district court to determine whether the work performed on the routes in this case went beyond routine maintenance and thus constituted trespass.

The trespass claim presents an issue of "scope," which was litigated in this Court in Sierra Club v. Hodel, 848 F.2d 1068 (10th Cir.1988). In Hodel, the issue was whether Garfield County could convert a one-lane dirt road on an established R.S. 2477 right of way into a two-lane gravel (later paved) road. Applying a state law definition of the scope of the right of way, the Court held that improvements on a valid R.S. 2477 right of way are limited to those "reasonable and necessary for the type of use to which the road has been put." Hodel, 848 F.2d at 1083. * * * In other words, the scope of an R.S. 2477 right of way is limited by the established usage of the route as of the date of repeal of the statute. That did not mean, however, that the road had to be maintained in precisely the same condition it was in on October 21, 1976; rather, it could be improved "as necessary to meet the exigencies of increased travel," so long as this was done "in the light of traditional uses to which the right-of-way was put" as of repeal of the statute in 1976.

The Hodel court also noted that "Utah adheres to the general rule that the owners of the dominant and servient estates 'must exercise [their] rights so as not unreasonably to interfere with the other.' " This requires a system of coordination between the holder of the easement and the owner of the land through which it passes. The Court thus concluded that the BLM needed to make an "initial determination" regarding the reasonableness and necessity of any proposed improvements beyond mere maintenance of the previous condition of the road. * * * [This is] consistent with holdings of circuit courts that changes in roads on R.S. 2477 rights of way across federal lands are subject to regulation by the relevant federal land management agencies. See Clouser v. Espy, 42 F.3d 1522, 1538 (9th Cir.1994) (holding that "regardless whether the trails in question are public highways under R.S. 2477, they are nonetheless subject to the Forest Service regulations"); see also United States v. Jenks, 22 F.3d 1513, 1518 (10th Cir.1994) (holding that the owner of a patent or common law

easement across national forest lands had to apply for a special use permit).
* * *

The Counties argue, in effect, that as long as their activities are conducted within the physical boundaries of a right of way, their activities cannot constitute a trespass. But this misconceives the nature of a right of way. A right of way is not tantamount to fee simple ownership of a defined parcel of territory. Rather, it is an entitlement to use certain land in a particular way. To convert a two-track jeep trail into a graded dirt road, or a graded road into a paved one, alters the use, affects the servient estate, and may go beyond the scope of the right of way. * * * This does not mean that no changes can ever be made, but that any improvements must be made in light of the traditional uses to which the right of way had been put, fixed as of October 21, 1976. Hodel, 848 F.2d at 1084. The Counties are correct that, under Hodel, the right-of-way holder may sometimes be entitled to change the character of the roadway when needed to accommodate traditional uses, but even legitimate changes in the character of the roadway require consultation when those changes go beyond routine maintenance. Just because a proposed change falls within the scope of a right of way does not mean that it can be undertaken unilaterally. * * *

We therefore hold that when the holder of an R.S. 2477 right of way across federal land proposes to undertake any improvements in the road along its right of way, beyond mere maintenance, it must advise the federal land management agency of that work in advance, affording the agency a fair opportunity to carry out its own duties to determine whether the proposed improvement is reasonable and necessary in light of the traditional uses of the rights of way as of October 21, 1976, to study potential effects, and if appropriate, to formulate alternatives that serve to protect the lands. The initial determination of whether the construction work falls within the scope of an established right of way is to be made by the federal land management agency, which has an obligation to render its decision in a timely and expeditious manner. * * * In the event of disagreement, the parties may resort to the courts.

* * *

IV. PRIMARY JURISDICTION OVER R.S. 2477 RIGHTS OF WAY

We turn now to the district court's holding that none of the fifteen contested routes falls within a valid R.S. 2477 right of way. We address first the question of whether the district court should have treated this dispute as an appeal of an informal, but legally binding, administrative adjudication, or instead should have treated it as a de novo legal proceeding. * * *

The difference is significant. If the doctrine of primary jurisdiction applies, * * * judicial review is limited to determining whether there was substantial evidence in the BLM proceeding to support the agency's determinations. If not, * * * the district court should have conducted a de novo proceeding * * * [in which] the parties were entitled to introduce evidence in court (including but not limited to the administrative record), and questions of fact would be decided by the court on a preponderance of the evidence standard. * * *

Primary jurisdiction is a prudential doctrine designed to allocate authority between courts and administrative agencies. An issue of primary jurisdiction arises when a litigant asks a court to resolve "[an] issue [ ] which, under a regulatory scheme, ha[s] been placed within the special competence of an administrative body." United States v. Western Pac. R.R. Co., 352 U.S. 59, 64 (1956). If the issue is one "that Congress has assigned to a specific agency," Williams Pipe Line Co. v. Empire Gas Corp., 76 F.3d 1491, 1496 (10th Cir.1996), the doctrine of primary jurisdiction allows the court to stay the judicial proceedings and direct the parties to seek a decision before the appropriate administrative agency. The agency is then said to have "primary jurisdiction."

* * *

* * *[N]othing in the terms of R.S. 2477 gives the BLM authority to make binding determinations on the validity of the rights of way granted thereunder, and we decline to infer such authority from silence when the statute creates no executive role for the BLM. This decision is reinforced by the long history of practice under the statute, during which the BLM has consistently disclaimed authority to make binding decisions on R.S. 2477 rights of way. Indeed, there have been 139 years of practice under the statute—110 years while the statute was in force, and 29 years since its repeal—and the BLM has not pointed to a single case in which a court has deferred to a binding determination by the BLM on an R.S. 2477 right of way. We conclude that the BLM lacks primary jurisdiction and that the district court abused its discretion by deferring to the BLM.

This does not mean that the BLM is forbidden from determining the validity of R.S. 2477 rights of way for its own purposes. The BLM has always had this authority. It exercises this authority in what it calls "administrative determinations." In its 1993 Report to Congress, the Department of the Interior explained that the BLM had developed "procedures for administratively recognizing and ... record[ing] this information on the land status records." 1993 D.O.I. Report to Congress, at 25. These procedures "are not intended to be binding, or a final agency action." Id. Rather, "they are recognitions of 'claims' and are useful only for limited purposes," namely, for the agency's internal "land-use planning purposes." Id. at 25–26. Nonetheless, they may reflect the agency's expertise and fact-finding capability, and as such will be of use to the court. * * *

Nothing in our decision today impugns the BLM's authority to make non-binding, administrative determinations, or the introduction and use of BLM findings as evidence in litigation.

V. LEGAL ISSUES ON REMAND

Because the BLM lacks primary jurisdiction over R.S. 2477 rights of way, a remand is required to permit the district court to conduct a plenary review and resolution of the R.S. 2477 claims in this case. On remand, the parties are permitted to introduce evidence regarding the validity and scope of the claims, including, but not limited to, the evidence contained in the administrative record before the BLM.

Bearing in mind the burden this places on the district court, and the importance of these issues to resolution of potentially thousands of R.S. 2477 claims in the State of Utah and elsewhere, this Court will proceed now to address some of the significant legal issues that have been briefed by the parties on appeal and ruled on by the court below. This should not be understood as a comprehensive catalog of applicable legal principles. Undoubtedly, new legal issues will arise in the course of the proceedings on remand. More importantly, as explained below, we are aware that some of the central legal concepts involved in this case cannot be resolved in the abstract, but must necessarily be fleshed out in the context of the actual facts of the case.

A. State or Federal Law

The central question in this case is how a valid R.S. 2477 right of way is acquired. As framed by the parties, the answer to this question turns on whether federal or state law governs the acquisition of rights of way under R.S. 2477. For reasons discussed below, we are more doubtful than the parties that the choice between federal and state law is outcome determinative. The principal difference between the federal and state standards, according to the parties, is whether acceptance of an R.S. 2477 right of way is dependent on actual "construction," meaning that "[s]ome form of mechanical construction must have occurred to construct or improve the highway," (the supposed "federal" standard adopted by the BLM), or whether it can be established by the "passage of vehicles by users over time" (the supposed "state" standard advocated by the Counties). * * * [I]t is far from clear that any of the R.S. 2477 claims under adjudication would pass the "usage" test and flunk the "construction" test, or vice versa. Much depends on questions of degree: what type, how frequent, and how well documented need the "passage of vehicles over time" have been to establish a right of way under state law, if applicable? How extensive must "construction" activities have been to establish a right of way under the BLM administrative definition? If the necessary extent of "construction" is the construction necessary to enable the general public to drive vehicles over the route, it may well turn out that the two standards will lead to the same results in most cases.

We nonetheless begin with this question: which law applies?

* * *

* * * [R.S. 2477's] language is short, sweet, and enigmatic: "And be it further enacted, that the right of way for the construction of highways over public lands, not reserved for public uses, is hereby granted." There is little legislative history. Interestingly, Sections 1, 2, 4, 5, and 9 of the Act make explicit reference either to state law or to the "local customs or rules of miners" in the district. * * * On the other hand, Sections 7, 10, and 11 make explicit reference to other federal laws. * * * Section 8 refers to neither state law nor federal law. * * * [In a prior decision, Sierra Club v.

Hodel, supra, we] suggested that "[t]he silence of section 8 reflects the probable fact that Congress simply did not decide which sovereign's law should apply."

The real question, we think, is not whether state law applies or federal law applies, but whether federal law looks to state law to flesh out details of interpretation. R.S. 2477 is a federal statute and it governs the disposition of rights to federal property, a power constitutionally vested in Congress. * * * As the Supreme Court has stated, "The laws of the United States alone control the disposition of title to its lands. The states are powerless to place any limitation or restriction on that control." United States v. Oregon, 295 U.S. 1, 27–28 (1935). "The construction of grants by the United States is a federal not a state question." Id. at 28.

Even where an issue is ultimately governed by federal law, however, it is not uncommon for courts to "borrow" state law to aid in interpretation of the federal statute. The Supreme Court has explained that "[c]ontroversies ... governed by federal law, do not inevitably require resort to uniform federal rules.... Whether to adopt state law or to fashion a nationwide federal rule is a matter of judicial policy 'dependent upon a variety of considerations always relevant to the nature of the specific governmental interests and to the effects upon them of applying state law.' " United States v. Kimbell Foods, Inc., 440 U.S. 715, 727–28 (1979). * * *

In determining when to borrow state law in the interpretation of a federal statute, the Supreme Court has instructed courts to consider: whether there is a "need for a nationally uniform body of law," whether state law would "frustrate federal policy or functions," and what "impact a federal rule might have on existing relationships under state law." Wilson, 442 U.S. at 672. * * * It follows that to the extent state law is "borrowed" in the course of interpreting R.S. 2477, it must be in service of "federal policy or functions," and cannot derogate from the evident purposes of the federal statute. State law is "borrowed" not for its own sake, and not on account of any inherent state authority over the subject matter, but solely to the extent it provides "an appropriate and convenient measure of the content" of the federal law. * * *.

To modern eyes, R.S. 2477 may seem to stand on its own terms, without need for reference to any outside body of law. At the time of its enactment, however, the creation and legal incidence of "highways" was an important field within the common law, with well-developed legal principles reflected in numerous legal treatises and decisions. * * * It is reasonable to assume that when Congress granted rights of way for the construction of highways across the unreserved lands of the West in 1866, it was aware of and incorporated the common law pertaining to the nature of public highways and how they are established.

In the decades following enactment of R.S. 2477, when disputes arose, courts uniformly interpreted the statute in light of this well-developed body of legal principles, most of which were embodied in state court decisions.

* * *

This did not mean, and never meant, that state law could override federal requirements or undermine federal land policy. For example, in an early decision, the BLM determined that a state law purporting to accept rights of way along all section lines within the county was beyond the intentions of Congress in enacting R.S. 2477. Douglas County, Washington, 26 Pub. Lands Dec. 446 (1898). The Department described this state law as "the manifestation of a marked and novel liberality on the part of the county authorities in dealing with the public land," and stated that R.S. 2477 "was not intended to grant a right of way over public lands in advance of an apparent necessity therefor, or on the mere suggestion that at some future time such roads may be needed." Id. at 447. * * * In none of the cases applying state law was there any suggestion of a conflict between the state law and any federal principles or interests. Rather, state law was employed as a convenient and well-developed set of rules for resolving such issues as the length of time of public use necessary to establish a right of way, abandonment of a right of way, and priorities between competing private claims.

We do not believe application of state law in this fashion offends the criteria * * * for appropriate borrowing of state law in the interpretation of federal statutes. The first question is whether there is a "need for a uniform national rule" regarding what steps are required to perfect an R.S. 2477 right of way. We think not. Although the substantive content of state law could in some cases conflict with the purposes of federal law * * *, we do not think uniformity for uniformity's sake is necessary in this area of the law. Indeed, there is some force to the view that interpretation of R.S. 2477 should be sensitive to the differences in geographic, climatic, demographic, and economic circumstances among the various states, differences which can have an effect on the establishment and use of routes of travel. * * * [I]n the southern Utah canyon country in which this case arises * * * [t]he sparse population, rugged terrain, scarcity of passable routes, seasonal differences in snow, mud, and stream flow, fragile and environmentally sensitive land, and paucity of towns or other centers of economic activity, could have an effect on the location of roads.

Moreover, for over 130 years disputes over R.S. 2477 claims were litigated by reference to non-uniform state standards, a fact that casts serious doubt on any claims of a need for uniformity today. * * *

We therefore conclude that federal law governs the interpretation of R.S. 2477, but that in determining what is required for acceptance of a right of way under the statute, federal law "borrows" from long-established principles of state law, to the extent that state law provides convenient and appropriate principles for effectuating congressional intent. The applicable state law in this case is that of the State of Utah, supplemented where appropriate by precedent from other states with similar principles of law.

B. Specific Legal Issues

We turn now to the criteria governing recognition of a valid R.S. 2477 right of way. * * *

1. Burden of Proof

The district court correctly ruled that the burden of proof lies on those parties "seeking to enforce rights-of-way against the federal government." Under Utah law determining when a highway is deemed to be dedicated to the use of the public, "[t]he presumption is in favor of the property owner; and the burden of establishing public use for the required period of time is on those claiming it." Leo M. Bertagnole, Inc. v. Pine Meadow Ranches, 639 P.2d 211, 213 (Utah 1981). Courts in other states have reached a similar conclusion. Because evidence in these cases is over a quarter of a century old, the burden of proof could be decisive in some cases.

This allocation of the burden of proof to the R.S. 2477 claimant is consonant with federal law and federal interests. As the district court noted, "[T]he established rule [is] that land grants are construed favorably to the Government, that nothing passes except what is conveyed in clear language, and that if there are doubts they are resolved for the Government, not against it." quoting United States v. Union Pac. R.R. Co., 353 U.S. 112, 116 (1957). * * * On remand, therefore, the Counties, as the parties claiming R.S. 2477 rights, bear the burden of proof.

2. The Public Use Standard

Under the common law, the establishment of a public right of way required two steps: the landowner's objectively manifested intent to dedicate property to the public use as a right of way, and acceptance by the public. * * * In the years after its enactment, R.S. 2477 was uniformly interpreted by the courts as an express dedication of the right of way by the landowner, the United States Congress. The difficult question was whether any particular disputed route had been "accepted" by the public before the land had been transferred to private ownership or otherwise reserved.

The rules for "acceptance" of a right of way by the public (whether under R.S. 2477 or otherwise) varied somewhat from state to state. Some states required official action by the local body of government before a public highway could be deemed "accepted." * * * In such states, the appropriation of public funds for repair was generally deemed sufficient to manifest acceptance by the public body. In most of the western states, where R.S. 2477 was most significant, acceptance required no governmental act, but could be manifested by continuous public use over a specified period of time. This was the common law rule. * * * In some states, the required period was the same as that for easements by prescription, in some states it was some other specified period, often five to ten years, and in some states it was simply a period long enough to indicate intention to accept. * * *

[The court then reviewed Utah law, and summarized as follows:] Acceptance of an R.S. 2477 right of way in Utah thus requires continuous public use for a period of ten years. The question then becomes how continuous and intensive the public use must be. The decisions make clear that occasional or desultory use is not sufficient. * * * [As] the Utah Supreme Court stated: "While it is difficult to fix a standard by which to measure what is a public use or a public thoroughfare, it can be said here that the road was used by many and different persons for a variety of purposes; that it was open to all who desired to use it; that the use made of it was as general and extensive as the situation and surroundings would permit, had the road been formally laid out as a public highway by public authority." Lindsay Land & Live Stock, 285 P. at 648.

The requirements for establishing acceptance of a right of way by user cannot, we think, be captured by verbal formulas alone. It is necessary to set forth the factual circumstances of the decided cases, both those recognizing and those not recognizing the validity of R.S. 2477 claims. On remand, the district court will have the difficult task of determining whether the Counties have met their burden of demonstrating acceptance under these precedents. * * *

3.   The "Mechanical Construction" Standard

* * *

Consistent with our conclusion that acceptance of the grant of R.S. 2477 rights of way is governed by long-standing principles of state law and common law, we cannot accept the argument that mechanical construction is necessary to an R.S. 2477 claim. Adoption of the "mechanical construction" criterion would alter over a century of judicial and administrative interpretation. This is not to say that evidence of construction is irrelevant. Construction or repair at public expense has sometimes been treated as a substitute for public use, as shortening the period of public use necessary for establishing acceptance, or as evidence of public use or lack thereof. Thus, although there are no Utah cases directly on point, we hold that evidence of actual construction (appropriate to the historical period in question), or lack thereof, can be taken into consideration as evidence of the required extent of public use, though it is not a necessary or sufficient element.

The BLM and SUWA defend their proposed "mechanical construction" standard primarily as dictated by the "plain meaning" of R.S. 2477, which grants the rights of way for the "construction" of highways. The BLM quotes the definition of "construction" from an 1860 edition of Webster's Dictionary as "[t]he act of building, or of devising and forming, fabrication." * * *

We are not persuaded. First, it would take more semantic chutzpah than we can muster to assert that a word used by Congress in 1866 has a "plain meaning" that went undiscerned by courts and executive officers for over 100 years. But even confining ourselves to the quoted dictionary definitions of "construction," we are left with a wide range of meanings, including "build," "form," and "make." If nineteenth-century pioneers made a road across the wilderness by repeated use—the so-called "beaten path"—this would fall squarely within the scope of the quoted definition. Such a road would be "formed" and "made" even if no mechanical means were employed. * * *

* * *

For this reason, we are skeptical that there is much difference, in practice, between a "construction" standard (if applied in light of contemporary conditions) and the traditional legal standard of continuous public use. If a particular route sustained substantial use by the general public over the necessary period of time, one of two things must be true: either no mechanical construction was necessary, or any necessary construction must have taken place. It is hard to imagine how a road sufficient to meet the user standard could fail to satisfy a realistic standard of construction. Thus, we do not necessarily disagree with the BLM's statement that:

A highway right-of-way cannot be established by haphazard, unintentional, or incomplete actions. For example, the mere passage of vehicles across the land, in the absence of any other evidence, is not sufficient to meet the construction criteria of R.S. 2477 and to establish that a highway right-of-way was granted.

* * * As the precedents in Utah and other states demonstrate, a road may be created intentionally, by continued public use, without record evidence of what the BLM defines as "mechanical construction." Such action is not haphazard, unintentional, or incomplete, though it might lack centralized direction; and the legal standard is not satisfied "merely" by evidence that vehicles may have passed over the land at some time in the past. That is a caricature of the common law standard.

Indeed, contrary to the apparent assumptions of the parties, it is quite possible for R.S. 2477 claims to pass the BLM's "mechanical construction" standard but to fail the common law test of continuous public use. See Town of Rolling v. Emrich, 122 Wis. 134, 99 N.W. 464, 464 (1904) (rejecting R.S. 2477 claim despite evidence that two men "cut out a road . . . through the 80 acres in question to haul logs upon") * * *. Large parts of southern Utah are crisscrossed by old mining and logging roads constructed for a particular purpose and used for a limited period of time, but not by the general public. Thus, we cannot agree with Appellees' argument that a "mechanical construction" standard is necessary to avoid recognition of "a multitude of property claims far beyond the scope of Congress's express grant in R.S. 2477." * * *

* * *

NOTES AND QUESTIONS

1. R.S. 2477 issues might be separated into two categories: first, the validity of the R.S. 2477 claim (the issue that occupies most of the court's opinion); and second, assuming the claim is valid, its scope, including the extent to which the holder might "improve" or "enlarge" it. On the trespass issue, the court seems to assume that the counties' R.S. 2477 claims are valid, and the only issue is scope. But what if the federal government believes a county's claim is invalid? Does the county have to notify the United States before going out to do "routine maintenance" of these claims? Does the court, in other words, encourage R.S. 2477 claimants like the counties here to fire up their bulldozers to "maintain" the

rights-of-way they claim, regardless of whether validity is at issue? To rip down "closed to vehicles" signs federal land managers have posted on federal lands that the counties think are subject to their R.S. 2477 claims? Or do they have to obtain permission from the federal land manager first? In short, who controls the federal land subject to the claim before the courts determine its validity—the claimant or the federal agency? Who has the burden of going to court, the county (or other R.S. 2477 claimant), or the United States (or other landowner seeking to contest such a claim)?

Upon remand, the district court judge made a pre-trial determination that, until Kane County proves its claim, the federal land managers may determine whether off-road vehicles ("ORVs") are permitted on the asserted R.S. 2477 roads. In August 2005, the county enacted an ordinance opening certain routes on federal lands to ORV use. However the federal land managers had closed those same areas to such uses. The Wilderness Society alleged that the county removed BLM signs restricting ORV travel and replaced them with county signs indicating the posted routes were open to ORVs. Wilderness Society v. Kane County, 470 F.Supp.2d 1300 (D.Utah 2006).

The Ninth Circuit recently reaffirmed the principle that rights-of-way through federal lands are subject to reasonable regulation by the United States. Hale v. Norton, 461 F.3d 1092 (9th Cir. 2006).

2. Why did the parties fight so hard over the primary jurisdiction issue? What difference did it make, especially since the court acknowledges that BLM can still make its own determinations about the validity of county right-of-way claims, and the courts can take them into account? For an extended argument in favor of primary jurisdiction here, see Bret C. Birdsong, *Road Rage and R.S. 2477: Judicial and Administrative Responsibility for Resolving Road Claims on Public Lands*, 56 HASTINGS L.J. 523 (2005).

3. Is the court saying state property law applies, or is the court saying federal law applies but it "borrows" state property law? What difference, if any, does it make? Does the result mean that the federal statute may be applied to federal lands in different ways in different states? Is uniformity in such things an important value that is undermined by this decision? Is there anything Utah can do to modify its state right-of-way law by statute to better tailor the R.S. 2477 claim analysis?

4. It seems likely that the evidence to be adduced on R.S. 2477 claims to meet the standard in Utah law (continuous use for ten years sometime prior to 1976) will often be stale or fragmentary, depending on old documents or fading memories. Does that suggest the burden of proof may be crucial to many outcomes? Who has the burden of proof, and by what reasoning?

5. All told, this ruling effectively creates a kind of World War I-style trench warfare over the existence of R.S. 2477 rights of way, with claimants and their opponents fighting yard by yard, applying vague standards to a thin and likely not very reliable historical record. And that war will take place directly in the federal district courts with full-blown trials, rather

than primarily in the agencies, with the courts merely reviewing records assembled by, and the findings of, the agency. Should Judge McConnell (often mentioned as a potential conservative nominee to the Supreme Court) have given more consideration to the workload of the courts or to the institutional strengths of specialist administrative tribunals in the Department of the Interior? Note that the court does cite an 1898 Interior Department opinion to show how R.S. 2477 borrows state law. Is the court consistent in its view of primary jurisdiction? Though there may not have been judicial opinions deferring to BLM determinations of R.S. 2477 rights-of-way, the Interior Department has been making such determinations for over a century.

6.   Can one make a claim for an R.S. 2477 right-of-way on a "single-track" foot or livestock trail? Or a dogsled trail in Alaska? If the answer is yes, and such a claim is established, what is its scope; that is, can it be widened into a trail suitable for motorized vehicles? Can a wagon trail be converted into an eight-lane highway? By what process, and who controls the decision?

7.   Judge McConnell acknowledges the concern of private property holders that "expansive R.S. 2477 definitions will undermine their private property rights by allowing strangers to drive vehicles across their ranches and homesteads." If you owned private property in rural Utah, which your predecessor in title obtained from the federal government under one of the homestead laws in 1908, and there was an old trail crossing the property that you believe dates back to the 1880s, should you be worried by this decision? Is this a case where environmental advocates usually friendly to government regulation of private property are taking positions that effectively protect private property rights? In some situations, the U.S. Forest Service has sought to argue that public highways have been established under R.S. 2477 in order to gain access over private land to national forests for timber and recreational use.

8.   Does this ruling make it possible to claim rights-of-way through national parks, wilderness areas and other protected areas? Canyonlands National Park, comprising 340,000 acres somewhat to the north of Kane and Garfield Counties, was created by Act of Congress in 1964; previously, it had been open public lands. Could the local county (or anybody, for on its face R.S. 2477 does not seem to restrict who may claim rights-of-way) assert a claim on a foot trail or wagon road that was in existence when the Park was created? If it succeeds, can it pave the road to stimulate tourist traffic?

9.   Why does the court employ the *Union Pacific R.R. Co.* canon of interpretation of grants in favor of the federal government and not the *Leo Sheep* version that is less deferential to U.S. interests?

b.   ANILCA PERMITS

Congress addressed the issue of access to non-federal land across certain kinds of federal land in two different parts of the Alaska National Interest

Lands Conservation Act (ANILCA) of 1980, 16 U.S.C. §§ 3170 and 3210, as follows:

§ 3170. Special access and access to inholdings

(a) Use of snowmachines, motorboats, airplanes, nonmotorized surface transportation, etc. for traditional activities and for travel.

Notwithstanding any other provision of this Act or other law, the Secretary shall permit, on conservation system units, national recreation areas, and national conservation areas, and those public lands designated as wilderness study, the use of snowmachines (during periods of adequate snow cover, or frozen river conditions in the case of wild and scenic rivers), motorboats, airplanes, and nonmotorized surface transportation methods for traditional activities (where such activities are permitted by this Act or other law) and for travel to and from villages and homesites. Such use shall be subject to reasonable regulations by the Secretary to protect the natural and other values of the conservation system units, national recreation areas, and national conservation areas, and shall not be prohibited unless, after notice and hearing in the vicinity of the affected unit or area, the Secretary finds that such use would be detrimental to the resource values of the unit or area. Nothing in this section shall be construed as prohibiting the use of other methods of transportation for such travel and activities on conservation system lands where such use is permitted by this Act or other law.

(b) Right of access to State or private owner or occupier.

Notwithstanding any other provisions of this Act or other law, in any case in which State owned or privately owned land, including subsurface rights of such owners underlying public lands, or a valid mining claim or other valid occupancy is within or is effectively surrounded by one or more conservation system units, national recreation areas, national conservation areas, or those public lands designated as wilderness study, the State or private owner or occupier shall be given by the Secretary such rights as may be necessary to assure adequate and feasible access for economic and other purposes to the concerned land by such State or private owner or occupier and their successors in interest. Such rights shall be subject to reasonable regulations issued by the Secretary to protect the natural and other values of such lands.

§ 3210. Access by owner to nonfederally owned land

(a) Notwithstanding any other provision of law, and subject to such terms and conditions as the Secretary of Agriculture may prescribe, the Secretary shall provide such access to nonfederally owned land within the boundaries of the National Forest System as the Secretary deems adequate to secure to the owner the reasonable use and enjoyment thereof: *Provided,* That such owner comply with rules and regulations applicable to ingress and egress to or from the National Forest System.

(b) Notwithstanding any other provision of law, and subject to such terms and conditions as the Secretary of the Interior may prescribe, the Secretary shall provide such access to nonfederally owned land surrounded by public lands managed by the Secretary under the Federal Land Policy and Management Act of 1976 (43 U.S.C. 1701–82) as the Secretary deems adequate to secure to the owner the responsible use and enjoyment thereof: *Provided*, That such owner comply with rules and regulations applicable to access across public lands.

NOTES AND QUESTIONS

1. A threshold question is whether these provisions, parts of a major piece of legislation that otherwise addresses only federal lands in Alaska, apply outside that state. The general assumption has been that § 3170 applies only in Alaska (because, among other things, it makes repeated reference to "conservation system units," a term of art in ANILCA applied to protected federal lands in Alaska). On the other hand, § 3210, added by amendment late in the congressional process, may apply outside of Alaska, although so far the courts have not definitively resolved this question. *Compare* Montana Wilderness Association v. United States Forest Service, 655 F.2d 951, 954 (9th Cir.1981) (holding that § 3210(a) applies to national forest lands in the lower forty-eight states, but suggesting, in dictum, that § 3210(b) applies only in Alaska, because ANILCA specifically defines "public lands" as certain lands "situated in Alaska"), *with* United States v. Srnsky, 271 F.3d 595 (4th Cir.2001) (questioning, in dictum, the Ninth Circuit's conclusion that subsection (a) applies outside of Alaska). The Forest Service has accepted the applicability of the ANILCA provision to all of its lands and adopted implementing regulations requiring permits. *See* 36 C.F.R. Parts 251(D) (access to non-federal lands); *see also* 36 C.F.R. § 212.6 (generic policy on ingress and egress). The Service now routinely applies the standards of these regulations in issuing, conditioning, and denying permits to inholders. A map and problem dealing with the Forest Service ANILCA regulations for right-of-way permits for access to inholdings is posted on this casebook's web site: www.law.indiana.edu/publicland

2. *Montana Wilderness Ass'n* upheld a claim by Burlington Northern Inc. (BN), which owned timberland checkerboarded within the Gallatin National Forest near Bozeman, Montana (the legacy of the Northern Pacific Land Grant Act of 1864). The court found that ANILCA § 3210(a) gave BN a right of access to its land, but did not address the extent to which BN's access could be regulated by the Forest Service in order to protect other values. BN was seeking to build an access road in order to remove timber from its land. Eventually the matter was mooted when BN and the Forest Service entered into, and Congress approved, large land exchanges that removed BN's inholdings from the forest. *See* Gallatin Range Consolidation and Protection Act of 1993, 107 Stat. 987; Gallatin Land Consolidation Act of 1998, 112 Stat. 2371.

3. Access-to-inholdings issues can arise when the government considers whether to preserve surrounding federal lands as roadless wilderness. A section of the Wilderness Act (16 U.S.C. § 1134(a)) specifically addresses

access to non-federal inholdings in federal wilderness areas, and is discussed briefly in Chapter 12A.

4.   These ANILCA provisions are rife with interesting interpretive questions. For example, the two sections plainly overlap to some extent, but are not easy to mesh together. Section 3170(a) is not limited to inholders, while §§ 3170(b) and 3210(b) both speak of access to nonfederal property interests (such as "valid" mining claims or occupancies) "effectively surrounded" or "surrounded" by certain kinds of federal lands. Boiled down, these statutory provisions recognize that inholders have some sort of "right" of access across surrounding federal lands, but that the federal land managers have considerable authority to regulate the exercise of that right to protect the federal lands. Section 3170(a) even acknowledges that the United States may "prohibit" access in certain circumstances. What are the dimensions of this "right of access," and how much can the federal land manager regulate the exercise of the right? May the Secretary specify the route of access? Require access by a route that is twice as costly as the inholder's preferred route, in order to avoid important wildlife habitat? May the Secretary control the means of access? Require access only by four-wheel drive vehicles, as opposed to passenger cars? By pack mule, as opposed to vehicle? By helicopter rather than across the surface?

5.   Might the general idea embodied in these statutes—that inholders have some sort of right to access their properties, but its exercise can be dictated substantially by the federal land manager—reflect or incorporate a kind of general federal common law of property that ought to be applied to access questions generally involving the federal lands? Or should access questions be determined, at least in part, by the particular statutes and terms under which the inholdings were created? For example, should access to state common school section inholdings be measured by a different legal standard from access to mining claims, or from access to inholdings created by patent under the Homestead Act?

6.   Litigation over access issues, many involving the ANILCA provisions, is proliferating. In Hale v. Norton, 476 F.3d 694 (9th Cir. 2007) (cert. pending as of this writing), the court held that an inholding in the Wrangell–St. Elias National Park and Preserve in Alaska had "limited access rights" under § 3170(a), and the National Park Service properly incorporated NEPA analysis in its decision about what kind of access is "adequate and feasible" when balanced against the agency's mission to "protect the natural and other values" of the federal lands. In Fitzgerald Living Trust v. United States, 460 F.3d 1259 (9th Cir. 2006), involving access to an inholding in a national forest in Arizona, the Court concluded that (a) the Homestead Act and the inholder's patent under that Act implied only a license for access, not an implied easement carrying with it a legal right of access; (b) no common law easement of necessity operated against the federal government, because ANILCA § 3210(a) applied here and granted a statutory right of access that eliminated the necessity for a common law right; and (c) the Forest Service's grant of a limited easement, upon payment of fair market value (set at $114 annually) and subject to other protective conditions, was proper. These holdings are consistent with

the Tenth Circuit's ruling in United States v. Jenks, 22 F.3d 1513 (10th Cir.1994).

7. In Adams v. United States (I), 3 F.3d 1254 (9th Cir.1993) and Adams v. United States (II), 255 F.3d 787 (9th Cir. 2001), the court held that an inholder on national forest land in Nevada was required by the terms of federal laws like ANILCA to apply for a special use authorization from the Forest Service for any use of a road through forest land which exceeded use of the road for travel by the general public, or for access which would cause surface-disturbing activities. Other cases support the idea that federal land managers have broad authority to regulate the manner and means of access regardless of the origin of the access right. *See, e.g.,* McFarland v. Kempthorne, 464 F.Supp.2d 1014 (D. Mont. 2006).

8. Roads have important implications for conservation in many ways, on wildlife dispersal and migration patterns, drainage patterns, and air and water quality. A whole new discipline has sprung up around the study of the ecological implications of roads and ways to make them more user friendly. A path-breaking, interdisciplinary book on the subject is ROAD ECOLOGY: SCIENCE AND SOLUTIONS (Forman & Sperling, eds. 2003). Federal land managers are beginning to pay attention to such matters in their plans, as are federal and state highway departments.

9. Wildlife refuges can also raise difficult access issues. In Coupland v. Morton, 5 Envtl. L. Rptr. 20504 (E.D.Va.1975), aff'd, 526 F.2d 588 (4th Cir.1975), the U.S. Fish and Wildlife Service severely restricted access to adjacent private land along a barrier island beach in a refuge because the increasing traffic was adversely affecting management. Plaintiff property owners challenged the restrictions on a variety of grounds, but the court denied relief. Later, however, political pressure forced the FWS to relax the access rules, and a few years later, Congress enacted a law permitting some full-time residents to commute across the refuge daily. 94 Stat. 958–59 (1980); see Michael J. Bean and Melanie J. Rowland, THE EVOLUTION OF NATIONAL WILDLIFE LAW 293–94 (3d ed. 1997).

B. DELEGATION

The Property Clause gives Congress power to make "all needful rules and regulations respecting" federal property, and therefore the power exercised by the executive branch to manage federal lands must somehow be delegated by Congress. Broad delegations have been common, and have been upheld in such historic cases as United States v. Grimaud, *supra* p. 126. More recently, the Supreme Court has affirmed the propriety of broad delegations, as long as the agency is given an "intelligible principle" to apply. Whitman v. American Trucking Ass'n, 531 U.S. 457 (2001). Moreover, "implied" delegations by acquiescence have also been upheld in United States v. Midwest Oil, *infra* p. 418.

A general delegation of authority to a cabinet-level officer or to an agency head is normally construed to include an implied power to subdelegate authority down through the department or agency. Subdelegations must, however, be express. In United States v. Gemmill, 535 F.2d 1145 (9th Cir.1976), for example, trespass convictions were overturned because power to close a part of a national forest had not been administratively subdelegated to the field official who had ordered the closure. Moreover, a Cabinet Secretary may not transfer jurisdiction from one agency to another inside his Department if it contradicts congressional direction.

In the past fifteen years, interest has grown in devolving or delegating management authority over particular tracts of public land to local or regional collaborative bodies. Indeed, this is a feature of both ecosystem management and cooperative federalism. See Keiter, *supra* p. 38 and Fischman, *supra* p. 201, respectively. In most cases, the parties seeking shared or delegated authority do not claim ownership of federal resources; they seek only a more formal and influential role in how the resources are managed. Collaborative management may be a good alternative to federal acquisition of nonfederal land. Often the result is that some management authority leaves the hands of established federal agencies and is given to ad hoc groups composed of a variety of interests, including private economic interests. In its more extreme forms, delegation may be a form of outsourcing resource management services. Congress increasingly has fashioned unconventional federal land management schemes in a number of geographic areas.

This section concerns two issues. The first is the extent to which subdelegations of decisionmaking authority can be made to nonfederal actors under existing, generally-worded statutes. This raises rather straightforward legal questions of statutory interpretation, as reflected in the following case. The second issue is whether this kind of devolution is a good idea as a matter of policy.

National Parks & Conservation Association v. Stanton

United States District Court, District of Columbia, 1999.
54 F.Supp.2d 7.

■ JUDGE KESSLER

Plaintiffs National Parks and Conservation Association ("NPCA"), Barry Harper, and the American Canoe Association ("ACA") bring this suit against Robert Stanton, Director of the National Park Service ("NPS"), and Bruce Babbitt, Secretary of the Department of the Interior ("Secretary"), challenging Defendants' plan for management of the Niobrara National Scenic River ("Niobrara"), located in Nebraska. The challenged management plan, under which NPS delegates all its responsibilities for managing the Niobrara to an independent local council over which NPS has virtually no control, is the first of its kind. * * *

The Niobrara, a unique river with abundant resources that runs through north-central Nebraska, is known for its historical, paleontological, archaeological, and ecological treasures. Its forests abound with ponderosa pine, American elm, bur oak, green ash, basswood, hackberry, and black walnut trees. There is striking bio-diversity among the vegetation, where

160 plant species from eastern, western, and northern forest ecosystems intermingle along the River valley. The Niobrara provides shelter and homes for bald eagles, turkeys, grouse, quails, doves, pheasants, ducks, and geese. It is also home to several threatened and endangered species, including the peregrine falcon, the interior least tern, the piping plover, and the whooping crane. Palaeontologists find a wealth of artifacts on the fossil beds along the Niobrara, including deposits from eighty species of extinct vertebrates. In one fossil excavation site, at least 146 vertebrate species were found. Of the 164 cataloged fossil excavation sites, 15 were rated as internationally significant, and 37 were rated nationally significant. The River was named one of the 10 best canoeing rivers in the nation by Backpacker magazine, and one of the eight special camping areas in the nation by Outside magazine.

One of the Niobrara's unique features is that it runs largely through private land. In 1991, Congress, despite local opposition, designated portions of the Niobrara to become components in the pre-existing national Wild and Scenic Rivers system. Niobrara Scenic River Designation Act of 1991, Pub.L. 102–50 ("NSRDA"); 16 U.S.C. § 1274(a)(117). Recognizing that the area along the River was largely privately-held, Congress limited the amount of land the federal government could acquire, and encouraged state and local involvement in the administration and management of the River locale. Congress also created the eleven member Niobrara Scenic River Advisory Commission ("Advisory Commission"), an advisory group representing local interests, for the purpose of aiding NPS in developing a management plan for the area.

As the agency responsible for overseeing the administration of the Niobrara, NPS developed, with the help of the Advisory Commission, a General Management Plan and Environmental Impact Statement ("GMP/ EIS"). The GMP/EIS outlined four management alternatives for administering the Niobrara * * *. [The NPS ultimately selected] Alternative B [, which] provided for management by a local council, which would include members from various county and state agencies, as well as local landowners and business people[.] * * *

* * * In July of 1997, NPS entered into the Interlocal Cooperative Agreement ("Interlocal Agreement") with local Nebraska governmental entities. The Interlocal Agreement established the Niobrara Council ("Council"), and outlined the Council's duties, which included: enter into agreements with NPS or the U.S. Fish and Wildlife Service ("FWS"); obtain and use funds from any source to perform its functions; coordinate management of the Niobrara with the responsible agencies; assist the four cooperating counties in developing zoning and other land protection methods; review county zoning ordinances and actions for consistency with the GMP; provide a forum for landowner/government conflict; work with landowners and provide technical assistance where there is no zoning; manage law enforcement, public access sites, visitor use levels, and other operational functions; retain the services of professionals as necessary to perform its duties; retain staff members to perform its functions; and acquire and manage real and personal property for staff office purposes

only. The Interlocal Agreement also noted that the Council should attempt to find outside sources of money, to avoid having NPS "dictate the decisions of the council."

* * *

The Council consists of fifteen members: four county commissioners (one from each participating county); four landowners (one from each participating county) two representatives of local Natural Resource Districts; one timber industry representative; one recreational business representative; one representative of the Nebraska Game and Parks Commission; one FWS representative; and one NPS representative. Decisions are reached through simple majority vote.

On August 6, 1997, the Council entered into a Cooperative Agreement with NPS, as called for in the ROD (Record of Decision, the decision document by which the National Park Service selected Alternative B). The Cooperative Agreement can be terminated by either party upon sixty days' notice, and can be modified by mutual written agreement. If the Council fails to manage and protect the Niobrara as set forth in the GMP/EIS, NPS has the authority to terminate the Agreement and implement one of the other Alternatives for managing the Niobrara. Under the GMP/EIS, the Council must carry out its activities to meet standards acceptable to NPS. Under the Cooperative Agreement, NPS must "consider for consistency with the GMP the advice and recommendations of the Council during and upon completion of its activities identified above."

Plaintiffs allege that although it has been over one and a half years since the Council was established, nothing has been done to protect or manage the Niobrara's resources. Plaintiffs challenge the decision to adopt Alternative B, the duties that have been delegated to the Council, and NPS' compliance with NEPA. Plaintiffs seek an injunction requiring NPS to administer the Niobrara itself, and requiring NPS to complete a more thorough EIS under NEPA. * * *

Plaintiffs argue that NPS' decision to adopt Alternative B for management of the Niobrara was an unlawful delegation of its responsibilities and authority. The Court must first examine the extent of NPS' existing statutory obligations before reaching the delegation issue. * * *

In 1968, Congress passed the Wild and Scenic Rivers Act to "preserve [the] selected rivers or sections thereof in their free-flowing condition to protect the water quality of such rivers and to fulfill other vital national conservation purposes". In 16 U.S.C. § 1274, Congress enumerated the rivers that would compose the Wild and Scenic Rivers system, and further indicated which agencies would manage those rivers. The Niobrara Amendment to this statute * * * [specifically delegates administration to the Secretary of the Interior.] 16 U.S.C. § 1274(a)(117) (1999). The duties of the Secretary of the Interior are further explained in 16 U.S.C. § 1281(c) (1999) (emphasis added):

> The Secretary of the Interior, in his *administration* of any component of the national wild and scenic rivers system, may utilize such general statutory authorities relating to areas of the national park system and

such general statutory authorities otherwise available to him for *recreation and preservation purposes and for the conservation and management of natural resources* as he deems appropriate to carry out the purposes of this chapter.

These statutes give the Secretary of the Interior sole responsibility for administering the lands included in the National Parks system and the National Wild and Scenic Rivers system. Basic rules of statutory construction provide that "absent ambiguity or unreasonable result, the literal language of the statute controls". The meaning of "administer" is perfectly clear in this context: it means "to manage . . . to direct or superintend the execution, use, or conduct of . . . to manage or conduct affairs". Thus, the Secretary, who is specifically charged with administering these lands and rivers, cannot wholly delegate his responsibility to a local entity which is not bound by the statutory obligations set forth above.

The creation of the Advisory Commission does not abrogate the Secretary's duties. The extensive legislative history shows that Congress was aware of the unique situation in the Niobrara (i.e., largely privately owned land), and strongly encouraged local participation in the management of the area. In recognition of this situation, Congress created the Advisory Commission to deflect local opposition to national designation and to aid NPS in developing a management plan for the area. But it is clear that in creating the Advisory Commission, Congress did not intend to undermine the Secretary's duties or shift them to any other entity. * * *

* * *

NPS cannot, under the unlawful delegation doctrine, completely shift its responsibility to administer the Niobrara to a private actor, particularly a private actor whose objectivity may be questioned on grounds of conflict of interest. "The relevant inquiry in any delegation challenge is whether Congress intended to permit the delegatee to delegate the authority conferred by Congress." There is no indication in the relevant statutes or the legislative history that Congress intended any variation on the doctrine of unlawful delegation.

Delegations by federal agencies to private parties are, however, valid so long as the federal agency or official retains final reviewing authority. The relevant inquiry in this case therefore becomes whether, in delegating its responsibility to the Council to administer the Niobrara, NPS retained sufficient final reviewing authority over Council actions to prevent a violation of the unlawful delegation doctrine.

According to the GMP, the Interlocal Agreement, and the Cooperative Agreement, Alternative B calls for management of the Niobrara by a local council, with NPS merely serving as liaison and providing technical support as needed. The Council is responsible for hiring staff, monitoring the River resources, evaluating access sites and land protection needs, providing educational and information services, providing law enforcement and emergency services, and maintaining roads, bridges, and other river access sites. These are all duties which fall squarely within the Secretary's responsibilities for managing the Niobrara. The Interlocal Agreement is, however, clear that it is the Council which shall manage the River. Moreover, the Council is encouraged to seek outside sources of funding to avoid having its decisions "dictated" by NPS. To further ensure that NPS does not "dictate" the decisions of the Council, NPS has only one voting member on the Council, and all decisions are made by majority vote. In short, it is clear that NPS retains virtually no final authority over the actions—or inaction—of the Council.

In their defense, Defendants argue that the relevant statutes encourage and authorize NPS to cooperate with local governments, and enter into cooperative agreements, in administering the Niobrara. * * * [A generally applicable portion of the Wild & Scenic Rivers Act provides]:

> The Federal agency charged with the administration of any component of the national wild and scenic rivers system may enter into written cooperative agreements with the Governor of a State, the head of any State agency, or the appropriate official of a political subdivision of a State *for State or local governmental participation in the administration of the component.* The States and their political subdivisions shall be encouraged to cooperate in the planning and administration of components of the system which include or adjoin State-or county-owned lands.

16 U.S.C. § 1281(e) (1999) (emphasis added).

> (1) The Secretary of the Interior, the Secretary of Agriculture, or the head of any other Federal agency, shall *assist, advise, and cooperate with States or their political subdivisions, landowners, private organizations, or individuals to plan, protect, and manage river resources.* Such assistance, advice, and cooperation may be through written agreements or otherwise. This authority applies within or outside a federally administered area and applies to rivers which are components of the National Wild and Scenic Rivers System and to other rivers. Any agreement under this subsection may include provisions for limited financial or other assistance to encourage participation in the acquisition, protection, and management of river resources.

16 U.S.C. § 1282(b)(1) (1999) (emphasis added).

Although NPS is given the authority to enter into cooperative agreements with local governments, there is nothing in any of the statutes or legislative history cited by either party to suggest that Congress wished to change the traditional role of NPS in managing lands and rivers under its stewardship. Furthermore, there is no precedent for the extent to which NPS has delegated its responsibilities to the Council. This is the first such agreement of its kind in NPS' history.

* * *

The Court concludes that Defendants' delegation of its statutory management duties to the Council violates the unlawful delegation doctrine because NPS retains no oversight over the Council, no final reviewing authority over the council's actions or inaction, and the Council's dominant private local interests are likely to conflict with the national environmental interests that NPS is statutorily mandated to represent. NPS lacks the authority to: appoint or remove members of the Council, aside from its own representative; determine which interests will be represented; select Council officers; establish Council sub-committees; determine the term limit for Council members; veto Council decisions which are contrary to the GMP; independently review Council decisions prior to implementation; and control Council funding. The delegation is also unlawful because the Council, made up almost wholly of local commercial and land-owning interests, does not share NPS' national vision and perspective. NPS controls only one of the 15 Council members, and is the only member, besides FWS, who represents national environmental concerns.

* * *

Defendants argue at length that they have supervisory power over the Council, that they are not bound by Council decisions, that they retain ultimate accountability and authority over management of the Niobrara, that they can review the Council's actions for consistency with the GMP, and that they can evaluate the Council's progress. Defendants offer no specifics to support their argument, and in fact, the exact nature and scope of the relationship between the Council and NPS remains vague and unclear. * * *

The tenuous relationship between the Council and NPS raises additional questions as to how exactly NPS intends to ensure compliance with all applicable federal laws (such as the APA; NEPA; the Freedom of Information Act; Land and Water Conservation Fund Act; National Historical Preservation Act.), considering that the Council is not a federal entity and thus not obligated to comply with these laws. Although NPS claims that it will ensure that all federal statutes are complied with, Defendants have offered no specifics, and presented no evidence, to support their argument that they would be able to ensure compliance, especially given that compliance would require extensive and *voluntary* participation by the Council.

In the end, Defendants' only authority over the Council appears to be its ability to terminate the Cooperative Agreement, a draconian remedy that NPS would be unlikely to exercise except in an extreme situation. This does not constitute the "final reviewing authority" required to prevent an unlawful delegation. Since it is clear that NPS has no "final reviewing authority" over the Council, the selection of Alternative B violates the unlawful delegation doctrine, constitutes an abuse of discretion, is not in accordance with the law, and is in excess of the Secretary's and NPS' statutory jurisdiction.

NOTES AND QUESTIONS

1. The Department did not appeal this decision. How might the Department "cure" the defects scored by the court? Would a sufficient cure be to give the head of the National Park Service, or the Secretary of the Interior, the right to overrule council decisions?

2.   Did the court give too short a shrift to the 60–day termination clause, which allowed the NPS to terminate for any reason? Why doesn't that maintain sufficient NPS oversight on the management of this area?

3.   Note that this stretch of the River was included in the national Wild & Scenic River System "over local opposition," as the court put it. That is, the designation of the Niobrara Scenic River thrust the NPS into a somewhat hostile world. Note also that the Congress had, in the court's words, "strongly encouraged local participation in the management of the area," and had created an Advisory Commission in the statute designating Niobrara Scenic River. The Advisory Commission, in turn, had recommended that a local council be created. Why, therefore, was it illegal for the NPS to try to secure local "buy-in" by creating the Council and vesting it with some management responsibility?

4.   Look closely at the makeup of the Council. Would the result have been the same if the NPS delegation had not been to an ad hoc public-private committee, but instead been to the local county, or by cooperative agreement to an ad hoc body composed exclusively of local governmental officials? See 16 U.S.C. § 1281(e), quoted in the opinion.

5.   If the delegation were held proper, who would have responsibility for complying with federal laws such as NEPA?

6.   Did the NPS cleverly invite defeat here, playing this situation both ways? The delegation was designed to placate the locals, but the ultimate result was a court decision that ringingly endorsed NPS's management authority.

7.   How should the NPS use the cooperative agreements described and encouraged by the laws at issue in the Niobrara case? Cooperative agreements are increasingly popular tools and they are a necessity for some under-funded programs? Moreover, President Bush pushed the use of "cooperative conservation" tools in a 2004 executive order. Executive Order 13352.

8.   Congress also has endorsed cooperative agreements to manage public lands in certain circumstances. The 1994 amendments to the Indian Self–Determination and Educational Assistance Act allow tribes to petition for shared management of federal lands. Pub. L. No. 93–638, *codified at* 25 U.S.C. 450–450e–1. After a decade of negotiation, the Salish and Kootenai tribes signed an agreement with the FWS in 2004 to conduct wildlife management, fire protection, visitor services, and other proprietary tasks for the National Bison Range, a refuge in Montana. The tribes have a good reputation for environmental protection and originally managed the land acquired for the Bison Range in 1908. On the other hand, "critics fear the move could lead to federal employees being displaced by tribal workers ... [and] set a precedent for wider privatization of federal parks and reserves." Mary Fitzgerald, *Wildlife Staff Protest Pact with Tribes*, WASH.POST, Oct. 19, 2004, at A21. *See* U.S. FWS, Fish and Wildlife Service and Confederated Salish and Kootenai Tribal Governments Sign Annual Funding Agreement, 70 Fed. Reg. 5205 (2005). The Bison Range management conflict boiled over in late 2006 when FWS officials announced that they would not renew

the management partnership. The Interior Department quickly overruled the FWS decision and announced that it would strive to work with the tribe to sign a new agreement. As of this writing, an investigation of the FWS allegations that the tribe did not meet its obligations under the agreement had not yet concluded. All parties acknowledge that poor relations between FWS employees and tribal workers exacerbated the situation. Jim Robbins, *Sharing of Bison Range Management Breaks Down*, N.Y.TIMES, Feb. 13, 2007.

The examples of Congress (rather than the Executive branch) fashioning ad hoc entities with the authority to manage federal lands seem to be growing, and the following summarizes some adopted in the last quarter century. These arrangements should be distinguished from the formation of mere "advisory councils" such as was directed in the Niobrara River legislation. Such purely advisory councils are common in federal legislation designating areas of federal lands for particular uses.

In 1986 Congress enacted the Columbia River Gorge National Scenic Area Act to protect scenic, recreational, and other interests in a large area of federal and non-federal land along the Columbia River. 16 U.S.C. §§ 544–544p. The statute directed the Forest Service to administer "Special Management Areas" (SMAs) consisting of mostly national forest land, and directed a regional agency known as the Columbia River Gorge Commission, created by a congressionally approved interstate agreement, to administer "General Management Areas" (GMAs) consisting of non-federal land. Nonfederal landowners in the SMAs can "opt out" by requiring the government to pay fair market value for their land within a period of time; if the government does not, the SMA provisions lapse. The commission administering the GMAs is specifically not to be considered a federal agency for purposes of any federal law. It consists of twelve voting members (one appointed from each of the three counties on each state's side of the River, and three appointed by each state's governor) and one nonvoting federal member appointed by the Secretary of Agriculture (the Forest Service being the principal federal land manager in the area). A management plan for the scenic area was required within three years, and had to be approved by the Secretary. Moreover, each county (or failing that, the Commission) had to adopt land use ordinances consistent with the plan (under guidelines developed by the Secretary in consultation with the Commission), with the Secretary policing compliance. Persons who were denied permits to develop their property by the Commission brought a broad-based facial attack on the constitutionality of the arrangement, but were rebuffed. *See* Columbia River Gorge United—Protecting People and Property v. Yeutter, 960 F.2d 110 (9th Cir.). *See* Michael C. Blumm & Joshua D. Smith, *Protecting the Columbia River Gorge: A Twenty-year Experiment in Land–Use Federalism*, 21 J. LAND USE & ENVTL. L. 201 (2006).

In 1996, Congress turned to a trust model for managing a portion of the National Park System. It created the Presidio Trust, a government corporation, to manage that part of the San Francisco Presidio (a former Army base at the south end of the Golden Gate, part of the Golden Gate National Recreation Area), which contains buildings and other structures of commercial value. 110 Stat. 4097–4104 (1996). A seven-member board composed of the Secretary of the Interior (or her designee) and six nonfederal members appointed by the President makes decisions for the Trust. The legislation directs the Trust to develop a comprehensive program for management of the facilities under its jurisdiction, to "reduce expenditures by the National Park Service and increase revenues to the Federal Government to the maximum extent possible." A review indicates that the trust is on track to become financially self-sufficient by 2013, and has improved the forests and buildings on the site. U.S. Government Accountability Office, Significant Progress Made in Preserving the Presidio and Attaining Financial Self–Sufficiency (GAO–02–87) (2001).

Building on the Presidio model, in 2000 Congress authorized the acquisition of the 95,000 acre Baca Ranch, part of an old Spanish land grant in a scenic caldera west of Los Alamos, New Mexico. 16 U.S.C. § 698v et seq. The legislation establishes this new federal land as the Valles Caldera National Preserve. Although part of a unit of the national forest system, the management of the Preserve was vested in a newly established government corporation known as the Valles Caldera Trust. A nine-member Board governs the trust. The board consists of the national forest supervisor, the superintendent of the adjacent Bandelier National Monument (part of the national park system), and seven nonfederal members appointed by the President in consultation with the New Mexico congressional delegation, each having a different area of expertise (forestry, livestock, wildlife, conservation, etc.). The purposes of the Preserve are to protect the area's scientific, scenic, geologic, watershed, fish, wildlife, historic, cultural, and recreational values, and to provide for multiple use and sustained yield of its renewable resources. The Trust is responsible for complying with federal environmental laws, and must administer the Preserve in accordance with laws pertaining to the national forest system, with a few exceptions. The statute requires the Trust to develop a program to provide for the operation of the Preserve as a working ranch, with public access for recreation, and to "optimiz[e] the generation of income based on existing market conditions, to the extent that it does not unreasonably diminish the long-term scenic and natural values of the area, or the multiple use and sustained yield capability of the land." Congress charged the Trust with attaining financial self-sufficiency by 2015. But the Trust is far from the ultimate goal of self-sufficiency. Since its founding, the Trust has received about $16 million in federal funding. In 2004, the Trust generated about $0.5 million in revenue, primarily from hunting and cattle grazing. In contrast to the Presidio, which has valuable San Francisco real estate, the Valles Caldera will have a difficult time leveraging its land to achieve fiscal self-sufficiency. U.S. Government Accountability Office, Valles Caldera: Trust Has Made Some Progress, But Needs To Do More To Meet Statutory Goals (GAO–06–98) 2005.

Two other recent unusual arrangements deserve mention. In 1996, Congress created the Tallgrass Prairie National Preserve, an 11,000 acre remnant of an ecotype that once covered 400,000 square miles in North America. A nonprofit entity had acquired the land, and the legislation set up a unique arrangement whereby title to the Preserve would remain in private hands, but the Preserve would be a unit of the National Park System. The Secretary administers the unit with the consent of the nonfederal landowner, consistent with the laws and regulations applicable to the Park System. The establishment legislation limited federal land acquisition authority in the area. It also called for preparation of a general management plan, and specified in some detail plan components on such matters as honoring existing mineral leases, grazing rights, hunting and fishing, and state fencing law. 16 U.S.C. §§ 698u.

In 1998, Congress enacted a statute authorizing a pilot project for three national forests in the northern Sierra Nevada of California to implement what had become known as the Quincy Library Group proposal. *See* 112 Stat. 2681. This group of representatives of fisheries, timber, environmental, county government, citizen groups, and local communities had developed a resource management program to promote both economic and ecological health for the area. National environmental groups opposed the legislation, which directs the Forest Service, after completing an environmental impact statement, to conduct a pilot project to "implement and demonstrate the effectiveness of the resource management activities" recommended by the group, to the extent they were consistent with applicable Federal law, and to report on the results. Though the Forest Service's EIS basically endorsed the Group's proposal, subsequent administrative and ecological imperatives, such as coordinated management of all eleven of the Sierra Nevada national forests and restrictions on timber harvesting in order to protect the California spotted owl, have dulled the impact of the Quincy Library collaboration. *See* Robert Keiter, KEEPING FAITH WITH NATURE 274–99 (2003).

NOTES AND QUESTIONS

1.   The emergence of public-private collaborations has scarcely been confined to federal lands and resources. Compare "negotiated rulemaking" that was somewhat in vogue in administrative law circles a few years back. There is a burgeoning general commentary on the subject; e.g., Jody Freeman, Collaborative Governance in the Administrative State, 45 U.C.L.A. L.Rev. 1 (1997) (collecting many sources). For a discussion of some recent federal lands collaborative exercises, see KEEPING FAITH WITH NATURE 273–327 (2003).

2.   Is there any doubt about Congress's ability to create these arrangements? If Congress has the power under the Property Clause to dispose of federal lands altogether, may it retain title yet vest management authority in nonfederal entities without federal supervision, or with minimal federal supervision? Are there some responsibilities which may not be delegated outside the government; i.e., that are inherently governmental? At the Niobrara Wild & Scenic River, for example, the NPS gave the Council

authority over "law enforcement." Is it problematic to have nongovernmental entities prosecute violations of federal law?

3. To some extent, these arrangements seek to provide alternative ways to balance national and local interests, a balance that is struck in somewhat different ways in the great federal land systems covered in this book (national parks, forests, wildlife refuges, and BLM lands). National environmental groups, for example, are generally skeptical of such arrangements, fearing that the national interest will be sacrificed in the zeal to get buy-in by local interests. Advocates of such arrangements sometimes accuse national groups of simply fearing a loss of their own influence. Can both be right?

4. Is there a value in having some uniformity and consistency of management across an entire national system of lands (e.g., national forests, national parks) by a single institution (the U.S. Forest Service; the National Park Service)? To the extent that is true, how big a threat to that value is the fragmentation inherent in the arrangements described above?

5. Conversely, is there a value in experimenting with different management models, and in giving institutions like the U.S. Forest Service and National Park Service some competition in how units of their systems are managed?

6. Is more formal collaborative management an appropriate policy in areas where significant amounts of nonfederal lands are involved (e.g., the Niobrara River corridor and the Columbia Gorge)? Or where peculiar local challenges exist (e.g., the management of more than one million square feet of commercial office space and rental housing in the Presidio)? Might it be less appropriate where the land is mostly or wholly federal (e.g., the Baca Ranch, after acquisition)? To a substantial extent the character of these various local arrangements reflects the attitudes of key members of the congressional delegations who as a matter of practical politics must sign off on authorizing legislation. At the Baca Ranch, for example, Senator Domenici would agree to support federal acquisition only if an alternative to conventional Forest Service management were devised. At the Tallgrass Prairie, the Kansas congressional delegation would not permit outright federal acquisition. In each case, conservation interests compromised on management arrangements in order to bring the areas under the protection of federal law.

7. Should federal policy move toward a paradigm where federal lands of high national interest (for example, "crown jewel" national parks) will be managed exclusively by the federal government, and areas of not so high national importance will be managed under more collaborative arrangements with state and local governments and private organizations?

8. How should generic federal environmental laws like the National Environmental Policy Act, the Endangered Species Act, and the Clean Water Act apply in these cases? Should the new managing entity be responsible for compliance? With or without the supervision of the federal agency involved?

C. EXECUTIVE WITHDRAWALS AND RESERVATIONS

In federal land law history, a "withdrawal" is a generic term referring to a statute, an executive order, or an administrative order that changes the designation of a described parcel of federal land from "available" to "unavailable" for certain kinds of activities, usually involving resource extraction or use. It is a protective measure to preserve the status quo and prevent specified future uses in specified land. A withdrawal can be made by Congress or the Executive, and it can be temporary or permanent. A "reservation" means a dedication of withdrawn land to a specified purpose, more or less permanently.* Whether a particular parcel is now or should remain open to mining, mineral leasing, logging, grazing, hunting and fishing, or intensive recreation is the key to many modern disputes on the federal public lands.

Executive withdrawals are now governed mostly by the provisions of the Federal Land Policy and Management Act of 1976, 43 U.S.C. § 1714 (FLPMA), discussed in detail further below. FLPMA now defines "withdrawal" in a considerably broader sense than was previously customary, to include reservations and transfers of jurisdiction among agencies. Specifically, 43 U.S.C. § 1702(j) defines withdrawal as

> withholding an area of Federal land from settlement, sale, location, or entry, under some or all of the general land laws, for the purpose of limiting activities under those laws in order to maintain other public values in the area or reserving the area for a particular public purpose or program; or transferring jurisdiction over an area of Federal land * * * from one department, bureau or agency to another department bureau or agency.

While Congress may have collapsed the concepts of withdrawal and reservation into the single notion of withdrawal in FLPMA, they may still have separate and legally significant meanings under older statutes that created vested property rights that even today may turn on subtle distinctions between withdrawal and reservation. For instance, R.S. 2477 permitted rights-of-way to be established over lands "not reserved for public uses." In Southern Utah Wilderness Alliance v. BLM, *supra* p. 224, the BLM had determined that a 1910 executive action designating the lands underlying the R.S. 2477 claims "withdrawn from settlement, location, sale or entry, and reserved for classification and appraisement with respect to coal values" reserved the lands and therefore removed them from the ambit of R.S. 2477 before the counties had alleged to establish the roads. The court disagreed: On its face, "withdrawn . . . and reserved" sounds like a reservation. But just because a withdrawal uses the term "reserved" does

---

* The word reservation is also used in federal land law in a different sense, referring to bilateral transactions. Thus, where a state cedes land or jurisdiction to the United States, it may "reserve" the right to tax activities on the granted land. *See* Chapter 3A. Or the United States may "reserve" subsurface mineral rights in a homestead patent, or a party conveying land to the U.S. may "reserve" mineral rights. *See* Chapter 7D.

not mean that it reserves land "for public uses." The court determined that the coal lands fell short of reservations because they were not permanent and did not dedicate lands to a particular purpose–they simply responded to a "perceived crisis" caused by excessive disposition of valuable coal. Do you think the 1910 presidential order was a withdrawal or a reservation? Is the purpose of the 1910 order a reservation "for public uses" of the coal?

In addition to the terms withdrawal and reservation, the term "classification" is also relevant here. It is often used to describe decisions of land management agencies, operating pursuant to broad statutory authority, to formally categorize (and recategorize) lands according to how they may be used. A rough rule of thumb is that withdrawals and reservations are usually large-scale and accomplished by Congress, the President, or cabinet secretaries, while classifications tend to be administrative fine-tuning by agency officials on a parcel-by-parcel basis. Examples of classifications include the Interior Department's designations of lands available for in lieu selection by states as illustrated by Andrus v. Utah, *supra* p. 90.

Bright lines do not always separate classifications, withdrawals, and reservations. Moreover, over the long history of federal lands, the sources of legal authority for making them are diverse, and the procedures to accomplish them may also vary. A rough division of authority between Congress and the President has grown up around specific statutes and long-term understandings.

Congress has itself retained the sole power to make certain kinds of withdrawals and reservations. National parks, for instance, may be created only by an Act of Congress. The same is true of other—but not all— elements of the national park system such as national preserves, national seashores and lakeshores, and national recreation areas. Designations of areas for inclusion in the National Wilderness Preservation System also require explicit legislation, but are ordinarily preceded by administrative studies and Presidential recommendations. Also, agencies may (and sometimes must) segregate and manage lands under their jurisdiction to preserve their wilderness qualities. *See* Chapter 12A, *infra*. Designation of stretches of rivers for inclusion in the national system of Wild & Scenic Rivers is handled in much the same way, although the Secretary of the Interior has been delegated limited power to include river reaches in the national system upon nomination by a State. Generally speaking, Congress may itself do directly what the executive may do (e.g., it may legislate national monuments or national wildlife refuges), and it always possesses the power to undo whatever it or the President has done.

Congress may also withdraw from disposition specific resources without reserving them for any particular use. The Mineral Leasing Act of 1920, 30 U.S.C. § 181 et seq., for example, withdrew oil, gas, coal, and like minerals on all public lands from the operation of the Mining Law of 1872 and associated acts, and made them subject to disposition only by leasing. Congress did much the same thing in 1947 and 1955 for common varieties of widely occurring minerals like sand, stone, gravel, clay, pumice, and cinders, making the minerals (but not the land) subject to disposition thereafter only by sale.

The Executive, exercising power delegated to it by Congress, may and frequently has withdrawn and reserved federal lands for certain purposes. The classic example grew out of the Forest Reserve Amendment of 1891, which authorized the President to withdraw and reserve public lands covered with timber or undergrowth. The grant was repealed in 1907 as to most western states, and some acreage returned to the public domain, but not before the Presidents Cleveland through Theodore Roosevelt had set aside most of the lands that now comprise the National Forest System. Withdrawals and reservations authorized by the Antiquities Act of 1906, 16 U.S.C. §§ 431433, and the Pickett Act of 1910, 43 U.S.C. §§ 141–142 (repealed 1976), both considered further below, are also important examples of such statutory delegations. Other less sweeping statutes have been adopted over the years to delegate withdrawal powers to the President and his subordinates for more limited purposes.

This section begins with the president's core constitutional powers and then discusses withdrawals under FLPMA. It concludes with the President's statutory power to establish national monuments under the Antiquities Act of 1906, which remains a surprisingly vital authority.

1.   THE PRESIDENT'S POWERS

Most withdrawals and reservations have resulted from either unilateral congressional action or from the Executive acting pursuant to congressionally-delegated authority. Despite the fact that the Constitution vests authority over public lands in Congress rather than the Executive, Presidents have long claimed and exercised an implied power to withdraw—and in some cases, to reserve—public lands in the public interest. For example, Presidents carved military reservations out of the public domain by executive order. (These actions were arguably justified by the Constitution's making the President "Commander in Chief" of the military. Article II, § 2.) Between 1855 and 1919, Presidents also set aside some twenty-three million acres of public lands for Indian reservations, a purpose less directly related to military exigency. Theodore Roosevelt began to reserve wildlife refuges beginning in 1903, despite the absence of statutory authorization. Eventually the executive's practice of withdrawals unsupported by express legislative authority came before the U.S. Supreme Court.

United States v. Midwest Oil Co.

Supreme Court of the United States, 1915.
236 U.S. 459.

■ JUSTICE LAMAR delivered the opinion of the court.

All public lands containing petroleum or other mineral oils and chiefly valuable therefor, have been declared by Congress to be "free and open to occupation, exploration and purchase by citizens of the United States * * * under regulations prescribed by law." Act of February 11, 1897, c. 216, 29 Stat. 526 [Oil Placer Act, which parroted the language of the Mining Law of 1872].

As these regulations permitted exploration and location without the payment of any sum, and as title could be obtained for a merely nominal amount, many persons availed themselves of the provisions of the statute. Large areas in California were explored; and petroleum having been found, locations were made, not only by the discoverer but by others on adjoining land. And, as the flow through the well on one lot might exhaust the oil under the adjacent land, the interest of each operator was to extract the oil as soon as possible so as to share what would otherwise be taken by the owners of nearby wells.

The result was that oil was so rapidly extracted that on September 17, 1909, the Director of the Geological Survey made a report to the Secretary of the Interior which, with enclosures, called attention to the fact that, while there was a limited supply of coal on the Pacific coast and the value of oil as a fuel had been fully demonstrated, yet at the rate at which oil lands in California were being patented by private parties it would "be impossible for the people of the United States to continue ownership of oil lands for more than a few months. After that the Government will be obliged to repurchase the very oil that it has practically given away." * * * "In view of the increasing use of fuel by the American Navy there would appear to be an immediate necessity for assuring the conservation of a proper supply of petroleum for the Government's own use * * * "and "pending the enactment of adequate legislation on this subject, the filing of claims to oil lands in the State of California should be suspended."

This recommendation was approved by the Secretary of the Interior. Shortly afterwards he brought the matter to the attention of the President who, on September 27, 1909, issued the following Proclamation:

"Temporary Petroleum Withdrawal No. 5."

"In aid of proposed legislation affecting the use and disposition of the petroleum deposits on the public domain, all public lands in the accompanying lists are hereby temporarily withdrawn from all forms of location, settlement, selection, filing, entry, or disposal under the mineral or nonmineral public-land laws. All locations or claims existing and valid on this date may proceed to entry in the usual manner after field investigation and examination."

The list attached described an area aggregating 3,041,000 acres in California and Wyoming—though, of course, the order only applied to the public lands therein, the acreage of which is not shown.

On March 27, 1910, six months after the publication of the Proclamation, William T. Henshaw and others entered upon a quarter section of this public land in Wyoming so withdrawn. They made explorations, bored a well, discovered oil and thereafter assigned their interest to the Appellees, who took possession and extracted large quantities of oil. On May 4, 1910, they filed a location certificate.

As the explorations by the original claimants, and the subsequent operation of the well, were both long after the date of the President's Proclamation, the Government filed, in the District Court of the United States for the District of Wyoming, a Bill in Equity against the Midwest Oil

Company and the other Appellees, seeking to recover the land and to obtain an accounting for 50,000 barrels of oil alleged to have been illegally extracted. * * *

* * * On the part of the Government it is urged that the President, as Commander-in-Chief of the Army and Navy, had power to make the order for the purpose of retaining and preserving a source of supply of fuel for the Navy, instead of allowing the oil land to be taken up for a nominal sum, the Government being then obliged to purchase at a great cost what it had previously owned. It is argued that the President, charged with the care of the public domain, could, by virtue of the executive power vested in him by the Constitution (Art. 2, § 1), and also in conformity with the tacit consent of Congress, withdraw, in the public interest, any public land from entry or location by private parties.

The Appellees, on the other hand, insist that there is no dispensing power in the Executive and that he could not suspend a statute or withdraw from entry or location any land which Congress had affirmatively declared should be free and open to acquisition by citizens of the United States. They further insist that the withdrawal order is absolutely void since it appears on its face to be a mere attempt to suspend a statute—supposed to be unwise—in order to allow Congress to pass another more in accordance with what the Executive thought to be in the public interest.

1.   We need not consider whether, as an original question, the President could have withdrawn from private acquisition what Congress had made free and open to occupation and purchase. The case can be determined on other grounds and in the light of the legal consequences flowing from a long continued practice to make orders like the one here involved. For the President's proclamation of September 27, 1909, is by no means the first instance in which the Executive, by a special order, has withdrawn land which Congress, by general statute, had thrown open to acquisition by citizens. [The Presidents have] during the past 80 years, without express statutory authority—but under the claim of power so to do—made a multitude of Executive Orders which operated to withdraw public land that would otherwise have been open to private acquisition. They affected every kind of land—mineral and nonmineral. The size of the tracts varied from a few square rods to many square miles and the amount withdrawn has aggregated millions of acres. The number of such instances cannot, of course, be accurately given, but the extent of the practice can best be appreciated by a consideration of what is believed to be a correct enumeration of such Executive Orders mentioned in public documents.

They show that prior to the year 1910 there had been issued

99 Executive Orders establishing or enlarging Indian Reservations;

109 Executive Orders establishing or enlarging Military Reservations and setting apart land for water, timber, fuel, hay, signal stations, target ranges and rights of way for use in connection with Military Reservations;

44 Executive Orders establishing Bird Reserves.

In the sense that these lands may have been intended for public use, they were reserved for a public purpose. But they were not reserved in pursuance of law or by virtue of any general or special statutory authority. For, it is to be specially noted that there was no act of Congress providing for Bird Reserves or for these Indian Reservations. There was no law for the establishment of these Military Reservations or defining their size or location. There was no statute empowering the President to withdraw any of these lands from settlement or to reserve them for any of the purposes indicated.

But when it appeared that the public interest would be served by withdrawing or reserving parts of the public domain, nothing was more natural than to retain what the Government already owned. And in making such orders, which were thus useful to the public, no private interest was injured. For prior to the initiation of some right given by law the citizen had no enforceable interest in the public statute and no private right in land which was the property of the people. The President was in a position to know when the public interest required particular portions of the people's lands to be withdrawn from entry or location; his action inflicted no wrong upon any private citizen, and being subject to disaffirmance by Congress, could occasion no harm to the interest of the public at large. Congress did not repudiate the power claimed or the withdrawal orders made. On the contrary it uniformly and repeatedly acquiesced in the practice and, as shown by these records, there had been, prior to 1910, at least 252 Executive Orders making reservations for useful, though non-statutory purposes.

This right of the President to make reservations—and thus withdraw land from private acquisition—was expressly recognized in Grisar v. McDowell, 6 Wall. 363, 381 (1867), where it was said that "from an early period in the history of the Government it has been the practice of the President to order, from time to time, as the exigencies of the public service required, parcels of land belonging to the United States to be reserved from sale and set apart for public uses." * * *

2. It may be argued that while these facts and rulings prove a usage they do not establish its validity. But government is a practical affair intended for practical men. Both officers, law-makers and citizens naturally adjust themselves to any long-continued action of the Executive Department—on the presumption that unauthorized acts would not have been allowed to be so often repeated as to crystallize into a regular practice. That presumption is not reasoning in a circle but the basis of a wise and quieting rule that in determining the meaning of a statute or the existence of a power, weight shall be given to the usage itself—even when the validity of the practice is the subject of investigation. * * *

3. These decisions do not, of course, mean that private rights could be created by an officer withdrawing for a Rail Road more than had been authorized by Congress in the land grant act. * * * Nor do these decisions mean that the Executive can by his course of action create a power. But they do clearly indicate that the long-continued practice, known to and acquiesced in by Congress, would raise a presumption that the withdrawals

had been made in pursuance of its consent or of a recognized administrative power of the Executive in the management of the public lands. This is particularly true in view of the fact that the land is property of the United States and that the land laws are not of a legislative character in the highest sense of the term (Art. 4, § 3) "but savor somewhat of mere rules prescribed by an owner of property for its disposal."

These rules or laws for the disposal of public land are necessarily general in their nature. Emergencies may occur, or conditions may so change as to require that the agent in charge should, in the public interest, withhold the land from sale; and while no such express authority has been granted, there is nothing in the nature of the power exercised which prevents Congress from granting it by implication just as could be done by any other owner of property under similar conditions. The power of the Executive, as agent in charge, to retain that property from sale need not necessarily be expressed in writing.

For it must be borne in mind that Congress not only has a legislative power over the public domain, but it also exercises the powers of the proprietor therein. Congress "may deal with such lands precisely as a private individual may deal with his farming property. It may sell or withhold them from sale." Camfield v. United States, 167 U.S. 524; Light v. United States, 220 U.S. 536. Like any other owner it may provide when, how and to whom its land can be sold. It can permit it to be withdrawn from sale. Like any other owner, it can waive its strict rights, as it did when the valuable privilege of grazing cattle on this public land was held to be based upon an "implied license growing out of the custom of nearly a hundred years." Buford v. Houtz, 133 U.S. 326. So too, in the early days the "Government, by its silent acquiescence, assented to the general occupation of the public lands for mining." Atchison v. Peterson, 20 Wall. 512. If private persons could acquire a privilege in public land by virtue of an implied congressional consent, then for a much stronger reason, an implied grant of power to preserve the public interest would arise out of like congressional acquiescence.

The Executive, as agent, was in charge of the public domain; by a multitude of orders extending over a long period of time and affecting vast bodies of land, in many States and Territories, he withdrew large areas in the public interest. These orders were known to Congress, as principal, and in not a single instance was the act of the agent disapproved. Its acquiescence all the more readily operated as an implied grant of power in view of the fact that its exercise was not only useful to the public but did not interfere with any vested right of the citizen.

4. The appellees, however, argue that the practice thus approved, related to Reservations—to cases where the land had been reserved for military or other special public purposes—and they contend that even if the President could reserve land for a public purpose or for naval uses, it does not follow that he can withdraw land in aid of legislation.

When analyzed, this proposition, in effect, seeks to make a distinction between a Reservation and a Withdrawal—between a Reservation for a purpose, not provided for by existing legislation, and a Withdrawal made in aid of future legislation. It would mean that a Permanent Reservation for a purpose designated by the President, but not provided for by a statute, would be valid, while a merely Temporary Withdrawal to enable Congress to legislate in the public interest would be invalid. It is only necessary to point out that, as the greater includes the less, the power to make permanent reservations includes power to make temporary withdrawals. For there is no distinction in principle between the two. The character of the power exerted is the same in both cases. In both, the order is made to serve the public interest and in both the effect on the intending settler or miner is the same. * * *

[T]hat the existence of [withdrawal] power was recognized and its exercise by the Executive assented to by Congress, is emphasized by [a] Report which the Secretary of the Interior made in 1902, in response to a resolution of the Senate calling for information "as to what, if any, of the public lands have been withdrawn from disposition under the settlement or other laws by order of the Commissioner of the General Land Office and *what, if any, authority of law exists for such order of withdrawal."*

The answer to this specific inquiry was returned March 3, 1902, (Senate Doc. 232, 57th Cong., 1st Sess., Vol. 17). On that date the Secretary transmitted to the Senate the elaborate and detailed report of the Commissioner of the Land Office, who in response to the inquiry as to the authority by which withdrawals had been made, answered that:

> "the power of the Executive Department of the Government to make reservations of land for public use, and to temporarily withdraw lands from appropriation by individuals as exigencies might demand, to prevent fraud, to aid in proper administration and in aid of pending legislation is one that has been long recognized both in the acts of Congress and the decisions of the court; * * * that this power has been long exercised by the Commissioner of the General Land Office is shown by reference to the date of some of the withdrawals enumerated. * * * The attached list embraces only such lands as were withdrawn by this office, acting on its own motion, in cases where the emergencies appeared to demand such action in furtherance of public interest and does not include lands withdrawn under express statutes so directed."
> * * *

This report refers to *Withdrawals* and not to *Reservations*. It is most important in connection with the present inquiry as to whether Congress knew of the practice to make temporary withdrawals and knowingly assented thereto. It will be noted that the Resolution called on the Department to state the extent of such withdrawals and the authority by which they were made. The officer of the Land Department in his answer shows that there have been a large number of withdrawals made for good but for non-statutory reasons. He knows that these 92 orders had been made by virtue of a long-continued practice and under claim of a right to take such action in the public interest "as exigencies might demand. * * * " Congress with notice of this practice and of this claim of authority, received the Report. Neither at that session nor afterwards did it ever repudiate the action taken or the power claimed. Its silence was acquiescence. Its acquiescence was equivalent to consent to continue the practice until the power was revoked by some subsequent action by Congress. * * *

■ JUSTICES DAY, McKENNA, and VAN DEVANTER, dissenting.

* * * [T]he lands here in controversy are situated in the state of Wyoming * * * [and] were withdrawn solely upon the suggestion that a better disposition of them could be made than was found in the existing acts of Congress controlling the subject. * * * [By the Property Clause of the Constitution] the power to dispose of lands belonging to the United States is broadly conferred upon Congress, and it is under the power therein given that the system of land laws for the disposition of the public domain has been enacted. * * *

It is true that many withdrawals have been made by the President and some of them have been sustained by this court, so that it may be fairly said that, within limitations to be hereinafter stated, Executive withdrawals have the sanction of judicial approval; but, as we read the cases, in no instance has this court sustained a withdrawal of public lands for which Congress has provided a system of disposition, except such withdrawal was—(a) in pursuance of a policy already declared by Congress as one for which the public lands might be used, as military and Indian reservations, for which purposes Congress has authorized the use of the public lands from an early day, or (b) in cases where grants of Congress are in such conflict that the purpose of Congress cannot be known, and therefore the Secretary of the Interior has been sustained in withdrawing the lands from entry until Congress had opportunity to relieve the ambiguity of its laws by specifically declaring its policy. * * *

The constitutional authority of the President of the United States (art. 2, §§ 1,3) includes the * * * duty to see that the laws are faithfully executed. * * * The Constitution does not confer upon him any power to enact laws or to suspend or repeal such as the Congress enacts. * * *

* * * [A] given withdrawal must have been expressly authorized by Congress, or there must be that clear implication of congressional authority which is equivalent to express authority; and when such authority is wanting there can be no Executive withdrawal of lands from the operation of an act of Congress which would otherwise control.

In our opinion, the action of the Executive Department in this case, originating in the expressed view of * * * the desirability of a different system of public land disposal than that contained in the lawful enactments of Congress, did not justify the President in withdrawing this large body of land from the operation of the law, and virtually suspending, as he necessarily did, the operation of that law, at least until a different view expressed by him could be considered by the Congress. * * *

NOTES AND QUESTIONS

1. What was the legal effect of "withdrawing" these federal lands from the operation of the 1897 Oil Placer Act? Is the President simply, and unilaterally, nullifying the operation of that Act on these withdrawn lands?

Is that consistent with the President's constitutional duty to "take Care that the Laws be faithfully executed"? Art. II, § 3.

2. The Court did not reach the question whether the President had authority to withdraw lands under his power as Commander in Chief, Article II, § 2, cl. 1, or under the basic executive authority, Article II, § 1, cl. 1 ("The executive Power shall be vested in a president * * * "). Would presidential power to make these withdrawals from mineral entry have been upheld on either of these two bases if no longstanding executive practice had existed? *Midwest Oil* continues to be cited in landmark cases construing presidential power. *See e.g.* Youngstown Sheet & Tube Co. v. Sawyer, 343 U.S. 579, 611, 655 n. 1, 661 n. 3, 689–93, 703 (1952). In Hamdan v. Rumsfeld, 126 S.Ct. 2749 (2006), the Court invalidated the military commissions President Bush established to try detainees of the "war on terror." Interpreting *Youngstown*, the Court determined that Congress constitutionally limits the President's war powers through legislation and that the President, even during war time, is not always authorized to take unilateral action.

Considering the issue here in the broader context of the Constitution's general allocation of authority between the Congress and the President, is there something special about federal real property that warrants altering this allocation? Does the decision rest, as Professor Harold Bruff has written, "on the premise that the [public] lands are initially infused with public not private rights, until Congress allows a conversion from public to private rights to occur, and it is actually perfected"? *Executive Power and the Public Lands*, 76 U. COLO. L.REV. 503, 508 (2005).

3. Were these withdrawals within the scope of implied authority created by the earlier kinds of withdrawals described in the majority opinion? That is, were the prior withdrawals made in the teeth of a congressional policy to the contrary, or were they consistent with or indirectly supported by acts of Congress? Consider separately Indian reservations, military reservations, and bird reserves. Is this where the majority and the dissent part company in their respective views?

4. Would the President be upheld if a withdrawal were made for a new purpose, such as a wilderness area, unrelated to those kinds of withdrawals to which Congress had given its "longstanding acquiescence"? More broadly, does this case suggest that the President did not need the authority granted by Congress in the 1891 Forest Reservation provision in order to withdraw federal lands from disposal to create national forests? Is the outcome really consistent with the principle announced by the majority that the Executive cannot "by his course of action create a power"? Recall that the Congress in 1907 repealed the President's power to created new national forests in some states. Would the Court's approach in *Midwest Oil* allow the President to ignore that repeal and create new national forests in those states today?

5. Why does the Court say that "no private interest was injured" by the withdrawal? Is the answer found in the 1909 Executive Order?

6. Suppose Congress enacts a statute prohibiting mining in national parks. Does *Midwest Oil* allow an exploitation-minded President nevertheless to issue an Executive Order "withdrawing" a particular national park from the operation of this statute? How does that differ from President Taft's withdrawal upheld in *Midwest Oil*? What does the majority mean when it says that "private rights" cannot be "created by an [executive] officer withdrawing for a Rail Road more than had been authorized by Congress in the land grant act"?

7. Theodore Roosevelt's unilateral reservations of land for wildlife refuges and coal surveys blazed the trail for Taft's order. Yet, in 1916, after he had left office, President Taft criticized Theodore Roosevelt's view that the President possesses broad residual power, calling it "an unsafe doctrine * * * that might lead under emergencies to results of an arbitrary character, doing irremediable injustice to private right." According to Taft, the executive

> can exercise no power which cannot be fairly and reasonably traced to some specific grant of power or justly implied and included within such express grant as proper and necessary to its exercise. Such specific grant must be either in the Federal Constitution or in an act of Congress passed in pursuance thereof. There is no undefined residuum of power which he can exercise because it seems to him to be in the general public interest.

William Howard Taft, OUR CHIEF MAGISTRATE AND HIS POWERS, *quoted in* John P. Roche and Leonard W. Levy, THE PRESIDENCY 23–25 (1964). Justice Jackson quipped, "It * * * seems that President Taft cancels out Professor Taft." Youngstown Sheet & Tube Co. v. Sawyer, 343 U.S. 579, 634 n. 1 (1952) (Jackson, J. concurring).

8. Professor Henry Monaghan has said that *Midwest Oil* is "occasionally cited as a decision—the *only* decision, I should add—in which the Supreme Court upheld presidential law-making contrary to the terms of an Act of Congress." Monaghan offered several possible explanations, including that *Midwest Oil* was confined to the exercise of power "necessarily incident to the President's role as 'chief administrator' in connection with government lands and perhaps other property." In Monaghan's view, however, the decision "has not been confined as a precedent to the notion of President as chief administrator." Instead, the Court has understood the decision "to sanction presidential conduct invading private rights if this conduct is supported by congressional acquiescence or tacit consent, and the question then becomes what congressional conduct suffices for that purpose." Mere congressional inaction is not enough, according to Monaghan; instead, " 'adjacent' congressional legislation must presume the validity of a prior presidential practice." Henry P. Monaghan, *Marbury and the Administrative State*, 83 COLUM. L.REV. 1, 44–47 (1983). *See also* Peter M Shane & Harold H. Bruff, SEPARATION OF POWERS LAW (2005).

In 1910, shortly after the Taft withdrawals, but before the decision in *Midwest Oil*, Congress enacted the Pickett Act of 1910, which provided, in pertinent part:

> The President may, at any time in his discretion, temporarily withdraw from settlement, location, sale, or entry any of the public lands of the United States, including Alaska, and reserve the same for water-power sites, irrigation, classification of lands, or other public purposes to be specified in the orders of withdrawals, and such withdrawals or reservations shall remain in force until revoked by him or by an Act of Congress. [43 U.S.C. § 141]

> All lands withdrawn under the provisions of this section and section 141 of this title shall at all times be open to exploration, discovery, occupation, and purchase under the mining laws of the United States, so far as the same apply to metalliferous minerals * * *. [43 U.S.C. § 142]

As Professor Robert Swenson observed, the Act reflected a general sentiment to support rather than undermine the conservation program that Roosevelt and Taft began. Congress could have taken back its prerogative to make all withdrawal decisions, but ultimately chose not to. Subsequent Congresses have likewise shown little appetite for overturning executive withdrawals. Robert Swenson, *Legal Aspects of Mineral Resources Exploitation, in* History of Public Land Law Development 735 (1970).

The Pickett Act was prospective only, and therefore the Supreme Court could not rely on it to uphold Taft's withdrawals. Although the Pickett Act was repealed by FLMPA in 1976, many withdrawals made under it are still in effect. Notice that while the Act gave the President very broad discretion to make withdrawals, its first sentence spoke of "temporarily" withdrawing lands. Yet the end of that same sentence provided that such withdrawals "shall remain in force until revoked" by the executive or Congress. As a result, Pickett Act withdrawals nearly four decades old were upheld in Mecham v. Udall, 369 F.2d 1, 4 (10th Cir. 1966). The Pickett Act was, however, subject to one important limitation: the President could not use it to withdraw federal lands from disposition of "metalliferous minerals" under the General Mining Law. So what was the President to do when he determined to withdraw a tract of federal lands from all mining, including for metalliferous minerals? Did there still exist an implied power along the lines sketched out in *Midwest Oil* to withdraw lands apart from the Pickett Act? This question was intensively debated inside the U.S. Department of Justice in 1940–41. Attorney General Robert Jackson (soon to become a Justice on the Supreme Court) initially came to the conclusion that the *Midwest Oil* authority no longer existed because the Pickett Act had occupied the field and recaptured Congress's authority. After strong objections from Secretary Harold Ickes and others, Jackson ultimately changed his mind, and issued an opinion in 1941 that affirmed the nonstatutory authority of the President to make "permanent" withdrawals of public lands, as opposed to the "temporary" withdrawals authorized by the Pickett Act.

Attorney General Jackson's opinion was neither approved nor rejected by the Congress. Nearly thirty years later, Secretary of the Interior Stewart Udall withdrew three million acres of federal land in Colorado, Wyoming, and Utah from, among other things, appropriation under the mining laws relating to "metalliferous minerals." Because of this feature, the Pickett Act could not be used as authority for the withdrawal. Portland General Electric Co. located mining claims for uranium (a metalliferous mineral) on some of the land in question after Udall made his withdrawal, and challenged the Secretary's authority to make it. The Secretary relied on *Midwest Oil*. In Portland Gen. Elec. Co. v. Kleppe, 441 F.Supp. 859 (D.Wyo.1977), the court, after briefly recounting the pertinent history, upheld the withdrawal. It relied in part on the legislative history of a 1958 statute placing express limits on the executive's power to withdraw lands for military purposes. The Senate Committee Report on this act noted that "Congress—applying the Midwest Oil yardstick—has perhaps, since 1941 remained silent, and has therefore indulged in a practice * * * equivalent to acquiescence and consent that the practice be continued until the power exercised is revoked." The 1958 legislation, according to the committee report, was "specifically aimed at breaking that silence * * * [and] signaling an end to the implied consent by direct congressional enactment limiting the power exercised." Because the 1958 act did *not* affect the executive's power over *non-military* withdrawals, like Udall's, and because a committee of Congress had been made aware of Secretary Udall's withdrawal and done nothing in response, the court concluded that "Congress had knowledge of and acquiesced in repeated assertions of the implied authority under which [these lands] were withdrawn."

The Pickett Act, and most other claimed sources for the power to withdraw federal lands, authorizes withdrawals for broadly expressed "public purposes." As *Midwest Oil* and *Portland General Electric* suggest, the most common reason for withdrawing federal lands has been to put them off limits to disposal. Especially since the decline and eventual abolition of homesteading, the Mining Law has prompted more withdrawals than any other purpose, although withdrawals can also be made to forestall mineral leasing (a subject explored further below), or other forms of exploitation. Sometimes it is not easy to discern what a particular withdrawal is withdrawing the lands in question from. Typical language of a withdrawal order is to withdraw federal lands "from settlement and entry, or other form of appropriation."

Because the mining industry has been the most frequent target of executive withdrawals, that industry has been in the forefront of a continuing debate, extending back more than a century, over uses and alleged abuses of the withdrawal power. Reservation of the national forests did not *ipso facto* affect the availability of land for hardrock mineral exploration, because Congress explicitly provided in the 1897 organic act for national forests that they generally remained open to the mining laws. Most subsequent withdrawals have, however, decreased the amount of land open to the mining industry. Consequently, the establishment of parks, refuges, monuments, wilderness areas, and other special purpose categories on which mining is forbidden or restricted have not been met with universal acclaim.

Preservationists and conservationists have long supported a vigorous executive withdrawal authority. They argue that the executive branch must have the legal authority (as well as the political will) to act to preserve federal land over the long term from disposal or intensive industrial development, and also to react quickly to emergency situations when imminent development threatens important wildlife and recreation resources. The minerals industries and their allies have sought strict limitations on executive discretion to withdraw. Generally speaking, the conservationists have won, although FLPMA, enacted in 1976, did make some attempt to reconcile the competing concerns, as discussed in detail below.

FLPMA's withdrawal provisions apply only prospectively. 43 U.S.C. § 1714(a). Although it repealed numerous older statutes dealing with withdrawals, including the Pickett Act, FLPMA did not disturb the many pre-FLPMA withdrawals that cover many millions of acres of federal lands. Thus issues relating to withdrawals made between the Pickett Act in 1910 and FLPMA in 1976 can remain alive, as *Portland General Electric Co.* demonstrates.

NOTE: THE PRESIDENT'S POWER TO GUIDE AGENCIES BY EXECUTIVE ORDER

Several times over the history of federal land and resources law, Presidents have issued executive orders to shape public land policy. Sometimes, as in the Antiquities Act, they act with clear statutory authority. At other times, however, as in Taft's withdrawal order upheld in *Midwest Oil*, they had no clear statutory mandate. There are several other examples of the latter, and some judicial discussion of the practice. For example, in National Wildlife Federation v. Babbitt, 24 E.L.R. 20200 (D.D.C.1993), the court had this to say:

Executive Order 11,990, issued by President Carter on May 24, 1977, requires that, "in carrying out the agency's responsibility for * * * land resources planning," each agency "shall take action to minimize the destruction, loss, or degradation of wetlands." Furthermore, agencies are required to avoid assisting construction in areas containing wetlands (permitting "construction" would include coal leasing) "unless the head of the agency finds (1) that there is no practicable alternative to such construction, and (2) that the proposed action includes all practicable measures to minimize harm to wetlands which may result from such use." * * * [Plaintiffs challenged the Interior Department's failure to conform to this Executive Order in adopting planning criteria for decisions on whether and how to lease federal coal.]

* * * It is now fairly well established that administrative action taken pursuant to an executive order is "agency action" within the meaning of APA § 706(2), so long as the executive order has the force of law and places substantive limits on agency discretion.

The court considers whether Executive Order 11,990 meets these two requirements. First, an executive order is to be "accorded the force and effect of a statute" when it has a "distinct statutory foundation." The President's proclamations and orders have the force and effect of laws when issued pursuant to a statutory mandate or delegation of authority from Congress. The President promulgated Executive Order 11,990, based on authority derived from the Constitution and unspecified statutes, "in furtherance of" NEPA, and in particular NEPA § 101(b)(3), *codified at* 42 U.S.C. § 4331(b)(3). The court is not faced with a situation where the President has acted in contradiction to a statute, or in the absence of legislative action. Rather, 42 U.S.C. § 4331(b) mandates ongoing executive action to promote the broad policies of NEPA. Congressional authorization for executive orders can be either "express or implied." The President acted under NEPA's implied authorization when he issued Executive Order 11,990. Consequently, the court finds that Executive Order 11,990 should be accorded "the force and effect of a statute."

* * * Executive Order 11,990 imposes a nondiscretionary duty on the heads of agencies to "take action to minimize the destruction, loss, or degradation of wetlands." EO 11,990 at § 1(a). In addition, the head of an agency may permit such damage or loss only after making a finding that "the proposed action includes all practicable measures to minimize harm to wetlands."

The Executive Order allows for some flexibility. In making this finding, "the head of the agency may take into account economic, environmental, and other pertinent factors." Id. In other words, measures to mitigate harm need only be "capable of attainment within relevant, existing constraints" to satisfy Executive Order 11,990. National Wildlife Federation v. Adams, 629 F.2d at 592.

However, the agency head is not free to do *nothing* to minimize harm to wetlands; nor free to permit damage to wetlands without having taken at least those mitigatory actions that are "capable of attainment within relevant, existing constraints"; nor free to permit damage to wetlands without making a finding that "all practicable measures to mitigate harm" have in fact been taken. These duties clearly place "substantive limits on agency action" and constitute "law to apply." Consequently, agency action pursuant to Executive Order 11,990 is subject to judicial review under the standards of 5 U.S.C. § 706(2).

In Minnesota v. Mille Lacs Band of Chippewa Indians, 526 U.S. 172 (1999), the Court held that an Executive Order issued by President Taylor in 1850, which terminated the Tribe's hunting, fishing and gathering rights secured by an 1837 Treaty, was ineffective because it had "no colorable source of authority" in either the Treaty, statutes, or the Constitution itself. For a valuable discussion of the President's authority to guide implementation of a statute, even when Congress has expressly delegated decision-making authority to an official below the President (such as the Secretary of Agriculture or the Interior), see Elena Kagan, *Presidential Administration,* 114 HARV. L.REV. 2245, 2250, 2320–64 (2001).

An important modern example of guiding public land policy through Executive Order involved regulating off-road vehicles (ORVs) on federal lands. In February 1972, President Richard Nixon issued Executive Order No. 11644, which directed the federal land management agencies effectively to "zone" the federal lands with respect to ORV travel. *See* 43 U.S.C. § 4321 note. Each agency head was to create a regulatory structure that would designate "specific areas and trails on public lands on which the use of off-road vehicles may be permitted, and areas in which the use of off-road vehicles may not be permitted," within a certain date. The Order contained general environmental criteria to be used in zoning the lands for ORV use, and required the agencies to carry out this task with full public participation. It recited that it was issued "by virtue of the authority vested in me as President of the United States by the Constitution of the United States and in furtherance of the purpose and policy of [NEPA]."

BLM regulations implementing the 1972 Executive Order were promptly challenged by environmental groups. In National Wildlife Federation v. Morton, 393 F.Supp. 1286 (D.D.C.1975), the court found that the BLM had "significantly diluted the standards emphatically set forth" in the Order and not followed it in several other respects. For example, BLM added a new substantive criterion ("[t]he need for public use areas for recreation use") that was not specified, and implicitly not allowed, in the Executive Order. The court also criticized BLM for engaging in "wholesale, blanket designation of 'open' lands" instead of evaluating "specific areas and trails to determine whether the use of ORV's should be permitted" with regard to the environmental criteria mandated by Executive Order 11644, and thus "violated the express requirements of" the Order. Tepid implementation of the Nixon Order led President Carter to issue another Executive Order early in his administration (No. 11989 (1977)) that required the federal land management agencies to ban ORVs from areas where the agency determines that continued use "will cause or is causing considerable adverse effects." For another case finding that these executive Orders have the force and effect of law and are enforceable by the courts, see Conservation Law Foundation v. Secretary of the Interior, 590 F.Supp. 1467, 1478 (D.Mass.1984), *aff'd*, 864 F.2d 954 (1st Cir.1989). Further consideration of off-road vehicle regulation and compliance with these Orders is found in Chapter 11.

Another, more common, kind of executive order seeks to guide agency action but expressly disclaims any toehold for judicial enforcement or review. These disclaimers are taken at face value by the courts. For example, in McKinley v. United States, 828 F.Supp. 888 (D.N.M.1993), the plaintiff cattle rancher sought to invoke an Executive Order to set aside a Forest Service decision reducing the amount of cattle he could graze on a national forest:

> Appellant also contends that the decision should be set aside because the Forest Service failed to comply with Presidential Executive order 12630, 53 Fed.Reg. 8859 (March 15, 1988), which requires federal agencies, in their predecisional analyses, to assess the impact of proposed actions on private property rights. Section 6 of E.O. 12630

expressly addresses judicial review and provides that "this order is intended only to improve the internal management of the Executive branch and is not intended to create any right or benefit, substantive or procedural, enforceable at law by a party against the United States, its agencies, its officers or any person." Section VIII of the Attorney General's Guidelines for the Evaluation of Risk and Avoidance of Unanticipated Takings (June 30, 1988) implementing E.O. 12630 also reiterates that intent and additionally provides that:

> Neither these Guidelines, the Appendix, nor the deliberative processes or products resulting from their implementation by agencies shall be treated as establishing criteria or standards that constitute any basis for judicial review of agency actions. Thus, the extent or quality of an agency's compliance with the Executive Order or these Guidelines shall not be justiciable in any proceedings for judicial review of agency action.

The appellant, therefore, has no basis to assert a claim against the Forest Service concerning compliance with E.O. 12630.

2.   MODERN WITHDRAWAL PRACTICE UNDER FLPMA

Congress, in FLPMA, sought to abolish the President's implied withdrawal power by taking the unusual step of naming a Supreme Court decision in a statute: "Effective on and after the date of approval of this Act, the implied authority of the President to make withdrawals and reservations resulting from acquiescence of the Congress (U.S. v. Midwest Oil Co., 236 U.S. 459) * * * [is] repealed." § 704, 90 Stat. 2792.

Does this kill it? How might it be revived? Is there, after *Midwest Oil*, the legal equivalent of a wooden stake through the heart that can get rid of implied executive power forever? If the Executive continues to withdraw land without other authority, and Congress with knowledge of the Executive's action does nothing, has the "power by acquiescence" revived? The answer to this question may be mostly academic, for FLPMA authorized broad executive withdrawals, including metalliferous minerals, in order to "maintain * * * public values" or reserve the area "for a particular public purpose or program."

Withdrawal process and limitations. FLPMA establishes rather detailed procedures for the withdrawal of Interior and Forest Service lands. These may be briefly summarized as follows: The Act allows the Secretary to make withdrawals of fewer than 5000 acres for up to twenty years. 43 U.S.C. § 1714(d). Most withdrawals in excess of 5000 acres are limited to an initial term of twenty years (but can be renewed) and are subject to a "congressional veto" within ninety days under complex procedures. Proposed withdrawals must be sent to Congress with a report that must detail answers to numerous questions, including a "clear explanation" of the reason for the withdrawal; what its effects will be, economically and environmentally; whether alternatives to the withdrawal exist and were considered; the extent to which the public and other governmental agencies were consulted; and detailed information on the geology and future mineral potential of the area proposed for withdrawal. *See* 43 U.S.C. § 1714(c)(2). The Secretary may make "emergency" withdrawals of any size for three years, in which case the report shall be furnished within three months after the withdrawal. *See* 43 U.S.C. § 1714(e).

Procedurally, a withdrawal is accomplished by the issuance of a public land order. Under FLPMA, withdrawal authority can be subdelegated within the Interior Department only to presidential appointees in the Office of the Secretary (e.g., the Under Secretary and Assistant Secretaries). 43 U.S.C. § 1714(a). Therefore, withdrawals made by line agencies such as the BLM or by officials in field offices are void. Regulations governing withdrawals are found at 43 C.F.R. Part 2300.

Review, revocation and termination of withdrawals. Primarily for the benefit of the minerals industry, one part of FLPMA's withdrawal procedures did attempt to get at the problem of the hodgepodge of past withdrawals. Specifically, § 1714(*l*) required the Secretary of the Interior by 1991 to review most existing withdrawals of lands from the mining and mineral leasing laws in the eleven western states in the lower forty-eight. The review was to lead to reports to the President and Congress with an eye toward lifting withdrawals for which the original purpose may long since have passed. This section forbade "termination" of any withdrawal made by Congress, and did not require the termination of other withdrawals, but did require a new determination of "whether, and for how long, the continuation of the existing withdrawal * * * would be, in [the Secretary's] judgment, consistent with the statutory objectives of the programs for which the lands were dedicated and of other relevant programs."

Perhaps to confuse future law students, however, FLPMA also speaks of the Secretary's power to "make, modify, extend, or *revoke* withdrawals." 43 U.S.C. § 1714(a) (emphasis added). Seizing on the difference between "termination" and "revocation" of withdrawals, the Department has claimed the power to revoke withdrawals in the ordinary course of business, apart from "terminating" them pursuant to the comprehensive review in 1714(*l*). In the early 1980s, the Reagan Administration's aggressive efforts to terminate protective classifications and revoke withdrawals on many millions of acres of federal land under these authorities led to the Supreme Court's decision in Lujan v. National Wildlife Federation, 497 U.S. 871 (1990), *supra* p. 210. Because the Supreme Court threw out the National Wildlife Federation's generic challenge on threshold grounds, the ultimate issue—how FLPMA, NEPA and the APA apply to withdrawal revocations and reclassifications—is still open to litigation in the context of individual revocation or reclassification decisions.

NOTE: IS A DECISION NOT TO AUTHORIZE AN ACTIVITY ON FEDERAL LAND A WITHDRAWAL?

Withdrawals are generally conceived as generic decisions to rule certain activities off limits on specific tracts of federal lands. FLPMA defines withdrawal in part as "withholding an area of Federal land from settlement, sale, location, or entry, under some or all of the general land laws."

43 U.S.C. § 1702(j). There are any number of situations in which the managing agency may exercise discretion and decide not to conduct particular activities on particular tracts of federal land. For example, the Department of the Interior may decide not to issue mineral leases or grazing permits, or the Forest Service may decide not to conduct timber sales, in a particular area, or even on a specific tract of land.

Back in the days when withdrawals were largely done informally, without public process, it did not matter whether such decisions were considered withdrawals, or simply exercises of agency discretion not to do something. Once FLPMA created a rather detailed process for making withdrawals, however, the issue has sometimes been litigated. The agency clearly has the power to decide not to go forward with leases or permits (so long as the decision is not arbitrary), whether or not the decision is considered a withdrawal. The issue is whether the somewhat cumbersome FLPMA withdrawal procedures (and possibly NEPA) must be followed when the agency says no to certain activities. The courts have not spoken consistently on the question.

Between 1977 and 1980 the Forest Service and the BLM withheld action on applications for oil and gas leases in national forest roadless areas while the lands were being studied for possible inclusion in the wilderness system. Mountain States Legal Foundation v. Andrus, 499 F.Supp. 383, 391, 395, 397 (D.Wyo.1980), held this inaction a "de facto withdrawal" of those lands that should have been subject to the FLPMA procedures, stating:

> the combined actions of the Department of the Interior and the Department of Agriculture fit squarely within the foregoing definition of withdrawal found in 43 U.S.C. § 1702(j). The combined actions of the Secretaries have (1) effectively removed large areas of federal land from oil and gas leasing and the operation of the Mineral Leasing Act of 1920, (2) in order to maintain other public values in the area, namely those of wilderness preservation. That's the plain meaning of Congress' definition of "withdrawal". * * *

> We conclude that it was the intent of Congress with the passage of FLPMA to limit the ability of the Secretary of the Interior to remove large tracts of public land from the operation of the public land laws by generalized use of his discretion authorized under such laws.

> We cannot allow the Defendants to accomplish by inaction what they could not do by formal administrative order.

But Bob Marshall Alliance v. Hodel, 852 F.2d 1223, 1229–30 (9th Cir.1988), rejected this analysis.

> We fail to see how a decision not to issue oil and gas leases on Deep Creek would be equivalent to a formal withdrawal. Kohlman cites only one case, Mountain States Legal Foundation v. Andrus, 499 F.Supp. 383 (D.Wyo.1980), as authority for the proposition that deferring action on oil and gas lease applications can constitute an unlawful administrative withdrawal. *Mountain States* is not binding on us and we do not find its reasoning persuasive. In that case, the court concluded that the Interior and Agriculture Departments had illegally

withdrawn over a million acres of land because they had failed to act on oil and gas lease applications and had thereby removed the land from the operation of the Mineral Leasing Act of 1920. Yet as the court acknowledged, the Mineral Leasing Act gives the Interior Secretary discretion to determine which lands are to be leased under the statute. 30 U.S.C. § 226(a). We have held that the Mineral Leasing Act "allows the Secretary to lease such lands, but does not require him to do so * * *. [T]he Secretary has discretion to refuse to issue any lease at all on a given tract." Thus refusing to issue the Deep Creek leases, far from removing Deep Creek from the operation of the mineral leasing law, would constitute a legitimate exercise of the discretion granted to the Interior Secretary under that statute.

NOTES AND QUESTIONS

1. Which position is correct? Is withdrawal the only method for implementing land management decisions such as withholding leases? Did Congress really intend to require that the FLPMA reporting and other processes be followed for every single decision rejecting some proposed activity on federal land? On the other hand, did Congress intend that generic policy decisions (such as no mineral leasing on an entire national forest) would escape these processes? Is it significant that operative words in the FLPMA definition of withdrawal (withholding an area from "settlement, sale, location, or entry") do not expressly include "leasing, contracting, or permitting"?

2. Can you reconcile the two approaches? Should a line be drawn somewhere between a decision rejecting a single or small number of lease applications in a relatively confined area of federal land, and a more generic policy decision putting a large area off limits? Has Congress already drawn such a line in the FLPMA definition of withdrawal? If so, where is it? Should the courts do it by interpretation?

3. Is the issue the same with regard to decisions not to sell timber off federal lands, or not to issue grazing permits, or rights-of-way, if not doing all of these things were within the discretion of the federal land manager?

4. There are actually at least three ways to put into effect a decision not to make a particular tract of land available for mineral leasing: (1) deciding not to grant any applications for leases; (2) withdrawing the area from mineral leasing in a FLPMA withdrawal order; and (3) declaring the land unavailable for leasing in the applicable land use plan for the area. Memorandum to Secretary from the Solicitor regarding Jack Morrow Hills Coordinated Activity Plan (Dec. 22, 2000). For authority that decisions in a land use plan putting some lands off limits to some actions is not a FLPMA "withdrawal," see Seattle Audubon Society v. Lyons, 871 F.Supp. 1291 (W.D.Wash.1994), *aff'd on other grounds*, 80 F.3d 1401 (9th Cir.1996).

NOTE: FLPMA WITHDRAWAL PROCEDURES AND THE LEGISLATIVE VETO

FLPMA generally calls for consultation between the executive and the Congress in withdrawal decisions. But in three situations the statute goes beyond mere reporting and consultation. First, 43 U.S.C. § 1714(c)(1) requires the Secretary to terminate a withdrawal the executive proposes to make if, within ninety days of the day notice of such withdrawal has been submitted to each house of Congress, "the Congress has adopted a concurrent resolution stating that such House [sic] does not approve the withdrawal." Second, 43 U.S.C. § 1714(e) allows for emergency withdrawals when "extraordinary measures must be taken to preserve values that would otherwise be lost." These withdrawals may be made on the Secretary's own initiative, "or when the Committee on Interior and Insular Affairs of either the House of Representatives or the Senate notifies the Secretary" that a qualifying emergency exists. Third, as part of the withdrawal review program addressed in the Lujan v. National Wildlife Federation case, *supra* p. 210, the statute provides that the Secretary may terminate withdrawals after reporting to Congress "unless [within ninety days of notice] the Congress has adopted a concurrent resolution" of disapproval. 43 U.S.C. § 1714(*l*)(2). [Concurrent congressional resolutions are not presented to the President for concurrence or veto, whereas joint resolutions are. The former raise the presentment clause issue discussed in the next paragraph.]

The constitutionality of these provisions is doubtful as a result of the post-FLPMA decision in Immigration and Naturalization Service v. Chadha, 462 U.S. 919 (1983), which held that somewhat similar statutory requirements requiring concurrence by less than the full Congress, and without an opportunity for the President to object, violated the constitutional requirements of bicameralism and presentment, U.S. Const. Art. I, § 7, cl. 2 (requiring that every "Bill" pass both houses and be presented to the President for veto or concurrence):

> In purely practical terms, it is obviously easier for action to be taken by one House without submission to the President; but it is crystal clear from the records of the Convention, contemporaneous writings and debates, that the Framers ranked other values higher than efficiency. The records of the Convention and debates in the States preceding ratification * * * [reflect] a determination that legislation by the national Congress be a step-by-step, deliberate and deliberative process.

> The choices we discern as having been made in the Constitutional Convention impose burdens on governmental processes that often seem clumsy, inefficient, even unworkable, but those hard choices were consciously made by men who had lived under a form of government that permitted arbitrary governmental acts to go unchecked. There is no support in the Constitution or decisions of this Court for the proposition that the cumbersomeness and delays often encountered in complying with explicit Constitutional standards may be avoided, either by the Congress or by the President. * * * With all the obvious flaws of delay, untidiness, and potential for abuse, we have not yet found a better way to preserve freedom than by making the exercise of power subject to the carefully crafted restraints spelled out in the Constitution.

462 U.S. at 959. In *dictum,* the Court approved "report and wait" provisions whereby proposed administrative action is reported to Congress and does not take effect until the end of a specified waiting period, 462 U.S. at 935 n. 9.

Two courts have confronted the issue whether FLPMA's provisions giving less than the full Congress a veto over executive withdrawal actions are constitutional. One decision came early in the Reagan Administration, before the Court decided *Chadha.* Interior Secretary James Watt announced plans to issue oil and gas leases in three wilderness areas in Montana that were legally open to mineral leasing through December 31, 1983. Invoking its statutory "emergency withdrawal" authority under FLPMA, the House Interior Committee voted along partisan lines to direct the Secretary to withdraw the areas from mineral leasing. Secretary Watt expressed doubt about the constitutionality of the Committee's action, but issued an order withdrawing the lands. Miners and conservative legal foundations challenged his order in court. The district court thought the issue was close, but upheld the withdrawal provisions on the seemingly artificial ground that, although a congressional committee could order a withdrawal, the Secretary retained power to set its duration. Pacific Legal Foundation v. Watt, 529 F.Supp. 982 (D.Mont.1981). This litigation, which included a brief subsequent opinion at 539 F.Supp. 1194 (D.Mont.1982), triggered a series of executive and congressional actions resulting in the withdrawal of all wilderness areas from mineral leasing through December 31, 1983. At that point, the statutory withdrawal in the Wilderness Act took effect.

The second case involved Secretary Watt's proposal to lease large tracts of federal coal in the Upper Great Plains. Once again the House Interior Committee, following on the heels of a General Accounting Office report that previous coal lease sales conducted by Secretary Watt had been $100 million below fair market value, voted to direct an emergency withdrawal of the lands under FLPMA. This time Secretary Watt, citing the Supreme Court's brand-new decision in *Chadha,* refused to make the withdrawal, and environmental groups sued, leading to the following opinion on plaintiffs' request for a preliminary injunction, addressing their likelihood of succeeding on the merits:

National Wildlife Federation v. Watt

United States District Court, District of Columbia, 1983.
571 F.Supp. 1145.

■ JUDGE OBERDORFER

* * * If Congress' authority to enact the procedure at issue here derives solely from Article I of the Constitution, or if the *Chadha* rationale applies to Article IV, Section 3, the Committee resolution will probably be held to be impermissible legislative activity. Plaintiffs' attempt to distinguish a section 204(e) withdrawal from a legislative veto on the grounds that the withdrawal is only temporary is unconvincing. A forced withdraw-

al, whether temporary or permanent, alters the legal rights and duties of the Secretary of the Interior, and this cannot be done, according to *Chadha*, without bicameral passage and presidential presentment.

[The Interior Department had adopted the following regulation in order to implement section 1714(e) of FLPMA:

When the Secretary determines, or when either one of the two Committees of the Congress that are specified in section 204(e) of the act (43 U.S.C. 1714(e)) notifies the Secretary, that an emergency exists * * * the Secretary shall immediately make a withdrawal which shall be limited in its scope and duration to the emergency. 43 CFR § 2310.5(a).]

Defendant's failure to follow his own regulation, or to rescind it after notice, comment, and reasoned determination, raises a more serious question. * * * [I]t will probably be held that defendant's decision not to follow his regulation, on the basis of informal, *ex parte*, unpublished legal opinions that the parallel provision of section 204(e) was void, violated those notice requirements. Reliance on such *ex parte* opinions without minimal testing by other interested persons does not satisfy the notice and comment requirements of APA. * * *

* * *

It may well be that when this Court, the Court of Appeals, or the Supreme Court has had comprehensive briefs and an adequate opportunity to consider all the relevant historical evidence about the drafting and context of Article IV, Section 3, as well as its application over the years, they will reach a conclusion contrary to the opinions relied upon by the defendant here. The Supreme Court has stated that Congress' proprietary interest in public lands gives it constitutional prerogatives which transcend those which it enjoys in its purely legislative role in respect of immigration. See, e.g., United States v. California, 332 U.S. 19, 27 (1947). Moreover, it is common historical knowledge that in the years before the Constitution was adopted (and for many years thereafter) Congress was in session for only brief periods and in recess for many months at a time. Public lands were matters of even greater public and political interest than they are now. It is not inconceivable that courts will decide from the text and context of Article IV, Section 3, that its Framers contemplated that Congress' proprietary power to "dispose of" public lands included the power to delegate power to dispose of public land to the Executive as a trustee. The Framers may well have contemplated that such an Article IV delegation might be subject to an express and narrow condition that a specified Committee of Congress could, during or in anticipation of a congressional recess, temporarily suspend that delegation in the manner now provided for in section 204(e) of the 1976 Act. Such a condition would be analogous to limitations traditionally imposed by settlors under familiar principles of trust law. * * *

[The court, reasoning that there was a probability that the plaintiffs would prevail on the merits, issued a preliminary injunction. Later, the court granted plaintiffs' motion for summary judgment. 577 F.Supp. 825 (D.D.C.1984).]

NOTES AND QUESTIONS

1. This case illustrates how shoes may end up on different feet: In *Midwest Oil*, the executive sought to put the brakes on congressionally-directed exploitation of federal natural resources. Here, a committee of Congress sought to forestall an exploitation-minded Secretary. Where did Secretary Watt go wrong, procedurally, in his zeal to issue the coal leases?

2. Are there grounds for distinguishing the public lands arena, and the FLPMA provisions, from the *Chadha* teachings? Should the Constitution be construed to permit Congress and/or one of its houses or committees to play an active, continuing role in setting federal natural resource policy through such devices as FLPMA creates in the withdrawal area, even when such a role is constitutionally inappropriate in other contexts? (*Chadha* involved deportation of aliens.)

3. Does or should it make any difference in analyzing this constitutional question that the United States is a landowner here as well as a sovereign regulator? That Congress is given explicit constitutional power to make "needful Rules and Regulations" respecting federal property? That, as illustrated by *Midwest Oil*, there is a long tradition of legislative-executive dialogue and cooperation on withdrawal questions? That withdrawal questions in and of themselves (unlike *Chadha*) do not involve questions of human rights nor resolve questions of property rights, but rather only determine what legal regime will apply to specific tracts of federal lands? Does the Court's reading of the Property Clause in this case mean that FLPMA can be distinguished from the statute at issue in *Chadha*? Can the analysis of section 1714(e) in *Pacific Legal Foundation*, giving the Secretary discretion over the duration of the withdrawal, be squared with the Supreme Court's decision in *Chadha*?

4. Can the emergency provision in section 1714(e) be distinguished from the two other legislative vetoes in the FLPMA withdrawal provisions? Is there a reason to defer to a congressional committee's declaration of an emergency requiring prompt action, when the executive can take that action much more promptly than the Congress can?

5. Even if the provisions are unconstitutional, there will remain the question whether they are severable from the rest of the statute. In *Chadha* itself, in part because the statute there at issue had a severability clause, the Court found the veto severable, allowing the rest of the Act to remain in force. Should, for example, the executive authority to make withdrawals in excess of 5000 acres be struck down, or should instead section 1714(c) be construed so that only the veto is severed, leaving in place the duty to report large withdrawals to Congress? If the veto provision is deemed not severable, then the executive would surely be tempted to revive *Midwest Oil* claims of implied executive authority to make withdrawals.

6. The court here suggests that the regulation must be formally stricken (by notice and comment rulemaking, presumably) before the

agency could ignore it. Can that be right? Is an agency bound to follow one of its own duly-adopted regulations that merely parrots a statute (here, giving a congressional committee authority to trigger a legislative withdrawal) even when the constitutionality of the statute is in grave doubt? Suppose in *Chadha* itself, the Attorney General had adopted a regulation announcing she would automatically implement any resolution passed by one house of Congress regarding a decision to deport or not to deport an alien. Would the Supreme Court have deferred to it? To date, the Interior Department has not revoked the regulation Judge Oberdorfer relied on; *see* 43 C.F.R. § 2310.5(a).

3.   WITHDRAWALS AND RESERVATIONS UNDER THE ANTIQUITIES ACT

Congress was motivated to enact the Antiquities Act of 1906 primarily out of a concern to protect archeological resources of the southwest, but it was carefully drafted so as to provide the opportunity for protection of other "objects of historic or scientific interest." Its core provision is 16 U.S.C. § 431:

> The President of the United States is authorized, in his discretion, to declare by public proclamation historic landmarks, historic and prehistoric structures, and other objects of historic or scientific interest that are situated upon the lands owned or controlled by the Government of the United States to be national monuments, and may reserve as a part thereof parcels of land, the limits of which in all cases shall be confined to the smallest area compatible with the proper care and management of the objects to be protected.

The use of the Act has been distinctly bipartisan, with some of the most vigorous uses of the act coming from Republicans like Teddy Roosevelt, Taft, and Hoover. All told, well over one hundred monument proclamations have been issued since 1906, protecting some eighty million acres of federal land. From the beginning, nearly all Presidents in the twentieth century exercised their Antiquities Act authority rather aggressively to protect many areas of federal land. Roosevelt kicked it off when the ink was barely dry by proclaiming Devil's Tower in Wyoming as the nation's first national monument. He followed this up with well over a dozen other proclamations, including one setting aside some 270,000 acres of the Grand Canyon as a National Monument. This proclamation eventually furnished the courts with their first opportunity to interpret the Act.

In Cameron v. United States, 252 U.S. 450 (1920), U.S. Senator Ralph Cameron resisted federal efforts to evict him from mining claims he had located along popular tourist sites around the south rim of the Grand Canyon. Among his defenses was that President Roosevelt's 1908 Order exceeded the authority under the Antiquities Act. The Court, speaking through Justice Van Devanter, would have none of it:

> To this we cannot assent. The act under which the President proceeded empowered him to establish reserves embracing "objects of historic or scientific interest." The Grand Canyon, as stated in his proclamation,

"is an object of unusual scientific interest." It is the greatest eroded canyon in the United States, if not in the world, is over a mile in depth, has attracted wide attention among explorers and scientists, affords an unexampled field for geologic study, is regarded as one of the great natural wonders, and annually draws to its border thousands of visitors.

Twenty-three years later, the second President Roosevelt invoked the Antiquities Act to create the Jackson Hole National Monument, composed of some 220,000 acres in northwest Wyoming. The State of Wyoming challenged the action, arguing that the area included within the Monument was "barren" of any of the features listed in the statute. State of Wyoming v. Franke, 58 F.Supp. 890 (D.Wyo.1945):

> [The United States introduced evidence of] trails and historic spots in connection with the early trapping and hunting of animals formulating the early fur industry of the West, structures of glacial formation and peculiar mineral deposits and plant life indigenous to the particular area, a biological field for research of wild life in its particular habitat within the area, involving the study of the origin, life, habits and perpetuation of the different species of wild animals, all of which it is claimed constitute matters of scientific interest within the scope and contemplation of the Antiquities Act.

The court concluded:

> If there be evidence in the case of a substantial character upon which the President may have acted in declaring that there were objects of historic or scientific interest included within the area, it is sufficient upon which he may have based a discretion. For example, if a monument were to be created on a bare stretch of sage-brush prairie in regard to which there was no substantial evidence that it contained objects of historic or scientific interest, the action * * * would undoubtedly be arbitrary and capricious and clearly outside the scope and purpose of the Monument Act.

> * * * [I]f the Congress presumes to delegate its inherent authority to Executive Departments which exercise acquisitive proclivities not actually intended, the burden is on the Congress to pass such remedial legislation as may obviate any injustice brought about as the power and control over and disposition of government lands inherently rests in its Legislative branch. What has been said with reference to the objects of historic and scientific interest applies equally to the discretion of the Executive in defining the area compatible with the proper care and management of the objects to be protected.

Many of the crown jewels of the national park system were first protected by executive action under the Antiquities Act, when Congress dragged its feet on legislative proposals. Besides the Grand Canyon and Jackson Hole (now mostly part of Grand Teton National Park), Death

Valley, Glacier Bay, Zion, Bryce Canyon, Capitol Reef, and several other large withdrawals were first made this way. Not only has Congress not interfered with these actions; in thirty cases it has later converted the monuments into national parks. In recognition of the value of executive action in FLPMA, Congress expressly forbade the Secretary of the Interior from "modify[ing] or revok[ing] any withdrawal creating national monuments" under the Antiquities Act. 43 U.S.C. § 1714(j). Of course, Congress can create national monuments itself. *See, e.g.*, 114 Stat. 1362 (2000) (Santa Rosa and San Jacinto Mountains National Monument); 96 Stat. 301 (1982) (Mount St. Helens National Volcanic Monument).

The most prominent exercise of Antiquities Act power was made by President Jimmy Carter. In late 1978, Congress seemed to put the finishing touches on a massive bill to protect upwards of one hundred million acres of federal land in Alaska. A deadline was looming, because the temporary, seven-year congressional withdrawal of eighty million acres in the 1971 Alaska Native Claims Settlement Act (ANCSA) was about to expire. Unyielding opposition to the legislation by the government of the state of Alaska and its congressional delegation stalled passage, and the state prematurely filed statehood land selections on lands the bill would protect, just before the expiration of the ANCSA withdrawal.

In a dramatic stroke on December 1, 1978, President Carter set aside fifty-six million acres of this Alaskan land as national monuments under the Antiquities Act, and affirmed Secretary of the Interior Cecil Andrus's temporary withdrawal, made two weeks earlier, of 105 million acres from state selection and resource exploitation. Taken together, these actions maintained the status quo of protection for these lands until Congress could finish its work on the legislation. It took two more years, but a lame duck President Carter signed the Alaska National Interest Lands Conservation Act (ANILCA) in December 1980. The Act rescinded the Carter withdrawals but included almost all the affected lands within various preservation systems.

The State of Alaska and several resource companies challenged the executive action on various grounds, including the propriety of applying the Antiquities Act to such large tracts. All were rejected by the Alaska district court, and not appealed. State of Alaska v. Carter, 462 F.Supp. 1155 (D.Alaska 1978). The Department had done its homework. It made a detailed record, with separate proclamations, each going to great pains to describe the areas and the facts justifying each withdrawal on the basis of "historic or scientific interest." For the maps and texts of the proclamations, which make surprisingly good reading, see 43 Fed.Reg. 57009–57131 (Dec. 1, 1978).

After nearly two decades of disuse, the Antiquities Act took a dramatic turn on center stage in September 1996. President Clinton used the Act to proclaim the 1.7 million acre Grand Staircase–Escalante National Monument in Southern Utah. (The GSENM has since been expanded to 1.9 million acres through land exchanges with Utah for its inholdings.) The monument included some of the most remote and unpopulated areas in the lower forty-eight states: Car and Driver magazine reported that one spot is more than fifty miles in any direction from the nearest paved road. The area long had been the target of proposals for developments such as coal mines and power plants, but its remoteness had left it largely unspoiled. The monument proclamation (which two of these editors helped craft) carefully described many "objects of historic and scientific interest" in the monument area, including "archaeological, geological, historical, paleontological, and botanical resources." In Utah Association of Counties v. Bush, 316 F.Supp. 2d 1172 (D. Utah 2004), the federal district court rejected all challenges to the creation of the Grand Staircase–Escalante National Monument in a lengthy opinion.

The GSENM was just a warm-up for President Clinton. In the last year of his term he proclaimed nineteen new and expanded three existing national monuments, covering nearly six million acres in total. Most of the early national monuments were managed by the U.S. Forest Service or the National Park Service; in the 1930s, all of the monuments then managed by the Forest Service were transferred to the National Park Service's care. The Antiquities Act does not require any particular agency to manage monuments, and President Clinton broke new ground by putting most of the monuments he created under the care of the Bureau of Land Management. In Mountain States Legal Foundation v. Bush, the D.C. Circuit dismissed a challenge to six of Clinton's national monuments for failure to present any specific facts warranting review of the President's action within the bounds of the Antiquities Act. 306 F.3d 1132 (D.C. Cir. 2002).

In addition to judicial challenges, opponents of national monuments have also tried altering legislation to prevent such proclamations. Congress has never substantially altered the Act, even though there have been numerous proposals to do so. However, some proclamations did ignite state-specific backlashes. In 1950 Congress exempted Wyoming from the Act's ambit in reaction to President Franklin Roosevelt's designation of the Jackson Hole National Monument, 16 U.S.C. § 431a. ANILCA's so-called "no more clause" provides that a withdrawal of more than 5,000 acres of public lands in Alaska shall expire after one year unless Congress has adopted a joint resolution of approval. 16 U.S.C. § 3213(a). This effectively restricts the use of the Antiquities Act.

Tulare County v. Bush

United States District Court, District of Columbia, 2002.
306 F.3d 1138 *cert. denied*, 540 U.S. 813.

■ JUDGE ROGERS

* * * In April 2000 President Clinton established by proclamation the Giant Sequoia National Monument pursuant to his authority under the Antiquities Act. Proclamation 7295, 65 Fed. Reg. 24,095 (Apr. 15, 2000). The Monument, which encompasses 327,769 acres of land in the Sequoia National Forest in south-central California, contains groves of giant sequoias, the world's largest trees, and their surrounding ecosystem.

Tulare County, which contains land near and within the Grand Sequoia National Monument ("Monument"), along with a number of other public and private entities that use the Monument area for business or recreational purposes (hereinafter "Tulare County"), filed a complaint seeking declaratory and injunctive relief. Tulare County alleged that the Proclamation violated various provisions of the Antiquities Act and the Property Clause of the Constitution, as well as the National Forest Management Act, the National Environmental Policy Act, and the parties' existing rights under a prior mediated settlement agreement. The district court, concluding that only facial review was appropriate, dismissed the complaint.

On appeal, Tulare County contends that in dismissing its complaint prior to discovery, the district court erred in failing to accept as true the facts alleged in the complaint and in limiting its review to the face of the Proclamation rather than reviewing the President's discretionary factual determinations. Tulare County does not contend that the President lacks authority under the Antiquities Act to proclaim national monuments like Giant Sequoia, as the Supreme Court has long upheld such authority. Rather, in Counts 1–4 of the complaint, Tulare County alleged that the Proclamation violated the Antiquities Act because it: (1) failed to identify the objects of historic or scientific interest with reasonable specificity; (2) designated as the basis for the Monument objects that do not qualify under the Act; (3) did not confine the size of the Monument "to the smallest area compatible with proper care and management of the objects to be protected," 16 U.S.C. § 431; and (4) increased the likelihood of harm by fires to any objects of alleged historic or scientific interest within the Monument rather than protecting those objects. * * *

Count 1 of Tulare County's complaint is premised on the assumption that the Antiquities Act requires the President to include a certain level of detail in the Proclamation. No such requirement exists. The Act authorizes the President, "in his discretion, to declare by public proclamation historic landmarks, historic and prehistoric structures, and other objects of historic or scientific interest." 16 U.S.C. § 431. The Presidential declaration at issue complies with that standard. The Proclamation lyrically describes "magnificent groves of towering giant sequoias," "bold granitic domes, spires, and plunging gorges," "an enormous number of habitats," "limestone caverns and ... unique paleontological resources documenting tens of thousands of years of ecosystem change," as well as "many archaeological sites recording Native American occupation ... and historic remnants of early Euroamerican settlement." By identifying historic sites and objects of scientific interest located within the designated lands, the Proclamation adverts to the statutory standard. Hence, Count 1 fails as a matter of law.

Count 2 alleges that the President has designated nonqualifying objects for protection. The Antiquities Act provides that, in addition to historic landmarks and structures, "other objects of historic or scientific interest" may qualify, at the President's discretion, for protection as monuments. 16 U.S.C. § 431. Inclusion of such items as ecosystems and scenic vistas in the Proclamation did not contravene the terms of the statute by relying on nonqualifying features. In Cappaert, 426 U.S. at 141–42, the Supreme Court rejected a similar argument, holding that the President's Antiquities Act authority is not limited to protecting only archeological sites.

As relevant to Count 3 of the complaint, the Proclamation states that the Monument's 327,769–acre size "is the smallest area compatible with the proper care and management of the objects to be protected." It also states that the sequoia groves are not contiguous but instead comprise part of a spectrum of interconnected ecosystems. Tulare County alleges that no one in the Clinton Administration "made any meaningful investigation or determination of the smallest area necessary to protect any specifically identified objects of genuine historic or scientific interest." Instead, it alleges, President Clinton "bowed to political pressure . . . in designating a grossly oversized Monument unnecessary for the protection of any objects of genuine historic or scientific interest." This allegation is a legal conclusion couched as a factual allegation. * * *

Contrary to the assumption underlying Count 3, the Antiquities Act does not impose upon the President an obligation to make any particular investigation. And to the extent that Tulare County alleges that the Proclamation designates land that should not be included within the Monument, the complaint fails to identify the improperly designated lands with sufficient particularity to state a claim. Id. Insofar as Tulare County alleges that the Monument includes too much land, i.e., that the President abused his discretion by designating more land than is necessary to protect the specific objects of interest, Tulare County does not make the factual allegations sufficient to support its claims. This is particularly so as its claim that the Proclamation covered too much land is dependent on the proposition that parts of the Monument lack scientific or historical value, an issue on which Tulare County made no factual allegations.

Count 4 of the complaint alleges that the Monument designation actually increases the risk of harm from fires to many of the objects that the Proclamation aims to protect. However, the Proclamation expressly addresses the threat of wildfires and the need for forest restoration and protection. The Proclamation observes that forest renewal is needed because environmental change "has led to an unprecedented failure in sequoia reproduction," and that "a century of fire suppression and logging" has created "an increased hazard of wildfires of a severity that was rarely encountered in pre-Euroamerican times." Count 4 contains no factual allegations, only conclusions, and it refers to current management rather than the designation under the Proclamation as the cause for likely increases in catastrophic fires.

* * *

Tulare County's remaining contentions, involving other federal statutes and contractual rights, fail as a matter of law. Contrary to Count 6 of the complaint, the Proclamation does not violate the National Forest Management Act of 1976 ("NFMA"), by unlawfully withdrawing land from the national forest system. The NFMA provides that no national forest land "shall be returned to the public domain except by an act of Congress." 16

U.S.C. § 1609(a). The Proclamation states that * * * "[n]othing in this proclamation shall be deemed to revoke any existing withdrawal, reservation, or appropriation; however, the national monument shall be the dominant reservation." The Proclamation thus conceives of the designated land as having a dual status as part of both the Monument and the Sequoia National Forest. The Proclamation is therefore wholly consistent with NFMA.

* * *

Accordingly, * * * we affirm the dismissal of the complaint.

NOTES AND QUESTIONS

1. What kinds of "objects of historic or scientific interest" can justify the designation of millions of acres of federal lands as national monuments? An entire functioning ecosystem? A prominent or unusual geological formation? An unusual biotic community? A collection of archeological sites which illustrate connections among prehistoric communities? Historic trails that may be visible over many miles? In fact, both President Carter's and President Clinton's national monument proclamations identified all of these things and more, and explained their significance and why it was important to protect them. Are there any limits? Do all federal lands have some scientific or historic value? In the *Tulare County*, the court remarked that including "such items as ecosystems and scenic vistas in the Proclamation did not contravene the terms of the statute by relying on nonqualifying features." Can a "scenic vista" be an "object of historic or scientific interest"? What if John Muir or Lewis & Clark had marveled at the majesty of a particular vista in their books or journals? Would that make it an "object" of "historic interest" such that the President could create a national monument to preserve it?

2. What about the statutory caution to preserve the "smallest area compatible with the proper care and management of the objects to be protected"? Although some argue the statutory text contemplates postage-stamp sized monuments around an archeological site or a particular scientific feature, from the beginning the Act has been applied to justify expansive protections. How much deference should the executive get from the courts in making these judgment calls about what area is required for "proper care and management of the objects to be protected"? And how much review will the courts provide of presidential determinations, according to the court here? According to what standard? Arbitrariness, capriciousness, abuse of discretion?

In *Tulare County*, the plaintiffs argued that President Clinton acted improperly by protecting a larger area instead of the isolated, non-contiguous sequoia groves. The court brushed the challenge aside, noting that the County had not "identified the improperly designated lands with sufficient particularity to state a claim." Who has burden to show the relevant facts? Is it enough that the proclamation said the sequoia groves were, as the court put it, "part of a spectrum of interconnected ecosystems"? Aren't almost all ecosystems interconnected in some sense?

3. President Clinton did not attempt to use the procedures of the National Environmental Policy Act in designating monuments. His lawyers maintained that NEPA applies only to federal agencies, and not to the President himself. The CEQ regulations agree that the term "federal agency" in NEPA does not include the President. 40 C.F.R. § 1508.12. Although the Department of the Interior and some other federal agencies were heavily involved in the drafting of the proclamations and assembling the record in support of them, they were acting at the President's explicit request.

4. Although many of the early proclamations were quite terse and did not contain much if any guidance on how the monuments were to be managed, the Carter and especially the Clinton proclamations contained quite a bit of detail on area management; e.g., defining the extent to which water was reserved as a matter of federal law, and the extent to which grazing, off-road vehicle travel, hunting and fishing, and other activities might be allowed. With only a couple of exceptions, all areas were withdrawn from mining and mineral leasing.

5. Can a Monument Proclamation be revoked? No President has ever done so, hence there is no law on this subject. The Attorney General has opined that proclamations cannot be revoked, because the Antiquities Act only authorizes the President to proclaim monuments, not "unproclaim" them. 39 Op. Atty. Gen. 185 (1938).

6. Can a President shrink the boundaries of a national monument? Many national monuments have been expanded by subsequent proclamations, and a few proclamations have taken acres out monument status. What does a President need to show, if anything, to cut acreage out of a monument? Must he make a showing that the earlier proclamation's judgment about the area reserved being the "smallest area compatible with the proper care and management of the objects to be protected" was erroneous? *See generally* Mark Squillace, *The Monumental Legacy of the Antiquities Act of 1906*, 37 Ga. L.Rev. 473 (2003).

7. In 2006 President Bush reserved the largest national monument ever under the Antiquities Act: Northwest Hawaiian Islands Marine National Monument. At nearly 140,000 square miles, it is the largest conservation area in the United States and the largest protected marine zone in the world. The monument is home to more than seven thousand marine species, one quarter of which are found nowhere else but the monument's extensive reef system. The National Oceanic and Atmospheric Administration manages the monument as part of its National Marine Sanctuaries System, in partnership with the FWS, which already managed part of the area in the National Wildlife Refuge System.

D. Land Exchanges, Sales, and Other Transfers

As Chapter 2 illustrates, the freewheeling era of federal land disposal led to a hodgepodge of land ownership patterns, particularly in the west.

One product of such patterns is burgeoning litigation over access questions, as recounted in Section A, above. Another product of federal land disposal has been difficulty in managing certain resources such as vegetation and wildlife that tend to follow ecosystem rather than ownership lines. Finally, states and railroad successors who find themselves checkerboarded or surrounded by federal lands often desire to block up their holdings to facilitate development of the resources they contain. These forces have gradually combined to produce a noticeable movement toward realigning landholdings along more rational lines. To some extent, ownership adjustment can be done by purchase and sale, although limitations on federal and state governmental budgets limit this option in many circumstances. Frequently a more attractive alternative is land exchanges.

Furthermore, there are some situations in which disposal or acquisition of federal land is desirable for other purposes. While the general federal policy now is to retain federal lands in federal ownership, Congress has seen fit to keep in place a number of mechanisms allowing disposal of federal lands in particular circumstances. Finally, the federal agencies retain power to acquire lands by the exercise of the power of eminent domain in many circumstances. This section will briefly cover these subjects, focusing on the method most used: exchanges.

1.   LAND ACQUISITIONS

Congress has not enacted any single statute laying out an overall land acquisition program. Instead, acquisitions by the federal land management agencies typically follow one of three patterns. First, Congress sometimes designates a special management area and authorizes the agency to acquire land within the boundaries. Second, the legislation may state a goal, such as preservation of waterfowl populations, and give the agency general authority to acquire land or interests in land to achieve that goal. Third, Congress has generally encouraged miscellaneous acquisitions for purposes of access or consolidation of existing holdings. Most federal land management agencies have generic acquisition authority by purchase, exchange, donation, or eminent domain. *See, e.g.,* 43 U.S.C. § 1715 (Forest Service and BLM). Federal land management agencies have varied authorities to acquire lands. For example, unless a specific park statute provides otherwise, the National Park Service may only acquire property within the boundaries of a national park; but the Service does have authority to make minor boundary adjustments with the written consent of the affected landowner. *See* 16 U.S.C. § 460l–9(c). The Bureau of Land Management, on the other hand, has broad authority to acquire lands or interests in lands by purchase, exchange, or donation, whenever consistent with the mission of the Department and with applicable land use plans. 43 U.S.C. § 1715(b). But it has only a narrow authority to acquire by eminent domain ("only if necessary to secure access to public lands, and then only if the lands so acquired are confined to as narrow a corridor as is necessary to serve such purpose"). *Id.* at § 1715(a).

Aside from ad hoc designations of new or expanded park and refuge system units, federal acquisition at present is mostly directed at enhancement of wildlife habitat and recreational opportunities. In the past, major federal land acquisition programs have resulted in the creation of the national forest system in the East and Midwest (under the Weeks Act) and in the national grasslands in the northern great plains. A few national parks consist almost exclusively of acquired lands; e.g., Redwood National Park along the northern California coast. The U.S. also acquires some lands via donation. Big Bend National Park, Great Smoky Mountains National Park, and Sevilleta National Wildlife Refuge are among the most spectacular examples.

Most federal land acquisitions are now financed by the Land and Water Conservation Fund (LWCF), established in 1965 as a "paper account" in the Treasury which may not be spent unless Congress appropriates funds from it. Congress does appropriate money from the account almost every year, though the amounts vary widely. The LWCF has underwritten acquisition of nearly five million acres of land (and interests in land, such as water rights and conservation easements) by federal, state, and local governments for outdoor recreation and wildlife purposes. More than half of that acreage has been included in federal conservation systems. It is treated in more detail in Chapter 11A.

2.   Land Sales

Federal law sharply circumscribes the sale of national park, national forest, and national wildlife refuge system lands. Disposition laws affecting the national forests include 16 U.S.C. § 519 (sale of "small areas of land chiefly valuable for agriculture"), and 16 U.S.C. § 478a (sales of no more than 640 acres for townsites). For national parks, see 16 U.S.C. § 430g–5(b) and § 4601–22(a).

Sales of BLM public lands are governed by FLPMA, which repealed various statutes authorizing sales of federal lands and substituted a single provision, 43 U.S.C. § 1713. All sales must be for fair market value. 43 U.S.C. § 1713(d).* Other substantive provisions for land sales are set out in § 1713(a):

(a) A tract of the public lands (except land in units of the National Wilderness Preservation System, National Wild and Scenic Rivers Systems, and National System of Trails) may be sold under this Act where, as a result of land use planning required under section 1712 of this title, the Secretary determines that the sale of such tract meets the following disposal criteria:

(1) such tract because of its location or other characteristics is difficult and uneconomic to manage as part of the public lands, and is not suitable for management by another Federal department or agency; or

---

* Proposed sales of more than 2,500 acres must be delayed for ninety days, during which time either House may veto such a sale. 43 U.S.C. § 1713(c). This legislative veto provision may well violate *Chadha,* and the severability issues are similar to those involving withdrawals.

(2) such tract was acquired for a specific purpose and the tract is no longer required for that or any other Federal purpose; or

(3) disposal of such tract will serve important public objectives, including but not limited to, expansion of communities and economic development, which cannot be achieved prudently or feasibly on land other than public land and which outweigh other public objectives and values, including, but not limited to, recreation and scenic values, which would be served by maintaining such tract in Federal ownership.

* * *

(e) The Secretary shall determine and establish the size of tracts of public lands to be sold on the basis of the land use capabilities and development requirements of the lands; and, where any such tract which is judged by the Secretary to be chiefly valuable for agriculture is sold, its size shall be no larger than necessary to support a family-sized farm.

Any lands *sold* under § 1713 must retain the minerals in federal ownership. 43 U.S.C. § 1719. The reservation of minerals does not apply to lands *exchanged* under FLPMA. Land sales are not currently an important source of governmental revenue. In Fiscal Year 2005, FLPMA § 1713 sales amounted to a bit over two million dollars.

FLPMA authorizes limited transfers of lands to state and local governments. 43 U.S.C. § 1721. The Recreation and Public Purposes Act, 43 U.S.C. § 869 (a separate act not repealed by FLPMA), allows the Secretary to give public land to local governments in certain circumstances. The federal government retains a reversionary interest in the event such lands are no longer used for the purposes for which they are granted. Local parks, school sites, and landfills seem to be the most common purposes underlying such grants. The City of Phoenix has the largest municipal park system in the nation thanks to this Act, which furnished the authority by which the Interior Department transferred ownership to the city of several small mountains within its borders. Concerned about possible BLM liability for improper waste disposal on such lands, Congress amended the Act in 1988 to grant immunity to the federal government in such circumstances. 102 Stat. 3813.

Occasionally, since the end of the disposal era in the 1930s, proposals are made to conduct major sales of federal lands. Most recently, the George W. Bush Administration has included in its budget proposals a program to sell federal lands in order to provide funds for public school systems in the Pacific Northwest whose revenue base has eroded by declining federal timber sales. The proposals have yet to overcome substantial opposition from editorial boards, county commissioners, hunters, anglers, and mainstream conservationists. In the early 1980s President Reagan issued an executive order to establish a Property Review Board to "review real property holdings of the federal government, * * * expedite the sale of unneeded property so that it can be put to more productive use, [and] use the proceeds from property sales to begin retiring the national debt." No.

12348, 47 Fed. Reg. 8547 (1982). At one point, Secretary of the Interior James Watt pushed for selling some thirty-five million acres of federally owned land (mostly BLM land), an area the size of Iowa. The Administration projected land sales returning $4 billion annually over a five-year period. The idea provoked controversy on many fronts, and the program never got off the ground; the Property Review Board was formally disbanded in 1984.

An important reason why BLM has not been very interested in simply selling land under the FLPMA land sales provisions is because the revenue generated by the sale goes directly to the federal treasury and is not available for use by the BLM unless and until it is appropriated by Congress. If, however, BLM exchanges rather than sells land, it directly benefits by acquiring property it can manage (such as endangered species habitat) in return. As a result, informal agency practice tended to favor exchanges over sales. But exchanges are difficult, time-consuming, and can be political hot potatoes. As one practitioner has noted, "every parcel of public land has its own constituency that will urge retention of that parcel in public ownership * * * [and m]any interests are aligned to oppose any sale or other disposition of resources from the public domain." Murray D. Feldman, *The New Public Land Exchanges: Trading Development Rights in One Area for Public Resources in Another*, 44 ROCKY MT. MIN. L. INST. 2–1, 2–38 (1998). Inevitably, questions about valuation are raised (appraisals hardly being an exact science), especially when BLM is disposing of land in a volatile economic climate, such as a fast-growing urban area where land values may change dramatically.

To address such concerns, Congress in 1998 enacted the Southern Nevada Public Land Management Act, 112 Stat. 2343. It aimed to provide for a more orderly method of disposing of surplus federal land for development purposes in the burgeoning Las Vegas, Nevada area (for the last several years, the fastest growing urban area in the Nation). The Act authorized BLM to auction off tracts of public lands available for disposal in the Las Vegas area, with most of the proceeds being retained by the BLM (rather than going into the Treasury, where congressional appropriations would be required to spend it). The law gave 10 percent of the proceeds to the Southern Nevada Water Authority for infrastructure needs, and 5 percent to the State for education purposes. The remaining 85 percent went to the BLM to acquire "environmentally sensitive land" or interests in land in the state (with priority to the Las Vegas area). In addition, the State and local governments may obtain any lands BLM would otherwise put up for sale for governmental purposes under the Recreation and Public Purposes Act, 43 U.S.C. § 869. The competitive auction process, furnishing the truest test of market value, reduced concerns about whether the federal government would receive fair return for the land sold. And, the revolving fund concept provided BLM and the local governments with incentives to put disposable land on the market.

Ironically, while making more urban development possible in Las Vegas, the Nevada Act may well increase substantially the total federal landholdings in Nevada, at 83 percent already the highest in the Nation.

The Act is, by far, the most important contemporary source of federal land sales. Since its inception, the Act has conveyed more than 31,000 acres of federal land fetching revenue of more than $2 billion.

It did not take Congress long to expand this basic idea across the West, for several other fast-growing Western cities still have substantial amounts of BLM land in the path of development. In 2000, Congress enacted the Federal Land Transaction Facilitation Act, 43 U.S.C. §§ 2301–2306, for the purpose, among others, of promoting "the reconfiguration of land ownership patterns to better facilitate resource management." It carried forward, with some modification, the model embodied in the Nevada Act for the eleven contiguous Western states plus Alaska, for a ten year period. It authorized competitive sale of BLM lands "identified for disposal under approved land use plans (as in effect on July 25, 2000)." The gross proceeds of these sales are deposited in a "Federal Land Disposal Account" and are made available, "without further Act of appropriation," to buy, from willing sellers, at a price not to exceed fair market value: (a) nonfederal inholdings in a wide but defined variety of federal lands managed primarily for conservation purposes; and (b) lands adjacent to such areas that contain "exceptional resources" where there is a "compelling need for conservation and protection under the jurisdiction of a Federal agency in order to maintain the resource for the benefit of the public." As with most federal land sales, mineral rights are reserved.

Because BLM land use plans in effect on July 25, 2000 may not precisely indicate how much land is "available for disposal," there are no firm figures on how much BLM land could be disposed of under this Act. The Clinton Administration insisted that the statute be limited to sale of lands identified in then-existing BLM plans because it did not want to open the door widely for wholesale privatization of federal lands. The Bush Administration has recommended that Congress lift the "existing plan" limitation, and also reduce the amount of receipts that could be spent on land acquisition to 60 percent from 80 percent. This could substantially expand the size of the privatization program, and would also give BLM more incentive to sell land because it could use receipts for things that resembled ordinary operating expenses

What do you think of this trend to create a revolving fund, bypassing the ordinary appropriations process, to use sales and purchases to better rationalize federal land holdings, primarily for the purpose of advancing conservation management? It is important to note that the proceeds of BLM land sales may be used to acquire inholdings or other lands for the benefit of the National Park Service, the Forest Service, and the Fish & Wildlife Service, as well as for the BLM. The legislation requires the Secretaries of Agriculture and the Interior to develop a procedure "prioritizing the acquisitions" considering, among other things, the date the inholding was established and the extent to which the acquisition will "facilitate management efficiency." It remains to be seen how much BLM's ardor to sell its land to fund acquisitions will be dampened by the fact that some benefits will inure to other agencies.

One of the concerns with respect to the revolving fund idea is that the Executive or the Congress will, in parlous budgetary times, be sorely tempted to divert the proceeds of the sale of federal lands into the federal treasury, and out of the revolving fund, to lower the federal deficit or justify more tax cuts. In fact, the white-hot Las Vegas real estate market has enabled the federal government to generate more than $2 billion in land sales at auction, many times what was anticipated when the Southern Nevada statute was adopted. The Bush Administration, seeking to close yawning budget deficits, has several times proposed to change the statutory formula to divert some money to other purposes, but the Nevada congressional delegation has objected and so far has prevailed. Another concern is that these public land sales revenues will tempt Congress to reduce appropriations for conservation land acquisition under the Land and Water Conservation Fund Act. The Federal Land Transaction Facilitation Act declared that funds made available from the sale of public lands shall be "supplemental" to (rather than a substitute for) funds appropriated under the LWCF Act. But this brave declaration does not legally bind future Congresses, which may choose to reduce LWCF appropriations.

3. Moving Federal Lands Around the Federal Family

Under the Federal Property and Administrative Services Act of 1949 (FPAS), 40 U.S.C. § 471 et seq., as amended, the General Services Administration (GSA) may dispose of excess or surplus government real estate to federal agencies, other public bodies, or private enterprises, in that order, for various purposes, but public domain, national forest, and national park lands are expressly excluded from disposition under the FPAS. 40 U.S.C. § 472(d)(1).

Federal land management agencies can take advantage of the FPAS to acquire land from other agencies for conservation purposes. The FPAS idea has been used to create urban "gateway" parks. In and around San Francisco, for instance, a variety of surplus military forts and reservations were turned over to the National Park Service for management as the Golden Gate National Recreation Area. The same thing happened in the New York City area with the Gateway National Recreation Area.

A somewhat similar process in recent years has added significant acreage to the federal conservation lands base. The Base Realignment and Closure (BRAC) process governs the downsizing of military bases in the post-Cold War era. There are several statutes involved. *See, e.g.*, 104 Stat. 1808–10 (1990). Several dozen military bases have been closed under the BRAC process. BRAC gives interested federal nonmilitary agencies an opportunity to apply for transfer of all or some of the land if it fits with their existing statutory mandate and is in the best interests of the government. In some instances, the land has been transferred to the federal land management agencies, primarily for wildlife conservation and parks purposes. *See*, e.g., Colorado's Rocky Mountain Arsenal National Wildlife Refuge on the former Army base.

Every so often, reformers propose massive reorganizations of public lands to consolidate public land systems along more rational lines. The most recent episode occurred when the Reagan Administration proposed a broad interagency land exchange between the Forest Service and the BLM. In January, 1985, it requested Congress to authorize a trade involving some thirty-five million acres. The plan was to consolidate large blocks of land under each agency in order to eliminate the costs resulting from virtually side-by-side BLM and Forest Service offices found in many regions. Also, the exchange would transfer most timber lands to the Forest Service and most grazing lands to the BLM to allow for greater specialization. In Washington State, for example, all BLM lands would be transferred to the Forest Service, while in Nevada nearly all Forest Service lands would go to the BLM. The maps describing the proposal thus portrayed neat, consolidated agency ownerships. There was one exception: a long, narrow tongue of Forest Service land extended down through BLM land in western New Mexico. The reason? Forest Service Chief Max Peterson, sensitive to hallowed agency traditions, was unyielding in his refusal to relinquish the place in Lincoln National Forest where Smokey Bear was found clinging to a charred tree in 1947. This interchange idea never gained much traction; the only significant implementation was in Nevada. There Congress approved a transfer of jurisdiction in which the Forest Service was the big winner; it gained 662,000 acres of BLM land, while the BLM picked up only 23,000 acres of former national forest land. *See* 102 Stat. 2749 (1988).

4.   LAND EXCHANGES

All the major federal land management agencies have traditionally been delegated power to exchange lands under their control for private lands; each empowering statute contains various conditions such as an "equal value" standard to prevent profiteering. Most such exchanges are undertaken to consolidate federal land holdings or acquire new lands of high conservation value. Because livestock graziers, recreationists, or other users of the public lands that go out of federal ownership in an exchange may be displaced, exchanges may provoke opposition. The BLM, given the checkerboard character of many of its lands, is the most active agency in promoting land exchanges.

Before the passage of FLPMA, Forest Service exchange authority was primarily found in the General Exchange Act of 1922, 16 U.S.C. § 485. While FLPMA did not repeal that statute, FLPMA did include a general exchange section governing both BLM and Forest Service lands. *See* 43 U.S.C. § 1716. Partly because of a growing recognition of the advantages of carefully crafted land exchanges, Congress in 1988 enacted the Federal Land Exchange Facilitation Act, or FLEFA, 102 Stat. 1086, which amended FLPMA in several respects. Generally, it streamlined the exchange process at several points, including land appraisals and arbitration of valuation disputes. Still, the amount of land exchanged each year remains fairly low. In F.Y. 2005, the United States disposed about 32,000 acres of land, worth about $12 million, through exchange.

A prominent factor that drives federal agencies to make land exchanges, as opposed to acquisitions and sales, is how the federal government handles money associated with sales and acquisitions. Specifically, proceeds from federal land sales go into the general federal treasury, not into agency coffers. Thus an agency has little incentive to sell land because it sees no direct benefit from it. Furthermore, money for federal land acquisitions almost always must be appropriated by Congress (there are very few revolving funds where federal land management revenues may be spent by the agency without congressional approval). Land exchanges are a way for the federal land management agency to get rid of land that it does not want (but which may have high value in the marketplace), for land that it desires for some purpose, and bypass the appropriations process.

FLPMA includes an "equal value" requirement and a mandate that exchange transactions be in the public interest, explained in the statute (43 U.S.C. § 1716(a)) as follows:

> when considering public interest the Secretary concerned shall give full consideration to better Federal land management and the needs of State and local people, including needs for lands for the economy, community expansion, recreation areas, food, fiber, minerals, and fish and wildlife and the Secretary concerned [must find] that the values and the objectives which Federal lands or interests to be conveyed may serve if retained in Federal ownership are not more than the values of the non-Federal lands or interests and the public objectives they could serve if acquired.

Does this definition of the public interest allow, or call for, stringent judicial review? That question, arising out of a slightly different statutory provision (contained in the Alaska National Interest Lands Conservation Act, or ANILCA), came before the court in the following case.

National Audubon Society v. Hodel

United States District Court, District of Alaska, 1984.
606 F. Supp. 825.

■ JUDGE FITZGERALD

On August 10, 1983, Deputy Under–Secretary of the Interior, William P. Horn, acting on behalf of then Secretary of the Interior James G. Watt (the Secretary), entered into a land exchange agreement with representatives of three Alaska Native Corporations * * * referred to collectively as the CIRI Group. The Secretary transferred to the Natives a portion of St. Matthew Island, a wilderness area in the Alaska Maritime National Wildlife Refuge, in exchange for various land interests in the Kenai and Yukon Delta National Wildlife Refuges. The driving force behind the land exchange was to enable the CIRI Group to lease the St. Matthew Island parcel to private companies for construction and operation of support facilities for oil exploration and potential oil development in the Navarin Basin in the Bering Sea. In making the exchange, the Secretary relied upon authorization granted in § 1302(h) [of ANILCA, 16 U.S.C. § 3192(h)]. The conveyance is for fifty years, or so long as commercial oil production activities occur in the Navarin Basin. * * *

[St. Matthew Island was established as a Wildlife Refuge in 1909, designated a Wilderness Area in 1970, and was made part of the Alaska Maritime National Wildlife Refuge in ANILCA. ANILCA authorized the Secretary, "notwithstanding any other provision of law," to exchange lands, "including lands within conservation system units [which include wilderness areas] * * *." Thus the inclusion of St. Matthew Island in the National Wilderness Preservation System in 1970, 84 Stat. 1104, did not rule out the exchange. Interestingly, the statute also prohibits the Secretary from executing an exchange to acquire inholdings in wilderness areas." [16 U.S.C. § 3192(a).] Many factors contribute to the island's value as a wilderness area, including its isolation, remoteness, distance from shipping lanes and aircraft routes, rugged and varied terrain, and unique bird and mammal populations. Aside from minor evidence of past human presence on the island, St. Matthew remains essentially natural in appearance.

[The Department of the Interior prepared a environmental impact statement (EIS) on its proposal to issue oil and gas leases on the Outer Continental Shelf in the Navarin Basin near St. Matthew Island. Two of the three scenarios outlined in the EIS for lease exploration and development involve locating support facilities on the Island. The preferred or primary scenario would involve using the Island for air support during the exploration phase. Then, if exploration identified oil and gas deposits in commercial quantities, a major storage, loading and processing terminal would be built on the Island to allow the resource to be shipped to its consumers.]

The exchange provision in § 1302(h) of ANILCA imposes two requirements before a land exchange may be approved. First, the Secretary must determine that the exchange will result in "acquiring lands for the purposes of [ANILCA]." Second, the exchange must further the "public interest" if the lands exchanged are of unequal value.

There are two principal documents in the record which explain the considerations and the rationale upon which the Secretary rested his decision to proceed with the challenged land exchange. These include (1) the Department of the Interior Record of Decision, and (2) the Public Interest Determination for the Proposed Acquisition of Inholdings in Kenai and Yukon Delta National Wildlife Refuges by Exchange for Lands on St. Matthew Island, Alaska.

According to these documents, the Secretary concluded that both requirements were met by the terms of the St. Matthew exchange. [Discussion of first requirement omitted.] * * *

Concerning the second requirement, the Secretary's Determination concludes that the St. Matthew Island exchange would * * * further the public interest. The Secretary offered seven major reasons for his conclusion:

(1) The exchange advances longterm CSU [eds: conservation system units, referring to federal lands put into protective status by ANILCA] and general wildlife conservation and management objectives by (a) preventing

the creation of over 100 Native inholdings within CSUs without permanent loss of a single CSU acre, (b) providing federal management and public enjoyment benefits which comport with congressional intent that CSU inholdings be eliminated primarily through land exchanges, and (c) improving the protection provided [to CSU lands by means of a] nondevelopment easement and permanent federal management * * *.

(2) The exchange as a whole also advances the public interest in CSU objectives during the short term because the United States will (a) secure land interests in over three times the CSU acreage it will be conveying, (b) obtain clear title to and interest in more biologically and recreationally significant lands in terms of wildlife habitat quality than would be temporarily conveyed out of federal ownership, and (c) secure greater environmental protection by reason of the nondevelopment easement acquired in one of the most important waterfowl nesting habitats at Kokechik Bay, more than outweighing the temporary wildlife disruption authorized on St. Matthew Island.

* * *

(6) * * * [The] use of the strategically located St. Matthew Island realty for a staging area for Navarin Basin energy development offers substantial environmental, human safety and economic public interest benefits because (a) the island's close location to the Navarin Basin provides critical time advantages in responding to environmental dangers and human safety emergencies when compared to other potential staging areas, and (b) the increased economic efficiency in offshore energy exploration and development allowed by St. Matthew Island's use may result in higher bidding revenues received on the lease sale and additional domestic oil and gas production. * * *

[The court rejected the argument of the CIRI Group that the Secretary's public interest determination is "committed to agency discretion by law" and therefore not judicially reviewable under the Administrative Procedure Act. The court concluded that the arbitrary and capricious standard applies.]

* * *

In authorizing the Secretary to make land exchanges of unequal value when in the "public interest," Congress did not impart what factors it intended the Secretary to consider in analyzing whether such an exchange is in the public interest. In his Public Interest Determination for the St. Matthew exchange, the Secretary * * * viewed this standard broadly, considering possible benefits to the nation's economic vitality and oil production capabilities as well as to its wilderness values. * * *

I conclude the Secretary's broad view of the public interest in the context of land exchanges is a reasonable and permissible construction of ANILCA § 1302(h)'s statutory language. "Public interest" exchanges under ANILCA are exceptions to the general congressional requirement that the Secretary only enter into exchanges of equal monetary value. It therefore was reasonable for the Secretary to conclude that Congress intended that he take non-monetary benefits into account in determining whether the overall public interest would be furthered by a given exchange. * * *

In broad terms, the Secretary has stated that his Public Interest Determination is based on "a qualitative comparison of the temporary short-term loss of approximately 4,110 acres of wildlife and wilderness habitat on St. Matthew Island with the permanent addition of over 14,000 acres of wildlife habitat to the NWR System." * * *

[The Secretary has] broad discretion * * *. [T]he court may not attempt to substitute its judgment for that of the Secretary. Rather, review of the Secretary's determination must focus on whether the decision rests on an adequate record and was reached after consideration of all relevant facts. * * *

A.   Prospective Benefits to Wildlife Conservation and Public Recreation

The Secretary declared in his document of decision that the Administrative Record demonstrated that the St. Matthew land exchange would clearly result in a "net benefit" to national wildlife and conservation values. * * *

In terms of acreage, the largest acquisition by the Secretary in the exchange amounts to approximately 8000 surface acres of waterfowl nesting habitat within the Yukon Delta NWR. Recognizing the importance of this nesting region in Alaska, Congress declared a primary purpose of the Yukon Delta NWR to be "to conserve fish and wildlife populations and habitats in their natural diversity including, but not limited to, shorebirds, seabirds, whistling swans, emperor, white-fronted and Canada geese, black brant and other migratory birds."

The site of the nondevelopment easement is in Kokechik Bay and the land is owned by Sea Lion Corp. [one of the CIRI Group]. The nondevelopment easement conveyed by Sea Lion Corp. to the Secretary under the exchange [gave the Secretary the power in perpetuity to prohibit Sea Lion Corp.] from developing *docking facilities, roads, canals, airstrips, utilities, transmissions lines, pipelines, tank facilities, structures not used for subsistence purposes, or excavations* or other topographical changes: *Provided,* that development on the Real Estate may be permitted with the prior written consent of the Secretary of the Interior or his designee. * * *

The lands subject to the nondevelopment easement contain excellent waterfowl nesting and brood rearing habitat. The most dense nesting concentrations of emperor geese [in the world] are found in this area. In addition, the Kokechik Bay region is the breeding ground for half the world's population of black brant. Cackling Canada geese also breed chiefly in the areas surrounding the Kokechik Bay.

There can be absolutely no doubt that the lands subject to the nondevelopment easement are important to conservation and management objectives in protecting the black brant and the Cackling Canada and emperor geese. My inquiry does not stop here, however. The Secretary's determination that the St. Matthew exchange is in the national interest rests in substantial part upon his conclusion that the nondevelopment easement acquired in Kokechik Bay added significant environmental protections in this region.

My review of the environmental protections already in place prior to the St. Matthew exchange has revealed that the lands subject to the nondevelopment easement are for the most part located within the Yukon Delta NWR. As such, they are governed by the requirements of § 22(g) of ANCSA. [Eds. ANCSA, the Alaska Native Claims Settlement Act of 1971, gave Alaska Natives the right to select up to forty-four million acres of land in Alaska.] This provision provides, in pertinent part, that:

> Notwithstanding any other provision of this chapter, *every patent* issued by the Secretary pursuant to this chapter—which covers lands lying within the boundaries of a National Wildlife Refuge on December 18, 1971—*shall contain a provision that such lands remain subject to the laws and regulations governing use and development of such Refuge.*

43 U.S.C. § 1621(g) (emphasis added).

When the Secretary conveyed these lands to the CIRI Group, he imposed covenants, pursuant to § 22(g)'s requirements, that subjected almost all of the lands to the laws and regulations of the National Wildlife Refuge System. The laws and regulations governing use and development of wildlife refuges provide that only activities which are "compatible" with the major purposes for which a particular refuge was established may be permitted by the Secretary. Although compatibility is not expressly defined in either the National Wildlife Refuge System Administration Act or ANILCA, implementing regulations for the administration of § 22(g) covenants state that compatibility means that proposed uses must not *"materially impair* the values for which the refuge was established." [43 CFR § 2650.4–6(b) (emphasis added).]

My reading of the language of § 22(g), which the Secretary properly inserted into the Kokechik Bay conveyances to the CIRI Group, suggests to me that these lands were already protected from incompatible uses even without the nondevelopment easement obtained by the Secretary. To this extent, I agree with Audubon's claim that the protections acquired under the easement were largely "redundant" of the environmental safeguards obtained through the § 22(g) covenants.

* * * Given the purpose for which the Yukon Delta NWR was established, there would seem to be considerable doubt as to whether docking facilities, roads, canals, airstrips, utilities, pipelines and the like would be compatible uses of the Kokechik Bay lands. Apart from that, the easement lands * * * are very important for subsistence uses by Native peoples. Certainly the sort of development precluded by the nondevelopment easement, if not so precluded, would have to be considered under [specific provisions in ANILCA expressly protecting subsistence uses against interference]. * * *

Finally, there is nothing that I have discovered in the Final Ascertainment Report that suggests the existence of any probable or potential threat of the kind of development prohibited by the nondevelopment easement obtained by the United States under the exchange. * * *

Thus it would be hard to find a more striking comparison between the potential or probable use of Kokechik Bay lowlands with the proposed use of CIRI's inholdings on St. Matthew Island. On St. Matthew Island construction of the type of facilities that would be barred by the nondevelopment easement in the Kokechik Bay lowlands is both certain and immediate. * * *

In sum, I have concluded that contrary to the Secretary's statement in his Public Interest Determination, the nondevelopment easement obtained under the exchange adds little to the environmental protections already in place for Kokechik Bay. Hence, the Secretary's conclusion that the acquisition of the nondevelopment easement significantly advances long term CSU and general wildlife conservation and management objectives is not borne out when the land status and legal restrictions otherwise applicable are examined. * * *

B.   Potential Dangers to St. Matthew Island's Wilderness Values

In concluding that relinquishing lands on St. Matthew Island to the CIRI Group for use as an oil support facility was in the public interest, the Secretary assumed that there was little possibility of long term environmental danger to the island's unique wilderness values. Being mindful of the narrow confines of the standard of review in this case, I nevertheless have found this determination fails to consider the relevant facts in the Secretary's own administrative record. My review of the record has also led me to conclude that the Secretary's determination that the placement of an oil support facility within the Alaska Maritime NWR would be compatible with this refuge's strict environmental objectives was a clear error of judgment.

* * * [C]ontrary to the Secretary's repeated descriptions of the potential environmental damage to St. Matthew's unique wilderness values as "temporary" and "remote," the administrative record reveals there is a substantial risk of significant short and long term injury to the island's wilderness qualities. Such prospective environmental degradation would conflict with the express goal of the Alaska Maritime NWR * * *.

The most ominous potential environmental destruction that might accompany development of St. Matthew will affect wildlife * * *. By FWS estimates, hundreds of thousands of seabirds nest in colonies on or immediately adjacent to the lands conveyed to the CIRI Group. * * * FWS * * * has estimated that the project will adversely affect nearly half a million nesting seabirds for a period of 80 to 100 years.

Of particular concern, the FWS report and the DEIS point to the frequent air traffic that will feed the support facility as especially dangerous to St. Matthew's seabird nesting colonies. Near flying aircraft inhibit breeding and initiate panic flights, potentially causing entire colonies to take to the air, knocking eggs and chicks into the ocean or leaving them vulnerable to predators. Continued disruption may cause reproduction failure, and, "in the worse case, colonies may be totally abandoned." * * *

In addition to a potential for serious long-term degradation to the seabird population of St. Matthew, the DEIS reveals that any major oil spill near the island is likely to cause substantial harm to the many whales that inhabit the island's waters. And by the FWS's own estimates, a major oil spill near the island is probable if pipelines eventually are used to transport oil to St. Matthew.

Although all of these facts appear on the face of the administrative record, the Secretary paid scant heed. Rather, he suggests in his Public Interest Determination that the St. Matthew Island stipulations for restoration and reconveyance assure that the land will be restored and returned to the National Wildlife and Wilderness System when use of the land as a support base for oil exploration or development comes to an end. He refers to the land transaction as a "temporarily conveyed use of federal ownership" and to the "temporary wildlife disruption authorized on St. Matthew Island" under the land use stipulations. * * *

The word "temporary" standing alone has little meaning. * * * The exchange provides by its terms that the conveyance to the CIRI Group is for 50 years, or if oil and gas have been produced in the Navarin Basin and the land has been used in connection therewith, then so long as may be necessary for completion of production. What is important are the consequences upon wildlife and wilderness habitats by the activity associated with the use of the land, and not whether that use may be characterized as "temporary." * * *

It is correct that the stipulations are useful to minimize harm to the wildlife and wilderness habitat on St. Matthew Island, but the stipulations cannot otherwise justify the Secretary's Public Interest Determination. That is, the Secretary cannot avoid consideration of potential environmental impacts * * * by suggesting that the stipulations will serve to mitigate the extent of the injury brought about by environmental impact.

My review of the underlying record has convinced me that the Secretary, by failing to consider the protections otherwise provided by law and by failing to consider relevant facts appearing of record, seriously overestimated the benefits to CSU and general wildlife conservation and management objectives advanced by this exchange. Additionally, by characterizing the effects on St. Matthew Island as temporary and by erroneously assuming that the land use stipulations would provide sufficient protection to wildlife and wilderness habitats, the Secretary failed to adequately consider the likely negative effects on St. Matthew Island. Finally, the Secretary's determination under ANCSA § 22(g) that a support base located within the Alaska Maritime NWR would be compatible with the environmental protection purposes of this refuge is contrary to the underlying record. The Secretary's Public Interest Determination thus constitutes a clear error of judgment. * * *

NOTES AND QUESTIONS

1. The "public interest" standard is frequently found, in one form or another, in modern statutes governing administrative agency decisions in a

wide variety of contexts. *See, e.g.*, Udall v. Federal Power Comm'n, 387 U.S. 428, 450 (1967) (an early landmark decision in modern environmental law, holding that the Federal Power Commission construed the public interest standard in the Federal Power Act too narrowly in connection with a proposed hydropower license, to exclude consideration of "the public interest in preserving reaches of wild rivers and wilderness areas, the preservation of anadromous fish for commercial and recreational purposes, and the protection of wildlife"). Will judicial reviewability of an agency's application of such a standard vary from statute to statute, even if the statutes have identical texts? Could, in fact, a "public interest" determination in another statute be held entirely unreviewable by a court?

2.   Must an agency prepare written findings and conclusions in making a decision as to what is in the "public interest" under the statute involved here? Even if not required, would an agency be advised to document its determination to better withstand judicial scrutiny? Here the Secretary did prepare such findings, which wasn't enough to ward off an adverse judicial decision. In contrast, the court in Lodge Tower Condominium Association v. Lodge Properties Inc., 880 F.Supp. 1370 (D.Colo.1995), *aff'd*, 85 F.3d 476 (10th Cir.1996), upheld a Forest Service exchange, relying heavily on the Forest Service's finding that "better land management" would result from exchanging two acres of federal land on a slope among condominiums at the Vail resort for 385 acres of private inholding (including wetlands, streams, and an endangered species of fish) in a nearby wilderness area. *See generally* John W. Ragsdale, Jr., *National Forest Land Exchanges and the Growth of Vail and Other Gateway Communities*, 31 URB. LAW. 1 (1999).

3.   Is the court here deferential enough to the Secretary? Does the Secretary have expertise that a federal district judge ought to respect, even if the Secretary is sitting in far-off Washington D.C. and the judge is sitting in Alaska, the site of the lands involved? Based upon the evidence set forth in the excerpted portions of the opinion, could the court have reached the opposite conclusion; namely, that the Secretary did not act arbitrarily and capriciously in approving the exchange? Upon review, could a court of appeals uphold either conclusion? (The decision here was not appealed.)

4.   A key question here was the meaning of the "compatibility" test for measuring proposed developments both at St. Matthew Island, and on the Alaskan Native inholdings sought to be removed from the Wildlife Refuge by the exchange. How does the Secretary interpret "compatibility"? How does the court? Is "compatibility" a question of fact, law, or is it mixed? A further discussion of compatibility is found in Chapter 10A.

5.   What if the Secretary had been more candid in his appraisal, admitting that the harm is substantial, and the value gained through acquiring the inholding is relatively small, but going on to argue that there is a strong national interest in developing all sources of domestic oil rather than rely on imports from unstable areas of the world. If the court were applying the FLPMA statutory standard of "public interest," would that approach survive judicial review?

6.   By a seemingly odd quirk, ANILCA does *not* require a "public interest" determination for exchanges where the lands are of *equal* value. 16 U.S.C. § 3192(h). Does this bear on the proper interpretation of "public interest" that must be determined when the lands are *unequal*? How should the Secretary weigh difficult-to-quantify values (protecting the environment, Native culture, subsistence values, the strategic value of domestic oil production) against monetary differences in value?

7.   Could the Secretary moot this case by restructuring the exchange to make it an "equal value" one? How would "equal value" be determined? By the marketplace? Is there a real market for this land? *See* Committee of 100 on Federal City v. Hodel, 777 F.2d 711, 720 n. 3 (D.C.Cir.1985) (upholding a proposed exchange of land involving the Park Service against an "equal value" challenge, and giving the agency "[g]reat deference * * * because the matter is one largely within the technical expertise of the agency"). Appraisals can be manipulated, and concern that the government has failed to obtain equal value in exchanges is periodically rehearsed in the press and elsewhere. *See, e.g.*, Tim Fitzgerald, Federal Land Exchanges: Let's End the Barter, p.8 (PERC Policy Series No.18 2000):

> Land exchanges are essentially barter-trade without a medium of exchange such as money. Those who engage in land exchanges therefore face the problem of finding some way to measure the value of different goods. Without the benefit of prices or some other standard, people with different products have a difficult time determining whether a trade makes sense for each person engaged in it—that is, whether it is fair.

8.   If the St. Matthews Island exchange had been an "equal value" exchange, then would the Secretary have the legal authority to count in the value the U.S. was obtaining an estimate of the increased revenues the U.S. would receive from oil industry royalty payments and increased taxes on profits that it could attribute to the oil industry having a more convenient staging area to produce oil from under the Bering Sea? (The Secretary here noted that the Island's use "may result in higher bidding revenues received on the lease sale and additional oil and gas production.")

9.   In Desert Citizens Against Pollution v. Bisson, 231 F.3d 1172 (9th Cir.2000), the plaintiffs challenged BLM's conveyance of 1745 acres of public land as part of an exchange with the private Gold Fields Co. The purpose was to allow the latter to put a landfill in Imperial County in southern California. The thrust of plaintiffs' complaint was that the exchange did not meet FLPMA's "equal value" standard because BLM had used an outdated appraisal. BLM defended the appraisal, which had concluded that the highest and best use of the federal land was either open space, or mine support, or wildlife habitat, at a value of $350 per acre, because there was no general market for use of the land as a landfill. In part this was because the parcels to be exchanged were surrounded by or adjacent to land already owned by Gold Fields, and were not large enough by themselves to support a landfill. Plaintiffs disputed this assumption (putting forward evidence that a landfill site would be worth several thousand dollars per acre) and the court agreed. Reversing the district

court, it held that the "BLM appraisal should have considered the landfill use as a possible highest and best use. Information available at the time of the appraisal made it reasonably probable that the property's potential use as a landfill was physically possible, legally permissible, and financially feasible." 231 F.3d at 1184. Although the parties had consummated the exchange the day after the district court had dismissed the case, the court ordered the exchange set aside.

10.   Should courts scrutinize federal-*private* exchanges more closely than federal-*state* exchanges? Is there more opportunity for abuse when private interests are involved than when all the land involved stays in some form of public ownership? If your answer is yes, into which category do federal-Alaskan Native (or Indian) exchanges such as that involved in National Audubon Society v. Hodel fit?

NOTE: FEDERAL–STATE LAND EXCHANGES

One consequence of the scattered, "in-place" character of grants of federal land to states is that some of them become inholdings within federal conservation areas which are later created. These inholdings create management problems of various kinds. If the inholdings are developed (especially with road access), management of the surrounding federal lands for conservation or wilderness purposes may be compromised. But restricting access to or activities on inholdings to keep with the character of surrounding federal lands could thwart the purpose of the grant of lands to the state (usually, to produce income for the common schools or other purposes). An obvious solution to this dilemma, with "win-win" potential, is a land exchange—the state conveys its inholdings to the federal government in return for federal land elsewhere. Because of the equal value requirement, such exchanges raise the important question of how to value the state inholdings, which are usually isolated, scattered, and without existing road access.

State inholding issues were most acute in Utah, where the state's four sections of inholdings in each township created what some called a "blue rash" (because typical land status maps show state sections in blue). In the mid–1980s the State proposed what it dubbed "Project Bold," an ambitious effort to achieve a comprehensive land exchange. While it foundered from opposition by a variety of disparate interests, it helped pave the way toward ultimate success. In 1993 Congress enacted a Utah-specific law (Pub. L. 103–93), which encouraged and created the framework for exchanging state inholdings out of national forests, national park system lands, and Indian reservations in the state. Implementation of this law had bogged down in what looked like interminable litigation over value when, in 1996, President Clinton created the Grand Staircase–Escalante National Monument. That 1.7 million acre federal monument on BLM land included within its outer boundaries nearly 180,000 acres of scattered state school sections, and in proclaiming the Monument, President Clinton committed his Administration to work to trade out these inholdings. In May 1998 the Utah governor and the Interior secretary announced a massive land exchange, billed as the largest single state-federal land exchange ever in the lower forty-eight states, in which the state relinquished all of its inholdings in the Grand Staircase–Escalante and all Utah units of the National Park System, and almost all of its inholdings in the Utah national forests and the Goshute and Navajo Indian reservations. All told, the exchange included 377,000 acres of state inholdings, plus an additional 66,000 acres in state mineral rights, in exchange for approximately 139,000 acres of federal land, mineral rights and money. Valuation issues were difficult, but resolution was, ironically, aided by the sweep of the effort, which allowed tradeoffs and compromises among various kinds of properties to arrive at a single deal, which was ratified by Congress without modification, in legislation signed into law. *See* Utah Schools and Land Exchange Act of 1998, 16 U.S.C. 431 note.

E. ORGANIC LEGISLATION FOR PUBLIC LAND SYSTEMS

In addition to the toolkit provided by FLPMA for consolidating, classifying, and protecting federal lands, each of the four major public land systems has its own legislative charter for management: an organic act. The first organic statute for a federal land system came along in 1897 as the "Petigrew Amendment to the Sundry Civil Act of June 4, 1897." That law subsequently came to be known as the Forest Service Organic Act, and it served as a basis for Gifford Pinchot to *organize* the forest reserves into a larger working system. Congress next pulled together the national parks into a system in 1916, and the national wildlife refuges in 1966. Organic acts help counteract what Herbert Kaufman called the "centrifugal tendencies" of large systems to serve local and particular needs rather than broad national objectives. Herbert Kaufman, THE FOREST RANGER 203–07 (1960). In contrast to establishment legislation, which addresses the status of a specific parcel of land (often called a "unit"), an organic act provides a comprehensive framework for unified management of a system of parcels.

Though the original organic acts all contained broad delegations of authority, they lacked detailed objectives, specific guidelines, footholds for judicial review, or roles for the public. However, between 1974 and 1997, Congress thoroughly overhauled existing organic legislation for all four (park, refuge, forest and BLM) major land systems, incorporating several common elements in each, which are discussed in this section. The resource-specific chapters that follow explore some of the particularities of each of these organic authorities. This subchapter describes their commonalities, which are fundamental to federal land management.

Professor Fischman has identified five hallmarks of modern organic legislation: purpose statements, designated uses, comprehensive planning, substantive management criteria, and public participation. These features compose a "table of elements" from which Congress has synthesized modern public land statutes, and also identify topics for reform of laws lacking effectiveness in key areas. The authority contained in an organic act is, however, not the exclusive authority or mandate for management of a public land system because each system has its share of idiosyncratic statutes, including some that govern particular areas or units.

Robert L. Fischman, The National Wildlife Refuges: Coordinating a Conservation System through Law

Pp.73–76 (2003).

The articulation of a systemic purpose remains the *sine qua non* of organic legislation. An organic act must generate a purpose to guide land management across an array of individual units in order to create a coordinated system. Otherwise, each unit proceeds in its own direction, in response to its own local circumstance. Unless a collection of public land units can align to become more than the sum of its parts, it cannot be considered a system. Without a mission, conservation systems generally suffer from the same maladies as the pre–1997 Refuge System:

> Management continuity to meet the long-term needs of wildlife are frequently sacrificed or subordinated ... to the demands of the local public. Lack of a congressional mandate in the form of system purposes is, in the bureaucratic world, akin to lack of identity.

Systemic purposes, however, usually must be defined in the most general of terms in order for them to speak to the diverse circumstances of far-flung lands. A conservation purpose for the Refuge System, for instance, must be applicable both to the Alaska Maritime National Wildlife Refuge, which extends over a thousand miles to encompass 2400 islands, and to Mason Neck National Wildlife Refuge, a bicycle ride away from Washington, D.C. Also, because Congress revisits organic legislation infrequently, purpose statements must be written somewhat vaguely to avoid locking in particular ecological understandings that may soon be superseded.

Nonetheless, most post–1970 organic acts, concerned with orchestrating individual land units into harmonious public land systems, contain missions with defined terms. A defined mission is particularly useful in resolving conflicts and ambiguities in establishment authorities. Although an organic act rarely contains all of the delegations of power to a land management agency, the systemic purpose serves as the interpretive pilot to guide implementation of other relevant laws.

To relate broad purposes to real management decisions, organic legislation typically designates particular uses to be prohibited, preferred, encouraged, or merely tolerated. The designated uses in an organic act often are the strongest indicators of the cultural values reflected in the system. In contrast to performance standards, which look objectively to effects of activities to decide what to allow, designated uses concentrate on the categories or types of the activities themselves. For instance, Refuge System legislation designates hunting as a use that receives special encouragement, in part because a hunting tax funds the purchase of many refuges and refuge expansions. This is a judgment based on concerns for tax fairness and the leadership role that hunters have played in the American conservation movement. It is not principally based on the effects of hunting on the land, waters, and wildlife of the refuges.

Though we often describe public land systems based on their designated use regimes (i.e., multiple use, dominant use, exclusive use), no modern organic legislation permits a use solely on the basis of the qualitative attributes of the use. Substantive management criteria demand that a use in a permitted category not exceed a particular effect level. For instance, the BLM must avoid "unnecessary or undue degradation" in allowing the multiple uses to occur on its lands. (43 U.S.C. § 1732(b).) However, organic legislation does sometimes outright prohibit an activity based on its type without regard to its effect. The category of new roads and buildings in wilderness areas is an example of this. (16 U.S.C. § 1133(c).)

Comprehensive planning is a key element in any organic act because it ensures that individual management decisions are made not haphazardly but rather to promote some greater goal namely, the system mission. It provides a framework within which individual unit administrators may make management decisions and segregate particular uses to appropriate zones. Planning facilitates the evaluation of cumulative effects from a projected series of small actions authorized over the term of the plan. Uniform, systemwide rules that govern planning exert a coordinating force on the diverse array of activities that may occur on land units. The comprehensive plan translates the general mission statements and broadly permissive designation of uses into prescriptions for a particular area over a particular time. It is the link between the systemic mandate and the local project.

The rise of substantive management criteria is an almost entirely new development of modern organic legislation. More than any other hallmark, the appearance of substantive management criteria characterizes the reforms of the 1970s. Substantive management criteria represent a reversal of the proprietary tradition, which relied on the "expert" judgment and location-specific experience of a unit administrator. Unlike designated uses (or, best technology standards in pollution control), substantive management criteria shift the discourse over conflicts away from judgments about the worthiness of an activity and toward measurable benchmarks of environmental consequences (e.g., whether the activity would exceed the threshold criterion of "unnecessary or undue degradation" of lands). In this way, substantive management criteria (like ambient standards in pollution control) are closely aligned with the utilitarian view that outcomes matter more than intentions. The rise of substantive management criteria with the use of the term "organic" legislation belies the cynical claims of Professors Fairfax and Popper that "our tools for thinking about public resources have not changed much in a century."

The statutory use of environmental criteria to condition land managers' discretion has changed the nature of public land law. Though we still distinguish among public lands systems by categorizing them as multiple or dominant use, substantive management criteria have joined the designated uses as a signature feature of organic acts. The Forest Service's diversity mandate, the BLM's no undue degradation criterion, and the National Park

Service's unimpaired standard reveal as much about these agencies' land management programs as do the terms "multiple" or "dominant" use. * * * [T]he 1997 mandate to maintain biological integrity, diversity, and environmental health is a distinctive milestone characterizing the Refuge System brand of conservation.

The final hallmark of modern organic legislation is public participation. Public participation requirements transformed administrative law in the 1970s. Natural resources law did not escape this transformation, which contributed to the revision of systemic legislation. Public land management agencies today must provide stakeholders opportunities to contribute to decisions about individual projects, comprehensive plans, and system-wide policies. For instance, the National Environmental Policy Act provides citizens avenues to contribute to and comment on mandated environmental impact analyses for agency proposals for action. Though the organic acts themselves generally contain few directly applicable provisions relating to appeals, information disclosure, advisory committee activity, and judicial review, these avenues for public participation are all maintained through administrative law statutes and judicial doctrines. Much of this hallmark is folded into organic acts by reference to these other statutes and doctrines.

A deeper understanding of organic acts may aid in the application of lessons from natural resources law to pollution control law. An important criticism of the Environmental Protection Agency's (EPA's) piecemeal pollution control authorities is that they are myopic to the distant long-term: they fixate on the specific, close-up problems but lack clear vision for integrated environmental quality improvement. In response, critics often propose more comprehensive, coordinated management, through an "integrating" statute for the EPA. Another way to think about these proposals is to consider what an organic act for a system of pollution control might look like. Rather than orchestrating a tangle of unit establishment mandates, an EPA organic act would have to integrate a tangle of media-, pollutant-, sector-, and (sometimes) place-specific pollution control mandates.

NOTES AND QUESTIONS

1. The 1916 "Act to Establish a National Park Service" not only created the new agency, but also provided an organic authority to organize the somewhat disparate park units into a national park system. *See* 16 U.S.C. §§ 1–3. Amendments to that act in 1978 modernized the framework for park system management and growth. The Bureau of Land Management's organic act is the Federal Land Policy and Management Act of 1976, 43 U.S.C. §§ 1701–82. The U.S. Fish & Wildlife Service's organic act for the national wildlife refuge system consists of legislation adopted in 1966 and substantially overhauled in 1997, 16 U.S.C. §§ 668dd & ee. The national forest system's organic act of 1897 was updated by the Multiple Use/Sustained Yield Act in 1960, the Forest and Rangeland Renewable Resources Planning Act of 1974, and the National Forest Management Act of 1976. 16 U.S.C. §§ 47–82, 528–31, 551.

2. The judiciary does not appear to attach special significance to whether statutory guidance appears in an agency's organic act instead of in other legislation. Many areas of the public lands (such as individual national parks) have specific establishment statutes that apply only to them, and such specific statutory guidance controls over the general terms of the organic act when the two differ. *See* 16 U.S.C. § 668dd(a)(4)(d); Robert L. Fischman, *The Problem of Statutory Detail in National Park Establishment Legislation and its Relationship to Pollution Control Law*, 74 DENV. U. L.REV. 779 (1997). Should subsequent organic legislation trump earlier terms of establishment statutes that are no longer consistent with a system's purpose? Alternatively, should courts engage in "centripetal interpretation" to lessen the tensions among system units in favor of the organic mandates? Many national wildlife refuges were created to promote increased populations of snow geese and wood ducks at a time when those waterfowl species were rare. Now that they have fully recovered, should refuges shift focus to provide different habitat types that might benefit different suites of species? *See* Vicky Meretsky et al., *New Directions in Conservation for the National Wildlife Refuge System*, 56 BIOSCIENCE 135 (2006).

3. The courts and Congress do not always hew to the terminology described above. *See* National Park Mining Regulation Act of 1976, Pub. L. No. 94–429, § 2 (referring to the "individual organic Acts for the various areas of the National Park System"); Sierra Club v. U.S. Forest Service (referring to the establishment statute for a national forest wildlife preserve as the "Norbeck Organic Act"). The term "organic" to describe a law is also used for statutes conferring powers of government on an agency, municipality, or territory. Although a statute creating a new state is sometimes called an organic act, the term "enabling act" is more common. Robert L. Fischman, *The National Wildlife Refuge System and the Hallmarks of Modern Organic Legislation*, 29 ECOLOGY L.Q. 457, 502–503 (2002).

4. From time to time over the past three decades Congress has considered but never enacted an organic act for the EPA. Does the failure of efforts to enact an organic act for the EPA suggest important differences between the pollution control and the resource management branches of environmental law?

Comprehensive Planning

The federal government has long employed plans to rationalize the management of natural resources. The earliest systematic effort came in the 1930s with the National Resources Planning Board. Marion Clawson, NEW DEAL PLANNING: THE NRPB (1981). The Forest Service also employed economic plans to govern commodity disposal before the modern era of organic legislation. Organic legislation now requires comprehensive unit-level plans for each of the four major public land systems to contain several common elements: 1) consideration of permitted uses; 2) public participation; 3) interdisciplinary analysis; 4) consideration of applicable or overlapping state/local plans; and 5) zoning maps defining which regions are slated for more intensive development, protective prescriptions, or visitor facilities. In a thorough analysis of the Forest Service's first generation of forest planning, Charles Wilkinson and H. Michael Anderson made the following observations:

> For many reasons, planning on the public lands is inevitably imprecise. The plans must cover large areas of land and there is usually uncertainty over location of some resources, especially minerals and wildlife. Valuation of some resources, such as recreation and preservation, is difficult. Barriers to development, such as fragile soil conditions, may not be apparent until the implementation stage of the plan. Changing demands for various resources and the occurrence of natural phenomena such as insect infestation, droughts, and forest fires, add to the difficulty. For these and other reasons, planning on the federal lands has properly been called "an inexact art." * * *

Charles F. Wilkinson & H. Michael Anderson, *Land and Resource Planning in the National Forests*, 64 OR. L.REV. 1, 10–12 (1985).

Comprehensive planning was to be the linchpin that held together all of the elements of organic legislation. However, the past decade has witnessed a decline in the importance of conventional comprehensive planning. Comprehensive planning owes as much to the NEPA idea of bounded rationality as it does to organic legislation. A recent trend in planning is to use environmental assessments to find no significant impact from plans rather than prepare EISs. One wonders why agencies should bother with planning if the plans have no significant impact. As recently as ten years ago, most agencies prepared EISs for all the comprehensive plans mandated by organic laws. Agencies have pulled back from EIS preparation, in part, based on the uncertainty about which authorized activities will actual occur during the plan's life and what the site-specific impact might be. That certainly makes environmental analysis at the larger scale more difficult. Does it justify failure to prepare an EIS?

Planning may take place at a national, system-wide level, or by region, but usually it occurs at the level of a specific geographic unit such as a particular national park, wildlife refuge, national forest, or BLM planning area. Only the national forests have a statutory requirement for certain kinds of system-wide planning. The Forest and Rangeland Renewable Resources Planning Act of 1974 (usually called the Resources Planning Act or RPA), 88 Stat. 476, requires the Forest Service to prepare system-wide five year program documents, based on decennial assessments of conditions in the system. *See* 16 U.S.C. § 1602. These documents have generally been regarded as too general to be of much use, and Congress has endorsed agency suspensions of this requirement. *See* Pub.L. No. 106–291, § 321. Even where not mandated to do so by statute, agencies may prepare "vision documents" looking at their entire systems, and the Government Performance and Results Act (GPRA), 31 U.S.C. § 1101, enacted in 1993, requires all federal agencies to develop strategic plans that contain specific benchmarks for measuring progress toward long-term, programmatic goals.

Even unit-level plans may be too general for some uses, especially judicial review. Consider the following case.

Norton v. Southern Utah Wilderness Alliance

Supreme Court of the United States, 2004.
542 U.S. 55.

■ JUSTICE SCALIA delivered the opinion of the Court.

[Portions of this opinion dealing with final agency actions reviewable by courts are excerpted in Chapter 4, *supra* p. 224. This portion of the case deals with the binding nature of comprehensive plans under organic legislation.]

[The Southern Utah Wilderness alliance (SUWA) claims that] BLM failed to comply with certain provisions in its land use plans, thus contravening the requirement that "[t]he Secretary shall manage the public lands . . . in accordance with the land use plans . . . when they are available." 43 U.S.C. § 1732(a); see also 43 CFR § 1610.5–3(a) (2003) ("All future resource management authorizations and actions . . . and subsequent more detailed or specific planning, shall conform to the approved plan"). The relevant count in SUWA's second amended complaint alleged that BLM had violated a variety of commitments in its land use plans, but over the course of the litigation these have been reduced [effectively to one] * * * that "in light of damage from ORVs in the Factory Butte area," a sub-area of Henry Mountains open to ORV use, "the [plan] obligated BLM to conduct an intensive ORV monitoring program." Brief for SUWA 7–8. This claim is based upon the plan's statement that the Factory Butte area "will be monitored and closed if warranted." * * *

The statutory directive that BLM manage "in accordance with" land use plans, and the regulatory requirement that authorizations and actions "conform to" those plans, prevent BLM from taking actions inconsistent with the provisions of a land use plan. Unless and until the plan is amended, such actions can be set aside as contrary to law pursuant to 5 U.S.C. § 706(2). The claim presently under discussion, however, would have us go further, and conclude that a statement in a plan that BLM "will" take this, that, or the other action, is a binding commitment that can be compelled under § 706(1). In our view it is not—at least absent clear indication of binding commitment in the terms of the plan.

FLPMA describes land use plans as tools by which "present and future use is *projected*." 43 U.S.C. § 1701(a)(2) (emphasis added). The implementing regulations make clear that land use plans are a preliminary step in the overall process of managing public lands—"designed to guide and control future management actions and the development of subsequent, more detailed and limited scope plans for resources and uses." 43 CFR § 1601.0–2 (2003). The statute and regulations confirm that a land use plan is not ordinarily the medium for affirmative decisions that implement the agency's "project[ions]." Title 43 U.S.C. § 1712(e) provides that "[t]he Secretary may issue management decisions to implement land use plans"—the decisions, that is, are distinct from the plan itself. Picking up the same theme, the regulation defining a land use plan declares that a plan "is not a final implementation decision on actions which require further specific plans, process steps, or decisions under specific provisions of law and regulations." 43 CFR § 1601.0–5(k) (2003).

* * *

The San Rafael plan provides an apt illustration of the immense scope of projected activity that a land use plan can embrace. Over 100 pages in length, it presents a comprehensive management framework for 1.5 million acres of BLM-administered land. Twenty categories of resource management are separately discussed, including mineral extraction, wilderness protection, livestock grazing, preservation of cultural resources, and recreation. The plan lays out an ambitious agenda for the preparation of additional, more detailed plans and specific next steps for implementation. Its introduction notes that "[a]n [ORV] implementation plan is scheduled to be prepared within 1 year following approval of the [San Rafael plan]." Similarly "scheduled for preparation" are activity plans for certain environmentally sensitive areas, "along with allotment management plans, habitat management plans, a fire management plan, recreation management plans ..., cultural resource management plans for selected sites, watershed activity plans, and the wild and scenic river management plan." The projected schedule set forth in the plan shows "[a]nticipated [i]mplementation" of some future plans within one year, others within three years, and still others, such as certain recreation and cultural resource management plans, at a pace of "one study per fiscal year."

Quite unlike a specific statutory command requiring an agency to promulgate regulations by a certain date, a land use plan is generally a statement of priorities; it guides and constrains actions, but does not (at least in the usual case) prescribe them. It would be unreasonable to think that either Congress or the agency intended otherwise, since land use plans nationwide would commit the agency to actions far in the future, for which funds have not yet been appropriated. Some plans make explicit that implementation of their programmatic content is subject to budgetary constraints. While the Henry Mountains plan does not contain such a specification, we think it must reasonably be implied. A statement by BLM about what it plans to do, at some point, provided it has the funds and there are not more pressing priorities, cannot be plucked out of context and made a basis for suit under § 706(1).

Of course, an action called for in a plan may be compelled when the plan merely reiterates duties the agency is already obligated to perform, or perhaps when language in the plan itself creates a commitment binding on the agency. But allowing general enforcement of plan terms would lead to pervasive interference with BLM's own ordering of priorities. For example, a judicial decree compelling immediate preparation of all of the detailed plans called for in the San Rafael plan would divert BLM's energies from other projects throughout the country that are in fact more pressing. And while such a decree might please the environmental plaintiffs in the present case, it would ultimately operate to the detriment of sound environmental management. Its predictable consequence would be much vaguer plans from BLM in the future—making coordination with other agencies more difficult, and depriving the public of important information concerning the agency's long-range intentions.

We therefore hold that the Henry Mountains plan's statements to the effect that BLM will conduct "use supervision and monitoring" in designated areas—like other "will do" projections of agency action set forth in land use plans—are not a legally binding commitment enforceable under § 706(1). That being so, we find it unnecessary to consider whether the action envisioned by the statements is sufficiently discrete to be amenable to compulsion under the APA.

NOTES AND QUESTIONS

1.   Notice the slight differences in wording between FLPMA and the BLM regulations cited in the first paragraph of the decision ("in accordance with," and "conform to"). Are the differences legally significant? Is the Court correct in interpreting these standards to "prevent BLM from taking actions *inconsistent with*" management plans (emphasis added)?

2.   Suppose a plan promulgated by BLM in 1999 says that a particular 10,000 acre tract of BLM land will be closed to oil and gas leasing. If the Secretary decides in 2001 to issue oil and gas leases in the area, must the plan first be amended, with attendant NEPA compliance and opportunity for public comment? (Notice that NEPA would presumably apply independently to the federal "action" of issuing an oil and gas lease on federal lands. That being the case, is there anything lost by saying the plan does not constrain the Secretary's decision?)

3.   If a land use plan designates an area as closed to ORVs, and BLM fails to post signs or enforce against ORV intrusions in the area, can conservationists sue to enjoin the BLM to carry out its plan, unless it goes through the necessary process to change the plan?

4.   What does this decision leave of the federal land planning process? Are plans' statements about actions the agency will take in the future exhortatory only? The Court seems to say there may be two situations where a plan's statement about future action is enforceable: (1) where the action "merely reiterates duties the agency is already obligated to perform;" and (2) and "perhaps," where "language in the plan itself creates a binding commitment on the agency." Regarding the first, if the agency says it will impose restrictions on, say, off-road vehicles in order to comply with the statutory command that it prevent "unnecessary or undue degradation," may the courts enforce that promise? Regarding the second, if you are an agency official, under what circumstances (if ever) would you want to put something in the plan that creates a binding, judicially enforceable commitment?

5.   The organic acts for both the national wildlife refuge and national forest systems contain language similar to FLPMA on the binding effect of plans. The U.S. Fish & Wildlife Service must manage refuges "in a manner consistent with the plan and shall revise the plan at any time if the Secretary determines the conditions that affect the refuge or planning unit

have changed significantly." (16 U.S.C. § 668dd(e)(1)(E)). The National Forest Management Act requires that all "permits, contracts [including timber sale contracts], and other instruments for the use and occupancy of National Forest System lands shall be consistent with the land management plans." 16 U.S.C. § 1604(i). The cryptic National Park System planning statute does not expressly make plans legally binding. 16 U.S.C. § 1a 7.

6. In combination with *Ohio Forestry, supra* p. 216, which found many aspects of public land planning unripe for challenge until implemented by particular projects, *SUWA* promises to immunize much of agency planning from judicial oversight. Is this a good idea? Courts now generally resist involvement in planning disputes because they regard the controversies as broad policy disagreements. Are disputes over specific project authorizations more sharply defined? What is gained by delaying review of a flawed plan until such time as a particular project is ready to move forward, at least if the project is fairly certain to move forward?

7. The federal land planning process, at least as currently implemented, has long provoked critics. *See, e.g.*, Richard Behan, *RPA/NFMA—Time to Punt*, J. FORESTRY 802 (Dec. 1981). Former BLM Director Frank Gregg once noted the irony of our "child-like faith in planning" for federal lands, at a time when centralized planning in formerly communist countries has been so discredited. Remarks to Congressional Research Service Symposium on the Future of Multiple–Use Sustained–Yield, Washington D.C. (March 6, 1992). Does the emphasis on planning simply reflect the lack of a societal consensus on how these lands and associated resources should be managed, and thus constitutes the second-or third-best alternative of all the major interests involved in federal land management?

A New Paradigm for Planning?

The most elaborate unit-level planning occurs for national forests under regulations required by the National Forest Management Act. The most recent revision of the planning regulations, dealt with in greater detail in chapter 8, announces a transformational change in planning for public lands.

National Forest System Land Management Planning Final Rule Preamble

70 Fed. Reg. 1023 (Jan. 5, 2005).

This final rule embodies a paradigm shift in land management planning based, in part, on the Forest Service's 25 years of experience developing plans under the 1982 planning rule. Having assessed the current system's flaws and benefits during this extended period, the Forest Service believes it is time to think differently about National Forest System (NFS) planning and management. Thus, based on the agency's expertise and experience, the Forest Service created this final rule to enable a better way to protect the environment and to facilitate working with the public.

* * *

[P]lans under this final rule will be more strategic and less prescriptive in nature than under the 1982 planning rule. Emphasizing the strategic nature of plans under this rule is the most effective means of guiding NFS management in light of changing conditions, science and technology. Specifically, plans under this final rule will not contain final decisions that approve projects or activities except under extraordinary circumstances. Rather, as described further below, plans under this final rule will contain five components, which set forth broad policies to help guide future decisions on the ground: The plan components are desired conditions, objectives, guidelines, suitability of areas, and special areas.

* * *

During the 15–year life expectancy of a plan, information, science, and unforeseen circumstances evolve. It must be possible to adjust plans and the plan-monitoring program and to react to new information and science swiftly and efficiently. An environmental management system (EMS) approach will enhance adaptive planning and should be part of the land management framework.

* * *

- Plan components.

* * * Under this final rule, plans have five principal components (§ 219.7(a)(2)): desired conditions, objectives, guidelines, suitability of areas, and special areas.

- Desired Conditions.

Desired conditions are the social, economic, and ecological attributes toward which management of the land and resources of the plan area is to be directed. Desired conditions are long-term in nature and aspirational, but are neither commitments nor final decisions approving projects and activities. Desired conditions may be achievable only over a period longer than the 15 years covered by the plan. Increased attention to fire regimes provides an example of the role of "desired conditions." The Forest Service is challenged with unnatural fuel levels throughout the NFS. Much of the western United States is currently in a severe drought cycle, and fuel reduction is needed. To facilitate moving toward a healthier and more natural condition on the land, a plan could contain, for example, desired conditions that include a description of desired fuel loading, along with a description of desired tree species, structure, distribution, and density closer to what would have occurred under natural fire regimes.

The agency, working with the public, also may seek to achieve or maintain desired conditions for attributes, such as quietness, or a sense of remoteness, or attributes of our cultural heritage. Desired conditions also have a key role to play for wildlife habitat management. During plan development, it is difficult to envision all the site-specific factors that can influence wildlife. For example, in the past plans might have included standards precluding vegetation treatment during certain months or for a buffer for activities near the nest sites of birds sensitive to disturbance during nesting. However, topography, vegetation density, or other factors may render such prohibitions inadequate or unduly restrictive in specific situations. A thorough desired condition description of what a species needs is often more useful than a long list of prohibitions. Thorough desired condition descriptions are more useful because they provide a better starting point for project or activity design, when the site-specific conditions are better understood and when species conservation measures can be most meaningfully evaluated and effectively applied. Again, a description of what the agency, working with the public, wants to achieve is key.

- Objectives.

Objectives are concise projections of intended outcomes of projects and activities to contribute to maintenance or achievement of desired conditions. Objectives are measurable and time-specific and, like desired conditions, are aspirational, but are neither commitments nor final decisions approving projects and activities. * * *

- Guidelines.

Guidelines provide information and guidance for the design of projects and activities to help achieve objectives and desired conditions. Guidelines are not commitments or final decisions approving projects and activities. Guidelines should provide the recommended technical and scientific specifications to be used in the design of projects and activities to contribute to the achievement of desired conditions and objectives. They are the guidance that a project or activity would normally apply unless there is a reason for deviation. If deviation from plan guidelines is appropriate in specific circumstances, the rationale for deviation should be based on project or activity analysis and explained fully in the project decision document. However, deviation does not require an amendment to the plan.

* * *

- Land management plans, adaptive management, and environmental management systems.

This final rule requires each national forest, grassland, prairie, or other comparable administrative unit to develop and implement an EMS based on the international consensus standard published by the International Organization for Standardization as "ISO 14001: Environmental Management Systems—Specification With Guidance For Use" (ISO 14001). Each unit's EMS * * * will identify and prioritize environmental conditions; set objectives in light of Congressional, agency, and public goals; document procedures and practices to achieve those objectives; and monitor and measure environmental conditions to track performance and verify that objectives are being met. Agency management personnel will regularly review performance, and information about environmental conditions will be regularly updated to continually improve land management and environmental performance.

The administrative units' EMS will be a systematic approach to identify and manage environmental conditions and obligations to achieve improved performance and environmental protection. Each unit's EMS will identify and prioritize environmental conditions; set objectives in light of Congressional, agency, and public goals; document procedures and practices to achieve those objectives; and monitor and measure environmental conditions to track performance and verify that objectives are being met. Agency management personnel will regularly review performance, and information about environmental conditions will be regularly updated to continually improve land management and environmental performance.

By systematically collecting and updating information about environmental conditions and practices (for example, through monitoring, measurement, research, and public input), the units' EMS will provide a foundation for effective adaptive management, plan amendments, or even changing specific project or work practices. The agency expects that, whenever possible, EMS and land management plan documentation will be coordinated and integrated to avoid unnecessary duplication.

The units' EMS will more efficiently meet legal obligations, will improve public participation in the land management planning process, and enhance the agency's ability to identify and respond to public input. Creating a transparent and consistent framework that describes how units are managed will improve the public's ability to effectively participate in land management. The units' EMS will not replace any legal obligations that the agency has under NFMA, MUSYA, NEPA, or any other statute, nor will the EMS diminish the public's ability to participate in the land management process or its rights under any law. To the contrary, EMS will significantly improve the public's ability to effectively participate in the process.

The agency chose ISO 14001 as the EMS model for several reasons. First, it is the most commonly used EMS model in the United States and around the world. This will make it easier to implement and understand (internally and externally) because there is a significant knowledge base about ISO 14001. Second, the National Technology and Advancement Act of 1995 (NTAA) (Pub. L. 104–113) requires that Federal agencies use or adopt applicable national or international consensus standards wherever possible, in lieu of creating proprietary or unique standards. The NTAA's policy of encouraging Federal agencies to adopt tested and well-accepted standards, rather than reinventing-the-wheel, clearly applies to this situation where there is a ready-made international and national EMS consensus standard (through the American National Standards Institute) that has already been successfully implemented in the field for almost a decade. Third, it has been a long-standing policy that Federal agencies implement EMS to improve environmental performance. * * *

The implementation of ISO 14001 in NFS administrative units will have to reflect the legal and public obligations of the agency, as well as the environmental conditions and issues relevant to land management, such as sustainability and long-term issues, including cumulative effects. For example, while ISO 14001 requires implementing organizations to identify their "environmental aspects," administrative units implementing their EMS under this rule will include the concept of environmental conditions in land management planning in this step. Another example reflecting the legal and public obligations of the agency is that the units' EMS must include the public participation requirements of this rule, which are much stronger than the public communication provisions of ISO 14001. Therefore, the agency will interpret and implement ISO 14001 in a manner consistent with the agency's legal obligations, its duty to the public, and the unique circumstances of land management.

* * *

National Environmental Policy Act and National Forest Management Act Planning

The application of NEPA to the planning process as identified in this final rule is the next iterative step in an evolution that began with the promulgation of the 1979 planning rule, revised in 1982. In developing the NEPA provisions of this final rule, the Department took into account the nature of the five plan components under this final rule, experience the agency has gained over the past 25 years from developing, amending, and revising land management plans; the requirements of NEPA and NFMA, the Council on Environmental Quality (CEQ) regulations, and the comments by the Supreme Court in Ohio Forestry Ass'n v. Sierra Club and Norton v. Southern Utah Wilderness Alliance regarding the nature of plans themselves.

* * * Over the course of implementing NFMA during the past 25 years, the agency has learned that environmental effects of projects and activities cannot be meaningfully evaluated without knowledge of the specific timing and location of the projects and activities.

At the time of plan approval, the Forest Service does not have detailed information about what projects and activities will be proposed over the 15–year life of a plan, how many projects will be approved, where they will be located, or how they will be designed. At the point of plan approval, the Forest Service can only speculate about the projects that may be proposed and budgeted and the natural events, such as fire, flood, insects, and disease that may occur that will make uncontemplated projects necessary or force changes in the projects and the effects of projects that were contemplated. Indeed, the Forest Service has learned that over the 15–year life of a plan it can only expect the unexpected.

In the course of completing NEPA analysis on the first generation of NFMA plans, the Forest Service also became more aware of the difficulties of scale created by the size of the national forests and grasslands. The National Forest System includes 192 million acres, and individual planning units, such as the Tongass National Forest, may be as large as 17 million acres. These vast landscapes contain an enormous variety of different ecosystems, which will respond differently to the same management practices. * * * The result is that it is usually infeasible to do environmental analysis for a national forest as a whole that is sufficiently site-specific to allow projects to be carried out without further detailed NEPA analysis after the plan has been approved.

* * *

* * * As applied to the final rule, land management plans under this final rule, as evidenced by their five components, are strategic and aspirational in nature and generally will not include decisions with on-the-ground effects that can be meaningfully evaluated and that may be major. * * * While a plan includes desired conditions, goals, and objectives, the Forest Service does not actively prepare to make a decision on an action aimed at achieving desired conditions, goals, or objectives until the agency proposes projects and activities. Thus, the decision to adopt, amend, or revise a plan, therefore, is typically not the point in the decisionmaking process at which the agency is proposing an action likely to have a significant effect on the human environment. The approach in this final rule is consistent with the nature of Forest Service land management plans acknowledged in Ohio Forestry Ass'n v. Sierra Club, 523 U.S. 726 (1998). * * * The Supreme Court repeated its description of plans as merely strategic without any immediate on the ground impact in the recent SUWA decision described above. Both cases reinforce the observations of the FS in reflecting on 25 years of completing EISs for plans, and buttress the approach to planning and NEPA compliance described in the final rule.

In accordance with NFMA, NEPA, and the CEQ regulations, this final rule will ensure that Forest Service NEPA analysis will be timed to coincide with those stages in agency planning and decisionmaking likely to have a significant effect on the human environment. The final rule emphasizes the clear distinction between the mere adoption, revision or amendment of a plan and projects and activities having on-the-ground environmental effects. In this final rule, the Department is clarifying the nature of National Forest land management plans, and based on the nature of plans, specifying that plans, plan amendments, and plan revisions may be categorically excluded from NEPA documentation as provided in agency NEPA procedures. * * *

NOTES AND QUESTIONS

1.   The planning rule preamble contains an extensive discussion of *Ohio Forestry* and *SUWA*. Did the Supreme Court provide the agency here a roadmap for downplaying the significance of planning as a legal instrument, enforceable in court, for managing the national forests? Is the general thrust of this rule to take the courts out of the forests, and restore maximum discretion to the agency? Is that such a bad thing? Will it make federal land management decision-making more "political" or less so? More or less fact-or science-based? More or less responsive to different constituencies?

2.   Is the reform consistent with the thrust of NEPA? The Forest Service planning statutes? What would you advise conservationists unhappy with this reform to do? Do you agree that the EMS approach will not

"diminish the public's ability to participate in the land management process"? Do the EMS tasks like monitoring, measurement, research, and public input create another, duplicate layer of administrative formalities for the Forest Service? How will EMS improve forest management efficiency? Does it cure "paralysis by analysis"?

3.   One frequent criticism of NEPA analysis is that it often occurs too late in the decision-making process to change the course of an agency's agenda. Does the new regulation exacerbate this problem? What are the gains to comprehensive environmental consideration in return?

4.   Will the EMS improve transparency of agency decision-making? The Service promises "impartial and objective audits, management reviews, and public disclosure of the results of those reviews." 70 Fed. Reg. at 1041–1042. Audits generally confirm the accuracy of financial statements. How would this apply to forest management? Will the audit tool require the Forest Service to quantify all of its considerations in making a resource allocation (such as a timber sale)? How do you think such audits should be structured? (The rule does not answer this question.) Such audits hold potential to supplement (or replace) NEPA and other litigation tools as a means for interested parties to secure review of agency decisions.

5.   More broadly, does the new Forest Service planning rule embody a paradigm shift regarding the perceived utility, or lack thereof, of the "rational planning" model in managing complex natural resources for a variety of purposes? Should other land management agencies follow the lead of this new rule? The Forest Service's embrace of a private-sector tool for continuous improvement (EMS) is consistent with a general theme in public administration to borrow models from the business world. Is that a good idea? How effectively will EMS achieve the adaptive component of ecosystem management? It may be helpful at this point to review Professor Keiter's description of ecosystem management, *supra* p. 38.

6.   As this book went to press, U.S. District Court Judge Phyllis Hamilton enjoined the 2005 rule for violations of the APA, NEPA, and ESA. Citizens for Better Forestry v. U.S. Dept. of Agriculture, 481 F.Supp.2d 1059 (N.D.Cal. 2007). The court did not address whether the rule met the standards of the NFMA. The APA violation stemmed from provisions in the 2005 final rule that were not "logical outgrowths" of the proposed rule and did not represent a natural evolution in the drafting of standards. The court took particular note of the Forest Service's claim that the EMS approach, which was not in the proposed rule, represents a "paradigm shift" for the agency. The APA requires the agency to afford the public an opportunity to comment on the merits of the EMS approach before it becomes a final rule. The court also found improper the Forest Service's use of a categorical exclusion to satisfy the CEQ regulations that call for an EA or EIS for programmatic rules and changes. The court held that the 2005 rule may have significant effects on the environment. Therefore the agency should have, at minimum, prepared an EA. Similarly, because the 2005 rule may affect listed species or critical habitat, the Forest Service violated section 7 of the ESA by not initiating consultation.

Public Participation

An important feature of all modern resource planning systems is that they provide opportunity for effected interests and the general public to participate in federal land planning. For example, FLPMA (43 U.S.C. § 1712(f)) provides typical instructions:

> The Secretary shall allow an opportunity for public involvement and by regulation shall establish procedures, including public hearings where appropriate, to give Federal, State, and local governments and the public, adequate notice and opportunity to comment upon and participate in the formulation of plans and programs relating to the management of the public lands.

Combined with the NEPA requirement that the general public have an opportunity to comment on draft analyses before the agency makes "any irreversible and irretrievable commitments" to a particular course of action, the organic acts have supported the search for the public interest in resource management. Consider how NEPA and FLPMA limit the BLM in its public participation procedures in the following case.

Western Watersheds Project v. Kraayenbrink

United States District Court, District of Idaho, 2006.
2006 WL 2348080, 63 ERC 1730 (No. CV–05–297–E–BLW).

■ JUDGE WINMILL

FACTUAL BACKGROUND

This action challenges amendments to BLM grazing regulations that had last been subject to major revision in 1995. The BLM asserts that the changes were necessary to "improv[e] the working relationship with permittees and licensees and increas[e] administrative efficiency and effectiveness, including resolution of legal issues."

The plaintiffs (hereinafter collectively referred to as WWP) claim that the changes violate NEPA and FLPMA, and must therefore be enjoined. The BLM counters that the regulations are proper and should be allowed to take effect on August 11, 2006.

* * *

The Final Rule makes two major changes to the public participation process. First, the BLM modified the definition of "interested publics." Under the old definition, an individual or group that submitted a written request to the BLM to be involved in the decision-making process as to a specific allotment would be put on a list of "interested publics" and receive notice of issues arising concerning that allotment—including notice of day-to-day management issues. Under the new rule, the group would be dropped from that list if it received notice but did not comment.

* * *

The second major change in public input comes from a narrowing of the BLM's duty to consult, cooperate, and coordinate (CCC) with the interested public. Under the old rules, the BLM's CCC duties ran to the interested public, the affected ranchers, and the state whenever the BLM issued, renewed, or modified a grazing permit for a certain allotment. The new rules no longer require the BLM to CCC with the interested public on the following decisions: (1) adjustments to allotment boundaries; (2) changes in active use; (3) emergency allotment closures; (4) issuance or renewal of individual permits or leases; and (5) issuance of nonrenewable grazing permits and leases. For these matters, the interested public would be cut out of the discussions between the BLM and the ranchers at the formulation stage of decisions.

The BLM's CCC duties will continue to apply to longer-range decisions such as developing allotment management plans, range development planning and apportioning additional forage. See FEIS at p. 4–28 (explaining that "[t]he proposed regulation would foster increased administrative efficiency by focusing the role of the interested public on planning decisions and reports that influence daily management, rather than on daily management decisions themselves").

Importantly, the new regulations effectively eliminate public oversight of temporary nonrenewable (TNR) permits. Under the existing regulations, the BLM was required to consult with the interested public, see 43 C.F.R. § 4130.6–2(a), and issue a proposed decision (that could be protested) before issuing the TNR. See 43 C.F.R. §§ 4160.1, 4160.2. Under the new regulations, the TNR permits will go into effect immediately without notice or consultation with members of the public.

* * *

The new public input provisions will have a substantial impact on WWP. WWP has "interested publics" status on hundreds of BLM allotments encompassing at least 50 million acres of public lands in Idaho, Nevada, Utah and other states. Given its wide involvement, WWP cannot respond to every BLM notice, and its failure to respond would result in it being dropped from the notice list for each corresponding allotment. Moreover, the BLM's CCC duties would no longer apply to WWP for those day-to-day decisions listed above and the issuance of TNR permits.

* * *

ANALYSIS

* * *

One reason advanced by the BLM for this change involves the cost of maintaining a list of "interested publics" that must get "periodic mailings at taxpayer expense" but have not "participated . . . in years." See FEIS at p. 5–95. The BLM does not list the specific costs it incurs, beyond noting that it has incurred "substantial expenses" in supporting public participation generally and that "[s]ome of these resources have been devoted to tasks such as maintaining lists" of persons that have not participated in years. Id.

It is impossible to evaluate this claim without knowing the specific costs involved. The cost of "maintaining" a list is not apparent. Certainly there is a cost for mailing notices to the "interested publics" but the FEIS does not discuss the number, bulk, or frequency of mailings. Indeed, at another section of the FEIS, the BLM contradicts itself by asserting that the "modification of the definition [of interested publics] would result in some *minor* administrative cost savings associated with maintaining the interested public mail list and in mailing costs." See FEIS at p. 4–27 (emphasis added).

This contradictory and vague discussion of costs in the FEIS prevents the public and Court from evaluating the BLM's claim that the new regulations will save costs. This compels the Court to conclude that WWP has a strong chance of prevailing on its argument that the BLM's cost rationale was not sufficiently discussed in the FEIS.

The BLM has advanced other reasons for the changes, including the following:

> BLM believes that in-depth involvement of the public in day-to-day management decisions is neither warranted nor administratively efficient and can in fact delay BLM remedial response actions necessitated by resource conditions. Day-to-day management decisions implement land use planning decisions in which the public has already had full opportunity to participate. Also, such in-depth public involvement can delay routine management responses, such as minor adjustments in livestock numbers or use periods to respond to dynamic on-the-ground conditions. Cooperation with permittees and lessees, on the other hand, usually results in more expeditious steps to address resource conditions and can help avoid lengthy administrative appeals.

See FEIS at pp. 5–24 to 5–25.

Public participation is, by nature, messy. To manage it, agencies must be "given ample latitude to adapt their rules and policies to changed circumstances." Motor Vehicle Mfers., 463 U.S. 29, 42 (1983). At the same time, the agency's management of public input cannot defeat NEPA's purpose of "ensuring that the agency will have ... detailed information concerning significant environmental impacts, and ... that the public can ... contribute to that body of information...." San Luis Obispo Mothers for Peace v. Nuclear Regulatory Commission, 449 F.3d 1016, 1034 (9th Cir.2006). The BLM itself recognized this when proposing the 1995 regulations: "Experience has shown that the greater and more meaningful the participation during the formulation of decisions and strategies for management, the higher the level of acceptance and thus the lower the likelihood of a protest, an appeal, or some other form of contest." See 60 Fed.Reg. 9894, 9924 (1995).

The FEIS concludes that the changed rules on public input will have only a minimal effect on public input. However, a group like WWP that monitors hundreds of allotments will now have to comment on every management issue or risk losing its status as an "interested public." Such groups will either have to monitor fewer allotments, thereby reducing the information transmitted to the BLM, or comment indiscriminately at every opportunity, diluting the value of their input.

Either way, the changes would appear to substantially affect both the amount and quality of public input. The FEIS reasons that groups like WWP will still receive notice of proposed decisions and can file protests and appeals. However, a proposed decision carries with it an inevitable momentum favoring that result, an effect NEPA seeks to avoid by "ensur[ing] that federal agencies are informed of environmental consequences before making decisions. . . ." Citizens for Better Forestry v. United States, 341 F.3d 961, 970 (9th Cir.2003). Thus, getting notice of a proposed decision does not mitigate the harm of being precluded from the formulation process.

Moreover, the interested public will not receive proposed TNR permit decisions under the new regulations—the TNRs could be issued immediately. In the past, the BLM has often used TNR permits to increase grazing levels above prior limits. See WWP v. Bennett, 392 F.Supp.2d 1217 (D.Id. 2005). Thus, this is no obscure change—it will freeze the public out of the formulation of TNR permits, a process the BLM has used frequently to increase grazing.

* * *

While the analysis of WWP's chance of success has proceeded to this point under NEPA, the same analysis can be made under the Federal Land Policy and Management Act (FLPMA). Public input has the same elevated role in FLPMA that it has under NEPA. FLPMA requires the BLM to give "the public adequate notice and an opportunity to comment upon the formulation of standards and criteria for, and to participate in, the preparation and execution of plans and programs for, and the management of, the public lands." See 43 U.S.C. § 1739(e).

This statutory language values public input on long-range issues ("preparation of plans and programs") as well as on day-to-day issues ("the management of" and "execution of" those long-range plans). This same language promotes early public participation at the "formulation" stage, before the decision is made. The changes made by the BLM appear to violate these FLPMA provisions.

* * *

These circumstances show that the balance of hardships tips favors WWP. The record reveals no need to quickly limit public input.

Finally, the public interest is advanced by enjoining limits on public input. For all of these reasons, the Court will enjoin those new BLM regulations governing public participation.

NOTES AND QUESTIONS

1. Recent Supreme Court cases, especially *SUWA* and *Ohio Forestry*, downplay the significance of (and therefore the opportunities for challenges

to) broad-scale planning. One result is a reduction in public participation at the planning level. The 2005 Forest Service planning rule reflects this change by reducing the number of firm commitments in and limiting the environmental review of plans. These cases and regulations locate the proper place for participation at the more specific project implementation level. Does the BLM grazing rule account for this development in the law of planning? Or, does it simply attempt to squeeze out public participation in grazing decisions?

2.   What substantive input can the public offer the BLM on grazing decisions specific to a particular allotment? Is the public in a position to know anything better than the rancher on the ground or the BLM land managers?

3.   The 2006 BLM rule challenged in *Western Watersheds* suggested that focusing cooperation on permittees "usually results in more expeditious steps to address resource conditions and can help avoid lengthy administrative appeals." Yet, the 1995 rule stated that: "Experience has shown that the greater and more meaningful the participation during the formulation of decisions and strategies for management, the higher the level of acceptance and thus the lower the likelihood of a protest, an appeal, or some other form of contest." 60 Fed. Reg. 9894, 9924. Is it possible to reconcile these two statements from the BLM?

4.   What would it take for the BLM to justify restrictions on public participation on the basis that the bother and delay seldom result in correspondingly meaningful improvements to proposed decisions?

CHAPTER 6

THE WATER RESOURCE

The water resource is the appropriate starting place for studying specific federal public resources, for all other resource uses are dependent upon the availability of water. Mineral extraction and processing often require significant quantities. Water itself, in the form of geothermal steam or as hydropower, is an energy resource. Western farmers rely on expansive irrigation systems—as much as 80% of all developed water supplies in the eleven western states is used for irrigation. Grass and trees and fish and wildlife all need water. And so do rafters and kayakers and other recreationists. Finally, water is an essential part of ecosystems that society wishes preserved for future generations.

Acquisition of water rights has traditionally been principally a matter of state law, but this is largely due to federal restraint. As a constitutional matter, valid federal water laws are supreme: The Property, Commerce, Spending and Treaty Clauses give Congress ample authority to legislate on issues relating to water. Large-scale water resources development is mainly a creature of federal money, if not federal law. While Congress has not generally legislated a federal water law (state law for the most part defines water rights connected with federal dams and related facilities), federal land management agencies frequently hold water rights bottomed on federal law, as explained below. Congress can also affect state water law and water rights perfected under such law when it acts to regulate navigation, to prevent floods, to control water pollution, or to protect endangered species.

Water policy on the federal lands involves more than the distribution of water among competing users. Land management practices often determine the character of the streams and lakes within a watershed. Timber harvesting can cause stream blockages and erosion, and affect the temperature, quantity, and quality of run-off. Overgrazing destroys groundcover and causes soil compaction; rainfall, instead of being absorbed and cooled by spongy soils, runs off in sheets, carrying soil with it and carving out gullies and arroyos. Mineral development can drastically affect hydrologic conditions; large open-pit gold mines in Nevada pump huge volumes of groundwater to dewater the pits and allow mining to continue. This can dry up some surface streams and greatly increase the supply in others. Development projects of all sorts usually require road systems, which can cause severe erosion. Land and resource planners therefore must give

Portions of the discussion in this chapter are drawn, with permission, from Chapter 9 of Joseph L. Sax, Barton Thompson, John D. Leshy, and Robert Abrams, LEGAL CONTROL OF WATER RESOURCES (West. Pub. Co., 4d ed. 2006).

prime consideration to protection of watercourses if downstream consumptive users, wildlife, and recreationists are to have adequate supplies of water.

The federal government influences national water policy in numerous ways that do not necessarily involve federal land law, but which often complicate resource decisions on the federal lands. Space and relevancy considerations prevent discussion of most of the legal issues that can arise; in particular, this chapter does not attempt to duplicate a course in water law. It is limited to aspects of water allocation that are intimately tied to the protection and development of the federal lands. Section A examines the law governing water rights for purposes related to federal lands. It focuses mostly on the doctrine of federal reserved water rights, and how such rights are established, adjudicated and protected. It also examines other means for the federal government to secure water rights and otherwise protect its interests in water in relation to federal lands. Section B contains materials on a subject of growing importance: the federal hydropower licensing process, which has special provisions to protect areas of federal lands.

A. The Acquisition of Water Rights on Federal Lands

1. The Origins of Water Law on Federal Lands

Water law defines legal rights to a limited, fluid, and largely renewable resource. Geographic variations in the quantity of water available, competition among the many various uses, and differing political and social contexts have resulted in two basic types of state water rights systems. Under English common law, the owner of land adjacent to a watercourse (a "riparian" owner) acquired water rights in the stream as part of the estate in real property. Each riparian owner was entitled to the "natural flow" of the stream. None could use the water for consumptive purposes other than such modest "natural uses" as household or stock-watering; nor could a riparian owner use the water off the riparian land. Instream, nonconsumptive uses (such as for mills) were permitted since the natural flow would be preserved. The English Rule of riparian rights came to be regarded as unsuited to the demands of industry, commerce, and agriculture where water is relatively scarce.

In the United States, the English "natural flow" doctrine evolved into a "reasonable use" doctrine. This version of riparianism permits consumptive uses if they are reasonable and do not unreasonably damage other riparian owners. These water rights are relative—they continually expand and contract in response to changing conditions. A very broad, "totality of the circumstances" set of criteria determines reasonableness. *See, e.g.*, Restatement, Second, Torts §§ 850–59.

Another system of water rights, the prior appropriation doctrine, emerged out of the gold fields of California in the mid-nineteenth century. This doctrine was thought better suited not only for mining but also for those lands (most of those west of the 100th meridian) which receive less than 20 inches of precipitation per year, and which therefore cannot sustain crops without artificial irrigation. Under this system an appropriator—whether or not the owner of riparian land—could obtain a vested property right superior to all later users by diverting water out of the stream and putting it to a beneficial use, a term that generally includes domestic, agricultural and industrial uses. The catchphrases of this legal system are "first in time, first in right" and "use it or lose it." On paper, the prior appropriation doctrine is a usufructuary system, requiring application of water to beneficial use in order to protect and maintain the right. Also, again on paper, the doctrine calls for no balancing of equities or proration among various users in times of shortage—the senior right-holder must be fully satisfied before any junior users get water. (Both of these hard-edged concepts have been softened considerably in practice.) Use in the appropriation doctrine is not limited to riparian land, not even to the watershed of origin, because miners and farmers often needed to transport water far away from the stream.

Most of the inland Rocky Mountain states are pure "Colorado doctrine" states, recognizing only water rights established by prior appropriation. A number of other western states (California, Kansas, Nebraska, North Dakota, Oklahoma, Oregon, South Dakota, Texas, and Washington) originally adopted what came to be known as the "California doctrine," which recognizes both riparian and appropriative rights. But all of the states in this latter group have, with very limited exceptions (mostly in California), since moved to a pure appropriation system. The result is that, generally speaking, the prior appropriation doctrine now holds sway in all states west of the 100th meridian.

The western states have, on paper, fairly elaborate systems for adjudicating and supervising water rights. Beginning with Wyoming in 1890, most of them established administrative agencies to issue and oversee water permits. Fairly early on, states provided for general stream adjudications in which courts could determine all rights, by priority, within entire watersheds. The reality of water rights administration in the states fell far short of the promise; in many states, even today, water rights are mostly unadjudicated and uncertain.

The traditional prior appropriation doctrine, which allocated water on a laissez-faire basis to the first consumptive user, has been modified in various respects. Most states now allow new appropriations only upon a governmental agency finding that they are in the "public interest." Similarly, just about all states have abandoned the old idea that one could not legally protect a stream-flow (as opposed to a water right based on diversion of water from the stream). Today it is more and more common for minimum stream flows to be legally established, by a variety of means, for protection of fish, wildlife, recreation, and the aesthetic qualities of streams and lakes. Water allocation is, however, still heavily influenced by deeply-entrenched state laws that have distributed most western water on a first-come, first-served basis to users who have actually diverted water from a watercourse and applied it to specified beneficial uses.

The following excerpt provides some history of federal policy toward water allocation in the Western states.

California v. United States

Supreme Court of the United States, 1978.
438 U.S. 645.

■ JUSTICE REHNQUIST delivered the opinion of the Court.

* * *

* * * [R]eclamation of the arid lands began almost immediately upon the arrival of pioneers to the Western States. Huge sums of private money were invested in systems to transport water vast distances for mining, agriculture, and ordinary consumption. Because a very high percentage of land in the West belonged to the Federal Government, the canals and ditches that carried this water frequently crossed federal land. In 1862, Congress opened the public domain to homesteading. And in 1866, Congress for the first time expressly opened the mineral lands of the public domain to exploration and occupation by miners. Mining Act of 1866. Because of the fear that these Acts might in some way interfere with the water rights and systems that had grown up under state and local law, Congress explicitly recognized and acknowledged the local law:

> "[W]henever, by priority of possession, rights to the use of water for mining, agricultural, manufacturing, or other purposes, have vested and accrued, and the same are recognized and acknowledged by the local customs, laws, and the decisions of courts the possessors and owners of such vested rights shall be maintained and protected in the same." § 9, 14 Stat. 253.

The Mining Act of 1866 was not itself a grant of water rights pursuant to federal law. Instead, as this Court observed, the Act was " 'a voluntary recognition of a preexisting right of possession, constituting a valid claim to its continued use.' " United States v. Rio Grande Dam & Irrig. Co. Congress intended "to recognize as valid the customary law with respect to the use of water which had grown up among the occupants of the public land under the peculiar necessities of their condition."

In 1877, Congress took its first step toward encouraging the reclamation and settlement of the public desert lands in the West and made it clear that such reclamation would generally follow state water law. In the Desert Land Act of 1877, Congress provided for the homesteading of arid public lands in larger tracts

> "by [the homesteader's] conducting water upon the same, within the period of three years [after filing a declaration to do so], *Provided however* that the right to the use of water by the person so conducting the same * * * shall not exceed the amount of water actually appropriated, and necessarily used for the purpose of irrigation and reclamation: *and all surplus water over and above such actual appropriation and use, together with the water of all, lakes, rivers and other sources of*

water supply upon the public lands and not navigable, shall remain and be held free for the appropriation and use of the public for irrigation, mining and manufacturing purposes subject to existing rights." Ch. 107, 19 Stat. 377 (emphasis added).

This Court has had an opportunity to construe the 1877 Desert Land Act before. In California Oregon Power Co. v. Beaver Portland Cement Co., 295 U.S. 142 (1935), Mr. Justice Sutherland explained that, through this language, Congress "effected a severance of all waters upon the public domain, not theretofore appropriated, from the land itself." The non-navigable waters thereby severed were "reserved for the use of the public under the laws of the states and territories." *Id.*, at 162. Congress' purpose was not to federalize the prior-appropriation doctrine already evolving under local law. Quite the opposite:

"What we hold is that following the act of 1877, if not before, all non-navigable waters then a part of the public domain became *publici juris*, subject to the plenary control of the designated states, including those since created out of the territories named, with the right in each to determine for itself to what extent the rule of appropriation or the common-law rule in respect of riparian rights should obtain. For since 'Congress cannot enforce either rule upon any state,' Kansas v. Colorado, 206 U.S. 46, 94, the full power of choice must remain with the state. The Desert Land Act does not bind or purport to bind the states to any policy. It simply recognizes and gives sanction, in so far as the United States and its future grantees are concerned, to the state and local doctrine of appropriation, and seeks to remove what otherwise might be an impediment to its full and successful operation."

Nineteenth century homestead policy initially dovetailed with the twentieth century reclamation policy, because more federal acreage was patented under the homestead laws after the Reclamation Act of 1902 took effect. The face of the West has been fundamentally reshaped by the large reclamation dams that supply subsidized federal water to western irrigators, large and small. Generally speaking, water rights for federal reclamation projects are obtained under state law, pursuant to section 8 of the Reclamation Act, 43 U.S.C. § 383, although exceptions to this deference may be created by "clear congressional directives." California v. United States, 438 U.S. 645 (1978). A major exception is along the lower Colorado River, where federal statutes have been construed to give the Secretary of the Interior sweeping authority to allocate water to states and private users. *Id.* at 674. Many federal reclamation projects have been at least partially located on federal land, and some major National Recreation Areas created by Congress have reclamation project reservoirs as their centerpiece; for example, Lake Mead National Recreation Area and Glen Canyon National Recreation Area (Lake Powell).

2.   FEDERAL RESERVED WATER RIGHTS

While Justice Rehnquist's majority opinion in California v. United States saw a "consistent thread of purposeful and continued deference to state water law by Congress," a separate doctrine evolved around the turn of the twentieth century. In United States v. Rio Grande Dam & Irrigation Co., 174 U.S. 690 (1899), the federal government sued to stop construction of a private dam across the Rio Grande River in the territory of New Mexico. Reversing the lower court's decision dismissing the suit, a unanimous Supreme Court acknowledged that local law generally controls, but said (174 U.S. at 703):

> [Y]et two limitations [on state power] must be recognized: First, that, in the absence of specific authority from Congress, a state cannot by its legislation destroy the right of the United States, as the owner of lands bordering on a stream, to the continued flow of its waters; so far at least as may be necessary for the beneficial uses of the government property. Second, that it is limited by the superior power of the General Government to secure the uninterrupted navigability of all navigable streams within the limits of the United States.

Nine years later, the Supreme Court built the first-mentioned limitation into the doctrine of federal reserved water rights in Winters v. United States, 207 U.S. 564 (1908). In *Winters,* the United States, as trustee for the Indian tribes occupying the Fort Belknap reservation in Montana, sought to enjoin upstream defendants on the Milk River from withdrawing water that was required for an irrigation project on the reservation. The defendants had appropriated water under Montana law after the reservation was established in 1888 but before 1898, when the Indian irrigation project was constructed. The Court tersely held that the creation of the Fort Belknap reservation not only set aside land but also impliedly reserved a sufficient quantity of water, as of the date of the reservation, to fulfill the purposes of the reservation (207 U.S. at 577): "The power of the Government to reserve the waters and exempt them from appropriation under the state laws is not denied, and could not be. United States v. Rio Grande Ditch [sic] & Irrig. Co. That the Government did reserve them we have decided * * *. This was done May 1, 1888 * * *."

Winters superimposed a federal water right, implied from setting aside federal land, on a state system that based water rights on prior appropriation. The two rights do not mesh easily; the federal right is established without application of water to a beneficial use—a hallmark of prior appropriation law. Much of the jurisprudence that has developed around the *Winters* doctrine has come in the context of Indian water rights. In this section, however, we will consider the doctrine only as it relates to non-Indian federal land interests. Until the 1950s, *Winters* was thought to be a doctrine of Indian water rights only, but in 1955 the Supreme Court suggested that it could apply to other federal lands that were reserved for particular purposes. Federal Power Comm'n v. Oregon, 349 U.S. 435 (1955). This suggestion ripened into a holding eight years later.

Arizona v. California

Supreme Court of the United States, 1963.
373 U.S. 546.

[The Colorado River and its tributaries are a principal source of water for seven states in the arid Southwest. Arizona invoked the original jurisdiction of the Supreme Court by filing an action against the State of California to determine each state's right to the water allocated to the lower Colorado River basin by the Colorado River Compact of 1922. The case was referred to a special master to take evidence and recommend a decree. Although the primary controversy concerned the amount of water each state had a legal right to use, the United States as intervenor asserted federal reserved rights for both Indian and non-Indian federal lands along the lower Colorado River. Near the end of its lengthy opinion largely affirming the recommendations of the special master, the Court held, per Justice Black (373 U.S. at 595, 597–98, 601)]:

In these proceedings, the United States has asserted claims to waters in the main river and in some of the tributaries for use on Indian Reservations, National Forests, Recreational and Wildlife Areas and other government lands and works. * * *

* * *

Arizona's contention that the Federal Government had no power, after Arizona became a State, to reserve waters for the use and benefit of federally reserved lands rests largely upon statements in Pollard's Lessee v. Hagan. * * * But those cases involved only the shores of and lands beneath navigable waters. They do not determine the problem before us and cannot be accepted as limiting the broad powers of the United States to regulate navigable waters under the Commerce Clause and to regulate government lands under Art. IV, § 3, of the Constitution. We have no doubt about the power of the United States under these clauses to reserve water rights for its reservations and its property.

Arizona also argues that, in any event, water rights cannot be reserved by Executive Order. Some of the reservations of Indian lands here involved were made almost 100 years ago * * *. In our view, these reservations, like those created directly by Congress, were not limited to land, but included waters as well. * * * We can give but short shrift at this late date to the argument that the reservations either of land or water are invalid because they were originally set apart by the Executive.[102]

* * *

The Master ruled that the principle underlying the reservation of water rights for Indian Reservations was equally applicable to other federal establishments such as National Recreation Areas and National Forests. We agree with the conclusions of the Master that the United States

---

102. *See* United States v. Midwest Oil Co., 236 U.S. 459, 469–75 (1915); Winters v. United States.

intended to reserve water sufficient for the future requirements of the Lake Mead National Recreation Area, the Havasu Lake National Wildlife Refuge, the Imperial National Wildlife Refuge and the Gila National Forest.

———————

The holding that the reserved rights doctrine extends to non-Indian federal land, including that withdrawn or reserved by Executive Order, gives nearly all categories of federal land some claim to water rights based on federal law. A survey of these federal water rights is set out further below. In the following case, a unanimous Supreme Court provided additional guidance on the dimensions of the *Winters* doctrine outside the Indian context.

Cappaert v. United States

Supreme Court of the United States, 1976.
426 U.S. 128.

■ CHIEF JUSTICE BURGER delivered the opinion of the Court.

The question presented in this litigation is whether the reservation of Devil's Hole as a national monument reserved federal water rights in unappropriated water.

Devil's Hole is a deep limestone cavern in Nevada. Approximately 50 feet below the opening of the cavern is a pool of 65 feet long, 10 feet wide, and at least 200 feet deep, although its actual depth is unknown. The pool is a remnant of the prehistoric Death Valley Lake System and is situated on land owned by the United States since the Treaty of Guadalupe Hidalgo in 1848, 9 Stat. 922. By the Proclamation of January 17, 1952, President Truman withdrew from the public domain a 40–acre tract of land surrounding Devil's Hole, making it a detached component of the Death Valley National Monument. The Proclamation was issued under the American Antiquities Preservation Act, 16 U.S.C. § 431, which authorizes the President to declare as national monuments "objects of historic or scientific interest that are situated upon the lands owned or controlled by the Government of the United States. . . ."

The 1952 Proclamation notes that Death Valley was set aside as a national monument "for the preservation of the unusual features of scenic, scientific, and educational interest therein contained." The Proclamation also notes that Devil's Hole is near Death Valley and contains a "remarkable underground pool." Additional preambulary statements in the Proclamation explain why Devil's Hole was being added to the Death Valley National Monument:

* * *

"WHEREAS the geologic evidence that this subterranean pool is an integral part of the hydrographic history of the Death Valley region is further confirmed by the presence in this pool of a peculiar race of desert fish, and zoologists have demonstrated that this race of fish, which is found nowhere else in the world, evolved only after the gradual drying up of the Death Valley Lake System isolated this fish population from the original ancestral stock that in Pleistocene times was common to the entire region; and

"WHEREAS the said pool is of such outstanding scientific importance that it should be given special protection, and such protection can be best afforded by making the said forty-acre tract containing the pool a part of the said monument. . . ."

* * *

The Cappaert petitioners own a 12,000–acre ranch near Devil's Hole, 4,000 acres of which are used for growing Bermuda grass, alfalfa, wheat, and barley; 1,700 to 1,800 head of cattle are grazed. The ranch represents an investment of more than $7 million; it employs more than 80 people with an annual payroll of more than $340,000.

In 1968 the Cappaerts began pumping groundwater on their ranch on land 2-1/2 miles from Devil's Hole; they were the first to appropriate groundwater. The groundwater comes from an underground basin or aquifer which is also the source of the water in Devil's Hole. After the Cappaerts began pumping from the wells near Devil's Hole, which they do from March to October, the summer water level of the pool in Devil's Hole began to decrease. * * *

* * *

[In 1970, when the Cappaerts sought permission from the Nevada State Engineer to change the use of water from several of their wells, the United States protested on the basis that continued pumping could injure the desert pupfish. The State Engineer rejected the protest. The United States filed suit in federal court to limit the Cappaerts' pumping. The lower courts issued the injunction sought by the United States, and the Supreme Court granted certiorari.]

This Court has long held that when the Federal Government withdraws its land from the public domain and reserves it for a federal purpose, the Government, by implication, reserves appurtenant water then unappropriated to the extent needed to accomplish the purpose of the reservation. In so doing the United States acquires a reserved right in unappropriated water which vests on the date of the reservation and is superior to the rights of future appropriators. Reservation of water rights is empowered by the Commerce Clause, Art. I, § 8, which permits federal regulation of navigable streams, and the Property Clause, Art. IV, § 3, which permits federal regulation of federal lands. The doctrine applies to Indian reservations and other federal enclaves, encompassing water rights in navigable and nonnavigable streams.

Nevada argues that the cases establishing the doctrine of federally reserved water rights articulate an equitable doctrine calling for a balancing of competing interests. However, an examination of those cases shows they do not analyze the doctrine in terms of a balancing test. For example, in Winters v. United States, the Court did not mention the use made of the water by the upstream landowners in sustaining an injunction barring their diversions of the water. The "Statement of the Case" in *Winters* notes that the upstream users were homesteaders who had invested heavily in dams to divert the water to irrigate their land, not an unimportant interest. The Court held that when the Federal Government reserves land, by implication it reserves water rights sufficient to accomplish the purposes of the reservation.

In determining whether there is a federally reserved water right implicit in a federal reservation of public land, the issue is whether the Government intended to reserve unappropriated and thus available water. Intent is inferred if the previously unappropriated waters are necessary to accomplish the purposes for which the reservation was created. See, e.g., Arizona v. California; Winters v. United States. Both the District Court and the Court of Appeals held that the 1952 Proclamation expressed an intention to reserve unappropriated water, and we agree.[5] The Proclamation discussed the pool in Devil's Hole in four of the five preambles and recited that the "pool . . . should be given special protection." Since a pool is a body of water, the protection contemplated is meaningful only if the water remains; the water right reserved by the 1952 Proclamation was thus explicit, not implied.

Also explicit in the 1952 Proclamation is the authority of the Director of the Park Service to manage the lands of Devil's Hole Monument "as provided in the act of Congress entitled 'An Act to establish a National Park Service, and for other purposes,' approved August 25, 1916 (16 U.S.C. §§ 1–3). . . ." The National Park Service Act provides that the "fundamental purpose of the said parks, monuments, and reservations" is "to conserve the scenery and the natural and historic objects and the wild life therein and to provide for the enjoyment of the same in such manner and by such means as will leave them unimpaired for the enjoyment of future generations." 16 U.S.C. § 1.

The implied-reservation-of-water-rights-doctrine, however, reserves only that amount of water necessary to fulfill the purpose of the reservation, no more. Arizona v. California. Here the purpose of reserving Devil's Hole Monument is preservation of the pool. Devil's Hole was reserved "for the preservation of the unusual features of scenic, scientific, and educational interest." The Proclamation notes that the pool contains a "a peculiar race of desert fish . . . which is found nowhere else in the world" and that the "pool is of . . . outstanding scientific importance." The pool need only be preserved, consistent with the intention expressed in the Proclamation, to the extent necessary to preserve its scientific interest. The fish are one of the features of scientific interest. The preamble noting the scientific

5. The [lower courts] correctly held that neither the Cappaerts nor their predecessors in interest had acquired any water rights as of 1952 when the United States' water rights vested. Part of the land now comprising the Cappaerts' ranch was patented by the United States to the Cappaerts' predecessors as early as 1890. None of the patents conveyed water rights because the Desert Land Act of 1877, 43 U.S.C. § 321, provided that such patents pass title only to land, not water. Patentees acquire water rights by "bona fide prior appropriation," as determined by state law. * * * Neither the Cappaerts nor their predecessors in interest appropriated any water until after 1952.

interest of the pool follows the preamble describing the fish as unique; the Proclamation must be read in its entirety. Thus, as the District Court has correctly determined, the level of the pool may be permitted to drop to the extent that the drop does not impair the scientific value of the pool as the natural habitat of the species sought to be preserved. The District Court thus tailored its injunction, very appropriately, to minimal need, curtailing pumping only to the extent necessary to preserve an adequate water level at Devil's Hole, thus implementing the stated objectives of the Proclamation.

* * *

No cases of this court have applied the doctrine of implied reservation of water rights to groundwater. Nevada argues that the implied-reservation doctrine is limited to surface water. Here, however, the water in the pool is surface water. The federal water rights were being depleted because, as the evidence showed, the "[g]roundwater and surface water are physically interrelated as integral parts of the hydrologic cycle." Here the Cappaerts are causing the water level in Devil's Hole to drop by their heavy pumping. It appears that Nevada itself may recognize the potential interrelationship between surface and groundwater since Nevada applies the law of prior appropriation to both. Thus, since the implied-reservation-of-water-rights doctrine is based on the necessity of water for the purpose of the federal reservation, we hold that the United States can protect its water from subsequent diversion, whether the diversion is of surface or groundwater.[7]

Petitioners in both cases argue that the Federal Government must perfect its implied water rights according to state law. They contend that the Desert Land Act of 1877, 43 U.S.C. § 321, and its predecessors severed nonnavigable water from public land, subjecting it to state law. That Act, however, provides that patentees of public land acquire only title to land through the patent and must acquire water rights in nonnavigable water in accordance with state law. California Oregon Power Co. v. Beaver Portland Cement Co. 295 U.S. 142, 162 (1935). * * *

* * *

We hold, therefore, that as of 1952 when the United States reserved Devil's Hole, it acquired by reservation water rights in unappropriated appurtenant water sufficient to maintain the level of the pool to preserve its scientific value and thereby implement Proclamation No. 2961. Accordingly, the judgment of the Court of Appeals is

---

7. Petitioners in both cases argue that the effect of applying the implied reservation doctrine to diversions of groundwater is to prohibit pumping from the entire 4,500 square miles above the aquifer that supplies water to Devil's Hole. First, it must be emphasized that the injunction limits but does not prohibit pumping. Second, the findings of fact in this case relate only to wells within 2-1/2 miles of Devil's Hole. No proof was introduced in the district Court that pumping from the same aquifer that supplies Devil's Hole, would significantly lower the level in Devil's Hole. Nevada notes that such pumping "will in time affect the water level in Devil's Hole." There was testimony from a research hydrologist that substantial pumping 40 miles away "[o]ver a period of perhaps decades [would have] a small effect."

Affirmed.

NOTES AND QUESTIONS

1. In most situations, statutes, executive orders, or other documents effecting federal land reservations are *silent* on water. Therefore, as in *Winters* itself, the federal reservation of water is implied. How strong was the implication that water was reserved in the order reserving the Devil's Hole? Same result if the underground pool and the pupfish had not been mentioned in the Proclamation reserving Devil's Hole?

2. What result if the Cappaerts had begun pumping in 1950? Actually, the Cappaerts acquired some of their land from the federal government in a 1969 land exchange. The deed from the United States made their title expressly "subject to vested and accrued water rights." Does that help justify the decision? After the Court ruled, the Cappaerts sold 13,000 acres to a developer for a retirement community. The Nature Conservancy stepped in to buy the land from the developer and sold it back to the United States in 1984 to establish Ash Meadows National Wildlife Refuge. Is acquisition of land a better solution to the pupfish problem than assertion of a water right?

3. By characterizing the underground pool as surface water, the Supreme Court avoided the question whether the *Winters* doctrine applies to groundwater. (The Ninth Circuit had held that the pool was groundwater, and was reserved. *See* 508 F.2d 313, 317 (1974).) The question is of considerable moment because groundwater is heavily used in many parts of the country. A number of western states, such as Nevada, apply the prior appropriation doctrine to groundwater, but the priority system may be uncoordinated with the allocation of surface water. Other western states, and most non-western states, apply groundwater allocation doctrines that are different from surface water doctrines.

The old English common law rule applicable to groundwater was a capture rule, misleadingly called "absolute ownership." This doctrine, still generally followed in most parts of Texas, Indiana and a handful of other states, allows landowners to extract groundwater from beneath their land without restriction, unless it is for malicious purposes. The "American rule" followed in many states modifies the English doctrine, and allows landowners to extract groundwater for "reasonable uses," with reasonableness being primarily determined by whether the water is being used on the land from which it is pumped. If it is conveyed off the land to the injury of others who are extracting water from the same underground source, it is per se unreasonable. A few states follow a version of "correlative rights," which favors on-land use like the American rule, but which apportions the water in the aquifer among overlying landowners in "fair and just proportion," usually based upon the amount of acreage owned.

4. Does the principle behind the federal reserved water rights doctrine support its application to groundwater? State courts addressing the question in the context of Indian water rights have split on the question. *Compare* In re General Adjudication of All Rights to Use Water in the Big

Horn River System, 753 P.2d 76 (Wyo.1988), *aff'd on other grounds by an equally divided court sub nom.* Wyoming v. United States, 492 U.S. 406 (1989) (no), *with In re* Gila River System, 989 P.2d 739 (Ariz.1999), cert. denied, 530 U.S. 1250 (2000) (yes).

5. Groundwater aquifers have widely varying rates of replenishment, or "recharge." Suppose that the recharge rate here is very low, such that pumping *any* water from the aquifer that supports the pool at Devil's Hole would lower the level of the water in the pool and threaten the pupfish. Suppose also that the aquifer is very large, extending under several hundred square miles of surface, much of it privately owned. Does *Cappaert* mean that no groundwater pumping can occur? See footnote 7 in the Court's opinion.

6. Assuming the pupfish is listed as an endangered species, may the Endangered Species Act come into play here, totally apart from the water rights context? That is, would the Cappaerts be liable for a "take" under section 9 of the Act if they continued to pump and dried up the pool?

7. A *Cappaert*-type problem may be raised in connection with geothermal (hot water or steam) resources. For example, proposed geothermal development in a national forest adjacent to Yellowstone has been opposed by Park Service officials because of concern that geothermal wells would adversely affect Yellowstone's fragile "plumbing." Does the United States have a reserved right to the geothermal resource, with a priority date of 1872, when Yellowstone National Park was established? What do you need to know to answer that question? Reconsider it after reading the next case.

Classic prior appropriation doctrine had little room for instream uses. Even where states move to establish minimum stream-flow levels, such protections are usually accorded junior priority and must give way to senior rights in years of low flows. On many streams, such junior priorities may be of little use where most flows have been appropriated by senior consumptive users. The following case reflected the Forest Service's attempts to obtain federal instream water rights with senior priority dates.

United States v. New Mexico

Supreme Court of the United States, 1978.
438 U.S. 696.

■ JUSTICE REHNQUIST delivered the opinion of the Court.

[The state of New Mexico initiated in state court a general adjudication of water rights on the Rio Mimbres in the southwestern part of the state. The United States participated and claimed reserved water rights for use in the Gila National Forest.]

The question posed in this case—what quantity of water, if any, the United States reserved out of the Rio Mimbres when it set aside the Gila National Forest in 1899—is a question of implied intent and not power.

* * * The Court has previously concluded that whatever powers the States acquired over their waters as a result of congressional Acts and admission into the Union, however, Congress did not intend thereby to relinquish its authority to reserve unappropriated water in the future for use on appurtenant lands withdrawn from the public domain for specific federal purposes.

Recognition of Congress' power to reserve water for land which is itself set apart from the public domain, however, does not answer the question of the amount of water which has been reserved or the purposes for which the water may be used. Substantial portions of the public domain *have* been withdrawn and reserved by the United States for use as Indian reservations, forest reserves, national parks, and national monuments. And water is frequently necessary to achieve the purposes for which these reservations are made. But Congress has seldom expressly reserved water for use on these withdrawn lands. If water were abundant, Congress' silence would pose no problem. In the arid parts of the West, however, claims to water for use on federal reservations inescapably vie with other public and private claims for the limited quantities to be found in the rivers and streams. This competition is compounded by the sheer quantity of reserved lands in the Western States, which lands form brightly colored swaths across the maps of these States.[4]

The Court has previously concluded that Congress, in giving the President the power to reserve portions of the federal domain for specific federal purposes, *impliedly* authorized him to reserve "appurtenant water then unappropriated *to the extent needed to accomplish the purpose of the reservation.*" *Cappaert* (emphasis added). While many of the contours of what has come to be called the "implied-reservation-of-water doctrine" remain unspecified, the Court has repeatedly emphasized that Congress reserved "only that amount of water necessary to fulfill the purpose of the reservation, no more." *Cappaert.* Each time this Court has applied the "implied-reservation-of-water doctrine," it has carefully examined both the asserted water right and the specific purposes for which the land was reserved, and concluded that without the water the purposes of the reservation would be entirely defeated.

This careful examination is required both because the reservation is implied, rather than expressed, and because of the history of congressional intent in the field of federal-state jurisdiction with respect to allocation of water. Where Congress has expressly addressed the question of whether federal entities must abide by state water law, it has almost invariably

---

4. The percentage of federally owned land (*excluding* Indian reservations and other trust properties) in the Western States ranges from 29.5% of the land in the State of Washington to 86.5% of the land in the State of Nevada, an average of about 46%. Of the land in the State of New Mexico, 33.6% is federally owned. Because federal reservations are normally found in the uplands of the Western States rather than the flatlands, the percentage of water flow originating in or flowing through the reservations is even more impressive. More than 60% of the average annual water yield in the 11 Western States is from federal reservations. The percentage of average annual water yield range from a low of 56% in the Columbia–North Pacific water-resource region to a high of 96% in the Upper Colorado region. In the Rio Grande water-resource region, where the Rio Mimbres lies, 77% of the average runoff originates on federal reservations.

deferred to the state law. Where water is necessary to fulfill the very purposes for which a federal reservation was created, it is reasonable to conclude, even in the face of Congress' express deference to state water law in other areas, that the United States intended to reserve the necessary water. Where water is only valuable for a secondary use of the reservation, however, there arises the contrary inference that Congress intended, consistent with its other views, that the United States would acquire water in the same manner as any other public or private appropriator.

* * *

[The state courts held that the United States had no federal reserved right to an instream flow on the national forest for "aesthetic, environmental, recreational, or 'fish' purposes." They also held that no water had been reserved for stock-watering on the national forest.]

The United States contends that Congress intended to reserve minimum instream flows for aesthetic, recreational, and fish-preservation purposes. An examination of the limited purposes for which Congress authorized the creation of national forests, however, provides no support for this claim. In the mid and late 1800's, many of the forests on the public domain were ravaged and the fear arose that the forest lands might soon disappear, leaving the United States with a shortage both of timber and of watersheds with which to encourage stream flows while preventing floods. It was in answer to these fears that in 1891 Congress authorized the President to "set apart and reserve, in any State or Territory having public land bearing forests, in any part of the public lands wholly or in part covered with timber or undergrowth, whether of commercial value or not, as public reservations." Creative Act of March 3, 1891, § 24, 16 U.S.C. § 471 (repealed 1976).

The Creative Act of 1891 unfortunately did not solve the forest problems of the expanding Nation. To the dismay of the conservationists, the new national forests were not adequately attended and regulated; fires and indiscriminate timber cutting continued their toll. To the anguish of Western settlers, reservations were frequently made indiscriminately. President Cleveland, in particular, responded to pleas of conservationists for greater protective measures by reserving some 21 million acres of "generally settled" forest land on February 22, 1897. President Cleveland's action drew immediate and strong protest from Western Congressmen who felt that the "hasty and ill considered" reservation might prove disastrous to the settlers living on or near these lands.

Congress' answer to these continuing problems was three-fold. It suspended the President's Executive Order of February 22, 1897; it carefully defined the purposes for which national forests could in the future be reserved; and it provided a charter for forest management and economic uses within the forests. Organic Administration Act of June 4, 1897, 16 U.S.C. § 473 et seq. In particular, Congress provided:

> *"No national forest shall be established, except to improve and protect the forest within the boundaries, or for the purpose of securing favorable conditions of water flows, and to furnish a continuous supply of timber*

for the use and necessities of citizens of the United States; * * * §§ 16 U.S.C. § 475 (emphasis added).

The legislative debates surrounding the Organic Administration Act of 1897 and its predecessor bills demonstrate that Congress intended national forests to be reserved for only two purposes—"[t]o conserve the water flows, and to furnish a continuous supply of timber for the people."[14] 30 Cong.Rec. 967 (1897) (Cong. McRae). See United States v. Grimaud, 220 U.S. 506, 515 (1911). National forests were not to be reserved for aesthetic, environmental, recreational, or wildlife-preservation purposes.

> "The objects for which the forest reservations should be made are the protection of the forest growth against destruction by fire and ax, and preservation of forest conditions upon which water conditions and water flow are dependent. The purpose, therefore, of this bill is to maintain favorable forest conditions, without excluding the use of these reservations for other purposes. They are not parks set aside for nonuse, but have been established for economic reasons." 30 Cong.Rec. 966 (1897) (Cong. McRae).

Administrative regulations at the turn of the century confirmed that national forests were to be reserved for only these two limited purposes.

Any doubt as to the relatively narrow purposes for which national forests were to be reserved is removed by comparing the broader language Congress used to authorize the establishment of national parks. In 1916, Congress created the National Park Service and provided that the

> "fundamental purpose of the said parks, monuments, and reservations ... is to conserve the scenery and the natural and historic objects and the wild life therein and to provide for the enjoyment of the same ... unimpaired for the enjoyment of future generations." 16 U.S.C. § 1.

* * *

National park legislation is not the only instructive comparison. In the Act of Mar. 10, 1934, 16 U.S.C. § 694, Congress authorized the establishment within individual national forests of fish and game sanctuaries, *but*

---

14. The Government notes that the Act forbids the establishment of national forests except *"to improve and protect the forest within the boundaries,* or for the purpose of securing favorable conditions of water flows, and to furnish a continuous supply of timber," and argues from this wording that "improvement" and "protection" of the forests form a third and separate purpose of the national forest system. A close examination of the language of the Act, however, reveals that Congress only intended national forests to be established for two purposes. Forests would be created only "to improve and protect the forest within the boundaries," or, *in other words,* "for the purpose of securing favorable conditions of water flows, and to furnish a continuous supply of timber."

This reading of the Act is confirmed by its legislative history. Nothing in the legislative history suggests that Congress intended national forests to be established for three purposes, one of which would be extremely broad. Indeed, it is inconceivable that a Congress which was primarily concerned with limiting the President's power to reserve the forest lands of the West would provide for the creation of forests merely "to improve and protect the forest within the boundaries"; forests would be reserved for their improvement and protection, but only to serve the purposes of timber protection and favorable water supply. * * *

only with the consent of the state legislatures. * * * If, as the dissent contends, Congress in the Organic Administration Act of 1897 authorized the reservation of forests to "improve and protect" fish and wildlife, the 1934 Act would have been unnecessary. Nor is the dissent's position consistent with Congress' concern in 1934 that fish and wildlife preserves only be created "with the approval of the State legislatures."

As the dissent notes, in creating what would ultimately become Yosemite National Park, Congress in 1890 explicitly instructed the Secretary of the Interior to provide against the wanton destruction of fish and game inside the forest and against their taking "for the purposes of merchandise or profit." * * * By comparison, Congress in the 1897 Organic Act expressed no concern for the preservation of fish and wildlife within national forests generally. * * *

Not only is the Government's claim that Congress intended to reserve water for recreation and wildlife preservation inconsistent with Congress' failure to recognize these goals as purposes of the national forests, it would defeat the very purpose for which Congress did create the national forest system. * * * The water that would be "insured" by preservation of the forest was to "be used for domestic, mining, milling, or irrigation purposes, under the laws of the State wherein such national forests are situated, or under the laws of the United States and the rules and regulations established thereunder." Organic Administration Act of 1897, 16 U.S.C. § 481. As this provision and its legislative history evidence, Congress authorized the national forest system principally as a means of enhancing the quantity of water that would be available to the settlers of the arid West. The Government, however, would have us now believe that Congress intended to partially defeat this goal by reserving significant amounts of water for purposes quite inconsistent with this goal.

In 1960, Congress passed the Multiple–Use Sustained–Yield Act of 1960, 16 U.S.C. § 528 et seq., which provides:

> "It is the policy of Congress that the national forests are established and shall be administered for outdoor recreation, range, timber, watershed, and wildlife and fish purposes. The purposes of sections 528 to 531 of this title are declared to be supplemental to, but not in derogation of, the purposes for which the national forests were established as set forth in the [Organic Administration Act of 1897.]"

The Supreme Court of New Mexico concluded that this Act did not give rise to any reserved rights not previously authorized in the Organic Administration Act of 1897. * * * While we conclude that the Multiple–Use Sustained–Yield Act of 1960 was intended to broaden the purposes for which national forests had previously been administered, we agree that Congress did not intend to thereby expand the reserved rights of the United States.[21]

* * *

21. The United States does not argue that the Multiple–Use Sustained–Yield Act of 1960 reserved additional water for use on the national forests. Instead, the Government argues that the Act confirms that Congress *always* foresaw broad purposes for the na-

As discussed earlier, the "reserved rights doctrine" is a doctrine built on implication and is an exception to Congress' explicit deference to state water law in other areas. Without legislative history to the contrary, we are led to conclude that Congress did not intend in enacting the Multiple–Use Sustained–Yield Act of 1960 to reserve water for the *secondary* purposes there established.[22] A reservation of additional water could mean a substantial loss in the amount of water available for irrigation and domestic use, thereby defeating Congress' principal purpose of securing favorable conditions of water flow. Congress intended the national forests to be administered for broader purposes after 1960 but there is no indication that it believed the new purposes to be so crucial as to require a reservation of additional water. By reaffirming the primacy of a favorable water flow, it indicated the opposite intent.

What we have said also answers the Government's contention that Congress intended to reserve water from the Rio Mimbres for stockwatering purposes. The United States issues permits to private cattle owners to graze their stock on the Gila National Forest and provides for stockwatering at various locations along the Rio Mimbres. The United States contends that, since Congress clearly foresaw stockwatering on national forests, reserved rights must be recognized for this purpose. The New Mexico courts disagreed and held that any stockwatering rights must be allocated under state law to individual stockwaterers. We agree.

While Congress intended the national forests to be put to a variety of uses, including stockwatering, not inconsistent with the two principal purposes of the forests, stockwatering was not itself a direct purpose of reserving the land.[23] * * *

tional forests and authorized the Secretary of the Interior as early as 1897 to reserve water for recreational, aesthetic, and wildlife-preservation uses. As the legislative history of the 1960 Act, demonstrates, however, Congress believed that the 1897 Organic Administration Act only authorized the creation of national forests for two purposes—timber preservation and enhancement of water supply—and intended, through the 1960 Act, to *expand* the purposes for which the national forests should be administered.

Even if the 1960 Act expanded the reserved water rights of the United States, of course, the rights would be subordinate to any appropriation of water under state law dating to before 1960.

22. We intimate no view as to whether Congress, in the 1960 Act, authorized the subsequent reservation of national forests out of public lands to which a broader doctrine of reserved water rights might apply.

23. As discussed earlier, the national forests were not to be "set aside for nonuse," 30 Cong.Rec. 966 (1897) (Cong.

McRae), but instead to be opened up for any economic use not inconsistent with the forests' primary purposes. Ibid. One use that Congress foresaw was "pasturage." Ibid. See also id., at 1006 (Cong. Ellis); id., at 1011 (Cong. De Vries). As this Court has previously recognized, however, grazing was merely one use to which the national forests could possibly be put and would not be permitted where it might interfere with the specific purposes of the national forests including the securing of favorable conditions of water flow. Under the 1891 and 1897 forest Acts, "any use of the reservation for grazing or other lawful purpose was required to be subject to the rules and regulations established by the Secretary of Agriculture. To pasture sheep and cattle on the reservation, at will and without restraint, might interfere seriously with the accomplishment of the purposes for which they were established. But a limited and regulated use for pasturage might not be inconsistent with the object sought to be attained by the statute." United States v. Grimaud, 220 U.S. 506, 515–516

Congress intended that water would be reserved only where necessary to preserve the timber or to secure favorable water flows for private and public uses under state law. This intent is revealed in the purposes for which the national forest system was created and Congress' principled deference to state water law in the Organic Administration Act of 1897 and other legislation. The decision of the Supreme Court of New Mexico is faithful to this congressional intent and is therefore

Affirmed.

■ JUSTICE POWELL, with whom JUSTICE BRENNAN, JUSTICE WHITE, and JUSTICE MARSHALL JOIN, dissenting in part.

I agree with the Court that the implied-reservation doctrine should be applied with sensitivity to its impact upon those who have obtained water rights under state law and to Congress' general policy of deference to state water law. I also agree that the Organic Administration Act of 1897 cannot fairly be read as evidencing an intent to reserve water for recreational or stockwatering purposes in the national forests.[1]

I do not agree, however, that the forests which Congress intended to "improve and protect" are the still, silent, lifeless places envisioned by the Court. In my view, the forests consist of the birds, animals, and fish—the wildlife—that inhabit them, as well as the trees, flowers, shrubs, and grasses. I therefore would hold that the United States is entitled to so much water as is necessary to sustain the wildlife of the forests, as well as the plants. * * *

* * * Although the language of the statute is not artful, a natural reading would attribute to Congress an intent to authorize the establishment of national forests for three purposes, not the two discerned by the Court. The New Mexico Supreme Court gave the statute its natural reading in this case when it wrote:

(1911). See also Light v. United States, 220 U.S. 523 (1911).

1. I express no view as to the effect of the Multiple–Use Sustained–Yield Act of 1960 on the United States' reserved water rights in national forests that were established either before or after that Act's passage. Although the Court purports to hold that passage of the 1960 Act did not have the effect of reserving any additional water in then-existing forests, this portion of its opinion appears to be dicta. As the Court concedes, "The United States does not argue that the Multiple–Use Sustained–Yield Act of 1960 reserved additional water for use on the national forests." Likewise, the State argues only that "[n]o reserved rights for fish or wildlife can be implied in the Gila National Forest *prior to the enactment of the Multiple–Use Sustained–Yield Act of June 12, 1960. . . . .*"(emphasis supplied). Indeed, the State has gone so far as to suggest that passage of the 1960 Act may well have expanded the United States' reserved water rights in the national forests, presumably with a priority date for the additional reserved rights of 1960. Read in context, the New Mexico Supreme Court's statement that the 1960 Act "does not have a retroactive effect nor can it broaden the purposes for which the Gila National Forest was established under the Organic Act of 1897," appears to mean nothing more than that the 1960 Act did not give the United States additional reserved water rights *with a priority date of before 1960*—a proposition with which I think we all would agree. But there never has been a question in this case as to whether the 1960 Act gave rise to additional reserved water rights with a priority date of 1960 or later in the Gila National Forest.

"The Act limits the purposes for which national forests are authorized to: 1) improving and protecting the forest, 2) securing favorable conditions of water flows, and 3) furnishing a continuous supply of timber."

Congress has given the statute the same reading, stating that under the Organic Administration Act of 1897 national forests may be established for "the purposes of improving and protecting the forest or for securing favorable conditions of water flows, and to furnish a continuous supply of timber...."

* * * [The Court] decides that the Act should be read as if it said national forests may "be created only 'to improve and protect the forest within the boundaries,' or, *in other words,* 'for the purpose of securing favorable conditions of water flows, and to furnish a continuous supply of timber.'" (emphasis in original). The Court then concludes that Congress did not mean to "improve and protect" any part of the forest except the usable timber and whatever other flora is necessary to maintain the watershed. This, however, is not what Congress said.

The Court believes that its "reading of the Act is confirmed by its legislative history." The matter is not so clear to me. From early times in English law, the forest has included the creatures that live there. Although the English forest laws themselves were not transplanted to the shores of the new continent, the understanding that the forest includes its wildlife has remained in the American mind. In establishing the first forest reservations, the year before passage of the Organic Act of 1891, Congress exhibited this understanding by directing the Secretary of the Interior to "provide against the wanton destruction of the fish ... and game found within said reservation, and against their capture or destruction, for the purposes of merchandise or profit." Act of Oct. 1, 1890, § 2, 26 Stat. 651.

* * *

One may agree with the Court that Congress did not, by enactment of the Organic Administration Act of 1897, intend to authorize the creation of national forests simply to serve as wildlife preserves. But it does not follow from this that Congress did not consider wildlife to be part of the forest that it wished to "improve and protect" for future generations. It is inconceivable that Congress envisioned the forests it sought to preserve as including only inanimate components such as the timber and flora. Insofar as the Court holds otherwise, the 55th Congress is maligned and the Nation is the poorer, and I dissent.[5]

Contrary to the Court's intimations, I see no inconsistency between holding that the United States impliedly reserved the right to instream

---

5. No doubt it will be said that the waterflow necessary to maintain the watershed including the forest will be sufficient for the wildlife. This well may be true in most national forests and most situations. But the Court's opinion, as I read it, recognizes no reserved authority in the Federal Government to protect wildlife itself as a part of the forest, and therefore if and when the need for increased waterflow for this purpose arises the Federal Government would be powerless to act. Indeed, upstream appropriators could be allowed to divert so much water that survival of forest wildlife—including even the fish and other life in the streams—would be endangered.

flows, and what the Court views as the underlying purposes of the 1897 Act. The national forests can regulate the flow of water—which the Court views as "the very purpose for which Congress did create the national forest system," only for the benefit of appropriators who are downstream from the reservation. The reservation of an instream flow is not a consumptive use; it does not subtract from the amount of water that is available to downstream appropriators. Reservation of an instream flow therefore would be perfectly consistent with the purposes of the 1897 Act as construed by the Court.[6]

I do not dwell on this point, however, for the Court's opinion cannot be read as holding that the United States never reserved instream flows when it set aside national forests under the 1897 Act. The State concedes, quite correctly on the Court's own theory, that even in this case "the United States is not barred from asserting that rights to minimum instream flows might be necessary for erosion control or fire protection on the basis of the recognized purposes of watershed management and the maintenance of timber." Thus, if the United States proves, in this case or others, that the reservation of instream flows is necessary to fulfill the purposes discerned by the Court, I find nothing in the Court's opinion that bars it from asserting this right.

NOTES AND QUESTIONS

1.   Examine the 1897 statute governing forest reservations closely. How does Justice Rehnquist interpret the phrase "improve and protect the forest within the boundaries"? Justice Powell? Does the former lose sight of the forest for the trees, as it were, or did Congress do so in 1897?

2.   In *Cappaert* the water reserved was described as the amount of water necessary to serve the purposes for which the land was reserved. In *New Mexico,* the adjective "primary" is added as a modifier of "purposes." Is this significant?

3.   Note that the Court was unanimous in holding that the 1897 Act did not reserve water for stockwatering and recreational uses, even though both are common uses of the national forests. In the absence of congressional action, what options are open to the Forest Service if it wishes to secure water for wildlife, grazing and recreation? Besides condemnation of water rights obtained under state law, the Forest Service can seek to become a state law appropriator, if unappropriated water is available. That and other strategies are considered further below. Also considered below are the application of *Winters* and *New Mexico* to a variety of other federal reservations, including national parks, wildlife refuges, wild and scenic rivers, and wilderness.

---

6. It is true that reservation of an instream flow might in some circumstances adversely affect appropriators upstream from the forest. There would be no inconsistency with the 1897 Act, however, for that Act manifestly was not intended to benefit upstream appropriators.

4. Does the Gila National Forest have reserved rights dating back to the 1960 Multiple–Use Sustained–Yield Act ("MUSYA")?

5. How does the federal reserved rights doctrine apple to the George Washington National Forest in Virginia, or other federal lands in riparian law jurisdictions? Should the underlying state law matter in determining whether federal water rights are created or what form they might take? The position of the United States is that federal reserved water rights "extend to acquired lands as well as public domain. [F]ederal water rights may be asserted without regard to state law to [satisfy] specific congressional directives or authorizations that override inconsistent state law * * * [or to fulfill] primary purposes for the management of federal lands * * * that would be frustrated by the application of state law." Federal "Non–Reserved" Water Rights, 6 Op. Off. Legal Counsel 328 (1982).

The application of the *Winters* doctrine in eastern riparian jurisdictions has not been developed in any reported cases (nor, for that matter, has any case we know of squarely addressed the interface between the doctrine and riparian rights recognized in California). Indeed, an informal survey in the Department of the Interior did not uncover a single instance in which the National Park Service has ever asserted a federal reserved water right in the East. Most federal lands now found in riparian jurisdictions were acquired for particular purposes; for example, national forests, parks, or wildlife refuges. A number of segments of eastern rivers have been designated under the federal Wild & Scenic Rivers Act.

In pure riparian jurisdictions, federal lands adjoining streams would presumably be entitled to the same water rights under state law as any riparian land. But might federal reserved water rights be superior to state law riparian rights in certain situations? Conceptually, there are some similarities between riparian rights and federal reserved rights. Neither is dependent upon putting water to actual use; both are related to land ownership. But there are some differences. Federal reserved water rights come into being at some fixed date (when land is reserved or withdrawn for particular purposes), and can be quantified on the basis of the amount of water necessary to carry out those purposes. Riparian rights are more indefinite and inchoate in quantity, being dependent upon reasonableness of uses along the stream at any one point in time. Academic commentary on the subject is limited.

3. RESERVED WATER RIGHTS BY FEDERAL LAND CATEGORY

This subsection briefly explores some kinds of reserved rights claims connected with non-Indian federal lands and programs, building on the teachings of Arizona v. California, Cappaert v. United States, and United States v. New Mexico. As you might suspect, the array of management categories and purposes of federal reservations are quite broad. In the wake of *New Mexico*, the Solicitor of the Department of the Interior issued a comprehensive Opinion that addressed the reserved rights and other water rights claims of the Interior Department's land managing agencies. 86 Interior Dec. 553 (1979). Some of the material in this note is drawn from that Opinion. For a useful collection of western state perspectives on the

scope and nature of non-Indian federal reserved rights claims, both generally and through a state-by-state survey, see D. Craig Bell and James Alder,
Federal Non–Indian Claims To Water (Western States Water Council,
1999). Military reservations generally fall within the principles of *Winters*,
but there is little reported litigation and commentary on their claims.

a. NATIONAL FORESTS

As Justice Rehnquist suggested at the beginning of his opinion in *New
Mexico*, the most hotly contested federal non-Indian reserved rights have
been in the national forests. This is probably because the national forest
system is extensive (comprising nearly two hundred million acres of land)
and dominates the headwaters of most important western rivers. *New
Mexico* settled some basic questions about national forest reserved water
rights, but left a number of other questions open.

For example, what is the precise holding of *New Mexico* regarding the
effect of the Multiple–Use Sustained–Yield Act of 1960 ("MUSYA")? Footnote 21 of the Court's opinion reveals that the United States did not argue
that MUSYA created a 1960 reservation of water, but rather that it simply
confirmed the 1897 Organic Act's reservation of water for broad purposes.
Compare the first footnote in Powell's dissent. Can the United States still
argue for reserved rights based on MUSYA alone? For a negative answer,
see United States v. City and County of Denver, 656 P.2d 1, 24–27
(Colo.1982); United States v. City of Challis, 988 P.2d 1199 (Idaho 1999).

Many of the national parks were created by Congress in areas that had
earlier been reserved from the public domain as national forests. If a
national forest had been created in 1898, and the area had been designated
a national park in 1930, what is the scope and priority date of the park's
water right? *See* United States v. City and County of Denver, 656 P.2d 1,
30 (Colo.1982) (holding that the park water right has the date of the forest
reservation "to the extent that the purposes of the national forests and
national parks overlap," but that "[r]eservation of water for other purposes
* * * will have a priority date from the time the national park was
established").

Does the Forest Service have federal reserved rights for water flows to
maintain stream channels and associated riparian areas? Note that securing "favorable conditions of water flows" was one of the two 1897 Organic
Act purposes *New Mexico* had recognized for the national forest system.
The Forest Service has argued that

> recent advances in the science of "fluvial geomorphology" have shown
> that strong, recurring instream water flows are necessary to maintain
> efficient stream channels and to secure favorable conditions of water
> flows, and that diversions of water within the national forests by
> private appropriators reduce stream flows and threaten the equilibri-
> um that preserves natural stream channels.

United States v. Jesse, 744 P.2d 491, 498 (Colo.1987) (paraphrasing the
brief for the United States). In *Jesse*, the Colorado Supreme Court remanded for a factual trial on such claims. After a lengthy hearing involving

many expert witnesses and more than a thousand exhibits, the Colorado trial court ruled that the Forest Service had failed to show that the water rights claimed were necessary to secure favorable water flows. The Forest Service did not appeal, but sometimes makes similar claims elsewhere.

Is the existence or scope of the reserved water right here determined by what modern science shows about the need for scouring flows to maintain healthy river channels, improve the reliability of flows and reduce downstream flooding? Or is it determined by what Congress intended when it authorized the reservation of national forests in part to maintain "favorable conditions of water flows"?

What would be the effect on water management if the Forest Service were to be awarded reserved water rights for channel maintenance? Would it have any adverse effects on downstream junior appropriators? Upstream appropriators? Inholders in the national forests, or those who divert from streams on the national forests?

b. NATIONAL PARKS

Recall that the Supreme Court's opinion in United States v. New Mexico in 1978 compared and contrasted the 1897 Organic Act applying to the national forest system with the counterpart 1916 Organic Act applying to the national park system. What water does the 1916 Act implicitly reserve, for what purposes? Instream flows for ecosystem maintenance? Water to sustain natural features like geysers in Yellowstone or Yosemite Falls? What about water for national park employees' residences? Water for campgrounds or service stations for park visitors? Water to grow hay for feeding the horses and mules maintained by national park concessioners?

National Park water rights tend not to be so controversial because (1) parks are popular cultural icons; (2) parks are often important contributors to local economies; (3) most park water uses are either nonconsumptive (instream flows for environmental health) or do not consume much (campgrounds, hotels); and (4) many parks are in headwaters or mountainous areas and thus preserve flows for uses downstream.

Cappaert-style concerns continue to crop up in Nevada, this time from proposals to pump groundwater in rural areas to meet burgeoning population growth. Las Vegas's water district, the Southern Nevada Water Authority, is planning to pump and export groundwater from valleys a couple of hundred miles north and east of the City. In the spring of 2006, the U.S. Geological Survey reported that certain creeks in Great Basin National Park were "likely susceptible" to the effects of large-scale groundwater withdrawals east of the Park. A month later the U.S. Department of Interior dropped its protest to the project, after the Authority agreed to permit conditions by which it would pay for drilling monitoring wells (at locations selected by Interior). The Authority agreed to reduce (or even eliminate) groundwater withdrawals or shift them to other locations if the monitoring wells indicate a potentially damaging drop in the water table. Local ranchers and conservationists continued to fight the project, raising the specter of another Owens Valley (a rural valley in eastern California that was dried up by diversions to Los Angeles in the early 20th century). Further to the south, the National Park Service filed objections in 2006 to a proposal for pumping 5000 acre-feet of groundwater to supply a proposed development of up to 85,000 homes (and 16 golf courses) fifty miles north of Las Vegas. The Service fears possible impacts on its federal reserved water rights in the Lake Mead National Recreation Area some forty miles away.

c. NATIONAL WILDLIFE REFUGES

The national wildlife refuge system consists of not only refuges but wildlife ranges, game ranges, wildlife management areas, and waterfowl production areas managed by the Fish & Wildlife Service. Arizona v. California recognized reserved water rights for wildlife refuges along the lower Colorado River. Many of these areas were originally established by individual Presidential or Secretarial Orders.

The Deer Flat National Wildlife Refuge was created by Executive Order in 1937 encompassing some 94 islands along 110 miles of the Snake River. An important component of the Pacific Flyway, more than 100 species of land and water birds, migratory and non-migratory, make use of the islands. The Order withdrew "all islands [in the designated area] as a refuge and breeding ground for migratory birds and other wildlife." Otherwise the Order, which also speaks of the islands as a "sanctuary for migratory birds," is silent on water. Does the Order reserve enough water, expressly or impliedly, in order to keep the islands as islands and thus help forestall predation against birds by coyotes and other predators? United States v. Idaho, 23 P.3d 117, 126 (Idaho 2001), answered the question in the negative, finding that "an expectation that the islands would remain surrounded by water * * * does not equate to an intent to reserve a federal water right to accomplish that purpose." The court went on to find it "inconceivable that President Roosevelt in 1937, in the context of the dust bowl years, intended to give preference to waterfowl * * * over people." Why would a nonconsumptive use of water for instream flows necessarily prefer birds over people? The United States did not seek review in the United States Supreme Court.

In the National Wildlife Refuge System Improvement Act of 1997, Congress provided that, "[i]n administering the System, the Secretary shall * * * acquire, under State law, water rights that are needed for refuge purposes." 16 U.S.C. § 668dd(a)(4)(G). The same section goes on to provide that nothing in the Act shall "create a reserved water right, express or implied, in the United States for any purpose," nor shall it "affect any water right in existence on October 9, 1997 [the date of enactment]." 16 U.S.C. § 668dd(n). Are reserved rights created prior to enactment still valid? Is that 1997 action by Congress relevant to the issue in the Deer Flat case? (The Idaho Supreme Court did not refer to it.) Which way does it cut? What rights would a refuge created by executive order in 1999 have if the purpose of the refuge is to "preserve the flora and fauna of the White River floodplain"?

d. WILDERNESS AREAS

Like most other statutes undergirding federal land reservations, the Wilderness Act of 1964 says very little about water,[*] other than a general disclaimer (found in other federal statutes as well) that nothing in it "shall constitute an express or implied claim or denial on the part of the Federal Government as to exemption from State water laws." 16 U.S.C. § 1133(d)(6).

The extent to which designation of wilderness areas reserves water has been embroiled in sometimes bitter controversy for decades. In 1979, the Solicitor of the Department of the Interior concluded that designation of wilderness areas reserves water rights necessary to carry out the preservation-oriented purposes of the Act, including science, education, inspiration and recreation. 86 Interior Dec. at 609–10. After President Reagan took office in 1981, the Forest Service failed to file claims for water rights in twenty-four national forest wilderness areas in an ongoing Colorado adjudication. This led to protracted but ultimately inconclusive litigation brought by environmentalists. See Sierra Club v. Block, 622 F.Supp. 842, 850–51, 862 (D.Colo.1985), 661 F.Supp. 1490 (D.Colo.1987), *vacated sub nom.* Sierra Club v. Yeutter, 911 F.2d 1405 (10th Cir.1990). In the midst of the litigation, a new Interior Solicitor issued a new opinion, approved by the Justice Department, which reversed the 1979 Opinion. *See* 96 Interior Dec. 211 (1988). That did not end things. Early in the Clinton Administration, the Attorney General, on advice of the Solicitor and the General Counsel of Agriculture (where the Forest Service is housed), vacated both the 1989 Opinion and the wilderness portion of the 1979 Opinion.

The reasons for all this fuss are not immediately apparent. Wilderness areas by definition are to be left alone for the forces of nature to operate in them unimpaired. Any water rights they have are to maintain natural flows, i.e., involve no artificial diversion or consumption. These areas are, moreover, usually at high altitudes, at or near the tops of watersheds, where instream flows pose no threat to other, more conventional uses. Finally, because the Wilderness Act did not become law until 1964, and most wilderness areas were designated by Congress even later, wilderness water rights have a relatively late priority date. The controversy seems more about principle than anything else.

However, sometimes wilderness water rights do have practical consequences. In Idaho, one wilderness area subject to litigation was not at the top of the watershed. In fact, there were some small communities upstream of the wilderness that had appropriated water from the streams. If the wilderness designation reserved all the water, it would seem to rule out any even modest expansions of the upstream water rights to accommodate a growing population. Does preserving an area in its natural condition (the purpose of wilderness designation) mean preserving all the water, or might

---

[*] It contains a provision authorizing the President to approve water projects in wilderness areas—areas which are otherwise off limits to development, including roads or other obvious imprints of human activity. See 16 U.S.C. § 1133(d)(4). The legislative history suggests this was to allow "minor" projects, but the provision has never been used even for that purpose.

some flexibility be found to allow some new upstream appropriations? Might the matter be handled by interpreting the upstream towns' pre-existing appropriations as in effect appropriating water for future population growth? If so, then the subsequent federal wilderness designation downstream might be interpreted as reserving all the water other than what was already appropriated for future use.

In the most definitive judicial ruling to date, the Idaho Supreme Court in 1999 held, three to two, that wilderness designation did not reserve unappropriated water within wilderness areas. Potlatch Corp. v. United States, 12 P.3d 1260 (2000). Like practically everything else connected with this issue, this decision had a tangled and contentious history. The same court had earlier held (also by a three-to-two vote) the opposite—that water was reserved by wilderness designation. This led to a spirited, and ultimately successful, electoral campaign to throw the author of that opinion off the bench, in a campaign in which a central issue was her opinion in that case. After she was defeated, but before she left the bench, another member of the court, the Chief Justice, switched her vote in the matter and the court reversed its decision. It was not the first time a state Supreme Court Justice had lost reelection over a water rights matter. See Hon. Gregory J. Hobbs, Jr., *State Water Politics Versus an Independent Judiciary: The Colorado and Idaho Experiences*, 5 U. DENVER WATER L.REV. 122 (2001).

e.   WILD & SCENIC RIVERS

The Wild and Scenic Rivers Act contains an express, though negatively phrased, assertion of federal reserved water rights:

> *Designation* of any stream or portion thereof as a national wild, scenic or recreational river area *shall* not *be construed as a reservation of the waters of such streams for purposes* other than those specified in this chapter, or *in quantities* greater than *necessary to accomplish these purposes.*

16 U.S.C. § 1284(c) (emphasis added). The Act's announced policy was to preserve "certain selected rivers" which "possess outstandingly remarkable scenic, recreational, geologic, fish and wildlife, historic, cultural, or other similar values" in their "free-flowing condition" and to protect the rivers "and their immediate environments" for the "benefit and enjoyment of present and future generations." 16 U.S.C. § 1271.

How much water is reserved by this Act? All the natural flows in the designated rivers? If something less than all the flows, how much less? *See* Potlatch Corp. v. United States, 12 P.3d 1256 (Idaho 2000) (rejecting the argument of forest products and mining companies that the Act does not reserve water, the court finding it would be "anomalous" to conclude that an act "expressly created to preserve free-flowing rivers failed to provide for the reservation of water in the rivers"). Note that rivers may be protected under the Wild and Scenic Rivers Act even if the federal government does not own any of the land within the designation. Compare the Supreme Court's summary description, in its unanimous decision in *Capp-

aert, that the United States may reserve "appurtenant water" when withdraws land from the public domain and reserves it for a federal purpose. Is the Wild & Scenic Act a case of Congress reserving "non-appurtenant" water?

f. BUREAU OF LAND MANAGEMENT ("BLM") PUBLIC LANDS

The BLM-managed federal lands are, with some exceptions, the residual public domain left after disposition into non-federal ownership, or after reservation for specific purposes and transfer for management by other federal agencies like the Forest Service, Park Service, and Fish & Wildlife Service. For that reason, they are generally regarded as having no federally reserved water rights. In 1976, Congress for the first time gave BLM an organic management statute, the Federal Land Policy and Management Act ("FLPMA"), 43 U.S.C. §§ 1701 et seq. While this Act set forth broad purposes for which these lands were to be managed, it did not in and of itself reserve water. Sierra Club v. Watt, 659 F.2d 203, 206 (D.C.Cir.1981). The court there expressed "substantial agreement" with the government's argument in its brief:

> Under the controlling decisions of the Supreme Court, the distinction between reservation[s] and unreserved public lands is fundamental. Reserved rights attach only to the former, and then only when water is necessary to fulfill the primary purpose of the reservation. No water is reserved for uses that are merely permissive upon a reservation. *A fortiori*, then, no reserved rights arise under [FLPMA], for no reservation of land is effected.

Id. The court also focused on one of FLPMA's savings clauses (§ 701(g)), which reads that nothing in FLPMA "shall be construed as * * * *expanding* or diminishing *Federal* or State jurisdiction, responsibility, interests, or rights in water resources development or control * * *.*" 43 U.S.C. § 1701 (note) (emphasis added). The court interpreted the italicized provisions as meaning that no federal water rights were reserved in the statute.

FLPMA essentially calls for BLM public lands to be managed for the same purposes as the national forests: multiple uses including mining, grazing, recreation, timber, and watershed protection, among others. Does it make sense that BLM has no reserved rights for these uses, but the Forest Service does for some of them? Does Congress have to act consistently in directing management of federal lands and associated water?*

BLM has one recognized category of reserved rights, growing out of a 1926 Executive Order (commonly called Public Water Reserve No. 107) that

---

* The inconsistency was dramatized in a 1988 statute approving a Forest Service–BLM exchange of management jurisdiction over nearly 700,000 acres of land in Nevada. BLM picked up 23,000 acres of former national forest land, and lost about 662,000 acres to the Forest Service. See Pub. L. 100–550, 102 Stat. 2749 (1988). On the new national forest land, Congress "expressly reserve[d] the min- imum quantity of water necessary to achieve the primary purposes" for which national forests were established, with a priority date as of the date of transfer. On the new BLM land, Congress "expressly relinquishe[d] all Federal reserved water rights created by the initial withdrawal from the public domain * * *." Id. § 8.

reserved lands around every "spring or waterhole" on public lands "for public use." 43 U.S.C. § 300 (repealed prospectively by FLPMA, leaving existing withdrawals intact). The idea behind the Executive Order was to prevent private monopolization of scarce water sources on the arid western public lands. There has been some debate about how broad "public use" ought to be defined—for example, whether it includes fish propagation or fire control as well as stockwatering and human consumption. *See, e.g.*, In re Snake River Basin Adjudication, 959 P.2d 449 (Idaho 1998).

4. MODERN CONGRESSIONAL AND EXECUTIVE PRACTICE IN FEDERAL LAND RESERVATIONS

Recall that United States v. New Mexico justified giving reserved rights claims careful scrutiny because they were for the most part implied from congressional enactments: "Where Congress has expressly addressed the question of whether federal entities must abide by state water law, it has almost invariably deferred to the state law." 438 U.S. at 696.

This is not completely accurate. Congress expressly addresses water rights in various federal resource management statutes. Sometimes it has, to be sure, expressly deferred to state water law. But it also has crafted disclaimers, such as the one used in the Wilderness Act of 1964 and several other statutes: "Nothing in this [Act] shall constitute an express or implied claim or denial on the part of the Federal Government as to exemption from State water laws." 16 U.S.C. § 1133(d)(6). What does this language mean? It asserts no claim of exemption, yet also asserts no denial of a claim of exemption. Is it calculated, as Yogi Berra supposedly said, to "leave the status quo right where it is"—a status quo that includes the implied reservation of water doctrine?

Since United States v. New Mexico was decided, an even more variegated picture has emerged. Responding to the criticism that it ought to specifically address water in making changes to the statutory management direction for particular public lands and resources, Congress has in the last two decades often done just that. The result has not, however, been "almost invariabl[e]" deference to state water law. Consider a 1987 statute establishing a national monument, national conservation area, and wilderness on federal lands in New Mexico:

> Congress expressly reserves to the United States the minimum amount of water required to carry out the purposes [of this Act]. * * * Nothing in this section shall be construed as establishing a precedent with regard to future designations, nor shall it affect the interpretation of any other Act or any designation made pursuant thereto.

101 Stat. 1539, 1549. How should a court go about determining how much water is reserved by this statute? Why do you suppose Congress included the second sentence? Was it to make sure that no negative inference is drawn from the express reservation of water here when construing whether water is implicitly reserved in another statute that is silent on water?

Consider this 1988 statute designating wilderness areas in national park units in the State of Washington:

Subject to valid existing rights, within the areas designated as wilderness by this Act, Congress hereby expressly reserves such water rights as necessary, for the purposes for which such areas are so designated. The priority date of such rights shall be the date of enactment of this Act.

102 Stat. 3961, 3968. How much water is reserved? Is groundwater as well as surface water reserved? Because this statute does not use the "minimum amount necessary" language found in the New Mexico statute of a year earlier (quoted in the preceding paragraph), does this statute reserve more than the minimum? Does the absence of "no precedent" language (such as was included in the New Mexico statute) allow a court to infer that silence in similar statutes does *not* imply a reservation of water? *See also* 16 U.S.C. § 410aaa–76 (designation of California desert areas as wilderness reserved "a quantity of water sufficient to fulfill the purposes" of wilderness designation, and included "no precedent" language). For other examples, see John Leshy, *Water Rights for New Federal Land Conservation Programs: A Turn-of-the-Century Evaluation*, 4 Water L.Rev. 271, 277 (2001).

Congress has not always reserved water in modern statutes, but when it has not, it has often gone to some lengths to explain why it isn't. Consider the law creating the Hagerman Fossil Beds National Monument in Idaho in 1988 (102 Stat. 4571, 4576, § 304):

Congress finds that there are unique circumstances with respect to the water or water-related resources within the Monument designated by this title. The Congress recognizes that there is little or no water or water-related resources that require the protection of a federal reserve [sic] water right. Nothing in this title, nor any action taken pursuant thereto, shall constitute either an expressed or implied reservation of water or water right for any purpose.

Congress has not always in recent years been able to fashion agreement on specific language that addresses water (other than a disclaimer) in legislating on federal land management issues. Where agreement cannot be reached, enactment of legislation may be delayed even if there is consensus on other parts of it. This was the case in Colorado, where for about a decade Congress could not resolve how to address water in designating new wilderness areas in the State, despite broad agreement over the other features. So long as litigation raged inconclusively over whether already designated wilderness areas in Colorado carried with them reserved water rights, silence or a disclaimer was not an acceptable option to either wilderness advocates or water developers. The stalemate was finally broken with an agreement enacted into law in the Colorado Wilderness Act of 1993. The compromise expressly rejected the reservation of water in the newly designated areas, but provided an alternative mechanism to protect the water at stake—control of land access to those areas by the federal land managers. 107 Stat. 756, 762–63. Control of water through control of access to federal lands is discussed at the end of this subchapter.

The Executive Branch has also caught the fever of expressly addressing water in new land reservations. All of President Carter's seventeen Alaska national monuments (covering fifty-six million acres of federal land) expressly reserved water. *See, e.g.*, 43 Fed. Reg. 57,035, 57,036 (Dec. 5, 1978) (Denali National Monument) ("There is also reserved all water necessary to the proper care and management of those objects protected by this monument and for the proper administration of the monument in accordance with applicable laws"). Almost all of President Clinton's nearly two dozen national monument proclamations addressed water, though not in a uniform way. Clinton's 1996 Proclamation creating the nearly two million acre Grand Staircase–Escalante National Monument in southern Utah (the largest in the lower 48 states) says this about water:

> This proclamation does not reserve water as a matter of Federal law. I direct the Secretary to address in the management plan [for the new monument that the proclamation directed be prepared within three years] the extent to which water is necessary for the proper care and management of * * * this monument and the extent to which further action may be necessary pursuant to Federal or State law to assure the availability of water.

Proc. No. 6920, 61 Fed. Reg. 50223 (1996). What result if the proclamation—which carefully describes the geologic, archeological, and biological "objects of historic or scientific interest" that qualified the area for safeguarding under the Antiquities Act—had been silent on water?

While there is no uniformity in the results, express reservations of water are becoming common. In effect, water is being considered along with boundaries, management, and other policies as part of the political process. In many situations, the actual, on-the-ground impact of reservations on other water users may be minimal. There are several reasons for this: The priority date for the reservation is recent and junior to other established uses. Second, most federal reserved water rights involve so-called "in situ" or instream uses of water. Being non-consumptive, such uses do not foreclose, and indeed protect, opportunities for diversion and consumptive uses of water downstream. Third, while the quantity of reserved water for such purposes as wilderness would seem to be very great—possibly the entire flow of water in the streams—the real impact on existing uses is usually small or nonexistent. Most wilderness areas and many other federal land reservations are at high elevations in unpopulated areas, and there are usually few practicable future diversion opportunities upstream to be restricted. Admittedly, some federal reservations may pose more serious problems. For example, many wetlands providing bird habitat were established relatively early in the 20th century for the primary purpose of wildlife protection, and they often are located in low-lying areas below irrigated farmland using water from creeks feeding into the refuges.

5. ADJUDICATING FEDERAL WATER RIGHTS: THE MCCARRAN AMENDMENT, STATE WATER ADJUDICATIONS AND RELATED ISSUES

Many federal reserved water rights have not yet been formally claimed or adjudicated. Often federal reserved water is being put to use, but there has been no need or occasion to adjudicate or otherwise officially establish the right. For example, the United States is often using instream flows for various purposes, but there are no competing claims for such flows, and/or no adjudication has ever required such claims to be made. Many federal reservations (such as of some national parks and many national forests) include the headwaters of watersheds, where federally reserved instream flows have only positive effects on downstream diversions (by preserving the water flows). Many other federally reserved uses (for campgrounds, for example) are for relatively small amounts of water that do not threaten uses under state law. Only when federal uses are threatened by various developments (such as by Cappaert's pumping) does the United States usually take steps to protect them.

Federal reserved rights claims can, however, put a cloud on state water management and administration. Some state law appropriations involve storage or diversions on or above federal reservations, such as those on national forest lands in the Colorado Rockies that feed the growth of crops and people along Colorado's Front Range.

The so-called McCarran Amendment, 43 U.S.C. § 666(a), enacted in 1952 as a rider on a Department of Justice appropriation act, provides a limited waiver of sovereign immunity by the United States in water rights litigation in state courts:

> Consent is given to join the United States as a defendant in any suit (1) for the adjudication of rights to the use of water of a river system or other source, or (2) for the administration of such rights, where it appears that the United States is the owner of or is in the process of acquiring water rights by appropriation under State law, by purchase, by exchange, or otherwise, and the United States is a necessary party to such suit. * * *

These deceptively simple words have provoked several U.S. Supreme Court decisions. In United States v. District Court In and For Eagle County, 401 U.S. 520 (1971), the Court held that the "or otherwise" language meant that federal reserved rights are subject to adjudication in state courts. The McCarran Amendment does not, however, divest the federal courts of federal question jurisdiction over federal water rights claims; thus, the state and federal courts have concurrent jurisdiction over these claims. Federal courts can still entertain suits involving federal water rights. *See, e.g.,* United States v. Alpine Land & Reservoir Co., 174 F.3d 1007 (9th Cir.1999) (federal court properly enjoined, at the request of the Nevada State Engineer, a state court proceeding initiated by a county seeking to overturn the State Engineer's decision on a water rights transfer involving the federal Fish & Wildlife Service, because under the applicable decree the federal district court exercises appellate jurisdiction over decisions of the State Engineer involving federally decreed water rights).

Nevertheless, the Supreme Court has made it clear in numerous decisions that, other factors being roughly equal, state court jurisdiction is preferred. The Court has explained that state courts may be better equipped than the federal courts to exercise jurisdiction over all water rights, state and federal. *See, e.g.,* Colorado River Water Conservation Dist. v. United States, 424 U.S. 800 (1976); Arizona v. San Carlos Apache Tribe of Arizona, 463 U.S. 545 (1983). In the one victory the federal government has had in recent decades under the McCarran Amendment, the Court ruled that the waiver of federal sovereign immunity is not broad enough to subject the United States to pay filing fees for its claims. United States v. Idaho, 508 U.S. 1 (1993).

The Amendment has been interpreted to extend only to *general* stream adjudications; that is, only to comprehensive proceedings in which the state joins all potential water rights claimants in a watershed, and not to actions that might be filed against the United States by individual water users. The central idea behind the provision is that the U.S. will not be an obstacle to a State's desire to adjudicate comprehensively all the water rights in a particular stream or watershed. Further, because the McCarran Amendment waives sovereign immunity only in a "suit," it is generally understood not to allow states to join the United States in state *administrative* proceedings concerning water rights, even ones that adjudicate rights and are subject to judicial review.

Nevertheless, the line between a general adjudication and one that singles out the federal claims can be blurry, as is the line between judicial proceedings and administrative proceedings. For example, the Ninth Circuit rejected a vigorous challenge by the United States that the Oregon general stream adjudication system was neither comprehensive nor judicial enough to meet McCarran's terms. Under that system, the Oregon state water rights agency would actually be conducting the litigation under minimal judicial supervision. Moreover, it would be adjudicating primarily federal water rights, because under the Oregon stream adjudication statute, all other water users merely had to register their water rights, which the court would accept at face value, unless successfully challenged by the United States. Finally, hydrologically related groundwater was not included in the adjudication. The court brushed aside the federal objections, essentially reading the McCarran Amendment as creating a strong presumption in favor of state court adjudications, and reasoning that, because the features of the Oregon system to which the U.S. objected were all in place when Congress adopted the Amendment in 1952, Congress must have contemplated that the Oregon system met its terms. See United States v. Oregon, 44 F.3d 758 (9th Cir.1994). Mindful of its dismal track record in the Supreme Court, the United States did not seek certiorari.

How big is a "river system or other source" embraced within the McCarran Amendment? In United States v. District Court for Eagle County, 401 U.S. 520 (1971), the Court firmly rejected the United States' argument that Colorado could not join it under the McCarran Amendment in a proceeding to adjudicate only a tributary of the Colorado River. On the other hand, the Idaho Supreme Court ruled that a McCarran Amendment adjudication in that state had to include the Snake River and all of its tributaries within Idaho, which included almost all the streamflow in the entire state. See In re General Adjudication of Snake River Basin Water System, 764 P.2d 78 (Idaho 1988).

When Does the Executive Branch Have a Duty to File Reserved Rights Claims in Adjudications?

If Congress intended to create reserved rights and the Executive fails to assert them in a general stream adjudication, is a judicial remedy available? The federal Administrative Procedure Act has been interpreted to create a strong presumption of reviewability of agency action, but one of its exceptions involves matters in which "agency action is committed to agency discretion by law." *See* 5 U.S.C. § 702(a)(2). The Supreme Court has said that if the statute under which the agency is acting "is drawn so that a court would have no meaningful standard against which to judge the agency's exercise of discretion," the matter is committed to the agency's discretion and not subject to judicial review. Heckler v. Chaney, 470 U.S. 821, 830 (1985).

Like most other statutes, treaties, or executive orders under which *Winters* claims might be made, the Wilderness Act says nothing about asserting federal reserved water rights. In fighting a Sierra Club challenge to its failure to file water rights claims for wilderness areas in a state court general stream adjudication, the federal government argued, among other things, that its action was unreviewable under Heckler v. Chaney. Although the Tenth Circuit ultimately dismissed the Sierra Club's case as not ripe, Sierra Club v. Yeutter, 911 F.2d 1405 (10th Cir.1990), it seemed to suggest that judicial review was available under certain circumstances because the Wilderness Act

> does provide guidelines the agency must follow: the agency cannot abandon, by action or inaction, the statutory mandate to preserve the wilderness characteristics of the wilderness areas. To the extent the Forest Service's inaction implicates this command of the Wilderness Act, the *Chaney* presumption of unreviewability is rebutted and we may review the agency's action.

Id. at 1414 n.5. The court concluded that judicial intervention was not warranted on the facts before it because the Sierra Club had not drawn a sufficient connection between the failure to file a claim for a federal reserved right for wilderness areas and harm to "wilderness water values." The court elaborated by noting, first, that "federal reserved water rights, as creatures of federal law, are protected from extinguishment under state law by the Supremacy Clause." Second, even if federal reserved water rights lost their early priority date because they were not timely filed under the rules of the Colorado adjudication, there may be no appropriations under state law that would or even could create adverse impacts on wilderness water values that a federal reserved right for wilderness would prevent. The court also acknowledged the Forest Service's argument that "there are either adequate administrative controls in place that will prevent diversions above or within wilderness area or that geographical features render such diversions or projects impractical in areas within or above the wilderness areas." These multiple contingencies underscore "the speculative and hypothetical nature of this issue." The court left open the possibility of revisiting the matter in the future:

> When and if a water development claim that may threaten wilderness water values is filed, and the Forest Service does not assert a federal reserved water right based on the Wilderness Act, and furthermore such failure to assert the reserved water right is irreconcilable with the Forest Service's duty to protect wilderness characteristics, then the

Sierra Club may either intervene in the state water proceeding as appropriate under state law or may seek judicial review of the Forest Service's failure to act in federal court. At that time the record will be more fully developed and the courts can better determine whether the Forest Service's proposed alternatives to the use of wilderness water rights are adequate to reconcile its actions with its obligations under the Act. If the proposed alternatives are not adequate, appropriate corrective orders can be issued.

Id. at 1418–19.

Suppose the federal government does not file a claim for a reserved right, and a new appropriation is approved under state law that allows a major diversion upstream from the federally reserved area, and the federal agency is otherwise powerless to prevent it. If the Sierra Club renews its suit against the federal agency, what "appropriate corrective orders" can the court issue? Does the Tenth Circuit require too much vigilance on the part of friends of federal reserved water rights outside the federal agencies?

Congress has sometimes directly addressed the problem of federal agency reluctance to make reserved water rights claims. A 1990 statute designating wilderness areas in Arizona not only expressly reserved water, but directed the Secretary of the Interior "and all other officers of the United States" to "take steps necessary to protect" the federally reserved water rights, including "filing * * * a claim for the quantification of such rights in any present or future appropriate stream adjudication * * *." 104 Stat. 4469, 4473, § 101(g)(2); *see also* California Desert Protection Act of 1994, 108 Stat. at 4498.

The Black Canyon of the Gunnison River in Colorado was made a national monument in 1933 by lame-duck President Herbert Hoover. In 1978, the Colorado Water Court decreed the United States a federal reserved water right for the monument, priority date 1933, to carry out the monument purposes (which emphasized preservation of scenic and conservation values), but the court postponed quantifying the right. Shortly before the Clinton Administration left office in January 2001, it filed an application for a 300 cfs (cubic feet per second) base flow, and higher peak and shoulder seasonal flows geared to natural runoff. A number of protests were filed. Ultimately the Bush Administration and the State agreed to a decree that gave the national monument a year-round base flow of the lesser of 300 cfs or natural flow, with a priority date of 2003, which could only be enforced by a state agency, the Colorado Water Conservation Board. Conservation interests promptly brought an action in federal court challenging the deal, and they moved for a stay of proceedings in state water court until the federal case is resolved. The water court granted the stay, and the Colorado Supreme Court affirmed. In re Application for Water Rights of the United States, 101 P.3d 1072 (2004). The court held that the McCarran Amendment does not allow state courts to review federal agencies' decision-making as to what kinds of claims to make, and because the federal court is the exclusive forum to hear those claims, the water court acted within its discretion in staying the proceedings. The court noted, among other things, that if the water court were to proceed to quantify the

Black Canyon right on the less protective basis the U.S. was now asking for, "res judicata would bar the United States from later claiming a broader reserved right even if the federal court were to decide that the United States violated federal law when it amended its application" to reduce its claim. Justice Hobbs, joined by Justice Kourlis, dissented, reasoning that the federal court would, in ruling on plaintiffs' claims, have to decide what federal law required in the way of water to carry out the purposes of the Black Canyon reservation. Because the federal court proceeding "transparently involve[d] quantification" of the national monument water right, the dissent argued it was a matter appropriate for state court jurisdiction under the McCarran Amendment, which "prefers deferral of the federal court to the state court, not the other way around."

In 2006 the federal court upheld the conservationists' challenge to the Bush settlement with the state of Colorado. High Country Citizens' Alliance v. Norton, 448 F.Supp.2d 1235 (D. Colo. 2006) found that the settlement (1) violated the National Environmental Policy Act (NEPA) because it was undertaken without analysis of its environmental effects or public participation; (2) was an unlawful delegation to the State of responsibility for performing duties that Congress had placed on the federal executive (among other things, the state officials may not "share the [federal] agency's 'national vision and perspective' "); (3) was an unlawful disposition of federal property without congressional authorization; and (4) violated the federal officials' "nondiscretionary duties to protect the Black Canyon's resources" created by statutes like the National Park Organic Act.

One of the United States' argument in defense of its settlement was that it merely compromised an uncertain claim to water. The court found it uncontroverted that the Monument "requires a greater quantity than" the 2003 settlement would give it. "It is of no consequence that the exact quantity of water the water court will award is unknown because it is evident that the federal Defendants contracted to give up what Congress specifically authorized: a 1933 reserved water right to the quantity of water needed by the canyon." The court underscored that the compromise deprived the Park Service "of ever exercising a right to peak and shoulder flows of the Gunnison River." The court concluded that it was "nonsensical" for the government to enter into an agreement that relinquished "a 1933 priority to the full quantity of water necessary for the preservation of the Black Canyon."

Federal Participation in State Administrative Proceedings

Recall that in *Cappaert*, the National Park Service had appeared before the State Engineer to protest Cappaert's application to change the use of water from its wells. The State Engineer rejected the protest, and the State later sought to dismiss the federal court litigation on res judicata or collateral estoppel grounds, because the United States had failed to appeal the rejection through the state court system. The Court would have none of it:

> [T]he United States was not made a party to the state administrative proceeding; * * * it did not assert any federal water-rights claims, nor did it seek to adjudicate any claims until the hydrologic studies * * * had been completed. * * * The State Water Engineer's decree explicitly stated it was "subject to existing rights."

426 U.S. at 146–47. This leaves open a number of questions. Can a federal official waive the sovereign immunity of the United States in proceedings that do not conform to the McCarran Amendment simply by making a general appearance before a State Engineer? Could the Nevada State Engineer have demanded that the National Park Service become a formal "party" to the proceeding in order to protest the Cappaert application? Could it have required the Park Service to put on proof of its water rights as a precondition to protest? Could the State Engineer have, in the course of deciding whether the Cappaert application would adversely affect the federal water right, determined the scope and quantity of the federal water right? If so, is the federal government bound by that determination unless it appeals through the state court system?

To the extent that a federal appearance before a state agency may bind the United States, would you advise federal agencies *not* to participate in such proceedings? If the federal agencies do not participate, however, state water administrators may not gain notice that their decisions could conflict with federal water rights claims. It is possible that, with notice, the state could avoid the conflict. Does this suggest that states should allow the federal agencies to make a special appearance without waiving federal immunity?

Settling Federal Reserved Rights Claims Associated with Federal Lands

Although litigation goes forward on many fronts, a growing number of non-Indian federal reserved rights claims have been settled. For example, in the 1990s in Montana, water rights for five National Park Service units (including Yellowstone and Glacier), three National Wildlife Refuges, a BLM wilderness, and a Wild & Scenic River unit were all worked out without going to trial. Most such settlements involve variations on the following theme: The United States agrees to subordinate its federal reserved rights to at least some appropriations initiated under state law after the federal reservation was made, in return for which the state agrees to cap further appropriations and to manage groundwater outside the boundaries of the federal reservation to protect wetlands and other water-dependent resources inside the reservation. In essence, the United States gives up some priority in return for state cooperation, rather than leaving matters to litigation under the *Cappaert* decision.

In August 2004, Idaho and the United States reached a settlement quantifying reserved rights claims for 444 miles of Wild & Scenic Rivers and 32 tributary streams and lakes in the Hells Canyon National Recreation Area, decreeing instream flows at various levels in specific time periods, but subordinating the federal water rights to existing water rights and uses and to certain specified future rights and uses. A link to the agreement can be found at http://www.idahorivers.org/news.htm.

As court decisions provide a better fix on the contours of these rights, federal agencies assemble the information necessary to quantify them, states discover what little threat many of these rights pose to state water right holders, and all continue to suffer from the expense and length of adjudications, the settlement fever is likely to spread.

6.   BEYOND THE RESERVED RIGHTS DOCTRINE: OTHER MEANS OF PROTECTING FEDERAL INTERESTS IN WATER

Many uses of federal lands that might involve the consumption of significant amounts of water are generally understood not to be covered by the federal reserved rights doctrine. For instance, mineral developers on federal land obtain any needed water rights under state law. United States v. City and County of Denver, 656 P.2d 1, 33–34 (Colo.1982), held that reservation as a hot spring did not reserve the water for geothermal energy production. Ski areas located on federal land also obtain any water needed for snow-making or domestic and sanitation uses under state law. What may the federal government do when it wants or needs water in order to carry out federal programs, such as those for conservation or recreation, where protection of stream-flows is required? The following explores alternative methods for federal agencies to protect water found on federal lands, other than asserting reserved rights.

a.   CONTROLLING WATER BY REGULATING ACCESS TO FEDERAL LAND

In some circumstances, the federal government may be able to protect water resources found on federal land by controlling land access rather than by claiming water rights. This was the approach used in § 8 of the 1993 Colorado Wilderness Act, 107 Stat. 756, 762. The national forest lands it designated as wilderness were located in headwaters areas with "few, if any, opportunities for diversion, storage, or other uses of water occurring outside such lands that would adversely affect the wilderness values of such lands." Id. § 8(a)(1)(A). Therefore Congress chose to "protect the wilderness values of the lands designated * * * by means other than those based on a Federal reserved water right." Id. § 8(a)(2). The Act said the executive shall not "fund, assist, authorize, or [otherwise permit] * * * the development * * * or enlargement of any water resource facility within the [wilderness] areas" designated by the Act. Id. § 8(c). It protected, within carefully defined limits, access to maintain existing water resource facilities located on the lands. Id. § 8(d)–(f).

Federal law generally gives federal land managing agencies broad power to permit or deny the use of federal lands for water development purposes. The right-of-way provisions of the Federal Land Policy and Management Act, for example, fairly bristle with environmental regulatory power, giving both the BLM and the Forest Service wide authority to grant, deny, or condition access to federal lands for various purposes, including water development. 43 U.S.C. §§ 1761–71. It may not be very problematic, politically or legally, to exercise this regulatory authority to prevent new non-federal water developments where new, or transfers of existing, appropriations under state law are involved.

Washoe County v. United States, 319 F.3d 1320 (Fed. Cir. 2003), involved the denial of a right-of-way permit across federal lands for a pipeline to move groundwater pumped from under private land and secured by a state law water right from a rural area to Reno. The court found no constitutional taking of property because the United States neither physically appropriated the water right nor denied the applicant meaningful access to water, and the government had no obligation to assist the holder of the water right in putting the water to its most profitable use. In 2006, the BLM did issue a permit for a scaled-down version of the pipeline project. The Pyramid Lake Paiute Tribe appealed the decision, expressing concern that, among other things, the groundwater pumping facilitated by the pipeline could reduce groundwater within its reservation.

But it can be controversial for a federal land managing agency to regulate access to federal land in such a way as to limit existing (often longstanding) uses supported by state water rights. The most prominent modern instance has been the so-called "bypass flows" controversy in Colorado. Many years ago non-federal water developers had built, under term-limited Forest Service permits, dams and diversion facilities on national forest land in Colorado's Front Range to supply downstream towns and farms. The developers obtained permanent water appropriations under state law (subject to maintaining beneficial use). When these federal permits expired in the 1970s, the Forest Service, responding to changing public values and a more sophisticated knowledge of environmental health, announced it would renew them only if some flows were restored to natural streams below the diversion facilities. Providing such "bypass flows" reduced the amount of the diversion by as much as 50–80% in dry years, according to the permittees. To the Forest Service, this was environmentally sound land management, and well within its legal authority. To the holders of state law appropriations/federal permits, it was confiscation of their state water rights without compensation.

On the law, the Forest Service had the better of it. *See, e.g.*, Nevada Land Action Ass'n v. U.S. Forest Serv., 8 F.3d 713, 719 (9th Cir.1993) (upholding federal authority to consider water flows in making decisions about the use of federal lands). Had the Forest Service been able to show that the flows were required to meet the standards of the Clean Water Act or the Endangered Species Act, the case would have been even more compelling. County of Okanogan v. National Marine Fisheries Serv., 347 F.3d 1081 (9th Cir. 2003) (upholding the exercise of authority reserved in federal rights-of-way permits for irrigation ditches to limit stream diversions to protect endangered species); PUD No. 1 v. Washington Dept. Of Ecology, 511 U.S. 700, 720–21 (1994) (Clean Water Act authorizes regulating flow levels to protect water quality, and such regulation may limit the exercise of water rights obtained under state law).

But politics took a different course. Not surprisingly, the attitudes of the Clinton and Bush Administrations differed markedly. The former often exercised authority to protect water in renewing permits for private water diversion and storage facilities on national forest lands, and the latter generally shrank from doing so—and even repealed a provision of the Forest Service Handbook that called for requiring bypass flows. Trout Unlimited v. United States Department of Agriculture, 320 F.Supp.2d 1090 (D.Colo.2004), overturned a Forest Service decision not to require bypass flows as a condition to renewal of a right-of-way for a reservoir on federal land. The court found that the decision failed to minimize damage to fish and wildlife habitat and protect the environment. Despite the war of words and policies, negotiations have led to some compromise over bypass flows in particular situations.

What is the right policy answer here? State law water rights do not insulate appropriators from the need to comply with other laws, such as zoning and environmental statutes. Moreover, the existence of state law water rights, no matter how longstanding, typically do not provide a defense against the application of new zoning or environmental quality standards to the uses made of that water, even if the effect is to reduce water diversions and use. Should federal land permitting requirements be regarded any differently? If federal permission to use federal land is granted for a specific term, but the permittee then perfects a state law water right without a term limit, should the state law water right in effect make that use of federal land permanent? Does it make any difference that the permittee may have a reasonable expectation, grounded in long tolerant federal policy, that it could continue to operate the project as it always had? That the permittee had a substantial investment in the water project?

Potential collisions between federal land use controls and state law water rights can be found in many contexts. In the Northern Great Plains, for example, the U.S. Fish & Wildlife Service has acquired easements from farmers to preserve so-called "prairie potholes," wetland areas vital for migratory birds. The easements typically contain a commitment by the farmer to maintain the lands as a waterfowl production area "by not draining or permitting the draining of any surface water by ditching or any other means." Assuming these acquired easements do not create federal reserved rights, and assuming that state law does not acknowledge *in situ* water rights for such purposes, and/or does not coordinate groundwater and surface water doctrines, how can the United States protect itself if the farmer subject to such an easement obtains a state permit and begins pumping groundwater and draining the wetlands? In United States v. Vesterso, 828 F.2d 1234 (8th Cir. 1987) the court held that federal law made unlawful the construction of ditches that drained wetlands protected by federal easements, rejecting the argument that state water law—pursuant to which the State Water Commission had permitted the construction to proceed—should control.

If a state law appropriation can no longer be exercised as it customarily has been because of a new but otherwise lawful federal land use restriction, does the appropriator have a remedy? In Hunter v. United States, 388 F.2d

148 (9th Cir. 1967), the U.S. sued to enjoin Hunter from grazing and watering his cattle within the boundaries of Death Valley, a unit of the National Park System, without a permit from the National Park Service, which managed the area. One of Hunter's defenses was that, prior to the area being made part of the National Park System, he had perfected a valid state law water right at springs and a stream on the federal land, and these water rights entitled him to continue to graze cattle there. The Ninth Circuit acknowledged he had valid water rights, but rejected the defense. It did say, however, that he "should be allowed a right of way over [Monument] lands to divert the water * * * elsewhere if he is able"; otherwise, his water right would simply lapse for non-use. *Id.* at 154–55 n. 4 (9th Cir. 1967). Ranchers with state law water rights to support livestock grazing on federal land still occasionally argue that their water rights give them authority over federal land uses, but these claims do not get sympathetic treatment in the courts. *See, e.g.*, Colvin Cattle Co. v. United States, 468 F.3d 803 (Fed.Cir. 2006). A few questions about whether a state law water right has been taken by the denial of a permit to graze are still in litigation. See Hage v. United States, 51 Fed. Cl. 570 (2002).

b. CLAIMING WATER RIGHTS UNDER STATE LAW

United States v. New Mexico stated that when no federal reserved water right exists to support a desired federal use, the inference is that "the United States would acquire water in the same manner as any other public or private appropriator." 438 U.S. at 702 (1978). This section will explore what that means. At first blush, the matter seems straightforward: The United States would look exclusively to state law for water rights. Federal lands in a riparian jurisdiction would enjoy riparian rights like those of any of its riparian neighbors. In prior appropriation jurisdictions, the United States could appropriate water just like all other users. Federal rights to groundwater would also be governed by state law. (Of course, the United States government could also, like other governmental entities, acquire needed water rights by condemnation or eminent domain.)

There are, however, complications. While the states wield considerable influence in the federal legislature, the converse is not so true. In the politically delicate area of water rights, states may feel, and respond to, pressure to discriminate against federal agencies, especially if doing so would advantage state water users. The United States may also have different water needs that are not as readily recognized under state law as more conventional uses. These things may compromise the ability of the United States to obtain rights to water it needs under state law.

Many federal water needs for federal lands involve protection of instream flows for conservation and recreation. Historically, state prior appropriation systems did not recognize instream flow water rights for these purposes, although today almost all of them do. Even where a state recognizes some form of instream flow protection, however, a state may not be eager to grant the United States an instream flow appropriation on federal land. The following unanimous opinion explores these questions:

State v. Morros

Supreme Court of Nevada, 1988.
766 P.2d 263.

■ Per Curiam

[The BLM applied for and received from the State Engineer a water right under state law for Blue Lake for public recreation and fishery purposes. The Forest Service applied for and received water rights under state law for recreation, stockwatering, and wildlife purposes. Various protestants, including the State Board of Agriculture, appealed.]

* * *

The Blue Lake application is for a water right to the waters of Blue Lake *in situ*, in place as a natural body of water. The BLM manages the land surrounding the lake and desires this water right to assure maintenance of the pool of Blue Lake for public recreation and fishery purposes. The Board of Agriculture contends that Nevada water law absolutely requires a physical diversion of water to obtain a water right, and that the district court therefore erred in affirming the state engineer's grant of a right to the water of Blue Lake *in situ*.

[After analyzing Nevada statutes, the court concluded that state law no longer requires a physical diversion in order to appropriate water.]

* * *

The Board of Agriculture also contends that the grant of a water right for Blue Lake to a United States agency is against the public interest in Nevada and that pursuant to NRS 533.370(3) the state engineer should have denied the application on that basis.[12] We see no threat to the public interest, however, in the grant of a water right to Blue Lake for public recreation purposes to a public agency such as the BLM. The BLM manages the land surrounding the lake for recreation and seeks a non-consumptive water right that will not reduce the amount of water presently available for other uses. Livestock and wildlife retain access to the water of Blue Lake under the district court's order.

* * *

The district court relied on this court's holding in Prosole v. Steamboat Canal Co., 37 Nev. 154, 140 P. 720 (1914), as authority for reversing the state engineer's grant of permits to the BLM and United States Forest Service to develop the new water sources for stock and wildlife watering. In *Prosole*, this court held that the person who "applies the water to the soil, for a beneficial purpose," is the actual appropriator and the owner of the water right, even if someone else, such as a canal company, diverts the water from its natural course.

---

12. NRS 533.370(3) provides, in pertinent part, that where a proposed appropriation "threatens to prove detrimental to the public interest, the state engineer shall reject the application and refuse to issue the permit asked for."

The BLM and Forest Service intend to provide the water requested in the applications to the livestock of grazing permit holders on federal range lands. Wildlife would also have access to the water. The district court reasoned that since the federal agencies owned no livestock, the United States could not put the water to beneficial use. Rather, the court stated, owners of livestock actually put water appropriated for stockwatering to beneficial use. The district court concluded that therefore under *Prosole* the United States could not appropriate water for stockwatering. The district court applied the same reasoning to wildlife watering. The court noted that the United States does not own the wildlife which is to receive water, because no one "owns" animals in the wild.

We conclude that the district court applied *Prosole* in an excessively rigid fashion. The proposed new water sources are dedicated to providing water to livestock and wildlife. These are beneficial uses of water. Nevada law and longstanding custom recognize stockwatering as a beneficial use of water.

Wildlife watering is encompassed in the NRS 533.030(2) definition of recreation as a beneficial use of water. Nevada law recognizes the recreational value of wildlife, and the need to provide wildlife with water. Sport hunting, a common use of wildlife, is a form of recreation. The legislative history of NRS 533.030(2) indicates that the legislature intended the provision to include watering under the rubric of recreation as a beneficial use of water. * * * It follows that providing water to wildlife is a beneficial use of water.

In managing federal grazing lands, the United States acts in a proprietary capacity. The new water sources covered by the applications at issue will permit better use of areas of the public range where grazing is limited by the lack of watering places, a problem recognized by this court. Congress has mandated development of water sources for livestock and wildlife as a component of the federal land management program. See 43 U.S.C. §§ 1751(b) and 1901 to 1904. Thus, the United States acts in its proprietary capacity as a landowner when federal agencies seek to appropriate water under state law for livestock and wildlife watering. Although the United States does not own the livestock and wildlife, it owns the land on which the water is to be put to beneficial use. In addition, the United States benefits as a landowner from the development of new water sources on federal land.

The United States is recognized as a "person" for the purpose of water appropriation in Nevada. The district court correctly stated that the United States "is to be treated as a person * * * it is not to be feared, given preferential treatment and certainly not discriminated against." Recently, the California Supreme Court held that the United States could not be denied the same riparian water rights for national forest lands that private riparian landowners enjoy under California water law. In re Water of Hallett Creek Stream Sys., 749 P.2d 324, cert. denied sub nom. California v. United States, 488 U.S. 824 (1988). *Hallett Creek* supports the principle that the United States is entitled to equal treatment under state water law.

The Board of Agriculture argues that * * * ownership of [these] water rights by the United States is against the public interest. The Board of Agriculture states that once the water is subject to federal control it will not be available for other uses at a later date. While this may be true, it is inherent in the prior appropriation system of water rights, and we cannot discriminate against the United States on that basis.

Under NRS 533.010, therefore, applications by United States agencies to appropriate water for application to beneficial uses pursuant to their land management functions must be treated on an equal basis with applications by private landowners. Although the United States owns no livestock and does not "own" wildlife, it owns land and may appropriate water for application to beneficial uses on its land. The district court erred in deciding that the United States could not obtain water rights for stockwatering and wildlife watering, and the portion of its order denying those applications is vacated.

* * *

NOTES AND QUESTIONS

1. Would the result in *Morros* have been the same if the Nevada statute had not defined the U.S. as a "person" for purposes of the state prior appropriation system? Suppose the Nevada state legislature responded to this decision by enacting a statute that only a state agency can appropriate instream flows under state law, even on federal lands. Some states have such laws. Suppose the state legislature simply did not recognize instream flow appropriations under state law, by anyone. What can BLM do in those states if it wants to protect instream flows or lake levels on federal lands for recreational and fishery purposes?

2. It is unclear whether the second part of *Morros*, that the BLM could hold a water right for stockwatering on federal lands, is still good law in Nevada. A 1995 Nevada statute, enacted in response to new federal rules governing livestock grazing on federal lands, provided that permits to appropriate water for livestock purposes on public lands can only be issued to those "legally entitled to place livestock on the public lands." Nev. Rev. Stat. § 533.503. The Nevada Attorney General advised the State Engineer that this prohibited the issuance of new water appropriations for livestock watering to BLM, and the State Engineer denied nine pending BLM applications in 1997. Upon challenge by the United States, the Nevada Supreme Court reversed, interpreting the statute to allow BLM to appropriate water for livestock watering, reasoning that it could issue itself a grazing lease for its own land and then apply for water, and that seemed an unnecessary step. United States v. State Engineer, 27 P.3d 51 (Nev. 2001). After this decision, the state legislature amended the statute to add the criterion that the applicant must have a "legal or proprietary interest in the livestock." Nev. Rev. Stat. § 533.503(1)(a)(1) (2003).

3. The Arizona legislature took the campaign against federal land managers one step further. In 1995 it enacted legislation allowing only

ranchers, and not federal land managing agencies like the BLM or the U.S. Forest Service, to hold livestock water appropriations on federal land. Moreover, Arizona sought to apply this rule retroactively—to strip the BLM and the Forest Service of livestock watering appropriations they had previously perfected when state law did not discriminate against the federal government. The Arizona Supreme Court struck down this feature of the law as a violation of the state constitution's due process clause. San Carlos Apache Tribe v. Superior Court, 972 P.2d 179, 189 (Ariz.1999) ("[l]egislation may not disturb vested substantive rights by retroactively changing the law that applies to completed events").

4. In neither the Nevada nor the Arizona situation did the United States rely on the Supremacy Clause of the U.S. Constitution. One reason for this is that the BLM had adopted a regulation providing that rights to use water for livestock water on public land "shall be acquired, perfected, maintained and administered under the substantive and procedural laws of the State within which such land is located." 43 C.F.R. § 4120.3–9. The regulation went on to provide: "To the extent allowed by the law of the State within which the land is located, any such water right shall be acquired, perfected, maintained and administered in the name of the United States." *Id.* Could the United States repeal this regulation and argue that, because Congress had authorized BLM to permit livestock grazing on federal lands it manages, and it had the constitutional power to control water use on federal lands, the Supremacy Clause trumps state legislation that interferes with this federally authorized use? What might stop the United States from making this argument?

5. As the court noted in *Morros*, the California Supreme Court has addressed the right of the United States as landowner to claim riparian water rights under state law. *In re* Water of Hallett Creek Stream System, 749 P.2d 324 (Cal. 1988). The United States claimed, on behalf of the U.S. Forest Service, unexercised riparian water rights under state law to be exercised in the future for the "secondary" use of "wildlife enhancement," a use not embraced within the federal reserved water right under the *New Mexico* decision. The court noted that the United States had not heretofore claimed such rights on its reserved lands in California, and the claims could have "far-reaching consequences" because the federal government owned nearly half the land in the Golden State.

The state resisted, arguing, among other things, that Congress had, in nineteenth century federal statutes like the Desert Land Act, "voluntary relinquished all proprietary claims to the western waters, except for reserved water rights." *Id.* at 328. The court rejected the argument, pointing out that the U.S. Supreme Court had, in *California Oregon Power Co.*, (described in California v. United States, *supra* p. 489) construed the federal statutes as leaving it up to each state "to determine for itself" what water law doctrine to follow. The California Supreme Court then construed its prior decisions as recognizing that "riparian rights exist in federal lands located in California as surely as they inhere in private lands. We have never in California predicated the recognition of riparian water rights on the identity of the riparian owner, and we perceive no principled reason to do so now." *Id.* at 334.

The court went on to address whether unexercised riparian rights held by the U.S. as landowner were subordinate to the rights of appropriators under state law. The court construed the Desert Land Act as answering that question in the affirmative for ordinary public domain lands. But, reversing the lower courts, it held that the Desert Land Act did not apply on federally reserved lands, and thus its provision "subordinating water rights in public domain lands to the vested rights of appropriators established under state law has no effect on riparian rights in federally held reserved lands." *Id.* 336. Therefore, the court concluded, the state law riparian water rights of the U.S. on its reserved national forest lands in California are as fully immune from defeasance as the riparian rights of a private owner. *Id.*

If the California Supreme Court had come out the opposite way on this point—holding that under California law the U.S. had no riparian water rights on its reserved land—would the U.S. Supreme Court have had jurisdiction to take the case and reverse the result? In this connection, consider that, under the *Hallett Creek* decision, state law riparian rights held by the U.S. on its unreserved public domain lands along California streams may in some circumstances be subordinated to state law appropriative rights, even though riparian rights held by persons who acquire those lands from the federal government may not be so subordinated. Is there any legal justification for this discrimination against the federal government in water rights matters? Although there is constitutional authority for limiting the ability of the states to discriminate against the United States in certain matters, it seems that neither the United States nor its agencies are "persons" protected against state discrimination by the equal protection clause.

c. FEDERAL NON–RESERVED WATER RIGHTS

Beyond federal reserved water rights and water rights obtained under state substantive and procedural law, is there a "third way" the federal government can satisfy its water needs? In 1978, shortly after the Supreme Court's decision in *New Mexico*, Interior Department Solicitor Leo Krulitz issued an opinion which claimed the existence of "federal non-reserved water rights." As its label suggested, this new federal right did not arise from a reservation, but rather from actual use of water to carry out a federal program or purpose. In that respect the right mimicked state law appropriative rights, for its foundation was the application of the water to a beneficial use. But this new right was not constrained by how state law defined beneficial use, nor was it subject to state procedural requirements. The Krulitz opinion provided a basis for the U.S. Forest Service or the BLM to claim an instream flow for habitat protection where the *New Mexico* test for a federal reserved right could not be satisfied and where the state that did not recognize appropriations of instream flows.

The basic legal argument to support federal non-reserved rights goes like this: Congress has delegated its broad power under the Property

Clause to federal land managing agencies like the U.S. Forest Service and the BLM. When these agencies act to fulfill their statutorily prescribed federal land management responsibilities, they have, unless Congress provides otherwise, sufficient authority to meet these responsibilities. Therefore, if the requirements of state water law are an obstacle to effective exercise of the federal power, the Supremacy Clause empowers the federal agencies to override state water law.

The Krulitz opinion was not warmly received. The most trenchant objection to the Krulitz opinion was not the power it claimed, but that it had not persuasively demonstrated that Congress had actually delegated this power to federal land managing agencies in particular statutes. The Krulitz claim that BLM could claim non-reserved rights on federal public lands was not long-lived. A new Solicitor of the Interior rejected it in what came to be known as the Coldiron opinion. See 88 Interior Dec. 1055 (1981). Shortly thereafter the Department of Justice's Office of Legal Counsel addressed the matter in a lengthy opinion signed by Assistant Attorney General Theodore Olson. While Olson found that Congress had not, in FLPMA, given BLM the authority to preempt state water law, he left no doubt that Congress could do so—the key question was "not generally whether Congress has the power to establish federal rights to unappropriated water, but whether it has exercised that power." Federal "Non–Reserved" Water Rights, 6 Op. Off. Legal Counsel 328, 362 (1982).

In 2000, Congress adopted a version of a "federal non-reserved right" (though it did not label it as such) in expanding the Great Sand Dunes National Monument in Colorado and converting it to a national park. Scientists had learned that the sand dunes ecosystem was dependent on continuing water flows, and so water became an important issue in the Congress. The legislation authorized the Secretary of the Interior to secure a water right to protect the dunes, to be appropriated through state law processes and in accordance with the state law priority system. But the right is to be defined and quantified according to the standard set in the federal statute—namely, whatever unappropriated surface and groundwater is shown to be necessary to protect the dunes ecosystem. And the water right will be held in the name of the National Park Service, even though state law requires a state agency to hold an instream flow water right. *See* 16 U.S.C. § 410hhh–7(b)(2). For a full discussion and an argument that this "third way" approach has great potential for addressing the legitimate needs of both the states and the federal land management agencies in future federal land conservation designations, see John D. Leshy, *Water Rights for New Federal Land Conservation Programs: A Turn-of-the-Century Evaluation*, 4 U. DENV. WATER L.REV. 273–289 (2001).

No federal statute expressly delegates to any land management agency the authority to establish water rights unilaterally as a matter of federal law. On the other hand, the organic statutes of the principal agencies all require, in varying language, that the agencies protect fish and wildlife, encourage outdoor recreation, and preserve watershed values. Given the traditional primacy of state control over water, does the BLM have delegated authority to set instream flows with a modern priority date? Does the

Forest Service or the Park Service? Does the result change, for each of those agencies, when it is managing a wilderness area under the Wilderness Act? When it is managing a segment of a river under the Wild and Scenic Rivers Act?

A number of federal regulatory statutes such as the Endangered Species Act do not expressly create federal water rights, but the constraints they place on natural resources management and development can have the effect of "reserving" water for federally-mandated uses, apart from state law. *See, e.g.*, Riverside Irrig. Dist. v. Andrews, 758 F.2d 508 (10th Cir.1985). Other federal laws can implicate water use involving federal property, without giving rise to federal water rights claims. In Bijou Irrigation District v. Empire Club, 804 P.2d 175 (Colo.1991), the Colorado Supreme Court rejected the effort by the District to add recreation as a beneficial use for water stored in its reservoir, on the ground that such use was beyond the scope of the federal right of way granted to the District for the reservoir site.

B. FEDERAL HYDROPOWER LICENSING

The federal government has assumed broad navigation-related responsibilities since the beginning of the Republic. *See, e.g.*, Gibbons v. Ogden, 22 U.S. (9 Wheat.) 1 (1824). Over the years federal involvement has mushroomed into far-flung programs for water resources regulation and flood control administered by several federal agencies.

The Federal Power Act, the last great Progressive Era piece of natural resources legislation, created the Federal Power Commission (now the Federal Energy Regulatory Commission ("FERC")) and gave it authority to license hydropower developments on navigable waters and their tributaries. Such licenses were good for up to fifty years. Many of these licenses are for projects found wholly or partially on federal land, and from the beginning the Act has had special provisions to protect federal lands and other resources. The next case discusses one key provision, the so-called "mandatory conditioning" authority given to federal land management agencies in section 4(e) of the Act, 16 U.S.C. § 797(e).

Escondido Mutual Water Co. v. La Jolla Band of Mission Indians

Supreme Court of the United States, 1984.
466 U.S. 765.

■ JUSTICE WHITE delivered the opinion of the Court.

[FERC issued a new license to an existing hydropower facility located on or near several Indian reservations in southern California, but did not include in the license several conditions offered by the Secretary of the Interior. Section 4(e) of the Act authorizes the Commission

> To issue licenses ... for the purpose of constructing ... dams ... or other project works ... upon any part of the public lands and reservations of the United States ... Provided, That licenses shall be issued within any reservation only after a finding by the Commission that the license will not interfere or be inconsistent with the purpose for which such reservation was created or acquired, and shall be subject to and contain such conditions as the Secretary of the department under whose supervision such reservation falls shall deem necessary for the adequate protection and utilization of such reservations....

Another section of the Act defines "reservations" to mean "national forests, tribal lands embraced within Indian reservations, military reservations, and other lands and interests in lands owned by the United States, and withdrawn, reserved, or withheld from private appropriation and disposal under the public land laws." 16 U.S.C. § 796(2). Thus, while the case concerned Indian reservations, the Court's opinion applies to non-Indian federal reservations as defined in the Act.]

* * *

* * * [T]he Commission ruled that § 4(e) of the FPA did not require it to accept without modification conditions which the Secretary deemed necessary for the adequate protection and utilization of the reservations.[8] Accordingly, despite the Secretary's insistence, the Commission refused to prohibit the licensees from interfering with the Bands' use of a specified quantity of water, * * * [and o]ther conditions proposed by the Secretary were similarly rejected or modified. Second, * * * [the Commission also ruled] that its § 4(e) obligation in that respect applies only to reservations that are physically occupied by project facilities. * * *

* * *

* * * The mandatory nature of the language chosen by Congress appears to require that the Commission include the Secretary's conditions in the license even if it disagrees with them. Nonetheless, petitioners argue that an examination of the statutory scheme and legislative history of the Act shows that Congress could not have meant what it said. We disagree.

We first note the difficult nature of the task facing petitioners. Since it should be generally assumed that Congress expresses its purposes through the ordinary meaning of the words it uses, we have often stated that " '[a]bsent a clearly expressed legislative intention to the contrary, [statutory] language must ordinarily be regarded as conclusive.' " Congress' apparent desire that the Secretary's conditions "shall" be included in the license must therefore be given effect unless there are clear expressions of legislative intent to the contrary.

Petitioners initially focus on the purpose of the legislation that became the relevant portion of the FPA. In 1920, Congress passed the Federal

---

8. The Commission concluded that § 4(e) required it "to give great weight to the judgments and proposals of the Secretaries of the Interior and Agriculture" but that under § 10(a) it retained ultimate authority for determining "the extent to which such conditions will in fact be included in particular licenses."

Water Power Act in order to eliminate the inefficiency and confusion caused by the "piecemeal, restrictive, negative approach" to licensing prevailing under prior law. Prior to passage of the Act, the Secretaries of the Interior, War, and Agriculture each had authority to issue licenses for hydroelectric projects on lands under his respective jurisdiction. The Act centralized that authority by creating a Commission, consisting of the three Secretaries,[14] vested with exclusive authority to issue licenses. Petitioners contend that Congress could not have intended to empower the Secretary to require that conditions be included in the license over the objection of the Commission because that would frustrate the purpose of centralizing licensing procedures.

Congress was no doubt interested in centralizing federal licensing authority into one agency, but it is clear that it did not intend to relieve the Secretaries of all responsibility for ensuring that reservations under their respective supervision were adequately protected. In a memorandum explaining the administration bill, the relevant portion of which was enacted without substantive change,[15] O.C. Merrill, one of the chief draftsmen of the Act and later the first Commission Secretary, explained that creation of the Commission "will not interfere with the special responsibilities which the several Departments have over the National Forests, public lands and navigable rivers." With regard to what became § 4(e), he wrote:

> "4. Licenses for power sites within the National Forests to be subject to such provisions for the protection of the Forests as the Secretary of Agriculture may deem necessary. Similarly, for parks and other reservations under the control of the Departments of the Interior and of War. Plans of structures involving navigable streams to be subject to the approval of the Secretary of War.
>
> "This provision is for the purpose of preserving the administrative responsibility of each of the three Departments over lands and other matters within their exclusive jurisdiction."

* * *

* * * It is thus clear enough that while Congress intended that the Commission would have exclusive authority to issue all licenses, it wanted the individual Secretaries to continue to play the major role in determining what conditions would be included in the license in order to protect the resources under their respective jurisdictions. The legislative history concerning § 4(e) plainly supports the conclusion that Congress meant what it said when it stated that the license "shall ... contain such conditions as the Secretary ... shall deem necessary for the adequate protection and utilization of such reservations." * * *

---

14. In 1930, the Commission was reorganized as a five-person body, independent from the Secretaries.

15. Between 1914 and 1917, four bills dealing with the licensing of hydroelectric projects were introduced into Congress, none successfully. In 1918, a bill prepared by the Secretaries of War, the Interior, and Agriculture, at the direction of President Wilson, was introduced. It contained the language of the § 4(e) proviso basically as it is now framed. Because of the press of World War I and other concerns, the legislation was not enacted until 1920.

Petitioners next argue that a literal reading of the conditioning proviso of § 4(e) cannot be squared with other portions of the statutory scheme. In particular, they note that the same proviso that grants the Secretary the authority to qualify the license with the conditions he deems necessary also provides that the Commission must determine that "the license will not interfere or be inconsistent with the purpose for which such reservation was created or acquired." 16 U.S.C. § 797(e). Requiring the Commission to include the Secretary's conditions in the license over its objection, petitioners maintain, is inconsistent with granting the Commission the power to determine that no interference or inconsistency will result from issuance of the license because it will allow the Secretary to "veto" the decision reached by the Commission. * * *

This argument is unpersuasive because it assumes the very question to be decided. All parties agree that there are limits on the types of conditions that the Secretary can require to be included in the license:[17] the Secretary has no power to veto the Commission's decision to issue a license and hence the conditions he insists upon must be reasonably related to the protection of the reservation and its people. The real question is whether the Commission is empowered to decide when the Secretary's conditions exceed the permissible limits. Petitioners' argument assumes that the Commission has the authority to make that decision. However, the statutory language and legislative history conclusively indicate that it does not; the Commission "shall" include in the license the conditions the Secretary deems necessary. It is then up to the courts of appeals to determine whether the conditions are valid.

Petitioners contend that such a scheme of review is inconsistent with traditional principles of judicial review of administrative action. If the Commission is required to include the conditions in the license even though it does not agree with them, petitioners argue, the courts of appeals will not be in a position to grant deference to the Commission's findings and conclusions because those findings and conclusions will not be included in the license. However, that is apparently exactly what Congress intended. If the Secretary concludes that the conditions are necessary to protect the reservation, the Commission is required to adopt them as its own, and the court is obligated to sustain them if they are reasonably related to that goal, otherwise consistent with the FPA, and supported by substantial evidence. The fact that in reality it is the Secretary's, and not the Commission's, judgment to which the court is giving deference is not surprising since the statute directs the Secretary, and not the Commission, to decide what conditions are necessary for the adequate protection of the reservation. There is nothing in the statute or the review scheme to indicate that Congress wanted the Commission to second-guess the Secretary on this matter.

In short, nothing in the legislative history or statutory scheme is inconsistent with the plain command of the statute that licenses issued

---

17. Even the Secretary concedes that the conditions must be "reasonable and supported by evidence in the record."

within a reservation by the Commission pursuant to § 4(e) "shall be subject to and contain such conditions as the Secretary . . . shall deem necessary for the adequate protection and utilization of such reservations." Since the Commission failed to comply with this statutory command when it issued the license in this case, the Court of Appeals correctly reversed its decision in this respect.

The Court of Appeals also concluded that the Commission's § 4(e) obligations to accept the Secretary's proposed conditions and to make findings as to whether the license is consistent with the reservation's purpose applied to the Pala, Yuima, and Pauma Reservations even though no licensed facilities were located on these reservations. Petitioners contend that this conclusion is erroneous. We agree.

Again, the statutory language is informative and largely dispositive.
* * *

If a project is licensed "within" any reservation, the Commission must make a "no interference or inconsistency" finding with respect to "such" reservation, and the Secretary may impose conditions for the protection of "such" reservation. Nothing in the section requires the Commission to make findings about, or the Secretary to impose conditions to protect, any reservation other than the one within which project works are located. The section imposes no obligation on the Commission or power on the Secretary with respect to reservations that may somehow be affected by, but will contain no part of, the licensed project works.

The Court of Appeals, however, purported to discover an ambiguity in the term "within." Positing that the term "reservations" includes not only tribal lands but also tribal water rights, the Court of Appeals reasoned that since a project could not be "within" a water right, the term must have a meaning other than its literal one. This effort to circumvent the plain meaning of the statute by creating an ambiguity where none exists is unpersuasive.

There is no doubt that "reservations" include "interests in lands owned by the United States" [quoting 16 U.S.C. § 796(2)] and that for many purposes water rights are considered to be interests in lands. But it does not follow that Congress intended the "reservations" spoken of in § 4(e) to include water rights. The section deals with project works to be located "upon" and "within" a reservation. As the Court of Appeals itself indicated, the section does tend to "paint a geographical picture in the mind of the reader," and we find the Court of Appeals' and respondents' construction of the section to be quite untenable. Congress intended the obligation of the Commission and the conditioning power of the Secretary to apply only with respect to the specific reservation upon which any project works were to be located and not to other reservations that might be affected by the project.

The Court of Appeals sought to bolster its conclusion by noting that a literal reading of the term "within" would leave a gap in the protection afforded the Bands by the FPA because "a project may turn a potentially useful reservation into a barren waste without ever crossing it in the geographical sense—e.g., by diverting the waters which would otherwise flow through or percolate under it." Ibid. This is an unlikely event, for in this respect the Bands are adequately protected by other provisions of the statutory scheme. First, the Bands cannot be deprived of any water to which they have a legal right. The Commission is expressly forbidden to adjudicate water rights, 16 U.S.C. § 821, and the license applicant must submit satisfactory evidence that he has obtained sufficient water rights to operate the project authorized in the license, 16 U.S.C. § 802(b). Second, if the Bands are using water, the rights to which are owned by the license applicant, the Commission is empowered to require that the license applicant continue to let the Bands use this water as a condition of the license if the Commission determines that the Bands' use of the water constitutes an overriding beneficial public use. 16 U.S.C. § 803(a). The Bands' interest in the continued use of the water will accordingly be adequately protected without requiring the Commission to comply with § 4(e) every time one of the reservations might be affected by a proposed project.

* * *

The scheme crafted by Congress in this respect is sufficiently clear to require us to hold that the Commission must make its "no inconsistency or interference" determination and include the Secretary's conditions in the license only with respect to projects located "within" the geographical boundaries of a federal reservation.

* * *

NOTES AND QUESTIONS

1.   What are the substantive limits on the Secretary's authority to prescribe conditions and insist that they be included in the license? Suppose a hydro facility located on federal land diverts water out of a river, dewatering it. The water is returned to the river downstream from the federal reservation. Could the Secretary impose a condition that requires the licensee to limit the amount of water diverted, in order to maintain a minimum level of stream-flow to protect the environment of the federal reservation?

2.   May the Secretary impose such a condition if the diversion limitation so interferes with the economics of the project that it makes it unprofitable? Does the licensee have any recourse? Where? With the Commission? The Court of Appeals? The Congress? Who ultimately decides whether such conditions are within the Secretary's statutory authority?

3.   What are the geographic limits on the Secretary's conditioning authority? When is a project license issued "within any reservation," in terms of the statute? Consider these variations on the example in paragraph 1: (a) The diversion facility is located upstream from the boundary of the federal reservation, but the diverted water is transported across the federal reservation in a pipe. (b) All the project facilities are located downstream from federally reserved land, but the reservoir behind the dam backs up occasionally into a federal reservation. (c) All project facilities are

located upstream of federally reserved land, but the operation of the facility occasionally releases high volumes of water that inundate a downstream federal reservation. (d) The project facilities are all located in a national forest, but a downstream national park, which contains no project facilities, is adversely affected by project diversions.

4.   The Court made clear that the Secretary's conditioning authority does not extend to protect stream-flow where the project is not within a federal reservation, and it offered reasons why the downstream reservations may be "adequately protected by other provisions of the statutory scheme." If a downstream national park (which does not contain any project facilities) is threatened by hydropower project diversions upstream, what other means does it have to protect itself? Might a federal reserved water right protect it? How, and under what conditions?

5.   City of Tacoma v. FERC, 460 F.3d 53 (D.C. Cir. 2006), involved a challenge to the scope of the Interior Secretary's authority under section 4(e). At issue was re-licensing of the city's Cushman Project.

> * * * Out of all the various facilities that constitute the Cushman Project, the lower of the two generating plants, an access road, and a transmission line are within the boundary of the reservation, but the generating plant is on land Tacoma owns in fee. Therefore, only the transmission line and the access road are "within" the reservation for purposes of the FPA, but this is sufficient.

> FERC concluded that Interior's authority to impose section 4(e) conditions was limited to mitigating the relatively small impact the transmission line and access road had (and would have) on the reservation, and it did not extend to the much greater impact the dams and water diversion had (and would have) on the reservation. * * * FERC stated:

> "Interior's theory could lead to any number of results that would be inconsistent with the letter and intent of section 4(e). For example, if a project is located entirely on private land with the exception of a small segment of a power line that crossed the corner of a reservation, Interior's theory would allow it to set minimum instream flows and impose other conditions on aspects of the project that have absolutely no impact on the reservation. . . . We do not interpret section 4(e) to require such [an] outcome[ ]."

> FERC cited *Escondido* in support of this conclusion, but *Escondido* actually suggests a different rule.

> The Supreme Court in *Escondido* considered whether Interior could impose section 4(e) conditions "any time a reservation is 'affected' by a licensed project even if none of the licensed facilities is actually located on the reservation." The Court rejected this argument, stating, "Congress intended . . . the conditioning power of the Secretary [of the Interior] to apply only with respect to [a] . . . reservation upon which any project works were to be located." Significantly, the Court referred to *any* project works, which would seem to include, contrary to FERC's conclusion, even "a small segment of a power line that crosse[s] the corner of a reservation." Later in its opinion, the Court stated, "[I]t is

clear that Congress concluded that reservations were not entitled to the added protection provided by the proviso of § 4(e) unless *some* of the licensed works were actually within the reservation." *Escondido,* 466 U.S. at 784 (emphasis added). "[S]ome" means "some"; it does not mean "all," or even "a lot." The issue under consideration in *Escondido* was whether Interior can impose license conditions based on the *indirect* effects a project has on a reservation. Therefore, the implication of the court's statements is that Interior can do so provided that at least "some" or "any" part of the licensed facilities is on reservation land.

This conclusion is consistent with the plain meaning of the statutory language. All the parties agree Tacoma's Cushman Project is "within [a] reservation" at least to the extent of the access road and transmission line, and section 4(e) provides that licenses issued "within [a] reservation" "shall be subject to and contain such conditions as the Secretary [of the Interior] . . . shall deem necessary for the adequate protection and *utilization* of such reservation." 16 U.S.C. § 797(e) (emphasis added). This language nowhere limits Interior's regulatory authority to those portions of the project that are on the reservation. On the contrary, so long as some portion of the project is on the reservation, the Secretary is authorized to impose any conditions that will protect the reservation, including *utilization* of the reservation in a manner consistent with its original purpose.

We conclude, therefore, that the Secretary of the Interior is not limited in this proceeding to mitigating the impact the access road and the transmission line will have on the reservation. Instead, he may impose license conditions that are designed to mitigate the effect of the project on the Skokomish River to the extent doing so is reasonably related to protecting the reservation and the Tribe. Moreover, the FPA gives FERC no discretion to reject Interior's section 4(e) conditions, though FERC is "free to express its disagreement" with the conditions "in connection with the issuance of the license" or "on [judicial] review," and it also has the option of not issuing the license. * * *

Is there a better reading of *Escondido* that would have supported FERC? Does *City of Tacoma* allow the Secretary of the Interior to use a small handle to leverage major changes in FERC permits without regard for whether they are in the best interests of federal energy policy?

6.   The Federal Energy Regulatory Commission is an independent regulatory agency, part of the so-called fourth branch of government. It has authority to represent itself in court, but when matters in which it is involved get to the Supreme Court, if its recommended position is in conflict with those of other parts of the Executive Branch, the Solicitor General of the United States decides what the position of the U.S. will be before the court. In *Escondido,* however, the Solicitor General permitted both the Commission and Interior to appear before the court, arguing inconsistent positions.

7.   Look closely at the definition of "reservation" in the Act, quoted in the bracketed introduction to the opinion. Most federal land managed by

the Bureau of Land Management is not considered "reserved" for purposes of the federal reserved water rights doctrine. But might it be considered "reserved" under this definition? The Solicitor of the Department of the Interior concluded, in an opinion issued in January 2001, that the answer was yes, because once BLM land was withdrawn generally from disposal (as President Roosevelt did in the mid–1930s), it qualified for "reservation" status under the Federal Power Act, even if it did not for purposes of the federal reserved water rights doctrine.

8. In section 241 of the Energy Policy Act of 2005, Congress substantially reformed the 4(e) conditioning authority. First, it gave the hydropower license applicant (and "any party to the licensing proceeding") a right "to a determination on the record, after an opportunity for an agency trial-type hearing of no more than 90 days, on any disputed issues of material fact with respect to" any conditions the federal resource agency may propose to include in the license. Congress required the resource agencies to establish jointly, by rule, "procedures for such expedited trial-type hearing[s], including the opportunity to undertake discovery and cross-examine witnesses."

Second, it allowed the applicant or any other party to the license proceeding to propose alternative 4(e) conditions, which FERC is obliged to accept, if the Secretary of Commerce, Agriculture or the Interior (whichever has supervision over the reservation and the § 4(e) conditioning authority) determines that the applicant's alternative "provides for the adequate protection and utilization of the reservation," and will either "cost significantly less to implement" or "result in improved operation of the project works for electricity production."

Third, it required the pertinent Secretary, whether the resource agency's or any proposed alternative condition is accepted, to supply a written statement explaining the basis for her decision regarding which condition to accept, which "must demonstrate that the Secretary gave equal consideration to effects of the condition adopted and alternatives not accepted on energy supply, distribution, cost, and use; flood control; navigation; water supply; and air quality (in addition to the preservation of other aspects of environmental quality)" and to submit "all studies, data, and other factual information available to the Secretary and relevant to [her] decision."

Fourth, it gave FERC, if it found the Secretary's final condition "would be inconsistent with the purposes" of the Act, to refer the dispute to the FERC's Dispute Resolution Service, which is to issue a "non-binding advisory" within ninety days, which the Secretary "may accept" unless she finds the recommendation "will not adequately protect the reservation."

How, if at all, do these reforms affect the substantive authority of the resource agencies to impose binding conditions on the applicant? Proponents of the measure justified the amendments to the FPA in the name of streamlining and efficiency. Are these reforms likely to make the process more efficient? Likely to improve the bargaining leverage of FERC or the applicant vis-à-vis the resources agencies? Likely to politicize the process within the resource agencies and the Cabinet Departments of which they are a part? Similar changes were made in the "fishway" prescription authority of section 18, explained in the following case.

———

Two other parts of the Federal Power Act give federal fish agencies an important role in federal hydropower licensing, on and off federal lands. They are explored in the following case.

American Rivers, et al. v. Federal Energy Regulatory Commission

United States Court of Appeals for the Ninth Circuit, 1999.
201 F.3d 1186.

■ JUDGE WARDLAW

At stake in these consolidated petitions is the continued operation of two hydroelectric power facilities located in Lane County, Oregon along a twenty-five mile stretch of the McKenzie River. The petitioners, a coalition of conservation/environmental organizations and the Oregon Department of Fish and Wildlife, challenge the decision of the Federal Energy Regulatory Commission ("FERC" or the "Commission") to reissue a hydropower license to the incumbent licensee, the Eugene Water and Electric Board ("EWEB"). Specifically, the petitioners contend that the Commission granted the disputed license * * * in violation of sections 10(j) and 18 of the FPA. * * *

The license under review authorizes the continued operation of the 14.5–megawatt Leaburg Hydroelectric Project and the 8–megawatt Walterville Hydroelectric Project for a duration of 40 years. The Leaburg and Walterville facilities have operated since 1930 and 1911, respectively. * * * After the licenses expired, EWEB managed both developments under separate annual licenses by operation of FPA section 15(a) [which directs the Commission to issue annual licenses to the existing licensee on the same terms as the original license while the renewal application is pending].

The Leaburg development, the project's upstream facility, consists of a dam, canal, powerhouse facilities, a tailrace, and a power substation. The dam creates a fifty-seven acre backwater called Leaburg Lake which extends approximately 1.5 miles upstream. On each side of the dam are fish ladders, only one of which is operational. On the upstream side of the dam, intake gates divert water through a downstream migrant fish screen into the five-mile Leaburg power canal. The diverted water passes through the power plant forebay into the two-turbine Leaburg powerhouse. The water returns to the McKenzie River through a 1,100–foot tailrace. The bypassed reach of the McKenzie between the entrance to the Leaburg canal and the point where the diverted water rejoins the river is 5.8 miles long.

Six miles downstream, headworks divert water from the McKenzie into the unscreened, four-mile Walterville power canal. The Walterville canal feeds into a single-turbine powerhouse from which water returns to the McKenzie through a two-mile tailrace. The Walterville canal bypasses a 7.3 mile stretch of the McKenzie.

The Director issued the disputed license on March 24, 1997, pursuant to the FPA * * * [which] authorizes the Commission to issue such licenses subject to conditions that the Commission finds best suited for power development and other public uses of the nation's waters. In the mid–1980's, Congress amended these provisions to realize an increased sensitivity to environmental concerns, directing the Commission to devote greater consideration to a project's overall effect on fish and wildlife. *See* Electric Consumers Protection Act of 1986 ("ECPA"). The new license reflects many of these concerns and would require EWEB to construct several new facilities and provide other measures for the benefit and protection of the fish populations that pass through and reside in the project area.[7] From a power standpoint, the new license authorizes EWEB to increase the project's generation capacity from 22.5 megawatts to 23.2 megawatts. Under the terms of the license, EWEB would achieve this increased generation capacity by raising the water level at Leaburg Lake by 18 inches, constructing fixed sill dams or other diversion structures at the head of the Walterville power canal, replacing the turbine runners at both powerhouses, and excavating the Walterville tailrace. The license also would increase the minimum flows[8] in the bypassed reaches below the diversions of both developments to 1,000 cubic feet per second.

* * *

The Commission's staff * * * examined the conditions submitted by the state and federal fish and wildlife agencies under color of FPA sections 10(j) and 18.[10] The staff adopted many of the fifty-six recommendations designated pursuant to section 10(j). The final environmental impact statement, however, stated that twenty-one of the fifty-six recommendations were outside the scope of section 10(j). The Commission's staff concluded that these recommendations either did not serve to protect fish and wildlife resources or conferred final authority over the level of enhancement and

7. For instance, the license orders EWEB to install a new fish screen at the Walterville power canal intake to enhance the passage of downstream migrating fish. EWEB also must construct a tailrace barrier at the Leaburg development, replace the tailrace barrier at Walterville, and modify the left-bank fish ladder and reconstruct a newly designed right-bank ladder at the Leaburg dam. The license also requires EWEB to operate the project according to scheduled ramping rates designed to prevent the stranding of fish. In addition, EWEB is to augment spawning gravel downstream of Leaburg dam to enhance salmonid spawning gravel and monitor the success of fish habitat enhancement measures.

8. Minimum instream flow represents the amount "of water that must remain in the bypassed section of the stream and that thus remains unavailable to drive the generators."

10. Under section 10(j) of the FPA, the Commission may impose conditions on licensees "based on recommendations received pursuant to the Fish and Wildlife Coordination Act (16 U.S.C. § 661 et seq.) from the National Marine Fisheries Service, the United States Fish and Wildlife Service, and State fish and wildlife agencies." 16 U.S.C. § 803(j)(1). Section 18 of the FPA requires the Commission to include in a license "fishways" prescribed by the Secretaries of Interior or Commerce. *See* 16 U.S.C. § 811 (1994).

project operations upon the agencies rather than the Commission. The final environmental impact statement nevertheless considered and adopted many of these submissions under FPA sections 10(a) and 4(e) which grant the Commission broader latitude to balance environmental and development interests. The Commission's staff also recommended the outright adoption of the federal agencies' section 18 conditions which required implementation of fish ladders and fish screens but determined that the remaining conditions lodged under color of section 18 did not constitute "fishway prescriptions." Again, the Commission analyzed and adopted many of these measures under sections 10(a) and 4(e).[11]

* * *

Two months after the section 10(j) dispute resolution meeting between the resource agencies and Commission staff, the Secretary of Interior filed modifications to its section 18 prescriptions for the Director's consideration. These modified prescriptions met with substantially the same results as the resource agencies' earlier submissions. Like the Commission staff before him, the Director found that the Secretary's prescriptions relating to fish ladders and fish screens constituted section 18 fishways but nevertheless did not incorporate the submissions as prescribed, electing instead to establish a plan under which EWEB would "consult with the agencies in developing final designs and monitoring plans for Commission approval." As to the remaining prescriptions, the Director held that the submissions, even as modified, were beyond the scope of section 18. The Director explicitly stated for the record the basis for the rejection or reclassification of most of the submissions.

* * *

* * * [P]etitioners challenge the Commission's construction of the FPA, raising two questions under related, but markedly different, statutory sections. These challenges again engender *de novo* review and require two distinct iterations of the *Chevron* standard. First, we consider whether the FPA authorizes the Commission to decide that a fish and wildlife agency recommendation submitted pursuant to section 10(j) does not qualify for treatment under that section. Second, we examine whether the Commission may reject a "fishway prescription" proposed by the Secretary of Commerce or the Secretary of Interior under FPA section 18. These are not inconsequential questions. Both questions present this Court with issues of first impression in our Circuit, and both beget answers bearing significantly on the hydropower relicensing process.

11. These measures included conditions that recommended: imposition of fish mortality standards at the fish screens of Leaburg and Walterville and at the Leaburg rollgates; construction of tailrace barriers; delays in raising the Leaburg Lake water level; delays in the construction of diversion structures at Walterville; the salvage of fish prior to any new construction at Walterville's tailrace; annual inspection of the Walterville tailrace; agency control over final design and monitoring of fishways; and agency enforcement of the licensee's duty to maintain fishways in efficient operating condition. The Director eventually adopted many of the reclassified recommendations or ordered EWEB to conduct studies regarding their feasibility.

As previously explained, the FPA establishes an elaborate regulatory regime which charges the Commission with responsibility to balance the interests of hydropower licensees and other participants in the licensing process. The processes required by section 10(j) represent a vital part of that regime. Subsection 10(j)(1), as amended by the ECPA, instructs:

> (1) That in order to adequately and equitably protect, mitigate damages to, and enhance, fish and wildlife (including related spawning grounds and habitat) affected by the development, operation, and management of the project, each license issued under this subchapter shall include conditions for such protection, mitigation, and enhancement. Subject to paragraph (2), such conditions shall be based on recommendations received pursuant to the Fish and Wildlife Coordination Act (16 U.S.C. 661 et seq.) from the National Marine Fisheries Service, the United States Fish and Wildlife Service, and State fish and wildlife agencies.

16 U.S.C. § 803(j)(1). Subsection 10(j)(2), however, specifies that the Commission should attempt to reconcile agency recommendations with the requirements of the FPA. *See* 16 U.S.C. § 803(j)(2). If, after giving due weight to these recommendations, the Commission does not adopt them, in whole or in part, the statute requires the Commission to publish the following findings (with a basis for each of the findings):

> (A) A finding that adoption of such recommendation is inconsistent with the purposes and requirements of this subchapter or with other applicable provisions of law.

> (B) A finding that the conditions selected by the Commission [protect and mitigate damage to fish and wildlife].

Id.

Here, our *Chevron* analysis begins and ends with the statute itself. We detect in section 10(j) the type of clear congressional mandate that suffices to curtail a *Chevron* query at step one. * * *

* * *

* * * Section 10(j) and section 4(e), the provision at issue in *Escondido,* set forth very different roles for the Commission to play in the hydropower licensing process. Congress provided in subsection 10(j)(2) a mechanism for the Commission to employ when it disagrees with a submitted agency condition, unlike the pre-license certification scheme Congress set forth in FPA section 4(e). That mechanism, the publication of findings, clearly qualifies the mandatory clause of subsection 10(j)(1) and is expressly contemplated in the phrase "[s]ubject to paragraph (2)" that prefaces the mandatory language. The ordinary meaning of "subject to" includes "governed or affected by." We therefore interpret "subject to paragraph (2)" to mean precisely what it says: subsection 10(j)(1) is governed or affected by subsection 10(j)(2). Moreover, were we to read subsection 10(j)(1) as conferring final authority over the section 10(j) process upon the resource agencies, we impermissibly would be making surplusage of subsection 10(j)(2). * * * In sum, the divergent structures of § 10(j) and § 4(e), the plain meaning of the prefatory phrase "subject to," and the abecedarian principle of giving effect to every subsection convince us that *Escondido* is inapposite here.

* * *

* * * In denying the petitions insofar as they challenge the Commission's understanding of its statutory mandate under section 10(j), our holding is narrow. We conclude that section 10(j) clearly vests in the Commission the discretion as to how or whether it will incorporate a section 10(j) recommendation received from a listed agency. As noted above, we express no opinion on the merits of the Commission's environmental findings. Moreover, we stress that nothing we have said should be construed as eviscerating the pro-environmental object beneath the ECPA amendments. The Commission must afford "*significant* deference to recommendations made by state (and federal) fish and wildlife agencies for the 'protection, mitigation, and enhancement' of fish and wildlife." *Kelley* [v. FERC], 96 F.3d at 1486 (emphasis added). Nevertheless, Congress clearly has ordained that this deference must yield to the Commission's reasoned judgment in those instances where the parties cannot agree. Under *Chevron,* "that is the end of the matter." 467 U.S. at 842.

* * *

* * * Section 18 directs that the Commission "shall require the construction, maintenance, and operation by a licensee at its own expense of . . . such fishways as may be prescribed by the Secretary of the Interior or the Secretary of Commerce, as appropriate."* 16 U.S.C. § 811. Conspicuously absent from this provision is a qualifying clause, such as the one in FPA subsection 10(j)(2), which expressly enables the Commission to reject a recommendation submitted under color of section 10(j). Ignoring this structural distinction, the Commission argues that we must not disturb its section 18 "findings" because the Commission fully explained on the record its reasons for rejecting the fishway prescriptions. This argument misses the mark. Section 18 on its face simply does not contemplate the two-pronged approach set forth in subsection 10(j)(2). Although the presence of a qualifying clause in subsection 10(j)(2) does not foreclose the Commission's professed authority to reject fishways prescribed by either the Secretary of Interior or Secretary of Commerce, the absence of a similar provision in section 18 suggests more than mere legislative oversight. Clearly, if Congress had wanted findings under section 18, it knew how to ask for them.

Taking a different tack, the Commission cautions that its statutory mission would be compromised if it were left without authority to determine whether a submission prescribes a fishway or instead constitutes a recommendation more appropriately evaluated under FPA sections 10(j) or 10(a). * * *

* * *

---

* [Eds. Interior and Commerce divide jurisdiction over various kinds of fish, which is why the statute refers to them both in § 18]

* * *[T]he Commission attempts to distinguish *Escondido,* insisting that its reasoning does not apply when what the Secretaries prescribe does not constitute a fishway.

The Commission's efforts to distinguish *Escondido* cannot withstand scrutiny. * * *

* * *

[Among other things, t]he Commission * * * relies upon a strained reading of a post-ECPA congressional clarification of the Commission's authority regarding fishways contained in the Energy Policy Act of 1992 (the "Energy Act"), 106 Stat. 2776 (1992). In the Energy Act, Congress explicitly considered and rejected amendments to section 18 that would have limited the Department of the Interior's authority to prescribe fishways. The Commission had asked Congress for a statutory grant of authority to consider and balance the Department of Interior's recommendations for fishways with other values. Congress rejected this approach. More significantly, Congress overturned the Commission's own rulemaking efforts to define fishway prescriptions. *See* 106 Stat. 3008 ("§ 1701(b)"). The Commission initially had adopted a restrictive definition of fishways that included only facilities "used for the upstream passage of fish" through a hydropower project. 56 Fed.Reg. 23,108, 23,146 (May 20, 1991). In response to public outcry over this definition, the Commission subsequently amended its rule on rehearing to embrace both upstream and downstream passage. *See* 56 Fed.Reg. 61,137, 61,140–45 (Dec. 2, 1991). Congress promptly rejected and overturned the amended regulatory definition as still too narrow, providing:

> The definition of the term "fishway" contained in 18 C.F.R. 4.30(b)(9)(iii), as in effect on the date of enactment of this Act [Oct. 24, 1992], is vacated without prejudice to any definition or interpretation by rule of the term 'fishway' by the Federal Energy Regulatory Commission for purposes of implementing section 18 of the Federal Power Act. Provided, that any future *definition* promulgated by regulatory rulemaking shall have no force or effect unless concurred in by the Secretary of the Interior and the Secretary of Commerce: Provided further, That the items which may constitute a 'fishway' under section 18 for the safe and timely upstream and downstream passage of fish shall be limited to physical structures, facilities, or devices necessary to maintain all life stages of such fish, and project operations and measures related to such structures, facilities, or devices which are necessary to ensure the effectiveness of such structures, facilities, or devices for such fish.

§ 1701(b) (emphasis in original).

Despite this explicit rejection of the Commission's proposed fishways definitions, the Commission seizes upon a perceived ambiguity in the limiting clause at the end of § 1701(b) which sets forth the items which may constitute a fishway. The Commission argues that this final clause does not specify which agency is to determine whether a given prescription "constitutes a fishway under section 18." In light of this omission, the Commission, EWEB, and industry amici extensively cite the legislative history, attempting to educe from the record some indicia of support for their position. * * *

* * *

The Commission has gone too far. The Energy Act conference report * * * clearly stated that the roles of the Commission and the Secretaries of Interior and Commerce "would continue to be as [they were] prior to [the passage of § 1701]. Nothing in this amendment is intended to limit the roles or authorities of either the Secretaries or the Commission." As noted above, prior to the passage of § 1701(b), *Escondido* delineated the respective roles of the Secretaries and the Commission under the statute. In other words, no matter how selectively the Commission quotes the legislative record and no matter how many inferential deductions it makes, there is no escaping the simple fact that *Escondido* has set forth the analytic framework which authoritatively animates the statutory scheme, both then and now. * * * We, too, find *Escondido* controlling in the section 18 context and therefore hold that the Commission may not modify, reject, or reclassify any prescriptions submitted by the Secretaries under color of section 18. Where the Commission disagrees with the scope of a fishway prescription, it may withhold a license altogether or voice its concerns in the court of appeals, but at the administrative stages, "it is not the Commission's role to judge the validity of [the Secretary's] position-substantially or procedurally."

We note the Commission's argument that an unqualified reservation of prescription authority for the Secretaries invites a unilateral fishways determination by two agencies which do not concern themselves with the delicate economic versus environmental balancing required in every licensing. We acknowledge, as pointed out by the Commission, that the prescribing federal agencies have not promulgated regulations to guide license applicants and others in utilizing this section of the law. Nevertheless, Congress was acutely aware of the Secretaries' omission when it passed § 1701 and * * * [even if] we might disagree with Congressional failure to require such regulations, * * * [that] does not authorize us to rewrite section 18.

* * * We deny the petitions insofar as they challenge * * * FERC's authority to reclassify, reject, or modify section 10(j) recommendations. Nevertheless, in light of the statutory scheme, its legislative history, and the precedent which binds this Court, we grant the petitions to the extent they challenge the Commission's construction of section 18. * * *

NOTES AND QUESTIONS

1.   Note the specific measures recommended by the fish agencies, characterized as "fishways." Do all of these fit the definition of "fishway" enacted by Congress in the 1992 Energy Policy Act, quoted in the court's opinion? Are they related to "structures, facilities, or devices" for fish? Who makes this determination? The fish agencies? FERC? The court of appeals?

2.   What does the Commission need to show in order to reject Interior Department recommendations under section 10(j)? Is it enough that the recommended conditions are expensive to implement? That their costs outweigh their benefits? That they will reduce licensee profits?

3.   In section 241 of the Energy Policy Act of 2005, Congress substantially reformed the section 18 "fishway" conditioning authority, in a manner comparable to its reforms of section 4(e) discussed above. Specifically, it (a) allowed the applicant or any other party to obtain an "agency trial-type hearing" to resolve "disputed issues of material fact" regarding the fishway prescription, including opportunities to undertake discovery and cross-examine witnesses; (b) allowed the applicant or other parties to propose alternative conditions; (c) required the Secretary to give these alternatives serious consideration and make a record and provide an explanation of her choice; and (d) gave FERC the right to refer disagreements to advisory dispute resolution.

4.   Is all this complexity in the licensing scheme good policy? The Commission cannot fail to include license conditions the Interior Secretary* recommends under section 4(e), or fishways recommended by fish agencies under section 18, and yet the Commission must make its own determination as to whether licensing the project is a good idea, environmentally or otherwise. Arguing that it, and not the Secretary of the Interior, should have ultimate authority over these projects, the Commission has repeatedly tried, so far without success, to persuade Congress to overturn this aspect of *Escondido*. Environmentalists, tribes and others have resisted cutting back on the Interior Department's role.

5.   The Federal Power Act also poses interesting issues of state versus federal authority. Most prominently, the always delicate interplay of federal authority and state water rights is handled quite differently in the context of hydropower licensing from how it is handled in federal reclamation law. This is so even though section 27 of the Federal Power Act, 16 U.S.C. § 821, is textually very similar to section 8 of the Reclamation Act. Distinguishing California v. United States, the Supreme Court has reaffirmed that FERC need not follow or give deference to state water law in licensing hydroelectric power projects. California v. FERC, 495 U.S. 490 (1990). On the other hand, a federal hydropower licensee must obtain a state certification under § 401 of the Clean Water Act before FERC can issue a hydropower license. *See* PUD No. 1 v. Washington Dept. of Ecology, 511 U.S. 700 (1994).

Wisconsin Public Service Corp. v. Federal Energy Regulatory Commission

United States Court of Appeals, Seventh Circuit, 1994.
32 F.3d 1165.

■ JUDGE CUDAHY

[FERC (by a vote of 3–2) included "reopener" clauses in two licenses. The licensees sought judicial review to overturn the clauses. The clauses stated:

---

* If the reservation involved is national forest land, the Secretary of Agriculture has authority to formulate conditions under section 4(e).

The License shall, for the conservation and development of fish and wildlife resources, construct, maintain, and operate, or arrange for the construction, maintenance, and operation of such reasonable facilities, and comply with such reasonable modifications of the project structures and operation, as may be ordered by the Commission upon its own motion or upon the recommendation of the Secretary of the Interior or the fish and wildlife agency or agencies of any State in which the project or a part thereof is located, after notice and opportunity for hearing.]

* * *

A fundamental objection of the petitioners to the Commission's reservation of fishways under the authority of Section 18 is that this invites a unilateral determination by another agency, the Department of the Interior, based upon its view of some future conservation or wildlife need, which is not balanced against the allegedly delicate economics of these water power projects. For example, the Commission staff estimated that the cost of energy from the Otter Rapids Project would be only two-tenths of a mill ($.0002) per kilowatt hour (or about $1,000 a year) less than alternative electric energy available in the region. Therefore, there would be no reasonable basis upon which the putative project licensee could estimate the future impact of a requirement to install fishways on the economics of the project. Hence, there was no rational basis on which the putative licensee could determine whether to accept the license with a fishway reservation.

This is certainly not an inconsequential issue. But * * * there can be no guarantee of profitability of water power projects under the Federal Power Act; profitability is at risk from a number of variable factors, and values other than profitability require appropriate consideration.

* * * The petitioners here contend that the Commission's reservation with respect to fishways to be exercised (or not) at some unspecified date in the future and to provide for the installation of a fishway of presently unknown design, cost and potential impact on other aspects of the project * * * provides the licensee with no reasonable or rational basis for evaluating the potential effect of a prescription. But this argument was made and rejected in *State of California v. FPC*, 345 F.2d 917 (9th Cir.), *cert. denied,* 382 U.S. 941 (1965) * * * [where] the Commission, acting under Section 10 of the Act, included a reopener clause in its license allowing it to re-evaluate after twenty years the minimum flow requirements that it had imposed on the licensee. * * *

The petitioners attempt to distinguish *California v. FPC* on a number of grounds. First, they point out that the Commission in that case was reserving its own authority and discretion as opposed to discretion vested in the Secretary of the Interior. But Congress, in its concern for environmental and conservation values, specifically elected to vest this authority in the Secretary of the Interior, perhaps in the belief that he would give the values in question a stronger priority than FERC, which might be more interested in energy economics. Second, petitioners claim that the reservation in *California v. FPC* was intended to address reasonably foreseeable circumstances. But here the reservation was intended to address circumstances, perhaps less foreseeable but nonetheless specifically contemplated by Congress. Third, they point out that in *California v. FPC* future action would be tested for consistency with the FPA, including its effect on project economics. This may be the case but again Congress addressed the situation here specifically with the provisions contained in Section 18. Fourth, the petitioners argue that in *California v. FPC*, as opposed to the present case, there would ultimately be a showing based on substantial evidence that the action was necessary and desirable. In the case before us, the Commission has given strong assurances to the petitioners that there would be a hearing at the time that Interior requested fishway installation. But, in any event, the need for fishways, here under Section 18, was a matter delegated to the Secretary of the Interior by the Congress. Fifth, the petitioners argue that in *California v. FPC* the licensee retained a right to challenge the validity of the action taken by the Commission. Here the petitioners can certainly raise the issue whether an ordered fishway accords with the sort of improvement contemplated by Congress.

The heart of the petitioners' argument is essentially that it is unfair to require them to decide whether or not to proceed with their water power projects when this license provision prevents them from knowing, before they undertake the activity, what their costs will be and therefore whether the activity will be commercially viable. But they ground their argument entirely on the statute; they do not raise a due process objection, and we can see nothing in the statutory scheme to distinguish this case from *California v. FPC*. The FPA cannot be read to require the Commission to protect the economic viability of all hydroelectric projects. Moreover, Section 18 specifically, and by its very terms provides for a reservation condition such as the one applied in this case. Therefore, we believe that *California v. FPC* and cases which follow it are controlling.

* * * The Commission should not be left with the untenable choice of either requiring petitioners to construct potentially needless fishways at the time of licensing or effectively eliminating the possibility of restoring migratory fish runs to the Wisconsin River. Therefore, the reservation of authority to impose a future requirement seems an appropriate measure for the protection of the public interest.

As we have noted, we think that the potential impact of the cost of the fishway on the economics of a relatively marginal power generating project may be a significant issue. However, there is no indication from this record that this is a generally applicable problem and it is certainly one that Congress can deal with within rather broad limits. In addition, we would emphasize that the Commission has committed itself to conduct hearings at such future time as fishways may have to be ordered. What precisely will be the scope of these hearings we cannot address at this point. However, we emphasize that our approval of the Commission's construction of the statute here is significantly dependent upon its commitment to conduct such hearings.

Petitioners also challenge the Commission's interpretation of Section 18 on the ground that it conflicts with the requirement for "reasonable" terms of licenses contained in Section 15. Section 15 provides that a new license be issued to an original licensee at the end of the original license term on "reasonable" terms. Petitioners argue that the possibility that the Commission's prescription of a fishway may make the project uneconomic at some future date renders the reservation an unreasonable term. Petitioners emphasize in this branch of their argument that the case for unreasonableness rests in considerable measure with the Commission's interpretation that it may not question Interior's determination of need nor may it weigh the need for a fishway against economic viability. If however, there is unreasonableness in this provision, it is the unreasonableness of Congress in enacting Section 18 rather than that of the Commission in interpreting the section. The purported "unreasonableness" springs from congressional emphasis on the priority to be given conservation considerations. There are a variety of unknown future contingencies under which the petitioners accept a license. One of the more notable of these presumably is the level of flow in the Wisconsin River in future years. By adding to the natural contingencies which must attach to any project envisioning operation over a long period of years a requirement for the construction of a fishway we do not believe that either Congress or the Commission has acted unreasonably. Reasonableness is a term of notable flexibility in both the legislative and the administrative lexicon and we do not believe that the present requirements exceed the usual and normal limits of the term.

The petitioners also challenge the Commission's construction of the FPA as being in conflict with certain requirements of the Administrative Procedure Act. They claim that there is no evidence in the record that at any time in the future a fishway will be necessary in connection with either of the two projects. We think that Congress in enacting Section 18, or its equivalent over the years has already made a finding, in effect, that a fishway may become necessary with respect to any water power project affecting fish migration in a river. Congress has delegated to the Secretary of the Interior the authority to make a determination when and if a fishway may become necessary. We can hardly expect the Commission at the present time to make a finding which would be meaningful with respect to an uncertain future event.

Also the petitioners complain that the reservation of Section 18 prescriptive authority is not necessary in light of the Commission's general authority to insert a standard reopener clause permitting it to consider and resolve fishway issues at an appropriate time and in an appropriate way. We think again that Congress has already decided this in the quite special case of a fishway prescription. In so doing, Congress has apparently given great weight to conservation objectives in the preservation of means for fish to pursue their migratory inclinations.

In addition, we believe that the Commission has proffered adequate reasons for the inclusion of the Section 18 reservation. As noted, Congress since 1906 had enacted provisions for fishway prescriptions similar to the present provisions of Section 18. This presumably indicates a longstanding congressional concern with conservation considerations involving fish migration. The Commission seems to us to have given a reasonable construction to these longstanding provisions. If there are complaints as to their economic impact they must be addressed to the Congress.

* * *

NOTES AND QUESTIONS

1. How awkward is the "reopener" provision for the licensee? Is the reservation of authority to prescribe a "fishway" at some point over the thirty-to fifty-year term of the license a sword of Damocles that could spell the end of a profitable facility? Should the "fish agencies" be required to decide at the time of the licensing (or relicensing) whether a fishway is a good idea, and to make a definitive decision whether to require it, rather than leave the matter open? Elsewhere these materials address other situations where agencies reserve the authority to make further decisions about natural resource development "downstream" from the initial decision. Consider, for example, the offshore oil and gas leasing situation and the *Mobil Oil* case, *supra* p. 347; and the "no surface occupancy" leasing stipulation discussed in the NEPA materials, *supra* p. 257.

2. Note that the court says the issue of a future fishway prescription on profitability is not "inconsequential." But is it legally relevant to Interior's authority to prescribe it? What is the court's answer to the licensee's concern?

3. The court points out that the licensee does not argue that this uncertainty deprives it of "due process," only that the "reopener" is not authorized by statute. Could the licensee frame a credible due process argument here? Does the court here provide clues as to whether the fish agencies have any obligation to consult with FERC, the license applicant or the public in formulating fishway prescriptions? Recall that the Energy Policy Act of 2005 addressed the matter, see *supra* p. 541 and 549.

4. Suppose there are two different FERC-licensed hydro facilities on a particular river, both built without fish passage facilities, and which effectively block all areas upstream to anadromous fish passage. The license for the one closest to the mouth of the river comes up for renewal in 2020. The other facility further upstream is before FERC now for relicensing. The long term goal of the fish agencies is to restore anadromous fish runs in the watershed, but it may not make sense to require fishways now for the upstream facility, because until the downstream facility has fish passage facilities they are worthless. On the other hand, if the upstream facility is given a thirty-to fifty-year license now without fishway prescriptions, it could seriously delay implementation of the restoration goal. A possible solution might be to include a fishway prescription in the license for the upstream facility, but delay implementation for many years until fishways are installed on the downstream facility. But from the standpoint

of the licensee's security, how different is that from the "reopener" clause? Furthermore, might conditions change between now and then, and more information and understanding might be gained over the interim which could change the perception of what kinds of fishways are needed at the upstream facility?

NOTE: DECOMMISSIONING AND DAM REMOVAL

Many dams constructed in the twentieth century under FERC licenses drastically diminished fish populations, despite the occasional installation of fish ladders and other mitigating devices. By the time many licenses came up for renewal, hydropower had become a much less important source of electricity in much of the country. (Because the "fuel"—falling water—is "free" and because such facilities can be turned on and off with a push of the button, hydropower remains a valuable source of "peaking" power to meet periods of high demand.) In an environmentally conscious era what had once seemed unthinkable became a subject of serious debate: Dam removal as an element of fish-friendly river restoration. Interior Secretary Babbitt began raising the issue in public speeches, saying that dams are not like the pyramids of Egypt:

> We have plenty of powerful stakeholders willing to reassert the known, traditional benefits of dams—irrigation, hydropower [and] urban water authorities [and] engineers. But the process of putting a value on the native life intrinsic to watersheds and ecosystems is something new * * *. My parents' generation gloried in the construction of dams across America's rivers. My generation saw how those rivers were changed, deformed, killed by dams. [The next] generation must help decide if, how and where those dams stand or fall.

"Dams Are Not Forever," Address to Ecological Society of America, August 4, 1998. Most serious attention focused on smaller, obsolete dams that had little economic value but were significant obstructions to fish, many of which were FERC-licensed. (There was also talk of removing even huge dams like Glen Canyon, which were built by the federal government and do not operate under FERC license.)

Dam removal can pose complications other than legal, and the engineering and environmental costs associated with dam removal might sometimes be significant. For example, a dam captures sediment behind it, which over decades can mount up to a large volume of material. These sediments may harbor heavy metals or other noxious substances. If a dam is removed, sediments might have to be removed too (an expensive process) or otherwise isolated or managed.

In 1997, FERC broke new ground by issuing an order denying a new license and ordering the Edwards Dam on the Kennebec River in Maine removed. *See* Edwards Mfg. Co., 81 F.E.R.C. ¶ 61,255 (Nov. 25, 1997). Although the licensee challenged the FERC's authority to require dam removal, ultimately the case was settled when several industries along the river agreed to contribute to the costs of removal and related costs as elements of mitigation for other developments of their own on the Kennebec. This resolution has left open a number of legal issues regarding FERC's authority to take such a step.

In the next couple of decades, several hundred FERC licenses will expire, so the issues will almost certainly arise again. Among the questions raised are whether, if FERC denies a license, it retains any regulatory authority at the site, and whether it has authority to order removal of the dam, and to require the licensee to pay the costs. FERC has adopted a lengthy policy statement addressing these questions; 69 F.E.R.C. ¶ 61,336. The issues basically involve statutory construction. The Federal Power Act seems clearly to contemplate that license renewals may be denied, but it is silent on what happens in that eventuality. Furthermore, the Act contains other provisions that muddy the waters somewhat.

In Wisconsin v. FERC, 104 F.3d 462 (D.C.Cir.1997), the States of Wisconsin and Michigan, intervenors in the proceeding before FERC to transfer a hydropower license from one entity to another, argued that the Commission should have inquired into the financial capability of the transferee to operate the dams, "particularly in light of the expected cost of future environmental measures likely to be required for the dams' continued operation." The states were concerned because an existing fisheries restoration plan could require the installation of costly fish passage facilities in the future, and that might make the dams "economically unviable," which could lead the licensee to abandon the facilities, and which could put the cost burden on state taxpayers. The court refused, finding it within FERC's discretion not to make the financial inquiry. It said, among other things:

> At this point, neither FERC nor Wisconsin or Michigan can predict with any certainty whether, and in what form, such requirements may eventually be imposed. Moreover, as FERC noted, the transferee has agreed to comply with all the terms and conditions of the licenses, which would include any environmental measures that may become necessary, and neither Wisconsin nor Michigan has presented any evidence that calls into question [the licensee's] commitment or ability to do so. * * * In the absence of any evidence to suggest that the projects were likely to become marginal or to be abandoned by the transferee, FERC could reasonably conclude that consideration of the impact of future environmental controls on the projects' economic viability was better deferred until such measures were actually imposed at the time of relicensing, and that the possibility that the projects might be decommissioned due to their economic unviability was too speculative to warrant requiring [the applicant] to submit additional financial documentation.

One way to think about these issues is to compare a hydro facility to, for example, a coal-fired power plant or a nuclear plant. When these other generating facilities reach the end of their useful life, it seems to be taken for granted that regulatory authorities can require that they be dismantled, the sites reclaimed, and any waste and other materials properly stored or disposed of at the operator's expense. Should hydro facilities be treated any differently, as a matter of policy? Should the Commission require operators to pay an annual surcharge to be put in a fund to provide for dam removal costs when the time comes? Is the Court in the *Wisconsin* case ducking this important issue? If the FERC concludes, fifteen years from now, that the projects ought to be decommissioned and the new owners argue they cannot afford to bear the costs of decommissioning, can FERC require them to bear it anyway?

In August 2004, agreement was reached among key players to complete implementation of legislation enacted by Congress in 1992 that called for removal of two large dams on the Elwha River on the north side of Washington's Olympic Peninsula. The project will cost nearly $200 million, mostly funded by the federal government. Starting in early 2008, the 108–foot Elwha Dam and 210–foot Glines Canyon Dam, built in 1913 and 1927, respectively, will be dismantled in stages to open 70 miles of prime salmon and steelhead spawning habitat eliminated when the dams were built. The upper part of the upstream reservoir is located in Olympic National Park, as is nearly all of the watershed. The removal process is complicated by the fact that some 18 million cubic yards of sediment have been trapped behind the dams (particularly Glines Canyon, the upstream one) since the dams were built. The current plan calls for 8 million cubic yards of that sediment to be left deposited in terraces along the sides of the canyon slope, to be as consistent as possible with the natural landform. The amount of sediment involved is perhaps a thousand times greater than that released in any other dam removal to date, which will provide a good opportunity to help understand the geomorphological processes involved, and the biological processes in reviving a fishery.

CHAPTER 7

THE MINERAL RESOURCE

Historically, mining was the most lucrative and therefore the most preferred use of the federal lands. Federal mineral development also furnished the context for some of the most colorful and famous (or infamous) episodes in federal land history: the California gold rush, the Teapot Dome scandal of the 1920s, the uranium boom on the Colorado Plateau in the 1950s, the gold boom in northern Nevada in the 1980s, and, recently, the coalbed methane boom in Wyoming's Powder River basin.

Earlier chapters have highlighted some of the legal issues involved in federal mineral development. After Congress abandoned an early attempt at leasing federal minerals (*Gratiot*), the federal government acquiesced to miners' customs developed in the California gold rush. State property and water laws incorporated these customs. Subsequently Congress largely incorporated these principles in the Mining Law of 1872. Within a few decades, however, the goal of all-out privatization of federal mineral resources gave way to reservations of minerals for development under governmental supervision. This led to controversies over withdrawal policies (*Midwest Oil*) culminating in the Mineral Leasing Act of 1920, which put the important fossil fuels and fertilizer minerals firmly under governmental control (*United States ex rel. McLennan*).

Withdrawal issues continue to be important, as do questions about the extent to which state law has been preempted (*Granite Rock*). There may also be questions about governmental regulation "taking" private property rights perfected in federally-owned minerals and when evolving governmental regulatory policies may give private contractors, such as mineral lessees, contract remedies against the government (*Mobil Oil*). Today, debate about mining on federal lands mostly concerns regulating its adverse effects on the environment or other resources and amenities, and this emphasis is reflected in what follows.

This chapter sets out the general framework for how decisions are made to move forward with development of federal minerals. Section A deals with the Mining Law of 1872, the embodiment of frontier free enterprise. A potent political symbol as well as the legal means for obtaining public hardrock minerals, it remains by far the most prominent of the great nineteenth-century disposal laws still on the books. Section B examines the separate and contrasting system of mineral leasing, used today for the disposition of fossil fuels, geothermal resources, and fertilizer minerals onshore; and, for all minerals on the Outer Continental Shelf. Since 1920, federal statutes governing coal, oil and gas, oil shale, potash, potassium, sodium, sulfur, and (since 1970) geothermal energy have retained federal ownership and control of the land overlying those resources. Section C looks briefly at the third system of federal mineral disposition—competitive sale—which is used for common minerals such as sand, gravel, and building stone. The final section addresses legal issues growing out of so-called "split estates," where the U.S. owns either the minerals or the surface estate, but not both.

A. HARDROCK MINERALS: THE GENERAL MINING LAW OF 1872

The Mining Law contains this clarion call of entrepreneurship (30 U.S.C. § 22):

Except as otherwise provided, all valuable mineral deposits in lands belonging to the United States, both surveyed and unsurveyed, shall be free and open to exploration and purchase, and the lands in which they are found to occupation and purchase, by citizens of the United States and those who have declared their intention to become such, under regulations prescribed by law, and according to the local customs or rules of miners in the several mining districts, so far as the same are applicable and not inconsistent with the laws of the United States.

As originally enacted, the Mining Law offered would-be mineral developers generous terms: Whoever discovers and develops a valuable mineral deposit on federal lands may mine that deposit virtually free of charge and competition, and may receive fee simple title (a "patent" purchased at $2.50 or $5 per acre) to the land containing the deposit. The system is based on self-initiation; historically, miners needed no federal permission to prospect and locate mining claims on federal lands and extract minerals from those claims.

Over the years, other concerns have been brought to bear that destroyed this original, somewhat elegant simplicity. Many public lands and many different kinds of minerals are no longer subject to the Mining Law. Even where it still applies, the right accorded the discoverer of the mineral has become less absolute; access and development are conditioned and controlled by newer statutes and regulations. As explained further below, the patent provision appears to be on its way out. Nevertheless, while the Mining Law has been limited and amended in many ways, its basic architecture has stubbornly survived a century of attempts to repeal it.

The Mining Law contains a wealth of arcana and complexity. It may have been the subject of more U.S. Supreme Court decisions (mostly from the late nineteenth century) than any single federal statute other than the Internal Revenue Code. Accordingly, there is an enormous literature on the Mining Law. The most comprehensive is a six-volume treatise produced by the Rocky Mountain Mineral Law Foundation, AMERICAN LAW OF MINING 2d (updated annually). John Leshy's book, THE MINING LAW: A STUDY IN PERPETUAL MOTION (1987), deals with an array of Mining Law issues from both an historical and contemporary reform perspective. The proceedings of the Rocky Mountain Mineral Law Institute, collected in annual volumes, generate a sizeable portion of the legal literature on hardrock mining. This chapter will touch on only the highlights. The Environmental Working Group maintains a comprehensive website, http://www.ewg.org/mining, about the number and location of mining claims around the West, with maps, detailed information about claimholders, and other interesting facts.

1. WHAT MINERALS ARE LOCATABLE UNDER THE MINING LAW?

The statutory reference in 30 U.S.C. § 22 to "all valuable mineral deposits in lands belonging to the United States" has been limited by Congress and the courts in several ways. When the Mining Law was adopted, it applied to all minerals except coal, which had already been made subject to sale at public auction by the Coal Act of 1864, 13 Stat. 205 (later modified by the Coal Lands Act of 1873, 17 Stat. 607). Coal was made a leasable mineral under the Mineral Leasing Act of 1920.

Oil and gas have posed special problems. In 1897, Congress passed the Oil Placer Act, 29 Stat. 526, confirming the status of oil, gas, and oil shale as locatable minerals under the Mining Law. The executive withdrawals of millions of acres of federal lands from petroleum location led to the famous decision in United States v. Midwest Oil Co., *supra* Chapter 5, and eventually to passage of the Mineral Leasing Act of 1920, 30 U.S.C. §§ 181 et seq. That landmark statute removed all the major fuel and fertilizer minerals from the scope of the General Mining Law. The Geothermal Steam Act of 1970, 30 U.S.C. §§ 1001–1025, makes federal geothermal resources leasable. Other minerals have been placed in the leasable category by special statutes. Leasable minerals are discussed in Section B of this chapter.

Besides locatable and leasable minerals, there is a third category—minerals (usually very common, widely occurring minerals) available only by competitive sale. The Materials Disposal Act of 1947, 30 U.S.C. §§ 601–602, as amended by the Common Varieties Act of 1955, 30 U.S.C. § 611, provides for sale of sand, stone, gravel, pumice, cinders, and other designated "common" minerals, unless the deposit "has some property giving it distinct and special value," id. § 601, in which case it may still be located under the Mining Law. The sales system is discussed in Section C of this chapter.

But apart from the minerals specifically dealt with by Congress, and in light of the truism that everything that is not animal or vegetable is mineral, there sometimes remains, even in modern times, a question as to what a mineral is for purposes of the 1872 Act.

Andrus v. Charlestone Stone Products Co.

Supreme Court of the United States, 1978.
436 U.S. 604.

■ JUSTICE MARSHALL delivered the opinion of the Court.

The question presented is whether water is a "valuable mineral" as those words are used in the mining law. * * * The claim at issue in this case, known as Claim 22, is one of a group of 23 claims near Las Vegas,

Nev., that were located in 1942. In 1962, after respondent had purchased these claims, it discovered water on Claim 22 by drilling a well thereon. This water was used to prepare for commercial sale the sand and gravel removed from some of the 23 claims. [In what was a garden variety challenge brought by the federal government to the validity of claim 22, the Ninth Circuit inexplicably held, *sua sponte*, that Claim 22 was valid because water is a valuable mineral under the 1872 Act. The Supreme Court granted certiorari.] * * *

We may assume for purposes of this decision that the Court of Appeals was correct in concluding that water is a "mineral," in the broadest sense of that word, and that it is "valuable." * * *

This Court long ago recognized that the word "mineral," when used in an Act of Congress, cannot be given its broadest definition. * * * As one court observed, if the term "mineral" in the statute were construed to encompass all substances that are conceivably mineral, "there would be justification for making mine locations on virtually every part of the earth's surface," since "a very high proportion of the substances of the earth are in that sense 'mineral.'" Rummell v. Bailey, 320 P.2d 653, 655 (1958). See also Robert L. Beery, 25 I.B.L.A. 287, 294–296 (1976) (noting that "common dirt," while literally a mineral, cannot be considered locatable under the mining law) * * *.

The fact that water may be valuable or marketable similarly is not enough to support a mining claim's validity based on the presence of water. Many substances present on the land may be of value, and indeed it seems likely that land itself—especially land located just 15 miles from downtown Las Vegas—has, in the Court of Appeals' words, "an intrinsic value." Yet the federal mining law surely was not intended to be a general real estate law; as one commentator has written, "the Congressional mandate did not sanction the disposal of federal lands under the mining laws for purposes unrelated to mining."

In order for a claim to be valid, the substance discovered must not only be a "valuable mineral" within the dictionary definition of those words, but must also be the type of valuable mineral that the 1872 Congress intended to make the basis of a valid claim. * * *

Our opinions thus recognize that, although mining law and water law developed together in the West prior to 1866, with respect to federal lands Congress chose to subject only mining to comprehensive federal regulation. When it passed the 1866 and 1870 mining laws, Congress clearly intended to preserve "pre-existing [water] right[s]." * * *

* * * [W]ithout benefit of briefing, the court below decided that "it would be incongruous * * * to hazard that Congress was not aware of the necessary glove of water for the hand of mining." Congress was indeed aware of this, so much aware that it expressly provided a water rights policy in the mining laws. But the policy adopted is a "passive" one; Congress three times (in 1866, 1870, and 1872) affirmed the view that private water rights on federal lands were to be governed by state and local law and custom. It defies common sense to assume that Congress, when it

adopted this policy, meant at the same time to establish a parallel federal system for acquiring private water rights, and that it did so *sub silentio* through laws designed to regulate mining. In light of the 1866 and 1870 provisions, the history out of which they arose, and the decisions construing them in the context of the 1872 law, the notion that water is a "valuable mineral" under that law is simply untenable.

The conclusion that Congress did not intend water to be locatable under the federal mining law is reinforced by consideration of the practical consequences that could be expected to flow from a holding to the contrary.

Many problems would undoubtedly arise simply from the fact of having two overlapping systems for acquisition of private water rights. Under the appropriation doctrine prevailing in most of the Western States, the mere fact that a person controls land adjacent to a body of water means relatively little; instead, water rights belong to "[t]he first appropriator of water for a beneficial use," but only "to the extent of his actual use." * * *

With regard to minerals located under federal law, an entirely different theory prevails. The holder of a federal mining claim, by investing $100 annually in the claim, becomes entitled to possession of the land and may make any use, or no use, of the minerals involved. See 30 U.S.C. § 28. Once fee title by patent is obtained, even the $100 requirement is eliminated.

One can readily imagine the legal conflicts that might arise from these differing approaches if ordinary water were treated as a federally cognizable "mineral." A federal claimant could, for example, utilize all of the water extracted from a well like respondent's, without regard for the settled prior appropriation rights of another user of the same water. Or he might not use the water at all and yet prevent another from using it, thereby defeating the necessary Western policy in favor of "actual use" of scarce water resources. As one respected commentator [Professor Frank Trelease] has written, allowing water to be the basis of a valid mining claim "could revive long abandoned common law rules of ground water ownership and capture, and * * * could raise horrendous problems of priority and extralateral rights." We decline to effect so major an alteration in established legal relationships based on nothing more than an overly literal reading of a statute, without any regard for its context or history.

A final indication that water should not be held to be a locatable mineral derives from Congress' 1955 decision to remove "common varieties" of certain minerals from the coverage of the mining law. 30 U.S.C. § 611. This decision was made in large part because of "abuses under the general mining laws by * * * persons who locate[d] mining claims on public lands for purposes other than that of legitimate mining activity." * * * Apparently, locating a claim and obtaining a patent to federal land was so inexpensive that many "use[d] the guise of mining locations for nonmining purposes," including the establishment of "filling stations, curio shops, cafes, * * * residence[s][and] summer camp[s]."

It has long been established that, when grants to federal land are at issue, any doubts "are resolved for the Government, not against it." United States v. Union Pacific R. Co., 353 U.S. 112, 116 (1957). *A fortiori,* the

Government must prevail in a case such as this, when the relevant statutory provisions, their historical context, consistent administrative and judicial decisions, and the practical problems with a contrary holding all weigh in its favor. * * *

NOTES AND QUESTIONS

1.   Nothing in the Mining Law requires the locator to identify, at the time the claim is located, the mineral or minerals which are the object of the enterprise. Typically, a claimant has to identify the minerals only when someone (the government or a rival locator) challenges the validity of the claim. How might that feature of the law create problems for state and other regulators of resource use?

2.   Professor Michael Braunstein has written:

[T]he question of what constitutes a mineral for purposes of the mining law retains great vitality. This is because the mining law is more generous to private claimants of publicly owned minerals than alternative schemes of disposition. If the claimant is able to obtain title to the minerals under the mining law, he does so without charge by or permit from the government. If the minerals are obtained pursuant to one of the alternative schemes of disposition, however, the claimant must first obtain permission from the government to mine, for these other schemes all vest substantial discretion in the government concerning whether mining will be permitted. Moreover, under these schemes, the miner is required to pay a royalty or rent to the government for the privilege of mining government owned minerals. If the minerals are obtained under the mining law, however, no rent or royalty is due. * * *

The determination of whether a substance is a mineral is not a question of fact, but a conclusion of law. * * * For a court to make this determination, it must first decide that the transfer of the substance and the lands containing it from public to private ownership under the mining law is appropriate in light of contemporary concerns and policies. Indeed, the question of whether a substance is a mineral is almost entirely a question of policy and only incidentally a question of chemistry.

Michael Braunstein, *All That Glitters: Discovering the Meaning of Mineral in the Mining Law of 1872*, 21 LAND & WATER L.REV. 293, 301 (1986). Is Braunstein correct when he states that judicial categorization of a substance as a "mineral" depends on a policy determination based on "contemporary concerns"? Or, should courts use a more historical approach and decide what Congress attempted to achieve at the time it enacted a statute?

3.   It is not always apparent that the Department of the Interior or the courts apply the test advocated by Professor Braunstein. Here are some examples from what is a very lengthy list of cases on the subject of what is and is not a qualifying mineral: United States v. Toole, 224 F.Supp. 440 (D.Mont.1963) (peat and organic soil not a mineral); Richter v. Utah, 27

L.D. 95 (1898) (guano is a mineral). *See also* Dunluce Placer Mine, 30 L.D. 357 (1900) (stalactites, stalagmites, and other "natural curiosities" not minerals); Hughes v. Florida, 42 L.D. 401 (1913) (shell rock not a mineral); Earl Douglass, 44 L.D. 325 (1915) (fossil remains of prehistoric animals not minerals); United States v. Elkhorn Min. Co., 2 IBLA 383 (1971) (radon gas not a mineral); United States v. Barngrover, 57 I.D. 533 (1941) ("drilling mud" is a mineral). *See also* 76 Stat. 652 (1962) (petrified wood shall not be deemed a valuable mineral deposit under the Mining Law, but the Secretary "shall provide by regulation that limited quantities of petrified wood may be removed without charge from those public lands which he shall specify").

4. Section D of this chapter shows that the question of what is a mineral may be answered in different ways in different contexts. Recall that the Stock–Raising Homestead Act of 1916 reserved minerals from disposition. Watt v. Western Nuclear, Inc., *infra* p. 664, held that gravel is a mineral for purposes of the Stock–Raising Homestead Act; United States v. Union Oil Co. of California, *infra* p. 567, held that geothermal energy, of which water is a main component, is also a mineral for the purposes of the 1916 law. Does it make sense to use different definitions of "mineral" for the 1872 and 1916 laws?

2. What "Lands Belonging to the United States" Are Open to Claim Location?

Despite the sweep of the statutory language, hardrock mineral activity is prohibited on a substantial proportion of the "lands belonging to the United States." The most severe limitation on mining locations is by legislative or executive withdrawals of federal land from the Mining Law. (Withdrawals are discussed in Chapter 5.) Even without a formal withdrawal, many federal lands are not open to Mining Law activities. In Oklahoma v. Texas, 258 U.S. 574 (1922), the two states and the federal government all disputed ownership of the bed of the Red River forming part of the states' common boundary. The Court first ruled that part of the riverbed belonged to the United States, because the river was not navigable when Oklahoma became a state. The Court then turned to whether this federally owned land was "belonging to the United States" within the meaning of the Mining Law. Speaking unanimously through Justice Van Devanter, it said no, explaining:

> [30 U.S.C. § 22] is not as comprehensive as its words separately considered suggest. It is part of a chapter relating to mineral lands which in turn is part of a title dealing with the survey and disposal of "The Public Lands." To be rightly understood it must be read with due regard for the entire statute of which it is but a part, and when this is done it is apparent that, while embracing only lands owned by the United States, it does not embrace all that are so owned. Of course, it has no application to the grounds about the Capitol in Washington or to the lands in the National Cemetery at Arlington, no matter what their mineral value; and yet both belong to the United States. And so of the lands in the Yosemite National Park, the Yellowstone National

Park, and the military reservations throughout the Western States. Only where the United States has indicated that the lands are held for disposal under the land laws does the section apply; and it never applies where the United States directs that the disposal be only under other laws.

Id. at 599–600.

This decision reflects the seemingly sensible policy that if federal lands are not generally open to disposal, the Mining Law—which can lead to such disposal through the process of patenting mining claims—should not apply unless an explicit decision is made to have it apply. Oklahoma v. Texas creates, in other words, a basic presumption that the Mining Law is inapplicable to federal lands not otherwise available for disposal of fee title. This meant that, as the disposal era drew to a close, lands remained open to the Mining Law only if Congress explicitly mandated that result. Congress has provided that perhaps 400 million acres of federal land (mostly those managed by the BLM and the Forest Service) are still open to the Mining Law, unless otherwise withdrawn by executive or legislative action.

The legal principle announced in Oklahoma v. Texas has continued vitality. As Department of the Interior Instructions put it in 1941 (57 Interior Decisions 365, 372–73), "public lands reserved or withdrawn for sundry public uses and purposes * * * which do not in terms expressly include mineral lands * * * are not subject to the operation of the mineral land laws." *See* Brown v. United States Dep't of the Interior, 679 F.2d 747 (8th Cir.1982) (relying on Oklahoma v. Texas to hold the Mining Law inapplicable in units of National Park System absent an express authorization from Congress); Pathfinder Mines Corp. v. Hodel, 811 F.2d 1288, 1291 (9th Cir.1987) (holding that a federal "Game Preserve" was not open to mining claim location even though the proclamation that designated it was silent on the subject, because "the express purposes of the Game Preserve are incompatible with entry under the [Mining Law]"). It means also that acquired lands (about 10 percent of all federal lands, including, most prominently, Eastern national forests) are generally off limits to the Mining Law, because these lands are not available for disposal. The 1947 Mineral Leasing Act for Acquired Lands, 30 U.S.C. 351–359, provides that minerals subject to leasing on ordinary federal lands are also subject to lease on acquired lands. Somewhat oddly, there is no generic law which authorizes the development of hardrock minerals on federal acquired lands.

Finally, because of the *pedis possessio* doctrine (discussed *infra* p. 567), mining claims may not, in some situations, be validly located on federal lands which are already subject to mining claims. For all these reasons, and especially because there is no central repository of withdrawals, it can be difficult to determine whether a particular tract of federal land remains open to the Mining Law. Miners have often regretted their failure to consult the record systems in BLM state offices before expending their efforts.

3. How Is a Mining Claim Located?

One of the many quaint features of the Mining Law (and one of the many that have been much litigated) is that several different types of mining claims may be located. There are two types of mineral claims—lode and placer—and there are nonmineral mining claims as well—millsites and tunnel sites. State law also plays a prominent role in the location process, for it controls locations to the extent it is not inconsistent with federal law. Butte City Water Co. v. Baker, 196 U.S. 119, 126 (1905). A starting point is 30 U.S.C. § 28:

> The miners of each mining district may make regulations not in conflict with the laws of the United States, or with the laws of the State or Territory in which the district is situated, governing the location, manner of recording, amount of work necessary to hold possession of a mining claim, subject to the following requirements: The location must be distinctly marked on the ground so that its boundaries can be readily traced. All records of mining claims * * * shall contain the name or names of the locators, the date of the location, and such a description of the claim or claims located by reference to some natural object or permanent monument as will identify the claim. * * *

Typically, state statutes require: (1) a valuable discovery; (2) prompt posting at or near the place of discovery to give notice; (3) development work to determine the character and extent of the deposit; (4) marking on the ground to establish the boundaries of the claim; and (5) recording of a notice or certificate, usually with the county clerk or recorder. For a long time, most states' laws required actual excavation of a pit on the claim. In the *Lucky Mc* case in the next subsection, for example, Arizona state law required the claimant to drill a ten-foot hole on each claim, even though the holes had absolutely nothing to do with the exploration, which was being carried out at much greater depths. All these anachronistic, environmentally damaging state laws seem now to have been repealed.

The two main kinds of mineral claims are lode and placer. The original Mining Law of 1866 authorized only lode claims, while an 1870 amendment authorized placer claims. Classically, "lodes" referred to aggregations or veins of mineral embedded in rock, while "placer" referred to mineral deposits in gravels or other loose sediments. Nature does not always draw such neat lines, of course, so there are ambiguous situations and the judicial results are unpredictable. *See* Globe Mining Co. v. Anderson, 318 P.2d 373 (Wyo.1957) (widespread horizontal deposit containing scattered mineralized zones deemed a lode). The leading Mining Law treatise calls the legal distinction between lode and placer claims an "historical accident." 1 American Law of Mining § 32.02[1].

The distinction is nevertheless important, because the Mining Law carefully specifies different criteria for the boundaries of lode and placer claims. *Lode* claims may not exceed 1500 feet in length or 300 feet on each side of the middle of the vein, and the end lines of the claim must be parallel. 30 U.S.C. § 23. There is no requirement that lode claims conform to survey lines, and lode claims are often irregular in shape. *Placer* claims must conform "as near as practicable" to survey lines where the area has been surveyed. 30 U.S.C. § 35. Otherwise no provisions govern the shape of the exterior boundaries of placer claims. A single claimant cannot locate a placer claim of more than 20 acres, 30 U.S.C. § 35, but associations of persons may locate placer claims of 20 acres per person, not to exceed a claim of 160 acres for an association of eight or more people. 30 U.S.C. § 36. Misidentification of a lode as a placer, or vice versa, is a ground for invalidating the claim. Cole v. Ralph, 252 U.S. 286, 295 (1920).

> The result is, for the unwary, a classic trap. For the prudent sophisticate, the result is often an additional expense for locating both types of claims on the same ground to avoid pitfalls. But the Law sets a trap for the prudent but unsophisticated, for the placer claim must be filed first; otherwise, filing it might be construed as an abandonment of the lode claim. These contortions serve absolutely no useful purpose.

John Leshy, THE MINING LAW, at 94.

Before 1976, recordation of mining claims was governed solely by state laws, which typically require filing with the county clerk or recorder, but contain no mechanism to determine whether a claim had been abandoned. By 1970, an estimated six to ten million inactive claims existed on the public lands and the Public Land Law Review Commission recommended federal recordation. Congress included a requirement in the Federal Land Policy and Management Act (FLPMA) that all claims be recorded with the Bureau of Land Management, or "conclusively" be deemed abandoned. 43 U.S.C. § 1744(c). Staying true to the maxim that nothing regarding the Mining Law ever follows the simplest path, this requirement apparently does not displace state recordation laws. *See* 43 U.S.C. § 1744(d). FLPMA also requires that every mining claimant annually file a statement of an intention to hold the claim upon penalty of losing the claim. The federal recordation requirement has weeded out a large number of stale or abandoned mining claims. As of September 2005, about 210,000 unpatented mining claims were properly recorded with BLM.

Millsites are nonmineral claims, located for the purpose of accommodating mineral processing and ancillary facilities on federal lands. Millsites are limited to five acres each, must be *noncontiguous* to mining claims, and must be located on *nonmineral* federal land open to the Mining Law. This puts an awkward burden on a millsite locator, who must show, if challenged, that the land located for a millsite does *not* contain minerals. The need for large acreages to locate processing facilities and tailings and waste rock piles has created a problem for the modern mining industry. With development of the ability to extract fine particles of widely disseminated gold deposits from rock through cyanide heap-leaching, it is now standard practice to move hundreds of tons of material to produce ounces of gold. Where to put those tons of waste rock and overburden is a problem.

The Bush (II) administration has taken several steps to accommodate the need for processing and waste facilities near mines. These steps have overturned prior decisions or liberalized longstanding practice under the Mining Law. For instance, a 2003 Solicitor's Opinion rescinded an affirmation by the Solicitor in the Clinton Administration of early interpretations of the Mining Law that limited millsites to no more than one per each mineral claim. The 2003 Opinion concluded that the Mining Law places no limits on the amount of public land that mining companies can claim for ancillary facilities like tailings piles and waste dumps.

The Solicitor responsible for the rescinded opinions, John Leshy, later characterized the debate over these issues this way:

> The mill site imbroglio is emblematic of a larger issue: namely, how to interpret this old Mining Law. Some members of the mineral law community see the Mining Law as almost infinitely flexible, so long as the flexibility runs in one direction—to serve the interests and needs of the domestic mining industry. [The Clinton Administration's] perspective has been different. Doubtless a basic purpose of the Mining Law was to promote the development of federal minerals, but if the enacting Congress had wanted the Executive Branch to bend every effort toward that end, it needed to say nothing more than that. As we all know, however, Congress instead chose to include exquisite (or mind-numbing, depending upon your perspective) details in the law. We concluded that Congress did not intend the statutory mill site acreage limitation to be ignored to give miners a right to claim (and patent) an unlimited amount of public land acreage for waste dumps and spoil piles.

Public Lands at the Millennium, 46 ROCKY MT. MIN. L. INST. 1, 1–13 to1–14 (2000).

4. WHAT ARE A MINING CLAIMANT'S RIGHTS BEFORE DISCOVERY? THE *PEDIS POSSESSIO* DOCTRINE

A mining claim is not valid against the United States until the physical steps of location have been completed *and* a valuable mineral deposit has been discovered. "Location is the act or series of acts whereby the boundaries of the claim are marked, etc., but it confers no right in the absence of discovery, both being essential to a valid claim." Cole v. Ralph, 252 U.S. 286, 296 (1920). The statute itself expressly requires that discovery precede claim location. *See* 30 U.S.C. § 23 ("[N]o location of a mining claim shall be made until the discovery of a vein or lode within the limits of the claim located."). Prior to discovery, courts have devised some limited protections for claim locators who are exploring in good faith, against others who try to "jump" their claims. The following case, which addresses mining claims located for petroleum, was decided a year before Congress removed fossil fuels from the ambit of the Mining Law and made them subject to leasing. But its interpretation of the Mining Law remains a bedrock precedent.

Union Oil Co. v. Smith

Supreme Court of the United States, 1919.
249 U.S. 337.

■ JUSTICE PITNEY delivered the opinion of the Court.

[Two rival groups of oil prospectors filed separate claims on the same ground. The defendant Union Oil argued it had located the ground first, many years before the plaintiff came on the scene.] * * * No discovery of oil or other minerals had ever been made upon the ground by either of the claimants or by any other person. But at the time plaintiff and his associates located [their claim on the ground,] defendant, although not then actually occupying this ground, was in actual occupation of a contiguous claim of 160 acres known as the "Sampson claim," upon which it then was drilling and afterwards continued to drill a well for the discovery of oil, the well being 1,000 feet distant from the boundary line of the disputed claim. Defendant claimed the right of possession of five contiguous claims, including [the one also claimed by the plaintiff] under locations regularly made in all respects save discovery. * * *

[I]t is clear that in order to create valid rights or initiate a title as against the United States a discovery of mineral is essential. * * * Nevertheless, [30 U.S.C. § 22] extends an express invitation to all qualified persons to explore the lands of the United States for valuable mineral deposits, and this and the following sections hold out to one who succeeds in making discovery the promise of a full reward. Those who, being qualified, proceed in good faith to make such explorations and enter peaceably upon vacant lands of the United States for that purpose are not treated as mere trespassers, but as licensees or tenants at will. For since, as a practical matter, exploration must precede the discovery of minerals, and some occupation of the land ordinarily is necessary for adequate and systematic exploration, legal recognition of the *pedis possessio* of a bona fide and qualified prospector is universally regarded as a necessity. It is held [by state and lower federal courts] that upon the public domain a miner may hold the place in which he may be working against all others having no better right, and while he remains in possession, diligently working towards discovery, is entitled—at least for a reasonable time—to be protected against forcible, fraudulent, and clandestine intrusions upon his possession. * * *

And it has come to be generally recognized that while discovery is the indispensable fact and the marking and recording of the claim dependent upon it, yet the order of time in which these acts occur is not essential to the acquisition from the United States of the exclusive right of possession of the discovered minerals or the obtaining of a patent therefore, but that discovery may follow after location and give validity to the claim as of the time of discovery, provided no rights of third parties have intervened. * * *

To what extent the possessory right of an explorer before discovery is to be deduced from the invitation extended in [30 U.S.C. § 22], to what extent it is to be regarded as a local regulation of the kind recognized by that section and the following ones, and to what extent it derives force from the authority of the mining states to regulate the possession of the public lands in the interest of peace and good order, are questions with which we are not now concerned. Nor need we stop to inquire whether the right is limited to the ground actually occupied in the process of exploration, or extends to the limits of the claim. These questions and others that suggest themselves are not raised by the present record * * *. Whatever the nature and extent of a possessory right before discovery, all authorities agree that such possession may be maintained only by continued actual occupancy by a qualified locator or his representatives engaged in persistent and diligent prosecution of work looking to the discovery of mineral. * * * [The Court concluded that Union Oil had no rights in the disputed claim because it was not in actual occupancy of it, even though it was engaged in exploratory drilling on the contiguous "Sampson" claim.]

NOTES AND QUESTIONS

1.   Given the clarity of the Mining Law that discovery must precede claim location (30 U.S.C. § 23), how could the Court conclude here that "the order of time in which these acts occur is not essential"? Is the result consistent with the intent of the enacting Congress? By what reasoning? Should a court feel free to refashion statutes that contain anachronistic notions of resource development?

2.   The last paragraph of the foregoing excerpt from *Union Oil* noted, but did not choose among, three possible sources of the *pedis possessio* doctrine: (1) implied from federal law, or federal common law filling in the Mining Law's interstices; (2) the customs of miners, incorporated into the federal statute; or (3) state police power to help keep the peace in mining country (*cf.* Omaechevarria v. State of Idaho, *supra* p. 139).

3.   What rights, if any, does *pedis possessio* give the claimant against the United States? For example, what would be the effect on a prospector if the United States were to withdraw the area from mining prior to discovery? *See, e.g.*, United States v. Carlile, 67 I.D. 417 (1960) (no vested rights).

4.   *Union Oil* gave the Supreme Court's imprimatur to the *pedis possessio* doctrine, but it did not provide much guidance on its contours. The following decision by a state supreme court addressed the scope of the doctrine in the context of a modern exploration project covering a wide area.

Geomet Exploration, Limited v. Lucky Mc Uranium Corp.

Supreme Court of Arizona, 1979.
601 P.2d 1339, *cert. dismissed*, 448 U.S. 917 (1980).

■ JUSTICE HAYS

* * * By use of modern scintillation equipment in September of 1976, plaintiff/appellee, Lucky Mc Uranium Corporation, detected "anomalies" (discontinuities in geologic formations) indicative of possible uranium deposits in * * * land in the federal public domain. In November, 1976, Lucky proceeded to monument and post 200 claims (4,000 acres), drill a 10–foot hole on each claim, and record notices pursuant to [state law].

Subsequently, defendant/appellant, Geomet, peaceably entered some of the areas claimed by Lucky and began drilling operations. Employees of

Geomet were aware of Lucky's claims but considered them invalid because there had been no discovery of minerals in place and Lucky was not in actual occupancy of the areas Geomet entered.

Lucky instituted a possessory action seeking damages, exclusive possession and a permanent injunction against trespass by Geomet or its employees. There was insufficient evidence to establish a valid discovery, but the trial court found that Lucky was entitled to exclusive possession and a permanent injunction. * * *

Additionally, the court found that Geomet had entered the land in bad faith, knowing that Lucky was claiming it.

We must decide a single issue: Should the actual occupancy requirement of *pedis possessio* be discarded in favor of constructive possession to afford a potential locator protection of contiguous, unoccupied claims as against one who enters peaceably, openly, and remains in possession searching for minerals?

PEDIS POSSESSIO

Mineral deposits in the public domain of the United States are open to all citizens (or those who have expressed an intent to become citizens) who wish to occupy and explore them "under regulations prescribed by law, and according to the local customs or rules of miners in the several mining districts, so far as the same are applicable and not inconsistent with the laws of the United States." 30 U.S.C. § 22.

The doctrine of *pedis possessio* evolved from customs and usages of miners * * *. Regardless of compliance with statutory requisites such as monumenting and notice, one cannot perfect a location, under either federal or state law, without actual discovery of minerals in place. Best v. Humboldt Placer Mining Co., 371 U.S. 334 (1963). Until discovery, the law of possession determines who has the better right to possession. * * *

If the first possessor should relax his occupancy or cease working toward discovery, and another enters peaceably, openly, and diligently searches for mineral, the first party forfeits the right to exclusive possession under the requirements of *pedis possessio*. Cole v. Ralph, 252 U.S. 286, 295 (1920). * * *

Conceding that actual occupancy is necessary under *pedis possessio,* Lucky urges that the requirement be relaxed in deference to the time and expense that would be involved in actually occupying and drilling on each claim until discovery. Moreover, Lucky points out that the total area claimed—4,000 acres—is reasonable in size, similar in geological formation, and that an overall work program for the entire area had been developed. Under these circumstances, Lucky contends, actual drilling on some of the claims should suffice to afford protection as to all contiguous claims. Great reliance is placed on MacGuire v. Sturgis, 347 F.Supp. 580 (D.Wyo.1971), in which the federal court accepted arguments similar to those advanced here and extended protection on a group or area basis. Geomet counters that *MacGuire* is an aberration and contrary to three Wyoming Supreme Court cases upholding the requisite of actual occupancy.

To adopt the premise urged by Lucky eviscerates the actual occupancy requirement of *pedis possessio* and substitutes for it the theory of constructive possession even though there is no color of title. We are persuaded that the sounder approach is to maintain the doctrine intact. * * *

We have canvassed the Western mining jurisdictions and found the requirement of actual occupancy to be the majority view.

There are always inherent risks in prospecting. The development of *pedis possessio* from the customs of miners argues forcefully against the proposition that exclusive right to possession should encompass claims neither actually occupied nor being explored. We note that the doctrine does not protect on the basis of occupancy alone; the additional requirement of diligent search for minerals must also be satisfied. The reason for these dual elements—and for the policy of the United States in making public domain available for exploration and mining—is to encourage those prepared to demonstrate their sincerity and tenacity in the pursuit of valuable minerals. If one may, by complying with preliminary formalities of posting and recording notices, secure for himself the exclusive possession of a large area upon only a small portion of which he is actually working, then he may, at his leisure, explore the entire area and exclude all others who stand ready to peaceably and openly enter unoccupied sections for the purpose of discovering minerals. Such a premise is laden with extreme difficulties of determining over how large an area and for how long one might be permitted to exclude others.

We hold that *pedis possessio* protects only those claims actually occupied (provided also that work toward discovery is in progress) and does not extend to contiguous, unoccupied claims on a group or area basis. * * *

Finally, Lucky asserts that Geomet cannot invoke *pedis possessio* because Geomet, knowing that Lucky claimed the area, entered in bad faith. Lucky relies principally on Bagg v. New Jersey Loan Co. [354 P.2d 40 (Ariz. 1960)] and Woolsey v. Lassen, 371 P.2d 587 (Ariz. 1962). It is true that a potential locator must enter in good faith.

There is language in our decisions that appears to indicate that mere knowledge of a prior claim constitutes bad faith. Although we are sure that our holdings were sound in the cases Lucky cites, certain statements may have been an inadvertent oversimplification of the issue of good faith and we take this opportunity to clarify the point.

In general terms, good faith may be defined as honesty of purpose and absence of intent to defraud. * * *

Both *Bagg* and *Woolsey* dealt with those who had discovered minerals in place and were in actual occupancy when others attempted to usurp their claims. These facts immediately distinguish them from the instant case, in which Lucky had neither made discovery nor was in actual occupancy of the areas Geomet entered. * * *

In summary, both cases differ significantly from this case in their factual framework and did not depend for their resolution solely upon the element of knowledge. We stand by our conclusions in those cases but wish to emphasize that mere knowledge of a previous claim, in and of itself, does not constitute bad faith.

Since Geomet's entry concededly was open and peaceable, we hold that the entry was in good faith. * * *

NOTES AND QUESTIONS

1. The Supreme Court granted Lucky Mc's petition for a writ of certiorari to review the Arizona Supreme Court's decision. Immediately thereafter, industry representatives urged Lucky Mc to dismiss its petition because of fears about how the Court might dispose of the case; e.g., it might extend the strict *pedis possessio* rule to all states. Eventually Lucky Mc dismissed its already-granted petition voluntarily. It was not clear whether the Court would have had jurisdiction to decide the case in any event. Specifically, is the *pedis possessio* doctrine one of federal or state law? If no rights of the U.S. are implicated absent a discovery on a claim, are such disputes between rival claimants governed by federal law, or only by state common law rules of "possession"? If it is a rule of state law, does the U.S. Supreme Court have jurisdiction to review it? Is the Arizona Supreme Court bound by decisions of other courts, including the United States Supreme Court, on this issue? Note that the Arizona court found the view of other state courts persuasive, and rejected a contrary federal district court decision in Wyoming.

2. What if Geomet had done no more than post an armed guard on each claim? Note that in the Arizona Supreme Court's view, "occupancy alone" is not enough to gain protection of the *pedis possessio* doctrine.

3. Is *pedis possessio* the kind of open-ended doctrine that should expand its coverage to meet the needs of new technologies and changing times? Should courts adopt the more liberal rule of MacGuire v. Sturgis (the Wyoming decision discussed by the Arizona Supreme Court)? How does one "occupy" 4000 acres?

4. What does *Lucky Mc* say about a prospector's security of possession over a large area that is typical of a modern exploration project? An experienced mining lawyer has suggested that legislative reform may be necessary:

> The complete exploration necessary to make an actual discovery of such a mineral as uranium at great depth requires a rather extensive accumulation of capital, engineering, and technological experience and expertise, and a substantial organization. Once such a deposit is found, it requires even greater capital, engineering skill, and technological resources to develop and produce it, process it, and ultimately to market it. Unless a party is able to perform all of these functions himself, he is not likely to be in a position to fail to adhere to the current customs because at some stage of the sequence of location, exploration, discovery, production, processing, and marketing, he invariably will have to enter into an arrangement or accommodation

with some other member of the industry who has elected to abide by those customs. * * *

Protection of possessory interests prior to discovery * * * is needed, but it probably is not afforded by the traditional application of pedis possessio. With the location of the claims and the existence of a proper plan for their exploration, the courts might liberalize the doctrine to grant that protection. However, the court decisions to date have not indicated the judiciary feels such a change would be proper. Therefore, operators at this time are in continuous jeopardy of loss of claims, but they really have little choice until the laws have been altered or broadened by legislation or judicial application.

Terry Fiske, *Pedis Possessio: Modern Use of an Old Concept,* 15 Rocky Mtn. Min. L. Inst. 181, 215–16 (1969).

5. Why doesn't Congress fix the problem? What should a legislative fix look like? If Congress did away with the occupancy requirement altogether, would this result in a few aggressive companies indefinitely tying up very large tracts of federal lands with mining claims? Who might object to such an approach? How would "mom-and-pop" prospectors respond to such a proposal? How would it affect those with a penchant for claim-jumping? What position do you think environmentalists would take?

6. As Union Oil Co. v. Smith shows, the courts have sometimes been willing to adjust their interpretations of the Mining Law to accommodate what they perceive to be the needs of the mining industry. As *Lucky Mc* shows, however, there are limits on judicial willingness to be creative in accommodating an ancient statute to changed conditions. But even when the rules in the law books do not keep pace with mining technology, mining companies can reach informal (albeit legally unenforceable) accommodations in the field to minimize conflict. *See* William Marsh & James M. King, *Staking Mining Claims on Revoked Public Land Withdrawals: Issues and Alternative Strategies,* 30 Rocky Mtn. Min. L. Inst. 9–1, 9–29 to 9–30 (1985):

Widely publicized mining claim staking rushes in areas of high mineral potential are usually closely monitored by local law enforcement agencies. Law enforcement personnel will prevent (and rightfully so) any affirmative efforts to exclude rival claimants except perhaps verbal and written admonitions to "stay off my claim." Experience has shown that such admonitions are totally ignored. Even in the absence of law enforcement agencies, an aura of conviviality rather than hostility seems to develop. Physical violence between rival claimants is eschewed, and would certainly be viewed with a jaundiced eye in the courts.

It is not only possible but almost universally the case that multiple rivals are "occupying" the same parcel of land while diligently (feverishly might be a more accurate description) seeking a discovery. Under these circumstances, it would seem that no such diligent occupant is entitled to any rights under the doctrine of *pedis possessio* as against another such diligent occupant, recognizing that both of them might gain *pedis possessio* rights as against a less enthusiastic participant.

As between two or more such diligent occupants, utilizing the traditional analytical framework, correlative rights should be determined on the basis of the first rival to couple the notice posting and discovery requirements in states where applicable law permits the locator a specified period within which to mark the boundaries of his claim and record a certificate of location.

5. GAINING RIGHTS AGAINST THE UNITED STATES: DISCOVERY OF A VALUABLE MINERAL DEPOSIT

The key term in the Mining Law that determines whether a miner has acquired a property right against the United States is "discovery." Because Congress did not provide a definition for "discovery," the Interior Department has filled in the legislative lacuna. The first excerpt, below, is a determination made by the Secretary of the Interior in ruling on the validity of a patent application. The second excerpt is a Supreme Court decision grappling with the same problem.

Castle v. Womble

Opinion of the Secretary of the Interior, 1894.
19 L.D. 455.

[On July 2, 1889, Martin Womble filed a patent application to gain title to federal land under the homestead/preemption laws. These laws did not apply to federal lands that are mineral in character. Womble's application was opposed by Walter Castle who, along with others, had located the Empire Quartz mining claim on some of the same land in 1890. Lower-ranking officials in the Interior Department concluded that Castle and his colleagues had made a valuable discovery, and denied Womble's application, and he appealed to the Secretary.]

The law is emphatic in declaring that "no location of a mining claim shall be made until the discovery of the vein or lode within the limits of the claim located." * * * And this Department [has previously said that discovery] * * * "is a prerequisite to the location, and, of course, entry of any mining claim. Without compliance with this essential requirement of the law no location will be recognized, no entry allowed.["] Has such discovery been made in this case?

In the case of Sullivan [v.] Iron Silver Mining Co. (143 U.S. 431) [1892], it was commonly believed that underlying all the country in the immediate vicinity of land in controversy was a horizontal vein or deposit, called a blanket vein, and that the patent issued was obtained with a view to thereafter develop such underlying vein. The supreme court, however, said * * * that this was mere speculation and belief, not based on any discoveries or tracings, and did not meet the requirements of the statute, citing Iron Silver Mining Co. v. Reynolds (124 U.S. 374) [1888].

In the last cited case the court, on page 384, says that the necessary knowledge of the existence of minerals may be obtained from the outcrop of the lode or vein, or from developments of a placer claim, previous to the application for patent, or perhaps in other ways; but hopes and beliefs cannot be accepted as the equivalent of such proper knowledge. In other words, it may be said that the requirement relating to discovery refers to present facts, and not to the probabilities of the future.

In this case the presence of mineral is not based upon probabilities, belief and speculation alone, but upon facts, which * * * show that with further work, a paying and valuable mine, so far as human foresight can determine, will be developed.

After a careful consideration of the subject, it is my opinion that where minerals have been found and the evidence is of such a character that a person of ordinary prudence would be justified in the further expenditure of his labor and means, with a reasonable prospect of success, in developing a valuable mine, the requirements of the statute have been met. To hold otherwise would tend to make of little avail, if not entirely nugatory, that provision of the law whereby "all valuable mineral deposits in lands belonging to the United States * * * are * * * declared to be free and open to exploration and purchase." For, if as soon as minerals are shown to exist, and at any time during exploration, before the returns become remunerative, the lands are to be subject to other disposition, few would be found willing to risk time and capital in the attempt to bring to light and make available the mineral wealth, which lies concealed in the bowels of the earth, as Congress obviously must have intended the explorers should have proper opportunity to do.

Entertaining these views, your judgment is affirmed.

United States v. Coleman

Supreme Court of the United States, 1968.
390 U.S. 599.

■ Justice Black delivered the opinion of the Court.

In 1956 respondent Coleman applied to the Department of the Interior for a patent [fee simple title] to certain public lands based on his entry onto and exploration of these lands and his discovery there of a variety of stone called quartzite, one of the most common of all solid materials. It was, and still is, respondent Coleman's contention that the quartzite deposits qualify as "valuable mineral deposits" under 30 U.S.C. § 22 * * *. The Secretary of the Interior held that to qualify as "valuable mineral deposits" under 30 U.S.C. § 22 it must be shown that the mineral can be "extracted, removed and marketed at a profit"—the so-called "marketability test." Based on the largely undisputed evidence in the record, the Secretary concluded that the deposits claimed by respondent Coleman did not meet that criterion. * * * The Secretary denied the patent application, but respondent Coleman remained on the land, forcing the Government to bring this present action in ejectment in the District Court against respondent Coleman and his lessee, respondent McClennan. The respondents filed a counterclaim seeking to have the District Court direct the Secretary to issue a patent to them. * * * We granted the Government's petition for certiorari because of the importance of the decision to the utilization of the public lands.

We cannot agree with the Court of Appeals and believe that the rulings of the Secretary of the Interior were proper. The Secretary's determination that the quartzite deposits did not qualify as valuable mineral deposits because the stone could not be marketed at a profit does no violence to the statute. Indeed, the marketability test is an admirable effort to identify with greater precision and objectivity the factors relevant to a determination that a mineral deposit is "valuable." It is a logical complement to the "prudent-man test" which the Secretary has been using to interpret the mining laws since 1894. Under this "prudent-man test" in order to qualify as "valuable mineral deposits," the discovered deposits must be of such a character that "a person of ordinary prudence would be justified in the further expenditure of his labor and means, with a reasonable prospect of success, in developing a valuable mine * * *." Castle v. Womble, 19 L.D. 455, 457 (1894). This Court has approved the prudent-man formulation and interpretation on numerous occasions. Under the mining laws Congress has made public lands available to people for the purpose of mining valuable mineral deposits and not for other purposes. The obvious intent was to reward and encourage the discovery of minerals that are valuable in an economic sense. Minerals which no prudent man will extract because there is no demand for them at a price higher than the cost of extraction and transportation are hardly economically valuable. Thus, profitability is an important consideration in applying the prudent-man test, and the marketability test which the Secretary has used here merely recognizes this fact.

The marketability test also has the advantage of throwing light on a claimant's intention, a matter which is inextricably bound together with valuableness. For evidence that a mineral deposit is not of economic value and cannot in all likelihood be operated at a profit may well suggest that a claimant seeks the land for other purposes. Indeed, as the Government points out, the facts of this case—the thousands of dollars and hours spent building a home on 720 acres in a highly scenic national forest located two hours from Los Angeles, the lack of an economically feasible market for the stone, and the immense quantities of identical stone found in the area outside the claims—might well be thought to raise a substantial question as to respondent Coleman's real intention.

Finally, we think that the Court of Appeals' objection to the marketability test on the ground that it involves the imposition of a different and more onerous standard on claims for minerals of widespread occurrence than for rarer minerals which have generally been dealt with under the prudent-man test is unwarranted. As we have pointed out above, the prudent-man test and the marketability test are not distinct standards, but are complementary in that the latter is a refinement of the former. While it is true that the marketability test is usually the critical factor in cases involving nonmetallic minerals of widespread occurrence, this is accounted for by the perfectly natural reason that precious metals which are in small supply and for which there is a great demand, sell at a price so high as to leave little room for doubt that they can be extracted and marketed at a profit. * * *

NOTES AND QUESTIONS

1. Was the Secretary in Castle v. Womble trying to expand or relax the concept of "discovery" as a substitute for the *pedis possessio* doctrine? That is, was he trying to protect explorers so as to encourage exploration? What is the difference between *pedis possessio* and discovery, so far as a claimant's rights against the United States are concerned?

2. How much latitude would a Secretary of the Interior have today to change the definition of discovery under the Mining Law? Does *Coleman* lock the marketability test into place, or is the Interior Department free to alter its longstanding interpretation?

3. Discovery was important in *Coleman* because he sought a patent, to gain fee title to the land (as well as the mineral). Patenting seems to be on its way out, see *infra* p. 589, but discovery is still important in many modern contexts. Consider this: Tex located a mining claim on federal land in 1880 and scratched out a marginal living by mining gold from it until 1900, when he died. His descendants have held onto the claim and recorded it with the BLM pursuant to FLPMA but have never patented it nor done any further mining. In 1990 the Secretary of the Interior withdrew the land in question from the Mining Law in order to protect wildlife habitat, subject to valid existing rights. Is Tex's mining claim a valid existing right? What information do you need to answer the question?

4. Does *Coleman* necessarily follow from Castle v. Womble? Is it "imprudent" to stake a claim to a low-grade deposit that might increase in value as higher grade ores are depleted, or as mineral processing technology develops to make it profitable to mine? *See* Hallenbeck v. Kleppe, 590 F.2d 852, 859 (10th Cir.1979) ("A private litigant cannot locate claims upon public lands and then simply wait until the minerals are in sufficient demand to be marketed at a profit"). Is profitability relevant because it makes it more likely a deposit will in fact be developed? Is it a way to test the good faith of the mining claimant, as a way to determine whether the claimant really has mineral development, versus some other use, in mind for the land?

5. The price of many hardrock minerals has fluctuated rather dramatically through history. If Helen locates a claim on a copper deposit that could be profitably mined if copper sold for 80 cents per pound, and the current market price is 60 cents, has Helen made a discovery? What if the price is $1.00 when Helen locates the claim, but the average price over the last ten years was 60 cents? *See, e.g.*, In re Pacific Coast Molybdenum, 90 I.D. 352 (1983) (historic and reasonably anticipated price ranges may be relevant). To bring some uniformity to what had been a highly subjective determination, BLM in the Clinton Administration adopted a policy for determining discovery that uses the average of (a) the mineral price for three years before, and (b) the price of the mineral on the futures market three years ahead of the pertinent date. Is there a better approach?

6. *Excess reserves.* Baker applied for a patent of five mining claims he located on a volcanic cinder deposit. Each claim contained enough cinders to satisfy the entire known market (for landscaping, primarily) for 60 years; together, the five would satisfy all the market for 300 years. The Interior Department issued Baker patents on two claims and denied discovery on three, on the ground he had "too much" of the mineral to show a discovery on all five claims. Baker sued and won. Baker v. United States, 613 F.2d 224 (9th Cir.1980). In 1996, the Interior Solicitor issued a legal opinion (M#36984, "Excess Reserves under the Mining Law"), which argued that this decision had been limited by a subsequent 9th Circuit decision, and concluded that BLM could contest the validity of mining claims for industrial minerals for lacking a discovery when the mineral deposits within the claim exceed the market demand for the mineral for the reasonably foreseeable future, taking into account other resources in the mining area held by the claimant. BLM followed this with a directive that defined "reasonably foreseeable future" as forty years. BLM Instruction Memorandum No. 98–167 (1998).

7. What about proving discovery on a mineral deposit that spans multiple claims? The Mining Law requires a discovery "within the limits of the claim located." 30 U.S.C. § 23. The courts have often stated that a discovery must be shown on each claim—that claims cannot be aggregated to show a single discovery. *See* Cole v. Ralph, 252 U.S. 286, 295 (1920); Lombardo Turquoise Milling & Mining Co. v. Hemanes, 430 F.Supp. 429 (D.Nev.1977), *aff'd mem.*, 605 F.2d 562 (9th Cir.1979). John Leshy has noted that

> * * * this rule runs head on into the modern imperative that many individual claims be grouped in order to justify a single mining operation. A prudent person would not endeavor to extract copper or uranium from a low-grade deposit if only 20 acres could be mined; in fact, an aggregated group of twenty or more claims is usually necessary to provide the economics of scale required to operate a mine involving a low-grade deposit successfully. * * * [However] no one has ever squarely raised the issue in the context of a large, low-grade mineral deposit.

The Mining Law 175.

8. The *Coleman* test is applied less strictly when the contest is between rival claimants and the government is not a party. The reasoning seems to be that, because no disposition of federal lands is involved, such private disputes do not implicate the broader public concerns that are at stake when a claimant is seeking to gain rights against the United States to public lands and minerals. *See, e.g.,* Boscarino v. Gibson, 672 P.2d 1119, 1122–24 (Mont.1983). In a dispute between two rival claimants, where the U.S. is not involved, discovery serves the same function as the *pedis possessio* doctrine. This was illustrated in a case that reached a Mining Law nadir of sorts. Amax Exploration, Inc. v. Mosher, Civ. R–86–162 BRT (D.Nev.1987) (unreported). Various locators of the same ground sued each other to quiet title and to get "punitive damages for bad faith claim jumping." After a long trial, the court ruled, among other things, that no

party had made an actual discovery of a valuable mineral deposit and that no party's occupation of the ground was sufficient to establish *pedis possessio* protection. The court's melancholy conclusion: "The best the court can do for the parties in this case is to declare * * * that the land remains in the public domain open to peaceable exploration by the parties or by any other citizen."

9. What factors are *not* relevant to "marketability" or "profitability"? What is the relevance to discovery of the distance to mills or markets? Or, of alternative capital investment opportunities? Is any profit sufficient, or should the locator have to demonstrate a rate of profit equivalent to that experienced by other industries? As explained in more detail below, the BLM, the Forest Service, the Environmental Protection Agency, and the states have been regulating hardrock mining operations on unpatented claims with increasing stringency. Requirements to reclaim land and to protect against impairment of water quality are now fairly common. Must the costs of complying with these environmental regulatory requirements be included in the discovery determination? *See* United States v. Kosanke Sand Corp., 80 I.D. 538, 546 (1973) ("To the extent federal, state, or local law requires that anti-pollution devices or other environmental safeguards be installed and maintained * * * [such expenditures] may properly be considered * * * with the issue of marketability.").

10. *Comparative Value Test.* Should other values of the land, such as wildlife habitat or recreational use, be accounted for in the discovery determination? Some cases have held claimants to a higher discovery standard on some categories of federal lands. *See, e.g.,* Converse v. Udall, 399 F.2d 616, 622 (9th Cir.1968) ("The prudent man test has long been strictly applied against one who asserts discovery on national forest lands, when the contest is between him and the government."). Conservation organizations raised the issue in a claim contest involving Misty Fjords National Monument, set aside by ANILCA in 1980. The Act withdrew the area from mining but recognized valid existing claims. In ruling on whether certain claims within the Monument were valid, the Interior Board of Land Appeals rejected the conservationists' argument:

> Appellants * * * suggest "a stronger showing of marketability is required for important recreation areas, such as Misty Fjords, than for other public lands." It is true that a number of cases in the past have indicated that a higher standard of proof is required for claims located in national forests than for other public lands. In actual practice, the Board has long since abandoned this position. We take this opportunity to expressly repudiate it. * * *

> As a conceptual matter, the theory that the situs of the land alters the nature of the test applied is untenable. Where the mining laws apply, they necessarily apply with equal force and effect, regardless of the characteristics of the land involved. The test of discovery is the same whether the land be unreserved public domain, land in a national forest, or even land in a national park.

In re Pacific Coast Molybdenum Co., 90 I.D. 352, 361–63 (1983).

This has not ended the matter, however. Some federal mineral legislation permits the location of mining claims only on land that is "chiefly valuable" for certain minerals. See, e.g., 30 U.S.C. § 161, enacted in 1892, which provides that "any person authorized to enter lands under the mining laws of the United States may enter lands that are chiefly valuable for building stone under the provisions of the law in relation to placer mineral claims." In 1998, in a case involving the validity of mining claims located for an allegedly unique kind of building stone, Secretary of the Interior Babbitt ruled that whether a discovery existed depended in part on an analysis of the comparative value of the land for building stone as opposed to other uses. (The mining claims were in and along a stream that had high scenic and recreational value.) United States v. United Mining Corp., 142 IBLA 339 (1998). The Secretary rested the need for comparative value on the statutory limitation to lands "chiefly valuable," and left open whether the test might apply elsewhere as well.

NOTE: THE PROBLEM OF "COMMON VARIETIES"

In the *Coleman* case, the government also argued that Coleman's quartzite deposits were a "common variety" of stone within the meaning of 30 U.S.C. § 611, and thus could not furnish the basis for a valid mining claim under the mining laws. The Court agreed:

> We believe that the Secretary of the Interior was also correct in ruling that "[i]n view of the immense quantities of identical stone found in the area outside the claims, the stone must be considered a 'common variety'" and thus must fall within the exclusionary language of § 3 of the 1955 Act, 30 U.S.C. § 611, which declares that "[a] deposit of common varieties of * * * stone * * * shall not be deemed a valuable mineral deposit within the meaning of the mining laws * * *." Respondents rely on the earlier 1892 Act, 30 U.S.C. § 161, which makes the mining laws applicable to "lands that are chiefly valuable for building stone" and contend that the 1955 Act has no application to building stone, since, according to respondents, "[s]tone which is chiefly valuable as building stone is, by that very fact, not a common variety of stone." This was also the reasoning of the Court of Appeals. But this argument completely fails to take into account the reason why Congress felt compelled to pass the 1955 Act with its modification of the mining laws. The legislative history makes clear that this Act (30 U.S.C. § 611) was intended to remove common types of sand, gravel, and stone from the coverage of the mining laws, under which they served as a basis for claims to land patents, and to place the disposition of such materials under the Materials Act of 1947, 61 Stat. 681, 30 U.S.C. § 601, which provides for the sale of such materials without disposing of the land on which they are found.

390 U.S. at 603–04.

The status of common minerals under the Mining Law, and under the laws which provided that lands "mineral in character" were not available for homesteading or other land disposal laws, long was a problem. It was easy to show a "discovery" of a valuable deposit of sand, gravel, building stone, clay, and other widely occurring substances. Could the same law that applied to these substances simultaneously work effectively for precious metals and other substances? The Department of the Interior and the courts tried various stratagems over the years to make them both work. Remnants of the problem still exist today, but as the Court pointed out in *Coleman*, Congress solved most of it by legislating that only "uncommon varieties" of such substances (those with a "distinct and special value") may be located under the Mining Law. "Common varieties" could only be disposed of by competitive sale. *See infra* p. 661.

The advantage of free minerals provides a powerful incentive to argue that one's claim contains "uncommon varieties;" hence, there has been considerable litigation over whether a substance has "distinct and special value." *See* Boyle v. Morton, 519 F.2d 551 (9th Cir.1975) (red, gold and pink decomposed granite a "common variety"); Brubaker v. Morton, 500 F.2d 200 (9th Cir.1974) (ditto for brightly colored stone). The government and the courts seem to be losing patience with such arguments. *See, e.g.,* United States v. McPhilomy, 270 F.3d 1302 (10th Cir.2001) (upholding conviction of theft of government property where defendants were found not to be acting in good faith, even though they were acting on an attorney's advice, when they located a mining claim and then removed common varieties of stone). In 1990 the Forest Service adopted regulations to tighten the test for "uncommon varieties." *See* 36 C.F.R. § 228.41(d) (containing a detailed set of definitions, such as "any mineral used in manufacturing, industrial processing, or chemical operations for which no other mineral can be substituted due to unique properties giving the particular mineral a distinct and special value;" "clays having exceptional qualities suitable and used for production of aluminum, ceramics, drilling mud, taconite binder, foundry castings, and other purposes for which common clays cannot be used;" and "[s]tone recognized through marketing factors for its special and distinct properties of strength and durability [but not appearance] making it suitable for structural support and used for that purpose").

DISCOVERY OF FUEL MINERALS: URANIUM AND OIL SHALE

Two mineral ores present special problems for applying the Mining Law. Rising petroleum prices have revived interest in both uranium and oil shale as alternative energy sources.

Uranium. Although its radioactivity sets it apart from most other minerals, uranium is a metalliferous mineral subject to location under the Mining Law. It sparked a great rush in the 1950s, with old-time prospectors, weekend explorers, and large mining companies all competing for discoveries in several regions of the West, most notably the Colorado Plateau. Reminiscent of the California Gold Rush and succeeding strikes in the 19th century, enthusiasm was rampant. The Colorado Supreme Court captured the prevailing ethos in Smaller v. Leach, 136 Colo. 297, 316 P.2d 1030 (1957):

Since Hiroshima was leveled in World War II the world has seen the rise of the atomic era. The active search for the wonder elements uranium and thorium has thrilled as well as disturbed mankind. It has already wrought wondrous economic changes in many sectors of our state as well as other parts of the west and has brought the hope and partial realization of medical relief, scientific advances and cheap power to the world along with the threat of destruction by atom and H bombs. It has in the instant case turned brother against brother in a bitter quest for riches by one and the hope of sustaining integrity as well as securing wealth in the other. Our mining laws were developed years ago, first out of customs and laws of the miners and their courts, later out of Acts of the Congress and the State Legislature. Since their adoption we have had the uranium rush which, because this mineral is not usually located like other minerals have been in the past, presents difficulties. True it is that lodes of primary uranium ores have been found and may be noted by outcrops as well as radio activity; yet many secondary ores of this metal have been created by deposits of thermal waters or other means spreading the element in not only cracks, fissures, faults and fossilized trees, but also along stream and river channels and in old lake beds where no outcrops may exist. One of the most successful ways of discovering uranium, therefore, has been by means of radio detecting instruments and other modern scientific means such as fluorescent lights, photographic film, electroscope tests and even surface growing plant life. The scintillator and Geiger Counter allowing gamma ray measurements have become as familiar in the west today as the gold pan and pick and shovel were in an earlier period. The old form of grubstake agreement whereby the man who had no time or aptitude for prospecting could furnish the burro, beans and bacon to another for a half share of any discoveries made, has its modern day version in the loaning to a friend, for the weekend, of one's scintillator or counter on shares of whatever is found. And, weekend instrument prospectors have made some of our largest and best discoveries. * * *

The technology of exploration has caused courts some difficulties in determining when discovery had occurred. In Globe Mining Co. v. Anderson, 78 Wyo. 17, 318 P.2d 373, 380 (1957), an action to quiet title to lode mining claims, the Wyoming Supreme Court refused to "recognize the readings of electrical instruments such as scintillation and Geiger counters as sufficient to support discovery. * * * [S]uch counters while helpful in prospecting for uranium cannot be relied upon as the *only* test." In several disputes between rival claimants (where the U.S. was not a party), some courts retreated somewhat from this view. *See* Rummell v. Bailey, 7 Utah 2d 137, 320 P.2d 653 (1958), (valid discovery could be based on radiometric detection plus geological analysis of the immediate vicinity, particularly when there are known, physically discovered deposits nearby); Dallas v. Fitzsimmons, 137 Colo. 196, 323 P.2d 274 (1958) (radiometric results, in combination with other evidence of assaying and the type of rock in place, satisfy the definitional requirements of discovery).

More recently, the price of uranium jumped from $7 per pound in 2001 to more than $50 in 2007. Over a similar time frame, the number of companies looking for uranium has increased by an order of magnitude, to more than 200. This has spurred a revival of the uranium fever: uranium "discoveries" now account for a substantial number of new mining claims recorded at the BLM.

Oil shale. For much of the twentieth century, the immense deposits of oil shale in western Colorado, eastern Utah, and southern Wyoming captured the imagination of energy planners, the mining industry, the federal and state governments, and many others. Hundreds of billions of barrels of petroleum are locked in the rocks of the Green River Formation laid down in lake beds in an earlier age. The problem has always been that extracting the oil from the rock is difficult and itself takes considerable amounts of energy. (The known technologies for doing so require mining the shale, crushing it, and heating it to 900 degrees Fahrenheit in a retort.) Despite these obstacles, the lure of the "rock that burns" has led to predictions, tirelessly offered for many decades, that oil shale development was right around the corner. The cruel fact remains, however, that the cost of developing oil shale has remained prohibitive, absent large government subsidies.

Until 1920, oil shale was subject to the Mining Law of 1872. In that year, the Mineral Leasing Act made it leasable but contained a savings clause that preserved "valid claims existent on February 25, 1920, and thereafter maintained in compliance with the laws under which initiated, which claims may be perfected under such laws, including discovery." 30 U.S.C. § 193. Several thousand previously-located oil shale mining claims, mostly in Western Colorado, fell under that awkwardly worded clause. Because oil shale had never (and still has not) been commercially produced in significant quantities, it would seem to have been easy to conclude that a "prudent person" would find unjustified, in the words of Castle v. Womble, the "further expenditure of * * * labor and means, with a reasonable prospect of success, in developing a valuable mine." Nevertheless, the Secretary of the Interior in 1927 succumbed to the naive belief that "there is no possible doubt of its value and of the fact that it constitutes an enormously valuable resource for future use by the American people." Therefore, he ruled, oil shale claims could be patented in the "present situation" despite the fact that there "has been no considerable production." Freeman v. Summers, 52 L.D. 201, 206 (1927). Patents were issued in the following three decades for oil shale claims covering some 350,000 acres of federal land. Committees of Congress held hearings in 1930 and 1931 on the patentability of oil shale, but no legislation was enacted to disturb the Secretary's practice.

In the early 1960s, Secretary of the Interior Stewart Udall, mindful that commercial production of oil shale had still not occurred, was determined to end the practice of patenting, and the Department of the Interior began a major effort to challenge the validity of the remaining oil shale claims. Eventually the Interior Board of Land Appeals overruled Freeman v. Summers, finding that it was inconsistent with the Mining Law because there did not appear "as a *present* fact * * * a reasonable prospect of success in developing an operating mine that would yield a reasonable profit." The matter came before the U.S. Supreme Court in Andrus v. Shell Oil Co., 446 U.S. 657 (1980). In a 6–3 decision (with a vigorous dissent), the Court concluded that the legislative history of the savings clause in the 1920 Mineral Leasing Act and subsequent developments prevented the Department from "imposing a present marketability requirement on oil shale claims." 446 U.S. at 672–73. A footnote to this statement in the Court's opinion cautioned that "[t]his history indicates only that a present marketability standard does not apply to oil shale. It does not affect our conclusion in United States v. Coleman that for other minerals the Interior Department's profitability test is a permissible interpretation of the 'valuable mineral' requirement." 446 U.S. at 673 n.11. Consequently, this decision has had no demonstrable impact on the discovery test applied to other minerals.

It speaks volumes about the Mining Law—ironically, a law designed in large part to foster more security for miners—that the validity of oil shale claims were still being litigated more than eighty years after they were located. In Marathon Oil Co. v. Lujan, 937 F.2d 498 (10th Cir. 1991), the court upheld the issuance of a writ of mandamus to compel the Department to take action on other pending patent applications for oil shale claims. And still more oil shale claims were at issue in Cliffs Synfuel Corp. v. Norton, 291 F. 3d 1250 (10th Cir. 2002). Plainly the Mining Law has generated many more dollars in attorneys' fees than barrels of shale oil.

When oil prices climbed to more than $60 a barrel in 2006, it was predictable that proponents of the coming "boom" in oil shale production would re-emerge. The Department of Energy predicts that the U.S. could produce up to ten million barrels of crude oil a day from the oil shale in Colorado, Utah, and Wyoming. Few take such estimates seriously because, per pound, oil shale contains 10 percent of the energy of crude oil and 15 percent that of coal, and it is not clear whether any technique can be devised that would produce more energy than the production process consumes. The latest idea, undergoing examination by Shell Oil, involves heating a 1000–foot–thick section of oil shale to 700 degrees, maintaining that temperature for three years, and then drilling wells to extract the oil presumably liberated from the rock. The heat would come from electricity, which would require the construction of large (coal-fired) power plants. Congress has remained stubbornly optimistic. Section 369 of the Energy Policy Act of 2005 declared that development of oil shale "should occur, with an emphasis on sustainability, to benefit the United States while taking into account affected States and communities," and called for a commercial oil shale leasing program (following preparation of a programmatic EIS).

6. HOLDING AND PRIVATIZING MINING CLAIMS
Holding Claims: The Assessment Work Requirement

Miners' local rules invariably required a miner to continue to develop his claim after he made a discovery, in order to assure maximum development of the resource, and protect against "speculators." The Mining Law codified this practice by providing that an unpatented claim will be forfeited unless "not less than $100 worth of labor shall be performed or improvements be made during each year." 30 U.S.C. § 28. Assessment work was not required during the exploration phase, before discovery, Union Oil Co. v. Smith, 249 U.S. 337, 352–53 (1919), but cautious claimants tended to do it on all claims, so as not to have to admit they did not have a discovery. The consequences for failing to do assessment work are not completely clear. 30 U.S.C. § 28 enunciates a "resumption" doctrine, providing that if the claimant fails to do the required assessment work, the land claimed "shall be open to relocation in the same manner as if no location of the same had ever been made, *provided that the original locators*, their heirs, assigns, or legal representatives, *have not resumed work upon the claim after failure and before such location.*" (Emphasis added.) The assessment work requirement was widely ignored, even though the required dollar amount of work, unchanged since 1872, was rendered increasingly inconsequential by inflation. The Department of the Interior had authority to raise the amount ("not less than"), but never tried to do so.

Until FLPMA became law in 1976, assessment did not have to be reported to the federal government. The following opinion explores the consequences if a mining claimant fails to file in compliance with FLPMA's requirements, the nature of the private property interest in an unpatented mining claim, and the extent to which Congress can change the requirements for existing claim-holders to retain their rights without running afoul of the 5th Amendment.

United States v. Locke

Supreme Court of the United States, 1985.
471 U.S. 84.

■ JUSTICE MARSHALL delivered the opinion of the Court.

* * * From the enactment of the general mining laws in the nineteenth century until 1976, those who sought to make their living by locating and developing minerals on federal lands were virtually unconstrained by the fetters of federal control. * * *

By the 1960s, it had become clear that this nineteenth century laissez faire regime had created virtual chaos with respect to the public lands. In 1975, it was estimated that more than six million unpatented mining claims existed on public lands other than the national forests; in addition, more than half the land in the National Forest System was thought to be covered by such claims. Many of these claims had been dormant for decades, and many were invalid for other reasons, but in the absence of a federal recording system, no simple way existed for determining which public lands were subject to mining locations, and whether those locations were valid or invalid. As a result, federal land managers had to proceed slowly and cautiously in taking any action affecting federal land lest the federal property rights of claimants be unlawfully disturbed. Each time the Bureau of Land Management (BLM) proposed a sale or other conveyance of federal land, a title search in the county recorders office was necessary; if an outstanding mining claim was found, no matter how stale or apparently abandoned, formal administrative adjudication was required to determine the validity of the claim.

After more than a decade of studying this problem in the context of a broader inquiry into the proper management of the public lands in the modern era, Congress in 1976 enacted the Federal Land Policy and Management Act [FLPMA]. Section 314 of the Act establishes a federal recording system that is designed both to rid federal lands of stale mining claims and to provide federal land managers with up-to-date information that allows them to make informed land management decisions. For claims located before FLPMA's enactment, the federal recording system imposes two general requirements. First, the claims must initially be registered with the BLM by filing, within three years of FLPMA's enactment, a copy of the official record of the notice or certificate of location. Second, in the year of the initial recording, and "prior to December 31" of every year after that, the claimant must file with state officials and with BLM a notice of intention to hold the claim, an affidavit of assessment work performed on the claim, or a detailed reporting form. Section 314(c) of the Act provides that failure to comply with either of these requirements "shall be deemed conclusively to constitute an abandonment of the mining claim * * * by the owner."

The second of these requirements—the annual filing obligation—has created the dispute underlying this appeal. Appellees, four individuals engaged "in the business of operating mining properties in Nevada," purchased in 1960 and 1966 ten unpatented mining claims on public lands near Ely, Nevada. These claims were major sources of gravel and building material: the claims are valued at several million dollars, and, in the 1979–1980 assessment year alone, appellees' gross income totaled more than one million dollars. Throughout the period during which they owned the claims, appellees complied with annual state law filing and assessment work requirements. In addition, appellees satisfied FLPMA's initial recording requirement by properly filing with BLM a notice of location, thereby putting their claims on record for purposes of FLPMA.

At the end of 1980, however, appellees failed to meet on time their first annual obligation to file with the Federal Government. After allegedly receiving misleading information from a BLM employee, appellees waited until December 31 to submit to BLM the annual notice of intent to hold or proof of assessment work performed required under section 314(a) of FLPMA, 43 U.S.C. § 1744(a). As noted above, that section requires these documents to be filed annually "prior to December 31." Had appellees checked, they further would have discovered that BLM regulations made quite clear that claimants were required to make the annual filings in the proper BLM office "on or before December 30 of each calendar year." 43 CFR § 3833.2–1(a) (1980) (current version at 43 CFR 3833.2–1(b)(1) (1984)). Thus, appellees' filing was one day too late.

This fact was brought painfully home to appellees when they received a letter from the BLM Nevada State Office informing them that their claims had been declared abandoned and void due to their tardy filing. In many cases, loss of claim in this way would have minimal practical effect; the claimant could simply locate the same claim again and then rerecord it with BLM. In this case, however, relocation of appellees' claims, which were initially located by appellees' predecessors in 1952 and 1954, was prohibited by the Common Varieties Act of 1955, 30 U.S.C.A. § 611; that Act prospectively barred location of the sort of minerals yielded by appellees' claims. Appellees' mineral deposits thus escheated to the Government.

[The claimants sued, and prevailed in the lower court on a "takings" claim and on the argument that they had "substantially complied" with the FLPMA filing requirement. Justice Marshall's opinion rejected the "substantial compliance" argument, noting that while the statutory phrase "prior to December 31" may be "clumsy," its "meaning is clear." It also identified some fourteen other federal statutes that contemplated action "prior to December 31." Moreover, the statute clearly expressed congressional intent to "extinguish those claims for which timely filings were not made," regardless of the magnitude or justification for the failure. The opinion then addressed the constitutional issue.]

* * * The framework for analysis of this question, in both its substantive and procedural dimensions, is set forth by our recent decision in Texaco, Inc. v. Short, 454 U.S. 516 (1982). There we upheld a state statute pursuant to which a severed mineral interest that had not been used for a period of 20 years automatically lapsed and reverted to the current surface owner of the property, unless the mineral owner filed a statement of claim in the county recorder's office within two years of the statute's passage.

Under Texaco, we must first address the question of affirmative legislative power: whether Congress is authorized to "provide that property rights of this character shall be extinguished if their owners do not take the affirmative action required by the" statute. Even with respect to vested property rights, a legislature generally has the power to impose new regulatory constraints on the way in which those rights are used, or to condition their continued retention on performance of certain affirmative duties. As long as the constraint or duty imposed is a reasonable restriction designed to further legitimate legislative objectives, the legislature acts within its powers in imposing such new constraints or duties. * * *

This power to qualify existing property rights is particularly broad with respect to the "character" of the property rights at issue here. Although owners of unpatented mining claims hold fully recognized possessory interests in their claims, we have recognized that these interests are a "unique form of property." * * * The United States, as owner of the underlying fee title to the public domain, maintains broad powers over the terms and conditions upon which the public lands can be used, leased, and acquired. See, e.g., Kleppe v. New Mexico, 426 U.S. 529, 539 (1976). * * * Claimants thus take their mineral interests with the knowledge that the Government retains substantial regulatory power over those interests. * * *

Against this background, there can be no doubt that Congress could condition initial receipt of an unpatented mining claim upon an agreement to perform annual assessment work and make annual filings. That this requirement was applied to claims already located by the time FLPMA was enacted and thus applies to vested claims does not alter the analysis, for any "retroactive application of [FLPMA] is supported by a legitimate legislative purpose furthered by rational means.* * *" The purposes of applying FLPMA's filing provisions to claims located before the Act was passed—to rid federal lands of stale mining claims and to provide for centralized collection by federal land managers of comprehensive and up-to-date information on the status of recorded but unpatented mining claims—are clearly legitimate. In addition, § 314(c) is a reasonable, if severe, means of furthering these goals; sanctioning with loss of their claims those claimants who fail to file provides a powerful motivation to comply with the filing requirements, while automatic invalidation for noncompliance enables federal land managers to know with certainty and ease whether a claim is currently valid. Finally, the restriction attached to the continued retention of a mining claim imposes the most minimal of burdens on claimants; they must simply file a paper once a year indicating that the required assessment work has been performed or that they intend to hold the claim. Indeed, appellees could have fully protected their interests against the effect of the statute by taking the minimal additional step of patenting the claims [that is, purchasing fee simple title from the government for a nominal fee]. As a result, Congress was well within its affirmative powers in enacting the filing requirements, in imposing the penalty of extinguishment set forth in § 314(c), and in applying the requirements and sanction to claims located before FLPMA was passed.

We look next to the substantive effect of § 314(c) to determine whether Congress is nonetheless barred from enacting it because it works an impermissible intrusion on constitutionally protected rights. * * * Regulation of property rights does not "take" private property when an individual's reasonable, investment-backed expectations can continue to be realized as long as he complies with reasonable regulatory restrictions the legislature has imposed. * * *

[JUSTICE O'CONNOR concurred separately, agreeing with the result, but noting that the issue of whether BLM's actions had estopped it from extinguishing "a property interest that has provided a family's livelihood for decades" was still open on remand. Justice POWELL dissented, finding the statutory phrase "prior to December 31" unconstitutionally vague in light of the "natural tendency to interpret this phrase as 'by the end of the calendar year.'" JUSTICE STEVENS, joined by JUSTICE BRENNAN, also dissented, finding the "unique factual matrix" here—an ambiguous statute, substantially complied with, where the agency had allegedly not alerted claimholders sufficiently, and a valuable active mine was at stake—justified finding substantial compliance with the statute.]

NOTES AND QUESTIONS

1. Upon remand, the principal case was settled on a basis that allowed the Lockes to continue to mine their claims, suggesting that the

entire exercise had been a test case (on rather extreme facts) to establish the federal government's authority to apply new filing requirements to existing claimants. We will explore below whether and the extent to which *Locke* has application to environmental regulation of mining claims.

2. The mining claims at issue in *Locke* were located many years prior to enactment of FLPMA and its annual filing requirement. Does the prior existence of the claims lessen the power of the government to impose an additional burden—enforceable by the penalty of loss of the property interest—on the claimant? Does it make any difference why the government was imposing the new requirement? In *Locke*, what was the government's purpose in imposing the recordation and annual filing requirements? Is the filing requirement here any different from an ordinary statute of limitations? That is, are the Lockes in any different situation from a person injured allegedly by another's negligence, who fails to file a tort action until one day after the limitation period expires?

3. In 1992, by a rider on an appropriation bill, the Congress instituted a $100 "claim maintenance fee" for holders of unpatented claims, in lieu of assessment work. 30 U.S.C. §§ 28f–28k. Failure to pay "shall conclusively constitute a forfeiture of the * * * claim [and it] shall be deemed null and void by operation of law." *Id.* at 28i. Miners holding ten or fewer claims have the option of doing the assessment work and so certifying. Faced for the first time with the need to pay money to hold claims, many claimants abandoned ship, and the number of active mining claims almost immediately dropped by more than half. Challenges to the new fee on various constitutional grounds all failed. *See, e.g.*, Kunkes v. United States, 78 F.3d 1549 (Fed.Cir.1996). The fee was originally imposed only for six years, but Congress has renewed it, and raised it to $125 per claim per year.

Privatizing: Patenting Claims

From 1872 until 1994, a holder of an unpatented claim could seek fee title (through a "patent") to the federal land (as well as minerals) embraced in the claim. In 1994 Congress called a halt to the practice, by including a rider on the Interior Department's annual appropriation bill that prevented the acceptance of new patent applications. Congress could restart the issuance of patents by simply failing to include the rider in any year's appropriation bill, but in recent years its inclusion has been rather automatic.

Before the moratorium, lode claims were patentable for $5.00 per acre, while placer claim patents cost $2.50 per acre. 30 U.S.C. §§ 29, 37. Also, claimants could patent parcels of federal lands (maximum five acres per mineral claim) for use as a millsite. 30 U.S.C. § 42. The applicant for the patent has the burden of proof as the "proponent of an order" under the Administrative Procedure Act. 5 U.S.C. § 556(d). The claimant must meet the *Coleman* test for value as of the date of the application for patent. Best v. Humboldt Placer Mining Co., 371 U.S. 334 (1963). If the land was withdrawn after the claim had been located, the claimant must also show a discovery as of the date of the withdrawal. Thus, "even if at one time there was a valid mineral prospect on claimed land, changed economic conditions can destroy" the original discovery. Bales v. Ruch, 522 F.Supp. 150, 153 (E.D.Cal.1981).

The patent ordinarily grants a fee simple absolute right. Some statutes carved out exceptions to this rule for special areas. For example, patents issued for designated wilderness areas include only the minerals, not the surface estate. 16 U.S.C. § 1133(d)(3). This restriction on existing claims is not a taking. See Swanson v. Babbitt, 3 F.3d 1348 (9th Cir.1993), discussed further below.

The high-water mark for the issuance of patents under the Mining Law was 1892, when 3,242 patents were issued. Patent issuance steadily dwindled after World War II because, with the end of the disposition era and the advent of the *Coleman* test, the Department of Interior developed "a grudging and somewhat tightfisted approach toward claims under the mining laws." Peter Strauss, Mining Claims on Public Lands: A Study of Interior Department Procedures, 1974 Utah L.Rev. 185, 187. Starting about 1950 the Department granted fewer than 200 patents per year on average. In all, the Department has issued approximately 65,000 mineral patents, totaling about three million acres of land, an area about the size of Connecticut.

Patenting has never been necessary in order to extract minerals from mining claims. In fact, the Supreme Court long ago said: "The patent adds little to the security of the party in continuous possession of a mine he has discovered or bought." Chambers v. Harrington, 111 U.S. 350, 353 (1884). Many large mines are found on mining claims that have never been patented; it is not unusual for a mine to include a combination of state, private (patented mining claims), and federal (unpatented mining claims) land. A patented claim becomes private property fully subject to the laws of the state on such subjects as land use regulation and taxation. But the U.S. Supreme Court long ago recognized that a state also has the power to tax a miner's interest in an *unpatented* claim on federal lands. Forbes v. Gracey, 94 U.S. 762 (1876).

The courts have generally held that a decision to grant a patent does not involve discretion: if the claimant can show the requirements of the law (primarily, proper location and maintenance of the claim, and a discovery of a valuable mineral deposit), then the Secretary must issue the patent. Therefore, NEPA does not apply to the decision whether to grant a patent. South Dakota v. Andrus, 614 F.2d 1190 (8th Cir.1980).

In recent decades, criticism mounted that the patenting feature of the law was out of step with modern federal land policy. In May 1994, what may have been the most valuable patent application in history ended up on Secretary Babbitt's desk, a consolidated application from American Barrick involving dozens of mining claims covering a huge deposit in Nevada containing an estimated $10 billion worth of gold. After a careful examination determined that all the requirements of law had been met (and after the company tendered the $9000 the Mining Law required it to pay the U.S. Treasury), the Secretary signed the patent, but chose not to do it in the privacy of his office. Instead, he held a press conference where the backdrop was a gigantic check made out to the mining company in the amount of $10 billion and signed "the American taxpayer," and he took the opportunity to roundly criticize the Mining Law and the failure of Congress to reform it. A few months later, Congress began the practice of including annual moratoria on new patent applications in the Interior Appropriation bill. The first few years there was a political skirmish over renewing the moratorium, but in recent years the provision has been included without fuss. It therefore appears that, barring some major change in sentiment, the era of patenting is finally over; to borrow from T.S. Eliot, not with a bang but with a whimper.

In Swanson v. Babbitt, 3 F.3d 1348 (9th Cir.1993), the court held that legislation eliminating the longstanding legal right of a miner on federal land to gain fee title to mining claims was not a taking, even as applied to a miner who had already applied for, but had not yet gained approval of, a patent. The court said that Swanson had no vested right to a patent when the legislation was enacted, because the Department had determined to contest the application on the ground that it did not meet the requirements of existing law. It quoted Cameron v. United States, 252 U.S. 450, 460 (1920): "Of course, the land department has no power to strike down any claim arbitrarily, but so long as the legal title remains in the Government it does have power, after proper notice and upon adequate hearing, to determine whether the claim is valid and, if it be found invalid, to declare it null and void."

7. INROADS ON THE FREEDOM OF THE MINING CLAIMANT

For a long time hardrock miners hastened to assume (and some unreconstructed mining claimants still fervently believe) that the Mining Law creates an absolute immunity from regulation. They pointed to the provision in the Mining Law that offered mining claimants, upon locating a valuable lode or placer claim (that is, after discovery), "the exclusive right of possession and enjoyment of all the surface included within the lines of their locations." 30 U.S.C. § 26. They urged that this provision gave the miner absolute control over the federal land embraced within the claim, with no "balancing" of relative values, and with no obligation to control environmental impacts. This extreme view, along with the many defects in the Law, long fueled efforts (so far unsuccessful) to replace the Mining Law with a leasing system.

But claimants' rights were never so absolute. The 1872 Act itself states that claimants were subject to "regulations prescribed by law." 30 U.S.C. § 22. The courts long implied limitations on the rights of mining claimants. Subsequent statutes like the Forest Service Organic Act of 1897, 16 U.S.C. §§ 478, 551, and Federal Land Policy and Management Act of 1976, 43 U.S.C. § 1732(b), give federal land management agencies express regulatory power over activities on mining claims (beyond the power to withdraw federal lands from the operation of the Mining Law) to protect the environment and other resources. This subsection examines the limitations of the unpatented right and the processes for challenging unpatented mining claims.

United States v. Rizzinelli

United States District Court, District of Idaho, 1910.
182 Fed. 675.

■ JUDGE DIETRICH

The defendants are charged with the maintenance of saloons upon mining claims within the limits of the Coeur d'Alene National Forest without a permit * * * in violation of the rules and regulations of the Secretary of Agriculture. The claims were duly located, subsequent to the creation of the forest reserve, and they are possessory only, no application for patent ever having been made. * * *

[T]he Secretary of Agriculture * * * formulated an elaborate set of regulations, published in what is known as the "Use Book". The particular rules alleged to have been ignored by the defendants are as follows:

"Reg. 6. Permits are necessary for all occupancy, uses, operations or enterprises of any kind within national forests, whether begun before or after the national forest was established, except: (a) Upon patented lands; (b) upon valid claims for purposes necessary to their actual development and consistent with their character; (c) upon rights of way amounting to easements for the purposes named in the grants; (d) prospecting for minerals, transient camping, hunting, fishing, and surveying for lawful projects."

"Reg. 19. The following acts within national forests are hereby forbidden: * * * (c) Erecting or conducting telephone, telegraph, or power lines, hotels, stores, sawmills, power plants, or other structures, or manufacturing or business enterprises, or carrying on any kind of work, except as allowed by law and national forest regulations, and except upon patented lands or upon a valid claim for the actual development of such claim, consistent with the purposes for which it was initiated."

* * * The defendants here have the possessory title only. They have a distinct but qualified property right, and, even if we assume that their interest is vested, it is one which may be abandoned at any moment, or forfeited. The primary title, the paramount ownership, is in the government, and upon abandonment by the locator, or his failure to comply with the conditions upon which his continuing right of possession depends, the entire estate reverts to the government; all the time, it retains the title, with a valuable residuary and reversionary interest. * * * [W]hatever [this interest] may be, [the United States] has the right to protect and obviously the interest which it retains is the entire estate, less that which is granted by the terms of [30 U.S.C. § 22], providing that locators shall have "the exclusive right of possession and enjoyment of all the surface of their locations." * * * The inquiry is substantially limited to the meaning of the phrase "exclusive enjoyment," for, notwithstanding the existence of the Coeur d'Alene forest reserve, it is conceded that the defendants are entitled to the exclusive possession of their claim not only as against third persons, but as against the United States. * * * The government inserts, after the word "enjoyment," the phrase "for mining purposes," and the defendants

the phrase "for all purposes." No other language is suggested, and, indeed, no middle ground appears to be possible; the "enjoyment" is either for mining purposes alone, or for all purposes without qualification or restriction. Under a familiar rule of statutory construction, the necessity of reading into the statute one or the other of these two phrases to make it complete, and its adaptability to either of them, of itself operates strongly to determine the question in favor of the government, for it is well settled that in public grants nothing passes except that which is clearly and specifically granted, and all doubts are to be resolved in favor of the government. But, independent of this rule, considerations pertinent to the construction of private grants and contracts clearly lead to the conclusion that the right of enjoyment which Congress intended to grant extends only to mining uses. The general purpose of the mineral laws is well understood; it was to encourage citizens to assume the hazards of searching for and extracting the valuable minerals deposited in our public lands. In form the grant is a mere gratuity; but, in considering the propriety of such legislation, it may well have been thought that by reason of the stimulus thus given to the production of mineral wealth, and rendering the same available for commerce and the arts, the public would indirectly receive a consideration commensurate with the value of the grant. In that view doubtless the legislation has for a generation been generally approved as embodying a wise public policy. But under what theory should the public gratuitously bestow upon the individual the right to devote mineral lands any more than any other public lands to valuable uses having no relation to mining, and for what reason should we read into the statute such a surprising and unexpressed legislative intent?

With much earnestness the consideration is urged that it has become more or less customary to erect valuable buildings upon lands embraced in mineral claims to be used for purposes having no necessary relation to mining operations, and that great hardship would ensue and important property rights would be confiscated if the locator's "enjoyment" of the surface be limited to uses incident to mining. But even if it be true, as suggested, that in many localities sites for dwelling houses and business structures could not be conveniently obtained except upon lands containing valuable mineral deposits and embraced in located claims, the fact is without significance and lends no support to the defendants' contention.
* * *

Holding, therefore, that the right of a locator of a mining claim to the "enjoyment" of the surface thereof is limited to uses incident to mining operations, no serious difficulty is encountered in reaching the further conclusion that forest reserve lands embraced in a mining claim continue to constitute a part of the reserve, notwithstanding the mineral location, subject, of course, to all the legal rights and privileges of the locator. The paramount ownership being in the government, and it also having a reversionary interest in the possessory right of the locator, clearly it has a valuable estate which it is entitled to protect against waste and unlawful use. It is scarcely necessary to say that it is the substantial property right of the government, and not the extent to which such right may be infringed in the present case, that challenges our consideration. The burden imposed upon the principal estate by the construction and maintenance of a little saloon building may be trivial, and the damage wholly unappreciable. But that is not to the point. If a worthless shrub may as a matter of legal right be destroyed in the location of a saloon, the entire claim may be stripped of its timber, however valuable, to give place for other saloons and other structures having no connection with the operation of the mine. To concede any such right at all is necessarily to concede a right without limit; there is no middle ground. It is therefore repeated that, subject to the locator's legitimate use for mining purposes, the government continues to be the owner of the land, and is interested in conserving its value and preventing injury and waste. * * * [The convictions for maintaining saloons on mining claims were affirmed.]

NOTES AND QUESTIONS

1. Note Rizzinelli's argument urged "[w]ith much earnestness" that what he did was "more or less customary." What does that suggest about the uses to which many mining claims are actually put?

2. If Rizzinelli had obtained a patent on the claim, could he have operated a saloon on the land?

3. If the only thing Rizzinelli was doing on the claim was operating a saloon, could the government have challenged the validity of his claim for lack of discovery? Why do you suppose it did not?

4. Could another person have "jumped" Rizzinelli's claim; i.e., was Rizzinelli protected by the *pedis possessio* doctrine?

United States v. Curtis–Nevada Mines, Inc.

United States Court of Appeals, Ninth Circuit, 1980.
611 F.2d 1277.

■ JUDGE HUG

* * * Curtis states that he located and filed [203 mining claims on federal land managed by the BLM and the Forest Service, covering some thirteen square miles] after stumbling upon an outcropping of valuable minerals while on a deer hunting trip. He states that, within this 13–mile area, he has located gold, platinum, copper, silver, tungsten, pitchblende, palladium, triduim [sic], asmium [sic], rhodium, ruthenium, scandium, vanadium, ytterbium, yttrium, europium, and "all the rare earths." These minerals he maintains have a value in the trillions. The mining activity of the appellees was very limited. At the time this litigation was instituted there was only one employee, who performed chiefly caretaking duties such as watching after equipment and preventing the public from entering the claims.

Hunters, hikers, campers and other persons who had customarily used the area for recreation were excluded by * * * Curtis [, who had] posted "no trespassing" signs on the claims and constructed barricades on the Blackwell Canyon Road and the Rickey Canyon Road, which lead up into the mountains and provide access to the Toiyabe National Forest. After receiving numerous complaints, the United States filed this action asserting the rights of the general public to the use of the surface of the mining claims. * * *

Section 4(b) of the [Surface Resources Act of 1955] provides in pertinent part:

> Rights under any mining claim hereafter located under the mining laws of the United States shall be subject, prior to issuance of patent therefor, to the right of the United States to manage and dispose of the vegetative surface resources thereof and to manage other surface resources thereof (except mineral deposits subject to location under the mining laws of the United States). Any such mining claim shall also be subject, prior to issuance of patent therefor, to the right of the United States, its permittees, and licensees, to use so much of the surface thereof as may be necessary for such purposes or for access to adjacent land: *Provided, however,* That any use of the surface of any such mining claim by the United States, its permittees or licensees, shall be such as not to endanger or materially interfere with prospecting, mining or processing operations or uses reasonably incident thereto * * *.

30 U.S.C. § 612(b).

As noted by the district court, the meaning of "other surface resources" and of "permittees and licensees" is somewhat ambiguous. The principal issues in this case are whether recreational use is embodied within the meaning of "other surface resources" and whether the phrase "permittees and licensees" includes only those members of the public who have specific written permits or licenses. * * *

[The 1955] Act was corrective legislation, which attempted to clarify the law and to alleviate abuses that had occurred under the mining laws [citing the House Committee Report on the 1955 Act]. * * *

* * * As a practical matter, mining claimants could remain in exclusive possession of [their claims] without ever proving a valid discovery or actually conducting mining operations. This led to abuses of the mining laws when mining claims were located with no real intent to prospect or mine but rather to gain possession of the surface resources. Furthermore, even persons who did have the legitimate intent to utilize the claim for the development of the mineral content at the time of the location often did not proceed to do so, and thus large areas of the public domain were withdrawn, and as a result these surface resources could not be utilized by the general public for other purposes.

It was to correct this deficiency in the mining law that Congress in 1955 enacted the Multiple Use Act. Some of the abuses and problems that the legislation was designed to correct are detailed in House Report 730:

> The mining laws are sometimes used to obtain claim or title to valuable timber actually located within the claim boundaries. Frequently, whether or not the locator so intends, such claims have the effect of blocking access-road development to adjacent tracts of mer-

chantable Federal timber, or to generally increase costs of administration and management of adjacent lands. The fraudulent locator in national forests, in addition to obstructing orderly management and the competitive sale of timber, obtains for himself high-value, publicly owned, surface resources bearing no relationship to legitimate mining activity.

Mining locations made under existing law may, and do, whether by accident or design, frequently block access: to water needed in grazing use of the national forests or other public lands; to valuable recreational areas; to agents of the Federal Government desiring to reach adjacent lands for purposes of managing wild-game habitat or improving fishing streams so as to thwart the public harvest and proper management of fish and game resources on the public lands generally, both on the located lands and on adjacent lands.

Under existing law, fishing and mining have sometimes been combined in another form of nonconforming use of the public lands: a group of fisherman-prospectors will locate a good stream, stake out successive mining claims flanking the stream, post their mining claims with "No trespassing" signs, and proceed to enjoy their own private fishing camp. So too, with hunter-prospectors, except that their blocked-out "mining claims" embrace wildlife habitats; posted, they constitute excellent hunting camps.

The effect of nonmining activity under color of existing mining law should be clear to all: a waste of valuable resources of the surface on lands embraced within claims which might satisfy the basic requirement of mineral discovery, but which were, in fact, made for a purpose other than mining; for lands adjacent to such locations, timber, water, forage, fish and wildlife, and recreational values wasted or destroyed because of increased cost of management, difficulty of administration, or inaccessibility; the activities of a relatively few pseudominers reflecting unfairly on the legitimate mining industry.

H.R.Rep. No. 730 at 6, U.S.Code Cong. & Admin.News, pp. 2478–79. * * *

* * * Curtis assert[s] that recreational uses are not encompassed within the meaning of "other surface resources" in § 612(b). However, as the district court properly held, the phrase "other surface resources" was clearly intended to include recreational uses. It is apparent from the [legislative history] that recreation was one of the "other surface resources" to which 30 U.S.C. § 612(b) refers. * * * It is therefore a surface resource that the United States has a right to manage and that the United States and its permittees and licensees have a right to use so long as the use does not "endanger or materially interfere with prospecting, mining or processing operations or uses reasonably incident thereto." 30 U.S.C. § 612(b).

The remaining question * * * concerns the identification of the "permittees and licensees" of the United States entitled to use the surface resources. The district court held that the "permittees and licensees" are only those who have specific written permits or licenses from any state or federal agency allowing those persons to engage in any form of recreation on public land. * * *

* * * [I]n the management of public lands, the United States has historically allowed the general public to use the public domain for recreation and other purposes, and often without a specific, formal permit. Such access has been described as an implied license.

Originally, grazing of livestock was such a use that was allowed without a formal permit. In McKee v. Gratz, 260 U.S. 127 (1922), the Court applied this concept of an implied license to include a license to use large tracts of uncultivated lands for recreational uses. Mr. Justice Holmes in the opinion of the Court stated:

> The strict rule of the English common law as to entry upon a close must be taken to be mitigated by common understanding with regard to the large expanses of unenclosed and uncultivated land in many parts at least of this country. Over these it is customary to wander, shoot and fish at will until the owner sees fit to prohibit it. A license may be implied from the habits of the country.

Id. at 136. * * *

[U.S. Forest Service and BLM] regulations confirm a traditional policy for the use of public lands allowing the public to use lands within the public domain for general recreational purposes without holding a written, formal permit, except as to activities which have been specifically regulated.

The Surface Resources Act was designed to open up the public domain to greater, more varied uses. To require that anyone desiring to use claimed lands for recreation must obtain a formal, written license would greatly restrict and inhibit the use of a major portion of the public domain. [In a footnote, the court cited a Department of Agriculture report that several million acres were covered by mining claims but few were producing minerals.] It is doubtful that Congress would intend that such use be dependent upon a formal permit, because the federal agencies do not generally issue or require permits for recreational use of public lands. To require a formal written permit would either put the public in a position of having to obtain permits but having no place from which to obtain them, or it would require the government to institute procedures to issue permits, a process which the government argues is burdensome and unnecessary.

One of the clear purposes of the 1955 legislation was to prevent the withdrawal of surface resources from other public use merely by locating a mining claim. * * *

Consequently, in light of the historical background of the use of the public domain for many purposes without express written permits or licenses we do not find in the legislative history of the 1955 act an intent to so limit the meaning of "permittees and licensees." Most assuredly, the B.L.M. or the Forest Service can require permits for public use of federal lands in their management of federal lands; however, they need not do so as a prerequisite to public use of surface resources of unpatented mining claims.

It should be noted that mining claimants have at least two remedies in the event that public use interferes with prospecting or mining activities. Section 612(b) provides that "any use of the surface * * * shall be such as not to endanger or materially interfere with prospecting, mining or processing operations or uses reasonably incident thereto." The mining claimant can protest to the managing federal agency about public use which results in material interference and, if unsatisfied, can bring suit to enjoin the activity. Secondly, a claimant with a valid claim can apply for a patent which, when granted, would convey fee title to the property.

In the present case, appellees have not presented any evidence that the public use of land included within their unpatented mining claim has "materially interfered" with any mining activity. Absent such evidence, section 612(b) applies in this case to afford the general public a right of free access to the land on which the mining claims have been located for recreational use of the surface resources and for access to adjoining property. Therefore, we reverse the portion of the judgment that requires specific written permits or licenses for entry onto the mining claims, and we remand this case to the district court for entry of an injunction consistent with the views expressed in this opinion.

NOTES AND QUESTIONS

1. What is the legal status of a casual recreational hiker on federal land managed by the Forest Service or the BLM?

2. Why didn't the U.S. contest the validity of these claims for lack of discovery? Was the claimant's motivation to keep the public off his claims suggested by the fact that he was on a deer hunting trip when he allegedly discovered minerals he valued "in the trillions" of dollars (and subsequently put little effort into extracting this fabulous treasure)?

3. Why was the 1955 Act even necessary? Did the federal government already have the power to prevent miners from using their claims for purposes other than mining, in ways that interfered with other uses of the federal lands? Isn't that the holding of *Rizzinelli*? The Senate Committee Report on the 1955 Act had this to say: "Strict Federal enforcement of existing laws * * * could, in theory at least, have eliminated many of the abuses * * *. But the existing legal and administrative machinery has been slow and cumbersome, and personnel for adequate enforcement insufficient." S. REP. 84–554 at 5 (1955).

4. What surface uses are "reasonably incident to mining" under the 1955 Act? A residential structure may qualify in some circumstances. United States v. Langley, 587 F.Supp. 1258 (E.D.Cal.1984). But what about "a mobile home, several vehicles—both operable and inoperable—assorted animals including a bull, cows, chickens and several dogs, a sweat lodge, a chicken coop or enclosure, and a garden"? *See* Bales v. Ruch, 522 F.Supp. 150 (E.D.Cal.1981) (no). In 1996, the Department of the Interior adopted new regulations to detail what claimants could and could not do on their mining claims. These "use and occupancy" regulations also increased

penalties for violators and streamlined enforcement mechanisms. 43 C.F.R. § 3715.

5.   Exactly what does "manage the vegetative resources" mean, and what is the scope of the authority it confers? For example, can a mining claimant clearcut an area of national forest, if removing the timber is reasonably incident to mining? Can the holder of an unpatented claim cut timber for sale to a third party? Can the holder cut timber for construction of a residence or graze stock for the miner's own domestic purposes?

NOTE: PROCESSES FOR CHALLENGING THE VALIDITY OF UN- PATENTED MINING CLAIMS

The hundreds of thousands of unpatented mining claims on federal land are a cloud on government title and can create serious land management problems for land managers. Moreover, because mining claims are still relatively easy to locate and maintain (if you're willing to pay $125 per year), they are a tempting lure to those who seek ends other than mining. One of the more colorful episodes in Mining Law history was the saga of Ralph Cameron. He located mining claims in popular tourist areas on the southern flank of the Grand Canyon before it was withdrawn from the Mining Law, in order to mine gold from the tourists' pockets, as Professor David Getches once put it. It was only after decades of litigation that challenges to his claims eventually succeeded.

The Mining Law is silent on the authority of the federal government to contest the validity of mining claims other than through its review of a claimant's application for a patent, or fee title. In Cameron v. United States, 252 U.S. 450 (1920), Cameron (by then a U.S. Senator from Arizona) argued that the Department of the Interior had no authority to bring an administrative contest against his claims. The Court (speaking through Justice Van Devanter) found support for the Department's right to challenge claims in statutes giving the Department general supervisory power over the federal lands, noting that holding to the contrary "would encourage the use of merely colorable mining locations in the wrongful private appropriation of lands belonging to the public." 252 U.S. at 463.

Another time-honored Mining Law tactic is that practiced by so-called "nuisance" or "strike" claimants, who locate claims mostly in the hope of being bought out by legitimate miners who otherwise would face costly litigation to oust them:

> The master of this gambit, a figure properly placed alongside Ralph Cameron in the first rank of Mining Law manipulators, was Merle Zweifel. Until his flamboyance, greed, and disarming candor about the game he was playing attracted so much attention that he could no longer be tolerated, the "old prospector," as he styled himself, filed several million mining claims on federal land all over the west. (He himself put the figure at 30 million acres, which included an unspecified amount of land claimed on the outer continental shelf.) When Congress authorized the Central Arizona Project, part of which required construction of an aqueduct from the Colorado River to Phoenix

and Tucson, the old prospector was there, filing claims on 600,000 acres along the aqueduct route. When interest in oil shale development began to revive on Colorado's west slope after 1960, Zweifel surfaced with 465,000 acres of mining claims in the Piceance Basin. Acknowledging that he would never actively explore the land (because that would damage the scenery, he said) he exploited the Law's offer of free access to the federal lands with a vengeance, though the character of his claims reflected the German meaning of his name—doubt. His "real goal in life," he was reported as saying, was to "discredit bureaucrats and their hypocritical ways," though he also admitted that fighting large companies "is an enjoyment I can't pass up," and that, finally, "I do have a lust for money."

John Leshy, THE MINING LAW 79. His tactics were so outrageous that the Department of the Interior was moved to bypass its own administrative contest procedures and instead to bring wholesale challenges against Zweifel's claims directly in federal court, in a quiet title action. Zweifel challenged this tactic, arguing that the Department had to use its complicated and lengthy administrative contest procedures instead (making essentially the opposite argument from the one Ralph Cameron had urged several decades earlier). The Tenth Circuit rejected his claims in United States v. Zweifel, 508 F.2d 1150 (10th Cir.1975). It held that the United States could elect to proceed administratively or judicially, that primary jurisdiction did not require a remand because the question was legal and the Department had already made up its mind, and that the government had met its burden of establishing prima facie the invalidity of the claims. After Zweifel passed on, one of his colleagues sued the Secretary of Interior for damages resulting from the invalidation of large numbers of claims. Among other things, the complaint requested damages of "$1,346,390,400.00 due to breach of contract" and "three hundred billion dollars in damages due to breach of fiduciary duty, bad faith and unfair dealing." Relief was denied. Roberts v. Clark, 615 F.Supp. 1554 (D.Colo.1985).

Although the attempts at under-the-table appropriation are seldom as blatant or baseless as Zweifel's, abuses of the Mining Law have been common since its inception and continue today. An adroit mining claimant took advantage of federal laxity in failing to make a timely withdrawal and located mining claims at Yucca Mountain, the site of the federal government's planned high-level nuclear waste repository in Nevada. It reportedly cost the Department of Energy upwards of $100,000 to buy out the claimant rather than suffer delay while litigating him out. In a study of 240 western mining claims, selected at random, the GAO found in 1974 that only one was being mined and only three had ever been mined. The BLM and Forest Service employees still must evict occasional "snowbirds" who like to winter on their mining claims on federal lands in the southwest, and continue the seemingly never-ending process of rooting out thousands of "miners" from prime recreation spots, survivalist enclaves, and hippie communes in remote areas all over the West.

The Department of the Interior has taken the position that only a person with "title to or an interest in land" may contest a mining claim.

See, e.g., In re Pacific Coast Molybdenum Co., 68 IBLA 325 (1982). Besides the United States, this includes a rancher who has grazing privileges on the land, but does not include a hiker or camper or other recreational user of the land. The Department does, however, allow recreational users and others some rights to "protest" and appeal denials of their protests in some circumstances. *See, e.g.,* Scott Burnham, 94 I.D. 429, 442–43 (1987). In Wilderness Soc'y v. Dombeck, 168 F.3d 367 (9th Cir.1999), the court ruled that an organization representing recreational users had standing to challenge the determination to grant mineral patents in a wilderness area. On the other hand, High Country Citizens Alliance v. Clarke, 454 F.3d 1177 (10th Cir.2006), held that neither local governments nor environmental groups could challenge an Interior Department decision to issue a patent to a mining company because they did not own a competing property interest in federal land, and thus were foreclosed from review by the terms of the Mining Law and the Administrative Procedure Act.

8. MODERN ENVIRONMENTAL REGULATION OF OPERATIONS ON UNPATENTED MINING CLAIMS

More than a century after enactment of the Mining Law of 1872, the two principal agencies that manage federal lands on which hardrock mining activities occur finally adopted regulations providing for environmental regulation of those activities. Because their statutory authority and their regulations are somewhat different, these materials consider them separately, starting with the U.S. Forest Service. Keep in mind that other agencies, especially the EPA, also regulate mining pollution, wherever it occurs. Mining operations are also regulated by states (as in *Granite Rock*), and may be subject to liability for cleaning up contamination under the Comprehensive Environmental Response, Compensation, and Liability Act (CERCLA, or Superfund), 42 U.S.C. §§ 9601–9657.

a. Forest Service Regulation

Authority for administering the Mining Law has always been lodged in the Interior Department (now through the BLM), even on lands managed by other federal agencies, such as the national forests. When Congress transferred most management authority over the national forests to the Secretary of Agriculture in 1905, it left the Department of the Interior with some authority over mineral activity, although the boundaries between Interior and Agriculture's authority were never sharply drawn. 16 U.S.C. § 472.

In the late 1960s and early 1970s, two conservation battles over mining—an ASARCO proposal to build an access road to a molybdenum claim deep in the White Cloud Mountains in Idaho, and a dispute over development in the Stillwater minerals complex in the Custer and Gallatin National Forests in Montana—drew the Forest Service into the business of regulating the environmental impact of hardrock mining on the national forests. In 1974 the agency promulgated regulations under the aegis of two sections of its 1897 Organic Act. First, 16 U.S.C. § 478:

Nor shall anything herein prohibit any person from entering upon such national forests for all proper and lawful purposes, including that of prospecting, locating, and developing the mineral resources thereof. Such persons must comply with the rules and regulations covering such national forests.

Second, 16 U.S.C. § 551:

The Secretary of Agriculture shall make provisions for the protection against destruction by fire and depredations upon the * * * national forests * * * and he may make such rules and regulations * * * as will insure the objects of such reservations, namely, to regulate their occupancy and use and to preserve the forests thereon from destruction * * *.

The stated purpose of these regulations is to ensure that hardrock mining activities are "conducted so as to minimize adverse environmental impacts on National Forest System surface resources." 36 C.F.R. § 228.1. They require claimants to file a notice of intent with the local district ranger before commencing any operation that might cause surface disturbance. If the district ranger determines that such operations will "likely cause significant disturbance of surface resources," the miner must then file a plan of operations. *Id.* § 228.4(a). The ranger reviews and revises the submitted plan with the operator until both agree upon an acceptable plan. The regulations direct the ranger to make an initial response within thirty days if possible, and not later than ninety days. The final operating plan must include surface environmental protection and reclamation requirements, as well as a bond to cover the costs of damage or unfinished reclamation. Pending final approval of the plan, the district ranger may allow mining to proceed so long as it is conducted to minimize environmental impacts. The regulations also provide for access restrictions, periodic inspection by the Forest Service, and remedies for noncompliance. *See* 36 C.F.R. §§ 228.1–228.15. The special restrictions on mining in Forest Service wilderness areas are covered in Chapter 12.

Miners questioned the authority for and extent of these regulations from the outset.

United States v. Weiss

United States Court of Appeals, Ninth Circuit, 1981.
642 F.2d 296.

■ JUDGE ANDERSON

* * * The appellants are owners of unpatented placer mining claims located within the St. Joe National Forest in Idaho. [They proceeded with mining operations without complying with the Forest Service regulations requiring an approved operating plan. The United States sued to require their compliance.] * * * Appellants' contention on appeal is that the regulations have not been promulgated pursuant to adequate statutory authority. * * *

* * * Under §§ 478 and 551, the Secretary may make rules and regulations for the protection and preservation of the national forests, and persons entering upon national forest land must comply with those rules and regulations. The authority of the Secretary to regulate activity on national forest land pursuant to these sections has been upheld in a variety of non-mining instances. See United States v. Grimaud, 220 U.S. 506 (1911) (regulations concerning sheep grazing in national forests); McMichael v. United States, 355 F.2d 283 (9th Cir.1965) (regulations prohibiting motorized vehicles in certain areas of national forest). That authority has also been sustained to prohibit non-mining activity upon unpatented mining claims. United States v. Rizzinelli, 182 F. 675 (D.Idaho 1910). However, the precise issue of whether these statutory provisions empower the Secretary to regulate mining operations on national forest land does not appear to have been decided before. * * *

We believe that the Act of 1897, 16 U.S.C. §§ 478 and 551, granted to the Secretary the power to adopt reasonable rules and regulations regarding mining operations within the national forests.

* * * The fact that these regulations have been promulgated many years after the enactment of their statutory authority does not destroy the Congressional authorization given. The failure of an executive agency to act does not forfeit or surrender governmental property or rights. In this situation, a mining claimant may not claim any sort of prescriptive right which would prevent the government from protecting its superior vested property rights.

In analyzing the issue before us, we are keenly aware of the important and competing interests involved. Mining has been accorded a special place in our laws relating to public lands. The basic mining law of 1872 encouraged the prospecting, exploring, and development of mineral resources on public lands. * * *

On the other hand, our national forests have also been a fundamental part of the use of our public lands. National forests were established to improve and protect our forest land, to secure "favorable conditions of water flows, and to furnish a continuous supply of timber for the use and necessities of citizens of the United States; * * *" 16 U.S.C. § 475. The object of the Organic Administration Act of 1897 was "to maintain favorable forest conditions, without excluding the use of reservations for other purposes. They are not parks set aside for nonuse, but have been established for economic reasons. 30 Cong.Rec. 966 (1897) (Cong. McRae)." United States v. New Mexico, 438 U.S. 696, 708 (1978).

Moreover, while locators were accorded the right of possession and enjoyment of all the surface resources within their claim, the "primary title, the paramount ownership is in the government * * * it retains the title, with a valuable residuary and reversionary interest." United States v. Rizzinelli, 182 F. at 681 (D.Idaho, 1910). "The paramount ownership being in the government, and it also having a reversionary interest in the possessory right of the locator, clearly it has a valuable estate which it is entitled to protect against waste and unlawful use." Id. at 684.

We believe that the important interests involved here were intended to and can coexist. The Secretary of Agriculture has been given the responsibility and the power to maintain and protect our national forests and the lands therein. While prospecting, locating, and developing of mineral resources in the national forests may not be prohibited nor so unreasonably circumscribed as to amount to a prohibition, the Secretary may adopt reasonable rules and regulations which do not impermissibly encroach upon the right to the use and enjoyment of placer claims for mining purposes.[5]

NOTES AND QUESTIONS

1.   In Okanogan Highlands Alliance v. Williams, 236 F.3d 468 (9th Cir.2000), environmentalist plaintiffs and a nearby Indian tribe challenged a Forest Service decision to approve an open pit gold mine on national forest land in northern Washington. One contention was that the Organic Act and 36 C.F.R. § 228.1 required the Forest Service to select the most environmentally preferable, but still profitable, project alternative identified in the EIS prepared on the proposal. The court said no. It noted that although the regulation required mining activities to be conducted "so as to *minimize adverse environmental impacts* on National Forest System surface resources," (emphasis added), 16 U.S.C. § 478 provides that 16 U.S.C. § 551 shall not be construed to "prohibit any person from entering upon such national forests for all proper and lawful purposes, including that of prospecting, locating, and developing the mineral resources thereof." The court continued:

> This circuit recognizes that 16 U.S.C. §§ 478 and 551 together evidence the "important and competing interests" of preserving forests and protecting mining rights. *United States v. Weiss.* * * * The statutory text, therefore, does not support Plaintiffs' assertion that, when the Forest Service is forced to choose between project alternatives, environmental interests always trump mining interests.

> Neither does 36 C.F.R. § 228.1 require the result Plaintiffs seek. To be sure, the regulation states that the purpose of the "rule and procedures" promulgated to govern mining operations in National Forest lands is to ensure that mining operations "minimize adverse environmental impacts." The regulation, however, sets no substantive standards that Defendants could violate. Rather, it merely explains the purpose of the *remaining* regulations, which do set substantive standards. And Plaintiffs do not claim that Defendants have violated any of those substantive standards.

> For those reasons, we hold that the Forest Service's selection of Alternative B did not violate the Organic Act or 36 C.F.R. § 228.1.

5. We emphasize that the reasonableness of the regulations has not been put into issue. Although authority exists for the promulgation of regulations, those regulations may, nevertheless, be struck down when they do not operate to accomplish the statutory purpose or where they encroach upon other statutory rights. Appellants have not attempted to comply with the regulations; therefore, those issues are not before us on this appeal.

236 F.2d at 478 (emphasis added).

Look closely at 16 U.S.C. §§ 478 and 551, quoted before the *Weiss* case, above. Do they really require balancing mineral and environmental values? Could they be fairly be interpreted in the way the *Okanogan* plaintiffs advocated? Could the Forest Service now adopt regulations requiring the selection of the most environmentally preferable alternative? Could a court require such a result in an appropriate case?

2. In Clouser v. Espy, 42 F.3d 1522 (9th Cir.1994), the court rejected a miner's argument that the Forest Service lacked authority to regulate the means of transportation to cross national forest lands in order to gain access to the claims:

> Plaintiffs assert—no doubt correctly—that the means of access permitted materially affects the commercial viability of mining claims. Under the legal standard applied by the Department of the Interior to determine whether a putative claim is "valid," validity depends in part on commercial viability. On this basis, plaintiffs argue that adjudication of questions concerning access materially affects claim validity. They therefore contend that adjudication of such issues is committed to the exclusive jurisdiction of the Department of the Interior since, the parties agree, Interior is the agency authorized to adjudicate the validity of mining claims.
>
> * * * In light of the broad language of [16 U.S.C.] § 551's grant of authority, [16 U.S.C.] § 478's clarification that activities of miners on national forest lands are subject to regulation under the statute, and [a] substantial body of case law, there can be no doubt that the Department of Agriculture possesses statutory authority to regulate activities related to mining * * * in order to preserve the national forests.

As noted above, plaintiffs argue that because the permissibility of motor-vehicle access may affect whether a claim is deemed to be "valid," the issue of access is different from other matters that the Forest Service may permissibly regulate. Plaintiffs contend that means of access go to the validity of the claim and, as such, are committed to the jurisdiction of Interior. Rejecting this argument, the district court wrote:

> I find that it is the nature of the issue presented (i.e. mode of access), not the *effect* of the determination which determines the appropriate agency forum. Thus, the fact that the Forest Service's rejection of a particular method of access may have a "material impact" on the mining claim activity does not *transform* the determination from one within the province of the Forest Service to one within the exclusive province of the Interior Department. (emphasis in original).

We concur in this conclusion. Virtually all forms of Forest Service regulation of mining claims—for instance, limiting the permissible methods of mining and prospecting in order to reduce incidental environmental damage—will result in increased operating costs, and thereby will affect claim validity, for the reasons explained above. However, the above case law makes clear that such matters may be regulated by the Forest Service, and plaintiffs have offered no compelling reason for distinguishing means of access issues from other such forms of regulation.

42 F.3d at 1528–30.

Assuming the U.S. Forest Service (or the BLM) may impose reasonable environmental mitigation measures as part of the plan approval process, what if the cost of complying with such measures makes a marginal mining operation (as on an low-grade deposit in difficult, remote terrain) uneconomic to pursue? May the requirement be imposed anyway, if it means no mining will occur? Does that result square with *Weiss* or *Okanogan Highlands Alliance*?

3.   The Forest Service regulations skirt the issue whether the agency can forbid mining altogether by refusing to approve otherwise suitable plans of operations. 36 C.F.R. § 228.5(a). Do any of the above cases shed any light on this issue? In United States v. Brunskill, 792 F.2d 938, 941 (9th Cir.1986), the court declined to decide whether the Forest Service was entitled to disapprove outright a proposed mining plan, explaining that the claimant there had not appealed the agency's rejection of its proposed operating plan.

4.   In United States v. Shumway, 199 F.3d 1093 (9th Cir.1999), Judge Kleinfeld wrote a paean to the Mining Law, calling it a "powerful engine driving exploration and extraction of valuable minerals," and noting with satisfaction that "[d]espite much contemporary hostility to [it] * * * and high level political pressure by influential individuals and organizations for its repeal, * * * it remains the law." The Shumways had located millsites in the Tonto National Forest. The Forest Service had for many years approved plans of operations for their small scale mining operation, but friction developed between the claimants and the Forest Service in the late 1980s. The Shumways did not post a larger performance bond the agency demanded, and were ordered to cease operations. Finally in 1995, the United States sued to evict them from the millsites. The district court had granted summary judgment to the government. In the meantime, the Shumways' application to patent the millsites was pending before the Interior Department. Finding that the "owner of a mining claim owns property, and is not a mere social guest * * * to be shooed out the door when the [government] chooses," the Ninth Circuit held that the district court erred in granting summary judgment because it found several genuine issues of fact in the record, including "whether the government improperly increased the bond amount to an arbitrary figure," and whether their "equipment and materials were 'junk.'" Describing the claimants' interest in the millsites as "property," the opinion concluded: "Like someone who proposes to operate a nursing home in an area zoned for single family residential and light retail, regulations may prohibit [the Shumways'] proposed use, but it does not follow that they forfeit their interests in the real estate." Is the analogy apt? Is it clear their interest in their claims is property?

5. In United States v. Doremus, 888 F.2d 630 (9th Cir.1989), the court rejected a mining claimant's argument that the Forest Service must prove that the claimant's logging activities were not "reasonably incident" to mining under 30 U.S.C. § 612(c) in order to prohibit them, even though the activities did not fall within the operating plan the Forest Service approved. It agreed with the district court that "the operating plan itself becomes the definition of what is reasonable and significant conduct under the circumstances," and held that "therefore any violation of the operating plan was *per se* unreasonable under the statute." The court also rejected the miner's argument that it could cut down trees on the claim even though this was not called for under the approved plan:

> [A]lthough appellants have a right [under 30 U.S.C. § 612(c)] to dispose of vegetative resources where such disposal is "reasonably incident" to their mining operation, they may not exercise that right without first obtaining approval of their operation in the manner specified in 36 C.F.R. Part 228. If appellants believed that their operation required the removal of trees and that the plan failed to accommodate that need, their remedy was to appeal the plan prior to commencing operations. Appellants may not blithely ignore Forest Service regulations and argue afterward that their conduct was "reasonable."

888 F.2d at 634.

b. BLM Regulation

The BLM's principal statutory authority to regulate hardrock mining operations on the federal lands it manages is found in FLPMA, 43 U.S.C. § 1732(b) (emphasis added):

> * * * *Except as provided in* section 314 [43 U.S.C.A. § 1744, dealing with recordation of mining claims], section 603 [43 U.S.C.A. § 1782, dealing with the BLM wilderness study], and subsection (f) of section 601 of this Act [43 U.S.C.A. § 1781(f), dealing specially with the California Desert Conservation Area] and in *the last sentence of this paragraph,* no provision of this section or any other section of this Act shall in any way amend the Mining Law of 1872 or impair the rights of any locators or claims under that Act, including, but not limited to, rights of ingress and egress. *In managing the public lands the Secretary shall, by regulation or otherwise, take any action necessary to prevent unnecessary or undue degradation of the lands.*

How broad is this authority to regulate hardrock mining activities on unpatented claims? Is the BLM statutory authority stronger, weaker, or about the same as that of the Forest Service? Although the ("except as provided in ... last sentence") phrasing is somewhat tortuous, putting the two quoted sentences together means that the second sentence expressly, if backhandedly, "amend[s] the Mining Law of 1872 [and] impair[s] the rights of any locators or claims under that Act."

What is "unnecessary or undue degradation" ("UUD")? Does it include, for example, the failure to reclaim a large open pit? Even if the cost of backfilling it is prohibitive? Does this statutory standard in effect mandate the application of something like "best available control technologies," a familiar standard under environmental regulatory laws like the Clean Air and Clean Water Acts? Note that FLPMA imposes this standard for stewardship on the BLM for all of its activities, and other chapters of this book address it in the context of grazing, off-road vehicle use, and wilderness management.

The BLM's implementation of this authority has hardly followed a straight line. BLM first promulgated regulations to govern hardrock mining activities in late 1980. Found at 43 C.F.R. Part 3809, and therefore known as the "3809 regulations," they generally tracked the Forest Service's regulations, although significantly, unlike the latter, they (a) did not require plans of operations to be submitted for approval for mines that disturb fewer than five acres of ground per year; and (b) did not require the filing of reclamation bonds for all operations. Both of these exceptions were roundly criticized by environmentalists, the General Accounting Office, and representatives in Congress. The sub-five-acre threshold exempted as many as 2000 mining operations each year; such mines needed only provide a simple notice to the BLM. Between 150 and 300 operations submitted plans of operations each year.

The following case discusses the two rules that succeeded the 1980 regulation. It also interprets the meaning of UUD in the context of BLM's regulation of hardrock mining.

Mineral Policy Center v. Norton

U.S. District Court, District of Columbia, 2003.
292 F. Supp. 2d 30.

■ JUDGE KENNEDY

Plaintiffs * * * challenge the revision of federal mining regulations promulgated by defendant, Bureau of Land Management ("BLM"), United States Department of the Interior ("Interior"), on October 30, 2001. According to plaintiffs, the regulations, codified at 43 C.F.R. § 3809 ("2001 Regulations") "substantially weaken, and in many instances eliminate, BLM's authority to protect the public's lands, waters, cultural and religious sites, and other resources threatened by industrial mining operations in the West." Plaintiffs therefore contend that the regulations run counter to BLM's statutory duty, as set forth in its guiding statute, the Federal Land Policy and Management Act, 43 U.S.C. §§ 1701 et seq. (2000) ("FLPMA"), to "take any action necessary to prevent unnecessary or undue degradation of the [public] lands." 43 U.S.C. § 1732(b). Accordingly, plaintiffs ask this court to vacate and remand any portion of the 2001 Regulations not in accordance with federal law.

* * *

FLPMA establishes standards for BLM to regulate hardrock mining activities on the public lands. Such regulation is vital. BLM administers roughly one-fifth of the land mass of the United States and, while the surface area of the land physically disturbed by active mining is comparatively small, the impact of such mining is not. Mining activity emits vast quantities of toxic chemicals, including mercury, hydrogen, cyanide gas, arsenic, and heavy metals. The emission of such chemicals affects water quality, vegetation, wildlife, soil, air purity, and cultural resources. The emissions are such that the hardrock/metal mining industry was recently ranked the nation's leading emitter of toxic pollution.

FLPMA thus attempts to balance two vital—but often competing—interests. On one hand, FLPMA recognizes the "need for domestic sources of minerals, food, timber, and fiber from the public lands," 43 U.S.C. § 1701(a)(12), and, on the other hand, FLPMA attempts to mitigate the devastating environmental consequences of hardrock mining, to "protect the quality of scientific, scenic, historical, ecological, environmental, air, and atmospheric, water resource, and archeological values," id. § 1701(a)(8). * * *

The heart of FLPMA amends and supersedes the Mining Law to provide: "In managing the public lands the Secretary shall, by regulation or otherwise, take any action necessary to prevent unnecessary or undue degradation of the lands." 43 U.S.C. § 1732(b) (emphasis added) * * * Also important for our purposes, FLPMA: (1) requires that the Secretary "manage the public lands under principles of multiple use and sustained yield," 43 U.S.C. § 1732(a); (2) encourages the "harmonious and coordinated management of the various resources without permanent impairment of the productivity of the land and the quality of the environment," id. § 1702(c); and (3) "declares that it is the policy of the United States that ... the United States receive fair market value for the use of the public lands and their resources unless otherwise provided for by statute," id. § 1701(a)(9).

The 1980, 2000, and 2001 Regulations

After FLPMA was enacted in 1976, BLM commenced a rulemaking to implement it. BLM issued its proposed rules on December 6, 1976, and finalized them on November 26, 1980. These rules, commonly known as the "1980 Regulations," established "procedures to prevent unnecessary or undue degradation ["UUD"] of Federal lands which may result from operations authorized by the mining laws." * * * These rules governed the mining industry for quite some time.

In the 1990s, however, Interior conducted a comprehensive review of the 1980 Regulations, and on January 6, 1997, commenced a rulemaking to amend them. During the rulemaking period, Congress intervened by * * * [directing] the National Research Council ("NRC") of the National Academy of Sciences to review the adequacy of existing state and federal regulation of hardrock mining on federal lands, without regard to Interior's proposed amendments. Congress also prohibited Interior from promulgating a new rule until after publication of the NRC report. The NRC published its report, entitled Hardrock Mining on Federal Lands, in late September 1999 ("NRC Report"). In support of this publication, later that year, Congress provided that the rule to emerge from Interior's rulemaking process must not be "inconsistent with the recommendations contained in the National Research Council report."

Interior finally amended the 1980 Regulations in 2000. The 2000 Regulations * * * adopted the NRC Report's recommendations—but differed in fundamental ways from the previous 1980 Regulations. 65 Fed.Reg. 69,998 (Nov. 21, 2000). Most importantly, the 2000 Regulations replaced the 1980 Regulations' UUD "prudent operator" standard with a new and more restrictive UUD standard, commonly referred to as the "substantial irreparable harm" or "SIH" standard.

The "substantial irreparable harm" standard is so named because in the 2000 Regulations, for the first time, BLM stated that it would deny a plan of operations, i.e., a mining permit, if the plan failed to comply with performance standards or would result in "substantial irreparable harm" to a "significant" scientific, cultural, or environmental resource value of the public lands that could not be "effectively mitigated." Thus, under the 2000 Regulations, BLM asserted its authority to deny a mining permit, simply because a potential site was unsuitable for mining because of, for instance, the area's environmental sensitivity or cultural importance.

These 2000 Regulations were short lived, however. On March 23, 2001, after a change in the Administration, Interior published a Notice in the Federal Register stating its intention to amend the regulations once again.

In so doing, the Interior Solicitor issued a legal opinion examining FLPMA and concluding that the 2000 Regulation's SIH standard was ultra vires, a conclusion with which the Interior Secretary agreed. The 2001 Regulations thus abolished the 2000 Regulations' SIH standard. 66 Fed. Reg. at 54,837–8. What was left after the revision was a standard more akin to the "prudent operator" standard utilized by the 1980 Regulations. Compare 65 Fed.Reg. at 70,115, with 66 Fed.Reg. at 54,860. The stated reason for the elimination of the SIH standard was that Interior determined that the standard's "implementation and enforcement ... would be difficult and potentially subjective, as well as expensive for both BLM and the industry," and that "other means" would "protect the resources covered by the SIH standard." Interior further determined that the SIH standard would precipitate a "10%–30% decline overall in minerals production."

The 2001 Regulations provide:

Unnecessary or undue degradation means conditions, activities, or practices that:

(1) Fail to comply with one or more of the following: the performance standards in § 3809.420, the terms and conditions of an approved plan of operations, operations described in a complete notice, and other Federal and state laws related to environmental protection and protection of cultural resources;

(2) Are not "reasonably incident" to prospecting, mining, or processing operations as defined in § 3715.0–5 of this chapter; or

(3) Fail to attain a stated level of protection or reclamation required by specific laws in areas such as the California Desert Conservation Area, Wild and Scenic Rivers, BLM-administered portions of the National Wilderness System, and BLM-administered National Monuments and National Conservation Areas.

43 C.F.R. § 3809.5.

The 2001 Regulations retained other provisions of the 2000 Regulations, however. Notably, for instance, Interior adopted all of the NRC's UUD recommendations, including requiring: (1) financial guarantees to cover commensurate reclamation costs for all mining activities disturbing the public lands or resources, even those affecting areas of less than five acres, 43 C.F.R. §§ 3809.552; and (2) plans of operation for all mining activities other than those defined as "Casual use" and "exploration," even where the disturbed area is less than five acres, id. at § 3809.1–.21. These 2001 Regulations are presently at issue before this court.

In this case, plaintiffs challenge Interior's decision to rescind a validly-issued rule and replace it with the 2001 Regulations. Rescission of agency rules that previously met Congress's legislative mandate are judged by the rulemaking record. That is, " '[a]n agency's view of what is in the public interest may change, either with or without a change in circumstances. But an agency changing its course must supply a reasoned analysis.' " Motor Vehicle Mfrs. Ass'n of U.S., Inc. v. State Farm Mut. Auto. Ins. Co., 463 U.S. 29, 57. An agency must therefore "examine the relevant data and articulate a satisfactory explanation for its action including a 'rational connection between the facts found and the choice made.' " Motor Vehicle Mfrs. Ass'n, 463 U.S. at 43.

As noted above, plaintiffs' essential argument is that the 2001 Regulations run contrary to key provisions of FLPMA. They contend that the 2001 Regulations * * * fail to meet BLM's statutory mandate to "take any action necessary to prevent unnecessary or undue degradation of the [public] lands." 43 U.S.C. § 1732(b). Plaintiffs argue that in promulgating the 2001 Regulations, BLM essentially abdicated its duty to prevent "undue degradation" and instead, revised its definition of "unnecessary or undue degradation" to limit its authority to prevent only operations that are "unnecessary" for mining. Plaintiffs maintain that by reading "undue degradation" as superfluous to the statute, defendants contravene the plain language of FLPMA, in violation of the APA.

* * *

In response to plaintiffs' claims, Interior offers three essential arguments. First, Interior asserts that the 2000 and 2001 Regulations are not as different from one another as plaintiffs contend. Interior maintains that "[t]he only change between the 2000 and 2001 rules in Interior's definition of UUD is the elimination of the provision defining UUD as 'substantial irreparable harm to significant scientific, cultural, or environmental resource values' because Interior determined the SIH proviso was contrary to statutory authority, subjective, potentially cumulative, and overbroad." Second, Interior argues that no party in these rulemakings ever identified or defined the harm ostensibly prevented by the 2000 Regulations' SIH proviso. And third, Interior maintains that, in this case, plaintiffs espouse mere policy preferences for less or no mining on the public lands, untethered to the requirements of FLPMA or the Mining Law. Each claim will be explored in turn.

A. Interior's Duty to Prevent Unnecessary or Undue Degradation of the Public Lands

FLPMA mandates that the Secretary of the Interior "shall, by regulation or otherwise, take any action necessary to prevent unnecessary or undue degradation of the [public] lands." 43 U.S.C. § 1732(b). The proper interpretation of this statutory mandate is the question now before this court.

1. Interior Must Prevent Both "Undue Degradation" and "Unnecessary Degradation" to the Public Lands.

The 2000 Regulations explicitly adopted the view that Congress had authorized the Secretary to prohibit mining activities found unduly degrading, although potentially lucrative. This view was succinctly expressed in the preamble to the 2000 Regulations, which states:

> Congress did not define the term "unnecessary or undue degradation," but it is clear from the use of the conjunction "or" that the Secretary has the authority to prevent "degradation" that is necessary to mining, but undue or excessive. This includes the authority to disapprove plans of operations that would cause undue or excessive harm to the public lands.

65 Fed.Reg. 69,998 (Nov. 21, 2000).

Interior's interpretation of FLPMA's UUD standard potentially changed in 2001, however. Before the 2001 Regulations were promulgated, Interior's Solicitor, William G. Myers III, wrote an opinion in which he reviewed the meaning of the words "unnecessary" and "undue," as well as FLPMA's legislative history. Based on this analysis, Solicitor Myers determined that the terms "unnecessary" and "undue" were not two distinct statutory mandates, as the 2000 Regulations presumed, but were instead "two closely related subsets or equivalents." (Solicitor's Opinion) (finding that "unnecessary" and "undue" "may be reasonably viewed as similar terms (the second term defining the first) or as equivalents").

Based on this interpretation of the UUD standard, Solicitor Myers determined that as long as a proposed mining activity is "necessary to mining," the BLM has no authority to prevent it. ("FLPMA amends the Mining Law only as provided in four limited ways, and preventing necessary and due degradation is not one of them."). Solicitor Myers found that:

> A definition that is more restrictive—that prevents degradation that would be caused by an operator who is using accepted and proper procedures in accordance with applicable federal and state laws and regulations when such degradation is required to develop a valuable

mineral deposit—would inappropriately amend the Mining Law and impair the rights of the locator.

Accordingly, Solicitor Myers provided that the 2000 Regulations' SIH standard could not be sustained; BLM could not disapprove of an otherwise allowable mining operation merely because such an operation would cause "substantial irreparable harm" to the public lands. The Solicitor thus concluded that "relevant legal authorities require removal of the 'substantial irreparable harm' criterion from both the definition of 'unnecessary or undue degradation' in § 3809.5 and the list of reasons why BLM may disapprove a plan of operations in § 3809.411(d)(3)(iii) of the 2000 regulations, 65 Fed.Reg. 69,998, 70,115, 70,121 through the rulemaking process currently underway within the Department." Id. at 15.

Plaintiffs challenge the Solicitor's interpretation and argue that, based upon FLPMA's statutory language, it is clear that Congress intended to prevent "unnecessary degradation" as well as "undue degradation." Thus, according to plaintiffs, under FLPMA "BLM must prevent undue degradation, even though the cause of the degradation may be necessary for mining."

Upon careful consideration, the court agrees with plaintiffs' view. The court finds that the Solicitor misconstrued the clear mandate of FLPMA. FLPMA, by its plain terms, vests the Secretary of the Interior with the authority—and indeed the obligation—to disapprove of an otherwise permissible mining operation because the operation, though necessary for mining, would unduly harm or degrade the public land.

Three well-established canons of statutory construction compel the court's conclusion. First, it is well settled that the language of the statute should govern. As stated by the Supreme Court: "The starting point in interpreting a statute is its language, for 'if the intent of Congress is clear, that is the end of the matter.'" Good Samaritan Hosp. v. Shalala, 508 U.S. 402, 409 (1993) (quoting Chevron, 467 U.S. at 842).

The second rule is that when construing a statute, the court is "obliged to give effect, if possible, to every word Congress used." Murphy Exploration & Prod. Co. v. U.S. Dep't of Interior, 252 F.3d 473, 481 (D.C.Cir.2001). The court should "disfavor interpretations of statutes that render language superfluous."

Third and finally, it is clearly established that "[i]n statutory construction the word 'or' is to be given its normal disjunctive meaning unless such a construction renders the provision in question repugnant to other provisions of the statute," In re Rice, 165 F.2d 617, 619 n. 3 (D.C.Cir.1947) . . . or "the context dictates otherwise," Reiter, 442 U.S. at 339.

Applying these well-established canons to the matter at hand, FLPMA provides that the Secretary "shall by regulation or otherwise, take any action necessary to prevent unnecessary *or* undue degradation of the lands." 43 U.S.C. § 1732(b) (emphasis added). Accordingly, in this case: (1) the disjunctive is used, (2) the disjunctive interpretation is neither "at odds" with the intention of the FLPMA's drafters * * * nor contrary to the statute's legislative history; and (3) the "or" separates two terms that have different meanings. Consequently, the court finds that in enacting FLPMA, Congress's intent was clear: Interior is to prevent, not only unnecessary degradation, but also degradation that, while necessary to mining, is undue or excessive.

2. Plaintiffs Have Not Shown that the 2001 Regulations Fail to Prevent Unnecessary or Undue Degradation.

With that resolved, the question now before this court is whether the 2001 Regulations effectuate that statutory requirement. * * * Put another way, the court must determine whether the 2001 Regulations reasonably interpret and implement FLPMA, as properly understood.

Plaintiffs contend that the 2001 Regulations ignore FLPMA's "undue" language and essentially limit BLM's authority to prevent only surface disturbance greater than necessary. Plaintiffs insist that "if an activity such as locating a waste dump on top of a Native American sacred site or dewatering an entire drinking water aquifer is 'necessary for mining,' and the mining company pledged to meet a few technical requirements, the BLM would be powerless to protect those resources."

Interior, on the other hand, maintains that, despite the elimination of the 2000 Regulations' SIH standard, and the Solicitor's understanding that the terms "undue" and "unnecessary" "overlap in many ways," the 2001 Regulations nevertheless prevent UUD, as properly defined by this court.

Specifically, Interior argues that it will protect the public lands from any UUD by exercising case-by-case discretion to protect the environment through the process of: (1) approving or rejecting individual mining plans of operations; (2) regulating in response to the requisite Notices that operators must submit before commencing exploration activities not requiring a plan of operations; (3) requiring financial guarantees for costs for mining activities; and (4) linking performance standards to those set forth in existing laws and regulations. These existing laws and regulations include: the Endangered Species Act; the Archeological Resources and Protection Act; the Clean Water Act; the Comprehensive Environmental Response, Control and Liability Act; Interior's authority under FLPMA to withdraw public land from mining entry; and Interior's authority under FLPMA to formally designate and withdraw from mining "areas of critical environmental concern."

Plaintiffs, in response, have been unable to present evidence to contradict or undermine Interior's claim. Plaintiffs have not shown that, by the exercise of case-by-case discretion, Interior will fail to prevent unnecessary or undue degradation.

The court thus finds that, in promulgating FLPMA, Congress tasked the Secretary of Interior with preventing both "unnecessary" as well as "undue" degradation to the public lands. The court finds further, however, that the terms "unnecessary" and "undue," which are not defined in the FLPMA, are themselves ambiguous. In tasking the Secretary to prevent "unnecessary or undue" degradation, Congress left two broad gaps for the

Secretary to fill, which the Secretary has elected to fill through the exercise of her discretion, on a case-by-case basis.

Because FLPMA is silent or ambiguous with respect to what specifically constitutes "unnecessary or undue degradation," and the means Interior should take to prevent it, the court shall review Interior's actions under the second prong of *Chevron*. Consequently, the court must determine, not whether the 2001 Regulations represent the best interpretation of the FLPMA, but whether they represent a reasonable one. Here, upon careful consideration, the court finds that they do. Plaintiffs have neither demonstrated that the 2001 Regulations fail to prevent unnecessary or undue degradation of the public lands, in contravention of FLPMA, nor that Interior, in promulgating the 2001 Regulations, toiled under an erroneous view of its own authority. The 2001 Regulations are neither "procedurally defective" nor "arbitrary or capricious in substance," nor "manifestly contrary" to the FLPMA. United States v. Mead Corp., 533 U.S. 218, 227 (2001). Thus, the regulations must be accorded due deference. Accordingly, the first of plaintiffs' challenges must fail. * * *

NOTES AND QUESTIONS

1. Who actually won this case? Why do you think it was not appealed by any of the parties? Once the court found the 2001 Solicitor's Opinion to be an erroneous interpretation of FLPMA, why didn't it provide a remedy? What would you advise environmental advocates do now? What would you advise Interior to do now, when it next faces a decision whether to approve a proposed new mine on BLM lands, where opponents say it will cause unacceptable impacts?

2. The BLM's 2000 SIH regulation was based on a 1999 Solicitor's Opinion. Who is right on the interpretation of FLPMA's "unnecessary or undue degradation" standard—the 1999 Solicitor or the 2001 Solicitor? The 1999 opinion concluded that the Secretary of the Interior had a right to reject plans of operations for proposed mines which would cause substantial and irreparable harm to significant scientific or cultural resource values of the public lands that could not be effectively mitigated. What difference does it make whether "or" means "or" or "and"? How much deference should the 1999 Opinion receive from the courts, in light of the fact that the BLM interpreted the phrase in formal regulations in 1980 in a different way? How much deference should the 2001 Opinion receive, in light of the fact that it reverses the 1999 Opinion? Suppose the next presidential administration wants to take another look at this issue. How would you advise it to go about that reexamination, to get maximum deference from the courts? Do another rulemaking? Accompany it with a draft Solicitor's Opinion and seek public comment on that as well?

3. The proposed Glamis gold mine in the desert of Imperial County, California, illustrates what a difference the regulatory definitions of UUD can make. In January 2001, the Interior Department rejected the Glamis plan of operations because of an unmitigable conflict with important Quechan Tribal cultural resources. In November 2001 the Department

announced its decision to rescind the rejection and reconsider Glamis' application to mine. BLM has still not made a final decision on the Glamis mine. It has issued a mineral report which finds that the mining claims there are supported by a valid discovery, if new California laws that require backfilling of open pits and protection of sacred sites are preempted. If these state laws apply, the Glamis claims lack a discovery.

4. In the meantime, the Glamis Gold Co., which is Canadian, has sought compensation for being so far thwarted in its development plans, under a provision of the North American Free Trade Agreement (NAFTA) which allows compensation in certain circumstances where a host state stops a foreign company from developing because of environmental or other regulations. The U.S. State Department is, so far, resisting the claim for compensation, and further proceedings are pending.

5. In Reeves v. United States, 54 Fed. Cl. 652 (2002), the plaintiff had located, in 1996, forty mining claims in an area of Utah that BLM had, in 1980, designated as a wilderness study area (WSA). Applicable provisions of FLPMA had been interpreted to leave WSAs open to new mining claim location, but subject any activities on these claims to a "non-impairment-of-wilderness-suitability" standard. The court rejected the claimant's argument that he had a compensable property right to have his mining plan of operations approved even though the BLM had decided his proposed operation did not comply with that standard.

6. Great Basin Mine Watch v. Hankins, 456 F.3d 955 (9th Cir.2006), involved conservationist challenges to BLM's separate approvals, with separate EISs, of Newmont Mining Company's proposed expansion of its open-pit gold mining and processing facilities on the Carlin trend in northern Nevada (slated to involve about 1400 acres, somewhat over half of those on public land) and a new underground mine in the same area. The Carlin trend produces more gold than almost any other region in the world. The court held the approval did not violate the Clean Water Act because, among other things, while the state of Nevada could apply an anti-degradation policy to the withdrawal of groundwater here, it chose not to do so. The court held that BLM's NEPA compliance was deficient. While the two projects had independent utility, and therefore did not need to be analyzed in a single EIS, the EISs together failed adequately to analyze the cumulative effects (particularly on air quality and waste rock and hazardous waste disposal) of these two proposals along with existing and reasonably foreseeable mines in this area. Finally, the court upheld BLM's decision regarding the bonding or financial assurance to cover the costs of environmental mitigation in the event of a default. The BLM required Newmont to provide nearly $29 million in bonding to cover the first phase of activity. The court found that BLM's regulations allow for phased bonding, and that BLM's calculation of the bond amount is entitled to substantial deference, particularly since BLM's regulations require it to review the amount and terms of the bonds "at least annually."

NOTE: REGULATING HARDROCK MINING IN NATIONAL PARKS

In 1976, in response to controversies over ongoing mining activities in Death Valley and what was then Mt. McKinley (since changed to Denali)

National Parks, Congress enacted the Mining in the Parks Act, 16 U.S.C. §§ 1901 et seq. (MPA). Hardrock mining occurred in a few parks because mining claims had been located on the lands before they were withdrawn. The Act governs activities "resulting from the exercise of valid existing mineral rights on patented or unpatented mining claims within any area of the National Park System," and makes such activities "subject to such regulations prescribed by the Secretary of the Interior as he deems necessary or desirable for the preservation and management of those areas." 16 U.S.C. § 1902. Except for valid existing rights, exploration, mining, and patenting of hardrock minerals within the national park system are prohibited. The Park Service's regulations are quite detailed and stringent. 36 C.F.R. Pt. 9.

The Park Service has used its authority under the MPA to prevent miners from operating on mining claims without first obtaining approval of an operations plan. United States v. Vogler, 859 F.2d 638 (9th Cir.1988), upheld this power even over claims patented before the unit entered the Park System. The Ninth Circuit has also held that the Secretary has discretion under the Act to decide when and under what conditions to conduct a field inspection and mineral examination to determine the value of a discovery prior to approving plans of operations. *See* Northern Alaska Environmental Center v. Lujan, 872 F.2d 901 (9th Cir.1989) (the Secretary may, considering the relatively extreme climatic conditions in Alaska, "channel his limited resources to on-site mineral examinations of isolated claims or to areas previously not subjected to mining operations").

NOTE: REFORMING THE MINING LAW

Calls for reform of the Mining Law date back over a century. Factions inside the mining industry have long advocated legislation to mitigate *pedis possessio* uncertainties and provide more security of tenure during the exploration phase. Proposals have long been offered to eliminate such litigation-prone features as the distinction between lode and placer claims and extralateral rights, and to substitute uniform location procedures for the patchwork of state laws. Until the 1960s, Mining Law reform was an internecine struggle, and proponents of major reform (usually the larger mining companies) could never muster enough political support to overcome the resistance of "mom-and-pop" prospectors and miners.

In the modern era, reformers are led by environmental groups and fiscal conservatives, who emphasize the relative lack of environmental safeguards on hardrock mining, the fact that hardrock miners pay no rental or royalty, the Law's opportunity for privatization of federal lands for a nominal fee, its numerous opportunities for abuse for purposes that have nothing to do with mining, and the inability of the federal agencies to rid their lands of stale or nuisance claims. Until the late 1980s, most reformers supported total abolition of the location system, substituting a fully discretionary leasing system modeled on the Mineral Leasing Act. Leasing proposals received serious attention in the mid–1970s, attracting the support of Presidents Nixon and Carter and key members of Congress. But reform efforts have never found a political formula to overcome substantial divisions in the Congress. The House has generally favored tough reform by a substantial margin, but the power of western Senators has kept the Senate from finding sixty votes (necessary to overcome a filibuster which diehard Mining Law supporters would mount if necessary) to pass meaningful reform. Defenders of the system continue to emphasize the need they perceive for the federal government to maintain incentives for hardrock mineral development. They especially oppose a discretionary leasing system, which they argue would destroy the opportunity for initiative built into the location system. Hardrock minerals, they maintain, are more elusive to find than the more widely occurring bedded minerals like coal and phosphate that are subject to the federal Mineral Leasing Act.

In the late 1980s, the reform effort—moribund for a decade—was resuscitated. The Reagan Administration's issuance of patents for several thousand acres of old oil shale claims in western Colorado combined with several reports of environmental and patenting abuses put the issue back before Congress. This time a number of environmental groups indicated a willingness to support major reform within the confines of the location system, rather than support all-out leasing. In 1993–94 it seemed that reform was at last at hand. For the first time in history, reform bills passed both Houses of Congress, but the two chambers could not resolve their differences and the effort died in the waning days of the 104th Congress. The next year, the Republicans took over both Houses, and eventually included a pale version of Mining Law reform (which did almost nothing to address the basic issues, and was opposed as "sham reform" by environmentalists and the Administration) in a massive omnibus "budget reconciliation bill" that was vetoed by President Clinton.

The Bush (II) Administration stated that it supported reform of the Mining Law, including the authorization of a production payment system, but never made it a legislative priority. Partly as a result, the General Mining Law continues to change only incrementally, through administrative interpretations and legislative riders.

B.   MINERAL LEASING

A leasing disposition system for some non-metalliferous minerals developed separately from the location system for hardrock minerals as much because of history as geology. Congress created a sale system for coal in 1864, before it enacted the first Mining Law. The age of petroleum dawned a few years before the 1872 Mining Law; the Law's application to petroleum was, as illustrated in Union Oil v. Smith, fraught with problems. Moreover, as demonstrated in *Midwest Oil*, *supra* p. 418, the federal government realized by 1909 there was little sense in giving away oil reserves one day and buying them back for the Navy the next.

Leasing was not an innovation. It had been the practice of the young United States with lead mines in what is now the Midwest for several decades in the early 1800's, and had been upheld by the U.S. Supreme

Court in United States v. Gratiot, *supra* p. 118. But the modern template is the Mineral Leasing Act of 1920 (MLA), as amended, 30 U.S.C. § 181 et seq. The MLA became the basic model for the Outer Continental Shelf Lands Act of 1953 (with substantial amendments in 1978), 43 U.S.C. §§ 1331–1343, and the Geothermal Steam Act of 1970, 30 U.S.C. §§ 1001– 1025. The MLA's sections on coal leasing were tightened by the Federal Coal Leasing Amendments Act of 1976, Pub.L.No. 94–377. The MLA's sections on oil and gas leasing were revised by the Federal Onshore Oil and Gas Leasing Reform Act of 1987, Pub.L.No. 100–203.

Today, the leasable minerals include the fossil fuel minerals (oil, gas, oil shale, coal, native asphalt, bituminous rock, and solid and semi-solid bitumen); the fertilizer and chemical minerals (phosphate, potassium, sodium, and, in a few states, sulfur); all minerals (but in practice, principally oil and gas) on the outer continental shelf; and geothermal resources. The Mineral Leasing Act for Acquired Lands applies to the same minerals as the MLA and simply extends its principles to acquired federal lands. 30 U.S.C. §§ 351 et seq. Hardrock minerals are leasable by regulation on acquired national forest lands and on the outer continental shelf. Minor acts cover a variety of special situations. The Environmental Working Group hosts a comprehensive website about federal oil and gas leasing in twelve western states in the lower forty-eight, with detailed information about lessees, maps, and other interesting facts. *See* http://www.ewg.org/ oil_and_gas.

In 2006, mineral leasing yielded a little more than $12 billion for the federal treasury. Of that total figure, about $3.6 billion came from onshore leasing of coal, oil, and gas, the focus of the discussion below. Federally owned, onshore oil and gas contribute 11 and 5 percent of the U.S. domestic production, respectively; but they constitute larger proportions of the nation's "proved reserves" (60 and 53 percent, respectively). Federal control of coal is even more important because leasing decisions can determine whether isolated private parcels can be mined with the economies of scale necessary for profitable operations. Nearly half of U.S. coal production now comes from federal lands.

1.   MINERAL LEASING SYSTEMS IN A NUTSHELL

Generalization about mineral leasing can be somewhat hazardous because the major acts are not identical, and special provisions abound. But certain common features distinguish leasing from location systems:

a.   There is no right of self-initiation. Permission must be obtained from the federal government to prospect, develop, or produce leasable minerals.

b.   The United States has broad discretion whether to offer lands for lease. *See* Ash Creek Mining Co. v. Lujan, 969 F.2d 868 (10th Cir.1992) (Wyoming had no standing to complain of the Secretary's decision to exchange federal coal rather than lease it, because leasing is a decision within the discretion of the executive and federal courts lack authority to order federal lands to be leased). The government may make determinations not to lease informally (by simply rejecting requests to lease), or formally through the land and resource planning process, or through the withdrawal process.

c.   The United States also has broad power to control mineral development through lease terms and stipulations, and leases typically contain provisions to protect other competing resources and the environment.

d.   The United States can require diligent development of the resource leased, on pain of forfeiture of the lease.

e.   The United States typically must put mineral resources up for competitive bid and may not accept less than fair market value for the resource. The lease offer specifies the royalty rate the lessee will pay on the unit of production (e.g., twenty percent of the value of resource produced). A minimum royalty rate is set by statute and varies somewhat from mineral to mineral. Bidders compete against each other in the amount of "bonus" or cash payment they are willing to offer the government to secure the lease. In addition to the bonus bid and the royalty, lessees must pay an annual rental on a per acre basis.

2.   COMPETITION IN FEDERAL MINERAL DEVELOPMENT

All offshore oil and gas leasing has always been by competitive bidding, although the form and content of the bidding process can vary dramatically. *See* Watt v. Energy Action Ed. Found., 454 U.S. 151 (1981). Onshore leasing systems, however, originally distinguished between areas where a good deal of information existed about likely mineral occurrence, and areas of unknown potential. In the former areas, no exploration permits were thought necessary. Leases were obtained only through competitive bidding. Where knowledge was lacking, the applicable statutes authorized the federal government to issue "prospecting permits" that authorized exploration for a period of time. If the permittee discovered a "valuable deposit" or "commercial quantities" of the mineral, it would become entitled to a so-called "preference right lease," without competitive bidding. (The showing required bears a strong resemblance to the "discovery" requirement under the Mining Law.) The return to the government from noncompetitive leases was significantly less than when leases were put up for bid. The justification for this lower return was to provide an incentive for exploration.

Congress has abandoned that distinction for the most important minerals, oil, gas, and coal. In 1987, Congress reformed the onshore oil and gas leasing system to require all areas to be offered for competitive bidding. Only if an offered tract draws no bids can it thereafter be leased noncompetitively with a statutory minimum royalty. Congress abandoned prospecting permits and moved to competitive leasing for coal in 1975. The issuance of prospecting permits followed by the opportunity to obtain a preference right lease still exists in geothermal leasing and in the fertilizer minerals. How this works is illustrated further below in the *Kerr–McGee* case, in the section on environmental regulation of lease activities.

Where competitive bidding is followed, the BLM, at the request of a private party or on its own initiative, publishes a notice to offer specific lands for lease. Persons may then submit bids in accordance with highly detailed requirements. Leases are issued to the qualified bidder with the highest bonus bid, but the United States may reject all bids, the most common basis being the inadequacy of the bids. The royalty is fixed by the BLM in advance; typical royalties are 12.5 to 25 percent for oil and gas, depending upon the amount of production; at least 12.5 percent for surface-mined coal; and 10 to 15 percent for geothermal steam. The Minerals Management Service (MMS), an agency in the Department of the Interior, collects royalties and administers leases. The Federal Oil and Gas Royalty Management Act in 1982 and the Federal Oil and Gas Royalty Simplification and Fairness Act of 1996 significantly revised royalty law. 30 U.S.C. §§ 1701–57. Consideration of the complexities of royalty management is beyond the scope of these materials. However, the sheer scale of the money at stake generates considerable litigation and scandal. Most recently, mistakes in drafting lease agreements in the 1990s and lax royalty auditing in the mid–2000s have cost the federal government billions of dollars. Edmund L. Andrews, *U.S. Drops Bid Over Royalties from Chevron*, N.Y.Times, Oct. 31, 2006, at A1.

The term of the mineral lease varies according to the mineral. Coal leases have an initial term of twenty years, 30 U.S.C. § 207(a). Oil and gas leases have primary terms of ten years. In most situations, a lease term is automatically extended beyond the primary term by production in "paying quantities," which also bears more than passing resemblance to the Mining Law's concept of discovery.

The various mineral leasing statutes generally contain limitations on the size of individual mineral leases, which vary according to the mineral. For example, a 2,560–acre limit applies to geothermal leases, while oil shale leases may encompass 5,120 acres. There are no limits on the size of individual coal leases, but they cannot be combined into a logical mining unit of more than 25,000 acres. The mineral leasing statutes also limit the total acres that a lessee can maintain under all leases. *See* 30 U.S.C. § 184. Leases must include provisions for rents and royalties, and they also require diligent development of the resource, with statutory and administrative requirements varying by mineral.

3.   What Is "Fair Market Value"?

One of the advantages of leasing over the General Mining Law's disposal system is the revenue and royalties that compensate the public for the minerals removed. An ongoing struggle in administering leasing, however, has been ensuring a fair return to the U.S. Treasury when so much money is at stake, and where the bidders wield great political power. From the Teapot Dome scandal to the current controversies over lessee underpayments, the question of what is a fair value for minerals never recedes from legal contention. Echoes of the marketability test from the General Mining Law can be heard in disputes like the one below, concerning coal leasing in the single most productive area of the country: the Powder River Basin.

Leasing of federal minerals has had an occasionally colorful history. Leasing under the 1920 Mineral Leasing Act got off to a particularly rocky start. Naval Petroleum Reserves had been established in California and Wyoming in the previous decade. Shortly after passage of the Mineral Leasing Act, Congress gave the Secretary of the Navy extensive jurisdiction over the reserves. Soon after taking office in 1921, President Warren Harding issued a secret executive order transferring jurisdiction over the reserves to Secretary of the Interior Albert B. Fall, a former Senator from New Mexico. Later investigation revealed that Fall then secretly, without competitive bidding, leased all of the Wyoming reserve (known as "Teapot Dome," after a rock formation in the vicinity) and much of the California reserve to his friends in the oil industry. Fall received large amounts of cash from these friends at the same time, contending that they were loans. A jury disbelieved him, and he became the first American cabinet officer to serve a prison term for crimes committed in office. Fall v. United States, 49 F.2d 506 (D.C.App.1931). Interestingly, the oil company executives who bribed him (or, if Fall was to be believed, made innocent loans to him) were acquitted of bribery. The trials are recounted in C.G. Haglund, *The Naval Reserves*, 20 GEO. L.J. 293 (1932). The Wyoming leases were eventually canceled on fraud grounds by the Supreme Court. *See* Mammoth Oil Co. v. United States, 275 U.S. 13 (1927).

Oil and gas leasing again became enmeshed in controversy a few decades later. The problem was caused when Congress narrowed the circumstances in which the Department could issue competitive oil and gas leases. In the 1950s, competition grew dramatically for areas put up for lease which under the statute could only be issued to "the person first making application." The Department's solution to this dilemma, in the face of congressional refusal to change the system, was to adopt a lottery. It collected all the applications that poured in on the date the Department said it was going to receive applications for particular tracts and pulled one out of a drum to receive the noncompetitive lease. The D.C. Circuit court upheld the practice:

> The history of the administration of the statute furnishes compelling proof, familiar to the membership of Congress, that the human animal has not changed, that when you determine to give something away, you are going to draw a crowd. It is the Secretary's job to manage the crowd while complying with the requirement of the Act. * * * We cannot say that [the lottery] is an impermissible implementation of the statutory purpose.

Thor–Westcliffe Development, Inc. v. Udall, 314 F.2d 257, 260 (D.C.Cir. 1963). Eventually Congress reformed the system. The 1987 Reform Act led to adoption of an all-competitive bidding system for onshore oil and gas. The Act provided that the Secretary must accept the highest bid for each parcel so long as it is not less than the national minimum acceptable bid.

In 1982 the Department of Interior sold coal leases in the Powder River Basin area of Montana and Wyoming. The sale involved approximately 1.6 billion tons of coal distributed over 23,000 acres of public land. Due to the timing and scale of the sale, however, the federal government earned relatively little in bonus bids. The controversial sale spurred the following litigation.

National Wildlife Federation v. Burford

United States Court of Appeals, Ninth Circuit, 1989.
871 F.2d 849.

■ JUDGE HUG

The National Wildlife Federation ("NWF"), Montana Wildlife Federation, Northern Plains Resource Council, and the Powder River Basin Resource Council appeal the district court's entry of summary judgment on count 1 of their amended complaint. Count 1 alleged that the Secretary of the Interior violated 30 U.S.C. § 201(a)(1) by accepting coal lease bids that fell below fair market value ("FMV"). The district court properly held that NWF had standing to bring its suit and properly concluded that the Secretary and acted within the law in selling the leases. We affirm the summary judgment.

* * *

* * * 30 U.S.C. § 201(a)(1) provides that no bid on land offered for leasing "shall be accepted which is less than the fair market value, *as determined by the Secretary*, of the coal subject to the lease" (emphasis added). The Secretary "shall award leases * * * by competitive bidding." Defined in 43 C.F.R. § 3400.0–5(n) (1981), fair market value is "that amount in cash, or on terms reasonably equivalent to cash, for which in all probability the coal deposit would be sold or leased by a knowledgeable owner willing but not obligated to sell or lease to a knowledgeable purchaser who desires but is not obligated to buy or lease."

In light of the language contained in section 201(a)(1) and the interpretative regulation, NWF's task is to show that DOI did not receive FMV for its leases in the Powder River Basin area. Since agency action is presumed to be justified, and the Secretary need present only a reasonable explanation for his actions, NWF's burden of proof is considerable.

The district court, after a careful review of the administrative record, concluded that the Secretary acted reasonably, although possibly not supremely wisely, in accepting the Powder River lease bids. He found specifically that the shift to an entry level bid ("ELB") system which allowed lower initial bids than the prior minimum acceptable bid ("MAB") system,* was satisfactorily explained in the record by information attesting to declining coal prices; that FMV refers to receipt of a fair return, and not to the procedures used; * * * that nine of the eleven tracts up for lease

---

* [Eds. Under the ELB system, the Department accepted all bids for consideration no matter how low. Under the MAB system the Department established a threshold amount, with all bids below that amount rejected from further consideration.]

received high bids that met or exceeded the pre-sale estimates of FMV[3]; and that the process used to calculate the pre-sale FMV figures, which involved approximately 4,000 hours of work, was not unsound.

NWF raises two major attacks on the district court's finding of reasonableness. First, it contends that the shift to the ELB system was irrational and insufficiently explained in the record. The ELB procedure guaranteed, according to NWF, the receipt of less than FMV. Second, NWF argues that the MABs used in the sales were skewed by the DOI's reliance on a prior coal lease sale not comparable to the Powder River Basin sale. Use of these MABs as benchmarks of FMV, consequently, was improper.

The claim based on deficiencies in the ELB system is unpersuasive. First, the ELB system is not in itself arbitrary or capricious. The basis for the bidding procedure, as NWF repeatedly points out, is the presumption of competitive bidding. As section 201(a)(1) makes clear, leases shall be sold by the Secretary "by competitive bidding." The Secretary contends the ELB system stimulates competitive bidding. The Secretary can hardly be faulted for using a sales system whose purpose is to implement the statute's mandate. Second, the shift from the MAB to ELB procedure did not constitute an abrupt or unexplained departure from settled policy. As the administrative record shows, DOI had begun to consider use of the ELB system in coal lease sales in 1981. The decision to implement this system in the Powder River lease sale occurred as a result of studies suggesting a decline in the western coal market. The use of the ELB to stimulate competitive bidding at the time of a softening market cannot be said to be arbitrary and capricious. Finally, despite whatever flaws may have existed in the ELB system, actual high bids on nine out of the eleven available tracts met or exceeded the presale estimate of FMV. It is the result of the bidding procedure that is important: whether the high bid represented fair market value.

NWF's second contention is that the MABs used in the pre-sale estimates were defective, and did not represent fair market value. NWF claims that in calculating presale FMV, DOI used data from one prior sale, the "AB" sale, that was not comparable while ignoring data from a comparable sale, the "CD" sale. Choice of comparable sales figures and the calculation of MABs is a technical issue subject to analysis by trained

---

3. The Secretary accepted bids on ten of the eleven tracts. One bid was rejected. The single accepted bid that fell below the pre-sale FMV estimate involved the Little Rawhide Creek tract. The Secretary accepted this bid on the grounds that the Little Rawhide Creek tract constituted a potential bypass tract. A bypass tract consists of "an isolated coal deposit that cannot * * * be mined economically and in an environmentally sound manner either separately or as part of any logical mining unit other than that of the applicant." 43 C.F.R. § 3400.0–5(d) (1981). This type of tract appeals, in other words, only to a single bidder who owns an adjacent tract. The one bidder on the Little Rawhide Creek tract, Meadowlark Farms, Inc., owns the land to the north and east of the tract. The Secretary determined that, even if adjacent unleased federal coal were included with the tract, the Little Rawhide Creek tract could not, standing alone, offer the possibility of a profitable return to a potential buyer. In light of this fact, and the fact that NWF has not shown that any mining unit other than Meadowlark Farms could economically mine the tract, the Secretary reasonably decided to accept the tendered bid as a special circumstance.

specialists. The reviewing court's task is not to resolve disagreements between differing technical perspectives. Instead, its duty "is the limited one of ascertaining that the choices made by the [Secretary] were reasonable and supported by the record * * *. That the evidence in the record may support other conclusions, even those that are inconsistent with the [Secretary's], does not prevent us from concluding that his decisions were rational and supported by the record." Lead Indus. Ass'n, Inc. v. EPA, 647 F.2d 1130, 1160 (D.C.Cir.), cert. denied, 449 U.S. 1042 (1980). The administrative record suggests that the Economic Evaluation Committee's appraisal of the AB sales led to the conclusion that the AB figures best suited the type of the leases available in the Powder River Basin. DOI had a reasonable basis for its Powder River MABs and for its conclusion that the lease price for the tracts which equaled or exceeded the pre-sale MABs represented fair market value.

Finally, NWF contends that a variety of procedural irregularities corrupted the bid process. NWF states that pre-bid pricing leaks to industry representatives, the Secretary's quick announcement that the sale was successful, and other events of a similar nature irretrievably corrupted the sale. Although these irregularities may have occurred, NWF has not met its burden of showing that the leases did not sell for a fair return as a result of these problems. Given that the pre-sale FMV figures were reasonable and that nine out of the ten leases went to bidders who met or exceeded those figures, NWF's procedural argument is unpersuasive.

NWF has not demonstrated that DOI received less than FMV for its Powder River leases and that the Secretary's decision to accept the leases was arbitrary or capricious. The district court's summary judgment ruling, consequently, is AFFIRMED.

NOTES AND QUESTIONS

1. "Fair market value" (FMV) is a rather common statutory mandate to govern sales or grants of federally-owned natural resources. Sometimes, as here, procedures like competitive bidding are required to help ensure its receipt. In such cases, is FMV determined solely by the level of bidding? At least if there is fair competition, bidding determines "market" value, but is "market" value always "fair"? If, as the court indicated here, the market for coal in the region was "soft" or "softening," does offering leases for sale achieve FMV? Is the key decision *when* to hold the sale (in a booming or depressed market), rather than what kinds of bids to accept? Is there a difference between achieving FMV and maximizing returns to the federal treasury? Are there any grounds on which a court might second-guess the Secretary on FMV, given the text of the Mineral Leasing Act, which refers to "fair market value, *as determined by the Secretary*" (emphasis added)?

2. Neither the rest of the Act nor the legislative history sheds much light on how FMV should be determined. A large body of case law exists to define FMV in both the taxation and eminent domain areas, and the U.S. Supreme Court has said that the same standards apply in both. Great

Northern R. Co. v. Weeks, 297 U.S. 135, 139 (1936). A standard definition is contained in a manual prepared to guide federal land acquisition:

> "Fair market value" is defined as the amount in cash, or on terms reasonably equivalent to cash, for which in all probability the property would be sold by a knowledgeable owner willing but not obligated to sell to a knowledgeable purchaser who desired but is not obligated to buy. In ascertaining that figure, consideration should be given to all matters that might be brought forward and reasonably be given substantial weight in bargaining by persons of ordinary prudence, but no consideration whatever should be given to matters not affecting market value.

Uniform Appraisal Standards For Federal Land Acquisitions 3–4 (Interagency Land Acquisition Conference 1973). Does this help provide a basis for judicial review of Secretarial determinations of FMV in coal lease sales? On another occasion, the Supreme Court described the application of such a test as "at best, a guess by informed persons." United States v. Miller, 317 U.S. 369, 374–75 (1943).

3.   In another case raising separate legal issues about this same coal lease sale, the court provided some useful background on the matter:

> In April and October 1982, the Department held coal lease sales in the Powder River Basin in Southeast Montana and Northeast Wyoming that were widely criticized for allegedly obtaining far less than fair market value. Department rules previously required bids to be evaluated against an independent assessment of the fair market value of a given lease prepared by the U.S. Geological Survey. The Department formally deleted this requirement the day before the first sale. A report by House Appropriations Committee staff estimated that the Department sold the leases for $60 million less than fair market value, while a General Accounting Office ("GAO") study calculated the underpayment at $100 million. * * * This scandal led to the suspension of nearly all federal coal lease sales for almost four years. In July 1983, Congress established the Commission on Fair Market Value Policy for Federal Coal Leasing (the "Linowes Commission") to review the Department's coal valuation procedures and make recommendations for improvements.

National Wildlife Federation v. Babbitt, 24 ELR 20200, 20201 (D.D.C. 1993). The "Linowes Commission" (named after its chair) issued a 500–page report, containing thirty six recommendations for improvement. Report to Congress: Commission on Fair Market Value Policy for Federal Coal Leasing (1984). The report contained the following conclusions, among many others:

> [F]lexibility in lease sale scheduling is desirable. The Government should seek to sell more coal when price signals indicate a greater need for Federal coal and seek to sell less when lower prices indicate less demand. [*Id.* at 492]

> [L]easing level decisions should be made in a broader context than the effect on Federal revenues alone. The purpose of the Federal coal

leasing program is to make the maximum contribution of Federal coal to the Nation's welfare. Besides earning revenues, this purpose includes providing coal to consumers at low prices, protecting the environment, furthering national security goals of reducing energy imports, conserving the Nation's coal resources, and treating residents of coal–producing areas fairly. The Federal Government's management of its coal resource differs from private resource management in that a much wider range of objectives is sought and must be reconciled. [*Id.* at 486]

[C]ompetition [has been] the exception rather than the rule in Federal coal leasing. * * * In some ways, current sale procedures of the Interior Department resemble negotiations, especially for maintenance and bypass tracts. ["Maintenance" tracts are those that by themselves do not contain enough coal to operate a profitable mine; they must be combined with other tracts not offered in the lease sale. "Bypass" tracts are those that are encompassed within an existing mine, and are of interest only to the company operating the mine.] * * * Despite Government efforts, a substantial number of tracts are still not likely to attract competitive bidding. For these tracts, there may be no alternative to negotiation, whether it is done informally within existing sale procedures or formally through new statutory authority to negotiate. Negotiated coal lease sales require strong public confidence in the negotiators. Interior Department officials expressed concern that unreasonable public expectations might put them in a difficult position as negotiators. [*Id.* at 507–08]

Because many Federal leases will not attract competition, the appraisal process plays a critical role in helping the Government receive fair market value. The two most widely used methods of appraisal are comparable sales analysis and capitalization of projected income—also known as discounted cash flow (DCF) analysis. Both the DCF and comparable sales methods have been used * * *. At one time or another, each has been considered the preferable approach by the Department. * * * [U]navoidably, there will be circumstances where neither comparable sales methods nor DCF methods can be expected to work well. * * * [T]he inexact character of coal lease appraisals makes it all the more imperative that a set of procedures be established to ensure the unbiased nature and professional independence of the appraisal effort. [*Id.* at 510–11]

On the Powder River lease sale that triggered the controversy, the Commission concluded:

[T]he Interior Department probably did not receive fair market value, [but] the Commission did not attempt to quantify the amount that should have been obtained. However, the Commission concluded that the Interior Deperment [sic] probably offered excessive amounts of Federal coal reserves in a declining market and that this, in turn, probably lessened the prospect of receiving fair market value. At the very least, the Interior Department made serious errors in judgment in its procedures for conducting the 1982 Powder River lease sale and failed to provide a sound rationale for many of its actions. [*Id.* at 536]

Neither the district court nor the court of appeals in the principal case addressed this finding in upholding the Department of the Interior. Does this episode, with its rich, expert documentation of the failure of the Department to receive FMV, suggest that the courts cannot, or lack the appetite to, play a meaningful role in these economic matters?

4. A legacy of the checkerboard pattern of federal land grants is found in the "bypass" tract problem discussed in footnote 3 of the court's opinion and in the excerpts from the Linowes Commission report. How can the Secretary meet the FMV requirement in that context, where the universe of potential bidders is practicably limited to one? Where the "market" value of the coal on such a tract may be sharply limited, how does the Secretary determine what is "fair"? By appraisal only? Would the Secretary be justified in raising the royalty rate on the coal in the bypass situation, in part because of lack of competition, and in part because the existing operator already has infrastructure in place, and therefore would have a higher profit margin on the bypass tract? For example, if the standard coal lease provided for a 12.5 percent royalty, could the Secretary charge 20 percent for a bypass coal tract?

5. How similar a challenge is it for a public agency to determine a FMV, compared to determining whether a discovery under the Mining Law meets the marketability test? The volatility of commodity prices and the risk spreading that is a part of modern business management make both challenging speculations. What lessons, if any, does the FMV problem hold for hardrock mining reform?

4. MINERAL LEASING AND ENVIRONMENTAL REGULATION

Generally, the Department of the Interior's Bureau of Land Management is responsible for issuing and supervising activities on mineral leases, even on lands managed by other agencies (the U.S. Forest Service being the principal one affected). In some cases, such as in mineral leases on acquired lands or oil and gas leases on national forests, the BLM is required by statute to obtain the consent of the surface managing agency (usually, the U.S. Forest Service) before issuing a lease. Even where the surface managing agency does not have a statutory veto, BLM's custom has long been not to issue leases over its objection.

The various mineral leasing acts generally give the Secretary ample authority to include lease provisions to protect the environment. Recall the discussion of this issue in *Ventura County, supra* p. 181, and see also the note on SMCRA, below. Although lease terms and regulations dealing with environmental matters were once vague and difficult to enforce, that picture has changed dramatically in the last few decades.

Kerr–McGee Corp. v. Hodel

U.S. District Court, District of Columbia, 1986.
630 F.Supp. 621.

■ JUDGE PARKER

Plaintiffs contend that on January 10, 1983, the Secretary of Interior wrongfully denied their applications for phosphate leases thus depriving them of vested rights to engage in phosphate mining. In response to those allegations, the federal defendants and the intervenors contend that the applications were denied because the reclamation technologies relied upon and proffered by the plaintiffs were inadequate to ensure restoration of the mined portions of the Osceola Forest to the purposes for which they were acquired and the historical uses to which they had been put, as required by the Mineral Leasing Act for Acquired Lands, 30 U.S.C. §§ 351 *et seq.* (1982). Specifically, the Secretary found that plaintiffs had not discovered "valuable deposits" of phosphate as required under the Act, because the costs of reclamation would be prohibitively high. * * *

The Osceola National Forest was established in 1931 by President Herbert Hoover pursuant to the Creative Act of 1891. The vast majority of the Forest was acquired under the authority of the Weeks Act of 1911. The primary purposes behind the acquisition and development were timber production, water shed protection, fish and wildlife protection, and preservation and maintenance of recreational opportunities. Osceola Forest consists of nearly 158 thousand acres located in North–Central Florida. Included within that acreage are cypress swamps, pine lands, unique hardwood wetlands, and upland hardwood forests. Highly diverse creek and river systems, within the area serve as a source of high quality surface and ground water, and provides an important water shed for North–Central Florida. The Forest also provides a home for important varieties of fish and wildlife species and for a number of valued and certain limited [sic] and endangered species.

The authority for phosphate leasing on federal land and the limits on the Interior Secretary's ability to lease, depends upon whether the lands are classified as "public domain" or "acquired" lands. Public domain lands are lands that have never left the control of the United States. The Mineral Leasing Act, 30 U.S.C. §§ 181, 211(b) *et seq.*, authorizes the Secretary to lease phosphate deposits on those lands. Public domain lands comprise a very limited portion of the Osceola National Forest.

For acquired lands, lands that have been either granted or sold to the United States, the source of mineral leasing authority stems from the Mineral Leasing Act for Acquired Lands, 30 U.S.C. § 352. That section provides in relevant part:

> No mineral deposit covered by this section shall be leased except with the consent of the head of the executive department ... having jurisdiction over the lands containing such deposit ... and subject to such conditions as that official may prescribe to insure the adequate utilization of the lands for the primary purposes for which they have been acquired or are being administered....

The Act also establishes the authority and conditions under which the Interior Secretary may issue phosphate leases. And, as is the case here, the Secretary must secure the consent of other departments or agencies which, because of concurrent jurisdiction over the lands, may impose requirements or stipulations. The Forest includes a significantly larger proportion of acquired lands as compared with public domain lands.

During the mid-to-late 1960s, the plaintiffs applied to the Interior Department for permits to prospect for phosphate deposits on acquired lands. The permits were issued by the Department's Bureau of Land Management pursuant to the Mineral Leasing Act for Acquired Lands and were made expressly subject to all regulations, then existing or subsequently enacted, including Special Stipulations required by the Forest Service, Department of Agriculture. * * *

Subsequently, between 1969–1972, the plaintiffs applied to Interior for preference right leases to mine phosphate on the lands embraced by their prospecting permits alleging discovery of "valuable deposits" within the meaning of section 211(b) of the Mineral Leasing Act. Thereafter, the United States Geological Survey certified that valuable deposits had been discovered and recommended that leases be issued. The certifications were based on quality and quantity standards that had been applied by the Interior Department for some time * * * [which were exclusively on the] basis of physical characteristics, namely, the quality, quantity, thickness and extent of a deposit. This approach was used without regard for mining and marketing costs or other factors bearing upon the economic feasibility of mine development. During this period, there was no regulation, decision, opinion or instruction reflecting a departmental interpretation of the term as used in the Act, or purporting to recognize the propriety of the practice.

[After the applications for preference right leases were filed, the Department undertook additional studies on the impact of phosphate mining in the area on the environment, including an EIS under NEPA, followed by a Supplement to the EIS. The Department also promulgated new regulations in 1976 which provided that an application for a preference right lease must, in order to satisfy the "valuable deposit" test, "show that there is a reasonable expectation that ... revenues from the sale of the mineral will exceed ... costs of developing the mine, and extracting, removing and marketing the mineral."]

* * *

On February 4, 1982, the Forest Service [submitted to the Bureau of Land Management the stipulations that would be attached to the preference right lease, should one be issued. The key one,] Stipulation No. 4, specified that:

> The lessee shall, except for permanent lakes created by mining, reestablish watercourses, soil stability and productivity, approximate landforms and elevations, and wetland and upland of similar vegetative communities and species diversity in approximate proportions as those existing prior to mining. *The purpose of reclamation is to reestablish plant and aquatic communities with similar interspersion of community types, i.e., pine flatwoods, cypress swamps, creek swamps and lakes.* The soil medium shall be *reestablished* to support forest tree growth by: (a) providing a ratio of clay to sand in a mixture that will retain sufficient moisture and nutrients in the root zones of forest trees

making up the vegetative community; (b) by returning overburden, including topsoil, over the clay and sand mixture. (emphasis added).

* * * [The Interior Department's 1974 EIS] was pessimistic on the possibility of reclamation of native species following phosphate mining, particularly with reference to swamp hardwood plant communities. * * * [The Supplement to the EIS prepared in 1979 expressed] doubt about the success of reclamation efforts based on the then present state of technological knowledge. * * * It also concluded that research was needed to provide techniques for reestablishing the plant species and vegetative community types then found. Otherwise, it reaffirmed the pessimism on revegetation of native species as was noted in the 1974 Final Environmental Statement. * * *

[In 1982 the Interior Secretary established an interagency task force to once again assess reclamation technology. This group] concluded that no new technology had been developed since the 1979 Supplemental ES and that technology capabilities were insufficient to ensure a reasonable likelihood of the successful reclamation of mined areas consistent with the requirements established for mining in Osceola. * * * [Its report recommended] that all pending lease applications in Osceola National be rejected. [In January 1983 Secretary Watt rejected the lease applications based on his] determination that:

* * * [A] mineral deposit discovered under a prospecting permit must be of "such a character and quantity that a prudent person would be justified in the further expenditure of his labor and means with a reasonable prospect of success in developing a valuable mine." The Forest Service, as prescribed by law, has established reclamation stipulations which were used in processing [plaintiffs'] preference right lease applications. The Department of the Interior has performed studies which indicate current technology is not capable of meeting the prescribed reclamation standards. The fact that no reclamation technology exists which can reclaim these lands precludes the possibility that this phosphate deposit could meet the valuable deposit test.

* * * Although Kerr–McGee and Global dispute the Environmental Assessment team's conclusion as to the feasibility of reclamation of Osceola lands following phosphate mining, they have not identified or referred to any significant and factual data which were not considered in the preparation of the 1983 Environmental Assessment report. * * *

* * * [I]t appears that mineral development is incompatible with the primary purposes and uses of the forest and has a great potential of destroying the natural resources of the Forest. Strip mining, the technique used to secure the phosphates, [is] highly destructive of natural resources. In the process, the forest area to be mined is leveled, cleared of all vegetation and trees, and wetland areas are drained. The overburden has a depth of 20 to 60 feet. Electrical powered walking draglines, resembling giant scoops, strip the overburden and dig the mining cuts to remove the phosphate matrix averaging 8 to 10 feet thick from the earth. The mining cuts formed by these draglines average 150–200 feet wide and several thousand feet in length.

The acquired lands of the United States which are included in the Osceola Forest may be leased for mineral development only upon conditions imposed by the Mineral Leasing Act for Acquired Lands, 30 U.S.C. § 351 *et seq.* Section 3 of the Act, vests in the Interior Secretary the authority to issue a mineral lease with the consent of the head of the executive department having jurisdiction over the lands where the mineral deposits are located. The latter may prescribe such conditions as necessary "to insure the adequate utilization of the lands for the primary purposes for which they have been acquired or are being administered." 30 U.S.C. § 352. The determination of what conditions should be imposed if a mineral lease is issued on national forest land is thus committed by law to the Secretary of Agriculture.

Applicants such as Kerr–McGee and Global, to ensure their entitlement to phosphate leases, are required to demonstrate the discovery of "valuable deposits" of phosphates on the lands covered by their prospecting permits 30 U.S.C. § 211(b). * * * In determining whether a prospecting permittee has discovered a "valuable deposit" of phosphate, the cost of compliance with lease terms is an important element which must be considered, and if the applicant lacks the technological capability to comply with prescribed lease terms, he cannot satisfy the test and is not entitled to a lease. Natural Resource Defense Council, Inc. v. Berklund, 458 F.Supp. 925, 936–37 (D.D.C.1978), *aff'd,* 609 F.2d 553 (D.C.Cir.1979). The restoration technologies necessary to insure the adequate utilization of the Osceola Forest for its primary purposes did not exist in January 1983 or in 1984, and did not exist at any earlier time. To demonstrate the discovery of "valuable deposits" of phosphates, Kerr–McGee and Global must comply with the terms and conditions imposed by the Forest Service and are required to show the economic and technological feasibility of reclaiming the lands covered by the lease applications.

Until February 1982, when the Forest Service submitted to the Bureau of Land Management the final stipulations to be attached to any leases which might be issued to phosphate lease applicants in the Forest, the Interior Secretary could not determine whether the plaintiffs had satisfied the "valuable deposit" test, and no lease entitlement was vested in the plaintiffs. The earlier practices of the Department of Interior in issuing phosphate preference right leases before 1970 did not alter or change the statutory requirements and did not establish a legal standard which the Interior Secretary was bound to recognize in determining plaintiffs' lease entitlement. Nor did the prior determination of the Geological Survey * * * in 1969 and 1970, that Kerr–McGee had discovered valuable phosphate deposits on lands covered by its prospecting permits, vest any right to receive leases for which it made application. The same is true for any subsequent determination of the Geological Survey * * * or any other departmental finding made between 1969 and 1983. None of those determinations precluded the Interior Secretary from subsequently finding that the requisite discovery had not been shown.

The January 10, 1983, decision of the Secretary of Interior was not arbitrary and capricious but, rather, was justified and supported by substantial and credible evidence.

NOTES AND QUESTIONS

1.   A few days after Secretary Watt rejected the lease applications in January 1983, President Reagan vetoed a bill that would have (a) prohibited mining in the Osceola National Forest, (b) required the Secretary to make the "valuable deposit" determination without taking into account the cost of compliance with environmental statutes and regulations, and (c) required compensation to the plaintiffs for any deposits deemed "valuable." In September 1984, the President signed the Florida Wilderness Act of 1983, which effectively prohibited mining in the area absent a Presidential recommendation and congressional concurrence. *See* 98 Stat. 1665 (1984). Judge Parker's decision, issued in February 1986, did not address that Act. The D.C. Circuit subsequently vacated Judge Parker's decision and dismissed the case as moot because of the wilderness legislation. The court said that Kerr–McGee could seek a remedy for an alleged taking of property in the claims court, but it "intimate[d] no views" on any taking questions. 840 F.2d 68 (D.C.Cir.1988). Kerr–McGee filed suit in the Court of Federal Claims, which issued a preliminary ruling that the government should have allowed Kerr–McGee to offer evidence that it could meet the reclamation stipulations mandated by the Forest Service. 32 Fed.Cl. 43 (1994). After more inconclusive litigation, the parties reached a settlement that packaged resolution of this dispute with an unrelated Superfund case involving the same parties, and the matter was brought to an end more than thirty years after the initial applications for phosphate prospecting permits were filed.

2.   If this dispute had come along after the Supreme Court's decision in the *Mobil Oil* case, *supra* p. 347, could Kerr–McGee have made out a case for rescission and restitution? A big difference here, however, is that Kerr–McGee had not given the U.S. any significant money for the prospecting permit, which it received without competition.

3.   Does Kerr–McGee have an equitable argument that it is being jerked around by the government? Notice that the Forest Service did not formulate the reclamation standard for inclusion in the lease until 1982, well over a decade after the prospecting permits were issued. Should the BLM or the Forest Service have thought about whether or not phosphate-mined areas could be reclaimed *before* the prospecting permit was issued? (This situation shows the value of the idea behind NEPA. Had that statute been in effect when the federal government was considering issuing the prospecting permits, it might have forced the government to address the problem of reclamation then.)

4.   Or did Kerr–McGee assume the risk of being subject to unachievable reclamation standards when it took the prospecting permit not knowing what reclamation standard was going to be applied to it?

5.   The district court here rejected the argument that the "earlier practices of the Department * * * establish[ed] a legal standard which the Interior Secretary was bound to recognize in determining plaintiffs' lease entitlement." It also found that determinations made by the U.S. Geological Survey that Kerr–McGee had discovered valuable phosphate deposits did not preclude the Secretary, before the leases were actually issued,

"from subsequently finding that the requisite discovery had not been shown." Does the court too lightly dismiss the fact that the government appeared to change its interpretation of the "valuable deposit" test after the prospecting permits had been issued, and before the decision was made on the preference right lease? When Kerr–McGee took the permit, did it have a legitimate expectation that it need only show that the phosphate it discovered was of mineable quality and quantity in order to get a preference right lease? If the Department does change its mind, should it be held to a stricter standard of review, especially if its changes undercut the reasonable expectations of those doing business with the government?

6. Even if Kerr–McGee could have avoided the new standard for determining "valuable deposit," would it still have had a problem with the lease stipulation that required it to reclaim the land, when that seems impossible or at least very difficult? Was its ultimate, inescapable problem that the statute, 30 U.S.C. § 352, made the prospecting permit and the lease subject to "such conditions as that [agency] may prescribe to insure the adequate utilization of the lands for the primary purposes for which they have been acquired or are being administered"?

7. Does 30 U.S.C. § 352 in effect require a comparative value analysis (compare the comparative value test for discovery under the Mining Law, *supra* p. 579) or an analysis of the compatibility of mining with the primary purposes for which the land was required (compare the compatibility test involved in the St. Matthews Island case, *supra* p. 455)?

Natural Resources Defense Council, Inc. v. Berklund, 609 F.2d 553 (D.C.Cir.1979), involved a situation somewhat similar to the *Kerr–McGee* case. The mineral was coal, however, and the federal lands involved were not acquired, so the governing statute was the coal section of the Mineral Leasing Act. It does not contain a provision equivalent to that centrally involved in *Kerr–McGee*, namely, giving the surface managing agency the right to prescribe conditions in the lease "to insure the adequate utilization of the lands for the primary purposes for which they have been acquired." Instead, the applicable statute provided that the Department had to determine whether the prospecting permittee had discovered "commercial quantities" of coal; if so, the statute provided that it "shall be entitled to a lease." The same regulations that reformed the "valuable deposit" test for phosphate addressed in *Kerr–McGee* also applied to the "commercial quantities" test for coal. Specifically, they required a permittee to show a reasonable expectation that its revenues will exceed development and operating costs, and defined the latter to include the cost of "complying with existing governmental regulations, reclamation and environmental standards, and proposed lease terms." 43 C.F.R. § 3521.1–1(c)(2)(vi)(1978).

Plaintiff environmental groups argued that the Secretary had authority to reject lease applications by prospecting permittees. The court said no, finding "the plain meaning of the statute as well as undisturbed administrative practice for nearly 60 years leaves the Secretary no discretion to deny a [preference right] lease to a qualified applicant." It went on, however, to give the plaintiffs at least some of what they sought, by a more indirect means:

> [Under its new regulations Interior now] requires a demonstration that the estimated revenues can reasonably be expected to exceed estimated costs. Those costs can include the costs of complying with lease terms demanding complete reclamation and safeguards against environmental harm. Even after a lease is granted the awardee may be precluded from harming the environment if the agency disapproves his mining plan. These costs can be figured into the assessment of commercial quantities, covered in stringent lease provisions, or adopted as criteria for measuring proposed mining plans. * * * [The court will not] rewrite [the statute] to undermine the property rights of prospecting permittee lease applicants. * * * [Although Congress has changed the law so that no more prospecting permits for coal will be issued, f]or the some 183 lease applications outstanding under the former version of the provision, the property rights anticipated by permittee applicants cannot be diminished.

Id. at 558–59.

NOTES AND QUESTIONS

1. In *Berklund*, even accepting the court's conclusion that the Secretary has no discretion to deny a preference right lease once commercial quantities of coal are shown, could the Secretary exercise his broad authority over lease terms to include such stringent conditions to protect the environment that the permittee would flunk the "commercial quantities" test?

2. Could the Secretary, as an alternative, simply include a sufficiently high rental or royalty rate in the preference right lease to discourage the prospecting permittee from taking the lease? The leasing statutes typically require a rental and a royalty at "not less than" a specified statutory minimum, but do not contain a maximum, and leave the rate-setting to the discretion of the Secretary. *See, e.g.*, 30 U.S.C. § 212 (phosphate). But is it arbitrary or an abuse of discretion for the Secretary to set a higher rental or royalty rate for preference right leases than for other leases, if the only reason to do so is avoid issuing the lease non-competitively? Can you think of any other reasons for setting a higher rental or royalty rate for preference right as opposed to other leases?

3. The issue of determining economically valuable mineral deposits can also arise in another context, at the back end of the lease. That is, federal leasing statutes (and many leases of minerals in private contexts) have a fixed (primary) term and extend beyond the primary term for so long thereafter as the leased mineral is produced in "paying" or "commercial" quantities. *See, e.g.*, 30 U.S.C. § 207(a) (coal). Such a lease is generally regarded as conveying a determinable fee—an estate that terminates upon the occurrence of a possible event. Does "paying quantities" mean that the expenses of production are weighed against the value of the

minerals produced? What expenses? The cost of exploration as well as the cost of production? What about overhead and management costs? Environmental costs? Obviously, lessees may have a strong interest in holding on to a marginal lease, anticipating higher mineral prices, while lessors may have a strong competing interest in recapturing the lease for re-leasing to someone else, or using the land for other purposes.

4.   What did the D.C. Circuit mean in *Berklund* when it cautioned that the "property rights anticipated by permittee applicants cannot be diminished"? Notice that the Court did not say that the permittees *had* property rights, only that they were "anticipated." Is that a distinction without a difference?

5.   Review question: Consider whether and how the discretion of the Secretary differs in each of these decisions: (1) whether to withdraw lands from mineral leasing or from the Mining Law; (2) whether to offer federal lands for competitive coal or oil and gas leasing; (3) whether to issue "preference right" phosphate leases on previously granted prospecting permits; (4) what kinds of stipulations or terms to include in mineral leases; (5) whether to approve proposed plans of operations under the Mining Law, and (6) whether to issue patents under the Mining Law.

Copper Valley Machine Works, Inc. v. Andrus

United States Court of Appeals, District of Columbia Circuit, 1981.
653 F.2d 595.

■ JUDGE MACKINNON

The principal issue in this appeal is whether a restriction in a drilling permit prohibiting summer drilling in the interest of conservation worked a "suspension of operations and production" that would extend the life of an oil and gas lease under section 39 of the Mineral Leasing Act of 1920, as amended, 30 U.S.C. § 209.

Effective February 1, 1966, the Secretary of Interior issued oil and gas lease A–063937 to run for an initial "period of ten years and so long thereafter as oil or gas is produced in paying quantities."

Near the end of the primary lease term, Copper Valley Machine Works, Inc. (Copper Valley), the designated operator of the lease * * * [filed with the United States Geological Survey, an agency of the Department of the Interior that then regulated operations on federal oil and gas leases,] an application for a permit to drill. On January 30, 1976 [the day before the lease was to expire] the drilling permit application was approved, "subject to conditions attached to the permit and conditions and requirements described below: * * * 10. The approved application and development plan provides for operation *during the winter season only,* as approved by the appropriate surface managing agency." (emphasis added). This "winter season only" restriction was considered "necessary because the lease itself was issued without any stipulations for protection of the tundra/permafrost environment during the months of summer thaw."

The events that then led to this dispute are described in a memorandum from the Acting Director of the Geological Survey to the Secretary of Interior:

> The well was commenced on January 31, 1976 (the expiration date of the primary term), and reached a depth of 100 feet before having to shutdown for the 1976 summer season. Following the summer shutdown from May to November 1976, operations were recommenced on February 5, 1977, and after reaching a depth of 1,070 feet on March 20, 1977, electric logs were run in the well. After evaluating the electric logs and examining the samples, the Supervisor concluded that the operator had satisfied the "diligent drilling" requirements of 43 CFR 3107.2–3,[3] and recommended to BLM that the lease be extended to January 31, 1978.
>
> After the 1977 summer shutdown, the Supervisor advised the operator and the lessee that the lease would expire January 31, 1978, absent a well physically and mechanically capable of production in paying quantities by that date.
>
> On January 20, 1978, the operator wrote the Supervisor and requested that the lease be extended for twelve (12) months to compensate for the two periods of summer shutdown in 1976 and 1977. The Supervisor considered this letter to be *an application to the Secretary* for an extension of [the] lease * * * pursuant to 43 CFR 3103.3–8[4] [Emphasis added].

Although acknowledging that Copper Valley had been "unable to conduct operations on a full-time basis since January of 1976 by the imposition of the requirement that operations would be permitted only during the winter months," the Acting Director recommended that no extension of the lease be granted or recognized.

On May 22, 1978, the Secretary of Interior followed the Acting Director's recommendation, ruling that

3. 43 C.F.R. § 3107.2–3. *Period of extension.*

Any lease on which actual drilling operations, or for which under an approved cooperative or unit plan of development or operation, actual drilling operations were commenced prior to the end of its primary term and are being diligently prosecuted at that time, *shall be extended for 2 years* and so long thereafter as oil or gas is produced in paying quantities.

(Emphasis added.)

4. 43 C.F.R. § 3103.3–8 provides:

Suspension of operations and production.

(a) * * * As to oil and gas leases, no suspension of operations and production will be granted on any lease in the absence of a well capable of production on the leasehold, except where the Secretary directs a suspension in the interest of conservation. * * *

(b) The term of any lease will be extended by adding thereto any period of suspension of all operations and production during such term pursuant to any direction or assent of the Secretary.

(c) A suspension shall take effect as of the time specified in the direction or assent of the Secretary. Rental and minimum royalty payments will be suspended during any period of suspension of all operations and production directed or assented to by the Secretary * * *.

the lease is considered to have expired by operation of law as of midnight, January 31, 1978, absent the existence of a well on that date which had been determined by the Supervisor as capable of producing in paying quantities. The reasons for the denial [of extension] are that (1) the lessee accepted the imposed restriction that drilling could be conducted only during the winter season without complaint until 11 days preceding the lease expiration date and (2) the 2–year lease extension earned by drilling across the end of the primary term of January 31, 1976, afforded sufficient additional time, despite the restriction, in which to have completed a well that was physically capable of production in paying quantities. * * *

[Copper Valley then sued, but the district court rejected its argument] that the Secretary's refusal to permit another 12 months of operations was unlawful. Copper Valley relied on section 39 of the Mineral Leasing Act of 1920, as amended, which provides in part:

> In the event the Secretary of Interior *in the interest of conservation,* shall direct * * * *the suspension of operations and production* under any lease granted under the terms of this Act, any payment of acreage rental or of minimum royalty prescribed by such lease likewise shall be suspended during such period of suspension or operations and productions; *and the term of such lease shall be extended by adding any such suspension * * * thereto.*

30 U.S.C. § 209 (emphasis added). * * *

Copper Valley's principal contention on appeal is that the drilling permit's "winter season only" restriction, by preventing drilling operations for 6 summer months a year, worked a "suspension of operations and production" "in the interest of conservation" and therefore, under § 209, mandated an automatic extension of the lease for a period equal to the length of the suspension. The Government responds that the drilling restrictions did not create suspensions within the meaning of § 209.

A. "In the Interest of Conservation"

* * * The parties agree that carrying on drilling operations during the summer months would have substantially damaged the permafrost character of the leasehold area. Preventing such damage is obviously in the interest of conservation if that term is to receive its ordinary meaning. While the prevention of environmental damage may not have been the "conservation" that Congress principally had in mind in 1933 when it passed § 209,[6] suspending operations to avoid environmental harm is definitely a suspension in the interest of conservation in the ordinary sense of the word. And there was no indication that Congress intended that

---

6. A congressional report accompanying the bill that became § 209 stated:

[I]t is * * * a matter of public knowledge that there has existed for some time past, and still exists, a condition of over-production [of petroleum and natural gas]. This condition has resulted in the adoption by the Interior Department of an administrative policy of conservation of oil and gas.

H.R.Rep. No. 1737, 72nd Cong., 1st Sess. 3 (1932).

"conservation" be given any interpretation other than its ordinary meaning.[8] * * *

The Secretary asserts that § 209 "was designed by Congress to cover only unanticipated interruptions of drilling." Under this view, whether a § 209 suspension has occurred depends on whether the "winter season only" restriction was a surprise to Copper Valley. It is in this context that the Secretary emphasizes that the lease gave "notice that drilling activities would be subject to restriction," that Copper Valley "did not protest against the restriction until two years after the permit was issued," and that Copper Valley "continued to pay rent during the thaw months without attempting to assert that the drilling permit condition was a surprise." We find it unnecessary to consider whether summary judgment was appropriate on the question whether Copper Valley could foresee the suspension of drilling, for we reject as unpersuasive the Secretary's attempt to narrow the scope of the plain terms of § 209.

As indicated in note 6, § 209 was enacted in a period when the Secretary was suspending the drilling operations of oil and gas lessees in order to alleviate the problem of excess petroleum production. The congressional report explained that the bill

> relieve[s] lessees of coal and oil lands from the necessity of paying prescribed annual acreage rental, during periods when operations or production is suspended, in the interest of conservation, either by direction or assent of the Secretary of the Interior, and [provides] that the period of such suspension shall be added to the term of the lease. * * *

H.R.Rep. No. 1737, 72nd Cong., 1st Sess. 2–3 (1932).

Because some of the oil and gas lessees who benefited from the lease extensions and rent moratoriums of § 209 might have been surprised by the petroleum glut and the Secretary's ensuing suspensions, the Government contends that the section, which by its terms applies to any Secretary-imposed "suspension of operations and production," actually applies only to those suspensions that are the product of unanticipated events. To state this contention is to suggest its refutation. The plain meaning of a statute cannot be overcome by speculation as to some unstated purpose. Nothing in the legislative history of § 209 suggests, much less establishes, the narrow interpretation the Secretary would have us adopt. * * * The Secretary's speculation, suspect on its own terms, has no support in the legislative history and cannot modify the statute's plain terms.

* * *

8. This conclusion is consistent with Gulf Oil Corp. v. Morton, 493 F.2d 141 (9th Cir.1973). The court in *Morton* interpreted § 5(a)(1) of the Outer Continental Shelf (OCS) Lands Act, 43 U.S.C. § 1334(a)(1), a provision similar to 30 U.S.C. § 209. Section 5(a)(1) authorizes the Secretary of Interior to provide, "in the interest of conservation," for the "suspension of operations or production." The court rejected the oil company's argument that "interest of conservation" is confined to conservation of oil and gas, id. at 145, and concluded the Secretary was empowered to suspend drilling operations to prevent undue harm to the marine environment.

The Secretary also contends that Copper Valley's interpretation of § 209 could double the term of all leases on Alaskan tundra, contrary to the congressional intent that the term of a non-producing non-competitive lease be limited to 10 years, with the possibility of a single 2–year extension. 30 U.S.C. § 226(e). Contrary to the Secretary, we perceive no conflict between Copper Valley's reading of § 209 and a sensible reading of § 226(e). Without undertaking to decide that issue, which is not before us, we note that § 226(e) gives the lessee a minimum number of years in which to develop the resources subject to his lease. Section 209, consistent with this policy, extends the life of the lease to the extent that the lessee is deprived of his full term by the Secretary's suspension of drilling operations in the interest of conservation. Far from undermining § 226(e), § 209 effectuates the policy it reflects. The law was intended to apply uniformly throughout the United States and give lessees in Alaska the same full term of enjoyment as lessees in the lower 48 states. If climatic conditions in Alaska cause the Secretary to order a suspension in the interest of conservation it is not to be considered as being any the less a suspension because the reason that prompted its imposition was foreseeable. * * *

* * * The Secretary * * * has arbitrarily ignored the language of § 209. Ordinarily this agency conduct would call for a remand for proper application of the appropriate legal standards, if the agency under the law could reasonably adhere to the result its challenged decision has reached. On the undisputed facts here, however, we conclude that no reasonable interpretation of § 209 can deny Copper Valley the extension it claims. Accordingly, the judgment of the district court granting summary judgment for the Secretary should be vacated and the district court in accordance with the foregoing opinion should grant the motion of Copper Valley for summary judgment in its favor.[12]

■ JUDGE PRATT, concurring in the remand

* * * Congress intended the term "conservation" in § 209 to refer to the conservation of mineral resources, and not to more general environmental protection measures which may restrict production. The history of the 1933 statute shows that the concept of mineral conservation was advanced repeatedly by the bill's sponsors and managers, and was agreed to by opponents. * * * The majority reads "conservation" in its modern sense, and inadequately weighs the special meaning of the term "conservation" intended by Congress.

12. We cannot join the speculation [in the concurring opinion] that ordering a lease extension in this case will "create significant new land title difficulties in areas which have been subject to leasing, make new investment in oil exploration substantially more risky and expensive, and shortchange the United States as lessor, by conferring an unbargained-for windfall on the holders of existing leases." The Secretary has not acquainted us with these asserted problems. If conditions in Alaska require a special exception from § 209's plain meaning and policy then Congress is free to create one. In any event, were speculation within our province, we would venture that assuring oil and gas lessees, through lease extensions, the full exploration period that Congress has given them would *promote* new investment in oil exploration and benefit the United States. The United States is not shortchanged in the process; it is merely held to the lease terms specified in its statutory bargain.

The Interior Department, which had authored and advocated the 1933 and 1946 statutes, interpreted § 209 to apply only to mineral conservation. This example of contemporaneous construction by the responsible cabinet officer is strong evidence of the original meaning, especially where Congress reenacts the statute consistently with that construction. The Department acted consistently with this interpretation in subsequent administrative adjudication and rulemaking. * * *

I think a remand appropriate[,] however, for the Secretary * * * to decide explicitly whether winter-only drilling restrictions are "suspensions" under § 209, and to state the policy and legal reasons for his choice among plausible interpretations of § 209.

There are sound practical and legal reasons for this approach. We know little more about Alaskan drilling than the fact that it is expensive and difficult. By pronouncing a rule at sharp variance with present practice in Alaska, we may create significant new land title difficulties in areas which have been subject to leasing, make new investment in oil exploration substantially more risky and expensive, and shortchange the United States as lessor, by conferring an unbargained-for windfall on the holders of existing leases. These are cogent reasons for seeking a careful exercise of the Secretary's expert judgment before deciding the interpretive issue presented here. Udall v. Tallman, 380 U.S. 1, 16–18 (1965). By pronouncing a flat rule before the Secretary has acted, we may significantly impede Alaskan oil development vital to meeting the Nation's current and future energy needs. I doubt Congress intended that result.

NOTES AND QUESTIONS

1.   The "winter-only" restriction responds to climatic conditions in Alaska. The oil industry has made great strides in the last few decades reducing the impact of its operations on the fragile Arctic environment. Operating in the winter allows access and other activities to take place on snow and ice, which is much less damaging than operating directly on the tundra vegetation, where scars in the permafrost may never heal. Unfortunately, the winter "season" in northern Alaska has been shortening. Since 1970, this frozen season for mining has shrunk in half, from about 200 to 100 days. Andrew C. Revkin, *Alaska Thaws, Complicating the Hunt for Oil*, N.Y. TIMES, Jan. 13, 2004.

2.   Note carefully the mechanism by which the Secretary imposed the "winter-only" restriction on the lessee. If the restriction had been *in the lease itself*, would that change the result? Would it then have been a "suspension of operations" in the "interest of conservation" that would have extended the lease term? If, in other words, the lessee had entered the lease with full knowledge of the restriction, is it unfair to the lessee to enforce it?

3.   Does the Secretary have authority to put such a restriction in the lease itself? Section 30 of the Mineral Leasing Act provides, in part, that "[e]ach lease shall contain * * * such other provisions as [the Secretary] may deem necessary * * * for the protection of the interests of the United

States * * * and for the safeguarding of the public welfare." 30 U.S.C. § 187. Is that sufficient authority to support such a restriction in the lease?

4.   The statute provided that the lease was to be for a primary term of ten years, and extended so long thereafter as oil or gas is produced in paying quantities. 30 U.S.C. § 226(e). If the seasonal restriction means that the lease can be explored only six months a year, does that effectively mean that the primary term is only five years, and thus inconsistent with the statute?

5.   Judge Pratt, concurring, seems to conclude that the "winter-only" restriction was not "in the interest of conservation" according to what Congress intended by "conservation" in 1933. If so, then why would he remand the issue to the Secretary? Does the Secretary have any authority to extend the lease term under his view of the statute?

6.   In Getty Oil v. Clark, 614 F.Supp. 904 (D.Wyo.1985), *aff'd sub nom.* Texaco Producing, Inc. v. Hodel, 840 F.2d 776 (10th Cir.1988), the court upheld a decision by Interior's Board of Land Appeals vacating the BLM's approval of an application for a permit to drill (APD) on a lease issued prior to 1970. Distinguishing *Copper Valley*, the court held that the Secretary could reserve, in a suspension order issued at *lessee*'s request, authority to reject future requests for APDs upon a finding of unacceptable environmental impacts, without automatically extending the lease term. The court left open the question whether the lessee had a "valid existing right" to drill on the lease.

These cases hint at a common problem touched on elsewhere in these materials, made particularly acute by the emergence of the modern environmental movement; namely, do rights of users of federal lands ever vest to the extent that newer, tougher environmental standards may not be imposed on them? This problem, inherent in making a transition from one policy or set of management standards to another, can arise in any number of different situations, from timber sale contracts to grazing permits, from mineral leases to rights-of-way. It can occur either when Congress legislates a new set of statutory standards, or when the executive branch itself determines that new policies are appropriate and that it has authority in existing law to implement them.

The legal issues can be analyzed from a number of different perspectives. For example, the government's role as resource owner can be considered a proprietary one, in which leases/permits/contracts determine what rights are conveyed, and a similar analysis can be employed to determine when rights "vest" so as to be immune from subsequent regulatory change other than through a "sovereign act." *Cf. Mobil Oil, supra* p. 347. Or a "takings" analysis might be employed to determine the extent of governmental regulatory power over private property interests in federal resources. Furthermore, questions about the degree of deference to be given to an agency in interpreting a statute it is charged with administering may also come into play. Finally, notions of estoppel and fair play, whether articulated or not, can be brought to bear. Consider, for example, the Interior Department's successful effort to inject "marketability" notions into the "prudent person" Mining Law discovery test for minerals other than oil shale (United States v. Coleman, *supra* p. 575), with its failed attempt to overrule its previously generous concept of "discovery" under the Mining Law in the context of oil shale (Andrus v. Shell Oil Corp., *supra* p. 584).

NOTE: THE SURFACE MINING CONTROL AND RECLAMATION ACT

The Surface Mining Control and Reclamation Act of 1977 (SMCRA, pronounced "smack-ra"), 30 U.S.C. §§ 1201–1328, was signed by President Carter after President Ford had earlier vetoed similar legislation. SMCRA applies almost exclusively to coal, and applies to all surface coal mining operations in the country (not just those on federal lands) that remove more than 250 tons per year. Among other things, the lengthy Act sets very specific environmental protection performance standards for such mining operations and establishes requirements for reclamation. It has been called "by far the most detailed and complex U.S. legislation established to regulate a single industry." Carl Zipper and Richard Roth, *Book Review*, 31 NAT. RES. J. 707 (1991). For example, all strip-mined land must be restored to its "approximate original contour" with some exceptions, and reclamation plans must be approved prior to the starting up of new mines. SMCRA established a new federal agency, the Office of Surface Mining (OSM), in the Department of the Interior to oversee implementation of the Act. The extensive regulations, first adopted in 1979 (and modified several times since), are located at 30 C.F.R. Parts 700–707, 730–845.

SMCRA requires the Secretary of the Interior to promulgate and implement a regulatory program for coal mining on federal lands that incorporates the general standards of the Act and considers any unique characteristics of particular federal lands. 30 U.S.C. § 1273(a). Cases involving SMCRA disputes on federal (as opposed to private) land are relatively few. Geographical and political differences account for much of this disparity. Most western public land states had relatively complete state reclamation standards prior to SMCRA, and those states generally supported passage of the Act. Additionally, most coal production in the western United States comes from large mines primarily located in the plains region, where huge coal seams are relatively close to the surface. In contrast, smaller, more numerous mines are much more common in the East, and eastern operators are subjected to more OSM inspections and enforcement actions than western operators.

SMCRA withstood constitutional challenges in two companion cases involving private lands. Hodel v. Virginia Surface Mining & Reclamation Association, Inc., 452 U.S. 264 (1981); Hodel v. Indiana, 452 U.S. 314 (1981). The Court upheld congressional Commerce Clause authority to regulate surface mining, finding that the Act did not usurp state sovereignty in violation of the Tenth Amendment, and also held that the Act on its face did not effect a taking of property.

Regulation of mining operations under SMCRA can occur in a variety of ways. Surface coal mining on private lands within a state is controlled either by a state program approved by the Secretary of the Interior or by the federal program in instances where a state fails to submit an adequate surface coal mining program. 30 U.S.C. §§ 1253, 1254. States with approved programs may enter into cooperative agreements with the Secretary of the Interior providing for state regulation of surface coal mining operations on public lands within the state. *Id.* § 1273(c). The Secretary has approved the state programs of all major western coal producing states.

Subject to "valid existing rights," SMCRA ended coal surface mining within the boundaries of several different federal lands systems, including national parks, wildlife refuges, wilderness areas, and wild and scenic rivers. 30 U.S.C. § 1272. The same section also establishes a procedure to designate lands (federal or non-federal) unsuitable for all or certain kinds of surface mining operations. It instructs the Secretary to "conduct a review of Federal lands" to determine unsuitability of surface coal mining on lands otherwise available for such mining, and allows citizens to petition the Secretary for such a determination. An area "may" be designated unsuitable if mining operations would be incompatible with state or local land use plans, could result in significant damage to the environment or other values, or could endanger life or property. In one of the few instances where SMCRA applies to other minerals, 30 U.S.C. § 1281 allows the Secretary, after review, to declare federal lands unsuitable for mining minerals *other* than coal.

5.   NEPA AND PLANNING FOR ONSHORE OIL AND GAS LEASING

The major impetus for reforming the onshore oil and gas leasing system in the 1980s came from the perception that the federal government was giving away valuable leases without competition, and from the problems of fraud and abuse growing out of the unwieldy lottery. As the bills traveled through the congressional thicket, however, environmentally-minded representatives weighed in with proposals to require decisions on oil and gas leasing to consider more closely impacts on the environment and competing uses of federal land. The House-passed bill included several such provisions, but the Senate bill did not. The Administration and the oil industry opposed them, and most were dropped in the conference committee convened to reconcile the two versions, with the proviso that the National Academy of Sciences study the integration of oil and gas leasing and federal land planning and environmental protection and report back to Congress.

The Reform Act did give the Forest Service a statutory veto over BLM's issuance of oil and gas leases on national forest land, and required both agencies to "regulate all surface-disturbing activities" conducted under oil and gas leases and to "determine reclamation and other actions as required in the interests of conservation of surface resources." No permit to drill may be granted "without the analysis and approval by the [appropriate agency] of a plan of operations covering proposed surface-disturbing activities within the leased area." Bonding is required to "ensure the complete and timely reclamation of the lease tract, and the restoration of any lands or surface waters adversely affected by lease operations." 30 U.S.C. § 226(g).

The most controversial litigation over the federal onshore oil and gas leasing program has concerned how to integrate the requirements of NEPA and the federal land planning statutes with the oil and gas leasing program. The panel of the National Academy of Sciences/National Research Council convened at the direction of Congress provided an overview of the issues as follows:

> Oil and gas activities on the federal lands proceed through four stages of federal authorizations—land use planning, leasing, exploration (* * * [including] permits to drill exploration wells), and development (permits to drill production wells, pipeline rights-of-way, and facility use permits). * * * Although the potential for oil and gas is recognized during land use planning, the volume, extent, and specific location of the resources, and the consequent surface impacts from their exploration and development, are commonly unknown.

> This informational problem poses the question of whether the surface impacts of oil and gas exploration and development can be fairly and adequately identified during planning to ensure that those activities are afforded equitable consideration with other federal land uses and values—that those activities are neither prematurely excluded from, or indiscriminately included on, federal lands by inadequately informed planning decisions. * * *

>   * * *

> Finally, even if the assumption is made that exploration and development will ensue, the type and level of impacts from production are not known when planning occurs. Producing fields vary wildly in size—from a few hundred acres and a handful of wells to more than 75,000 acres and 21 wells. Within the field, impacts will correspond to such factors as whether the terrain is flat or hilly * * *, what the wellhead density and concomitant number of connecting service roads and gathering lines will be * * *, and what additional facilities may be needed (e.g., dehydration plants, injection wells for disposal of produced water or reinjection for pressure maintenance, or preparation plants to remove hydrogen sulfide from sour gas).

National Research Council, Land Use Planning and Oil and Gas Leasing on Onshore Federal Lands 10–13 (1989). The report repeated the oft-cited rule of thumb that only one in ten leases ever proceeds to well drilling, and only one in ten of drilled leases ultimately produces commercial quantities of oil or gas.

The following two cases examine the current NEPA practices of the BLM, first at the planning stage and then at leasing. They describe some of the environmental concerns surrounding leasing in two of the most important regions of the country for onshore energy material mining: the North

Slope of Alaska and the Powder River Basin of Wyoming and Montana. Most importantly, the opinions summarize the tangled case law dealing with the timing of environmental analysis in mineral leasing. Consider how well the NEPA model of evaluation addresses the characteristics identified in the National Research Council report.

The oil resource of the National Petroleum Reserve in Alaska holds the potential to fill the Trans–Alaska pipeline as the Prudhoe Bay deposit declines in production. It is therefore exceedingly important to the companies that have invested in the infrastructure of the pipeline and to the state of Alaska, which derives almost all of its revenue from oil production.

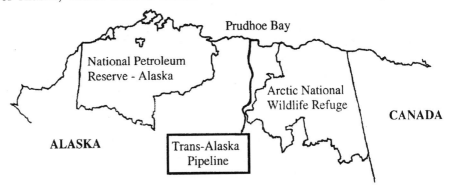

Northern Alaska Environmental Center v. Kempthorne

United States Court of Appeals, Ninth Circuit, 2006.
457 F.3d 969.

■ CHIEF JUDGE SCHROEDER

In this litigation, a group of environmental plaintiffs have challenged the adequacy of the Final Environmental Impact Statement ("FEIS") prepared by the Bureau of Land Management ("BLM") for its plan to offer long term oil and gas leases in the NWPA [Northwest Planning Area in Alaska]. The leases would enable the oil companies to undertake exploration to determine what sites, if any, can be developed for productive drilling. The National Environmental Policy Act ("NEPA") requires an assessment of the effects of major federal action on the surrounding environment.

* * *

The plaintiffs' main contention is that the analysis undertaken for the EIS was inadequate, because it lacked site specific analysis for particular locations where drilling might occur. The government responds, we conclude cogently, that no such drilling site analysis is possible until it is known where the drilling is likely to take place, and that can be known only after leasing and exploration. The government points out that the environmental consequences at specific sites can be assessed in connection with later applications for permits for drilling at those sites, and that no permits should issue without extensive site specific analysis of adverse environmental effects and of the mitigation measures appropriate to minimize them. On that basis, we affirm the district court's grant of summary judgment in favor of the government.

BACKGROUND

President Harding established the Naval Petroleum Reserve on Alaska's North Slope in 1923. It was fifty years later, in 1976, that the National Petroleum Reserve Protection Act ("NPRPA") transferred authority over the Reserve to the Secretary of Interior. The Reserve was subsequently renamed the National Petroleum Reserve–Alaska ("NPR–A"). It remains the largest single unit of public land in the United States and covers 23.6 million acres. It is also an important habitat for vegetation, fish, and wildlife.

The NPR–A prohibited petroleum exploration until 1980 when Congress, driven by the fuel crisis of the previous decade, directed the Secretary to carry out an "expeditious program of competitive leasing of oil and gas" on the Reserve. The Congressional Act also recognized the subsistence interests of Native American tribes in the area and the need to protect the environment. In 1998, the BLM opened up 4.6 million acres, or 87 percent of the Northeast Planning Area of the Reserve to oil and gas leasing, while carving out various special areas as off limits to leasing. The Northeast Planning Area is also the subject of litigation in the district court.

The portion of the NPR–A at issue here is the Northwest Planning Area, consisting of 8.8 million acres to the west of the Northeast Planning Area. * * *

DEVELOPMENT OF THE FEIS

The BLM published a draft EIS for the NWPA in January 2003 and received considerable critical comment. The BLM published the Final EIS in December 2003 to open parts of the NWPA to leasing. The FEIS adopted the Preferred Alternative of the draft EIS, opening the BLM administered lands in the NWPA to leasing subject to certain significant limitations. The BLM would defer for 10 years any leasing on the western most portion of the NWPA, consisting of approximately 17 percent of the proposed area; the FEIS identified the Kasegaluk Lagoon as a special area because of important migratory bird and marine mammal habitat. It imposed no surface occupancy restrictions along the coastal areas and deep water lakes, comprising about 16 percent of the area, and imposed stipulations on development that included set back restrictions and seasonal prohibitions on exploration and development in several of the areas richest in wildlife resources.

Under the plan, the leases are to be offered as individual parcels that vary in size and are identified by number. At the time this record was developed, only a relatively small proportion of the parcels had received bids and only a few leases had been issued. Of the 488 parcels available for leasing, approximately 120 received bids. No exploration had begun.

In assessing the environmental impact of the leasing program for purposes of preparing the FEIS, the BLM had no way of knowing what, if any, areas subsequent exploration would find most suitable for drilling. Thus, it did not do an analysis of any specific parcels.

The BLM did do an analysis of the possible effects of drilling in the climatic environment of the region. That analysis projected two hypotheticals, representing each end of the available spectrum of possibilities. On the basis of experiences in drilling elsewhere in Alaska, the BLM projected types of drilling and patterns of development that might ensue, if, under the first scenario, half of the available parcels were leased for exploration, but no actual development occurred, and, in the second scenario, if the total resources available in the area were to be discovered and developed.

The FEIS conducted an analysis under each scenario for each of the natural resources affected in the area, as, for example, water, wildlife, and specific bird species. Because the analysis was based upon hypothetical future projections of what might be undertaken in the exploration and development phases, and was conducted on a resource by resource basis, the EIS did not attempt to examine the impact on specific parcels. That is what gives rise to this litigation.

* * *

With respect to the need for site specific analysis in the EIS, our law under NEPA makes it clear that there must be such analysis whenever there is an "irretrievable commitment of resources" by a federal agency to a project. See Conner v. Burford, 848 F.2d 1441 (9th Cir.1988). There is no question here that approval of the leasing program represents an irretrievable commitment of resources. The issue is whether it was sufficiently site specific.

Plaintiffs' major contention is that "site specific" in this context requires an analysis of the environmental effect with respect to each parcel involved in a possible lease for exploration and development. The problem is that until the lessees do exploratory work, the government cannot know what sites will be deemed most suitable for exploratory drilling, much less for development. We are left with a "chicken or egg" conundrum in that if plaintiffs' interpretation of its requirements were adopted, NEPA could never be satisfied in the circumstances of this case.

Our task, however, is to give effect to Congressional intent as expressed not only in NEPA, but also in the 1976 and 1980 enactments relating to the Alaska Reserve. The government's resolution of the problem of how to give appropriate effect to all the relevant statutes in this case was to consider hypothetical situations that represented the spectrum of foreseeable results, once all phases of the program were completed. We cannot say that this resolution, as set forth in the FEIS, is arbitrary or capricious under our circuit's law.

Conner v. Burford is one of our seminal cases considering the procedures for evaluating the environmental effects of leasing programs to develop oil and gas resources. In that case the government instituted programs to sell oil and gas leases without preparing any EIS at all. Two types of leases were involved. One, the so called "no surface occupancy" or "NSO" leases, forbid any use, or even occupancy of the surface of the national forest land being leased, without BLM approval of the specific, surface-disturbing activity the lessees planned to undertake. We held that such leases themselves involved no "irretrievable commitment of resources" and no EIS was required at the leasing stage.

The second and more numerous type of leases in *Conner* were "non NSO" leases. They authorized the lessees to undertake development subject to government regulation of surface disturbing activities such as roads and drilling. The government could not totally preclude such activities, however, and for that reason we held an EIS was required for non NSO leases.

Plaintiffs place principal reliance on *Conner*, but we do not believe it advances their position in this case. Here the leases are more like the "non NSO leases" in *Conner*. The government can condition permits for drilling on implementation of environmentally protective measures, and we assume it can deny a specific application altogether if a particularly sensitive area is sought to be developed and mitigation measures are not available. The government cannot, however, consistent with current statutory imperatives, forbid all oil and gas development in Alaska's NWPA. The leasing program thus does constitute an irretrievable commitment of resources. An EIS is undeniably required, and, indeed one has been prepared.

The issue here is plaintiffs' contention that the EIS is insufficient because it does not undertake a parcel by parcel analysis of surfaces that will eventually be explored and developed. As to this contention, *Conner* is of no assistance to plaintiffs, for we did not discuss the degree of site specificity required in the EIS. The only question was whether one had to be completed at all.

We recognize that in arguing that this EIS analysis should have been parcel specific, the plaintiffs raise legitimate concerns about the uncertainty at this stage of gauging the adverse effects that future development may have on this environment. Similar concerns, however, are inherent in any program for the development of natural resources. This is because such projects generally entail separate stages of leasing, exploration and development. At the earliest stage, the leasing stage we have before us, there is no way of knowing what plans for development, if any, may eventually materialize.

Such concerns underlay our decision in *Conner* and inform our decision today. They become critically important when dealing in the environmental context of Northern Alaska. Indeed, the D.C. Circuit addressed them in North Slope Borough v. Andrus, 642 F.2d 589, 600 (1980), when it upheld an EIS prepared for off shore exploration of resources under the Beaufort Sea, off the Northeast Planning Area. The D.C. Circuit explained that uncertainty is an inherent problem with multi-stage projects such as oil and gas programs, which include separate leasing, exploration, and development stages. The court went on to say that "[t]he Secretary [of Interior] plainly cannot be expected or required to wait until the totality of environmental effects is known." The D.C. Circuit concluded that when an agency complies in good faith with the requirements of NEPA and issues an EIS indicating that the agency has taken a hard look at the pertinent environmental questions, its decision should be afforded great deference. The same holds true for the instant case. There is no basis for holding that the analysis in the EIS was arbitrary, capricious, or done in bad faith.

NEPA applies at all stages of the process, however. Any later plan for actual exploration by lessees will be subject to a period of review before being accepted, rejected or modified by the Secretary. See 43 C.F.R. § 3162.3–1(c). Plaintiffs will have an opportunity to comment on any later EIS. In addition, before any activity for exploration or development occurs, permits from several agencies may be required and additional permit conditions imposed for the protection of land, water and wildlife resources. Id.

For these reasons we conclude that the government was not required at this stage to do a parcel by parcel examination of potential environmental effects. Such effects are currently unidentifiable, because the parcels likely to be affected are not yet known. Such analysis must be made at later permitting stages when the sites, and hence more site specific effects, are identifiable.

We do not agree, however, with the government's further suggestion that any challenge to the sufficiency of the EIS at this stage is premature. The government overreaches when it suggests that the Tenth Circuit's decision in Park County Resource Council v. United States Department of Agriculture, 817 F.2d 609 (1987) precludes any challenge to an FEIS at the leasing stage. The Tenth Circuit held that plaintiffs in that case could, at the permit stage, challenge the earlier approval of the leasing program that was instituted without preparation of any EIS. The court held the plaintiffs were not required to make the objection at the earlier stage. The Tenth Circuit therefore recognized that the failure to prepare an EIS could be raised at either stage.

Park County is consistent with our decision in *Conner*. It is also consistent with our decision today that plaintiffs are entitled to raise a challenge to the sufficiency of the EIS at this stage, but that their particular challenge to site specificity lacks merit, and that they will be able to raise more focused criticisms of site analysis at the exploration and permit stages of the leasing program.

Pennaco Energy, Inc. v. U.S. Department of the Interior

United States Court of Appeals, Tenth Circuit, 2004.
377 F.3d 1147.

■ JUDGE BRISCOE

Plaintiff Pennaco Energy, Inc. (Pennaco), brought this suit * * * against the United States Department of the Interior (DOI) to challenge a decision of the Interior Board of Land Appeals (IBLA). The challenged IBLA decision reversed a decision of the Bureau of Land Management (BLM) to auction three oil and gas leases (successfully bid upon by Pennaco). The IBLA concluded the requirements of the National Environmental Policy Act (NEPA) had not been satisfied prior to issuing the leases and remanded the matter to the BLM for additional appropriate action. * * *

* * *

Oil and gas leasing decisions

The DOI manages the use of federal oil and gas resources through a three-phase decision-making process. At the earliest and broadest level of decision-making, the DOI develops land use plans-often referred to as resource management plans (RMPs). * * * Under the Federal Land Policy and Management Act (FLPMA), "[t]he Secretary [of Interior] shall manage the public lands under principles of multiple use and sustained yield, in accordance with the land use plans . . . when they are available." 43 U.S.C. § 1732(a).

Once an RMP has been issued, "subsequent more detailed or specific planning, shall conform to the [RMP]." 43 C.F.R. § 1610.5–3(a). In the context of oil and gas development, the BLM is initially charged with determining whether the issuance of a particular oil and gas lease is consistent with the RMP. The lessee must obtain BLM approval of an Application for Permit to Drill (APD) before commencing any "drilling operations" or "surface disturbance preliminary thereto." 43 C.F.R. § 3162.3–1(c).

BLM's decision to auction leases

At issue in this case is whether the BLM satisfied the NEPA prior to auctioning three oil and gas leases on February 1, 2000, for the development of tracts of land in the Powder River Basin in Wyoming. In August 1999, interested parties nominated 49 parcels of land for inclusion in the next available oil and gas lease sale. It is undisputed that the planned use of the leases was the extraction of coal bed methane (CBM). It is also undisputed that a CBM exploration and development boom is occurring in the Powder River Basin. The hotly contested issue underlying this case is whether the environmental impacts of CBM development are significantly different than the environmental impacts of non-CBM oil and gas development.

On September 28, 1999, Richard Zander, the acting field manager of the BLM Buffalo Field Office, prepared separate but identical Interim Documentation of Land Use Conformance and NEPA Adequacy worksheets (DNAs) for each of the 49 nominated parcels. DNAs are forms designed to allow BLM employees to determine whether they properly can rely on existing NEPA documents. In this case, Zander concluded that two existing NEPA analyses (the Buffalo Resource Management Plan EIS (Buffalo RMP EIS) and the Wyodak Coal Bed Methane Project Draft EIS (Wyodak DEIS)) satisfied the NEPA requirements with regard to issuance of the leases.

The first document relied upon by Zander, the Buffalo RMP EIS, was published in October 1985 in conjunction with the development of the Buffalo RMP. In the Buffalo RMP EIS, the BLM discussed the potential environmental impacts of oil and gas development within the Buffalo

Resource Area, an area encompassing the three parcels at issue in this case. However, the Buffalo RMP EIS did not specifically address CBM extraction.

The second document relied upon by Zander, the Wyodak DEIS, was published in May 1999. Unlike the Buffalo RMP EIS, the Wyodak DEIS addressed the potential environmental impacts of CBM mining. However, as the Wyodak DEIS was a *post*-leasing project level study, the BLM did not consider whether leases should have been issued in the first place. Further, the geographic scope of the Wyodak DEIS did not encompass two of the three parcels at issue in this case.

Having concluded the NEPA requirements were satisfied in regard to the proposed leases, Zander further concluded that issuance of the leases conformed to the Buffalo RMP. Thus, the BLM auctioned the leases at a competitive sale on February 1, 2000, and Pennaco was the successful bidder.

* * *

This case requires us to apply the arbitrary and capricious standard of review to an IBLA decision very limited in its sweep. The IBLA did not determine what the NEPA required, but only that existing NEPA analyses were not sufficient to allow the BLM to take a "hard look" at the environmental impacts of the proposed CBM development. Therefore, the narrow question before us is whether the IBLA acted arbitrarily and capriciously in deciding that the leases at issue should not have been issued before additional NEPA documentation was prepared.

* * *

Water Quantity

The administrative record * * * contains evidence to support the IBLA's conclusion that water production associated with CBM extraction is significantly greater than water production associated with non-CBM oil and gas development. The Buffalo RMP Draft EIS, in addressing non-CBM development, stated that the "[m]ining would have little effect on regional groundwater systems." Further, the Buffalo RMP Draft EIS predicted the effects of non-CBM development on water resources would be the same if no development was undertaken. In comparison, there is ample evidence in the record that the process of CBM extraction involves bringing significant amounts of groundwater to the surface. A March 1990 EA for Eastern Campbell and Western Johnson Counties, Wyoming, estimated that water production rates associated with CBM projects could be up to 2,000 barrels per day per well (1 barrel equals 42 gallons). The Wyodak DEIS projected CBM related water flow based on an estimated average discharge of 12 gallons per minute of water per well, or 17,280 gallons per day, per well. In the Wyodak DEIS, the BLM discussed the potential for flooding and erosion related to waterflow from CBM development.

* * *

[In a 2001 statement to Congress, BLM assistant secretary Tom Fulton] stated:

The CBM extraction process involves pumping water from the coal seams to the surface in order to reduce the water pressure that traps the gas in the coal. This releases the methane. Managing the water produced with methane is a challenge to the oil and gas industry, as well as Federal and State regulators. We must work together to find innovative solutions to address the surface water issues and the potential impacts to the entire land and water system.

Further, the IBLA cited several newspaper articles that addressed the potential impacts of CBM development. Some of the articles addressed concerns associated with the drawing of large quantities of sub-surface water to the surface during the CBM extraction process. * * *

* * *

After reviewing the entire record, we conclude it contains substantial evidence to support the IBLA's conclusion that CBM development poses unique environmental concerns related to water discharge that were not addressed by the Buffalo RMP EIS. * * *

Air Quality

We further conclude the record contains substantial evidence to support the IBLA's conclusion that CBM development poses unique environmental concerns related to air quality that were not addressed in the Buffalo RMP EIS. The Buffalo RMP DEIS predicted the effects of non-CBM oil and gas development on air quality would be the same as if no development was undertaken. In comparison, the Wyodak DEIS predicted the operation of natural-gas fired compressors, required to move CBM gas from the wellhead to pipelines, would release a number of emissions. Although the Wyodak DEIS predicted that most of the emissions would not significantly impact air quality, it acknowledged the incomplete combustion of natural gas would result in the emission of formaldehyde, a known carcinogen. The Wyodak DEIS characterized the emission of formaldehyde as a "risk" and recommended steps to minimize the risk.

* * *

In this case, the IBLA concluded the Wyodak EIS had one significant shortcoming. The Wyodak EIS was a post-leasing analysis and, therefore, the BLM did not consider pre-leasing options, such as not issuing leases at all. In the Wyodak EIS, the BLM acknowledged its limited discretion in regard to the Wyodak project. The Wyodak EIS provides:

None of the stipulations imposed (on the leases within the project area) would empower the Secretary of the Interior to deny all drilling activity because of environmental concerns where leases have been issued with surface occupancy rights.

Provisions that expressly provide Secretarial authority to deny or restrict lease development in whole or in part would depend on an opinion provided by the U.S. Fish and Wildlife Service (USFWS) regarding impacts to endangered or threatened species or habitats of species that are listed or proposed for listing.

This language reflects that lessees already had acquired certain rights, subject only to stipulations contained in their leases. Similarly, 43 C.F.R. § 3101.1–2 provides:

A lessee shall have the right to use so much of the leased lands as is necessary to explore for, drill for, mine, extract, remove and dispose of all the leased resource in a leasehold subject to: Stipulations attached to the lease; restrictions deriving from specific, nondiscretionary statutes; and such reasonable measures as may be required by the authorized officer to minimize adverse impacts to other resource values, land uses or users not addressed in the lease stipulations at the time operations are proposed. To the extent consistent with lease rights granted, such reasonable measures may include, but are not limited to, modification to siting or design of facilities, timing of operations, and specification of interim and final reclamation measures.

The BLM Handbook for Planning for Fluid Mineral Resources puts it this way:

The BLM has a statutory responsibility under NEPA to analyze and document the direct, indirect and cumulative impacts of past, present and reasonably foreseeable future actions resulting from Federally authorized fluid minerals activities. By law, these impacts must be analyzed before the agency makes an irreversible commitment. In the fluid minerals program, this commitment occurs at the point of lease issuance. Therefore, the EIS prepared with the RMP is intended to satisfy NEPA requirements for issuing fluid mineral leases.

Therefore, in light of the Wyodak EIS' failure to consider the pre-leasing options, we conclude the IBLA did not act arbitrarily and capriciously in deciding that the Wyodak EIS did not adequately supplement the Buffalo RMP EIS

Park County

Finally, we note that Pennaco relies heavily on *Park County,* 817 F.2d 609. In *Park County,* the plaintiffs (environmental interest groups) claimed the BLM "unlawfully issued an oil and gas lease, and thereafter unlawfully approved an [APD] filed by the Marathon Oil Company, in contravention of ... NEPA." In recounting the facts, we noted that prior to issuing the lease in question the BLM had prepared an "extensive" EA which addressed the "issuance of federal oil and gas leases" in the Shoshone National Forest where the tract at issue was located. The EA exceeded 100 pages and addressed various leasing alternatives, including "issuance of no leases." The EA concluded that merely issuing the leases would create no environmental impacts, and a FONSI was issued with respect to the lease issuance. Approximately three years after issuance of the FONSI and the sale of the lease, Marathon submitted an APD. In response, the BLM and the Forest Service prepared a comprehensive EIS with respect to the drilling application.

The *Park County* plaintiffs challenged both the adequacy of the pre-drilling EIS and issuance of the oil and gas lease prior to preparation of an EIS. We concluded plaintiffs' challenge to the adequacy of the pre-drilling EIS had been rendered moot by the lessee's development and subsequent abandonment of the site in question. On the other hand, we concluded the challenge to issuance of the lease was not moot because the lease remained operative. We employed a *reasonableness* standard to review the BLM's issuance of a FONSI and concluded:

> [I]n light of the substantial EA, of the mitigating lease restrictions requiring further environmental appraisal before any surface disturbing activities commence, of the nebulousness of future drilling activity at the time of leasing, and of the continuing supervision of the federal agencies involved over future activities, the agency's decision in this case that the lease issuance itself was not a major federal action significantly affecting the quality of the human environment was not unreasonable.

Id. at 624 (emphasis added).

* * *

This case differs significantly from *Park County.* First, in *Park County,* plaintiffs challenged an agency decision to issue an oil and gas lease prior to preparation of a comprehensive EIS. We concluded that the BLM's decision to not prepare an EIS at the leasing stage was "not unreasonable." In comparison, the question before us is *not,* as Pennaco suggests, whether the documents relied upon by the BLM pass muster. The central issue is whether the IBLA's determination that the documents did not "pass muster" was arbitrary and capricious. In *Park County,* this court did not conclude the agency would have abused its discretion if it decided that an EIS was necessary at the pre-leasing stage.

Moreover, in *Park County,* we relied in part on the fact that the BLM issued a FONSI after having prepared an "extensive" EA that addressed the potential environmental impacts of issuing the leases and considered the option of not issuing leases. In comparison, in this case, the BLM did not prepare such an EA, did not issue a FONSI, and did not prepare any environmental analysis that considered not issuing the leases in question. Instead, the BLM determined, after filling out DNA worksheets, that previously issued NEPA documents were sufficient to satisfy the "hard look" standard. DNAs, unlike EAs and FONSIs, are not mentioned in the NEPA or in the regulations implementing the NEPA. *See* 40 C.F.R. § 1508.10 (defining the term "environmental document" as including environmental assessments, environmental impact statements, findings of no significant impact, and notices of intent). As stated, agencies may use non-NEPA procedures to determine whether new NEPA documentation is required. For reasons discussed above, however, we conclude the IBLA's determination that more analysis was required in this case was not arbitrary and capricious.

We REVERSE and REMAND to the district court with instructions to reinstate the IBLA's decision.

NOTES AND QUESTIONS

1. What is the right approach here, as a matter of policy? What are the relevant considerations in formulating a policy? How important to

national policy is providing a lessee some certainty about what development activities the lease authorizes? Is the government engaged in a shell game to avoid performing a site-specific environmental analysis until it is too late to bar development? What is the solution to this double bind?

2. Can you reconcile the holdings in the two court decisions? Is this an example of different circuits making different law? Were leasing decisions in the two cases at the same stage in the multi-step process? Do they help resolve the issue of what kind of environmental analysis is appropriate at the steps of: planning/authorizing leasing, actual leasing, exploration, and development?

3. Did the 1980 legislation on NPR–A leasing amend NEPA? The *Northern Alaska* court discusses *North Slope Borough*, which allowed the Interior Department to defer detailed NEPA analysis until post-leasing decision-making. But, the underlying law of off-shore leasing explicitly reserves the right of the United States to deny the lessee permission to drill in order to accommodate environmental values. 43 U.S.C. § 1334(a). *See Mobil Oil*, *supra* p. 347. Does the absence of a similar provision in the onshore mineral leasing legislation suggest that the court should demand more environmental analysis at the leasing stage (except on "no surface occupancy" stipulation leases)?

The *Northern Alaska* court notes that later plans for actual exploration and development in the NPR–A will require site-specific environmental analysis. But, can regulation of these post-leasing activities be so stringent as to impose impracticable costs? In *Pennaco Energy*, the Wyodak RMP EIS explicitly identified the limitations of post-leasing environmental regulation. These limitations on oil and gas activities are reminiscent of Forest Service control of hardrock mining through plans of operation, *supra* p. 601.

4. The BLM has now leased some 5 million acres of the NPR–A north*west* area. However, Judge Singleton sent the agency back to the drawing board in its plan to lease the 4.6 million-acre north*east* quadrant of the NPR–A. National Audubon Society v. Kempthorne, No. 1:05–cv–00008–JKS (D.Alaska Sept. 25, 2006). He found that the EIS for the north*east* quadrant did not adequately consider the cumulative effects of drilling (especially on biologically sensitive Teshekpuk Lake) in combination with the approved leasing of the north*west* zone. Rather than appeal the decision, the BLM has decided to supplement the EIS in order to evaluate the cumulative effects of more drilling in the NPR–A.

5. In 2005 the BLM completed an EA/FONSI in response to *Pennaco Energy* and is pressing forward with the leases. *Pennaco Energy* has become a NEPA blueprint for CBM development across the West. The BLM is in the process of updating old RMPs to consider the special problems caused by the unanticipated boom in CBM mining. The agency also plans more EAs and more leases. The *Pennaco Energy* court interprets *Park County* as standing for the proposition that leasing may require an EIS, but that a mitigated FONSI specifying preconditions for granting an APD may also suffice under certain circumstances. How is that different from the *Northern Alaska* court's use of *Park County*? You might want to review the

brief discussion of *Conner* and *Park County* in context of NEPA's limitation on irreversible and irretrievable commitments of resources prior to environmental evaluation. Chapter 4, *supra* p. 257.

6.   The boom in CBM development, especially in the Powder River Basin, continues to raise unresolved environmental issues, and frequently pits ranchers against drillers. This chapter considers conflicts between lessees and surface owners in greater detail in Section D, *infra*, on split-estate lands. Many ranch operations have been disrupted by briny water generated by CBM development. *See* Keith G. Bauerle, *Reaping the Whirlwind: Federal Oil and Gas Development on Private Lands in the Rocky Mountain West*, 83 DENV. U. L.REV. 1083 (2006).

7.   The Energy Policy Act of 2005, Pub.L.No. 109–58, contained provisions designed to have federal agencies "ensure expeditious compliance" with NEPA and "any other applicable environmental and cultural resources laws" to "ensure timely actions on oil and gas leases and applications for permits to drill" on federal lands. In response to industry complaints that BLM had not been processing applications for permits to drill quickly enough (because of NEPA compliance, among other things), the Act called on the Interior Secretary to "develop and implement best management practices" to improve oil and gas lease administration and adopt regulations setting "specific timeframes for processing leases and applications." The Act also established rebuttable presumptions for categorically excluding drill permits that limit surface disturbance to less than five acres under certain circumstances.

8.   The Forest Service deals with the same difficult timing issues in performing NEPA analysis for oil and gas leasing. Wyoming Outdoor Council v. U.S. Forest Service, 165 F.3d 43 (D.C.Cir.1999), upheld the Forest Service's interpretation of its own regulations that identify the findings it must make before authorizing the BLM to lease specific parcels. The court allowed the Forest Service to authorize leasing without verifying that the NEPA analysis in the underlying unit plan adequately considered the impacts. The Forest Service did promise it would undertake this prior to actual lease issuance. The court concluded that while the environmentalists' more stringent interpretation might be the "most natural" way to read the regulations, the regulations were ambiguous and the Forest Service reading was not plainly erroneous.

NOTE: OIL AND GAS LEASING ON THE OFFSHORE LANDS

Decisions such as Pollard v. Hagan, 44 U.S. (3 How.) 212 (1845), *supra* p. 70, had left open the question whether states owned the submerged lands offshore, beyond the tide lines. Few cared before the advent of offshore drilling technology, but as it emerged, the matter became worth litigating. In 1947, the Supreme Court ruled that the offshore lands were and always had been owned by the United States as a feature of national sovereignty. United States v. California, 332 U.S. 19 (1947).

The coastal states made ownership of these submerged lands a significant political issue in the 1952 presidential election, and Congress responded in 1953 by ceding to the coastal states ownership of the seabed resources in the three-mile belt seaward of the coast. Submerged Lands Act of 1953, 43 U.S.C. §§ 1301–1315. A few months later, Congress asserted federal "jurisdiction, control, and power of disposition" over the "subsoil and seabed of the outer Continental Shelf" beyond the three-mile limit. Outer Continental Shelf Lands Act of 1953 (OCSLA), as amended, 43 U.S.C. §§ 1331–1343, at § 1332(a).

The United States asserted a different kind of jurisdiction in the Fishery Conservation and Management Act of 1976 (FCMA), 16 U.S.C. §§ 1801–1882. While not claiming ownership per se, Congress decreed that all living resources between three and 200 miles offshore, with a few exceptions, could be harvested or exploited only in accordance with a new federal-regional regulatory scheme. Congress has also cooperated with and financed states in imposing controls over developments in and around the tidal margins by means of the Coastal Zone Management Act (CZMA), 16 U.S.C. §§ 1451–1464. The Marine Sanctuaries Act (MSA), 16 U.S.C. §§ 1431–1434, and other more specialized laws, such as the Marine Mammal Protection Act of 1972 (MMPA), 16 U.S.C. § 1361 et seq., also aim to protect the coastal and marine environments.

There is no single management system for the federal offshore lands. Navigation is subject to Coast Guard regulations, and obstructions to navigable capacity must be cleared by the Army Corps of Engineers. Offshore oil and gas and other subsea mineral deposits can be leased by Interior's BLM, and supervised by Interior's Minerals Management Service (MMS), an agency created in the 1980s in part to exercise regulatory supervision (formerly exercised by the United States Geological Survey) over offshore mineral leases. Fisheries resources are largely within the ambit of the National Oceanic and Atmospheric Administration, located in the Department of Commerce, but inshore fisheries of the same fish plus other species are subject to regulation by the Fish and Wildlife Service, located in the Department of the Interior. Offshore regulation may also be affected by international treaty obligations.

The various forms of jurisdiction and sovereignty that the United States has asserted over offshore areas do not amount to a claim of fee ownership of the underlying lands, nor to an assumption of complete, exclusive jurisdiction over the waters. For example, Treasure Salvors, Inc. v. Unidentified Wrecked and Abandoned Sailing Vessel, 569 F.2d 330 (5th Cir.1978), involved a contest between the government and treasure seekers who had located an ancient Spanish galleon off Florida. The United States claimed that both OCSLA and the 1906 Antiquities Act, 16 U.S.C. §§ 431–433, vested ownership of the sunken ship in it. The court held that the former asserted jurisdiction for purposes of controlling exploitation of the natural resources of the OCS, which did not include wrecked ships; and the latter was inapplicable because, the court said rather dubiously, the seabed was not "controlled" by the United States.

Deep-water off-shore drilling is a comparatively new phenomenon. Platforms had been constructed in shallow water off Santa Barbara as early as 1897, but it was not until the middle of the twentieth century that any

platform was constructed out of sight of land. Since then, rapid technological advances have enabled drillers to prospect and produce in ever-deeper
waters and more forbidding conditions like the North Sea. But advanced
technology can also produce new risks; more difficult operations raise the
possibility of major blowouts and oil spills threatening ecologically fragile
coastal areas and other offshore resources. Nevertheless, the offshore
industry in the U.S. has had a remarkable environmental record, with very
few problems since a 1969 blowout in Santa Barbara. That widely-publi-
cized incident led to a skein of litigation. *See, e.g.,* Sun Oil Co. v. United
States, 572 F.2d 786 (Ct.Cl.1978) (the Secretary could suspend operations
in the interest of conservation, broadly defined, but only for a limited time;
otherwise, the lessee's interest would be "taken").

More enduringly, the Santa Barbara incident helped give birth to
NEPA, which has since become the main ground of litigation for plaintiffs
opposed to further lease sales. Resource conflicts on the OCS raise issues
conceptually similar to those common on the onshore lands. For instance,
the St. Georges Bank lease sale off Massachusetts posed the specter of oil
spills harming the fishery in the area, once said to be one of the world's
most productive. Massachusetts v. Watt, 716 F.2d 946 (1st Cir.1983).
Leasing in the area was stopped by environmental concerns; ironically, the
fishing industry then so over-exploited the fishery that it collapsed. Other
conflicts involve lease sales harming endangered species, such as whales
and other wildlife, North Slope Borough v. Andrus, 642 F.2d 589 (D.C.Cir.
1980), or subsistence hunting and fishing rights, Amoco Prod. Co. v. Village
of Gambell, 480 U.S. 531 (1987).

Congress enacted significant amendments to OCSLA in 1978, primarily
to strengthen environmental regulation. 43 U.S.C. § 1334(a) authorizes the
Secretary to cancel any lease where: "(i) continued activity * * * would
probably cause serious harm to * * * [the] environment; (ii) the threat of
harm or damage will not disappear or decrease to an acceptable extent
within a reasonable period of time; and (iii) the advantages of cancellation
outweigh the advantages of continuing such lease or permit in force."

Congress also required payment of compensation to the lessee if the
lease is canceled under certain circumstances (43 U.S.C.
§ 1334(a)(2)(C)). Specifically, the lessee is entitled to receive the lesser
of (1) the fair value of the canceled rights as of the date of cancellation,
taking account of both anticipated revenues from the lease and anticipated costs, including costs of compliance with all applicable regulations and operating orders, liability for cleanup costs or damages, or
both, in the case of an oil spill, and all other costs reasonable anticipated on the lease, or (2) the excess, if any, over the lessee's revenues,
from the lease (plus interest) of all consideration paid for the lease and
all direct expenditures made by the lessee after the date of issuance of
such lease and in connection with exploration or development, or both,
pursuant to the lease (plus interest). For leases issued prior to the 1978
amendments, the standard of compensation is (1), the fair value of the
canceled rights.

LAND USE PLANNING AND OIL AND GAS LEASING ON ONSHORE FEDERAL LANDS 129 (National Research Council 1989).

A leading decision construing the Act, as amended, is Secretary of the Interior v. California, 464 U.S. 312 (1984). It concerned a new twist on the age-old problem of state vs. federal law. The Supreme Court held that the contested lease sales did not "directly affect" California's coastal zone and thus, under the Coastal Zone Management Act, 16 U.S.C. § 1456(c), the Secretary did not have to find the lease sales (as opposed to approval of subsequent plans to explore for or develop petroleum resources) "consistent" with California's coastal zone plan. Congress reversed this result by legislation in 1990. Pub. L. No. 101–508. Environmental and "not in my back yard" concerns about coastal protection led Congress to legislate moratoria on OCS leasing in many coastal areas of the United States. Today, in fact, the central Gulf of Mexico coast (the location of nearly all the current offshore oil industry) and most of the Alaskan coast are the only large OCS areas open to new federal oil and gas leasing.

GEOTHERMAL RESOURCES

Various elements cooperate to produce geothermal power accessible for use on the surface of the earth. Magma or molten rock from the core of the earth intrudes into the earth's crust. The magma heats porous rock containing water. The water in turn is heated to temperatures as high as 500 degrees Fahrenheit. As the heated water rises to the surface through a natural vent, or well, it flashes into steam.

Geothermal steam is used to produce electricity by turning generators. In recommending passage of the Geothermal Steam Act of 1970, the Interior and Insular Affairs Committee of the House reported: "[G]eothermal power stands out as a potentially invaluable untapped natural resource. It becomes particularly attractive in this age of growing consciousness of environmental hazards and increasing awareness of the necessity to develop new resources to help meet the Nation's future energy requirements. The Nation's geothermal resources promise to be a relatively pollution-free source of energy, and their development should be encouraged."

United States v. Union Oil Co. of California, 549 F.2d 1271 (9th Cir.1977).

Areas of the western United States with high concentrations of federally owned lands often have geological conditions favorable to the existence of developable geothermal resources, such as comparatively recent volcanism and a relatively shallow mantle. Some of the areas with potential are protected in national parks; e.g., Yellowstone and Mount Lassen. The Geothermal Steam Act of 1970, 30 U.S.C. §§ 1101–1126, defines the geothermal resource as:

(i) all products of geothermal processes, embracing indigenous steam, hot water and hot brines; (ii) steam and other gases, hot water and hot brines resulting from water, gas, or other fluids artificially introduced into geothermal formations; (iii) heat or other associated energy found in geothermal formations; and (iv) any by-product derived from them.

"Byproduct" means any minerals (exclusive of oil, hydrocarbon gas, and helium) which are found in solution or in association with geothermal steam and which have a value of less than 75 per centum of the value of the geothermal steam or are not, because of quantity, quality, or technical difficulties in extraction and production, of sufficient value to warrant extraction and production by themselves.

30 U.S.C. §§ 1001(a) and (b). In some ways, exploitation of the geothermal resource resembles the development of hydroelectric generating facilities more than mineral development. The object is direct production of energy, not fuel or mineral extraction, and the medium is water convection. The federal mode of allocation and regulation under the 1970 Act, however, allocates and regulates geothermal production under a system comparable to that used for leasable minerals, as opposed to that used for hydroelectric licensing. For materials on the latter, see Chapter 6.

Currently, the United States leases approximately 500,000 acres for geothermal development under 400 leases. Most of the electric production from these leases occurs in California. Almost half of the existing geothermal power plants in the United States receive energy from federal leases.

Perhaps the most interesting and important set of issues involves federalism, and the extent to which state or federal law allocates rights to this fugacious resource, which can be found in common pools underlying both federal and state/private lands. The question can be further complicated depending upon whether state law treats the geothermal resource as a mineral resource, or as a water resource. Geothermal resources may be hydrologically interconnected with other water systems. Questions about the interaction of state and federal law where groundwater or geothermal development of non-federal lands threatens to interfere with geothermal resources on federal land are explored in Chapter 12, *infra* p. 1087.

C.   Federal Minerals That Are Subject to Sale

As noted earlier, there is a third category and system for disposing of federal minerals—very common, widely occurring minerals are available for disposition only by competitive sale. The Materials Disposal Act of 1947, 30 U.S.C. §§ 601–604, as amended by the Common Varieties Act of 1955, 30 U.S.C. § 611, provides for sale of sand, stone, gravel, pumice, cinders, and other designated "common" minerals, unless the deposit "has some property giving it distinct and special value," *id.* § 601, in which case it may still be located under the Mining Law. "Vegetative materials" found on the public lands and not subject to disposal under other laws, such as those governing commercial timber, are also subject to sale under these provisions. The Materials Disposal Act requires that such sales must usually be made to the highest responsible qualified bidder after advertising, with certain exceptions (such as where it is "impracticable to obtain competition"). Sales must not be "detrimental to the public interest," and must be for "adequate compensation therefor, to be determined by the Secretary." Regulations governing these sales are found at 43 C.F.R. Parts 3600, 3610.

The Secretary of the Interior exercises a great deal of discretion in choosing whether to put up these materials for bid.

What Happens When Different Minerals Are Targets of Development on the Same Federal Lands?

The same federal land may be valuable for different minerals; e.g., some strata may contain gold, others coal or oil. The same mineral deposit may contain both coal and methane gas. Common minerals like gravel or stone may be found in lands where other minerals are found. Interesting legal questions sometimes arise in these situations, especially to the extent different legal regimes apply to different minerals. For example, there had long been uncertainty, and conflicting legal opinion, about whether the Department of the Interior could sell common variety mineral materials (such as sand and gravel) from federal land that had been claimed under the Mining Law. The mining claimant has no right under the Mining Law to sell these materials, which are sometimes a main component of the overburden removed in order to develop locatable minerals. A 1999 Solicitor's Opinion resolved the past inconsistencies by concluding that the Secretary has authority under the Materials Act of 1947 to dispose of these materials where it can be done without endangering or materially interfering with prospecting, mining, or reasonably related uses. Disposal of Mineral Materials from Unpatented Mining Claims, M–36998 (1999).

Where the different minerals are subject to the same law, the matter is usually straightforward. Precious metals like lead, zinc, and silver are often found in association with each other. All are subject to the Mining Law of 1872, and a claim under that law embraces all the valuable minerals subject to that law found within the claim. Federal land may be claimed under the Mining Law but also contain coal, oil or gas, or another leasable mineral. Here a special federal statute, the Multiple Mineral Development Act of 1954, 30 U.S.C. §§ 521–531, establishes an uneasy compromise that is aimed at promoting compatible dual development. Special rules are provided for geothermal areas. *See, e.g.*, 30 U.S.C. § 1003(a).

Complications occur when both minerals are subject to leasing under different sections of the Mineral Leasing Act. This issue has come to the fore in the Powder River Basin in Wyoming as a result of a boom in coalbed methane activity that began in the late 1990s. The federal government issued many oil and gas leases on minerals it owned in the Basin in the 1960s and 1970s. The expectation at the time was that there would be wildcat exploration for any deep oil and gas deposits that might exist; no one at the time the leases were issued anticipated that the gas found in shallow coal beds might be exploitable. The leases themselves simply leased "gas," without regard to the depth or formation where it might be found. Sometime thereafter, the federal government issued separate coal leases to exploit the large and shallow coal deposits. More recently, the technology was developed to extract gas from the coal-beds. If the coal is mined first, the gas is lost to the atmosphere. If the gas is extracted first, the coal can later be mined. The problem becomes, then, a problem of timing. The different holders of the different mineral leases may not always see eye to eye on the matter. Holders of gas leases argue that they have priority because their leases were issued first. Therefore, if they are not willing or able to extract gas before the coal lessee was ready to mine the coal, they claim a right by their lease priority either to stop the coal mining or extract compensation from the coal owner for the lost gas. The coal lessee wants to avoid that situation, of course, and wants the federal government, as owner of both resources, to step in to force the gas lessee to develop the gas in a manner compatible with the coal lessee's schedule for mining the coal. The Department's authority in this matter turns on the terms of both leases, and the Department's regulations.

D. Split Estates: Issues Where Mineral Interests are Separated from Surface Interests

"The meek shall inherit the earth, but not the mineral rights."

—John Paul Getty (1892–1976), quoted in Robert Lenzner, The Great Getty (1985).

1. Federal Minerals Under Private Surface

For most of the disposition era, the railroad, statehood, homestead, and other statutes that authorized disposition of federal land were usually not applicable to federal "mineral lands," or federal lands that were "mineral in character." Such lands were not, in other words, available for selection or disposition under those statutes; instead, they were subject to the Mining Law of 1872.

Of course, it was not always easy to tell which of the lands that homesteaders wanted to settle upon, or that were within the in-place grants to the states or railroads, were "mineral in character." The rule that emerged was simple: The critical determination was usually made at the point in time that the land was surveyed, which was necessary before the land could be actually conveyed. If the land was deemed mineral in character then, the homesteader could not gain title. If land subject to an in-place grant was determined to be mineral in character at the time the lands were surveyed, in lieu selection rights were provided instead. *See* Andrus v. Utah, *supra* p. 90. In either case, if the land was deemed not to be mineral in character, and was then conveyed out of federal ownership, and it turned out later the land contained minerals, the grant was not affected and the grantee took the minerals. Burke v. Southern Pac. R. Co., 234 U.S. 669 (1914).

In 1957 a divided U.S. Supreme Court belatedly recognized an exception to that general notion. It held that a grant of a right of way to a railroad to build the first transcontinental railroad did not include the rights to minerals underneath the right of way. United States v. Union Pacific R. Co., 353 U.S. 112 (1957). This decision left undisturbed the holding in *Burke* in other contexts. Justice Douglas, writing for the majority in *Union Pacific*, explained that the process for determining "mineral in character" before issuance of patent was "obviously inappropriate" for the right of way for the railroad roadbed itself, because "the route of the railroad had to be determined by engineering considerations which could not allow for the extensive detours that avoidance of land containing minerals would make necessary." Therefore the result most faithful to the intent of the Congress was to deny the railroad the minerals underneath the right of way. 353 U.S. at 116–17. There was a vigorous dissent.

Shortly after the turn of the twentieth century, the policy of separating mineral lands from other lands began to change. Starting in 1909, some statutes authorized disposition of federal land without regard to whether it was mineral in character, and instead reserved to the United States all or some minerals in that land. This is the primary reason that, in addition to the minerals underlying the federal lands and the continental shelf, the United States also owns or controls the rights to minerals under more than 60 million acres of land surface it does not own, mostly in eleven western states. While it is convenient to refer to the "surface" and "subsurface estates" in this split estate context, in reality the surface owner has title to the subsurface as well, except for whatever minerals are reserved.

This movement to reserve *minerals* instead of *mineral lands* from disposition responded to a number of concerns. It sought to satisfy the pressure to make more western federal lands available for settlement and other disposition. It also grew out of a growing conviction that the United States should retain ownership of valuable (e.g., fossil fuel) minerals that the government might need. Indeed, President Taft's withdrawal leading to the *Midwest Oil* decision came the same year as the first statutory mineral reservation. The withdrawals were obstacles to disposition for non-mineral purposes. The split estate compromise allowed agricultural land to remain available for disposition.

The first important express general reservation of minerals in a public land disposition statute was in the Coal Lands Act of 1909, 30 U.S.C. § 81. It required coal to be reserved in subsequent agricultural patents. Congress quickly followed with the Agricultural Entry Act of 1914, 30 U.S.C. §§ 121–123 (reserving oil, gas, and other specified minerals) and the most important one, the Stock–Raising Homestead Act of 1916, 43 U.S.C. §§ 291–301 (reservation of "coal and other minerals"). Over 33 million acres were patented under the 1916 Act. Some of these acts allowed issuance of a patent without the mineral reservation if the recipient could show the land to non-mineral in character; that kind of provision was of limited assistance to patentees because of the difficulty of proof. The Stock–Raising Homestead Act did not include such an option.

The issues that arise under these reservations tend to divide into two categories: First, what substances are actually reserved? And second, what are the rights of the two estate owners vis-à-vis each other, when the mineral owner seeks to develop the reserved mineral estate?

a.   WHAT MINERALS ARE RESERVED?

Watt v. Western Nuclear, Inc.

Supreme Court of the United States, 1983.
462 U.S. 36.

■ JUSTICE MARSHALL delivered the opinion of the Court.

The Stock–Raising Homestead Act of 1916, the last of the great homestead acts, provided for the settlement of homesteads on lands the surface of which was "chiefly valuable for grazing and raising crops" and "not susceptible of irrigation from any known source of water supply." 43 U.S.C. § 292. Congress reserved to the United States title to "all the coal and other minerals" in lands patented under the Act. 43 U.S.C. § 299. The question presented by this case is whether gravel found on lands patented under the Act is a mineral reserved to the United States. * * *

In March 1975 respondent Western Nuclear, Inc. (Western Nuclear), acquired a fee interest in a portion of the land covered by [a 1926 Stock–Raising Homestead Act patent]. Western Nuclear is a mining company that has been involved in the mining and milling of uranium ore in and around Jeffrey City since the early 1950s. In its commercial operations Western Nuclear uses gravel for such purposes as paving and surfacing roads and shoring the shaft of its uranium mine. In view of the expense of having gravel hauled in from other towns, the company decided that it would be economical to obtain a local source of the material, and it acquired the land in question so that it could extract gravel from an open pit on the premises.

After acquiring the land, respondent obtained * * * a [state] permit authorizing it to extract gravel from the pit located on the land. Respondent proceeded to remove some 43,000 cubic yards of gravel. * * *

On November 3, 1975, the Wyoming State Office of the BLM served Western Nuclear with a notice that the extraction and removal of the gravel constituted a trespass against the United States[.] * * *

After a hearing, the BLM determined that Western Nuclear had committed an unintentional trespass. Using a royalty rate of 30 cents per cubic yard, the BLM ruled that Western Nuclear was liable to the United States for $13,000 in damages for the gravel removed from the site. [The IBLA and then the federal district court affirmed, but the court of appeals reversed, holding that the gravel extracted by Western Nuclear was not a mineral reserved to the United States by the Act.]

In view of the importance of the case to the administration of the more than 33 million acres of land patented under the SRHA, we granted certiorari. We now reverse.

As this Court observed in a case decided before the SRHA was enacted, the word "minerals" is "used in so many senses, dependent upon the context, that the ordinary definitions of the dictionary throw but little light upon its signification in a given case." Northern Pacific R. Co. v. Soderberg, 188 U.S. 526, 530 (1903). In the broad sense of the word, there is no doubt that gravel is a mineral, for it is plainly not animal or vegetable. But "the scientific division of all matter into the animal, vegetable or mineral kingdom would be absurd as applied to a grant of lands, since all lands belong to the mineral kingdom." While it may be necessary that a substance be inorganic to qualify as a mineral under the SRHA, it cannot be sufficient. If all lands were considered "minerals" under the SRHA, the owner of the surface estate would be left with nothing.

Although the word "minerals" in the SRHA therefore cannot be understood to include all inorganic substances, gravel would also be included under certain narrower definitions of the word. For example, if the term "minerals" were understood in "its ordinary and common meaning [as] a comprehensive term including every description of stone and rock deposit, whether containing metallic or non-metallic substances," gravel would be included. If, however, the word "minerals" were understood to include only inorganic substances having a definite chemical composition, gravel would not be included.

The various definitions of the term "minerals" serve only to exclude substances that are not minerals under any common definition of that word. Cf. United States v. Toole, 224 F.Supp. 440 (D.Mont.1963) (deposits of peat and peat moss, substances which are high in organic content, do not constitute mineral deposits for purposes of the general mining laws). For a substance to be a mineral reserved under the SRHA, it must not only be a mineral within one or more familiar definitions of that term, as is gravel, but also the type of mineral that Congress intended to reserve to the United States in lands patented under the SRHA. Cf. Andrus v. Charlestone Stone Products Co., 436 U.S. 604 (1978).

The legal understanding of the term "minerals" prevailing in 1916 does not indicate whether Congress intended the mineral reservation in the SRHA to encompass gravel. On the one hand, in Northern Pacific R. Co. v. Soderberg, this Court had quoted with approval a statement in an English case that "everything except the mere surface, which is used for agricultural purposes; anything beyond that which is useful for any purpose whatever, whether it is *gravel,* marble, fire clay, or the like, comes within the word 'mineral' when there is a reservation of the mines and minerals from a grant of land." 188 U.S., at 536 (emphasis added). * * *

On the other hand, in 1910 the Secretary of the Interior [held that land alleged to be chiefly valuable for sand and gravel was not "mineral in character" which would have excluded it from homestead entry.] Zimmerman v. Brunson, 39 Pub. Lands Dec. 310, *overruled,* Layman v. Ellis, 52 Pub. Lands Dec. 714 (1929). Zimmerman claimed that gravel and sand found on the property could be used for building purposes and that the property therefore constituted mineral land, not homestead land. In refusing to cancel Brunson's homestead entry, the Secretary explained that "deposits of sand and gravel occur with considerable frequency in the public domain." He concluded that land containing deposits of gravel and sand useful for building purposes was not mineral land beyond the reach of the homestead laws, except in cases in which the deposits "possess a peculiar property or characteristic giving them a special value."

Respondent errs in relying on *Zimmerman* as evidence that Congress could not have intended the term "minerals" to encompass gravel. Although the legal understanding of a word prevailing at the time it is included in a statute is a relevant factor to consider in determining the meaning that the legislature ascribed to the word, we do not see how any inference can be drawn that the 64th Congress understood the term "minerals" to exclude gravel. It is most unlikely that many members of

Congress were aware of the ruling in *Zimmerman*, which was never tested in the courts and was not mentioned in the reports or debates on the SRHA. Even if Congress had been aware of *Zimmerman*, there would be no reason to conclude that it approved of the Secretary's ruling in that case rather than this Court's opinion in *Soderberg*, which adopted a broad definition of the term "mineral" and quoted with approval a statement that gravel is a mineral.

Although neither the dictionary nor the legal understanding of the term "minerals" that prevailed in 1916 sheds much light on the question before us, the purposes of the SRHA strongly support the Government's contention that the mineral reservation in the Act includes gravel. * * * Congress' underlying purpose in severing the surface estate from the mineral estate was to facilitate the concurrent development of both surface and subsurface resources. While Congress expected that homesteaders would use the surface of SRHA lands for stock-raising and raising crops, it sought to ensure that valuable subsurface resources would remain subject to disposition by the United States, under the general mining laws or otherwise, to persons interested in exploiting them. It did not wish to entrust the development of subsurface resources to ranchers and farmers. Since Congress could not have expected that stock-raising and raising crops would entail the extraction of gravel deposits from the land, the congressional purpose of facilitating the concurrent development of both surface and subsurface resources is best served by construing the mineral reservation to encompass gravel. * * *

Given Congress' understanding that the surface of SRHA lands would be used for ranching and farming, we interpret the mineral reservation in the Act to include substances that are mineral in character (i.e., that are inorganic), that can be removed from the soil, that can be used for commercial purposes, and that there is no reason to suppose were intended to be included in the surface estate. This interpretation of the mineral reservation best serves the congressional purpose of encouraging the concurrent development of both surface and subsurface resources, for ranching and farming do not ordinarily entail the extraction of mineral substances that can be taken from the soil and that have separate value.[14]

Whatever the precise scope of the mineral reservation may be, we are convinced that it includes gravel. * * * Insofar as the purposes of the SRHA are concerned, it is irrelevant that gravel is not metalliferous and

---

14. * * * We note that this case does not raise the question whether the owner of the surface estate may use a reserved mineral to the extent necessary to carry out ranching and farming activities successfully. Although a literal reading of the SRHA would suggest that any use of a reserved mineral is a trespass against the United States, one of the overriding purposes of the Act was to permit settlers to establish and maintain successful homesteads. There is force to the argument that this purpose would be defeated if the owner of the surface estate were unable to use reserved minerals even where such use was essential for stock-raising and raising crops.

In this case, however, respondent cannot rely on any right it may have to use reserved minerals to the extent necessary for ranching and farming purposes, since it plainly did not use the gravel it extracted for any such purpose. The gravel was used for commercial operations that were in no way connected with any ranching or farming activity.

does not have a definite chemical composition. What is significant is that gravel can be taken from the soil and used for commercial purposes. * * *

It is also highly pertinent that federal administrative and judicial decisions over the past half-century have consistently recognized that gravel deposits could be located under the general mining laws until common varieties of gravel were prospectively removed from the purview of those laws by the Surface Resources Act of 1955, 30 U.S.C. § 611. While this Court has never had occasion to decide the appropriate treatment of gravel under the mining laws, the Court did note in United States v. Coleman, 390 U.S. 599, 604 (1968), that gravel deposits had "served as a basis for claims to land patents" under the mining laws prior to the enactment of the Surface Resources Act of 1955.

The treatment of gravel as a mineral under the general mining laws suggests that gravel should be similarly treated under the SRHA, for Congress clearly contemplated that mineral deposits in SRHA lands would be subject to location under the mining laws, and the applicable regulations have consistently permitted such location. * * *

Finally, the conclusion that gravel is a mineral reserved to the United States in lands patented under the SRHA is buttressed by "the established rule that land grants are construed favorably to the Government, that nothing passes except what is conveyed in clear language, and that if there are doubts they are resolved for the Government, not against it." United States v. Union Pacific R. Co., 353 U.S. 112, 116 (1957). In the present case this principle applies with particular force, because the legislative history of the SRHA reveals Congress' understanding that the mineral reservation would "limit the operation of this bill *strictly to the surface of the lands*." H.R.Rep. No. 35, at 18 (emphasis added). In view of the purposes of the SRHA and the treatment of gravel under other federal statutes concerning minerals, we would have to turn the principle of construction in favor of the sovereign on its head to conclude that gravel is not a mineral within the meaning of the Act.

For the foregoing reasons, we hold that gravel is a mineral reserved to the United States in lands patented under the SRHA. * * *

■ JUSTICE POWELL, with whom JUSTICE REHNQUIST, JUSTICE STEVENS, and JUSTICE O'CONNOR join, dissenting.

The Court's opinion may have a far-reaching effect on patentees of, and particularly successors in title to, the 33,000,000 acres of land patented under the Stock–Raising Homestead Act of 1916 (SRHA). * * * [T]he Court adopts a new definition of the statutory term: "[T]he Act [includes] substances that are mineral in character (i.e., that are inorganic), that can be removed from the soil, that can be used for commercial purposes, and that there is no reason to suppose were intended to be included in the surface estate."

This definition compounds, rather than clarifies, the ambiguity inherent in the term "minerals." It raises more questions than it answers. Under the Court's definition, it is arguable that all gravel falls within the mineral reservation. This goes beyond the Government's position that gravel *deposits* become reserved only when susceptible to commercial exploitation. And what about sand, clay, and peat? As I read the Court's opinion it could leave Western homesteaders with the dubious assurance that only the dirt itself could not be claimed by the Government. It is not easy to believe that Congress intended this result. * * *

The first attempt by the Department of the Interior to acquire ownership of gravel on SRHA lands did not occur until this case began in 1975. One would think it is now too late, after a half-century of inaction, for the Department to take action that raises serious questions as to the nature and extent of titles to lands granted under SRHA.[20] Owners of patented land are entitled to expect fairer treatment from their Government. In my view, the Department should be required to adhere to the clear intent of Congress at the time this legislation was adopted. I would affirm the judgment of the Court of Appeals.

NOTES AND QUESTIONS

1.   Who is right here, the majority or the dissent? Can Congress use the same word ("mineral") to mean different things in different statutes? Is the pivotal issue whether the Congress that enacted the Stock–Raising Homestead Act in 1916 was *aware* of the 1910 Departmental decision in Zimmerman v. Brunson holding that ordinary gravel was not a mineral for purposes of the Mining Law?

2.   Is the dissent saying that the government ought to be estopped from changing its mind? Do you agree that it is "not easy" to believe that the Congress intended to leave Western homesteaders without title to the sand and gravel underneath their property?

3.   Congress reserved the minerals in part because it did not, in Justice Marshall's words, "wish to entrust the development of subsurface resources to ranchers and farmers." Is it ironic that in this case the patentee's successor wants to develop the minerals, but is found not to have the legal authority to do so?

4.   The gravel deemed reserved to the U.S. in the principal case is subject to competitive sale rather than to leasing under the Mineral Leasing Act or to claim location under the Mining Law.

20.   The Department is in no position to adopt a new policy for land patents long granted. See Andrus v. Shell Oil Co., 446 U.S. 657 (1980). Its prior actions have caused the population generally, including respondent, to understand that gravel was not a reserved mineral. [As the district court observed:] "Until [1975], it was the practice of the Wyoming Highway Department, construction companies, and the ranchers owning the surface estate to treat the gravel as part of the surface estate, the gravel being sold or used by the rancher with the approval of the [Bureau of Land Management]." As Justice Rehnquist stated for the Court in Leo Sheep Co., supra:

"Generations of land patents have issued without any express reservation of the right now claimed by the Government. Nor has a similar right been asserted before. * * * This Court has traditionally recognized the special need for certainty and predictability where land titles are concerned, and we are unwilling to upset settled expectations. * * * "

5. Relying on *Western Nuclear*, the court in Hughes v. MWCA, 12 Fed.Appx. 875 (10th Cir.2001), held that "scoria," a form of volcanic cinder which became valuable in the 1970s for use in landscaping and as gas barbecue briquettes, was a mineral reserved by the United States in the Stock–Raising Homestead Act. It went on to hold that the deposit of scoria at issue was a common variety subject to sale by the United States, rejecting the argument of the surface owner that it was entitled to mine and sell it because it had located mining claims on the deposit.

6. Gravel may not be a "mineral" in other mineral reservations, especially those not made under a specific statute whose legislative history and context help in construing the term. *See, e.g.*, United States v. Hess, 194 F.3d 1164 (10th Cir.1999).

7. In United States v. Union Oil Co. of California, 549 F.2d 1271 (9th Cir.1977), the question was whether geothermal resources were reserved to the United States in the Stock–Raising Homestead Act. The court noted that:

> [t]here is no specific reference to geothermal steam and associated resources in the language of the Act or in its legislative history. The reason is evident. Although steam from underground sources was used to generate electricity at the Larderello Field in Italy as early as 1904, the commercial potential of this resource was not generally appreciated in this country for another half century. No geothermal power plants went into production in the United States until 1960. Congress was not aware of geothermal power when it enacted the Stock–Raising Homestead Act in 1916; it had no specific intention either to reserve geothermal resources or to pass title to them.

> * * * The Act reserves to the United States "all the coal and other minerals." All of the elements of a geothermal system—magma, porous rock strata, even water itself—may be classified as "minerals." When Congress decided in 1970 to remove the issue from controversy as to future grants of public lands, it found it unnecessary to alter the language of existing statutory "mineral" reservations. It simply provided that such reservations "shall hereafter be deemed to embrace geothermal steam and associated geothermal resources." Geothermal Steam Act of 1970, 30 U.S.C. § 1024. Thus, the words of the mineral reservation in the Stock–Raising Homestead Act clearly are capable of bearing a meaning that encompasses geothermal resources.

Is the court here saying that the geothermal resource is a mineral? Compare Andrus v. Charlestone Stone Products Co., 436 U.S. 604 (1978), *supra* p. 559 (reversing a 9th Circuit decision rendered a few months after this case, and holding water is not a mineral under the Mining Law of 1872). Might the meaning of "mineral" change appreciably between 1872 and 1916? The court in Rosette Inc. v. United States, 277 F.3d 1222 (10th Cir.2002), reached the same result as the Ninth Circuit in *Union Oil* and distinguished *Charlestone* because different statutes were involved.

8. What is really at stake in these cases; i.e., what difference does the result make in terms of future geothermal resource development? In

Rosette, the holder of the Stock–Raising Homestead patent was extracting hot water from a well and using it to heat greenhouses where it grew roses for commercial distribution. (It irrigated the roses with cooler water drawn from another well.) The United States sought to collect royalties and damages, claiming it owned the geothermal resource. The court said that while Rosette might, consistent with the patent, be able to use the heated water from geothermal resources to water livestock or irrigate forage crops, it could not use it for "the commercial activity of heating greenhouses to produce roses for sale."

9. In Amoco Production Co. v. Southern Ute Indian Tribe, 526 U.S. 865 (1999), the Supreme Court held that the reservation of "coal" to the United States in the Coal Lands Acts of 1909 and 1910 did not reserve coalbed methane (CBM) gas within the coal formations. (In 1938, the United States had conveyed all the interests in land it owned in the area to the tribe; therefore, if the U.S. had reserved the coalbed methane, the tribe succeeded to that ownership.) The majority opinion said:

> [The question] is not whether, given what scientists know today, it makes sense to regard CBM gas as a constituent of coal but whether Congress so regarded it in 1909 and 1910. * * * We are persuaded that the common conception of coal at the time Congress passed [those statutes] was the solid rock substance that was [then] the country's primary energy resource. * * * Congress [then] viewed CBM gas not as part of the solid fuel resource it was attempting to conserve and manage but as a dangerous waste product, which escaped from coal as the coal was mined. * * * [While t]here is some evidence of limited and sporadic exploitation of CBM gas as a fuel prior to passage of the 1909 and 1910 Acts * * * there is every reason to think [Congress] viewed the extraction of CBM gas as drilling for natural gas, not mining coal. The distinction is significant because the question before us is not whether Congress would have thought that CBM gas had some fuel value, but whether Congress considered it part of the coal fuel. * * * Because we conclude that the most natural interpretation of 'coal' as used in the 1909 and 1910 Acts does not encompass CBM gas, we need not consider the applicability of the canon that ambiguities in land grants are construed in favor of the sovereign or the competing canons relied on by petitioners.

526 U.S. at 873–74. Is *Amoco Production Co.* consistent with *Union Oil* and *Western Nuclear*?

10. In BedRoc Ltd., LLC v. United States, 541 U.S. 176 (2004), the Court held that sand and gravel were not "valuable minerals" reserved to the United States in patents issued under an obscure federal statute that authorized disposal of certain public lands in Nevada (the Pittman Underground Water Act of 1919). The statute in question is of trivial importance in the panoply of public land laws; before its repeal in 1964 (subject to valid existing rights), only a handful of patents were issued under it. Still, the case produced some interesting opinions. Chief Justice Rehnquist, joined by Justices O'Connor, Scalia and Kennedy, held that the Pittman Act's reservation of "valuable minerals" did not include sand and gravel. He distin-

guished Watt v. Western Nuclear because there the statute reserved "minerals," omitting the adjective "valuable." Rehnquist pointed out that four justices (including himself and O'Connor) had "vigorously disagreed" with the majority in Western Nuclear, and said "we share the concerns expressed" in that dissent, but, while "declin[ing] to overrule our recent precedent," the Court would not "extend [its] holding to conclude that sand and gravel are 'valuable minerals.'" Sand and gravel were so abundant and Nevada was so undeveloped in 1919 that Congress could not have regarded them as valuable, he reasoned, but he did not examine the legislative history of the Pittman Act. Justice Thomas, joined by Justice Breyer, thought that Chief Justice Rehnquist loaded too much freight on the word "valuable," and that no distinction could fairly be drawn between the statute here and the statute in *Western Nuclear*. Justice Stevens (who had dissented in *Western Nuclear*), joined by Justices Souter and Ginsburg, dissented here as well. Citing then-Justice Rehnquist's dictum in *Leo Sheep, supra* p. 375, of the "need for certainty and predictability where land titles are concerned," Justice Stevens thought *Western Nuclear* ought to be followed because it "has been settled law for two decades," and no meaningful difference could be drawn between the two statutes. He pointed out that the legislative history of the Pittman Act quite clearly ties its reservation of minerals to that made in the Stock–Raising Homestead Act which was addressed in *Western Nuclear*, and he berates the plurality opinion for ignoring that fact.

b. PROTECTING THE ENVIRONMENT AND SURFACE VALUES IN DEVELOPING FEDERALLY RESERVED MINERALS

Statutes reserving minerals in federal ownership typically made the mineral estate dominant and the surface estate servient. Thus the Stock–Raising Homestead Act of 1916 reserved not only the minerals but also "the right to prospect for, mine, and remove the same," and "to reenter and occupy so much of the surface * * * as may be required for all purposes reasonably incident to the mining or removal of the * * * minerals." 43 U.S.C. § 299. When Congress enacted these statutes reserving minerals early in this century, all the reserved minerals (except coal) were subject to the Mining Law of 1872. Many of the minerals were later made subject to leasing under the Mineral Leasing Act of 1920; common varieties of widely occurring minerals like sand and gravel were made subject to sale in 1947. In both situations the government retains considerable control over whether the reserved mineral shall be available for development, and the terms (including environmental restrictions) upon which development shall proceed.

Some of the minerals the U.S. reserved (such as gold and silver reserved under the broad "minerals" reservation of the 1916 Act) are, however, still subject to the self-initiation feature of the Mining Law. This means that the initial decision to locate claims and start mineral activity lies with mining claimants rather than the government, and the government's power to control whether and how the reserved federal minerals will be developed is somewhat more ambiguous.

Even though the federal reserved mineral estate includes a right to develop the minerals, Congress never freed mining activity from all restraint in split estate situations. The Stock–Raising Homestead Act, for example, required the mineral developer to compensate the surface owner for "crops" and other "improvements" damaged by mining operations. The Supreme Court held that this provision did not require compensation for any impairment of surface resources that did not strictly qualify as a growing crop or a permanent, agriculturally-related improvement. Kinney–Coastal Oil Co. v. Kieffer, 277 U.S. 488 (1928).

> The mineral reservation could create serious problems for farmers, ranchers, and even suburbanites in areas that were once privatized under laws like the Stock–Raising Homestead Act. [O]ne can envisage an entire residential subdivision on Stock–Raising Homestead Act lands. There are many such developments today, and more are being built. In come the prospectors, bearing not only their 1916 picks and shovels, but their modern day bulldozers and draglines. They may not harm the permanent improvements; that much is clear. And they must make restitution for damages to "crops." So they set to work in the lawn areas of the suburb, and perhaps also in the parks, greenbelts, and other "unimproved" areas.

Willis V. Carpenter, *Severed Minerals as a Deterrent to Land Development*, 51 U. Denv. L. Rev. 1, 24–25 (1974). In rare instances, such as underneath the metropolitan Tucson area, Congress has withdrawn federal minerals from location and leasing.

Of course, the degree of disruption depends upon the mineral involved and the method used to extract it. Oil and gas activity may involve only limited, tolerable intrusions on the surface estate. Surface mining of coal and other accessible deposits may virtually destroy the surface. As that technique gained favor because of its cost and safety advantages, Congress moved in 1949 to enlarge the liability of the developer of federally-reserved minerals by requiring payment for damage to the value of the land for grazing caused by "strip" or "open-pit" mining. 30 U.S.C. § 54.

Modern environmental concern for protection of surface values has combined with rancher concern for their way of life to lead to increasing legislative solicitude for the surface estate. The Federal Land Policy and Management Act (FLPMA), for example, not only codified a sweeping power of withdrawal, but also subjected reserved federal mineral interests to the planning dictates of the act (by defining public lands subject to FLPMA as including "any * * * interest in land" owned by the United States and managed by the BLM). 43 U.S.C. § 1702(e). FLPMA also allows future patents to be issued without reservations of minerals. And it permits present surface owners to apply for title to the reserved minerals, but they must pay fair market value for them. 43 U.S.C. § 1719(b)(2). In both cases, if mineral deposits are unknown, minerals will remain with the United States unless the BLM finds that the federal reservation "is interfering with or precluding appropriate non-mineral development of the land and that such development is a more beneficial use of the land than mineral development." 43 U.S.C. § 1719(b)(1).

The most notable example of extending protection to surface owners overlying federally reserved coal is found in the Surface Mining Control and Reclamation Act of 1977. There Congress decided that the surface owner must give written consent before the federal government can enter into a coal lease "to be mined by methods other than underground mining techniques." 30 U.S.C. § 1304. "Surface owner" is defined as a person who for at least three years has held title to the surface, and who either lives on the land, personally conducts farming or ranching operations on it, or derives a significant portion of her income from such operations. *Id.*

Because the consent of the surface owner can be purchased by one desiring to obtain a federal coal lease, this provision in effect can operate to transfer a portion of the value of the coal underneath the land from the federal government (which presumably will receive lower bids for the coal) to the surface owner. This may especially be true in cases where the surface owner gives non-transferable consent to a particular company because that effectively discourages others from bidding on the coal lease. As a result, the provision effects one of the largest privatizations of interests in federal land in a half-century.

In 1993, Congress once again returned to the matter of protecting the surface owner, this time amending the Stock–Raising Homestead Act to require the mineral developer, among other things, to gain approval in advance from the Secretary of the Interior of a surface use plan, and to post a bond. 43 U.S.C. § 299(b)-(p). In response to a rising chorus of complaints from ranchers and other surface owners of split estate lands, Section 1835 of the Energy Policy Act of 2005 requires the Secretary of the Interior to "undertake a review of the current policies and practices" for managing federally reserved oil and gas "and their effects on the privately owned surface."

The federal government owns mineral rights under forty-three percent of all private land in Wyoming. In response to the 2005 boom in leasing federal oil and gas underlying private lands, Wyoming enacted new legislation giving the surface owners greater leverage in negotiating the terms of surface disturbance and damage assessment. Wyo.Stat.Ann. § 30–5–402. The BLM has said it is not bound by state law where federally reserved minerals are involved, and a court battle seems likely.

In a context where both the surface estate and the mineral estate are privately owned, such legislative readjustments of the initial allocation of rights may raise constitutional questions. Recall that two of the classic takings cases in American constitutional law arose in a split-estate context, testing (with opposite results) the authority of the state legislature to adjust the rights of the coal owner and the surface owner. Pennsylvania Coal v. Mahon, 260 U.S. 393 (1922); Keystone Bituminous Coal Ass'n v. DeBenedictis, 480 U.S. 470 (1987). Where the federal government has retained title to the reserved minerals, however, it can of course limit or otherwise impose restrictions on its own interests without raising constitutional questions. But if it has already disposed of the reserved mineral by lease or other means, any new restrictions imposed after the fact may require compensation for property or contract rights.

NOTE: DETERMINING WHETHER FEDERAL RIGHTS ARE RESERVED IN DISPOSITIONS

In a broad sense, the federal mineral reservations addressed here are a species of federal reserved rights akin to federal reserved water rights usually associated with federal land withdrawals *See* Chapter 6. In other contexts, however, claims of federal reservations have been rejected. *See, e.g.*, Leo Sheep v. United States, Chapter 2, *supra* p. 375 (easement for public access for recreation purposes held not reserved). Can these differing outcomes be reconciled? Is there a single rule or canon of construction that can, or should, be applied to all claims of federal reserved rights? Or must each be examined on an ad hoc basis, controlled by its specific statute or order? Should the courts adopt a presumption that Congress intended, in privatizing federally owned resources, to reserve such rights as are appropriate for the reasonable, long term protection and preservation of resources on the public lands? Should wildlife, recreation, and preservation be considered as resources under such a formulation?

2. PRIVATE MINERALS UNDER FEDERAL SURFACE

This category of split estates may be found in a variety of situations. In the West, federal land purchases or exchanges, done for such purposes as consolidating former checkerboard patterns of ownership or acquiring land with high public values into federal ownership, have sometimes resulted in the federal government acquiring only surface ownership. For example, the holder of a railroad land grant or its successor may reserve the minerals while conveying the surface to the federal government. In the eastern part of the country, when the federal government embarked on a major program of acquiring lands for national forests under the Weeks Act of 1911, 16 U.S.C. §§ 513–518, 521, the private sellers often reserved mineral rights, sometimes in perpetuity and sometimes for a period of years. The same thing happened with many federal acquisitions under the Bankhead–Jones Farm Tenant Act of 1937, involved in the next principal case. Reserved private mineral interests can be found under lands managed by the National Park Service and the U.S. Fish & Wildlife Service. The Forest Service estimates that approximately six million acres in the national forest system have reserved nonfederal mineral rights. The National Park Service estimates that some five million acres of land it manages (and about two-thirds of the individual units) contain private mineral rights, either in fee simple inholdings or reserved mineral interests.

a. WHAT MINERALS ARE RESERVED?

In this context, too, questions sometimes arise about what minerals are reserved and the scope of the mineral reservation. The first question is resolved by the terms of the deed or conveyance that reserved the minerals (unlike the situation of reserved federal minerals explored above, where the issue is usually one of statutory interpretation). Some courts answer the question of what minerals are reserved in a particular deed by looking to the amount of destruction that would be caused by mineral extraction. In Downstate Stone Co. v. United States, 712 F.2d 1215 (7th Cir.1983), the question was whether the privately-owned mineral estate of "all minerals" included the right to extract limestone, a common mineral, the quarrying of which often involves destruction of the surface. The court determined that, under either federal or state law, the parties to the deed creating the estate did not intend to allow surface destruction so that limestone was not included in the grant.

Similarly, in United States v. Stearns Coal & Lumber Co., 816 F.2d 279 (6th Cir.1987), the parties agreed that Kentucky law controlled construction of a deed conveying land to the Forest Service and reserving minerals to the seller. On the merits, the court held that the deed did not reserve to the mineral owner the right to strip mine coal without permission of the Forest Service, explaining in part that under the provisions of the deed, "strip mining would not be a reasonable use of the surface because * * * the parties did not contemplate that [the mineral rights holder] could totally destroy the surface." 816 F.2d at 283.

The Interior Department's Office of Surface Mining sometimes finds itself on the front lines of making these determinations. This is because the Surface Mining Control and Reclamation Act (SMCRA) provides, with certain exceptions, subject to "valid existing rights," that no coal mining which disturbs the surface "shall be permitted * * * on any federal lands within the boundaries of any national forest." 30 U.S.C. § 1272(e)(2). In Belville Mining Co. v. United States, 763 F.Supp. 1411 (S.D.Ohio 1991), the court engaged in a detailed review of the mineral reservations contained in deeds to four different tracts of land acquired by the Forest Service under the Weeks Act. It concluded that on three of the tracts, the reservations allowed strip mining. It also found that, because the OSM had concluded in 1988 that the mineral rights holder possessed "valid existing rights" under SMCRA for all four tracts, and the holder had relied on that determination by "devoting considerable resources" to securing a permit to mine from the state, OSM had no power to revoke that determination. On appeal, the Sixth Circuit affirmed the rulings as to the first three tracts but reversed as to the fourth, finding that OSM had adequate inherent, statutory, and regulatory authority to reverse its policies. 999 F.2d 989 (6th Cir.1993).

b.   AUTHORITY OF THE UNITED STATES TO CONTROL DEVELOPMENT OF RESERVED MINERAL RIGHTS

The materials that follow focus on the authority of the federal government to regulate development of reserved minerals in nonfederal ownership, especially where such development threatens surface values. As the following case indicates, sometimes a key question is whether state or federal law applies.

Duncan Energy Company v. United States Forest Service

United States Court of Appeals, Eighth Circuit, 1995.
50 F.3d 584.

■ JUDGE JOHN R. GIBSON

* * * Meridian owns mineral rights on land within the Little Missouri National Grasslands area, which is part of the Custer National Forest in

North Dakota. The United States owns the surface estate.[1] Duncan has an exploration agreement with Meridian.

Since 1984, Meridian and its predecessor, Milestone Petroleum, have explored for oil and gas within the Custer National Forest without incident. Meridian submitted surface use plans to the Forest Service for review and obtained special use letters of authorization before developing its mineral estates. The Forest Service Regional Office reviews surface use plans by applying the standards and guidelines set forth in the Custer National Forest Land and Resource Management Plan. The Forest Service surveys resources in the area of proposed operations, analyzes potential effects, and determines whether there may be reasonable alternatives and mitigation measures. Following this review, the Forest Service issues a letter of authorization which establishes conditions and protective measures for surface use.

In 1984, the United States Forest Service and Meridian's predecessor, Milestone Petroleum, entered into a Memorandum of Understanding, which provided that the Forest Service would process a surface use plan within ten working days of the receipt of the complete surface use plan. Since 1984, Meridian has submitted fifteen surface plans to the Forest Service before drilling; the Forest Service has processed only two of the plans in fewer than ten days.

On October 15, 1992, the Forest Service and Duncan met to discuss well location, access, and road specifications for Duncan's anticipated drilling. The Forest Service suggested a different access route from that proposed by Duncan, and the access road was staked as the Forest Service suggested. On October 22, the Forest Service and several of Duncan's contractors met for an on-site surface inspection of the well location and staked access route. On December 7, 1992, Duncan submitted a surface use plan for a well site. The Forest Service advised Duncan's contractor that the surface use plan contained an inaccurate map of the proposed access route based on the October 22 meeting, and Duncan submitted a corrected map on December 24, 1992. The Forest Service then conducted an environmental analysis of the well and access route, consisting of a review of reports submitted by Duncan's contractors and consultation with the United States Fish and Wildlife Service and the North Dakota Department of Fish and Game. The Forest Service began to prepare an analysis document, which sets forth terms and conditions for the use of the federal surface.

---

1. The United States originally patented the land in question to Northern Pacific Railroad Company as a part of a railroad land grant. In 1916, the railroad deeded the land to various farmers, reserving "all minerals of any nature whatsoever * * * together with the use of such of the surface as may be necessary for exploring for and mining or otherwise extracting and carrying away the same." In 1937, the United States acquired the surface estate pursuant to the Bankhead–Jones Farm Tenant Act, subject to the mineral reservation in the 1916 deed. Meridian eventually acquired the mineral rights and Meridian executed an oil and gas exploration agreement with Duncan on September 30, 1992.

Over the next two months, Duncan contacted the Forest Service to check the status of the Forest Service's authorization. Duncan wanted to begin drilling, as its contract with Meridian required it to drill seven wells within one year or incur liquidated damages. During this time, Duncan learned that the Forest Service believed that the Memorandum of Understanding did not apply and that the Forest Service was considering whether the more extensive National Environmental Policy Act procedures applied. Under NEPA, Duncan could not drill until the Forest Service completed an area-wide environmental impact study and a site-specific environmental impact statement, which might take two to three years. See 42 U.S.C. § 4332(2)(C) (1988).

On March 4, 1993, Duncan sent a letter to the Forest Service stating that it had an absolute right to access and drill the site. Duncan requested that the Forest Service immediately issue a special use permit and comply with the 1984 Memorandum of Understanding. Duncan threatened to access the well as originally proposed if the Forest Service did not immediately approve the staked route. On March 16, 1993, Duncan submitted a revised map for the access route to the Forest Service. Because the new route varied two-tenths of a mile from the staked route, the Forest Service informed Duncan that it must complete the necessary environmental surveys for the new road, but that it would complete its analysis of the original route by the following week.

On Friday, March 19, 1993, at 4 o'clock p.m. Duncan telephoned the Forest Service to say that it would begin constructing the new road the next morning. The Forest Service visited the site the next morning and found that Duncan had begun constructing the road. Duncan completed all road construction by March 27. On April 6, 1993, Duncan placed the drill rig on the site, over the Forest Service's written objection. After Duncan asserted that the Forest Service was bound by the ten-day period stated in the Memorandum of Understanding, the Forest Service formally terminated the Memorandum on April 15, 1993.

Meanwhile, on March 29, 1993, Duncan filed suit against the Forest Service seeking a declaratory judgment that the Service could not prohibit access to or regulate the exploration and development of the privately owned oil and gas estate. The Forest Service filed an answer and a counterclaim asserting that Duncan had improperly used federal surface without obtaining the necessary authorization. The Forest Service requested a permanent injunction barring Duncan from further ground disturbing activity at the well site and on other National Forest System lands without the Forest Service's express written authorization.

* * *

Under North Dakota law, the mineral estate is dominant, carrying "inherent surface rights to find and develop the minerals." Hunt Oil Co. v. Kerbaugh, 283 N.W.2d 131, 135 (N.D.1979). The mineral developer's rights, however, are not unrestricted. The mineral developer's rights "are limited to so much of the surface and such use thereof as are *reasonably necessary* to explore, develop, and transport the minerals." Id. Thus, North

Dakota law does not preclude the Forest Service from requiring that only reasonable use be made of the federal surface lands. *Hunt Oil* established that the mineral developer's right of access is subject to a standard of reasonableness:

> [I]f the manner of use selected by the dominant mineral lessee is the only reasonable, usual and customary method that is available for developing and producing the minerals on the particular land then the owner of the servient estate must yield. However, if there are other usual, customary and reasonable methods practiced in the industry on similar lands put to similar uses which would not interfere with the existing uses being made by the servient surface owner, it could be unreasonable for the lessee to employ an interfering method or manner of use.

Id. at 136–37.

Although North Dakota law protects the surface owner's property rights by limiting the mineral holder to the "reasonable use" of the surface, North Dakota law does not * * * cloak the Forest Service with the specific authority to approve surface use plans. Indeed, there is not even specific authority to allow a surface owner to enjoin the unreasonable use of the surface. *Hunt Oil* does not discuss injunctive relief. North Dakota's Oil and Gas Production Compensation Act requires only that the mineral developer "give the surface owner written notice of the drilling operations contemplated at least twenty days prior to the commencement of the operations," and provides a damages remedy. N.D.Cent.Code § 38–11.1–05 (1987).

Nevertheless, the Forest Service contends that federal law gives it the authority to approve surface use plans. Duncan responds * * * that Congress has not given the Forest Service the authority to regulate outstanding mineral rights, as it has given the National Park Service. See 16 U.S.C. § 1902.

Congress has the power under the property clause to regulate federal land. * * * Under the Bankhead–Jones Farm Tenant Act, Congress directed the Secretary of Agriculture "to develop a program of land conservation and land utilization." 7 U.S.C. § 1010. The Act directs the Secretary to make rules as necessary to "regulate the use and occupancy" of acquired lands and "to conserve and utilize" such lands. 7 U.S.C. § 1011(f). The Forest Service, acting under the Secretary's direction, manages the surface lands here as part of the National Grasslands, which are part of the National Forest System. See 16 U.S.C. § 1609(a). Congress has given the Forest Service broad power to regulate Forest System land.

* * *

* * * The only issue before us is the Forest Service's ability to regulate surface access to outstanding mineral rights. The Forest Service recognizes that it cannot prevent Duncan, as the owner of the dominant mineral estate, from exploring for or developing its minerals. * * *

[The court then considered and rejected several specific arguments by Duncan that the special use regulations and other sources show that the Forest Service has no regulatory authority here. The court then addressed the Forest Service Manual.] Although the Forest Service Manual does not cite the special use regulations, the substance of the manual is consistent with the regulations. For example, the Manual requires the mineral estate owner to submit "an operating plan for the exercise of outstanding mineral rights," including methods for controlling environmental degradation. The Manual authorizes the Forest Service to send a letter of authorization after reviewing the plan to determine whether it "[u]ses only so much of the surface as is prudently necessary for the proposed operations." Although the Manual says that the Forest Service should meet with the mineral owner to negotiate modifications, it provides for "appropriate legal action" if the mineral owner deviates from the operating plan. * * *

* * * For these reasons, we are convinced that the Forest Service has the limited authority it seeks here; that is, the authority to determine the reasonable use of the federal surface.

If North Dakota law is read to allow developers unrestricted access after twenty days' notice and no injunctive relief for the surface owner, North Dakota law is inconsistent with the special use regulations. State law may be pre-empted in two ways:

> If Congress evidences an intent to occupy a given field, any state law falling within that field is pre-empted. If Congress has not entirely displaced state regulation over the matter in question, state law is still pre-empted to the extent it actually conflicts with federal law, that is, when it is impossible to comply with both state and federal law, or where the state law stands as an obstacle to the accomplishments of the full purposes and objectives of Congress.

Silkwood v. Kerr–McGee Corp., 464 U.S. 238, 248 (1984).

In addition, under choice-of-law principles, when determining whether to apply federal or state law, federal courts will apply federal law "when the case arises from or bears heavily upon a federal regulatory program." United States v. Albrecht, 496 F.2d 906, 910 (8th Cir.1974).

Allowing unrestricted access after twenty days' notice would impede Congress' objective of protecting federal lands and abrogate a congressionally-declared program of national scope. If North Dakota law is read to allow a developer unrestricted access after twenty days' notice, North Dakota law is preempted or falls under choice-of-law principles.

Accordingly, the judgment of the district court is reversed, and the case is remanded to the district court with instructions to enter summary judgment for the United States and an order declaring that Duncan violated Forest Service regulations by proceeding with mineral development absent Forest Service authorization of the surface use plan. The Forest Service's request for a permanent injunction is best considered by the district court on remand. * * *

NOTES AND QUESTIONS

1. Duncan Energy is between a rock and a hard place: Forest Service delays may cause breach and termination of its contract with Meridian, but some "reasonable" delay is inevitable if the agency can regulate and condition Duncan's surface entry. Is this dilemma the fault of the Forest Service or of Duncan?

2. Is there an argument that the NEPA process does not apply here, if it would result in delaying the Forest Service consideration of Duncan's plans "unreasonably"? Could the court, in other words, hold that the Forest Service has authority to regulate Duncan's activities to some extent in order to protect the surface estate, but cannot use regulatory processes such as a full-blown EIS process if it would greatly delay the exercise of that regulatory authority?

3. What about the relation between federal and state law here? The split estate here was not created under federal law; the federal government originally issued a fee simple deed for this land. The estate was later split by the Northern Pacific Railroad, under state law. That being the case, why doesn't state law control the definition of the respective rights of the mineral owner and the surface owner? Before the Forest Service acquired the surface, state law governed that issue. Why does the Forest Service have more authority than its predecessor in title to the surface could convey? Has the Court in *Duncan Energy* effectively used federal law to make the surface estate dominant in contravention of North Dakota law?

4. While states for a long time generally applied the principle that the reserved mineral estate was dominant and the surface estate was servient, in more recent years a number of states, like the Congress, have moved to provide more protection for the surface owner. North Dakota itself, the scene of *Duncan Energy*, has enacted a statute that requires the mineral developer to pay the surface owner for all value lost as a result of the mineral development, N.D.Cent.Code § 38–11.1–01. Its constitutionality was upheld in Murphy v. Amoco Prod. Co., 729 F.2d 552 (8th Cir.1984). Other states (led, somewhat surprisingly, by wild and woolly Texas, Getty Oil v. Jones, 470 S.W.2d 618 (1971)) have judicially developed an "accommodation doctrine." As described by Andrew Mergen, it "requires the mineral owner to act with prudence and to have due regard for the interests of the surface owner in exercising its right to use the surface to explore for and extract minerals." *Surface Tension: The Problem of Federal/Private Split Estate Lands*, 33 LAND & WATER L.REV. 419, 433 (1998);. *See, e.g.*, Flying Diamond Corp. v. Rust, 551 P.2d 509, 511 (Utah 1976) ("wherever there exists separate ownerships of interest in the same land, each should have the right to the use and enjoyment of his interest in the property to the highest degree possible, not inconsistent with the rights of others"). In states following this idea, the conflict with the federal interest in protecting the surface may narrow or disappear entirely.

Agency Split Estate Regulations and Application

1. *National Forest System.* Somewhat curiously, the Forest Service has bifurcated its regulatory approach to privately reserved mineral interests. One set of regulations applies to "reserved" mineral rights, which are defined as those reserved by the seller in the conveyance of the surface to the United States. 36 C.F.R. § 251.15 (2000). The Forest Service regulates "outstanding" mineral rights, which were severed from the surface *before* the United States acquired the property, under its generic "special use" regulations. 36 C.F.R. § 251.110. The mineral rights involved in *Duncan Energy* were "outstanding," having been severed before the U.S. acquired the property.

The Forest Service regulations applicable to "reserved" mineral interests require, among other things (and with some exceptions): (a) prior written notice to the agency, including submission of "satisfactory evidence of authority to exercise such rights;" (b) limitation of surface occupancy and disturbance to that "necessary in bona fide [mineral activities]"; (c) obtaining a permit, posting a bond, repairing or replacing any improvements damaged or destroyed, and "restor[ing] the land to a condition safe and reasonably serviceable for authorized programs of the Forest Service;" and (d) making "reasonable provisions * * * for the disposal of * * * deleterious materials * * * in such manner as to prevent obstruction, pollution, or deterioration of water resources."

2. *National Park System.* The Park Service has comprehensive regulations that govern mining in the parks, to implement the Mining in the Parks Act of 1976, 16 U.S.C. §§ 1901–12. But the statute and the regulations apply only to patented and unpatented federal mining claims. A number of individual park enabling acts contain specific provisions relating to the regulation of private mineral rights. In 1978, the Park Service adopted regulations that govern the development of nonfederal oil and gas rights throughout the national park system. 36 C.F.R. § 9(B) (2000). These take the same basic approach as the Forest Service regulations, requiring advance approval of a plan of operations and a bond, but are far more detailed. Many oil and gas operations in park units are grandfathered or otherwise largely exempt from these regulations, however. For minerals other than oil and gas, the Park Service attempts to use special use permits or other means to protect the parks.

In Dunn McCampbell Royalty Interest, Inc. v. National Park Service, 964 F.Supp. 1125 (S.D.Tex.1995), *aff'd*, 112 F.3d 1283 (5th Cir.1997), the owner of a severed mineral estate within the Padre Island National Seashore claimed an "unfettered right" to "destroy," if necessary, the surface lands to develop the minerals. It argued for application of state law and claimed a taking of its property interest if the Park Service regulated its oil/gas actively. The district court held the challenge to the regulations on their face was time-barred by the generic six year statute of limitations on civil actions against the United States. In the alternative it held the regulations a valid exercise of Park Service authority, and preempted any inconsistent state law. The takings claim was transferred to the court of claims. Over a dissent, the Fifth Circuit affirmed, without reaching the question of the validity of the regulations because the Park Service had not taken any action against plaintiff. The National Park Service in February 2004 approved an oil company's plan to drill for natural gas on the Padre Island National Seashore. The agency said the activity is an exercise of the company's valid existing rights grandfathered by the legislation creating the Seashore; that it would have only minimal impact on wildlife, including the endangered Kemp Ridley sea turtle which nests there; and that it would supervise the drilling closely. Section 373(b) of the Energy Policy Act of 2005 expressed the "sense of Congress that * * * any regulation of the development of * * * minerals [at] Padre Island National Seashore should be made as if [the] lands retained the status that the lands had on September 27, 1962," just before Congress designated the lands as the Seashore.

Directional drilling technology enables owners of oil/gas rights underneath federal land to access from adjacent private land. Though the technology costs more than vertical drilling, it allows development without treading on federal surface resources. The NPS regulations allow directional drillers to operate outside of park boundaries without plans of operations if the NPS determines that the operations pose no significant threat to park resources. A district court remanded a Park Service decision to allow directional wells adjacent to Big Thicket National Preserve without approving plans of operations. The Sierra Club argued that air pollution and noise from the drilling operations would harm the park. While the NPS did consider these impacts in its environmental assessments, it failed to justify with reasoned analysis its conclusions that the impacts: 1) would not impair park resources or values; and 2) are not significant impacts justifying preparation of environmental impact statements. Sierra Club v. Mainella, 459 F.Supp.2d 76 (D.D.C. 2006).

3. *National Wildlife Refuges.* The U.S. Fish & Service has brief and rather modest regulations on the exercise of reserved mineral rights on refuge system lands, even though oil and gas operations are fairly common and refuge managers cite them as a frequent cause of adverse impact on refuge objectives. 50 C.F.R. § 29.32. The regulations seek to prevent interference with operations on and damage to the refuge. However, conditions on drilling are limited to those that are "practicable." And, physical occupation of the refuge while engaging in mining "must be kept to the minimum space compatible with the conduct of efficient mineral operations." *Id.*

4. *BLM-managed public lands.* The BLM does not have regulations specifically addressing the exercise of reserved mineral rights on BLM lands. But FLPMA's command to prevent "unnecessary or undue degradation," provides a standard for BLM's stewardship responsibility. 43 U.S.C. § 1732(b).

CHAPTER 8

THE TIMBER RESOURCE

Federal policy toward wood production from federal lands is primarily implemented through the U.S. Forest Service's management of the national forest system. Since the 1970s, that policy has undergone profound change. For the first seven decades of the national forests' existence, congressional directives were generally understood to mean that the Forest Service was to harvest timber on the national forests where, when and how it thought best. The principal governing law was the Organic Act of 1897, 16 U.S.C. §§ 475–482 (§ 476 repealed 1976), setting general guidelines for administering the forests; and, later, the Multiple–Use, Sustained–Yield Act of 1960, 16 U.S.C. §§ 528–531. Each granted nearly unfettered authority, and the courts did not much intrude: Forest Service powers and discretion were routinely upheld in the few cases challenging them; *e.g.*, Light v. United States and United States v. Grimaud, *supra* p. 126. Timber litigation consisted of a miscellany of timber theft convictions and private contract disputes until the rise of the modern environmental movement, beginning about 1970.

This historical autonomy was due in large part to the rich tradition nurtured in the Forest Service by Gifford Pinchot from the time he became the head of the Forestry Division in the Department of Agriculture in 1898. Though he originally had no trees to manage, Pinchot's brand of conservation and silviculture (the branch of forestry dealing with growing and tending trees) effectively became official federal policy in 1905, when Congress transferred the forest reserves from the Interior to the Agriculture Department, and formally created the U.S. Forest Service to manage them. Even today, Pinchot's name is commonly invoked within the Forest Service and in congressional hearings.

The Forest Service gained its share of detractors over the years, especially as annual harvests from the national forests shot up with the demands of World War II and the postwar construction boom. Since the early 1990s, however, in one of the most sweeping changes in modern federal land policy, the annual timber cut has declined sharply as a result of several factors. They include: (a) limitations brought about by endangered species concerns; (b) the maturation of the Forest Service planning process under the National Forest Management Act of 1976; (c) a near-halt in the building of new roads on national forest lands; (d) growing public opposition to clearcutting as a timber management tool; and (e) a migration of the core of the domestic timber industry from the public lands of the northwest to private tree farms in the southeast. This evolution is illustrated by statistics showing annual timber production from the national forests in selected years over the twentieth century: From Pinchot's day in the first decade of the twentieth century, the cut remained relatively consistent at about 1 billion board feet annually for a few decades, climbing to 2 billion board feet in 1940. During World War II, the harvest rose to about 4 billion board feet. In the postwar boom years, the cut shot up, reaching 12 billion board feet by the mid–1960s, where it remained until about 1990. Then, as a result of the forces just mentioned, the annual harvest steadily fell to about 3 billion board feet in 2002. Through all this, although the Forest Service concedes that its track record includes some serious professional and political misjudgments, most knowledgeable critics (from any direction) recognize that the agency's history and heritage have given it a professional tradition uncommonly respected among governmental institutions.

From the days of near-complete deference and autonomy, federal timber policy is now governed by detailed legal standards, defined by legislation, further elaborated on by administrative rules, and enforced by the courts. A recent Chief of the Forest Service has noted that "[a]gency decisionmakers spend as much or more time with lawyers as with natural resource management personnel." Jack Ward Thomas, *Stability and Predictability in Federal Forest Management: Some Thoughts from the Chief*, 17 PUB. LAND. & RESOURCES L.REV. 9, 19 (1996). Elsewhere in this book some of the pertinent issues have been explored, including NEPA, the planning process, and limitations imposed in contracts, such as timber sales contracts. This chapter looks at others in some detail. Section A analyzes traditional forest practices under the rubric of multiple use-sustained yield, a longstanding touchstone of federal forest management. Section B examines the transition, sparked by the *Monongahela* decision, from the traditional system. Section C focuses on the dominant statute, the National Forest Management Act of 1976, which is now best understood as the Forest Service's organic act. Section C also covers important current controversies over wildfire management and roadless area protection in the national forests. Section D addresses the dynamic controversy, culminating in the Northwest Forest Plan, over logging in the old-growth forests of the Pacific Northwest—the leading modern development involving the national forests and among the most significant in public land law as a whole. While this chapter does not have a separate section on timber lands administered by the Bureau of Land Management ("BLM"), the most valuable BLM forest holdings—some three million timber-rich acres forfeited from the Oregon & California Railroad grant ("the O&C Lands")—are subject to the Northwest Forest Plan.

A.   TRADITIONAL FOREST SERVICE MANAGEMENT

1.   THE MULTIPLE-USE, SUSTAINED-YIELD ACT OF 1960

Although the 1897 Forest Service Organic Act referred primarily to management for timber, water, and protection of the forests, 16 U.S.C. § 476, the Forest Service in fact managed its lands to serve a broader number of uses from its inception. Grazing interests had been an important presence on national forest land from the beginning. Visionaries like Aldo Leopold and Bob Marshall labored from within to expand recreational opportunities in national forests, and to promote the protection of wildlife. By the 1950s, the wilderness movement had begun to make its presence felt. At the same time, the traditional users—timber operators and reclamation interests—argued for greater protection for their particular needs. As these cross-currents swirled about the agency in the middle of the twentieth century, it decided to go to Congress for ratification, delicately arguing both that new legislation was desirable to clarify the agency's mission, and that it had possessed such broad authority all along.

The result was the Multiple–Use, Sustained–Yield Act of 1960 ("MUSY"), 16 U.S.C. § 528–31, the key provision of which listed five uses alphabetically. In a classic case of political optics elevating form over substance, the Forest Service's draft of the statute (accepted by Congress) took pains to show its sensitivity to recreation by modifying the word with the adjective "outdoor," in order to allow it to be listed first:

> It is the policy of the Congress that the national forests are established and shall be administered for outdoor recreation, range, timber, watershed, and wildlife and fish purposes. The purposes of this Act are declared to be supplemental to, but not in derogation of, the purposes for which the national forests were established as set forth in the Act of June 4, 1897. [16 U.S.C. § 528]

> The Secretary of Agriculture is authorized and directed to develop and administer the renewable surface resources of the national forests for multiple use and sustained yield of the several products and services obtained therefrom. In the administration of the national forests due consideration shall be given to the relative values of the various resources in particular areas. The establishment and maintenance of areas of wilderness are consistent with the purposes and provisions of sections 528 to 531 of this title. [16 U.S.C. § 529]

> As used in this Act, the following terms shall have the following meanings:

> (a) "Multiple use" means: The management of all the various renewable surface resources of the national forests so that they are utilized in the combination that will best meet the needs of the American people; making the most judicious use of the land for some or all these resources or related services over areas large enough to provide sufficient latitude for periodic adjustments in use to conform to changing needs and conditions; that some land will be used for less than all of the resources; and harmonious and coordinated management of the various resources, each with the other, without impairment of the productivity of the land, with consideration being given to the relative values of the various resources, and not necessarily the combination of uses that will give the greatest dollar return or the greatest unit output.

> (b) "Sustained yield of the several products and services" means the achievement and maintenance in perpetuity of a high-level annual or

regular periodic output of the various renewable resources of the national forests without impairment of the productivity of the land. [16 U.S.C. § 531]

The BLM formally received its multiple use mandate in the Federal Land Policy and Management Act ("FLPMA") in 1976. FLPMA's definitions of these two concepts generally track those quoted above, although there are some interesting differences in the definition of "multiple use." *See* 43 U.S.C. § 1702(c), (h). FLPMA lists not five but an open-ended number of uses; i.e., "including, but not limited to, recreation, range, timber, minerals[*], watershed, wildlife and fish, and natural scenic, scientific and historical values." It also speaks of meeting "the present *and future* needs of the American people," and of coordinating management of the various resources "without *permanent* impairment of the productivity of the land *and the quality of the environment.*" (differences from the MUSY Act italicized).

The 1960 Act preserved the autonomy that the Forest Service had enjoyed since its inception. With little "law to apply," few judicial decisions have addressed agency implementation of these broad concepts. An early one came in connection with the largest single timber sale ever entered into by the Forest Service. In 1968, it sold 8.7 billion board feet of timber from the Tongass National Forest in southeast Alaska to U.S. Plywood–Champion Papers, Inc. The transaction encompassed more than 99% of the commercial forest lands (more than 4.5 million acres of the 16 million acre national forest), and called for harvest over a period of 50 years. The Sierra Club challenged the sale on several grounds, one of which was the MUSY Act. In Sierra Club v. Hardin, 325 F.Supp. 99, 122–24 (D.Alaska 1971), the court denied relief:

> Plaintiffs introduced substantial testimony as well as documentary evidence, much of it in the form of offers of proof, to show that the Tongass National Forest is being administered predominantly for timber production. While the material undoubtedly shows the overwhelming commitment of the Tongass National Forest to timber harvest objectives in preference to other multiple use values, Congress has given no indication as to the weight to be assigned each value and it must be assumed that the decision as to the proper mix of uses within any particular area is left to the sound discretion and expertise of the Forest Service. Accordingly, evidence was admitted only for the purpose of showing that the Forest Service failed to give ["due consideration" under 16 U.S.C. § 529] to any of the competing uses or that it took into consideration irrelevant matters which it should not have considered. The court must presume * * * that the Forest Service did give due consideration to the various values specified in the Multiple Use–Sustained Yield Act.

---

* Minerals were included in the BLM definition, but not the Forest Service's, because under the terms of the 1905 Act transferring the Forest Service to the Department of Agriculture, 16 U.S.C. § 472, the BLM oversees the development of minerals on the national forests. As illustrated by various materials in Chapter 7, however, the Forest Service regulates mining activities in order to protect the other resources of the forests.

The district court's decision was vacated and remanded by the court of appeals. Sierra Club v. Butz, 3 Envtl. L. Rptr. 20292 (9th Cir. 1973). The court explained:

> [A] report by A. Starker Leopold and Reginald H. Barrett to U.S. Plywood–Champion Papers, Inc., * * * [analyzed] the manner in which the sales contract should be carried out, with due consideration given to social values other than the economic yield of pulp or lumber. It was the view of this team of experts that "the basic precepts on which the original timber sale contract were based are not today acceptable." It recommended "that the company explore with the Forest Service the possibility of revising the cutting plan to provide more adequate protection for the wide spectrum of ecologic values that is characteristic of Southeastern Alaska." * * *

> The [lower] court, at 325 F.Supp. 123 n. 48, discussed what should be regarded as "due" consideration under the Act and concluded that what was intended was that the Forest Service should "apply their expertise to the problem after consideration of all relevant values." It concluded that "some" consideration was sufficient. (For the purposes of this order we accept this interpretation, with the caution that "due consideration" to us requires that the values in question be informedly and rationally taken into balance. The requirement can hardly be satisfied by a showing of knowledge of the consequences and a decision to ignore them.) * * *

> In our judgment the [Leopold–Barrett] report tendered upon this motion may be found to bear upon the stated issues: Whether the Forest Service in truth had knowledge of the ecological consequences of the contract and cutting plan to which it agreed; whether in reaching its decision it failed to consider the available material (the report appends a 10–page list of material cited in the report in existence at the time the contract was entered into); further, a relevant question may be whether consideration was given to alternatives (such as those recommended by the report), which, while giving prime consideration to timber values, would still afford protection to the other values to which due consideration must be given.

NOTES AND QUESTIONS

1. How can a concededly "overwhelming commitment" to timber production on the Tongass National Forest be consistent with "multiple use"? Could the Service legally decide to cut every tree in the Tongass National Forest? Could it legally decree that no trees at all will be cut? As the district court observed, only a little more than one quarter of the Tongass National Forest contained commercial stands of timber. Even though the Forest Service sold practically all this timber in this sale, nearly three-quarters of the land area in the Tongass National Forest was arguably left for other uses. Is that relevant to the issue here? How useful is "due consideration" as a standard of judicial review?

2. Timber harvesting in the Tongass National Forest has been the source of continual judicial and congressional attention ever since 1973, under statutes more specific than MUSY, such as the Tongass Timber Reform Act, 16 U.S.C. § 539(d). *See, e.g.*, Hoonah Indian Assn. v. Morrison, 170 F.3d 1223 (9th Cir.1999).

3. A widely cited case discussing MUSY is Perkins v. Bergland, 608 F.2d 803, 806 (9th Cir. 1979), dealing with regulation of livestock grazing on national forests, where the court described the "so-called standards" in the MUSY Act as "contain[ing] the most general clauses and phrases * * * [which] can hardly be considered concrete limits upon agency discretion. Rather it is language which 'breathe[s] discretion at every pore.' "

4. "Multiple use" has a powerful emotional and political content in federal land management as a shorthand for emphasizing the traditional uses: mining, livestock grazing, and timber harvesting. As controlling law, however, it is far less significant today than before enactment of many modern statutes. The Forest Service and BLM planning mandates and NEPA together ushered in a new management era for these agencies, ending their near-plenary discretion in making MUSY decisions. While the modern statutes may be more procedural than substantive (and while the courts may give a higher level of scrutiny to agency process than agency outcomes), the fact remains that the "multiple use" federal lands are now more or less formally zoned, with particular areas being managed for some dominant uses. Congress has directly played a role in this zoning process, by designating large tracts of Forest Service (and, increasingly, BLM) lands as wilderness areas, wild & scenic rivers, national recreation areas, national conservation areas, and the like. There have also been numerous executive actions with similar effect, such as designations of national monuments and areas of critical environmental concern, withdrawals, and zoning through the federal land planning process.

5. Even on lands nominally still subject to "multiple use" management, laws like the National Forest Management Act, explored in the next section, provide much more specific guidance for taking account of differing resources and values. Furthermore, in recent years, partially in response to the need to comply with the Endangered Species Act, all of the federal land management agencies have begun to move toward something that has come to be known by many as "ecosystem management." For the Forest Service and BLM, ecosystem management evidently is a variant of, or gloss upon, multiple use management. Professor Keiter explains ecosystem management in the excerpt, *supra* p. 38. *See also* Oliver A. Houck, *On the Law of Biodiversity and Ecosystem Management*, 81 MINN. L.REV. 869 (1997) (studying the experience of the Forest Service and the BLM, and concluding that "however high we raise our sights towards managing the whole, the requirement of individual species will remain the bottom line, or we will have no bottom line, and the entire effort will fail.").

6. All this raises the question whether multiple-use/sustained yield—in its classic formulation as allowing consideration of a wide variety of uses, without any one having priority—has any meaning anymore, or any future. How is sustainability to be defined? How is it to be demonstrated and

evaluated by land managers? How great a commitment should be made to commodity users who depend on federal resources, and how can these local needs be balanced with broader national interests? What pricing system for resource uses and outputs is fair and of greatest national benefit?

2. THE RESOURCES PLANNING ACT OF 1974

Congress's tradition of a "hands-off" approach toward Forest Service timber harvesting continued after MUSY. In 1974, at the request of professional foresters inside and outside the agency, legislation did address important questions of long-range funding and planning but, once again, there was no toehold for meaningful judicial review.

With a few important exceptions, Congress has generally refused in public natural resource law to create "revolving funds" whereby financial receipts from federal resource programs are returned directly to the federal land management agency for its use. Instead, the federal land management agencies, like most other federal agencies, receive their operating funds through the annual congressional appropriations process. The Forest Service has long regarded itself as disadvantaged by the ups-and-downs of that annual exercise. In the Forest and Rangeland Renewable Resources Planning Act of 1974 ("RPA"), as amended, 16 U.S.C. §§ 1601–1613, Congress embarked on what proved to be a hopelessly idealistic effort to bring more rationality to the process. It acknowledged that forest lands are capital assets and that the agency requires reliable estimates of future funding to plan for timber management practices such as reforestation.

The RPA directs the Forest Service periodically to prepare three planning documents: (1) an Assessment describing the renewable resources of all the nation's forest and range lands (every ten years); (2) a Program, with a planning horizon of at least forty-five years, proposing long-range objectives and setting out the specific costs for all Forest Service activities (every five years); and (3) an Annual Report evaluating Forest Service activities in comparison with the objectives proposed in the Program. In addition, the RPA requires the President to submit two documents to Congress: (1) a Statement of Policy, which is based upon the Program and which can be modified by Congress, to be used in framing future budget requests for Forest Service activities (every five years); and (2) a Statement of Reasons, an explanation accompanying any annual proposed budget which does not request funds necessary to achieve the objectives of the Statement of Policy.

This was the triumph of rational planning over political imperatives. Despite high expectations, the RPA has not fundamentally altered the Forest Service budget or budgetary politics in the White House or Congress. Budget proposals and appropriations almost immediately dropped below the amounts recommended in the 1975 Program and the resulting 1976 Statement of Policy. When President Carter's proposed 1979 budget fell well short of the funding envisioned by the Statement of Policy (intended to guide future budget requests), the National Wildlife Federation sued, taking the position that the President's Statement of Reasons did not explain the shortfall to the extent required by the RPA. In particular, the Federation objected to low budget levels for programs such as recreation and reforestation. The D.C. Court of Appeals held that the action was properly dismissed:

> Sometimes the great public importance of an issue militates in favor of its prompt resolution. At other times, however, the public interest dictates that courts exercise restraint in passing upon crucial issues. We think such restraint is necessary where, as here, appellants ask us to intervene in wrangling over the federal budget and budget procedures. Such matters are the archetype of those best resolved through bargaining and accommodation between the legislative and executive branches. We are reluctant to afford discretionary relief when to do so would intrude on the responsibilities including the shared responsibilities of the coordinate branches.

National Wildlife Federation v. United States, 626 F.2d 917 (D.C.Cir.1980). (The opinion includes a useful description of the RPA's provisions.) Other courts have since held that RPA goals are not binding on national forest planners. *See* Wind River Multiple–Use Advocates v. Espy, 835 F.Supp. 1362 (D.Wyo.1993), aff'd 85 F.3d 641 (table) (10th Cir.1996) (upholding a forest plan setting 12 million board feet ["mmbf"] as the timber harvesting objective instead of the RPA-derived goal of 46 mmbf, because, in accordance with Forest Service regulations, the incorporation of the RPA objectives in the forest plan is "anything but mandatory"). The Forest Service continues to issue periodic Assessments under the RPA, but it has stopped producing a Program, as congressional appropriations riders have blocked work on it. Instead, the Forest Service produces Strategic Plans pursuant to the Government Performance and Results Act (GPRA), 5 U.S.C. § 306.

Although Congress and the Executive have never met the financial defined in the five-year Programs, it is possible, but difficult to demonstrate, that the Act's national planning process may have caused the Forest Service to improve its long-range planning. Overall, though, the RPA may be best understood as the last gasp of the era of unfettered Forest Service discretion. The following material shows that, even before the RPA was enacted, events were moving quickly toward greater congressional and judicial involvement in the management of the national forests.

B. The Watershed: Clearcutting, the *Monongahela* Decision, and the Passage of The National Forest Management Act of 1976

A major controversy over the practice of "clearcutting" in the late 1960s and early 1970s reshaped federal timber policy and the perception of the Forest Service by Congress, the courts and the public. Clearcutting means the complete removal of timber from an area, somewhat like shaving the land. It is an economically efficient method of providing a large flow of timber from the national forests. It can also have severe impacts on wildlife, water, soils, and the beauty of forest landscapes.

After World War II, increased demand for timber brought more intensive management to the national forest system. Clearcutting was accelerated in forests where it was already an existing practice. In some forests it was employed for the first time. Heavy management expenditures associated with increased logging, especially in areas where tree densities and growth rates were limited, meant that the Forest Service's costs of administering its sales and associated roadbuilding exceeded timber revenues in some areas. Furthermore, local resentment grew, especially in areas near the Bitterroot National Forest in Montana and the Monongahela National Forest in West Virginia. Lengthy hearings before a subcommittee of the U.S. Senate in the spring of 1972 culminated in a report setting out broad rules for timber harvesting in general and clearcutting in particular.

These "Church guidelines," named after subcommittee chairman Sen. Frank Church of Idaho, amounted to something of a breakthrough: Congress was beginning to get involved in the specifics of national forest logging. But the guidelines were not legally binding,* and did not dissuade environmental interests from challenging the practice of clearcutting in court. The setting for this carefully targeted test case was the acquired national forest lands in the East, where many argued clearcutting was especially inappropriate. Clearcutting the mixed hardwood stands in many Eastern forests resulted in forest type conversion to pine stands, reducing the overall diversity of species.

West Virginia Div. of Izaak Walton League of America, Inc. v. Butz

United States Court of Appeals, Fourth Circuit, 1975.
522 F.2d 945.

■ JUDGE FIELD

Alleging that the Forest Service was entering into contracts for the sale of timber in the Monongahela National Forest of West Virginia the terms of which violated the Organic Act of 1897 (hereinafter "Organic Act"), the plaintiffs instituted this action seeking both declaratory and injunctive relief. Specifically, the plaintiffs challenged three proposed timber sales * * *. Under the sales contracts * * * 428 acres were to be harvested by clearcutting in units ranging in size from five to twenty-five acres. * * * [I]n the clearcut area all merchantable timber would be cut and none of the trees would be individually marked. The plaintiffs charged that the contracts with respect to the 428 acres violated the sales provision of the Act, 16 U.S.C. § 476, which reads in pertinent part as follows:

> "For the purpose of preserving the living and growing timber and promoting the younger growth on national forests, the Secretary of Agriculture, * * * may cause to be designated and appraised so much of the dead, matured or large growth of trees found upon such national

---

* The Church guidelines were, however, ultimately incorporated, with some modifications, into the NFMA of 1976, 16 U.S.C. §§ 1604(g)(3)(E), (F), discussed further below.

forests as may be compatible with the utilization of the forests thereon, and may sell the same. * * * Such timber, before being sold, shall be marked and designated, and shall be cut and removed under the supervision of some person appointed for that purpose by the Secretary of Agriculture * * *.''

* * * [The parties stipulated] that the three contracts in question were representative of other contracts for the sale of timber in the Monongahela National Forest and that they involved the sale and cutting of trees, some of which were neither dead, physiologically matured nor large. It was further [agreed] that the Forest Service was selling timber pursuant to procedures under which each tree was not individually marked prior to cutting, although the boundaries of cutting areas were marked. * * * [T]he district court granted the plaintiffs' motion for summary judgment. In doing so, the court declared that the practice, regulations and contracts of the Forest Service which (1) permit the cutting of trees which are not dead, mature or large growth, (2) permit the cutting of trees which have not been individually marked and (3) allow timber which has been cut to remain at the site violate the provisions of the Organic Act. The court enjoined the Forest Service from contracting for or otherwise allowing the cutting of timber in the Monongahela National Forest in violation of the Organic Act. * * *

* * *

The Service takes the position that ''large growth of trees'' signifies a sizeable stand or grouping of trees, and that the district court erroneously converted this phrase into ''large growth trees'' which in effect requires that each individual tree be identified as ''large''. We think the district court correctly construed this statutory phrase. The stated purpose of ''promoting the younger growth'' clearly refers to the characteristics of the individual trees, and in our opinion the use of the phrase ''large growth of trees'' in the latter part of the same sentence likewise refers to the individual trees, the words ''large growth'' being used in contradistinction to the prior reference to ''younger growth.'' To accept this contention that ''large growth of trees'' means a sizeable stand or group of trees would treat the words ''dead and mature'' as surplusage, and violate the ''well known maxim of statutory construction that all words and provisions of statutes are intended to have meaning and are to be given effect, and words of a statute are not to be construed as surplusage''. Wilderness Society v. Morton, [*supra* p. 235]. The interpretation urged by the defendants would lead to the absurd result that while in small areas of the forest the authority of the Secretary would be restricted, he would nevertheless be free to cut any trees he might desire from a sizeable stand or group of trees (defined by the Government as ten acres or more), regardless of whether the individual trees in such group or stand were small or large, young or old, immature or mature. In our opinion such a paradoxical result would be at odds with the purpose of the Organic Act as well as the plain language of the statute.

The Service further contends that in treating ''mature'' trees as only those which are physiologically mature, the court ignored other accepted silvicultural tests of maturity. Here again we agree with the district court that the language of the statute means physiological maturity rather than economic or management maturity. A tree is physiologically mature when because of age and condition its growth begins to taper off or it loses its health and vigor, and while age and size are indicators of physiological maturity, they are not exclusively so. From the economic viewpoint a tree is considered mature when it has the highest marketable value, and management maturity is defined as the state at which a tree or stand best fulfills the purpose for which it was maintained, e. g., produces the best supply of specified products. We think unquestionably that in using the word "mature" Congress was referring to physiological maturity. This appears to be the meaning of "mature" in forestry terminology today, and was the accepted meaning of the word at the time the Organic Act was passed by the Congress. * * * Since Congress used the word in its physiological sense at the time of the passage of the Organic Act, we know of no canon of statutory construction which would justify or require that its meaning be changed merely because during the intervening years the timber industry has developed the commercial concept of economic or management maturity. * * *

Turning to that part of Section 476 which requires that the timber "before being sold, shall be marked and designated", we find the statutory language to be simple and unambiguous. The term "marked" in the context of forestry is well defined and means "selection and indication by a blaze, paint * * * or marking hammer on the stem of trees to be felled or retained". "Designate", on the other hand, is a much broader term and merely means to "indicate". The two words are not synonymous or interchangeable and in using them conjunctively it is evident that Congress intended that the Forest Service designate the area from which the timber was to be sold and, additionally, placed upon the Service the obligation to mark each individual tree which was authorized to be cut. This plain reading of the statutory language is buttressed by reference to the statement of Gifford Pinchot, the first Chief of the Forest Service, in his 1898 Surveys of Forest Reserves:

> "In reserves where timber is sold it will be necessary to indicate unmistakably before the cutting what trees are to be cut and afterwards to ascertain that these trees, and these only, have been taken."

Typical of the instructions with respect to sales of timber in Forest Reserves shortly after passage of the Act were those issued by the Secretary of the Interior on February 27, 1902:

> If the application (to cut timber) is approved, the head ranger or supervisor (with assistance, if necessary) will mark at once all trees to be cut. This is imperative in all cases involving living timber.

> The marking of standing timber must be done with the "U.S." stamping hammer, and all trees must be marked near the ground in order that the stumps may afford positive evidence of the marking.

This emphasis placed on such selective marking by those who urged the passage of the Organic Act and were charged with the responsibility of its implementation is entitled to particular weight.

* * *

While we base our decision primarily upon a literal reading of the statute we find convincing support for our conclusion in the background and legislative history of the Organic Act. * * *

* * *

This legislative history demonstrates that the primary concern of Congress in passing the Organic Act was the preservation of the national forests. While the Act as finally passed rejected the position of the extremists who wished to forbid all cutting in the forests, it specifically limited the authority of the Secretary in his selection of timber which could be sold. He could select the timber to be cut only from those trees which were dead, physiologically mature or large, and then only when such cutting would preserve the young and growing timber which remained. Following the addition of "large growth of trees" to the bill, the sponsors repeatedly made it clear that the Act would permit the sale only of the individual trees which met its specific requirements which, in the words of Senator Pettigrew, were "the large trees, the dying trees and trees that will grow no better in time." * * *

* * *

The appellants also rely upon the subsequent legislation, together with administrative interpretations and practices of the Forest Service, which they contend support their interpretation of the Organic Act. We find it unnecessary to comment upon any of the legislation with the exception of the Multiple–Use Sustained–Yield Act of 1960. * * *

* * *

The language of the Multiple–Use Act is broad and ambiguous, and from our review of the material at hand we are satisfied that in enacting this legislation Congress did not intent to jettison or repeal the Organic Act of 1897. We are equally satisfied that this Act did not constitute a ratification of the relatively new policy of the Forest Service which applied the principles of even-aged management and clearcutting in all of the national forests.

It is apparent that the heart of this controversy is the change in the role of the Forest Service which has taken place over the past thirty years. For nearly half a century following its creation in 1905, the National Forest System provided only a fraction of the national timber supply with almost ninety-five per cent coming from privately owned forests. During this period the Forest Service regarded itself as a custodian and protector of the forests rather than a prime producer, and consistent with this role the Service faithfully carried out the provisions of the Organic Act with respect to selective timber cutting. In 1940, however, with private timber reserves badly depleted, World War II created an enormous demand for lumber and this was followed by the post-war building boom. As a result the posture of the Forest Service quickly changed from custodian to a production agency. It was in this new role that the Service initiated the policy of even-aged management in the national forests, first in the West and ultimately in the Eastern forests, including the Monongahela. The appellants urge that this change of policy was in the public interest and that the courts should not permit a literal reading of the 1897 Act to frustrate the modern science of silviculture and forest management presently practiced by the Forest Service to meet the nation's current timber demands. Economic exigencies, however, do not grant the courts a license to rewrite a statute no matter how desirable the purpose or result might be. * * *

We are not insensitive to the fact that our reading of the Organic Act will have serious and far-reaching consequences, and it may well be that this legislation enacted over seventy-five years ago is an anachronism which no longer serves the public interest. However, the appropriate forum to resolve this complex and controversial issue is not the courts but the Congress. * * *

Affirmed.

NOTES AND QUESTIONS

1. The *Monongahela* court cites Wilderness Society v. Morton (the trans-Alaska pipeline case) for the principle that the judiciary cannot rewrite old statutes that have become anachronistic with respect to current technology. But *Wilderness Society* involved a statute that specified a particular number of feet as the maximum for a right-of-way. Does the 1897 Organic Act provide greater room for reasonable interpretation? Was the long-standing, professionally accepted interpretation of the term "large growth," for instance, really beyond the pale? If this case had come after the 1984 *Chevron* precedent, would *Monongahela* have come out differently? Why didn't the court cite Union Oil Co. v. Smith (interpreting the General Mining Law to allow location before discovery), *supra* p. 567? Is *Union Oil* more similar than *Wilderness Society* to the *Monongahela* problem? When should courts engage in flexible interpretations to save the viability of old statutes? How actively should courts attempt to fulfill the aims of old statutes? See generally Guido Calabresi, A COMMON LAW FOR THE AGE OF STATUTES (1982).

2. Among the most vehement opponents of the *Monongahela* decision was the forestry profession, which continues to guard the independence of its judgment from judicial meddling. Immediately following the *Monongahela* decision, the Society of American Foresters invoked the emergency procedures of its bylaws and passed the following position:

The Concern of the Forestry Profession

Forestry professionals have been severely limited in the application of scientific forestry practice by the Fourth Circuit Court of Appeals' interpretation of the Organic Act of 1897, which provides for the administration of the national forests. This interpretation makes impossible the full attainment of the provision of the Multiple Use-Sustained Yield Act that there be a "high-level annual or regular periodic output of the various renewable resources of the national forests...." Because of the complexity and diversity of the nation's forests, the Society of American Foresters, which represents the profession of forestry in the United States as it has since 1900, finds the implications of this decision unduly restrictive. The decision will impede the Society of American Foresters in attaining its objectives: to advance the science, technology, practice and education of professional forestry in America and to use the profession's knowledge and skills to benefit society.

The Scientific Base for Forest Resources Management

The Court's restrictive interpretation of the 1897 Act prohibits full application of the large body of special knowledge about the forests of this country, practically all of which was developed since the Act was written. The established principles and practices in forest resources management are the result of more than sixty years of organized research in this country and centuries of forest management experience in Europe and Asia. * * *

* * *

Remedial Action

The Society of American Foresters agrees with the statement by the Fourth Circuit Court of Appeals that its interpretation of the Act "will have serious and far-reaching consequences...." The Society also agrees with the Court that "the appropriate forum to, resolve this complex and controversial issue is not the courts but the Congress." Accordingly, the Society recommends that remedial legislation be enacted immediately to resolve the problems resulting from this latest interpretation of the Act.

In preparing remedial legislation, the Society of American Foresters cautions that forest management prescriptions cannot be written inflexibly into law without adversely affecting many forest environments and resources. Furthermore, rigid forest management prescriptions will prevent or delay implementation of the results of research. Finally, excessive legal restrictions will hamper forestry professionals in attaining the high-level sustained yields of the various renewable resources from the national forests which are required by the public and already mandated by the Congress.

Impact of the Monongahela Decision of August 21, 1975: Position of the Society of American Foresters, 73 JOURNAL OF FORESTRY 758 (1975).

Are foresters and other resource managers always better served by more discretion? Sometimes, political "cover" can be helpful for a manager who wants to say "no" to an activity endorsed by local congressional representatives, or economically powerful interests. Is it always enough to rely on professional judgment?

3.   Almost immediately a district judge in Alaska followed the Fourth Circuit decision. Zieske v. Butz, 406 F.Supp. 258 (D.Alaska 1975) (enjoining clearcutting by Ketchikan Pulp Company under a Forest Service contract), and several other cases sought to apply it to other forests. Seeing the handwriting on the wall, the Forest Service, forestry profession, and forest products industry turned to Congress for a repeal of the offending provision in the 1897 Organic Act. Environmentalists used the clearcutting issue as a lever to open a broad-ranging congressional debate on all forest management practices. Legislation introduced by Senator Jennings Randolph of West Virginia, chair of one of the key committees of jurisdiction, would have severely restricted Forest Service timber operations, while other bills supported by industry would have done little more than remove the strictures of the 1897 Act. The legislation that finally emerged from Congress fourteen months after the Fourth Circuit decision was, like all major legislation, a compromise, but it was one so comprehensive as to amount to a new organic act for the Forest Service. The definitive description comes from the seminal article by Charles F. Wilkinson and H. Michael Anderson, *Land and Resource Planning in the National Forests*, 64 Or. L.Rev. 1, 10–12 (1985):

> By 1976 the mood of Congress had shifted dramatically in the wake of the clearcutting controversy. Upon introducing his bill, [Minnesota Senator Hubert] Humphrey observed that the MUSY Act had not succeeded and that a "fundamental reform" was needed. Humphrey stated: "We have had 15 years since the 1960 Multiple Use and Sustained Yield Act was passed. Much has happened, and as we look at what has transpired, the need for improvement is evident." He identified the central problem as the predominance of timber production over protection of other resources. Humphrey declared: "The days have ended when the forest may be viewed only as trees and trees viewed only as timber. The soil and the water, the grasses and the shrubs, the fish and the wildlife, and the beauty that is the forest must become integral parts of resource managers' thinking and actions." During the Senate hearings Humphrey observed that the Forest Service's record had brought into question the extent to which the agency could be trusted to guard and manage public resources. He proposed that the NFMA legislation be shaped to prevent the Forest Service from "turning the national forests into tree production programs which override other values." Senator Randolph and other members of Congress shared Humphrey's views.

NOTE: THE ROLE OF THE NATIONAL FORESTS IN AMERICAN FOREST POLICY

The National Forest Management Act of 1976 repealed the 1897 provisions at issue in the Fourth Circuit *Izaak Walton* case, and is laced with qualifying language, but it addressed on-the-ground forestry issues with a specificity unthinkable in earlier times. Before we turn to the details of that statute, it is useful to set out some general background on the place of the national forests in American forest policy.

TIMBER AREA AND VOLUME STATISTICS BY OWNERSHIP CLASSES

In billion cubic feet

Ownership classes	Commercial area held million acres	Total softwood growing stock volume			Total hardwood growing stock volume		
		Inventory (volume)	Growth	Removals	Inventory (volume)	Growth	Removals
National Forests	97	228	3.3	0.3	32	0.6	0.1
Other Public	51	52	1.2	0.6	39	.9	0.4
Forest Industry	66	66	3.5	3.7	33	.9	.9
Other Private	291	146	5.7	5.6	260	7.5	4.4
National Total	504	492	13.7	10.1	364	10.0	5.8

Note: Data may not add to totals because of rounding.

Source: Department of Agriculture, Forest Service, W. Brad Smith, Patrick D. Miles, John S. Vissage, and Scott A. Pugh, Forest Resources of the United States, Tables 11, 18, 23, 34, and 35 (2005).

———————

Commercial forest land traditionally has been defined as land capable of producing at least 20 cubic feet of timber per acre per year. The "other public" lands category in the table includes state, county, and municipal lands, and about eight million acres of BLM lands.

1. *Timber Inventory and Timber Types.* As the left column on the table shows, national forests account for about 19% of the Nation's commercial timber land, but that figure is misleading because it does not measure the amount of inventory, or volume of wood, on those acres. Although the inventory of hardwood timber on national forest lands is not a significant part of the nation's total standing hardwood timber, the Forest Service presides over almost half of the Nation's inventory of softwood timber. Softwood timber, which is in greater demand than hardwood, is the primary source of construction lumber and is thus essential to the housing industry.

2. *Old Growth Forests.* As the two columns on the left show, the forest industry owns 66 billion cubic feet of softwood timber on 66 million acres, or about 1000 cubic feet per acre. But, on national forest lands, the softwood inventory per acre is well over twice that found on private industry lands: the inventory of 228 billion cubic feet of timber on 97 million acres averages out to 2,351 cubic feet per acre. The disparity is even greater for "other private" lands (miscellaneous private holdings of 20 acres or more), which hold an average of only 502 cubic feet per acre.

These disparities exist largely because most private lands have been cut over and no large old-growth trees remain. Some private lands have been harvested by "cut and run" or "highgrading" practices, in which the best timber was cleared and no reforesting undertaken. In contrast, many of the federal lands have never been cut at all, leaving massive stands of old-growth timber intact. These valuable stands, especially in the national forests of the Pacific Northwest, include magnificent virgin fir, redwood, cedar, and pine forests. These trees are straight, large, and provide the highest quality lumber. Harvesting them is said by some to be the solution for meeting the Nation's growing demand for timber. Others argue that such stands are unique ecological resources that cannot be replaced for generations, if ever, and should be preserved.

3. *Intensive Management.* The second and third columns from the left on the table show that the annual growth rate for softwood industry lands is about 5.3% (amounting to 3.5 billion cubic feet from an inventory of 66 billion cubic feet) while the growth rate for national forest lands is about 1.5% (3.3 billion cubic feet on an inventory of 228 billion cubic feet). Industry lands produce more growth because more intensive management practices are employed. High yield management is based on growing "thrifty, young trees," starting with the prompt planting of seedlings, sometimes genetically improved. Years later, precommercial and commercial thinning removes some trees to provide more light and soil to those remaining; fertilizers and other enhancement methods are also commonly employed. A short "rotation" period (the time over which an area of forest is harvested) is used so that the intensive management cycle can be repeated. (When Weyerhauser Company correctly called itself "The Tree Growing Company," a Sierra Club representative replied "Yes. They grow small trees.")

The federal old-growth forests have low growth rates because they have attained an age when annual growth tapers off. Indeed, some old growth forests actually have a negative growth rate: the slow growth of the live trees does not equal the annual mortality rate of wood fiber through rot and disease. Environmental aesthetics and silviculture collide over whether and at what rate these ancient stands should be liquidated:

> * * * [T]he legal profession has a similar kind of responsibility in its own canons of ethics as the members of the medical and forestry professions have with respect to the public health. This responsibility includes ensuring not only that laws are not permitted that allow forests to be wasted, but that the forests be adequately protected so that man may always enjoy all their qualities. One must question the views of many lawyers who believe that more old growth forests should be put into withdrawals or reserves by laws attempting to preserve them forever in their untouched state. Such a goal is patently ridiculous and indicates that law schools need to teach prospective members of the legal profession a few facts of life about the ecology of plants. All trees have a date certain with death, just like every person. Trees were placed here by higher laws than man's for serving the human race, and they must continue to do so through protection, management and renewal, the principal purposes of the forestry profession.
>
> When there are homeless people in the world, there is no more of a right to waste wood than there is a right to waste food when there are hungry people. Whether people like it or not, the old forest must make way for the new.

Perry Hagenstein, *The Old Forest Maketh Way for the New*, 8 ENVTL. L. 479, 494–95 (1978). For an argument that old growth is necessary for the stability of forest ecosystems as a whole, *see* Glenn Patrick Juday, *Old*

Growth Forests: A Necessary Element of Multiple Use and Sustained Yield National Forest Management, 8 ENVTL. L. 497 (1978).

4. *Rate of Removal.* Although old-growth removal is itself a subject of controversy, some critics in the timber industry believe that Forest Service harvesting schedules are too conservative on all lands. The rate at which the softwood inventory is removed annually can be obtained by dividing the fourth column on the table by the second column. The rate of removal on Forest Service lands (just over one-tenth of one percent) is much less than that on industry lands (5.6%) for a variety of reasons. (Even before the recent drop in the national forest timber cut, the industry's rate of removal was many times higher than the Forest Service's.) One factor is the Forest Service's use of a long rotation period; for example, the rotation period for Douglas fir is 100 years in many national forests compared with periods of 60, 50 or even 40 years on intensively managed private Douglas fir forests. In addition, Forest Service long-range projections sometimes build in conservative assumptions; for example, computer analyses may assume less than maximum returns from practices such as thinning and genetic improvement. Since the present harvest cannot exceed future growth potential, these conservative projections tend to keep annual removal lower than it otherwise might have been.

5. *"Other Private" Forests.* The table also indicates that almost 60% of commercial forest land is located in non-industry private holdings. Most studies conclude that improving management practices on those lands is one way to help meet market demands and lessen the pressure on federal lands in the future. Coordinating silvicultural practices on these small, widely-dispersed holdings is, however, no easy matter.

6. *Timber–Dependent Communities.* About one-fifth of federal commercial timberlands are located in the Great Lakes Area, New England, and the South. In those areas, as well as in many regions in the west, the economies of numerous small communities are partially or heavily dependent on jobs created by timber harvesting on federal lands. Accelerated cutting of old growth can result in a drastic decline in harvest when the last old growth is cut, severely harming local economies, because timber harvesting must cease or decrease when the large stands are gone. This has led to the Forest Service's policy of non-declining even flow, a conservative version of sustained yield management that requires a relatively level annual cut to avoid the "boom and bust" cycle that would occur if old-growth timber is harvested on an accelerated basis. The excerpt in Chapter 1 from the Sonoran Institute's report, "Prosperity in the 21st Century West: The Role of Protected Lands," points out that very few western counties are now economically dependent on traditional resource extraction industries like mining and logging.

7. *Timber Management Practices.* How to harvest is as divisive an issue as whether to harvest. Modern forestry tries to see that streams are protected from fallen timber; that yarding (physically removing the cut timber from the logging site) is carried on with minimum erosion or damage to the remaining stand; that slash (residue such as limbs and stumps) is properly disposed; and that restocking occurs promptly and

efficiently. Many argue that such practices do not go far enough; clearcutting in particular continues to stir ire. Another delicate issue is road building, which can cause as much or more erosion damage as timber harvesting.

C. THE NATIONAL FOREST MANAGEMENT ACT

The logging controversy that led to the NFMA spurred Congress to focus its attention on creating substantive standards for timber harvesting on the national forests. Much of the litigation and regulation spurred by this organic act focuses on the Service's timber program. Therefore, this section begins with an examination of the NFMA provisions relating to harvesting, water and soil conditions, biological diversity, and several other substantive criteria.

The first step toward fully implementing NFMA was for the Forest Service to prepare detailed regulations. The statute created a Committee of Scientists to play a significant role in that process, and final regulations were promulgated in 1979. During much of the 1980s, the Forest Service was engaged in preparing the first generation of forest plans for most of the National Forest System. These plans involved extensive public participation, and many of them were subject to appeals on various issues by various interests up through the agency's administrative appeals system. A number of these plans were challenged in federal court, usually (but not always) by environmental protection advocates. These challenges typically alleged violations of the NFMA, NFMA regulations, NEPA, the Administrative Procedure Act, and the Endangered Species Act.

The Supreme Court, in Ohio Forestry Ass'n v. Sierra Club, 523 U.S. 726 (1998), *supra* p. 216, put a stop to most but not all "pre-implementation" challenges to Forest Service land use plans by ruling them unripe for review. Now challenges to Forest Service policies and actions have to be made, not by addressing the forest-wide plans directly, but by seeking judicial review of specific projects, such as timber sales. Some of the pre-*Ohio Forestry* cases discussed in this section might well have been dismissed on ripeness grounds if they had been brought after 1998. Although their value as precedent is thereby somewhat weakened, they still contain valuable indicia of judicial attitudes toward forest planning.

The Forest Service regulations have played a key role in agency timber practices and judicial review. The original 1979 regulations—the highlight of which was the emphasis on the protection of biodiversity—remained in place with minor changes (especially in 1982) until the late 1990s, when the Forest Service undertook a major overhaul of its planning process to make ecological sustainability the first priority. The agency promulgated new rules in 2000. The Bush Administration promptly delayed implementation of those rules pending further study and then adopted new rules in 2005. The 2005 rules lack the kind of specific requirements found in the 1979 and 2000 regulations and will provide few opportunities for judicial review. We will compare these versions of the rules in part 4, below.

We conclude this subchapter with a look at two of the most contentious current controversies vexing national forest management under the NFMA: controlling wildfire and protecting roadless areas.

1. Timber Harvesting Methods and Physical Suitability

In broad terms, timber harvests for a national forest are calculated in this manner. First, planners determine what land is suitable for timber management. They must exclude, for example: (a) land allocated to other uses (such as wilderness); (b) noncommercial timberland (traditionally defined as land growing less than twenty cubic feet of wood per acre annually) and (c) land not suitable for harvesting due to inaccessibility or to fragile slope or soil conditions. The land left available for harvest after such exclusions is the suitable land base, or inventory.

Second, the Forest Service must calculate the amount of timber that may be harvested from the inventory. This is the "allowable cut," usually expressed as an annual volume harvesting target. The two primary factors used to calculate the allowable cut are (a) the volume of timber available in the inventory, and (b) the rotation period, i.e., the time over which a stand will be harvested before a second harvesting schedule can begin. If, for example, estimated volume is 500 mmbf and a conservative rotation period of 100 years is used, the annual allowable cut will be 5 mmbf. The volume and rotation period calculations both depend in part upon the estimated rate of growth in the future. If optimistic projections for stand management (e.g., thinning, fertilization, reforestation, and use of genetically superior stocks) are used, the volume will be higher, and so will be the resulting harvest level. Thus, if substantial stand improvement measures are assumed, this might lead to a timber volume estimate of 750 mmbf, which means that the annual cut can be set at 7.5 mmbf, still using the same rotation period of 100 years. In the same way, if a broader definition of suitability is used, more timber may be included in the inventory, which will make the volume higher, and the annual allowable cut higher. Shortening the rotation period has the same effect; that is, the allowable cut increases.

After the allowable cut is set, planners must determine harvesting methods (clearcutting or selective cutting; timber removal by tractor, cable, balloon, or helicopter) and the process for regenerating the stand.

It should not be surprising that the calculation of the allowable cut is an issue often contested in the planning process. The allowable cut has historically tended to be a central premise for managing national forests, and the central organizing principle for many Forest Service field offices. Acre for acre, commercial timber is the most valuable commodity resource in the National Forest System. Even as emphasis on the wildlife, recreation, and preservation resources was growing, the operative slogan of many forest rangers was still GOTAC ("get out the allowable cut"). This attitude has been changing considerably, from within and without the agency, as the materials that follow reflect.

Very few lawsuits have involved direct challenges to allowable cut determinations. These matters are inordinately complex due to the quantity of data, the imprecision of projections of future timber growth, the necessity for numerous professional judgments on economic and silvicultural issues, and the intricacies of computer programs. Lawyers must develop legal arguments and marshal the evidence, but the work of foresters and economists is more likely to determine the outcome of litigation. NFMA planning does not displace NEPA; the NFMA requires forest plans to be prepared "in accordance with" NEPA, 16 U.S.C. § 1604(g)(1); and the Forest Service generally has used a single process to meet planning and NEPA requirements, although recently the Bush Administration has reformed the planning process so as to sever NEPA from it. An overview of planning on the national forests, as well as on other federal lands, was set out in Chapter 5E.

Clearcutting, which triggered the *Monongahela* litigation that led to the National Forest Management Act, is one of three variants of what silviculturalists call "even-aged management." As applied to old growth forests, clearcutting—where all or substantially all trees are harvested from a given area—aims at producing a new forest in which all of the trees in a given area will be of roughly the same age. The other two variants are the "seed tree" method and "shelterwood" or "shade tree" cutting, which leave some trees per acre, usually for regenerations or to provide some filtered sunlight for the young trees. Seed tree and shelterwood cutting both eventually result in an even-aged forest because the veteran trees originally left standing are usually removed in an early second harvest. Selective cutting, the other means of timber harvesting in which trees are removed individually or in small groups, differs from even-aged management in that it produces a diversified forest. Both even-aged management and selective harvesting are discussed further in Sierra Club v. Espy, which follows.

Clearcutting often has economic advantages over selection harvesting. Yarding costs are lower; road engineering and construction costs are diminished because logging roads need not be maintained for future use; and administrative costs of preparing sales are lower. Clearcutting also has some environmental advantages. Even-aged management can be conducted with a less extensive road system, thus causing less soil erosion. Further, large trees are subject to windthrow, or blowdown; selection cutting lessens protection and leaves the remaining trees vulnerable to wind damage. In addition, some animals such as deer, black bear, and ruffed grouse thrive on the sunlight and browse created by clearcuts. In some cases, clearcutting may prevent the spread of insects or disease.

Moreover, some tree species in some climates cannot regenerate under a selection regime. The economically valuable Douglas fir, for example, is "shade-intolerant": it cannot grow without direct sunlight. There are few young Douglas firs in old-growth forests. Without clearcutting, no new Douglas fir forest will replace the old and another species such as hemlock will become dominant. Such forests may have depended upon cycles of fire to be reestablished under natural conditions.

Clearcutting also has prominent environmental disadvantages, some which remain long after the harvest. Beauty is subjective, but most agree that a clearcut area is an insult to the eye, an ugly practice that no amount of blending with the natural terrain can much change. The difference between a second-growth managed forest and a varied, virgin stand is, according to some, the difference between a tree farm and a cathedral. Even-age management has serious impacts on wildlife and soil conditions. Species of birds, insects, bats, and small animals live in the old trees. Some forms of nitrogen-fixing bacteria, which provide essential nutrients for the soil, live only in dead or down timber. Ultimately, the productivity of the soil in old growth forests depends on the generations of trees that have rotted back into the earth. No forester can be certain of the long-range result if the process stops: it may take hundreds of years to learn the answer.

Clearcutting also has serious effects on water resources. The erosion can turn a pure mountain stream chocolate at the time of the cut and lesser erosion can continue in later years. Water temperature and runoff are affected: with no cover, snow will melt earlier in the season, increasing the spring flow and leaving unnaturally low and warm water in the summer and fall. Buffer zones and conservative clearcutting schedules can alleviate, though not eliminate, some of these conditions.

The drafters of the NFMA rejected a proposal to limit all clearcuts on national forest lands to 25 acres. Instead, 16 U.S.C. § 1604(g)(3)(F) provides that the regulations adopted by the Forest Service shall:

insure that [even-aged management shall be used] only where—

(i) for clearcutting, it is determined to be the optimum method, and for other such cuts it is determined to be appropriate, to meet the objectives and requirements of the relevant land management plan;

(ii) the interdisciplinary review as determined by the Secretary has been completed and the potential environmental, biological, esthetic, engineering, and economic impacts on each advertised sale area have been assessed, as well as the consistency of the sale with the multiple use of the general area;

(iii) cut blocks, patches, or strips are shaped and blended to the extent practicable with the natural terrain;

(iv) there are established according to geographic areas, forest types, or other suitable classifications the maximum size limits for areas to be cut in one harvest operation, including provision to exceed the established limits after appropriate public notice and review by the responsible Forest Service officer one level above the Forest Service officer who normally would approve the harvest proposal: *Provided,* That such limits shall not apply to the size of areas harvested as a result of natural catastrophic conditions such as fire, insect and disease attack, or windstorm; and

(v) such cuts are carried out in a manner consistent with the protection of soil, watershed, fish, wildlife, recreation, and esthetic resources, and the regeneration of the timber resource.

In addition to the special attention given to clearcutting, the NFMA sets requirements for all timber harvesting, clearcutting included, with an emphasis on impacts to watersheds. Land that does not meet these "physical suitability" standards must be classified as unsuitable and excluded from the inventory. The provisions for physical suitability, 16 U.S.C. § 1604(g)(3)(E), which extend to logging road construction, a major cause of erosion, require that the regulations and the forest plans shall:

> insure that timber will be harvested from National Forest System lands only where—
>
> (i) soil, slope, or other watershed conditions will not be irreversibly damaged;
>
> (ii) there is assurance that such lands can be adequately restocked within five years after harvest; [and]
>
> (iii) protection is provided for streams, streambanks, shorelines, lakes, wetlands, and other bodies of water from detrimental changes in water temperatures, blockages of water courses, and deposits of sediment, where harvests are likely to seriously and adversely affect water conditions or fish habitat * * *

The following opinion construes these NFMA provisions. Controversy over logging in the four east Texas national forests led to an epic battle that bounced around the federal courts for over a decade. Like many of the eastern national forests, the federal land ownership is highly fragmented. These piney woods harbor some of the last good habitat for the endangered red-cockaded woodpecker. Conversion of mature pine forests in the southeast to short-rotation period plantations has eliminated most of the habitat for this rare bird.

Sierra Club v. Espy

United States Court of Appeals, Fifth Circuit, 1994.
38 F.3d 792.

■ JUDGE HIGGINBOTHAM

The district court issued a preliminary injunction barring the Forest Service from conducting even-aged management in any of the four Texas national forests. The injunction was based on the district court's finding of probable success on plaintiffs' claims under two statutes: the National Forest Management Act, and the National Environmental Policy Act. The government and the timber industry intervenors bring this interlocutory appeal challenging the district court's order.

We disagree with the district court's insistence that NFMA restricts even-aged management to exceptional circumstances. We are persuaded that the district court erected too high a barrier to even-aged management. The standard that even-aged management may be used only in exceptional circumstances goes to the heart of the finding by the district court of a likelihood of success on the merits and upsets the delicate balance struck by Congress between friends and foes of this harvesting method. We must vacate the preliminary injunction and remand.

* * *

The government challenges the district court's interpretation of NFMA. Specifically, the government argues that the district court erred when it held that even-aged logging practices could only be used in exceptional circumstances. To hold otherwise, the district court reasoned, would violate the statutory provision that requires the Forest Service to use even-aged management only where "such cuts are carried out in a manner consistent with the *protection* of soil, watershed, fish, wildlife, recreation, and esthetic resources, and the regeneration of the timber resource." 16 U.S.C. § 1604(g)(3)(F)(v) (emphasis added). This duty to protect, the court held, "reflects the truism that the monoculture created by clearcutting and resultant even-aged management techniques is contrary to NFMA-mandated bio-diversity."

The district court's holding that NFMA requires even-aged management be used only in exceptional circumstances is in tension with Texas Comm. on Natural Resources v. Bergland, 573 F.2d 201 (5th Cir. 1978) (*TCONR I*). There we found that Congress, after hearing testimony on both sides of the clearcutting issue, struck a delicate balance between the benefits of clearcutting and the benefits of preserving the ecosystems and scenic quality of natural forests. Specifically, NFMA "was an effort to place the initial technical, management responsibility for the application of NFMA guidelines on the responsible government agency, in this case the Forest Service. The NFMA is a set of outer boundaries within which the Forest Service must work." We then cautioned the Forest Service that clearcutting could not be justified merely on the basis that it provided the greatest dollar return per unit output; "[r]ather[,] clearcutting must be used only where it is essential to accomplish the relevant forest management objectives." We concluded by noting that "[a] decision to pursue even-aged management as the over-all management plan under the NFMA is subject to the narrow arbitrary and capricious standard of review."

TCONR I recognized that the Forest Service may use even-aged management as an overall management strategy. That even-aged management must be the optimum or appropriate method to accomplish the objectives and requirements set forth in an LRMP does not mean that even-aged management is the exception to a rule that purportedly favors selection management. Similarly, the requirement that even-aged logging protect forest resources does not in itself limit its use. Rather, these provisions mean that the Forest Service must proceed cautiously in implementing an even-aged management alternative and only after a close examination of the effects that such management will have on other forest resources.

The conclusion that even-aged management is not the "exception" to the "rule" of uneven-aged management is supported by NFMA's legislative history. On three separate occasions, Congress rejected amendments [by Senator Jennings Randolph of West Virginia] that would have made

uneven-aged management the preferred forest management technique.
* * *

TCONR [used by the court to denote the plaintiffs Texas Committee on Natural Resources, Sierra Club, and The Wilderness Society collectively] points out that since the Randolph amendments would have required the use of uneven-aged management, they are not relevant on the issue of whether uneven-aged management is preferred. While TCONR correctly distinguishes the district court's holding from Senator Randolph's attempts to bar even-aged management, TCONR fails to persuade on the issue of whether rejection of congressional efforts to restrict even-aged logging sends a legislative message. That no amendment was specifically offered and rejected that proposed a preference for uneven-aged logging does not change the fact that legislators were loath to deprive the Forest Service of the option to select even-aged management. The final outcome of NFMA reflects those concerns.

* * *

The directive that national forests are subject to multiple uses, including timber uses, suggests that the mix of forest resources will change according to a given use. Maintenance of a pristine environment where no species' numbers are threatened runs counter to the notion that NFMA contemplates both even-and uneven-aged timber management. Indeed, NFMA regulations anticipate the possibility of change and provide that "[r]eductions in diversity of plant and animal communities and tree species from that which would be expected in a natural forest, or from that similar to the existing diversity in the planning area, may be prescribed only where needed to meet overall multiple-use objectives." 36 C.F.R. § 219.27(g); *see also* 16 U.S.C. § 1604(g)(3)(C) (LRMP must ensure research and evaluation of effects of each management system to assure no "*substantial and permanent* impairment" of land productivity) (emphasis added); 16 U.S.C. § 1604(g)(3)(E)(i) (LRMP must provide that timber be harvested only where "soil, slope, or other watershed conditions will not be *irreversibly* damaged") (emphasis added). That protection means something less than preservation of the status quo but something more than eradication of species suggests that this is just the type of policy-oriented decision Congress wisely left to the discretion of the experts—here, the Forest Service.

The Forest Service's discretion, however, is not unbridled. The regulations implementing NFMA provide a minimum level of protection by mandating that the Forest Service manage fish and wildlife habitats to insure viable populations of species in planning areas. 36 C.F.R. § 219.19. In addition, the statute requires the Forest Service to "provide for diversity of plant and animal communities." 16 U.S.C. § 1604(g)(3)(B). This diversity mandate itself has been the subject of considerable debate. The regulations define diversity as "[t]he distribution and abundance of different plant and animal communities and species within the area covered by a land and resource management plan." 36 C.F.R. § 219.3. At least one court has recognized the difficulty in requiring a precise level of diversity: "The agency's judgment in assessing issues requiring a high level of technical expertise, such as diversity, must . . . be accorded the considerable respect that matters within the agency's expertise deserve.''

We need not take this opportunity to define precisely the "outer boundaries" of NFMA's protection and diversity requirements, because we find that the timber sale EAs fall clearly within such boundaries. Each EA considered no action, even-aged management, and uneven-aged management alternatives. Although it is true that when all nine sales are taken together even-aged management emerges as the preferred alternative,[3] each sale varies as to the extent of its usage. For instance, in Compartment 32, forty-six percent of the acres scheduled to be harvested will be harvested using selection management. The remaining acres will be harvested by seed tree cutting. In Compartment 98, twenty-three percent of the acres scheduled to be harvested will be harvested using selection cutting. The remaining acres will be harvested using the seed tree method. Finally, in Compartment 57, the Forest Service chose to harvest sixty acres of timber using group selection, an uneven-aged management method. Even this limited interspersing of even-and uneven-aged management helps assure a mix of early and late successional habitats.

Moreover, the EAs do not ignore old growth ecosystems. The Compartment 32 EA, for example, discusses the old growth component of the forest. Compartment 32 contains 964 acres of federal land and approximately 2,000 acres of privately owned land. The EA notes that no stands in the compartment were selected for old growth designation because of the fragmented ownership of the compartment. This determination cannot be said to be arbitrary or capricious.

* * *

3.   The following chart details, by compartment, the number of acres to be cut and the timber method employed.

Compartment	Even-aged Management		Uneven-aged Management
	Seed Tree	Clearcut	
32	120		101
51	222		
57			60
66	165		
79	193		
93	275	27	
98	143		43
110	93	14	
113	70		

Given these goals, the Forest Service's selection of an even-aged management alternative in Compartment 93 cannot be said to be arbitrary or capricious. Under the selected alternative, the numbers of fox squirrel and pileated woodpecker decrease. However, other species would increase; namely, white-tailed deer, eastern wild turkey, red-cockaded woodpecker, yellow-breasted chat, eastern bluebird, bobwhite quail, and the six-lined racerunner. Under the selection management alternative, only the pileated woodpecker would increase in numbers. All other listed MIS would decrease, though all existing species would be maintained at viable population levels. The Forest Service is charged with managing the ever-changing resources of the national forests. In the absence of forest management, trees would grow older, the character of plant and animal diversity would change, and some wildlife species would decline in numbers. Harvesting trees using even-aged management techniques necessarily results in younger stands. Wildlife dependent on younger stands would flourish at the expense of species dependent on older growth forests. Harvesting trees using uneven-aged management techniques results in denser forests. Wildlife dependent on such cover would flourish at the expense of wildlife dependent on forest clearings. These forest dynamics make clear that protecting forest resources involves making trade-offs. We may believe that protection afforded by selection management is more desirable than that afforded by even-aged management; however, in the nine sales before the court, the agency's determination as to the appropriate level of protection was not unreasonable. We therefore defer to the agency's determination.

[The court also ruled that the agency had complied with NEPA].

NOTES AND QUESTIONS

1.   Is the court correct in interpreting the NFMA as a kind of "dispute resolution" document? Can that be a surrogate for a balancing approach that leads to broad agency discretion that courts will almost always affirm? Does the legislative history support that? Do terms like "optimum" and "protection" establish firm standards or are they softened by the statutory context and legislative history? The court found that "these provisions mean that the Forest Service must proceed cautiously in implementing an even-aged management alternative" and give "close examination" of the effects on other forest resources. Did the court require that here? Does the opinion strike the same, or more, or less deferential stance to expert judgment as compared to *Monongahela*? Is it possible to apply a single approach to harvesting to all national forests, from western Washington to east Texas to Ohio?

2.   In footnote 3, the court shows the different methods of harvesting by acre. Does this show an excessive commitment to even-aged management or clearcutting? Note that the statute requires that clearcutting be the "optimum" method and that other forms of even-aged management (including seed tree logging) be "appropriate"? Did the Forest Service meet those standards? Suppose that the amount of acres dedicated to clearcutting and seed tree cutting were reversed. Would that suggest enough of an

imbalance that the court should remand for further explanation? Chattooga River Watershed Coal. v. United States Forest Service, 93 F.Supp.2d 1246, 1249 (N.D. Ga. 2000), took roughly the same approach as Sierra Club v. Espy. Sierra Club v. Thomas, 105 F.3d 248, 250–51 (6th Cir. 1997), *rev'd on other grounds sub nom.* Ohio Forestry Assn. v. Sierra Club, *supra* p. 216, described institutional pressures driving the Forest Service toward intensive harvesting and found that "the planning process was improperly predisposed toward clearcutting. The resulting plan is arbitrary and capricious because it is based upon this artificial narrowing of options."

3. Since the adoption of the NFMA, the Forest Service has overhauled its clearcutting program. Many fewer clearcuts are used and, when they are, they are smaller and designed to eliminate the traditional square-cornered look in order to appear more natural (though even the most committed "timber beast" is likely to concede that a clearcut designed to look like a fire or a rock slide still looks mostly like a clearcut).

4. On the physical suitability provisions, did the record support the court's findings on the statutory terms "irreversibly damaged" and "substantial and permanent impairment"? Do those provisions have any teeth? Are the data on the different impacts on various species of wildlife persuasive?

5. After the circuit court remanded this litigation back to the district court, an unusual (for public land law) trial ensued. A new district court judge found that the east Texas logging program failed to meet a number of NFMA's substantive criteria, including the physical suitability provisions. Sierra Club v. Glickman, 974 F. Supp. 905 (E.D. Tex. 1997). Based on these findings from trial, the circuit court then affirmed the sweeping lower court injunction against the logging. It upheld the ruling that the NFMA physical suitability provisions were substantive and that the agency-sponsored logging practices were causing substantial and permanent soil damage. Sierra Club v. Peterson, 185 F.3d 349 (5th Cir.1999). Later, in en banc review, the court vacated the decision on the ground that no final agency action existed. Though the plaintiffs did identify specific timber sales, they ultimately failed to convince the court to review a *program* of even-aged management in the Texas forests. Sierra Club v. Peterson, 228 F.3d 559 (5th Cir.2000). Judge Higginbotham, who wrote the 1994 decision excerpted above, concurred.

6. What does the physical suitability "assurance" that the lands "can be adequately restocked within five years" mean? The Knutson–Vandenberg Act of 1930, 16 U.S.C. §§ 576(a)-(c), authorizes the Forest Service to require deposits from timber operators to cover reforestation costs. That program has been less than entirely successful: there has long been a backlog of millions of national forest acres that have not been restocked. Although the NFMA authorized an expenditure of $200 million per year to eliminate the backlog, in subsequent years Congress has not appropriated sufficient funds to do this. If Congress fails to make funds available for this purpose, could a court use the physical suitability section to enjoin further timber sales until the backlog has been eliminated? The decision in Big Hole Ranchers Ass'n v. United States Forest Service, 686 F.Supp. 256

(D.Mont.1988), gave the agency broad discretion, finding that the issue was not whether restocking "would" occur within five years but rather whether it "could" occur. Ayers v. Espy, 873 F.Supp. 455 (D.Colo.1994), found that a Forest Service harvesting program violated the five-year restocking requirement.

2.   THE DIVERSITY MANDATE

This is one of the most hotly contested provisions of the NFMA. To some extent its thrust is similar to, and overlaps with, the objectives of the Endangered Species Act. Section 1604(g)(3)(B) requires that Forest Service land management plans shall

> provide for diversity of plant and animal communities based on the suitability and capability of the specific land area in order to meet overall multiple-use objectives, and within the multiple-use objectives of a land management plan adopted pursuant to this section, provide, where appropriate, to the degree practicable, for steps to be taken to preserve the diversity of tree species similar to that existing in the region controlled by the plan. * * *

To preserve diversity of species, the Forest Service promulgated regulations that designated "indicator species" to serve as proxies for large numbers of species; in other words, rather than inventorying all species—which would be impossible—planners attempted to assure suitable habitat for the indicator species. Many of the early skirmishes took place in the Pacific Northwest. Especially controversial was the designation of the northern spotted owl, which uses old-growth Douglas fir as a preferred habitat, as an indicator species in the Pacific Northwest. The timber industry argued that proposed forest plans may remove too much valuable timber land from the inventories in order to protect the spotted owl; environmentalists believed that more land should be set aside. This led to much litigation, proposals for legislative "fixes," and public controversy. Although the dispute became enmeshed in the Endangered Species Act once the owl was listed as endangered, a good deal of the litigation actually centered on the "diversity" requirement of the NFMA. The northern spotted owl saga is discussed below, in section D. Partly in response to the indicator species litigation, the 2005 revision to the forest planning regulations revoked this particular path to meeting the NFMA diversity mandate.

The following case, which arose in the Upper Great Lakes region, deals with modern ecological methodology and demonstrates how diversity of species is ultimately about land.

Sierra Club v. Marita

United States Court of Appeals, Seventh Circuit, 1995.
46 F.3d 606.

■ JUDGE FLAUM

* * *

The present case concerns management plans developed for two forests: Nicolet National Forest ("Nicolet") and Chequamegon (She–WA–megon) National Forest ("Chequamegon"). Nicolet spreads over 973,000 acres, of which 655,000 acres are National Forest Land, in northeastern Wisconsin, while Chequamegon encompasses 845,000 publicly-owned acres in northwestern and north-central Wisconsin.[4] Collectively, the Nicolet and the Chequamegon contain hundreds of lakes and streams, thousands of miles of roads and trails, and serve a wide variety of uses, including hiking, skiing, snowmobiling, logging, fishing, hunting, sightseeing, and scientific research. The forests are important for both the tourism and the forest product industries in northern Wisconsin.

In the late 1970s and early 1980s, the Nicolet and Chequamegon Forest Supervisors and interdisciplinary teams each began drafting a forest management plan for their respective forests. These plans were expected to guide forest management for ten to fifteen years beginning in 1986. Drafts of * * * [b]oth plans were followed by a period of public comment, pursuant to 16 U.S.C. § 1604(d), which resulted in a number of changes to both plans.

---

4. Until the mid–1800s, both the Nicolet and Chequamegon were old-growth forests consisting primarily of northern hardwoods. Pine logging around 1900, hardwood logging in the 1920s, and forest fires (caused by clear cutting) significantly affected the landscape. Government replanting and forest-fire control efforts beginning in the 1930s have reclaimed much of the land as forest. The forests now contain a mixture of trees that markedly differs from the forests' pre–1800 "natural" conditions but is also more diverse in terms of tree type and age.

The Regional Forester issued final drafts of both plans on August 11, 1986, as well as final environmental impact statements ("FEIS") and RODs ["records of decision"] explaining the final planning decisions. [Following exhaustion of administrative remedies, plaintiffs sued.]

* * *

The Sierra Club's primary contention concerned the Service's failure to employ the science of conservation biology, which failure led it to violate a number of statutes and regulations regarding diversity in national forests. Conservation biology, the Sierra Club asserted, predicts that biological diversity can only be maintained if a given habitat is sufficiently large so that populations within that habitat will remain viable in the event of disturbances. Accordingly, dividing up large tracts of forest into a patchwork of different habitats, as the Nicolet and Chequamegon plans did, would not sustain the diversity within these patches unless each patch were sufficiently large so as to extend across an entire landscape or regional ecosystem. Hence, the Sierra Club reasoned, the Service did not fulfill its mandates under the NFMA, NEPA and MUYSA to consider and promote biological diversity within the Nicolet and the Chequamegon.

[The court of appeals found the claim ripe, an outcome that now likely would be different because of *Ohio Forestry, supra* p. 216.]

* * *

The Sierra Club claims that the Service violated the NFMA and NEPA by using scientifically unsupported techniques to address diversity concerns in its management plans and by arbitrarily disregarding certain principles of conservation biology in developing those plans. The Sierra Club asserts that the Service abdicated its duty to take a "hard look" at the environmental impact of its decisions on biological diversity in the forests on the erroneous contentions that the Sierra Club's proposed theories and predictions were "uncertain" in application and that the Service's own methodology was more than adequate to meet all statutory requirements. According to the Sierra Club, the Service, rather than address the important ecological issues the plaintiffs raised, stuck its head in the sand. The result, the Sierra Club argues, was a plan with "predictions about diversity directly at odds with the prevailing scientific literature."

Several statutes and regulations mandate consideration of diversity in preparing forest management plans. Section 6(g) of the NFMA, the primary statute at issue, directs the Secretary of Agriculture in preparing a forest management plan to, among other things,

> provide for diversity of plant and animal communities based on the suitability and capability of the specific land area in order to meet overall multiple-use objectives, and within the multiple-use objectives of a land management plan adopted pursuant to this section, provide, where appropriate, to the degree practicable, for steps to be taken to preserve the diversity of tree species similar to that existing in the region controlled by the plan[.]

16 U.S.C. § 1604(g)(3)(B).

A number of regulations guide the application of this statute.* The most general one stipulates that:

> Forest planning shall provide for diversity of plant and animal communities and tree species consistent with the overall multiple-use objectives of the planning area. Such diversity shall be considered throughout the planning process. Inventories shall include quantitative data making possible the evaluation of diversity in terms of its prior and present condition. For each planning alternative, the interdisciplinary team shall consider how diversity will be affected by various mixes of resource outputs and uses, including proposed management practices.

36 C.F.R. § 219.26. Another regulation addresses the substantive goals of the plan:

> Management prescriptions, where appropriate and to the extent practicable, shall preserve and enhance the diversity of plant and animal communities, including endemic and desirable naturalized plant and animal species, so that it is at least as great as that which would be expected in a natural forest and the diversity of tree species similar to that existing in the planning area. Reductions in diversity of plant and animal communities and tree species from that which would be expected in a natural forest, or from that similar to the existing diversity in the planning area, may be prescribed only where needed to meet overall multiple-use objectives * * *.

36 C.F.R. § 219.27(g); *see also* 36 C.F.R. § 219.27(a)(5) (requiring that all management prescriptions "provide for and maintain diversity of plant and animal communities to meet overall multiple-use objectives"). Diversity is defined for the purposes of these regulations as "[t]he distribution and abundance of different plant and animal communities and species within the area covered by a land and resource management plan." 36 C.F.R. § 219.3.

Regulations implementing the NFMA with regard to the management of fish and wildlife resources are more specific still. First,

> [f]ish and wildlife habitat shall be managed to maintain viable populations of existing native and desired non-native vertebrate species in the planning area * * *. In order to ensure that viable populations will be maintained, habitat must be provided to support, at least, a minimum number of reproductive individuals and that habitat must be well distributed so that those individuals can interact with others in the planning area.

36 C.F.R. § 219.19. In order to perceive the effects of management on these species, the Service must monitor the populations of specially selected "management indicator species" ("MIS"). 36 C.F.R. § 219.19(a)(1). The selection of MIS must include, where appropriate, "endangered and threatened plant and animal species" identified on state and federal lists for the area; species with "special habitat needs that may be influenced significant-

---

* [Ed.] All of the regulations cited in the opinion have since been deleted in the Forest Service 2005 planning regulations. See, infra, p. 735.

ly by planned management programs; species commonly hunted, fished or trapped, non-game species of special interest; and additional * * * species selected because their population changes are believed to indicate the effects of management activities on other species * * * or on water quality." *Id.*

The NFMA diversity statute does not provide much guidance as to its execution; "it is difficult to discern any concrete legal standards on the face of the provision." Wilkinson and Anderson, *supra* at 296. However, "when the section is read in light of the historical context and overall purposes of the NFMA, as well as the legislative history of the section, it is evident that section 6(g)(3)(B) requires Forest Service planners to treat the wildlife resource as a controlling, co-equal factor in forest management and, in particular, as a substantive limitation on timber production." *Id.*

* * *

The Service addressed diversity concerns in the Nicolet and Chequamegon in largely similar ways * * *. The Service defined diversity as "[t]he distribution and abundance of different plant and animal communities and species within the area covered by the Land and Resource Management Plan." The Service assumed that "an increase in the diversity of habitats increases the potential livelihood of diverse kinds of organisms."

The Service focused its attention first on vegetative diversity. Diversity of vegetation was measured within tree stands as well as throughout the forest, noting that such diversity is "desirable for diverse wildlife habitat, visual variety, and as an aid to protecting the area from wildfire, insects, and disease." The Service assessed vegetative diversity based on vegetative types, age class structure of timber types, within-stand diversity of tree species, and the spatial distribution pattern of all these elements across the particular forest. The Service also factored in other considerations, including the desirability of "large areas of low human disturbance" and amount of "old-growth" forest, into its evaluations. Using these guidelines, the Service gathered and analyzed data on the current and historical composition of the forests to project an optimal vegetative diversity.

The Service assessed animal diversity primarily on the basis of vegetative diversity. Pursuant to the regulations, the Service identified all rare and uncommon vertebrate wildlife species as well as those species identified with a particular habitat and subject to significant change through planning alternatives. The Service grouped these species with a particular habitat type, identifying 14 categories in the Nicolet and 25 (reduced to 10 similar types) in the Chequamegon. For each of these habitat types, the Service selected MIS (33 in the Nicolet and 18 in the Chequamegon) to determine the impact of management practices on these species in particular and, by proxy, on other species in general.[5] For each MIS, the Service calculated the minimum viable population necessary in order to ensure the continued reproductive vitality of the species. Factors involved in this calculation included a determination of population size, the spatial distribu-

---

5. A number of the MIS selected were also chosen because their endangered status required the Service to monitor them directly.

tion across the forest needed to ensure fitness and resilience, and the kinds, amounts and pattern of habitats needed to support the population.

Taking its diversity analysis into consideration, along with its numerous other mandates, the Service developed a number of plan alternatives for each of the forests (eight in the Nicolet and nine in the Chequamegon). Each alternative emphasized a different aspect of forest management, including cost efficiency, wildlife habitat, recreation, and hunting, although all were considered to be "environmentally, technically, and legally feasible." In the Nicolet, the Service selected the alternative emphasizing resource outputs associated with large diameter hardwood and softwood vegetation; in the Chequamegon an alternative emphasizing recreational opportunities, quality saw-timber, and aspen management was chosen.

The Sierra Club argues that the diversity statute and regulations * * * required the Service to consider and apply certain principles of conservation biology in developing the forest plan. These principles, the Sierra Club asserts, dictate that diversity is not comprehensible solely through analysis of the numbers of plants and animals and the variety of species in a given area. Rather, diversity also requires an understanding of the relationships between differing landscape patterns and among various habitats. That understanding, the Sierra Club says, has led to the prediction that the size of a habitat—the "patch size"—tends to affect directly the survival of the habitat and the diversity of plant and animal species within that habitat.

A basic generalization of conservation biology is that smaller patches of habitat will not support life as well as one larger patch of that habitat, even if the total area of the smaller patches equals the total area of the large patch. This generalization derives from a number of observations and predictions. First, whereas a large-scale disturbance will wipe out many populations in a smaller patch, those in a larger patch have a better chance of survival. Second, smaller patches are subject to destruction through "edge effects." Edge effects occur when one habitat's environment suffers because it is surrounded by different type of habitat. Given basic geometry, among other factors, the smaller the patch size of the surrounded habitat, the greater the chance that a surrounding habitat will invade and devastate the surrounded habitat. Third, the more isolated similar habitats are from one another, the less chance organisms can migrate from one habitat to another in the event of a local disturbance. Consequently, fewer organisms will survive such a disturbance and diversity will decline. This third factor is known as the theory of "island biogeography." Thus, the mere fact that a given area contains diverse habitats does not ensure diversity at all; a "fragmented forest" is a recipe for ecological trouble. On the basis of these submissions, the Sierra Club desires us to rule that

> [t]o perform a legally adequate hard look at the environmental consequences of landscape manipulation across the hundreds of thousands of hectares of a National Forest, a federal agency must apply in some reasonable fashion the ecological principles identified by well accepted conservation biology. Species-by-species techniques are simply no longer enough. Ecology must be applied in the analysis, and it will be used as a criterion for the substantive results. (Nicolet Appellant's Br. at 7)

As a way of putting conservation biology into practice, the Sierra Club suggested that large blocks of land (at least 30,000 to 50,000 acres per block), so-called "Diversity Maintenance Areas" ("DMAs"), be set aside in each of the forests. The Sierra Club proposed and mapped three DMAs for the Nicolet and two for the Chequamegon. In these areas, which would have included about 25% of each forest, habitats were to be undisturbed by new roads, timber sales, or wildlife openings. Neither forest plan, however, ultimately contained a DMA; the Chequamegon Forest Supervisor initially did include two DMAs, but the Regional Forester removed them from the final Chequamegon plan.

The Sierra Club contends that the Service ignored its submissions, noting that the FEISs and RODs for both the Nicolet and the Chequamegon are devoid of reference to population dynamics, species turnover, patch size, recolonization problems, fragmentation problems, edge effects, and island biogeography. According to the Sierra Club, the Service simply disregarded extensive documentary and expert testimony, including over 100 articles and 13 affidavits, supporting the Sierra Club's assertions and thereby shirked its legal duties.

The Service replies that it correctly considered the implications of conservation biology for both the Nicolet and Chequamegon and appropriately declined to apply the science. The Service asserts that it duly noted the "concern [of the Sierra Club and others] that fragmentation of the * * * forest canopy through timber harvesting and road building is detrimental to certain plant and animal species." The Service decided that the theory had "not been applied to forest management in the Lake States" and that the subject was worthy of further study. However, the Service found in both cases that while the theories of conservation biology in general and of island biogeography in particular were "of interest, * * * there is not sufficient justification at this time to make research of the theory a Forest Service priority." Given its otherwise extensive analysis of diversity, as well as the deference owed its interpretation of applicable statutory and regulatory requirements, the Service contends that it clearly met all the "diversity" obligations imposed on it.

* * *

The Sierra Club's arguments regarding the inadequacy of the Service's plans and FEISs can be distilled into five basic allegations, each of which we address in turn. First, the Sierra Club asserts that the law "treats ecosystems and ecological relationships as a separately cognizable issue from the species by species concepts driving game and timber issues." The Sierra Club relies on the NFMA's diversity language to argue that the NFMA treats diversity in two distinct respects: diversity of plant and animal communities and diversity of tree species. *See* 16 U.S.C. § 1604(g)(3)(B). * * * The Sierra Club concludes from these statutes and regulations that the Service was obligated to apply an ecological approach to forest management and failed to do so. In the Sierra Club's view, MISs and population viability analyses present only half the picture, a picture that the addition of conservation biology would make complete.

The Sierra Club errs in these assertions because it sees requirements in the NFMA * * * that simply do not exist. The drafters of the NFMA diversity regulations themselves recognized that diversity was a complex term and declined to adopt any particular means or methodology of providing for diversity. Report of the Committee of Scientists to the Secretary of Agriculture Regarding Regulations Proposed by the United States Forest Service to Implement Section 6 of the National Forest Management Act of 1976, 44 Fed.Reg. 26,599, 26,609 (1979). We agree with the district court that "[i]n view of the committee's decision not to prescribe a particular methodology and its failure to mention the principles that plaintiffs claims were by then well established, the court cannot fairly read those principles into the NFMA * * *." Thus, conservation biology is not a necessary element of diversity analysis insofar as the regulations do not dictate that the service analyze diversity in any specific way.

Furthermore, the Sierra Club has overstated its case by claiming that MIS and population viability analyses do not gauge the diversity of ecological communities as required by the regulations. Except for those species to be monitored because they themselves are in danger, species are chosen to be on an MIS list precisely because they will indicate the effects management practices are having on a broader ecological community. Indeed, even if all that the Sierra Club has asserted about forest fragmentation and patch size and edge effects is true, an MIS should to some degree indicate their impact on diversity. *See* Report of the Committee of Scientists, 44 Fed.Reg. at 26,627 (noting that MIS are chosen "because they indicate the consequences of management on other species whose populations fluctuate in some measurable manner with the indicator species"). The Sierra Club may have wished the Service to analyze diversity in a different way, but we cannot conclude on the basis of the records before us that the Service's methodology arbitrarily or capriciously neglected the diversity of ecological communities in the two forests.

In a second and related argument, the Sierra Club submits that the substantive law of diversity necessitated the set-aside of large, unfragmented habitats to protect at least some old-growth forest communities. * * * Diversity, the Sierra Club asserts, requires the Service to maintain a range of different, ecologically viable communities. Because it is simply not possible to ensure the survival of any old-growth forest communities without these large, undisturbed patches of land, the Service has therefore reduced diversity. The Service was thus bound to protect and enhance the natural forest or explain why other forest uses prevented the Service from doing so. The Sierra Club believes the Service did neither.

The Sierra Club asserts that the diversity regulations require a certain procedure and that because the substantive result of the Service's choices will produce, in the Sierra Club's view, results adverse to "natural forest" diversity, the Service has violated its mandate. However, as the Service points out, the regulations do not actually require the promotion of "natural forest" diversity but rather the promotion of diversity at least as great as that found in a natural forest. [36 C.F.R. § 219.27(g).] The Service maintains that it did provide for such diversity in the ways discussed above.

Additionally, the Service did consider the maintenance of some old-growth forest, even though the Sierra Club disputes that the Service's efforts will have any positive effects. And to the extent the Service's final choice did not promote "natural diversity" above all else, the Service acted well within its regulatory discretion. *See* Sierra Club v. Espy, 38 F.3d 792, 800 (5th Cir.1994) ("That [NFMA diversity] protection means something less than the preservation of the status quo but something more than eradication of species suggests that this is just the type of policy-oriented decision Congress wisely left to the discretion of the experts—here, the Forest Service."). * * *

* * *

Fourth, the Sierra Club contends that the rejection of its "high quality" science argument on the basis of "uncertainty" in the application of conservation biology was unscrupulous. The Sierra Club asserts that conservation biology represented well-accepted and well-respected science even at the time the Service developed its management plans in the mid–1980s and that this evidence was before the Service when it drafted the forest plans. Thus, if the Service's only argument against applying the "high quality" science of conservation biology was its uncertainty, the Service has utterly failed to respond to the challenge of conservation biology.

A brief look at available evidence suggests that the district court's understanding of uncertainty was correct and the Service's explanation principled. The Service, in looking at island biogeography, noted that it had been developed as a result of research on actual islands or in the predominantly old-growth forests of the Pacific Northwest and therefore did not necessarily lend itself to application in the forests of Wisconsin. Literature submitted by the Sierra Club to the Service was not unequivocal in stipulating how to apply conservation biology principles in the Nicolet and Chequamegon. Likewise, a Sierra Club group member suggested during meetings regarding the Chequamegon that "the Forest Service should be a leader and incorporate this concept into the Plan. He indicated that it would set a precedent for other Forests and Regions." The Chequamegon Forest Supervisor also originally decided to include the DMAs in his forest plan not because science so compelled but as a way to research an as yet untested theory. Even recent literature has recognized that "new legislation may be necessary" in order to force the Service to adopt conservation biology. Robert B. Keiter, Conservation Biology and the Law: Assessing the Challenges Ahead, 69 Chi.Kent L.Rev. 911, 916 (1994). Perhaps the Service "ha[s] the ability to reinterpret [its] own governing mandates to give species protection priority over visitor services and other concerns," *id.* at 921, but that is not and was not required.

The amici scientific societies suggest that the district court misunderstood the nature of scientific uncertainty. Their argument on this point boils down to the assertion that all scientific propositions are inherently unverifiable and at most falsifiable. * * *

Amici, like the Sierra Club, misapprehend the "uncertainty" of which the Service and the district court spoke. We agree that an agency decision to avoid a science should not escape review merely because a theory is not certain. But, however valid a general theory may be, it does not translate into a management tool unless one can apply it to a concrete situation. The Service acknowledged the developments in conservation biology but did not think that they had been shown definitively applicable to forests like the Nicolet or the Chequamegon. Thus, circumstances did not warrant setting aside a large portion of these forests to study island biogeography and related theories at the expense of other forest-plan objectives. Given that uncertainty, we appropriately defer to the agency's method of measuring and maintaining diversity.

* * *

The creation of a forest plan requires the Forest Service to make trade-offs among competing interests. The NFMA's diversity provisions do substantively limit the Forest Service's ability to sacrifice diversity in those trades * * *. However, the Service neither ignored nor abused these limits in the present case. * * *

Affirmed.

NOTES AND QUESTIONS

1. The large record on the science of conservation biology compiled by the plaintiffs and the participation of scientific societies as amici give this the feel of a test case where plaintiffs sought to reorient national forest management. Was it a good litigation strategy to ask the courts in effect to bless a specific scientific school of thought and mandate its use in managing national forests? Was the court being asked to act as a "science court" and decide among differing scientific theories? Can courts do that easily? Should they? Should the courts have applied the standard test for determining the admissibility of scientific evidence? *See* Daubert v. Merrell Dow Pharmaceuticals, Inc., 509 U.S. 579, 592–95 (1993).

2. Did the plaintiffs pick the wrong place to litigate this? Regardless of the acceptance and credibility of conservation biology as a general school of thought, what does the court's opinion indicate about the state of knowledge and analysis of that school of thought as applied to the forests of the upper Midwest?

3. Was this really a dispute about two competing scientific theories? What scientific school of thought did the Forest Service follow, if any? Was the Forest Service position that it rejected the teachings of conservation biology, or was it that it wanted to apply those teachings in a way the plaintiffs disagreed with? From the standpoint of legal strategy, which would be the best course?

4. What are the legal footholds for incorporating the science of conservation biology into national forest management? Look first at the "diversity" provision of the NFMA, 16 U.S.C. § 1604(g)(3)(B). Does it require that the U.S. Forest Service should obey, or try to mimic, the laws

of nature in managing the forests? Or does management mean, inevitably, some manipulation of the natural world that will change the mix and diversity of species found there?

5. Now look at the various regulations quoted by the court. How much flesh do they put on the bones of the statute? Do they embrace the principles of conservation biology? The regulations dealing with diversity were repealed in 2005. See the discussion below of revisions in the Forest Service planning regulations.

6. Does the Forest Service ever have a legal (and judicially enforceable) obligation to conduct experiments on alternative management strategies to help advance science? Do the adaptive planning provisions of the 2005 planning rule, discussed in chapter 5E, *supra*, create new obligations for experimentation?

7. Suppose that the Forest Service had adopted the conservation biology-oriented approach proposed by the plaintiff. If a timber company sued to overturn the agency action, what would be the result?

8. The district court decision in the *Marita* case found that the "Service did not act arbitrarily or capriciously, etc., in failing to base its diversity analysis on the principles of conservation biology set forth by plaintiffs." But the court dropped an unusual footnote at the end of the sentence:

> Note the use of the past tense in this sentence. The court has been presented with information relating to the state of scientific knowledge as of the early 1980s and therefore knows nothing of what may have developed in this area since then. Thus, the court's conclusions regarding the rationality of defendants' mid 1980s analysis of biological diversity do not necessarily apply to its subsequent analyses.

Sierra Club v. Marita, 845 F. Supp. 1317, 1330 n. 8 (E.D. Wis.1994). Did the court in 1994 sense the progress that conservation biology had made in gaining acceptance of its theories for land management? Should a court today approve a decade-old plan that no longer represents a reasonable application of science? Is it a general principle of administrative law that, in order to avoid arbitrary and capricious decisionmaking, an agency must use the best available science? Is it possible that climate change will make it much more difficult to make predictions about how ecosystems will respond to management? If so, should the courts give the federal land managing agencies more deference?

9. Even before the court of appeals decided *Marita*, the Forest Service began to respond to the growing stature of conservation biology. In 1990 the Chief directed the Wisconsin national forests to establish a committee of experts to address biodiversity concerns. The result was a series of meetings culminating in a 1994 report recommending that the Nicolet and Chequamegon be managed, in part, for protecting biological diversity on an ecosystem scale. In 2004 the Forest Service adopted a new LRMP for the combined Nicolet and Chequamegon. The 2004 LRMP was guided by the same LRMP rule as the 1986 plans but it purports to provide "management direction which will increase the amount of large forest patches over

the long term." Though it falls short of establishing DMAs, it does contain many references to conservation biology principles. Did the Sierra Club lose the battle in court but win the war outside of it? Is this an example of the courts serving as poor drivers of social and scientific change?

Beyond the large question about the acceptability of conservation biology addressed in *Marita*, the methodology the Forest Service has used to assess and conserve biodiversity has been much litigated. Diversity may be protected by statute, but gathering on-the-ground data is time-consuming and burdensome. The following cases address this contentious matter.

Inland Empire Public Lands Council v. United States Forest Service

United States Court of Appeals, Ninth Circuit, 1996.
88 F.3d 754.

■ Judge Hall

The United States Forest Service proposed eight timber sales in the Upper Sunday Creek Watershed region of the Kootenai National Forest in northwest Montana. * * * Plaintiffs, a number of environmental groups, challenged the sale first in administrative hearings and ultimately in district court, claiming that the Service's analysis of the sale's impact on seven species—the lynx, boreal owl, flammulated owl, black-backed woodpecker, fisher, bull charr, and wet-sloped cutthroat trout—was inadequate under both the National Forest Management Act and the National Environmental Policy Act of 1969. [The Forest Service designated all of these species as either "sensitive" or "indicator" species.] The district court concluded that the Service's analysis was sufficient * * *. In this expedited appeal, Plaintiffs now argue [that NEPA was violated and that] the Service failed to comply with 36 C.F.R. § 219.19, which requires a minimum level of population viability analysis * * *. [The court's discussion of NEPA is omitted.]

* * *

* * * Plaintiffs claimed that the Service fell short of what the NFMA required because it never examined the species' population size, their population trends, or their ability to interact with other groups of the species living in neighboring patches of forest. The district court rejected this argument on summary judgment, reasoning that Plaintiffs were quibbling over the choice of scientific methodologies, a decision to which a reviewing court should defer.

* * *

As noted above, the NFMA imposes substantive duties on the Forest Service, one of which is the duty to "provide for diversity of plant and animal communities." 16 U.S.C. § 1604(g)(3)(B). Regulation 219.19, one of the many regulations promulgated to ensure such diversity, states in relevant part that:

> Fish and wildlife habitat shall be managed to maintain viable populations of existing native and desired non-native vertebrate species in the planning area. For planning purposes, a viable population shall be regarded as one which has the estimated numbers and distribution of reproductive individuals to insure its continued existence is well distributed in the planning area. In order to insure that viable populations will be maintained, habitat must be provided to support, at least, a minimum number of reproductive individuals and that habitat must be well distributed so that those individuals can interact with others in the planning area.

36 C.F.R. § 219.19. This duty to ensure viable, or self-sustaining, populations, applies with special force to "sensitive" species. Because neither party disputes the Service's ultimate obligation to ensure viable populations, the key to this appeal is deciding what type of population viability analysis the Service must perform in order to comply with Regulation 219.19.

Each party suggests its own answer. The Forest Service proposes that its "habitat viability analyses" were sufficient. For four of the species (the black-backed woodpecker, lynx, fisher, and boreal owl), the Service did the following: It consulted field studies that disclosed how many acres of territory an individual of each species needed to survive and the percentage of that acreage that was used for nesting, feeding, denning, etc. (e.g. a lynx needs a 200 acre territory, 20 acres—or 10%—of which must be suitable for denning). The Service then assumed that these percentages would hold true regardless of the size of the individual's territory (e.g. that a lynx would need 10% of whatever acreage of territory it inhabited to be denning habitat). The Service examined each proposed alternative to see how many acres of each type of relevant habitat would remain after the timber was harvested (e.g. Alternative 1 would leave 2,000 acres of denning habitat). It next determined what percentage of the decision area that the remaining types of habitat constituted (e.g. decision area was 10,000 acres so that remaining denning habitat is 20% of the decision area). The Service concluded a species would remain viable as long as the threshold percentage of each type of habitat remaining in the chosen alternative was greater than the percentage required for that species to survive (e.g. the lynx population would remain viable because Alternative 1 left 20% denning habitat and a lynx needs only 10% of its territory to be suitable for denning).

* * *

Plaintiffs contend that the Service's manifold "habitat viability analyses" are insufficient. They argue that Regulation 219.19 also requires the Service to examine: (1) the population of each species; (2) the population dynamics (trends, etc.) of each species; and (3) whether the species could travel between different patches of forest ("linkages"). Plaintiffs claim that their form of analysis is the minimum required by law.

In deference to an agency's expertise, we review its interpretation of its own regulations solely to see whether that interpretation is arbitrary and capricious. This is especially true when questions of scientific methodology are involved. * * * Thus, we will uphold the Forest Service's interpretation "unless it is plainly erroneous or inconsistent with the regulation."

We start, as we must, with the plain language of the Regulation. The Regulation specifically provides that the Forest Service may discharge its duties though habitat management as long as "habitat [is] provided to support, *at least,* a minimum number of reproductive individuals and that habitat [is] well distributed so that those individuals can interact with others in the planning area." 36 C.F.R. § 219.19 (emphasis added).

We do not believe that the habitat management analysis conducted in this case for the black-backed woodpecker, lynx, fisher, and boreal owl was in any way "plainly erroneous" or "inconsistent" with this regulatory duty. Regulation 219.19 ultimately requires the Forest Service to maintain viable populations. In this case, the Service's methodology reasonably ensures such populations by requiring that the decision area contain enough of the types of habitat essential for survival. In applying this methodology, the Service recognizes that decision areas are artificial boundaries that change depending on the project at issue, and that the species inhabiting these areas pay no attention to such boundaries.

We recognize that the Service's methodology necessarily assumes that maintaining the acreage of habitat necessary for survival would in fact assure a species' survival. The Service is entitled to rely on reasonable assumptions in its environmental analyses. We find the above-stated assumption eminently reasonable and therefore do not find that the Forest Service's habitat analyses for the black-backed woodpecker, lynx, fisher, and boreal owl were arbitrary or capricious.

[The court held that the similar analysis of the flammulated owl, an indicator species, was also reasonable.]

* * *

We therefore affirm the district court's conclusion that the Service's population viability analysis was not "arbitrary and capricious."

NOTES AND QUESTIONS

1. In Sierra Club v. Martin, 168 F.3d 1 (11th Cir.1999), the court reached the opposite result.

We do agree with the Forest Service that the combination of §§ 219.26 and 219.19 require it only to collect inventory data on MIS rather than on all species in the Forest. To read § 219.26 to require inventory data on *all* species obviates the need for MIS and reduces § 219.19 to nonsense. On the other hand, the Forest Service and Timber Intervenors' interpretation of § 219.26—that they need not collect data on MIS either—would consign that regulation to a similar fate. By their reading, § 219.26 would have no meaning despite its explicit requirement that quantitative inventory data be used to measure forest diversity. Interpreting a regulation in a manner that robs it of all meaning is unacceptable. * * *

We believe that the regulations are harmonious when read together. MIS are proxies used to measure the effects of management strategies on Forest diversity; Section 219.19 requires that the Forest Service monitor their relationship to habitat changes. Section 219.26 requires the Forest Service to use quantitative inventory data to assess the Forest Plan's effects on diversity. If § 219.19 mandates that MIS serve as the means through which to measure the Forest Plan's impact on diversity and § 219.26 dictates that quantitative data be used to measure the Plan's impact on diversity, then, taken together, the two regulations require the Forest Service to gather quantitative data on MIS and use it to measure the impact of habitat changes on the Forest's diversity. To read the regulations otherwise would be to render one or the other meaningless as well as to disregard the regulations' directive that population trends of the MIS be monitored and that inventory data be gathered in order to monitor the effects of the Forest Plan.

Turning now to the instant case, it becomes clear that the Forest Service's approval of the timber sales without gathering and considering data on the MIS is arbitrary and capricious. The regulations require that MIS be monitored to determine the effects of habitat changes. The timber projects proposed for the Chattahoochee and Oconee National Forests amount to 2,000 acres of habitat change. Yet, despite this extensive habitat change and the fact that the some MIS populations in the Forest are actually declining, the Forest Service has no population data for half of the MIS in the Forest and thus cannot reliably gauge the impact of the timber projects on these species.

See also Utah Environmental Congress v. Bosworth, 439 F.3d 1184 (10th Cir. 2006), which follows *Martin* in holding that the Forest Service regulations require the Forest Service to acquire and analyze actual, quantitative population data of its management indicator species.

2.   Which court is correct? Do you agree with the 11th Circuit that to read the regulations as requiring only habitat monitoring for MIS would render the MIS tool meaningless? Did Martin give enough deference to the Forest Service?

3.   Look closely at the Forest Service's regulations, § 219.19 and 219.26 (quoted in *Marita*), and how they define "viability" of species and otherwise set requirements for protecting biodiversity. Do the regulations turn the concept of diversity in the statute into something like a duty to preserve self-sustaining populations of all or most species found in the national forests? Those regulations were repealed in 2005, leaving the statutory language in 16 U.S.C. section 1604(g)(3)(B) as the standard. How should the "hard population data" issue be analyzed now?

4.   Is there a separation of powers consideration lurking here? The Forest Service has much to do—run campgrounds, rescue careless visitors,

supervise ranchers and miners, etc. If it has to run the wildlife surveys the plaintiffs want in these cases, it may not be able to meet some of its other responsibilities. Should that be a relevant factor to a court addressing this issue?

5. For further commentary on diversity requirements under the NFMA, *see* Greg D. Corbin, *The United States Forest Service's Response to Biodiversity Science*, 29 Envtl. L. 377, 414 (1999), where a lawyer-biologist concluded that:

> How to manage the national forest system for biodiversity is a complex and perplexing question. Both Congress and the first Committee of Scientists recognized that the answer to that question lay in the future, and that science would provide guidelines from which management decisions are made. In the nearly twenty-five years since Congress passed NFMA, researchers and land managers have amassed a substantial body of knowledge around the broad concepts adopted by the first Committee. With those requirements in place, and a knowledge base to draw from, the Forest Service has come under ever-increasing pressure to apply contemporary scientific understanding to its forest management activities. Instead of embracing scientific advances, however, the Forest Service has argued for its own interpretation of how best to manage the national forest system. * * * The Forest Service may view the absence of any meaningful or enforceable standard as necessary to achieve the regulatory flexibility to manage the national forests, but Congress did not adopt this view when it passed NFMA.

3. Other NFMA Provisions

a. ECONOMIC SUITABILITY: THE "BELOW-COST TIMBER SALES" ISSUE

Considered as a whole, annual timber sale revenues from the national forest system usually exceed the costs of managing the system. Most of the profitable sales, however, take place in the humid, timber-rich Pacific Northwest. Sales in other regions, especially in the Rocky Mountains, are often below-cost—the government's costs of growing and selling trees exceed revenues from timber sales—due to a more arid climate and lower-quality commercial timber land. Roadbuilding is a large cost constituent. But roads can be used for nontimber purposes such as recreation and wildlife management as well. Most studies have found, however, that even when appropriate portions of road costs are allocated to nontimber benefits, many timber sales still fail to pay their way. Industry argues that below-cost sales are necessary to support local communities dependent on a continuing flow of timber from national forests. Fiscal conservatives, who dislike subsidies, and environmentalists, who oppose extending road systems into roadless areas where many of the proposed below-cost sales are proposed, join in objecting to the practice.

During the congressional hearings leading to the NFMA, eminent economist Dr. Marion Clawson and others objected to uneconomical sales.

The Senate bill included a reasonably strict cost-benefit analysis, the House version did not directly deal with the issue, and the conference of the two chambers mediated the differences by drafting an "economic suitability," or "marginal lands" provision, which became 16 U.S.C. § 1604(k):

> In developing land management plans pursuant to this [Act], the Secretary shall identify lands within the management area which are not suited for timber production, considering physical, economic, and other pertinent factors to the extent feasible, as determined by the Secretary, and shall assure that, except for salvage sales or sales necessitated to protect other multiple-use values, no timber harvesting shall occur on such lands for a period of 10 years. Lands once identified as unsuitable for timber production shall continue to be treated for reforestation purposes, particularly with regard to the protection of other multiple-use values. The Secretary shall review his decision to classify these lands as not suited for timber production at least every 10 years and shall return these lands to timber production whenever he determines that conditions have changed so that they have become suitable for timber production.

In Thomas v. Peterson, 753 F.2d 754 (9th Cir.1985), the court rejected the argument that federal law prohibited timber harvesting and associated road construction where the value of the timber to be harvested is less than the cost of the road construction. The court did not address § 1604(k), but examined a provision of the RPA of 1974, which contained a congressional declaration that the national forest transportation system should "meet anticipated needs on an economical and environmentally sound basis." 16 U.S.C. § 1608(a). The court said:

> Plaintiffs * * * cite Forest Service regulations, Congressional committee reports, Congressional testimony, unenacted bills, and Forest Service practices, all of which evince a concern for economically efficient management of the National Forests, for avoiding costs not justified by benefits, for obtaining fair market value in the sale of National Forest resources, and for recovery of the costs of National Forest roads and other management expenses. These sources merely counsel economic prudence. They do not evidence a statutory requirement that timber roads be built only when the proceeds of the timber sales will defray construction costs.

> The Forest Service interprets "economical" to permit consideration of benefits other than timber access, such as motorized recreation, firewood gathering, and access to the area by local residents. An agency's interpretation of the statute that it is charged with administering is entitled to substantial deference, see Udall v. Tallman, 380 U.S. 1, 16 (1965), and will be upheld unless unreasonable. Here it is clearly reasonable.

In Citizens for Environmental Quality v. United States, 731 F.Supp. 970 (D.Colo.1989), the court remanded a plan to the Forest Service to explain more fully why it allowed timber production goals to play a heavy role in determining the suitability of lands for timber production. The court said that § 1604(k) provides the Forest Service with ample discretion to consider both economic and other pertinent factors in identifying land suitable for timber production. * * * However, * * * if production goals are to be given greater weight in the suitability analysis, then adequate reasons must be set forth for so doing. * * * In the instant case, no such justification has been set forth.

How should the brief mention of economic factors in section 1604(k) be construed? Should the section be read to require a cost-benefit analysis? Does it prohibit making lands available for timber harvest where the cost of preparing for the sale and extracting the timber exceed the value of the timber? Does it contain enough "meat" to provide for meaningful judicial review, or should the matter left to the discretion of the U.S. Forest Service? Might some timber sales be so uneconomic that the courts are justified in stepping in?

Section 1604(*l*) directs the Forest Service to establish a process for comparing costs and receipts for timber sales and to report annually to Congress on below-cost sales—but sets no substantive standards. Following enactment, the Committee of Scientists, a group of leading experts designated by Congress to propose NFMA rules to the Forest Service, concluded that below-cost sales must be limited by some "rules of reason." The Forest Service has continued making below-cost sales in areas of marginally productive timber, although it has taken steps to reduce the practice, which remains a point of significant controversy. In its 1998 report to Congress, the Forest Service calculated that timber sales lost $88.6 million during 1997. About 60% of this loss was the result of road construction. But the Service also justified the poor return on the expense of timber treatments aimed at improving forest health rather than just maximizing profit. The Service asserted that if the clean water, habitat, and recreational benefits of the more expensive practices were quantified, they would justify the expenses.

As a matter of legislative policy, should Congress prohibit or more directly limit below-cost timber sales on the national forests? Should an exception be made for timber-dependent communities, where local mills need a relatively continuous supply of timber or they will shut down?

b. ROTATION AGE AND CULMINATION OF MEAN ANNUAL INCREMENT ("CMAI")

After the Service establishes a suitable inventory, it must set a harvesting schedule. Section 1604(m) prohibits cutting unless "stands of trees * * * generally have reached the culmination of mean annual increment of growth," with narrow exceptions. Is this a restatement, in modern technical language, of the requirement of the 1897 Organic Act, as interpreted in the *Monongahela* decision that only "dead, matured, or large growth of trees" can be harvested? The provision does appear to adopt a substantive limitation on logging based on when trees reach biological maturity, rather than at the earlier point of economic maturity (except that 1604(m) speaks in terms of "stands" instead of individual trees). Its application is, however, complicated by the state of the forestry art: To take one example, the "rotation age for ponderosa pine on [on class of site] varies from 39 to 107 years, depending on the unit of measurement employed and the utilization standards assumed." Samuel Trask Dana & Sally Fairfax, FOREST AND RANGE POLICY 331 (2d ed. 1980). In Lamb v. Thompson, 265 F.3d 1038 (10th Cir.2001), the court held that a Forest Service decision to make an exception to CMAI must be subject to public participation. It went on to find that the CMAI requirement had not been met in the preparation of the forest plan before it, but was ultimately satisfied by a brief mention of the CMAI issue in an environmental assessment the Forest Service prepared on the particular timber sale being challenged.

c. SUSTAINED YIELD AND THE CONCEPT OF NONDECLINING EVEN FLOW ("NDEF")

In its broadest sense, sustained yield means only that the forest be managed so that timber can be produced in perpetuity. It does not tell us how much timber might be cut each year. Suppose, for example, a national forest has a managed, second-growth timber inventory of 100 mmbf, that the annual growth is 1 mmbf, and that the rotation cycle is 100 years. The "sustained yield" requirement could be met if all 100 mmbf were cut in 1990 and the ground were replanted, because the stand would regenerate and 100 mmbf would again be available for harvest in 2090. At that point, there could be another wholesale cut, and so on. The example is the extreme, but the same reasoning applies to a schedule of 50 mmbf twice a century, 10 mmbf every 10 years, and other variations. This has led some critics to describe "sustained yield" timber management as almost bereft of meaning. *See, e.g.*, Richard Behan, *Political Popularity and Conceptual Nonsense: The Strange Case of Sustained Yield Forestry*, 8 ENVTL. L. 309 (1978).

Nondeclining even flow is an awkward descriptor for the most conservative variant of sustained-yield management. It requires that the same level of harvest be maintained *annually in perpetuity*. Thus, in the example above, since annual growth is one mmbf and the rotation period is 100 years, the amount that can be removed annually forever is one mmbf per year.

Now suppose, instead of the hypothetical second-growth forest just described, a forest of the same size and with a similar capacity for growth—with similar soil conditions, slopes, moisture, and exposure to sunlight—except that it is a virgin, old-growth forest. In the old-growth forest, with giant "overmature" trees, the timber inventory will be much greater and may approach, say, 500 mmbf on the same number of acres as the managed forest. Management of such old-growth stands in national forests in some areas of the Northern Rocky Mountains and Pacific Northwest has been at the cutting edge of controversy between industry and environmentalists. If NDEF is *not* followed in this hypothetical old growth forest, and a conservative "conversion period" of 100 years is used to achieve a managed forest, then an accelerated harvest of 5 million board annually can be employed. Then, after 100 years, when the conversion period is completed and the old-growth is liquidated, the harvest must "fall down" to an average of 1 mmbf each year.

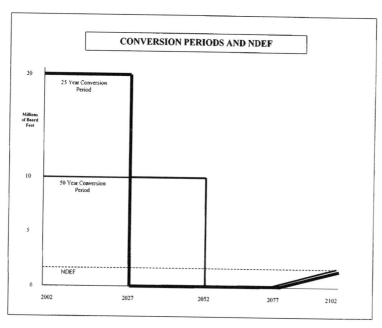

If NDEF is employed, the annual harvest of the old-growth stand cannot exceed the amount that can be produced annually in perpetuity, which cuts the annual yield to 1 mmbf. This conservative, level harvesting schedule means no fall-down in later years to disrupt local communities. But it also means that old-growth forests will be liquidated much more slowly. Indeed, in some cases, the numbers are such that there will always be a considerable amount of old growth in the forest. The computer modeling methods by which the formulae, economic projections, exceptions, and silvicultural assumptions are factored into the calculations are complex, and the method is less than an exact science. Almost everyone agrees, however, that application of NDEF results in significantly smaller present harvests of old-growth stands.

The definition of "sustained yield" in the MUSY Act (which applies to all renewable resources, and not just timber) neatly straddles the issue by referring to "achievement and maintenance in perpetuity of a high-level *annual or regular periodic output * * *.*" 16 U.S.C. § 531(b). Congress set a considerably more rigorous standard as applied to timber in the NFMA, 16 U.S.C. § 1611, by codifying NDEF in this fashion:

(a) The Secretary of Agriculture shall limit the sale of timber from each national forest to a quantity equal to or less than a quantity which can be removed from such forest annually in perpetuity on a sustained-yield basis: *Provided,* That, in order to meet overall multiple-use objectives, the Secretary may establish an allowable sale quantity for any decade which departs from the projected long-term average sale quantity that would otherwise be established: *Provided further,* That any such planned departure must be consistent with the multiple-use management objectives of the land management plan. * * * In addition, within any decade, the Secretary may sell a quantity in excess of the annual allowable sale quantity established pursuant to this section * * * [for] any national forest so long as the average sale quantities of timber from such national forest over the decade covered by the plan do not exceed such quantity limitation. * * *

(b) Nothing in subsection (a) of this section shall prohibit the Secretary from salvage or sanitation harvesting of timber stands which are substantially damaged by fire, windthrow, or other catastrophe, or which are in imminent danger from insect or disease attack. The Secretary may either substitute such timber for timber that would otherwise be sold under the plan or, if not feasible, sell such timber over and above the plan volume.

Has Congress chosen NDEF in this language? The section begins with a pure NDEF formulation: The Forest Service cannot exceed a level of cut that can be removed "annually in perpetuity on a sustained-yield basis." But notice the qualifiers and exceptions. Do they swallow the rule set out before the first proviso? In the late 1970s, President Carter proposed a departure from NDEF for the 1980s to bring more lumber on the market to reduce housing costs as an inflation-fighting tool. Was that permitted under this language?

As of 2007, with the greatly reduced annual cut on the national forests, NDEF has much less significance than it did when the NFMA was enacted. Of course, if efforts are made to increase the harvest, NDEF will likely again play an important role.

4.   REVISION OF THE FOREST SERVICE PLANNING REGULATIONS

The Clinton Administration undertook two major rulemaking efforts involving the national forests: a revision of the Forest Service Planning Regulations, discussed here; and the roadless area initiative, which is taken up in subsection 6. The Bush Administration replaced both rules, but it allowed planning already initiated under the old rules to continue under them.

The planning regulations implement the NFMA and, as such, control or implicate most decisionmaking within the Forest Service. The agency produced its original regulations in 1979 with (as required by a distinctive provision of the NFMA) the advice of a Committee of Scientists. Amendments in 1982 included the diversity provisions first proposed by the Committee of Scientists and quoted in the *Marita* case (*see supra* p. 713). Because the diversity requirement for indicator and sensitive species affected so much habitat, these provisions became central to the Forest Service timber program and laid the foundation for the long journey toward protection of the Northern spotted owl and the old-growth forests it inhabits.

a.   THE 2000 REGULATIONS

By the late 1980s, there was widespread agreement that the Forest Service planning system needed an overhaul. Planning had become too time consuming and expensive, too dependent upon computer programming for setting the timber cut, too unresponsive to public input, and too little-used—the plans, once all the effort to formulate them had been expended, mostly took up shelf space. Several efforts to amend the planning regulations in the early and mid–1990s bore no fruit. In 1997, Agriculture Secretary Glickman appointed a new Committee of Scientists and in 2000, the Forest Service issued new planning regulations based substantially on the Committee's recommendations. 65 Fed.Reg. 67514.

The 2000 planning regulations addressed a wide range of issues including public participation, increased efficiency, and collaborative decision-making. The most important and controversial changes called for more extensive use of scientific and ecological principles, including rigorous requirements of monitoring, evaluation and independent scientific review. The two most divisive issues involved ecological sustainability and species viability.

The 2000 Forest Service planning regulations went beyond other versions of "sustainability," which is often defined as the objective of sustaining, for future generations, ecological, economic and social values. The regulations gave primacy only to ecological sustainability:

> The first priority for planning to guide management of the National Forest System is to maintain or restore ecological sustainability of national forests and grasslands to provide for a wide variety of uses, values, products, and services. The benefits sought from these lands depend upon long-term ecological sustainability. Considering increased human uses, it is essential that uses of today do not impair the functioning of ecological processes and the ability of these natural resources to contribute to sustainability in the future.

36 C.F.R. § 219.2 (2000).

Giving primacy to ecological sustainability received extensive criticism, centering on the belief that it departed from the Forest Service's multiple use statutory mandate and would have deflated the production of commercial products from the national forests. Supporters of the ecological sustainability approach believe that healthy national forest ecosystems can and will produce many economic and social benefits—and that such benefits of necessity depend upon the integrity of the water, soil, vegetation, and air that healthy ecosystems provide. Refining the idea of sustainability in this way, they believe, gives an edge to the sustainability doctrine (often referred to as vague) and offers more specific guidance to land managers than multiple use-sustained yield.

Species diversity was the driving force for measuring ecological sustainability—and national forest management in general—under the 2000 regulations. Current scientific knowledge is not yet at the stage when it can accurately assess the integrity of whole ecosystems. More is known, however, about biological diversity. Of the different aspects of biological diversity—ecosystem, species, and genetic—far more information exists about species diversity. Section 219.20(b)(2), which was just one element of an elaborate five-page ecological sustainability section, began as follows:

> Plan decisions affecting species diversity must provide for ecological conditions that the responsible official determines provide a high likelihood that those conditions are capable of supporting over time the viability of native and desired non-native species well distributed throughout their ranges within the plan area.

On the adoption of the 2000 regulations, *see* Charles Wilkinson, *A Case Study in the Intersection of Law and Science: The 1999 Report of the Committee of Scientists*, 42 ARIZ. L.REV. 307 (2000).

NOTES AND QUESTIONS

1.   Did the 2000 rule quoted above give unreviewable discretion to the "responsible official"? How would a court review a challenge to a timber sale under the 2000 standard? How does it compare to § 219.19 from the 1982 rule, quoted in *Marita*, supra p. 713?

2.   Does the Forest Service have the authority to promulgate regulations making ecological sustainability the "first priority" in the national forests? The NFMA explicitly retains the multiple-use mandate, directing the agency to "provide for multiple use and sustained yield of the products and services obtained [from the national forests] in accordance with the Multiple–Use Sustained Yield Act of 1960." 16 U.S.C. § 1604(e)(1). Critics of the 2000 regulations argue they fly in the face of the MUSY Act, which had long been applied to allow extensive commodity use (livestock grazing, timber harvesting) on the national forests. On the other hand, MUSY itself is premised on a notion of sustainability and the NFMA states as a matter of policy that Forest Service management should "meet the requirements of our people in perpetuity." 16 U.S.C. § 1600(7). Further, the national forests must be managed according to many other statutes, including NEPA, the Clean Water Act, the Clean Air Act, and the ESA, all of which can be described as consistent with sustainability.

3.   As a matter of policy, should the national forests be managed according to ecological sustainability with a heavy emphasis on biodiversity, especially species diversity? Would the 2000 regulations make the national forests a "dominant use" system, where all actions must be compatible with ecological baseline standards? On compatibility tests and dominant use, see discussion in chapter 10 on the national wildlife refuges. Did the 2000 regulations call for too much science or ask too much of science?

4.   Should these decisions be left to Congress rather than the Forest Service? *See* George Hoberg, *Science, Politics, and U.S. Forest Service Law: The Battle over the Forest Service Planning Rule*, 44 NAT. RESOURCES J. 1 (2004) (arguing, among other things, that the Committee of Scientists and Clinton Administration should have sought congressional endorsement rather than making the changes administratively) and Michael J. Mortimer, *The Delegation of Law–Making Authority to the United States Forest*

Service: Implications in the Struggle for National Forest Management, 54
Admin. L.Rev. 907 (2002).

5. In Sierra Club v. Marita, *supra* p. 713, the court ruled that existing
law does not require the Forest Service to manage the National Forests in
accordance with the science of conservation biology. The 2000 regulations,
including the emphasis on species diversity, are rife with conservation
biology. Does the *Marita* reasoning mean that the Forest Service exceeded
its authority by relying so heavily on conservation biology? Or are these
matters left to the discretion of the Forest Service under the *Chevron*
principle?

6. Professor Holly Doremus has charged that "[c]onservation-orient-
ed scientist-advocates have sometimes exaggerated the role of scientific
data in their calls for resource protection," and cites as an example the role
of the two Committees of Scientists that advised the Forest Service in both
the late 1970s and again in the late 1990s. Holly Doremus, *Science Plays
Defense: Natural Resource Management in the Bush Administration*, 32
Ecology L.Q. 249, 259–60 (2005). Is the task of defining the meaning of
"diversity" in the NFMA through regulation principally a scientific determination? Diversity is a term used by scientists, but its meaning varies
depending on its application. The NFMA's vagueness in the meaning of
"diversity" in 1976 allowed subsequent developments in conservation biology to receive attention through rulemaking. Would it have been better for
Congress to have specified in detail the understanding of diversity in 1976,
before conservation biology got off the ground as a field?

b. THE 2005 REGULATIONS

The George W. Bush Administration quickly suspended the 2000
regulations, believing them too burdensome, expensive, and difficult to
administer and that the emphasis on ecological sustainability was bad
policy. It allowed planning to continue under the 1982 regulations, and
then developed a new rule on the subject in 2005. 70 Fed. Reg. 1023 (2005).
The 2005 rule, which bears virtually no resemblance to either the 1982 or
2000 regulations, jettisoned the idea of ecological sustainability and called
for streamlined forest planning that sets broad strategic goals and makes
essentially no hard decisions. The preamble leaves no doubt about the
boldness of the new system:

> This final rule embodies a paradigm shift in land management plan-
> ning based, in part, on the Forest Service's 25 years of experience
> developing under the 1982 planning rule. Having assessed the current
> system's flaws and benefits during this extended period, the Forest
> Service believes it is time to think differently about National Forest
> System (NFS) planning and management. * * *

> * * *

> * * * [P]lans under this final rule will be more strategic and less
> prescriptive in nature than under the 1982 planning rule. Emphasizing
> the strategic nature of plans under this rule is the most effective
> means of guiding NFS management in light of changing conditions,

science, and technology. Specifically, plans under this final rule will not contain final decisions that approve projects or activities except under extraordinary circumstances.* * *

The rule deemphasized science and imposed few if any substantive standards. *See* Barry R. Noon et al., *Conservation Science, Biodiversity, and the 2005 U.S. Forest Service Regulations*, 19 Conservation Biol. 2359 (2005). With regard to biodiversity, the 1982 regulations required that, through the use of indicator species, "fish and wildlife habitat shall be managed to maintain viable populations of existing native and desired non-native vertebrate species" and that the agency "must insure that viable populations will be maintained." The 2005 rule included diversity as one factor lumped in with general multiple-use management:

§ 219.10   Sustainability.

* * *

(a) Sustaining social and economic systems. The overall goal of the social and economic elements of sustainability is to contribute to sustaining social and economic systems within the plan area. * * *

(b) Sustaining ecological systems. The overall goal of the ecological element of sustainability is to provide a framework to contribute to sustaining native ecological systems by providing ecological conditions to support diversity of native plant and animal species in the plan area. * * *

(1) Ecosystem diversity. Ecosystem diversity is the primary means by which a plan contributes to sustaining ecological systems. Plan components must establish a framework to provide the characteristics of ecosystem diversity in the plan area.

(2) Species diversity. If the Responsible Official determines that provisions in plan components, in addition to those required by paragraph (b)(1) of this section, are needed to provide appropriate ecological conditions for specific threatened and endangered species, species-of-concern, and species-of-interest, then the plan must include additional provisions for these species, consistent with the limits of agency authorities, the capability of the plan area, and overall multiple use objectives.

Rather than being bound by the best available science (as is the case, for example, under the Endangered Species Act and Clean Water Act), the 2005 rule states:

219.11   Role of science in planning.

(a) The Responsible Official must take into account the best available science. For purposes of this subpart, taking into account the best available science means the Responsible Official must: (1) Document how the best available science was taken into account in the planning process within the context of the issues being considered; (2) Evaluate and disclose substantial uncertainties in that science; (3) Evaluate and disclose substantial risks associated with plan components based on that science; and (4) Document that the science was appropriately interpreted and applied. * * *

(b) To meet the requirements of paragraph (a) of this section, the Responsible Official may use independent peer review, a science advisory board, or other review methods to evaluate the consideration of science in the planning process.

NOTES AND QUESTIONS

1.   Is anything left of the diversity requirement? The remainder of the 2005 regulations also seems to contain little if any prescriptive language. Between them, do the 2005 rule and the *Ohio Forestry* case eliminate the role of judicial review in planning? If so, is that a loss from the perspective of good resource management? Does it promote more experimentation and adaptive management? Have we gotten to the point that, given the time and expense of federal court review, regulations for a modern land management agency should be general policy statements that will not lead to the courthouse?

2.   After the *Ohio Forestry* case, few plan provisions are subject to facial challenge in court. Judicial review, however, continues to be available for individual projects, and the courts occasionally enforce provisions in plans that they regard as binding the agency, in the context of specific actions taken to carry out the plan. *See, e.g.,* Neighbors of Cuddy Mountain v. United States Forest Service, 137 F.3d 1372 (9th Cir. 1998). The 2005 rule states that henceforth plans are to be "more strategic and less prescriptive in nature" and "will not contain final decisions that approve projects or activities except under extraordinary circumstances." Does that mean they are not likely to contain "law to apply" for judicial review? Most plans approved as of the beginning of 2007 continued to use the 1982 rule because the 2005 rule allowed individual forests to continue with the older rule to complete planning already underway. Therefore, judicial tests of forest plans under the 2005 rule are still years off.

3.   Is the reform consistent with the thrust of the National Forest Management Act? What would you advise conservationists unhappy with this reform to do?

4.   At the end of the day, with this revision, and following the upheaval and congressional intervention in national forest management that began with the *Monongahela* case in 1975, does the Forest Service have the same vast discretion to manage the national forests that it enjoyed for the first three quarters of the twentieth century? Is that a good or bad thing? Consider the observations of Andrew Orlemann:

> If one views the Forest Service as an elite, efficient, conscientious agency seemingly fettered in its professional management by endless lawsuits, [then a loose] regulation is probably a reasonable one. It should provide the agency with more opportunities to apply its expertise to national forest management without the interference of public interest group generated injunctions. If, on the other hand, one views the Forest Service as an incompetent bureaucracy staffed by the

proverbial timber beast, [then a loose] regulation is probably less than ideal. It does not provide very many specific requirements by which the Forest Service can be monitored by the interested public.

Do the Proposed Forest Service Regulations Protect Biodiversity? An Analysis of the Continuing Viability of "Habitat Viability Analysis", 20 J. LAND RESOURCES & ENVTL. L. 357 (2000). Do you agree with his characterizations?

5. The portion of the 2005 planning rule dealing with planning as strategic, continuous improvement of management "systems" is covered in chapter 5, *supra* p. 474.

6. As this book went to press, U.S. District Court Judge Phyllis Hamilton enjoined the 2005 rule for violations of the APA, NEPA, and ESA. Citizens for Better Forestry v. U.S. Dept. of Agriculture, 481 F.Supp.2d 1059 (N.D. Cal. 2007), discussed *supra* p. 480. In a prior, unreported decision, Judge Hamilton had dismissed the plaintiffs' NFMA claims as unripe under the *Ohio Forestry* standard because there were no site-specific actions directly associated with the challenged LRMP. Citizens for Better Forestry v. U.S. Dept. of Agriculture, 2006 WL 1072043 (N.D.Cal. 2006).

7. The administrative appeals processes in the Forest Service differ from those in the BLM in the Department of the Interior, where most appeals of agency decisions go to a hearings officer and then to the Interior Board of Land Appeals. The review procedures in the Forest Service dispense with formal hearings and appellate-type legal appeals, such as those handled by the IBLA. Instead, Forest Service appeals are handled by agency line officers (and sometimes by the Undersecretary of Agriculture), and are less formal and quicker. For a discussion of the Forest Service appeals process, and the 1992 Appeals Reform Act, see Earth Island Institute v. Ruthenbeck, 459 F.3d 954 (9th Cir. 2006) (overturning a number of appeals rule changes as violating the 1992 law).

Appeals of specific projects are governed by 36 CFR Part 215. There is just one level of appeal—for example, a decision by a forest supervisor goes to the regional forester. The reviewing official can hold a "meeting"—not a "hearing"—and the reviewing official must render a decision within 45 days. There is no discretionary appeal beyond that point and the decision of the reviewing officer is final agency action for the purpose of judicial review. Under the 2005 planning regulations, forest plans and amendments may be contested by an expedited process called "objection," in which an objector may file a "concise statement" with the reviewing official. That official's decision is final agency action. 36 CFR § 219.13. An objection process is also used for issues under the Healthy Forest Restoration Act discussed immediately below, *see* 36 CFR § 218. The procedures are somewhat more extensive for appeals by holders of written instruments, which are usually private law matters, such as contract disputes between timber companies and the agency. *See* 36 CFR § 251.80.

5.   WILDFIRE MANAGEMENT

In December 2003 President Bush signed into law the Healthy Forest Restoration Act, 117 Stat. 1887, 16 U.S.C. §§ 6501 et seq. The HFRA responds to increasing episodes of wildfires in the West and a growing understanding that nearly a century of fire suppression had caused a dangerous buildup in forest fuels. There is no doubt about the need to respond to the threat of catastrophic fires as evidenced by the Yellowstone fire of 1988 and the devastating fire seasons of 2000 and 2002 that afflicted every western state. Environmentalists objected to the HFRA, however, because they feared it would lead to unnecessary logging—with the Forest Service too often choosing commercial thinning over controlled burns and responding to industry's interest in large-diameter trees whose removal would not be essential to true fuel reduction.

A key part of the HFRA, 16 U.S.C. § 6512, authorizes "fuel reduction projects" and expedites (some say "short-circuits") the environmental review process, opportunities for public participation, and administrative appeals in connection with certain broadly-defined forest treatment projects, including timber harvesting, for the purpose of fuel reduction. The total area of such projects may not exceed twenty million acres of federal land, and may not be carried out in wilderness, wilderness study areas, or some other protected areas.

Professor Robert B. Keiter offered these perspectives in *The Law of Fire: Reshaping Public Land Policy in an Era of Ecology and Litigation*, 36 Envtl. L. 301, 344–48 (2006):

> [The HFRA] represents the first serious congressional effort to articulate a federal fire policy for the public lands. Adopted in the aftermath of three extraordinarily destructive fire seasons, Congress confronted mounting political pressures to reduce the risk of catastrophic fire near the ever-growing wildland-urban interface zones. The resulting HFRA brought various political factions together in compromise legislation that incorporated several Bush Administration-supported legal reforms, yet still minimized intrusions into environmentally sensitive areas and retained important legal safeguards. * * *

> * * * Significantly, the HFRA does not acknowledge that fire constitutes an important ecological process that belongs on the landscape, and only once mentions prescribed fire as an acceptable strategy for addressing wildfire risks on wildland-urban interface lands or elsewhere. The overriding sense is that the agencies must undertake aggressive management actions to reduce the likelihood of catastrophic fires.

> The HFRA's primary wildfire control strategy is the hazardous fuel reduction project. The statute affirmatively directs the agencies to implement hazardous fuel reduction projects, which will generally involve tree and brush removal. * * *

> The HFRA may legitimately be seen as taking federal forest management policy toward restoration, but its revisions to legal requirements have potentially troubling implications. With its emphasis on restoration, Congress has reaffirmed that forest management entails more than commodity production and that ecological considerations must be factored into the management equation. The HFRA not

only exempts various preserved lands from hazardous fuel projects, but it also contains detailed new prescriptive limitations on cutting ecologically important old growth components. But to achieve its restoration objectives, the HFRA plainly contemplates active forest management through hazardous fuel projects and applied silvicultural assessments—provisions that could accelerate timber cutting levels and rekindle smoldering antagonisms between the agencies and environmental groups. In addition, the HFRA revises NEPA compliance obligations and reduces administrative appeal avenues, thus eliminating important legal oversight opportunities in the name of decision making efficiency. The HFRA's more ecologically sensitive and prescriptive restoration provisions, in short, are counterbalanced by a renewed congressional commitment to timber cutting and to minimizing the law's role in this process.

—————

Fuel reduction sales under the HFRA and salvage sales are likely to dominate Forest Service litigation in the upcoming years. After a century of aggressive suppression, there is broad agreement about the need for reducing the accumulated fuel in federal forests. However, sharp disputes arise over whether controlled burns or logging should be employed and whether some projects advertised as necessary for fuel reduction are in fact carried out mainly for commercial purposes. In the meantime, heavy fuel loads and increased residential development surrounding federal lands continue to press the issue of treatment. Federal expenditures for fighting fire continue to climb; 2006 was the most expensive year to date with $2 billion (40 percent of the total Forest Service budget) spent to fight fires that burned nearly 10 million acres.

After fires burn, there is little agreement on the best treatment of forests. Salvage sales—the logging of trees that are dead or dying as a result of fire, blowdown, or insect infestation—present particularly contentious issues. Silviculturally and economically, the sales often make sense and the NFMA has several special exceptions for salvage sales. *See* 16 U.S.C. sections 1604(g)(3)(F)(iv) (size of clearcuts); 1604(k) (physical and economic suitability); 1604(m)(1) (culmination of mean annual increment); 1611(b) (nondeclining even flow). Ecologically, however, the down timber, if not removed by salvage sales, will return nutrients to the soil and provide other environmental benefits. Further, the logging and roading, especially in fire-scarred terrain, may cause significant erosion and surface disturbance. A leading report of independent scientists, headed by Professor Robert Bechta of Oregon State University, "recommends minimal intrusion into severely burned areas and no salvage logging in sensitive areas including severely burned areas and erosive sites." *See* Blue Mountains Biodiversity Project v. Blackwood, 161 F.3d 1208, 1213 (9th Cir. 1998).

Salvage sales now make up about one-third of all Forest Service timber sales. There is time pressure from the commercial side because the wood may begin to rot within a year or two. Industry has proposed legislation allowing for expedited consideration of salvage sales, but it has not passed. Opposition to this approach is be due in part to the excesses of the "Salvage Rider," which was enacted as part of the 1995 Rescissions Act and remained in force from its passage in July, 1995 through December, 1996. This short-term rider allowed high-yield, expedited salvage sales with curtailed environmental compliance and judicial review. Today, generally, the Forest Service must comply with the NFMA, ESA, NEPA, the Northwest Forest Plan, and other applicable laws in making salvage sales.

Ecology Center, Inc. v. Austin

United States Court of Appeals, Ninth Circuit, 2005.
430 F.3d 1057, cert. denied 127 S.Ct. 931 (2007).

■ JUDGE FLETCHER

* * *

I

In 2000, wildfires burned approximately 74,000 acres on the Lolo National Forest. While the fires caused considerable damage to the forest, they also created habitat for species that are dependent upon post-fire habitats, such as the black-backed woodpecker.

In response to the 2000 fires, the Forest Service began developing the Lolo National Forest Post Burn Project and preparing the requisite Environmental Impact Statement ("EIS"). The Forest Service considered four alternatives in detail, including a "no action alternative." In July 2002, the Forest Service selected a slightly modified version of "Alternative Number Five" for the Project. This alternative involves, *inter alia*, commercial thinning of small diameter timber and prescribed burning in old-growth forest stands, as well as salvage logging of burned and insect killed timber in various areas of the forest.

* * *

II.

* * *

A. "Treatment" of Old–Growth Habitat

The Project involves what the Forest Service characterizes as rehabilitative "treatment" of old-growth (and potential old-growth) forest stands; this treatment entails the thinning of old-growth stands via commercial logging and prescribed burning. The Forest Service cites a number of studies that indicate such treatment is necessary to correct uncharacteristic forest development resulting from years of fire suppression. The Service also points out that the treatment is designed to leave most of the desirable old-growth trees in place and to improve their health.

Ecology Center highlights the scientific uncertainty and debate regarding the necessity, design, and long-term effects of such old-growth treatment. In particular, Ecology Center alleges that the treatment of old-growth forest harms species that are dependent upon old-growth habitat. For example, Ecology Center claims that, even if treatment leaves most old-growth trees in place, it removes or alters other essential elements within old-growth habitat and disturbs bird species currently nesting or foraging within targeted stands.[2] Although treatment may be designed to restore old-growth to "historic conditions," Ecology Center points out this can be a misleading concept: for example, information regarding historic conditions is incomplete; altering particular sections of forest in order to achieve "historic" conditions may not make sense when the forest as a whole has already been fundamentally changed; many variables can affect treatment outcomes; and the treatment process is qualitatively different from the "natural" or "historic" processes it is intended to mimic.

While Ecology Center does not offer proof that the proposed treatment causes the harms it fears, the Service does not offer proof that the proposed treatment benefits—or at least does not harm—old-growth dependent species. Ecology Center argues that because the Forest Service has not assessed the effects of old-growth treatment on dependent species, the Service cannot be reasonably certain that treating old-growth is consistent with NFMA's substantive mandate to ensure species diversity and viability. As a result, especially given the scientific uncertainty surrounding the treatment of old-growth stands, the Forest Service's decision to treat additional old-growth stands was arbitrary and capricious.

Although the Forest Service points to a report which notes that two species of woodpecker were observed foraging in treated old-growth forest, it does not otherwise dispute the charge that it has not directly monitored the impact of treating old-growth on dependent species. Instead, the Service maintains that it need not do so because (1) it has observed the short-term effects of thinning old-growth stands via commercial logging and prescribed burning on forest composition, (2) it has reason to believe that certain old-growth dependent species would prefer the post-treatment composition of old-growth forest stands, and (3) its assumption that treatment does not harm old-growth dependent species is therefore reasonable. The Service further argues that we must defer to its methodological choices regarding what to monitor and how to assess the impact of old-growth treatment.

An agency's choice of methodology is entitled to deference. However, there are circumstances under which an agency's choice of methodology, and any decision predicated on that methodology, are arbitrary and capricious. * * * While the Service's predictions may be correct, the Service has not yet taken the time to test its theory with any "on the ground analysis," id., despite the fact that it has already treated old-growth forest elsewhere and therefore has had the opportunity to do so. Just as it would be

---

2. For example, the pileated woodpecker is dependent upon old-growth snags (standing dead trees), but treatment involves timber harvesting, which "creates the potential for snag loss." Although the Service acknowledges this danger, it believes that proposed "snag mitigation measures," combined with the potential for snag-creation during the prescribed burning process, will offset most of the snag loss caused by logging.

arbitrary and capricious for a pharmaceutical company to market a drug to the general population without first conducting a clinical trial to verify that the drug is safe and effective, it is arbitrary and capricious for the Forest Service to irreversibly "treat" more and more old-growth forest without first determining that such treatment is safe and effective for dependent species. This is not a case in which the Forest Service is asking for the opportunity to verify its theory of the benefits of old-growth treatment. Rather, the Service is asking us to grant it the license to continue treating old-growth forests while excusing it from ever having to verify that such treatment is not harmful.

The Service argues that under *Inland Empire Public Lands Council v. U.S. Forest Serv.*, we must defer to its decision to monitor only the effect of treatment on forest composition, instead of also monitoring the effect of treatment on dependent species. However, Inland Empire is inapposite here. In that case, we permitted the Service to determine that it was complying with its duty to maintain species viability by using a "proxy-on-proxy" method for monitoring species population. *But see Idaho Sporting Congress*, 305 F.3d at 972–73 (finding use of proxy-on-proxy approach arbitrary and capricious where there is evidence that the "methodology does not reasonably ensure viable populations of the species at issue"). Under the proxy-on-proxy approach, the Service does not ensure that it is maintaining species viability by directly monitoring species populations. Instead, the Service designates certain "management indicator species" as proxies for other species with comparable habitat needs. It then designates certain kinds of habitat as proxies for the management indicator species. Finally, it assumes that a species' viability is maintained so long as the requisite amount of the species' habitat is maintained. Here, the Service is not simply maintaining the amount of old-growth habitat necessary to support old-growth dependent species—it is altering the composition of old-growth habitat through an invasive process.

Although the Service concedes that the opinions of well-qualified experts vary with respect to the appropriateness of management activities in old-growth areas, it also argues that it must have the "discretion to rely on the reasonable opinions of its own qualified experts even if, as an original matter, a court might find contrary views more persuasive." However, this is not a case in which different experts have studied the effects of commercial thinning and prescribed burning in old-growth forests and reached different conclusions. Here, experts have differing hypotheses regarding the effects that treating old-growth has on dependent species, yet the Forest Service proposes to continue treating old-growth without first taking the time to observe what those effects actually are. In light of its responsibilities under NFMA, this is arbitrary and capricious.

* * *

B. Salvage Harvesting of Black–Backed Woodpecker Habitat

* * *

[The court found that the decision to log in the habitat of black-backed woodpeckers, designated by the Forest Service as a "sensitive species," was arbitrary and capricious: "Because the Forest Service failed to provide the factual basis for its analysis and failed to adequately explain its decision, we cannot be reasonably certain that the salvaging—which the Service concedes may harm individual black-backed woodpeckers—will not jeopardize the black-backed woodpeckers' viability."]

C. Soil–Quality Analysis

Ecology Center next challenges the Forest Service's soil quality analysis. Under the applicable Regional Soil Quality Standard, the Forest Service cannot allow an activity that would create detrimental soil conditions in fifteen percent of the activity area. Ecology Center claims that the methodology the Forest Service used to determine what percentage of soil is in a detrimental state in each activity area was insufficiently reliable because the Service estimated soil conditions on the basis of maps, samples from throughout the Forest, aerial reconnaissance, and computer modeling, but did not verify those estimates by directly observing soil conditions in the activity areas.

We addressed a nearly identical claim, involving the same Regional Soil Quality Standard, in Lands Council [v. Powell, 379 F.3d 738, 752–53 (9th Cir. 2004)]. In that case, "based on samples from throughout the Forest, and aerial photographs, the Forest Service estimated the quality of the soils in the Project area using a spreadsheet model." *Id*. at 752. We held that the "Forest Service's reliance on the spreadsheet models, unaccompanied by on-site spot verification of the model's predictions, violated NFMA." *Id*. at 752–53. * * *

* * *

2. On–Site Verification of Soil Conditions

First, the Service points to the transects it conducted during the BAER [Burned Area Emergency Rehabilitation Report] assessment of the 2000 fires' aftermath. However, during the Project development, one of the Service's own experts pointed out that the transects targeted burned areas, not proposed harvest units; as a result, most of the activity areas were not transected. Thus, the BAER transects do not distinguish this case from Lands Council, where the Service similarly "did not test much of the activity area." *Lands Council*, 379 F.3d at 752, as amended by 395 F.3d at 1034.

Second, the Forest Service argues that its soil analysis is nonetheless sufficiently reliable because it utilized data from areas with ecological characteristics similar to the proposed harvest units. Lands Council expressly rejected this same argument. Id. ("The Forest Service concedes that it did not test much of the activity area, but argues that because it tested similar soils within the Forest, and similar soils act the same way, then the methodology is sound."). We note that comments on the Project by the Service's own expert support this holding: Region Scientist Nesser argued that the Service's conclusions regarding soil conditions in the activity areas were "not credible" because the Service did not test the activity areas themselves, as the Standard requires.

Third, the Service points to some informal field reports contained in the record, some of which indicate that a small percentage of the activity areas were observed directly. The record provides little information that enables us to assess the reliability or significance of these reports; for example, we do not know the qualifications of the persons conducting the field review, the methodology utilized, or whether the field observations confirmed or contradicted the Service's estimates. Moreover, the final EIS repeatedly explains that the Service will conduct field testing to verify its estimates prior to any ground-breaking activities, and there is no indication in the draft EIS or final EIS that the Forest Service actually consulted and relied upon any of the field reports it now cites when it was making its selection amongst the Project alternatives. Thus, we cannot conclude that these reports distinguish this case from Lands Council.

Finally, we consider whether the Service's plan to verify soil conditions in the activity areas after authorizing the Project, but before actually commencing harvesting activities, satisfies NFMA and NEPA. The fact that the Service plans to conduct on-site verification prior to any harvesting implies that even the Service recognizes that its soil-quality estimates need to be verified. Thus, we conclude that the Forest Service's decision to authorize the Project first and verify later does not distinguish this case from Lands Council, and that the Project violates NFMA. We also conclude that the Service's plan to verify its estimates post-decision fails to satisfy NEPA, because "NEPA requires consideration of the potential impact of an action before the action takes place."

III

The Forest Service's selection of Modified Alternative Number 5 for the Lolo National Forest Post–Burn Project violates both NEPA and NFMA. We reverse the district court's summary judgment in favor of the Forest Service, and direct the district court to enter summary judgment on behalf of Ecology Center. We remand this case to the Forest Service for further proceedings consistent with this opinion.

REVERSED AND REMANDED.

■ JUDGE McKEOWN, dissenting.

The Ninth Circuit, like the other circuits, repeats frequently the legal mantras of administrative review in the context of environmental decisions: "arbitrary and capricious," "hard look," and "no second guessing." These standards are easy to articulate, but it is more difficult to know when we have crossed the line from reviewer to decisionmaker. In this case, we have gone too far.

* * *

* * * In faulting the Forest Service's soil quality analysis and concluding that old-growth forest will not be impaired, the majority changes our posture of review to one where we sit at the table with Forest Service scientists and second-guess the minutiae of the decisionmaking process.

My concern is perhaps best illustrated in the majority's application of *Lands Council* to the soil quality analysis issue. In *Lands Council*, we addressed the Forest Service's analysis of disturbed soil conditions in a watershed restoration project in the Idaho Panhandle National Forest. The Forest Service had taken soil samples from throughout the forest but not in the activity area. Based on these samples and aerial photographs, it calculated the impact of the watershed restoration project on soil quality in the activity area.

In *Lands Council*, we rejected the Forest Service's choice of scientific methodology because it did not walk or test soil in the activity area. We concluded that the "Forest Service's reliance on the spreadsheet models, unaccompanied by on-site spot verification of the model's predictions, violated NFMA." Given the specific record and circumstances in *Lands Council*, this resolution may have made perfect sense. But in the abstract, without the ability to compare the record in *Lands Council* with the record here, there is no legal basis to conclude that the NFMA requires an on-site analysis where there is a reasonable scientific basis to uphold the legitimacy of modeling. NFMA does not impose this substantive requirement, and it cannot be derived from the procedural parameters of NEPA.

Application of *Lands Council* makes even less sense in this specific case. Here, the Forest Service conducted exactly the kind of on-site analyses found lacking in Lands Council—soil samples in activity areas. The record lists five activity areas surveyed in soil sample transects and details the walkthrough of a number of activity areas. The majority concedes that these on-site analyses exist but criticizes them for being too few and of poor quality. Resting on this characterization, the majority rejects the Forest Service's soil analysis on the ground that it was "nearly identical" to the one we found lacking in *Lands Council*.

Lands Council makes compliance with NFMA and NEPA a moving target. If one reads *Lands Council* to require on-site analysis in every case, which I respectfully suggest is an over-reading of the case, the circumstances here comply with that dictate. Yet the majority now says, without support in the record and absent a challenge by Ecology Center at the administrative level, that the on-site analysis was insufficient and that we do not possess enough information to know if the inspectors were qualified. From this judgment, we are left to conclude that not only does the court of appeals set bright-line rules, such as requiring an on-site, walk the territory inspection, but it also assesses the detail and quality of that analysis—even in the absence of contrary scientific evidence in the record. * * *

* * *

Nor do I think it appropriate to analogize the Forest Service process to the separate and wholly inapposite regime of the Food and Drug Administration ("FDA"). The majority writes that "it would be arbitrary and capricious for a pharmaceutical company to market a drug to the general population without first conducting a clinical trial" just as the Forest

Service cannot be permitted to "treat more and more old-growth forest without first determining that such treatment is safe and effective for dependent species." Without commenting on the obvious differences between humans and trees (and in fact acknowledging the importance of both to our environment), this analogy underscores the degree to which the majority inserts itself into the internal judgments of the Forest Service. The FDA process dictates a substantive and specific administrative course of action in terms of clinical trials and other requirements as a prelude to the approval of drugs and medical devices. Neither NEPA nor NFMA serve that function in the environmental context. To import the notion of clinical trials from the FDA context to soil sampling in federal forests is a leap too far.

Apparently we no longer simply determine whether the Forest Service's methodology involves a "hard look" through the use of "hard data," but now are called upon to make fine-grained judgments of its worth. In reaching this conclusion, the majority takes aim at two firmly established lines of precedent in administrative law. First, this view is contrary to the basic principle that we reverse agency decisions only if they are arbitrary and capricious. This standard of review does not direct us to literally dig in the dirt (or soil, as it were), get our fingernails dirty and flyspeck the agency's analysis. Yet the majority does exactly that by rejecting the Forest Service's soil analysis field checks and its observations and historical data in treated old-growth forests. The majority's rationale cannot be reconciled with our case law requiring "[d]eference to an agency's technical expertise and experience," particularly "with respect to questions involving engineering and scientific matters." * * *

* * *

NOTES AND QUESTIONS

1. Here, the *Ecology Center* court—this time writing after the Bush (II) Administration eliminated sections 219.19 and 219.26 of the NFMA regulations—applies the kind of rigor found in Sierra Club v. Martin and the cases following it. Does the diversity language in the NFMA, now standing alone, support the result? Is *Ecology Center* consistent with Inland Empire Public Lands Council v. Forest Service, *supra* p. 723?

2. Even though Sierra Club v. Marita defers to the agency, and *Ecology Center* does not, both courts seem to demand on-the-ground data (field work) to show that it makes sense to apply a theory to a particular place. What should courts demand from land management agencies to justify a resource management decision? Should courts ask more of plaintiffs seeking to challenge an agency action as failing to properly apply current science?

3. Another salvage case, Earth Island Institute v. United States Forest Service, 442 F.3d 1147 (9th Cir.2006), also enjoined timber sales, finding violations of NEPA and the NFMA—but the now-repealed regulations were in effect for those sales. As a matter of policy, given the amount

of data collecting involved in assuring sufficient habitat for sensitive and indicator species, should the courts leave it the Forest Service to decide how many person-hours to allocate to these matters in light of overall agency responsibilities? Is the answer different for scheduled rather than for salvage timber sales? In Sierra Club v. Bosworth, 465 F. Supp.2d 931 (N.D. Cal. 2006), District Judge Charles Breyer, following *Earth Island*, struck down proposed Forest Service fuel reduction sales within and adjacent to the Giant Sequoia National Monument on NEPA grounds and made these observations:

> In *Ecology Center*, the court addressed whether an EIS adequately addressed the environmental effects on the black-backed woodpecker of a post-wildfire logging project in the Lolo National Forest. The court concluded that "[t]he EIS fails to adequately explain the basis for the Forest Service's conclusion that eliminating a portion of the newly-created habitat will not adversely affect the black-backed woodpeckers' viability." The EIS at issue there stated that "even though salvaging post-fire habitat may negatively impact individual black-backed woodpeckers, it will 'not likely result in a trend towards federal listing.' "The court stated that "[w]ithout more, this general statement regarding the possible impact and risk involved do[es] not constitute a 'hard look' absent a justification regarding why more definitive information could not be provided." The Forest Service's conclusion here is eerily similar to that which the *Ecology Center* court ruled to be insufficient to constitute a hard look. *See* October Ice SIR at (concluding that the Ice Project "may affect individual fisher but would not likely result in a trend toward federal listing or loss of viability of the fisher").
>
> Moreover, the Ninth Circuit recently identified "a disturbing trend in the [Forest Service's] recent timber-harvesting and timber-sale activities." *Earth Island*, 442 F.3d at 1177–78 (listing eight cases since 2002 where courts found the Forest Service to have violated environmental laws relating to logging projects). Noting the "substantial financial interest in the harvesting of timber," the court stated: "We regret to say that in this case, like the others just cited, the [Forest Service] appears to have been more interested in harvesting timber than in complying with our environmental laws." It appears from the record before the Court that, like in *Earth Island* and the cases cited therein, the Forest Service's interest in harvesting timber has trampled the applicable environmental laws.

6.   THE NATIONAL FOREST ROADLESS RULE

The Clinton Administration undertook a major initiative in national forest management that had ramifications for timber production. The objective was to promulgate a national rule that would govern management of more than 58 million acres (or 30%) of the national forest system. The main provisions were that, with some exceptions, there would be no roadbuilding and no timber harvesting in the remaining roadless areas. The widely-debated rule was adopted through Administrative Procedure Act notice-and-comment rulemaking, accompanied by an environmental impact statement under NEPA. How to manage of these lands, including whether to designate some of them as wilderness, had been a major point of contention since the early 1970s.

The rule, which went into effect in early 2001, summarized the purpose of the regulation as follows:

> The Department of Agriculture is responsible for managing National Forest System resources to sustain the health, diversity, and productivity of the nation's forests and grasslands to meet the needs of present and future generations. * * * In the future, expanding urban areas and increased fragmentation of private lands make it likely that the largest and most extensive tracts of undeveloped land will be those in public ownership.

> This final rule prohibits road construction, reconstruction, and timber harvest in inventoried roadless areas because they have the greatest likelihood of altering and fragmenting landscapes, resulting in immediate, long-term loss of roadless area values and characteristics. Although other activities may also compromise roadless area values, they resist analysis at the national level and are best reviewed through local land management planning. Additionally, the size of the existing forest road system and attendant budget constraints prevent the agency from managing its road system to the safety and environmental standards to which it was built. Finally, national concern over roadless area management continues to generate controversy, including costly and time-consuming appeals and litigation.* * *

66 Fed. Reg. 3244 (January 12, 2001).

The agency identified, and discussed at length, the values that often characterize the roadless areas: high quality or undisturbed soil, water, and air; sources of public drinking water; diversity of plant and animal communities; and habitat for threatened, endangered, proposed, candidate, and sensitive species and for those species dependent on large, undisturbed areas of land. Roadless areas function as biological strongholds and refuges for many species; areas for primitive, semi–primitive, non–motorized, and semi–primitive motorized classes of dispersed recreation; reference landscapes of relatively undisturbed areas to serve as a barometer to measure the effects of development on other parts of the landscape; natural appearing landscapes with high scenic quality; and traditional cultural properties and sacred sites.

The regulations themselves were very short. Key provisions follow.

36 C.F.R.§ 294.12 Prohibition on road construction and road reconstruction in inventoried roadless areas.

(a) A road may not be constructed or reconstructed in inventoried roadless areas of the National Forest System, except as provided in paragraph (b) of this section.

(b) Notwithstanding the prohibition in paragraph (a) of this section, a road may be constructed or reconstructed in an inventoried roadless area if the Responsible Official determines that one of the following circumstances exists:

(1) A road is needed to protect public health and safety in cases of an imminent threat of flood, fire, or other catastrophic event that, without intervention, would cause the loss of life or property;

(2) A road is needed to conduct a response action under the Comprehensive Environmental Response, Compensation, and Liability Act (CERCLA) or to conduct a natural resource restoration action under CERCLA, Section 311 of the Clean Water Act, or the Oil Pollution Act;

(3) A road is needed pursuant to reserved or outstanding rights, or as provided for by statute or treaty;

(4) Road realignment is needed to prevent irreparable resource damage that arises from the design, location, use, or deterioration of a classified road and that cannot be mitigated by road maintenance. Road realignment may occur under this paragraph only if the road is deemed essential for public or private access, natural resource management, or public health and safety;

(5) Road reconstruction is needed to implement a road safety improvement project on a classified road determined to be hazardous on the basis of accident experience or accident potential on that road;

(6) The Secretary of Agriculture determines that a Federal Aid Highway project, authorized pursuant to Title 23 of the United States Code, is in the public interest or is consistent with the purposes for which the land was reserved or acquired and no other reasonable and prudent alternative exists; or

(7) A road is needed in conjunction with the continuation, extension, or renewal of a mineral lease on lands that are under lease by the Secretary of the Interior as of January 12, 2001 or for a new lease issued immediately upon expiration of an existing lease. Such road construction or reconstruction must be conducted in a manner that minimizes effects on surface resources, prevents unnecessary or unreasonable surface disturbance, and complies with all applicable lease requirements, land and resource management plan direction, regulations, and laws. Roads constructed or reconstructed pursuant to this paragraph must be obliterated when no longer needed for the purposes of the lease or upon termination or expiration of the lease, whichever is sooner. * * *

36 C.F.R § 294.13 Prohibition on timber cutting, sale, or removal in inventoried roadless areas.

(a) Timber may not be cut, sold, or removed in inventoried roadless areas of the National Forest System, except as provided in paragraph (b) of this section.

(b) Notwithstanding the prohibition in paragraph (a) of this section, timber may be cut, sold, or removed in inventoried roadless areas if the

Responsible Official determines that one of the following circumstances exists. The cutting, sale, or removal of timber in these areas is expected to be infrequent.

(1) The cutting, sale, or removal of generally small diameter timber is needed for one of the following purposes and will maintain or improve one or more of the roadless area characteristics as defined in § 294.11.

(i) To improve threatened, endangered, proposed, or sensitive species habitat; or

(ii) To maintain or restore the characteristics of ecosystem composition and structure, such as to reduce the risk of uncharacteristic wildfire effects, within the range of variability that would be expected to occur under natural disturbance regimes of the current climatic period; * * *

36 C.F.R § 294.14 Scope and applicability.

(a) This subpart does not revoke, suspend, or modify any permit, contract, or other legal instrument authorizing the occupancy and use of National Forest System land issued prior to January 12, 2001. * * *

NOTES AND QUESTIONS

1. What policy arguments are made for keeping roadless areas roadless? Is this purely an environmental issue? A spiritual one? An economic one?

2. If the main focus is to stop further roadbuilding, why is timber harvesting also prohibited? Is that prohibition adequately justified in the preamble?

3. Is the policy in this rule consistent with multiple use principles? Why or why not?

4. One question is whether such decisions should be made at the local level (by individual national forests) or at the national level? What are the arguments for keeping it local?

5. Nine lawsuits were filed in various jurisdictions by a variety of opponents of the new rule. The first court to exercise review enjoined implementation of the rule, finding various procedural shortcomings, primarily involving NEPA compliance. But the Ninth Circuit upheld the rule, finding sufficient NEPA compliance, and reinstated the roadless rule, over a sharp dissent by Judge Kleinfeld. Kootenai Tribe v. Veneman, 313 F.3d 1094 (9th Cir. 2002).

The plot thickened when District Judge Brimmer issued a lengthy opinion that disagreed with the Ninth Circuit and enjoined the rule, finding a violation not only of NEPA but the Wilderness Act as well. Wyoming v. United States Dep't of Agric., 277 F.Supp.2d 1197 (D. Wyo. 2003). Environmental intervenors appealed to the Tenth Circuit, but the Bush Administration did not, and instead filed an amicus brief arguing that the court lacked jurisdiction to hear the environmentalists' appeal. Ultimately, after the Forest Service adopted a new roadless rule, discussed below, the Court of Appeals dismissed the appeal as moot, 414 F.3d 1207 (10th Cir. 2005).

6.   In Idaho ex rel. Kempthorne v. United States Forest Service, 142 F.Supp.2d 1248 (D.Idaho 2001), the environmentalist intervenors argued that no EIS was required for the Roadless Rule because it did not "commit resources to some affirmative human development of the environment, does not change existing environmental conditions, and does not alter the environmental status quo." The court disagreed, concluding that "changing or limiting existing active management in the national forest, drastically alters the current status quo * * * by preventing the enactment of land management techniques that provide for road construction, reconstruction or timber harvesting." 142 F.Supp.2d at 1259. Is it a misuse of NEPA for opponents of roadless area protection to argue that its procedures should be strictly followed, so as to throw out a rule that has stronger environmental protection as its goal?

Strategically, was it wise for the environmentalist intervenors to argue that NEPA did not apply here at all, because the proposal did not change the status quo in roadless areas? Might it, if accepted, create a precedent undesirable for environmental interests in the long run? That is, usually environmentalists advocate expanding the coverage of NEPA; here they are arguing the opposite. Suppose a license for an environmentally destructive dam comes up for renewal. Can the dam operator argue that NEPA doesn't apply because renewal will not change the status quo?

The Bush Administration reopened public comment on the roadless policy in 2001, proposed regulations in 2004, and published a new rule in May, 2005. 70 Fed. Reg. 25654 (2005), revising 36 C.F.R. Part 294. The preamble emphasized the need for local input, especially by the states:

> USDA is committed to conserving and managing inventoried roadless areas and considers these areas an important component of the NFS. The Department believes that revising 36 CFR part 294 by adopting a new rule that establishes a State petitioning process that will allow State-specific consideration of the needs of these areas is an appropriate solution to address the challenges of inventoried roadless area management on NFS lands.

> States affected by the roadless rule have been keenly interested in inventoried roadless area management, especially the Western States where most of the agency's inventoried roadless areas are located. Collaborating and cooperating with States on the long-term strategy for the conservation and management or inventoried roadless areas on NFS lands allows for the recognition of local situations and resolutions of unique resource management challenges within a specific State. Collaboration with others who have strong interest in the conservation and management of inventoried roadless areas also helps ensure balanced management decisions that maintain the most important characteristics and values of those areas. * * *

The 2005 rule established a voluntary process in which governors may petition the Forest Service and recommend management requirements for some or all of the roadless areas in the state. The petitions had to be filed within 18 months of the publication date of the rule.

NOTES AND QUESTIONS

1. Reaction among the governors was mixed. The Governor of Oregon petitioned the U.S. Department of Agriculture asking that the state be allowed simply to request the Clinton roadless rule be left in place, but the Department promptly rejected the petition. Governor Richardson of New Mexico petitioned to protect all the roadless areas in his state. The governors of Colorado, Idaho and Montana all created avenues for public input and ultimately petitioned to protect most of their roadless areas. The Attorneys General of California, New Mexico, Washington, and Oregon brought a NEPA lawsuit to void the Bush rule and reinstate the Clinton rule.

2. The suit brought by California, Washington, New Mexico, and Oregon received a ruling in September, 2006. People ex rel. Lockyer v. U.S. Department of Agriculture, 459 F.Supp.2d 874 (N.D. Cal. 2006), where Magistrate Judge Elizabeth D. LaPorte issued summary judgment in favor of the plaintiff states, enjoined implementation of the 2005 rule, and reinstated the 2001 rule. The court ruled that the Forest Service failed to engage in proper consultation under section 7 of the ESA and that the agency was required to prepare an EIS and could not employ a categorical exclusion under NEPA regulations. An appeal is expected. Opponents of the roadless rule have gone back to court in Wyoming, seeking to reinstate the injunction against the Clinton rule they previously obtained.

3. What is the best approach—the 2001 rule, the 2005 rule, leaving the roadless areas to planning in individual forests, or something else? Given this brouhaha, why has Congress not stepped in? Should it?

D. THE NORTHWEST FOREST PLAN: A STUDY IN SCIENCE, LAW, AND POLITICS

The Northwest Forest Plan, the most ambitious exercise in ecosystem management yet undertaken and perhaps the most prominent controversy ever to emerge under the ESA, was born in efforts to protect the northern spotted owl. Not bad for a bird that stands about 18 inches tall, with a 40–inch wingspan. Largely because of its secretive, nocturnal nature, not much was known about it before the late 1980s. A few thousand breeding pairs occupy several million acres of old growth Douglas fir forests in the Pacific Northwest, about 65 percent of which is national forest land, another 25 percent other federal land, and about 10 percent state, tribal, or privately-owned land. In the early 1980s, the Forest Service designated the northern spotted owl as an indicator species. The Forest Service has traditionally produced about half of the total timber harvest in the National Forest

System from the forests of Oregon and Washington. The matter soon moved to the front pages:

> In 1986, the spotted owl and biological diversity surged into the public consciousness when the Forest Service released proposed management guidelines on the spotted owl. The guidelines called for 550 spotted owl habitat areas, each holding up to 2200 acres of old growth. Logging of old growth would continue apace, at the rate of 60,000 acres per year. Even by conservative estimates, the proposal would have allowed the harvesting of 25 percent of all existing spotted owl habitat within fifteen years and approximately 60 percent after fifty years. This spotted owl management plan—as controversial an issue as the Forest Service has ever addressed—generated 40,000 letters from the public. Both industry and environmentalists went up in arms, industry leaders claiming that the proposal would cost thousands of jobs, environmentalists pointing to studies showing that the plan might well end the spotted owl's chances for survival within just twenty-five years.
>
> The Forest Service released its final spotted owl guidelines in 1988. These called for protection of 3000 acres for each nesting site—ten times the area recommended by the original task force in the 1970s— and stipulated that the Forest Service would review the adequacy of these measures within five years. During the administrative appeals from the 1988 plan, however, new scientific evidence showed that more would be needed to protect the northern spotted owl—and its ancient forest habitat. * * *

Charles F. Wilkinson, CROSSING THE NEXT MERIDIAN: LAND, WATER, AND THE FUTURE OF THE WEST 161 (1992).

Doubting that the Forest Service would provide sufficient protection under the NFMA, environmentalists petitioned to list the owl under the ESA. The might of the timber industry initially prevailed and the U.S. Fish & Wildlife Service declined to list the species. But then Judge Thomas Zilly ordered that the bird be listed in Northern Spotted Owl v. Hodel, 716 F.Supp. 479 (W.D. Wash. 1988), *supra* p. 285:

> The Court will reject conclusory assertions of agency "expertise" where the agency spurns unrebutted expert opinions without itself offering a credible alternative explanation. * * * Here, the Service disregarded all the expert opinion on population viability, including that of its own expert, that the owl is facing extinction, and instead merely asserted its expertise in support of its conclusion.
>
> The Service has failed to provide its own or other expert analysis supporting its conclusions. Such analysis is necessary to establish a rational connection between the evidence presented and the Service's decision. Accordingly, the United States Fish and Wildlife Service's decision not to list at this time the northern spotted owl as endangered or threatened under the Endangered Species Act was arbitrary and capricious and contrary to law.

After the stinging remand, the Fish and Wildlife Service listed the northern spotted owl as threatened. But the number of lawsuits increased as the Forest Service attempted to maintain levels of logging. The blunder-buss came in 1991, when Judge William Dwyer enjoined all Forest Service timber sales in spotted owl habitat until the agency developed a spotted owl management plan consistent with the diversity regulation adopted pursuant to the NFMA, 36 CFR § 219.19. Judge Dwyer left no doubt that politics had been trumping science and law:

> More is involved here than a simple failure by an agency to comply with its governing statute. The most recent violation of NFMA exemplifies a deliberate and systematic refusal by the Forest Service and the FWS to comply with the laws protecting wildlife. This is not the doing of the scientists, foresters, rangers, and others at the working levels of these agencies. It reflects decisions made by higher authorities in the executive branch of government.

Seattle Audubon Society v. Evans, 771 F. Supp. 1081 (W.D. Wash. 1991), *aff'd.* 952 F.2d 297 (9th Cir. 1991). In 1993, the Clinton Administration came into office with much of the timber supply from the Northwest shut down until the government came up with a plan sufficient to lift Judge Dwyer's injunction. The President soon convened a "Timber Summit" in Portland.

Steven Lewis Yaffee, THE WISDOM OF THE SPOTTED OWL: POLICY LESSONS OF A NEW CENTURY

Pp. 141–143 (1994).

In the early days of the administration, it was clear that President Clinton needed all the political capital he could muster to promote a variety of initiatives, including deficit reduction, economic stimulus, and health care reform, and early political fiascoes presented the image of a weakened and disorganized administration that was very willing to compromise its objectives in the face of political opposition.

Yet the magnitude of the political dilemma facing administration was matched by an opportunity to forge the political will to settle the owl dispute. While President George Bush had derided the preservationists as those "spotted owl people," candidate Bill Clinton pledged to convene a multiparty working group to resolve the controversy within the first 100 days of his administration, and he was true to his word. Scheduled for April 2, 1993, the forest conference represented the first step by the Clinton administration to legitimize a compromise solution to the controversy.

* * *

Held in Portland, Oregon, the forest conference was remarkable in several ways. It showcased the President and Vice–President of the United States, along with three cabinet secretaries, sitting around a conference table for a full day, talking domestic policy with those who ostensibly would be most directly affected by any course of action, while the rest of the nation had the opportunity to watch the proceedings on national television. Reflecting the lauded style of an earlier televised conference on the economy held in Little Rock, Arkansas, the forest conference suggested that the top levels of government took the issue seriously, and viewed it as a complex problem needing a serious solution to get beyond the gridlock that had prevailed for the preceding few years.

Just as remarkable was the set of individuals who were not visibly participating in the dialogue at the conference: the agencies and the Northwest Congressional delegation, some of the major historic players in the dispute. The symbolism was unmistakable: Here was a conference focused largely on the future of national forest management in the Pacific Northwest, and the chief of the FS and the elected representatives of the region's population were not at the table. While the agencies and members of Congress were present as invited members of the audience, the team planning the event orchestrated it to focus on a small set of experts and a larger set of Pacific Northwest residents who were personally affected by any outcome. This approach reduced the amount of grandstanding at the conference, offset the need for many participants to define past actions, and focused many of the presentations on the kind of personal stories cherished by the President and loved by the media. From the strategic perspective of the administration, it also had the potential of focusing follow-up activities on solving a recast problem rather than on justifying past positions. The handpicked panelists included twenty-one representatives of timber (split approximately evenly between labor and management), four fisheries groups, nine environmentalists, six scientists, a handful of local and state government representatives, two economists, two sociologists, one vocational counselor, and the Archbishop of Seattle.

The conference also was notable for explicitly reframing the controversy as something bigger than the spotted owl issue. The problem was defined as: how to protect a broad range of environmental values within the old growth ecosystem while dealing humanely within a regional economy that was undergoing a normal process of transformation. While the needs of some 480 old growth dependent species were aired (and the threat of 480 more spotted owl controversies described), more important was a discussion of the impacts of timber activities on salmon and other fisheries. The Congressional delegation had tried in preconference negotiating sessions to keep the salmon issue off the table, but presentations at the conference made the very logical connection that one segment of the economy may well benefit from changes in other segments of the economy: Salmon stocks could improve as logging declined and management practices changed.

* * *

In concluding the conference, President Clinton called on his cabinet secretaries to craft a "balanced and comprehensive long-term" plan to end the stalemate and to complete it within sixty days. He reiterated the theme of compromise: "I don't want this situation to go back to posturing and positioning. To the politics of division that has characterized this issue in the past. I hope we can stay in the conference room and out of the courtroom." Clinton established five principles to guide the construction of a plan:

- The needs of loggers and timber communities had to be addressed.
- Forest health had to be protected.
- The plan had to be scientifically sound.
- A sustainable and predictable level of timber had to be provided.
- The government had to speak with a single voice.

The administration sprung into action in order to put in place a plan that would meet the president's formulation. It will depend on one's perspective as to whether the work of the Forest Ecosystem Management Assessment Team ("FEMAT"), described as follows, amounted to the zenith of principled, excellent, applied science or whether it was "Scientists Gone Wild."

Kathie Durbin, TREE HUGGERS: VICTORY, DEFEAT & RENEWAL IN THE NORTHWEST ANCIENT FOREST CAMPAIGN

Pp. 201–06 (1996).

Scientists began assembling in the pink marble U.S. Bancorp Tower in Downtown Portland in late March of 1993. They had two months to produce a blueprint for the survival of the Northwest's old-growth forests and all the creatures that inhabited them. As if that weren't challenge enough, President Clinton wanted a plan that would allow federal timber to flow again, and soon.

* * *

Initially, the Clinton administration envisioned a team of about 15. Assistant Interior Secretary George Frampton worked with Thomas to pick the core group. But as the scope and complexity of the task began to sink in, more scientists were enlisted. By the end, there were more than 100. Eventually, the unwieldy group was given an unwieldy name: the Forest Ecosystem Management Assessment Team, or FEMAT for short.

Everyone on the team was invited to take part in discussions, with final decisions left to [soon-to-be Forest Service Chief Jack Ward Thomas's] discretion. It was a heavy responsibility, even for someone with his knowledge and political acumen. He eventually named a core group of a dozen scientists to advise him on important issues.

Early on, the administration decided the scientists' work would be done in secret, without public involvement or press access. The reason offered was that time was so short they could not afford distractions. The shroud of secrecy surrounding the deliberations heightened media curiosity and fed the rumor mill.

* * *

The scientists began by reviewing all the previous studies that had brought the federal government to this moment. There were nearly 50.

They singled out the ones that could pass muster scientifically for further consideration. Eventually, they chose eight options for detailed evaluation.

The first computer runs predicting timber harvest levels under the eight options jolted even Thomas. Protecting all those plants and animals, with a moderately high level of certainty that none of them would go extinct in the foreseeable future, meant that very little logging could occur in the owl region. "We were shocked there was so little wiggle room," Thomas said later.

In early May, the various FEMAT working groups presented their work to the full team during an all-day session in Portland. Several administration officials and government lawyers also attended. During the presentations, it became clear to Thomas that none of the eight options were politically viable. None articulated a core philosophy or vision of how the forests should be managed for future generations. More to the point, only two options would produce more than 1 billion board feet of timber, and both of those were likely to be rejected by Judge Dwyer. Others clustered at 600 to 700 mmbf. Option 1, the greenest, came in at just 200 mmbf—virtually a zero cut.

* * *

Still, [University of Washington forestry professor Jerry] Franklin's concepts pointed to a way out of the impasse, a way to leave habitat reserves open to some kind of management and to ratchet up the timber yield, however slightly. The scientists decided to write a new option that would allow thinning of trees up to 80 years old within old-growth reserves—*if* it would hasten the development of old-growth characteristics within these younger stands. They also decided to allow salvage logging in the reserves—*if* it could be shown to promote "forest health."

Under this option there would be no new inviolate reserves. And at least a quarter of the remaining old growth would stay in the "matrix," the area open to modified clearcutting. * * *

It was given that the plan would have to protect dwindling wild salmon runs if the administration hoped to stave off future endangered species listings. The scientists redrew the old-growth reserves, concentrating them in watersheds critical to the survival of salmon. They theorized that these reserves could do double duty as habitat for land species—spotted owls, marbled murrelets, and salamanders.

No logging or road-building would be allowed within these "key watersheds" until the agencies formally studied them. Roadless areas within key watersheds would remain roadless. Even small streams would be protected by buffer zones. * * *

To accommodate Bruce Babbitt's fascination with consensus groups * * * the team drew 10 enormous "adaptive management areas," ranging in size from 80,000 to 400,000 acres. Within them, foresters would be encouraged to conduct large-scale experiments in ecosystem management, with local citizens closely involved in designing the experiments.

Computer runs showed that by leaving 25 percent of the old growth in the matrix, and by allowing thinning and salvage logging even in the reserves, the federal agencies could sell about 1.2 billion board feet of timber annually.

The scientists christened this new strategy Option 9.

To those following the evolution of the forest issue, this new timber yield figure was not a shock. "We all knew going in that an ecologically credible plan would not produce more than 1 billion board feet," Frampton said.

* * *

Thomas knew Clinton would pick Option 9 because, among the options that could pass muster with Judge Dwyer, it was the one that would allow him to sell the most timber. He also knew the president had hoped for a plan that would allow him to sell much more. But Option 9 was the best he had been able to deliver. "Do I think there was false hope created? Yes," Thomas said later. "But no one should have been surprised by 1.2 billion board feet."

* * *

On July 1, five weeks late, President Clinton unveiled Option 9 in a somber press conference fed by closed-circuit television to the Northwest. The president looked downcast and uncomfortable. With Vice President Gore and several Cabinet members and congressional Democrats flanking him, he apologized to the people of the Northwest for not offering a plan that provided more timber. He explained that his scientific and legal advisors had told him this plan was the best that could be managed under existing law. He admitted that the timber industry would be disappointed with timber sale levels and that environmentalists would be disappointed because the plan lacked some of the protections they had sought.

Then he borrowed a line from Oregon Governor Barbara Roberts: "I can only say that as with every other situation in life, we have to play the hand we were dealt. We are doing the best we can with the facts as they now exist in the Pacific Northwest. If these were easy questions, they would have been answered long ago."

Interior Secretary Bruce Babbitt then made a promise he would live to regret. "I'm confident we can move 2 billion board feet into communities of the Northwest in the coming year," he said. "It's our intent to sit down with groups in the Northwest and ask them not to debate Option 9 but to talk about implementation."

The subtext was clear: Bill Clinton had done all he was going to do on behalf of the old-growth forests. He had done it reluctantly, to get the federal timber sale program out of the courts. Now it was time to mitigate the political damage.

NOTES AND QUESTIONS

1. Assuming Durbin's account to be accurate, what roles did science and politics play in the development of Option 9? Was it a case (as

recommended by some, e.g., Kai N. Lee, COMPASS AND GYROSCOPE: INTEGRATING SCIENCE AND POLITICS FOR THE ENVIRONMENT (1993)) of using science to point the direction but then invoking democracy—i.e., politics—to make adjustments based on social and economic circumstances? Or did science predominate? Or did politics? If the latter, which politics?

2.   In 1994, the Forest Service and the BLM completed the NEPA analysis and issued a Record of Decision adopting Option 9, and that Record of Decision became the Northwest Forest Plan. Judge Dwyer then upheld the validity of the plan and, after all parties appealed, the Ninth Circuit affirmed. Seattle Audubon Society v. Lyons, 871 F. Supp. 1291 (W.D. Wash. 1994), aff'd sub nom. Seattle Audubon Society v. Moseley, 80 F.3d 1401 (9th Cir. 1996). The Northwest Forest Plan covers all national forests and BLM lands in western Washington, western Oregon, and northwestern California.

Lauren M. Rule, *Enforcing Ecosystem Management under the Northwest Forest Plan: The Judicial Role*
12 FORDHAM ENVTL. L. REV. 211, 222–27 (2000).

The Northwest Forest Plan calls for an ecosystem management approach to managing federal forests within the range of the northern spotted owl. The Plan attempts to "respond to multiple needs, the two primary reasons being the need for forest habitat and the need for forest products," through a system of land allocations, an ACS [Aquatic Conservation Strategy], requirements to survey a variety of species, and a monitoring program. The first part of the Plan assigns all 24.4 million acres of federal land covered by the Plan to one of seven land allocations. Five of these seven categories are various types of reserves, with either no timber harvest allowed or harvesting that would enhance late-successional or old-growth forest characteristics.** The Plan allocates 18.8 million acres to these five designations, 78 percent of the total lands covered by the Plan. By setting up a system of reserves, the Plan establishes a landscape-level approach to help protect and restore biodiversity. One of the goals of ecosystem management is to have managers incorporate into their analyses a holistic view of natural systems covering large areas, rather than solely focusing on individual parts of the forest. The Plan assigns the remaining 5.5 million acres to the two land allocations that allow for timber harvest. This land will provide most of the 1.1 billion board feet of timber that the agencies can harvest annually. By managing for timber harvest and protection of species, the Plan attempts to fulfill the ecosystem management goal of integrating the human and biological dimensions of natural resource management to achieve sustainability of all resources.

The second component of the Plan, the ACS, is designed to restore and maintain the health of aquatic ecosystems and applies to all of the Forest Service and BLM administered lands. Managers must conduct Planning

---

** [Ed.] The plan defined late-successional forests as 80–200 old and old-growth forests as 200 or more years old with large trees and complex structure.

for this strategy at four spatial scales: region (Pacific Northwest), river basin, watershed, and individual site. While the FEMAT report stated that the most comprehensive analyses are conducted at the watershed level, the report stressed that "information collected at the finer scales provides early warning of likely future problems at the broader scales." Ecosystem management emphasizes the importance of assessing effects of projects at various scales, from the landscape level down to the specific site level. This helps agencies manage for the complexity of the ecosystem, and therefore helps to protect species.

The ACS requires the agencies to restore or maintain healthy aquatic ecosystems by restricting timber harvests in riparian areas and important watersheds to those that provide benefits to the aquatic ecosystem, and by requiring managers to conduct watershed analyses and watershed restoration projects. When doing watershed analyses, managers must consider both the short-term and long-term effects of timber sales and other projects. In the short-term, agencies need to assure against losses of diversity and ecological processes; in the long-term, they must achieve restoration and appropriate conditions at the landscape scale. This type of analysis aims to protect and restore biodiversity, which is a critical factor in sustaining the health and productivity of ecosystems. By assessing the short-term effects of projects, managers can determine whether that project will imperil a localized population of a species, possibly threatening the existence of that species.

The third aspect of the Northwest Forest Plan requires agencies to conduct surveys for hundreds of species. Ecosystem management requires a thorough understanding of the environment and its complexity. To preserve species, thereby preserving biodiversity, managers must improve their understanding of the relationships among organisms and between organisms and their environment. Surveys are the primary method of increasing knowledge about the ecosystem and the relation of species to their environment. Surveys provide baseline information about where species exist and what type of habitat they require, allowing managers to plan projects, like timber sales or herbicide spraying, while protecting species, a key element of ecosystem management.

The Plan's survey requirements cover 414 species, each of which falls into one of four survey categories. "Category one" surveys do not require field surveys, but require that project planners use the information about known species sites when designing activities to ensure protection for that species.

The "category two" surveys require field surveys of project areas before any ground-disturbing activity occurs. The Plan requires that the agencies conduct surveys for several species of salamanders and the red tree vole before any ground-disturbing activities are implemented by the agency in 1997 or thereafter. Surveys for other category two species must occur prior to ground-disturbing activities that are implemented in 1999 or thereafter. * * * When surveyors locate "category two" species, the agencies must develop management standards to manage the species' habitat at those sites.

"Category three" and "category four" surveys extend over broader landscapes and are not connected to specific planning activities * * *.

The fourth component of the Northwest Forest Plan incorporates the strategy of adaptive management through the use of monitoring and evaluation. The Plan calls for agencies to monitor their actions, providing feedback to land managers who will evaluate the findings and determine whether to change their plans or actions, based on the evaluations. This accomplishes the ecosystem management goal of adjusting to new information by giving managers the flexibility to revise plans in order to move toward desired objectives or conditions.

From the beginning, the timber harvest, which had averaged about four billion board feet annually during the 1980s, failed to meet the plan's annual goal of one billion board feet (painfully low from the timber industry's standpoint), much less than Interior Secretary Babbitt's estimate of two billion board feet in the first year. "In the first two years after announcement of the plan, approximately one-quarter of a billion board feet was sold. The following few years have been closer to their targets, but the roughest test may come [in the future], when many of the sales with relatively low controversy will be complete, leaving some very tough decisions for future programs." BIOREGIONAL ASSESSMENTS: SCIENCE AT THE CROSSROADS OF MANAGEMENT AND POLICY 107–08 (K. Norman Johnson et al., eds. 1999).

The courts enjoined numerous sales on the basis of NEPA and violations of the plan's Aquatic Conservation Strategy (ACS) and Survey and Management requirements. *See, e.g.*, Oregon Natural Resources Council Action v. United States Forest Service, 59 F. Supp.2d 1085, 1088 (W.D. Wash. 1999), where Judge Dwyer struck down sales because surveys had not been conducted and emphasized the importance of the "Survey and Management" requirements: "The plan sets aside certain reserves and requires that known sites of certain rare species be protected. But for many species, surveys are the principal means of ensuring that their viability will not be ended by logging. By requiring surveys for those species before ground-disturbing activities * * * are implemented * * *, the plan allows measures to be taken to protect any sites that are found." In Pacific Coast Federation of Fishermen's Ass'n. v. National Marine Fisheries Service, the court, among other ACS violations, found error because the agencies disregarded short-term (less than ten years) degradation caused by timber sales:

> [under agency practices,] only degradations that persist more than a decade and are measurable at the watershed scale will be considered to degrade aquatic habitat. This generous time frame ignores the life cycle and migration cycle of anadromous fish. In ten years, a badly degraded habitat will likely result in the total extinction of the subspecies that formerly returned to a particular creek for spawning.

265 F.3d 1028, 1037 (9th Cir. 2001).

The low level of harvested timber under the plan continued into the 2000s and the timber companies considered it a "broken promise." In response, the Forest Service and BLM revisited the ACS and Survey and Management provisions in order to expedite sales. The 2004 amendments entirely eliminated the Survey and Management standard, one of the four main components of the Northwest Forest Plan and designed to protect rare and uncommon species.

Environmentalists sued and the court found three NEPA violations in Northwest Ecosystem Alliance v. Rey, 380 F. Supp.2d 1175 (W.D. Wash. 2005). First, the agencies assumed that some species covered by Survey and Management would be added by forest supervisors and BLM state directors to the "Special Species Status" Program but did not, during the NEPA process, analyze the effects if species were not added to the SSS Program. Second, the court found that the agencies failed sufficiently to analyze their assumption that species previously covered by Survey and Management would be protected by the large amount of late-successional and old-growth forest land set aside as reserves and comprising approximately 80% off all land covered by the plan. A primary flaw was the failure of the Final EIS to analyze satisfactorily the original FEMAT analysis that led to the Survey and Management provisions:

> [T]he FEMAT team's and the Agencies' respective analysis in 1994 was thorough. They never definitively stated that the Reserves were so degraded that they were non-functional LSOG ["late-successional and old growth"] forests. However, they did conclude that these non-vertebrate species had a less than desired likelihood of persistence under the Reserve system. While the Agencies are correct that part of the concern over these species' viability was due to a lack of information, the Survey and Manage standard was introduced to address both this lack of information and the concern that these species would not persist under the Reserve system. Further, even though the Survey and Manage standard was only a part of the overall strategy to protect these species, it was a necessary part to satisfy the Plan's "foundational objectives."

* * *

Counsel also argued that apart from this more general new information, the Agencies have the discretion to change their opinion about the best way to balance the Plan's two goals. While true, this misses the point. The point is not that the Agencies can or cannot chose to eliminate the Survey and Manage standard in an effort to re-balance the Plan's goals (which is an issue beyond the scope of NEPA). Rather, the point under NEPA is that the Agencies' analysis of the environmental impacts of eliminating the standard is premised on an assumption that is inconsistent with their own prior analysis and therefore appears to lack support. Even if including the Survey and Manage standard as a part of the Plan was a policy choice by the Agencies in 1994, just as eliminating the standard is the Agencies' policy choice in 2004, the Agencies have an obligation under NEPA to disclose and explain on what basis they deemed the standard necessary before but assuming it is not now. In sum, the 2004 SEIS failed to provide a thorough analysis of this issue to permit the public and the decision-makers to make a reasonably informed decision.

The third NEPA violation concerned the agencies' finding that the Survey and Management Standard impeded hazardous fire treatments. The court found that the agencies failed to disclose flaws in their methodology for calculating the need for, and cost of, the treatments. While the Survey and Manage provisions remain in place for the time being as a result of the *Northwest Ecosystem* ruling, the administration released a new draft SEIS in 2006 to respond to the decision.

As for the ACS, the strategy was working well in terms of stream conditions:

> The ACS met its expectation that watershed condition should begin to improve in the first decade of the NWFP. Conditions of watersheds in the NWFP have improved at least somewhat since the NWFP was implemented and the proportion of watersheds with improving conditions was significantly greater than those that declined. A primary reason for this improvement was an increase in the number of large trees in riparian areas and a decrease in the extent of clearcut harvesting in riparian zones. This general trend should be expected to continue, and may actually accelerate in the future, if the ACS continues to be implemented as originally intended.

Gordon H. Reeves et al., *The Aquatic Conservation Strategy of the Northwest Forest Plan*, 20 CONSERVATION BIOL. 319, 327 (2006). The 2004 amendments, however, provided that consistency with the ACS would be measured at the watershed, not the project, level. As a result, under the 2004 amendment, the agencies could issue timber sales that might cause negative short-term, localized effects so long as they are not measurable at the watershed scale. This effectively overturned the 2001 *Pacific Coast* interpretation of the ACS. The Fish and Wildlife Service issued two no-jeopardy biological opinions (BOs) on the 2004 amendments.

A salmon fishing federation brought suit and U.S. Magistrate Judge Mary Alice Thieler, in a formal opinion, recommended to District Court Judge Ricardo Martinez (who has not ruled as of this printing) that the amendment be struck down:

> * * * [I]n their final BOs, the consulting agencies essentially defer analysis to future site-specific consultations. In adopting a wholesale deferral of analysis to the project level, it cannot be said that the agencies satisfied their [ESA] burden to "make certain" that the proposed action is not likely to jeopardize listed species or destroy or adversely modify critical habitat. Additionally, as noted by plaintiffs, site-specific § 7 consultations will focus on a smaller area than the entire NFP and, based on the ESA's definition of cumulative effects, assess only those prior federal projects that have undergone consultation. Deferral, therefore, also necessarily improperly curtails the discussion of cumulative effects. * * *

* * * [I]t appears that the 2004 BOs premised their no-jeopardy findings, at least in significant part, on the assumption that the analytical process would be applied at the site-specific level. Yet, critically, the BOs fail to address the potential impact posed by projects proceeding without application of that discretionary process. The 2004 BOs, therefore, lack a "rational connection between the facts found and the choice made." [*Pacific Coast*], 265 F.3d at 1034.

Pacific Coast Federation of Fishermen's Associations v. National Marine Fisheries Service, Case No. CO4–1299–RSM (W.D. March 28, 2006).

NOTES AND QUESTIONS

1. Is this a case of science and law run amok? The courts have found that the Forest Service and BLM must comply with the plan itself, the ESA, and the NFMA. As noted in the Rule article, the objective of the plan is to "respond to multiple needs, the two primary reasons being the need for forest habitat and the need for forest products." The second need is plainly not being met. How should judges treat that in their opinions? How should the agencies view the two objectives in administering, and perhaps amending, the plan?

2. How broad is the agencies' substantive authority to change the plan? In approving the plan, Judge Dwyer pointedly observed that "If the plan as implemented is to remain lawful the monitoring, watershed analysis, and mitigating steps called for [by the plan] will have to be faithfully carried out, and adjustments made if necessary. * * * As written, it is legally sufficient. It remains, of course, to be carried out." But now a major legal change has taken place since Judge Dwyer handed down his initial injunction in *Seattle Audubon* in 1991: a principal basis for the ruling—36 C.F.R. § 219.19, the rigorous Forest Service diversity provision from the 1982 regulations—has since been repealed. Does that make the plan easier to amend? Is the authority to amend in any event very broad in light of the dual "forest habitat" and "forest products" objectives?

3. Do the 2004 changes to the NWFP require greater justification because they modify a prior agency position? In other words, if the 2004 modifications were part of the original FEMAT-based plan, would Judge Dwyer have approved them in the first place as within the Forest Service discretion?

4. A group of researchers recently conducted a comprehensive examination of Forest Service court cases during the agency's most intensive years of litigation activity. Among other things, the authors found that the agency won 57.6% of all cases, lost 21.3%, settled 17.6%, and saw 3.6% withdrawn. The article, which includes useful charts and graphs, concludes as follows:

> This study analyzed a census of legal challenges to Forest Service national forest management initiated from 1989 to 2002; it represents the most complete picture of national forest litigation assembled to date. The results confirm many policymakers' and stakeholders' per-

ceptions: three of every four cases involve parties seeking less resource use; Region 6, the Pacific Northwest, experienced almost a quarter of all litigation; and NEPA was the statutory basis in nearly 7 of every 10 cases.

Our study did not address the overall impact of litigation of Forest Service land management decisions, but it is important to remember that the 729 cases we examined did not represent 729 land management projects or plans. Many lawsuits involved multiple projects, and many cases established a legal precedent that directed future Forest Service land management decisions. The Forest Service makes thousands of management decisions each year (the precise number for our period is unknown). We still cannot estimate the total percentage of projects that were subject to litigation.

Our findings also revealed some unexpected results. Litigation increased during these 14 years; however, a decrease occurred after 2000. Although logging was the focus of most lawsuits, other management activities accounted for more than 60% of cases. Many statutes besides NEPA, NFMA, and ESA provided the statutory basis for plaintiffs' challenges. Forest Service success varied widely based on the statute involved in the lawsuit and the Forest Service activity litigated. Most importantly, this study documented the prevalence of settlements in national forest management cases. More than one of every six cases resulted in a settlement between the Forest Service and the party bringing the lawsuit. It appears, then, that both the Forest Service and its litigant adversaries view settlements as an important dispute-resolution tool.

Denise M. Keele, Robert W. Malmsheimer, Donald W. Floyd, and Jerome E. Perez. 2006. Forest Service Land Management Litigation 1989–2002. *Journal of Forestry* 104(4):196–202

CHAPTER 9

THE RANGE RESOURCE

A. INTRODUCTION

Livestock grazing has been a source of controversy over management of vast tracts of federal lands for a very long time. Early contests pitted cattle raisers against sheepherders (*see* Omaecheverria v. Idaho, *supra* p. 139) and farmers (sodbusters) against ranchers. Shortly after the turn of the twentieth century, the young U.S. Forest Service took very modest steps to bring the livestock grazing industry on national forests under some regulation, leading to landmark legal opinions in *Grimaud* and *Light*, *supra* p. 126. Although most ranchers acquiesced in the Taylor Grazing Act in 1934, continuing resentment toward federal regulation led right-wing Senator Pat McCarran of Nevada to lead a spirited (and to some observers, downright mean) five-year effort to starve the then-infant Bureau of Land Management into submission in the 1940s, an episode recounted in E. Louise Peffer's masterly account, THE CLOSING OF THE PUBLIC DOMAIN 247 (1951)[1].

Ranching is at the core of the "western" self-image of rugged independence and self-reliance that has been burned on the national consciousness by innumerable novels, movies and television shows. But livestock grazing can significantly impact other uses and values of the federal lands, and governmental decisions about where and how many head of cattle or sheep will be allowed to graze on federal lands can be controversial. Ranchers were at the vanguard of the Sagebrush Rebellion of the late 1970s and the County Supremacy movement of the 1990s. University of Wyoming Law Professor Debra L. Donahue has published a comprehensive survey of the law, economics, and politics of public land livestock grazing. THE WESTERN RANGE REVISITED (1999). Her book is critical of the ranchers' hold on federal lands and unabashedly opposed to public land livestock grazing; perhaps needless to say, it has sparked some criticism of her employment by the state university in what is, after all, the Cowboy State, but it has not muted her voice. *See* Donahue, *Western Grazing: The Capture of Grass, Ground, and Government*, 35 ENVTL. L. 721, 790–91, nn.477, 482 (2005).

Acre for acre, livestock grazing is in fact the most widespread extractive use of the federal lands, found on more than a *quarter of a billion* acres, or a land area 2½ times that of the state of California. It is concentrated (and this chapter focuses primarily) on about 158 million

---

1. A measure of McCarran's single-minded championing of the rancher was his conducting a hearing on public lands grazing fees on May 11, 1945, V–E Day, with the hearing record utterly silent on the liberation of Europe from the Nazis. William Voigt Jr., PUBLIC GRAZING LANDS: USE AND MISUSE BY INDUSTRY AND GOVERNMENT 276–77, 286–87 (1976).

acres of federal lands managed by the BLM, almost all in the eleven western states of the lower forty-eight. About 18,000 permittees hold BLM-issued grazing leases and permits. The current maximum authorized use, for all these combined, is around 12.7 million "animal unit months" (AUMs) of forage harvesting. (An AUM is the amount of forage eaten by one cow, or five sheep or goats, grazing for one month—or about 750–800 pounds of grass.) Grazing is also an important use of some 100 million acres of the national forests, with about 7,000 permittees authorized to use a maximum of about 9.2 million AUMs on these lands. In total, then, perhaps 20,000 livestock operators use the federal lands (several thousand hold permits to graze livestock on both BLM and Forest Service lands). Livestock grazing is permitted in some wildlife refuges. Previously established livestock grazing is also allowed to continue in some wilderness and national park system areas; e.g., Grand Teton National Park.

While the number of acres involved is vast, the amount of meat produced is, compared to total national meat production, quite small[2]. Beef cattle producers with permits to graze on federal land comprise about three percent of the beef producers, and federal lands provide about two percent of the total feed consumed by beef cattle in the Nation. Even regionally the public lands play a small role. In 1994, the Department of the Interior estimated that stopping all grazing on all federal lands would eliminate only about eight percent of the cows and less than one percent of the sheep in the 11 western states, causing a regional job loss at 18,300 (about one percent of total agricultural employment in the region, and less than one-tenth of one percent of total westwide employment), with only "slight" effect on beef prices. Department of the Interior, Rangeland Reform Draft Environmental Impact Statement 4–118 to 4–121 (1994).

Who are grazing permittees? A good question, about which there is relatively little hard information. Ample anecdotal evidence supports the notion that traditional ranching families, descendants of homesteaders, are being steadily displaced with hobbyists, wealthy professionals, and others looking for a lifestyle in pursuit of the cowboy myth. Bradley J. Gentner and John A. Tanaka, *Classifying Federal Public Land Grazing Permittees*, 55 J. RANGE MANAGEMENT 2–11 (Jan. 2002), report the results of a random survey of 2000 U.S.F.S. and BLM grazing permittees (about ten percent of the total number) with a fifty-four percent response rate. About half of the respondents were what the authors called "hobbyists," who got most of their income elsewhere. The other half, who depended upon ranching for most of their income, subdivided into "dependent family ranchers," "diversified family ranchers," corporate ranchers, and sheepherders. Other studies have suggested that the federal land grazing industry is quite concentrated, with the largest 20 BLM permittees controlling nearly 21 million

2. Sources vary somewhat on the total number of permittees, acres, AUMs, and meat production traceable to federal lands grazing. Part of the difficulty of making precise calculations is that many livestock forage on public lands only part of the year, or part of their lives; for example, about one-third of the beef cattle found in the western states graze at least part of the year on federal rangelands. Professor Donahue's discussion of grazing statistics, present and historical, is found in THE WESTERN RANGE REVISITED 250–63 (1999).

acres, and the 500 largest permittees (about three percent of the total) controlling more than one-third of the total AUMs.

Range conditions in the more arid parts of the west are not very good and have long been so, given the unforgiving character of much of the land. Most of the lands now managed by the BLM were never very productive of vegetation. Many had, besides aridity, poor soil and rugged terrain. Those factors exacerbate the effects of overuse and render restoration difficult. On millions of acres of public lands, grazing has eroded sparse topsoil, scoured and fouled streams, and replaced native grasses with exotic species. Cheatgrass is one; imported to the west more than a century ago, it is now found on 25 million acres of range in the Intermountain West, an area the size of Kentucky. It forms dense, fire-susceptible mats that can wipe out sagebrush, which has led to serious decline of the sage grouse. (BLM in the late 1990s established a Great Basin Restoration Initiative to try to restore some native grasses, but progress is slow.) Regulation has in some cases stemmed the environmental deterioration and has, along with efforts of individual ranchers, even resulted in some improvement. But heavy grazing use takes a toll, and today much of BLM's grazing lands bear little resemblance vegetatively to "potential natural, or climax" plant communities. BLM's surveys of riparian-wetland areas show that only forty percent of the areas surveyed are in "proper functioning condition."

Meanwhile, demands for other uses and values of federal lands are increasing. Some ranchers are responding by working to make their operations more compatible with these new imperatives, and some environmental groups work with ranchers to try to show that working ranches can be compatible with healthy environments. *See generally* Ranching West of the 100th Meridian (Richard L. Knight et al., eds. 2002). But a wide gulf remains between the more outspoken ranchers and their more severe critics, as the following two excerpts show. First, from Ron Micheli, *Response to "Role of Land Treatments on Public and Private Lands,"* in Developing Strategies for Rangeland Management 1421 (1984):

In addition to cattle production, [the nation's cattlemen] are interested, as conservationists, in fish and wildlife, improved water quality, erosion control, and aesthetics. The cattlemen often do not get credit for the contributions they make to such benefits which accrue to the general public. * * * [T]he grazing of rangelands can have positive influences on the vegetative and soil resources, rather than all negative impacts in uncontrolled situations, which are occurring less today. Some positive impacts of grazing * * * include:

- Grazed plants are often more productive than those ungrazed.
- Grazing reduces excessive accumulation of dead vegetation and mulch that may inhibit new growth.
- Grazing tramples seed into the ground.

* * * [R]angelands properly used can maintain or improve the plant communities * * * [and] prolonged nonuse can result in range deterioration as surely as overuse will. * * * [T]here are many ways to improve rangelands other than reduction in cattle numbers.

The late Edward Abbey had a much different take on the subject, colorfully expressed in *Even the Bad Guys Wear White Hats*, HARPER'S (Jan. 1986), at 51:

> There are some Western cattlemen who are nothing more than welfare parasites. They've been getting a free ride on the public lands for over a century, and I think it's time we phased it out. I'm in favor of putting the public lands livestock grazers out of business. First of all, we don't need the public lands beef industry. * * * More than twice as many beef cattle are raised in the state of Georgia than in the sagebrush empire of Nevada. And for a very good reason: back East, you can support a cow on maybe half an acre. Out here, it takes anywhere from twenty-five to fifty acres. In the red rock country of Utah, the rule of thumb is one section—a square mile—per cow. * * * [E]liminating that industry should not raise supermarket beef prices very much. Furthermore, we'd save money in the taxes we now pay for various subsidies to these public lands cattlemen. Subsidies for things like "range improvement"—tree chaining, sagebrush clearing, mesquite poisoning, disease control, predator trapping, fencing, wells, stock ponds, roads. * * * Moreover, the cattle have done, and are doing, intolerable damage to our public lands. * * * Overgrazing is much too weak a term. Most of the public lands in the West, and especially in the Southwest, are what you might call "cowburnt." * * * These are places denuded of forage, except for some cactus or a little tumbleweed or maybe a few mutilated trees like mesquite, juniper, or hackberry.

For a long time the government did little to rein in the ranchers on the public lands, and conservation groups did not become engaged in the issue. As a result, other than the Taylor Grazing Act of 1934, there was almost no legislation, and very little litigation, involving livestock grazing on federal lands until enactment of the Federal Land Policy and Management Act in 1976.

B. THE NATURE OF THE GRAZING INTEREST ON FEDERAL LANDS

Until passage of the Taylor Grazing Act in the depth of the Great Depression, ranchers were deemed to have permission, though it did not rise to the stature of a legal "right," to run their herds on the public lands. Congress had never legislated otherwise, state law tended to encourage full and free use of federal lands, and the U.S. Supreme Court had noted that congressional acquiescence in local practices conferred an implied license to graze that prevailed until federal legislation decreed otherwise. The legal position of ranchers was thus not very different from the miners' in the gold rush era before Congress enacted the Mining Law in 1866–1870–1872 (*see supra* p. 109).

Free grazing brought ranchers west, and they built their operations around it. The Homestead Act and other disposal statutes were used to obtain fee title to "base property" of 160, 320, or 640 acres, typically on bottom land along a creek. Water rights were established to water stock, to grow hay to tide livestock over the winter, and for subsistence farming. In many parts of the arid west, a ranch could not be profitable unless it encompassed several hundred or even several thousand acres, and so early settlers tended to select lands to homestead on the basis of the availability of nearby federal land for grazing. This led to the typical situation where ranchers own in fee far fewer acres than the public lands they graze. In some parts of the west, it is common for a single ranch to have permits or leases to use BLM lands, national forest lands, and state lands (often checkerboarded with BLM and, to a lesser extent, national forest lands). Livestock may spend harsher winter months on lower elevation BLM lands, and summer months foraging on higher elevation national forest lands once the snow melts. Their dependency on access to the federal lands led many ranchers to regard themselves as having genuine, alienable, and inheritable property interests in those publicly-owned lands that could not, or at least should not, be diminished by governmental action.

The courts never went that far. But they did acknowledge that live-stock owners had an implied license to use the public domain. Indeed, this license was powerful enough to carry with it a license to cross the *private* lands of others with their livestock in order to gain access to the public lands. In Buford v. Houtz, 133 U.S. 320 (1890), cattlemen (successors to the Central Pacific Railroad grant) owned 350,000 acres interspersed among more than 600,000 acres of public land in northern Utah. They sought to enjoin sheepherders from trespassing on their fee lands to reach the public lands. The Court denied relief, reasoning that otherwise, plaintiff ranchers would monopolize grazing on the public lands, and thwart the implied license the sheepherders also possessed to use those same public lands:

> We are of opinion that there is an implied license, growing out of the custom of nearly a hundred years, that the public lands of the United States, especially those in which the native grasses are adapted to the growth and fattening of domestic animals, shall be free to the people who seek to use them where they are left open and unenclosed, and no act of government forbids this use. For many years * * * [many livestock have used] the public lands without charge, * * * hindrance or obstruction. The government of the United States, in all its branch-es, has known of this use, has never forbidden it, nor taken any steps to arrest it. No doubt it may be safely stated that this has been done with the consent of all branches of the government, and, as we shall attempt to show, with its direct encouragement. * * *
>
> The value of this privilege grew as the population increased, and it became a custom for persons to make a business or pursuit of gather-ing herds of cattle or sheep, and raising them and fattening them for market upon these unenclosed lands of the government of the United States. Of course the instances became numerous in which persons purchasing land from the United States put only a small part of it in cultivation, and permitted the balance to remain unenclosed and in no way separated from the lands owned by the United States. All the neighbors who had settled near one of these prairies or on it, and all

the people who had cattle that they wished to graze upon the public lands, permitted them to run at large over the whole region, fattening upon the public lands of the United States, and upon the unenclosed lands of the private individual, without let or hindrance. The owner of a piece of land, who had built a house or enclosed twenty or forty acres of it, had the benefit of this universal custom, as well as the party who owned no land. Everybody used the open unenclosed country, which produced nutritious grasses, as a public common on which their horses, cattle, hogs and sheep could run and graze.

The invitation to use the forage on the public domain initially gave rise to classic illustration of the "tragedy of the commons." (In fact, Garrett Hardin used overgrazing as the paradigm case in his classic article, *The Tragedy of the Commons, supra* p. 35.) Without controls, each rancher's private self-interest was to run as many head as possible on the "free" range before somebody else did. The consequence was severe overgrazing and degradation of the forage-producing capacity of the land. As Phillip Foss noted in his classic study, POLITICS AND GRASS 3–4, 74, 77 (1960) (emphasis in original):

> Competition for water and the scant grass and browse of this free land was chiefly responsible for the range wars and the "romantic" legend of the guntoting cowboy. Stockmen attempted to reserve grazing rights for themselves by homesteading waterholes, by acquiring land along creeks, by checkerboard patterns of ownership, and by various other devices * * * [which] all had as their objective the free and exclusive use of parts of the public domain. This kind of finagling does not necessarily imply that the early stockmen were rogues or possessed of any particularly sinister or wicked intent. Most of the land so manipulated was of such low productivity that homestead tracts were too small to provide a reasonable living. Consequently, stockmen and farmers were forced to supplement their homestead with "free land" or go bankrupt. * * *

> There were two general results of this "free land" situation. First, squabbles over range and water continued interminably and even the most powerful operators lived an uncertain economic existence. Second, the "free land" *had* to result in overgrazing. Cattlemen and sheepmen could not be expected to withhold stock from government range to prevent overgrazing when they knew that other stockmen would get the grass they left. Overgrazing permitted an accelerated rate of erosion by removing the forage that held moisture and soil. Erosion of soil led to still greater erosion with the result that the carrying capacity of the range decreased and floods and desert land increased.

> Overgrazing caused millions of acres of grassland to become desert. Lands which produced native grasses "up to your stirrups" within the lifetime of persons now living became, and remain today, virtual deserts.

In arid areas dramatic, apparently permanent changes in entire ecosystems were wrought by livestock in a few years toward the end of the nineteenth century. Environmental historian Donald Worster has likened this "invasion" by millions of introduced forage animals beginning in the late nineteenth century to the "explosive, shattering effect of all-out war." UNDER WESTERN SKIES: NATURE AND HISTORY IN THE AMERICAN WEST 45 (1992). The drastic decline in forage (coupled with some particularly harsh winters in the north in the mid–1880s, and with drought in the southwest in 1893) led to dramatic declines in herd size. According to Donald J. Pisani, the number of cattle in Wyoming alone plummeted from 1.5 million in 1885 to 900,000 in 1886 to 300,000 in the mid–1890s. TO RECLAIM A DIVIDED WEST: WATER, LAW, AND PUBLIC POLICY, 1848–1902 226–27 (1992). Worster wrote that the collapse of what he calls the "laissez-faire commons" was one of the greatest losses of animal life in the history of pastoralism. Worster, at 41–42. Sheep came to outnumber cattle in most western states (the proportion was not reversed until after World War II). Donahue, THE WESTERN RANGE REVISITED 251.

The unreserved public domain was carved up by the creation of national forest reserves in the 1890's and early 1900's, and grazing in national forests came under some primitive regulation. The Forest Service policy favored those who lived inside the forest reserve, maintained ranches inside the reserve, or were in the "immediate vicinity" of the reserve. But the Forest Service also "tried to balance the interests of current range users with a preference for small users over large ones," in an attempt to give new settlers with small herds "access to the national forests, even if that meant reducing the share of forage allocated to large ranchers with priority," which naturally created some controversy. Over time, existing users were favored more than new users. *See* Leigh Raymond, PRIVATE RIGHTS IN PUBLIC RESOURCES 115–117 (2003). Grazing on the unreserved public lands, however, remained free and unregulated. Partly because of this differential, national forest lands were far more productive by the mid–1930's than the public domain lands.

State regulation provided the only controls on the public domain before 1934, but state law in this era was almost exclusively concerned with encouraging private grazing and keeping the peace, and not with protecting the health of the resource. Eventually the failure of state law to protect the range, coupled with drought conditions, led to the passage of the Taylor Grazing Act of 1934. Shortly thereafter, the Grazing Service was created inside the Department of the Interior to implement it. In 1946, the Grazing Service was merged with the General Land Office and the Bureau of Land Management was born.

1.   INTRODUCTION TO THE TAYLOR GRAZING ACT (TGA)

The TGA directed the national government to start supervising livestock grazing that had gone on for decades on public lands throughout the West. While henceforth all livestock grazing on the public lands had to be authorized by federal permit, Congress did not leave the matter of who should get the permits entirely to the discretion of the Secretary of the Interior. Its approach was concisely summarized this way by the urbane Justice Breyer in his opinion for a unanimous Supreme Court in Public

Lands Council v. Babbitt, 529 U.S. 728, 733, 736 (2000) (the main part of the opinion is set out further below):

The Taylor act seeks to "promote the highest use of the public lands." 43 U.S.C. § 315. Its specific goals are to "stop injury" to the lands from "overgrazing and soil deterioration," to "provide for their use, improvement and development," and "to stabilize the livestock industry dependent on the public range." 48 Stat. 1269. The Act grants the Secretary of the Interior authority to divide the public range lands into grazing districts, to specify the amount of grazing permitted in each district, to issue leases or permits "to graze livestock," and to charge "reasonable fees" for use of the land. It specifies that preference in respect to grazing permits "shall be given . . . to those within or near" a grazing district "who are landowners engaged in the livestock business, bona fide occupants or settlers, or owners of water or water rights." § 315b. And, as particularly relevant here, it adds:

> "So far as consistent with the purposes and provisions of this subchapter, grazing privileges recognized and acknowledged shall be adequately safeguarded, but the creation of a grazing district or the issuance of a permit . . . shall not create any right, title, interest, or estate in or to the lands." *Ibid.*

The Taylor Act delegated to the Interior Department an enormous administrative task. To administer the Act, the Department needed to determine the bounds of the public range, create grazing districts, determine their grazing capacity, and divide that capacity among applicants. It soon set bounds encompassing more than 140 million acres, and by 1936 the Department had created 37 grazing districts. The Secretary then created district advisory boards made up of local ranchers and called on them for further help. Limited department resources and the enormity of the administrative task made the boards "the effective governing and administrative body of each grazing district."

By 1937 the Department had set the basic rules for allocation of grazing privileges. Those rules recognized that many ranchers had long maintained herds on their own private lands during part of the year, while allowing their herds to graze farther afield on public land at other times. The rules consequently gave a first preference to owners of stock who also owned "base property," *i.e.,* private land (or water rights) sufficient to support their herds, *and* who had grazed the public range during the five years just prior to the Taylor act's enactment. They gave a second preference to other owners of nearby "base" property lacking prior use. And they gave a third preference to stock owners without base property, like the nomadic sheep herder. Since lower preference categories divided capacity left over after satisfaction of all higher preference claims, this system, in effect, awarded grazing privileges to owners of land or water. See Foss, (quoting Grazing Division Director F.R. Carpenter's remarks that grazing privileges are given to ranchers "not as individuals, nor as owners of livestock," but to "build up [the] lands and give them stability and value").

As grazing allocations were determined, the Department would issue a permit measuring grazing privileges in terms of "animal unit months" (AUMs), *i.e.*, the right to obtain the forage needed to sustain one cow (or five sheep) for one month. Permits were valid for up to 10 years and usually renewed, as suggested by the Act. But the conditions placed on permits reflected the leasehold nature of grazing privileges; consistent with the fact that Congress had made the Secretary the landlord of the public range and basically made the grant of grazing privileges discretionary. The grazing regulations in effect from 1938 to the present day made clear that the Department retained the power to modify, fail to renew, or cancel a permit or lease for various reasons.

First, the Secretary could cancel permits if, for example, the permit holder persistently overgrazed the public lands, lost control of the base property, failed to use the permit, or failed to comply with the Range Code. * * * Second, the Secretary, consistent first with 43 U.S.C. § 315f, and later the land use planning mandated by 43 U.S.C. § 1712 * * * was authorized to reclassify and withdraw land from grazing altogether and devote it to a more valuable or suitable use. * * * Third, in the event of range depletion, the Secretary maintained a separate authority, not to take areas of land out of grazing use altogether as above, but to reduce the amount of grazing allowed on that land, by suspending AUMs of grazing privileges "in whole or in part," and "for such time as necessary." * * *

NOTES AND QUESTIONS

1.   Is the Taylor Grazing Act an environmental regulatory statute? A pro-ranching statute? Something in between? What guidance does it provide the Secretary in resolving conflicts that arise between protecting environmental health on the federal lands and the interests of the rancher?

2.   The Taylor Act generally authorized the creation of grazing districts and the issuance of grazing *permits* in them. *See* 43 U.S.C. § 315b. The Act also authorized the issuance of grazing *leases* on isolated or disconnected public lands. 43 U.S.C. § 315m. Some cases and parts of the Taylor Act (e.g., 43 U.S.C. § 315m, proviso) refer also to federal grazing *licenses*. Generally speaking, the differences among these terms have no legal significance. This chapter uses grazing *permits* in a generic sense to cover grazing leases and grazing licenses as well.

3.   Formally, the TGA was a major shift: It ended the tradition of free uncontrolled use of public lands by any grazier and substituted a new regimen of express allocation of public land forage. But at least in its early days the on-the-ground change wrought by the TGA was not so great. Ranchers remembering the open and bureaucracy-free grazing commons did not readily welcome what many saw as unjustifiable government interference into private affairs. Their strong interest combined with the brand-new federal Grazing Service's weak institutional status meant that implementation of the Act was through a system of semi-self-government. The holders of federal permits, through Stockmen's Advisory Boards and less formal means, dominated the administration of grazing districts for

decades. BLM district officers often tended to act more as agents for the ranching industry than as regulators of it. Some of those holding BLM grazing permits and leases still believe today that they are entitled, by law, equity, or policy, to higher priority than any other resource use or consideration on federal lands. Their ranching enterprise is built upon federal land availability, and they have been quite successful in defending it.

4.   The basic issue in allocating public land forage was whether to favor those with property in the vicinity, or to use priority of use as the standard. For the details of the struggle over this inside and outside the Department from enactment of the TGA to adoption of the Federal Range Code in 1938, *see* Leigh Raymond, PRIVATE RIGHTS IN PUBLIC RESOURCES 126– 52 (2003). Raymond characterizes the struggle as between a Lockeian vision, based on historic use, and a Hegelian notion of defining the grazing privilege through reconciliation of opposing principles. *Id.* at 151–52. As Justice Breyer indicated, the Interior Department ultimately construed the "preference" for the most part to displace those graziers who did not own "base property" or fee land in the vicinity of the public lands. In the end, "many prior users, especially nomadic range users lacking private land, were excluded * * *." *Id.* at 151. *Cf.* Garcia v. Andrus, 692 F.2d 89, 93 (9th Cir.1982) (grazing lessee who loses a partial interest in his "base property" loses priority to renew his grazing lease "in a proportionate amount").

5.   Still, perhaps a bigger loser was the health of the rangeland. Ferry Carpenter, the first Director of the Grazing Service, acknowledged that even though the TGA was designed to reverse the degradation of the public rangelands by ending the commons, the practicalities of adjusting to the new regime would inevitably mean some overallocation of the forage resource. As he put it:

> If we try to get these districts under regulations as hastily as many people think we should we will hamper and hamstring the livestock and hammer the heads of the operators unmercifully. If we go at it slow we will continue to hammer the public domain. Well, as the public domain range is less articulate than the stockmen, we have chosen to hammer the public domain.

Transcript of statewide meeting in Oregon, Dec. 15, 1934, quoted in Raymond at 216, n. 93.

2.   THE GRAZIER'S LEGAL INTEREST IN THE PUBLIC LANDS

As we have seen in other chapters of this book, the nature and quantum of private rights (if any) in federal lands and resources varies. Mining claims, oil and gas leases, and timber contracts all can give their holders some sort of property interest in federal minerals and timber. As shown in the excerpt of Justice Breyer's opinion in the *Public Lands Council* case, Congress expressly addressed this issue in the Taylor Grazing Act, 43 U.S.C. § 315b: "[T]he issuance of a [grazing] permit * * * shall not create any right, title, interest, or estate in or to the lands." While the Taylor Act was aimed in part at "stabiliz[ing] the livestock industry dependent on the public range," it thus fell far short of being a sort of "Magna Carta" for grazing that the 1872 Mining Law came to be regarded for hardrock miners. Most important, TGA permits do not rise to the status of a legal interest that can be obtained in a federal mineral lease or a timber sale contract.

Because ranchers in the arid west had long invested time, energy and money to build ranching enterprises that depended on the availability of public lands forage, Congress's denial of property rights in grazing permits might seem at odds with English philosopher John Locke's labor theory of property rights. *See* SECOND TREATISE OF GOVERNMENT § 27 (c. 1699) ("[w]hatsover, then, he removes out of the state that nature has provided and left it in, he has mixed his labour with, and joined to it something that is his own, and thereby makes it his property"). What do you suppose motivated Congress in the TGA to draw the line as firmly as it did against a property right?

Although livestock grazing permits do not give ranchers a *property* interest in federal lands, courts sometimes acknowledged that ranchers deserve some protection in particular contexts. For example, in Red Canyon Sheep Company v. Ickes, 98 F.2d 308 (D.C.Cir.1938), a permittee who had "long been grazing" sheep on public lands was permitted to object to a proposal to exchange the public lands it was grazing for fee land owned by another within a national forest, under a special statute that authorized the exchange so long as the public lands were "unreserved and unappropriated." within the meaning of the exchange statute. The Court observed:

> * * * We recognize that the rights under the Taylor Grazing Act do not fall within the conventional category of vested rights in property. Yet, whether they be called rights, privileges, or bare licenses, or by whatever name, while they exist they are something of real value to the possessors and something which have their source in an enactment of the Congress. The jurisdiction of equity is flexible and should not be confined to rigid categories so that the granting of an injunction will depend upon nomenclature rather than upon substance. * * *
>
> [T]he right to hunt upon public waters bears a striking analogy to the right or privilege of grazing upon the public lands. Neither is an interest in the land itself, and both are subject to restriction or withdrawal, the one by game laws, and the other by laws in the interest of the protection of the public domain; yet both are of value to the persons possessing them.

The same circuit took a much less charitable view of the rancher's interest a quarter century later. LaRue v. Udall, 324 F.2d 428 (D.C.Cir. 1963). The facts were similar to *Red Canyon Sheep*—the Secretary of the Interior proposed to exchange public lands, on which LaRue grazed livestock under a Taylor Act permit, for lands owned by a defense contractor in Nevada. The Court upheld the Secretary's view that the statutory standard (which authorized such exchanges when the "public interest" would be served) "need not be related exclusively to conservation of Federal grazing resources nor need it be shown that a proposed exchange will promote range management." The court went on to reject another argument the rancher put forward:

> Appellants also assert that their grazing unit has been and is pledged as security for *bona fide* loans, and that therefore the Secretary may

not terminate their grazing permit. As a basis for the assertion they rely upon the language we have italicized in the following portion of § 3 of the Taylor Grazing Act (43 U.S.C.A. § 315b): "* * * *no permittee complying with the rules and regulations laid down by the Secretary of the Interior shall be denied the renewal of such permit, if such denial will impair the value of the grazing unit of the permittee, when such unit is pledged as security for any bona fide loan. * * *"*

Their contention is that if the Secretary may not refuse to renew a permit when the permittee's grazing unit is pledged as security for a *bona fide* loan, "he can hardly bring about the same result indirectly by terminating a permit prior to the expiration of the term * * *." As the context shows[*], the provision relied upon by the appellants is one of the factors to be considered by the Secretary in establishing preferences between conflicting applications for permits on the federal range. By no means should it be construed as providing that, by maintaining a lien on his grazing unit, a permittee may also create and maintain a vested interest therein which will prevent the United States from exchanging it under § 8(b). * * *

Appellants' reliance on the Fifth Amendment disregards the provision of § 3 of the Act (43 U.S.C. § 315b) that

> * * * So far as consistent with the purposes and provisions of this chapter, grazing privileges recognized and acknowledged shall be adequately safeguarded, but the creation of a grazing district or the issuance of a permit pursuant to the provisions of this chapter shall not create any right, title, interest, or estate in or to the lands.

The command of Congress that grazing privileges shall be adequately safeguarded "so far as consistent with the purposes and provisions of this chapter" does not mean that a grazing permit is to prevent the Government's exercise of the right of exchange, which is "one of the provisions of this chapter."

Eventually, the U.S. Supreme Court turned its authoritative gaze upon the question of whether any property interest exists in federal grazing permits.

United States v. Fuller

Supreme Court of the United States, 1973.
409 U.S. 488.

■ JUSTICE REHNQUIST delivered the opinion of the Court.

Respondents operated a large-scale "cow-calf" ranch near the confluence of the Big Sandy and Bill Williams Rivers in western Arizona. Their

---

* [Eds. The passage quoted in italics in the *Larue* opinion appears in the middle of 43 U.S.C. § 315b, three long sentences and some twenty-two lines before that section's concluding statement that the issuance of a grazing permit "shall not create any right, title, interest, or estate in or to the lands." The quoted passage concludes a sentence that begins, "[p]reference shall be given in the issuance of grazing permits to" landowners, etc.

In context, the quoted passage effectively discourages the Secretary from issuing a grazing permit to another rancher higher on the preference ladder if the consequence would be to impair the value of an existing permittee's grazing unit, if that existing permittee is in compliance with all rules and regulations and has used the permit as collateral for a bona fide loan.]

activities were conducted on lands consisting of 1,280 acres that they owned in fee simple (fee lands), 12,027 acres leased from the State of Arizona, and 31,461 acres of federal domain held under Taylor Grazing Act permits issued in accordance with § 3 of the Act, 43 U.S.C. § 315b. The Taylor Grazing Act authorizes the Secretary of the Interior to issue permits to livestock owners for grazing their stock on Federal Government lands. These permits are revocable by the Government. The Act provides, moreover, that its provisions "shall not create any right, title, interest, or estate in or to the lands." Ibid.

The United States, petitioner here, condemned 920 acres of respondents' fee lands. At the trial in the District Court for the purpose of fixing just compensation for the lands taken, the parties disagreed as to whether the jury might consider value accruing to the fee lands as a result of their actual or potential use in combination with the Taylor Grazing Act "permit" lands. The Government contended that such element of incremental value to the fee lands could neither be taken into consideration by the appraisers who testified for the parties nor considered by the jury. Respondents conceded that their permit lands could not themselves be assigned any value in view of the quoted provisions of the Taylor Grazing Act. They contended, however, that if on the open market the value of their fee lands was enhanced because of their actual or potential use in conjunction with permit lands, that element of value of the fee lands could be testified to by appraisers and considered by the jury. The District Court substantially adopted respondents' position, first in a pretrial order and then in its charge to the jury over appropriate objection by the Government. * * *

Our prior decisions have variously defined the "just compensation" that the Fifth Amendment requires to be made when the Government exercises its power of eminent domain. The owner is entitled to fair market value, United States v. Miller, 317 U.S. 369, 374 (1943), but that term is "not an absolute standard nor an exclusive method of valuation." * * *

The record shows that several appraiser witnesses for respondents testified that they included as an element of the value that they ascribed to respondents' fee lands the availability of respondents' Taylor Grazing Act permit lands to be used in conjunction with the fee lands. Under the District Court's charge to the jury, the jury was entitled to consider this element of value testified to by the appraisers. This Court has held that generally the highest and best use of a parcel may be found to be a use in conjunction with other parcels, and that any increment of value resulting from such combination may be taken into consideration in valuing the parcel taken. Olson v. United States, 292 U.S. 246, 256 (1934). The question presented by this case is whether there is an exception to that general rule where the parcels to be aggregated with the land taken are themselves owned by the condemnor and used by the condemnee only under revocable permit from the condemnor.

To say that this element of value would be considered by a potential buyer on the open market, and is therefore a component of "fair market value," is not the end of the inquiry. In United States v. Miller, *supra*, this Court held that the increment of fair market value represented by knowledge of the Government's plan to construct the project for which the land was taken was not included within the constitutional definition of "just compensation." * * *

* * * A long line of cases decided by this Court dealing with the Government's navigational servitude with respect to navigable waters evidences a continuing refusal to include, as an element of value in compensating for fast lands that are taken, any benefits conferred by access to such benefits as a potential portsite or a potential hydro-electric site.

These cases go far toward establishing the general principle that the Government as condemnor may not be required to compensate a condemnee for elements of value that the Government has created, or that it might have destroyed under the exercise of governmental authority other than the power of eminent domain. If * * * the Government need not pay for value that it could have acquired by exercise of a servitude arising under the commerce power, it would seem *a fortiori* that it need not compensate for value that it could remove by revocation of a permit for the use of lands that it owned outright.

We do not suggest that such a general principle can be pushed to its ultimate logical conclusion. In United States v. Miller, supra, the Court held that "just compensation" did include the increment of value resulting from the completed [federal] project to neighboring lands originally outside the project limits, but later brought within them. * * *

"Courts have had to adopt working rules in order to do substantial justice in eminent domain proceedings." United States v. Miller, *supra*, at 375. Seeking as best we may to extrapolate from these prior decisions such a "working rule," we believe that there is a significant difference between the value added to property by a completed public works project, for which the Government must pay, and the value added to fee lands by a revocable permit authorizing the use of neighboring lands that the Government owns. The Government may not demand that a jury be arbitrarily precluded from considering as an element of value the proximity of a parcel to a post office building, simply because the Government at one time built the post office. But here respondents rely on no mere proximity to a public building or to public lands dedicated to, and open to, the public at large. Their theory of valuation aggregates their parcel with land owned by the Government to form a privately controlled unit from which the public would be excluded. If * * * a person may not do this with respect to property interests subject to the Government's navigational servitude, he surely may not do it with respect to property owned outright by the Government. * * * We hold that the Fifth Amendment does not require the Government to pay for that element of value based on the use of respondents' fee lands in combination with the Government's permit lands.

* * * The provisions of the Taylor Grazing Act quoted supra make clear the congressional intent that no compensable property right be created in the permit lands themselves as a result of the issuance of the permit. Given that intent, it would be unusual, we think, for Congress to

have turned around and authorized compensation for the value added to fee lands by their potential use in connection with permit lands. We find no such authorization in the applicable congressional enactments.

Reversed.

■ Justice Powell, with whom Justices Douglas, Brennan, and Marshall join, dissenting.

I dissent from a decision which, in my view, dilutes the meaning of the just compensation required by the Fifth Amendment when property is condemned by the Government. * * *

The Government's role here is not an ambiguous one—it is simply a condemnor of private land which happens to adjoin public land. If the Government need not pay location value in this case, what are the limits upon the principle today announced? Will the Government be relieved from paying location value whenever it condemns private property adjacent to or favorably located with respect to Government property? Does the principle apply, for example, to the taking of a gasoline station at an interchange of a federal highway, or to the taking of a farm which in private hands could continue to be irrigated with water from a federal reservoir? * * *

NOTES AND QUESTIONS

1. What precisely is the legal interest a rancher has in a grazing permit? A protectable privilege? A license subject to administrative curtailment "in the public interest"? Does the answer depend on why the question is asked? Might a permit be "property" for some purposes even if it falls short of being "property" requiring just compensation if taken by the government?

2. About three-fourths of the "base property" Fuller held in fee was condemned by the government. As a result of this decision, Fuller was not allowed to recover the value that the permit might have added to that portion of the "base property." If Fuller had purchased the base property after enactment of the Taylor Grazing Act in 1934, what would a "willing buyer-willing seller" sale price have been based on? Phillip Foss's leading study confirmed what the appraisers said in their testimony in the *Fuller* case; namely, "grazing permits are ordinarily capitalized into the value of the ranch so that * * * a ranch buyer actually pays for both the private and public lands contained in the ranch unit." P. Foss, Politics and Grass 197 (1960); *see also* L. Allen Torell & Marc E. Kincaid, *Public Land Policy and the Market Value of New Mexico Ranches, 1979–1994*, 49 J. Range Management. 270 (1996) (ranches with federal land grazing permits tend to sell for more than the base property is worth, and more than the earning potential of the livestock enterprise). The fact that the federal grazing permit may have a substantial value in the private marketplace, even though it is not a compensable property right, helps account for the tenaciousness of ranchers in dealing with threats to their federal land grazing privileges.

3. Dissenting Justice Powell compared the situation in *Fuller* with government condemnation of private land near a federal interstate highway interchange, where presumably the U.S. would have to pay for the value as enhanced by the interchange. Are the situations comparable? If compensation were provided here, would it violate the (arguably plain) intent of Congress as expressed in section 3 (43 U.S.C. § 315b) of the Taylor Grazing Act?

4. What might account for the curious lineup of Justices in *Fuller,* with the majority comprised mostly of conservatives (normally thought to be more zealous in advocating and protecting property rights), and the dissent mostly of liberals (usually considered less zealous on the subject)?

5. Arguments for some sort of protected property interest in grazing permits are still made but routinely rejected. *See, e.g.,* Diamond Bar Cattle Co. v. United States, 168 F.3d 1209, 1215–16 (10th Cir.1999) (even more than a century of grazing use does not give any sort of prescriptive or appropriative rights to the land or to grazing privileges). Judge Loren Smith, widely known for his vigorous defenses (and expansive interpretations) of property rights, conceded that while the permit may have value to the rancher, "value itself does not create a compensable property right, no matter how seemingly unjust the consequences", Hage v. United States, 51 Fed. Cl. 570 (2002). The plaintiff in that case, the late Wayne Hage, was a well-known firebrand rancher who wrote STORM OVER RANGELANDS: PRIVATE RIGHTS IN PUBLIC LANDS (1989), the title of which said it all.

6. Ranchers who graze livestock on federal land sometimes acquire water rights under state law in springs and other sources of water on federal lands. If a rancher with such water rights loses her federal grazing permits, the water rights might be rendered useless, unless she can transfer their use to a place off federal land. Ranchers have tried, with little success, to argue that these state law water rights are taken when the federal grazing permit is denied, or that they carry with them some sort of right to graze cows on federal land. *See* Colvin Cattle Co. v. United States, 468 F.3d 803 (Fed. Cir. 2006).

7. Federal law does provide some, albeit limited, protection to ranchers who invest in their ranching operations on federal land. For example, three years after *Fuller,* Congress enacted FLPMA, which contained this subsection:

> Whenever a permit or lease for grazing domestic livestock is canceled in whole or in part, in order to devote the lands covered by the permit or lease to another public purpose, including disposal, the permittee or lessee shall receive from the United States a reasonable compensation for the adjusted value, to be determined by the Secretary concerned, of his interest in authorized permanent improvements placed or constructed by the permittee or lessee on lands covered by such permit or lease, but not to exceed the fair market value of the terminated portion of the permittee's or lessee's interest therein. Except in cases of emergency, no permit or lease shall be canceled under this subsection without two years' prior notification.

43 U.S.C. 1752(g). Does this modify the principle or result of *Fuller*? Had it been in effect when Fuller's base property was condemned, could Fuller have recovered anything under it? What? FLPMA's next subsection, § 1752(h), which provides that "[n]othing in this Act shall be construed as modifying in any way law existing on October 21, 1976, with respect to the creation of right, title, interest or estate in or to the public lands or lands in National Forests by issuance of grazing permits and leases." The key language—"right, title, interest, or estate in or to the [public] lands"—is lifted verbatim from the TGA, 43 U.S.C. § 315b. If a rancher sells her "base property," she has some risk of losing the grazing privilege that has attached to it, even if the purchaser defaults and reconveys the property to the rancher. *See* Bischoff v. Glickman, 54 F. Supp.2d 1226 (D. Wyo. 1999), *aff'd w/o op.*, 216 F.3d 1086 (10th Cir. 2000).

8. Permittee ranchers were in the vanguard of the 1970s Sagebrush Rebellion and the 1990s County Supremacy movement, partly as a protest to the government's efforts to reduce permitted numbers of grazing animals. For somewhat different reasons, a small but hardy band of free-market economists supports the ranchers' claims for federal divestiture and privatization, arguing that economic efficiency would thereby be promoted. One of these, Gary Libecap, concluded in Locking up the Range 102 (1981):

> * * * Assigning title to existing [BLM grazing] permittees is the least costly way of granting private property rights. Title can be subsequently traded at low cost to others (including conservation and wildlife groups). Limited areas of great amenity value, where exclusion is for some reason difficult, can be retained under state or federal control. However, most of the 174 million acres administered by the Bureau of Land Management are not affected by those strict conditions and are amenable to private ownership. Recognizing existing uses of the range in assigning title is consistent with U.S. and state policies which have historically recognized prior appropriation claims for water, farmland, and hard-rock minerals.
>
> Well-defined private rights capture individual incentive and initiative for using rangeland efficiently. Further, they insure response by profit-maximizing land owners to changing market demands for range use. Finally, they allow the U.S. to avoid socially costly scientific management programs advocated by the BLM. Private property rights are the necessary conditions for restoring and maintaining the productive value of a land area larger than New England and the Mid–Atlantic states combined which has been much maligned and fought over for one hundred years.

3. Administration of the TGA

Soon after taking office, the Clinton Administration decided to reform public lands grazing management. After an effort to get statutory changes failed to overcome a filibuster by rancher supporters in the Senate, the Administration used the rulemaking process to put in place some procedural and structural reforms. One key element was abolition of rancher-dominated grazing advisory councils, and substitution of state-wide or area "resource advisory councils," or RACs (pronounced "racks"), which were required to have a membership balanced among affected interests. Another was the preparation of fundamentals of rangeland health and standards and guidelines that would govern grazing in individual geographic areas. Still other elements are described in the next case.

Public Lands Council v. Babbitt

United States Supreme Court, 2000.
529 U.S. 728.

■ JUSTICE BREYER delivered the opinion of the Court.

This case requires us to interpret several provisions of the 1934 Taylor Grazing Act, 48 Stat. 1269, 43 U.S.C. § 315 *et seq.* The Petitioners claim that each of three grazing regulations [adopted as a part of Rangeland Reform] * * * exceeds the authority that this statute grants the Secretary of the Interior. We disagree and hold that the three regulations do not violate the Act. * * *

[Excerpts from Justice Breyer's introductory description of the Taylor Grazing Act are set out at p. 774 *supra.* Those excerpts ended with the observation that the Secretary had long maintained authority under the TGA and its implementing regulations to *suspend* or approve the non-use of AUMs of grazing privileges "in whole or in part," and "for such time as necessary." The opinion continued:] Indeed, the Department so often reduced individual permit AUM allocations under this last authority that by 1964 the regulations had introduced the notion of "active AUMs," *i.e.,* the AUMs that a permit *initially* granted *minus* the AUMs that the department had "suspended" due to diminished range capacity. Thus, three ranchers who had initially received, say, 3,000, 2,000, and 1,000 AUMs respectively, might find that they could use only two-thirds of that number because a 33% reduction in the district's grazing capacity had led the Department to "suspend" one-third of each allocation. The "active/suspended" system assured each rancher, however, that any capacity-related reduction would take place proportionately among permit holders, and that the Department would try to restore grazing privileges proportionately should the district's capacity later increase.

In practice, active grazing on the public range declined dramatically and steadily (from about 18 million to about 10 million AUMs between 1953 and 1998) * * *

Despite the reductions in grazing, and some improvements following the passage of the Taylor Act, the range remained in what many considered an unsatisfactory condition. In 1962, a congressionally mandated survey found only 16.6% of the range in excellent or good condition, 53.1% in fair condition, and 30.3% in poor condition. Department of Interior Ann. Rep. 62 (1962). And in 1978 Congress itself determined that "vast segments of the public rangelands are . . . in an unsatisfactory condition." [Public Rangeland Improvement Act, or PRIA, 43 U.S.C. § 1901(a)(1).]

* * * FLPMA strengthened the Department's existing authority to remove or add land from grazing use, allowing such modification pursuant to a land use plan, while specifying that existing grazing permit holders would retain a "first priority" for renewal so long as the land use plan continued to make land "available for domestic livestock grazing." § 1752(c).

In 1978, the Department's grazing regulations were, in turn, substantially amended to comply with the new law. As relevant here, the 1978 regulations tied permit renewal and validity to the land use planning process, giving the Secretary the power to cancel, suspend, or modify grazing permits due to increases or decreases in grazing forage or acreage made available pursuant to land planning. * * *

That same year Congress again increased grazing fees for the period 1979 to 1986. See Public Rangelands Improvement Act of 1978, 43 U.S.C. § 1905. However neither [FLPMA nor PRIA] * * * significantly modified the particular provisions of the Taylor Act at issue in this case.

This case arises out of a 1995 set of Interior Department amendments to the federal grazing regulations. 60 Fed.Reg. 9894 (1995) (Final Rule). The amendments represent a stated effort to "accelerate restoration" of the rangeland, make the rangeland management program "more compatible with ecosystem management," "streamline certain administrative functions," and "obtain for the public fair and reasonable compensation for the grazing of livestock on public lands." The amendments in final form emphasize individual "stewardship" of the public land by increasing the accountability of grazing permit holders; broaden membership on the district advisory boards; change certain title rules; and change administrative rules and practice of the Bureau of Land Management to bring them into closer conformity with related Forest Service management practices.

Petitioners Public Lands Council and other nonprofit ranching-related organizations with members who hold grazing permits brought this lawsuit * * * challenging 10 of the new regulations. [The district court found 4 of 10 unlawful, but the court of appeals upheld three of the four, one judge partially dissenting.**] Those three * * * (1) change the definition of "grazing preference"; (2) permit those who are not "engaged in the livestock business" to qualify for grazing permits; and (3) grant the United States title to all future "permanent" range improvements. * * * We granted certiorari to consider the ranchers' claim that these three regulatory changes exceed the authority that the Taylor Act grants the Secretary.

The ranchers attack the new "grazing preference" regulations first and foremost. Their attack relies upon the provision in the Taylor Act stating that "grazing privileges recognized and acknowledged shall be adequately safeguarded...." 43 U.S.C. § 315b. Before 1995 the regulations defined the term "grazing preference" in terms of the *AUM-denominated*

** [Eds. The United States did not seek Supreme Court review of the one issue it lost in the court of appeals–the legality of issuing grazing permits for "conservation non-use." That issue is discussed *infra* p. 835.]

amount of grazing privileges that a permit granted. The regulations then defined "grazing preference" as

> "the total number of animal unit months of livestock grazing on public lands apportioned and attached to base property owned or controlled by a permittee or lessee." 43 CFR § 4100.0–5 (1994).

The 1995 regulations changed this definition, however, so that it now no longer refers to grazing privileges "apportioned," nor does it speak in terms of AUMs. The new definition defines "grazing preference" as

> "a superior or priority position against others for the purpose of receiving a grazing permit or lease. This priority is attached to base property owned or controlled by the permittee or lessee." 43 CFR § 4100.0–5 (1995).

The new definition "omits reference to a specified quantity of forage." 60 Fed.Reg. 9921 (1995). It refers only to a priority, not to a specific number of AUMs attached to a base property. But at the same time the new regulations add a new term, "permitted use," which the Secretary defines as

> "the forage allocated by, or under the guidance of, an applicable land use plan for livestock grazing in an allotment under a permit or lease and is expressed in AUMs." 43 CFR § 4100.0–5 (1995).

This new "permitted use," like the old "grazing preference," is defined in terms of allocated rights, and it refers to AUMs. But this new term as defined refers, not to a rancher's forage priority, but to forage "allocated by, or under the guidance of *an applicable land use plan*." *Ibid.* (emphasis added). And therein lies the ranchers' concern.

The ranchers refer us to the administrative history of Taylor Act regulations, much of which we set forth in Part I. In the ranchers' view, history has created expectations in respect to the security of "grazing privileges"; they have relied upon those expectations; and the statute requires the Secretary to "safeguar[d]" that reliance. Supported by various farm credit associations, they argue that defining their privileges in relation to land use plans will undermine that security. They say that the content of land use plans is difficult to predict and easily changed. Fearing that the resulting uncertainty will discourage lenders from taking mortgages on ranches as security for their loans, they conclude that the new regulations threaten the stability, and possibly the economic viability, of their ranches, and thus fail to "safeguard" the "grazing privileges" that Department regulations previously "recognized and acknowledged."

We are not persuaded by the ranchers' argument for three basic reasons. First, the statute qualifies the duty to "safeguard" by referring directly to the Act's various goals and the Secretary's efforts to implement them. The full subsection says:

> "*So far as consistent with the purposes and provisions of this subchapter*, grazing privileges recognized and acknowledged shall be adequately safeguarded, *but* the creation of a grazing district or the issuance of a permit pursuant to the provisions of this subchapter shall *not* create

any right, title, interest or estate in or to the lands." 43 U.S.C. § 315b (emphasis added).

The words "so far as consistent with the purposes ... of this subchapter" and the warning that "issuance of a permit" creates no "right, title, interest or estate" make clear that the ranchers' interest in permit stability cannot be absolute; and that the Secretary is free reasonably to determine just how, and the extent to which, "grazing privileges" shall be safeguarded, in light of the Act's basic purposes. Of course, those purposes include "stabiliz[ing] the livestock industry," but they also include "stop[ping] injury to the public grazing lands by preventing overgrazing and soil deterioration," and "provid[ing] for th[e] orderly use, improvement, and development" of the public range. 48 Stat. 1269.

Moreover, Congress itself has directed development of land use plans, and their use in the allocation process, in order to preserve, improve, and develop the public rangelands. *See* 43 U.S.C. §§ 1701(a)(2), 1712. That being so, it is difficult to see how a definitional change that simply refers to the use of such plans could violate the Taylor Act by itself, without more. Given the broad discretionary powers that the Taylor Act grants the Secretary, we must read that Act as here granting the Secretary at least ordinary administrative leeway to assess "safeguard[ing]" in terms of the Act's other purposes and provisions. Cf. §§ 315, 315a (authorizing Secretary to establish grazing districts *"in his discretion"* (emphasis added), and to "make provision for protection, administration, regulation, and improvement of such grazing districts").

Second, the pre–1995 AUM system that the ranchers seek to "safeguard" did not offer them anything like absolute security—not even in respect to the proportionate shares of grazing land privileges that the "active/suspended" system suggested. As discussed above, the Secretary has long had the power to reduce an individual permit's AUMs or cancel the permit if the permit holder did not use the grazing privileges, did not use the base property, or violated the Range Code. And the Secretary has always had the statutory authority under the Taylor Act and later FLMPA to reclassify and withdraw range land from grazing use, see 43 U.S.C. § 315f (authorizing Secretary, "in his discretion, to examine and classify any lands ... which are more valuable or suitable for the production of agricultural crops ... or any other use than [grazing]"); §§ 1712, 1752(c) (authorizing renewal of permits "so long as the lands ... remain available for domestic livestock grazing *in accordance with land use plans*" (emphasis added)). The Secretary has consistently reserved the authority to cancel or modify grazing permits accordingly. Given these well-established pre–1995 Secretarial powers to cancel, modify, or decline to review individual permits, *including the power to do so pursuant to the adoption of a land use plan,* the ranchers' diminishment-of-security point is at best a matter of degree.

Third, the new definitional regulations by themselves do not automatically bring about a self-executing change that would significantly diminish the security of granted grazing privileges. The Department has said that the new definitions do "not cancel preference," and that any change is "merely a clarification of terminology." 60 Fed.Reg. 9922 (1995). It now assures us through the Solicitor General that the definitional changes "preserve all elements of preference" and "merely clarify the regulations within the statutory framework." *See* Brief in Opposition 13, 14.

The Secretary did consider making a more sweeping change by eliminating the concept of "suspended use"; a change that might have more reasonably prompted the ranchers' concerns. But after receiving comments, he changed his mind. *See* 59 Fed.Reg. 14323 (1994). The Department has instead said that "suspended" AUMs will

> "continue to be recognized and have a priority for additional grazing use within the allotment. Suspended use provides an important accounting of past grazing use for the ranching community and is an insignificant administrative workload to the agency." Bureau of Land Management, Rangeland Reform § 94: Final Environmental Impact Statement 144 (1994).

Of course, the new definitions seem to tie grazing privileges to land-use plans more explicitly than did the old. But, as we have pointed out, the Secretary has since 1976 had the authority to use land use plans to determine the amount of permissible grazing, 43 U.S.C. § 1712. The Secretary also points out that since development of land use plans began nearly 20 years ago, "all BLM lands in the lower 48 states are covered by land use plans," and "all grazing permits in those States have now been issued or renewed in accordance with such plans, or must now conform to them." Brief for United States 26. Yet the ranchers have not provided us with a single example in which interaction of plan and permit has jeopardized or might yet jeopardize permit security. An *amicus* brief filed by a group of Farm Credit Institutions says that the definitional change will "threate[n]" their "lending policies." But they do not explain *why* that is so, nor do they state that the new definitions will, in fact, lead them to stop lending to ranchers.

We recognize that a particular land use plan could change pre-existing grazing allocation in a particular district. And that change might arguably lead to a denial of grazing privileges that the pre–1995 regulations would have provided. But the affected permit holder remains free to challenge such an individual effect on grazing privileges, and the courts remain free to determine its lawfulness in context. We here consider only whether the changes in the definitions by themselves violate the Taylor Act's requirement that recognized grazing privileges be "adequately safeguarded." Given the leeway that the statute confers upon the Secretary, the less-than-absolute pre–1995 security that permit holders enjoyed, and the relatively small differences that the new definitions create, we conclude that the new definitions do not violate that law.

The ranchers' second challenge focuses upon a provision of the Taylor Act that limits issuance of permits to "settlers, residents, and other *stock owners....*" 43 U.S.C. § 315b (emphasis added). In 1936, the Secretary, following this requirement, issued a regulation that limited eligibility to those who "ow[n] livestock." But in 1942, the Secretary changed the regulation's wording to limit eligibility to those "engaged in the livestock business," and so it remained until 1994. The new regulation eliminates the words "engaged in the livestock business," thereby seeming to make eligible otherwise qualified applicants even if they do not engage in the livestock business. *See* 43 CFR § 4110.1(a) (1995).

The new change is not as radical as the text of the new regulation suggests. The new rule deletes the entire phrase "engaged in the livestock business" from § 4110.1, and seems to require only that an applicant "own or control land or water base property...." *Ibid.* But the omission, standing alone, does not render the regulation facially invalid, for the regulation cannot change the statute, and a regulation promulgated to guide the Secretary's discretion in exercising his authority under the Act need not also restate all related statutory language. Ultimately it is *both* the Taylor Act and the regulations promulgated thereunder that constrain the Secretary's discretion in issuing permits. The statute continues to limit the Secretary's authorization to issue permits to "bona fide settlers, residents, and *other stock owners.*" 43 U.S.C. § 315b (emphasis added).

Nor will the change necessarily lead to widespread issuance of grazing permits to "stock owners" who are not in the livestock business. Those in the business continue to enjoy a preference in the issuance of grazing permits. The same section of the Taylor Act mandates that the Secretary accord a preference to "landowners engaged in the livestock business, bona fide occupants or settlers." * * *

The ranchers' underlying concern is that the qualifications amendment is part of a scheme to end livestock grazing on the public lands. They say that "individuals or organizations owning small quantities of stock [will] acquire grazing permits, even though they intend not to graze at all or to graze only a nominal number of livestock—all the while excluding others from using the public range for grazing." The new regulations, they charge, will allow individuals to "acquire a few livestock, ... obtain a permit for what amounts to a conservation purpose and then effectively mothball the permit."

But the regulations do not allow this. The regulations specify that regular grazing permits will be issued for livestock grazing, or suspended use. New regulations allowing issuance of permits for conservation use were held unlawful by the Court of Appeals, see 167 F.3d, at 1307–1308, and the Secretary did not seek review of that decision. * * *

The ranchers' final challenge focuses upon a change in the way the new rules allocate ownership of range improvements, such as fencing, well drilling, or spraying for weeds on the public lands. The Taylor Act provides that permit holders may undertake range improvements pursuant to (1) a cooperative agreement with the United States, or (2) a range improvement permit. 43 U.S.C. § 315c. The pre–1995 regulations applicable to cooperative agreements gave the United States full title to "nonstructural" improvements, such as spraying for weeds, and to "non-removable improvements," such as wells. 43 CFR § 4120.3–2 (1994). But for "structural or removable improvements," such as fencing, stock tanks, or pipelines, the regulations shared title between the permit holder and the United States "in proportion to the actual amount of the respective contribution to the initial construction." *Ibid.* And for range improvements made pursuant to permit, the pre–1995 regulations gave the permittee "title to removable range improvements." § 4120.3–3(b).

The 1995 regulations change the title rules for range improvements made pursuant to a cooperative agreement, but not the rules for improvements made pursuant to permit. For cooperative agreements, they specify that "title to permanent range improvements" (authorized in the future) "such as fences, wells, and pipelines ... shall be in the name of the United States." 43 CFR § 4120.3–2(b) (1995).

The ranchers argue that this change violates 43 U.S.C. § 315c, which says:

> "No permit shall be issued which shall entitle the permittee to the use of such [range] improvements constructed *and owned* by a prior occupant until the applicant has paid to such prior occupant the reasonable value of such improvements...." (Emphasis added.)

In their view, the word "owned" foresees ownership by a "prior occupant" of at least some such improvements, a possibility they say is denied by the new rule mandating blanket Government ownership of permanent range improvements.

The Secretary responds that, since the statute gives him the power to *authorize* range improvements pursuant to a cooperative agreement—a greater power, § 315c, he also has the power to set the terms of title ownership to such improvements—a lesser power—just like any landlord. Under this reading, the subsequent statutory provision relating to "ownership" simply provides for compensation by some future permit holder *in the event* that the Secretary decides to grant title.

As detailed above, the Secretary did grant ownership rights to range improvements under certain circumstances prior to 1995. We see nothing in the statute that prevents him from changing his mind in respect to the future. And the Secretary has now changed his mind for reasons of administrative convenience and because what he takes as the original purpose of this provision (assuring that, in 1934, ranchers would pay compensation to nomadic sheep herders) is no longer important. In any event, the provision retains even the "contemplation of ownership" meaning stressed by the ranchers, for permit holders may still "own" removable range improvements, such as "corrals, creep feeders, and loading chutes, and temporary structural improvements such as troughs for hauled water," 43 CFR § 4120.3–3(b) (1995), which could be transferred to a new permit holder and thus compel compensation under § 315f.

In short, we find nothing in the statute that denies the Secretary authority reasonably to decide when or whether to grant title to those who make improvements. And any such person remains free to negotiate the terms upon which he will make those improvements irrespective of where title formally lies, including how he might be compensated in the future for the work he had done, either by the Government directly or by those to whom the Government later grants a permit. Cf. 43 U.S.C. § 1752(g) (requiring the United States to pay compensation to a permittee for his "interest" in range improvements if it cancels a permit).

The judgment of the Court of Appeals is *Affirmed*.

■ JUSTICE O'CONNOR, with whom JUSTICE THOMAS joins, concurring.

I join in the Court's opinion. I write separately * * * [to observe that a] permit holder may bring an as-applied challenge to the Secretary's action [on the ground that it failed to adequately safeguard the permit holder's grazing privileges, and that the agency rules as applied are arbitrary and capricious].

NOTES AND QUESTIONS

1.   Look closely at the purposes of the TGA. The court of appeals had determined that the TGA's goal of stabilizing the livestock industry is "secondary" to the goals of protecting and restoring the rangeland and providing for its orderly use. 167 F.3d 1287, 1298 n.5 (10th Cir. 1999). Does the Supreme Court endorse that view? Or are the goals of equal stature? Notice how this issue ties into the TGA's directive that grazing privileges be "adequately safeguarded."

2.   On the first issue (whether the grazing preference reforms adequately safeguard the grazing privileges), what is really at stake? The ranchers were not arguing that they had a property interest in the AUMs that had been allocated to them under their preference. And they were not denying the authority of the BLM to reduce their grazing privileges in order to protect rangeland health. So what were they arguing? What did they say they had, and how did it limit BLM's authority, if at all? Is this all about optics rather than substance? A tempest in a teapot?

3.   As Justice Breyer noted, the level of use authorized in the permits often exceeds the amount of use actually authorized, with the rest in a "suspended" category. BLM grazing permits in FY 2005 included about 2 million AUMS in the "suspended" category, and about 12.7 million in the active category. Why did ranch lending institutions feel, according to their amicus brief, that the new policy threatened them? Do you suppose their loans were predicated on the basis of authorized use, or actual use?

4.   Justice Breyer noted that grazing on the public range has steadily declined, being cut almost in half, to ten million AUMS, in the last half of the twentieth century. Sheep herds tended to decline much more steeply, helped along by the grazing preference system of the TGA, because sheepherders tended to be nomadic, without "base property." Some of the decline has been voluntary, the result of marginal ranchers going out of business or cutting back on their operations as a result of competition from other sources of meat, domestic and foreign. Some has been the result of regulatory restrictions by federal land managers or the result of litigation, mostly tied to compliance with the Endangered Species Act.

5.   Both Justice Breyer's opinion and Justice O'Connor's concurrence recognize that ranchers remain free to challenge individual BLM decisions to deny or reduce their grazing privileges, either through FLPMA's land

use planning process or otherwise. If BLM decides that rangeland health requires reducing the number of livestock to be grazed in an area, what does the rancher have to show to overturn the BLM decision?

6. In challenging BLM's deletion of the requirement that permittees be "engaged in the livestock business," what are ranchers worried about? What is wrong, or threatening, about an organization like The Nature Conservancy buying a ranch and running a few cattle on the public lands while it works to restore rangeland health? Ranchland purchases by conservation organizations to reduce or retire grazing on public lands is dealt with in the concluding pages of this chapter.

7. On the third issue—title to certain range improvements being in the United States—note that the change was prospective, applying only to range improvements built in the future. Did this feature eliminate any argument that ranchers were being treated unfairly? On the title question, the policy issue here is similar to that raised in connection with ownership of water rights perfected to support grazing on the public lands. *See* Chapter 6, *supra* p. 526.

8. Why do you suppose the Supreme Court granted certiorari in this case? There were no conflicts among the lower courts, and ultimately the Court seemingly had little difficulty unanimously affirming the Tenth Circuit.

9. The 1995 grazing regulations require each state BLM office to prepare "standards and guidelines" ("S&Gs") for rangeland health, in consultation with the local Resource Advisory Council, or RAC. These were subject to approval by the Secretary. In early 2001, the Interior Solicitor opined (and the Secretary concurred) that the proposed New Mexico S&Gs had to be rejected because they were inconsistent with the rangeland reform regulations and applicable law. ("Proposed New Mexico Standards and Guidelines for Grazing Administration; Evaluation and Recommendations," January 11, 2001.) The New Mexico S&Gs would have required BLM to consider socioeconomic impacts in determining whether federal rangeland is in a healthy condition. The Solicitor's Opinion pointed out that this could "dictate a BLM decision to put more livestock on public lands that are already in poor ecological condition, in order to serve short-term local economic needs." That, the Opinion continued, violates several laws, including FLPMA's definition of "multiple use" ("without permanent impairment of the productivity of the land and the quality of the environment"), and its mandate to avoid "unnecessary or undue degradation of the lands." The Opinion concluded that socioeconomic factors may inform the choice of options for improving rangeland health, but may not be used at the initial stage of assessing the condition of the range.

10. What the ranchers lost in court they succeeded in getting back from the Bush Administration. In July 2006, the BLM promulgated new grazing regulations that made a number of changes, including rolling back the regulations upheld in the *Public Lands Council* case. *See* 71 Fed. Reg. 39402–39509 (2006). For example, the new regulations (a) enlarge the definition of grazing "preference" to embrace a quantity of grazing (measured in AUMs, or animal-unit-months); (b) allow the rancher to gain a

share of title to rangeland improvements, and to establish water rights on the public lands exclusively in their own name (Forest Service policy on range improvements is not so favorable to ranchers); (c) water down the Clinton Administration rule by requiring BLM to assemble data through "monitoring" before it can order improved grazing practices to protect rangeland health; (d) reduce the opportunity for the public to have input in agency grazing decisions at various points in the process; and (e) make it more difficult to interrupt grazing in the administrative appeals process. The BLM would still be required to make determinations about the health of the land in renewing grazing permits, although it now must consider the economic, social and cultural impacts of grazing decisions. Shortly after the regulations became final, a federal district judge in Idaho preliminarily enjoined those parts that cut back on public participation in grazing decisions. Western Watersheds Project v. Kraayenbrink, 2006 WL 2348080 (D.Id. 2006), discussed in Chapter 5, *supra*, at p. 481. A few weeks later the same judge also preliminarily enjoined provisions of the new BLM regulations that (a) changed the use of the Fundamentals of Rangeland Health, the criteria for judging range condition, and (b) allowed ranchers to share ownership of certain of permanent range improvements. Maughan v. Rosenkrance, 2006 WL 2348077 (D. Idaho 2006). The court found a strong likelihood that plaintiffs would prevail on the merits of their claim that NEPA was violated because the evidence showed that BLM did not fully consider advice from its own experts who maintained the regulatory changes would adversely effect wildlife and riparian conditions. This advice had been rendered before the draft EIS was published, but removed from the public documents and not addressed until BLM made available an addendum eight months after the final EIS was issued which partially addressed the points the experts had raised. The court found an injunction appropriate because BLM had scheduled rangeland health assessments on more than a million acres of Idaho grazing land over the next few months, as well as a number of range improvements. Further proceedings in the district court are pending as of this writing.

NOTE: GRAZING FEES

The price for leasing public rangeland traditionally has been a political lightning rod, especially for ranchers, with two interrelated constants: First, the fee has always been considerably lower than the going rate for comparable lands in private ownership, and second, raising the fee even to keep pace with inflation has proved stubbornly difficult.

The Forest Service first charged a nominal fee for grazing on national forests in 1906, and it was upheld in United States v. Grimaud, *supra* p. 126 (and provoked a proposal that the western states secede from the Union, *see* Donahue, p. 28). Not until 1931 was a new formula employed on the national forests; the grazing fee then increased slowly but steadily up to $0.56 per animal-unit-month (AUM) by 1968, still well below market levels.

Nothing was charged for grazing the public lands "common" until two years after the Taylor Act (which authorized the Secretary to charge "reasonable fees") was passed in 1934. The initial charge of a nickel an AUM (upheld against a rancher's challenge in Brooks v. Dewar, 313 U.S. 354 (1941)) was in effect until 1946, and had risen to only $0.33 twenty years later, when a joint fee study by the Secretaries of Agriculture and Interior concluded that the fee on BLM and national forest lands should be increased to $1.23 per AUM over ten years. This fee schedule was implemented, though interrupted by four moratoria on annual increases.

FLPMA, enacted in 1976, contained a generic policy statement that the United States should "receive fair market value of the use of the public lands and their resources unless otherwise provided for by statute," 43 U.S.C. § 1701(a)(9). But the same Act mandated another study of the grazing fee by both agencies. 43 U.S.C. § 1751(a). When it concluded that the fee system should collect fair market value, Congress ignored it and, in the Public Rangelands Improvement Act of 1978, 43 U.S.C. § 1905(a), tied the grazing fee to the price of cattle and the cost of production—the lower the price, the lower the fee—and capped any adjustment up or down in any year at twenty-five percent of the previous year's fee. In 1980, the fee was $1.89, but it dropped to $1.35 per AUM in 1985. Secretary of the Interior Babbitt early on announced an intention to impose higher grazing fees, but bowed to congressional opposition. In early 2007, the federal agencies announced that the grazing fee would fall to the minimum allowed by law, $1.35 per AUM, fifty-four cents below the fee charged more than a quarter of a century earlier, and a small fraction of grazing fees on comparable private lands ($13 per AUM by one estimate). State land intermingled with federal grazing land is usually leased at much higher rates.

The low grazing fees have led some ranchers to "rent" all or part of their federal grazing permit allotments to other ranchers, at higher rates than the federal fee. The BLM's regulations generally prohibit "subleasing" the permit without also subleasing the base property. They define "subleasing" as where a grazing permittee allows grazing on the federal lands covered by his permit "by livestock that are not owned or controlled by the permittee * * *." 43 C.F.R. §§ 4140.1(a)(6); 4100.0–5 (2001). Some subleases are formalized by "livestock pasture agreements" that purport to give the permittee "control" over the livestock to meet the terms of the regulations.

Professor Coggins criticized many aspects of public rangeland management, including the subsidized fee, in a series of articles; e.g., Coggins and Margaret Lindeberg–Johnson, *The Law of Public Rangeland Management II: The Common and the Taylor Act*, 13 ENVTL. L. 1, 74–75 (1982). Its problem, he argues, is that the subsidy is capitalized into the purchase price and mortgage value of the base ranch, leading the subsidy recipients to resist fiercely any cuts in their permitted AUMs, even when the reductions would ultimately redound to the ranchers' economic benefit.

NOTE: ENFORCING THE RANGE CODE

The BLM administers the preference system and otherwise regulates public land livestock grazing through what has come to be known, rather formidably, as the Range Code, even though it is merely a set of ordinary federal regulations formulated shortly after passage of the Taylor Grazing Act, and now found, as amended, at 43 C.F.R. §§ 4110–4170. For decades BLM did little to enforce many of its requirements. In the middle 1970s, the Department of the Interior suspended the grazing permit of a large ranch in Wyoming for two years for illegally spraying herbicide on public lands. On appeal, the rancher argued that the Department had no authority to suspend grazing privileges as a penalty. In rejecting that argument, the Tenth Circuit Court of Appeals "treated this as a question of first impression," noting "a surprising dearth of prior prosecutions along this line." Diamond Ring Ranch, Inc. v. Morton, 531 F.2d 1397 (10th Cir.1976). Section 1752(a) of the Federal Land Policy and Management Act of 1976 confirmed the *Diamond Ring* result by giving the government express authority to cancel, suspend, or modify a grazing permit or lease for any violation of a grazing regulation or of any terms contained in a permit or lease.

Each grazing permit under the Taylor Act is supposed to specify the kind and number of livestock allowed to graze, and the time of year a particular allotment can be grazed. 43 U.S.C. § 315b; 43 C.F.R. subpart 4130 (2001). Trespass—referring both to grazing animals in excess of the permitted number, and permitting them to graze on federal lands where or when they are not supposed to graze—has historically been a common problem on public rangelands. Enforcement is, by most accounts, spotty. Proof can be difficult because of intermingled land ownerships and the tradition of open rangeland still observed in parts of the west. BLM's attempts to deal with these problems have sometimes encountered difficulty, requiring considerable persistence. The Forest Service trespass regulations prohibit "[p]lacing or allowing unauthorized livestock to enter or be in" national forests. 36 C.F.R. § 261.7(a) (2001). The Eighth Circuit held that intent is not an element of the offense, United States v. Larson, 746 F.2d 455, 456 (8th Cir.1984), but the Ninth Circuit later held that the "Government must prove that the defendant willfully acted to allow his cattle to enter the National Forest, or willfully failed to prevent their entering when he had a clear opportunity to do so" in order to establish a criminal trespass. United States v. Semenza, 835 F.2d 223, 225 (9th Cir.1987).

Although the long history of private grazing on federal lands and the relationship between ranchers and federal land managers make the latter not the most aggressive regulators, sometimes efforts to enforce grazing regulations escalate. After BLM charged a Wyoming rancher with trespass more than two dozen times on 17 different allotments, a senior political appointee engineered a settlement that led to a critical Interior Inspector General report. Meanwhile, the rancher sued the government alleging that federal land managers had violated federal racketeering laws and committed *Bivens* constitutional torts by, he alleged, (1) retaliating against him for excluding federal officials from his private property by charging him with violating the terms of his grazing permits, and (2) attempting to extort from him a right of way for the public to cross his private lands. *See* Robbins v. BLM, 252 F. Supp.2d 1286 (D.Wyo. 2003), *aff'd* 433 F.3d 755

(10th Cir. 2006), *cert. granted*, 127 S.Ct. 722 (2006). Other ranchers have become folk heroes for resisting federal managers' efforts to curb their grazing. One was Kit Laney in Catron County, New Mexico, who spent well over a decade resisting federal regulation in court, eventually serving five months in federal prison after being found guilty of assaulting a Forest Service employee. Upon his release, he announced he was moving to Argentina. Laney's ranch, the Diamond Bar, first established by his great-grandfather in 1883, includes 115 acres of fee property and permits to graze 144,000 acres of national forest, about eighty-five percent of it inside the Gila Wilderness, the first wilderness area protected by Forest Service administrative designation at the instigation of Aldo Leopold nearly a century ago. Country western performer Michael Martin Murphey wrote a song, Storm Over the Rangeland, celebrating the defiance of Nevada rancher Wayne Hage. Supreme Court Justice Sandra Day O'Connor wrote in her reminiscence about growing up on a public lands ranch how her family gave up running cattle after armed agents seized a neighbor's herd for grazing without a permit. That neighbor, Luther W. "Wally" Klump, went on to serve more than a year in prison for contempt of court by defying a federal court order to remove cows from a BLM grazing allotment before eventually relenting, apparently ending fifteen years of litigation. *See* Dennis Wagner, Jailed Rancher Won't Budge Over Grazing, Arizona Republic, April 20, 2004; Klump v. United States, 50 Fed. Cl. 268 (2001), *aff'd* 30 Fed. Appx. 958 (Fed. Cir. 2002).

C.   RANGE ALLOCATION AND ANALYSIS UNDER FLPMA

As the foregoing materials indicate, BLM's control over private grazing operations on public lands has historically been considerably short of stellar, particularly from a resource protection standpoint. While the Taylor Act survived the onslaught of new federal lands statutes enacted in the 1970s, other statutes adopted in that era have ushered in a new (and for some ranchers, a painful) era of public range management, the ultimate effects of which are still being played out. We have explored two of the most important statutes—NEPA and the ESA—earlier, in Chapter 4. Here we take a quick look at NEPA's application before turning to FLPMA.

1.   NEPA

NEPA was seized on by environmentalists in the early 1970s as the best hope of bringing more environmental sensitivity to livestock grazing on BLM lands. In Natural Resources Defense Council, Inc. v. Morton, 388 F.Supp. 829 (D.D.C. 1974), *aff'd per curiam*, 527 F.2d 1386 (D.C.Cir. 1976), the court said BLM had to do more than prepare a programmatic EIS on its entire livestock grazing program in order to comply with NEPA. The court noted that plaintiffs "do not ask that impact statements be filed for every license or permit issued or renewed by the BLM. Nor do they seek an immediate injunction of the licensing program which could admittedly have a most deleterious effect on the entire livestock industry." The court itself did not specify the appropriate coverage for EISs:

> The crucial point is that the specific environmental effects of the permits issued, and to be issued, in each district be assessed. It will be initially within the BLM's discretion to determine whether to make this specific assessment in a separate impact statement for each district, or several impact statements for each district, or one impact statement for several districts or portions thereof, or indeed by other means. So long as the actual environmental effects of particular permits or groups of permits in specific areas are assessed, questions of format are to be left to defendants.

While this case was pending before the district court, BLM released a report compiled by a team of BLM resource managers, examining the environmental effects of livestock grazing in Nevada on the public lands. The court summarized its results this way:

> "Uncontrolled, unregulated or unplanned livestock use is occurring in approximately 85 percent of the State and damage to wildlife habitat can be expressed only as extreme destruction." [Report] at 13. Over-grazing by livestock has caused invasion of sagebrush and rabbitbrush on meadows and has decreased the amount of meadow habitat available for wildlife survival by at least 50 percent. The reduced meadow area has caused a decline in both game and non-game population. Id. at 26. In addition, there are 883 miles of streams with deteriorating and declining wildlife habitat, thus making it apparent, according to the report, that grazing systems do not protect and enhance wildlife values.[22]

NOTES AND QUESTIONS

1. If you were Director of BLM and you were asked to approve release of the report at that time, would you have done so (if you could have found an excuse to delay it)? Why or why not?

2. How should BLM go about complying with NEPA on a program involving some 18,000 permittees and 160 million acres of public land? Are individual EISs on individual permits out of the question? (By comparison, the entire federal government has in recent years prepared roughly 300 EISs every year.) In this connection, many studies have concluded that the cost of administering the public lands grazing program (including preparation of environmental documents and other processes involved in permit issuance and administration, and associated management costs such as predator control) far exceeds the revenues the government derives from grazing permits. *See* Donahue, The Western Range Revisited 277–79.

3. Eventually BLM reached an agreement with NRDC, approved by the court, under which it committed to prepare well over one hundred site-specific EISs on its grazing program on a specific schedule over a several

---

22. Whether the original deterioration occurred before or during BLM management is irrelevant since the crucial questions are whether it can be allowed to continue and whether it will be exacerbated by continued grazing.

year period. With some delays and other bumps along the way, the EISs were eventually completed, and documented what many observers had understood all along; namely, (a) many of the public grazing lands remain in less than healthy condition compared to their historic potential; (b) one clear cause for this condition is overgrazing; and (c) improvement in range condition depends largely upon reducing the number of grazing animals and limiting the areas available for grazing.

4. NEPA has been used from time to time by environmental groups as a tool to achieve grazing reform on the ground, at least temporarily. In Idaho Watersheds Project v. Hahn, 307 F.3d 815 (9th Cir. 2002), for example, the trial court found that BLM had violated NEPA in issuing 68 grazing permits covering about one million acres of public lands in the Owyhee Resource Area in the sculpted and arid canyonlands in the southwestern corner of Idaho. Apparently BLM's grazing administration in this area had been somewhat casual (the court of appeals described it as not very "rigorous"), because BLM learned, after the Clinton Administration adopted new Rangeland Reform regulations in 1995, that most of the local ranchers using federal lands for grazing either had no federal grazing permits at all, or were relying on permits that had expired. BLM issued new permits in 1997, relying for NEPA compliance on an EIS BLM had prepared in 1981 on its resource management plan for the Owyhee area. The district court found that continued grazing had caused "new and significant environmental impacts" not addressed in the 1981 EIS. But it rejected plaintiffs' request for a complete cessation of grazing until an adequate EIS was prepared, and instead entered an injunction that adopted interim grazing restrictions it solicited from the BLM range specialist, calling for such things as maintaining a minimum "stubble height" of four inches in "[k]ey herbaceous riparian vegetation," maintaining fifty percent of the "current annual twig growth" within reach of livestock on "[k]ey riparian browse vegetation," and limiting streambank damage attributable to grazing livestock to less than ten percent of any stream segment. The court of appeals affirmed, rejecting a variety of arguments by the BLM and the area ranchers, and commending the district judge for doing "an admirable job of ensuring an equitable result in a difficult situation," and giving "due regard to protection of the environment and the welfare of the affected ranching families."

2. FLPMA

FLPMA grew out of the recommendations of the landmark Public Land Law Review Commission in its report, One Third of the Nation's Lands, which generally supported multiple use and achieving fair market value for disposing of the lands' resources, and also recommended that "delicate" or "frail" or "deteriorated" lands be "classified not suitable for grazing." FLPMA gave BLM for the first time express, permanent authority to manage its lands for multiple use and sustained yield. It also created a resource planning process for BLM lands.

In enacting FLPMA (and the Public Rangelands Improvement Act, or PRIA, two years later), Congress essentially found that the public rangelands are in unhealthy condition, are deteriorating, and should be improved. In general, however, FLPMA did not thoroughly overhaul the law of livestock grazing or the legal relationship between the permittee and the government. It clarified and confirmed the government's authority in many important respects while leaving in place the Taylor Grazing Act's basic structure. It reconfirmed the TGA's admonition that "grazing permits do not carry any right, title, interest or estate in public lands." 43 U.S.C. § 1752(h). All the rangeland provisions of FLPMA are expressly made applicable to livestock grazing on the national forests as well as on BLM lands.

A subsection of FLPMA, 43 U.S.C. § 1752(a), sets ten years as the usual term for grazing permits or leases. A shorter term is allowed if the land is pending disposal, if it will be put to some other public purpose within ten years, or if it is "in the best interest of sound land management to specify a shorter term." *Id.* § 1752(b). In practice, nearly all permits are for ten year terms. FLPMA addresses the renewal of grazing permits this way (43 U.S.C. § 1752(c)):

> So long as (1) the lands for which the permit or lease is issued remain available for domestic livestock grazing in accordance with land use plans prepared pursuant to [FLPMA, for BLM, and the NFMA, for the Forest Service], (2) the permittee or lessee is in compliance with the rules and regulations issued and the terms and conditions in the permit or lease specified by the Secretary concerned, and (3) the permittee or lessee accepts the terms and conditions to be included by the Secretary concerned in the new permit or lease, the holder of the expiring permit or lease shall be given first priority for receipt of the new permit or lease.

How much protection does this provision give to a rancher seeking renewal? A rancher-lawyer has offered some policy arguments for favoring existing permittees:

> Priority renewal does have advantages. A permittee becomes intimately familiar with the range. * * * [H]igh turnover of federal graziers does not permit them to get to know the range nearly as well. Only long use can teach an operator where the thicket is that hides the stubborn bull late in the fall. The seasonal pattern of drying up of the range and waterholes must be known to fully utilize the range resource. If the first areas to dry are not used early in the season, they will be wasted. The rancher who expects to use the same range for many years in the future will be careful not to hurt the resource. The range cattle themselves get to learn the range. An old range cow can find hidden waterholes and meadows that a new cow would not. And with the first snows of fall, the old cows will lead the herd back to the home ranch.

Marc Valens, Federal Grazing Lands: Old History, New Directions (1978) (unpublished manuscript).

Regarding setting the appropriate level of grazing, FLPMA has this to say (43 U.S.C.A. § 1752(e)):

The Secretary concerned shall also specify [in the permit] the number of animals to be grazed and the seasons of use and * * * he may reexamine the condition of the range at any time and, if he finds on reexamination that the condition of the range requires adjustment in the amount or other aspect of grazing use, that the permittee or lessee shall adjust his use to the extent the Secretary concerned deems necessary. Such readjustment shall be put into full force and effect on the date specified by the Secretary concerned.

a. FLPMA PLANNING AND GRAZING MANAGEMENT ON A BROAD SCALE

Because the great bulk of BLM land is devoted to livestock grazing, planning as it relates to the forage resource has remained the subject of considerable attention. The following case (sometimes called the Burns decision, after the judge who rendered it) is perhaps the most detailed examination of BLM's planning responsibilities in relation to grazing.

Natural Resources Defense Council, Inc. v. Hodel

United States District Court, District of Nevada, 1985.
624 F. Supp. 1045.

■ JUDGE BURNS

This is a complex case of first impression, brought by environmental organizations seeking to overturn certain decisions made by the Bureau of Land Management (BLM) relating to livestock grazing on public lands in the Reno, Nevada area. The plaintiffs challenge the BLM's land use plan as being in conflict with Congressional statutory mandates, and as being arbitrary and capricious as a matter of administrative law. * * *

The BLM lands are divided for grazing purposes into districts, and subdivided into planning areas, such as the "Reno Planning Area" which is the subject of this action. The Reno Planning Area encompasses an overall area of just over 5 million acres, about 700,000 of which are under BLM supervision. The planning areas are further divided into grazing allotments, for which the BLM issues grazing permits or licenses. * * *

* * * [BLM began] in the late 1970s to lay the groundwork for a comprehensive grazing management plan and EIS for the Reno area. The agency began gathering inventory data, listing the available resources in portions of the planning area. Agency specialists then began preparation of the Management Framework Plan (MFP)*, which [took several months and was accompanied by NEPA compliance. The draft plan and EIS was published, and public comment taken, and then] * * * a final land use plan

---

* [Eds.: The management framework plans were pre-FLPMA plans; BLM calls its post-FLPMA plans "resource management plans," or RMPs. MFPs remain in force until they are replaced by RMPs. *See* 43 U.S.C. § 1732(a). Somewhat confusingly, BLM and the Forest Service also prepare Allotment Management Plans (AMPs), discussed in the *Oregon Natural Desert Association* case, *infra* p. 812.]

for grazing in the Reno planning area [was issued] on December 21, 1982.
* * *

Plaintiffs first correctly point to the legislative histories of the Taylor Grazing Act, FLPMA, and PRIA, to demonstrate Congress' general concern about overgrazing by livestock, and to indicate that reductions in livestock levels were one of the methods mentioned by Congress to prevent further deterioration of rangelands. Plaintiffs then cite portions of the record, including the DEIS, which indicate that there has been overuse of some portions of the Reno area by livestock. The conclusion plaintiffs say should then follow is that BLM has violated the law, and that the relatively modest improvements predicted from the MFP are insufficient to comply with the statutory mandates.

The facts established by the enormous record in this case do show that there has been overgrazing in the Reno area, but that in only four allotments could it be *conclusively* determined that the overgrazing was due to livestock use. On eight allotments the overuse could have resulted from a combination of livestock, deer, and wild horses; on the three remaining allotments there was no livestock grazing whatsoever. Thus, overgrazing due to livestock was not endemic to the entire Reno area.

A second important point to note in this context is that even where overgrazing is found to exist, the remedy is not necessarily the immediate removal of livestock. I give due weight to the proposition put forth by defendants' experts that other methods, such as vegetation manipulation and seeding, fencing, water development, or other range improvements or grazing systems may serve to address problems of selective overgrazing without a mandatory reduction in livestock use. * * * While reductions in AUMs for livestock may be one accepted method of addressing range deterioration, as recognized by Congress (see 43 U.S.C. § 1903(b)), it is not the only method.

A third important point here concerns the quality of data available to the BLM for making livestock management decisions. * * * [T]he BLM reached the decision that in order to defend its actions against attack from ranching interests it would need a solid data base upon which to ground livestock reduction orders. * * * Perkins v. Bergland, 608 F.2d 803, 807 (9th Cir.1979). As explained by defendants' experts, in order for the BLM to be certain of the proper livestock carrying capacity of a given allotment the agency must have: (1) actual use data (what kinds of animals grazed where and for how long), (2) how much vegetation has been consumed (utilization data), and (3) the overall effect of the specified grazing (trend). * * * The BLM said it lacked the first type of data for much of the Reno area and felt (at least after 1981) that in its absence it should refrain from immediate changes in livestock numbers, and concentrate its efforts on other techniques of range management.

Plaintiffs claim that the BLM is allowing overgrazing to continue. In reality, however, their complaint is with the *methods* selected by the BLM to allocate the resources within its control. Rather than immediate reductions in livestock numbers, the BLM chose to install range improvements and grazing systems on the areas ("I" allotments) that the BLM says are in need of the greatest attention. Moreover, the MFP does call for a significant reduction in livestock numbers, although this is to take place over a longer period of time than plaintiffs insist on. Finally, the MFP is predicted to bring about an overall improvement in the rated quality of many of the allotments. In sum, it is not entirely certain that the BLM has allowed continued overgrazing or deterioration of resources, in violation of statutory mandates.

The * * * MFP does result in limited improvements in overall ecological and forage conditions in the Reno area. Plaintiffs characterize the BLM's management as "do nothing", but in reality it appears that the real argument is that the BLM does not do what plaintiffs want, namely redress range conditions through immediate reduction or elimination of livestock grazing.

It must be noted that it is yet too early for a court to evaluate a claim that the BLM has not complied with its own plan, or that it has not taken the steps promised in the MFP. * * *

Plaintiffs argue that FLPMA and PRIA provide "standards" against which the court can determine whether the MFP is "arbitrary, capricious or contrary to law." The declarations of policy and goals in 43 U.S.C. §§ 1701(a), 1732, 1901, 1903 and ancillary provisions contain only broad expressions of concern and desire for improvement. They are general clauses and phrases which "can hardly be considered concrete limits upon agency discretion. Rather, it is language which 'breathes discretion at every pore.'" Perkins v. Bergland, 608 F.2d at 806. Although I might privately agree with plaintiffs that a more aggressive approach to range improvement would be environmentally preferable, or might even be closer to what Congress had in mind, the Ninth Circuit has made it plain that "the courts are not at liberty to break the tie choosing one theory of range management as superior to another." Perkins v. Bergland, 608 F.2d at 807. The modest plans adopted by the BLM for dealing with range conditions in the Reno area are not "irrational" and thus cannot be disturbed by the court.

The real question posed in this section of the case is what are BLM land use plans supposed to look like? That is, what kind of detail must the MFP contain to qualify as a legitimate land use plan required by Congress? FLPMA and PRIA refer to the importance of land use planning in several places. See 43 U.S.C. §§ 1701(a)(2), 1712, 1732(a), 1901(b). But nowhere in the statutes did Congress describe in detail what sort of information must be included in a land use plan. * * *

* * * It is therefore a reasonable assumption that Congress intended the BLM to continue its practice of setting grazing capacity at the permit-decision stage, and that land use planning (as required by 43 U.S.C. § 1712) deal with broader issues. These broader issues might include long-term resource conflicts, long-term range trends, planning of range improvements, and concentrating the BLM's limited resources on certain key areas.

This is the type of planning adopted by the BLM in this case. Clearly, the agency will continue to set grazing capacity on an on-going basis when it issues or renews grazing permits or licenses. A land use plan need not encompass every localized decision that must be made in the foreseeable future. Indeed, the legislative history indicates that Congress recognized "land use planning as dynamic and subject to change with changing conditions and values." [quoting House Committee Report on what became FLPMA] * * *

The present BLM regulations cited by plaintiffs do not compel a contrary interpretation. * * * BLM district managers * * * know that after the first five years they must begin reducing livestock AUMs to meet the 30,618 level they have set as a long term goal, and that total consumption must not exceed 59,344 AUMs for all species. If they fail to take these long term limits into account in issuing grazing permits after the first five years of the plan then they may be liable to an enforcement action by plaintiffs, or others with a similarly deep concern for the environment.

* * * FLPMA and PRIA demand no more. The type of "planning" envisioned by plaintiffs, wherein the plan would effectively contain allotment management plans for each unit in the Reno area, allocating forage to each consumer species for each of the next ten years or more, is not a plan. It is an administrative straight-jacket which eliminates the room for any flexibility to meet changing conditions. In the absence of more directive legislation, or mandate from my appellate superiors, I will not command such a requirement. * * *

Defendant's * * * affidavits * * * are persuasive in refuting the notion that there is such a thing as an *a priori* "carrying capacity" or grazing capacity for any one piece of land. Consider a hypothetical allotment which could support 100 head of cattle in one year, and not show signs of downward trend. However, in the following year, depending on only one variable such as climate[,] the same allotment could perhaps support only 80 head. Conversely, with the addition of certain range improvements that would improve dispersal of the livestock on the allotment, the same parcel could in the following year perhaps support 120 head without signs of deterioration. Each of these permutations could be further affected by other variables such as usage by wild horses, or mule deer, precipitation or temperature patterns, seeding, encroachment of inferior types of forage, changes in seasons of use, and so on. * * * Unrealistic, then, is plaintiffs' theory that there is a fixed and immutable level of acceptable livestock use that can be administratively determined for years into the future. * * *

Although the BLM had trend data for most of the area, such data alone is [sic] not useful for setting livestock grazing levels because a declining trend can be due to a wide number of factors, only one of which is overuse by livestock. Further, although the BLM had some utilization data (showing how much forage was consumed in a given plot) it was not able to conclusively determine actual use by livestock. The actual use by real numbers of cattle is not always the same as the authorized use contained in permits. [citing BLM affidavit] * * *

Because of these and other difficulties, the BLM decided to revamp its methodology of setting grazing levels, based primarily on continued monitoring over longer periods of time, and not based on one-point-in-time studies * * *. A new monitoring system for Nevada was developed by a joint task force and was adopted in 1981. * * * [T]his change in methodology took place around the time that Mr. Watt became Secretary of the Interior, and the ultimate result of the decision was the continuation of existing grazing levels in the Reno area. But there is no direct evidence in this record that the change in methodology was primarily prompted by a political decision to postpone any adjustments in allocation that would adversely affect ranching interests. * * *

* * * If it were possible to glean more precise standards from the statutes or regulations, against which these policy decisions could be measured, then I might be more able to discern a pattern of illegal or arbitrary conduct, and to fashion appropriate relief. That is not the case before me. * * * The administrative record in this case does at least contain plausible support for defendants' position that existing monitoring data for the Reno area was not reliable for purposes of setting fixed grazing levels. While the BLM probably *could* have made defensible livestock adjustments where their data showed overutilization, poor range condition, and downward trend, this court cannot say it was "irrational" for them to refrain from doing so without the sort of monitoring data they desired. At this point, judicial inquiry is at an end. * * *

CONCLUSION

* * * [T]he role plaintiffs would have me play in this controversy is an unworkable one. Plaintiffs are understandably upset at what they view to be a lopsided and ecologically insensitive pattern of management of public lands at the hands of the BLM, a subject explored at length by many commentators. Congress attempted to remedy this situation through FLPMA, PRIA and other acts, but it has done so with only the broadest sorts of discretionary language, which does not provide helpful standards by which a court can readily adjudicate agency compliance. * * * [P]laintiffs ask me to become—and defendants urge me not to become—the rangemaster for about 700,000 acres of federal lands in western Nevada. * * * Fortunately, for reasons set out in this opinion which (to me) are legally correct, I am able to resist the invitation * * *.

NOTES AND QUESTIONS

1. The Ninth Circuit affirmed this decision with a brief opinion, noting:

> Reduced to its essence, the NRDC's challenge to the EIS and the final land use plan is a challenge to the BLM's policy decision to postpone livestock grazing adjustments until reliable data was [sic] available. While we sympathize with the NRDC's strong desire to preserve the environment, we agree with the district court that we cannot label this policy decision as either irrational, or contrary to law. Thus, "[a]t this point, judicial inquiry is at an end."

819 F.2d 927, 930 (9th Cir. 1987). The opinion also contained this footnote (*id.* n.1):

The NRDC complains that the district court incorrectly assumed that the BLM sets grazing capacity on an on-going basis when it issues or renews grazing permits or licenses. We agree with the BLM that this assumption was not essential to the district court's conclusion that [FLPMA and PRIA] "demand no more" than broad objective-oriented land use plans. * * *

2. Regarding the alleged lack of data, the district court referred in various places to BLM's claimed lack of data on such things as the actual (as opposed to authorized) level of livestock grazing, the amount of forage consumed, the environmental impacts of grazing on specific allotments or specific areas, and the environmental effects of adjustments in grazing levels. Does either court in this case *require* the BLM to *gather* such data? Should the courts at least require BLM to gather data as to the actual level of livestock grazing going on? Does FLPMA (or NEPA) require gathering of relevant data?

3. After the Supreme Court's decision in Norton v. SUWA, *supra* p. 471, can a court enforce an agency promise in a plan to do more monitoring? Is it lawful for a federal land management agency to put its head in the sand and ignore whatever problems might exist on its lands? As long as the federal land manager does not have, and does not take steps to produce, reliable information to show that problems exist, is the agency immune from judicial interference? Is that good policy? What other remedies exist?

4. On the other hand, if a federal land management agency may be said to have a legally enforceable duty to gather relevant data, how can that idea be cabined within reasonable bounds? Does the agency have a duty to commission studies to learn exactly how many species exist and what might be the effect of proposed actions on each?

5. Suppose the BLM had, on the basis of the limited data it had here, gone ahead and provided in the final plan for reductions in the authorized level of livestock grazing. Would that have been arbitrary and capricious?

6. Recall that BLM is also under a mandate to achieve "sustained yield" of the forage resource, defined in FLPMA as "the achievement and maintenance in perpetuity of a high-level annual or regular periodic output of the various renewable resources of the public lands consistent with multiple use." 43 U.S.C. § 1702(h). Did the BLM comply with this mandate in the Reno Planning Area? Recall also the generic mandate of FLPMA, 43 U.S.C. § 1732(b), that "[i]n managing the public lands the Secretary shall, by regulation or otherwise, take any action necessary to prevent unnecessary or undue degradation of the lands." Did the BLM comply with this mandate in the Reno Planning Area?

7. One might question, after the Supreme Court's 1998 decision in Ohio Forestry Ass'n v. Sierra Club, *supra* p. 216, whether NRDC's facial challenge to BLM's plan would be ripe if brought today. If NRDC had to bring the challenge to the plan in the context of a renewal of a specific grazing permit, might that have made its case more appealing, by providing a real, on-the-ground factual context in which to judge BLM's action (or inaction)? On the other hand, would the result in one permit-specific

challenge necessarily dictate the outcome of challenges that might be brought to other grazing permits in the same planning area?

8. In that part of his opinion addressing plaintiffs' claim of inadequate compliance with NEPA, Judge Burns held that an alternative of completely banning grazing on BLM land in the Reno area was not reasonable and did not require consideration. He noted, among other things, that

> Livestock grazing has been going on in the Reno planning area, on public lands, for more than a century, [and it is] an important priority in the overall resource picture of this area. * * * NEPA does not require examination of alternatives that are so speculative, contrary to law, or economically catastrophic as to be beyond the realm of feasibility. The complete abandonment of grazing in the Reno planning area is practically unthinkable as a policy choice; it would involve monetary losses to the ranching community alone of nearly 4 million dollars and 290 jobs, not to mention unquantifiable social impacts. Of course, compared with the economy of the Reno area as a whole, ranching plays only a negligible role. Nevertheless, eliminating all grazing would have extreme impacts on this small community.

Senator Harry Reid of Nevada, who has supported efforts to reform rangeland practices, has said that one large Las Vegas hotel employs more people than the entire agriculture industry in Nevada.

9. Judge Burns expressed reluctance to become "rangemaster" of BLM lands in the Reno area. In Washington v. Washington State Commercial Passenger Fishing Vessel Ass'n, 443 U.S. 658 (1979), the Supreme Court held that the trial court was justified in assuming the role of "fishmaster" in the Columbia River basin to protect Indian treaty fishing rights and "has the power to undertake the necessary remedial steps and to enlist the aid of the appropriate federal law enforcement agents in carrying out those steps." 443 U.S. at 696. Should the court's decision whether or not to become a "rangemaster" depend on whether the agency is implementing and complying with the law? On the seriousness of the abuses? On the complexity of the situation?

The Forest Service also has broad planning responsibilities through which it must address livestock grazing on federal lands under its jurisdiction, as the following case illustrates.

Central S.D. Co-op. Grazing Dist. v. Secretary of Agriculture

United States Court of Appeals for the Eighth Circuit, 2001.
266 F.3d 889.

■ JUDGE BEAM

[The 116,000 acre Fort Pierre National Grassland in North Dakota was established in the 1930s on federal land acquired from failed homesteaders.

Part of the movie Dances With Wolves was filmed there. Under the National Forest Management Act,] a forest plan identifies suitable grazing lands, while permits to graze, if appropriate under that general plan, are issued pursuant to an appropriate site-specific project analysis. * * * Grazing permits "convey no right, title, or interest" in lands or resources, 36 C.F.R. § 222.3(b), and are subject to modification according to changes in management needs or resource conditions, 36 C.F.R. § 222.4(a)(7) & (8).

In this case, the Grazing District is an association that has a permit to graze cattle upon the Grasslands. In 1984, after completion of an EIS, the Forest Service adopted and approved the Nebraska National Forest Land and Resource Management Plan (Nebraska Forest Plan) to regulate use of the Grassland's resources. This plan emphasizes wildlife habitat, directing the Forest Service to "[a]lter grazing systems, season of use, and stocking levels to enhance wildlife habitat." It also requires the Forest Service to have developed residual cover[4] guidelines for the sharp-tailed grouse and greater prairie chicken "by [the] close of FY 1988." In 1985—prior to having considered all resource factors, seeking involvement of all interested parties, or conducting the requisite NEPA analysis—the Forest Service authorized the issuance of permits to graze cattle on the Grasslands at a maximum stocking rate of 70,436 Animal Unit Months (AUMs)[5]. Documentation incorporated into the Grazing District's grazing agreement indicated that proper range condition analyses needed to be conducted, that when residual cover requirements were established, the permits would be subject to them and that as monitoring and evaluation were conducted, the stocking levels could be revised.

After extensively studying the impact of grazing on the wildlife habitat [using many different techniques from 1985 to 1997 to monitor resource conditions on the Grasslands], the Forest Service ultimately determined that the 1985 stocking level made it impossible to satisfy the Nebraska Forest Plan's requirements for "long-term rangeland health and productivity, wildlife habitat, woody draw habitat, and soil and water protection." Therefore, in accordance with the NFMA and NEPA, the Forest Service prepared an Environmental Assessment in which it considered maximum grazing levels of 55,440 (an alternative considered at the request of the Grazing District), 45,211, 15,070, and 51,558 AUMs, along with a no-grazing alternative. In 1998, after giving public notice and receiving comments, the Forest Service issued a decision notice establishing the total maximum stocking level for the Grasslands at 51,558 AUMs and made a finding of no significant impact for the selected level.

The Grazing District subsequently filed a complaint seeking judicial review of this agency action. Both the Grazing District and Forest Service filed simultaneous motions for summary judgment. The district court

---

4. "Residual cover" refers to the height and density of residual vegetation when measured in the fall after the grazing season has ended.

5. An AUM is defined by the Natural Resources Conservation Service as a 1000-pound cow with a calf less than six months old.

granted summary judgment in favor of the Forest Service. * * * [The court rejected plaintiff's NEPA challenge both for lack of standing and on the merits.]

The Grazing District argues that the Forest Service's habitat suitability index was such an unreliable measure of sharp-tailed grouse nesting habitat that it rendered decisions stemming therefrom arbitrary and capricious. The index compares levels of residual cover that remained after grazing with levels of cover in ungrazed areas in order to assess whether habitat for management indicator species, such as the sharp-tailed grouse, achieved at least 40% of potential. * * * [T]he Grazing District's underlying assumption [was] that the Forest Service should have included the effect of visual obscurity on sharp-tailed grouse populations in its index. However, the Grazing District misapprehends the index, which was designed to assess the effect of grazing on the level of residual cover, not on the grouse population. The Forest Service obtained from other sources data regarding what constitutes habitat suitability and need not have included in chart-form what it knew from its other sources to be the case. For instance,

> Plains sharptail nesting cover tends to be more grassy and less shrubby than that of the prairie sharptail of the Great Lakes States. The lack of good quality nesting and brood-rearing cover generally is limiting for sharp-tailed grouse throughout their range. Plains sharp-tailed grouse are generally limited by intensive grazing and conversion of rangeland to cropland. Grazing reduces the quantity of residual vegetation. Residual herbaceous vegetation is important nesting cover because little current growth is available in early spring when most nests are constructed.

Bart L. Prose, *Habitat Suitability Index Models: Plains Sharp–Tailed Grouse*, U.S. Fish Wildl.Serv.Biol.Rep. 82(10.142), 9, (1987) (citing various authorities). * * *

Furthermore, the Grazing District ignores the Forest Service's charge to protect the Grasslands habitat for fauna other than the sharp-tailed grouse, along with flora and other resources. As the Environmental Assessment points out:

> Through visual observations, erosion and gullies were noticed due to a lack of vegetative cover and a lower range condition. If livestock continue to graze at this [initial] level, resource conditions will degrade. If intensive grazing continues during a prolonged drought, the vegetative composition will decrease to a lower level of condition and the overall rangeland health declines.

The Forest Service's habitat suitability index was not defective for the purpose it was used and does not undermine other data the Forest Service relied upon. Nor was the index the primary tool used in the Forest Service's decision-making, but was merely "one of many considerations . . . along with many other pieces of information, both biological and social." The Forest Service accounted for discrepancies to which the Grazing District directs us and was entitled to rely upon its experts and data even though there may have been some conflicting data. * * * That the sharp-tailed grouse *can* nest in more heavily grazed areas misses the point since the Forest Service seeks to improve the habitat overall. The index was a reasonable tool among others employed and does not render the chosen stocking level arbitrary and capricious.

Also unpersuasive is the Grazing District's assertion that the Forest Service's reliance on a "one-point-in-time" range vegetation inventory violated the National Forest Management Act and rendered its choice of stocking levels arbitrary and capricious. The NFMA's general criteria require that, in developing and maintaining land management plans, the Forest Service use "a systematic interdisciplinary approach to achieve integrated consideration of physical, biological, economic, and other sciences." 16 U.S.C. § 1604(b).

The Grazing District claims that "inherent inadequacies of one point in time inventories as measures of overall stocking levels have been recognized by the scientific community and in court," citing *Hodel,* 624 F.Supp. at 1061. However, *Hodel* did not indicate that all one-point-in-time inventories were categorically unreliable, but that, there, the data obtained from a one-point-in-time study "was not ultimately used ... because it yielded inconsistent results." *Id.* Yet those inconsistencies were "due in part to an insufficient number of samples, errors in identifying plant species, and assumptions built into the model." *Id.* Furthermore, that conclusion was not reached by a court, but by the Bureau of Land Management, an agency to whose decision the trial court deferred. *Id.* * * *

The Grazing District refers us to the testimony of Dr. Jim Johnson of South Dakota State University to make its point that the Forest Service failed to consider the "best available information" regarding the relationship between the Grasslands' condition to stocking levels. Dr. Johnson testified:

> In order to perfectly [sic—"correlate" may be the missing word, eds.] the range condition to stocking rates, we would also need grazing history, trend, and utilization data on a pasture by pasture basis. However, experiences of range scientists and producers in South Dakota strongly support the validity of using the Suggested Initial Stocking Guides as a good approximation of where stocking levels should be to improve range or maintain high range conditions.

Our standard for agency action is not one of perfection, but whether the agency acted arbitrarily and capriciously. We find that the Forest Service has not.

The Grazing District also contends that the NFMA, 16 U.S.C. § 1610, required the Forest Service "to use information available from third parties." * * * Section 1610 states that, in carrying out her land management duties, "the Secretary of Agriculture shall utilize information and data available from other Federal, State, and private organizations and shall avoid duplication and overlap of resource assessment and program planning efforts of other Federal agencies." Although this is likely an efficiency provision, the Forest Service did look to available data from other agencies and private organizations. The statute does not require the Forest Service to adhere to the letter of each datum, which, judging from the various reports in this matter, would likely be virtually impossible. Furthermore, judging from Dr. Johnson's testimony, it appears that the Forest Service did rely on the best *available* data. The Forest Service did not contravene section 1610.

For the reasons we have outlined, we affirm the district court's grant of summary judgment in favor of the Forest Service.

NOTES AND QUESTIONS

1. In the NEPA portion of the opinion not included in the above excerpt, the court noted that actual use of forage had not been above 52,400 AUMs since 1989, or about the level that the Forest Service established in the decision being challenged. Why, then, do you suppose the plaintiffs challenged it?

2. How can *Hodel* and *S.D. Co-op. Grazing Dist.* be reconciled? Both involved agency planning processes and grazing levels. Is it that the agency always (or usually) wins; i.e., that the deference principle is very strong? That the courts feel ill-equipped to delve into the details of federal land management? Especially when very large tracts of federal lands are involved? (The Reno Planning Area contains about six times as much federal land as the Fort Pierre National Grassland.)

3. Another way of comparing the two cases is to look at the quantity and type of information available to each agency. The Forest Service had the benefit of more than a dozen years of monitoring data that focused primarily on the relationship of grazing to a couple of species of wildlife. If BLM had had the same kind of focused information in the Reno planning area, might it have been able to reduce livestock grazing? Did, in other words, the Forest Service do its homework, and the BLM did not? Note that the Forest Service set the maximum stocking rate at 70,436 AUMs in 1985, in the court's words, "prior to having considered all resource factors, seeking involvement of all interested parties, or conducting the requisite NEPA analysis."

4. All told, does *Hodel* suggest that FLPMA's planning process has no or at best limited utility when it comes to addressing and setting appropriate levels of livestock grazing? Does the South Dakota case suggest otherwise about the Forest Service planning process? Is the issue the design and details of the planning process, or do factors of agency tradition, culture, and political will predominate regardless of process and facts?

b.   ALLOTMENT MANAGEMENT ON A FINE SCALE

The environmentalists' strategy in *NRDC v. Hodel* sought to use the agency's planning processes along with NEPA as a way to limit the adverse environmental impacts of public lands grazing. The effort was carried out at a broadbrush level, not focusing on individual permits. In part this strategy was dictated by the sheer magnitude of the federal land grazing enterprise, involving many thousands of operations and some quarter of a billion acres. The *Hodel* decision showed the limitations of that strategy. In fact, a free-market advocate who worked in the Interior Department for many years argues that BLM made "few changes in grazing practices" as a result of NEPA compliance and the planning process. Robert H. Nelson, *How to Reform Grazing Policy: Creating Forage Rights on Federal Range-lands*, 8 FORDHAM ENVTL. L. REV. 645, 655–56 (1997); *see also* Donahue, THE WESTERN RANGE REVISITED 54–65 (1999). After *Hodel*, environmental advocates showed more interest in looking at the grazing management process from a micro, "bottom-up" perspective.

Along this line, Professor Joseph Feller has described how grazing levels are usually determined in practice by the federal agencies:

> Although the permit or the AMP should prescribe the terms and conditions necessary to ensure proper management of livestock grazing on an allotment, in reality many management decisions are made on an annual basis. For example, although the permit specifies a number of livestock, the BLM annually determines how many livestock will actually graze on an allotment. The actual number allowed to graze may be less than the number in the permit either because the permittee has requested voluntary "non-use" of all or a part of the permitted number, or because the BLM has concluded that the allotment in its current condition cannot actually support the permitted number. On many allotments, the BLM also issues an annual grazing schedule specifying which pastures on an allotment will be grazed and which will be rested that year, and the dates of use and numbers of livestock for each of the pastures that will be grazed. Where an AMP is in place, this annual grazing schedule should be, but sometimes is not, consistent with the AMP.

> In principle, these annual decisions provide the flexibility needed to adapt the permitted numbers, and the terms and conditions of the permit or AMP, to changing and unpredictable circumstances, particularly variations in rainfall. In practice, these annual decisions sometimes supplant the permit and the AMP as the mechanisms for prescribing the management of an allotment. *The number of livestock specified in the permit often substantially exceeds the number that the permittee ever actually places on the allotment or that the allotment could accommodate without resource damage. In such a case, the permit acts as a blank check, allowing the permittee and the BLM to agree privately each year on how many livestock will actually graze.* Further, on many allotments without an AMP, the permit contains only the minimum specifications (number and kind of livestock and dates of use of the allotment), leaving all other management prescriptions to the annual grazing schedule.

Grazing Management on the Public Lands: Opening the Process to Public Participation, 26 LAND & WATER L.REV. 569, 575–76 (1991) (emphasis added). The extent to which the courts will review these informal agency decisions setting grazing levels is addressed in the next two cases.

Oregon Natural Desert Association v. U.S. Forest Service

United States Court of Appeals, Ninth Circuit, 2006.
465 F.3d 977.

■ JUDGE PAEZ

This appeal presents the narrow question whether the United States Forest Service's issuance of annual operating instructions ("AOIs") to permittees who graze livestock on national forest land constitutes final agency action for purposes of judicial review under the Administrative Procedure Act ("APA"), 5 U.S.C. §§ 702–706. * * * We conclude that the Forest Service's action in issuing the AOIs is "final agency action" under § 704 and therefore that plaintiffs' claims are ripe for judicial review.

FLPMA authorizes the Forest Service to allow livestock grazing on specified allotments[1] within a national forest. The Forest Service authorizes and manages grazing on specified allotments by issuing (1) a grazing permit pursuant to 43 U.S.C. § 1752(a) and 36 C.F.R. § 222; (2) an Allotment Management Plan ("AMP") pursuant to 43 U.S.C. § 1752(d) and 36 C.F.R. § 222.1(b); and (3) AOIs.[2] A grazing permit is a "document authorizing livestock to use National Forest System or other lands under Forest Service control for the purpose of livestock production." 36 C.F.R. § 222.1(b)(5); 43 U.S.C. § 1702(p). A permit grants a license to graze and establishes: (1) the number, (2) kind, (3) and class of livestock, (4) the allotment to be grazed, and (5) the period of use. The Forest Service sets these parameters based on its assessment of the land's ability to sustain average levels of livestock use according to the applicable land and resource management plan. The Forest Service generally issues permits for ten-year periods. The Forest Service is also required to prepare an AMP for each allotment. An AMP is "a document that specifies the program of action ... to meet[, *inter alia*,] the multiple-use, sustained yield, economic, and other needs and objectives as determined for the lands involved" and includes provisions relating to grazing objectives "as may be prescribed by the [Forest Service], consistent with applicable law," 36 C.F.R. § 222.1(b); 43 U.S.C. §§ 1702(k)(1), 1752(d), including the applicable forest plan. While a forest plan is an overarching land management directive for an entire forest-wide unit within the National Forest System, the AMP is a land management directive for a specific allotment within a national forest that the Forest Service has designated for livestock grazing. The AMP must be consistent with the applicable forest plan. *See* 16 U.S.C. § 1604(I).

Finally, as reflected in the administrative record, prior to the beginning of a grazing season, the Forest Service issues an AOI to grazing permit holders. Whereas the AMP relates the directives of the applicable

1. An allotment is a "designated area of land available for livestock grazing." 36 C.F.R. § 222.1(b)(1). The administrative record reflects that the Forest Service divides an allotment into several smaller "units," or pastures.

2. Prior to 2004, the Forest Service called AOIs "annual operating plans." We refer to these documents as AOIs regardless of whether the Forest Service issued the document prior to the change in name.

forest plan to the individual grazing allotment, and the grazing permit sets grazing parameters through a ten-year period, the AOI annually conveys these more long-term directives into instructions to the permittee for annual operations. * * * The AOI consists of a signed agreement between the Forest Service and permit holder. According to its explicit terms, the AOI is made part of the grazing permit and governs the permit holder's grazing operations for the next year[3].

Because an AOI is issued annually, it is responsive to conditions that the Forest Service could not or may not have anticipated and planned for in the AMP or grazing permit, such as drought conditions, timing and duration of rainfall over the grazing season, success or failure of habitat restoration projects, water quality, or degree of risk to threatened or endangered species affected by grazing. With this contextual background in mind, we review briefly the statutory basis for ONDA's claims and the district court's jurisdictional ruling.

In 1988, Congress designated stretches of the North Fork Malheur and Malheur Rivers in the Blue Mountains of eastern Oregon as wild and scenic river corridors under the Wild and Scenic Rivers Act of 1968 ("WSRA"). The 1990 Malheur National Forest Land and Resource Management Plan ("Malheur Forest Plan" or "Forest Plan") designates more than 10,000 acres of national forest land on and adjacent to the North Fork Malheur and Malheur River corridors as livestock grazing allotments. [Plaintiffs (collectively, "ONDA") charged that the Forest Service issued AOIs during the period 2000–2004 to grazing permit holders for pastures on six allotments along roughly forty miles of the protected river corridors that violated the WSRA, NFMA, NEPA and the agency's own regulations.]

* * * [T]he Forest Service and the intervenors moved to dismiss for lack of jurisdiction because the AOIs at issue did not constitute final agency actions reviewable under 5 U.S.C. § 706(2)(A). * * * [After affirming the district court's decision that the AOIs are agency actions, the court turned to whether it was "final" agency action within the meaning of the APA. It applied the two-part test of Bennett v. Spear, 520 U.S. 154 (1997) for determining whether an agency action is final; namely, that it represents the consummation of the agency's decisionmaking process and that it is one "by which rights or obligations have been determined, or from which legal consequences will flow." First, it addressed the "consummation" issue, as follows:]

An AOI sets forth the Forest Service's annual determinations regarding how much grazing particular units (pastures) within a given allotment can sustain in the upcoming season. As demonstrated by the record, in establishing the terms of an AOI, the Forest Service considers such matters as changes in pasture conditions, new scientific information, new rules that

---

3. The administrative record contains a number of pre–2004 AOIs that include a provision stating: "[t]his Annual Operating Instruction is made part of Part 3 of your Term Grazing Permit" and "[t]his signed AOI is your agreement to comply with the following provisions, as well as other instructions given to you, your employees, and contractors by the district ranger." * * * [T]he Forest Service eliminated these statements from the 2004 AOIs.

have been adopted during the previous season, or the extent of the permit holder's compliance with the previous year's AOI. The AOI is a critical instrument in the Forest Service's regulation of grazing on national forest lands.

Indeed, when the Forest Service takes a site-specific action within the Malheur Forest, such as issuing a grazing permit for an allotment within the forest, the Forest Service's actions must comply with the standards and conditions set out in the Malheur Forest Plan as well as applicable federal environmental law. Although the Forest Service generally implements Forest Plan standards on designated grazing allotments with an AMP, none of the allotments involved in this litigation has a current AMP.[9]

Where an AMP does not exist for an allotment, the Forest Service has integrated the Forest Plan's terms directly into the grazing permits each year through the AOI. For example, in 1996, the Forest Service issued three grazing permits for different pastures within the Bluebucket Allotment. The permits identify the general statutory and regulatory framework that governs the actions of the individual permit holders so that livestock grazing will be consistent with the Malheur Forest Plan. Part III of each grazing permit provides: "prior to completion and implementation of the scheduled individual AMP's, we will be working with you through the Annual Operating Plans [i.e., AOIs] to bring management of the Bluebucket Allotment into consistency with the terms of the Malheur [Forest Plan]." Thus, here, the Forest Service directly "put[s] the [allotment management] decision[s] into effect" through an AOI. *Idaho Watersheds Project [v. Hahn]*, 307 F.3d [815] at 828 [9th Cir. 2002)].

In *Idaho Watersheds Project,* we held that the BLM's issuance of a grazing permit was a final agency action because "the initial agency decisionmaker arrived at a definitive position and put the decision into effect by issuing the ... permits." Here, as in *Idaho Watershed Project,* the Forest Service arrived at a definitive position to allow grazing in the Malheur National Forest and put that decision into effect by issuing grazing permits. In issuing the permits, the Forest Service reserved the right to impose additional terms and conditions in light of its annual assessment of changed pasture conditions, new scientific information, new rules, and past compliance by the permit holder. As noted, the Forest Service puts these additional modifications or restrictions into effect by issuing an AOI. As the record reflects, when viewed in its proper context, the AOI represents the consummation of the Forest Service's annual decisionmaking process regarding management of grazing allotments.[10]

9. Other than the Bluebucket Allotment, for which the Forest Service prepared an AMP over twenty years ago, none of the allotments at issue in this appeal has an AMP. Each permit states that the Forest Plan has "scheduled" an AMP; however, the record does not reflect that the Forest Service has complied with these schedules. In one case, the Dollar Basin/Star Glade Allotment, the Forest Service has not completed an allotment analysis—a step preceding development of an AMP—since 1965.

10. To suggest that the AOIs are merely part of the Forest Service's "day-to-day operation," see Dissenting Opinion at 11857, relegates them to an insignificant role in the Forest Service's management of the grazing lands under its control. In light of the substantive legal constraints imposed by the

Moreover, after the Forest Service issues an AOI, the grazing permit holder is authorized to begin the new grazing season under its terms and conditions[11]. Because the AOI is the only substantive document in the annual application process, it functions to do more than make minor adjustments in the grazing permit as the Forest Service asserts; pragmatically, it functions to start the grazing season. In short, the AOI is the Forest Service's "last word" before the permit holders begin grazing their livestock. Cf. Ecology Ctr., Inc. v. USFS, 192 F.3d 922, 925 (9th Cir.1999) (holding that monitoring and reporting under NFMA were not agency actions that consummated the Forest Service's decisionmaking process because they were "only steps leading to an agency decision, rather than the final action itself").

The Forest Service does not contest that an AOI is the Forest Service's "last word" before a permit holder begins grazing his livestock. Rather, the Forest Service asserts that an AOI merely implements other decisions that the Forest Service has already made (i.e., the Forest Plan, AMPs, and grazing permits), and therefore is not, in itself, a final agency action. This argument, however, mis-characterizes the role of an AOI in the Forest Service's management of the public range. * * * It is correct, as the Forest Service argues, that, in obtaining a grazing permit, the applicant agrees to comply with the Forest Plan and other applicable federal environmental requirements. However, as the administrative record demonstrates, an AOI is the only instrument that instructs the permit holder how those standards will affect his grazing operations during the upcoming season. Although the permit holder has already agreed to abide by applicable federal environmental law in signing the term grazing permit, that acknowledgment does not diminish the force of an AOI as consummating the Forest Service's annual decisionmaking process. In sum, the issuance of an AOI represents the consummation of the Forest Service's determination regarding the extent, limitation, and other restrictions on a permit holder's right to graze his livestock under the terms of the permit.[12] * * *

[The court then turned to whether the AOI is an action "by which rights or obligations have been determined, or from which legal conse-

---

AOIs, we are not persuaded by the dissent's argument.

11. As documented in the administrative record, every spring, the Forest Service initiates consultation with the permit holder regarding the issuance of the AOI for the forthcoming grazing season. At the end of this consultation process, the Forest Service sets the terms and conditions for grazing in any particular allotment. Without the AOI, the permit holder would not know where within the allotment to graze, how many head to graze when, or any specific conservation measures that the Forest Service deemed warranted for the upcoming season.

12. * * * In *Montana Wilderness,* we held that trail maintenance did not constitute

final agency action for purposes of judicial review under the APA. 314 F.3d 1146, 1150 (9th Cir.2003), *vacated on other grounds by SUWA.* * * * [W]e noted that the Forest Service's trail maintenance activities "implement[ed] its trail management and forest plans adopted for the study area." *Id.* We concluded that "the maintenance of trails designated by those plans [was] merely an interim aspect of the planning process, not the consummation of it." *Id.* Here, the AOIs are not part of an interim planning process. Instead, as even the dissent seems to acknowledge, the AOIs represent the consummation of a process, which results in the imposition of enforceable rights and obligations on the permittee.

quences will flow."] * * * If a permittee does not comply with the directives in the AOI, the Forest Service can issue a Notice of Non–Compliance (NONC) to the permit holder. * * *

The legal effect of an AOI is also demonstrated by the Forest Service's use of the AOI to impose standards promulgated in the wake of the 1998 listing of the bull trout, a native salmonid species, as a threatened species under the ESA. As documented in the record, the Forest Service issued a grazing permit to Coombs Ranch for the Dollar Basin/Star Glade Allotments in 1996. The permit stated that no AMP existed for the allotments, but that the Forest Service was scheduled to develop one. It also stated that, in the meantime, the Forest Service would use the AOI "to bring management of the [allotments] into consistency with the terms of the Malheur [Forest Plan]." In 1998, the Fish and Wildlife Service ("FWS") listed the bull trout as a threatened species under the ESA, 63 Federal Reg. 31,647 (June 10, 1998), which triggered the Forest Service's duty under the ESA to consult with FWS to insure that any agency action, such as authorization of grazing, on Forest Service land would not likely jeopardize the threatened species or its habitat.

Since the 1998 listing, the relevant AOIs have incorporated bull trout standards and objectives. * * * Because the Forest Service issued most of the grazing permits underlying the AOIs challenged in this litigation prior to the bull trout listing and there are no current AMPs for the allotments, the AOI was the Forest Service's principal means of imposing the new bull trout standards on the permit holders from 1998 forward. By restricting the rights of and conferring duties on a grazing permit holder to bring the Forest Service's annual authorization of grazing into compliance with ESA requirements, the AOI is the Forest Service's definitive statement that fixes the legal relationship between the Forest Service and the permit holder. The utilization of an AOI in this manner further supports our conclusion that an AOI is a final agency action. * * *

Finally, the Forest Service argues that "[w]ithout the AOIs, the permittees would still be authorized to graze in accordance with the terms and conditions of the permit." The Forest Service's position is contradicted by the terms of the grazing permit itself and Forest Service practice. The permit does not authorize the permit holder to graze continuously for the permit's ten-year duration. Rather, the permit authorizes the permit holder to graze livestock only after the Forest Service has approved the permittee's annual application. In practice, the Forest Service approves the application in conjunction with issuance of the AOI. Although the annual application calls for basic information, it is the AOI that indicates the detailed terms and conditions by which the Forest Service expects the permit holder to graze his livestock in the upcoming season. The Forest Service's argument is not supported by the terms of the permit or by the record.

The record supports the conclusion that an AOI is a discrete, site-specific action representing the Forest Service's last word from which binding obligations flow. * * * [It] imposes substantial and intricate legal obligations on the permit holder. For these reasons, we hold that an AOI is a final agency action subject to judicial review under § 706(2)(A) of the APA.

REVERSED AND REMANDED.

■ Judge Fernandez, Dissenting:

As I see it, the final agency action took place when the Forest Service issued the permits to allow grazing by certain numbers of livestock for certain periods on designated land allotments. * * * [I]n a sense, every step by an agency or by a permittee * * * is the result of a then final decision and can have legal, as well as physical, consequences. Thus, a somewhat narrower and more pragmatic approach is required. * * * However final an action might look on its face, if it is merely implementing an earlier truly final determination, it is not final action for APA review purposes. * * * AOIs are merely a way of conducting the grazing program that was already authorized and decided upon when the permits were issued. The AOIs reflect nothing more sophisticated or final than the "continuing (and thus constantly changing) operations" of the Forest Service in reviewing the conditions of the land and its resources, and assuring that the mandated grazing programs go forward without undue disruption of the resource itself. Whether the decisions are by AOIs, or by phone calls, or by encounters in the field, or otherwise, they merely address day-to-day resource management and feeding of livestock. Review of that sort of decision is not contemplated by the APA. In fact, the Supreme Court has frowned upon broad programmatic attacks on agency action because, among other things, those would empower courts "to determine whether compliance was achieved—which would mean that it would ultimately become the task of the supervising court, rather than the agency, to work out compliance with the broad statutory mandate, injecting the judge into day-to-day agency management." *Norton v. S. Utah Wilderness Alliance*, 542 U.S. 55, 66–67 (2004). * * *

In pragmatic terms, if every AOI for every permit in every allotment every year is to be open to litigation by ONDA, and others, it is a little difficult to see how the grazing program can continue, if the purpose of the program is to feed animals. They need to eat *now* rather than at the end of some lengthy court process. But, I fear that what is really afoot is an attack by ONDA on the whole grazing program. * * * [B]road attacks of that sort are neither within the purpose nor a proper use of APA review. See S. Utah Wilderness Alliance, 542 U.S. at 64; *Nat'l Wildlife Fed'n*, 497 U.S. at 891. I do not think that we should let ourselves be ensnared by ONDA's little springe.

NOTES AND QUESTIONS

1. Under the dissent's view (that is, if the Forest Service had prevailed and the district court had been upheld), would effective judicial review of federal agency grazing decisions have been impossible? That is, could the agency have simply provided for livestock grazing in the most general terms in the resource management plan, simply not updated its allotment management plan, and then made the basic grazing decisions in

annual operating instructions not reviewable in court? (With one exception, none of the allotments here had AMPs prepared, despite the fact that the court acknowledged they were required.) Would a better approach be for conservationists to seek a court order compelling the agency to prepare AMPs, and then seek review of them?

2.   Or are most of the key federal decisions involving livestock grazing on the public land in fact made in the AOIs, so that if effective judicial review is going to take place at all, it must be there? Is the basic message of Supreme Court decisions like *Lujan I* and *II* and Norton v. SUWA, *supra* Chapter 4A(1), that the courts should stay away from reviewing broader agency policy decisions, and get involved at the ground level when disputes are real and fact-specific? If so, then why does the dissenting judge cite *Lujan* and Norton v. SUWA as support for concluding that these ground level decisions are unreviewable?

3.   On the other hand, does the dissenting judge have a good point, that the prospect of throwing open the courthouse doors to review of thousands of individual AOIs issued annually by the BLM and the Forest Service is a daunting one, which could require the federal courts to be "masters of the public range"? Does the majority have a response to this practical concern?

4.   In Forest Guardians v. U.S. Forest Service, 329 F.3d 1089 (9th Cir. 2003), the court rejected an environmentalist challenge to grazing levels set in allotment management plans for parts of the Apache–Sitgreaves National Forest in Arizona. While the agency's new plan did reduce from historic levels the overall amount of authorized grazing, one of the challenges was that the agency had allocated one hundred percent of the available forage— that is, the amount of forage it decided could be grazed without damage to the environment—to cattle over the entire ten-year permit term, even though wild ungulates like deer and elk were known to inhabit the allotments. The Forest Service's defense was that it would consider actual levels of deer and elk use through active monitoring of the allotments, and would limit the number of livestock appropriately either at the beginning of the grazing season, or halfway through the season, depending on climactic conditions, wild ungulate use, and other factors. Forest Guardians argued that the Forest Plan and the Forest Service's grazing regulations require that grazing permits specify the maximum number of cattle that can graze on the allotment without causing unacceptable damage. Therefore, said Forest Guardians, the agency's decision to allocate all of the forage to cows, knowing that deer and elk will consume some of it, sets a livestock grazing level that violates the National Forest Management Act.

In a 2–1 decision, the majority concluded that the Service's "interpretation of the Forest Plan to allow for maximum allocation to livestock with adjustments based on monitoring" deserves substantial deference, and can be seen as appropriate because it is "very difficult to estimate climactic changes or to assert with any confidence how the wild ungulate population will change[.] * * * [Because r]equiring the Service to come up with a single estimate that can cover a ten-year time period would be unreasonable, if not pure folly,'' the Service's approach was not plainly erroneous, according to the court.

The Forest Service conceded it had allowed the area to be badly overgrazed in the past, which led Forest Guardians to argue that the agency's monitoring program deserved no respect because it was a "proven failure" which should not be relied on as a management strategy. The majority responded:

> It was rational for the Service to conclude that, although there had been failures in the past, monitoring was the only way to effectively predict wild ungulate use of the land. The past failure of monitoring to prevent overgrazing does not change this result, because there is no evidence that the monitoring program itself was the but-for cause of that overgrazing. An agency's actions need not be perfect; we may only set aside decisions that have no basis in fact, and not those with which we disagree. Thus, even if we were to conclude that the Service could develop a better system of predicting wild ungulate use, or even preventing overgrazing, we are not permitted to substitute our judgment for the agency's.

329 F.3d at 1099–1100. Judge Paez dissented from this portion of the opinion, finding that the Forest Plan and the agency's regulations "make clear that the Service must determine the maximum 'stocking rate' and 'grazing capacity'—i.e., how many livestock *and* wild ungulates can graze on the land without damaging vegetation or related resources—*prior to* issuing the grazing permits." They also contemplate that the Service "should use monitoring to assess the allotments *after* it has determine their grazing capacity, and should not use monitoring to determine grazing capacity." 329 F.3d at 1101 (emphasis in original). Does the court in *Forest Guardians* effectively insulate the agency from judicial review of its decisions setting grazing levels? Is *Forest Guardians* consistent with *ONDA*? Does the latter limit the impact of the former, by making clear that, whatever the plan says, the agency's ongoing decisions on the amount of grazing are subject to judicial review? But, given the practical difficulties of invoking the judicial process at the fine-grained level of relatively informal decisions made seasonally (or even more often), is the net result that public land livestock grazing decisions may usually, or often, remain beyond effective judicial scrutiny?

5. The flamboyant James Watt, Secretary of the Interior in the early days of the Reagan Administration, tried a somewhat different approach to the grazing issue. Under his leadership, the Department amended the Range Code to authorize the BLM to delegate substantial legal authority (as well as practical control) to the ranchers themselves, in the form of so-called "Cooperative Management Agreements," or CMAs. Conservationists promptly challenged the program, a district court threw out the regulations, and the government did not appeal. Excerpts from Judge Ramirez's opinion (Natural Resources Defense Council v. Hodel, 618 F. Supp. 848 (E.D. Cal. 1985)) follow:

> The regulation establishing the CMA program authorizes the BLM to enter into special permit arrangements with selected ranchers who

have demonstrated "exemplary rangeland management practices." "Exemplary practices" are not defined in the regulation, rather, the choice of ranchers is apparently within the discretion of BLM officials.

The expressed purpose of the CMA program is to allow these ranchers the heretofore *verboten* opportunity to "manage livestock grazing on the allotment as they determine appropriate." 48 Fed.Reg. at 21823–24. The BLM is bound by the terms of a CMA for ten years. * * * The rule envisions periodic evaluations and provides for cancellation or modification only in the event of unauthorized transfers, violation of whatever terms and conditions the Secretary inserts in the CMA, or violation of regulations unrelated to overgrazing.

* * * [BLM's instructions regarding CMAs show] that CMA permittees shall not be subject to evaluation before "the end of the first 5 years" at which time a "joint evaluation" will take place. The permittee is automatically entitled to a CMA renewal (transforming it into a fifteen-year contract) if the mutual examination reveals that the agreement's objectives are being met. If the objectives have *not* been realized after five years, the permittee is nevertheless entitled to an additional five years within which to comply. The BLM, therefore, forfeits any remedy for the rancher's failure to meet objectives except that of denying renewal of the CMA after ten years of non-compliance. This is secure tenure indeed. * * *

Plaintiffs' principal contention is that the CMA regulation * * * is a naked violation of defendants' affirmative duties under the Taylor Grazing Act, FLPMA, and PRIA. The Court agrees. The CMA program disregards defendants' duty to prescribe the manner in and extent to which livestock practices will be conducted on public lands. The program also overlooks defendants' duty of expressly reserving, in all permits, sufficient authority to revise or cancel livestock grazing authorizations when necessary.

* * * [A]ny defense of the [CMA] program begins on the shakiest of legs since the dominant message and command of defendants' Congressional mandate is that *defendants* shall prescribe the extent to which livestock grazing shall be conducted on the public lands. The apparent goal and inevitable result of the CMA program is to allow ranchers, for a term of at least ten years, to rule the range as they see fit with little or no governmental interference. * * * Had Congress left a gap in its regulatory scheme which allowed defendants to decide whether individual ranchers should be entrusted with such decisions, this Court would be in no position to second guess the *wisdom* of the CMA program. However, Congress, in directing that the Secretary prescribe the extent of livestock practices on each allotment, precluded such entrustment, apparently because after years of rancher dominance of range decisions, it found substantial evidence of rangeland deterioration.

* * * Defendants' assertion that the CMA regulation is valid because it requires specification of "performance standards" is without merit. The statute requires specification of numbers and seasons, not general-

ized standards or responsibilities. CMAs, by definition and in practice, fail to comply with this Congressional mandate. * * *

The CMA regulation and program falls far short of the standard set by Congress in FLPMA. * * * The statutes cannot be reasonably interpreted to allow defendants to tie their own hands with respect to their authority to modify, adjust, suspend, or cancel permits. Nor is there any statutory provision creating exceptions for "exemplary" ranchers or those grazing livestock on public lands which, in defendants' view, require no improvement. Permittees must be kept under a sufficiently real threat of cancellation or modification in order to adequately protect the public lands from overgrazing or other forms of mismanagement. Any other interpretation of Congressional intent is inconsistent with the dominant purposes expressed in the Taylor Grazing Act, FLPMA, and PRIA. * * * It is for Congress and not defendants to amend the grazing statutes. In the meantime, it is the public policy of the United States that the Secretary and the BLM, not the ranchers, shall retain final control and decisionmaking authority over livestock grazing practices on the public lands. * * *

CONCLUSION

The problems facing defendants in managing the public lands are gigantic. * * * [P]rivate business and ranching values are sometimes in basic conflict with environmental quality and other societal values. But nothing in this opinion should be construed as a finding by this Court that defendants have consciously compromised one set of values in favor of another. Rather, the assumption throughout has been that defendants and plaintiffs merely possess opposing views as to the best way to strike a proper balance between competing interests. * * * [T]he Court recognizes that Congress has left most grazing management judgments to the discretion of defendants. * * * [But] Congress has already spoken clearly on the subject over which defendants and plaintiffs debate. * * *

Did the district court give appropriate deference to the agency interpretation of statutes it administers? Was BLM's mistake here that it tried to formalize what critics of the federal grazing program argue is in fact the case, that the ranchers and not the government make the basic determinations about where and how many cattle to graze? Is it really necessary for the government to specify the number of cows allowable in a particular area of public lands? Why can't the agency allow some room for rancher judgment to operate in these circumstances? Is the rancher always and totally motivated by maximizing the number of cows in the short term, to the long-term detriment of the range? Should Congress authorize a program by which BLM can delegate management authority to "exemplary" ranchers? Or should it simply give ranchers the opportunity to buy the public lands they are ranching?

In Idaho, a determined group of rangeland reformers has brought a series of cases seeking to use NEPA and FLPMA to curb grazing in particular allotments. The following case is an example.

Western Watersheds Project v. Bennett

United States District Court for the District of Idaho, 2005.
392 F. Supp.2d 1217.

■ JUDGE WINMILL

* * * Plaintiff WWP challenges the BLM's issuance of grazing permits for allotments on the Jarbidge Resource Area. WWP contends that the BLM's issuance of the permits was arbitrary and capricious under the Administrative Procedures [sic] Act (APA) because the BLM failed to follow the requirements of the National Environmental Protection [sic] Act (NEPA) and the Federal Land Policy and Management Act (FLPMA).

The BLM has divided the public lands it manages into administrative segments known as Resource Areas. The Jarbidge Resource Area (JRA) comprises about 1.7 million acres of land in southern Idaho. Congress has required that each Resource Area be governed by a Resource Management Plan. The BLM manages the JRA according to the terms of the Jarbidge Area Resource Management Plan and its accompanying Environmental Impact Statement and Record of Decision (JRA RMP–EIS), completed in 1987.

To manage cattle grazing, the BLM has created grazing allotments that cover the entire JRA. Recently, the BLM renewed ten-year grazing permits for 28 of these allotments, and it is that action that WWP challenges here. WWP seeks to halt the grazing to improve the condition of the rangeland.

When the JRA RMP–EIS was issued in 1987, it described a bleak landscape. Only 16% of the rangeland was in "fair" or better condition, while 48% was in "poor" condition. Recognizing that grazing was part of the problem, the RMP ROD stated that "wildlife goals and watershed needs will be satisfied prior to allowing increases in livestock use."

In the same vein, the RMP ROD stated that increased grazing "would not be authorized unless monitoring studies indicate that the basic soil, vegetation and wildlife resources are being protected and additional forage is available." Consistent with this, the RMP–EIS directs that "[p]riority for habitat management will be given to habitat for listed and candidate Threatened, Endangered, and Sensitive species."

One of the sensitive species designated by the BLM in the JRA is the sage grouse. Sage grouse were "originally spread over most of the [JRA] area." More recently, however, the BLM has observed that their numbers have declined dramatically: "Over the last 20 to 50 years there has been an 85% reduction in the number of sage grouse male attendance at known leks [eds.: a traditional place where males assemble during the mating season and engage in competitive displays to attract females] . . . and a subsequent overall population reduction." The number of occupied leks "decreased

37% over the last 20 to 50 years." The causes of this decline include "overgrazing of sagebrush habitats," along with wildfires, habitat fragmentation, drought, invasion of exotic plants, and conversion of sagebrush habitat to agriculture.

The alarming decline of the sage grouse is occurring at the same time that the BLM is documenting problems with the JRA rangeland. Since 1999, the BLM has determined that all 28 of the grazing allotments at issue here fail to meet the ecological standards of the Fundamentals of Rangeland Health (FRH). These regulations set minimum criteria for the condition of environmental resources, requiring, for example, that watersheds and riparian areas be in proper functioning condition, that water quality meets legal standards, and that adequate habitat is being maintained for wildlife.

For example, after examining 14 allotments * * * the BLM determined that for each, (1) FRH standards were not being met and (2) livestock grazing practices were a significant factor in the failure to meet those standards.

Despite the deterioration of these 14 allotments caused by grazing, the BLM has approved increased grazing on 9 of these allotments, and approved maintaining the past level of grazing on the other five. No reductions in grazing are planned.

On a 15th allotment—Juniper Butte—the BLM found FRH violations and concluded that grazing was a factor in those violations although the BLM could not determine if it was a significant factor. The BLM approved an increase in grazing on this allotment.

On another 13 allotments * * * the BLM found FRH violations but concluded that grazing was not a significant factor in those violations. For 11 of these allotments, the BLM has approved an increase in grazing while for the remaining 2 allotments, the BLM approved maintaining grazing at past levels. [The court's discussion of NEPA is omitted.] * * *

The BLM argues that "this case is about the significant increase in forage production on the [JRA] that has occurred over the last 30 years...." The BLM estimates that "in some areas, forage has increased approximately 300% following the seeding of crested wheatgrass."

Yet despite this increased forage, all 28 of the allotments at issue have FRH violations, and the sage grouse is in steep decline. While the increase in forage is beneficial, it is a means to an end—a means of curing FRH violations and stemming declines in wildlife populations—not the end itself. * * *

The BLM also asserts that each Final Grazing Decision specifically addressed the FRH violations and proposed mitigation measures for the specific allotments being reviewed. That is certainly a step in the right direction. From the Court's review of the record, it is apparent that the BLM and its Interdisciplinary Team have worked hard to craft mitigation measures for each allotment. The Court certainly does not mean to denigrate those efforts. However, even the BLM does not argue that the mitigation measures will be immediately effective. In the interim, grazing is increasing, putting increased pressure on the rapidly declining sage grouse population.

There is also a real question about the whether the mitigation measures will actually be implemented. For example, the BLM states in the Simplot EA that an "optimum level" of a crucial mitigation measure—monitoring—"would be dependent on funding."

Most importantly, however, the BLM's incremental allotment-by-allotment approach leaves it unable to answer a simple, yet crucial, question: What is the cumulative environmental impact of increasing grazing on 21 of 28 allotments in the face of widespread FRH violations and a dramatic decline of a sensitive species? That question cannot be answered because nobody has looked at the big picture here.

The BLM argues that grazing is not being increased, and is in fact reduced by 8% in the Final Grazing Decisions. The BLM arrives at this figure by comparing the grazing levels approved in the Final Grazing Decisions with the actual grazing levels a year earlier.

The problem with this analysis is that the BLM has authorized past grazing increases by issuing Temporary Nonrenewable Permits (TNRs) without complying with NEPA or FLPMA. If the grazing levels authorized by the Final Grazing Decisions in the 28 allotments at issue are compared with the last levels authorized by a NEPA document, grazing has increased by 83%. That is the most accurate comparison in a NEPA review. The BLM's comparison, in contrast, begins with a blind acceptance of years of TNR grazing increases that were never properly evaluated. The Court therefore rejects the BLM's argument that grazing has dropped by 8%.
* * *

FLPMA

FLPMA directs the BLM to develop and maintain comprehensive Resource Management Plans (RMPs) that govern all aspects of public land management, including grazing administration. 43 U.S.C. § 1712 (2000). Grazing permits must be consistent with RMPs. 43 U.S.C. § 1732(a); 43 C.F.R. § 1601.0–5(b), 4100.0–8. RMPs constrain grazing permits by determining where grazing will or will not be allowed and by setting environmental standards that all grazing permits must meet.

As discussed above, the BLM manages the JRA pursuant to the JRA RMP–EIS. That document is designed to order priorities, and it clearly places wildlife interests ahead of grazing increases: "[W]ildlife goals and watershed needs will be satisfied prior to allowing increases in livestock use." To drive home this point, the JRA RMP–EIS states that increased grazing "would not be authorized unless monitoring studies indicate that the basic soil, vegetation and wildlife resources are being protected and additional forage is available." If any doubt remained, it was clarified by the direction that "[p]riority for habitat management will be given to habitat for listed and candidate Threatened, Endangered, and Sensitive species."

The BLM argues that these provisions merely list discretionary guidelines rather than mandatory requirements. The Court disagrees. The plain language of the provisions speaks in terms of requirements, not suggestions. For example, the JRA RMP–EIS does not suggest that priority for habitat management "may" be given to habitat for Sensitive species—rather, it requires that such priority "will" be given.

The BLM also argues that the land use plan provisions are not enforceable under Norton v. Southern Utah Wilderness Alliance, 542 U.S. 55 (2004). That case, however, dealt with claims that an agency had failed to act, while this case involves agency action that is inconsistent with the land use plan. On that point, *Norton* stated that agency action inconsistent with the plan "can be set aside as contrary to law pursuant to 5 U.S.C. § 706(2)."

There is no doubt that the sage grouse, a sensitive species, is in rapid decline, and that FRH violations exist on all the allotments. Under these circumstances, the JRA RMP–EIS requires the BLM to ensure that wildlife protection takes priority over increases in grazing levels.

The BLM argues that it did act to protect wildlife by adopting Management Guidelines in the EAs that approved the increased grazing levels. The Court disagrees for two reasons.

First, these Guidelines are discretionary. The title "Guidelines" demonstrates that they are goals, not requirements. As an example, one Guideline suggests that monitoring should be done, but then qualifies that by noting that the "optimum level" of that monitoring "would be dependent on funding." This is not a mandatory mitigation measure. Moreover, the actual grazing practices are changed year-to-year in the Annual Grazing Plans for each permit without public input. Thus, a requirement one year could be downgraded to a mere suggestion the next.

Second, the Guidelines have been adopted without the monitoring required by the JRA RMP–EIS. The monitoring requirements are triggered by the decline in a sensitive species combined with continuing FRH violations. Yet the Allotment Assessments show that for many allotments where the BLM has found FRH violations caused by livestock grazing, the BLM has failed to do any monitoring for sensitive species.

For example, the BLM has approved an increase in grazing for the Cedar Creek, Pigtail Butte, Flat Top, Noh Field, North Fork Field, Winter Camp, and Desert 71 allotments. For each of these allotments, as discussed above, the BLM has found FRH violations, and found that grazing is a significant factor in those violations. The BLM has also found on each of these allotments that "[a] number of species presently designated as sensitive species are present in the allotment."

All of these findings require, under the JRA RMP–EIS, that the BLM conduct monitoring for sensitive species before approving increased grazing. However, that monitoring has not been done. Each of the Allotment Assessments for the allotments listed above contain an identical statement that "for the most part, the allotment has not been inventoried for sensitive species." *Id.* Moreover, this failure may continue in the future since, as discussed above, an "optimum level" of monitoring "would be dependent on funding."

For all of these reasons, the Court finds that the BLM has violated FLPMA's consistency requirement—that is, the requirement that the agency's action (the BLM's approval of the grazing permits) be consistent with the land use plan (the JRA RMP–EIS). The Court will therefore grant WWP's motion for partial summary judgment on its fifth claim for relief.

Injunctive Relief

* * * Here, serious environmental concerns are arrayed against substantial commercial interests. * * * Here, the Court is faced with * * * violations of FLPMA and, according to the BLM's own findings, violations of the FRH regulations. These violations occur simultaneously with the decline in the population of a sensitive species * * *.

These circumstances require the immediate issuance of an injunction. The Court will therefore enjoin all grazing on the 28 allotments at issue until a single EIS is completed and a Record of Decision or Final Grazing Decision is rendered.

NOTES AND QUESTIONS

1. Although the sage grouse is in serious decline, the U.S. Fish & Wildlife Service determined in 2005 not to list it as threatened or endangered under the ESA. This meant that the ESA was not implicated in this decision. How did the sage grouse's condition affect the way the court applied FLPMA here?

2. Does a picture emerge from the BLM's administration of grazing in the Jarbidge Area, and from other materials in this chapter on BLM grazing administration, of a wide gulf between paper planning and NEPA documents and what is actually happening on the ground? For example, was BLM actually proposing to increase grazing here, or not? What measures can the courts take to close this gap between what's on paper and what's happening on the ground?

3. What does BLM need to do now, on remand, to bring this grazing into compliance with FLPMA? May BLM simply amend the Jarbidge Plan to remove the requirement for monitoring?

4. Thereafter, plaintiffs and four of the largest cattle operations struck an unusual deal whereby the plaintiffs agreed not to litigate further if the ranchers agreed to reduce grazing slightly in some areas to protect sage grouse habitat, and to abide by the outcome of the EIS process and neither seek *nor accept* (if it were to be enacted by Congress) legislative relief from the NEPA process.

5. In Western Watersheds Project v. U.S. Forest Service, 2006 WL 292010, 2006 WL 1697181 (D. Idaho 2006), the federal court found that the Forest Service had violated NEPA and the National Forest Management Act in preparing an EIS covering four grazing allotments. Among other things, the agency had failed to discuss publicly the "capability" and "suitability" determinations the Forest Service had used in its internal decisionmaking process, and had failed to fully explain its adaptive management strategy. The court found irreparable harm because there was a

history of grazing-induced problems and serious degradation of riparian conditions and habitat of several sensitive species of fish, and enjoined grazing on some of the allotments until the Forest Service remedied the violations. Congress's appropriation rider forbidding injunctions against grazing permit renewals where the agency has not completed NEPA analysis (*see infra* p. 829) did not apply because here the question was the adequacy of the NEPA analysis, not delay in completing it.

Does FLPMA ever require the BLM to say no to grazing on some public lands? The next case, known colloquially as the *Comb Wash* decision, is a rare example of a discussion of BLM's obligation under FLPMA to assess the continuing viability of grazing on certain public lands.

National Wildlife Federation v. BLM
(The Comb Wash Case)

Interior Board of Land Appeals, 1997.
140 IBLA 85.

■ JUDGE HARRIS

[Environmentalists challenged BLM's renewal of a grazing permit for an area in southern Utah that included Comb Wash, which drained streams from five scenic canyons. The BLM had prepared a Resource Management Plan (RMP) and accompanying EIS for the 1.8 million acre Resource Area (an area more than one-third the size of Massachusetts), of which the 72,000 acre Comb Wash was a part. The challenge was based on both FLPMA and NEPA; the Board's discussion of NEPA is omitted.] * * *

Numerous BLM witnesses confirmed the following facts about the Proposed RMP/FEIS:

(1) That it is not useful or does not provide the detailed information necessary to determine whether to graze the canyons;

(2) That it does not contain an analysis of the 1990 proposed grazing plan or grazing system being implemented by issuance of the annual grazing authorizations nor does it contain information regarding the available forage, condition of the vegetation, or condition of the riparian areas in the canyons; and

(3) That it lacks any discussion of the relative values of the resources in the canyons and no balancing of the harms and benefits of grazing the canyons. * * *

[The Administrative Law Judge analyzed] the evidence relating to BLM's decision-making process * * * as follows:

The Area Manager, Mr. Scherick, correctly believed that he had discretion under the RMP to allow or disallow grazing on the Comb Wash allotment. He testified that, in exercising this discretion, he had not considered the relative values of the resources in the canyons because consideration of those values would take place during the activity planning stage (formation of the new AMP). But a new AMP has not yet been developed * * *.

Mr. Scherick also admitted that neither he nor any document, including the Proposed RMP/FEIS, weighs the benefits and harms of grazing the canyons. In authorizing grazing in the canyons, Mr. Scherick simply relied upon the information and recommendations provided to him by Mr. Curtis, the range conservationist responsible for the allotment.

Contrary to the evidence and Mr. Scherick's belief, Mr. Curtis thought that the RMP had already considered the impacts of grazing on the allotment's resources and determined that the allotment should be grazed, regardless of the recognized conflict with recreational uses and the need for adjustment confirmed by monitoring. He therefore felt it was not his responsibility to consider those impacts. Mr. Scherick's reliance upon Mr. Curtis, who believed that the decision to graze had already been made and was still binding, does not constitute a rational basis for determining whether the canyons should be grazed.

Furthermore, Mr. Curtis, an expert in range management only, does not have the expertise necessary to understand all the impacts of grazing in the canyons. Yet, he testified that he relied solely upon the utilization data, the Proposed RMP/FEIS, and ocular observations to determine the specific terms under which grazing would be allowed. There is some question whether he also sought and relied upon advice from experts in archaeology and other fields, but he provided no documentation and little evidence of the context or content of any discussions with those experts.

Mr. Curtis' reliance upon the Proposed RMP/FEIS is unavailing, as [everyone involved] admitted that the Proposed RMP/FEIS does not contain the detailed information necessary for determining whether or not to graze the canyons. * * *

In sum, BLM's decision to graze the canyons was not reasoned or informed, but rather based upon Mr. Curtis' misinterpretation of the RMP and a totally inadequate investigation and analysis of the condition of the canyons' varied resources and the impacts of grazing upon those resources.

We agree with that analysis. * * * FLPMA does not require a "specific" public interest determination for grazing. However, FLPMA's multiple-use mandate requires that BLM balance competing resource values to ensure that public lands are managed in the manner "that will best meet the present and future needs of the American people." 43 U.S.C. § 1702(c) (1994). Indeed, all parties agree that BLM must conduct some form of balancing of competing resource values in order to comply with the statute. * * * [Here BLM] failed to engage in any reasoned or informed decision-making process concerning grazing in the canyons in the allotment. That process must show that BLM has balanced competing resource values to ensure that the public lands in the canyons are managed in the manner that will best meet the present and future needs of the American people. * * *

NOTES AND QUESTIONS

1. If you were representing the affected rancher here, what sort of reasoned decisionmaking analysis would you suggest BLM follow on remand if it wants to conclude that grazing should still be allowed in these canyons? Should it focus on the economic benefit to the rancher and say that whatever environmental harm results is tolerable? Say that the area has already been so hammered by cows that things can't get worse? Is the Board saying anything more than that BLM must have *some* reason, and *some* factual basis, for going forward with the grazing permit renewal here?

2. If Judge Burns (the trial judge in NRDC v. Hodel, *supra* p. 800) had confronted this record in considering whether BLM should renew a specific grazing permit in part of the Reno Planning Area, would he have decided it the same way as the IBLA? Did he look at FLPMA the same way the IBLA did?

3. The lack of focused analysis revealed in the *Comb Wash* case is quite common in BLM's administration of its grazing program. That is, the environmental evaluation contained in the resource management plans typically covers several hundred thousand or even several million acres in a single document, which is simply too broad-brush to be very informative at the level of an individual canyon or riparian area. This makes many grazing permit renewals vulnerable to attack on both FLPMA and NEPA grounds, if the *Comb Wash* decision is followed. The BLM is left with a dilemma: The paperwork necessary to show FLPMA and NEPA compliance is expensive, especially compared to the economic value of the resource at stake. Congress has never been generous with BLM's budget and its staff is thin compared to the U.S. Forest Service.

4. Starting in 1999, with a glut of permit renewals coming due and BLM's NEPA compliance in some disarray, Congress began providing relief in the form of riders on the Interior Appropriations bill directing that expiring grazing permits be renewed under the same terms and conditions until the Secretary can finish the applicable paperwork, "at which time such permit or lease may be canceled, suspended or modified, in whole or in part, to meet the requirements of such applicable laws and regulations." The version in effect as of this writing, applicable through fiscal year 2008, also makes explicit that the "priority and timing for completing required environmental analysis of grazing allotments" is in the federal land manager's "sole discretion." 117 Stat. 1307 (2003). For an illustration of how this short-circuits judicial review, see Great Old Broads for Wilderness v. Kempthorne, 452 F. Supp. 2d 71 (D.D.C. 2006). In late 2004, Congress authorized the Forest Service to use categorical exclusions under NEPA to authorize continued grazing on up to 900 Forest Service allotments through fiscal year 2007 if "monitoring indicates that current grazing management is meeting, or satisfactorily moving toward, objectives" in the applicable resource management plan, "as determined by the Secretary."

118 Stat. 3103 (2004). As of this writing, BLM is also considering expanding its use of categorical exclusions in grazing management.

5.   While a site-specific approach can be a tool to protect the health of federal rangeland, it has its limitations. Most prominently, bringing these specific challenges is labor-and resource-intensive for conservation interests. The area involved in *Comb Wash* is a tiny fraction of the total area of BLM land that is grazed. Second, there is no guarantee of success, and a victory may only put the matter back in the agency's hands to come up with a better justification for renewal. Third, the livestock industry has many friends in the Congress, so that a legislative "fix" is an ever-present possibility.

6.   *Comb Wash* remains a rare if not unique case of using FLPMA to force BLM to take more steps to justify continued livestock grazing on its lands. Nevertheless, in recent years BLM and the U.S. Forest Service have begun to pay closer attention to livestock grazing in riparian (stream-influenced) areas, which tend to be favored by wildlife, livestock and recreationists. State fish and game agencies as well as environmentalists have urged the federal land managers to regulate grazing in riparian zones more heavily to protect these other values. A report of a committee of the National Research Council, *Riparian Areas: Functions and Strategies for Management* (National Academy Press, 2002), usefully summarizes the science and the law applicable to riparian area protection and livestock grazing.

7.   The Endangered Species Act and the Wild & Scenic Rivers Act have proved somewhat more promising as tools to restrict livestock grazing on environmental grounds. *See, e.g.*, Chapter 5, *supra* p. 319; Chapter 12, *infra* p. 1101. The Clean Water Act has been tried, but so far without much success. *See* Oregon Natural Desert Ass'n v. Dombeck, 172 F.3d 1092 (9th Cir.1998), *cert. denied*, 528 U.S. 964 (1999) (cows, even cows that "discharge" directly into streams, are not point sources under the Clean Water Act). Some argue that other parts of the Clean Water Act, in particular those that call for control of total maximum daily loads (TMDLs) of pollution, whether from point or nonpoint sources, have more promise. *See, e.g.*, Peter M Lacy, *Addressing Water Pollution From Livestock Grazing after ONDA v. Dombeck: Legal Strategies under the Clean Water Act*, 30 Envtl. L. 617 (2000).

D.   Voluntary Retirements of Grazing Permits and the Economics of the New West

As wrangling between federal lands ranchers and environmental advocates continues, a promising non-regulatory solution has emerged—voluntary buyouts by conservation interests (in both the public and private nonprofit sectors), who purchase federal land grazing permits (with or without the accompanying "base property" held in fee simple), and offer to relinquish the permits if the federal land manager will retire the public lands subject to these permits from livestock grazing. These marketplace-based "purchases and retirements" appear to offer great benefits, environmental and otherwise. They lead to restoration of the health of riparian areas and wildlife populations. They give the government land managers more flexibility to cope with drought, fire, and insect outbreaks. They may achieve tangible, visible environmental improvements in a short time in a less contentious way than pitched battles over regulation. Economists have advocated grazing buyouts since the 1950s. *See, e.g.*, Robert H. Nelson, *How to Reform Grazing Policy: Creating Forage Rights on Federal Rangelands*, 8 FORDHAM ENVTL. L.REV. 645, 656–57 (1997).

Buyouts also often make sense for ranchers, who increasingly find themselves operating at the margin in many places. The global market for beef that has emerged in recent years has led to diminishing economic returns for remote, marginal, independent operations like those generally found on the public lands of the West. Considered strictly as meat-producing enterprises, the profit margin for ranches is low compared to almost all other investments. *See* E.T. Bartlett *et al.*, *Valuing Grazing Use on Public Land*, 55 J. RANGE MANAGEMENT 426 (2002). Sometimes, in fact, grazing allotments with high biological or recreational value are the most marginal and troublesome to manage for livestock. Grasses may be sparse, access may be difficult, recreationists may leave gates open, regulations may be enforced more stringently, and controversy may be greater. Ranchers sometimes find it simpler to cash out of such allotments, retire debts, and either retire from ranching altogether or reorganize the ranch around less highly contested pastures.

In recent years there has been something of a boomlet in such efforts; for example: In Idaho, with support from the Shoshone–Bannock Tribes and the state Department of Game and Fish, the Bonneville Power Administration used fish restoration funds to buy and retire grazing permits on 49,000 acres of national forest in the Elk Creek drainage, prime habitat for salmon, steelhead, bull trout and westslope cutthroat. Clark County, Nevada, bought and retired grazing permits on about 400,000 acres of public lands as part of a Desert Tortoise Habitat Conservation Plan designed to remove obstacles to more development in Las Vegas. Further north, in and around Great Basin National Park, the Conservation Fund, with the support of several private foundations, worked with ranchers and federal managers to retire permits on more than 100,000 acres of BLM, National Park, and National Forest lands, a transaction supported by the Nevada Cattleman's Association, the Nevada Commission on Tourism, and the U.S. Fish and Wildlife Service. Overall, since 1992 the Conservation Fund has helped acquire grazing rights to more than 2 million acres of federal land in seven western states for about $10 million. In Utah, four allotments totaling 125,000 acres of important bighorn sheep habitat within the Desolation Canyon Wilderness Study Area along the Green River in northeastern Utah were retired by BLM after sheep ranchers there were compensated by the Utah Division of Wildlife Resources.

Such transactions suggest that permit purchase and retirement is an ecologically responsible, socially compassionate, and politically acceptable policy of enormous potential. Many more similar transactions may be possible, with the promise of solving many contentious resource and value conflicts across the West, but for one major problem: Those committing funds for these deals have no assurance under current laws and policies that the federal lands on which the grazing permits are purchased and relinquished will be permanently retired from grazing. Simple relinquishment of the permits leaves the federal land managers with discretion to reopen the federal lands involved for grazing by other operators. The federal land is, in other words, itself not permanently "retired" from grazing; only those particular permits are retired.

Usually, as part of these transactions, the public land managers have taken steps to amend the pertinent land use plan for the area involved, to provide that grazing shall not be restored on that area. These "grazing withdrawals by plan amendments" are, however, good only for the life of the plan. As we have seen, BLM and Forest Service plans may generally be amended at any time; in fact, the law requires the Forest Service to reexamine its plans at specific intervals. What one plan amendment accomplishes can be undone by another. The bottom line is that amending the plan to retire the area from grazing adds only a procedural hurdle should the federal land managers determine to make these public lands once again available for livestock. The underlying discretion to allow grazing remains intact, and with it a risk to those funding the buyouts.

Moreover, while these consensual transactions would seem to have something for everybody, in fact the potential availability of the lands for future grazing can be a significant local issue. Neighboring ranchers may seek to expand their operations by introducing their livestock on the public lands being retired. Others in the local community (local businesses which depend on a viable local ranching industry, local governments who believe their tax revenues may be adversely affected by grazing retirements, and those who strongly identify with the ranching culture) may be strongly opposed to permanent retirements, which they may see as dooming a locally important economic sector as well as a treasured culture. And the ranchers' trade associations, like the Public Lands Council, tend to see their clients as those ranchers who want to stay in business, not those who want to get out, and they regard buyouts as threatening their very existence.

When the Grand Canyon Trust bought and then sought to retire grazing permits in the Grand Staircase–Escalante National Monument in southern Utah in the early 2000s, opponents (including county governments, using money supplied by the state of Utah from a "constitutional defense fund," engineered by a state representative from southern Utah, a former BLM land manager) filed protests and administrative appeals with BLM and, when these failed, a lawsuit. It challenged the wisdom of retiring several hundred thousand acres of public land from livestock grazing, which the suit contends would "leav[e] a void in the economy of each county and contribut[e] to a reduction in taxable income." Kane County Commissioner Mark Habbeshaw described the Trust's action more cosmically as a "stepping stone" to "put[ting] an end to livestock grazing in the United States."

Still, while BLM decided the Trust can hold grazing permits, it dragged its feet on amending the land use plan to retire the land from grazing. Insecurity over the permanence of such purchases and retirements casts a cloud on funding potential, and prevents the emergence of a much larger market for grazing permits. Funders of buyouts are concerned that their objective—to restore health to tracts of public lands by permanently retiring grazing from them—may be later nullified by discretionary decisions by federal land managers.

One piece of the Clinton Administration's Rangeland Reform would have authorized the issuance of grazing permits for "conservation use," which was really "livestock non-use." It would have allowed a conservation group who bought out a rancher's grazing permit to apply to BLM to put the grazing permit, which it would continue to hold, into "conservation use" status for up to ten years, the duration of the permit. As part of its general attack on Rangeland Reform, a ranchers' trade association challenged the legality of this approach. The Tenth Circuit held it illegal, and the United States did not seek review in the U.S. Supreme Court. The following are excerpts from the Tenth Circuit's discussion (Public Lands Council v. Babbitt, 167 F.3d 1287 (10th Cir. 1999)):

> The 1995 regulations added "conservation use" as a permissible use of a grazing permit. See 43 C.F.R. § 4100.0–5 (1995) (defining "grazing permit" as a document that specifies "all authorized use [of public lands within a grazing district] including livestock grazing, suspended use, and conservation use"). "Conservation use" means "an activity, excluding livestock grazing, on all or a portion of an allotment" for the purpose of protecting the land and its resources, improving rangeland conditions, or enhancing resource values. Conservation use may be approved for a period of up to ten years-i.e., for the entire duration of the permit. See id. § 4130.2(g)(1). According to the Secretary, conservation use will be initiated by request of the permittee and will not be forced on an unwilling permittee. Allotments in conservation use will not be subject to grazing fees since no forage will be consumed by livestock. BLM will not consider allowing another operator to use any resulting forage. * * *

> Section three of the TGA authorizes the Secretary "to issue or cause to be issued permits to graze livestock" on the public lands. 43 U.S.C. § 315b. In the 1995 regulations, the Secretary has authorized the issuance of grazing permits or leases for "livestock grazing, suspended use, and conservation use." 43 C.F.R. § 4130.2(a) (1995). Conservation use, in turn, is defined as "an activity, *excluding livestock grazing*, on all or a portion of an allotment" for conservation purposes. 43 C.F.R. § 4100.0–5 (1995) (emphasis added). Thus, the Secretary has authorized the issuance of a grazing permit to an individual or group who will not graze livestock for the entire duration of a permit.

> The Secretary makes several arguments in support of the new regulation allowing "conservation use" permits. First, he points out (and PLC agrees) that resting land is a perfectly acceptable practice on the public range and is done with regularity in order to prevent permanent

destruction of the lands. Indeed, under the pre–1995 regulations, active use could "be suspended in whole or in part on a temporary basis due to drought, fire, or other natural causes, or to facilitate installation, maintenance, or modification of range improvements." 43 C.F.R.§ 4110.3–2(a) (1994). The Secretary asserts that the issuance of grazing permits for conservation use merely reflects "a longstanding grazing management practice consistent with the resumption of grazing."

The Secretary further argues that the issuance of permits for conservation use is authorized by the TGA, FLPMA, and PRIA. The Secretary points to section two of the TGA, which provides, "The Secretary shall . . . do any and all things necessary to accomplish the purposes of this [Act]." 43 U.S.C. § 315a. One of the purposes of the TGA is "to preserve the land and its resources from destruction or unnecessary injury." Id. The Secretary asserts that issuance of permits authorizing conservation use is fully consistent with this mandate. Moreover, FLPMA charges the Secretary with "manag[ing] the public lands under principles of multiple use and sustained yield." 43 U.S.C. § 1732(a). Multiple use requires that the Secretary consider, among other things, "the long-term needs of future generations for renewable and non-renewable resources." 43 U.S.C. § 1702(c). The Secretary argues that the issuance of conservation use permits helps achieve the goal of multiple use. Similarly, the Secretary contends that conservation use is a mechanism to achieving PRIA's goal of "manag[ing], maintain[ing], and improv[ing] the condition of the public rangelands so they become as feasible as possible for all rangeland values." 43 U.S.C. § 1901(b)(2).

Notwithstanding the reasonable arguments that the Secretary presents, we are not persuaded. The question before us is not whether the Secretary possesses general authority to take conservation measures- which clearly he does-but rather, whether he has authority to take the specific measure in question, i.e., issuing a "grazing permit" that excludes livestock grazing for the entire term of the permit. We conclude at the first step of the *Chevron* analysis that Congress has spoken directly to this precise question and answered it in the negative. Our decision rests on the plain language of the relevant statutes. The TGA provides the Secretary with authority to issue "permits to graze livestock on . . . grazing districts." 43 U.S.C. § 315b. That statute does not authorize permits for any other type of use of the lands in the grazing districts. FLPMA and PRIA confirm that grazing permits are intended for grazing purposes only. Both those statutes define "grazing permit and lease" as "any document authorizing use of public lands . . . *for the purpose of grazing domestic livestock.*" 43 U.S.C. §§ 1702(p), 1902(c) (emphasis added). Thus, the TGA, FLPMA, and PRIA each unambiguously reflect Congress's intent that the Secretary's authority to issue "grazing permits" be limited to permits issued "for the purpose of grazing domestic livestock." None of these statutes authorizes permits intended exclusively for "conservation use." The Secretary's assertion that "grazing permits" for use of land in "grazing districts" need not involve an intent to graze is simply untenable.

The TGA authorizes the Secretary to establish grazing districts comprised of public lands "which in his opinion are chiefly valuable for grazing and raising forage crops." 43 U.S.C. § 315. When range conditions are such that reductions in grazing are necessary, temporary non-use is appropriate and furthers the preservation goals of the TGA, FLPMA, and PRIA, even when that temporary non-use happens to last the entire duration of the permit. * * * The presumption is, however, that if and when range conditions improve and more forage becomes available, permissible grazing levels will rise. * * * The Secretary's new conservation use rule reverses that presumption. Rather than annually evaluating range conditions to determine whether grazing levels should increase or decrease, as is done with temporary non-use, the Secretary's conservation use rule authorizes placement of land in non-use for the entire duration of a permit. This is an impermissible exercise of the Secretary's authority under section three of the TGA because land that he has designated as "chiefly valuable for grazing livestock" will be completely excluded from grazing use even though range conditions could be good enough to support grazing. Congress intended that once the Secretary established a grazing district under the TGA, the primary use of that land should be grazing.

Thus, when the Secretary issues a permit under section three of the TGA, the primary purpose of the permit must be grazing. If range conditions indicate that some land needs to be rested, the Secretary may place that land in non-use on a temporary basis, in accordance with Congress's grants of authority that the Secretary manage the public lands "in a manner that will protect the quality of scientific, scenic, historical, ecological, environmental, [and other] values," 43 U.S.C. § 1701(a)(8), or he may reduce grazing on that land * * * [or] employ other means to ensure that the resources of the public range are preserved. * * *

In short, it is true that the TGA, FLPMA, and PRIA, give the Secretary very broad authority to manage the public lands, including the authority to ensure that range resources are preserved. Permissible ends such as conservation, however, do not justify unauthorized means. We hold that the Secretary lacks the statutory authority to issue grazing permits intended exclusively for conservation use. Because there is no set of circumstances under which the Secretary could issue such a permit, the new conservation use regulation is invalid on its face.

NOTES AND QUESTIONS:

1. Is this analysis persuasive? The Taylor Grazing Act does not mandate the Secretary to require grazing on public land within a grazing district; instead, it merely "authorize[s]" the Secretary to issue grazing permits within these districts. 43 U.S.C. § 315b. Tracing the history of this provision, Professor Donahue shows that the "chiefly valuable for grazing"

language basically reflected a widespread contemporary assumption that these arid lands were not much good for anything else, and not that grazing itself was an especially valuable use. In fact, the prime mover in Congress, Edward Taylor of Colorado, said that much of the western range was "a very poor quality of grazing land," and an Oregon Congressman put it more bluntly, saying "much of [the public domain] is not worth a damn, even for grazing." *See* THE WESTERN RANGE REVISITED 193–198 (1999). Under this interpretation, the only legal significance of putting land in a grazing district is that it puts it off limits to disposal, arguably appropriate because it has no real value. Being within a grazing district should not, under this view, affect how the lands are managed.

2.   Should the U.S. have appealed this issue to the U.S. Supreme Court, as a counter to the livestock industry's appeal of the three counts it lost? What might have been the outcome there, given the Court's disposition of the issues it did review?

_____

The Interior Solicitor addressed BLM's authority to act on requests for voluntary retirement of livestock grazing in an opinion issued January 19, 2001. It noted that both FLPMA and the Public Rangelands Improvement Act specifically provided for the possibility of retiring public land from grazing. FLPMA gives an existing permittee first priority for renewal "[s]o long as [among other things] the lands for which the permit or lease is issued remain available for * * * grazing in accordance with land use plans" prepared under FLPMA. 43 U.S.C. § 1752(c). PRIA has as its major goal improving conditions on the public range with an important exception; namely, "[e]xcept where [FLPMA's] land use planning process * * * determines otherwise or the Secretary determines, and sets forth his reasons for this determination, that grazing uses should be discontinued (either temporarily or permanently) on certain lands." 43 U.S.C. § 1903(b). The Solicitor opined that the decision to retire lands from grazing is a straightforward "multiple use/sustained yield" decision. It does not have to be based on a finding of "unnecessary or undue degradation," but rather may be made simply upon a determination that the public lands should be devoted to other uses. Although the Solicitor did not directly address grazing districts or the "chiefly valuable" language of the TGA, the Opinion generally concluded that grazing retirement decisions were "within the sound discretion of the Secretary on the basis of information revealed in the administrative record (including appropriate NEPA analysis), and the requirements of other laws, such as the Endangered Species Act."

The Bush (II) Administration's Solicitor, the former Executive Director of the Public Lands Council (the ranching trade association which led the legal challenge to Clinton's Rangeland Reform), issued an opinion that, while not overruling the January 2001 Opinion, sought to make it more difficult to retire public land from grazing. It found that "[t]here must be a proper finding that lands are no longer chiefly valuable for grazing in order to cease livestock grazing within grazing districts." The finding must be based on analysis and the rationale must be expressed in a record of decision. Authority for the BLM to Consider Requests for Retiring Grazing Permits and Leases on Public Lands, M #37008 (Oct. 4, 2002). Because the TGA assumes that lands in grazing districts are considered "chiefly valuable for grazing," *see* 43 U.S.C. § 315, a retirement decision requires a formal process that finds the lands to be retired are no longer "chiefly valuable" for such a purpose and need to be excised from grazing district.

This conclusion was at substantial variance from historic practice. There seems to have been no serious study of the suitability of lands for grazing when grazing districts were initially established under the TGA, and no systematic "chiefly valuable" findings were made. Dozens of grazing districts encompassing many millions of acres of public lands were put in grazing districts within a few months in early 1935. Moreover, as it retired public land from grazing for a myriad of purposes since 1935, the Department has never made a "not chiefly valuable" determination.

In May 2003, the Solicitor issued a "clarification" of M#37008, retreating to the position that a "chiefly-valuable-for-grazing determination is required only when the Secretary is considering creating or changing grazing district boundaries * * * [and] is not required nor appropriate when establishing grazing levels within a district." Although the clarification removed one procedural roadblock to grazing retirements, the Solicitor continued to discourage the practice, emphasizing that eliminating grazing can "disrupt the orderly use of the range, breach the Secretary's duty to adequately safeguard grazing privileges, be contrary to the protection, administration, regulation and improvement of public lands within grazing districts, hamper the government's responsibility to account for grazing receipts, [and] impede range improvements * * *."

NOTES AND QUESTIONS

1. As a matter of policy, should such buyouts be preferred over more regulatory solutions? If the government or private entities decide to pay ranchers in order to improve the health of public lands, how much does it undermine the government's will to regulate the use of public lands to protect their health? And how much does it undermine a rancher's willingness to improve grazing practices? *See* John D. Echeverria, *Regulating Versus Paying Land Owners to Protect the Environment*, 26 J. Land Res. & Envtl. L. 1 (2005). Whatever might be appropriate as a matter of generic public policy, can a special case be made for buying out public land grazing permits, given the peculiar and long history of the use of the public lands for livestock grazing, and the stubborn resistance to regulatory solutions? Or is compensation particularly inappropriate here, given that stubborn resistance and the fact that ranchers have never had a legally compensable property interest in their grazing permits?

2. Should the federal land manager automatically or routinely retire the land when the permittee offers to relinquish the permits? Is that an inappropriate delegation of decisionmaking authority over public lands to a private entity? If the federal land manager should make an independent

decision about whether to retire the land from grazing or issue the permit to another, what criteria should apply to such a decision? Health of the land? Health of the local community? Economic value of alternative uses?

3.   Has FLPMA's multiple use/sustained yield mandate and its resource planning process overtaken or supplanted the "chiefly valuable" determination required by the TGA? Does such a determination make sense anymore, if it ever did? Is that the basic difference between the Clinton and Bush Administration's Solicitor's Opinions discussed above? Should conservationists press the BLM to begin making such determinations, in the expectation that many lands now grazed might in fact be "chiefly valuable" for other purposes, like wildlife habitat?

4.   Can the Secretary "withdraw" lands from grazing use through the FLPMA withdrawal procedure? Notice, however, that withdrawals are generally good only for twenty years, and can be revoked sooner (although they can also be renewed). How is a withdrawal different from simply excising the area from a grazing district under the TGA?

5.   What does BLM need to show to retire public land from grazing upon the application of a conservation buyer of a grazing permit? What does it need to open public land so retired back up to grazing again, upon the application of a neighboring rancher?

6.   BLM's 2006 grazing regulations eliminated what had been a three-year limit on the length of time BLM could grant "temporary nonuse" of a grazing permit. (The limit had been imposed in Clinton's Rangeland Reform, at the same time it added the alternative of "conservation non-use," subsequently invalidated by the federal court of appeals.) Historically, in exercising their broad discretion, federal land managers have tended to allow rancher-permittees to run fewer livestock than specified in their permits, or no livestock at all, for periods of many years, without losing their preference. Whether the agencies will be willing to treat conservation-oriented permittees with the same regard is not yet clear. In 2005, a partnership of the Grand Canyon Trust and the Conservation Foundation purchased the Kane and Two Mile Ranches on the Arizona Strip north of the Grand Canyon for $4.5 million. The ranches include about 1,000 acres of fee land and hold grazing preferences and permits on more than 800,000 acres of BLM, U.S. Forest Service, and state land. The Trust is seeking to reduce the amount of grazing on the public land for conservation purposes, but obviously wants to avoid any action by the federal land managers to rescind its permits for noncompliance, nullify its preference, and allow the public land to be grazed by other ranchers. Although there is, to the knowledge of these editors, no reported decision ever cancelling a grazing permit for nonuse, federal agencies may be inclined to be tougher on conservation-oriented permittees (demanding total technical compliance with permit terms and conditions) than on other, more conventional ranchers, though this of course is not easy to prove.

7.   If you were a private philanthropist or foundation interested in furnishing funds for conservation-oriented buyouts, what kind of assurance would you ask for to ensure that the lands were retired from grazing?

8.   What happens to a rancher's permit, and preference, if BLM orders cattle to be removed from an allotment to help meet the requirements of the Endangered Species Act; e.g., to protect the desert tortoise? If the permit comes up for renewal, may BLM renew it even though no livestock will actually be put out on the public land so long as the desert tortoise remains listed under the ESA?

9.   The Taylor Grazing Act requires permittees to be "stock owners." 43 U.S.C. § 315b. In the *Public Lands Council* case, the Supreme Court upheld BLM's elimination of its regulatory requirement that a permittee be "engaged in the livestock business." But the statutory requirement of "stock owner" remains. If a conservation-oriented permittee sold her herd and took voluntary non-use for a period of several years, might she fail to qualify as a "stock owner"? Would it be sufficient if she owned stock that grazed on private land, but not public land?

10.   Although grazing retirements are usually dealt with under generic public land laws, the issue has not entirely escaped the attention of Congress, which has sometimes responded with *ad hoc* statutory enactments to solve immediate problems. At Great Basin National Park, for example, the Nevada delegation successfully sponsored a provision in 1996 to allow grazing permittees to donate or exchange their permits inside the Park, but the statute cautioned that exchanges should not be approved if it would "result in overgrazing of Federal lands." *See* 16 U.S.C. § 410mm–1(f). At Arches National Park two years later, Congress specially authorized retirement of a grazing allotment in a canyon that was being added to the Park. *See* 16 U.S.C. § 272b. In the California Desert legislation adopted in 1994, Congress directed that the Secretary give priority to acquiring base property from willing sellers, even as it grandfathered the "privilege of grazing domestic livestock on lands within the [new Mohave National Park] at no more than the current level, subject to applicable laws and National Park Service regulations." 16 U.S.C. § 410aaa–5.

11.   What might generic legislation look like that would facilitate voluntary buyouts? Should it simply create a mechanism for permanent withdrawal of federal lands from livestock grazing where a conservation group buys out a rancher? Reconsider the question in note 2 about whether this is an objectionable "buying" of a permanent management status on public lands. Should the government make efforts to mitigate so-called "third party effects" (for example, loss of business to local rancher-supply stores) when it retires public lands from grazing?

12.   Conservation-friendly alternatives may exist to retiring public land from grazing completely and permanently; e.g., reducing livestock numbers, or putting the public land in some sort of "grass bank" status, ungrazed and held in reserve for use by other ranchers in the vicinity where their own allotments are insufficient because of drought or other conditions. From a conservation standpoint, grass banks carry risk, especially considering the federal government's historic tenderness to ranchers. In 2004, for example, the U.S. opened lands enrolled in the Department of Agriculture's Conservation Reserve Program (environmentally sensitive croplands that producers agree to retire in return for receiving cash

payments from the federal treasury) to livestock grazing because of severe drought. BILLINGS GAZETTE, June 25, 2004.

The Future of Public Lands Grazing:
Cows Versus Condos and the Rise of the Amenity Buyer

As ranching grows ever more marginal in parts of the arid West, and ranchers come under more pressure to find alternative sources of income, there is the pressure to subdivide and sell the base property for development or sale as "ranchettes." In what has been dubbed the "cows versus condos" debate, some conservationists argue that encouraging continued public land ranching is better for the environment, for maintaining plant and wildlife habitat and open spaces, than development of base property. Others argue that the choice is rarely that stark, and the environmental pluses versus minuses are controlled by local specific factors.

Some studies have attempted to sketch the dimensions of the issue. For example, the American Farmland Trust attempted to locate "prime" ranchlands with significant ecological value that were vulnerable to sprawl and development over the next two decades. These tended to be in high mountain valleys and mixed grasslands surrounding major mountain ranges. Montana and Idaho contain the greatest amount (five million acres each) followed by Colorado (4.8 million acres). Ten of the 25 counties (of 263 counties in the seven state area) with the highest acreage of strategic ranchland at risk are in the area around Yellowstone National Park. Strategic Ranchland in the Rocky Mountain West: Mapping the Threats to Prime Ranchland in Seven Western States (American Farmland Trust).

A related report, "Ranchland Dynamics in the Greater Yellowstone Ecosystem" (William R. Travis, Center of the American West), looked at rates and patterns of ranch ownership change in the area around Yellowstone. About 1.5 million acres of ranchland (more than one quarter of the total) changed hands at least once between 1990 and 2001. Forty per cent of the purchasers were amenity buyers (acquiring a ranch for ambience, recreation and other amenities, not primarily for agricultural production), about a quarter were traditional ranchers, and the rest were investors, developers, or unclassified. The trend has greatly accelerated during recent years, with the emergence of a globe-trotting class of wealthy people looking for retreats close to wild lands. The result is that most ranching landscapes in scenic western regions like Greater Yellowstone are now strongly affected, if not dominated, by amenity and investment ownership. Acreage-wise, amenity buyers are much more dominant than nonprofit conservation groups (the latter own only two percent of the acreage, although this does not include acreage in conservation easements).

The rapidly growing number of private amenity owners raises a number of questions about the future of the federal land grazing program. Amenity owners can turn cows into condos by subdividing their base property—the demand has been strong and there are few significant regulatory restraints on subdivision and development in many areas. They may also have varied goals. Some have a broad conservation vision, with sophisticated management to protect wildlife and ecological processes, leading them to seek to permanently reduce livestock grazing on the public lands where they have grazing permits (or, as Ted Turner has done on some of his western ranches, to reintroduce native species like bison or wolves). Others seek recreation, scenery and privacy, confining ecological improvements to things like elk habitat or trout streams (perhaps with introduced, non-native trout), and decreasing public access to their lands or nearby public lands, which may shut out hunters, anglers, and hikers. Others seek a ranching hobbyist "lifestyle," and hire ranch managers (with varying levels of conservation sensibilities) to run their cattle operations.

For several years environmental activist Andy Kerr (through the National Public Lands Grazing Campaign (NPLGC)) has been promoting legislation that would authorize the use of federal funds to pay ranchers a fixed price ($175 an AUM, considerably above the current average value on the open market) to voluntarily give up their federal grazing permits and permanently retire the lands from livestock grazing. Kerr argues that even though the initial price tag is not cheap (about $1.5 billion if every public land rancher took the buy-out), the federal government would save substantial costs in administering the grazing program, carrying out fire and weed and predator control and other subsidies provided ranchers. A report issued by the Government Accountability Office in September 2005 (Livestock Grazing: Federal Expenditures and Receipts Vary, Depending on the Agency and the Purpose of the Fee Charged) reported that grazing fees cover about one-sixth of the annual cost of managing the program ($21 million compared to $144 million). NPLGC believes total annual federal grazing program costs might approach $500 million if all the subsidies were accounted for.

Kerr's proposal has critics across the spectrum. Critics of ranching don't like the idea of using federal funds to buy out what are not property rights. Some believe it would accelerate the conversion of cows to condos. Ranching traditionalists fear the loss of their culture, and argue the buyout does not address third-party effects. Some argue the Campaign ignores evidence that (a) public rangelands are not deteriorating any more; (b) restoring these western lands to their natural condition is unscientific and unrealistic because we don't know what "natural" is, and the invasion of exotic species like noxious weeds is irreversible; and (c) many other uses (like condos) are more ecologically harmful. Amidst the brouhaha, one recent commentator concluded that prospects for significant change in federal grazing policy are low, for several reasons: (a) Despite the vast land area involved, nationally the issue is low-stakes; (b) the aggregate subsidy provided to livestock operators on public lands is very small compared to the federal budget; and (c) most of the land is remote and it has proved very difficult to generate national public, media, or legislative concern to overcome the entrenched defenses of regional interests. Charles Davis, *The Politics of Grazing on Federal Lands: A Policy Change Perspective, in* PUNCTUATED EQUILIBRIUM AND THE DYNAMICS OF U.S. ENVIRONMENTAL POLICY 232–252 (Robert Repetto ed., 2006).

CHAPTER 10

THE WILDLIFE RESOURCE

The American public's attitude toward wildlife as a resource has gradually evolved from one of putting food on the table to one of recreational, scientific, and aesthetic interest. In the process, with population growth and the spread of human-dominated landscapes, wildlife management and protection has more and more become controlled by law. The twentieth century saw the evolution of wildlife law from a set of relatively narrow hunting and fishing rules established under state law to a more comprehensive scheme which emphasizes maintenance and enhancement of quality habitat, with federal law playing a more prominent role. Despite the increasing prominence of federal law, state fish and game departments remain key actors in wildlife management. In federal law, "wildlife" (or "fish and wildlife") typically means all wild animals.

The initial mission of state fish and game agencies was to protect the wildlife resource by curbing more pernicious abuses, but during most of the nineteenth century, the few rudimentary state wildlife statutes were ineffective for lack of wardens or other enforcement mechanisms. The reservation of national forests and parks beginning in the late nineteenth century, while not motivated by a concern for protecting wildlife, did just that by providing large, relatively undisturbed regions of prime wildlife habitat. The irrepressible Teddy Roosevelt took a more direct step by asking Congress to create federal game refuges shortly after he became President in 1901. One Congressman described the proposal as "the fad of game preservation run stark raving mad." When the bill died, Roosevelt took matters into his own hands, asking: "Is there any law that will prevent me from declaring Pelican Island a Federal Bird Reservation?" When told not, he responded: "Very well, then I so declare it." With his Pelican Island Bird Refuge Proclamation of March 14, 1903, a national program for protecting wildlife habitat was born. Congress then followed up, first by delegating express authority to the President to do what Roosevelt had already begun to do, and later by statutorily establishing specific refuges. It was not until 1966, however, that Congress consolidated the various wildlife and game areas into the National Wildlife Refuge System.

Federal wildlife law began to evolve in other contexts around the turn of the twentieth century. Congress had long legislated for wildlife conservation in the territories, and in 1900 it ventured into general wildlife regulation with passage of the Lacey Act, 16 U.S.C. §§ 701, 3371–3378, and 18 U.S.C. § 42. That Act bolstered state wildlife laws by forbidding interstate transportation or sale of animals taken illegally in the state of origin. The Migratory Bird Treaty Act of 1918 (MBTA), 16 U.S.C. §§ 703–711, took a much bolder step, creating a national program for managing migratory bird populations. Directly preempting state law, the MBTA employed the Department of the Interior as a national game agency, establishing hunting seasons and bag limits and regulating methods of taking. The Supreme Court, speaking through Justice Holmes, upheld the Act in Missouri v. Holland, 252 U.S. 416 (1920).

For the next several decades, Congress only sporadically and rather haphazardly showed concern for national wildlife regulation. The Bald Eagle Act of 1940, 16 U.S.C. §§ 668–668d, flatly banned killing or molesting bald (and, since 1962, golden) eagles except with federal permission. (It authorized permits to meet the religious needs of Indians and for the protection of domestic livestock against the depredations of golden eagles.) In 1958 Congress commanded federal agencies to ensure that "wildlife conservation" receives "equal consideration" and coordination with "other features of water-resource development programs," and required reports on plans for mitigation of wildlife habitat losses due to federal water projects. Fish and Wildlife Coordination Act, 16 U.S.C. §§ 661–667e. The Anadromous Fish Conservation Act of 1965, 16 U.S.C. §§ 757a–757f (anadromous fish, e.g. salmon, spawn in fresh water but live most of their lives in the oceans) simply directed the Secretary of the Interior to conduct studies and make appropriate recommendations "regarding the development and management of any stream or other body of water for the conservation and enhancement of anadromous fishery resources." Nevertheless, in one of the landmark judicial decisions in the early days of the modern environmental movement, the Supreme Court, speaking through Justice Douglas, relied on it to set aside a Federal Power Commission license to construct a dam. Udall v. FPC, 387 U.S. 428 (1967).

With the rise of the modern environmental movement, the legislative pace quickened dramatically. Primitive versions of an Endangered Species Act were enacted in 1966 and 1969. They were followed by the Wild and Free–Roaming Horses and Burros Act of 1971 (WF–RHBA), discussed in Chapters 3 and 9, and then the Marine Mammal Protection Act of 1972 (MMPA). The latter declared a moratorium on all taking of or commerce in all marine mammals, with exceptions, such as incidental taking of porpoises by tuna fishermen. The next year saw a dramatic strengthening of the Endangered Species Act (ESA), 16 U.S.C. §§ 1531–1543, making it what some call the most stringent wildlife law ever enacted by any country.

Missouri's challenge to the Migratory Bird Treaty Act that culminated in Missouri v. Holland was a typical state reaction to the growth of federal wildlife law. State hunting and fishing license fees generate considerable revenues. State fish and game departments, supported by hunting and fishing organizations, fiercely protect traditional state prerogatives, and their efforts have not been without some success. Federal law governing (or prohibiting) the take of wildlife applies to preempt state law only for certain species or in certain specific situations, or on certain land systems, such as the national park system. This has left states as the principal arbiters of most hunting, fishing, and trapping on the two largest systems of federal lands, the national forests and BLM-managed public lands. Even there, however, federal authority over wildlife remains important, because federal land managers now generally follow Aldo Leopold's premise that healthy wildlife populations are most effectively achieved by assuring healthy habitat; thus, the best wildlife management is in essence good land management. *See* Aldo Leopold, GAME MANAGEMENT (1933).

As in most areas of natural resources management, divergent viewpoints on wildlife management philosophy are common. For example, David S. Favre, in *Wildlife Rights: The Ever–Widening Circle*, 9 ENVTL. L. 241 (1979), makes a case for according wildlife species certain legal rights:

> Arguably, a major stumbling block to recognizing wildlife rights is the problem of how humans can presume to know animals' best interests when animals cannot communicate with humans. With the possible exception of the most intelligent animals, it may be questionable whether humans can ever truly know what a particular animal or species desires or needs. However, the presumption that certain interests are so fundamental that all humans should be accorded legal rights to protect these interests, whether or not they individually ask for them, should be extended to wildlife. As humans have both a self-interest and a moral obligation to recognize the rights of other human beings, they have an equivalent interest and obligation to recognize the interests of wildlife since the stability and integrity of the ecosystem is at stake. Moreover, the moral burden demanding this recognition is particularly great when human activities cause serious intrusions upon the interests of the wildlife community. Given the reasonable presumption that humans should recognize the fundamental interests of wildlife, important questions remain: What are wildlife's interests? What rights should wildlife be accorded? After these rights are granted, how will conflicts between human rights and wildlife rights be resolved?

Is wildlife a resource like petroleum, to be valued only for what it can do for us? Is there an intermediate position between pure utilitarian valuation and Professor Favre's assertion of rights for wildlife? Reconsider the land ethic of Aldo Leopold, excerpted in Chapter 1.

Toward the other end of the spectrum, Susan M. Schectman, *The "Bambi Syndrome:" How NEPA's Public Participation in Wildlife Management is Hurting the Environment*, 8 ENVTL. L. 611 (1978), concludes:

> * * * Non-native burros and native deer have increased in important scenic areas to the point where severe impacts are occurring to flora, fauna, and soil. Proper wildlife management requires reduction, and as a practical matter this can only be accomplished by shooting. * * * But attempts to reduce the herds have been delayed by NEPA actions and lengthy public involvement procedures. * * *

> A common complaint was that the "Bambi Syndrome" subverted the involvement process. The public was concerned with individual animals and not their ecosystem as a whole, and seemed to respond more to emotional media presentations than technical assessments prepared by the managers. Skepticism towards the managers and emotionalism created by Walt Disney-like misconceptions of wildlife jeopardized the information function. The sentimental value of individual wildlife to

the public became clear, but the decision-makers obtained few valuable comments or feasible alternatives; many suggested alternatives ranged from the emotional to the fanciful to the irrational. While the information function was partially served, managers felt that the public was often not interested in staff assessments and that the public input was simply not valuable enough to deserve a great deal of effort. In no case did the public suggest a feasible alternative that the staff had not previously considered. The public's "Bambi Syndrome" was simply incompatible with sound resource management. * * *

Are cultural or religious preferences for wildlife antithetical to sound resource management? Is there a place for nonnative wild horses on public lands to symbolize public images of the "wild west"? Does widespread national support for wolf reintroductions on public land contradict the existence of a "Bambi syndrome"?

The constitutional underpinnings of federal law over wildlife were discussed in Chapter 3, and the Endangered Species Act was discussed in Chapter 4. Section A of this chapter addresses the National Wildlife Refuge System, managed by the U.S. Fish & Wildlife Service (FWS) in the Department of the Interior. Section B examines wildlife controversies in the national parks, national forests and on the BLM public lands. Section C looks at the Migratory Bird Treaty Act. An excellent introduction to these issues is found in Michael J. Bean & Melanie J. Rowland, THE EVOLUTION OF NATIONAL WILDLIFE LAW (3d ed. 1997). *See also* George Cameron Coggins & Robert Glicksman, 3 PUBLIC NATURAL RESOURCES LAW, ch. 18.

A. THE NATIONAL WILDLIFE REFUGE SYSTEM

1. HISTORY AND ISSUES OF ADMINISTRATION

Portions of the following summary of refuge law and history borrow heavily from two texts by Professor Fischman, THE NATIONAL WILDLIFE REFUGES (2003) and *The Significance of National Wildlife Refuges in the Development of U.S. Conservation Policy*, 21 J. LAND USE & ENVTL. L. 1 (2005).

When Theodore Roosevelt established Pelican Island as the first "bird reserve," he placed management in the hands of the Bureau of Biological Survey, located in the Department of Agriculture. In 1940 Franklin Roosevelt merged the Biological Survey and the Bureau of Fisheries into a U.S. Fish and Wildlife Service (FWS), under the Department of the Interior, where it remains today. The FWS has managed the system since then, with the exception of the big game ranges, which were not transferred over from the BLM until the 1970s.

The following chart traces the growth of the system. The early decades manifest steady growth mostly at the behest of the President. Even when Congress passed legislation establishing refuges, it generally acted to endorse reservations already made by the President. The first significant legislative innovation was the Migratory Bird Conservation Act of 1929, which authorized acquisition of lands to serve as avian refuges. 16 U.S.C. § 715–715r. It required the permission of the state in which the property was located, and established the first multi-refuge management purpose: acquired refuges should serve as "inviolate sanctuaries" for migratory birds. Beyond that basic mission, however, the 1929 Act contained no management mandates for refuge administration. And, in subsequent years, Congress progressively whittled away at the hunting restrictions in the "inviolate sanctuaries." Hunting of migratory game birds may now occur on up to 40 percent of an area established under the MBCA. 16 U.S.C. § 668dd(d)(1)(a).

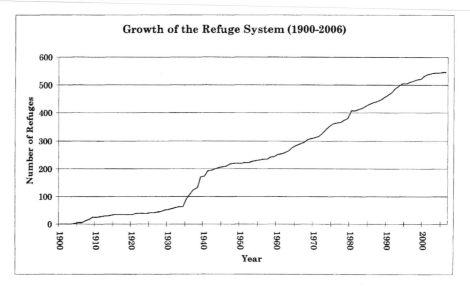

The 1929 law merely authorized spending—it did not actually appropriate money for acquisition. Funds to purchase refuges in the early years of the Great Depression were scarce. In the early 1930s, waterfowl populations declined precipitously and Biological Survey research succeeded in mapping the four north-south flyways used by birds in their seasonal migration across the continent. Congress responded with the Migratory Bird Hunting Stamp Act of 1934. 16 U.S.C. § 718–718(h). It created a dedicated fund for acquiring waterfowl habitat refuges from the sales of federal stamps that all waterfowl hunters would be required to affix to their state hunting licenses. The law, therefore, is commonly called the Duck Stamp Act. Ninety percent of the Duck Stamp fund revenues were earmarked for acquisition of habitat and the remainder for refuge management.

Since 1934, the federal government has collected more than a half billion dollars from duck stamp sales. Periodic congressional appropriations and loans (later forgiven) have bolstered the fund's stamp income. Along with the Land and Water Conservation Fund Act of 1964, 16 U.S.C. §§ 460l–4 to 460l–11, which collects receipts from motorboat fuels tax and payments for federal offshore oil and gas leases, the Duck Stamp Act funding mechanism remains the major source of money for purchasing expansions to the Refuge System. A quick glance at a map of today's refuge system confirms the legacy of the research findings and funding mechanism of the 1930s: refuges are concentrated in four corridors. Thus, the geometry of the refuge system conservation shifted from the enclave points on the map to the flyway lines across the country.

With assured acquisition funding, the growth of the Refuge System accelerated and created a strong constituency for refuge management among the hunters who made the annual, mandatory contributions. Although reservation of public domain would remain an important source of refuges, particularly in Alaska, land acquisition would be the dominant engine of growth in the number of refuges after 1934. The result of this history is that the most prevalent purpose for refuges is to contribute to the conservation of "the continental migratory waterfowl population." On the other hand, from the perspective of area, the relative importance of acquisition is very low. After the establishment of the huge refuges in Alaska in 1980, the proportion of reserved public domain grew to 97 percent of the Refuge System.

The bewildering taxonomic diversity of units in the Refuge System owes much to acquisition funding mechanisms. Many of the units purchased with Duck Stamp Act monies were named migratory bird refuges. After a 1958 amendment to the Duck Stamp Act, the FWS began acquiring waterfowl production areas, typically small wetlands or prairie potholes, which are exempt from the "inviolate sanctuary" mandate of the Migratory Bird Conservation Act. Refuges reserved or transferred from existing public lands might be designated any of a wide variety of names (e.g., wildlife refuge, game range, wildlife and fish refuge, migratory waterfowl refuge, migratory bird refuge) depending on the source (e.g., Congress, the President, the Secretary of the Interior) and the particular purpose of the establishment. In addition, the Department of the Interior has long accepted donations for refuge lands.

After the push for migratory waterfowl, the next impetus for refuge system growth came in the 1960s as Congress recognized the larger variety of species than just birds, big game, and fish that needed protection from extinction. The Endangered Species Preservation Act of 1966 sought to protect species, regardless of their popularity or evident value, principally through habitat acquisition and reservation. In doing so, the law provided the first statutory charter for the refuge system as a whole. Indeed, the part of the 1966 law dealing with the refuges is often called the Refuge Administration Act. Pub. L. No. 89–669, 16 U.S.C. § 668dd. This law was of a piece with the larger nature preservation trend sweeping natural resources law in the 1960s, as evident in the 1964 Wilderness Act and the 1968 Wild and Scenic Rivers Act. It coincided with the second, less dramatic growth spurt of new refuges, as shown by the chart.

The 1966 statute consolidated the conservation land holdings of the FWS into the "National Wildlife Refuge System." The law also mandated a uniform management rule. It formally closed the refuges to private activities except where opened by the FWS on a finding that an allowed use would be compatible with the purpose of the refuge. The compatibility criterion, established by statute in 1966, would become a byword of international sustainable development in the 1980s.

A new wave of science influenced refuge management in the late 1960s. In 1967, E.O. Wilson and Robert MacArthur published their path-breaking monograph, The Theory of Island Biogeography. Application of this new theory revealed refuges as akin to small, isolated island sanctuaries, vulnerable to species extinctions regardless of how well they are managed. The theory taught that refuges, even if maintained in pristine condition, were not sufficient to prevent species extinction unless they were large enough and linked to other protected areas. Small pockets of species do not persist long anywhere.

The rise of ecology as a scientific basis for management in the 1960s is exemplified in the Leopold reports solicited by the Secretary of the Interior. In 1963, Professor A. Starker Leopold, a son of the famous Aldo, led a committee to recommend that the national parks be managed to maintain and restore native species in their natural, biotic associations. This recommendation was updated and applied to the refuge system in a similar, 1968 report. The 1968 Leopold committee report described the long-range systemic goal for the refuges to serve as show places for the full spectrum of native wildlife. The committee proposed "to add a 'natural ecosystem' component to the program of refuge management." In this recommendation, the Leopold committee sought an overarching, guiding principle that would provide a uniform direction for system management and respond to growing ecological concerns about the viability of isolated reserves. Though it anticipated by three decades the formal FWS adoption of an ecosystem management policy, it nudged the refuges toward the forefront of conservation. The Keiter excerpt in Chapter 1 considers ecosystem management.

The refuge system spent the 1970s and 1980s lagging behind the enormous changes that affected other federal lands. With the exception of the 1980 Alaska National Interest Lands Conservation Act, Congress enacted few significant legislative reforms specific to the refuges. In the 1970s, the Forest Service and Bureau of Land Management (BLM) lands received completely new statutory charters governing land management (NFMA and FLPMA) and the National Park Service obtained a substantial revision of its legislative mandate. But the FWS limped along with its 1966 framework.

As with other federal lands, the refuges began to shift toward a more ecological approach to management as a result of scientific developments, environmental statutes (such as NEPA and the ESA), and the opening of the courts to hear citizen environmental complaints. Nonetheless, conditions on the refuges were poor. A combination of austere funding, lax oversight, limited jurisdiction, and local political pressure gave rise to widespread incompatible uses on refuges. In 1989 the Government Accountability Office (then called the General Accounting Office) found incompatible uses harming conservation goals on 59 percent of refuges. Among the most commonly occurring secondary activities were mining, off-road vehicle use, power boating, military exercises, grazing, logging, hunting, and rights of way use.

In response to the GAO report, a law suit, and several follow-up studies that confirmed the major problems with incompatible uses, President Clinton continued the long tradition of presidential initiative. He issued an executive order in 1996 establishing a firmer management framework for conserving the refuge system. The next year Congress enacted the 1997 Refuge Improvement Act as a charter for the refuge system, displaying all five of the hallmarks of modern organic legislation noted in Chapter 5E. Pub.L.No. 105–57.

a. PURPOSE STATEMENT

The 1997 conservation mandate finally provided a unifying mission for a system that retains a disparate set of establishment purposes for individual refuges. Until then, only individual refuges had purposes. The Act sets a goal of conservation, defined in ecological terms. 16 U.S.C. § 668dd(a)(2). This is a very different conception of conservation from the progressive-era, multiple-use, sustained yield missions that sought to conserve a steady stream of commodities to be extracted from the public lands. It also embraces a broader land (and water) ethic that extends to plants and habitat than the earlier refuge goals, which focused on animals ("wildlife") almost exclusively. The statutory mission directs the FWS "to sustain and, where appropriate, restore and enhance healthy populations of fish, wildlife, and plants utilizing ... methods and procedures associated with modern scientific resource programs." 16 U.S.C. § 668ee. Moreover, refuge administration now recognizes a key lesson of conservation biology: nature reserves need to be interconnected. The 1997 statute envisions the refuge system as a "national network" of lands and waters to sustain plants and animals. This realigns the geometry of refuge conservation from linear flyways to a more complex web of relationships.

b. DESIGNATED USES

The 1997 Refuge Improvement Act constructs a dominant use regime where most activities must either contribute to the system goal, or at least avoid impairing it. The primary uses that dominate the system are individual refuge purposes and the conservation mission. This clear command to maintain ecological functions (rather than resource outputs) on the refuges represents the current trend for all public land management. Secondary uses are the "priority public uses" of wildlife-dependent recreation, which the statute defines as "hunting, fishing, wildlife observation and photography, or environmental education and interpretation." 16 U.S.C. § 668ee. Secondary uses may be permitted where they are compatible with primary uses. The statute affirmatively encourages the FWS to promote secondary uses on refuges. Tertiary uses are other recreational activities, such as snowmobiling, boating, and biking that may be allowed on refuges where they are compatible with the primary uses and do not conflict with secondary uses. Finally, economic activities, such as logging and farming, may occur only where they contribute to a primary use and do not conflict with a secondary use. A big exception to this hierarchy is for "refuge management activities," which generally are conducted by the federal government. The appropriate uses policy of the FWS, however, expands this category outside of the hierarchy to include state fish and game activities, such as predator control, under certain circumstances. FWS Manual part 603 § 1.2(B).

c. COMPREHENSIVE PLANNING

The Refuge Improvement Act requires a comprehensive conservation plan (CCP) for each refuge unit (usually a single national wildlife refuge or cluster of them). The CCPs zone refuges into various areas suitable for different purposes and set out desired future conditions. Following the model established by the NFMA, the Improvement Act requires the Service to prepare a CCP for each unit outside of Alaska within 15 years and to update each plan every 15 years, or sooner if conditions change significantly. 16 U.S.C. § 668dd(e)(1). In contrast, the Alaska refuges' comprehensive conservation plans, the BLM resource management plans, and the NPS general management plans have no statutory schedule for periodic revision. Planning tends to focus on habitat management and visitor services. The planning policy models its procedure on adaptive management. FWS Manual part 602. Once approved, the CCP becomes a source of management requirements that bind the FWS, 16 U.S.C. § 668dd(e)(1)(E), though judicial enforcement may be limited by Norton v. SUWA, *supra* p. 471.

d. SUBSTANTIVE MANAGEMENT CRITERIA

This is the hallmark where the 1997 Act advanced organic legislation the furthest beyond congressional precedent. Congress imposed many substantive management criteria, some of which are unprecedented in public land law. First, the Act expanded the compatibility criterion as a basic tool for determining what uses are allowed on refuges. The FWS may not permit uses to occur where they are incompatible with either the conservation mission or individual refuge purposes. And, compatibility determinations must be put in writing. 16 U.S.C. § 668dd(d)(3). The statute requires the Secretary, in implementing the compatibility provisions of the NWRSIA, to (a) estimate the "timeframe, location, manner, and purpose of each use"; (b) determine the "effects of each use;" and (c) provide for "the elimination or modification of any use as expeditiously as practicable after a determination is made that the use is not a compatible use." 16 U.S.C. § 668dd(d)(3)(B)(i)-(ix). We will consider compatibility in greater depth below in Subsection 4.

Second, the 1997 law requires that the Service maintain "biological integrity, diversity, and environmental health" on the refuges. 16 U.S.C. § 668dd(a)(4)(B). This is the closest Congress has ever come to requiring a land system to ensure ecological sustainability. Other path-breaking criteria include a duty to acquire water rights needed for refuge purposes, biological monitoring, and a stewardship responsibility. 16 U.S.C. § 668dd(a)(4).

e. PUBLIC PARTICIPATION

NEPA procedures structure much of the public participation anticipated by the Act in key decisions, such as comprehensive plan adoption and compatibility determination. Even visitor service plans and other specific programming decisions receive public scrutiny under FWS implementing policies.

Like practically all legislation, the 1997 NWRSIA was the product of political compromise. In this case, the primary players were environmentalists, who wanted strong protection for wildlife habitat and the ecological health of refuges, and sport hunters and anglers, who wanted to ensure that their interests would receive some priority consideration in refuge management. The broad architecture of the compromise, fashioned in a series of meetings among the contending interests in Secretary of the Interior Babbitt's office, was rather elegant: The environmentalists secured strong, bottom-line protection for the ecological health of refuges while the sport hunters and anglers attained priority through creation of the "wildlife-dependent recreational uses" category, subject to compatibility with the ecological mission. The losers in the process were non-wildlife-dependent recreational users, other users like graziers (who were subjected to more stringent compatibility rules) and animal rights sympathizers (whose cause was set back by the priority positioning of hunting and angling on the refuges).

2. State Law and Refuge System Goals

Professor Fischman has documented the solicitousness with which Congress treated the states in the 1997 Act and its implementing policies:

> The legislative history * * * adumbrates coordination of refuges with state programs. Indeed, the Act itself requires coordination with states in the administration of the System generally and in planning. This partnership with states is, of course, limited by federal preemption of state law that conflicts with FWS management control on refuges. For instance, a state may not impose its own hunting/trapping regulations or property law restrictions on the Refuge System under circumstances where they would frustrate decisions made by the Service or Congress.
>
> Nonetheless, the FWS has always worked closely with states, especially on hunting and fishing issues, where states have traditionally exercised comprehensive, default management. Coordination Areas, where states manage federal Refuge System lands, are the most extreme example of Service deference to state wildlife programs. However, even on national wildlife refuges, the Service continually renews its commitment to respond to state interests. Service policy emphasizes state participation in most refuge decision-making, especially for comprehensive conservation planning [and for determination of appropriate uses].

The National Wildlife Refuges 88. Nonetheless, there are circumstances where state wildlife management and refuge conservation conflict. Consider the following controversy in the National Elk Refuge (NER), which Congress established in 1912. Numerous species make the NER their home during part or all of the year, including birds, bison, mule deer, bighorn sheep, pronghorn antelope, moose, wolves, coyotes, badgers, and black and grizzly bears. But it is the elk that most people come to see and around which the litigation revolves.

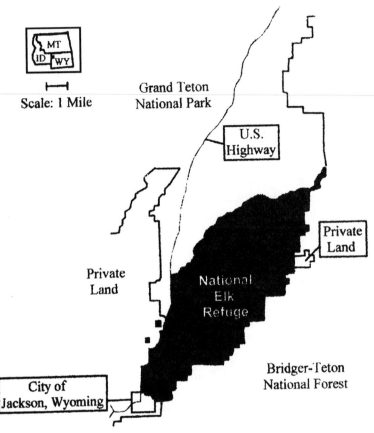

State of Wyoming v. United States

United States Court of Appeals for the Tenth Circuit, 2002.
279 F.3d 1214.

■ JUDGE BALDOCK

Once again a federal court is called upon to unravel a congressionally-legislated Federal–State standoff. The National Elk Refuge (NER), a part of the National Wildlife Refuge System (NWRS), encompasses approximately 24,700 acres of wilderness north of Jackson Hole, Wyoming, in the greater Yellowstone area. Brucellosis, a serious disease that causes miscarriage, is endemic to free-ranging elk in the greater Yellowstone area and a threat to Wyoming's domestic cattle industry. * * * [T]he State challenges the FWS's refusal to permit the State to vaccinate elk on the NER with a brucellosis vaccine known as "Strain 19." According to the FWS, after several years of research and study, the biosafety and efficacy of Strain 19 vis-à-vis elk remain unproven. The State disagrees.

Resolution of this matter ultimately rests upon our construction of the National Wildlife Refuge System Improvement Act of 1997 (NWRSIA) (codified at 16 U.S.C. §§ 668dd–668ee). Unfortunately, the NWRSIA does not (nor does any Federal law) directly address the problem of brucellosis in wildlife, or establish clear priority between wildlife and domestic livestock when interests involving the two conflict. In the jurisdictionally-fragmented Yellowstone area, however, one thing is certain: Wildlife management policies affecting the interests of multiple sovereigns demand a high degree of intergovernmental cooperation. Such cooperation is conspicuously absent in this case.

Brucellosis is a disease caused by Brucella abortus, a bacterial borne pathogen which infects the reproductive organs and lymphatic systems of ungulates.[2] Brucellosis most often produces spontaneous abortion in female ungulates during the first pregnancy following infection. A small percentage of infected ungulates may develop inflamed joints resulting in arthritis and lameness. The disease also may produce sterility in infected males. Research has shown that female ungulates are largely responsible for the spread of brucellosis to other susceptible hosts. Aborted fetuses, vaginal fluids, newborn young, birth by-products, and milk from infected females all are contaminated with the Brucella bacteria. The disease spreads most commonly when ungulates consume infected tissue or contaminated feed or water.[3]

Authorities first detected brucellosis in elk in the greater Yellowstone area around 1930. Today, brucellosis infects approximately thirty percent of the elk in western Wyoming. Thus, significant levels of brucellosis still occur in the feed ground elk population on the NER. Experts estimate that the annual elk calf loss due to brucellosis-related abortions on the NER is seven percent of the calf crop.

The concentration of free-ranging elk herds on Wyoming and NER winter feed grounds appears to perpetuate brucellosis. The feed grounds, which host around 25,000 elk each winter, are prime locations for the transmission of brucellosis because the herds are in close contact during the critical birthing period. Because natural winter habitat in the region is not adequate to sustain the elk herds at their current numbers, closing the feed grounds would foster competition [eds.: with livestock], which appears to increase the risk of brucellosis transmission.

The primary significance of brucellosis-related abortions in Wyoming's elk herds is the potential for transmission of the disease to domestic cattle. Elk and other wildlife in the greater Yellowstone area do not respect jurisdictional boundaries. Instead, wildlife wanders freely across the region's public and private lands. * * *

2. An ungulate is defined as "a hoofed mammal." Random House Dictionary 2069 (2d ed. 1987).

3. Humans are susceptible to infection from the Brucella bacteria as well. The symptoms of undulant fever, as the disease is known in humans, are flu-like. Most cases of undulant fever, however, are caused by Brucella melitensis, which is found primarily in sheep and goats. The risk of human infection by elk or cattle is possible, but more remote.

But see Parker Land and Cattle Co. v. United States, 796 F. Supp. 477, 487 (D.Wyo.1992) (describing incident where ranch hand contracted undulant fever while assisting in the delivery of calves; "several courses of medication" proved effective in combating the disease). Cooked meat poses no threat of transmitting brucellosis and is considered safe for human consumption. See Smith & Roffe, supra, at 74, 76–77.

No documented cases of elk infecting domestic cattle with brucellosis under natural conditions exist. But see Parker Land and Cattle Co. v. United States, 796 F. Supp. 477, 488 (D.Wyo.1992) (concluding that a brucellosis outbreak in Wyoming cattle "was most likely caused by contact with infected elk or bison, as those are the only two known sources of the disease in the entire State of Wyoming"). Scientists at Texas A & M University, however, have transmitted brucellosis from elk to cattle in confined conditions. Thus, the impetus behind Wyoming's desire to eradicate brucellosis in elk is the potential for economic loss to its domestic cattle industry. * * *

Despite disagreement over how effective the Strain 19 vaccine is in immunizing elk from brucellosis, experts agree that vaccinating cattle with Strain 19 plays an important role, together with test-and-removal of infected animals, in eradicating brucellosis from cattle herds. * * *

[In 1985,] the State began vaccinating elk with Strain 19 on state feed grounds, apparently with some success. By the early 1990's, Wyoming reported that its vaccination program had resulted in a seventy percent calving success rate for vaccinated elk, as compared to a thirty percent calving success rate for unvaccinated elk. By 1998, the State was vaccinating elk on twenty-one of twenty-two state feed grounds without notable adverse consequence. Since 1985, however, at least four documented incidents of brucellosis in Wyoming cattle have occurred. The source of the disease in these cases remains unidentified.

* * *

* * * [In 1998, the Wyoming governor offered] to undertake a vaccination program of elk on the NER at the State's own expense, and to "indemnify and hold harmless" the FWS from any claims arising out of the program. This time the Director responded, denying the State of Wyoming the authority to conduct a Strain 19 vaccination program on the NER:

> As you know, the Service disagrees that Wyoming has adequately demonstrated the effectiveness of the Strain 19 program. While we have no doubt that Wyoming has been successful at vaccinating elk [on state feed grounds], there are not adequate data to indicate whether or not the lowered seroprevalence is attributable to vaccination. Feed-line management on the Refuge, which minimizes the time that animals are concentrated on the feed line through the use of alfalfa pellets rather than hay also appears to have lowered seroprevalence according to Service data. However, in both cases (Wyoming vaccination and Refuge feed-line management), there are inadequate data to ensure that these particular management actions are solely responsible for or simply correlate with observed changes in seroprevalence. In the case of the State's feed grounds, the Service would be far less skeptical of the vaccine's effect if rigorous clinical trials had demonstrated efficacy under controlled conditions....
>
> The Service is willing to implement a vaccination program once adequate, scientifically sound data demonstrate that any proposed vaccine

is both safe and effective. We believe such a vaccine does not exist at this time, but we continue to support its development. . . .

Therefore, given the points raised in this letter outlining the Service's concerns for vaccination of elk with Strain 19, the Service does not authorize Wyoming to conduct a vaccination program on the Refuge at this time. . . .

[Wyoming filed suit, claiming the state had a "sovereign right" to manage wildlife within its borders, including to vaccinate elk on the NER. The district court dismissed the case.] * * * The State asserts a concurrent, if not exclusive, right to manage wildlife on the NER, including a right to vaccinate elk on the NER with Strain 19, free from federal interference. The FWS counters by asserting exclusive unlimited discretion under the NWRSIA to manage wildlife on the NER in any manner the Secretary deems appropriate, free from state interference. Unfortunately, we do not believe this case is as clear cut and easily resolved as the parties urge.

[The court first addressed and rejected Wyoming's constitutional argument for control over wildlife on federal lands.] * * * [W]e believe the point painfully apparent that the Tenth Amendment does not reserve to the State of Wyoming the right to manage wildlife, or more specifically vaccinate elk, on the NER, regardless of the circumstances. * * * The remedy the State seeks must come, if at all, not from the Constitution but from Congress. To what extent Congress sought to exercise its power under the Property Clause in enacting the NWRSIA is the inquiry to which we turn next.

* * *

While plainly vesting the FWS with authority to administer the Act and manage the NWRS, the NWRSIA makes numerous mention of the need for cooperation between the FWS and the States to achieve the Act's objectives. At its outset, the NWRSIA directs that the FWS "shall" (1) "complement efforts of States and other Federal agencies to conserve fish and wildlife and their habitats;" (2) "ensure effective coordination, interaction, and cooperation with owners of land adjoining refuges and the fish and wildlife agency of the States in which the units of the System are located;" and (3) "ensure timely and effective cooperation and collaboration with Federal agencies and State fish and wildlife agencies during the course of acquiring and managing refuges." Id. § 668dd(a)(4)(C), (E), (M).

* * *

Notably for purposes of this case, the NWRSIA concludes with an opaque provision termed "State authority:"

Nothing in this Act shall be construed as affecting the authority, jurisdiction, or responsibility of the several States to manage, control, or regulate fish and resident wildlife under State law or regulations in any area within the System. Regulations permitting hunting or fishing of fish and resident wildlife within the System shall be, to the extent practicable, consistent with State fish and wildlife laws, regulations, and management plans.

Id. § 668dd(m). The State of Wyoming primarily relies on the first sentence of this "saving clause" to support its claimed right to vaccinate elk on the NER with the Strain 19 brucellosis vaccine. According to the State, Congress specifically included the saving clause in the NWRSIA to "reserve[] to the States the right to manage wildlife on refuge lands within their borders." Consequently, the State opines the FWS exceeded its authority under the NWRSIA when it refused to permit the State to vaccinate elk on the NER. * * *

* * *

Initially, we note that this is not a case in which the State of Wyoming seeks to invade "an area where the federal interest has been manifest since the beginning of our Republic." Compare United States v. Locke, 529 U.S. 89, 99 (2000) (recognizing the long-standing federal interest in the regulation of maritime commerce). Rather, as the Secretary of the USDI recognizes, wildlife management is a field which the States have traditionally occupied. Even today, the Secretary generally acknowledges that "State jurisdiction remains concurrent with Federal authority." 43 C.F.R. § 24.3(c); see also id. § 24.3(b) ("Despite the existence of constitutional power respecting fish and wildlife on Federally owned lands, Congress has, in fact, reaffirmed the basic responsibility and authority of the States to manage fish and resident wildlife on Federal lands."). According to the Secretary, "Federal authority exists for specified purposes while State authority regarding fish and resident wildlife remains the comprehensive backdrop applicable in the absence of specific, overriding Federal law." Id. § 24.1(a) * * *

The first sentence of the NWRSIA's saving clause, viewed in isolation, seems to support our assumption that even after the NWRSIA, the State retains the absolute right to manage wildlife on the NER free from federal intervention: "*Nothing in this Act* shall be construed as affecting the authority, jurisdiction, or responsibility of the several States to manage, control, or regulate fish and wildlife under State law or regulations in any area within the System." 16 U.S.C. § 668dd(m) (emphasis added). The State's sweeping interpretation of the first sentence in § 668dd(m) is not without force, and our assumption might be plausible if we interpreted the sentence in isolation. Such an interpretation of the saving clause, however, simply is not feasible in light of established rules of construction requiring us to consider the NWRSIA in its entirety, mindful of congressional purposes and objectives.

Unquestionably, the NWRSIA inspirits a "cooperative federalism," calling for, at a minimum, state involvement and participation in the management of the NWRS as that system affects surrounding state ecosystems. * * *

Still, the NWRSIA requires the FWS in developing conservation plans for a refuge to act in conformity with State objectives only "to the extent practical." Id. § 668dd(e)(1)(A)(iii); id. § 668dd(e)(3). The NWRSIA's legislative history confirms this, stating the Act requires that "to the extent practicable, the FWS should seek opportunities to coordinate the management of National Wildlife Refuges with the management of fish and wildlife resources generally by the State or States in which the refuges are located." H.R. Rep. No.105–106, at 8. Even the second and final sentence of the NWRSIA's saving clause, which appears to contradict its first sentence, requires only that "regulations permitting hunting or fishing of fish and resident wildlife within the system shall be, to the extent practicable, consistent with State fish and wildlife laws, regulations, and management plans." 16 U.S.C. § 668dd(m) * * *.

The legislative history behind § 668dd(m) lends little support to the State of Wyoming's claim that the saving clause unconditionally reserves to it the "sovereign" right to manage elk on the NER. * * * The discussion of the saving clause in the Senate Report together with the entire tone of the NWRSIA reveals that Congress was solicitous of state sensibilities and simply did not wish to face the Federal–State jurisdictional dilemma which the NWRSIA and its predecessor the NWRSAA created. Instead, Congress left the courts to resolve jurisdictional disputes on a case-by-case basis.

In the end, the proposition that the FWS lacks the power to make a decision regarding the health of wildlife on the NER when a State, for whatever reason, disagrees with that decision proves too much. * * * If we construed the NWRSIA to grant the State of Wyoming the sweeping power it claims, the State would be free to manage and regulate the NER in a manner the FWS deemed incompatible with the NER's purpose. But the Secretary alone is authorized, "under such regulations as he may prescribe," to "permit the use of any area within the System for any purpose . . . whenever he determines that such uses are compatible with the major purposes for which such areas were established. . . ." Id. § 668dd(d)(1)(A); see also id. § 668dd(d)(3)(A) (The Secretary shall not permit a use of a refuge "unless the Secretary has determined that the use is a compatible use.").

Yet, the NWRSIA's saving clause is not meaningless. Section 668dd(m) convinces us that Congress did not intend to displace entirely state regulation and management of wildlife on federal public lands, especially where such regulation and management bears directly upon the well being of state interests arising outside those public lands. In other words, Congress rejected complete preemption of state wildlife regulation within the NWRS. Rather, we believe Congress intended ordinary principles of conflict preemption to apply in cases such as this. * * *

Consistent with our construction of the NWRSIA, we hold that the FWS's decision to refuse to permit the State to vaccinate elk on the NER with Strain 19 based upon efficacy and biosafety concerns was not, in itself, beyond the agency's statutory authority or ultra vires. * * *

At the prompting of the district court, the State of Wyoming amended its original complaint and grudgingly added Count III to its first amended complaint seeking review of the FWS's decision under the APA, 5 U.S.C. §§ 701–706. The State sought to overturn the FWS's decision under both § 706(2)(A) as "not in accordance with law," and § 706(2)(C) as "in excess of statutory jurisdiction." * * * We therefore focus on whether the FWS's decision was "arbitrary, capricious, an abuse of discretion, or otherwise not in accordance with law." 5 U.S.C. § 706(2)(A).

* * * We have seen that the FWS has the authority under the NWRSIA to make decisions binding on the State regarding wildlife management within the NWRS. But that authority is not unlimited as the district court seemed to suggest. Congress undoubtedly did not intend its call for "effective coordination, interaction, and cooperation with owners of land adjoining refuges and the fish and wildlife agencies of the State," 16 U.S.C. § 668dd(a)(4)(e), a theme running throughout the NWRSIA, to constitute merely a recommendation which the FWS might ignore with impunity.

Similarly, we reject any suggestion that Congress "committed to agency discretion by law" the FWS's decision to deny the State of Wyoming's request. * * * Congress throughout the NWRSIA has indicated an intent to circumscribe the FWS's discretion. The requirement that the FWS in developing a conservation plan for each refuge comply with State policies and objectives to the "extent" or "maximum extent practicable," id. §§ 668dd(e), undoubtedly places limits on the agency's discretion. See Random House Dictionary 1517 (2d ed. 1987) (defining "practicable" as "capable of being done, effected, or put into practice, with the available means").

Additionally, in determining whether a proposed "use" of a refuge constitutes a "compatible use," i.e., a use that "will not materially interfere with or detract from the fulfillment of the mission of the System or the purposes of the refuge," the NWRSIA directs the Secretary to exercise "sound professional judgment." 16 U.S.C. § 668ee(1). The NWRSIA defines the phrase "sound professional judgment" as "a finding, determination, or decision that is consistent with principles of sound fish and wildlife management and administration, available science and resources, and adherence to the requirements of this Act and other applicable laws." Id. § 668ee(3). The legislative history of § 668ee reveals that Congress expected "the FWS to be energetic and creative in seeking such resources, including partnerships with the States, local communities and private and nonprofit groups." H.R. Rep. No. 105–106, at 6. Thus, Congress rejected the idea that the FWS's exercise of "sound professional judgment" under the NWRSIA is unreviewable.

* * * [W]e believe the FWS's decision may be subject to a "thorough, probing, in-depth review" under the traditional agency review principles set forth in § 706(2)(A) of the APA. * * * Our decision to construe Count III of the first amended complaint in this manner, despite the State's inartful pleading, rests upon the following factors—

(1) the long-standing and increasingly urgent nature of the brucellosis problem in elk on the NER and its threat to Wyoming's domestic cattle and resident elk populations;

(2) the FWS's inability after more than a decade to reach any real consensus regarding the efficacy and biosafety of the Strain 19 vaccine as applied to elk on the NER;

(3) the "Catch-22" in which the State of Wyoming finds itself in struggling with the apparently discordant views over brucellosis control and eradication between the USDA and the FWS;

(4) the Congress' ongoing reluctance to address the brucellosis problem in wildlife; and

(5) the State of Wyoming's and FWS's bipolar claims of absolute power to decide the fate of elk on the NER. * * *

The State alleges that extending its vaccination program to the NER will not adversely affect the refuge because Strain 19 is a safe and effective means of containing brucellosis, and thus "neither the ecosystem nor the elk herds will be negatively impacted." The State further alleges that the FWS's program to control brucellosis on the NER has proven ineffective. * * *

Finally, the State alleges that the FWS has failed to conduct any independent studies on the efficacy and biosafety of Strain 19. Rather, according to the State, the FWS bases its criticism of Strain 19 solely on statistical analysis of limited depth and scope.

Accepting the foregoing allegation as true, we have little difficulty concluding that the State of Wyoming states a claim for relief in Count III of its first amendment complaint. If, as the State suggests, the Strain 19 vaccine is a safe and effective means of containing brucellosis in free-ranging elk, and the FWS has no viable alternative means of reducing the high rate of brucellosis-infected elk on the NER, then the FWS decision to deny the State's request to vaccinate elk on the NER with Strain 19 may very well be "arbitrary, capricious, an abuse of discretion, or otherwise not in accordance with law." 5 U.S.C. § 706(2)(A). Thus, we conclude that the district court erred in dismissing Count III for failure to state a claim upon which relief may be granted.

As we recently recognized, "habitat management is a delicate venture." Sierra Club–Black Hills Group v. United States Forest Serv., 259 F.3d 1281, 1286 (10th Cir.2001). To make matters worse, jurisdictional allocation regarding wildlife management within the NWRS is a legal quagmire. Unfortunately, the NWRSIA with its broad language and general directives is not particularly helpful in resolving any particular conflict, especially where resolution of that conflict, whether agreed upon or court ordered, will inevitably affect the interests of dual sovereigns. To that extent, wildlife management is inherently political. Thus, wildlife managers simply cannot view wildlife management in isolation, as the FWS appears to be doing in this instance. The FWS's apparent indifference to the State of Wyoming's problem and the State's insistence of a "sovereign right" to manage wildlife on the NER do little to promote "cooperative federalism." Given the NWRSIA's repeated calls for a "cooperative federalism," we find inexcusable the parties' unwillingness in this case to even attempt to amicably resolve the brucellosis controversy or find any common ground on which to commence fruitful negotiations.

To be sure, deference to agency action is appropriate "where that action implicates scientific and technical judgments within the scope of agency expertise." Sierra Club–Black Hills Group, 259 F.3d at 1286. The problem is that after an extended period of time, the FWS still appears unable or unwilling to make any judgment regarding the biosafety and efficacy of Strain 19 as applied to free-ranging elk. But the law requires answers. For instance, the FWS has never explained why the State's proposal would "stand as an obstacle to the accomplishment and execution" of federal objectives. Due to health and safety concerns, the FWS effectively pulled the plug on the State's vaccination of elk on the NER after a trial run from 1989–1991. That was over a decade ago and the FWS has yet to resolve these concerns.

* * * Given that the FWS effectively suspended the State's Strain 19 vaccination program on the NER over a decade ago due to health and safety concerns, the "temporary" nature of FWS's action has long since passed. Instead, in typical bureaucratic fashion, the FWS now claims that it needs an (1) elaborate efficacy study of Strain 19, (2) an environmental impact study, and (3) a comprehensive review of the State's proposed course of action as it affects the FWS's trust responsibilities to elk and other wildlife residing on the refuge. This proves too much too late in the day. If the executive and legislative branches of our Government will not act to resolve the brucellosis controversy in the State of Wyoming in what little time remains, the judicial branch may have to.

The State's apparent end purpose in pursuing this suit is to protect itself, its producer's domestic livestock, and its free-ranging elk from a threat arising out of the FWS's alleged lack of any meaningful program to combat brucellosis on the NER. Simplicity ends when we are faced with a situation where the program, or lack thereof, by one sovereign allegedly impairs the meaningful accomplishment of another sovereign's responsibilities. Unlike the district court, we do not read the NWRSIA as providing the FWS, through the Secretary of the USDI, with unlimited discretion to act or fail to act in a manner that threatens the well-being of a neighboring sovereign's livestock or game industry.

* * * We leave to the district court's discretion whether creation of that record requires a remand to the FWS. We also leave to the district court to determine in the first instance the appropriate level of deference, if any, to be given the FWS's position in this case. * * *

NOTES AND QUESTIONS

1. The court seems to acknowledge that USFWS has the authority to prohibit the state from vaccinating the elk on the NER with Strain 19. Yet it remands the case for a reconsideration of the USFWS decision. What would you now advise the USFWS to do, assuming that the agency leadership has dug in, and continues to oppose vaccinating the elk, firmly believing that the risk of elk infecting domestic cattle with brucellosis is very small? Could the agency simply beef up the record to support its opposition? Could it say that it will entertain the State's vaccination proposal seriously, but will do so in the format of preparing an EIS under NEPA? While the court is showing impatience here, can the court enjoin

the USFWS from preparing an EIS? Does the 1997 organic act require a compatibility determination before authorizing vaccination?

2. Notice that the federal government wears several hats here. The U.S. Department of Agriculture has authority over whether to certify Wyoming's cattle industry as "brucellosis-free." Without certification, livestock growers face restrictions on interstate sales and the costs of vaccinating cattle. If the Department of Agriculture believes there is a significant risk of elk-cattle transmission, does that affect the authority of the USFWS regarding elk vaccination on the NER? Is the court saying that the USFWS has a duty to spend federal money to investigate the efficacy of Strain 19? Can the FWS plead poverty if austerity budgets give it little flexibility to conduct studies? Suppose USFWS responds by asking the Congress to fund a $10 million, ten-year study of the effectiveness of Strain 19. If Congress provides the funds without changing the underlying legal regime, what does that do to the litigation? What effect on the litigation if Congress refuses to provide the funds?

After the circuit court issued its opinion, the United States settled with the state of Wyoming and agreed to conduct an environmental assessment of a vaccination program. After issuing a FONSI, elk vaccinations began in early 2003. But the vaccines were too late for Wyoming to retain its brucellosis-free certification. The U.S. Department of Agriculture revoked the certification in 2004. Wyoming regained its brucellosis-free status in 2006.

The NER is currently collaborating with its neighboring national park units on an EIS to consider a comprehensive bison and elk management plan that would determine how many elk the NER should accommodate during the winter. All of the options would reduce winter elk and bison numbers on the refuge. One option would phase out winter feeding. The state will continue to vaccinate on the refuge until the EIS is complete and an alternative is selected. The new management plan is expected in 2007.

3. Is the court correct when it states in the second paragraph of the excerpt that the 1997 Refuge Improvement Act does not "establish clear priority between wildlife and domestic livestock when interests involving the two conflict"? The Act requires each refuge to "fulfill the mission of the system." 16 U.S.C. § 668dd(a)(3). Does the mission speak to the relative priority of wildlife and livestock? Recall that the definition of "conservation" in the mission statement focuses on "healthy populations" of animals and plants. Does the high incidence of brucellosis in winter-fed elk suggest that that the feeding program violates the statutory mission?

The mission statement raises a host of questions: Which plant and animal populations is the FWS to sustain, restore, or enhance? Those that might be expected to have occurred prior to the arrival of Euro–Americans? Those that were present when the particular refuge was established? Those that are now present on the refuge? The populations that we prefer because they are endangered or provide game for hunters or for some other reason?

Gergely, et al., *A New Direction for the U.S. National Wildlife Refuges,* 20 NATURAL AREAS J. 107, 111–13 (2000).

4. If brucellosis is such an insidious, infectious disease that it threatens domestic livestock and the ranching industry, why does the USFWS resist vaccinating the elk for brucellosis? If the scientific evidence on efficacy of such a course is ambiguous, is it better to be safe than sorry? Who should bear the cost of rigorous scientific testing of the vaccine?

Is there something about the "wild" in "wildlife" that is antithetical to vaccination? Does the unnaturally high concentration of elk drawn to refuge feeding stations dispensing alfalfa pellets defeat this argument? The FWS finds non-fed elk in the area to have a prevalence rate of brucellosis of one to two percent, compared to a fed-elk prevalence rate in the refuge of twenty to thirty percent.

Is the brucellosis bacterium a species of wildlife entitled to protection for its own sake? *See* 16 U.S.C. § 668ee (defining "wildlife" to include "any member of the animal kingdom"). Should the refuges permit states to conduct insecticide spraying on refuge wetlands to control populations of mosquitoes? If so, how is that different from the brucellosis situation?

Pending litigation is currently challenging the winter feeding grounds that Wyoming operates on Forest Service and BLM lands without ever having been subject to NEPA analysis. The Refuge System laws do not apply to those feeding grounds, but the policy issues are similar. *See Robert Keiter & Peter Froelicher, Bison, Brucellosis, and Law in the Greater Yellowstone Ecosystem,* 28 LAND & WATER L.REV. 1 (1993) (recommending the phasing out of all winter feeding grounds). If winter feeding ends, ranchers will bear a higher cost as the elk graze on range used by their cattle. Is that a fair result? Another terrible disease, chronic wasting syndrome, is spreading throughout ungulates in the west. If it reaches the elk feeding grounds, mortality could result in fewer elk than would survive without the supplemental food.

5. Look at the "State authority" savings clause in the NWRSIA. 16 U.S.C. § 668dd(m). If the USFWS decides to allow public hunting or fishing on a national wildlife refuge (a matter discussed immediately below), must hunters or anglers have state licenses and conform to state seasons and bag limits? May the USFWS preempt such state laws? How? Could the FWS open the NER to hunting as an elk control mechanism and waive the state hunting license requirement? Does the court's interpretation of the savings clause rescue it from meaninglessness?

6. Why did the State frame its lawsuit in the broadest possible terms, asserting that it had primacy as a matter of constitutional law over wildlife on federal lands? After the unanimous decision in Kleppe v. New Mexico, *supra* p. 163, wasn't it clear that argument was a loser? Note that after "prompting" by the district court, the State "grudgingly" amended its complaint to challenge the USFWS decision as arbitrary and capricious under the APA.

7. Could the State have vaccinated the elk without this litigation if it did so when the elk wandered off the Refuge to private land? Would it have

made any difference whether the State knew the elk would likely wander back into the Refuge?

8. What does the "biological integrity, diversity and environmental health" mandate in the 1997 organic act 16 U.S.C. § 668dd(a)(4)(B) (and the FWS implementing policy) say about winter feeding of elk? Does the "un-naturalness" of the feeding program have any relevance in meeting the integrity, diversity, and health goals? What ought to be the desired future condition of the NER? The high concentrations of elk adversely affect plant communities on the refuge. What relevance should that have in deciding on elk population goals?

Professor Fischman has examined the mandate to maintain biological integrity, diversity, and environmental health. He concludes:

> There is no evidence in the legislative history that Congress sought to distinguish among or disaggregate the three terms. Yet, the terms together do not constitute a recognizable or coherent concept distinct from the meaning of the individual elements. The 2001 FWS policy on biological integrity, diversity, and environmental health defines three distinct yet largely overlapping categories.

Robert L. Fischman, *The Meanings of Biological Integrity, Diversity, and Environmental Health*, 44 NAT. RES. J. 989, 1005 & 1024 (2004).

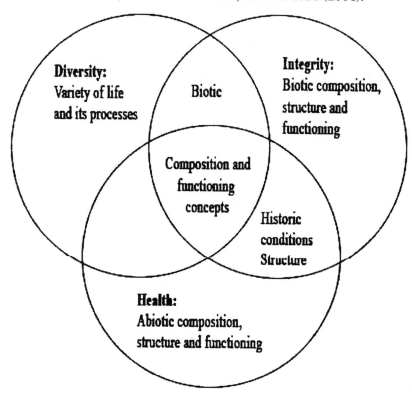

The core idea seems to be maintaining composition and function of ecosystems. That is a very ambitious task. Rather than compare refuge conditions to existing reference sites, the policy encourages managers to use historic conditions (for integrity and health) as a benchmark for success. How might this work, given the changes that have occurred in the refuge habitats over the past several hundred years? Is pre-European colonization a workable benchmark? What about the changes that occurred prior to European settlement, cause Native American hunting and fire management? How does the growing reality of human-induced climate change factor into the historic conditions standard?

In language reminiscent of the 1982 Forest Service rule that helped launch the northern spotted owl litigation halting timber sales in the Pacific Northwest, the FWS policy promises to assure that "densities of endangered or otherwise rare species are sufficient for maintaining viable populations." FWS Manual 601 § 3.14C. In contrast to NFMA, which speaks only of diversity (not integrity or health) and which qualifies the Forest Service's obligation with the phrases "where appropriate" and "to the degree practicable," 16 U.S.C. § 1604(g)(3)(B), the 1997 Refuge Improvement Act does not qualify the mandate at all (the Secretary must "ensure," period). 16 U.S.C. § 668dd(a)(4)(B). Can the FWS use this stringent mandate to justify termination of winter feeding if it can show that elk overcrowding adversely affects populations of rare riparian plants on the refuge?

Perhaps the most important consequence of the "biological integrity, diversity and environmental health" statutory mandate has been a broader geographic and temporal conservation focus in the refuge system. This has prompted the FWS to pay more attention to actions happening outside of refuges that might impact refuge resources. The external threat to public lands is one of the most serious hurdles to achieving the conservation mission on a scattershot system. Because refuges, compared to national forests and national parks, tend to concentrate in wet areas at the lower reaches of watersheds, the refuge system faces particularly difficult transboundary problems. Chemical run-off and soil erosion from upstream farming, oil and gas extraction, and residential development degrade refuges throughout the system. Is there anything the NER can do to improve winter elk habitat in the region? Improved winter habitat outside the refuge would relieve the NER from the problems of ungulate overcrowding at feeding stations.

Many decades ago a federal court of appeals acknowledged that federal power over migratory wildlife (under the Migratory Bird Treaty Act, see *infra* p. 895) authorizes the Secretary of the Interior to prohibit hunting of migratory waterfowl on nonfederal land adjacent to a national wildlife refuge. Bailey v. Holland, 126 F.2d 317 (4th Cir.1942). Protecting habitat and promoting environmental quality cannot be achieved with so simple and blunt a tool as a hunting ban. The 2001 FWS policy tells refuge managers to seek redress before local planning and zoning boards, and state administrative and regulatory agencies, if voluntary or collaborative attempts to forge solutions do not work. FWS Manual 601 § 3.20. Though tempered by cautionary language, these are nonetheless bold instructions for a traditionally timid agency. In 2004 FWS officials helped stop a 19,250–

seat concert amphitheater on a tract of land adjacent to the Minnesota Valley National Wildlife Refuge by testifying before the local county commissioners in opposition to a permit application. Should refuge managers get involved in local zoning matters? Should the NER manager campaign against conversions of ranches to residential developments that result in losses of winter elk range? Because many refuges in the lower 48 have a history of intensive use prior to establishment, their condition is far from the paragon of wilderness. Yet they may hold the potential to demonstrate to other landowners in a watershed how disturbed lands may still hold ecological potential. What relevance does this policy have for management of the NER? External threats to national parks are considered in Chapter 12B.

3. Individual Refuge Establishment Purposes

Refuges may be created or added to in several ways: by executive withdrawal, by act of Congress, by transfers from other federal agencies, and by purchase, donation, or exchange under various authorities such as the Migratory Bird Conservation Act, the Endangered Species Act, or the Land and Water Conservation Fund. Over the past century, a hodgepodge of refuge purposes, many now anachronistic, accumulated in the system. For instance, Blackbeard Island National Wildlife Refuge in Georgia is "for use as a bird refuge and as an experiment station for the acclimatization of certain foreign game birds" under Exec. Order No. 451 (Sept. 20, 1926), and Crab Orchard National Wildlife Refuge in Illinois is "for the conservation of wildlife, and for the development of the agricultural, recreational, industrial, and related purposes" under Pub. L. No. 80–361, 61 Stat. 770 (1947).

One of the principal challenges for achieving the modern System's ecological mission is how to overcome the centrifugal tendencies of individual purpose fulfillment. There is a tension between the 1997 restoration- and preservation-oriented view of the refuges as ecological networks, and the individual refuge purposes, which tend to be less beholden to the more modern ecological conceptions of conservation, and which often reflect political compromises necessary to establish particular refuges. The 1997 Act requires the system mission to yield only "if a conflict exists between the purposes of [an individual] refuge and the [system] mission." 16 U.S.C. § 668dd(a)(4)(D). Direct conflicts are rare. However, refuge managers have many competing priorities and limited funding. How should the FWS reconcile a systemic mission with individual refuge purposes that often reflect precise political compromises that were necessary to establish a refuge in the first place?

The FWS responds to this conundrum through its implementing policy, National Wildlife Refuge System Mission and Goals and Refuge Purposes, 71 Fed. Reg. 36,404, 36,405 (June 26, 2006), which states that the FWS's "first obligation is to fulfill and carry out the purpose(s) of each refuge." FWS Manual 601 § 1.5. Another section of the Goals and Refuge Purposes Policy makes even more clear that the systemic goals are to be achieved only "to the extent practicable" after the higher priority individual purposes. *Id.* at § 1.10. The decision to favor individual purposes over the system mission reflects a prioritization of more traditional "hook and bullet" objectives over the ecological principles of systemic organization.

For public land systems composed of units each established under its own authority for a specific purpose, such as the national parks and refuges, should there be some kind of commission to exercise ongoing review of old establishment purposes? Are organic acts for these systems less important in understanding management decisions than those of the Forest Service and BLM, whose individual units usually do not have individual purposes?

Some of the units of the Refuge system were originally established as "game ranges," with the dual and often conflicting purposes of grazing livestock and protecting wildlife. One such area was the Fort Peck Game Range (later redesignated the Charles M. Russell National Wildlife Range) in eastern Montana, created by a 1936 executive order (No. 7509). The order provided that the Range's "natural forage resources shall be first utilized for the purpose of sustaining in a healthy condition a maximum of" 400,000 sharptail grouse and 1,500 antelope as "primary" species, and "such nonpredatory secondary species in such numbers as may be necessary to maintain a balanced wildlife population." It went on to say that "all" the Range's forage resources "shall be available, except as herein otherwise provided with respect to wildlife, for domestic livestock" under secretarial regulation implementing the Taylor Grazing Act.

Does this language give wildlife a priority on the Game Range? All wildlife, or just the "primary" species? Do cows have equal priority? Does the Order basically leave it up to the Secretary to allocate the "natural forage resources" among these groups as she sees fit? In fact, the Secretary for a number of years gave cows and wildlife equal priority. Schwenke v. Secretary of the Interior, 720 F.2d 571, 574 n. 4 (9th Cir.1983). In 1976, Congress transferred game ranges and other conservation lands from shared jurisdiction with the BLM to the FWS alone, in order to secure better wildlife conservation. The *Schwenke* court construed the establishment language to give priority to the sharptail grouse and the antelope, up to the population numbers mentioned in the order; and after that, all wildlife and livestock had "equal priority in access to the forage resources of the Range." The court found that the 1976 statute, considered alone, did heighten the priority of wildlife over livestock in access to forage on the refuges subject to the transfer. However, because the 1976 law failed to revoke expressly the 1936 executive order creating the refuge, the individual purposes set out in the presidential document continued to control management of the refuge. The court held that the limited priority scheme established by the 1936 executive order still bound the Service despite "congressional intent to dictate a different priority." *Schwenke* at 576–77.

In the wake of *Schwenke*, what legal standards guide the refuge manager in her decision to allocate forage between cows and wildlife? Prior to 1985, FWS followed BLM's prior practice and allocated about sixty percent of the forage to livestock. In that year, the FWS completed an EIS on livestock grazing on the Range, and decided to alter the allocation so that wildlife got sixty three percent of the Range's forage and livestock thirty seven percent. NEPA compliance on the decision was upheld against attack in Schwenke v. Secretary of the Interior (II), 21 Envtl. L. Rptr. 20542 (D.Mont.1990). When establishing a new refuge, would you recommend that Congress or the President be as specific as possible in defining a compromise resource allocation? How much specificity might be possible, if the establishment could provoke opposition by those in the vicinity? Or, should establishment documents leave plenty of room for FWS adaptation to changing conditions?

Professors Coggins and Glicksman question the *Schwenke I* holding on the grounds that Congress, not the President, has superior constitutional power to set priorities for public lands. PUBLIC NATURAL RESOURCES LAW § 10D:6. Does the Property Clause (U.S. Const. art. IV, § 3) provide a constitutional basis for a rule of interpretation that would favor congressional instruments over presidential ones? Professor Fischman argues for a different rule to resolve these kinds of cases. He asserts that courts should employ canons of construction that favor more systemic rather than individualistic goals. THE NATIONAL WILDLIFE REFUGES 169–70. Does a proper understanding of organic legislation support a mode of interpretation that requires less than express revocation of old establishment documents in order to consolidate refuge management under systemic goals? If so, does the strengthening of organic legislation in the 1997 Act now tip the scales toward this mode of "centripetal interpretation"?

Should the *Wyoming* court have examined the establishment documents for the National Elk Refuge? Unlike the executive order in *Schwenke*, they do not specify a population target for elk.

4. THE COMPATIBILITY CRITERION

As noted earlier, the national wildlife refuges do not offer "refuge" in one commonly accepted meaning of the word: hunting, fishing, and trapping have become normal activities on refuge lands. Economic activities, from growing hay to mineral leasing, may also occur. Like other federal lands, some refuges are also threatened with degradation from too much recreational use.

The compatibility test did not provoke litigation until the mid–1970s. (Udall v. Tallman, *supra* p. 231, grew out of a controversy over the compatibility of oil and gas leasing in refuges, but no compatibility issues were involved in the case.) We have already seen one application of the "compatibility" standard, in National Audubon Society v. Hodel (St. Matthews Island exchange), *supra* p. 455, which arose in connection with whether a proposed exchange of Alaska Native inholdings inside refuges for other federal lands elsewhere met a statutory "public interest" test. Though the following court opinions predate the 1997 Act, they remain important for three reasons. First, they are the fullest explorations of the application of the compatibility standard. Second, they concern a refuge whose purpose derives from the most common establishment legislation, the Migratory Bird Conservation Act. Third, the Refuge Recreation Act of 1962 (RRA) remains unaltered by the 1997 Refuge Improvement Act except with respect to wildlife-dependent recreational activities. Waterskiing and some other forms of boating would be subject to the same RRA standards today as they were in 1978.

Defenders of Wildlife v. Andrus (Ruby Lake Refuge I)

United States District Court, District of Columbia, 1978.
11 Env't Rep. Cas. (BNA) 2098.

■ Judge Pratt

[In April 1978 the Fish & Wildlife Service adopted special regulations governing recreational boating in the Ruby Lake National Wildlife Refuge. Plaintiff filed this suit two months later, charging that the regulations violated the Refuge Recreation Act of 1962 (16 U.S.C. § 460k), and seeking injunctive relief against continued motorboat use in the Refuge.] * * *

Findings of Fact

I. *Ruby Lake National Wildlife Refuge.*

1.1   On July 2, 1938, by Executive Order No. 7923, President Franklin Roosevelt "reserved and set apart" the Refuge "as a refuge and breeding ground for migratory birds and other wildlife," in order to effectuate further the purposes of the Migratory Bird Conservation Act. The area so reserved and set apart * * * comprised all lands and waters within a described area of approximately 37,640 acres in Elko and White Pine Counties, Nevada. 3 Fed.Reg. 1639 (July 7, 1938).

1.2   Section 5 of the Migratory Bird Conservation Act, 15 U.S.C. § 715d, authorizes the United States to purchase, rent or otherwise reserve areas "for use as inviolate sanctuaries for migratory birds * * *." Section 6 of this Act, 16 U.S.C. § 715e, requires that easements and reservations retained by any grantor from whom the United States received title "shall be subject to rules and regulations prescribed by the Secretary of [Interior] for the occupation, use, operation, protection and administration of the areas as inviolate sanctuaries for migratory birds * * *."

1.3   The primary purpose for which the Refuge was established is for use as a refuge, breeding ground and inviolate sanctuary for migratory birds. * * *

1.6   The Refuge consists of 25,150 acres of wetlands and 12,468 acres of surrounding uplands. The wetlands portion of the Refuge consist of the 7,000–acre South Sump, which is the primary waterfowl nesting area, and the North and East Sumps, which are all maintained by a complex and intricate flowage of waters throughout the marsh basin. The average depth of water in the South Sump is approximately four feet, and in the North and East Sumps considerably less.

1.7   The management objectives of the Refuge are (1) to preserve, restore and enhance in their natural eco-systems all species of animals and plants that are endangered or threatened with becoming endangered on lands of the National Wildlife Refuge System; (2) to perpetuate the migratory bird resource for the benefit of people—to manage the refuge for an annual production of 5,000 canvasbacks and 5,000 redheads; (3) to preserve natural diversity and abundance of mammals and non-migratory birds on refuge land; and (4) to provide understanding and appreciation of fish and wildlife ecology and man's role in his environment, and to provide visitors with high quality, safe, wholesome, and enjoyable recreation which is fully compatible and consistent with, and which in no way harms or interferes with the area's primary purpose as a refuge and breeding ground for migratory birds and other wildlife.

1.8 All national wildlife refuges are maintained for the primary purpose of preserving, protecting and enhancing wildlife and other natural resources and of developing a national program of wildlife and ecological conservation and rehabilitation. These refuges are established for the restoration, preservation, development and management of wildlife and wildlands habitat; for the protection and preservation of endangered or threatened species and their habitat; and for the management of wildlife and wildlands to obtain the maximum benefits from these resources. 50 C.F.R. § 25.11(b).

II. *The Refuge Supports Canvasback and Redhead Ducks and a Diverse Population of Other Migratory Birds and Wildlife.*

2.1 The Refuge provides one of the most important habitats and nesting areas for over-water nesting waterfowl in the United States. The Refuge is particularly valuable to the canvasback and redhead duck, which use the area in approximately equal numbers for nesting and broodrearing during the spring, summer and early fall.

2.2 Continental populations of both the redhead and the canvasback duck are low and both species have suffered throughout their respective ranges from encroachment and habitat loss. In 1972, the annual winter waterfowl inventory conducted by the United States Fish and Wildlife Service showed an all time low of 179,000 canvasbacks. The redhead has faced intensive drainage programs in the prairie-parkland region of central North America, the major breeding area of this species. A more comprehensive program oriented towards habitat protection is necessary to conserve and protect these species.

2.3 The canvasback duck and the redhead duck have been listed as "migratory birds," as defined by Section 11 of the Migratory Bird Conservation Act, 16 U.S.C.A. § 715j, and are protected by the Migratory Bird Treaty Act, 16 U.S.C.A. §§ 703 to 711, and by [treaties between the U.S. and Great Britain (on behalf of Canada), Mexico, and Japan].

2.4 In addition to the canvasback and redhead duck, numerous species of waterfowl and other birds using the Refuge have been so designated as "migratory birds," including the prairie falcon, the peregrine falcon, the bald eagle, the golden eagle, the trumpeter swan, the white-faced ibis, the snowy egret, the great blue heron, the black-crowned night heron, the ruddy duck, the ringed-necked duck, the sandhill crane, the Canada goose, the coot and the cinnamon teal.

Conclusions of Law

III. *The Ruby Lake Special Regulations are Invalid in That They do not Include Appropriate Findings Necessary to Their Promulgation.*

3.1 On April 21, 1978, the Secretary of Interior promulgated the Ruby Lake Special Regulations, 50 C.F.R. § 25.34 (hereinafter referred to as "regulations").

3.2 These regulations permit year-round boating in an area designated as Zone 1 in the South Sump by boats without motors or boats with electric motors.

3.3 Beginning on July 1 on the east side and July 15 on the west side of an area designated as Zone 2 of the South Sump, and extending until December 31, boats without motors, boats with electric motors and boats with internal combustion motors of unlimited horsepower are permitted. No boat may exceed 20 miles per hour in any area or 5 miles per hour in areas so designated by the Refuge Manager.

3.4 Beginning on July 1 and extending until December 31, waterskiing is permitted on a designated area from 10 a.m. to 5 p.m. daily.

3.5 Beginning on August 1 and extending until December 31, boats without motors, boats with electric motors and boats with internal combustion motors of unlimited horsepower are permitted in an area designated as Zone 3 of the South Sump. No boat may exceed 20 miles per hour in any area or 5 miles per hour in areas so designated.

3.6 The Refuge Recreation Act of 1962 (16 U.S.C. § 460k) governs the Secretary's authority to permit recreation within the Ruby Lake National Wildlife Refuge and all other areas within the National Wildlife Refuge System, national fish hatcheries and other conservation areas administered by the Secretary for fish and wildlife purposes. The Refuge Recreation Act provides in pertinent part that:

> "In recognition of mounting public demands for recreational opportunities on areas within the National Wildlife Refuge System, * * * the Secretary of the Interior is authorized, as an appropriate incidental or secondary use, to administer such areas or parts thereof for public recreation when in his judgment public recreation can be an appropriate incidental or secondary use: Provided, That such public recreation use shall be permitted only to the extent that is practicable and not inconsistent with other previously authorized Federal operations or with the primary objectives for which each particular area is established: * * * And provided further, That none of the aforesaid refuges, hatcheries, game ranges, and other conservation areas shall be used during any fiscal year for those forms of recreation that are not directly related to the primary purposes and functions of the individual area *until the Secretary shall have determined*—
>
> (a) *that such recreational use will not interfere with the primary purposes for which the areas were established,* and
>
> (b) that funds are available for the development, operation, and maintenance of these permitted forms of recreation. This section shall not be construed to repeal or amend previous enactments relating to particular areas." (emphasis added)

3.7   In supporting enactment, Congressman Dingell stated on the floor of the House:

"The Secretary must make certain findings before he throws these areas open to public use; the bill requires him to find, for example, that there is sufficient money available to administer and protect these areas, and *he must find that the utilization for recreational use will not be harmful to the basic purpose of the refuges.*" 108 Cong.Rec. 5548 (April 2, 1962) (emphasis added).

3.8   In determining to permit recreational use of a National Wildlife Refuge, the burden of proof is necessarily on the Secretary to demonstrate that such use is incidental to, compatible with, and does not interfere with the primary purpose of the refuge as "an inviolate sanctuary for migratory birds."

3.9   The regulations violate the statutory standard because the Secretary failed to make the determination required by the statute that the permitted recreational use would not interfere with the Refuge's primary purpose as an "inviolate sanctuary for migratory birds."

3.10   The Refuge Recreation Act does not permit the Secretary to weigh or balance economic, political or recreational interests against the primary purpose of the Refuge.

3.11   When Congress has sought to authorize the weighing or balancing of competing interests it has done so explicitly.

3.12   Neither poor administration of the Refuge in the past, nor prior interferences with its primary purposes, nor past recreational uses, nor deterioration of its wildlife resource since its establishment, nor administrative custom or tradition alters the statutory standard. The Refuge Recreation Act permits recreational use only when it will not interfere with the primary purpose for which the Refuge "was established." The prior operation of the Refuge in a manner inconsistent with that purpose does not change the base point for applying the statute's standard. Past recreational use is irrelevant to the statutory standard except insofar as deterioration of the wildlife resource from prior recreational use serves to increase the need to protect, enhance and preserve the resource. Past recreational abuses may indeed require the Secretary to curtail recreational use to an even greater degree than mandated by the Refuge Recreation Act, in order to restore and rehabilitate the area promptly as required by the Secretary's existing regulations. 50 C.F.R. § 25.11(b).

IV.   *This Court Will Not Supply Findings to Support the Regulations on Behalf of the Secretary.* * * *

4.4   In adopting these regulations the Assistant Secretary balanced economic, political and recreational interests against the primary wildlife purpose of the refuge and reached a compromise.

4.5   The compromise reached by the Assistant Secretary in adopting these regulations was not supported by certain members of his staff. The former Refuge Manager, an expert in wildlife biology and management, testified in opposition to the regulation. The Deputy Associate Director for

Wildlife refused to [endorse] the regulations because in his opinion the regulations were not in the best interest of the Refuge and the resources for which it was established. * * *

[The court enjoined the regulations and ordered the Secretary to promulgate, within five days, new regulations "which permit secondary uses of Ruby Lake only insofar as such usages are not inconsistent with the primary purpose for which the refuge was established," and to "take all appropriate and necessary steps to enforce the resulting regulations."]

Defenders of Wildlife v. Andrus (Ruby Lake Refuge II)

United States District Court, District of Columbia, 1978.
455 F.Supp. 446.

■ Judge Pratt

[The Secretary quickly issued new regulations that differed from the old ones only in setting lower speed (but not horsepower) limits for powerboats. On August 18, 1978, the court threw out the new version and ordered yet another round of rulemaking. The opinion noted that approximately 30,000 boaters annually used the 7,000 acre South Sump that was the preferred nesting habitat for migratory birds. Boating was increasing dramatically; 19 percent per year in recent years. The opinion concluded:]

19.   If the regulations are permitted to continue in effect they will immediately and irreparably damage plaintiff's interests and the wildlife resources of the Refuge. The use of powerboats of unlimited horsepower on the Refuge (including for waterskiing) will directly and immediately harm the wildlife resources of the Refuge (i) by reducing submergent aquatic vegetation which is the principal food source for migratory waterfowl; (ii) by reducing macroinvertebrate populations which are the principal food sources for ducklings; (iii) by breaking up broods, by separating ducklings from their hen, by forcing broods out of brooding areas, and thereby reducing brood size; and (iv) by reducing the reproductive success of late nesting and re-nesting hens.

20.   Late nesting and re-nesting extends through September 1 of each season and occurs with sufficient frequency to be significant to the immediate and long-term productivity of the Refuge.

21(a) The level of boating use permitted by these regulations is not incidental to or compatible with, and will interfere with the primary purpose of[,] the Refuge.

(b) The suggestion that horsepower limitations would not be appropriate, and would not aid the primary purpose of the Refuge, is completely contrary to all reason and the facts of the record.

(c) The proposed speed limitations to be used in conjunction with [unlimited] horsepower are so obviously unenforceable that to rely on a speed limitation, even as high as twenty miles an hour, is unrealistic because of its very unenforceability.

Conclusions of Law

22. The regulations violate the statutory standard of the Refuge Recreation Act because the degree and manner of boating use which they would permit is not incidental or secondary use, is inconsistent, and would interfere with the Refuge's primary purpose.

23. The regulations violate the statutory standard of the Refuge Recreation Act because the degree and manner of boating use which they would permit is not practicable because of their unenforceability.

24. The Secretary's determination that the level of boating permitted by the regulations does not interfere with the Refuge's primary purpose is arbitrary and capricious.

25. Based on the record in this action, the use of boats with unlimited horsepower in the South Sump of the Refuge is inconsistent and interferes with its primary purpose as a refuge and breeding ground for migratory birds and wildlife.

NOTES AND QUESTIONS

1. What legal restrictions did the Refuge Recreation Act place on the Secretary? A typical dictionary definition is that "compatible" means "capable of existing together in harmony." Does that support the court's ruling here?

2. As a matter of law, was the unrestricted boating allowed by the Secretary prior to the 1978 regulations consistent with the statute? Note that the Refuge Recreation Act said public recreation use "shall be permitted only to the extent that is * * * not inconsistent with * * * the primary objectives for which each particular area is established * * * [and] until the Secretary shall have determined (a) that such recreational use will not interfere with the primary purposes for which the areas were established."

3. The 1966 National Wildlife Refuge Administration Act was worded somewhat differently, authorizing the Secretary to permit other uses "whenever he determines that such uses are compatible with the major purposes for which such areas were established." 16 U.S.C. § 668dd(d)(1). In Wilderness Society v. Babbitt, 5 F.3d 383 (9th Cir.1993), the court addressed whether the defendants' failure to examine the effects of cattle grazing in a wildlife refuge was "substantially justified" under the Equal Access to Justice Act, 28 U.S.C. § 2412(d)(1)(A). If it was not, the plaintiffs were eligible for attorneys fees under the Act after the government settled the lawsuit with the plaintiffs by agreeing to examine the compatibility of grazing with the Refuge's purposes. The court said:

> [T]he Service renewed annual grazing permits without regard to the incompatibility of grazing to the Refuge's purposes. As early as December 1989, the Service was aware that its grazing practices were damaging the Refuge. The Refuge Manager warned that "there is no question that current grazing practices causing this damage are negatively impacting fish and wildlife habitats and are (1.) in violation of

the refuge's executive orders and (2.) currently not compatible with the uses for which the refuges were established.''

The Refuge Manager's report did not foreclose the possibility that the Service could formulate a grazing plan that would be compatible with purposes of the Refuge. Based upon this report, however, the Service had a duty to investigate the compatibility of grazing with the Refuge's purposes prior to permitting grazing on the Refuge. Nonetheless, the Service continued its same practices, issuing grazing permits for 1990 without any compatibility determination. It made little headway in formulating a new management plan prior to the initiation of the Wilderness Society lawsuit in 1991. In light of the Refuge Manager's report, we cannot find that the Service's actions were substantially justified.

Absent the Refuge manager's December 1989 finding, was the Service's renewal of grazing permits without a finding of compatibility "substantially justified"? Judge Farris dissented from the court's ruling, construing the 1966 Refuge Act as "not specify[ing] that the Service has a duty to make a compatibility determination to permit the continuation of a preexisting use of the Refuge." Because grazing "had been permitted on the Refuge since 1936," Judge Farris opined that

> [w]ithout plain language or precedent to alert the Service to its "duty" under the Act, the Service was not unreasonable for continuing an age old practice while it formulated alternatives. * * * On the basis of a single memorandum, without benefit of trial, the majority confidently holds that the Service has breached its duty. I am troubled by the perverse incentives created by this holding and the adverse consequences it will have beyond this case. The majority tells all government agencies that if they discover a problem with one of their programs, they should never discuss it openly and frankly. If one member of an agency expresses an opinion, and the government does not immediately adopt his position, a court may later find that the agency illegally "disregarded" his advice. That is not and should not be the law.

The 1997 organic act provided that the Secretary "shall not initiate or permit a new use of a refuge or expand, renew, or extend an existing use of a refuge, unless the Secretary has determined that the use is a compatible use * * *," except that "[c]ompatibility determinations in existence on [the date of enactment] shall remain in effect until and unless modified." 16 U.S.C. § 668dd(d)(3)(A)(i) and (iv). If this language had been applied by the court in the *Wilderness Society* case, what would have been the result?

4.   The 1997 Refuge Improvement Act restated the compatibility test this way: " 'compatible use' means a wildlife-dependent recreational use or any other use of a refuge that, in the sound professional judgment of the Director, will not materially interfere with or detract from the fulfillment of the mission of the System or the purposes of the refuge." 16 U.S.C. § 668ee(1). "Sound professional judgment" was defined as "a finding, determination, or decision that is consistent with principles of sound fish and wildlife management and administration, available science and re-

sources, and adherence to the requirements of this Act and other applicable laws." *Id.* § 668ee(3).

One of the co-authors of this text opined that "[i]f this had been all that Congress chose to say on the question of compatibility, *Ruby Lake* would have been effectively overridden and the FWS would be free to do whatever it chose." Public Natural Resources Law § 14A.02. Do you agree? Would a failure to impose limits on speedboats have satisfied this standard? Note that the statute, somewhat unusually, refers to the "sound professional judgment" not of the Secretary of the Interior, but of the Director of the U.S. Fish & Wildlife Service. Like the Secretary, the Director is a political appointee, appointed by the President and subject to Senate confirmation. But unlike the Secretary, the Director is also required by statute to be, "by reason of scientific education and experience, knowledgeable in the principles of fisheries and wildlife management." 16 U.S.C. § 742b(b). Should this make a difference in how the statute is interpreted? If the Wilderness Society v. Babbitt grazing case were decided today, under the 1997 law, would you expect a different result?

Did the Ruby Lake court show sufficient deference to sound professional judgment? Note some wildlife professionals in the Department thought the first regulations were too weak, and that the "former Refuge Manager, an expert in wildlife biology and management, testified in opposition to the regulation." Is this relevant to the court's determination of whether the regulations were lawful? Conclusive on the point? The Assistant Secretary of the Interior (a political appointee with supervisory power over the Fish & Wildlife Service) made the final decision and, according to Judge Pratt's first opinion, "balanced economic, political, and recreational interests against the primary wildlife purpose of the refuge and reached a compromise." Was this relevant? Unwise? Unlawful?

5. The 1997 compatibility test eliminates the 1966 modifier of "major" on the establishment purposes against which a use is judged. It also adds the refuge system mission as an additional purpose, that an activity must not "materially interfere with or detract from." 16 U.S.C. § 668ee. Does the more recent language help or hinder the analysis?

What, for example, are the primary purposes of the Ruby Lake Refuge? Judge Pratt said (in finding 1.3 in his first opinion) that the primary purpose was as a "refuge, breeding ground and inviolate sanctuary for migratory birds." But Franklin Roosevelt's 1938 Executive Order established the Refuge "as a refuge and breeding ground for migratory birds *and other wildlife*" (emphasis added). Suppose speedboats did not threaten migratory birds (at least in seasons when the birds were not present on the Refuge) but did threaten other forms of wildlife. Does the Recreation Act's compatibility test require that speedboats be restricted? Does the 1997 compatibility criterion change the analysis of the situation where speedboat use did not threatened migratory birds but did threaten other wildlife?

6. The FWS policy implementing the compatibility standard prohibits uses that reasonably may be anticipated to fragment habitats. 65 Fed. Reg. 62,486. This is the most direct of any of the public land mandates to protect biological diversity or ecological integrity. This prohibition on fragmenta-

tion may prove to be a powerful limit on even secondary, priority public uses. Does the policy prevent the Ruby Lake Refuge from dividing the lake into zones, separated by dikes? From constructing a new "auto tour" road?

7. Today, the entire refuge is closed to boating from January 1 through June 14. The remainder of the year, boating is restricted to certain zones on the refuge, and subject to stringent limitations on the kind of motors (motorless, battery powered electric motors, or, from August 1 through December 31, boats propelled by motors with a total of ten horsepower or less).

8. Ruby Lake is typical of many of the refuges established to produce migratory birds: it is a highly manipulated system, with dikes, sump pumps, and other tools to put water and food in the right place at the right time for the birds. This is another good example the conflict between the wilderness vision of untainted nature and the refuge vision of "healthy populations." Is there a place for both kinds of nature protection on the federal public lands?

9. In McGrail & Rowley v. Babbitt, 986 F.Supp. 1386 (S.D.Fla.1997), *aff'd w/o opinion*, 226 F.3d 646 (11th Cir.2000), the court upheld the USFWS's denial of a permit to operate a commercial boat tour on Boca Grande Key in the Key West National Wildlife Refuge because it was incompatible with refuge purposes. Among other things, the plaintiff argued that the FWS was being inconsistent because it allowed another company to operate tours on another key in the Refuge. The FWS distinguished the two because it found the permitted tours were "passive and education oriented," and its customers apparently obeyed admonitions not to enter into closed areas. In contrast, the tours conducted by the company being denied permission were recreational, involving picnicking, kayaking, and wading, and passengers were supplied with sports equipment like Frisbees and paddleballs for use on the beach, and they had been observed entering closed areas. The court upheld the FWS, although it grumbled that it "might well have come to different conclusions" regarding the FWS decision to permit *any* commercial tours.

Where does recreational boating fit in? Might a speedboat operator on Ruby Lake claim that she is engaged in priority "wildlife-dependent recreational use" under the 1997 Act by occasionally fishing or observing wildlife (e.g., the flight of migratory birds disturbed by the boat)?

10. In addition to showing that a (nonwildlife-dependent) recreational activity will not interfere with the primary purpose of the refuge, the Refuge Recreation Act also requires that the Interior Secretary determine "that funds are available for the development, operation, and maintenance of these permitted forms of recreation." 16 U.S.C. § 460k(b). Does this provision prevent the FWS from committing to an authorization of a recreational activity beyond the end of the fiscal year? The refuge system receives the smallest appropriation for management of any of the four federal public land systems except the BLM. Austerity is widespread and chronic. Is a speed limit designed to protect birds effective if personnel to enforce it is lacking?

11. The Humane Society and similar groups tried to stop sport and other hunting in wildlife refuges before 1997, relying primarily on the *Ruby Lake* rationale, but failed. *See e.g.*, Humane Society v. Hodel, 840 F.2d 45 (D.C.Cir. 1988). As discussed earlier, the 1997 statute eases the compatibility determination for hunting and the other five wildlife-dependent recreational activities. It also requires a reevaluation of the compatibility of all uses whenever conditions change significantly or significant new information arises regarding the effects of the use. Under the Act the Service reevaluates most existing uses at least every ten years (except for wildlife-dependent recreational uses, where the limit is fifteen years) to determine whether they are still compatible with the mission of the System. 16 U.S.C § 668(d)(3)(B). The FWS implementing policy generally requires that where there is insufficient information to document compatibility, refuge managers should deny the use unless it is in a wildlife-dependent recreation category, in which case the refuge manager "should work with the proponent of the use to acquire the necessary information before finding the use not compatible based solely on insufficient available information." 65 Fed. Reg. 62,492 (2000).

Professor Fischman exhaustively documents the manifold ways in which the 1997 Act promotes wildlife-dependent recreational uses. The National Wildlife Refuges 94–98. Still, hunting opponents continue to challenge the FWS. Fund for Animals recently won an injunction on hunting on several refuges because the Service failed to consider the cumulative effects in its NEPA compliance. Fund for Animals v. Hall, 448 F.Supp.2d 127 (D.D.C. 2006) (overturning a series of regulations opening specific areas of the National Wildlife Refuge System to hunting). The Court suggested that the FWS needed to consider the cumulative impacts of hunting system-wide.

B. Wildlife Conservation and Management on Other Federal Lands

1. The National Park System

Unlike the refuge system, the national park system does not generally encourage hunting. In fact, the Park Service has a blanket rule against hunting, although some units of the park system are open to hunting by special legislative dispensation. The units permitting hunting are usually called national park "preserves" and are particularly common in Alaska. Fishing, on the other hand, principally "catch and release," is generally permitted in units of the national park system.

The National Park Service sometimes licenses hunting to control park wildlife populations, and this has occasionally been controversial. *See* Davis v. Latschar, 202 F.3d 359 (D.C.Cir.2000) (upholding a controlled deer hunt by park-employed shooters to control over-browsing). Often the national park wildlife cannot be isolated from the surrounding lands. The following case illustrates this situation around Yellowstone National Park, where ranchers, wildlife advocates, and state and federal agencies have long disagreed about how to manage bison.

Intertribal Bison Co-op. v. Babbitt

United States District Court, District of Montana, 1998.
25 F.Supp.2d 1135, *aff'd*, 175 F.3d 1149 (9th Cir.1999).

■ JUDGE LOVELL

* * * The Yellowstone National Park ("YNP") bison herd of 2,500 or more animals is at or above YNP carrying capacity. Particularly when the YNP bison herd exceeds Park capacity and when the Park experiences a harsh winter interfering with the herd's food supply within the Park, the herd tends to migrate north and west from the Park in search of additional forage. Uncontrolled migration of brucellosis-infected bison into Montana presents a danger to the Montana livestock industry and a health risk to humans. Migrating bison also present a significant risk of property damage outside the Park.

The YNP bison herd is genetically and numerically healthy and has recovered from the high mortality of the winter of 1996–97. The integrity and viability of the YNP herd is in no way threatened or endangered.

Genesis of 1996 Interim Plan

The size of the YNP bison herd has fluctuated repeatedly in this century. At the turn of the century the herd consisted of approximately 23 bison within the Park. The NPS imported domestic bison from Montana and Texas to enlarge the herd. The herd was managed as livestock, with YNP rangers cowboying the herd with the use of corrals and barns. By mid-century, the herd size was well over 1,000. The NPS reduced herd size to 397 animals in 1967. NPS then decided to discontinue its bison management program and allow the herd to roam free. In 1988 there were approximately 2,800 bison in the Park, and by 1995 the number reached approximately 3,900 bison.

As the YNP bison herd became larger, portions of the herd began to migrate out of the Park during harsh winters in search of food. As early as 1968, NPS embarked on a boundary protection program which involved NPS personnel shooting bison at the Park boundaries. NPS later discontinued this program, but eventually the State of Montana began a similar program on its side of the YNP boundary because of its concerns of private property damage, conflicts with humans, and disease transmission.

Montana has the right under its police powers to protect the health, safety, and welfare of its inhabitants by removing possibly infected YNP bison that migrate into Montana. *Fund for Animals, Inc. v. Lujan*, 794 F.Supp. 1015 (D.Mont.1991). In 1985 the Montana legislature authorized public hunting of migrating bison as a method of helping to control this problem. During the winter of 1988B89 large migrations of YNP bison resulted in the killing of 569 YNP bison within the State of Montana. Apparently because of negative publicity generated by these large-scale public hunts, Montana ended them and resumed control efforts of migrating bison through its agencies.

The State of Montana became increasingly dissatisfied with its boundary management role and the refusal of YNP to manage its bison. This culminated in suit against the federal government in 1995. That litigation was settled with an agreement between Montana and the United States to prepare an interim bison management plan. After preparation of an Environmental Assessment, a Finding of No Significant Impact, and final agreement by the State of Montana and the federal agencies, the 1996 Interim Plan was implemented.

The 1996 Interim Plan called for increased cooperation between the two governments and for increased responsibilities for boundary management by the NPS. Important features of the 1996 Interim Plan were that the NPS agreed to prevent bison from migrating onto private land in the Reese Creek area by capturing such bison, if necessary, and shipping them to slaughter. The 1996 Interim Plan called for increased tolerance of migrating bison on federal lands adjacent to YNP, and a program of capture and testing in the West Yellowstone area, with bison testing seronegative for brucellosis to be marked and released.

The 1996 Interim Plan also contained procedures for emergency situations. Such contingency plans were put into effect during the winter of 1996–97 when, due to harsh winter conditions, more YNP bison were destroyed than was previously contemplated.

As a result of the experience of the parties with the 1996 Interim Plan during the unusually harsh winter of 1996–97, which resulted in some 1,100 bison being killed by government personnel and an additional number dying due to weather conditions, the 1996 Interim Plan was modified. After reevaluating the circumstances of YNP bison and the proposed modifications to the Plan, the parties agreed to implement the modified plan in December, 1997 (the "1997 Interim Plan").

[The court then addressed the claims of the plaintiff Great Yellowstone Coalition in one of the cases consolidated before the court.] * * * [The] National Park Service Organic Act, 16 U.S.C. § 1[,] * * * provides that the fundamental purpose of the National Park Service is to "conserve the scenery and the natural and historic objects and the wildlife therein . . ." of the national parks. 16 U.S.C. '1. All parties agree that NPS must protect and conserve YNP bison.

Plaintiffs argue that NPS cannot destroy any YNP bison. NPS counters that part of its overall protection of the YNP bison herd may require it to destroy individual bison pursuant to the 1996 Interim Plan. NPS further argues that the alternative to the 1996 Plan is to return to indiscriminate destruction of bison as they leave the Park, as provided by the 1992 Interim Plan or as has occurred historically without the benefit of any federal-state cooperative agreement. NPS asserts that the Organic Act has provided it with broad discretion to manage and regulate the Park and its wildlife to best achieve the conservation mandate. NPS interprets its Congressional mandate to allow it to determine whether selective removal of individual bison protects and conserves the YNP bison herd. The court defers to reasonable agency interpretations of statute. *See Chevron, U.S.A., Inc. v. Natural Resources Defense Council, Inc.,* 467 U.S. 837, 843–44 (1984).

[Another section of the Park Service Organic Act, 16 U.S.C. § 3,] states that the Secretary of the Interior "may also provide in his discretion for the destruction of such animals and of such plant life as may be detrimental to the use of any of said parks, monuments, or reservation." 16 U.S.C. § 3. Plaintiffs argue that because this is the sole statute providing for destruction of wildlife in the Park, a finding of detriment is necessary before Park wildlife can be destroyed. NPS disagrees, taking the position that the conservation mandate of 16 U.S.C. § 1 provides NPS with the requisite authority to destroy wildlife in the Park. The court also notes that one other statute authorizes NPS to "sell *or otherwise dispose* of the surplus buffalo of the Yellowstone National Park herd...." 16 U.S.C. § 36 (emphasis supplied). * * *

There is no statutory requirement that the Secretary make a finding of detriment to justify the destruction of wildlife. The court agrees with NPS that pursuant to § 3 of the Organic Act and NPS policy a finding of detriment is necessary to justify a controlled harvest, but an explicit finding of detriment is not otherwise necessary to justify destruction of wildlife, especially when serving the broader conservation goals of section one of the Organic Act. It is significant that section three, unlike section one, permits destruction of YNP wildlife to serve non-conservation goals. For example, section three would permit destruction of wildlife when wildlife causes detriment to the physical facilities or structures in YNP. In this sense, section three is a broader statute because it extends beyond the conservation mandate of section one.

Plaintiffs rely on § 26 of the Yellowstone Act, which provides that "[a]ll hunting, or the killing, wounding or capturing at any time of any bird or wild animal, except dangerous animals, when it is necessary to prevent them from destroying human life or inflicting an injury, is prohibited within the limits of said park...." 16 U.S.C. § 26. This statute criminalizes poaching by members of the general public. However, this anti-poaching statute does not limit the authority of NPS to destroy YNP wildlife pursuant to properly prepared wildlife management plans, and if this were not the case there could never be controlled harvests of wildlife.

NOTES AND QUESTIONS

1. The court of appeals affirmed on the basis of the district court's opinion. In 2005 Montana returned to hunting as a tool to control the number of bison escaping Yellowstone in the winter. An official from Montana's Fish, Wildlife, and Parks Commission said that the hunt is a step toward treating bison as wildlife, "as opposed to a nuisance animal." *Montana Expands Hunt for Yellowstone Bison,* N.Y. TIMES, Nov. 13, 2006. How would Montana handle bison if it did treat the animals as nuisances? What does this imply about the status of bison as a "resource" in Yellow-

stone National Park and in Montana? What power does the NPS possess to protect bison outside of the park boundaries?

2. Is the Park responsible, legally or morally, for any damage caused by migrating bison outside the Park? Whether from brucellosis, or from trampling fences? Compare the "takings" litigation involving wild horses, Mountain States Legal Found. v. Hodel, *supra* p. 330.

3. What is the relationship between the 1872 Yellowstone Act and the 1916 Park Service Organic Act in resolving the bison case?

4. Plaintiffs in National Rifle Ass'n v. Potter, 628 F.Supp. 903 (D.D.C. 1986), failed in their attempt to overturn a regulation that restricted hunting and trapping in the national park system to areas where it was plainly mandated by federal legislation. Where park establishment legislation permits "hunting and fishing," the Park Service may prohibit trapping. Michigan United Conservation Clubs v. Lujan, 949 F.2d 202 (6th Cir.1991). The Refuge System similarly views trapping as distinct from hunting and fishing. The court in Alaska Wildlife v. Jensen, 108 F.3d 1065 (9th Cir. 1997), ruled that the NPS could allow commercial fishing in Glacier Bay National Park except in those areas of the Park designated as wilderness. But an NPS decision to ban commercial fishing in Everglades National Park was sustained in Organized Fishermen of Florida v. Hodel, 775 F.2d 1544 (11th Cir.1985).

5. The National Park Service is largely unaffected by state law in managing national parks by virtue of its preservation mandate in 16 U.S.C. § 1, the enclave status of a number of parks, and the longstanding prohibition against hunting in the parks. Its authority vis-à-vis state law may be somewhat more circumscribed on national monuments and other miscellaneous lands categories under its jurisdiction. *See, e.g.*, The Cape Hatteras National Seashore Act, 16 U.S.C. § 459a–1.

6. Sometimes the Park Service faces some truly exotic wildlife challenges. In recent years it has been trying, unsuccessfully, to eradicate oryx, imported by the state of New Mexico in the 1960s from southern Africa to enliven hunting, from the White Sands National Monument.

2. NATIONAL FOREST AND BLM PUBLIC LANDS

Grizzly bears don't vote, coyotes don't contribute to political campaigns, and all wildlife species are notoriously unresponsive to legal dictate. Hunters vote, pay the freight for fish and game agencies, and are politically powerful; consequently, wildlife regulation was primarily hunting and fishing regulation aimed at the satisfaction of participants in those sports. As a result, the law governing hunting and fishing on national forest and BLM-managed lands consists mostly of bodies of state administrative rules specifying who can shoot or angle for what species by what methods with what success at which times in what places. State wildlife agencies are financed by license fees and taxes paid directly and indirectly by sportsmen. State regulations have historically tended to favor encouragement of sport to the asserted detriment of "non-game" species and other values. This is changing, albeit slowly; stocking and artificial propagation of fish and wildlife are still usually undertaken primarily for the benefit of game species.

From its inception, the Forest Service regarded wildlife as one of the major forest resources to be managed and protected like timber or watershed resources. This understanding was formalized in the 1960 Multiple–Use Sustained–Yield Act, declaring that "fish and wildlife" is one of the five resources to which "due consideration shall be given." 16 U.S.C. §§ 528–529. Section 528 also disclaims any intent to affect "the jurisdiction or responsibilities of the several States with respect to wildlife and fish on the national forests." There has long been no doubt, however, that the Forest Service need not comply with state law when it takes wildlife for federal management purposes on lands under its jurisdiction. In Hunt v. United States, 278 U.S. 96 (1928), for example, the Court summarily rejected Arizona's claim that the Secretary of Agriculture could not kill excess deer in violation of state law on the Kaibab National Forest and Game Reserve.

Until the enactment of the Federal Land Policy and Management Act (FLPMA) in 1976, BLM had no generic legal mandate with respect to wildlife, and state hunting and fishing laws generally applied. FLPMA generally gives BLM authority over wildlife comparable to that of the Forest Service, for wildlife is one of BLM's multiple uses. *See* 43 U.S.C. § 1702(c).

The relationship between state and federal wildlife law on national forests and BLM lands is now set by FLPMA § 302(b), 43 U.S.C. § 1732(b). The tangled language and history of this provision is a measure of the states' concern with protecting their traditional authority over hunting and fishing on BLM and Forest Service "multiple use" lands. Indeed, the states' political power on this single issue nearly derailed, at the last minute, FLPMA itself, after six years of active congressional deliberation and compromise on a wide variety of issues. The following summary nicely illustrates how the legislative process can fail to yield crisp answers to politically controversial questions, especially those involving "states' rights."

a. *The statute.* After providing that the Secretary of the Interior "shall manage the public lands under principles of multiple use and sustained yield," and setting out other management prerogatives and restrictions, the statute continues, in 43 U.S.C. § 1732(b), by piling *proviso* upon *proviso*:

> *Provided further,* That nothing in this Act shall be construed as authorizing the Secretary [of the Interior or of Agriculture] * * * to require Federal permits to hunt and fish on public lands or on lands in the National Forest System and adjacent waters or as enlarging or diminishing the responsibility and authority of the States for management of fish and resident wildlife. However, the Secretary [of the Interior or of Agriculture] * * * may designate areas of public land and of lands in the National Forest System where, and establish periods when, no hunting or fishing will be permitted for reasons of public safety, administration, or compliance with provisions of applicable law.

Except in emergencies, any regulations of the Secretary concerned relating to hunting and fishing pursuant to this section shall be put into effect only after consultation with the appropriate State fish and game department.

b. *The House Committee Report.* The House-passed version of the bill permitted the secretary to close lands to hunting and fishing only for "reasons of public safety." The Committee report on that bill (H.Rep. No. 94–1163, 94th Cong., 2d Sess. 6 (1976)) explained that the bill

provides that hunting and fishing will be permitted in accordance with Federal and State laws and that no Federal permits for hunting or fishing are authorized by this section. It permits the Secretaries to close areas to hunting and fishing for reasons of public safety. The Secretaries are expected to use the authority granted by the bill to close areas only if essential to the public safety, and then only for the shortest periods needed to accomplish this purpose. Protection of the public safety includes prevention and avoidance of hazards to persons, animals, and property.

c. *The Senate Committee Report.* The Senate-passed version of the bill provided simply that nothing in the bill "shall be construed as authorizing the Secretary to require any Federal permit to hunt or fish on the [public lands]." The Committee Report (S.Rep. No. 94–583, 94th Cong., 1st Sess. 42 (1975)) explained:

" * * * [H]unting and fishing will continue under State control and State licenses or permits. Of course, this does not foreclose the Secretary's authority to limit access to [BLM and national forest] lands where necessary to protect the resources or users of the lands. This includes situations where there are fire hazards or where discharge of firearms would endanger human safety."

d. *The Conference Committee Report.* The Conference Committee's reconciliation of the differences between the House and Senate bills were explained in the Conference Committee Report (H.Rep. No. 94–1724, 94th Cong., 2d Sess. 60 (1976)) as follows:

The conferees authorize the two Bureaus to ban hunting and fishing for reasons of public safety, administration, and compliance with applicable law. The word "administration" authorizes exclusion of hunting and fishing from an area in order to maintain supervision. It does not authorize exclusions simply because hunting and fishing would interfere with resource-management goals.

e. *Floor Discussion.* Once the bill reported by the Conference Committee reached the floor of the House and the Senate, key legislators added some "spin" to the bill's impact on state-federal relations on hunting and fishing. Senator Lee Metcalf of Montana, Chairman of the Conference Committee, stated on the Senate floor (122 Cong.Rec. 34511 (1976)):

Mr. METCALF. * * * Unfortunately, in attempting to define the term "administration," the statement of managers confuses the issue and could be wrongly interpreted to prevent the Secretary from protecting the public lands.

Traditionally, the States have regulated fishing and hunting or resident species of wildlife. The BLM and the Forest Service have not attempted to manage resident species of wildlife, but have focused on management of their habitat. This bill does nothing to change that.

The language of the statement of the managers could be interpreted as so narrowing the definition of "administration" that the agency would be unable to close an area to hunting even where a number of species is drastically reduced. Carried further this language could be interpreted to mean that an area which was used for habitat research could not be closed to hunting or fishing "simply because hunting and fishing would interfere with resource management goals."

In this legislation for the first time we are giving BLM basic statutory authority to manage the public lands on a multiple-use basis. Two of those uses are hunting and fishing, but they should not take precedence over all other uses. Further, it makes no sense to give an agency authority and then to tie its hands.

When this matter was discussed by the conferees, the right—indeed the responsibility—of BLM and the Forest Service to manage wildlife habitat was agreed to by all. I believe the language in the statement of managers could be interpreted differently and thus does not accurately reflect the conferees' agreement on this issue.

On the House floor the next day, Representative John Melcher of Montana, Chairman of the Subcommittee of the House Interior Committee that handled the bill, engaged in the following colloquy with a key advocate for environmental interests, Representative John Seiberling of Ohio (122 Cong. Rec. 34217 (1976)):

Mr. SEIBERLING. * * * [I]n attempting to define the term "administration," the conference report language confuses the issues. * * * [T]he term "administration" * * * certainly would include the proprietary right of [federal] agencies as landlord to manage wildlife habitat, would it not?

Mr. MELCHER. Yes. The intent of the bill and the intent of the conference report is to assure that wildlife habitat management, and wildlife itself, are included in the management on our Federal lands.

We do not, however, intend to interfere with the States' prerogatives in setting the seasons for hunting of wildlife and wildfowl. On that score the Federal agencies go back to what has been left as State prerogatives, but the general management of wildlife habitat is expected, and also is a Federal responsibility.

Mr. SEIBERLING. I would certainly concur * * *. I would like to ask one further question. Would the gentleman agree that, consistent with the multiple-use policy of this legislation, management of wildlife habitat with that exception is a responsibility of the BLM and Forest Service on public lands?

Mr. MELCHER. Yes, we view wildlife as part of the resources on our Federal lands.

Mr. SEIBERLING. Therefore, I take it that the gentleman would agree that the BLM and the Forest Service could close lands under their jurisdiction to hunting and fishing for reasons related to the management of the wildlife habitat?

MR. MELCHER. Yes, I would agree to that, but we do expect to cooperate in all instances possible with the State Fish and Game Commissions to allow those authorities to set hunting seasons and to set requirements for hunting and fishing.

The meaning of this statutory section was quickly tested in court and ultimately led, after litigation that was, fittingly, as tangled as the legislative maneuvering that preceded it, to the next case. Two questions were raised in the litigation: (1) Did the Secretary of the Interior have authority under FLPMA § 302(b) to close federal BLM-managed lands in Alaska to a state wolf hunting program, and if so, (2) did NEPA apply to the Secretary's decision? Reproduced here is that portion addressing the FLPMA issue.

Defenders of Wildlife v. Andrus (Alaska Wolf Kill)

United States Court of Appeals, District of Columbia, 1980.
627 F.2d 1238.

■ Judge McGowan

On February 16, 1979, the Alaska Department of Fish and Game (ADFG) announced a program whose aim was to kill from aircraft 170 wolves (approximately sixty percent of the wolf population) in an area of 35,000 square miles in the interior part of the state. Many, perhaps most, of the wolves were to be killed on federal lands for which the Department of the Interior is responsible. On February 23, counsel for one of the appellees * * * asked the Department to prepare an environmental impact statement for Alaska's program before allowing it to begin. The Department, however, did not exercise whatever authority it may have to stop the program and did not prepare an impact statement. On March 12, appellees—organizations and individuals interested in the preservation of the environment in general and of wildlife in particular—filed a complaint asking for declaratory and injunctive relief against appellants—the Secretary and two other officials of the Department of the Interior.

The complaint predicted that, although the wolf hunt was proposed in order to increase the number of moose in the region by decreasing the numbers of their major predator, it would in fact weaken the moose herds by ending a "culling process [which] is natural selection in action, and [which] assures survival of the fittest moose . . ." and would devastate the wolf packs even beyond the ADFG's estimates. This interference with these two major species, the complaint continued, would disrupt the ecology of the entire area.

The complaint asserted that [FLPMA] authorizes the Secretary of the Interior to prevent the killing of wildlife on federal lands and requires him to evaluate whether he must intervene if he is fully to serve the environmental concerns of the Act. The complaint claimed as one of its "Violations of Law" that appellants failed to make that evaluation. * * *

On March 13, 1979, the United States District Court for the District of Columbia issued a temporary restraining order which enjoined appellants to "take all steps necessary to halt the aerial killing of wolves by agents of the State of Alaska" on the relevant federal lands. Although Alaska has apparently continued to kill wolves on its own lands, it has discontinued doing so on federal lands.

* * *

FLPMA * * * was enacted "to provide the first comprehensive, statutory statement of purposes, goals, and authority for the use and management of about 448 million acres of federally-owned lands administered by the Secretary of the Interior through the Bureau of Land Management." S.Rep. No. 94–583, 94th Cong., 1st Sess. 24 (1975). As such, it certainly imposes on the Secretary [as the district court found,] a general duty "to plan for and manage federal land and resources." However, the District Court's reasoning seems to us to upset an allocation of functions Congress carefully and explicitly made in FLPMA, for Congress there assigned the states the primary responsibility for the management of wildlife programs within their boundaries.

It is unquestioned that "the States have broad trustee and police powers over wild animals within their jurisdictions," Kleppe v. New Mexico, 426 U.S. 529, 545 (1976). Neither is it questioned that * * * Congress may, if it wishes, pre-empt state management of wildlife on federal lands [pursuant to the Property Clause]. Despite its ability to take control into its own hands, Congress has traditionally allotted the authority to manage wildlife to the states. For instance, in the Multiple Use–Sustained Yield Act of 1960, Congress declared:

> It is the policy of the Congress that the national forests are established and shall be administered for outdoor recreation, range, timber, watershed, and wildlife and fish purposes. * * * Nothing herein shall be construed as affecting the jurisdiction or responsibilities of the several States with respect to wildlife and fish on the national forests. * * *

16 U.S.C. § 528.[7]

* * *

7. When Congress has wished to change this traditional allocation of tasks, it has done so self-consciously and precisely, as the Endangered Species Act of 1973, 16 U.S.C. § 1531 et seq., demonstrates. * * * In the Act itself, Congress specifically provided:

> Any State law or regulation which applies with respect to the importation or exportation of, or interstate or foreign commerce in, endangered species or threatened species is void to the extent that it may effectively (1) permit what is prohibited by this chapter or by any regulation which implements this chapter, or (2) prohibit what is authorized pursuant to an exemption or permit provided for in this chapter or in any regulation which implements this chapter. This chapter shall not otherwise be construed to void any State law or regulation which is intended to conserve migratory, resident, or introduced fish or wildlife, or to permit or prohibit sale of such fish or wildlife.

Far from attempting to alter the traditional division of authority over wildlife management, FLPMA broadly and explicitly reaffirms it. [The court then proceeded to quote the statutory section and parts of the legislative history set out in the text, *supra*.]

The first quoted sentence of section 302(b) self-evidently places the "responsibility and authority" for state wildlife management precisely where Congress has traditionally placed it—in the hands of the states. The second quoted sentence of the section arguably permits ("may"), but certainly does not require ("shall"), the Secretary to supersede a state program, and even when he does so, it must be after consulting state authorities. We are simply unable to read this cautious and limited permission to intervene in an area of state responsibility and authority as imposing such supervisory duties on the Secretary that each state action he fails to prevent becomes a "Federal action." A state wildlife-management agency which must seek federal approval for each program it initiates can hardly be said to have "responsibility and authority" for its own affairs.

Appellees remind us that FLPMA directs the Secretary to "manage the public lands under principles of multiple use and sustained yield," 43 U.S.C. § 1732(a), and that

"multiple use" means * * * a combination of balanced and diverse resource uses that takes into account the long-term needs of future generations for renewable and nonrenewable resources, including, but not limited to, recreation, range, timber, minerals, watershed, wildlife and fish, and natural scenic, scientific and historical values. * * *

43 U.S.C. § 1702(c). * * *

Nevertheless, * * * Section 302(b) * * * expressly commands that "nothing in this Act" enlarges or diminishes the state's responsibility for managing wildlife. We are therefore unable to conclude that appellees' citations to FLPMA should alter our understanding of the Secretary's obligation to prepare an environmental impact statement when he declines to exercise the power which FLPMA arguably gives him to preempt state wildlife-management programs.[10] * * *

16 U.S.C. § 1535(f). Even in this Act, however, the House Committee report continued the comments quoted above by reaffirming the importance of state management of wildlife:

[T]he states are far better equipped to handle the problems of day-to-day management and enforcement of laws and regulations for the protection of endangered species than is the Federal government. It is true, and indeed desirable, that there are more fish and game enforcement agents in the state system than there are in the Federal government.

H.Rep. No. 93–412, 93d Cong., 1st Sess. 7 (1973).

10. It is possible to read appellees' complaint as alleging that the Secretary has violated duties under FLPMA quite apart from FLPMA's effect on his obligation to prepare an environmental impact statement. However, we do not understand the District Court to have done more than instruct the Secretary to halt the killing of wolves until he has prepared an environmental impact statement. Therefore, although our discussion of FLPMA has necessarily touched on the limited nature of the Secretary's obligations under the Act, we do not otherwise reach the question of whether he has violated it.

NOTES AND QUESTIONS

1.   Where does this decision leave matters (i.e., does the Secretary have authority under FLPMA to halt the wolf kill)? Did the court decide the question? Did the court hold that FLPMA furnished the Secretary with no authority, or no duty, to close the lands to the hunt?

2.   Would the result be the same if the plaintiffs had argued that the Secretary's failure to halt the wolf kill was a breach of his basic duty to protect the resources on the public lands and was thus arbitrary and capricious? See footnote 10. Another part of FLPMA, § 302(b), provides: "In managing the public lands the Secretary shall, by regulation or otherwise, taken any action necessary to prevent unnecessary or undue degradation of the lands." Do the "lands" include the wolves? If Alaska proposed to shoot every wolf on the BLM lands, could the Secretary have found that "undue degradation"?

3.   The district court had offered this view of FLPMA § 302(b):

[T]he Act must be construed to mean that the Secretary does have the authority to close the federal lands to the instant wolf kill. By providing that the states' responsibility was not diminished by the Act, Congress intended to preserve to the states their traditional control over sport hunting and fishing seasons and the licensing of such hunting and fishing. However, by authorizing the Secretary to close the federal lands to hunting for public safety, administration and law enforcement reasons, Congress intended to vest defendants with some authority over the use of federal lands for hunting. The administration of the public lands includes their administration for multiple-use purposes, such as wildlife preservation, so that the Secretary can prevent, under certain circumstances, hunting on federal lands when a multiple use such as wildlife is seriously threatened. The court will not at this time delineate the exact parameters of the Secretary's authority to close federal lands to non-sport, state licensed hunting. The court determines only that the Secretary has the authority to prevent persons from coming on federal lands to hunt wildlife for purposes other than sport or subsistence where, as plaintiffs have shown to be true in the instant case, such hunting presents a serious threat to the existence of a form of wildlife on these lands, at least until BLM has the opportunity to assess and consider the impact of the proposed hunt and seek the cooperation of the state game officials.

Defenders of Wildlife v. Andrus, 9 Env't Rep. Cas. 2111 (D.D.C.1977). Was the court of appeals just disagreeing with the district court here about whether the facts showed that the wolf hunt was, in the words of the district court, a "serious threat" to the continued existence of the wolves on federal land?

4.   FLPMA gives the federal officials power to close federal lands to hunting and fishing for "reasons of public safety, administration, or compliance with provisions of applicable law." What might be examples of each of these reasons for prohibiting hunting and fishing on federal lands otherwise authorized under state law? For example, could the Secretary close

lands to hunting because of a concern about endangered species? Fire danger? Disease spreading? What does "administration" mean in this context? Not enough personnel at hand to properly supervise and regulate activities on the ground?

5.   Is the statutory text dispositive? If not, does the legislative history clarify Congress's meaning? Or should the court resort to the history at all?

6.   The court reads the phrase "nothing in this Act shall be construed * * * as enlarging or diminishing the responsibility and authority of the States for management of fish and resident wildlife" as giving states "responsibility and authority for state wildlife management." Is that necessarily correct? Does it depend on what the prior jurisdictional relationships were? How does the FLPMA savings clause compare to the one in the refuge system organic act, analyzed in Wyoming v. United States, *supra* p. 852. 16 U.S.C. § 668dd(m).

7.   Suppose the Secretary of the Interior had proposed a BLM wolf kill program in order to promote caribou and moose populations or other values and uses of the public lands. Would he have to comply with state law? *Cf.* Hunt v. United States, 278 U.S. 96 (1928).

8.   Aside from history and tradition, what justification is there for state wildlife management jurisdiction on federal lands? The need for local decisions to control local resources? More or better management or enforcement personnel?

3.   Predator Control

Predator control to protect ranchers' livestock from depredation has had a long if not particularly illustrious history on federal lands. And, as the following case illustrates, it introduces yet another governmental agency into the mix—the Department of Agriculture's Animal and Plant Health Inspection Service (APHIS). The APHIS Animal Damage Control unit is now called "Wildlife Services."

Southern Utah Wilderness Alliance v. Thompson

United States District Court, District of Utah, 1993.
811 F.Supp. 635.

■ Judge Anderson

* * * The Dixie and Fishlake National Forests support numerous types of wildlife and serve as grazing areas for livestock. Historically, Animal Damage Management ("ADM") decisions in these forests have led to conflicts between the supporters of the wildlife and of the domestic populations, especially because the ADMs authorize Animal Damage Control ("ADC"), which involves the control and reduction of predator species population, such as cougars and coyotes, through non-lethal and lethal control methods. Despite these conflicts, ADC programs have been conducted successfully since 1973, excluding 1991 and 1992.

Various statutes, regulations, and plans guide the implementation of ADC programs. Federal authority for ADM programs emanates from the Animal Damage Control Act of 1931, 7 U.S.C. §§ 426 to 426b (the "ADCA"), which directs the Secretary of Agriculture to "conduct campaigns for the destruction" of animals injurious to agriculture and livestock on the national forest and the public domain. Authority to conduct ADC programs currently resides with the Animal and Plant Health Inspection Service—Animal Damage Control ("APHIS—ADC").

The National Forest Management Act, 16 U.S.C. § 1604(i) (1988) ("NFMA"), authorizes the Forest Service to manage land designated as National Forests and assess the environmental impact of ADC programs. The Forest Service Manual ("FSM") * * * provides further guidance for implementation of ADM programs. In the FSM, the Forest Service recognizes the authority of the APHIS–ADC to conduct animal damage management services. The FSM requires both the Forest Service and the APHIS–ADC to reduce the damage done to wildlife by predation and to conduct ADM activities when predation causes or threatens to cause damage to livestock.

This shared responsibility and coordinated effort is memorialized in a Memorandum of Understanding ("MOU") prepared at the national level between the Forest Service and the APHIS–ADC. The MOU details the respective authority of each division. Generally, the APHIS–ADC is responsible for documenting predation loss and conducting the actual predation control pursuant to the ADCA, and the Forest Service is responsible for managing the land under its jurisdiction and for insuring compliance with environmental statutes.

Notwithstanding federal jurisdiction in this area, the states retain a significant amount of authority. State law authorizes ranchers with livestock on national forest allotments to protect their herds from predation. State law plays an important role in predator control in other ways. For example, federal statutes provide that state civil and criminal jurisdiction extends to forest reserves. 16 U.S.C. § 480 (1988). This jurisdiction includes the application of state wildlife and game laws to hunting, trapping, and fishing activities on the national forests.

* * * [B]ecause of this overlapping authority and of the possible conflict in state and federal predator control programs, both the Dixie and the Fishlake National Forest Plans call for cooperation between the state and federal agencies responsible for predator control.

In establishing an ADC program, the Forest Service is subject to other statutory constraints [found in the NFMA, and in NEPA, and it must not be arbitrary and capricious under the Administrative Procedure Act]. * * *

On April 25, 1991, Thompson, the supervisor of the Dixie National Forest, issued a [decision] * * * which authorized a full range of non-lethal and lethal control methods, including aerial gunning, a type of lethal predator control in which predators are tracked and shot from a helicopter. The decision requires ranchers to use a combination of the following non-lethal control measures: using of guard dogs; changing bed grounds daily;

having the herder camp with the herd; disposing of dead sheep at least one-half mile away from the grazing band; using more than one herder with the band; avoiding areas where historically predation has been high; using experienced herders; and using more and better quality dogs. Under the [decision], the rancher must diligently apply non-lethal control measures before the Forest Service will authorize lethal control. When non-lethal measures prove ineffective, the forest supervisor then has available a full range of lethal control measures, including leghold traps and snares, hunting by calling and shooting, denning,[1] the use of hunting dogs, M–44s,[2] and the most objectionable measure, aerial gunning.[3] [Plaintiffs sought to enjoin the decision alleging numerous violations of law.] * * *

In establishing the need for injunctive relief, the court balances the last three requirements: (1) whether, in the absence of injunctive relief, Plaintiffs are threatened with irreparable injury; (2) whether Plaintiffs' potential injury outweighs any damage to Defendants; and (3) whether an injunction will be adverse to the public interest. Plaintiffs assert three types of irreparable harm: (1) that the ADCs threaten the viability of the coyote population; (2) that they lose enjoyment of recreational land and suffer psychological pain when lethal predator control is occurring; and (3) that the forest supervisors failed to follow NEPA * * *. Plaintiffs further contend that the permittees will suffer no further harm until spring because sheep predation ceases during the winter months. Contrariwise, the government asserts a long list of potential harms, including the threat to permittees' economic viability and the danger to wildlife from permittees' self-help efforts.

The court finds that the balance of harms does not "tip decidedly" in favor of Plaintiffs, but rather that it tips in favor of the permittees and the public. Injunctive relief would threaten permittees' interests in three ways. First, although predation loss varies from permittee to permittee, the record reveals a trend toward increased predation loss. This is evidenced by the fact that permittees are experiencing losses in allotments that have never suffered predation before. Second, actual losses to predation are much greater than confirmed losses. Various factors, including terrain and herd movement, make it impossible to assess the actual loss, but the court finds that predation loss is much greater than confirmed losses. Third, increased predation loss, the predominant reason why ranchers leave the sheep business, threatens the economic viability of the permittees.

Further, injunctive relief would not serve the public interest. The ADCA directs the Secretary of Agriculture to "conduct campaigns for the destruction" of animals injurious to agriculture and livestock on the national forest and the public domain. 7 U.S.C. §§ 426 to 426b (1988). By contrast, the State of Utah has protected two predators: (1) cougars and (2) black bears. The state, however, has not protected coyotes, but rather regulates coyotes as a predatory animal. Coyote regulation extends to federal lands, including national forest land. Because coyotes are a non-

---

1. Denning involves the killing of coyote pups in the den.

2. M–44s eject a cloud of sodium cyanide gas when activated by the coyote.

3. Aerial gunning is authorized only in the winter months and only in areas where other lethal methods have been unsuccessful.

protected predatory animal, ranchers suffering predation loss may practice predatory control methods against them. Thus, even if the court were to grant the injunction, the permittees may, by law, exterminate predators in order to protect their livestock. Therefore, injunctive relief could become a two-edged sword cutting against the public interest: first, by restricting the government from achieving its statutory objective; and second, by transferring the authority to conduct predator control to those ill-suited to conduct it, the permittees. This self-help situation would create a substantial risk of irreparable harm to the public interest.

Finally, Plaintiffs will suffer no irreparable injury because, despite its contrary contention, even with the ADC programs, the coyote population will remain viable. * * *

* * *

Plaintiffs argue that the EAs violate the APA because the respective forest supervisors have not established the need for the ADC program. Each forest supervisor must determine need based on studies conducted concerning that forest. Here, Plaintiffs contend, the forest supervisors have not assessed need beyond the word of the permittees.

Even then, Plaintiffs argue that the supervisors should establish some objective criteria for establishing need. For example, need for predator control might exist when the economic viability of the permittees is threatened by predation or when loss to predation reaches some percentage, such as five percent. Plaintiffs also assert that the ADCs have no rational basis because the need for the ADCs was never studied and is, therefore, uncertain, and because the effectiveness of the ADCs is open to dispute. In response, the government contends that the ADC programs are both necessary and effective.

Turning first to the need for the ADCs, the agency need not show that a certain level of damage is occurring before it implements an ADC program. In other words, it is not necessary to establish a criteria, such as economic viability of the permittees or percentage loss of a herd, to justify the need for an ADC. Chapter 2650.3 of the Forest Service Manual establishes a policy of animal damage management "when necessary to accomplish multiple-use objectives." This policy allows for control activities in two circumstances: (1) when predators threaten "public health or safety"; and (2) when predators "cause or threaten to cause damage to threatened or endangered animals or plants, other wildlife, permitted livestock, or other resources, on National Forest System lands or private property." Id. "In evaluating the need for and in conducting animal damage management programs", the forest supervisor is instructed to "weigh the social, esthetic [sic], and other values of wildlife along with economic considerations." Hence, to establish need for an ADC, the forest supervisors need only show that damage from predators is threatened.

In this case, the record indicates that actual predation damage was occurring in both the Dixie and Fishlake National Forests. Consequently, the need for the ADC program is established. Moreover, the forest supervisors sought public comment and considered the competing social and economic values in evaluating the need for an ADC. Therefore, Plaintiffs have failed to show that the ADC was not needed.

Similarly, although disagreement exists concerning the effectiveness of predator control programs, the record establishes a rational basis for effectiveness. The supervisors have consulted numerous studies that establish the effectiveness of ADC programs. Further, they have discretion to decide when enough information has been gathered. Accordingly, this court will not second-guess the assessment of the forest supervisors concerning the effectiveness of the ADCs.

Finally, Plaintiffs argue that the ADCs violate the APA because they are contrary to the NFMA. 16 U.S.C. § 1604(i) (1988). Under the NFMA, the Forest Service must act in accordance with the forest plan promulgated for each forest. The respective forest plans permit predator control if needed. Plaintiffs assert that the ADCs violate the forest plans because they contain no objective analysis of the need for predator control. The court, however, has already found that the need for the ADCs was established because of actual and threatened damage to livestock. Therefore, Plaintiffs have failed to show that the ADCs are inconsistent with the respective forest plans or that the programs endanger the diversity of wildlife in the forests.

The record supports the hardiness of the coyote and attributes this hardiness to the coyotes['] adaptability and rapid reproductive capability. To jeopardize the viability of the coyote population, seventy-five percent of that population would have to be eradicated yearly for fifty years. Under the worst case scenario, the cumulative impact on the coyote population will be no more than a forty percent loss. Id. Such losses will not endanger the coyote population. Therefore, the court finds that the ADCs as embodied in the EAs do not violate the APA. * * *

NOTES AND QUESTIONS

1. Should the court have demanded more evidence on the need for this program? More evidence that the program was effective?

2. Given the hardiness of the coyote, is the entire Animal Damage Control program a futile effort? Should the government acquiesce to the ebb and flow of predator-prey dynamics? To protect livestock, wolves, mountain lions, coyotes, bobcats, and eagles were largely eliminated around the Grand Canyon early in the 20th century, and the deer population exploded twenty-fold in fewer than two decades, leading to a government program to kill large numbers of deer. See Hunt v. United States, 278 U.S. 96 (1928). The reintroduction of wolves into Yellowstone National Park caused the coyote population to diminish substantially. Is there a policy justification any more for eliminating predators on the federal lands in order to protect livestock?

NOTE: PROTECTING SUBSISTENCE USES OF WILDLIFE RESOURCES ON FEDERAL LANDS

In some situations, federal lands support wildlife taken by subsistence hunters, fishers, and trappers. Besides Indian hunting, fishing, and gathering rights that are sometimes preserved on federal lands, a large number of rural Alaskans, mostly Native, rely on the subsistence take of fish, especially salmon, and big game. (An entire title of the Alaska National Interest Lands Conservation Act (ANILCA) is devoted to codifying a preference for rural Alaskans to engage in subsistence hunting and fishing on federal lands in Alaska. 43 U.S.C. §§ 3111–3126.) ANILCA not only establishes a preference for subsistence uses, id. § 3114, but also requires federal land management agencies to evaluate the effects on "subsistence uses and needs," and alternatives when "determining whether to withdraw, reserve, lease, or otherwise permit the use, occupancy, or disposition" of federal lands. *Id.* § 3120(a). Any such decision that would "significantly restrict subsistence uses" requires public notice and hearing and a determination that

> (A) such a significant restriction of subsistence uses is necessary, consistent with sound management principles for the utilization of the public lands, (B) the proposed activity will involve the minimal amount of public lands necessary to accomplish the purposes of such use, occupancy, or other disposition, and (C) reasonable steps will be taken to minimize adverse impacts upon subsistence uses and resources resulting from such actions.

In Hoonah Indian Ass'n v. Morrison, 170 F.3d 1223 (9th Cir.1999), the court upheld a Forest Service decision to go ahead with two timber sales despite objections from Native groups that subsistence resources would be significantly impaired. The Forest Service had estimated that the deer habitat capabilities in the area of the sales would decrease by two percent and seven percent, respectively. It went on to assume (as did the parties) that these sales would, in combination with other sales involving timber on both federal lands and lands owned by Native corporations, "significantly restrict subsistence uses." The court agreed with the U.S. that the word "necessary" in the statute does not prohibit timber sales that are within the agency's discretion. Instead, it interpreted the statute to mean that a "significant restriction of subsistence uses might [be] * * * necessary to conform to sound management principles for such 'utilization.'" Thus the Forest Service could find that the sale is necessary because the local economy was substantially dependent on a viable timber industry. The court also rejected the Natives' argument that the sales did not conform to the statutory requirement of involving the "minimal amounts of public lands necessary." The court said that the "measure of * * * what must be 'minimal' in the statutory language is 'the purposes of such ... disposition,' not minimization of impact on subsistence. The purpose of the disposition was to sell timber."

The program has been enmeshed in controversy for well over a decade. Consistent with its general tenderness toward state game and fish programs, Congress in ANILCA authorized the federal government to delegate responsibility for administering the preference to the state of Alaska, so long as it met the terms of the federal preference. The delegation was made shortly after ANILCA was enacted, but within a few years the Alaska Supreme Court ruled that the state constitution forbade the state from acknowledging a preference because it provided open access to fish and game. McDowell v. State, 785 P.2d 1 (Alaska 1989). The federal government then reassumed responsibility for administering the preference on federal lands, but initially took a narrow view of what constituted federal land to which the subsistence preference applied; specifically excluding most waters, which rendered the preference for subsistence fishing mostly meaningless. Alaska natives challenged the exclusion in federal court, and eventually the Clinton Administration reversed course, taking the position that reserved water rights were enough of a federal property interest to justify applying the subsistence preference to waters in or bordering federal conservation units (such as units of the national park, forest, and wildlife refuge systems) in the state. The Ninth Circuit eventually upheld this approach after tortuous litigation. *See* Katie John v. United States, 247 F.3d 1032 (9th Cir.2001) (en banc).

C. THE MIGRATORY BIRD TREATY ACT (MBTA)

One of the earliest of the federal wildlife laws is the Migratory Bird Treaty Act of 1918, 16 U.S.C. §§ 703–711, the statute deemed constitutional in the landmark case of Missouri v. Holland. Its key provision reads, in pertinent part:

> Unless and except as permitted by regulations made as hereinafter provided in this subchapter, *it shall be unlawful at any time, by any means or in any manner, to* pursue, hunt, *take*, capture, or kill, possess, offer for sale, sell, offer to barter, barter, offer to purchase, purchase, deliver for shipment, ship, export, import, cause to be shipped, exported, or imported, deliver for transportation, transport or cause to be transported, carry or cause to be carried, or receive for shipment, transportation, carriage, or export, *any migratory bird*, any part, nest, or egg of any such bird, or any product, whether or not manufactured, which consists, or is composed in whole or in part, of any such bird or any part, nest, or egg thereof, included in the terms of the [various treaties the U.S. has entered into with Great Britain (Canada), Mexico, Japan, and the former Soviet Union].

16 U.S.C. § 703 (emphasis added).

Though originally enacted to stem overhunting and implement existing treaties, the broad language and stringent liability regime of the MBTA continue to sustain its use as a cutting-edge legal tool. In recent years, plaintiffs have sought to use the MBTA to control activities that often result in bird death—such as farming, timber harvesting, and brush clearing. Consider the following two decisions interpreting the reach of the MBTA take prohibition.

Sierra Club v. Martin

United States Court of Appeals for the Eleventh Circuit, 1997.
110 F.3d 1551.

■ JUDGE BLACK

The United States Forest Service (Forest Service) and a group of timber contractors, including Bert Thomas, Cook Brothers Lumber Company, Inc., Parton Lumber Company, Inc., and Thrift Brothers Lumber Company, Inc. (collectively Timber Contractors), appeal the issuance of a preliminary injunction on May 8, 1996, ordering the Forest Service to stop all timber cutting and road building activities in seven timber projects in the Chattahoochee and Oconee National Forests in Georgia (collectively Chattahoochee). We reverse.

* * * In 1991, pursuant to the Chattahoochee's land and resource management plan, the Forest Service proposed to sell the rights to cut timber on seven parcels of land * * * [which] encompass approximately 2,103 acres out of the 846,000 acres that comprise the Chattahoochee. * * *. [This lawsuit was filed in 1996 by a coalition of national and Georgia-based environmental organizations, alleging violations of several federal statutes.]

The Chattahoochee is home to numerous species of neotropical migratory birds, which typically winter in Mexico or the Caribbean and spend the nesting season in the Chattahoochee. These birds include species designated for protection under the MBTA. Sierra Club asserted that the Forest Service's timber contracts violate the MBTA because they allowed timber cutting during the migratory bird nesting season and that tree cutting during nesting season would directly kill at least 2,000 to 9,000 neotropical migratory birds. The Forest Service did not dispute that cutting down a tree with an active nest directly killed migratory birds.[7] The district court held that the Forest Service's actions violated the MBTA because "thousands of migratory birds will be killed directly by cutting down trees with nests and juvenile birds in them." * * *

The MBTA, by its plain language, does not subject the federal government to its prohibitions. The MBTA makes it unlawful to "take" or "kill" birds. The penalties for violating its prohibitions are set forth in 16 U.S.C. § 707, which provides that a "person, association, partnership, or corporation" will be guilty of a misdemeanor or felony and subject to fine or imprisonment or both for violating the MBTA.[12] Sierra Club nonetheless

---

7. A Forest Service memorandum noted that tree cutting during nesting season would kill migratory birds: "The loss of individual nests and or birds is an un-avoidable cost of any type of land management activity, whether it be agricultural plowing, mowing, road maintenance, lawn maintenance, clearing land for construction, or cutting trees."

12. Section 707 provides, in relevant part:

(a) Except as otherwise provided in this section, any *person, association, partnership, or corporation* who shall violate any provisions of said conventions or of this subchapter, or who shall violate or fail to comply with any regulation made pursuant to this subchapter shall be deemed guilty of a misdemeanor and upon conviction thereof shall be fined not more than $500 or be imprisoned not more than six months, or both.

(b) Whoever, in violation of this subchapter, shall knowingly—

(1) take by any manner whatsoever any migratory bird with intent to sell, offer to sell, barter or offer to barter such bird, or

(2) sell, offer for sale, barter or offer to barter, any migratory bird shall be guilty of a felony and shall be fined not more than $2,000 or imprisoned not more than two years, or both.

16 U.S.C. § 707 (emphasis added).

asserts that because the prohibitions are stated broadly—that is, "it is unlawful" to "take" or "kill"—it should be unlawful for anybody, including federal agencies, to "take" or "kill" migratory birds. The MBTA, however, should be read as a whole to derive its plain meaning. The MBTA is a criminal statute making it unlawful *only* for persons, associations, partnerships, and corporations to "take" or "kill" migratory birds. Moreover, there is no expression of congressional intent which would warrant holding that "person" includes the federal government, thus enabling the United States to prosecute a federal agency, or a federal official acting in his official capacity, for taking or killing birds and destroying nests in violation of the MBTA. Congress has demonstrated that it knows how to subject federal agencies to substantive requirements when it chooses to do so. For example, the term "person" in the Endangered Species Act is defined to include "any officer, employee, agent, department, or instrumentality of the Federal Government." 16 U.S.C. § 1532(13).

The historical context of the MBTA's enactment further demonstrates that it does not apply to the federal government. In 1897, Congress established the National Forest System "[t]o conserve the water flows, and to furnish a continuous supply of timber for the people." *United States v. New Mexico*, 438 U.S. 696, 707 (1978). In light of that purpose, it is difficult to imagine that Congress enacted the MBTA barely twenty years later intending to prohibit the Forest Service from taking or killing a single migratory bird or nest "by any means or in any manner" given that the Forest Service's authorization of logging on federal lands inevitably results in the deaths of individual birds and destruction of nests. The application of the MBTA to the federal government would have severely impaired the Forest Service's ability to comply with the congressional directive to manage the national forests for timber production.

Congress's subsequent enactment of legislation relating to management of the National Forest System buttresses the conclusion that the MBTA does not apply to the federal government. In the NFMA, Congress expressed its intent that the Forest Service manage forests for multiple uses, including timber production. *See* 16 U.S.C. § 528 ("It is the policy of the Congress that the national forests are established and shall be administered for outdoor recreation, range, timber, watershed, and wildlife and fish purposes."). Through the NFMA, Congress has prescribed the procedures the Forest Service is to follow and the factors it is to consider in making land management decisions. In the process of complying with the NFMA, NEPA, and their implementing regulations, the Forest Service ensures that the impact of land management on migratory bird populations is considered in the context of ensuring viability of native species. 36 C.F.R. § 219.19. The viability regulation requires that, in the context of multiple use planning, habitat be provided within the forest to support a minimum number of reproductive individuals in order to "maintain viable populations of existing native and desired non-native vertebrate species in the planning area." *Id.* The Forest Service's compliance with the viability regulation is subject to judicial review in actions challenging timber sales brought under the APA. Congress intended that the Forest Service follow the NFMA's regulatory process, rather than the MBTA's criminal prohibitions, in addressing conservation of migratory birds.

The MBTA does not apply to the federal government. As no violation of the MBTA could occur by any formal action of the Forest Service, the Forest Service may not be enjoined under the APA.

Humane Society of the United States v. Glickman

United States Court of Appeals, District of Columbia Circuit, 2000.
217 F.3d 882.

■ JUDGE RANDOLPH

* * * At the center of the controversy is the Canada goose—*Branta canadensis*. With its black-stockinged neck and head and distinctive white cheek patch, its loud resonant honking calls, and its V-shaped flight formations, the Canada goose is a familiar sight throughout most of North America. The Mid–Atlantic population of Canada geese, one of eleven recognized races, winters in the coastal areas of Virginia, Maryland, Delaware, and New Jersey, and returns in the spring to the tundra zone of the Ungava Peninsula in Quebec, its traditional summer breeding grounds. In recent years, however, large flocks of Canada geese have stopped migrating, preferring to breed, nest and rear their young in the coastal states of the middle Atlantic region. The Commonwealth of Virginia has become a host to many of these full-time residents. In 1991, an estimated 66,169 Canada geese lived year round in Virginia. By 1998 Virginia's resident goose population had quadrupled to 254,000. In the same year, only 70,000 migratory Canada geese wintered over in Virginia, a number not much larger than the migratory population in the 1970s.

Residential owners, farmers, government officials and many others are deeply concerned about the exploding population of Canada geese. Browsing by Virginia's resident geese has reduced state-wide yields of cereal grains, peanuts, soybeans and corn. Goose droppings have spoiled water quality around beaches and wetlands, and interfered with the enjoyment of parks and ball fields. The geese have damaged gardens, lawns and golf courses. Their fecal deposits threaten to contaminate drinking water supplies. And they pose a hazard to aircraft. Resident geese are found at most of Virginia's airports and military bases. In 1995, a passenger jet hit ten Canada geese at Dulles International Airport, causing $1.7 million of wing and engine damage. Collisions have also occurred at other Virginia airports. And "Langley Air Force Base and Norfolk Naval Air Station have altered, delayed, aborted, and ceased flight operations because of Canada geese on their field."[2]

2. Resident Canada geese and the problems they cause are not confined to the east coast. The Washington Post reported that the Agriculture Department, having obtained a permit from FWS, is rounding up resident Canada geese and killing them in twelve counties surrounding Puget Sound in Washington State. *See* Ben White, *Honk if You Hate Goose Droppings,* WASH. POST, June 29, 2000, at A29.

In response to these problems and others, the Department of Agriculture, through its Animal Health and Inspection Service's Wildlife Services division, instituted an "Integrated Goose Management Program" in conjunction with Virginia state agencies. The plan called for various measures such as harassment, biological control, habitat alteration, repellents, nest and egg destruction, and capture and killing. The killings were to take place during the "summer molt"—between mid-June and late-July—when the resident geese cannot fly (the migratory geese are in Canada at this time of year). An Environmental Assessment, issued on January 29, 1997, reflected the Interior Department's longstanding position that the Migratory Bird Treaty Act restricted not only private parties and states, but also federal agencies. Hence a "federal Migratory Bird Depredation Permit ... would be required and obtained for the proposed action." Interior's Fish and Wildlife Service (FWS) is authorized to issue such depredation permits for migratory birds that "bec[o]me seriously injurious to the agricultural or other interests in any particular community." International Convention for the Protection of Migratory Birds, art. VII, 39 Stat. 1702, 1704 (1916) ("International Convention"), *referenced in* 16 U.S.C. § 704.

In 1997, the Director of FWS issued a memorandum to regional directors stating that federal agencies no longer needed to obtain a permit before taking or killing migratory birds. The Humane Society of the United States, Citizens for the Preservation of Wildlife, the Animal Protection Institute, and three individuals thereupon filed suit against the Secretaries of Agriculture and Interior and other officials in those departments seeking to enjoin implementation of the Goose Management Plan. The district court ruled that § 703 of the Migratory Bird Treaty Act restricted federal agencies * * * [and] enjoined the defendants "from conducting the Canada Goose Plan until such time as they shall obtain valid permits to do so pursuant to the" Act.

Although Virginia's Canada geese are year-long residents, they are members of a species that migrates and therefore fall within the category of "migratory birds" protected by the 1916 Treaty and the Act. *See* 50 C.F.R. § 10.13. Protected from whom? The district court thought § 703 of the Act gave the answer—from everyone in the United States, including federal agencies.

* * * As legislation goes, § 703 contains broad and unqualified language—"at any time," "by any means," "in any manner," "any migratory bird," "any part, nest, or egg of any such bird," "any product ... comprised in whole or part, of any such bird." The one exception to the prohibition is in the opening clause—"Unless and except as permitted by regulations made as hereinafter provided in this subchapter...." For migratory game birds, of which the Canada goose is one, the exception gives the Interior Department authority to regulate hunting seasons and bag limits. Article II of the Treaty itself required a closed season—no hunting of these birds—between March 10 and September 1, the typical period when the birds breed, molt and raise their young. In addition to issuing hunting regulations, the Secretary of the Interior may issue permits for killing Canada geese and other migratory birds if this is shown to be

"compatible with the terms of the [Migratory Bird] conventions." 16 U.S.C. § 704. As we have said, Article VII of the Treaty contemplated that permits allowing the killing of migratory birds would be available in "extraordinary conditions" when the birds have "become seriously injurious to the agricultural or other interests in any particular community," International Convention, art. VII, 39 Stat. 1704.

As § 703 is written, what matters is whether someone has killed or is attempting to kill or capture or take a protected bird, without a permit and outside of any designated hunting season. Nothing in § 703 turns on the identity of the perpetrator. There is no exemption in § 703 for farmers, or golf course superintendents, or ornithologists, or airport officials, or state officers, or federal agencies. In that respect, § 703 is rather like the statute in *United States v. Arizona,* 295 U.S. 174, 183–84 (1935), which also framed its prohibition in terms of the forbidden acts without mentioning the identity of the transgressor: there shall be no "construction of any bridge, dam, dike or causeway over or in any port, roadstead, haven, harbor, canal, navigable river or other navigable water of the United States until the consent of Congress shall have been obtained and until the plans shall have been submitted to and approved by the Chief of Engineers and by the Secretary of War." *Id.* at 184 (citing 33 U.S.C. § 401). The Court viewed the provision as restricting not only private parties, but also state and federal agencies, so that the Secretary of the Interior could not order the building of a dam without congressional authorization. "The plaintiff maintains that the restrictions so imposed apply only to work undertaken by private parties. But no such intention is expressed, and we are of opinion that none is implied. The measures adopted for the enforcement of the prescribed rule are in general terms and purport to be applicable to all. No valid reason has been or can be suggested why they should apply to private persons and not to federal and state officers." *Id.* at 184.

The defendants here, in order to promote their position that federal agencies are exempt from § 703, seek to introduce structural ambiguity into the Act, citing the criminal penalty provision of § 707(a):

> Except as otherwise provided in this section, any person, association, partnership, or corporation who shall violate any provisions of said conventions or of this subchapter, or who shall violate or fail to comply with any regulation made pursuant to this subchapter shall be deemed guilty of a misdemeanor and upon conviction thereof shall be fined not more than $15,000 or be imprisoned not more than six months, or both.

16 U.S.C. § 707(a). Federal agencies, they say, cannot be considered "persons" who may be held criminally liable for violating the Act or the Treaty. (They do not discuss whether federal officers carrying out the extermination of migratory birds could be considered "persons.") The defendants' reading of § 707(a) gains support from the canon that the term "person" does not ordinarily include the sovereign. *See United States v. Cooper Corp.,* 312 U.S. 600, 604 (1941).[4] And so we are willing to assume that the

---

4. The canon applies not only to the federal government but also to the States.   *See Vermont Agency of Natural Resources v. United States ex rel. Stevens,* 529 U.S. 1858

criminal enforcement provision could not be used against federal agencies. From this the defendants reason that Congress could not have intended to have § 703 restrict federal agencies because there would have been no means to enforce the restrictions; at the time of its enactment, they tell us, there was no provision in the Migratory Bird Treaty Act for injunctive relief. * * *

The argument goes nowhere. Even without a specific review provision, there still could have been a suit against the appropriate federal officer for injunctive relief to enforce § 703. *Missouri v. Holland,* for instance, was a "bill in equity brought by the State of Missouri to prevent a game warden of the United States from attempting to enforce the Migratory Bird Treaty Act." 252 U.S. at 430. * * * By 1903 the Court had determined that the "acts of all of [an agency's officers] must be justified by some law, and in case an official violates the law to the injury of an individual the courts generally have jurisdiction to grant relief." *American School of Magnetic Healing v. McAnnulty,* 187 U.S. 94, 108 (1902). Defendants are, in short, quite mistaken in supposing that § 703 could not be enforced against federal agencies except through the criminal provision contained in § 707(a).

Defendants' argument, and our assumption, that federal agencies are not "persons" within § 707(a)'s meaning therefore does not lead to the conclusion that Congress meant to exempt federal agencies from § 703. Indeed it would be odd if they were exempt. The Migratory Bird Treaty Act implements the Treaty of 1916. Treaties are undertakings between nations; the terms of a treaty bind the contracting powers. After ratification of the Treaty, President Woodrow Wilson affixed his signature to it and made it public, "to the end that the same and every article and clause thereof may be observed and fulfilled with good faith *by the United States* and the citizens thereof." 39 Stat. 1705 (italics added). If one year later, in 1917, Canadian authorities had started slaughtering eider ducks, no one would doubt that Canada would be guilty of violating Article IV of the Treaty, which protects these ducks. If some agency of the federal government did the same in Alaska, the United States too would be in violation of the Treaty. There is no reason to treat the Act differently from the Treaty since the legislation was meant to "give effect to the convention between the United States and Great Britain for the protection of migratory birds," ch. 128, 40 Stat. 755, 755 (1918). The Act incorporates the terms of the Treaty in determining, among other things, two critical issues: which birds are covered, *see* 16 U.S.C. § 703, and under what conditions the Interior Department may issue exemptions, *see id.* § 704. In short, the fact that the Act enforced a treaty between our country and Canada reinforces our conclusion that the broad language of § 703 applies to actions of the federal government.

Canada too understood that legislation implementing the Treaty applied to the sovereign. If Canadian authorities kill migratory birds without

---

(2000). Yet defendants maintain that States and state agencies are subject to the Act's restrictions.

a permit they violate not only the Treaty, but also Canada's Migratory Birds Convention Act. That Act "is binding on Her Majesty in right of Canada or a province." R.S.C., ch. 22, § 3 (1994). The Canadian Act, like its American counterpart, derives from Article VIII of the Treaty, which obligated both Contracting Powers to "propose to their respective appropriate law-making bodies the necessary measures for insuring the execution of the present Convention." International Convention, art. VIII, 39 Stat. 1704. That Canada treated this joint obligation to mean that implementing legislation would be binding on the sovereign indicates still further that § 703 restricts the actions of federal agencies in this country.

This too had been the longstanding conclusion of the Department of the Interior, which until 1997 had "historically interpreted the provisions of the MBTA as applying to actions of FWS employees themselves." Letter from Frank K. Richardson, Solicitor, U.S. Dep't of the Interior, to the Secretary of the Interior at 3 (May 31, 1985); *see also* 50 C.F.R. § 21.12. Although FWS has now changed its mind, neither Interior nor Agriculture asks us to defer to their interpretation of the Act, and for good reason. The Agriculture Department does not administer the Act and so its view of § 703's meaning is entitled to no special respect. For its part, the Interior Department conceded that the 1997 FWS change of heart, in a letter to regional offices, was not "a policy call on the part of the Service," nor "a 'filling in' of the 'gaps' in the" statute. *Christensen v. Harris County,* 529 U.S. 576 (2000), holds that: "Interpretations such as those in opinion letters—like interpretations contained in policy statements, agency manuals, and enforcement guidelines, all of which lack the force of law—do not warrant *Chevron*-style deference."

For many of the reasons we have mentioned, we disagree with the * * * holding in *Sierra Club v. Martin,* 110 F.3d 1551, 1555 (11th Cir. 1997), that § 703 does not apply to federal agencies. * * * [It rests] on the mistaken idea that in 1918, § 703 could be enforced only through the criminal penalty provision in § 707(a). The *Martin* opinion adds the thought that Congress could not have wanted the Act to apply to the Forest Service in the early 1900s because whenever it cut trees it might be destroying migratory birds or their nests, in violation of the Act. The *Martin* court's assumption that timber harvesting could violate the Migratory Bird Treaty Act is not shared by others. The Eighth Circuit in *Newton County,* following the lead of the Ninth Circuit in *Seattle Audubon Society v. Evans,* 952 F.2d 297, 302 (1991), held that § 703 does not prohibit "conduct, such as timber harvesting, that indirectly results in the death of migratory birds." 113 F.3d at 114. Even if the *Martin* court were correct about timber harvesting, its observation about the Forest Service ignores the facts that it was not until 1997 that the Interior Department asserted immunity for federal agencies; that before then the Fish and Wildlife Service interpreted the Act to apply to all federal agencies; that during the pre–1997 period the Forest Service, like other federal agencies, could obtain permits; and that—as the documents submitted in this case show—it was the *Martin* case and other pending litigation that "spurred" Interior to adopt the "new" interpretation.[7]

We conclude that because the Wildlife Services division of the Department of Agriculture did not obtain a permit from the Department of the Interior, its implementation of the Integrated Goose Management Plan by taking and killing Canada Geese violates § 703 of the Migratory Bird Treaty Act.

NOTES AND QUESTIONS

1. Note that two separate issues are raised here. One raised on the facts in *Martin* is whether the MBTA prohibits conduct like timber harvesting that indirectly or incidentally results in the death of migratory birds. It is addressed further below. The other is whether federal agencies are covered by the prohibition in the MBTA, which would seem to present a straightforward question of statutory construction. On that issue, the 11th Circuit and the D.C. Circuit take contrary positions. Which is more persuasive? The federal government took the position here that the MBTA did not apply to federal agencies but did apply to state and local governments. See footnote 4 in the *Humane Society* opinion. Is that a plausible position?

2. As a matter of policy, should the U.S. exempt itself from broad prohibitions it imposes on state or private actors? Should a court construing an ambiguous statute in these circumstances presume the federal agencies are covered (as a matter of fairness) or should it presume they are exempt (on the basis that waivers of sovereign immunity ought to be express)? In the wake of 9/11, Congress exempted the Defense Department from the MBTA after some environmental groups won a court injunction against military exercises that killed migratory birds. Pub.L. No. 107–314, Div. A, title III, § 315; Center for Biological Diversity v. Pirie, 191 F. Supp. 2d 161 (D.D.C. 2002).

3. If federal agencies are not themselves constrained by the MBTA, are their permittees and licensees (such as those harvesting timber under Forest Service contract) nevertheless liable? Or should the permit or license provided by the federal agency be construed as permission to take migratory birds? Note that the Act provides for the federal government to give permission to take migratory birds under regulations, but the Act gives that authority to the Secretary of the Interior. Thus the Secretary of Agriculture could not provide such permission (e.g., in a contract to harvest timber on national forest lands) without the concurrence of the Interior Secretary.

4. The scope of the MBTA has long caused conflicts among agencies within the executive branch. Wildlife advocates in the Interior Department have from time to time advocated fashioning a permit system under the MBTA that would allow the FWS to regulate all takes of migratory birds, by federal agencies or others. Other federal agencies resist the notion of

7. Nor did the *Martin* court acknowledge the Supreme Court's dictum in *Robertson v. Seattle Audubon Society,* 503 U.S. 429 (1992), that the Act applies to federal agencies.

seeking permission from another federal agency for conduct they otherwise have authority to pursue.

5.   In *Humane Society*, killing the geese was the object of the program. But in *Martin*, the timber harvesting only indirectly and unintentionally results in the death of migratory birds. Although *Martin* avoids answering the question because it holds federal agencies are not subject to the MBTA, some other courts have held that accidental killing of migratory birds violates the Act. *See* United States v. FMC Corp., 572 F.2d 902 (2d Cir.1978) (unintentional release of toxic substances by pesticide manufacturer into a lagoon frequented by migratory waterfowl held actionable, reasoning by analogy from situations where strict liability is imposed on those engaging in "extrahazardous activities"); United States v. Moon Lake Electric Assn., 45 F.Supp.2d 1070 (D.Colo.1999) (rural electric cooperative may be held liable under MBTA for failing to install inexpensive equipment on 2,450 power poles located near eagle, hawk, and owl habitat which has resulted in death or injury to birds).

6.   In this connection, it is worth comparing the MBTA with the ESA. In Seattle Audubon Society v. Evans, 952 F.2d 297, 302 (9th Cir.1991), the court pointed out that the ESA defines "take" to include "harass" and "harm," while these expansive words do not appear in the MBTA. Finding the differences "distinct and purposeful," the court concluded "[h]abitat destruction causes 'harm' to the owls under the ESA but does not 'take' them within the meaning of the [MBTA]." Note, however, that the MBTA prohibits killing protected birds "at any time, by any means or in any manner" except as permitted by Interior Department regulations. 16 U.S.C. § 703. Does that suggest *Seattle Audubon Society* is wrong? Compare the discussion of habitat modification as ESA "take" in the various opinions in Babbitt v. Sweet Home, *supra* p. 306.

7.   Should courts treat the scope of the MBTA differently depending on whether the case is a civil action for injunctive relief or a criminal prosecution?

> The MBTA's "plain meaning and legislative history" require a restrained interpretation. If interpreted broadly, the MBTA would resist principled limitation; prosecutorial discretion, extra-hazardous materials, and permit schemes all fail to provide a meaningful limit. Moreover, the fate of migratory birds does not depend upon such a strained interpretation of the MBTA. More recently minted environmental laws protect wildlife and seek to achieve a balance of various kinds of land use.

Benjamin Means, *Prohibiting Conduct, Not Consequences: The Limited Reach of the Migratory Bird Treaty Act*, 97 MICH. L.REV. 823, 841–42 (1998). What other "environmental laws" might address the habitat needs of neotropical migratory birds, such as non-endangered but declining warblers?

8.   Millions of migratory birds are fated to die from incidental or non-directed take. Domestic and feral cats kill hundreds of millions of migratory birds a year. Probably that many are killed by building window impacts.

Rough estimates of annual mortality from other causes include motor vehicles (57 million); pesticide ingestion and other forms of water contamination from irrigation return flows, such as gave rise to a notorious case at the Kesterson National Wildlife Refuge in California's Central Valley in the 1980s (67 million); communication towers (40–50 million); industrial spills and accidents (1.5 million or more; the Exxon Valdez oil spill killed several hundred thousand birds). Other significant causes include fishing bycatch (birds taken by nets, hooks, and longlines); electrocutions and power line impacts; wind generators, and aircraft bird strikes. Some of these causes are found on federal lands, while many others are not. At least some of these unintended causes of bird death are avoidable by various measures, including more bird-friendly design and operation. Although there are hundreds of millions of migratory birds, ninety of an estimated 836 species of migratory birds found in the U.S. are listed as endangered (seventy five) or threatened (fifteen) under the ESA, and another 124 are on the FWS list of non-game species of management concern, with some populations declining precipitously. Larry Martin Corcoran, *Migratory Bird Treaty Act*, 77 Denv. U. L.Rev. 315, 346–55 (1999) (collecting sources).

9. The MBTA poses this practical dilemma: if its command is interpreted sweepingly, much conduct that is regarded as part of ordinary modern life is criminal. Who should bear the responsibility to try to accommodate its requirements to that reality? The courts, by narrow interpretations? The Department of Justice by the exercise of prosecutorial discretion? The Interior Department, by crafting a regulatory (and permitting) scheme to cover some or all of these multitude of acts and practices that kill migratory birds? The Congress, through legislation modifying the Act?

10. The MBTA does not itself define "migratory bird," but refers to the underlying treaties for definition. These "several aged" treaties themselves may not clearly answer the question, but in Hill v. Norton, 275 F.3d 98 (D.C.Cir.2001), the court held that the Secretary of the Interior's refusal to include the mute swan on the list of protected birds was arbitrary and capricious.

NOTE: THE MBTA AS A NATIONAL HUNTING LAW

Under the MBTA, the FWS regulates hunting of migratory birds throughout the country through generic regulations governing such things as identification requirements, hunting methods, and the like. See 50 C.F.R. Parts 20 & 21. FWS also promulgates regulations annually prescribing season lengths, shooting hours, bag limits, and other such things, which are based on analysis of bird population data and recommendations of various interests, including states. 50 C.F.R. 20.100–.110. The Act preserves state regulation that is consistent with the treaties and the Act. 16 U.S.C. § 708.

Beyond these MBTA regulations, other federal laws like the Endangered Species Act may operate to restrict hunting opportunities on federal and non-federal lands. In the "sunrise hunting case," Defenders of Wildlife

v. Andrus, 428 F.Supp. 167 (D.D.C.1977), the court held that FWS regulations permitting waterfowl hunting from before sunrise until sunset were arbitrary, because the rulemaking proceedings "did not concern themselves with the amount, extent or nature" of the risk that hunters will misidentify their targets and mistakenly shoot endangered birds. The court said that the ESA does not necessarily require that "twilight shooting must be prohibited if protected species are subject to any killing by inadvertent action of hunters or otherwise," but the record must reflect that "hunting hours * * * are so fixed that such killing is kept to the minimum consistent with other obligations imposed on the Service by Congress."

In 1991 the Fish & Wildlife Service completed a lengthy effort to ban the use of lead shot in hunting waterfowl. According to many studies, lead shot results in substantial mortality to protected bird species through lead poisoning by ingestion. Alternative non-toxic shot (typically steel) is less preferred by hunters because it is less accurate, more costly, and causes more barrel wear or safety concerns. Litigation in the long-running dispute resulted in rulings upholding federal limitations on lead shot. *See, e.g.,* National Rifle Ass'n of America, Inc. v. Kleppe, 425 F.Supp. 1101 (D.D.C. 1976), *aff'd mem.*, 571 F.2d 674 (D.C.Cir.1978). Congress delayed the inevitable with annual appropriations riders that for years prevented the Interior Department from enforcing the regulations except in states that agreed to them. But the phase-out of lead shot for waterfowl and coot hunting was completed in 1991. Lead shot for upland game hunting, however, remains a source of environmental contamination and mortality for endangered California condors.

CHAPTER 11

THE RECREATION RESOURCE

This chapter examines a mélange of federal recreational policy topics. Section A treats federal acquisition of interests in land for recreational purposes. Section B examines management of the nation's flagship outdoor recreation destination, the national park system. Section C addresses an emerging category of land management, special recreational and conservation overlay designations like "national recreation areas." Section D addresses management of recreation on federal lands through fees, concessions, and permits. Section E focuses on one particular kind of intensive recreational use with significant environmental impacts and associated controversy—off-road vehicles. Section F describes the basis of federal liability under the Federal Tort Claims Act for mishaps to recreational licensees.

Measured by user days, the single greatest demand on the public lands is from persons seeking recreational opportunities. The burgeoning American penchant for refreshment of the spirit in the outdoors comes in varying forms, from motorized cross-country frolicking to quiet contemplation of nature. Exercised with varying degrees of intensity, it creates some of the most intractable land management problems of the modern era. Recreation is a resource like the more conventional ones: Congress has recognized that recreation is a valid and sometimes preferred land use and has often subsidized it. Recreation and American culture are intimately related. Preferred forms of recreation are influenced by available leisure time, prosperity, technology, and prevailing social mores.

Recreation is one of the "multiple uses" that statutes require the Forest Service and the BLM to provide. The Fish and Wildlife Service may allow recreational use on refuges when compatible with wildlife conservation. The 1997 National Wildlife Refuge System Improvement Act instructs the FWS to promote compatible "wildlife-dependent recreation." 16 U.S.C. § 668dd. Congress has charged the National Park Service with providing for "the enjoyment of the [national parks] in such manner and by such means as will leave them unimpaired for future generations." National Park Organic Act of 1916, 16 U.S.C. § 1.

Increasingly in modern times Congress has applied relatively new designations—such as national recreation area—to tracts of land managed by the NPS, the Forest Service, and the BLM. Each of these statutes varies in the extent to which it gives priority to recreation and excludes other multiple uses, but practically all are intended to elevate recreational use and management to a position of priority.

Recreational uses may conflict with each other, and create conflicts with other resource uses. Ski area proposals are fought by hikers, hunters, and bird-watchers; off-road vehicle enthusiasts are despised by many but may have no other large tracts of land available for their pursuit; increased sightseeing overwhelms parts of the "crown jewels" of the national park system; and so forth. As a general rule, the more mechanized or technologically advanced the form of recreation, the more potential for conflict and destruction it poses. Off-road vehicles, for example, are more dangerous to ecological stability than mountain bikes, but the latter may, in turn, have greater impact than hikers. Hotels cause more serious changes than tents. Quantity obviously is important as well: a horde of hikers can leave the terrain in worse condition than a single jeep. By the early 2000s, Forest Service Chief Dale Bosworth had identified recreation (especially motorized, off-road recreation) as one of the four major threats to the health of the national forest system.

Substantial economic interests are at stake in recreation management decisions made by federal land managers. The recreation industry includes, besides those operating concessions on federal lands, nearby resort operators, vehicle and equipment rental businesses, and manufacturers of motor homes, boats, off-road vehicles, skiing equipment, and other sporting goods. All have an interest in promoting recreational use of federal lands. Many settlements near the public lands are economically dependent on tourism; gateway communities like West Yellowstone, Montana and Gatlinburg, Tennessee would shrivel without the dollars brought in by recreation on nearby federal lands. For example, not counting the people who drive through and view the scenery, the Forest Service hosted 214 million recreationists in 2002, generating an estimated $100 billion. This reflects an eighteen-fold increase from 1946. A 2004 study estimated that the 37 million recreationists using the national wildlife refuges generated $1.37 billion of sales in regions surrounding the refuges and created 24,000 private sector jobs. Despite the imprecision of the monetary estimates, which can vary significantly by economic method used, these numbers dwarf timber and grazing programs on the public lands.

It should not be surprising that conflicts between recreation and other values or resources find their way to the courts. A number of cases in earlier chapters involve the recreation resource. In Leo Sheep Co. v. United States, *supra* at p. 375, the access rights at issue were intended for the benefit of hunters and anglers. The *Ruby Lake Refuge* cases, *supra* at p. 868, show the conflict between recreation and wildlife, with the latter itself furnishing the basis for two large but very different recreational industries, sport hunting and birdwatching. Recreational access sometimes requires resolving fundamental questions of federal authority and private rights, as in United States v. Curtis–Nevada Mines, Inc., *supra* at p. 594.

Jan G. Laitos & Thomas A. Carr, The Transformation on Public Lands

26 Ecology L.Q. 140, 178–84 (1999).

One of the major sociological and economic events in the twentieth century United States involves the dramatic increase in recreation, particularly outdoor recreation. By 1997, the Outdoor Recreation Coalition of America reported that more than 90 percent of Americans over the age of sixteen regularly participate in at least one outdoor recreational activity. Much of the increase has taken place on federal lands. * * *

But an overall increase in recreation does not explain why public lands have become recreation destinations. One needs to understand how traditional multiple-use public lands, such as Forest Service and BLM lands, have evolved from extractive uses to dominant, nonextractive, recreational uses. As discussed below, this change in use of public lands has been caused by psychological, sociological, economic, and legal factors.

1.   *Psychological and Sociological Factors*

As the century comes to a close, one is left with the impression that the physical environments preferred at the beginning of the century have been replaced by a totally different vision of what constitutes an ideal community. One hundred years ago a prosperous setting was one in which extractive industries flourished—timber was being turned into pulp and paper; copper was being mined; cattle and sheep were grazing. Today, Americans are more aware that these economic activities impact other sources of well being. What is often far more desirable than a steel mill or paper factory is a pristine natural environment where recreation can flourish, health is protected, air and water are unpolluted, and wildlife is abundant. Americans increasingly judge an area's desirability not by the quantity of commodity goods produced there, but by the environmental and recreational amenities it offers.

* * * Surveys reveal that outdoor recreation has become a significant part of the lives of over 75 percent of Americans. * * *

* * *

Various sociological and demographic changes have also served to stimulate the public's desire to use public lands for recreational purposes. Recreation requires leisure time, and Americans enjoy an average of nearly 40 hours of leisure a week, up from 35 hours in 1965. This country's population is increasing, and much of it is concentrated in urban areas, whose dwellers comprise the fastest growing segment of the population using public lands for recreational purposes. America also enjoys a high level of disposable personal income and an interstate highway system that provides low cost-access to recreation areas far from home. Rising discretionary purchasing power and mobility combine to give recreation-minded urban residents access to public lands and nearby communities.

2.   *Economic Factors Causing Increased Recreational Use of Public Lands*

For many years, the economic health of states in the West was tied closely to the commodity resources found on public lands—hardrock minerals, coal, oil and gas, water, forage for crops and livestock, and timber. But with the decline of traditional commodity resource use on public lands has come a different economic reality, linked not to extractive industries, but to the emerging recreation value of public lands. Four factors help to explain the dominance of recreation use.

First, one can argue that the recreation resource on public lands is a public good. Public goods generally have two characteristics: (1) they are difficult to exclude persons from; and (2) as a consequence they tend to be over-used. Unlike most commodity resources such as a mining deposit or an oil reservoir, the recreation resource usually has no borders (other than the boundary line separating public and private property). Moreover, no administrative mechanism exists to easily restrict the flow of persons wishing to engage in public-lands recreation. As a result, once one person is allowed to use BLM or Forest Service lands for recreational purposes, it is quite difficult to exclude others from taking full advantage of similar recreational opportunities. Since it would be incredibly expensive to put impenetrable fences around all public lands not already devoted to recreation, and since it could be administratively burdensome and politically unpopular to collect fees at fixed entrance points to limit those who wish to gain access to these lands, BLM lands and national forests effectively become "commons." Visitors can hike, bike, camp, swim, ride horses, or drive their all-terrain vehicles without asking permission, making a reservation, or paying a fee. As a result, the recreation resource on public lands, as a public good or commons, becomes over used.

Second, recreation has economic worth. The economic value of recreation in part takes the form of dollars that flow into the outdoor recreation equipment market. In 1996, the Outdoor Recreation Coalition of America estimated that retail sales of such equipment (e.g., mountain bikes, hiking and walking shoes, outerwear, skis, kayaks) totaled almost $5 billion. The outdoor recreation industry provided nearly 800,000 full-time jobs, for a total of $13 billion in annual wages. Of course, since these are national figures, one cannot presume that the economic benefits of the recreation industry are directed * * *where most public lands are located. Still, one can assume that a significant portion of the retail sales for outdoor recreational equipment takes place in, and therefore benefits the economies of, the public lands states.

Third, apart from spending money on (and thereby employing those who manufacture) recreation equipment, outdoor enthusiasts who buy such equipment often use it on the public lands. During their visit to public lands, these individuals typically spend money in surrounding communities. Thus, nearby communities reap an economic benefit from the active participants who come to public lands to fish, hunt, camp, hike, snowboard, and raft, as well as the tourists whose recreation consists only of taking a few steps from an automobile to observe or photograph natural beauty. Both types of recreation create income for communities that are gateways to public lands, thereby boosting their economies. In virtually all population centers near public lands, recreational activities and tourism provide significantly greater employment than commodity resource extraction. Most interior West states now count on recreation and tourism as the first or second largest part of their economies.

NOTES AND QUESTIONS

1.   Is the observation that recreation is the most common or most valuable use of public lands the same thing as saying that the public lands are now dominant-use systems for recreation? How does that square with laws addressed in prior chapters, like the mining law or organic legislation? Oil and gas leasing on multiple-use federal lands has increased in recent years. Does that mean that petroleum development is a dominant use?

2.   Laitos and Carr focus on increases in recreation on the multiple-use land systems. But dominant-use systems, such as the national wildlife refuges, have also experienced big increases in recreation. Conflicts among recreationists and the limits of recreational carrying capacity of even dominant use lands create tensions the law provides a framework for resolving.

3.   Another factor driving the increase in public land recreation is the decline in available private land as an alternative site for public outdoor recreation. The Forest Service predicts this trend will continue. USDA Forest Service Strategic Plan for Fiscal Years 2004–2008 29.

4.   Per capita visits to national parks have declined in recent years, after a half century of steady increases. Some have suggested that the popularity of sedentary activities involving electronic media is displacing outdoor recreation. Oliver Pergams & Patricia Zaradic, *Is Love of Nature in the US Becoming Love of Electronic Media?*, 80 J. Envtl. Mgt. 387 (2006); *Visitation to National Parks Dips*, Federal Parks and Recreation (Jan. 12, 2007). If true, how might the social trend affect public support for federal lands? *See also* Richard Louv, Last Child in the Woods: Saving Our Children from Nature-Deficit Disorder (2005).

5.   On the relationship between recreational resources on public lands and economic development in the surrounding region, a recent study by the Sonoran Institute, *supra* chap. 1, p. 48, suggests that regional economies dominated by logging, ranching, and mining on public lands remain stagnant or decline while economies focused on recreation thrive. The study finds that places attracting recreationists also attract migrants whose livelihoods are not location-dependent and retain educated youths who otherwise seek their fortunes elsewhere.

A.   Acquisition of Lands for Recreation: The Land and Water Conservation Fund

The Land and Water Conservation Fund, 16 U.S.C. §§ 460*l*–4 to 460*l*–11, is a keystone of federal recreational policy. The Fund is a paper account in the U.S. Treasury which is credited with federal receipts from oil and gas leasing on the Outer Continental Shelf, and some other, much smaller, sources of revenue. Since its inception in 1965, LWCF moneys have enabled federal agencies to purchase some 4.5 million acres of land and interests in land. LWCF grants to states have bought an additional 2.3 million acres for state and local government recreational land systems, and also fund recreation planning.

In contrast to true "revolving funds" like Duck Stamp receipts, *supra* p. 846, which are automatically available for spending by agencies without further action by Congress, LWCF money cannot be spent absent an appropriation by Congress. Appropriations out of the Fund have never equaled receipts credited to it. Of a total of $28.1 billion dollars credited to the Fund since 1965, only half has been appropriated. Sometimes spending out of the Fund has come in for political criticism; for example, in 1981 Secretary of the Interior James Watt, decrying "park barrel politics," called for a moratorium on further LWCF acquisitions. In the late 1990s, unaccustomed (if short-lived) budget surpluses led to sharp increases in appropriations to the LWCF for land acquisitions. More recently, appropriations have fallen steadily. The fund currently takes in about $900 million annually, but appropriations have declined to under $300 million annually. Jeffrey A. Zinn, Land and Water Conservation Fund (Congressional Research Service 2005).

Not surprisingly, the federal monies made available through the LWCF program for state and local recreational land acquisition come, as federal funds usually do, with strings attached. The primary string is, sensibly, to ensure that the money being made available will serve its statutory purpose.

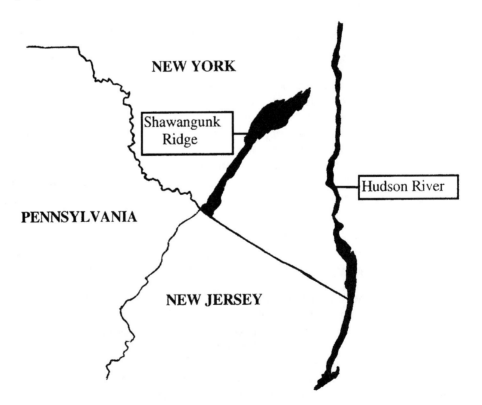

Friends of Shawangunks, Inc. v. Clark

United States Court of Appeals, Second Circuit, 1985.
754 F.2d 446.

■ Judge Oakes

This case presents the novel question whether amendment of a conservation easement acquired in part with federal funds under the Land and Water Conservation Fund Act of 1965 so as to permit expansion of a golf course with limited access constitutes a conversion "to other than public outdoor recreation uses" under section 6(f)(3) of the Act, 16 U.S.C. § 460*l*–8(f)(3).[1] The Secretary of the Interior, acting through the National Park Service's Acting Regional Director, determined that a section 6(f)(3) conversion would not occur. * * *

The Shawangunk Range, located in Ulster County, New York, is noted for spectacular rock formations, sheer cliffs, windswept ledges with pine barrens, fast-flowing mountain streams and scenic waterfalls, as well as a series of five mountain lakes, the "Sky Lakes." Of these, Lake Minnewaska is one, with extremely steep banks and many magnificent cliffs rising as high as 150 feet along its northern and eastern shores. Lake Minnewaska is situated approximately in the center on a general north-south line of 22,000 acres of permanent open space extending for some sixteen miles along the crest of the Shawangunks. Large tracts of land within the overall area are owned, maintained, and made available to the public for hiking and other limited recreational activities by, among others, the Village of Ellenville, the Palisades Interstate Park Commission (PIPC), the Mohonk Preserve, Inc., Mohonk Mountain Houses, Inc., and the Nature Conservancy.

In 1971, the State of New York purchased about 7,000 acres of land bordering Lake Minnewaska to the south and west for the formation of Minnewaska State Park. The park is under the jurisdiction and management of the PIPC, an interstate park commission formed by compact between the State of New York and the State of New Jersey.

In 1977, the PIPC added 1,609 acres of land to the park and purchased an approximately 239–acre conservation easement over Lake Minnewaska itself and certain land adjacent to it, all with the help of 50% federal matching funds from the Land and Water Conservation Fund. *See* 16 U.S.C. § 460*l*–8. The lands encumbered by the easement contain inter alia the lake itself, a nonoperating nine-hole golf course, a golf course pro shop, the water supply system for an adjacent resort building, and wooded land.

---

1. Section 6(f)(3) provides:

No property acquired or developed with assistance under this section shall, without the approval of the Secretary, be converted to other than public outdoor recreation uses. The Secretary shall approve such conversion only if he finds it to be in accord with the then existing comprehensive statewide outdoor recreation plan and only upon such conditions as he deems necessary to assure the substitution of other recreation properties of at least equal fair market value and of reasonably equivalent usefulness and location.

According to its terms, the easement is "for the purpose of, but not solely limited to, the conservation and preservation of unique and scenic areas; for the environmental and ecological protection of Lake Minnewaska and its watershed; and to prevent development and use in a manner inconsistent with the present use and operation of lands now owned and to be conveyed [to the PIPC] and to be part of Minnewaska State Park." It provides that the fee owner "shall not develop or erect new facilities within the described area; alter the landscape or terrain; or cut trees" but may

> operate, maintain and reconstruct existing facilities within the easement area, including, but not limited to buildings, roads, utilities and golf courses; provided that (a) Any reconstruction shall be in the same location and utilized for the same purpose as that which existed on the date hereof and that such reconstructed facilities shall be no larger in area than the facility being replaced.

In a limited exception to the prohibition against expanded or new construction, the PIPC agreed to the construction or reconstruction of several specific facilities, including "[t]he existing golf course pro shop and a golf course maintenance building" as well as "[a]n access road and parking lot for golf course patrons."

The Marriott Corporation, a national hotel and resort developer, acquired an option in 1980 to purchase approximately 590 acres, including the water and lands encumbered by the 239–acre easement. Marriott proposes to develop a resort facility, complete with a 400–room resort hotel and conference center, 300 condominium units, restaurants, ski facilities, and an expanded, professional grade 18–hole golf course. Eight golf course holes and related facilities, apparently with golf-cart roadways, would be constructed on property subject to the easement. * * *

Despite the Friends' arguments, the PIPC resolved on July 20, 1981, to amend the conservation easement to allow the Marriott Corporation to expand the golf course as proposed, drill wells within the easement area, increase the use of water from Lake Minnewaska, and utilize acreage encumbered by the easement for purposes of computing total average density of residential development. In consideration, Marriott agreed to extend the area covered by the easement, permit public access to footpaths through the easement area and adjacent lands owned by Marriott, maintain the lake level above an elevation of 1,646 feet, limit development on its other adjoining property, and open the golf course to the public twenty-five percent of the time. On October 20, 1981, [the Park Service notified] the PIPC that the contemplated amendment of the conservation easement did not constitute a section 6(f)(3) conversion and therefore did not require any federal authorization. This lawsuit followed.

* * * [The district court held] that the amendment did not constitute a conversion. The court reasoned that because the public had no access to the lands encumbered by the easement these lands "presently are not intended for outdoor, public, recreational use" within the meaning of the Land and Water Conservation Fund Act of 1965. Hence,

[w]hatever limited public access is contemplated by the terms of the proposed amendment to that easement, therefore, must be viewed as nothing less than a bonus to the public, and not as a diminution in, or conversion of, the availability of public, outdoor, recreation facilities.

We agree with the Friends that the district court wrongly decided that the easement lands presently are "not intended for outdoor, public, or recreational use." Rather, in light of the policies of the Department of the Interior and the purposes of the statute, we interpret section 6(f)(3) "public outdoor recreation uses" broadly, to encompass uses not involving the public's actual physical presence on the property. After all, Webster's Third New International Dictionary (1971) defines "recreation" as "refreshment of the strength and spirits after toil," *id.* at 1899; surely by exposing scenic vistas and serving as a buffer zone between Minnewaska State Park and developed areas, the easement area provides such refreshment. * * *

It is after all a "conservation" fund act. Conservation may include, though it is by no means necessarily limited to, the protection of a present resource in its natural state. Indeed, the Act's stated purposes include "preserving" the "quality" of outdoor recreation resources. 16 U.S.C. § 460*l*–4. The focus on preservation reappears in section 460*l*–9(a)(1), which authorizes allocation of funds for federal acquisitions both to protect endangered and threatened species and also, by reference to section 460k–1, to protect "natural resources."

Thus, contrary to the district court's holding, the easement area presently *is* used for "public outdoor recreation uses," as that term of art was conceived by Congress and has been interpreted by the Interior Department. Having made this determination, we are next faced with the question whether the amendment at issue here constitutes a "conversion" of that easement to other than outdoor, public, recreation uses within the meaning of section 6(f)(3). Though the nature of a conservation easement makes the application of the concept of conversion somewhat elusive, we conclude that the proposed amendment does constitute such a conversion. The property acquired by PIPC through its purchase of the easement was the right to prevent further development of the land underlying the easement. By the proposed amendment, Marriott, the holder of the fee, would be permitted to engage in precisely such development, changing both the character of the land and the population having access to it. By the amendment, in effect, PIPC would convey away its right to prevent any change in the character of the land subject to the easement. The view that such a change constitutes a "conversion" is supported by the Department of the Interior's own practice. In a May 15, 1978 Memorandum, [the pertinent Interior official] defined "conversion" to include instances in which "property interests are *conveyed* for non-public outdoor recreation uses." (Emphasis added.) It is plain that there is a conversion from public enjoyment of an unspoiled area to private golfing.

What is the consequence of this determination? The Secretary, in the words of section 6(f)(3), must determine that the conversion is "in accord with the then existing comprehensive statewide outdoor recreation plan" and grant his approval "only upon such conditions as he deems necessary to assure the substitution of other recreation properties of at least equal fair market value and of reasonably equivalent usefulness and location." These findings may seem simple, but they nevertheless must be made. [The pertinent NPS official who determined that Marriott's plan was not a conversion] did look to these very criteria [but] we cannot assume that he gave them the attention outlined in the above-mentioned Memorandum of May 15, 1978, which instructs regional directors to determine, for example, that "all practical alternatives to the conversion have been evaluated and rejected on sound bases," and that the fair market values of the property to be converted and of the property to be substituted have been established and compared. Thus, though [the pertinent federal official] reviewed the [state's environmental documentation on the project, and] implicitly found that the amended easement was "reasonably equivalent" to the original easement * * * we cannot assume, for example, that he made sure that *all* practical alternatives were considered and rejected (*e.g.*, whether the new golf holes could be built elsewhere on Marriott land), or that he established and compared the fair market values of the original and amended easements. We assume, rather, that [he] would engage in more careful scrutiny before approving a conversion than before determining, as he did here, that his approval was unnecessary.

Here we hold that the amended easement constitutes a conversion to "other than public outdoor recreation uses," 16 U.S.C. § 460*l*–8(f)(3), requiring the Secretary's approval. However, we would require approval by the Secretary in this case even if the Marriott Corporation planned to build a completely public outdoor recreation facility, because such a plan would be inconsistent with the original easement's prohibition of new facilities. Our reasoning runs as follows. The Act requires the Secretary to approve all "planning, acquisition, or development projects" before allocating federal funds. *Id.* § 460*l*–8(f)(1). It envisions that these "projects" will affect the future of the area acquired, preserving outdoor recreation opportunities for "present and future generations." *Id.* § 460*l*–4. Consistent with Congress's concern for lasting recreation opportunities, the Secretary approved federal funding for the Minnewaska easement in part because of the plans for the easement area's future—specific constraints on development and guarantees of environmental protection. Consequently, any future change that contravenes these plans retroactively calls into question the basis for the original federal funding. Such a change necessarily requires the Secretary's approval, whether or not the change falls within the Act's definition of a "conversion." Otherwise, the Secretary's initial approval of a "project" extending into the future would be meaningless. Once again, it would not be enough for the Secretary to find that federal approval is unnecessary; while the statutory criteria for approval would not apply to a change from one public use to another, positive approval is still required.

We recognize with Marriott the rather cumbersome process involving a considerable amount of time and effort that undertaking this development has entailed. * * * Unfortunately, or fortunately perhaps, the courts do not control the process, let alone establish it. When one undertakes to develop for private purposes a project involving the use of lands encumbered by a government interest, one's expectations are, or should be, that a certain amount of process and expense will be involved; presumably the anticipated rewards offset the cost and hassle, though surely the ultimate consumer will pay the cost of the benefit the process achieves, or there will be a hole in the developer's pocket. A court is left with the thought that one challenge of the years ahead is to cut down the process, thus lowering the cost, even while preserving the benefit. Meanwhile, the court's duty remains to follow the law as written and intended. * * *

* * * The district court should enter judgment prohibiting amendment of the easement without an appropriate determination by the Secretary as to the effect of conversion.

NOTES AND QUESTIONS

1. Was the court correct in equating "preservation" with "recreation"? How do you define recreation? Are there any realistic limits to such a definition? Is it appropriate to incorporate the broader purposes of the LWCF into the § 6(f)(3) conversion test?

2. The *Shawangunks* court concedes that the findings it requires of the Secretary "may seem simple." Are they; that is, is this litigation much ado about little? Note that § 6(f)(3) allows conversion only if the Secretary determines it is "in accord with the then existing comprehensive statewide outdoor recreation plan" and only upon "such conditions as [the Secretary] deems necessary to assure the substitution of other recreation properties of at least equal fair market value and of reasonably equivalent usefulness and location." Is the federal approval of the conversion the same as the NEPA process for considering a federal project? Does NEPA apply to the Secretary's determination?

3. What is suitable "mitigation land" here? What would be lost if the Marriott plan is implemented? How does one go about providing another scenic view of "reasonably equivalent usefulness and location" to that lost by development?

4. In the third paragraph from the end (beginning "Here we hold"), is Judge Oakes saying that the Secretary has a continuing responsibility to monitor and approve any changes in land use of any area acquired with Land & Water Conservation Fund monies, whether or not they remove land from public outdoor recreation uses? 16 U.S.C. § 460l–8(f)(1) says that the Secretary may make LWCF moneys available to the states "only for those planning, acquisition, or development projects that are approved by him." The original "project" approved by Secretary was acquisition of the conservation easement in 1977. If the easement was broadly worded to protect the environment and scenery, does any adjustment of its terms require a new approval from the Secretary?

5. In some respects, the LWCF is a "Lord of Today," a modern statute that will cast its influence far into the future. Long after the LWCF acquisition is made, the 6(f)(3) requirement remains, often hidden, ready to spring into action if the acquired land use changes. The LWCF strings attach to many places, even if the federal share of funding was small. Park

managers and developers must vigilantly investigate the funding history of public lands that may have been acquired piecemeal without central documentation. The 6(f)(3) lever turns up in unexpected places. In 2006 the Washington Post reported that, after getting state and city approval for the construction of a new baseball stadium in the Bronx, the Yankees needed the help of a D.C. law firm to lobby the Interior Department for the necessary LWCF approval. Apparently, a piece of the city park for the new stadium received some LWCF money in 1978. Judy Sarasohn, *N.Y. Yankees go Cap in Hand to Park Service*, WASH. POST, June 8, 2006.

6.   In Sierra Club v. Davies, 955 F.2d 1188 (8th Cir. 1992), plaintiffs sought to enjoin test drilling proposed to determine whether commercial mining of diamonds was feasible in the Crater of Diamonds State Park in Arkansas. The parkland had been purchased by the state in 1972, and four years later, it received a LWCF grant to develop the park's recreational facilities, which mainly involved allowing the public to search a diamond-bearing geologic formation for the gems. Therefore, the Secretary of the Interior had to approve any "conversion" of property developed with these funds to "other than public outdoor recreation uses." LWCF § 6(f)(3). The Park Service initially took the position (relying in part on *Shawangunks*) that the test drilling was a "conversion" within the meaning of the Act, and disapproved it because it "could have the potential of progressing into a full-blown commercial diamond mining operation." Following intervention by the Departmental Solicitor's Office in Washington, the Park Service reversed itself and approved the testing as a "temporary non-conforming use," noting that any subsequent testing or mining activity that would constitute a conversion would also need further approval. A divided court of appeals reversed a lower court decision and upheld the Department, deferring heavily to its application of the Act. The majority noted that the exploratory drilling would cause no permanent damage and "does not limit public uses of the park, except for the ten-to twelve-week period when a 5000 square foot region will be cordoned off." *Shawangunks* was distinguished because here "no change in the character of the land" would result.

A vigorous dissent argued otherwise. It noted that the LWCF Act contains no statutory exception for "de minimis" impacts or temporary non-conforming uses, and relied on *Shawangunks* for its conclusion that the test drilling would constitute a conversion under § 6(f)(3). Do you agree with the majority or the dissent? Which position is most consistent with *Shawangunks*?

7.   Is the holding of *Shawangunks* more about scenic preservation or private use? Conservation easements may not ensure public access and thus can be quite different from publicly owned fee simple absolute rights. Suppose, instead of an easement, the PIPC had purchased the land outright with LWCF money. Would the result have been different if the PIPC decided to lease the golf course to Marriott in order to improve and operate a public facility? Would the fees charged by Marriott for public use influence the 6(f)(3) analysis? The use of concessioners to operate developed recreational facilities has long been common and continues to increase.

8. In Idaho v. Hodel, 814 F.2d 1288 (9th Cir. 1987), the Coeur D'Alene Tribe sought forfeiture of a tract of land that had formerly been part of its reservation but then conveyed to the State of Idaho in 1908 to be "held, used, and maintained solely as a public park." The Tribe contended that the State's issuance of leases to private parties for waterfront cottages and permits to maintain float homes on a lake within the park violated the terms of the grant. Rejecting the tribe's claim, the court found that both state and national park managers had historically issued leases for cottages, and noted that while the federal government generally no longer leases cottage sites on its lands, that change in policy does not affect how the 1908 statute should be construed. The court also found persuasive that state courts had traditionally accorded city park commissioners substantial discretion in the administration of public parks, and it emphasized that 99.67 percent of the land in the park was not encumbered by the contested leases. Judge Reinhardt dissented, arguing that the court should apply "modern day notions of proper public park uses" in interpreting the 1908 grant, and that Idaho's leasing practice "constitutes the privatizing of public lands" and violates the terms of the grant. He also found deference to state park administrators inappropriate because (a) enforcement of federal law is at stake; (b) turning park land over to "private individuals for their exclusive enjoyment and preclud[ing] all public access to prime public lakefront property constitutes a wholly different and far less benign use" of public parkland than was involved in the state cases cited by the majority, and (c) although masked by the small percentage of total park area involved, the state leases effectively denied public access to about half the usable shoreline of the lake.

9. The Public Land Law Review Commission recommended that the federal government be "responsible for the preservation of scenic areas, natural wonders, primitive areas, and historic sites of *national significance*." ONE THIRD OF THE NATION'S LAND 197 (1970) (emphasis in original). Is the federal government's role properly limited to areas of "national significance"? Who determines what is nationally significant? Should LWCF monies be spent on state or regional parks?

10. The LWCF Act was preceded by the Recreation and Public Purposes Act of 1926, which authorizes the Secretary of the Interior to grant BLM land that lacks "national significance" to states, local governments, and nonprofit corporations "for any recreational or any other public purpose." 43 U.S.C. § 869(a). The Act, which remains on the books, is subject to several significant limitations; most important, the grant is conditional on the land being used for the purpose specified. If it is not, the grant may revert to the United States. 43 U.S.C. § 869–2. Such grants have been used for everything from landfills and golf courses to urban wilderness parks.

B. THE NATIONAL PARK SYSTEM

Conflicts often arise between those desiring solitary, active, non-commercial activities and those preferring more "civilized," sedentary forms of entertainment. For some, just the existence of the federal lands is sufficient; others are content to enter on their own legs, carrying their basic requirements on their backs. Most visitors, however, desire more in the way of creature comforts and the means to let them pursue their more intensive interests. Casual visitors desire centers where someone explains the land's attractions, boaters require ramps, downhill skiers need lifts, motorized vehicles need gasoline, and most want soft beds, good food, and bathrooms with plumbing. The land management agencies often contract with private concessioners to provide such services when consistent with federal policy. This section discusses recreation management in the national park system, which seeks to fill all of these roles as the flagship system for outdoor recreation in the United States.

First, however, it is useful to examine the tension that exists between recreational enjoyment of resources and preservation of those resources for the future. As we shall see, the National Park Organic Act embodies this tension.

Joseph L. Sax, Fashioning a Recreation Policy for Our National Parklands: The Philosophy of Choice and the Choice of Philosophy

12 Creighton L.Rev. 973 (1979).

A few years ago the National Park Service put forward a proposal for one of the less well-known areas that it manages. It recommended the construction of an aerial tramway to the top of Guadalupe Peak in Guadalupe Mountains National Park, the highest point of elevation in Texas. The plan seemed harmless enough. Guadalupe Peak is a place of considerable scenic merit, the park receives very few visitors, and it is located on the much-travelled road from El Paso to Carlsbad Caverns. Yet the tramway proposal elicited a surprisingly substantial and vehement opposition, and the Park Service soon shelved the plan.

The more one thinks about the Guadalupe incident, the more puzzling it becomes. For in one form or another it is repeated almost daily in the management of the public recreation lands. Should we permit the construction of a ski resort in a relatively pristine mountain valley? Should motor boats be permitted on the Colorado River in Grand Canyon? Should hotels be removed from the parks, or should they remain but without such facilities as swimming pools and tennis courts? These are all only particular instances of a general question that is a great deal more puzzling than it at first seems: What recreational policy ought we to want for the National Parks?

It is customary to believe that controversies of the sort just mentioned revolve around disputes over protection of the parks' natural resources, but a moment's reflection makes clear that environmental or scientific principles are rarely decisive. Every human use impairs the natural setting to some extent and whether a tramway impairs it "too much" is a question of policy, not of science. As with the question whether to build a road, to allow the noise of motorboats and snowmobiles, or even to establish a hiking trail, the issue we are really deciding is what kind of recreation we want to facilitate, and how much intrusion upon the untrammeled ecosystem we are prepared to tolerate for that purpose.

To be sure, some uses are far less disruptive than others, but to say that we want to minimize damage is to restate the problem rather than to solve it. Five hundred visitors a year on the river in Grand Canyon would put a great deal less pressure on the canyon ecosystem than 5,000 or the 15,000 whom we now permit to use it, and there is a great range of opinion on the point at which development, or use, becomes a spoiling factor. Some people don't want motors on wild river trips because they drown out the bird-song; others defend such trips as their only reasonable means of access to the place and find a good deal in the experience even at the expense of some quietude.

Just as these questions cannot be resolved as matters of science, neither can they be decided by economics. Should the Guadalupe Peak tramway have been built in response to public demand? The Park Service estimated that with the tramway, visitations to the Park would have increased from about 60,000 to some 500,000 persons per year. Demand is simply a measure of how people are willing to spend their time and money. No doubt many more people would be prepared to ride up Guadalupe Peak than can, or will, walk it. But just as clearly, there are many people who would patronize gambling casinos, race tracks, elegant restaurants or high rise condominia if we were willing to build them in the parks. There is demand, perfectly legitimate it may be assumed, for all these activities. Yet, at least so far, we have been unwilling to meet that demand in the parks.

Another common view is that parks should be reserved for activities that require the special resources parklands uniquely contain, or that cannot be provided by private enterprise. That position seems to explain why we have traditionally resisted building swimming pools, golf courses and tennis courts in the parks, but it does not adequately respond to the individual who aspires to play tennis in the grand setting of Yosemite Valley rather than to hike there. Nor does it explain whether those who like the solitude and silence of the parks should be preferred to those who find pleasure in a motorized, people-filled tramway or safari down the river. To assert that solitude is the essence of the park experience is to state a preference, not a fact. Each of these experiences is unique in its way, and unavailable in the private market.

Nor, finally, can we avoid the problem by asserting that government should simply hold parklands available and permit each of us to decide for ourselves how to enjoy them. This is another way of describing a policy of variety or diversity. But such a policy can only avoid preferences on the assumption of unlimited abundance. If there were many Yosemite Valleys, we could provide the Yosemite experience as everyone, in his own way, chose it. Of course there are not *many* Yosemites; and though the parks are varied enough to accommodate much diversity, someone—and not each visitor for him or herself—must decide what will happen in the one

Yosemite Valley, and the one Grand Canyon, that we do have. It is at these special kinds of places that conflict is at its most intense.

Management decisions must perforce be made, and those decisions themselves imprint an agenda on the landscape. * * * To a significant extent, management decisions effectively determine who the visitors will be, what they will do, and in what numbers, by choices that *must* be made, one way or the other.

To say that none of these management theories is decisive is not to suggest any of them is irrelevant. It is only to say that before we can think usefully about how much natural impairment we should tolerate, or where we want to draw the line in meeting demand, we need to decide what we are trying to achieve by having a public recreation policy.

If it were evident to everyone that the National Parks should be used simply to accommodate a portion of the enormous quantity of leisure time that Americans have to spend, a proposal to build a tramway that could increase recreational opportunities nearly ten-fold with a rather modest impact on the land would not have produced anything like the vigorous outcry it actually elicited. Nor would the familiar controversies over motorized recreation, ski resorts and commercial facilities in the parks have anything like the intensity that is now so evident. Beneath the multitude of specific disputes is a much deeper battle over the question whether park policy should reflect a preference for certain kinds of recreational experiences.

1. THE NPS ORGANIC ACT AND NATIONAL PARK ESTABLISHMENT STATUTES

Like the national wildlife refuges, each national park seeks to fulfill both the mission of the system as well as the individual purposes in the legislation establishing the unit. The following material explores conflicts about the meaning of those goals and the means of achieving them.

Southern Utah Wilderness Alliance v. Dabney

United States Court of Appeals, Tenth Circuit, 2000.
222 F.3d 819.

■ JUDGE EBEL

Plaintiff–Appellee Southern Utah Wilderness Alliance ("Wilderness Alliance") challenged portions of a National Park Service ("NPS") back-country management plan ("BMP") that affected access to areas of Canyonlands National Park in Utah. Wilderness Alliance alleged that the BMP violated * * * [among others] the National Park Service Organic Act ("the Organic Act" or "the Act"), 16 U.S.C. §§ 1–18(j); and the Canyonlands National Park Enabling Act, 16 U.S.C. § 271. Utah Shared Access Alliance ("Utah Shared Access"), a combination of groups supporting four-wheel drive vehicle recreation, intervened as defendants. On cross motions for summary judgment by Wilderness Alliance and the federal defendants, the district court * * * found in favor of Wilderness Alliance on its claim that the BMP's continued allowance of motorized vehicles on a ten-mile portion of the Salt Creek Jeep Road from Peekaboo Spring to Angel Arch was inconsistent with a clear legislative directive of Congress. * * * [The court] enjoined the NPS from allowing motorized vehicle travel in Salt Creek Canyon above Peekaboo Spring.

Utah Shared Access, the intervenor below, now appeals the district court's decision with respect to the ten-mile portion of the Salt Creek Road. Interestingly, the federal defendants did not appeal the district court's decision; however, they did submit a brief to this court "to advise the Court of the Department's views as to the proper legal construction of the [Organic] Act." In that brief, they take a position different from the position taken in the district court. * * *

In 1992, the NPS began developing a BMP for Canyonlands National Park and the Orange Cliffs Unit of Glen Canyon National Recreation Area in Utah. The goal of that plan as articulated by the NPS was "to develop backcountry management strategies to protect park resources, provide for high quality visitor experiences, and be flexible to deal with changing conditions." The plan was being developed in response to growing visitation to the areas, which had increased the impact on resources and diminished the quality of visitor experience.

One of the areas on which the plan was to focus was the area that is the subject of this appeal, a portion of Salt Creek Canyon. According to the NPS, the Salt Creek Road is a vehicle trail that runs in and out of Salt Creek, the only year-round, fresh water creek in Canyonlands National Park other than the Colorado and Green Rivers. There is no practical way to reroute the road to avoid the water course. To navigate this road safely, a high clearance four-wheel-drive vehicle and some experience in four-wheel driving, or the participation in a commercially guided tour, is necessary. The NPS found that it was receiving numerous requests every year for assistance in removing vehicles that broke down or became stuck on the Salt Creek Road. In addition, there were several instances every year of vehicles losing transmission, engine, or crankcase fluids in the water. The NPS became concerned with the adverse impacts inherent in the existence of a road and vehicle traffic in this narrow riparian corridor. A Notice of Intent to prepare a BMP was printed in the Federal Register. * * * The NPS solicited possible solutions to the problems in the area, and hosted public discussions in Utah and Colorado in late 1992 and early 1993.

* * * [Following publication of a draft environmental assessment, and numerous public meetings, NPS release a final BMP in early 1995 which] adopted an alternative that did not close the ten-mile portion of the Salt Creek Road; instead, it closed a one-half mile segment of the road and left the rest open to vehicles on a limited permit system.[3] Wilderness Alliance

---

3. The relevant portion of the BMP stated as follows:

Salt Creek and Horse Canyon four-wheel drive roads in the Needles District will

remain open to vehicular traffic, but travel will be by backcountry use permit only. A locked gate at the north end of the road (the location of the current subsequently filed a complaint [claiming, among other things, that] * * * by approving the BMP and sanctioning continued vehicle-caused degradation in that area, the NPS violated the * * * the Organic Act, and the Canyonlands National Park Enabling Act. Wilderness Alliance sought declaratory and injunctive relief. Utah Shared Access intervened as defendants, opposing the closure of Salt Creek Canyon to vehicle access.

The * * * [district court] ruled in favor of Wilderness Alliance on its challenge to the portion of the BMP that left the ten-mile segment of the Salt Creek Road from Peekaboo Spring to Angel Arch open to vehicles[, holding] * * * that the Organic Act and the Canyonlands enabling legislation preclude the NPS from authorizing activities that permanently impair unique park resources. It then determined, based on the administrative record, that such a permanent impairment would occur from the continued use by motorized vehicles of this ten-mile segment[, and] * * * enjoined the federal defendants from permitting or otherwise allowing motorized vehicle travel in Salt Creek Canyon above Peekaboo Spring. * * *

* * * When the question before us involves an agency's interpretation of a statute it administers, we utilize the two-step approach announced in *Chevron U.S.A., Inc. v. Natural Resources Defense Council, Inc.,* 467 U.S. 837, 842–43 (1984). When Congress has spoken to the precise question at issue, we must give effect to the express intent of Congress. *See Chevron,* 467 U.S. at 842–43. If the statute is silent or ambiguous, however, we defer to the agency's interpretation, if it is a permissible one. *See id.* at 843–44.

The provision of the Organic Act relating to the creation of the NPS and the purpose of the national parks it oversees provides:

> The service thus established shall promote and regulate the use of the Federal areas known as national parks ... by such means and measures as conform to the fundamental purpose of the said parks ... which purpose is to conserve the scenery and the natural and historic objects and the wild life therein and to provide for the enjoyment of the same in such manner and by such means as will leave them unimpaired for the enjoyment of future generations.

16 U.S.C.§ 1. Another provision of the Organic Act prohibits authorization of activities that derogate park values:

> The authorization of activities shall be construed and the protection, management, and administration of these areas shall be conducted in light of the high public value and integrity of the National Park System and shall not be exercised in derogation of the values and purposes for which these various areas have been established, except as

gate) will control access. Day use permits for Salt Creek and Horse Canyon will be limited to ten (10) permits for private motor vehicles (one vehicle per permit), two (2) permits for commercial motor vehicle tours (one vehicle per permit), one (1) or more permits for up to seven (7) private or commercial bicyclists, one (1) or more permits for up to seven (7) pack or saddle stock.... All permits are available through the advance reservation system. Unreserved permits or cancellations will be available to walk-in visitors.

may have been or shall be directly and specifically provided by Congress.

16 U.S.C. § 1a–1. The enabling legislation creating Canyonlands National Park provides: "In order to preserve an area in the State of Utah possessing superlative scenic, scientific, and archeologic features for the inspiration, benefit, and use of the public, there is hereby established the Canyonlands National Park ..." 16 U.S.C. § 271. That legislation also mandates that Canyonlands be administered, protected, and developed in accordance with the purposes of the Organic Act.

In the district court, the NPS asserted that the Organic Act and the enabling legislation creating Canyonlands National Park authorized a balancing between competing mandates of resource conservation and visitor enjoyment, and that its BMP represented a reasonable accommodation of conflicting mandates that should be afforded considerable deference. The district court reviewed the agency's interpretation in accordance with the analysis set forth in *Chevron* * * *. According to the district court, the first *Chevron* inquiry was determinative on the issue of continued vehicle access to the ten-mile portion of the Salt Creek Road. The court stated:

> Congress has issued a clear answer to the question of whether the Park Service is authorized to permit activities within national parks that permanently impair unique park resources. The answer is no. As set out in the statutes discussed above, the Park Service's mandate is to permit forms of enjoyment and access that are *consistent* with preservation and *inconsistent* with significant, permanent impairment.

Southern Utah Wilderness Alliance, 7 F.Supp.2d at 1211. Finding that the evidence in the administrative record showed that "the riparian areas in Salt Creek Canyon are unique and that the effects of vehicular traffic beyond Peekaboo Spring are inherently and fundamentally inimical to their continued existence," the district court held that the BMP was inconsistent with the "clear legislative directive" of Congress. *Id.*

On appeal, Utah Shared Access argues that the district court erred in resolving the issue under the first *Chevron* inquiry. Utah Shared Access argues that the district court should have reached the second *Chevron* inquiry because of ambiguities inherent in the relevant statutes and their application to the issue of vehicular access.[6] We agree.

* * *

6. Utah Shared Access also advances an argument that the Salt Creek Road was "grandfathered" in as a road and cannot be closed because it existed prior to the establishment of the park, and the park was established "subject to valid existing rights." 16 U.S.C. § 271. In support of its argument, Utah Shared Access cites language in the legislative history stating that road access to parts of Glen Canyon National Recreation Area is over jeep trails. We find this argument without merit. Utah Shared Access has not established that it had any legally cognizable right to use of this jeep trail at the time of the establishment of this park, or even that this particular portion of the jeep trail existed at that time. In any event, nothing in the statutory language indicates that a jeep trail cannot be closed if closure is deemed necessary for preservation. The legislative history is inconclusive at best on the issue, and thus carries little weight.

Although the Act and the Canyonlands enabling legislation place an overarching concern on preservation of resources, we read the Act as permitting the NPS to balance the sometimes conflicting policies of resource conservation and visitor enjoyment in determining what activities should be permitted or prohibited. *See* 16 U.S.C. § 1 ("to conserve ... and to provide for the enjoyment of...."); 16 U.S.C. § 271 ("to preserve ... for the inspiration, benefit, and use of the public....") * * * The test for whether the NPS has performed its balancing properly is whether the resulting action leaves the resources "unimpaired for the enjoyment of future generations." Because of the ambiguity inherent in that phrase, we cannot resolve the issue before us under step one of *Chevron;* instead we must reach step two.

The question for the court under step two of *Chevron* is "whether the agency's answer is based on a permissible construction of the statute." *Chevron,* 467 U.S. at 843. To resolve this question, we must first determine what the agency's position is. In its brief to this court and at oral argument, the NPS has advised us that the Department of the Interior "has conducted a substantive reassessment of the proper construction of the Organic Act." On the basis of that reassessment, the Department took the position in its brief to this court that the Act prohibits "permanent impairment of those resources whose conservation is essential to the fundamental purposes and values for which an individual park has been established." The Department also took the position that the NPS has discretion under the Act to determine what resources are essential to the values and purposes of a particular national park, and what constitutes the impairment of those resources. In supplemental authority provided to this court just prior to oral argument, the Department submitted Draft NPS Management Policies (the "Draft Policies"), which clarify its position further. The Draft Policies address impairment of resources in terms of the duration, extent, timing, and cumulative effect of various impacts on park resources and values. They also are based on a premise that the Organic Act forbids broader categories of impairment in addition to those considered as permanent. *See id.* In addition, the Draft Policies provide definitions for various terms in the Organic Act.

The Draft Policies propose to define "impairment of park resources and values" as "an adverse impact on one or more park resources or values that interferes with the integrity of the park's resources or values, or with the opportunities that otherwise would exist for the enjoyment of them by a present or future generation." The Draft Policies also propose to define "park resources and values" as "all the resources and values of a park whose conservation is essential to the purposes for which the area was included in the national park system ... and any additional purposes stated in a park's establishing legislation or proclamation."

The interpretation of the Act now offered by the Department and the NPS in this court and in the Draft Policies varies from the interpretation previously offered by the NPS in the district court.[8] We must determine

---

8. The position adopted in the Draft Policies apparently supplants the former position of the NPS and the Department of the Interior. Thus, the former position is one to which the agency no longer subscribes.

what weight to give the new interpretation. We conclude that there is currently no valid agency position worthy of deference.

An agency is free to change the meaning it attaches to ambiguous statutory language, and the new interpretation may still be accorded *Chevron* deference. * * *A position taken by an agency during litigation, however, is not sufficiently formal that it is deserving of *Chevron* deference. * * *

Similarly, agency policy statements, like litigation positions, do not usually warrant deference under step two of *Chevron*. *See Christensen v. Harris County,* 529 U.S. 576 (2000) (stating that agency interpretations contained in policy statements, agency manuals, and enforcement guidelines do not warrant *Chevron*-style deference).

A notice of availability of the Draft Policies, however, was published in the Federal Register and the public was given an opportunity to comment on them. *See* Notice of Availability of Draft National Park Service Management Policies, 65 Fed. Reg. 2984 (2000). Thus, the Draft Policies are unlike typical informal agency policy manuals. The fact that a notice regarding the Draft Policies appeared in the Federal Register and that they were subjected to comment procedures does not, however, automatically make them deserving of *Chevron* deference. The comments must still be considered and a rule must be properly adopted with a statement of its basis and purpose to complete the notice and comment rulemaking procedures. *See* 5 U.S.C. § 553(c). If the Draft Policies are finalized and adopted pursuant to the requisite rulemaking procedures, and then construed as substantive or legislative rules, they should be accorded *Chevron* deference; however, if, when ultimately finalized, they lack the requisite formality and are construed merely as interpretative rules, they should be examined under a less deferential standard that asks whether the agency's interpretation is "well reasoned" and "has the power to persuade." *See Chrysler Corp. v. Brown,* 441 U.S. 281, 301–02 (1979) (distinguishing between substantive rules and interpretative rules).

At this time, the agency's Policies are still only in draft form and have not yet been finalized or adopted by the agency; therefore, we cannot accord either *Chevron* deference or the lesser deference applicable to interpretative rules to the agency's interpretation of the Act. Having no current interpretation in front of us that has been formally adopted by the agency, we examine the Act and the district court's disposition without giving deference to any agency interpretation. * * *

The district court's legal interpretation of the Act was that the NPS is prohibited from permitting activities that result in "significant, permanent impairment." *Southern Utah Wilderness Alliance,* 7 F.Supp.2d at 1211. We agree that permitting "significant, permanent impairment" would violate the Act's mandate that the NPS provide for the enjoyment of the parks "in such manner and by such means as will leave them unimpaired for the enjoyment of future generations." 16 U.S.C. § 1. Although "significant, permanent impairment" may not be coterminous with what is prohibited by the Act because other negative impacts may also be prohibited, we find that it is within the range of prohibitions contemplated by Congress.

The district court determined that the administrative record demonstrated that permanent impairment would occur; however, the parties continue to dispute whether the impairment caused by vehicles would be permanent and how serious it would be. The administrative record includes the NPS's FONSI, which stated that any impairment would be temporary and minor. In its discussion of the evidence in the administrative record on impairment, the district court did not mention that finding by the NPS, which should be reviewed under the standard set forth in § 706(2) of the APA. Given the conflicting views regarding the level of impairment that vehicles would cause to the ten-mile segment of the Salt Creek Road, we remand for the district court to re-examine the evidence in the record regarding impairment, applying the appropriate standard to the NPS finding of temporary impairment.

On remand, the district court should not limit its analysis under step two of *Chevron* to whether the evidence demonstrates significant, permanent impairment. Rather, it should assess whether the evidence demonstrates the level of impairment prohibited by the Act. Moreover, by the time of trial, the Department of the Interior may have finalized and adopted its new NPS Management Policies. If the district court determines that those policies have been expressed in a binding format through the agency's congressionally delegated power, they should be considered legislative rules worthy of *Chevron* deference. If, however, the district court determines that they are merely interpretative rules, they should be evaluated pursuant to the less deferential standard articulated in * * * *Skidmore v. Swift & Co.*, 323 U.S. 134, 140 (1944).

Because we find error in the district court's conclusion that the activity at issue is explicitly prohibited by the relevant statutes, we find the district court abused its discretion in granting an injunction. We therefore vacate the district court's order enjoining the BMP's allowance of continued motorized vehicle use on the Salt Creek Road in Salt Creek Canyon above Peekaboo Spring.

The district court erred in finding that step one of *Chevron* was determinative with respect to the issue of vehicle access on the ten-mile segment of the Salt Creek Road. The analysis must proceed under step two of *Chevron,* and, in conducting that analysis, the district court must re-examine the evidence in the record regarding impairment caused by vehicles in that area, applying the appropriate standard to the NPS finding of temporary impairment. The district court must also determine the weight to be given to the position of the NPS as to the standards set forth in the Organic Act. * * *

NOTES AND QUESTIONS

1.   Look closely at the language in the Organic Act. Does it call for a balancing between recreational visitor use and preservation? Is one purpose

dominant over the other? Or is it ambiguous? In Sierra Club v. Babbitt, environmentalists challenged a Park Service decision to reconstruct a road providing one of the principal means of access into Yosemite National Park, arguing among other things that the project would permanently alter the Merced River canyon in the Park, and thus violate the Organic Act. The court found no violation:

> The Organic Act commits the NPS to the protection and furtherance of two fundamentally competing values; the preservation of natural and cultural resources and the facilitation of public use and enjoyment. These competing values of conservation and public use have been actively in conflict since before the establishment of the NPS. The Organic Act did not resolve the conflict in favor of one side or the other. Rather, the Organic Act acknowledges the conflict and, saying nothing about how to achieve resolution, grants deference to NPS in balancing the competing and conflicting values. * * * The Organic Act would serve as a basis for a cause of action were the NPS to allow use of a national park in a way that was not in the interests of either conservation or public enjoyment or in a way that was clearly against the interests of future generations. The current action does not fall in either category. The current action concerns how best to preserve access to the park while at the same time preserving the values for which the Yosemite Valley and the Merced River corridor were declared a national park.

69 F.Supp.2d 1202, 1246–47 (E.D.Cal.1999). Does this interpretation give the NPS greater management discretion than the other federal public land agencies? Is that appropriate? Is it consistent with the Salt Creek Canyon Road opinion in SUWA v. Dabney?

2. Is the question what adjective to put in front of "impairment"? "Permanent" or "significant" versus "temporary" or "minor"? Does the Act literally prohibit "any" impairment? Is that a reasonable construction, if it would outlaw many uses visitors routinely make of national parks? Would a "permanent, significant impairment" standard prohibit the Park Service from ever authorizing any new road or building construction in a park? See Robin W. Winks, *The National Park Service Act of 1916: "A Contradictory Mandate"?*, 74 Denv. U. L.Rev. 575 (1997).

3. Here the district court cited evidence in the administrative record that the riparian areas in Salt Creek Canyon are "unique." Is that relevant? Might every area in every park be considered unique? (Recall the maxim of property law, justifying specific performance in contracts to convey land, that all parcels of land are unique.) Does the Organic Act forbid the Park Service from building a road down to the bottom of the Grand Canyon from the South Rim in order to provide vehicular access to its depths? Does the Salt Creek Canyon Road present the same challenge?

4. Does the Act's reference to "future generations" provide a clue as to how it should be interpreted? Is it a permissible interpretation of the statute for the Park Service to say that if a use causes some impairment, but that impairment can be erased within a generation (say, twenty-five

years), it may be allowed? Would that be the only permissible interpretation?

5. Notice the interplay between the statute creating Canyonlands National Park and the generic National Park Organic Act. Does the former add anything to the latter? Note that the establishment act for Canyonlands uses the word "preserve" rather than the organic act's "conserve." 16 U.S.C. § 271d. This kind of overlapping statutory guidance, with more general legislation supplemented by specific legislation applicable to the particular area or unit at issue, is typical in federal land law. *See* Robert Fischman, *The Problem of Statutory Detail in National Park Establishment Legislation*, 74 DENV. U. L.REV. 779 (1997).

6. The National Park Service finally completed a rulemaking in July 2004 that prohibited motor vehicles on this portion of Salt Creek Canyon. 69 Fed. Reg. 32871 (2004). Interestingly, the NPS noted that the district court's initial injunction in 1998 provided an experiment in riparian restoration, but also suggested the difficulty of showing impairment while a longstanding activity continues. The judicial ban was the only period of significant duration without vehicular use in the canyon since the park's creation in 1964. The Service seized the opportunity to gather information on riparian conditions without the effects of vehicles, which showed such improvements as vegetation returning to vehicle tracks and water flows restoring a more natural river channel. The agency therefore made a finding of "impairment to park resources and values" from any vehicle use. Upon remand, the district court dismissed all of the challenges to the new rule. 387 F.Supp.2d 1178 (D.Utah 2005). However, litigation continues over whether a valid "highway" had been constructed in the canyon under the nineteenth century statute, R.S. 2477, before the Park was created. See Chapter 5, *supra* p. 386.

7. Is the court correct in its approach to the agency's rather inconsistent attempts to construe the statute? Might impairment have meant one thing in 1916, when the statute was enacted, and mean something else nearly a century later? If public opinion has shifted over that time about how "natural" it wants the parks kept, may the agency properly take that shift in values into account, or must the agency go back to Congress for more guidance? If the agency changes its interpretation of "impairment" over time, can it still receive the same amount of deference from the courts on its new interpretation as it would have with its original interpretation? If so, why doesn't it get deference here?

NPS Management Policies

The NPS Management Policies document is the Service's "official interpretation" of the 1916 Organic Act and the 1978 "Redwood" amendment, 16 U.S.C. § 1a–1. It fills the same role as the agency manuals do for the national forests and national wildlife refuges. Shortly before the Clinton Administration left office in early 2001, the draft policies discussed in *SUWA v. Dabney* were, after further modification, put in final form. In the fall of 2005, Deputy Assistant Secretary of the Interior Paul Hoffman stirred up considerable controversy by circulating a rewrite of the 2001 Management Policies that would have watered down the preservation mandate and elevated recreation and recreational development to a more comparable status. Hoffman was formerly head of the Chamber of Commerce in Cody, Wyoming (a gateway community to Yellowstone), where he often tangled with conservationists concerning park management. After protests by park defenders, including some members of Congress and an active group of retired Park Service employees, the Administration disavowed the draft. The Bush administration released its final, considerably milder, changes to the policies in 2006. Excerpts from the Management Policies (2006) follow:

1.4.2 "Impairment" and "Derogation": One Standard

Congress intended the language of the Redwood amendment to the General Authorities Act to reiterate the provisions of the Organic Act, not create a substantively different management standard. * * * For simplicity, Management Policies uses "impairment," * * * to refer to that single standard.

1.4.3 The NPS Obligation to Conserve and Provide for Enjoyment of Park Resources and Values

* * * [The Organic Act and the General Authorities Act] give the Service the management discretion to allow impacts to park resources and values when necessary and appropriate to fulfill the purposes of a park, so long as the impact does not constitute impairment of the affected resources and values. * * * The enjoyment that is contemplated by the statute is broad; it is the enjoyment of all the people of the United States and includes enjoyment both by people who visit parks and by those who appreciate them from afar. It also includes deriving benefit (including scientific knowledge) and inspiration from parks, as well as other forms of enjoyment and inspiration. Congress, recognizing that the enjoyment by future generations of the national parks can be ensured only if the superb quality of park resources and values is left unimpaired, has provided that when there is a conflict between conserving resources and values and providing for enjoyment of them, conservation is to be predominant. This is how courts have consistently interpreted the Organic Act.

* * *

1.4.5 What Constitutes Impairment of Park Resources and Values

The impairment that is prohibited by [the statutes] is an impact that, in the professional judgment of the responsible NPS manager, would harm the integrity of park's resources or values, including the opportunities that otherwise would be present for the enjoyment of those resources or values. Whether an impact meets this definition depends on the particular resources and values that would be affected; the severity, duration, and timing of the impact; the direct and indirect effects of the impact; and the cumulative effects of the impact in question and other impacts.

An impact to any park resource or value may, but does not necessarily, constitute an impairment. An impact would be more likely to constitute impairment to the extent that it affects a resource or value whose conservation is:

—necessary to fulfill specific purposes identified in the establishing legislation or proclamation of the park, or

—key to the natural or cultural integrity of the park or to opportunities for enjoyment of the park, or

—identified in the park's general management plan or other relevant NPS planning documents as being of significance.

* * *

An impact that may, but would not necessarily, lead to impairment may result from visitor activities; NPS administrative activities; or activities undertaken by concessioners, contractors, and others operating in the park. Impairment may also result from sources or activities outside the park.

1.4.6 What Constitutes Park Resources and Values

—The "park resources and values" that are subject to the no-impairment standard include:

—the park's scenery, natural and historic objects, and wildlife, and the processes and conditions that sustain them, including, to the extent present in the park: the ecological, biological, and physical processes that created the park and continue to act upon it; scenic features; natural visibility, both in daytime and at night; natural landscapes; natural soundscapes and smells; water and air resources; soils; geological resources; paleontological resources; archeological resources; cultural landscapes; ethnographic resources; historic and prehistoric sites, structures, and objects; museum collections; and native plants and animals;

—appropriate opportunities to experience enjoyment of the above resources, to the extent that can be done without impairing them;

—the park's role in contributing to the national dignity, the high public value and integrity, and the superlative environmental quality of the national park system. * * *

1.4.7 Decision-making Requirements to Identify and Avoid Impairments

Before approving a proposed action that could lead to an impairment * * * an NPS decisionmaker must consider the impacts of the proposed action and determine, in writing, that the activity will not lead to an impairment of park resources and values. If there would be an impairment, the action must not be approved. * * * [The] decisionmaker must use his or her professional judgment [and] consider [among other things, NEPA documents, relevant scientific studies, and public comments.] * * *

When an NPS decision-maker becomes aware that an ongoing activity might have led or might be leading to an impairment of park resources or values, he or she must investigate and determine if there is or will be an impairment. This investigation and determination may be made independent of, or as part of, a park planning process undertaken for other purposes. If it is determined that there is, or will be, an impairment, the decision-maker must take appropriate action, to the extent possible within the Service's authorities and available resources, to eliminate the impairment. The action must eliminate the impairment as soon as reasonably possible * * *.

NOTES AND QUESTIONS

1.   What is the difference between an impact and impairment under the 2006 policies? Which better describes motor vehicle use in Salt Creek Canyon? Does the "professional judgment" language in 1.4.5 insulate Park Service determinations from judicial review? Park values under 1.4.6 include an extremely broad array of attributes, including soundscapes and smell. How can the Park Service justify allowing any motor vehicles, including snowmobiles, under this standard?

2.   The NPS Management Policies now require written determinations that activities will not impair park resources. This follows Congress' 1997 organic mandate for the National Wildlife Refuge System to provide written compatibility determinations for refuge uses. Recall that a compatible use is one that "will not materially interfere with or detract from the fulfillment of the mission of the System" or the individual purpose of the unit. 16 U.S.C. § 668ee. *See supra* p. 867. Are the two standards (ensure compatibility and prevent impairment) the same? Note that while FWS refuge management activities are excluded from the compatibility requirement, NPS Management Policy 1.4.5 contains no such express exclusion for NPS management activities. Is that a good idea, or unduly burdensome for park superintendents attempting to respond to routine management imperatives?

3.   Does 1.4.7 create a judicially enforceable, affirmative duty to act when the Park Service receives a complaint about impairment? Is 1.4.7 a manifestation of Wilkinson's theory of a public trust responsibility that arises from the web of conservation statutes? *See* Wilkinson, Chapter 2 *supra* p. 84.

4.   Does 1.4.3 correctly characterize the case law interpreting 16 U.S.C. § 1? In particular, is it fair to state that Sierra Club v. Babbitt, the Yosemite N.P. road case, *supra* p. 929, interpreted the organic mandate to mean that "when there is a conflict between conserving resources and values and providing for enjoyment of them, conservation is to be predominant"?

5.   Like the national wildlife refuges, national parks face increasingly difficult conservation challenges from threats emanating outside of park boundaries. *See supra* p. 864. The Park Service has made great strides in

recognizing this problem and encouraging its officials to respond. The 1988 version of Management Policies (§ 1.4) stated that:

> the National Park Service does not support the creation of buffer zones around the parks or seek veto power over activities on adjacent lands, [but] it will work cooperatively with surrounding landowners and managers to help ensure that actions outside the parks do not impair park resources and values.

While the 2006 policy (§ 1.6) retains NPS's enthusiasm for cooperative approaches to landscape-level challenges, it also provides significantly greater encouragement for more assertive, and even adversarial, approaches:

> Superintendents will monitor land use proposals, changes to adjacent lands, and external activities for their potential impacts on park resources and values. * * * Superintendents will encourage compatible adjacent land uses and seek to avoid and mitigate potential adverse impacts on park resources and values by actively participating in the planning and regulatory processes of other federal agencies and tribal, state, and local governments having jurisdiction over property affecting, or affected by, the park. If a decision is made or is imminent that will result in unacceptable impacts on park resources, superintendents must take appropriate action, to the extent possible within the Service's authorities and available resources, to manage or constrain the use to minimize impacts.

Does the 2006 policy implicitly endorse the concept of buffer zones around parks to protect park resources?

6.   The only significant addition to national park organic legislation since the 1978 Redwood Amendment is the National Parks Omnibus Management Act of 1998 (which mostly dealt with concession reforms, discussed *infra*). It provided:

> The Secretary shall take such measures as are necessary to assure the full and proper utilization of the results of scientific study for park management decisions. In each case in which an action undertaken by the National Park Service may cause a significant adverse effect on a park resource, the administrative record shall reflect the manner in which unit resource studies have been considered.

16 U.S.C. § 5936. Are the Management Policies consistent with this statute? Does this statute reflect a congressional view that the Park Service has authority to take action that causes "a significant adverse effect on a park resource," as long as it does so with its eyes open? Another section of the 1998 law deals with monitoring external threats to parks. 16 U.S.C. § 5934.

Rationing Recreation

Grand Canyon river trips are in some ways a microcosm of the challenge of managing recreation throughout the national park system.

From John Wesley Powell's famous expedition down the river in 1869 until the mid–1960s, fewer than 1000 persons made the trip by water through the Grand Canyon. Improved technology, a dramatic increase in demand for outdoor adventure, and other factors combined in the mid–1960s to cause an explosion of interest. More than 1000 persons made the trip in the single year of 1966. Use exceeded 10,000 persons in 1971 and 16,000 in 1972, when the Park Service first placed limits on the number. The following case resulted.

Wilderness Public Rights Fund v. Kleppe

United States Court of Appeals, Ninth Circuit, 1979.
608 F.2d 1250, *cert. denied*, 446 U.S. 982 (1980).

■ JUDGE MERRILL

These cases involve the manner in which use of the Colorado River for rafting and boating is apportioned between concessioners approved by the National Park Service and noncommercial users. Permits from the National Park Service are required for river use and the dispute here concerns the apportionment made in granting permits.

In December, 1972, the Secretary of the Interior found that the boating and rafting use of the Colorado River in the Grand Canyon National Park had experienced such an increase that it posed a threat to the ecology of the river. A study was initiated for the purpose of ascertaining river capacity and it was decided that until completion of the study use of the river should be frozen at the 1972 level. Accordingly, river use was limited to 96,600 user days per year (a user day being one day spent on the river by one person). This total use was apportioned between two user groups in the ratio of actual 1972 use by each group: 89,000 user days or 92 percent of the total use was allotted to commercial concessioners of the Park Service who, for a fee, make guided trips through the canyon; 7,600 user days or 8 percent of the total was allotted to noncommercial users who apply for permits as private groups. Noncommercial users for the most part are experienced in river running and furnish their own equipment and supplies. Expenses are shared, as is the performance of the necessary duties involved. Permits for river use and the apportionment thereof have remained frozen at the 1972 level.

Appellants are, or represent, noncommercial river runners who, on various grounds, challenge the apportionment between commercial and noncommercial users. They assert that they, or those they represent, have applied for permits from the Park Service which were denied, the Service instead having granted permits to persons who used them for commercial purposes. In January, 1975, a member of Wilderness Public Rights Fund petitioned the Secretary for a change in the allocation system for the issuance of permits. The request was denied. [Separate law suits were filed by two different plaintiffs in two different states challenging the Park Service's allocation between commercial and non-commercial permittees. In one, brought by the Wilderness Public Rights Fund in the Northern District of California, the plaintiff argued that noncommercial users are entitled to priority over commercial users. In the other, brought by individuals in the District of Arizona, the plaintiffs argued that noncommercial users should have equal access with commercial users. In both the Park Service was victorious in the lower courts, and the appeals were consolidated.] * * *

A number of statutes and regulations bear on the issues of these actions. 16 U.S.C. § 1 creates the National Park Service (hereinafter NPS) in the Department of the Interior and directs it to "promote and regulate the use of the Federal areas known as national parks, monuments and reservations * * * by such means and measures as conform to the fundamental purpose of said parks, monuments and reservations * * *." That purpose is stated to be "to conserve the scenery and the natural and historic objects and the wild life therein and to provide for the enjoyment of the same in such manner and by such means as will leave them unimpaired for the enjoyment of future generations."

16 U.S.C. § 3 provides in part:

"The Secretary of the Interior shall make and publish such rules and regulations as he may deem necessary or proper for the use and management of the parks, monuments, and reservations under the jurisdiction of the National Park Service * * *. He may also grant privileges, leases, and permits for the use of land for the accommodation of visitors in the various parks, monuments or other reservations [herein provided for] but for periods not exceeding thirty years; and no natural curiosities, wonders, or objects of interest shall be leased, rented, or granted to anyone on such terms as to interfere with free access to them by the public."

Pursuant to this authority the Secretary has promulgated 36 C.F.R. § 7.4(h)(3) as follows:

"(3) No person shall conduct, lead, or guide a river trip unless such person possesses a permit issued by the Superintendent, Grand Canyon National Park. The National Park Service reserves the right to limit the number of such permits issued, or the number of persons travelling on trips authorized by such permits when, in the opinion of the National Park Service, such limitations are necessary in the interest of public safety or protection of the ecological and environmental values of the area."

The Concessions Policy Act, 16 U.S.C. § 20 provides in part: "It is the policy of the Congress that such development [concessions] shall be limited to those that are necessary and appropriate for public use and enjoyment of the national park area in which they are located * * *."

* * * Appellants contend that allocation between commercial and noncommercial use of the river is not an acceptable method of accomplishing a limitation of river use. They propose that anyone wishing to run the river should apply for a permit, leaving to him, if his application be granted, the choice between joining a guided party or a noncommercial party; that permits then be granted by lottery or on a first-come-first-served basis. They assert that the record establishes that such a method is

feasible. They contend that there is no justification for allocating between commercial and noncommercial use, and that to do so amounts to arbitrary action; that it denies them "free access" to the river contrary to 16 U.S.C. § 3 and permits development by concession to a degree in excess of that allowed by the Concessions Policy Act. We disagree.

The Secretary of the Interior, acting through the NPS, has the wide ranging responsibility of managing the national parks. 16 U.S.C. § 3. Pursuant to this authority, the NPS regulates use of the Colorado River through the permit requirement described in 36 C.F.R. § 7.4(h)(3), supra. In issuing permits, the Service has recognized that those who make recreational use of the river fall into two classes: those who have the skills and equipment to run the river without professional guidance and those who do not. The Service recognizes its obligation to protect the interests of both classes of users. It can hardly be faulted for doing so. If the overall use of the river must, for the river's protection, be limited, and if the rights of all are to be recognized, then the "free access" of any user must be limited to the extent necessary to accommodate the access rights of others. We must confine our review of the permit system to the question whether the NPS has acted within its authority and whether the action taken is arbitrary. Allocation of the limited use between the two groups is one method of assuring that the rights of each are recognized and, if fairly done pursuant to appropriate standards, is a reasonable method and cannot be said to be arbitrary. It is well within the area of administrative discretion granted to the NPS.

Throughout these proceedings Wilderness Public Rights Fund has persisted in viewing the dispute as one between the recreational users of the river and the commercial operators, whose use is for profit. It asserts that by giving a firm allocation to the commercial operators to the disadvantage of those who wish to run the river on their own the Service is commercializing the park. The Fund ignores the fact that the commercial operators, as concessioners of the Service, undertake a public function to provide services that the NPS deems desirable for those visiting the area. 16 U.S.C. § 20a. The basic face-off is not between the commercial operators and the noncommercial users, but between those who can make the run without professional assistance and those who cannot.

While the Concessions Policy Act, 16 U.S.C. § 20, supra, expresses the congressional intent that the granting of concessions shall be limited to "those that are necessary and appropriate for public use and enjoyment" of the park involved, the authority for the granting of concessions is given to the Secretary by 16 U.S.C. § 3, and there is no showing here of arbitrary action or abuse of that authority.

Appellants also complain that noncommercial applicants receive unfair and unequal treatment at the hands of the Service. They must apply to the Service for permits and thus must plan their trips well in advance. Deadlines must be met. The names of all in the proposed party (with signatures) must be set forth. Those who make the trip under guide may deal directly with the concessioners and make arrangements at the last minute. This comports with the NPS' right to regulate river trips in the interests of safety. 36 C.F.R. § 7.4(h)(3). We find nothing unreasonable in thus assuring, as matter of safety, that those who make the trip on their own without concessioners' supervision have undertaken the necessary preparation and possess the necessary skill to participate in the activities involved.

We conclude that allocation between the two classes of recreational users is not per se an arbitrary method of recognizing and accommodating the interests of the two classes. The question remaining is whether allocation has been fairly made pursuant to appropriate standards. * * *

Appellants challenge the method used by the Park Service in determining allocation between the classes of users for the reason that it is founded on 1972 data. It is asserted that since that year there has been a substantial increase in the demand for use by noncommercial users, and that to freeze allocation of use on the basis of seven-year-old data in the face of rapid change is arbitrary and unreasonable.

We are informed, however, that the study initiated by the National Park Service has now been completed and that the interim basis for allocation between the two classes of users—freezing at the 1972 level—is being abandoned. A proposed management plan for the river and a draft environmental impact statement have been completed and published. The allocation departs from the 1972 level of 92 percent user days for commercial operators and 8 percent user days for noncommercial river runners. Under the plan, 70 percent of the user days will be allocated for commercial trips and 30 percent for noncommercial trips. The period assigned for comment has expired and it is anticipated that a final plan will be forthcoming in a matter of weeks.

This renders moot challenges to the specifics of the interim management plan, now about to be superseded by a final plan. The basis for the claim of arbitrariness—that the freezing of use and allocation of use at the 1972 levels is, in 1979, unreasonable—falls from the case.

NOTES AND QUESTIONS

1.   Examine 16 U.S.C. § 3, quoted in the opinion. Does this give the Park Service plenary authority to require permits and otherwise regulate visitor conduct? Where in 16 U.S.C. §§ 1 or 3 does the Park Service find authority either (a) to limit the total number of raft trips; or (b) to allocate trips between commercial and non-commercial users? By issuing concession contracts to rafting companies, and limiting others, is the agency making a grant of "natural curiosities on such terms as to interfere with free access * * * by the public" (expressly forbidden by 16 U.S.C. § 3)? Does "free" mean "free" in the same sense that the *TAPS* case read "50 feet" to mean "50 feet"? *See* Wilderness Society v. Morton, *supra* p. 235.

2.   The court did not rule on the split of ninety-two percent for commercial uses and eight percent for non-commercial. Is that the kind of decision that should be left completely up to the agency? Or is this specific allocation so extreme that a court should require an especially strong

administrative record and a compelling explanation in support of the decision? If the 2006 Management Policies had been in place at the time of the NPS decision, would they have compelled a different result?

3.   Is allocation on the basis of "historical use" always rational? Are there other, better bases? Is the Park Service's legal obligation to ascertain and then meet the "public demand" for outdoor recreational experiences? How would Professor Sax propose to resolve this dispute? *See* excerpts *supra* p. 46 and 920. At least in areas of unique or scarce scenic or aesthetic resources like here, is some sort of rationing system inevitable? Should the NPS auction river trips to the highest bidders? How would that approach differ from concessioner agreements?

4.   What might be the Park Service's interest in encouraging commercial as opposed to non-commercial trips? Health and safety—risk management? Protecting the environment? Revenues? Could the Park Service ban *all* non-commercial trips? What would it need to show in order to do that? In Great American Houseboat Co. v. United States, 780 F.2d 741 (9th Cir. 1986), the court rejected an equal protection attack on a Forest Service regulation banning commercial (under a time-sharing scheme) but not individual use of houseboats on a recreational lake: "The commercial/personal use distinction served the legitimate statutory purpose of allowing the Forest Service to regulate and accommodate multiple uses on Shasta Lake and to avoid overcrowding * * * and a degrading of the quality of the recreational experience there." 780 F.2d at 748.

5.   Many persons who travel through the Grand Canyon on the river do so on craft powered by small outboard motors. In the late 1970s, a controversy briefly raged when the Park Service considered banning motorized trips. Motor trips are about twice as fast as oar-powered trips (nine versus eighteen days, approximately) and are also about half as expensive (because the cost to the visitor is measured mostly by time on the river). Park Service studies have generally shown that, so long as the carrying capacity of the river corridor is not exceeded, the only environmental difference between the two kinds of trips is the (relatively modest) noise of the motors; i.e., all other impacts are basically the same. May the Park Service ban motors to provide a quieter river experience, even if that tends to put these trips beyond the reach of middle-class people? Do the statutes provide any clue to answering that question, or is it a policy judgment for the agency that the courts should not interfere with?

6.   Is it relevant to the "oars/motors" controversy, or to the "commercial/private" dispute, that the rafting experience in the Grand Canyon is not entirely "natural"? The Colorado River in the Grand Canyon has been much manipulated by the Glen Canyon Dam upstream. The dam captures much of the sediment that formerly gave the River its eponymous red color. The water is not only clear but cold, a uniform 48 degrees Fahrenheit as released from bowels of Lake Powell behind the dam, compared to pre-dam temperatures as high as the 70s or even 80s in low flow periods. (The temperature change has substantially altered aquatic life in the Canyon.) Finally, the dam has evened out the flows to a much more dependably uniform level, which has also facilitated the growth of the rafting industry.

Mankind is increasingly manipulating nature practically everywhere federal lands are found, sometimes by design, sometimes inadvertently. How should that fact inform how those lands should be managed where the goal is to provide a "natural" recreational experience, or to preserve them (as addressed in the next chapter)?

7. In the fall of 2005, the Park Service completed a final EIS on its latest management plan for the Colorado. The preferred alternative splits the total number of user days about down the middle between commercial (115,500) and non-commercial (113,486) users; although the annual number of passengers is estimated at 17,606 commercial and 7,051 non-commercial, reflecting that non-commercial users spend more days on the river per trip. A lottery system would be used to allocate noncommercial permits. The plan allocates more days to non-commercial use without cutting back on the commercial allocation by modestly enlarging the total number of visitor-days permitted, shifting more use away from the peak summer season to the fall and spring seasons, limiting trip sizes and encouraging more oar-powered trips. The plan permits motors during the peak months (April 1 through September 15), with motor trips comprising a little more than half the launches in May–August.

2. RECREATION MANAGEMENT AND NEPA

The National Park Service's efforts to accommodate heavy visitor use demands while safeguarding the amenities of some of the country's most cherished lands have been much watched, debated, and, inevitably, litigated. The basis of the litigation has not, however, been limited to or even dominated by the National Park Organic Act. Instead, NEPA and the Wild & Scenic Rivers Act have played central roles. The Wild & Scenic Rivers Act issues are discussed in Chapter 12.

The NPS organic act (via the Redwood amendment) requires each park unit to prepare a general management plan (GMP) that includes:

(1) measures for the preservation of the area's resources;

(2) indications of types and general intensities of development (including visitor circulation and transportation patterns, systems and modes) associated with public enjoyment and use of the area, including general locations, timing of implementation, and anticipated costs;

(3) identification of and implementation commitments for visitor carrying capacities for all areas of the unit; and

(4) indications of potential modifications to the external boundaries of the unit, and the reasons therefor.

16 U.S.C. § 1a–7. This umbrella document should clearly define the direction for resource preservation and visitor use. NPS Management Policies § 2.3.1 (2006). As with all public land planning, NEPA is the principal vehicle for public participation and analysis. However, the Park Service has gone through several different approaches to engaging NEPA. Originally, the NPS prepared full EISs for only some GMPs. After an embarrassing episode involving the promulgation of a GMP for North Cascades National

Park with only an EA, the NPS modified its planning policy to require EISs for all GMPs. The current policy states that:

> In most cases, an environmental impact statement (EIS) will be prepared for general management plans. In a few cases, the regional director * * * may approve an exception to this general rule if:
>
> - completion of scoping demonstrates that there is no public controversy concerning potential environmental effects; and
> - the initial analysis of alternatives clearly indicates there is no potential for significant impact by any alternative.

NPS Management Policies § 2.3.1.7 (2006).

Increasingly, though, the NPS makes key park management decisions in various specialized plans tiered to the GMP. The following case illustrates this common approach and the NEPA difficulties that arise.

Sierra Club v. United States

United States District Court, Northern District of California, 1998.
23 F.Supp.2d 1132.

■ JUDGE [CHARLES] BREYER

The National Park Service describes Yosemite as a "premiere masterwork of the natural world." Any change to this masterwork should only take place after there has been strict compliance with all applicable environmental laws. It is in this context that plaintiff Sierra Club asks the Court to halt implementation of Phase One of the Yosemite Lodge Area Development Plan in Yosemite National Park. * * *

In January 1997, the Merced River in Yosemite Valley overflowed its banks during a severe flood. This flooding caused substantial damage to buildings in the Yosemite Lodge area, located near the base of Yosemite Falls. Fifty percent of the public lodging facilities and one hundred percent of employee housing were damaged or destroyed.

In response to the flood damage, the National Park Service ("NPS") quickly developed a plan to construct new lodge facilities nearby so that it could continue to accommodate the same number of overnight visitors in the area. In addition to proposing the new facilities, the NPS set out to make other structural changes that it believed would improve the visitor experience in the Yosemite Lodge area.

The present layout of the lodge area is as follows: the accommodations that comprise Yosemite Lodge lie just to the north of the Merced River. Most of the cabins or buildings lie within the 100–year floodplain of the river, many of which were damaged in the January 1997 flood. Just north of Yosemite Lodge lies Northside Drive, which provides access to the area for both daytime and overnight visitors. Adjoining Northside Drive is a parking lot for cars and tour buses. Further north is the trailhead which begins the hike to Upper Yosemite Falls, approximately 3.5 miles away. Visitors have a view of the falls from the lodge area, although this view is impeded somewhat by the lodge facilities, parking lots, and cars proceeding along Northside Drive.

The lodge development plan crafted by NPS in the wake of the floods envisions substantial structural changes in the area. First, NPS seeks to remove the damaged lodging facilities from the floodplain. Rather than reconstruct the facilities in the same location, where they would remain exposed to potential flood damage, the Park Service seeks to construct new facilities—284 motel rooms, 96 cottage rooms, and 60 cabins—to the north of the current location of Northside Drive, which falls outside the floodplain. In turn, the plan calls for Northside Drive and its adjoining parking lots to be re-routed to the south, closer to Merced River. The Park Service's stated purpose for re-routing the road is to improve views of Yosemite Falls and move traffic further away from the new lodge facilities. Much of the new Northside Drive would be built in the area where the flood-damaged buildings currently rest.

NPS conceived the lodge development plan in the context of the ongoing park-wide planning process that has been in motion for almost 20 years. This process began with the adoption of the 1980 General Management Plan ("GMP"), which [was accompanied by an EIS and called, among other things, for removal of] * * * lodging facilities from the Merced River floodplain to avoid potential damage to those facilities. * * *

NPS adopted another major planning document in 1992—the Concession Services Plan ("CSP") [also accompanied by an EIS]. The CSP amended the GMP, reducing the number of overnight visitors that the GMP sought to accommodate in the park, and * * * [w]ith respect to the Yosemite Lodge Area, * * * reiterated that facilities would be removed from the floodplain and envisioned construction of new facilities elsewhere. However, the type, number, and location of these new facilities were not specified. * * *

In 1996, NPS initiated the Valley Implementation Plan ("VIP"), which seeks to implement the broad directives of the GMP and CSP by detailing, on a site-specific basis, the development projects with respect to visitor accommodations throughout the park. The Park Service decided that it was necessary to conceive these site-specific proposals in the course of one large, park-wide planning process in order to ensure that the overall impact of development within the park could be adequately monitored. The VIP has not yet been completed; the Park Service envisions that a draft will be submitted for public comment some time in the next few months. As with prior park-wide planning documents, the VIP will be accompanied by an Environmental Impact Statement.

Development activities pertaining to the Yosemite Lodge area were originally included in the VIP. However, in the wake of the flood, NPS determined that it needed to expedite the construction process in order to accommodate the number of visitors envisioned in the previous park-wide planning documents. Therefore, it separated the lodge area from the VIP process and crafted the Yosemite Lodge Area Development Plan on an individual basis.

In April 1997, less than four months after the flood, NPS drafted an Environmental Assessment, which set forth an initial version of the plan. In July 1997, NPS issued a Finding of No Significant Impact ("FONSI") which determined that an Environmental Impact Statement was not required for the project. In response to public comments, NPS issued a modified FONSI, which sets forth the lodge development plan as described above.

* * *

[The court later, in a footnote, discussed the lodge development plan in relation to the GMP and CSP, as follows:] It is by no means clear that the lodge development plan is wholly consistent with the GMP and CSP. * * *[W]hile there is no language in the GMP that explicitly precludes the lodge development plan at issue in this case, the document certainly did not contemplate any construction project in the area—or anywhere else in the park for that matter—with any degree of specificity. It merely discussed, in general terms, the kinds of services and accommodations, and the number of lodging facilities, that would be maintained in various areas throughout the park.

An examination of the CSP * * * also reveals that the type of project envisioned by the lodge development plan was not specifically contemplated. Unlike the GMP, the CSP does specify that new construction would take place in the Yosemite Lodge area * * * [but] also states, however, that "[c]reating new disturbance in the valley to relocate lodging structures is not acceptable." Defendants explain that this statement indicates an unwillingness on the part of NPS to initiate construction on "undisturbed areas," and assert that much of the proposed development will take place on "previously disturbed and moderately degraded" woodland. However, defendants concede that the lodge development plan would cause 1.2 acres of previously undisturbed mixed conifer forest to be developed, and admit that this portion of the plan is inconsistent with the CSP. In light of this inconsistency, as well as the general terms in which the GMP and CSP addressed development in the Valley, it is not clear that the lodge development plan is consistent with prior park-wide planning documents. [end of footnote]

* * *

* * * The GMP and CSP lay out the goals of the Park Service with respect to the park in very broad terms. * * * However, neither document specifies how, when, or precisely where * * * construction [of facilities] would occur.

[The court went on to issue a preliminary injunction to halt phase 1 of the lodge development plan, finding that plaintiffs had showed a substantial likelihood of success that they would succeed on their NEPA claims that the NPS had "failed to consider the cumulative impact of the lodge development plan, as well as several reasonable alternatives to that plan."]

NOTES AND QUESTIONS

1. The NPS went back to fix its NEPA documentation and eventually produced a final master plan that has provoked continued controversy, this time mostly from people (including the local Member of Congress, who promptly introduced legislation to stop its implementation) who object to the removal of some visitor facilities from the Valley. The dimensions of the debate were captured in letters to the New York Times in January 2002. An opponent argued, among other things, that "[r]emoving a few hundred campsites, cabins and parking spaces would not result in a significant increase in the area available for nature," visitor demand for car-accessible Valley accommodations is very heavy, and that cabins "are the most affordable accommodation for middle-class families." A plan supporter argued that it would still leave 500 campsites in the Valley, and that visitors should "remember Yosemite for its waterfalls and vibrant meadows and not for its gridlock and asphalt."

Work on the Yosemite Lodge, road paving, and campground expansion was halted again in 2006 when a federal district court found that the NPS had failed to prepare a comprehensive management plan for the Merced River that complied with NEPA.

Is the NPS mired in a tangle of environmental evaluation, with overlapping plans for the Merced River, visitor implementation, concession services, and overall park management? Would the NPS have been able to proceed more efficiently if had comprehensively revised its GMP immediately after the flood to discuss all of the controversial aspects of rebuilding in the Merced Valley? What role, if any, should the GMP play in determining the size and footprint of park lodging?

2. In Sierra Club v. Lujan, 716 F.Supp. 1289 (D.Ariz.1989), the court preliminarily enjoined the NPS from proceeding with construction of a hotel complex at the North Rim of the Grand Canyon. The proposal apparently violated both the master plan for the Park and NEPA, in that the decision was made before an EA was prepared, and sites outside of the Park were not considered. More than ninety-nine percent of the Grand Canyon National Park is unroaded and has no developed visitor facilities. Nearly all the four million people who have visited the Park annually in recent years have concentrated in a small area along the South Rim of the canyon. Much the same is true of Yosemite; the vast majority of visitors and visitor facilities are in the Yosemite Valley, which is a small fraction of the Park's 700,000 acres. About ninety-five percent of Yosemite Park is in roadless wilderness. In these situations, should the Park Service attempt to diminish and disperse the crowds that congregate in these choice places by building or upgrading roads and providing new visitor facilities in what are now more remote regions of the Park? Or should the wilderness qualities of large areas of these parks be preserved? Is the answer to limit visitor use, a solution that is politically unpopular? Or is the problem in some of these places, as former Secretary of the Interior Babbitt was fond of saying, not too many people, but too many cars? If so, is the answer to require visitors to leave their cars (and provide lodging) at the periphery of the Parks, and use mass transit?

3.   Does the Organic Act allow the Park Service to decide to provide *no* visitor facilities in some of its units? In the Gates of the Arctic National Park and Preserve, one of the largest park units at almost 8 million acres (about the size of Connecticut and Massachusetts combined), and located north of the Arctic Circle in Alaska, the Park Service has decided to provide no developed visitor facilities. Visitors may go there (and may hire private guides), but they are on their own.

4.   Rationing recreational access at the other end of the use intensity spectrum also causes legal disputes. There are no roads to Alaska's spectacular Glacier Bay, and eighty percent of the park's visitors arrive on large, thousand-passenger cruise ships. The Park Service has for a couple of decades regulated the entry and activity of cruise ships and other vessels in Glacier Bay. The regulations are crafted in part to address endangered species concerns regarding humpback whales and Steller sea lions. NPS's 1984 Vessel Management Plan allowed 107 cruise ship entries per season. As demand continued to increase and cruise lines built ever more and larger ships, in the early and mid–1990s the NPS went through a public process of revising its VMP, accompanied by an environmental assessment that looked at alternatives including reducing as well as increasing entries, and ultimately decided in 1996 to increase the entry by thirty percent for the succeeding two years, with the possibility of further increases if certain conditions were met. Concluding that "Glacier Bay Park is too precious an ecosystem for the Parks Service to ignore significant risks to its diverse inhabitants and its fragile atmosphere," the court in National Parks & Conservation Ass'n v. Babbitt, 241 F.3d 722, 731, 739 (9th Cir. 2001), held that a full EIS should have been prepared under NEPA because of "the high degree of uncertainty and the substantial controversy regarding the effects" of the increase on the environment, and enjoined any increase in cruise ship entry until one was completed. Should the NEPA threshold be lowered for proposals that could affect "precious ecosystems" like the "crown jewels" of the national park system?

5.   Should there be hunting, fishing, and trapping in the national parks? National Rifle Ass'n v. Potter, 628 F.Supp. 903 (D.D.C.1986) upheld a Park Service regulation outlawing hunting and trapping in all units of the national park system except where specifically ordained by Congress. The opinion reviewed the history of Park Service policy toward hunting and trapping, and concluded (628 F.Supp. at 912):

> The Secretary and the Park Service have been charged by Congress with the responsibility for achieving the sometimes conflicting goals of preserving the country's natural resources for future generations while ensuring their enjoyment by current users. Notwithstanding his recent predecessors may have permitted hunting and trapping in selected park areas of their choosing, the present Secretary has re-examined the subject in the light of recent amendments to the Organic Act and has concluded that his primary management function with respect to Park wildlife is its preservation unless Congress has declared otherwise. The regulation thus issues rationally from that conclusion, and if relief is to be forthcoming, plaintiff must look to Congress for it, not the courts.

C. SPECIAL RECREATIONAL AND CONSERVATION OVERLAYS

With dramatic growth in recreation use on most federal lands in the last few decades and the rise of the modern environmental movement, increasing amounts of federal land—including much land formally subject to multiple use management (by the U.S. Forest Service and the BLM)—are being managed primarily for recreation and conservation purposes. Congress has confirmed this trend by specifically designating many areas of federal land for these dominant uses. Because conservation and recreation are so closely aligned in such statutes, the inclusion of the discussion in this chapter, rather than in the preservation chapter that follows, is somewhat arbitrary. The statutes overlay and modify the underlying statutory management framework, whether it is multiple-use or something else.

Congress has put a rather dizzying variety of different formal labels on such areas, such as national recreation areas (NRAs), national conservation areas (NCAs), special management areas, protection areas, scenic areas, and the like. The statutes are collected in various places, mostly in volume 16 of the U.S. Code. The areas may be small and urban, or large and rural, or many shades in between. All these area-specific federal statutes basically have in common is that their management is primarily for conservation and recreation use, and to that end, use of the land and associated resources is subject to restrictions.

There is no overarching "organic act" for this category of federal land, but the individual area statutes tend strongly to have a number of features in common (with some differences as they are tailored to local conditions). They generally (a) require the area to be managed to serve dominant conservation and/or recreational uses; (b) withdraw the lands involved from the Mining Law and the mineral leasing acts; (c) ban or severely restrict timber harvesting; and (d) may place some restrictions on grazing. (Some other uses may be allowed to the extent the agency finds them consistent or compatible with these dominant purposes.) Often the legislation calls for the agency involved to set the details of the management through a formal planning process (which will include such standard features as public participation, NEPA compliance, and, if appropriate, ESA consultation). These statutes do not entirely displace the underlying generic laws that otherwise apply. Thus an NRA in a national forest is still subject to the National Forest Management Act; one in the national park system is still subject to the Park Service Organic Act, etc. But to the extent there is a conflict between the area-specific statute and the generic one, the specific one controls. Thus, for example, while livestock grazing may be subject to relatively broad U.S. Forest Service management discretion on ordinary national forest lands, the agency's discretion may be more sharply circumscribed in a national recreation area.

The largest chunk of lands in this category is found under the formal label of National Recreation Areas. Congress created the first NRA for the National Park System in 1964 around Lake Mead, formed by Hoover Dam on the lower Colorado River. Many of the other early NRAs were also established around large reservoirs constructed by the federal government both in the Colorado River Basin (Flaming Gorge in Wyoming, 1968; Glen Canyon in Utah, 1972); and elsewhere (Whiskeytown–Shasta–Trinity in California, 1965; Bighorn Canyon in Montana and Wyoming, 1966; Hells Canyon in Oregon and Idaho, 1975). Beginning in 1972, Congress extended the NRA designation to urbanized areas around New York City and the San Francisco Bay, cobbling together scattered federal parcels (much of it formerly military land). These NPS units are Golden Gate NRA, California (16 U.S.C. §§ 460bb to 460bb–5) and Gateway NRA, New York and New Jersey, (16 U.S.C. §§ 460cc–2). The NRA designation has since proved popular enough to be extended to more than three dozen areas, many of them not associated with reservoirs and some of them embracing mostly nonfederal land. The establishment statutes are collected beginning at 16 U.S.C. 460n.

More recent congressional inventions are the National Conservation Area (NCA) (e.g., Red Rock Canyon in southern Nevada, 16 U.S.C. § 460ccc); the Riparian National Conservation Area (e.g., Gila Box in Arizona, 16 U.S.C. § 460ddd); and the Outstanding Natural Area (e.g., Yaquina Head in Oregon, 43 U.S.C. § 1783). Many of these are on BLM lands. In fact, the Nation's first NCA protected an area of BLM land, the King Range, along the northern California coast. Adopted near the dawn of the modern environmental movement in 1970, the King Range NCA legislation contained an early expression of dominant use conservation management. Its history is also fairly typical: An executive withdrawal first protected the area from disposal in 1929. The congressional designation first encompassed about 25,000 acres but has since been expanded to include 60,000 acres of isolated beaches and rugged mountains (rising to more than 4000 feet only three miles from the Pacific). 16 U.S.C. § 4604.

On national forest lands, Congress has used a variety of labels like special management area (e.g., Greer Spring, Missouri, 16 U.S.C. § 539h), recreation management area (e.g., Fossil Ridge, Colorado, 16 U.S.C. § 539i), protection area (e.g., Bowen Gulch, Colorado, 16 U.S.C. § 539j), scenic area (e.g., Columbia River Gorge, Oregon–Washington, 16 U.S.C. § 544–544m), scenic-research area (e.g., Cascade Head, Oregon, 16 U.S.C. § 541); scenic recreation area (e.g., Opal Creek, Oregon, 16 U.S.C. § 545b), national scenic area (e.g., Mount Pleasant, Virginia, 16 U.S.C. § 545); national forest scenic area (e.g., Mono Basin, California, 16 U.S.C. § 543); and national preserve (Valles Caldera, New Mexico, 16 U.S.C. § 698v).

Because all these areas have been individually established by Congress in legislation, they have relative permanence. Congress has also authorized executive branch agencies to put protective management (and a protective label) on areas of federal land. For example, the Federal Land Policy and Management Act of 1976 authorizes the Secretary of the Interior to designate areas of BLM-managed public land as "areas of critical environmental concern" and requires BLM to give them "priority." *See* 43 U.S.C. §§ 1702(a), 1711(a). The BLM may modify or abolish these areas without further action by Congress.

The general management standard for such areas (albeit with some variation from statute to statute) resembles to some extent the "dominant but not exclusive use" idea behind the "compatibility" test applied on national wildlife refuges. Two questions emerging with increasing frequency are how the test should be applied and what process should be used to make compatibility decisions. The next case is one of the few judicial explorations of the legal issues. *Caveat*: While most statutes designating these special areas have some features in common, there is no "organic" or generic Act, and at bottom the individual statutes are like snowflakes—no two seem to be identical.

Oregon Natural Resources Council v. Lyng

United States Court of Appeals, Ninth Circuit, 1989.
882 F.2d 1417.

■ JUDGE TROTT

[Plaintiff environmental groups sued to enjoin a Forest Service timber sale in a portion of the Hells Canyon NRA (HCNRA) and also sought an order requiring the Forest Service to promulgate regulations under the HCNRA Act.]

The Hells Canyon National Recreation Area was established by Congress in 1975. It encompasses 652,488 acres of land in Eastern Oregon and Western Idaho, most of which had been managed under the National Forest System. This land, which includes the deepest gorge in North America and the seventy-one mile segment of the Snake River between the Hells Canyon Dam and the Oregon–Washington border, became the Hells Canyon National Recreation Area. The specified purpose of the HCNRA Act is "[t]o assure that the natural beauty, and historical and archeological values" of this area "are preserved for this and future generations, and that the recreational and ecologic values and public enjoyment of the area are thereby enhanced. . . ."[1] 16 U.S.C. § 460gg(a).

1. Section 7 of the HCNRA Act provides a more detailed description of the Act's objectives:

[T]he Secretary shall administer the recreation area in accordance with the laws, rules, and regulations applicable to national forests for public outdoor recreation in a manner compatible with the following objectives:

(1) the maintenance and protection of the freeflowing nature of the rivers within the recreation area;

(2) conservation of scenic, wilderness, cultural, scientific, and other values contributing to the public benefit;

(3) preservation, especially in the area generally known as Hells Canyon, of all features and peculiarities believed to

be biologically unique including, but not limited to, rare and endemic plant species, rare combinations of aquatic, terrestrial, and atmospheric habitat, and the rare combinations of outstanding and diverse ecosystems and parts of ecosystems associated therewith;

(4) protection and maintenance of fish and wildlife habitat;

(5) protection of archeological and paleontologic sites and interpretation of these sites for the public benefit and knowledge insofar as it is compatible with protection;

(6) preservation and restoration of historic sites associated with and typifying the economic and social history of the region and the American West; and

The Act requires the Secretary to develop a "comprehensive management plan" ("CMP") that provides for a "broad range of land uses and recreation opportunities" in the HCNRA. 16 U.S.C. § 460gg–5. In accordance with NEPA, and after consulting with a large number of federal, state and local agencies, elected officials, and private organizations, the forest service prepared an Environmental Impact Statement ("EIS") to aid in formulating the CMP. The EIS, issued in May of 1981, identifies key issues and concerns pertinent to the management of the HCNRA and proposes seven alternative plans for managing the area. The CMP, finalized in 1984, designates "Alternative C" as the HCNRA management plan. This alternative allocates the HCNRA to seven land-use classifications. Twelve percent of HCNRA land, including the Duck Creek area at issue in this appeal, is designated as "dispersed recreation/timber management." This designation permits timber management but requires it to be consonant with providing "ample opportunities for dispersed recreation." Permissible timber management activities include salvage cutting and the harvest of between five and nine million board feet of timber each year.

In November of 1981 a violent storm toppled many trees in the HCNRA. During the following two summers bark beetles attacked storm-felled Engelmann Spruce trees in the Duck Creek area. By the summer of 1984, the bark beetle population had begun to attack standing green trees. The voracious beetles had infested virtually all large Engelmann Spruce trees in the Duck Creek area by the summer of 1987. Health and life departed from the Duck Creek area, which held an estimated twenty million board feet of dead and dying Engelmann Spruce timber by early 1988. Because Engelmann Spruce is a soft white wood that deteriorates quickly, salvage value of this specie [sic] declines rapidly after the year of infestation.

The Forest Service responded to the bark beetle epidemic, which has spread to other areas of the HCNRA, by preparing a site-specific "Environmental Assessment" ("EA") for the Duck Creek area. This EA, issued in February of 1988, identifies issues and opportunities related to the beetle problem and considers six alternative methods of managing the Duck Creek area's beetle-infected spruce. These methods range from taking no action to harvesting fifteen million board feet of timber. The EA designates "Alternative F" as the preferred alternative. On April 3, 1988, Robert Richmond, Supervisor of the Wallowa–Whitman National Forest, approved this alternative and concluded that its implementation would not have a significant impact on the quality of the human environment.

Alternative F calls for the harvest of approximately six million board feet of beetle-threatened, beetle-infected and dead trees from the Duck Creek area. The harvest is to be accomplished by cable logging and helicopter systems in order to protect wet areas and soils on steep ground

(7) such management, utilization, and disposal of natural resources on federally owned lands, including, but not limited to, timber harvesting by selective cutting, mining, and grazing and the continuation of such existing uses and developments as are compatible with the provisions of section 460gg to 460gg–13 of this title.

16 U.S.C. § 460gg–4.

and to avoid having to build a road system in the large, "unroaded" section of Duck Creek. The proposal leaves nearly sixty percent of the damaged timber unharvested in wildlife and visual areas and in riparian no-cut zones. The sawlog volume removed will postpone or defer cutting of an equal amount of volume on lower priority timber stands. * * *

[The timber was sold two days after this suit was filed. After initially granting a TRO against the logging, the trial court found for the defendants and dissolved the injunction, and the court of appeals refused to reinstate it pending appeal. The appeals court found that the agency had adequately complied with NEPA on the sale, and that the plaintiffs had not shown that the sale would violate the Clean Water Act or the state of Oregon's water quality standards. It then turned to the HCNRA establishment statute] * * *

Appellants allege that the timber sale violates the HCNRA Act in two respects. First, they state that section 8(f) of the Act limits timber harvesting to areas where such activity was occurring at the time of enactment. Second, they assert that section 10 of the Act compels the Secretary to promulgate regulations governing when, where, and how certain activities, including timber harvesting, may occur in the HCNRA.

[The district court had found plaintiffs barred from raising the § 8(f) claim by laches and failure to exhaust administrative remedies. It ruled against plaintiffs' § 10 claim on the merits. Without passing on the correctness of the first ruling, the court of appeals went directly to the merits on both claims.] * * *

* * * Section 8 is entitled "Management plan for recreation areas." 16 U.S.C. § 460gg–5. Section 8(f)[9] must thus be interpreted as part of a Congressional effort to describe the process by which the CMP is to be developed, the issues it must consider, and what may occur in the HCNRA while the CMP is under preparation. If section 8(f) is read in the context of section 8 as a whole, it becomes evident that section 8(f) addresses only that period of time between passage of the Act and development of the CMP and is not relevant to the Duck Creek Timber sale. Appellants argue that the legislative history of the Act supports their interpretation of section 8(f). Their arguments appear to have little force. Because the statute is clear on it[s] face, however, we need not be concerned with legislative history in interpreting its scope. * * *

We now turn to appellants' second contention, that section 10 of the Act directs the Secretary to promulgate regulations governing certain activities, including timber harvesting, in the HCNRA. In the almost fourteen years since enactment of the HCNRA Act, the Secretary has not

---

9. Section 8(f) reads:

(f) Continuation of ongoing activities[.] Such activities as are as compatible with the provisions of sections 460gg to 460gg–13 of this title, but not limited to, timber harvesting by selective cutting, mining, and grazing may continue during development of the comprehensive management plan, at current levels of activity and in areas of such activity on December 31, 1975. Further, in development of the management plan, the Secretary shall give full consideration to continuation of these ongoing activities in their respective areas. 16 U.S.C. § 460gg–5.

promulgated any rules and regulations. This court has concluded that it would not be consistent with the overall purpose of the HCNRA Act, protection of the HCNRA, to interpret section 10 as stripping the Secretary of his general regulatory authority over the HCNRA, leaving him without power to act until he promulgates regulations under section 10. If other regulations already apply to an activity in the HCNRA, we will not view section 10 as invalidating those regulations and requiring the Secretary "to take an additional, in fact, a redundant, affirmative step before he would be able to take *any* action to protect an area placed under his supervision."

Thus, the question we must answer is whether section 10 compels the Secretary to promulgate the regulations it describes when those regulations would not be duplicative of other rules already in effect in the HCNRA. We respond to this question in the affirmative. The language and legislative history of section 10 clearly reveal an intent to create a mandatory duty to promulgate regulations in the specified categories.

Section 10 reads:

The Secretary shall promulgate, and may amend, such rules and regulations as he deems necessary to accomplish the purposes of section 460gg to 460gg–13 of this title. Such rules and regulations shall include, but are not limited to—

(a) standards for the use and development of privately owned property within the recreation area * * *;

(b) standards and guidelines to insure the full protection and preservation of the historic, archeological, and paleontological resources in the recreation area;

(c) provision for the control of the use of motorized and mechanical equipment for transportation over, or alteration of, the surface of any Federal land within the recreation area;

(d) provision for the control of the use and number of motorized and nonmotorized river craft: *Provided*, That the use of such craft is hereby recognized as a valid use of the Snake River within the recreation area; and

(e) standards for such management, utilization, and disposal of natural resources on federally owned lands, including but not limited to, timber harvesting by selective cutting, mining, and grazing, and the continuation of such existing uses and developments as are compatible with the provisions of sections 460gg to 460gg–13 of this title.

16 U.S.C. § 460gg–7. Judge Panner perceived the phrase "as he deems necessary" to indicate that section 10 leaves the decision regarding whether to issue regulations to the Secretary's discretion. We do not believe that, read as a whole, the language of the section supports this view. The first sentence directs the Secretary to promulgate regulations but seems to limit that mandate to rules the Secretary decides are necessary to accomplish the purposes of the Act. The second sentence, however, extends that mandate beyond the confines of the Secretary's discretion to specific types of regulations. This interpretation makes grammatical sense. In both the first

and second sentences of section 10 the predicate nominative of the word "shall" is "rules and regulations": "shall" describes the Secretary's relationship to the regulations. * * *

Such legislative history as exists supports our interpretation of section 10. The House Report on the HCNRA Act states that section 10 "directs the Secretary to promulgate regulations needed to accomplish the intent of the legislation. Specific regulation [sic] are to include...." House Committee on Interior and Insular Affairs, H.R.Rep. No. 94–607, 94th Cong., 1st Sess. 12, reprinted in 1975 *U.S.Code Cong. & Admin. News* 2281, 2286. And the Senate Report, which summarizes section 10 by subsection rather than as a whole, also states that the Act "directs" the Secretary to promulgate the specified types of regulation. *See* [Sen.] Rep. No. 94–153, 94th Cong., 1st Sess. 8 (1975).

We thus find that section 10 compels the Secretary to promulgate nonduplicative regulations of the sort described by subsections 10(a) through 10(e). In addition, the Secretary has discretion to issue additional regulations that he deems necessary to accomplish the purposes of the Act. Section 10(e) mandates regulations for timber harvesting by selective cutting on federally owned lands. We therefore reverse the district court's ruling on the regulation issue and remand for issuance of an order directing the Secretary to promulgate the regulations required by section 10.

It is conceivable that had the regulations been issued they would have affected the Duck Creek timber sale. This fact would ordinarily cause us to ask the district court to determine whether the Secretary's failure to issue the relevant regulations requires that the Duck Creek sale be enjoined. Given that timber harvesting in the Duck Creek area resumed in late April, however, such a request might be pointless. We therefore ask the district judge to consider the necessity of an injunction only if the Duck Creek harvest has not been completed on the date this opinion is filed. * * *

NOTES AND QUESTIONS

1. Is this a "recreation" area statute or a "conservation" area statute? Is conservation the dominant purpose? If yes, is the label in the statute a misnomer? A harmless one? Some conservationists remain somewhat skeptical. Should they be, or should they welcome an NRA as an improvement over the flabby "multiple use" standard?

2. Is the compatibility judgment called for by § 7 of the HCNRA (reproduced in footnote 1 of the court's opinion) the same as the one used in wildlife refuges? *See supra*, p. 867. Is determining what is compatible with recreation easier or more difficult than determining what is compatible with wildlife? Does each call for a scientific, policy, or political judgment?

3. Apart from the order to prepare regulations, would the result have been any different here if this area had not been an NRA but rather had been subject to the multiple use/sustained yield standard that applies to

most national forest land? Does § 7(7) of the Act, quoted in footnote 1, give the Forest Service authority or direction to regulate hardrock mining activities more stringently than it does on ordinary national forest land? Could it, consistent with the Act, withdraw the entire NRA from the Mining Law? Prohibit all surface mining? Oust all livestock grazing? Sell no timber?

4. Did the court too quickly reject the plaintiffs' argument that section 8(f) of the HCNRA (quoted in footnote 9) prohibits expansion of timber harvesting into areas where it was not occurring when the HCNRA was enacted? The subsection allows continuation of timber harvesting (where compatible with the purposes of the HCNRA) *in areas of such activity* when the Act was passed and directs the Secretary to give "full consideration" to allow them to continue *in their respective areas*. Doesn't that at least permit an inference that timber harvesting is not allowed outside such "areas"?

5. Why do you suppose the Secretary had not prepared the regulations required by § 10 of the Act in the fourteen years it had been on the books? Should that failure have been sufficient ground to enjoin this sale? If the sale had not been to salvage dead, rapidly deteriorating timber, should it have been enjoined? In a previous case noted in this opinion, the Ninth Circuit had upheld the Forest Service's application of its generic regulations to a river guide service in Hells Canyon, notwithstanding the agency's failure to promulgate specific regulations dealing with the HCNRA. *See also* Hells Canyon Preservation Council v. United States Forest Service, 883 F.Supp. 534 (D.Or.1995) (relocation of road now in a wilderness area).

6. In October 1989, after the decision of the court of appeals here, the Forest Service adopted regulations governing Hells Canyon NRA. Among other things, they provide that timber shall be managed to "perpetuate healthy stands of diverse tree species and size and age classes and to emphasize stand condition, scenery, wildlife habitat, and recreation needs." Clearcutting is prohibited unless its use would "mitigate the situation" where timber has been "damaged by fire, insect, disease, or wind." 36 C.F.R. § 292.43(d). If these regulations had been in place when the principal case was litigated, what outcome?

7. Although mining is a prohibited or disfavored use in most if not all of these areas, mining issues occasionally arise—even on withdrawn lands. The statute creating the first NRA at Lake Mead provides that the area (which is managed by the Park Service) is to be administered generally for recreation, but that the Secretary may permit other specific uses (grazing, mineral leasing, and vacation cabin sites) "to such extent as will not be inconsistent with" recreational use or with reservoir operation. 16 U.S.C.A. § 460n–3. The Act did not define the "minerals" that could be leased. The court in Sierra Club v. Watt, 566 F.Supp. 380 (D.Utah1983), upheld an agency regulation allowing leasing of minerals in the NRA that would otherwise be locatable under the Mining Law as a reasonable interpretation of this statute.

8.   In all of the great national land management systems, there is a tension between the value of having readily understood, uniform laws and policies that apply across the entire system, and the value of being able to tailor laws and policies to local conditions. The National Park System, for example, is now a sprawling empire that embraces many different kinds of units: the crown jewel national parks, national battlefields, seashores, monuments, historic sites, recreation areas, and the like. In 1970 and 1978 Congress enacted legislation that the Park Service took as a directive to bring more uniformity to the system. Its implications were explored in Bicycle Trails Council of Marin v. Babbitt, 82 F.3d 1445 (9th Cir. 1996), where the court addressed plaintiffs' several challenges to the Park Service's limitation on the use of bicycles in the Golden Gate National Recreation Area in California's Bay Area. One of the arguments was that the Park Service had wrongfully decided to move toward a uniform policy throughout the national park system, that all lands were closed to bicycle use unless specifically opened. The court rejected the challenge, and in the process explained the old and new policies and the reasons behind the change:

> In 1964, NPS at its own initiative implemented a management by categories scheme by which units of the National Park System would be classified "natural," "historical," or "recreational,"[1] and by which management policies would be formed so as to regulate these three types of units in conformity with their differing classifications. The effect of this scheme would be, *inter alia,* that recreational units would be managed in a less restrictive and less resource-protective manner than units classified natural or historical. Under this scheme, NPS in 1966 decided to alter its longstanding policy regarding bicycle use in park units from one wherein all trails were closed unless designated open to one in which the old rule generally applied except in units classified as recreational, in which trails would be presumed open to bicycle use unless designated closed by the local park superintendent.
>
> By a series of amendments to the National Park Service Organic Act, 16 U.S.C. sections 1 et seq., Congress disapproved of this management by categories scheme and directed that all units of the national parks were to be treated consistently, with resource protection the primary goal, while retaining the flexibility for individual park units to approve particular uses consistent with their specific enabling legislation. Thus, NPS eliminated these management categories from its internal administration in 1978 and ultimately began promulgating regulations in the 1980's eliminating these categorical distinctions from the Code of Federal Regulations.
>
> The 1987 regulation, adopted pursuant to notice and comment, established a uniform rule for national park units wherein all bicycle use of

---

1. The "recreational" management category was an internal administrative construction and was not necessarily coextensive with those units that Congress in enabling legislation had named "Recreation Areas." However, GGNRA was both named a "Recreation Area" in its enabling legislation, 16 U.S.C. section 460bb, and deemed a recreational unit under NPS's taxonomy.

off-road areas would be prohibited unless local park superintendents designated particular trails to be open. (As noted, this had previously been the rule in all but the recreation units.) Local park officials determined that they would not enforce this rule in the GGNRA until it was determined which trails would be open and which closed to bicycle use. Thus, because of NPS's and the GGNRA Superintendent's exercise of prosecutorial discretion, the 1987 regulation was not enforced and bicyclists in fact retained access to all trails in the GGNRA pending the development of a trail use plan. Finally, after a long and contentious trail designation process, the 1992 trail plan was adopted (also pursuant to notice and comment) establishing which trails were to be open to bicycles and which trails were to be closed. * * *

Plaintiffs challenge the legality of the regulation on the theory that it is not based upon a permissible interpretation of the Organic Act. This challenge fails. A review of the Organic Act and the history of its amendments shows that NPS based its decision to eliminate the reference to management categories (and thus to eliminate the special "recreation" unit rule) in the 1987 regulation on a mandated, and certainly permissible, construction of the Organic Act and its amendments.

In response to congressional amendments to the Organic Act, NPS in 1978 began phasing out its usage of the "management categories" that had been earlier developed to allow for the different treatment of different classes of units in the National Park System. In the 1980's, NPS began eliminating such distinctions in its regulations. NPS interpreted Congress's amendments to the Organic Act to be clear in the message that NPS was not to single out a particular class of units of the park system (i.e. recreational units) for less protective treatment, but that instead NPS was to manage all units of the park system so as to effect the purpose of the Organic Act–primarily resource protection.

9. Another example of a court integrating special legislation adopted for a particular area with general legislation applicable across an entire land management system is Sierra Club–Black Hills Group v. U.S. Forest Service, 259 F.3d 1281 (10th Cir. 2001). Congress created the Norbeck Wildlife Preserve in 1920, and, as part of the Black Hills National Forest, the Forest Service manages 28,000 of the Preserve's 35,000 acres. At issue were timber sales the Forest Service authorized in the Preserve and how to mesh the National Forest Management Act's mandate regarding overall species diversity with the narrower statutory mandate of the Norbeck Preserve, "for the protection of game animals and birds and * * * as a breeding place thereof." 16 U.S.C. § 675. The court directed the Forest Service to reconsider the sales because the agency "cannot apply the NFMA mandate in a way that effectively abolishes the specific statutory mandates Congress has established" in what is now called the Norbeck Act. Because the latter "requires the protection of game animals and birds, not the overall protection of all plant and animal species," the agency "must justify the proposed timber harvests not by showing that optimal diversity is served generally, but by showing specifically that game animals and birds

are protected." Dissenting Judge Ebel would have found enough ambiguity in the Norbeck Act to justify deferring to the Forest Service's judgment. If there were a clear choice on the facts between promoting overall species diversity and promoting habitat for game, which side should environmental organizations be on? Should courts adopt a special canon of interpretation giving presumptive deference to organic legislation in the absence of a clear conflict with establishment legislation? *See* Chapter 5, *supra* p. 469.

10.   In the past couple of decades Congress has established about three dozen "National Heritage Areas" which altogether encompass more than 100 million acres (larger than California) and include within their boundaries over 45 million people. These are not units of the National Park System, although the National Park Service provides seed money, recognition, and technical assistance. Typically these areas do not contain much federal land, although they often contain land owned by state and local governments as well as the private sector. The general idea behind the designation is to commemorate, conserve, and promote areas of cultural, scenic, and/or historic significance. There is no "organic act" providing criteria for their designation or standards for their funding and operation. Usually the legislation designates a nonfederal management entity to coordinate and develop a management plan for the NHA which, upon approval by the Secretary of the Interior, becomes the blueprint for administration. Most NHAs are in the eastern part of the country, including such areas as Rivers of Steel in Pennsylvania, the Hudson River Valley in New York, and the National Coal Heritage in West Virginia (all designated by Pub.L. No. 104–333); the Motor Cities Automobile NHA in Michigan (designated by Pub.L. No. 105–355); and Atchafalaya National Heritage Area in Louisiana (designated by Pub. L. No. 109–338). Proponents of NHAs emphasize the opportunity to protect lands and traditions while promoting tourism and community revitalization. Opponents emphasize the cost to the federal government and the prospect that an NHA is an initial step that may lead to federal control over nonfederal lands. Carol Hardy Vincent and David Whiteman, Heritage Area: Background, Proposals, and Current Issues (Congressional Research Service 2004).

NOTE: NATIONAL TRAILS

National trails don't fit neatly into any particular category. They grew out of the 1968 National Trails System Act, 16 U.S.C. §§ 1241–1249, which begins with the statement (§ 1241(a)):

> In order to provide for the ever-increasing outdoor recreation needs of an expanding population and in order to promote presentation of, public access to, travel within, and enjoyment and appreciation of the open-air, outdoor areas and historic resources of the Nation, trails should be established (i) primarily, near the urban areas of the Nation, and (ii) secondarily, within scenic areas and along historic travel routes of the Nation, which are often more remotely located.

The Act creates several categories of national trails and offers federal assistance to state trail programs. Congress and the land management agencies have now designated hundreds of national trails under the law, but funding to build the paths and acquire property interests has been scant at best. See John S. Davis, *The National Trails System Act and the Use of Protective Federal Zoning*, 10 Harv. Envtl. L.Rev. 189 (1986).

The growing "rails-to-trails" movement seeks to implement Congress's direction in the National Trails System Act that federal agencies facilitate the conversion of unused railroad rights-of-way to trails. A section of the Trails Act provides that abandonment or discontinuance of a rail line should not be permitted if a "qualified" person wishes to operate a trail on the line, is willing to manage it, take legal responsibility for it, and pay any taxes on it. See 16 U.S.C. § 1247(d). The Supreme Court considered, but ultimately ducked, the question of whether such conversion constituted a "taking" of the right of owners of abutting property who hold a reversionary interest in the railroad right of way. Preseault v. ICC, 494 U.S. 1 (1990).

As a result, litigation over when rails-to-trails conversions are takings continues, and often turns on narrow questions of state law–such as the nature of the interest conveyed and standards for determining when interests have been abandoned. In *Preseault* itself, for example, even though the original grant to the railroad was by a deed that conveyed "fee simple," the Federal Circuit construed Vermont law to mean that it actually conveyed an easement only. Preseault v. United States, 100 F. 3d 1525 (Fed. Cir. 1996); 52 Fed. Cl. 667 (Ct. Fed. Cl. 2002). *Compare* Chevy Chase Land Co. v. United States, 355 Md. 110, 733 A.2d 1055 (1999) (conversion to trail usage was within the easement's scope) and Mauler v. Bayfield County, 309 F. 3d 997 (7th Cir. 2002) (former railway corridor was not subject to reversionary interest and thus subject to disposition under federal law); *with* Toews v. United States, 376 F. 3d 1371 (Fed. Cir. 2004) (rail-to-trail conversion effected a taking, because applicable California state law—while allowing a right of way for public transportation to be converted from one means of mechanical transportation to another—did not allow a conversion from transportation to park and recreation uses). *See generally* Danaya C. Wright & Jeffrey M. Hester, *Pipes, Wires, and Bicycles: Rails-to-Trails, Utility Licenses, and the Shifting Scope of Railroad Easements from the Nineteenth to the Twenty–First Centuries*, 27 Ecology L.Q. 351 (2000).

D. Managing Recreation on Federal Lands: Fees, Concessions and Permits

1. Recreation Fees

The Land and Water Conservation Fund Act limited the authority of federal land management agencies to charge fees for recreational access to many federal lands, 16 U.S.C. § 460*l*–6a. *See, e.g.*, United States v. Maris, 987 F.Supp. 865 (D.Or.1997) (merely driving through a national forest area is not a recreational "use" subject to user fee). Where federal land management agencies had authority to charge entrance, campground, and other fees, they had little incentive to do so. Longstanding federal law compelled agencies to deposit all recreation fees into the federal treasury, where they could not be spent by the agencies directly. Instead, agencies could spend only money appropriated by Congress.

Then, in 1996, looking for ways to meet the management burdens associated with burgeoning growth in federal land recreation demand, Congress adopted a three-year, recreational fee demonstration program. Pub. L. 104–134, section 315. Its key feature allowed federal agencies to retain one hundred percent of the recreation fees they generated, "without further appropriation," with eighty percent spent at the particular unit where they were collected. Congress extended the fee demonstration program several times.

Finally, in 2004, Congress created a more permanent program that superseded and extended the basic principles of the fee demonstration program. The Federal Lands Recreation Enhancement Act (FLREA), Pub. L. 108–447, *codified at* 16 U.S.C. §§ 6801 et seq., contains similar restrictions on use of the recreation fees as the older fee demonstration program: the agency keeps all of the revenue with sixty to eighty percent to be retained and used at the site collected. The remaining revenue may be used anywhere within the agency. Most of the money is used for facility maintenance, repair, and enhancement, but some funds can be put toward visitor services, habitat restoration, law enforcement, and administration of the program. Only the NPS and FWS may charge entrance fees. But all of the agencies may charge fees for visitor "amenities," such as access to interpretive centers, campgrounds, and motorized recreational vehicle trails. Supporters of the recreation fee programs cite the additional revenue available to agencies ($173 million in FY 2003, including $123 million generated from national parks), the fairness of charging users the costs of recreational services, and deterring criminal activity. Critics argue that the fees unfairly tax recreationists twice, promote commercial development, and discriminate against low-income people and low-impact recreation. These critics note that "the typical $5 fee for a day hike is more than double what a rancher pays to graze a cow on the same land for a month." Tony Davis, *Fed Up with Paying to Play*, HIGH COUNTY NEWS, Nov. 27, 2006. *See generally*, Carol Hardy Vincent, Federal Lands Recreation Enhancement Act (Congressional Research Serv. 2005).

The FLREA provides that receipts collected may not be taken into account in allocating revenues under various federal laws, including the Land & Water Conservation Fund Act. 16 U.S.C. § 1613. But, some fear that Congress will eventually reduce appropriated funds for federal land management agencies as they become more successful in generating revenue through fees. This would make agencies more reliant on visitors for funding, and the concern is that this will give the agencies a powerful incentive to attract visitation (on the theme park model), even if it is at the expense of sound resource management. Is there any way to prevent that scenario from unfolding, while still allowing agencies to charge fees and retain the revenues?

Among the most hotly debated aspects of the FLREA is the prohibition on BLM and Forest Service fees for parking, access to dispersed areas with little infrastructure, passing through areas, and using scenic overlooks. Critics charge that the land agencies do charge fees for access even where little or no services are provided. In perhaps the first judicial interpretation of FLREA, a district court upheld Forest Service parking fees within the Mt. Lemmon High Impact Recreation Area ("HIRA") along the Catalina Highway outside of Tucson. United States v. Wallace, 476 F.Supp.2d 1129 (D.Ariz.2007). The dispute centered around 16 U.S.C. § 6802(d)(1)(A), which prohibits the Service from collecting fees "solely for parking, undesignated parking, or picnicking along roads or trailsides." The Forest Service interpreted "solely" to modify all three activities identified in the quoted clause. The court accepted the Forest Service's application of the statute to allow fees for undesignated parking, where the parking was not the sole amenity available. The Forest Service legally combined all of the recreational amenities in the HIRA, including parking, and charged a single fee for access to the area through the Catalina Highway.

2.   RECREATION CONCESSIONS

The role of the private sector in providing recreation goods and services on federal lands is a subject of considerable contemporary debate. * * *Some critics have contended that the agencies responsible for our public lands have not sufficiently encouraged private investment in recreation development to accommodate growing public demand. Conversely, others have rallied behind a cry of opposition to "commercialization, privatization, industrialization, and 'Disneyfication' " of their national parks and forests.

The agencies themselves wrestle internally between the need to supplement meager federal appropriations for recreation and the underlying goal of natural resource protection. Pricing concerns, social equity, and perceived excessive development and commercialization are but a few of the issues agencies need to address as they weigh the pros and cons of increased privatization.

These are not new issues. Indeed, they have been at the forefront of public land recreation management for nearly 130 years.

Tom Quinn, Public Lands and Private Recreation Enterprise (USDA Forest Service 2002).

a.   THE NATIONAL PARK SERVICE

The legislation authorizing the world's first national park, Yellowstone, authorized the leasing of portions of the park for "the erection of buildings for the accommodation of visitors." 17 Stat. 33 (1872). Early leaders and promoters of the national park system sought to promote tourism to the parks as a way to build a constituency—public support—for the agency and its mission. Stephen Mather, first director of the National Park Service, said that "[s]cenery is a hollow enjoyment to a tourist who sets out in the morning after an indigestible breakfast and a fitful sleep in an impossible bed." Dennis J. Herman, *Loving Them to Death: Legal Controls on the Type and Scale of Development in the National Parks*, 11 STAN. ENVTL. L.J. 3, 3 (1992). Roads, railroads, grand hotels, and other developments to facilitate visitation and provide creature comforts were encouraged, often in places and ways deemed unacceptable by today's tastes. *See, e.g.*, Alfred Runte, NATIONAL PARKS: THE AMERICAN EXPERIENCE Ch. 5 (1979).

The strategy worked; the agency's public support is wide and deep, but there has been a cost in terms of overuse of developed areas and deterioration of park facilities and in some cases the parks themselves. What are parks for—private profit, public use, or both? Is there an inherent conflict between the two? In National Parks & Conservation Ass'n v. Kleppe, 547 F.2d 673, 676 (D.C.Cir. 1976) (addressing how much disclosure the Freedom of Information Act requires of financial data submitted to the Park Service by concessioners), the court observed:

> Concession activity in the national parks is a thriving business which is becoming increasingly dominated by large corporate concessioners. The relationship between the Park Service and the park concessioners is long-standing and has been fostered in large measure by various financial incentives aimed at maintaining the quality and continuity of goods and services available to park visitors.

Some concessions in federal recreation areas are indeed big business. The Park Service's nearly 600 concession contracts generate $800 million. The 52 largest contracts generate half of that revenue. National Park Service Concessions Program, Senate Comm. on Energy & Nat. Res., April 8, 2004. Some of the concessioners are effectively monopolies, and regulated by the federal agencies in a fashion similar to other "natural" monopolies like electrical utilities. Other concessioners are directly in competition with each other; e.g., nearly two dozen separate companies are licensed by the National Park Service to operate commercial river trips through the Grand Canyon.

Early on, the National Park Service offered "financial inducements to private contractors to convince them to provide and operate facilities in what were often remote locations." Amfac Resorts v. U.S. Dept. of the Interior, 282 F.3d 818 (D.C.Cir. 2002). A preference for renewal, so long as "full and satisfactory service to the public had been given," was one of these inducements. *Id.* The 1965 National Park Service Concessions Policy Act wrote the preference into law. Over the years, this preferential right of renewal came to be seen as drastically limiting competition and entrenching existing concessioners in place regardless of performance. Following many years of effort, with strong bipartisan support, Congress in 1998 finally enacted a sweeping overhaul of the Concessions Policy Act of 1965. The changes furthered competition in the award of concession contracts in the hopes of ensuring a better return to the government and better service for park visitors. For all but the smallest concessioners, the 1998 Act prospectively ended the preferential right of renewal. In *Amfac Resorts* the court rejected the concessioners' attempt to interpret the repeal as ineffective. Nonetheless, recent studies have found evidence that local service providers have not succeeded in challenging the domination of larger enterprises. Rick S. Kurtz, *The Federal Concessioner System*, 23 REV. POL'Y RESEARCH 373 (2006).

Capital improvements (such as hotels) constructed by park concessioners on federal land in the parks are the property of the United States. But concessioners have a monetary interest in facilities they construct pursuant to the concession contract. Therefore, if the contract expires or is terminated, they are entitled to receive from their successor concessioner, or the government, the value of the so-called "leasehold surrender interest." Disagreement between key members of Congress over how much of a lease surrender interest to recognize in concession contracts (when an existing concessioner loses the bid for a new contract, how much of the loser's investment in facilities should the winner have to pay?) nearly doomed the 1998 Act, but a last minute compromise paved the way to enactment by providing more specificity in the administration of these interests. The National Park Service's regulations to implement these changes were generally upheld against concessioner attack in *Amfac Resorts*. The 1998 legislation, dubbed the National Parks Omnibus Management Act of 1998, 16 U.S.C. §§ 5901–6011, also made a number of other important changes in concession policy, provided for science-based management of the system, sketched out a process for studying the additions to the national park system, and authorized a passport program for park visitors.

b. THE U.S. FOREST SERVICE AND SKI AREAS

The Forest Service has dramatically increased its reliance on concessioners in the past two decades. Today concessioners run some 2,000 national forest campgrounds. Downhill skiing concessions on national forests generate the greatest recreational revenue. Nearly all of the major ski areas in the West, and many in the East, are located at least partially on national forest land. There are about 200 downhill ski areas permitted on national forests. Until 1986, the Forest Service authorized these areas under an awkward "dual permit" arrangement.

The original 1897 Organic Act gave the Forest Service general authority to make rules and regulations governing occupancy and use of the forests. 16 U.S.C. § 551. The Forest Service often used this authority to regulate by permit such activities as livestock grazing and ancillary activities on mining claims. In 1915, Congress enacted a separate law that specifically authorized the Forest Service to issue permits for recreational facilities. 16 U.S.C. § 497. This law capped permits at 80 acres in size and thirty years in duration, and did not provide for exclusive occupancy; i.e., it forbade "preclud[ing] the general public" from enjoying the forests. The legislative history of the 1915 Act suggested congressional awareness of the agency's authority to issue revocable permits for recreational developments under the 1897 Act.

Under the "dual permit" system, the operator would receive a base 80–acre permit for the lodge and related facilities, and a revocable permit under the 1897 Act for the other several hundred acres typically required. At the dawn of the modern environmental movement, one of the Sierra Club's first uses of the courts challenged the legality of this arrangement in a highly publicized dispute over a proposal by Walt Disney Productions for development of the beautiful Mineral King valley in the southern Sierra Nevada range in California. In Sierra Club v. Hickel, 433 F.2d 24 (9th Cir. 1970), the court upheld the "dual permit" approach, rejecting the Club's argument that the acreage and term limits of the 1915 Act prevented the agency from using the 1897 Act. It found, among other things, that Congress had been made aware of the practice, and that its widespread use by the agency was "convincing proof of [its] legality."*

Even though no court had invalidated the "dual permit" scheme for ski areas, the ski industry remained nervous about making large investments on the shaky foundation of "revocable" permits. The National Forest Ski Area Act of 1986, 16 U.S.C. § 497b, changed the permit system. It removed the acreage limit on term permits for ski areas, extended the ordinary maximum term to 40 years, and allowed for renewal. But it also allowed permits to be cancelled by the Secretary of Agriculture on various grounds, such as upon a determination in forest plans "that the permitted area is needed for higher public purposes." Similarly, the Secretary can modify permits "from time to time * * * to accommodate changes in plans or operations in accordance with the provisions of applicable law." Permittees must also pay a fee "based on fair market value in accordance with applicable law." Existing "dual permit" facilities had three years to decide whether to convert their permits to the new system. This posed somewhat of a dilemma for ski operators, who had to decide whether the increased security of their basic tenure was worth acknowledging the agency's more explicit continuing regulatory authority and fair market value obligation in the new Act. The planning process for new ski areas can be quite involved, and is of course subject to NEPA. See Robertson v. Methow Valley Citizens Council, supra p. 258.

3.   RECREATIONAL PERMITTING ON NATIONAL FORESTS AND BLM PUBLIC LANDS

Recreation is one of the "multiple uses" for national forests and BLM lands. The MUSY mandate of FLPMA, along with the public land planning

---

* In the Mineral King case, the Ninth Circuit went on to reject the Club's other legal arguments. The case is better known as a landmark modern decision on standing to sue (under its caption in the U.S. Supreme Court, Sierra Club v. Morton, 405 U.S. 727 (1972)). See supra p. 208. The Club lost the immediate legal battle but ultimately won the war. On remand from the Supreme Court, the district court allowed the Club to amend its complaint to obtain standing and add new claims, including one under NEPA. The For-

est Service agreed to prepare an EIS, which further delayed matters. The project and the lawsuit were both eventually dropped; in 1978 the Valley was added to Sequoia National Park with this statutory explanation: "The Congress recognizes that the Mineral King Valley area has outstanding potential for certain year-round recreational opportunities, but the development of permanent facilities for downhill skiing within the area would be inconsistent with the preservation and enhancement of its ecological values." 16 U.S.C. 45(h).

process the statute creates, constitutes the essential guidance for BLM recreation planning. The 1897 Organic Act, the 1915 recreational permitting statute (discussed above in connection with ski areas), the 1960 MUSY Act, and the 1975 RPA (as modified by the 1976 National Forest Management Act) form an equivalent, if much less tidy, legal structure for Forest Service recreation management. Except for ski areas, recreational regulation on national forests is still governed largely by the terms of the 1897 and 1915 Acts.

A number of cases have addressed the Forest Service's exercise of its authority over "occupancy and use" under the 1897 Organic Act in connection with recreational activities, primarily concerning outfitters who provide services such as horses and canoes to recreationists. The Forest Service regulation requires a permit in order to "conduct[] any kind of work activity or service" on the national forests, 36 C.F.R. § 261.10(e), and the courts generally sustain convictions for violating this provision. *See, e.g.,* United States v. Brown, 200 F.3d 710 (10th Cir. 1999) (upholding conviction for violating the rule where outfitter dropped off rented snowmobiles at the edge of federal land). On the other hand, the Ninth Circuit has held that the regulation prohibits the specified activities "only when they are engaged in for consideration." United States v. Strong, 79 F.3d 925 (9th Cir. 1996) (relying on a provision of a USFS Special Uses Handbook). The federal agencies may enforce generic regulations promulgated under the Organic Act, even when the defendant is operating in an area subject to a special statute which authorizes protective regulations that the agency has not yet promulgated. *See* United States v. Hells Canyon Guide Service, Inc., 660 F.2d 735 (9th Cir. 1981) (affirming a permanent injunction against a guide who persisted in operating jet and float boats in Hells Canyon National Recreation Area without obtaining a permit from the Forest Service).

The question of how far either the U.S. Forest Service or the BLM can go in transferring what may effectively be a permanent or very long-term interest in federal lands under their supervision to a private recreational developer is not completely settled. But, agency discretion may cut both ways. Courts have vested the agency with broad authority to revoke special land use permits for resort facilities. In Mount Evans Co. v. Madigan, 14 F.3d 1444 (10th Cir. 1994), the court upheld a Forest Service decision not to rebuild the "Crest House" at the summit of Mount Evans after it was destroyed by fire. The structure had been built by a private company under permit from the Forest Service. The court held the decision not to rebuild was not committed entirely to agency discretion and was subject to judicial review, but the agency had not acted arbitrarily. This was so even though the court found that the record did not support a Forest Service determination of traffic counts on the summit before and after the fire "because the agency relied on a number of findings, not merely the number of visitors to Mount Evans' summit, to reach its decision."

In general, special use permits do not create protected, compensable property rights. For example, in Paulina Lake Historic Cabin Owners Ass'n v. United States Department of Agriculture Forest Service, 577 F.Supp.

1188, 1193 n. 2 (D.Or.1983), the court noted that the plaintiffs, owners of recreational cabins built on national forest land pursuant to a special use permit from the Forest Service, did not claim a property right in the permit, "[n]or would such an allegation be well-taken. The law is settled that special use permits create no vested property rights." The court analogized the special use permit to a grazing permit and cited United States v. Fuller, *supra* p. 778.

Like private developers, the United States often has problems with its contractors. Is there anything to prevent the federal agency from itself building a ski area, a resort, or dock facilities? Should the federal agency prefer to (a) provide these facilities itself, (b) favor a few large developers or operators, or (c) favor more numerous and potentially unruly small enterprises or individuals (such as individual dock owners)?

E. OFF-ROAD VEHICLE REGULATION

The public may visit most federal lands for recreational purposes, but the "right" to do so is merely a license, revocable at the will of Congress or at the informed discretion of an authorized land management agency. The upsurge in recreational use has spurred the development of new kinds of controls on intensive recreation, including rationing of recreational experiences, to protect the most popular areas from overuse. Federal efforts to limit recreational access can provoke opposition inside as well as outside of land management agencies, for they can undermine public support for agency programs. Restrictions on the recreational license are usually regarded as the last resort. Congress has seldom directly addressed this volatile issue. Conflicts between restrictive policies and the traditional right of free access are most acute with respect to off-road vehicles (ORVs), including jeeps, motorcycles, 4 X 4s, mountain bicycles, snowmobiles, as well as their aquatic counterparts, jet skis and other personal watercraft.

1. WHEELED ORVs

From their introduction into the mass consumer market in the early 1960s, annual ORV sales quickly exploded to more than seven million vehicles in 1970 and ten million vehicles in 1979. The public land agencies did not anticipate this surge in ORV and were slow to respond to its planning challenges.

> From 1982 to 2000, the number of people driving motor vehicles off road in the United States increased over 109 percent * * *. Recent decades have seen like advances in the power, range, and capabilities of OHVs [off-highway vehicles]. Whole new classes of vehicles have been introduced by manufacturers and are growing in popularity. From 1997 to 2001, the number of ATVs [all-terrain vehicles] in use increased by almost 40 percent * * *. These advances expand opportunities for Americans to enjoy Federal lands.

* * *

In addition, the line between highway vehicles and OHVs has blurred. Vehicles created for specialized off-road use, such as military vehicles, are now marketed and purchased as family cars. Some States have recently enacted statutes governing OHV use, including vehicle registration requirements, limits on operator age, training and licensing requirements, equipment requirements, sound restrictions, and safety requirements.

70 Fed. Reg. 68264 (Nov. 9, 2005).

ORVs pose a prominent danger to some federal lands, but regulating them is especially troublesome. As Jim Ruch, former BLM State Director for California, has said, "You can't understand true multiple-use management until you've stood on the top of a sand dune with the members of the Desert Lily Society coming up one side and, coming up the other, the Barstow Bombers." Enforcement of any regulatory system can be difficult because of the dispersed nature of the activity and the shortage of agency personnel even in heavily used areas.

The first major effort to regulate ORVs on federal lands started at the top: In February 1972, President Richard Nixon issued Executive Order No. 11644, which directed the federal land management agencies effectively to "zone" the federal lands with respect to ORV travel. The President directed each agency head to create a regulatory structure that would designate "specific areas and trails on public lands on which the use of off-road vehicles may be permitted, and areas in which the use of off-road vehicles may not be permitted," within a date certain. The Order contained general environmental criteria to be used in zoning the lands for ORV use and required the agencies to carry out this task with full public participation. It recited that it was issued "by virtue of the authority vested in me as President of the United States by the Constitution of the United States and in furtherance of the purpose and policy of [NEPA]." *See supra* p. 429, regarding the President's authority to issue such orders.

Only the BLM implemented this order with regulations specific to ORV use. The other principal federal land agencies—the Park Service, Fish & Wildlife Service, and Forest Service—chose instead to make ad hoc determinations of the suitability of ORV use in particular areas or, in the case of the Forest Service, to issue ORV plans for specific national forests that generally codify existing management practices. In response to this tepid implementation, early in his administration President Carter issued an Executive Order, No. 11989 (1977), which required the federal land management agencies to ban ORVs from areas where the agency determines that continued use "will cause or is causing considerable adverse effects." This Order failed to produce any significant progress in the agencies.

a. BLM

The BLM regulations implementing the 1972 Executive Order were promptly challenged by environmental groups. In National Wildlife Federation v. Morton, 393 F.Supp. 1286 (D.D.C.1975), the court found that the BLM had "significantly diluted the standards emphatically set forth in" the

Order and not followed it in several other respects. For example, the court cited BLM's adding a new substantive criterion ("[t]he need for public use areas for recreation use") that was not specified, and implicitly not allowed, in the Executive Order. Perhaps the most important defect identified by the court was the following (393 F.Supp. at 1295):

> Instead of evaluating with regard to the environmental criteria mandated by Executive Order 11644 specific areas and trails to determine whether the use of ORVs should be permitted, BLM has engaged in a wholesale, blanket designation of "open" lands. By doing so, it has violated the express requirements of Executive Order 11644.

The BLM eventually responded with new regulations that contained criteria for the designation of ORV use and routes on public lands that rather closely tracked the 1972 Executive Order criteria. *See* 43 C.F.R. pt. 8340. But BLM implementation of the Order and its regulations, particularly in the California Desert, continued to attract controversy.

David Sheridan described part of the BLM's problem:

> The process of designating areas or trails open or closed to ORV use is a laborious undertaking for an agency such as the BLM, which administers [more than two hundred] million acres of public land. The task is compounded by the fact that almost no control over ORV uses was exercised prior to Executive Order 11644, and hence behavior patterns of millions of ORV recreationists had already become established. In addition, BLM has fewer men and women per acre than the other land management agencies.

[Sheridan went on to describe the BLM's initial ORV regulation plan adopted in 1973 for the California Desert, the most intensively used ORV area in the nation:]

> It designates 3 percent of the [BLM land in the California Desert] as "closed" to ORVs, 6 percent as "open," and the remainder as "restricted," which means that ORV drivers are supposed to stay on existing roads and trails.
>
> The major flaw in this scheme is that it does not take into account BLM's lack of presence in the field. A person can drive all day in the desert on a motorcycle or in a four-wheel drive vehicle and never see a BLM sign or enforcement officer. Indeed, the BLM has only slightly more than a dozen rangers to patrol 12 million acres of land. * * *

OFF-ROAD VEHICLES ON PUBLIC LAND (1979)

As the BLM tried again to grapple with ORV use in the California Desert, it had in the meantime gained new management authority with passage of the Federal Land Policy and Management Act in 1976. Section 601 of FLPMA created the California Desert Conservation Area (CDCA), and directed BLM to promulgate a plan for managing it. 43 U.S.C. § 1781.*

---

* The California Desert Conservation Area near the Los Angeles/San Diego megalopolis poses some of the toughest recreational management issues on the federal lands. The story of the movement to protect it (which included the 1976 designation of the

Congress prefaced this section with special findings that, among other things, described the unique, "extremely fragile, easily scarred, and slowly healed" resources of the area, which were threatened by "pressures of increased use, particularly recreational use." It also found that

> the use of all California desert resources can and should be provided for in a multiple use and sustained yield management plan to conserve these resources for future generations, and to provide present and future use and enjoyment, particularly outdoor recreational uses, including the use, where appropriate, of off-road recreational vehicles.

In American Motorcyclist Ass'n v. Watt, 543 F.Supp. 789 (C.D.Cal. 1982), the court addressed that portion of the BLM's plan for the CDCA specifying that in so-called "Class L" areas, motorized vehicles will be allowed only on "approved routes of travel." At issue were the specific criteria set out in the plan by which the approved routes were to be selected. The applicable BLM regulations (43 C.F.R. § 8342.1) provided (court's emphasis added):

> The authorized officer shall designate all public lands as either open, limited, or closed to off-road vehicles. All designations shall be based on the protection of the resources of the public lands, the promotion of the safety of all the users of the public lands, and the *minimization of conflicts* among various uses of the public lands; and in accordance with the following criteria:
>
> (a) Areas and trails shall be located to *minimize damage* to soil, watershed, vegetation, air, or other resources of the public lands, and to prevent impairment of wilderness suitability.
>
> (b) Areas and trails shall be located to *minimize harassment* of wildlife or significant disruption of wildlife habitats. Special attention will be given to protect endangered or threatened species and their habitats.
>
> (c) Areas and trails shall be located to *minimize conflicts between* off-road vehicle use and other existing or proposed recreational uses of the same or neighboring public lands, and to ensure the compatibility of such uses with existing conditions in populated areas, taking into account noise and other factors.
>
> (d) Areas and trails shall not be located in officially designated wilderness areas or primitive areas. Areas and trails shall be located in natural areas only if the authorized officer determines that off-road vehicle use in such locations will not adversely affect their natural, esthetic, scenic, or other values for which such areas are established.

The BLM's California Desert Plan provided (court's emphasis added):

> In Multiple–Use Class L areas, vehicle access is limited to only those routes "approved" and marked as vehicle access routes. Routes not "approved" for vehicle access in most instances will be obliterated,

CDCA in FLPMA and a second statute enacted in 1994, which designated the Mohave National Park and Preserve and millions of acres of wilderness, see 16 U.S.C. §§ 410aaa- aaa83), is well told by the late lawyer/conservationist Francis Wheat, in CALIFORNIA DESERT MIRACLE (1999).

barricaded, signed, or shown "closed" on maps. "Approved" routes will be signed or otherwise marked or mapped so that those routes of travel which are clearly open will be readily identifiable.

Route Designation Factors—Multiple–Use Class L

Decisions on approval of vehicle routes for Class L *will be based* on an analysis of each situation, using the following decision criteria:

(1) Is the route new or existing?

(2) Does the route provide access for resource use or enjoyment?

(3) Are there alternate access opportunities?

(4) *Does the route cause considerable adverse impacts?*

(5) Are there alternate access routes which do not cause considerable adverse impacts?

The court concluded (543 F.Supp. at 797):

> The route designation criteria, as shown above, are presented in such a manner so as to appear to be the exclusive standard pursuant to which route designation decisions are to be made. Concededly, the criteria are phrased in a neutral, interrogative form, such that they do not explicitly require that a route be approved if certain conditions are satisfied. At the same time, however, the criteria do not explicitly *prohibit* route designation in any defined situation. Thus, the Plan criteria would permit agency officials to make route designations without the minimization of environmental impacts and conflicts between uses expressly required by 43 C.F.R. § 8342.1. Furthermore, the criteria, even though neutrally phrased, will very likely lead BLM officials responsible for implementing the Plan to conclude that routes should be approved absent a finding of "considerable adverse impacts." The "considerable adverse impacts" standard is qualitatively different than the minimization criteria mandated by § 8342.1 and in practice is almost certain to skew route designation decision-making in favor of ORV use.

> Defendants argue that various references in the Plan to E.O. 11,644, E.O. 11,989, and certain BLM regulations make it clear that the BLM does not intend to, or was not authorized to, apply the route selection criteria in a manner inconsistent with 43 C.F.R. § 8342.1. However, viewed in the context in which they appear, these references are not sufficient to counteract the impression, created in the presentation of the route designation criteria quoted above, that those criteria are to be the exclusive bases for route approval decisions. No mention of the executive orders or applicable BLM regulations is made in the text surrounding the criteria in the Plan. Furthermore, the Court has seen no language anywhere in the Plan which would alert a reader that the criteria presented in the Plan are inconsistent with 43 C.F.R. § 8342.1 or the executive orders. (If anything, the impression is given that the criteria faithfully implement these pre-existing directives.) Accordingly, I conclude that the Plan, viewed as a whole, is very likely to result in a

route selection process which does not comply in significant respects with the express standards set forth in 43 C.F.R. § 8342.1.

The court enjoined BLM "from approving any route of travel in Class L areas, on either a one-time or permanent basis, without complying with the selection criteria set forth in 43 C.F.R. § 8342.1." That scarcely ended the matter, as the next case shows.

Sierra Club v. Clark

United States Court of Appeals, Ninth Circuit, 1985.
756 F.2d 686.

■ JUDGE POOLE

* * * Dove Springs Canyon is located in the California Desert Conservation Area ("Desert Area"), established in 1976, 43 U.S.C. § 1781, under the Federal Land Policy Management Act ("the Act"), 43 U.S.C. § 1701 et seq. The Desert Area covers approximately 25 million acres in southeastern California, approximately 12.1 million of which are administered by the BLM. Dove Springs Canyon is comprised of approximately 5500 acres; 3000 acres are designated "open" for unrestricted use of ORVs.

Dove Springs Canyon possesses abundant and diverse flora and fauna. Over 250 species of plants, 24 species of reptiles, and 30 species of birds are found there. It also offers good habitat for the Mojave ground squirrel, the desert kit fox, and the burrowing owl. Because the rich and varied biota is unusual for an area of such low elevation in the Mojave Desert, the Canyon was once frequented by birdwatchers and naturalists, as well as hikers and fossil hunters.

Recreational ORV usage of Dove Springs Canyon began in 1965 and became progressively heavier in the ensuing years. By 1971, the Canyon was being used intensively by ORV enthusiasts. It became especially popular because the site's diverse terrain, coupled with relatively easy access, provides outstanding hill-climbing opportunities. By 1979, up to 200 vehicles used the Canyon on a typical weekend; over 500 vehicles used it on a holiday weekend. In 1973, the BLM adopted its Interim Critical Management Program for Recreational Vehicle Use on the California Desert ("Interim Program") which designated Dove Springs Canyon as an ORV Open Area, permitting recreational vehicle travel in the area without restriction.

Extensive ORV usage has been accompanied by severe environmental damage in the form of major surface erosion, soil compaction, and heavy loss of vegetation. The visual aesthetics have markedly declined. The character of the Canyon has been so severely altered that the Canyon is now used almost exclusively for ORV activities.

In July of 1980 Sierra Club petitioned the Secretary of the Interior to close Dove Springs Canyon to ORV use under the authority of Executive Order No. 11644, as amended by Executive Order No. 11989, and 43 C.F.R. § 8341.2 because of "substantial adverse effects" on the vegetation, soil and wildlife in the Canyon. The Secretary responded that the matter would be addressed in the California Desert Conservation Plan and Final Environmental Impact Statement ("the Final Plan").

The Final Plan approved by the Secretary in December 1980 maintained unrestricted ORV use in Dove Springs of 3000 of the 5500 acres. Sierra Club filed this action on January 6, 1981, alleging that the Secretary's failure to close Dove Springs violated Executive Order No. 11644, as amended by Executive Order No. 11989, and 43 C.F.R. § 8341.2; 43 U.S.C. § 1732(b), which requires the Secretary to prevent "unnecessary or undue degradation of the lands;" and 43 U.S.C. §§ 1781(b) and (d), which require the Secretary to maintain and conserve resources of the Desert Area under principles of "multiple use and sustained yield." * * * [The cited regulation] provides:

> Notwithstanding the consultation provisions of § 8342.2(a), where the authorized officer determines that off-road vehicles are causing or will cause considerable adverse effects * * * the authorized officer shall immediately close the areas or trails affected. * * * Such closures will not prevent designation * * *, but these lands shall not be opened to the type(s) of off-road vehicle to which it was closed unless the authorized officer determines that the adverse effects have been eliminated and measures implemented to prevent recurrence.

43 C.F.R. § 8341.2(a). * * * [T]he closure standard of the Executive Orders and the Regulation applies independently of the designation of the land as open under the Act, the issue before us is whether the damage to Dove Springs Canyon amounts to "considerable adverse effects" which require the Canyon's closure. The parties agree that there is no genuine issue as to the extent of the damage to the Canyon, and therefore resolution of this issue depends upon whether the Secretary's interpretation of this phrase or that of the Sierra Club is to control. * * *

The Secretary interprets "considerable adverse effect" to require determining what is "considerable" in the context of the Desert Area as a whole, not merely on a parcel-by-parcel basis. The Secretary contends such a broad interpretation is necessary and is consistent with 43 U.S.C. § 1781(a)(4) which expresses a congressional judgment that ORV use is to be permitted "where appropriate."

Sierra Club argues against the Secretary's interpretation. Sierra Club contends that the interpretation of the Executive Orders set forth by the Council on Environmental Quality (CEQ) in its August 1, 1977 memorandum is entitled to great deference, and that the CEQ's interpretation requires the closure of the Canyon. This argument fails on two grounds.

First, the CEQ's interpretation of the Executive Order does not directly conflict with the Secretary's interpretation of the regulation. While it states that "the term 'considerable' should be liberally construed to provide the broadest possible protection reasonably required by this standard," it does not purport to decide whether the term "considerable adverse effects" should be analyzed in the context of the entire Desert Area, or on a site-specific basis. Moreover, the memorandum acknowledges that the responsibility for closing particular areas rests with "responsible federal officials in the field" "[b]ased on their practical experience in the management of the public lands, and their first-hand knowledge of conditions 'on-the-ground.' "

Second, the authority of the CEQ is to maintain a continuing review of the implementation of the Executive Order. Executive Order No. 11644, § 8(b). The authority of the Secretary, on the other hand, is to promulgate regulations to provide for "administrative designation of the specific areas and trails on public lands on which the use of off-road vehicles may be permitted, and areas in which the use of off-road vehicles may not be permitted." *Id.* at § 3(a). Discretion rests with the Secretary, therefore, to determine whether and to what extent specific areas should be closed to ORV use. Thus, it is the Secretary's interpretation which is entitled to our deference.

Sierra Club argues that even if the CEQ's interpretation of the closure standard is not controlling, the Secretary's interpretation should not be adopted because it is unreasonable. Sierra Club insists that the sacrifice of any area to permanent resource damage is not justified under the multiple use management mandate of 43 U.S.C. § 1702(c) that requires multiple use "without permanent impairment of the productivity of the land and the quality of the environment." In further support of its position Sierra Club adverts to the requirement in the Act that the Secretary prevent "unnecessary and undue degradation" of the public lands, 43 U.S.C. § 1732(b). In addition, Sierra Club contends, when Congress established the Desert Area it intended the Secretary to fashion a multiple use and sustained yield management plan "to conserve [the California desert] resources for future generations, and to provide present and future use and enjoyment, particularly outdoor recreational uses, including the use, where appropriate, of off-road recreational vehicles." 43 U.S.C. § 1781(a)(4). Sierra Club argues that it is unreasonable for the Secretary to find ORV use "appropriate" when that use violates principles of sustained yield, substantially impairs productivity of renewable resources and is inconsistent with maintenance of environmental quality.

We can appreciate the earnestness and force of Sierra Club's position, and if we could write on a clean slate, would prefer a view which would disallow the virtual sacrifice of a priceless natural area in order to accommodate a special recreational activity. But we are not free to ignore the mandate which Congress wrote into the Act. Sierra Club's interpretation of the regulation would inevitably result in the total prohibition of ORV use because it is doubtful that any discrete area could withstand unrestricted ORV use without considerable adverse effects. However appealing might be such a resolution of the environmental dilemma, Congress has found that ORV use, damaging as it may be, is to be provided "where appropriate." It left determination of appropriateness largely up to the Secretary in an area of sharp conflict. If there is to be a change it must come by way of Congressional reconsideration. The Secretary's interpretation that this legislative determination calls for accommodation of ORV usage in the administrative plan, we must conclude, is not unreasonable and we are constrained to let it stand.

The court must review agency action to determine if it complies with the Secretary's interpretation of the Regulation. In Perkins v. Bergland, 608 F.2d 803 (9th Cir. 1979), we held that the scope of review of an agency's factual findings is very narrow where the Secretary has been vested with substantial discretion, as in the administration of public land. * * * We noted that the various goals of "multiple use," "sustained yield," and how "best [to] meet the needs of the American people," vested in the Secretary discretion to determine optimum means of administering forest and range land. We concluded that the agency's factual findings as to range conditions and carrying capacity would be overturned only if arbitrary and capricious.

Under the California Desert Conservation Area Plan, approximately 4 percent (485,000 acres) of the total acreage is now open to unrestricted ORV use. Dove Springs itself constitutes only 0.025 percent of BLM administered lands in the Desert Area. Although all parties recognize that the environmental impact of ORV use at Dove Springs is severe, the Secretary's determination that these effects were not "considerable" in the context of the Desert Area as a whole is not arbitrary, capricious, or an abuse of the broad discretion committed to him by an obliging Congress. * * *

NOTES AND QUESTIONS

1. Does BLM's experience in implementing the executive orders here, and the federal courts' responses, show the toothlessness of presidential executive orders in the face of agency inertia or opposition? Who is entitled to deference in interpreting and applying the executive order, the CEQ or the BLM?

2. How much deference should the BLM receive here? Would the result be the same if BLM *closed* Dove Springs Canyon to ORV use, while leaving other, less ecologically significant areas of the Desert open to unrestricted ORV use? Same result if BLM had left twenty-five percent of the Desert open to unrestricted ORV use? Fifty percent? Is there a principled basis on which the BLM, or the courts, could draw a line?

3. Congress's express purpose in creating the CDCA was to "provide for immediate and future protection and administration of the public lands in the California desert within the framework of a program of multiple use and sustained yield, and the maintenance of environmental quality." 43 U.S.C. § 1781(b). Did Congress really make a decision in FLPMA § 1781(a)(4), that heavy, destructive use of portions of the California Desert by ORVs was proper? Does the phrase "where appropriate" in that subsection (a)(4) congressional finding mean that heavy ORV use had to be "appropriate" *somewhere* in the Desert? Is the court saying that if ORV traffic is to be banned here it must be banned everywhere in the Desert, and that can't be what Congress had in mind? But if the congressional intent is cloudy, should the court—given the damage being caused—err on the side of protection, enjoin ORV traffic, and in effect remand the matter

to Congress to make its intentions more clear if it had something else in mind?

4.   Along the same lines, examine how the court deals with FLPMA's general statutory standards such as its mandate to prevent "unnecessary or undue degradation" (FLPMA § 302(b), 43 U.S.C. § 1732(b)). Is the court saying this mandate simply cannot meaningfully be applied to compel specific action with respect to ORV use? How does this compare to the court's application of the FLPMA standard in the regulation of hardrock mines on BLM land? See *Mineral Policy Center, supra* p. 608. Note that the court's opinion here erroneously sometimes (but not consistently) quotes the standard as "unnecessary *and* undue." Is that a Freudian slip? Does the "or" make a difference? (And speaking of Freud, do you suppose the name of the Canyon influenced plaintiffs' decision to make a federal case out of BLM's decision?)

5.   Similarly, what about FLPMA's mandate (in the definition of multiple use) to prevent "permanent impairment of the productivity of the land and the quality of the environment." 43 U.S.C. § 1702(c). What about BLM's duty under FLPMA to provide "sustained yield" of the renewable resources of the public lands? Why is the result in this case different from the Tongass logging case (Sierra Club v. Butz, *supra* p. 688), where the court of appeals vacated and remanded a lower court decision upholding a whole-hearted emphasis on logging? More generally, are all the grand statutory paeans to environmental quality and resource protection empty against the tide of massive amounts of mechanized recreation? Given those lofty goals, should the courts put the burden of legislative inertia on the side of the environment, or on the side of ORVs? That is, instead of allowing this kind of intensive, destructive, use until Congress expressly prohibits it, should the courts prohibit it until Congress expressly allows it?

6.   Perhaps the pinnacle of ORV use of the federal lands was the annual Barstow to Las Vegas off-road motorcycle race. Attracting thousands of participants, it was run on Thanksgiving weekend from 1967 to 1974. At that point BLM decided not to issue permits for it because of adverse impacts to desert resources. ORV enthusiasts nevertheless held annual, unsanctioned "protest" races along the same course on succeeding Thanksgiving weekends. In 1983, BLM amended the CDCA Plan to allow the race to resume with official sanction. The Plan amendment designated the 110–mile race course (covering some 2000 acres), and included mitigation measures. It was also accompanied by an EIS. When BLM followed up by issuing a permit for a 1983 race, the Sierra Club sued. The 1983 race was held before the court of appeals ruled. In Sierra Club v. Clark, 774 F.2d 1406 (9th Cir. 1985), the court followed the Dove Springs Canyon case and upheld the BLM. Among other things, the court seemed to accept a "if you can't lick 'em, join (and regulate) 'em" defense:

> While there is little doubt that negative impacts resulted from the 1983 race, so is there little doubt that harm would result if uncontrolled "protest rides" were to continue. The mitigation requirements seek to assure that impacts are minimized. These requirements are not static—they can be expanded to offer greater assurances of compliance and

lessen the potential for harm. The challenged amendment * * * seems a reasoned approach to a difficult balancing act mandated by Congress.

Is it proper to permit the race simply because the agency recognizes that it cannot effectively prohibit a "protest" race? Could the BLM have allowed the race to resume on the sole ground that it had insufficient manpower to enforce its protective regulations? Could the court have overturned the BLM decision allowing the race, and ordered the BLM to divert personnel from other tasks in order to prevent a "protest" race from occurring? The Barstow–Las Vegas race was run annually through 1990. Recurring problems of enforcing the mitigation requirements, compounded by the listing of the Desert Tortoise as an endangered species, finally prompted the BLM to suspend it.

7.   Could the federal agencies look to private land and private markets to satisfy the demand for ORV use? Should (or could) the BLM sell off Dove Springs Canyon to ORV enthusiasts and take this problem off its plate? Is there any reason to keep the lands public if they are to be devoted to such a single narrow use? Would that rationale justify selling off grazing or mining or timber land?

b.   NPS

Meanwhile, on a coast three thousand miles to the east, another federal agency, operating under a somewhat different statutory mandate, was grappling with ORV regulation.

Conservation Law Foundation of New England, Inc. v. Secretary of the Interior

United States Court of Appeals, First Circuit, 1989.
864 F.2d 954.

■ JUDGE CAFFREY

The Conservation Law Foundation of New England, Inc. ("CLF") appeals from the district court's ruling upholding the validity of the National Park Service's 1985 Management Plan ("the 1985 Plan"). The 1985 Plan allows for the restricted use of off-road vehicles ("ORVs")[1] on the Cape Cod National Seashore ("the Seashore"). CLF contends that ORV use under the 1985 Plan violates the Cape Cod National Seashore Act, 16 U.S.C. §§ 459b et seq., and Executive Order 11644, which deals with ORV use on public lands.

Congress enacted the Cape Cod National Seashore Act ("the Seashore Act") in 1961, establishing the Seashore as part of the National Park System. The Seashore includes 48 miles of ocean front and bayside beaches * * *. The National Park Service maintains six Seashore beaches and

---

1. The term "off-road vehicles" refers to vehicles that are capable of cross-country travel over natural terrain. These include jeeps, dune buggies, and other four-wheel drive vehicles.

provides facilities for a number of other recreational activities, including boating, fishing, bicycling, and horseback riding.

At the time the Seashore Act was enacted, limited ORV use existed on the Seashore. The National Park Service began to regulate such use in 1964, as the Seashore started to become one of the major ORV recreational areas in New England. By 1974, many miles of ORV trails covered the Seashore. [Eds.: According to the district court, ORV use on the beach escalated from 400 vehicles per year when the seashore was created in 1961 to almost 5000 vehicles per year in 1979. 590 F.Supp. at 1471.] In that year, the Park Service contracted with the University of Massachusetts to conduct a study ("the U.Mass. Study") on the effects of ORV use on the Seashore's ecosystems. The results of the five-year study were published in thirteen volumes, and documented certain adverse ecological effects resulting from ORV travel on the Seashore.

In response to the findings of the U.Mass. Study, the National Park Service promulgated new regulations ("the 1981 Plan") restricting ORV use on the Seashore. Under the 1981 Plan, all tidal flats and salt marshes were closed to ORV travel. All upland areas and dune trails were also closed, except for an access route to be used by commercial dune taxis and cottage residents, and an emergency bypass route. Other significant restrictions were also created. Following adoption of the 1981 Plan, ORV travel on the Seashore decreased considerably.

CLF filed this suit seeking to enjoin implementation of the 1981 Plan. * * * CLF argued that the 1981 Plan would cause significant damage to the coastal ecosystem and impermissible conflicts between ORV travel and other recreational activities on the Seashore, in violation of the Seashore Act and Executive Order 11644. The district court denied CLF's request for injunctive relief, but remanded the 1981 Plan to the Secretary for additional findings regarding whether[,] in relation to other protected uses of the Seashore[,] ORV use meets the definition of "appropriate public use" as set forth in the Act. * * *

The National Park Service adopted an Amended Management Plan ("the 1985 Plan") in August of 1985 further restricting ORV use at the Seashore. CLF then amended its complaint to challenge the 1985 Plan, and [both sides] moved for summary judgment[.] * * *

* * *

Section 7 of the Seashore Act provides for the development of the Seashore in certain limited circumstances. The statute provides in pertinent part:

In order that the seashore shall be permanently preserved in its present state, no development or plan for the convenience of visitors shall be undertaken therein which would be incompatible with the preservation of the unique flora and fauna or the physiographic conditions now prevailing or with the preservation of such historic sites and structures as the Secretary may designate: *Provided*, That the Secretary may provide for the public enjoyment and understanding of the unique natural, historic, and scientific features of Cape Code within the

> seashore by establishing such trails, observation points, and exhibits and providing such services as he may deem desirable for such public enjoyment and understanding: *Provided further, That the Secretary may develop for appropriate public uses such portions of the seashore as he deems especially adaptable for camping, swimming, boating, sailing, hunting, fishing, the appreciation of historic sites and structures and natural features of Cape Cod, and other activities of similar nature.*

16 U.S.C. § 459b–6(b)(1)(emphasis added). Under the express language of Section 7, development of the Seashore is permissible where it is ecologically compatible and where it is for an "appropriate" public use. It is crucial to observe, therefore, that despite the "preserved in its present state" language, the statute does not impose a ban on all development of the Seashore.

* * *

CLF argues that the defendants applied the wrong standard in determining whether ORV use is an appropriate public use of the Seashore under Section 7. CLF maintains that the crucial factor the agency must consider is whether the contemplated use would protect the traditional scenic value of the Seashore. Plaintiff seems to argue, moreover, that the "preserved in its present state" language of Section 7 means that the Secretary cannot authorize any development of the Seashore that would alter the scenery from its condition at the time the Seashore Act was enacted. According to this view, because parts of the Seashore may look different now than they did in 1961 due to ORV travel, the activity must be inappropriate *per se* as a public use. Nothing in the plain language of Section 7 or in the relevant legislative history persuades us that the Secretary should be constrained by this interpretation of the statute.

* * *

Executive Order No. 11644 * * * provides that ORV use on federal lands must be consistent with "the protection of the resources of the public lands, promotion of the safety of all users of those lands, and minimization of conflicts among the various uses of those lands." E.O. 11644 § 3(a). Section 3(a) of the Order requires that ORV trails be located in areas of the National Park System only "if the respective agency head determines that off-road vehicle use in such locations will not adversely affect their natural, aesthetic, or scenic values." *Id.* § 3(a)(4). Executive Order 11989, the 1977 amendment to Executive Order 11644, further provides that the agency head must,

> whenever he determines that the use of off-road vehicles will cause or is causing considerable adverse effects on the soil, vegetation, wildlife habitat or cultural or historic resources of particular areas or trails of the public lands, immediately close such areas or trails to the type of off-road vehicle causing such effects until such time as he determines that such adverse effects have been eliminated and that measures have been implemented to prevent future recurrence.

E.O. 11644 § 9(a). These provisions, then, restrict the Secretary's discretion regarding ORV use on the Seashore, along with Section 7 of the Seashore Act.

CLF maintains that Executive Order 11644 requires the defendants to close the Seashore to ORV use because of alleged ecological damage and aesthetic degradation at the Seashore. CLF challenges the Secretary's finding that current regulations on ORV use effectively protect the ecology of the Seashore and that limited ORV use does not adversely affect natural or scenic values at the Seashore. The plaintiff argues in particular that numerous violations of the National Park Service regulations cause considerable damage to the Seashore ecology and aesthetics, and require that a ban be imposed on ORV travel, unless the violations can be prevented.

The Secretary determined that limited ORV use under the 1985 Plan does not adversely affect natural, aesthetic or scenic values at the Seashore. We agree with the district court that there is adequate support for this determination. The defendants considered the protection of natural values in arriving at the current regulations restricting ORV use on the Seashore. The extent and location of ORV trails were set under the 1985 Plan consistent with these values. Though unregulated ORV travel on the Seashore might well threaten the natural or scenic values of the Seashore, the restrictions imposed under the 1985 Plan are substantial and were designed specifically to protect those values that would otherwise be at risk.

The Secretary also determined that ORV use has caused no significant ecological damage at the Seashore since the adoption of the 1981 Plan. The district court correctly explained in its June 27, 1984 decision that an agency's technical conclusions are to be upheld by a reviewing court where they are "founded on supportable data and methodology, and meet minimum standards of rationality." We agree with the district court that the defendants' conclusion regarding effective protection of the Seashore ecology under the Management Plan is based on supportable data and methodology, and meets minimum standards of rationality. Accordingly, the defendants' finding as to adequate ecological protection should not be disturbed.

It may be true, as CLF points out, that ORVs caused certain adverse effects at the Seashore prior to the adoption of the 1981 Plan. Those effects were addressed in the U.Mass.Study. What is at issue, however, is whether any significant ecological damage has occurred under the regulations that have been adopted and enforced since that time. Persuasive expert testimony submitted by the government supports its position that restrictions imposed originally under the 1981 Plan and then supplemented by the 1985 Plan have created effective protection of the Seashore ecology. The closure of the dune trails under the 1981 Plan, moreover, caused a significant decline in ORV use of the Seashore. In addition, the National Park Service has added a number of rangers to improve patrol of the Seashore. Finally, with the adoption of the 1985 Plan the government placed greater restrictions on ORV use of the Seashore. Though some ecological damage to the Seashore may have occurred prior to adoption of the 1981 Plan, we believe sufficient evidence exists to support defendants' conclusion that ORV use has caused no significant ecological damage at the Seashore since that time.

We therefore affirm the district court on the issue of ecological protection under the 1981 and 1985 Plans. * * *

■ JUDGE [STEPHEN] BREYER (concurring).

I agree with the panel that, given the statute's *proviso*, one cannot reasonably read it as imposing an absolute ban on ORVs, particularly since many fishermen and campers like to use them. I also agree with the panel's opinion; we cannot now say that the Interior Department's regulations are "arbitrary, capricious" or an "abuse of discretion." 5 U.S.C. § 706(2)(A). I add only that this latter question is quite a close one. The Conservation Law Foundation, in its brief, notes that recreational "vehicles are used by less than 2.5 percent of the summertime visitors to the Seashore." The government, in its brief, says that it has set aside 8 miles, of 48 Cape Cod National Seashore beachfront miles, or 16 percent of the beach, for ORV use. Although it seems fairly obvious that those who use ORVs need a length of coastline in which to use them, it is also fairly obvious that their use is often incompatible with the quiet enjoyment of the seashore that the Cape Cod National Seashore Act contemplated the vast majority of visitors would seek. At some geographical point, reserving miles of coastline for ORVs would amount to taking too much from too many for the enjoyment of too few. We here hold only that, giving full and appropriate weight to the judgment of the administrators, we cannot say, on the basis of the record before us, that 16 percent actually crosses the line marked by the statutory word "arbitrary."

NOTES AND QUESTIONS

1. Did the Park Service and the courts correctly interpret the Seashore Act as permitting ORV use? Examine the proviso at the end of § 7 of that Act. Notice the illustrative list of "appropriate public uses" does not specifically include ORVs, but does say the Secretary may allow "other activities of similar nature." Should the agency or the courts have demanded a more express statement by Congress that ORV use was appropriate on the Seashore before allowing it? Or did the court properly defer to the agency's interpretation here, that ORV use is not *per se* inappropriate? *Cf.* Judge Breyer's concurring opinion on this point, and compare the language of § 601 of FLPMA, dealing with the California Desert, which did refer specifically to ORV use, and which was heavily relied upon by the Ninth Circuit in the *Dove Springs Canyon* case. Do the 2006 NPS Management Policies help the agency determine what is appropriate? *See supra* p. 930.

2. How significant was the fact that the NPS had commissioned a study which documented the effects of ORV use here?

3. The plaintiff argued that there had been "numerous" violations of the Park Service regulations allowing limited ORV use, and therefore unless the agency could prevent such violations, all ORV use should be banned. Did the court adequately respond to that argument by noting that the NPS had "added a significant number of rangers to improve patrol of the Seashore"?

4.   Is a key question in this case—and in ORV regulation generally—whether most of the ORV damage occurred *before* or *after* regulatory efforts were undertaken? If the major damage has already occurred, is there much reason to ban or stringently regulate future ORV use? Does the answer depend upon how practicable it is to restore the area to its pre-ORV use condition? Recall that a similar issue is raised with respect to livestock grazing, where unregulated livestock use in the 1880s caused massive and seemingly irreversible change on some public rangelands.

5.   Should the federal agencies distinguish between ORV use for access purposes (for fishing, hunting, hiking, etc.) as opposed to use purely for the thrill of riding? Is Judge, now Justice, Breyer hinting in his concurring opinion that the NPS may be on stronger legal ground if it allows ORV use only for access for fishing and camping? Would regulators be able to meaningfully distinguish the two kinds of ORV uses? On the Cape Cod National Seashore, should the Park Service institute a shuttle to provide access to remote areas as a substitute for ORV use? Should ORV use for thrill-seeking be banned on federal lands, leaving it to the private market, and private property owners, to satisfy that demand?

6.   The California and Cape Cod situations both illustrate the power and importance of the Endangered Species Act. In California, the listing of the Desert Tortoise and rare desert plants have helped curb ORV use; on the east coast, the listing of the piping plover, a shorebird that frequents areas popular for ORVs, and some endangered plants have had the same effect. NEPA has also sometimes helped. For example, in Washington Trails Ass'n v. United States Forest Service, 935 F.Supp. 1117 (W.D.Wash. 1996), hikers persuaded the court to halt proposed trail reconstructions, which would make roadless areas more accessible to ORVs, on the ground that the agency violated NEPA by ignoring evidence indicating the possibility of significant environmental impacts.

c.   USFS

The U.S. Forest Service has also been caught up in these controversies. In Northwest Motorcycle Ass'n v. U.S. Dept. of Agriculture, 18 F.3d 1468 (9th Cir. 1994), the court upheld a Forest Service decision in a forest plan to close areas of a national forest to ORV use. The agency applied Executive Order 11644's directive to control ORVs in order to, among other things, minimize conflicts among various users. In meetings with various users, the Forest Service documented that, while ORV users did not perceive a conflict between their use and nonmotorized uses, nonmotorized users disagreed. The court ruled that the agency was "in the best position to determine the credibility of the comments offered by the public establishing the existence of 'user conflict,'" and need not await "actual physical altercations" in order to act. Furthermore, there was ample evidence that the closure was "for the protection of the resources on the land" as well as the safety of all land users.

In November 2005, the U.S. Forest Service issued major amendments to its regulations implementing the 1972 and 1977 Executive Orders. 70

Fed. Reg. 68264 (Nov. 9, 2005). The amendments tighten regulation to restrict ORVs to designated trails and roads. The rule's preamble noted:

Nationally, the Forest Service manages approximately 300,000 miles of NFS roads open to motor vehicle use, and about 133,000 miles of NFS trails. Only a portion of the trails are open to motor vehicles. This transportation system ranges from paved roads designed for passenger cars to single-track trails used by dirt bikes. Many roads designed for high-clearance vehicles (such as log trucks and sport utility vehicles) also allow use by all-terrain vehicles (ATVs) and other off-highway vehicles (OHVs) not normally found on city streets. Almost all NFS trails serve nonmotorized users, including hikers, bicyclists, and equestrians, alone or in combination with motorized users. NFS roads often accept nonmotorized use as well.

In addition to this managed system of roads and trails, many National Forests contain user-created roads and trails. These routes are concentrated in areas where cross-country travel by motor vehicles has been allowed, and sometimes include dense, braided networks of criss-crossing trail. There has been no comprehensive national inventory of user-created routes (and continuing proliferation of such routes has made a definitive inventory difficult), but they are estimated to number in the tens of thousands of miles.

Wilderness areas are closed to motor vehicles by statute. On some National Forests, and portions of others, motor vehicles are restricted by order to the established system of roads and trails. On other Forests, cross-country travel is not currently restricted.

Need for Revised Rule

Most National Forest visitors use motor vehicles to access the National Forests, whether for recreational sightseeing; camping and hiking; hunting and fishing; commercial purposes such as logging, mining, and grazing; administration of utilities and other land uses; outfitting and guiding; or the many other multiple uses of NFS lands. For many visitors, motor vehicles also represent an integral part of their recreational experience. People come to National Forests to ride on roads and trails in pickup trucks, ATVs, motorcycles, and a variety of other conveyances. Motor vehicles are a legitimate and appropriate way for people to enjoy their National Forests—in the right places, and with proper management.

Current regulations at 36 C.F.R. pt. 295, which provide for allowing, restricting, or prohibiting motor vehicle travel, were developed when OHVs were less widely available, less powerful, and less capable of cross-country travel than today's models. The growing popularity and capabilities of OHVs demand new regulations, so that the Forest Service can continue to provide these opportunities while sustaining the health of NFS lands and resources.

* * * [T]he magnitude and intensity of motor vehicle use have increased to the point that the intent of E.O. 11644 and E.O. 11989 cannot be met while still allowing unrestricted cross-country travel.

Soil erosion, water quality, and wildlife habitat are affected. Some National Forest visitors report that their ability to enjoy quiet recreational experiences is affected by visitors using motor vehicles. A designated and managed system of roads, trails, and areas for motor vehicle use is needed.

Current regulations prohibit trail construction (§ 261.10(a)) and operation of vehicles in a manner damaging to the land, wildlife, or vegetation (§ 261.13(h)). However, these regulations have not proven sufficient to control proliferation of routes or environmental damage. This insufficiency is due in part to the nature of OHV travel. The first vehicle driving across a particular meadow may not harm the land. However, by the time 50 vehicles have crossed the same path, there may be a user-created trail and lasting environmental impacts. Determining which particular vehicle caused the damage can sometimes represent a challenge to law enforcement officers.

* * *

Current agency policy varies from State to State and National Forest to National Forest. Sometimes one National Forest restricts motor vehicles to roads and trails, while an adjoining National Forest allows unrestricted cross-country travel. One State may prohibit ATVs on public roads, while an adjoining State generally allows such use. Revised regulations are needed to provide national consistency and clarity on motor vehicle use within the NFS. At the same time, the Department believes that designations of roads, trails, and areas for motor vehicle use should be made locally. The final rule provides a national framework under which designations are made at the local level.

* * * The agency must strike an appropriate balance in managing all types of recreational activities. To this end, a designated system of roads, trails, and areas for motor vehicle use, established with public involvement, will enhance public enjoyment of the National Forests while maintaining other important values and uses on NFS lands.

The new rule requires each national forest unit to identify and designate those roads, tails and areas that are open to motor vehicle use, after seeking public input and coordinating with other federal agencies, tribes, state and local governments. Unplanned, user-created routes are considered at the local level during the designation process and may be designated as open. The agency expects it will take four years to complete the designation process for all 155 national forests and 20 national grasslands, and one end result of this process is that each unit will publish a map. Once the designation process is complete, the forest prohibits motor vehicle use off these routes. The prohibition does not apply to snowmobiles. State, county, or other public roads will not be affected by or included in the process. The rule does not require units that already have established systems of roads, trails, and areas designed and managed for motorized use to change those plans.

The heart of the rule is 36 C.F.R. § 212.55, Criteria for designation of roads, trails, and areas.

(a) General criteria * * *.

In designating National Forest System roads, National Forest System trails, and areas on National Forest System lands for motor vehicle use, the responsible official shall consider effects on National Forest System natural and cultural resources, public safety, provision of recreational opportunities, access needs, conflicts among uses of National Forest System lands, the need for maintenance and administration of roads, trails, and areas that would arise if the uses under consideration are designated; and the availability of resources for that maintenance and administration.

(b) Specific criteria for designation of trails and areas.

In addition to the criteria in paragraph (a) of this section, in designating National Forest System trails and areas on National Forest System lands, the responsible official shall consider effects on the following, with the objective of minimizing:

(1) Damage to soil, watershed, vegetation, and other forest resources;

(2) Harassment of wildlife and significant disruption of wildlife habitats;

(3) Conflicts between motor vehicle use and existing or proposed recreational uses of National Forest System lands or neighboring Federal lands; and

(4) Conflicts among different classes of motor vehicle uses of National Forest System lands or neighboring Federal lands.

In addition, the responsible official shall consider:

(5) Compatibility of motor vehicle use with existing conditions in populated areas, taking into account sound, emissions, and other factors.

(c) Specific criteria for designation of roads.

In addition to the criteria in paragraph (a) of this section, in designating National Forest System roads, the responsible official shall consider:

(1) Speed, volume, composition, and distribution of traffic on roads; and

(2) Compatibility of vehicle class with road geometry and road surfacing.

(d) Rights of access.

In making designations pursuant to this subpart, the responsible official shall recognize:

(1) Valid existing rights. * * *

NOTES AND QUESTIONS

1. Of the roughly 215 million annual visits to national forests, somewhat less than 2 million (five percent) are for ORV use. Is that relevant to Forest Service decisionmaking? Off-road vehicle riders rose from an estimated 5 million in 1972 to more than 50 million in 2004. Some studies show a sizeable number occasionally stray from sanctioned routes. Some national forests have no full-time law enforcement officers; others have a handful at most, raising serious questions whether closure orders can be effectively enforced.

2. In some ways, what the Forest Service is now proposing to do is not much different from what Presidents Nixon and Carter contemplated in their Executive Orders in the 1970s. While those orders raised the profile of the issue, it obviously did not result in generally acceptable limits on ORV use on federal lands. Is there any reason to think the Forest Service will do better this time? Is the new rule easier to enforce with a thinly distributed enforcement staff? On the problems of patrolling national forests, particularly near growing residential areas, see Timothy Egan, *Rangers Take on Urban Woes in Wide Open Spaces*, N.Y.TIMES, July 26, 2006.

3. What should the U.S. Forest Service do if it decides for resource protection purposes to close a road under this process, and users protest that the road is a valid R.S. 2477 right-of-way, or that they have a valid right of access under the ANILCA access provisions? *See* Chapter 5A(2). Should the agency address whether a valid right-of-way exists? Should it accede to the claim and not enforce the closure? Or should it enforce the closure and prosecute offenders, allowing them to raise the validity of the claim in defense?

4. You represent conservationists seeking to maximize road closures, or you represent ORV users seeking to minimize them. What do you advise your clients to do in response to this rule?

2. SNOWMOBILES AND JET SKIS

Technological innovations continue to lead to new recreational stresses and controversies on federal lands; in the last few years, attention has turned to the snowmobile and personal watercraft (or "jet-ski"). Both devices often employ a noisy two-stroke engine that provides heretofore unavailable quick access to remote areas, but also shatters the tranquility many associate with the federal land recreation experience. The engine is also dirty: A coalition of environmental groups has calculated that in one hour a typical snowmobile produces more hydrocarbons than a typical automobile does in a year of average driving. In 1998, the California Air Resources Board found that a jet-ski operating for just two hours produced the same exhaust emissions as a 1998 passenger car operated for over 100,000 miles. Newer models, however, do operate more efficiently.

Environmentalists also claim that, because of snowmobiles, the west entrance to Yellowstone National Park had the highest carbon monoxide levels in the nation in the winter of 1996, and that snowmobile engines spewed out 50,000 gallons of raw gasoline in the Park. At the same time, a thriving winter economy based upon snowmobiles has grown up at the Park, creating a strong economic interest opposed to snowmobile regulation. The Park Service has been picking its way through this policy minefield for more than a decade, with no end in sight.

In 1997 the Interior Department settled a NEPA lawsuit brought by environmental groups by agreeing to complete an EIS on winter use in the area. At the end of that process, in December 2000, the NPS decided to phase out snowmobile use in Yellowstone National Park by the winter of 2003–04. The decision allowed continued winter use by snowcoaches while eliminating the impacts on park resources and values from snowmobile use. 65 Fed. Reg. 79024, 80908 (2000). Excerpts follow:

> In the winter of 1999–2000, 76,571 visitor-days of snowmobile use occurred in Yellowstone, representing over 60 percent of all [winter] visitors. * * * This motorized, oversnow use of the parks is a relatively recent development, with virtually no such use present in the parks in the 1970s.
>
> * * * [NPS has recently] conducted a survey of [the 44 units of the national park system] in which snowmobile use is currently allowed. * * * We learned * * * that much of the snowmobile use that occurs in the national park system is not consistent with management objectives or the protection of park resources and values, and is not in compliance with the requirements of the two executive orders and the NPS general regulations on snowmobile use.* * *
>
> NPS general regulations on snowmobile use, 36 C.F.R. § 2.18(c), state that:
>
> > The use of snowmobiles is prohibited, except on designated routes and water surfaces that are used by motor vehicles or motorboats during other seasons. Routes and water surfaces designated for snowmobile use shall be promulgated as special regulations. Snowmobiles are prohibited except where designated and only when their use is consistent with the park's natural, cultural, scenic and aesthetic values, safety considerations, park management objectives, and will not disturb wildlife or damage park resources.
>
> The NPS has determined that the snowmobile use occurring in [Yellowstone and other parks] * * * harms the integrity of the resources and values of the parks, and therefore constitutes an impairment. We have also determined that the snowmobile use * * * is inconsistent with the requirements of the Clean Air Act, Executive Orders 11644 and 11989, the NPS's general snowmobile regulations, and NPS management objectives for the parks. The types of impacts on which these determinations are based are summarized below.
>
> Natural Soundscapes. * * * [Studies demonstrate that, i]n open terrain with a quiet background, the sound of a single snowmobile is audible for about 4,120 feet * * * [and] a group of four snowmobiles for 7,510 feet[.] * * * By comparison, an automobile in the same circumstances is audible for 2,330 feet. According to daytime audibility

monitoring, in Yellowstone, snowmobile noise can be heard 95 percent of the time by visitors at Old Faithful[.] * * *

Wildlife. * * * Snowmobile use in the parks takes place during the season when animals are most stressed by high snow depths, extreme cold, and food shortages. Disturbance or harassment of wildlife during this sensitive time can adversely affect individual animals and, in some cases, populations as a whole. * * * Wildlife movements are * * * inhibited by traffic and snow berms created by plowing and grooming operations. * * *

Air Quality. * * * Even though snowmobiles are present in Yellowstone for only three months of the year and there are fewer of them than there are of other motor vehicles during the remainder of the year, the snowmobiles contribute more air pollution to the park than do other motor vehicles. The contribution from snowmobiles to total annual hydrocarbon emissions from all mobile sources can range from 68 percent to 90 percent at Yellowstone, depending on which emission factors are used to estimate emissions. Similarly, snowmobiles can contribute from 35 percent to 68 percent of total carbon monoxide annual emissions.* * * Employees at the entrance station have complained of adverse health effects from emissions from snowmobiles. * * * In 1993 and 1994, Yellowstone received over 1,200 complaint letters concerning employee and visitor health and excessive snowmobile pollution. * * * Snowmobiles can cause localized, perceptible decreases in visibility near the West Entrance and Old Faithful in Yellowstone[.] * * *

Water Quality. * * * Deposition of airborne pollutants from snowmobiles and snowplanes onto frozen lake surfaces and snowpack can lead to those pollutants entering groundwater and surface water when the snow and ice melts. * * * Concentrations of ammonium and sulfate at the sites in the snowpacked roadways between West Yellowstone and Old Faithful were greater than those observed at any of the 50 to 60 other snowpack-sampling sites in the Rocky Mountain region. * * *

Effects on Other Visitors. * * * Winter visitor surveys indicate that the most important factors for visitor enjoyment in the parks are opportunities to view scenery and wildlife, the safe behavior of others, and opportunities to experience clean air and solitude. * * * [S]nowmobiles can cause decreases in visibility and increased air pollution within the parks; disturb the natural presence and behavior of wildlife; interfere with the natural soundscapes of the parks, reducing a sense of solitude; and adversely affect public safety.

Safety Considerations. * * * In the last 10 years, eight fatalities in Yellowstone resulted from snowmobile accidents. In 1994, 44 percent of all park fatalities resulted from snowmobile accidents. During the past five winters, 92 percent of all incidents requiring response from an NPS ranger involved snowmobiles, which account for 61 percent of all winter users. During all of fiscal year 1998, snowmobilers, who represent two percent of all park visitors in the year, were involved in nine percent of Yellowstone's motor vehicle accidents. * * *

* * *

Snowcoaches [larger vehicles, often converted passenger vans, that, like snowmobiles, operate over snow on belts, but more slowly] have lower impacts on park resources and values than snowmobiles. For example, a single newer snowcoach, capable of carrying eight or more passengers, emits much lower levels of air pollutants and much less noise than a single snowmobile, which carries one or two passengers. Also, snowcoaches, operated by professional, trained drivers operating under NPS concession contracts or permits, are much less likely to be operated in a way that disturbs wildlife than snowmobiles. As a result, expanding the use of snowcoaches and eliminating most use of snowmobiles will make it possible to accommodate large numbers of winter visitors to the parks, while still preserving an enjoyable experience for most visitors and avoiding substantial adverse impacts on park resources.

If the NPS were to continue to allow snowmobiles in the parks * * * it would be necessary to establish very strict limitations on that use to remain consistent with the NPS Organic, the relevant Executive Orders, the NPS general snowmobile regulations, and other applicable requirements. Even with strict user limitations, however, snowmobiles would continue to have substantial adverse impacts on natural soundscapes, wildlife, air quality, the experience of other park visitors, and other park resources and values. The remaining impacts would be substantial enough that it might be necessary to also limit the number of other types of users, at least including snowcoach users, to ensure that overall winter visitor impacts would not unlawfully or unacceptably affect park resources and values. Rather than establishing limitations on both snowmobile and snowcoach users, the NPS prefers to eliminate most snowmobile use in the parks and allow unlimited access to the parks by snowcoach users and other visitors.

Other Legal Requirements. The NPS has been unable to find any evidence that the Service, before now, made the determinations required by Executive Order 11644—that snowmobile use in particular areas and on particular trails in these parks will not adversely affect the park's natural, aesthetic, or scenic values of the parks—before deciding to allow snowmobile use in the parks. Further, until making this proposal for new rules, the NPS has not complied with the requirement of that Executive Order that the Service rescind or amend the designation or areas open to snowmobile use as necessary to avoid adverse effects on the park's natural, aesthetic, or scenic values.

Also, prior to proposing this rule, the NPS has not complied with the requirement of Executive Order 11989 that the Service, whenever it determines that the use of snowmobiles will cause or is causing considerable adverse effects on the natural resources of a park, take steps to prevent those effects, including immediately halting that use.

The regulations themselves were published at 66 Fed. Reg. 7260 (2001), along with responses to comments and other relevant information. Excerpts follow:

> Some comments said we should not take away visitors' personal freedom to ride snowmobiles where and when they want to, leaving as their only option travel in snowcoaches driven by somebody else.

> NPS Response—We understand that many people enjoy the freedom snowmobiles provide. However, we must comply with the applicable legal requirements. Snowmobilers will continue to be able to ride snowmobiles where and when they want to on other lands, including nearby national forest lands that are open to snowmobile use. In other parks, when necessary to protect their resources and values, we have prohibited travel by individual motor vehicles, providing mass transit instead. This has been widely acceptable to visitors to those parks. We believe this change will be acceptable to visitors to these parks, too.

> Numerous comments urged us to require the use of cleaner and quieter snowmobiles rather than prohibiting the use of all snowmobiles.

> NPS Response—Some newer snowmobiles have promise for reducing some impacts, but not enough for the use of large numbers of those machines to be consistent with the applicable legal requirements. Cleaner, quieter snowmobiles would do little, if anything, to reduce the most serious impacts on wildlife, which are caused more by inappropriate use of snowmobiles than by the machines themselves. Quieter snowmobiles are still noisy, and are audible at a greater distance than 4–track conversion snowcoaches. Since snowcoaches carry many passengers and snowmobiles only one or two, snowcoaches can accommodate the same level of overall winter visitation with far fewer noise impacts on the natural soundscape and other visitors than even quieter snowmobiles. Also, the ultimate extent to which some new snowmobiles may produce less air pollution over their useful life is unclear in the absence of emission standards, testing, and certification. Under the Clean Air Act, the EPA has the authority to establish emission standards for snowmobiles, and it is at least two or three years away from setting any such standards, which then would not take effect for additional years. The need for us to comply with the applicable legal requirements does not allow for such a delay. * * *

> * * *

> [The Park Service also addressed economic impacts, and summarized a consultant's study it contracted for, which] estimates that the total adverse economic effect on businesses (mostly small businesses) will likely range from $4.8 million to $10 million annually. * * * Most affected will be 70 snowmobile rental businesses and 11 snowcoach tour companies, which could lose between $4.1 million to $4.4 million annually. Most are in West Yellowstone, Montana, with others in other gateway communities. Hotels, restaurants, gas stations, and retail establishments, again mostly in West Yellowstone but also in other gateway communities, will be less affected, and could lose between

$700,000 to $5.6 million annually. One local government, the city of West Yellowstone, will be an affected small entity, and could lose between $80,000 to $125,000 from reduced resort tax receipts. From a national perspective, these impacts do not constitute a significant impact to a substantial number of small entities. * * *

We have made several decisions on how to implement this action to mitigate any adverse economic impacts, especially those on small entities. To begin with, the elimination of snowmobiles will be phased over four winter seasons, allowing significant time for affected businesses to adjust to providing snowcoach service instead. Next, snowcoach access to the parks will require a concession permit from us. Permits will be awarded to numerous small businesses in the surrounding communities. We have already authorized existing snowmobile operators to add snowcoach service, and authorized existing snowcoach operators to add more coaches. Finally, we will join with the tourism offices of the affected states and counties, as well as destination marketing organizations, to market winter visitation to the parks under the new rules. We have committed $100,000 in fiscal year 2001 for this purpose.

NOTES AND QUESTIONS

1. The Clinton Administration rule called for a phase-out of snowmobiles in Yellowstone over three years, but the International Snowmobile Manufacturers' Association challenged it in Wyoming federal court, with the State of Wyoming intervening as plaintiff. Upon taking office, the Bush Administration promptly settled the lawsuit, agreeing to do a supplemental EIS and make a new decision. In 2003 the Interior Department decided to allow 950 snowmobilers to enter the Park each day. Conservation interests challenged this decision in federal court in the District of Columbia. The Manufacturers and the State of Wyoming intervened and sought to transfer the case to Wyoming to consolidate with the pending litigation there, but the court denied transfer because the Wyoming case challenged the Clinton rule and the D.C. case challenged the Bush rule. In late 2003, the D.C. District Court found the Department's "dramatic change of course, in a relatively short period of time and conspicuously timed with the change in administrations," had not been accompanied by an adequate, reasoned explanation for the change, in violation of NEPA and the APA, and reinstated the Clinton rule. Fund for Animals v. Norton, 294 F.Supp.2d 92 (D.D.C.2003).

The Wyoming District Court then granted a preliminary injunction against the Clinton rule, finding that the economic and related harms suffered by the plaintiffs is "far greater than that suffered by" the environmentalists from continuing a winter use policy that had been in effect in the Park for decades, and the increasing use of four-stroke snowmobiles will lessen the public health issues and respiratory problems of park rangers. International Snowmobile Manufacturers Ass'n v. Norton, 304 F.Supp.2d 1278 (D.Wyo.2004). The court found the plaintiffs likely to prevail on the merits because it appeared that the Park Service failed to take a "hard look" at all the relevant information (such as doubts about the feasibility of snowcoaches), that the Clinton Administration had a "prejudged political conclusion to ban snowmobiles in the parks," and it failed to provide the public and cooperating governmental agencies (like the states) with meaningful participation in the process. The Tenth Circuit denied a stay of that order, and the injunction against the Clinton rule, combined with the previous injunction against the Bush rule, left in place the pre–2001 winter use plan for the Park, which had essentially no regulation of snowmobiles. Further sparring in both Wyoming and D.C. federal courts followed. In 2004 the Park Service issued temporary rules capping snowmobile use to somewhat more than 700 per day, 69 Fed. Reg. 65348 (2004). Congress quickly endorsed the rules in an appropriation act rider, 118 Stat. 2809, 3074 (2004). In 2005, the Park Service launched a new process, with a new EIS, to prepare a winter management plan for snowmobiles in Yellowstone to be completed in the fall of 2007, 70 Fed. Reg. 36656 (2005). The preferred alternative of the draft EIS released in February 2007 called for 720 snowmobiles per day.

2.   Given the findings and conclusions expressed in the above excerpts, how would you have advised the NPS to go about reversing the ban on snowmobile use at Yellowstone? Is legislation necessary? Is repeal or revision of the Executive Orders dealing with off-road vehicles necessary in order to reverse the ban? Repeal or revision of the Management Policies interpreting the Organic Act? *See supra* p. 930. Is calling for new studies of the effects of snowmobiles a sufficient reason in and of itself to justify reversing the ban? Is it sufficient if the Administration decides it will await the development of new technology (e.g., four-stroke engines), which would presumably be much quieter and less polluting? In the meantime, snowmobile technology continues to evolve in other ways, with the machines gaining power, losing weight, and being able to handle ever deeper snow.

3.   In Voyageurs Region Nat'l Park Ass'n v. Lujan, 966 F.2d 424 (8th Cir. 1992), the court upheld a NPS decision to allow snowmobile use of a roadless area in Voyageurs National Park, relying heavily on the fact that the statute designating that particular Park authorized the Secretary to "include appropriate provisions for (1) winter sports, including the use of snowmobiles." 16 U.S.C. § 160h. Does that decision support or undercut a ban on snowmobiles at Yellowstone?

It was not until 2000 that the NPS began to address the emergence of personal watercraft (PWC, commonly called jet-skis) use system-wide. In that year the agency promulgated a rule explicitly closing the park system to PWC except where special rules are promulgated to allow and restrict it in particular areas. 65 Fed. Reg. 15077 (2000), codified at 36 C.F.R. §§ 1.4, 3.24, 13.1 (2001). The preamble to the final rule noted:

> Over the years, NPS areas have been impacted with new, and what often prove to be controversial, recreational activities * * * [which] tend to gain a foothold in NPS areas in their infancy, before a full

evaluation of the possible impacts and ramifications * * * can be initiated, completed and considered. PWC use fits this category.

PWC use * * * has been observed in about 32 of the 87 areas of the National Park System that allow motorized boating. PWCs are high performance vessels designed for speed and maneuverability and are often used to perform stunt-like maneuvers. * * * Over 1.3 million PWCs are in use today with annual sales of approximately 150,000 units. * * *

This rule takes a conservative approach to managing PWC use in areas of the National Park System based on consideration of the potential resource impacts, conflicts with other visitors' uses and enjoyment, and safety concerns. The rule prohibits PWC use in areas of the National Park System unless we determine that PWC use is appropriate for a specific area based on that area's enabling legislation, resources, values, other visitor uses, and overall management objectives. * * *

[There are] 1,782 federally managed man-made lakes and reservoirs. The NPS manages 82 of these lakes (4.6 percent). A number of the NPS managed lakes will have continued PWC use. Therefore, well over ninety-five percent of the federally managed recreation lakes will be unaffected by this rulemaking.

The 2000 rule stated that PWC use could only be designed in twenty one identified units. As of 2007, seven of those areas prohibit PWC and fourteen have rules allowing PWC under unit-specific conditions. Is the PWC issue significantly different in any way from the snowmobiling controversy? Does it matter whether the pertinent state has a credible claim to ownership of the bed of the waterway (e.g., if it might have been navigable at statehood)?

F.   FEDERAL LIABILITY FOR RECREATIONAL MISHAPS

Mountain climbing, motorcycle racing, and white water rafting pose obvious risks; hiking and camping in an area inhabited by grizzly bears can unnerve even the stout-hearted. Even hiking in canyons prone to flash flooding, swimming in unfamiliar places, or driving on primitive backcountry roads can be hazardous. People, especially those less experienced at such pursuits, have been killed or seriously injured when a recreational activity goes awry. Not infrequently, the injured claim that the United States as landowner and land manager is liable.

The United States has sovereign immunity from tort liability, but has waived it in specified circumstances in the Federal Tort Claims Act, 28 U.S.C. §§ 1291, 1346, 1402, 2401, 2402, 2411, 2412, 2671–80 (FTCA). Specifically, the FTCA allows recovery for

> personal injury or death caused by the negligent or wrongful act or omission of any employee of the Government while acting within the scope of his office or employment, under circumstances where the United States, if a private person, would be liable to the claimant in

accordance with the law of the place where the act or omission occurred.

Id. § 1346(b). The last-quoted clause makes federal liability somewhat dependent on state tort law. This has raised a number of issues. One is the extent to which the United States can be treated the same as a private party when it manages its lands for public recreational benefit. Another concerns the application and integration of state recreational use statutes which sharply limit private landowner liability. The next principal case grapples with these.

An important exception to the FTCA's waiver of federal sovereign immunity is that it does not extend to performance of "discretionary functions." That is, the FTCA prohibits any claim against the United States "based upon the exercise or performance or the failure to exercise or perform a discretionary function or duty on the part of a federal agency or an employee of the Government, whether or not the discretion involved be abused." 28 U.S.C. § 2680(a). Application of this concept has long bedeviled the courts; *see, e.g.,* Berkovitz v. United States, 486 U.S. 531 (1988). Its application to federal land management is considered further below.

Otteson v. United States

United States Court of Appeals, Tenth Circuit, 1980.
622 F.2d 516.

■ JUDGE SEYMOUR

* * * The tragic accident giving rise to this litigation occurred in San Juan National Forest in Colorado. The decedent Stacey Otteson was a passenger in a jeep returning from a pleasure trip. After traveling down a narrow dirt logging access road which reaches a dead end several miles beyond the point of the accident, the jeep was forced to return due to impassable snow and ice. On the way back, the jeep slid on an ice patch and rolled down an embankment. Stacey and the driver were killed, and two other passengers received minor injuries.

The estate of Stacey Otteson brought a wrongful death action against the United States under the Federal Tort Claims Act. It alleged that Stacey's death resulted from the government's negligent failure to maintain the road free from ice, to warn of hazards on the road, or to close it when it became unsafe. The government moved for summary judgment, contending it is immune from liability under the Tort Claims Act on two grounds: 1) it was performing a "discretionary function" in the design and maintenance of the road; and 2) a private individual would not be liable under the facts of the case and the law of the forum state. The trial court found the second contention dispositive and granted the government's motion. We affirm. * * *

The trial judge concluded that a private landowner is not liable for negligence to persons coming onto the land for recreational purposes under

Colorado's "sightseer statute".[1] Therefore, he found as a matter of law * * * that the government had not waived its immunity from liability in accordance with the Tort Claims Act.

On appeal, plaintiff contends that the sightseer statute should not have been applied to bar its claim because the government is not in the same position as the private parties to whom the statute applies. The purpose of the statute is to encourage private landowners to open their land to the public for recreational purposes. However, plaintiff asserts that the government has an independent duty to maintain the national forests as public recreational areas. Therefore, plaintiff argues that the government has a corresponding duty to maintain the roads in the national forests for recreational use. Plaintiff would have us equate this duty with that which a political subdivision has to maintain public roads.

Plaintiff's argument misconceives the purposes of the national forests, as set forth in the National Forests Acts [sic]. The recent Supreme Court case of United States v. New Mexico, 438 U.S. 696 (1978) [eds., *supra* p. 498], contains a thorough discussion of the legislative history and purposes of the national forest system. The Court there held that the Acts establishing the national forests had "only two purposes—'[t]o conserve the water flows and to furnish a continuous supply of timber for the people'. * * * National forests were not to be reserved for aesthetic, environmental, recreational, or wildlife-preservation purposes." *Id.* at 707, 708. While the Court noted that the Multiple–Use Sustained–Yield Act of 1960 broadened the purposes for which national forests are maintained to include recreation, the Court made clear that recreation was a secondary and supplemental purpose, and that a national forest could not be established for recreation alone. 438 U.S. at 713–715.

Bearing in mind the primary purposes for which national forests have been established, we now consider plaintiff's argument that the Forest Service has a duty to maintain roads in the national forests under the same standard imposed on a political subdivision. While it is true that Congress has stated recreation to be one of the uses for the national forest road system [16 U.S.C. § 532], the legislation and relevant regulations read as a whole clearly indicate that the roads are intended primarily to facilitate the harvesting, removal and management of timber. Although these provisions authorize the construction of roads of a higher standard than that needed

---

1. Sections 33–41–101 et seq. of the Colorado Revised Statutes (1973) provide that:

"33–41–101. Legislative declaration. The purpose of this article is to encourage owners of land within rural areas to make land and water areas available for recreational purposes by limiting their liability toward persons entering thereon for such purposes."
* * *
"33–41–103. Limitation on landowner's liability. (1) Subject to the provision of section 33–41–105, an owner of land who either di-

rectly or indirectly invites or permits, without charge, any person to use such property for recreational purposes does not thereby:

(a) Extend any assurance that the premises are safe for any purpose;

(b) Confer upon such person the legal status of any invitee or licensee to whom a duty of care is owed;

(c) Assume responsibility or incur liability for any injury to person or property or for the death of any person caused by an act or omission of such person."

for the harvesting and removal of timber, they do not require it. The road on which this accident occurred was constructed and maintained for logging.[5] We do not believe Congress intended to impose on the Forest Service the same standard of maintenance with respect to all logging roads that a political subdivision has regarding public thoroughfares. Therefore, we reject plaintiff's argument that the government should be treated as a political subdivision rather than a private landowner for purposes of the Tort Claims Act. * * *

Plaintiff's argument that the government should not be treated as a private party under the Colorado sightseer statute because it is somehow obligated to keep the national forests open to the public is unpersuasive. The Forest Service regulations allow each Forest Supervisor, among others, to close or restrict the use of forest areas and roads. If liability were imposed upon the government in cases such as this one, the Forest Service might well choose to close the forests to public use rather than bear the heavy burden of maintaining logging roads as public thoroughfares. This result is precisely what the Colorado sightseer statute was enacted to prevent. Thus, we hold that the government is entitled to the protection of the Colorado sightseer statute and is therefore only liable "[f]or willful or malicious failure to guard or warn against a known dangerous condition * * *." Colo.Rev.Stat. § 33–41–104(a). * * * Accordingly, the trial court judgment is affirmed.

NOTES AND QUESTIONS

1. Is the court's reasoning consistent with the historical policy of keeping national forest lands open for recreation? Recall that the Multiple–Use, Sustained Yield Act makes "outdoor recreation" one of the five co-equal authorized uses of the national forests, and that the National Forest Management Act requires forest plans to, *inter alia*, "provide for outdoor recreation," 16 U.S.C. § 1604(g)(3)(A). Do these statutes suggest the court's analysis in *Otteson* is wrong?

2. A policy statement in FLPMA directs the BLM to manage federal lands under its care "in a manner that will protect the quality of scientific, scenic, historical, ecological, environmental, air and atmospheric, water resource, and archeological values; that, where appropriate, will preserve and protect certain public lands in their natural condition; that will provide food and habitat for fish and wildlife and domestic animals; and that will provide for outdoor recreation and human occupancy and use." 43 U.S.C. § 1701(a)(8). What should be the result if a similar accident were to occur on BLM lands?

3. Note that in the *Otteson* situation the federal land management agency has an incentive to argue against recreation management responsi-

---

5. We need not decide what liability, if any, would be incurred by the Forest Service with respect to roads built to a standard higher than that required for logging. Thus this case is distinguishable from Miller v. United States, 597 F.2d 614 (7th Cir. 1979), cited by plaintiff. In *Miller,* the area in which the accident occurred was maintained by the government and included bathroom facilities and a boat dock.

bility, in order to minimize its exposure under the FTCA. Here, in other words, the Forest Service argues that its roads are built for logging, while in other contexts the agency argues that part of the cost of the roads is properly accountable to recreation. See the discussion of "below-cost" timber sales in Chapter 8, *supra* p. 722. Can the agency have it both ways?

4.   Note the close interplay between federal and state law here. Under the FTCA, do the state legislatures and courts hold the keys to the federal treasury? What prevents them from adopting broad rules of liability to unlock the federal treasury on behalf of their injured citizens? (The court here did not explain why it examined plaintiff's argument that the Forest Service should be subject to the same standard of liability as a political subdivision of the state. The FTCA expressly equates federal agency liability with that of a "private person" under state law, not a political subdivision. 28 U.S.C. § 1346(b).)

5.   Before the advent of state recreational use statutes, federal liability for recreational accidents was more common. Since 1960, nearly all states have responded to the collision between growth in outdoor recreation and expanding tort liability notions by adopting such statutes. The Colorado legislation in *Otteson* is typical. See Paul A. Svoboda, *Protecting Visitors to National Recreation Areas Under the FTCA*, 84 COLUM. L.REV. 1792, 1798 (1984).

6.   In some cases a state law other than the recreational use statute may apply. For example, in Miller v. United States, 597 F.2d 614 (7th Cir. 1979), involving a diving accident at a national wildlife refuge, the court held the state recreational use statute inapplicable, and instead applied a separate state law that governed private recreational facilities open for more than "casual" recreational use.

NOTE: FEES AND THE SIGHTSEER STATUTES

In Ducey v. United States, 713 F.2d 504 (9th Cir. 1983), the court considered the application of the Nevada recreational use statute in a suit against the United States seeking compensation for the deaths of three persons in a flash flood in Eldorado Canyon in the Lake Mead National Recreation Area. Decedents had been camping and boating. The Park Service had a ranger station, boat launching ramp, and comfort stations in the area, and a Park Service concessioner maintained and operated a cafe-store, boat slips, automobile fueling and boat service facilities, rental cabins, and trailer spaces. The decedents had paid no fees to the U.S.; two of them had paid rental fees to the concessioner for use of a boat slip, one had rented a trailer space, and all three had bought various goods at the concessioner's store. The concessioner was obligated to pay 1.25 percent of its gross receipts to the Park Service.

The Nevada statute was generally similar, but not identical, to the Colorado statute at issue in *Otteson*. It provided limited immunity for private property owners, except where permission to participate in recreational activities "was granted for a consideration." The Park Service argued that it had not received consideration, both because no fee was charged to enter the area, and because the payments to the concessioner were not "consideration" that should apply to the government. The court disagreed:

> First, the language of the consideration exception itself suggests a broad reading of section 41.510(3)(b). The exception is worded not in narrow terms of "fee" or "charge," but rather in the far more encompassing terms, "for a consideration." "Consideration" is a term of art, a word with a well-understood meaning in the law, embracing any "right, interest, profit or benefit." Used in a statute, it should be accorded that meaning. The statutory exception, then, is itself literally applicable to situations well beyond those involving a strict charging of a "fee" for "permission" to recreate. * * *

> The policy underlying the adoption of a consideration exception to the Nevada recreational use statute is to retain tort liability in actions involving recreational use of land where the use of the land for recreational purposes is granted not gratuitously but in return for an economic benefit. Since the potential for profit alone is thought sufficient to encourage those owners who wish to make commercial use of their recreational lands to open them to the public, the further stimulus of tort immunity is both unnecessary and improper. Furthermore, where a landowner derives an economic benefit from allowing others to use his land for recreational purposes, the landowner is in a position to post warnings, supervise activities, and otherwise seek to prevent injuries. Such a landowner also has the ability to purchase liability insurance or to self-insure, thereby spreading the cost of accidents over all users of the land.

The court also rejected the argument that the National Park Service was immune because the consideration was not paid to it:

> Subsection 41.510(3)(b) does not specify to whom consideration must be tendered. We think it a fair reading of the provision, however, that consideration must be tendered directly or indirectly to a person who has the power to grant or deny permission to participate in recreational activities. Since the concession agreement did not give ECR [eds.: the concessioner at Eldorado Canyon] the power to deny permission to recreate in Eldorado Canyon, the exception is applicable only if consideration was tendered, directly or indirectly, to the United States in return for permission to recreate in Eldorado Canyon. We conclude that this condition is met in this case.

> Before entering its concession agreement with ECR, the United States certainly was free to deny permission to recreate in Eldorado Canyon. * * * Thereafter, however, it was not. The concession agreement required the concessioner to provide and maintain facilities, to offer services, and to pay to the government a fixed percentage of all revenues from operations. Implicit in the agreement was a commitment on the government's part that users would be allowed to enter the area to use the concession facilities. Under these circumstances, we conclude that the consideration tendered here by the users to ECR was

in return for permission to participate in recreational activities in Eldorado Canyon in the sense of subsection 41.510(3)(b).

The court remanded for further proceedings on whether the United States was immune under the "discretionary function" exception. One judge dissented:

> I read the [Nevada] statute to mean quite clearly that the owner is exempt from liability unless he charges a *fee* for granting permission to participate in these recreational activities. Thus, I think that the attempt in the opinion to impose liability upon the owner in the event *any* transaction for consideration takes place while a person is on the property imposes a burden that is not intended by the statute. I cannot believe that the fact that the decedents may have bought coffee or a candy bar or paid a fee for a place to park a trailer should be allowed to negative the fact that they were given free access to the area.

NOTES AND QUESTIONS

1. What is the underlying purpose of the "consideration" requirement? Is the majority applying it in accordance with that purpose? Did the United States open this area to recreation to make money? Did it charge for any of the activities mentioned in the statute? Did it allow use of its lands "gratuitously"? When plaintiffs bought candy bars at the cafe-store, what were they paying for?

2. What will be the consequences under the FTCA and state sightseer statutes of the fact that many federal land management agencies now charge fees for admission to federal recreation areas? While fees bring in useful revenue, if they result in less immunity for the United States, they may prove to be a mixed financial blessing. Of course, the discretionary function defense will still be available, as explored below, which could blunt the effect of the U.S. not being able to defend on the basis of state sightseer statutes.

3. Should Congress enact uniform standards defining federal liability for recreational accidents on the public lands, rather than leaving the questions substantially up to state law? What standards would be appropriate?

The Discretionary Function Exception

The scope of the FTCA's "discretionary function" exception often determines whether the federal government is liable for a tort claim. The exception is particularly important in the federal lands context, as the following materials show.

Johnson v. United States

United States Court of Appeals, Tenth Circuit, 1991.
949 F.2d 332.

■ Judge Brorby

[Decedent and three companions hiked to the summit of Buck Mountain in Grand Teton National Park. The group descended in pairs in the late morning, and the two less experienced climbers, Feikin and the decedent Johnson, strayed from the trail and entered difficult terrain. Feikin became stuck on a ledge; the decedent continued on. Later that afternoon, the two experienced climbers (Macal and Wechner), who had descended without difficulty, decided to summon help. Macal went to the visitor's center where he reported to Park Ranger Springer at 4:30 P.M. that the other two climbers were off course. Springer radioed Ranger Harrington in the vicinity of Buck Mountain, who reported he had seen four climbers descending the mountain. Springer then told Macal to return to the trailhead to wait for his companions. At 8:45 P.M., Macal encountered Wechner, who reported that Feikin was still stuck on the ledge and the whereabouts of Johnson was unknown. It then became clear that the two other climbers Ranger Harrington had seen were not Feikin and Johnson. The Park Service was informed, and after consultations, rangers were dispatched at 9:30 P.M. to search for the missing men. Feikin was found and rescued in the early morning. Johnson, who had fallen on a hard snowslope and sustained a serious head injury about 3:15 P.M. the previous day, was not located until a helicopter search was undertaken at first light. He had died of hypothermia several hours earlier.] * * *

Plaintiff alleges that Ben Johnson would not have died but for the Park Service's negligent failure to: (1) adequately regulate a recreational climbing activity in Grand Teton National Park; (2) initiate a rescue effort after Macal's initial report; and (3) conduct a reasonable rescue effort after Macal's second report. In response to these allegations, Defendant filed a motion to dismiss, or, in the alternative, for summary judgment, asserting as a matter of law: (1) Plaintiff's action is jurisdictionally barred by the discretionary function exception to the FTCA, 28 U.S.C. 2680(a); and (2) the United States had no legal duty to rescue Ben Johnson. * * * Because we conclude the discretionary function exception deprived the district court of jurisdiction, we do not address the propriety of the district court's summary judgment rulings regarding legal duty, breach of duty or proximate cause.

* * * [The FTCA's] broad waiver of sovereign immunity is limited * * * by the discretionary function exception, which prohibits any claim against the United States "based upon the exercise or performance or the failure to exercise or perform a discretionary function or duty on the part of a federal agency or an employee of the Government, *whether or not the discretion involved be abused.*" *Id.* § 2680(a) (emphasis added). The discretionary function exception "marks the boundary between Congress' willingness to impose tort liability upon the United States and its desire to protect certain governmental activities from exposure to suit by private individuals." *United States v. S.A. Empresa de Viacao Aerea Rio Grandense (Varig Airlines)*, 467 U.S. 797, 808 (1984). Application of this exception is therefore a threshold issue—a jurisdictional issue which precedes any negligence analysis. * * *

* * * [T]he principles set forth in Berkovitz v. United States, 486 U.S. 531 (1988) * * * guide * * * application of the discretionary function exception. * * * We first consider whether the challenged action "is a matter of choice for the acting employee." Berkovitz, 486 U.S. at 536. If a statute, regulation, or policy prescribes a specific course of conduct, then an employee must "adhere to the directive" and no discretion is involved. *Id.* If, however, the challenged action is discretionary, we must then determine whether it is of the kind Congress intended to shield through the exception. *Id.* The Court concluded that Congress intended to shield only those "governmental ... decisions based on considerations of public policy"— decisions " 'grounded in social, economic and political policy.' " *Id.* at 537 (quoting *Varig,* 467 U.S. at 814). Accordingly, the discretionary function exception will not bar a negligence claim if the government's "policy leaves no room for an official to exercise policy judgment in performing a given act, or if the act simply does not involve the exercise of such judgment." *Id.* at 546–47.

Interestingly, no federal court has been asked to apply the discretionary function exception to circumstances similar to those presented here. Therefore, the issue of whether the National Park Service's climbing regulation and rescue decisions in Grand Teton National Park are shielded from liability is one of first impression. We do not approach this issue lightly—"exceptions to the FTCA are to be narrowly construed." For that reason, we must carefully apply the *Berkovitz* analysis to the unique facts of this case, examining separately Plaintiff's claims regarding (1) regulating climbing activity, and (2) initiating and conducting rescue efforts. We examine the regulation claim first.

Plaintiff challenges, inter alia, Park Service decisions not to require additional warnings regarding the potential danger of mountain climbing, not to require safety equipment use, not to test the competency of each mountain climber, and not to "clear" the mountains of all climbers before dark. They assert that these decisions regarding the nature and extent of mountain climbing regulations in Grand Teton National Park do not invoke the discretionary function exception * * *. We disagree.

* * * [N]o federal statutes or regulations apply to the National Park Service or to Grand Teton National Park which specify how mountain climbing should be regulated. The Park Service has never promulgated a formal mountain climbing policy or climbing regulations. The Park does, however, require climbers to obtain a permit before departing on a climb. The purpose of the permit system is to educate climbers via face-to-face ranger contact. When a permit is requested, rangers attempt to evaluate the climbers' capabilities, and suggest alternative climbs if appropriate. Rangers have no authority, however, to prohibit climbers from taking a particular route.

Within this broad statutory/regulatory framework, we first examine Plaintiff's assertion that Park Service decisions regarding climbing regulation are not insulated from liability. Plaintiff concedes these decisions involve an exercise of judgment or choice, and thereby satisfy the first *Berkovitz* prong. No statute, regulation, or policy specifically prescribes a course of action for the National Park Service to follow. Decisions as to the extent or nature of mountain climbing regulation are truly the product of the Park Service's independent judgment—they are discretionary.

Plaintiff argues, however, that these regulatory decisions fail the second prong of *Berkovitz*—they do not implicate social, economic, or political policy considerations. To the contrary, Superintendent Stark asserts that each of Plaintiff's contentions have been considered, but were rejected for the following social and economic policy reasons: (1) the inherent dangers of mountain climbing are patently obvious; (2) both manpower and economic resources should be conserved to preserve availability during emergency situations; (3) it would be impractical if not impossible to test competency, monitor equipment use, or "clear" the mountain given the limited available manpower and economic resources; and (4) many Park visitors value backcountry climbing as one of the few experiences free from government regulation or interference. Plaintiff has presented no evidence to dispute Superintendent Stark's assertions. We conclude that decisions if, when and how to regulate mountain climbing in Grand Teton National Park go to the essence of the Park Service's judgment in maintaining the Park according to the broad statutory directive. By their very nature, these decisions involve balancing competing policy considerations pertaining to visitor safety, resource availability, and the appropriate degree of governmental interference in recreational activity. The Park Service's actions, insofar as they relate to the regulation of mountain climbing in Grand Teton National Park, are therefore shielded from judicial review by the discretionary function exception.

Plaintiff's failure to warn claim should be analyzed separately from the alleged failure to adequately regulate mountain climbing. * * * "[A] decision not to warn 'still may be a policy decision *or part of a policy decision* protected by the discretionary function exception.'" [quoting Zumwalt v. United States, 928 F.2d 951, 955 (10th Cir. 1991).]

* * * [T]he record here indicates the Park Service's decision not to place additional warnings in the Teton Range, whether explicit or implicit, was part of the overall policy decision to limit governmental regulation of climbing, educate climbers via the permit system, and preserve the Park in accordance with the statutory directive. This decision cannot be divorced from the overall policy not to engage in strict regulation of climbing activity in the Park. "A decision that is a component of an overall policy decision protected by the discretionary function exception also is protected by this exception." *Zumwalt*, 928 F.2d at 955. * * * In the absence of facts indicating the failure to post additional warnings was a distinct, nonpolicy decision, we conclude that Plaintiff's failure to warn claim is barred by the discretionary function exception.

We now turn to the issue of whether Park Service decisions if, when and how to conduct rescue operations are shielded by the discretionary function exception. Fundamentally, Plaintiff alleges that the National Park Service was negligent in its response to Ben Johnson's plight. However, the dispositive threshold issue is not whether the Park Service was negligent, but rather what was the nature of the Park Service's decisions. In response to this issue, Plaintiff baldly asserts that "the rangers [sic] negligent actions in responding to Macal and Wechner 'simply did not involve the exercise of [social, economic and political] judgment,' " and, therefore, do not invoke the discretionary function exception. A closer analysis is in order.

Again, we must first determine whether the challenged action "is a matter of choice for the acting employee." *Berkovitz*, 486 U.S. at 536. In addition to the general statutory directive quoted above, the Secretary of the Interior is authorized, not mandated, to assist National Park visitors in emergencies. 16 U.S.C. § 12. No statute imposes a duty to rescue, nor are there regulations or formal Park Service policies which prescribe a specific course of conduct for search or rescue efforts. Instead, the decision if, when or how to initiate a search or rescue is left to the discretion of the SAR [search and rescue] team. Therefore, the rangers must act without reliance upon fixed or readily ascertainable standards when making a search or rescue decision in the field. Plaintiff wisely concedes that these decisions are discretionary and therefore satisfy the first prong of *Berkovitz*.

Plaintiff contends, however, that Park Service rescue responses do not involve the kind of discretionary judgment protected by the discretionary function exception. We therefore focus our attention on the second prong of the *Berkovitz* analysis—whether the decision if, when or how to initiate a search or rescue is the kind of decision the discretionary function exception was designed to shield. *Berkovitz*, 486 U.S. at 536. Congress intended that this exception protect from judicial second-guessing only those governmental actions and decisions based on public policy considerations. *Id.* at 536–37. The key to a proper construction of the discretionary function exception thus lies in the determination of whether a governmental decision is "*grounded* in social, economic, and political policy." *Varig*, 467 U.S. at 814 (emphasis added).

Governmental actions outside the regulatory context may be protected by the discretionary function exception. *Varig*, 467 U.S. at 810–14. Furthermore, "the nature of the conduct, rather than the status of the actor * * * governs whether the discretionary function exception applies in a given case." *Varig*, 467 U.S. at 813. The fact that the rangers, as employees, make nonregulatory search and rescue decisions is therefore inconsequential to our determination of whether those decisions are policy judgments. The nature of the rescue decision process is the critical inquiry: Do Park Service search and rescue decisions simply involve weighing safety considerations under an established program or do they involve the balancing of competing policy considerations?

Park Service search and rescue decisions are not guided by formal standards. Yet, these decisions are not arbitrary. The record demonstrates that Park rangers make individual search and rescue decisions based on the following considerations:

(1) Safety—It is a primary objective of the Park Service to protect the safety of both the visitors and the rangers. For this reason the rangers consider a variety of factors, including but not limited to, the nature of the

situation reported (e.g., lost, overdue, off route, injured),[8] the weather, the nature and difficulty of the terrain, the number of climbers, and the presence or absence of a leader at the scene.

(2) Human resources—The Park Service has limited manpower resources which it must allocate and deploy carefully. In June 1987, Grand Teton National Park had 17,197 visitors per day. Hikers and climbers accounted for 1,009 of these daily visitors. During this same period, forty seasonal and twelve permanent rangers (including the eighteen search and rescue rangers in the Jenny Lake Subdistrict) patrolled 332,331 acres— over 519 square miles of extremely rugged terrain.

(3) Economic resources—The Park Service has limited economic resources which it must use wisely. Search and rescue efforts are expensive. For example, a helicopter search costs $750 per hour.

(4) Governmental interference—The climbing community appreciates the inherent danger of the sport and is perceived to value the individual freedom of a backcountry experience.

We need not find evidence in the record that the rangers in this instance considered each of the identified policy factors. The discretionary function exception may apply in the absence of a conscious decision, so long as the Park Service's search and rescue program allowed room for the rangers to make independent policy judgments. * * * The record before us adequately supports our conclusion that the rangers' decision if, when or how to rescue inherently involves the balancing of safety objectives against such practical considerations as staffing, funding and minimizing government intrusion. As such, these decisions are grounded in social and economic policy, and thus are shielded from liability under the FTCA discretionary function exception. * * *

After careful examination of the record, we find nothing to contradict the government's evidence that Park Service search and rescue decisions are discretionary decisions requiring rangers to balance competing policy considerations. * * *

We recognize that in Plaintiff's view this is a harsh end. However, Plaintiff's entire case rests on the assertion that Park Service personnel could have communicated more accurately and responded more quickly. While this assertion may be true (i.e., the rangers' interview and response may have deviated from standards against which liability is measured where liability is available) it is not sufficient to establish FTCA liability. * * * Factual issues concerning negligence are irrelevant to the threshold issue whether the officials' actions are shielded from liability by the discretionary function exception. * * * The Park Service's conduct involved the permissible exercise of policy judgment, therefore governmental immunity is preserved under 28 U.S.C. § 2680(a) "whether or not the discretion involved be abused."

---

8. Because it is not uncommon for climbers to be overdue, unaccounted for, or off route, it is not Park policy to initiate a search or rescue effort based on a report that a climber is overdue, unaccounted for, or off route, or simply because another climber demands one.

NOTES AND QUESTIONS

1.   Should the Congress enact a statute (or should the federal land agencies adopt regulations) addressing such adventurous recreational activities as mountain climbing, river running, etc.? Do agencies like the Park Service already have statutory authority to do so? Do the agencies have any incentive to make detailed rules concerning dangerous recreational activities? Did the Park Service here in fact regulate by requiring a permit, and "face-to-face ranger contact," before undertaking a climb?

2.   Same result if the Park Service had been notified of a climbing accident, and the rangers had decided not to mount an immediate rescue because they wanted to attend a dinner honoring the retiring Park superintendent, or meet with a visiting dignitary (such as the chair of a congressional committee with jurisdiction over the Park Service)? Would that be a decision "grounded in social, economic, and political policy" protected by the "discretionary function" exception?

3.   Does the result in this case suggest that federal land management agencies have broad immunity, even from negligence in regulating or failing to regulate, under the "discretionary function" exception? If the plaintiff in *Otteson* had shown that the government's conduct would have made it liable under the Colorado "sightseer" statute, would the government have still won under that exception?

4.   Do federal agencies owe a duty to warn recreationists on federal lands that they might face dangerous conditions? In a later phase of the *Ducey* litigation discussed *supra* at p. 994, the district court ruled that the flood was not foreseeable and that the U.S. had no duty to warn the decedents and dismissed the case. In *Ducey II*, 830 F.2d 1071 (9th Cir. 1987), the appeals court reversed again. It found that the Park Service was "aware that a life-threatening, 100–year flood was long overdue," relying on statements of concern about flash flood danger made at public meetings by Park Service officials. Citing Nevada state law decisions, it found that the agency did have a duty to warn of a 100–year flood. It remanded the matter to the district court to determine whether the Park Service had given reasonable warnings, and if not, whether the warnings would have prevented the deaths. One judge dissented.

5.   In Tippett v. United States, 108 F.3d 1194 (10th Cir. 1997), the court applied the discretionary function exception to shield a decision by a park ranger not to move a moose that had been threatening snowmobilers on a winter day, in a suit by a snowmobiler injured when the moose charged him.

Reed v. U.S. Department of the Interior

United States Court of Appeals, Ninth Circuit, 2000.
231 F.3d 501.

■ JUDGE WOOD, JR.

Plaintiff-appellant Daniel Reed was severely injured in the early morning hours of September 2, 1996, when a car ran over the tent in which he was sleeping. At the time of the accident, Reed was attending an event known as the Burning Man Festival, which was held on the desolate Black Rock Desert playa[2] in Nevada. The playa is federally owned land managed by the Bureau of Land Management (BLM). [Reed sued under the FTCA; the district court granted summary judgment to the U.S., finding the discretionary function exception applied.] * * *

It may be helpful in viewing plaintiff's injuries in context to explain the Burning Man event. According to its promoters, the event began on a beach in San Francisco in 1986, but in 1990 was moved to the "vast and oceanic space" of the Black Rock Desert of Nevada near Gerlach. The San Francisco Examiner described the event as "based loosely on European pagan straw man festivals at which people gather to erect and burn a large human effigy as dedication to the earth's fertility." The Journal of the Burning Man describes the event as "ritualistic ... anarchic ... primal ... a radical communal experiment ... art ... the death of art ... dream-like ... surreal ... creative ... destructive ... absurd ... spiritual" and "real." The Journal tells us:

> Think of Burning Man as Disneyland turned inside out. But unlike an escapist fantasy produced by others, Burning Man is not vicarious. At Burning Man *you* are the fantasy. People do not come to this event to be distracted from themselves, they come here to discover and distill what they uniquely are. We will not tell you what it means, for Burning Man is based on your immediate experience.

(Emphasis in original.) The Journal advises attendees to "[c]ome prepared to camp here and confront your own survival." In answer to the question, "What is Burning Man?", the Journal states, "It's what you make it." Participants enter the event through the "Gate of Hell" on which is inscribed the admonition, "ABANDON HOPE YOU WHO ENTER HERE." The Burning Man 1996 Survival Guide handout warns: "All participants must take personal responsibility for their own survival, safety and comfort" and cautions participants to bring common sense as "the desert is notoriously unkind to fools." The Survival Guide also warns that "[t]here are no roads, signs or street lights" on the playa. The Pershing County Sheriff's Office issued a report on the 1996 festival, estimating that participants numbered approximately 7,000, with an additional 3,000 to 4,000 onlookers.

Reed, age 21, * * * pitched his tent near a few other tents on the playa several miles from the main camp. September 1, 1996, appears to be the day the event concluded, although the following day was designated as "clean-up day." Early on the morning of September 2, the car of another attendee, traveling across the playa, ran over Reed in his tent. Reed alleges that he suffered severe, permanent brain damage and was left permanently disabled. * * *

Reed contends that the following four actions by the BLM fall outside the scope of the discretionary function exception: (1) failing to warn, or to

---

2. A playa is "the flat-floored bottom of an undrained desert basin that becomes at times a shallow lake which on evaporation may leave a deposit of salt or gypsum."

require Burning Man organizers to warn, of the hazard of camping in an area subject to unrestricted night-time vehicular travel; (2) approving a site plan that failed to segregate cars from tents; (3) failing to monitor the event as prescribed by regulation and policy; and (4) failing to suspend the permit once public safety was in jeopardy.

With respect to the first two challenged actions, the first prong of the discretionary function test clearly is met. The BLM was granted discretion to determine whether to issue the permit or not and, if issued, to decide the restrictions to be applied. The agency is given specific authority to include in a recreation permit "such stipulations as the authorized officer considers necessary to protect the lands and resources involved and the public interest in general." 43 C.F.R. § 8372.5(b). As a practical matter, it could be no other way than by the exercise of discretion. No federal statute, regulation, or policy requires a particular course of action. * * * Even if the permit had been granted without any conscious policy decision (contrary to the facts of this case), the discretionary exception function would still apply. * * * The BLM, in its exercise of discretion, balanced competing public policy concerns, including concerns about public access, safety, resource allocation, and the environment * * *.

The record reveals that the government exercised its discretion in granting Burning Man the event permit. Even if the exercise of that governmental discretion was ill-advised, it does not make the discretionary function exception inapplicable. Even if the particular provisions included in the permit itself were not well-conceived or sufficient, that exercise of discretion is also beyond Reed's reach. After the BLM received the event application * * * [it] sent out letters to interested parties * * * seeking comments related to the proposed event. The comments received expressed concerns about safety, morality, and the environmental impact of the event. Following consideration of those comments, the BLM prepared an Environmental Assessment, which considered the possible impact of the event on the environment, but found that there would be no significant environmental impact. It noted that the area to be used was believed to be one of the largest, flattest dry lake beds in the world.[7] In its judgment, BLM considered that the Burning Man event had had no prior significant safety problems from 1992 through 1995. Even though the event was growing in size each year, the record shows that it also had a good compliance record with BLM licensing requirements. As part of the process, the promoters were required to submit a "site plan" with some indication of the physical layout for the event, bearing in mind the openness, vastness, and flatness of the area. The BLM reviewed the site plan submitted and, in its discretion, considered it adequate for the short-term recreational event.

The BLM also considered Congressional directives, as stated in the Federal Land Policy and Management Act of 1976, (FLPMA), to manage the land for multiple uses in a manner that would help meet the present and future needs of the citizens, including recreational uses. * * * Accord-

---

7. According to the BLM district manager, during the period of these events because the playa was so vast and flat, the area had been used in 1981 and 1997 to set new land speed records.

ing to a BLM district manager, the government land use plan in effect at the time Burning Man applied for its 1996 permit dictated that "as many recreational opportunities as possible" be provided, "without undue environmental degradation." And, of course, under the Constitution's First Amendment, the agency's discretion could not be used to abridge the legitimate rights of expression or association of the participants. The BLM was aware that many event participants pursued and encouraged an "alternative lifestyle," but it believed that the actions taken in the exercise of its discretion should not be affected by the personal philosophies of the participants. The BLM believed that the proposed policing strategies would be sufficient to handle any illegal activity that might occur. According to the record, there had been some use of alcohol and illegal drugs in the past but, in the BLM's judgment, there had been no serious problems. The provisions for policing were expected to be adequate. The BLM also took into consideration planned coordination with local law enforcement officials, in addition to the event's own acceptance of responsibility for the safety of its participants. There is no need to further explore all the details involved in the BLM's exercise of its discretion. Some would disagree with the manner of the agency's exercise of its discretion, but that is irrelevant.

Reed argues that, even though the BLM may have had discretion to issue the permit, "the decision to approve an event involving thousands of campers and cars without segregating them, or requiring Burning Man to do so, was not the kind protected by the discretionary jurisdiction exception, it violated standard, elementary objective, technical standards for events of this size." Reed is mistaken. This issue is the type of judgment the discretionary function exception was designed to shield. * * * There was one discretionary license issued for this event, and what its terms were and how those terms might be enforced were all discretionary. Reed's own argument shows the need for agency discretion. He disagrees with the way discretion was exercised, but the discretionary function exception makes that objection irrelevant.

Reed next argues that the BLM was required by regulation and policy to monitor the event and that its failure to do so falls outside the discretionary function exception. Under 43 C.F.R. § 2920.9–2, the BLM was required to "inspect and monitor . . . to assure compliance with the plan of management and protection of the resources, the environment and the public health, safety and welfare." Although Reed asserts that BLM agents chose not to monitor the event, in fact, they did monitor it. Rather, his real argument is that, because the agents left the site by 10:00 p.m. each evening, the agents failed to monitor in a reasonable manner. However, * * * the discretionary decisions made as to the precise *manner* in which the BLM should monitor events also fall within the exception. No regulation required twenty-four hour monitoring; in fact, the BLM Manual H–8372–1–Special Recreation Permit for Commercial Use, VIIA, states that the amount of monitoring should be "commensurate with the resource values at risk, the permittee's past record of compliance, the ability to obtain monitoring services through other means such as local police, other permittees, the public, and other factors." The decision as to the nature and extent of monitoring clearly involves both discretion on the part of BLM employees and a balancing of public policy concerns.

Finally, Reed contends the BLM had a duty to suspend the permit once public safety was in jeopardy, but failed to do so. * * * Both the regulations and the BLM Manual require not only a finding of a violation, but also a finding that the violation affects public health or safety. There were no set standards in place outlining what types of permit violations would be sufficient to justify permit suspension; the BLM Manual, H–8372–1, VIIC, states only that "[a]n example could be the lack of a required local license for food service." The decision to suspend the permit would necessarily include a discretionary balancing of policy considerations. * * * Therefore, again, the discretionary function exception applies.

This was a tragic accident. However, under the circumstances, the government is not liable for any of Reed's damages.

NOTES AND QUESTIONS

1. Did BLM do all it should have done here in connection with this event? What if the plaintiff could show there had been a history of safety problems at past Burning Man events, but BLM decided to go ahead and permit it anyway on the same terms as the past? Would that have changed the outcome?

2. Should BLM have required, as a condition of the permit, that the event sponsors purchase liability insurance to cover accidents like the one that injured Reed, to back up what the court called "the event's own acceptance of responsibility for the safety of its participants"? Does it have the authority to do that, under FLPMA? Even if that arguably might have a limiting effect on what the court called "the legitimate [first amendment] rights of expression or association of the participants"?

3. The January 22, 2002 Wall Street Journal reported that the Nevada Commission on Tourism is running a nationwide ad campaign touting Nevada as a "primal playground with more * * * tear-yourself-to-shreds terrain than any other place in this great nation," which can provide a "nice quiet place to get in touch with your inner masochist," and asked, "Ready to get medieval?"

CHAPTER 12

THE PRESERVATION RESOURCE

Preservation is as much a resource of the federal lands as the more traditional ones surveyed elsewhere in this book. A natural area is nonrenewable, at least for generations, if its essential qualities are destroyed. Preserving artifacts and other items of historical and scientific value are essential to pursuit of a civilized life. While the "outputs" or values of preservation are less susceptible to measurement in economic terms, contemporary society has, by a variety of mechanisms explored in this chapter, assigned preservation considerable, sometimes surpassing, importance.

Still, the preservation resource escapes easy definition. To many, it connotes leaving well enough alone; they emphasize the need to protect natural areas and certain objects and values from human manipulation, profit seekers and wrecking balls. To others, the concept is simply a means by which elitists lock up resources and put them off-limits to "productive" use. Increasingly, preservation focuses on the maintenance of ecosystem services, such as nutrient cycling and flood control. "Preserved" land, from this perspective, is not inert or unproductive. "Ecosystem services" focuses attention on the work that even undeveloped or "off-limits" land contributes to the common wealth.

The urge to preserve tangible things and areas of historic significance preceded the desire to set aside tracts of scenic, aesthetic, or ecological value. Famous battlegrounds, for instance, have long been of great popular interest; *e.g.*, United States v. Gettysburg Elec. Ry. Co., 160 U.S. 668 (1896), *supra* p. 120. Yellowstone National Park in 1872 became the first significant reservation of public land for scenic purposes, but it was initially to be a "pleasuring ground" rather than a strict preserve. And in fact Yellowstone and some other units of the National Park System were, over the years, festooned with roads, lodges, shops, sanitary facilities, and other amenities that many claim are antithetical to strict preservation. Nevertheless, that system still encompasses some of the most spectacularly pristine country in the nation; large amounts of land within it have been formally declared as wilderness and much of the remainder is managed primarily for maintenance of its prehistoric attributes.

Preservation is often associated with passive management. The Wilderness Act, for instance, defines its preserved domain as areas "where the earth and its community of life are untrammeled by man, where man himself is a visitor who does not remain." 16 U.S.C. § 1131(c). Although the basic thrust of preservation of much federal lands and resources is to "leave nature alone," that is often not possible. Human activities inside and outside protected areas can have significant effects. Active intervention may be required to preserve areas in the path of spreading invasive plants.

The Park Service kills deer at Gettysburg National Military Park in order to reduce overbrowsing that threatens to thwart the objective of "preserving the historic appearance of woodlots and cropfields, components of the landscape critical to the understanding and interpretation of the historic events that took place" in the park. Davis v. Latschar, 202 F.3d 359 (D.C.Cir.2000). In other places, drier weather, higher temperatures, glacial retreat, and rising sea levels may make the preservation of a historic "nature" impossible.

Two important federal preservation laws have already been addressed in these materials: The Endangered Species Act, addressed in Chapter 4, has become perhaps the most famous "preservation" law of all but will not be considered further here. Chapter 5 covered the Antiquities Act of 1906, by which presidents of both political parties have acted to preserve of some of our best-loved natural areas (and historic and scientific resources) as national monuments. The organic acts for the four principal federal land management agencies all contain preservationist elements and tools. In this final chapter we will cover some important preservation laws and issues not yet addressed.

Section A examines the designation and management of official wilderness areas under the Wilderness Act of 1964, 16 U.S.C. §§ 1131–1136. That law established the still-growing National Wilderness Preservation System ("NWPS") and contains the strictest legal preservation of natural areas. Disputes over the definition and uses of wilderness capture the most difficult questions about preservation. It is therefore the longest section of this chapter. Section B addresses the authority of federal land managers, particularly those in the NPS, to combat external threats to the scenic and ecological integrity of federal lands managed primarily for preservation and recreation. Section C deals with river preservation, a matter of intense popular concern since before Justice Holmes noted that a river "is more than an amenity, it is a treasure," New Jersey v. New York, 283 U.S. 336, 342 (1931). Section D examines protection of archaeological, cultural, and historical resources, and also examines related First Amendment issues. Though often excluded from studies of natural resources, these key attributes of public property present similar issues of scarcity and value. But they challenge conventional approaches to conservation.

What Roderick Nash said about the wilderness movement applies to resource preservation across the board:

> While the American conception of wilderness has almost always been a compound of attraction and repulsion, the relative strengths of these attitudes, both in single minds and in the national opinion, have not remained constant. Appreciation * * * [has grown] from an esoteric and eccentric notion into a broad public sentiment capable of influencing national policy and securing statutory protection for wild country.

WILDERNESS AND THE AMERICAN MIND (4d ed. 2001). The quickening of the trend toward preservation raises fundamental questions. Is "preservation" of a "natural" world even possible, given the relentless change and disequilibrium in nature, the spread of exotic species, and our unwitting manipulation of the global climate? Can and must preservation be justified by weighing costs and benefits? Should costs and benefits be measured over a longer time than the conventional marketplace tends to count these things? Should preservation be pursued for ecological reasons alone? Or, should it be premised on anthropocentric considerations, such as the role of wilderness in the American conception of freedom, as articulated by many preservationists, including the late Supreme Court Justice William O. Douglas?

A.   WILDERNESS PRESERVATION

1.   THE ORIGINS OF FEDERAL WILDERNESS PRESERVATION

Ability to see the cultural value of wilderness boils down, in the last analysis, to a question of intellectual humility. The shallow-minded modern who has lost his rootage in the land assumes that he has already discovered what is important.

—Aldo Leopold

The United States pioneered the idea and law of preserving natural areas in their pristine state as wilderness. It is now an international movement, despite its origins in the peculiar history of America. Perhaps the most widely quoted proponent was Henry David Thoreau who declared that "in wildness is the preservation of the world." Many aboriginal groups oppose the wilderness idea as one imposed by descendents of European colonizers who both literally and figuratively erased native peoples from the face of the land. Nonetheless, as section D shows (see, e.g., Lyng v. Northwest Indian Cemetery Protective Ass'n, infra p. 1116), wilderness designation today can help preserve important religious and cultural sites of tribes.

Early efforts at preservation focused on preserving scenic resources in unimpaired conditions. In 1864 Congress granted the Yosemite "gorge" and the Mariposa sequoia grove to the state of California for "public use, resort, and recreation." In 1872 it established Yellowstone National Park on two million acres of land. Though the National Park Service developed portions of these areas once it gained control of the system after 1916, many of the preserved park areas retained their value as wilderness.

The state of New York can claim credit for the earliest "wild" designation of public lands. The New York legislature created the Adirondack Preserve in 1885 and expanded it to a Park in 1892. Then in 1894, in the face of development pressures, the state amended its constitution to provide that the parklands "be forever kept as wild forest lands."

The federal government initially began designating areas for wild land preservation through administrative action. The Forest Service blazed the trail with "wilderness" and "primitive area" protection. Aldo Leopold of the Forest Service first succeeded in convincing the agency to set aside as wilderness 700,000 acres in the Gila National Forest in New Mexico in 1924. Arthur Carhart followed Leopold's lead for an area in Colorado. Leopold's writings, including A SAND COUNTY ALMANAC (1949) (excerpted in

Chapter 1, *supra* p. 30), formed an important part of the philosophical basis for later wilderness proposals. By the mid–1930s several dozen such areas had been established but—true to the Forest Service tradition of decentralized administration—field officials exercised considerable discretion, and, in some cases, allowed logging, grazing, and road building. Leopold defined wilderness as "a continuous stretch of country preserved in its natural state, open to lawful hunting and fishing, big enough to absorb a two weeks' pack trip, and kept devoid of roads, artificial trails, cottages, or other works of man." *The Wilderness and its Place in Forest Recreational Policy*, 19 J. FORESTRY 718 (1921).

Bob Marshall, a vigorous outdoorsman and co-founder (with Leopold) of the Wilderness Society who was influenced by the Adirondack reserve, became chief of the Forest Service's Division of Recreation in 1937. Among his many contributions to the wilderness movement during his brief two years in office (and his short life; he died at 38) were the so-called U Regulations in 1939, tightening the restrictions on uses in wilderness areas. Marshall wrote:

> [I] shall use the word *wilderness* to denote a region which contains no permanent inhabitants, possesses no possibility of conveyance by any mechanical means and is sufficiently spacious that a person in crossing it must have the experience of sleeping out. The dominant attributes of such an area are: First, that it requires any one who exists in it to depend exclusively on his own effort for survival; and second, that it preserves as nearly as possible the primitive environment. This means that all roads, power transportation and settlements are barred. But trails and temporary shelters, which were common long before the advent of the white race, are entirely permissible.

The Problem of Wilderness, 30 SCIENTIFIC MONTHLY 141, 141 (1930).

In a few instances prior to 1964, Congress had adopted acts requiring specific areas of federal lands to be managed as roadless and primitive; for example, the Shipstead–Nolan Act in 1930 contained what may have been the first express congressional recognition of the wilderness idea by mandating, subject to certain exceptions, that a certain area of the Superior National Forest in Minnesota remain "in an unmodified state of nature." 16 U.S.C. § 577b. But in the absence of a generic statutory foundation for formal wilderness areas in the forests, litigation was occasionally brought to challenge Forest Service restrictions on use of such areas. It was uniformly unsuccessful.

Wilderness received little attention during World War II, but the movement revived in the late 1940's and early 1950's, spearheaded by Howard Zahniser, Executive Director of the Wilderness Society. Zahniser and other advocates argued that congressional designation was essential because administrative wilderness could be administratively revoked at any time. In Oregon, the old-growth French Pete Valley was returned to general forest designation for potential logging. In New Mexico, the Gila Wilderness itself was partially opened. Other intrusions on wilderness areas drew regional and national attention. Controversy over the proposal to build the Echo Park Dam in Dinosaur National Monument along the Utah–

Colorado border—perhaps the single largest environmental controversy of the first two decades after World War II—demonstrated the emerging strength of the preservationists.

As Professor Nash explained WILDERNESS AND THE AMERICAN MIND (4d ed. 2001):

> The concept of a wilderness system marked an innovation in the history of the American preservation movement. It expressed, in the first place, a determination to take the offensive. Previous friends of the wilderness had been largely concerned with defending it against various forms of development. But the post-Echo Park mood was confident, encouraging a bold, positive gesture. Second, the system meant support of wilderness in general rather than of a particular wild region. As a result, debate focused on the theoretical value of wilderness in the abstract, not on a local economic situation. Finally, a national wilderness preservation system [created by congressional, rather than administrative, action] would give an unprecedented degree of protection to wild country.

In 1956 Senator Hubert Humphrey introduced the first wilderness bill into Congress. The Forest Service initially opposed wilderness bills, arguing that statutory wilderness was contrary to multiple use, sustained yield management. Passage of the Multiple–Use, Sustained–Yield Act of 1960 not only codified the agency's multiple use authority, but included a provision that "the establishment and maintenance of areas of wilderness are consistent with the purposes [of this Act]," 16 U.S.C. § 529. After that, Forest Service opposition abated. An even more serious threat to wilderness legislation was the opposition of Congressman Wayne Aspinall of Colorado, Chairman of the Interior Committee, who refused to let any wilderness legislation out of committee until conservationists agreed to support his pet proposal, the creation of the Public Land Law Review Commission. Once that was done, and after concessions were made to miners, ranchers, and other economic interests in amendments, the Wilderness Act—still one of the most idealistic pieces of federal legislation ever enacted—became law on September 3, 1964. Pub L. No. 88–577, 78 Stat 890 (codified as amended at 16 U.S.C. §§ 1331–1336).

Resource development is generally prohibited in wilderness areas. For that reason, timber companies, miners, utilities, power companies, and ranchers frequently oppose official wilderness designation, sometimes bitterly. Their objections are directed not only at the designation of wilderness per se, but also at studies by federal agencies of large tracts of lands for possible inclusion in the National Wilderness Preservation System ("NWPS"). During those often lengthy study periods, the land is for the most part "locked up" to avoid destruction of its wilderness characteristics, and the economic ramifications of these choices cannot be ignored.

The Forest Service previously had designated fifty-four places as "wilderness," "wild," or "canoe" areas. The Wilderness Act made them the initial units in the National Wilderness Preservation System. 16 U.S.C. § 1132(a). These "instant wilderness areas" totaled 9.1 million acres. The Act also required the Forest Service to study an additional 5.4 million acres of designated "primitive areas" and to report to the President within ten years on their suitability as wilderness. In turn, the President was to report his findings on the primitive areas to Congress. 16 U.S.C. § 1132(b). In the Department of Interior, ten-year studies for wilderness suitability were also required on all roadless areas over 5000 acres (and roadless islands of any size) in the National Wildlife Refuge System and the National Park System. 16 U.S.C. § 1132(c). These mechanisms for adding to the system are considered more fully in subsection 3, below.

While Congress did not disturb federal land agency authority to use existing law to manage areas in a roadless or primitive status, it took care in the Wilderness Act to provide that "no Federal lands shall be designated as 'wilderness areas' except as provided for in [the Wilderness Act] or by a subsequent Act [of Congress]." 16 U.S.C. § 1131(a). To quell longstanding interagency rivalries, the Act provided that any area included in the wilderness system would continue to be managed by the same agency that administered it before wilderness designation. 16 U.S.C. § 1131(b). To prove that neither conservationists nor Congress had yet learned all of the lessons of history, the Act did not expressly deal with the single largest block of federal lands, those managed by the BLM.

The definition of wilderness in 16 U.S.C. § 1131(c) reads precious little like an ordinary federal statute:

> A wilderness, in contrast with those areas where man and his own works dominate the landscape, is hereby recognized as an area where the earth and its community of life are untrammeled by man, where man himself is a visitor who does not remain. An area of wilderness is further defined to mean in this chapter an area of undeveloped Federal land retaining its primeval character and influence, without permanent improvements or human habitation, which is protected and managed so as to preserve its natural conditions and which (1) generally appears to have been affected primarily by the forces of nature, with the imprint of man's work substantially unnoticeable; (2) has outstanding opportunities for solitude or a primitive and unconfined type of recreation; (3) has at least five thousand acres of land or is of sufficient size as to make practicable its preservation and use in an unimpaired condition; and (4) may also contain ecological, geological, or other features of scientific, educational, scenic, or historical value.

The first sentence of the section defines wilderness in an ideal sense. The remainder of the section defines wilderness for legal purposes, and it is replete with qualifying phrases that depart from the ideal. The definition remains important as the guiding objective for wilderness management. 16 U.S.C. § 1133(d) generally mandates that, except where otherwise specified:

> each agency administering any area designated as wilderness shall be responsible for preserving the wilderness character of the area and shall so administer such area for such other purposes for which it may have been established as also to preserve its wilderness character. Except as otherwise provided in this chapter, wilderness areas shall be

devoted to the public purposes of recreational, scenic, scientific, educational, conservation, and historical use.

The definition is also important in guiding subsequent additions to the system, because they presumably qualify under it. In the end, however, wilderness designations are political judgments, and nothing except self-restraint prohibits Congress from following what former House Interior Committee Chair Morris Udall once described as former Secretary of the Interior James Watt's definition of wilderness: "a parking lot without stripes."

NOTES AND QUESTIONS

1. Does the definition of wilderness by itself outlaw mining, timber harvesting, or grazing? Does an area in the eastern U.S. that was logged fifty years ago, but which has now revegetated to such an extent that only a trained eye could distinguish it from virgin forest, qualify as wilderness under this definition? Do the wild upper slopes of a mountain near an urban area, which is within sight and earshot of urban civilization, qualify? This question of "purity" is considered further below.

According to his biographer, Zahniser carefully worded the first sentence of the wilderness definition to refer to untrammeled rather than undisturbed land so as not to exclude areas that had been altered by mining, grazing, and other uses. Untrammeled nicely orients the discussion toward the future rather than the past: wilderness must not be hampered or bound by management. "With 'untrammeled,' Zahniser reached deep into American ideas of freedom for a term that would liberate the land." Jon Christensen, *The Great Wilderness Compromise*, High Country News, Jan. 22, 2007. Mark Harvey, Wilderness Forever: Howard Zahniser and the Path to the Wilderness Act (2005).

2. Is the concept of wilderness, as defined in the Act, consistent with the "multiple use" concept? Note that Congress said it was even before the Wilderness Act was adopted; see 16 U.S.C. § 529, quoted above, part of the 1960 MUSY Act. Is that a correct interpretation of "multiple use"?

3. Some environmental philosophers and historians have attacked the wilderness idea as "perpetuat[ing] the pre-Darwinian myth that 'man' exists apart from nature." J. Baird Callicott, *A Critique of and an Alternative to the Wilderness Idea*, Wild Earth, Winter 1994–95, p. 54.

[T]he trouble with wilderness is that it quietly expresses and reproduces the very values its devotees seek to reject. The flight from history that is very nearly the core of wilderness represents the false hope of an escape from responsibility, the illusion that we can somehow wipe clean the slate of our past and return to the tabula rasa that supposedly existed before we began to leave our marks on the world. The dream of an unworked natural landscape is very much the fantasy of people who have never themselves had to work the land to make a living * * *. Only people whose relation to the land was already alienated could hold up wilderness as a model for human life in nature, for the romantic ideology of wilderness leaves precisely nowhere for human beings actually to make their living from the land.

This, then, is the central paradox: wilderness embodies a dualistic vision in which the human is entirely outside the natural. If we allow ourselves to believe that nature, to be true, must also be wild, then our very presence in nature represents its fall. * * * To the extent that we celebrate wilderness as the measure with which we judge civilization, we reproduce the dualism that sets humanity and nature at opposite poles.

William Cronon, *The Trouble with Wilderness, in* William Cronon, ed., UNCOMMON GROUND: RETHINKING THE HUMAN PLACE IN NATURE 69, 80–81 (1996). Professor Cronon, later in his essay, writes that "[a]ny way of looking at nature that encourages us to believe we are separate from nature as wilderness tends to do is likely to reinforce environmentally irresponsible behavior." *Id.* at 87. Do you agree? Does the Wilderness Act purport to establish a measure with which to judge civilization or the model for human beings to make their living from the land? Does the Wilderness Act need to answer these challenges? Do we hold other natural resource legislation, such as the Mining Law or the National Forest Management Act to the same standard? Can wilderness be justified as merely a reserve of lands to counterbalance the many areas (such as corn fields) where nature is so tightly controlled in the service of human commerce as to constrict its manifestation to a handful of species.

2. WILDERNESS MANAGEMENT

Most wilderness areas are not simply left alone after designation. Inevitably, some degree of human regulation or management is required. As demand for "wilderness experiences" grows, some areas may be "loved to death." Philosophical questions of purity become concrete when officials are faced with fires, insect attacks, rescue operations, trail maintenance, hunting, sanitation, and pack trains. Activities on adjacent lands also pose management problems.

Key restrictions and guidance on wilderness management are found in 16 U.S.C. § 1133(c) & (d). Here are reflected the political accommodations that had to be made to pass the Act. These protect some existing uses, and allow for limited commercial use and resource development in wilderness areas. The federal land agencies have adopted generic regulations governing wilderness area management that sometimes provide helpful guidance on answering some of the issues posed in this section. *See, e.g.,* 36 C.F.R. pt. 293 (national forest wilderness); 43 C.F.R. pt. 6300 (BLM wilderness).

Some of the exceptions and special provisions in the Wilderness Act apply to "wilderness areas designated by this chapter," (for example, subsection (d)(1)); while others apply to "wilderness areas in the national forests designated by this chapter" (for example, subsections (d)(3) and (4)); and still others apply to "national forest wilderness areas" (for example, subsection (d)(2)). Furthermore, every area added to the National Wilderness Preservation System is done so by statute. In these individual establishment statutes Congress sometimes incorporates, and sometimes varies, the generic management guidelines contained in the Wilderness Act. In recent years the trend for wilderness, like national park, establishment legislation has been toward increased congressional management mandates and exceptions from organic act provisions. This is creating greater variations among units in the system. Thus some care is required to determine exactly what restrictions apply where.

The management compromises and controversies in the Wilderness Act are covered in the symposium: *Wilderness Act of 1964: Reflections, Applications, and Prediction*, 76 DENV. U. L.REV. 331–679 (1999). The standard text on wilderness management is John C. Hendee et al., WILDERNESS MANAGEMENT (3d ed., 2005).

Perhaps more than any other affirmative attribute, wilderness is characterized by the absence of motorized equipment and mechanical transport. Section 1133(c) is a general prohibition:

> Except as specifically provided for in this chapter, and subject to existing private rights, there shall be no commercial enterprise and no permanent road within any wilderness area designated by this chapter and, except as necessary to meet minimum requirements for the administration of the area for the purpose of this chapter (including measures required in emergencies involving the health and safety of persons within the area), there shall be no temporary road, no use of motor vehicles, motorized equipment or motorboats, no landing of aircraft, no other form of mechanical transport, and no structure or installation within any such area.

The provision, which protects "existing private rights," is then qualified in several respects by section 1133(d). For example, § 1133(d)(1) says that within statutory wilderness, "the use of aircraft or motorboats, where these uses have already become established, may be permitted to continue subject to such restrictions as the [managing agency] deems desirable." "May" does not mean "shall" in this context, as the pilot in United States v. Gregg, 290 F.Supp. 706 (W.D.Wash.1968), discovered to his chagrin. He was fined for landing an airplane in a wilderness area contrary to Forest Service regulations. The court rejected his argument that because he had an established use, the Forest Service could not prohibit him from landing. The Forest Service policy is found at 36 C.F.R. § 293.6. Congress can ban motorized vehicles from state or private land within the boundaries of a federally designated wilderness; *see* Minnesota v. Block, *supra* p. 173. After a two-day trial, former race car driver Bobby Unser was fined $75 when he drove his snowmobile into a wilderness area in New Mexico and garnered considerable publicity in the late 1990s. The court rejected Unser's defense that he was lost, holding that the unlawful possession and operation of a motorized vehicle in national forest wilderness is an offense without a mens rea requirement. United States v. Unser, 165 F.3d 755 (10th Cir. 1999).

The agencies managing wilderness have some discretion to use motorized equipment for the "purpose" of the Act, including rescue missions, 16 U.S.C. § 1133(c). More controversial is the exception for controlling "fire, insects, and disease." The Act allows the federal managing agency to take "such measures * * * as may be necessary in the control of fire, insects, and diseases, subject to such conditions as the Secretary deems desirable." 16 U.S.C § 1133(d)(1). The Forest Service uses chain saws and other equipment to clear trails and construct some rough bridges; it fights some but not all fires; and it uses motorized equipment for rescue operations but not to bring out dead bodies where no "emergency" exists. This section, in conjunction with the Forest Service's effort to control the infestation of the southern pine beetle, led to the following opinions, which together comprised the seminal judicial discussion of agency management obligations in designated wilderness.

Sierra Club v. Lyng I

United States District Court, District of Columbia, 1987.
662 F.Supp. 40.

■ JUDGE GESELL

By a complaint filed July 12, 1985, Sierra Club and the Wilderness Society have challenged the legality of a program initiated by the United States Forest Service under direction of the Secretary of Agriculture to control infestations of the Southern Pine Beetle in federally designated Wilderness Areas located in Arkansas, Louisiana and Mississippi. * * *

[Plaintiffs alleged that the "extensive tree-cutting and chemical-spraying campaign involved" violated NEPA, the Endangered Species Act (because of the presence of the red-cockaded woodpecker in the areas), and the Wilderness Act. The district court had earlier enjoined much of the program pending preparation of an EIS. In this opinion the court addressed the application of 16 U.S.C. § 1133(d)(1), quoted above.]

* * * Plaintiffs' primary contention is that the Secretary is not authorized to undertake an insect control program in a designated Wilderness Area unless the Secretary can demonstrate that the program is necessary in the sense that it is effective, and that the program for the Southern Pine Beetle infestations which are under attack here must be restrained since the program is ineffective. They argue that the Wilderness Areas were being destroyed by extensive and continuing spot cutting of infestations pursuant to the Secretary's program without any appreciable success in curbing the pest and that wilderness values Congress sought to preserve as a matter of affirmative national policy were, as a consequence, being permanently injured. The complex life cycle of the Southern Pine Beetle, an indigenous, well-known pest, has been elaborately studied and plaintiffs offered considerable data indicating the program's dubious effectiveness.

The Secretary presents both a legal and factual opposition. First, he asserts that the Court has no authority to consider the motion since Section 4(d)(1) leaves all management decisions affecting Wilderness Areas to his nonreviewable discretion. It is further suggested that since a different program may emerge with the eventual publication of the EIS the Court is being asked to issue an advisory opinion. Factually, the Secretary contends the program is effective in the sense that although continued cutting of spot infestations would be required, the program has somewhat slowed the appearance of new infestations as more and more mature pine trees are cut down and destroyed.

The Wilderness Act, as the Secretary urges, clearly places broad discretion in the Secretary to manage designated Wilderness Areas. Each area differs. There are no standards indicated for control of fire, insects or disease. Technical information and research must in the end guide the Secretary in the sensitive task of keeping nature's precarious balance within each area stable. Resolution of these decisions through litigation is surely counterindicated except upon the most explicit showing of arbitrary irresponsibility.

However, a further circumstance overhangs this particular dispute which must be considered. The Southern Pine Beetle program is not limited to Wilderness Areas and indeed the purpose and effect of the program is solely to protect commercial timber interests and private property, including, of course, national forests in which more draconian steps can be taken to eliminate the beetle. The extensive cutting in the Wilderness Areas that was being carried out under the program until preliminarily enjoined was conducted solely to aid outside adjacent property interests, not to further wilderness interests or to further national wilderness policy.

Both plaintiffs and the Secretary agree that Congress also intended by Section 4(d)(1) to authorize the Secretary to take actions within Wilderness Areas where necessary to control fire, insects, or disease from spreading beyond the areas and harming adjacent or neighboring private or commercial interests. The legislative history sustains this view. Plaintiffs' case therefore poses the declared national policy to preserve pristine wilderness ecology and values into sharp juxtaposition with the program's effectiveness, or lack of effectiveness, in controlling the harm being caused by pine beetles on adjacent property. Management of wilderness areas as such is not involved and the program could not be approved as a wilderness-management program.

Unfortunately, the material submitted on the motion provides no clear answers to the dilemma suggested. Pine beetles have a considerable range of flight and studies leave in doubt the extent to which they may migrate to or from adjacent pine land. There is no way the Court can determine from the material submitted to what extent beetle migration out of these particular Wilderness Areas into commercial timber properties may be adequately controlled under the program. Nor is it clear whether adjacent properties can be equally well controlled against beetle infestation by measures taken outside of the Wilderness Areas that would be wholly inappropriate within the Wilderness Areas.

Thus this case does not involve the management of Wilderness Areas as such. Rather, it presents a different question, one that is not fully addressed by the Act itself. That question is whether the Secretary has been given the same Section 4(d)(1) broad management discretion previously noted when he takes actions within the Wilderness Areas for the benefit of outside commercial and other private interests. This question must be answered in the negative because in a situation like this the Secretary is not managing the wilderness but acting contrary to wilderness policy for the benefit of outsiders.

A fair reading of the Wilderness Act places a burden on the Secretary affirmatively to justify his actions under these circumstances. Where such actions are shown to contravene wilderness values guaranteed by the Wilderness Act, as they do here, then the Secretary must, when challenged, justify them by demonstrating they are necessary to effectively control the threatened outside harm that prompts the action being taken. Here the Secretary has not addressed this affirmative burden.

Plaintiffs have amply demonstrated that the Southern Pine Beetle program as carried out in these three Wilderness Areas was wholly antithetical to the wilderness policy established by Congress.

The destruction of many acres of pine trees by chain sawing, and chemical spraying accompanied by noise and personnel in a continuing process unlimited in scope, is hardly consonant with preservation and protection of these areas in their natural state. These are delicate, sensitive places where the often mysterious and unpredictable process of nature were [sic] to be preserved for the study and enjoyment of mankind. Congress directed that man must tread lightly in these areas, in awe and with respect. Ruthless intrusion in disregard for these values was condemned as a matter of national policy. While many facts remain unclear, the record before the Court suggests that within Wilderness Areas, as mature pines are destroyed by the beetle there will be less and less possibility of outbreaks infecting neighboring areas. Only a clear necessity for upsetting the equilibrium of the ecology could justify this highly injurious, semi-experimental venture of limited effectiveness.

The Secretary has failed to demonstrate that the Southern Pine Beetle program as carried out in the three Wilderness Areas is necessary to control the presence of that pest in neighboring pine forests or that it has in any way been more than marginally effective in doing so. There is little evidence relating to the effect of the program on the beetle's tendency, if any, to move out of the Wilderness Areas. Conversely, the Court has not received any material indicating whether adjacent pine land, which has been already infected by the beetle, could be managed with less effective controls in the absence of the accompanying Wilderness authority. Nor is the Secretary's weighing of alternatives apparent. The record strongly suggests that the beetle cannot be eradicated and the solution of the problem is long-term, dependent for its ultimate efficacy upon further research and scientific study.

While the Secretary's program covers the South, this particular case only concerns a limited aspect. Serious problems exist in other southern regions and indeed the United States District Court for the Eastern District of Texas has before it a challenge to the Southern Pine Beetle program as it affects five Wilderness Areas in Texas. That Court has also been awaiting the EIS. The problems in different regions in all probability vary and what may be a necessity in one Wilderness Area, or effective there, may not be so in another. The very generality of the Secretary's approach suggests inadequate sensitivity to his wilderness duties.

Because this Court's analysis raises issues not fully addressed in the papers and because it suggests a need to particularize any approach to the Southern Pine Beetle program in terms of each Wilderness Area, area by area, the Court has concluded that final resolution of the motion can most appropriately await the EIS. * * *

A little less than two months later, the Forest Service published a three-volume Final Programmatic EIS on "short-term beetle control" on national forest units in fourteen southern states (which included fifteen designated wilderness areas); and a "Record of Decision" ("ROD") setting out the agency's final decision. The court then took up the Wilderness Act issues again.

Sierra Club v. Lyng II

United States District Court, District of Columbia, 1987.
663 F.Supp. 556.

■ JUDGE GESELL

* * *

The Secretary's ROD greatly narrows the scope of the beetle control program in the Wilderness Areas from that in effect when this litigation began. The Forest Service previously authorized the cutting of thousands of acres of wilderness pineland in an attempt, among other things, to create "buffer" areas against the spread of beetles—a process seriously unsettling to the values underlying the Wilderness Act.

The Forest Service ultimately adopted the fourth of nine alternatives considered in detailing the FEIS, relating to beetle-control action within the Wilderness Areas.[1] Control efforts will be made under the program only: (1) to protect established woodpecker colony sites in immediate foraging areas; and (2) to protect "State and private lands, and high value Federal forest resources," excluding federal land being used for commercial timber operations. This alternative contemplates "spot-control" techniques confining cutting in the Wilderness Areas to edges contiguous to neighboring property. Cutting will be allowed only if a spot infestation of beetles is located within one-quarter mile of bordering non-wilderness lands, and a biological evaluation predicts the spot will expand into neighboring lands to be protected and cause unacceptable damage. A number of other cautionary

---

1. Less intrusive options considered were those of allowing no cutting, and of allowing cutting only for the benefit of essential woodpecker colony sites. The more intrusive options considered were to allow cutting in the one-quarter mile boundary area also to benefit Federal commercial timberland, and to allowing cutting throughout the wilderness. *See* ROD at 5–8.

factors must be considered in each site-by-site specific analysis prior to cutting.

The Forest Service emphasizes that under this selective approach, beetle control will be the exception; natural forces will be allowed "to play their role in the wilderness ecosystem," and "[i]t is only when these natural forces are predicted to threaten an essential [woodpecker] colony or cause unacceptable damage to specific resources adjacent to the wilderness that control in wilderness may be taken." It is emphasized that control efforts will be made only after detailed site-specific analysis.

Decisions on boundary cutting will take into account both the value of adjacent land and of the wilderness qualities damaged by control methods, and must be premised on a reasonable prediction that control will be effective. The Court has been assured, at argument on the motions, that no control efforts will be initiated in a Wilderness Area unless the owner of adjacent land to be protected has taken reasonable steps on the adjacent land to combat spread of the beetle and will continue such efforts. The public will be kept informed of control efforts and may object to site-specific control decisions. ROD.

* * *

Plaintiffs * * * persist in urging that the Secretary has not demonstrated that any boundary cutting of Wilderness Areas for the benefit of adjacent state and private timberland is "necessary" within the meaning of the Section.

Plaintiffs argue that no action by the Secretary can be deemed "necessary" unless the Secretary has first proven by scientific evidence that the contemplated spot-control cutting will be further effective in accomplishing the desired objectives. They seize on a dictionary definition of "necessary," arguing that it can only mean "essential to a desirable . . . end," and urge that if control measures intruding on wilderness values have not been scientifically proven effective, by definition they cannot be necessary—i.e., essential—to control beetles.

Plaintiffs suggest the Secretary has little or no basis for concluding that the various spot-control methods that may be employed in the program will have any significant effect in controlling the spread of beetles to contiguous areas, and they attack past studies of control methods as scientifically unsophisticated, emphasizing that only area-wide control efforts can check the beetles. They note that in the regions of the country where spot control is contemplated under the program, beetles are generally present in both wilderness and non-wilderness areas, in varying degrees. Thus, the beetle does not present a natural hazard present only in Wilderness Areas that uniquely threatens uninfested adjacent lands; rather, it is indigenous to pineland areas generally, with beetles spreading back and forth between wilderness and non-wilderness land. Plaintiffs conclude that if control methods are adopted at all, they must be designed to check spread of the beetle in an entire area of pineland, because there is no other way of scientifically ensuring that even successful spot control applied in the border of a Wilderness Area will have lasting protective benefit to adjacent lands.

The degree of effectiveness of the spot-control methods to be employed under the program does remain in doubt. The record establishes considerable differences of opinion among biologists and other scientists studying the problem. The Secretary stresses the narrowness of the control allowed under the program, and the fact that a site-specific analysis must be employed before each control effort is undertaken. He cites numerous prior control efforts as supporting his view that the methods of spot control employed in the program have efficacy, and has concluded that the program will minimize significant harm from the spread of beetles.

Whether the Secretary has met his burden, on this record, of justifying intrusion on wilderness values for the benefit of adjacent landowners depends initially upon how Section 4(d)(1)'s allowance of "necessary" measures is interpreted. If plaintiffs are correct that only measures which are proven to be fully successful in effectively preventing the spread of beetles in an entire area are to be allowed, then the Secretary has failed to meet his burden; he admits that effective area-wide control measures have not yet been identified. If the statute incorporates a less stringent necessity standard, however, the record will support the Secretary's judgment.

Plaintiffs read the Act too broadly. First, there is no ground for concluding the Congress used the term "necessary" in the absolute sense urged by plaintiffs. Under the statute, various measures are authorized to the extent that they "may be necessary in the control ... of insects...." The most natural reading of the Section focuses on the phrase "necessary in the control." In this context "necessary" simply embraces measures "needed to achieve a certain result or effect," *American Heritage Dictionary of the English Language* 877 (1981)—that is, measures that are needed as part of a program designed to control, in the sense of restrain or curb, beetle infestations.

The pertinent section of the statute is therefore most reasonably construed as allowing the Secretary to use measures that fall short of full effectiveness so long as they are reasonably designed to restrain or limit the threatened spread of beetle infestations from wilderness land onto the neighboring property, to its detriment.

The degree of efficacy of various control methods is not to be debated between various scientists and resolved before this Court. The Secretary's judgment that the control measures authorized are reasonably efficacious is entitled to respect under Section 10 of the Administrative Procedure Act, 5 U.S.C. § 706(2)(A) (1982), unless shown to be "arbitrary, capricious, an abuse of discretion, or otherwise not in accordance with law." Although the Secretary has not conducted the most elaborate studies of the proposed measures that are scientifically possible, and perhaps would have welcomed funds enabling him to do so, the Court is satisfied that his judgment is reasonable given the information now available from the past actual experience of the Forest Service in combating the beetle threat, and available scientific opinion. Of great importance is the fact that the effectiveness of these measures will ultimately be determined by specific study of each potential spot-control site, and a decision to cut does not rest upon the promulgation of the Secretary's underlying policy decision alone.

One further point must also be stressed. The Secretary's burden under Section 4(d)(1) affirmatively to justify control actions taken for the benefit of adjacent landowners is grounded on the need to ensure that wilderness values are not unnecessarily sacrificed to promote the interests of adjacent landowners which Congress authorized the Secretary to protect. The Secretary has now made clear that unless adjacent landowners and federal authorities responsible for neighboring lands are following all reasonable means for combating beetles, the well-settled policies governing preservation of Wilderness Areas will not be compromised. Vigorous control efforts along the borders of wilderness land will be undertaken, therefore, only when met by equally vigorous efforts on adjacent land, ensuring that the burden of beetle control will not fall disproportionately on the Wilderness Areas. Those who seek protection of their lands must demonstrate to the Forest Service a willingness to share the burden of acting in a manner that will minimize any necessary intrusions upon wilderness values.

There are no material facts in dispute. The Secretary has met his burden. The Secretary's action is rational and not arbitrary. It constitutes a proper exercise of his discretion and contemplates action consistent with the requirements of the Wilderness Act as interpreted by the Court. [Defendants' motion for summary judgment granted.]

NOTES AND QUESTIONS

1. The judicial intervention here seemed to have a significant impact on the agency's policy. For example, the court noted at one point in the second opinion that the Secretary's ultimate decision "pays close attention to the court's specification [in its first opinion] of the Secretary's burden." 663 F.Supp. at 560 n.10. The court's interpretation of the Wilderness Act was followed in a Texas case raising nearly identical issues. Sierra Club v. Lyng, 694 F.Supp. 1260, 1274 (E.D.Tex.1988), *aff'd in part, vacated in part on other grounds sub nom.* Sierra Club v. Yeutter, 926 F.2d 429 (5th Cir.1991).

2. What is or should be the obligation of the federal managing agency where natural forces operating within wilderness areas may have impacts beyond their borders? (In a sense, this is the reverse of the "external threats" problem discussed in section B of this chapter.) Is Judge Gesell correct in saying that the agency has less discretion, and the courts should give closer scrutiny, to management actions that are undertaken not to promote wilderness values, but instead to protect "outside commercial and other private interests"? Is it fair to reverse the burden of proof as a counterweight to pressure agencies will usually feel from outside commercial interests? How strong is the argument that treating timber infestations in wilderness promotes wilderness values by sustaining the political support of neighboring landowners who might otherwise oppose wilderness designations?

3.   Would the result in the second opinion have been the same if the Forest Service had not required rigorous control measures on the adjacent land outside the wilderness?

4.   Would it make a difference if the southern pine beetle were an exotic pest, imported from abroad, and thus posed an "unnatural" threat to wilderness? Suppose the infestation here involved mosquitoes carrying human pathogens, such as West Nile virus? Would the Forest Service have greater flexibility in mosquito control than in beetle infestation?

5.   Like insect infestation, wildfires occur naturally and such "disturbance regimes" are not necessarily welcomed by inholders or neighbors. Should the federal agencies fight fires in wilderness areas? Only those caused by human activity as opposed to natural forces (lightning)? Only those that could conceivably threaten persons and property outside the boundaries of the area? Many ecosystems are adapted to and require "disturbance regimes" for continued health.

6.   Proposals are occasionally made to seed clouds over wilderness areas in order to enhance precipitation to benefit water users downstream from wilderness areas. If the best scientific evidence is that such man-induced precipitation would generally not exceed variations in precipitation that could naturally occur in the wilderness, is such cloud-seeding lawful? Might it be lawful if it were done from airplanes but not if it were done from ground-based generators inside the wilderness areas?

The following case involves an even more direct challenge to the non-motorized character of wilderness lands. Cumberland Island Wilderness Area is typical of many Eastern wilderness areas that are in the midst of restoration to natural conditions after a period of development.

Wilderness Watch v. Mainella

United States Court of Appeals, Eleventh Circuit, 2004.
375 F.3d 1085.

■ JUDGE BARKETT

Cumberland Island, which features some of the last remaining undeveloped land on the barrier islands along the Atlantic coast of the United States, was declared by Congress to be a National Seashore in 1972. Ten years later, Congress designated as wilderness or potential wilderness some 19,000 acres, including most of the northern three-fifths of the island. Under the aegis of the Secretary of the Interior, the Park Service thus became responsible for administering the wilderness area "in accordance with the applicable provisions of the Wilderness Act." *Id.* at § 2(c). Today, visitors to Cumberland Island must leave their vehicles on the mainland and travel to the island by boat.

In addition to wilderness area, Park Service land includes several buildings and facilities on the southern end of the island as well as two historical areas on the northern and western coasts: Plum Orchard, just outside the wilderness boundary, and the Settlement, located in potential wilderness area.[3] Historically, these two locations have been reached via the "Main Road," a one-lane dirt road that has also been designated as part of the wilderness and potential wilderness areas.

Once federal land has been designated as wilderness, the Wilderness Act places severe restrictions on commercial activities, roads, motorized vehicles, motorized transport, and structures within the area, subject to very narrow exceptions and existing private rights. * * * Thus, aside from exceptions not relevant here, the statute permits the use of motor vehicles and transport only "as necessary to meet minimum requirements for the administration of the area for the purpose of this chapter." 16 U.S.C. § 1133(c).

Following the wilderness designation, the Park Service continued to use the existing one-lane dirt road to access the historical areas. Motorized transportation on Cumberland Island became a controversial issue in the 1990s, as the federal government sought to obtain remaining private tracts on the island and various groups called for greater public access to and support of the historical sites. An informal group of environmental organizations, historical societies, and local residents met several times in an attempt to discuss and ultimately to influence Park Service policy. Jack Kingston, the representative to Congress from the district including Cumberland, introduced legislation that would have removed the wilderness designation from the roads leading to the historical sites. This bill died in committee in 1998, but later that year the Park Service convened the first of two meetings with many of the same interested parties in an attempt to negotiate a solution to the conflict over its policies. In February 1999 the Park Service agreed to provide regular public access to Plum Orchard and the Settlement via Park Service motor vehicles until boat service could be established.

The Park Service claimed that it needed motorized access to the historical areas in order to "meet[ ] its obligations to restore, maintain, preserve and curate the historic resources . . . and permit visitor access and interpretation." The Service also claimed that permitting tourists to "piggyback" along on Park Service personnel trips to these locations would yield "no net increase in impact,"—that is, the number of trips and overall impact on the area would be no greater than if the Park Service were simply meeting its statutory obligations. *Id.* For the first two months, the Park Service used vehicles that held four passengers, but the agency soon acquired a fifteen-person van in order to accommodate larger numbers of visitors. The Park Service offered trips to Plum Orchard three times per week and to the Settlement once per month. Although the Park Service had not previously visited the sites on a regular schedule, the agency decided to

---

3. Plum Orchard, a mansion complex commissioned by Thomas Carnegie in the late nineteenth century, lies some two-and-one-half miles from the wilderness boundary on the western coast. The Settlement, the remnants of an area occupied by a group of freed slaves after the Civil War, lies another six miles north of Plum Orchard.

establish a regular schedule in order to accommodate the transportation of visitors.[6]

* * *

The Park Service, on the other hand, reads the statute to allow visitors to ride along with its employees as they travel to Plum Orchard and the Settlement to perform what they claim is administrative and maintenance work on those properties. The Service claims that the Act allows land designated as wilderness to be devoted to multiple purposes, citing as authority 16 U.S.C. § 1133(b), which provides that "wilderness areas shall be devoted to the public purposes of recreational, scenic, scientific, educational, conservation, and historical use." Thus, the Park Service argues, because it has a separate duty to preserve the historical structures at the Settlement, the "preservation of historic structures in wilderness (or, as here, potential wilderness) is in fact administration to further the purposes of the Wilderness Act."

This dispute thus requires us to interpret the limitations imposed on motor vehicle use under the Wilderness Act, in particular the requirement that motor vehicle use be restricted to the level "necessary to meet minimum requirements for the administration of the area," 16 U.S.C. § 1133(c). We must also determine the effect of the Act upon the Park Service's obligations to maintain the historical structures on Cumberland Island and whether the Act can accommodate the Park Service's decision to transport tourists for the purpose of visiting those structures.

* * *

As an initial matter, we cannot agree with the Park Service that the preservation of historical structures furthers the goals of the Wilderness Act. The Park Service's responsibilities for the historic preservation of Plum Orchard and the Settlement derive, not from the Wilderness Act, but rather from the National Historic Preservation Act (NHPA). The NHPA requires agencies to "assume responsibility for the preservation of historic properties" they control. Plum Orchard and the historic district containing the Settlement have both been listed in the National Register of Historic Places, though the congressional reports and early Park Service reports only mention Plum Orchard (which itself lies outside the designated wilderness area).

The agency's obligations under the Wilderness Act are quite different. The Wilderness Act defines wilderness as "undeveloped Federal land retaining its primeval character and influence, without permanent improvements or human habitation." 16 U.S.C. § 1131(c). A wilderness area should "generally appear[ ] to have been affected primarily by the forces of nature, with the imprint of man's work substantially unnoticeable." *Id.* Another section of the Act explicitly states that, except as necessary for minimal administrative needs that require occasional vehicle use, "there shall be . . .

6. In September 2002, four months after this litigation commenced, the Park Service established boat service to Plum Orchard and discontinued land transportation of tourists to that site. * * *

no structure or installation within any such [wilderness] area." 16 U.S.C. § 1133(c). As the Park Service notes, Section 1133(b) mentions "historical use" along with "recreational, scenic, scientific, educational, [and] conservation" uses. However, this list tracks the definition of wilderness areas in § 1131(c), which describes "a primitive and unconfined type of recreation" and "ecological, geological, or other features of scientific, educational, scenic, or historical value." 16 U.S.C. § 1131(c). Given the consistent evocation of "untrammeled" and "natural" areas, the previous pairing of "historical" with "ecological" and "geological" features, and the explicit prohibition on structures, the only reasonable reading of "historical use" in the Wilderness Act refers to natural, rather than man-made, features.

Of course, Congress may separately provide for the preservation of an existing historical structure within a wilderness area, as it has done through the NHPA. Congress wrote the wilderness rules and may create exceptions as it sees fit. Absent these explicit statutory instructions, however, the need to preserve historical structures may not be inferred from the Wilderness Act nor grafted onto its general purpose. Furthermore, any obligation the agency has under the NHPA to preserve these historical structures must be carried out so as to preserve the "wilderness character" of the area. *See* 16 U.S.C. § 1133(b) ("[E]ach agency administering any area designated as wilderness shall be responsible for preserving the wilderness character of the area and shall so administer such area for such other purposes for which it may have been established as also to preserve its wilderness character.")

This appeal turns not on the preservation of historical structures but on the decision to provide motorized public access to them across designated wilderness areas. The Wilderness Act bars the use of motor vehicles in these areas "except as necessary to meet minimum requirements for the administration of the area for the purpose of this chapter [the Wilderness Act]." 16 U.S.C. § 1133(c). The Park Service's decision to "administer" the Settlement using a fifteen-passenger van filled with tourists simply cannot be construed as "necessary" to meet the "minimum requirements" for administering the area "for the purpose of [the Wilderness Act]." 16 U.S.C. § 1133(c). The plain language of the statute contradicts the Park Service position. When interpreting the language of a statute, "we generally give the words used their ordinary meaning." If these words are unambiguous, our inquiry is complete, for "we must presume that Congress said what it meant and meant what it said." In no ordinary sense of the word can the transportation of fifteen people through wilderness area be "necessary" to administer the area for the purpose of the Wilderness Act.

The Park Service argues that these trips affect the wilderness no more than would a standard Park Service vehicle with no additional passengers. Thus, the agency argues that the "use of motor vehicles" remains the same as what would be minimally necessary for administration. There are several problems with this interpretation. Most obviously, it still runs counter to the plain meaning of the provision. Under an ordinary, common-sense reading, people "use" motor vehicles when they ride in the Park Service van, thereby increasing the "use of motor vehicles" beyond the minimum necessary for administration of the Wilderness Act. The Park Service wishes to define the term based on the number of vehicles used rather than on the number of people using them, but even so, the acquisition and use of a large passenger van for transporting tourists cannot reasonably be squeezed into the phrase "necessary to meet minimum requirements" of administration. The language in this subsection is quite categorical, providing for "*no* motor vehicle use" except "as necessary" and labels this a "*prohibition.*" 16 U.S.C. § 1133(c) (emphasis added). Moreover, the same subsection provides that there shall be "no other form of mechanical transport" beyond what is necessary for administration of the Wilderness Act. *Id.* A passenger van certainly provides more "transport" than would a Park Service vehicle without extra passengers.

In addition, the overall purpose and structure of the statute argue against the agency interpretation. The prohibition on motor vehicle "use" in the Wilderness Act stems from more than just its potential for physical impact on the environment. The Act seeks to preserve wilderness areas "in their natural condition" for their "use and enjoyment *as wilderness.*" 16 U.S.C. § 1131(a) (emphasis added). The Act promotes the benefits of wilderness "for the American people," especially the "opportunities for a primitive and unconfined type of recreation." *Id.* at § 1131(c). Thus, the statute seeks to provide the opportunity for a primitive wilderness experience as much as to protect the wilderness lands themselves from physical harm. Use of a passenger van changes the wilderness experience, not only for the actual passengers, but also for any other persons they happen to pass (more so than would be the case upon meeting a lone park ranger in a jeep). Of course, there is nothing wrong with appreciating natural beauty from inside a passenger van, and many other categories of public land administered by the federal government appropriately offer this opportunity. It simply is not the type of "use and enjoyment" promoted by the Wilderness Act.

Other documents in the record highlight the potential conflict between wilderness values and the transportation of passengers. The agency's Minimum Requirements Determination (MRD) for the Plum Orchard trips recognized "concerns over the van affecting the quality of the visitor experience for those seeking a wilderness experience." The House report accompanying the bill establishing the Cumberland wilderness area urged the Park Service to provide exclusive access to Plum Orchard by water "in the interests of minimizing unnecessary intrusion on wilderness values." H. Rep. No. 97–383 at 5. The agency itself previously stressed the need to limit mechanized transport to administrative purposes that promote wilderness values.

The language of the specific provision at issue and the overall purpose and structure of the Wilderness Act demonstrate that Congress has unambiguously prohibited the Park Service from offering motorized transportation to park visitors through the wilderness area.

* * *

NOTES AND QUESTIONS

1. Should the court have been more deferential to the Park Service's determination that the use of motorized vehicles was necessary to administer the Act? Did the court view the dispute through the eyes of the wilderness recreationists whose experience might be impaired by roads and motor vehicles?

2. How much deference should administering agencies have to tailor wilderness preservation to the particular needs of a place? How relevant is the history of Plum Orchard and "The Settlement"? Is there a better way to reconcile historical preservation with wilderness protection?

3. Wilderness Watch succeeded in generating an important Eleventh Circuit precedent in this case, but it did not ultimately prevail on the ground. Representative Jack Kingston, who represents coastal Georgia, succeeded in placing a rider on an omnibus spending bill that Congress rushed to enact at the end of 2004.

> In practice, the [2004] law means that motorized tours run by the island's only inn, Greyfield, and the National Park Service can continue unchallenged through the wilderness area and along the empty beach. It also allows for new enterprises, allowing a new inn or an artists' colony to be installed in an old mansion bordering the wilderness area.

* * *

> The new law directly affects only a small portion of the island—200 or so acres on the northern end, plus several miles of primitive one-lane roads. The land involved was considered "potential wilderness" because the former owners had rights to live there. The land remains under park service control.

> For the heirs of Thomas Carnegie—brother of Andrew—whose forebears, seeking coastal playgrounds, bought the plantations that had crumbled after the Civil War, the bill reflects the reality of the island's use. The Carnegie descendants who own Greyfield Inn, a private hotel on private land, take guests on tours in the back of an aging Land Rover.

* * *

> The National Park Service has played a shifting role in the long debate. The current superintendent, Jerre Brumbelow, favors the new law, saying it is "better than trying to force-feed a wilderness on top of so many long-term, non-conforming uses there." He added that an increasing number of African–Americans want to find their history in a 19th–century graveyard near the north end. He said they should not have to walk up to 17 miles to do so.

Felicity Barringer, *Georgia Islanders Take Lead in Feud Over Land Use*, N.Y.TIMES, Jan. 15, 2005. Do you agree with Superintendent Brumbelow? Does it matter whether the graveyard is accessible by boat? Would it make a difference if, instead of a graveyard, the attraction were a natural hot springs?

4.   In Barnes v. Babbitt, 329 F. Supp. 2d 1141, 1155 (D. Ariz. 2004), the court set aside an agency decision to allow repair and motorized use of a road to an inholding in a BLM wilderness area (which had fallen into disrepair and was unusable at the time the area was designated wilderness). Like the *Wilderness Watch* court, the judge did not bend a strict reading of the Wilderness Act to accommodate history and uses of the area:

> To support the BLM's decision to authorize repair and maintenance of roads in the Wilderness area and the use of motor vehicles and mechanized equipment, the IBLA found that "the Arrastra Wilderness is not a homogenous area 'where the earth and its community of life are untrammeled by man,' . . . but an area interlaced with the imprint of man." The IBLA concluded that the limited use of motor vehicles and maintenance of access roads in the area, as allowed by the [Range Improvement, or] RIM Plan Decision, would not compromise the wilderness characteristics of the area because those did not exist.
>
> In other words, the IBLA concluded that the conditions in the Arrastra Mountain Wilderness do not constitute "wilderness" as defined in the Wilderness Act so that the Act's prohibition against roads does not apply. Since the wilderness designation was determined by Congress, however, the IBLA was without authority to make a contrary determination. In addition, the record does not support the IBLA's conclusion. Because the IBLA's decision affirming the RIM Plan Decision was based, at least in part, on a finding that the Arrastra Mountain Wilderness is not a wilderness area as defined by § 1131(c), its decision is contrary to the Wilderness Act and the ADWA ["Arizona Desert Wilderness Act," establishing the wilderness area] and must be set aside.
>
> The IBLA also concluded that repair and maintenance of the five access routes does not constitute construction of roads, but merely the repair of existing roads. To qualify as a wilderness area, however, the Arrastra Mountain area must have been "roadless," meaning that it lacked roads that had been improved or maintained by mechanical means for relatively regular and continuous use. *See* 43 U.S.C. § 1782(a). An example provided of regular or continuous use is motor vehicle access to maintain established water sources. Although the access routes may have been used occasionally by motor vehicles, such as jeeps, before the wilderness designation, there is no evidence that the routes had been improved or maintained for regular or continuous use. The Final EIS for the Arrastra Mountain Wilderness area states that the areas considered for wilderness designation were "roadless." Therefore, the IBLA's conclusion that the area had pre-existing roads is contrary to the evidence and the determination made by Congress in designating the area as wilderness.
>
> The RIM Plan Decision allows grazing permittees to perform limited mechanized route maintenance and to have limited motorized access to range developments for repair and maintenance. Despite the limita-

tions, the anticipated motor vehicle use would be regular and continuous. As such, the access routes, once repaired and in use, would be "roads" within the meaning of the Wilderness Act. Therefore, because the repairs and maintenance of the access routes would constitute road construction in violation of the Wilderness Act, the IBLA's decision must be set aside.

The *Barnes* decision restricts the practices of ranchers holding grazing permits in wilderness areas as well as inholders. Does the *Barnes* court take an overly formalistic view of wilderness areas? Does congressional designation of a less-than-pristine area transform the land or uses into true wilderness? Should Congress have addressed the issue in the ADWA?

5.   What about the installation, with battery-powered motorized drills, of permanent climbing bolts in wilderness areas? Is a drill "motorized equipment"? Federal agencies generally believe so. Are the climbing bolts a "structure or installation"? Here the agencies have sometimes split. The current view seems to be that they are not prohibited across the board, although they may be regulated and even prohibited by local land managers.

6.   In the Americans with Disabilities Act of 1990, Congress "reaffirmed" that the Wilderness Act is not to be construed as "prohibiting the use of a wheelchair in a wilderness area by a [disabled] individual," and that federal land managers are not required to "construct any facilities or modify any conditions within a wilderness area in order to facilitate such use." 42 U.S.C. § 12207(c). Determining what constitutes "mechanical transport" can require some fine hairsplitting. Rowboats with swivel oarlocks, alpine skis with bindings, and even some climbing equipment might be considered such under an expansive view, but they are generally allowed in wilderness. Mountain bikes, not in use in 1964, are another story. The federal agencies ban the bikes (along with hang gliders) in wilderness, which has led the International Mountain Bike Association to join with ORV advocates to oppose some new wilderness areas.

In addition to the ban on motors and mechanized transport, commercial activities are generally off-limits in wilderness areas. Section 1133(c) contains a general proscription, "subject to existing private rights," on any "commercial enterprise * * * within any wilderness area." It also prohibits, among other things, any "structure or installation" within any such area "except as necessary to meet minimum requirements for the administration of the area." Section 1133(d)(5) provides that "[c]ommercial services may be performed" within wilderness areas "to the extent necessary for activities which are proper for realizing the recreational or other wilderness purposes of the areas." This applies to services provided by outfitters, guides, river-runners and the like.

Insect infestation (spruce bark beetles) and other effects of climate change are the greatest ecological threat to the Kenai National Wildlife Refuge in Alaska, where temperatures have been rising much more rapidly than in temperate regions. The following wilderness management case does not deal with responses to the deforestation in the manner of the Sierra Club v. Lyng litigation. It is, instead, about a common activity on wildlife refuges: stocking fish in lakes and streams.

The Wilderness Society v. U.S. Fish & Wildlife Service

United States Court of Appeals, Ninth Circuit, 2003.
353 F.3d 1051 (en banc).

■ JUDGE GOULD

We consider an action brought by the Wilderness Society and the Alaska Center for the Environment ("Plaintiffs") challenging a decision by the United States Fish and Wildlife Service ("USFWS"), to grant a permit for a sockeye salmon enhancement project ("Enhancement Project") that annually introduces about six million hatchery-reared salmon fry into Tustumena Lake, the largest freshwater lake in the Kenai National Wildlife Refuge ("Kenai Refuge") and the Kenai Wilderness. Plaintiffs assert that the USFWS permit for the Enhancement Project violated the Wilderness Act, 16 U.S.C. §§ 1131–1136, by offending its mandate to preserve the "natural conditions" that are a part of the "wilderness character" of the Kenai Wilderness, and by sanctioning an impermissible "commercial enterprise" within a designated wilderness area. * * * We conclude that the district court erred in finding that the Enhancement Project is not a "commercial enterprise" that Congress prohibited within the designated wilderness. We reverse and remand so that the final decision of the USFWS may be set aside, the Enhancement Project enjoined, and judgment entered for Plaintiffs.

* * *

In 1980, Congress enacted the Alaska National Interest Lands Conservation Act ("ANILCA") to control the management of Alaska refuge lands. ANILCA expanded the Kenai National Moose Range by nearly a quarter-million acres, renamed it the Kenai National Wildlife Refuge, and further set aside 1.35 million acres of the Refuge, including Tustumena Lake, as the Kenai Wilderness, a designated wilderness.

* * *

Tustumena Lake lies near the western edge of the Kenai Refuge and within the Kenai Wilderness. Tustumena Lake is the largest freshwater lake located within the Kenai Refuge and is the fifth largest freshwater lake in the State of Alaska. The lake's outlet is the Kasilof River, which drains into the Cook Inlet, a tidal estuary that flows into the Gulf of Alaska and the Pacific Ocean.

As a result of its remote location, the ecosystem around and within Tustumena Lake is in a natural state. This ecosystem supports several species of anadromous fish, including sockeye salmon, which spawn within the Kasilof River watershed. A commercial fishing fleet, operating outside the boundaries of the Kenai Refuge, intercepts and harvests these sockeye salmon during their annual run from the Gulf of Alaska back to the Kasilof River, Tustumena Lake, and other spawning streams.

The antecedents of the present Enhancement Project date back to 1974, when the Alaska Department of Fish and Game ("ADF & G") first conducted a sockeye salmon egg collection at Tustumena Lake as part of a research project designed to test the ability of the ecosystem to produce fish. The eggs were incubated at the Crooked Creek Hatchery, outside of the Kenai Refuge, and the resulting fry were stocked outside of the Kenai Refuge in the spring of 1975. In 1976, fry were first released into Tustumena Lake, and since have been released into Tustumena Lake in all but two subsequent years. The number of fry stocked yearly in Tustumena Lake has ranged from a low of 400,000 in 1978 to a high of 17,050,000 in 1984. Since 1987, the number of fry released annually into the lake has been slightly greater than 6 million.

* * *

* * * In 1993, ADF & G entered into a contract with the Cook Inlet Aquaculture Association ("CIAA") to staff and run * * * its hatchery programs.

The CIAA is a private, non-profit corporation "comprised of associations representative of commercial fishermen in the region" as well as "other user groups interested in fisheries within the region." * * * The CIAA relies on funding from two sources. First, the Cook Inlet commercial salmon industry imposes a voluntary two percent tax on the value of its fishermen's annual salmon harvest. Second, the CIAA generates income through producing hatchery-raised salmon from the surplus fry not used to stock Tustumena Lake.

* * *

* * * In August 1997, the final [Environmental Assessment] of the Enhancement Project was released. In a simultaneously released "Mitigated Finding of No Significant Impact," the USFWS concluded that "mitigative measures" contained in the Special Use Permit would minimize risks associated with the Enhancement Project, and that preparation of an Environmental Impact Statement was not required.

Also in August 1997, the Kenai Refuge Manager issued a Wilderness Act Consistency Review * * * [concluding] that the Enhancement Project was consistent with the Wilderness Act, which he viewed as a legislative compromise not reflecting absolute preservationist values. The Refuge Manager also suggested that, because the State of Alaska had previously administered the project, criticism that the Enhancement Project was a commercial enterprise raised "a distinction without a difference." In August 1997, the Refuge Manager also released a Compatibility Determination, which concluded that the Enhancement Project "cannot ... be considered as supporting refuge purposes, but neither can it be found incompatible with them."

After issuance of these documents, the USFWS on August 8, 1997, issued a Special Use Permit to the CIAA for the Enhancement Project.

Under the terms of this permit, each summer the CIAA establishes a temporary camp within the Kenai Wilderness at the mouth of Bear Creek, which flows into Tustumena Lake, and catches about 10,000 returning sockeye salmon, which yield about 10 million eggs. These eggs are transported to a hatchery outside the Kenai Wilderness. The following spring about six million salmon fry produced by the eggs are stocked and returned to the wilderness in Bear Creek.

* * *

* * * Section 4(c) of the Wilderness Act states that, subject to exceptions not relevant here, "there shall be no commercial enterprise ... within any wilderness area." 16 U.S.C. § 1133(c). The Wilderness Act does not define the terms "commercial enterprise" or "within." The district court considered these terms ambiguous and concluded that they do not bar the Enhancement Project.

Because no statutory or regulatory provision expressly defines the meaning of the term "commercial enterprise" as used in the Wilderness Act, we first consider the common sense meaning of the statute's words to determine whether it is ambiguous. Webster's defines "enterprise" to mean "a project or undertaking." Webster's defines "commercial" as "occupied with or engaged in commerce or work intended for commerce; of or relating to commerce." The American Heritage Dictionary of the English Language provides a strikingly similar definition, viewing "commercial" as meaning "1.a. of or relating to commerce, b. engaged in commerce, c. involved in work that is intended for the mass market." Black's Law Dictionary adds that "commercial" may be defined as "relates to or is connected with trade and traffic or commerce in general; is occupied with business or commerce." These definitions suggest that a commercial enterprise is a project or undertaking of or relating to commerce.

We also consider the purposes of the Wilderness Act. The Act's declaration of policy states as a goal the "preservation and protection" of wilderness lands "in their natural condition," so as to "leave them unimpaired for future use and enjoyment as wilderness and so as to provide for the protection of these areas, [and] the preservation of their wilderness character." 16 U.S.C. § 1131(a). The Wilderness Act further defines "wilderness," in part, as "an area where the earth and its community of life are untrammeled by man." *Id.* § 1131(c). These statutory declarations show a mandate of preservation for wilderness and the essential need to keep commerce out of it. Whatever else may be said about the positive aims of the Enhancement Project, it was not designed to advance the purposes of the Wilderness Act. The Enhancement Project to a degree places the goals and activities of commercial enterprise in the protected wilderness. The Enhancement Project is literally a project relating to commerce.

The structure of the relevant provisions of the Wilderness Act may also be considered. The Wilderness Act's opening section first sets forth the Act's broad mandate to protect the forests, waters and creatures of the wilderness in their natural, untrammeled state. 16 U.S.C. § 1131. Section 1133, devoted to the use of wilderness areas, contains a subsection entitled "[p]rohibition provisions." *Id.* § 1133(c). Among these provisions is a broad prohibition on the operation of all commercial enterprise within a designated wilderness, except as "specifically provided for in this Act." *Id.* The following subsection of the Act enumerates "special provisions," including exceptions to this prohibition. *Id.* § 1133(d). This statutory structure, with prohibitions including an express bar on commercial enterprise within wilderness, limited by specific and express exceptions, shows a clear congressional intent generally to enforce the prohibition against "commercial enterprise" when the specified exceptions are not present. There is no exception given for commercial enterprise in wilderness when it has benign purpose and minimally intrusive impact.

The language, purpose and structure of the Wilderness Act support the conclusion that Congress spoke clearly to preclude commercial enterprise in the designated wilderness, regardless of the form of commercial activity, and regardless of whether it is aimed at assisting the economy with minimal intrusion on wilderness values.

Because the aim of Congress in the Wilderness Act to prohibit commercial enterprise within designated wilderness is clear, we do not owe deference to the USFWS's determination regarding the permissibility of the Enhancement Project if it is a commercial enterprise.

The district court grounded its decision in part on an assessment that the impact on wilderness of millions of fry unseen beneath the waters of Bear Creek and Tustumena Lake was not terribly intrusive on wilderness values and that the project would hardly be noticed by those visiting the wilderness. The district court also was impressed that the CIAA was a nonprofit entity, that the State of Alaska heavily regulated the Enhancement Project, and that commercial effects of the project generally occurred years after the collection of salmon eggs and later release of the fry and were realized by commercial fishermen who sought their catch outside the wilderness bounds.

We thus deal with an activity with a benign aim to enhance the catch of fishermen, with little visible detriment to wilderness, under the cooperative banner of a non-profit trade association and state regulators. Surely this fish-stocking program, whose antecedents were a state run research project, is nothing like building a McDonald's restaurant or a Wal–Mart store on the shores of Tustumena Lake. Nor is it like conducting a commercial fishing operation within designated wilderness, which we have previously proscribed. Nor is the project like cutting timber, extracting minerals, or otherwise exploiting wilderness resources in a way that is plainly destructive of their preservation.

Conversely, the challenged activities do not appear to be aimed at furthering the goals of the Wilderness Act. The project is not aimed at preserving a threatened salmon run. Looked at most favorably, for the proponents of the fish-stocking project, it might be concluded that the project only negligibly alters the wild character of Tustumena Lake and is not incompatible with refuge values, though those issues are disputed. And it might also be considered that, to the extent the project is a servant of commerce, it may pose a threat to the wild, even if it operates under the eye of state and federal regulators.

* * *

In light of Congress's language and manifest intent, we conclude that the most sensible rule of decision to resolve whether an activity within designated wilderness bounds should be characterized as a "commercial enterprise" turns on an assessment of the purpose and effect of the activity. *See Sierra Club v. Lyng,* 662 F.Supp. 40, 42–43 (D.D.C.1987). * * * [In *Lyng*], the district court stressed that the "purpose and effect of the program [was] solely to protect commercial timber interests and private property," and imposed an affirmative burden on the Secretary of Agriculture to justify the eradication program in light of wilderness values.

* * *

The primary purpose of the Enhancement Project is to advance commercial interests of Cook Inlet fishermen by swelling the salmon runs from which they will eventually make their catch. The Enhancement Project is operated by an organization primarily funded by a voluntary self-imposed tax instituted by the Cook Inlet fishing industry on the value of its salmon catch. In the words of the Kenai Refuge Manager, in a memorandum to the Department of Interior's Regional Solicitor:

> The *primary purpose of the enhancement activity is to supplement sockeye catches* for East Side Cook Inlet set-net commercial fishermen, and for lower Cook Inlet enhancement projects. * * * *The activity is no longer experimental in nature, nor is restoration of fish stocks an objective. It is strictly an enhancement effort to increase the number of sockeye salmon available to the commercial fishery.*

(emphasis added). * * * This primary purpose is not contradicted by evidence that the Enhancement Project serves other secondary noncommercial purposes, including providing a general benefit to the fishery commonly used by commercial and recreational fishermen alike. Incidental purposes do not contradict that the Enhancement Project's principal aim is stock enhancement for the commercial fishing industry.

The primary effect of the Enhancement Project is to aid commercial enterprise of fishermen. More than eighty percent of the salmon produced by the Enhancement Project are caught by commercial fishermen, who realize over $1.5 million in additional annual revenue from project-produced fish. * * * In light of this primary effect, any incidental benefit to sport fishermen or others is not controlling. The incidental benefit that the program may provide to recreational and sport fishermen is subordinate to the primary benefit conferred on the commercial fishing industry.

In light of the unmistakable primary purpose and effect of the Enhancement Project, we reject arguments advanced by the USFWS that were credited by the district court. The district court reasoned in part that the CIAA is itself a nonprofit organization. But the non-profit status of the CIAA cannot be controlling because its non-profit activities are funded by the fishing industry and are aimed at providing benefits to that industry.

The CIAA's continued funding and operation is dependent upon the revenues of commercial fishermen, and we have previously recognized that even non-profit entities may engage in commercial activity.

In addition, the district court relied on the involvement of the State of Alaska, which previously had run the stocking project to research the viability of artificially enhancing salmon runs. But prior management activity and present regulatory control by the State of Alaska is irrelevant to assessing the primary purpose and effect of the current Enhancement Project. When the State had direct control of operations, the project's primary purpose was research-oriented. * * * But now the project, as run by the CIAA, is aimed at enhancing salmon runs to increase the catch of commercial fishermen. The purpose of the project has changed from research on techniques to practical operations to swell the catch of fish and the commerce thereon. * * *

Furthermore, the essential nature of the Enhancement Project is not changed merely because the commercial benefit derived from the Enhancement Project is conferred when fishermen make their salmon catch outside the bounds of the Kenai Wilderness. It is correct that what the Wilderness Act bars is the operation of a "commercial enterprise ... *within* any wilderness area." 16 U.S.C. § 1133(c) (emphasis added). But it is not disputed that substantial and essential parts of the Enhancement Project's operation, the collection of eggs taken to a hatchery and the stocking of six million fry returned to Bear Creek, occur within the Kenai Wilderness.

Implicit in the justifications urged for the project is the premise that we may recognize that the benign purposes of the project should be permitted to continue because the Wilderness Act resulted from a "compromise" of the legislature. But regardless of any tradeoffs considered by Congress in enacting the Wilderness Act, we interpret and apply the language chosen by Congress, for that language was chosen in order to incorporate and effectuate those tradeoffs. The plain language of the Wilderness Act states that there shall be *"no* commercial enterprise" within designated wilderness. 16 U.S.C. § 1133(c) (emphasis added). This mandatory language does not provide exception to the prohibition on commercial enterprise within wilderness if aimed at achieving a benign goal for commerce with modest impact on wilderness. That compromises may have been made in the legislative process does not alter an analysis of Congress's words of proscription based on traditional canons of statutory construction.

* * *

As an alternative holding in support of our decision, even if we were to assume that the Wilderness Act's prohibition on commercial enterprise within the wilderness is ambiguous, we would reach the same conclusion that the Enhancement Project offends the Wilderness Act. Assuming ambiguity in the scope of the prohibition, under *Mead* agency action is not entitled to heightened *Chevron* deference unless the agency can demonstrate that it has the general power to "make rules carrying the force of law" and that the challenged action was taken "in the exercise of that authority." Administrative interpretations not meeting these standards are entitled not to deference, but to a lesser "respect" based on the persuasiveness of the agency decision.

Applying *Mead,* we conclude that this case involves only an agency's application of law in a particular permitting context, and not an interpretation of a statute that will have the force of law generally for others in similar circumstances. The issuance of a permit by a federal agency cannot in this case be characterized as the exercise of a congressionally delegated legislative function.* * *

* * *

Under *Mead* and *Skidmore,* the weight that we are to give an administrative interpretation not intended by an agency to carry the general force of law is a function of that interpretation's thoroughness, rational validity, and consistency with prior and subsequent pronouncements. *Mead* adds as other relevant factors the "logic[ ] and expertness" of an agency decision, the care used in reaching the decision, as well as the formality of the process used. Even if we assume the Wilderness Act's prohibition on commercial enterprise to be ambiguous, the USFWS's permitting of the Enhancement Project "goes beyond the limits of what is ambiguous and contradicts what in our view is quite clear." Whatever else might be done permissibly within wilderness in extraordinary circumstances for purposes relating to conservation or preservation of the wilderness, we conclude that it is "quite clear" that conduct with the primary purpose and effect to aid commercial enterprise cannot be countenanced.

* * *

NOTES AND QUESTIONS

1. Is the interpretation of "commercial enterprise" offered here reasonable? Is the court correct to employ the "purpose and effect" test? Did the court apply the test correctly in this situation, or overemphasize the "purpose" part? Should the interpretation of "commercial" turn on the physical impact of the enterprise in the wilderness, or the degree of "psychological intrusion"? Should the Court have deferred to the agency, especially since this seemed to be a case of first impression, with an ambiguous statute? (That was essentially the approach of the district court, and the majority of the Ninth Circuit panel which first heard this case, before it was reviewed en banc.)

2. Is there a reasoned basis for distinguishing between logging inside a wilderness and the salmon enhancement project at issue here?

3. Is this decision consistent with the Sierra Club v. Lyng cases where the Forest Service was able to act within wilderness areas in order to protect commercial timber outside of the wilderness? Here, the wilderness supports a valuable fishery outside of the protected area. If the FWS had prepared a more thorough EIS, would the result have been different?

Would this case have come out differently if the fish stocking were for sport rather than commercial fishing?

4. The Wilderness Act does not explicitly authorize land managing agencies to issue regulations to carry out the Act. If it did, would the result have been the same? Even though the Act may not authorize regulations, could the FWS here, with more careful attention to the issues presented, have made a persuasive case that issuing the permit was consistent with the Wilderness Act?

5. Why should commercial enterprises be per se incompatible with wilderness? Would the Wilderness Act be improved if it prohibited only activities that physically degraded the ecosystem? Is the cultural component of wilderness significant here? What exactly is so objectionable about using the prime ecosystem of Tustumena Lake to increase fish stocks?

6. Several years before the *Wilderness Society* case, the Ninth Circuit found that the same Wilderness Act provision banned commercial fishing from the wilderness areas in Glacier Bay National Park, notwithstanding long-established practices. Alaska Wilderness Alliance v. Jensen, 108 F.3d 1065 (9th Cir. 1997).

7. In High Sierra Hikers Ass'n v. Blackwell, 390 F.3d 630 (9th Cir. 2004), the court upheld an injunction against the U.S. Forest Service, based on inadequate compliance with NEPA, in renewing special use permits to outfitters taking large pack groups with stock animals into wilderness. The court upheld the agency's finding under the Wilderness Act that allowing large pack groups was a "necessary" commercial service under § 1133(d)(5), but faulted the agency for failing to show that the number of permits granted was no more than necessary to achieve the goals of the Act. The court also found that renewal of permits "in the face of documented damage resulting from overuse does not have rational validity." 390 F.3d at 648.

8. Would the commercial-use ban prohibit a "bioprospector" from collecting microbes in order to study whether their organic material, for example, DNA, offers templates for pharmaceuticals or other useful products? Does the answer turn on whether the research actually yields a commercial product?

Researchers generally must secure permits from the managing agency before conducting studies on public lands. But the research phase of bioprospecting may be a prelude to commercial development. While this has not yet come up for wilderness, the Park Service, which bans "sale or commercial use" of national park resources (36 C.F.R. § 2.1(c)(3)), has grappled with this issue. In Edmonds Institute v. Babbitt, 93 F.Supp.2d 63 (D.D.C. 2000), a court upheld a research agreement between the U.S. and a private biotechnology company, Diversa, to explore the thermal features of Yellowstone for valuable microbes:

> This novel agreement, officially termed a Cooperative Research and Development Agreement ("CRADA"), was the first of its kind to involve a national park. The Statement of Work in the CRADA explains how Yellowstone and Diversa will cooperate in researching

and cataloguing the Park's biological diversity. * * * Following an initial survey, sites will be "prioritized and systematically sampled by [Diversa] scientists," using techniques to be "jointly selected by [the park] and [Diversa] to ensure that there is no significant impact to park resources or other appropriate park uses." Once raw samples have been extracted from the selected sites, nucleic acids will be isolated, purified and used to create a library of genetic information. The resulting gene libraries will be the starting point for the discovery and cloning of biocatalytic and bioactive compounds, which will be evaluated for potential commercial applications. These libraries of genetic information will also be available to Park scientists for their own research. * * *

* * *

* * * Diversa will make annual payments of around $20,000 to the defendants, as well as provide research equipment and other support for Yellowstone's use and benefit. More importantly, however, Diversa will pay royalties to Yellowstone on any future commercial use or product derived from the company's bioprospecting activities in the Park. Although the specifics are not public, Yellowstone has indicated that it will receive royalties of between .5% and 10% depending upon the nature of the raw material and the final product. By virtue of the CRADA, Yellowstone will share in any revenues generated by future beneficial applications or products developed from Diversa's research at Yellowstone.

Notwithstanding the novelty of the Yellowstone–Diversa CRADA itself, this agreement is not the first time that the National Park Service has permitted scientific research and collection of microbial specimens from Yellowstone's thermal features. To the contrary, the earliest research permit authorizing collection of microbial samples from Yellowstone was in 1898. Indeed, in recent years, the number of annual requests by researchers for access to Yellowstone has averaged 1,500, with some 250–300 research permits issued each year (between 40 and 50 of which are for microbial research projects). * * *

Prior to the CRADA, Diversa or other researchers were free to remove any specimen within the purview of their permit and develop it as they wished. If such development led to commercial uses, the Park Service never saw any proceeds from the derivative products. Thus, recognizing that resources yielding potentially valuable properties were being removed from Yellowstone with no remuneration to Yellowstone or the American people, officials at Interior began to consider a resource management scheme, patterned on the successes of Costa Rica and other nations, which would use bioprospecting to provide funds and incentives for the conservation of biological diversity. * * *

Edmonds Institute, 93 F.Supp.2d at 64–66. For a subsequent decision addressing how much information about particular benefit-sharing agreements is disclosable under the Freedom of Information Act, see Edmonds Institute v. Department of the Interior, 460 F.Supp.2d 63 (D.D.C. 2006).

The 1998 National Parks Omnibus Management Act specifically authorizes the Secretary of the Interior to "enter into negotiations with the research community and private industry for equitable, efficient benefits-sharing arrangements." 16 U.S.C. § 5935(d). Congress has not issued a similar instruction for the national wilderness preservation system. Do non-park wilderness areas have management authority to enter into revenue-, equipment-, and information-sharing agreements with commercial enterprises? How real is the risk that such an arrangement would commercialize the wilderness areas or parks? What is the long term policy implication of giving the federal land managing agency a financial interest, something akin to a "profit motive," in allowing scientific research that may have commercial value? Compare the discussion of recreation fees, where the land managing agencies are given a financial incentive to charge recreational visitors, Chapter 11, *supra* p. 957. The National Park Service released a draft environmental impact statement in the fall of 2006 on its system-wide research policy, with a preferred alternative of evaluating benefit-sharing for research case by case. Jim Robbins, *The Search for Private Profit in the Nation's Public Parks*, N.Y.TIMES, Nov. 28, 2006.

NOTE: MINING AND WILDERNESS

The Wilderness Act, 16 U.S.C. § 1133(d), created a twenty-year window for the mining industry to prospect and gain mineral rights under the General Mining Law of 1872 in national forest wilderness areas that had not already been withdrawn. The Act also allowed new mineral leases to be issued until 1984. The limited "window of opportunity" for the mining industry in certain wilderness areas expired of its own terms on January 1, 1984, at which point the minerals in wilderness areas were "withdrawn from all forms of appropriation under the mining laws and from disposition under all laws pertaining to mineral leasing and all amendments thereto." Congress has occasionally made some exceptions, for example, withdrawing the Boundary Water Canoe Area Wilderness from mining in 1978. On the other hand, Congress provided that a "special management zone" in The River of No Return Wilderness in Idaho remains open to locations for cobalt indefinitely.

Almost no mineral leases were ever issued in statutory wilderness areas despite this twenty-year window. Successive Secretaries of the Interior, in other words, exercised their discretion under the mineral leasing acts against leasing. There has been little hardrock mining in wilderness areas. The Interior Solicitor, noting the limited extent of mining activities in wilderness areas, has surmised that "possible causes include poor mineral prospects, stringent regulation of proposed mineral operations (Forest Service regulations on the subject are found at 36 C.F.R. § 228.15), and the reluctance of the mining industry to risk adverse public reaction by opening major mining operations in wilderness areas." 86 I.D. 89, 110 n. 50 (1979). Costs associated with accessibility to remote areas in rugged terrain doubtless also played a role. In Clouser v. Espy, 42 F.3d 1522 (9th Cir. 1994), the court found "no doubt whatever that the Forest Service enjoys the authority to regulate means of access," and upheld the Forest Service's policy of refusing to approve motorized access to mining claims "unless and until claim validity is established." It also endorsed the Forest Service regulations limiting access to those means "customarily used with respect to other such claims," and limiting mechanized transport and motorized equipment to situations where they are "essential" to mining activities. Finally, the court upheld the Forest Service's application of its regulations to require the use of pack animals for access, upon its finding that motorized access was not "essential" for the miner to use a small dredge in a proposed mining operation four miles into the wilderness, and was not "customary" because the access trails in question had been closed to traffic for a decade.

The Geothermal Steam Act excludes from leasing national parks, recreation areas, and wildlife refuges but does not mention wilderness areas. 30 U.S.C. § 1014(c). The Wilderness Act itself was enacted six years before the Geothermal Act, and therefore is silent on geothermal leasing. Whether leasing is allowed in congressionally-designated wilderness areas is not an idle inquiry: there are known geothermal resources in wilderness areas and developers have applied, unsuccessfully, for leases. Because other mineral leasing is now generally prohibited in wilderness areas, geothermal leasing would seem to be politically if not legally untenable in such areas.

Overall, there has been very little mineral activity in wilderness areas. Mineral potential of roadless areas that are candidates for congressional designation can, of course, be a key political issue when Congress deliberates over adding new areas to the system, and Congress has frequently gerrymandered the boundaries of designated wilderness to avoid areas that have mineral potential.

NOTE: GRAZING AND WILDERNESS

Under 16 U.S.C. § 1133(d)(4), "the grazing of livestock, where established prior to September 3, 1964, *shall* be permitted to continue subject to such reasonable regulations as are deemed necessary." (emphasis added) Does this provision, unlike the discretionary language used for aircraft and motorboats, create a right where none existed before? Michael McCloskey argued no, in *The Wilderness Act of 1964: Its Background and Meaning*, 45 OR. L.REV. 288, 311–12 (1966):

> Traditionally, under the law grazing permits are held not as a matter of right but merely as a matter of privilege, with the administering agency having the right to discontinue permits on their expiration. Does this provision establish any statutory rights in existing permittees? The fact that the continuance of grazing is made subject to reasonable regulation by the secretary implies there was no intent to establish definite rights. Indeed, if there had been any intent to change the basic law on this point, there would have been considerable debate. There was none. Under the "reasonable regulations" that the Forest

Service has prepared for its manual, continuance of grazing will be contingent on being consistent with wilderness values and maintenance of soil values. What the draftsmen of this section probably intended, then, was merely to make it clear that the existence of the Wilderness Act *per se* would not preclude continuance of grazing. The Forest Service would still have the authority to decide whether grazing on a given site was desirable and at what levels of stocking.

Are you persuaded by this argument? Can the managing federal agency restrict or prohibit livestock grazing in a wilderness area in order to preserve wilderness character? Can it do so for reasons *unrelated* to wilderness?

In the Colorado Wilderness Act of 1980, Congress declared that, "without amending the Wilderness Act of 1964, with respect to livestock grazing in wilderness areas," the Act's provisions on livestock grazing "shall be interpreted and administered in accordance with the guidelines contained in" the House Report (No. 96–617) accompanying the Act. 94 Stat. 3271, § 108 (1980). The Report basically said that existing grazing uses may continue in wilderness areas, but reductions in grazing intensity may be made through agency planning processes to improve poor range conditions. Reductions may not be made, however, *solely* because the area in which grazing is permitted has been designated as wilderness. The guidelines also nudged the Forest Service to be tender toward existing grazing practices, structures, facilities, and use of motorized equipment in wilderness areas.

Subsection 1133(d)(4) speaks of grazing established *prior to* enactment of the Wilderness Act. About half of the national forest wilderness areas have some livestock use; the proportion for BLM is almost certainly substantially higher. Can the federal land management agencies allow grazing in wilderness where the use was *not* established prior to the Act? Is grazing of domesticated livestock per se incompatible with the statutory definition of wilderness?

Aldo Leopold opined that "cattle ranches [in wilderness] would be an asset from the recreational standpoint because of the interest which attaches to cattle grazing operations under frontier conditions," and that ranchers themselves would benefit from protection against "settlers and the hordes of motorists" which follow the construction of roads in formerly wild country. Leopold, The Wilderness and Its Place in Forest Recreation Policy, 19 J. Forestry 721 (1921). The late Wallace Stegner, a strong wilderness advocate, once wrote:

> I have known enough range cattle to recognize them as wild animals; and the people that herd them have, in the wilderness context, dignity and rareness; they belong on the frontier, moreover, and have a look of rightness. The invasion they make on the virgin country is sort of an invasion that is as old as Neanderthal man, and they can in moderation, even emphasize a man's feeling of belonging to the natural world.

The Wilderness Idea, in WILDERNESS: AMERICA'S LIVING HERITAGE 100 (D. Brower ed. 1961).

In Forest Guardians v. Animal & Plant Health Inspection Serv., 309 F.3d 1141 (9th Cir. 2002), the court held that the Forest Service may institute lethal control of mountain lions in wilderness areas in order to protect livestock grazing, even where it was not practiced before the area was designated wilderness. In a terse opinion, it held that the Act did not expressly prohibit such predator control, and found that the authorization to allow pre-existing grazing to continue implicitly allowed such predator control. Can you make arguments against that result?

NOTE: OTHER WILDERNESS MANAGEMENT ISSUES

Logging

Somewhat curiously, the Wilderness Act does not expressly refer to timber harvesting even though it was a major issue leading up to enactment. The legislative history, the general provisions of the Act, and the ban on roads and motorized equipment all make clear, however, that commercial logging is a prohibited activity. *See* Lyng v. Northwest Indian Cemetery Protective Ass'n, 485 U.S. 439, 443 (1988) (wilderness "means commercial activities such as timber harvesting are forbidden"). Several courts have enjoined timber harvests in areas being considered for wilderness designation on the ground that wilderness suitability would be destroyed by logging.

Access to Non–Federal Inholdings

16 U.S.C. § 1134(a) requires the Secretary of Agriculture to give a non-federal property owner (state or private) whose land is "completely surrounded" by national forest wilderness, "such rights as may be necessary to assure adequate access" to the land, "or the [inholding] * * * shall be exchanged for" federal land of "approximately equal value" elsewhere in the state. Somewhat curiously, the latter clause is not clear on whether the choice to provide access or an exchange is the Forest Service's or the inholder's. The Ninth Circuit determined that "the Secretary has the option of exchanging land of equal value so that the wilderness may be preserved." Montana Wilderness Ass'n v. U.S. Forest Service, 655 F.2d 951, 957 n. 12 (9th Cir.1981).

16 U.S.C. § 1134(b) requires the Secretary of Agriculture to "permit ingress and egress * * * by means which have been or are being customarily enjoyed with respect to other such areas similarly situated" to "valid mining claims or other valid occupancies * * * wholly within a designated national forest wilderness area * * *." But it also says that the Secretary shall impose "reasonable regulations consistent with the preservation of the area as wilderness."

Water Resources

In the deliberations leading up to enactment of the Wilderness Act, traditional water resource development interests in the west (sometimes known as "water buffaloes") fought for the opportunity to build water projects inside wilderness areas. Wilderness advocates resisted, and the congressional compromise left the President (rather than the agency head or Cabinet officer) with the discretion, "under such regulations as he may deem desirable, [to] authorize" water resource development projects and ancillary facilities, including roads, "upon his determination that such use or uses in the specific area will better serve the interests of the United States and the people thereof than will its denial." 16 U.S.C. § 1133(d)(4). The authority has never been exercised, although former President Gerald Ford reportedly thwarted a proposed water project in a wilderness area near Vail, Colorado (where he maintained a residence) by lobbying a successor, Ronald Reagan, not to invoke the provision. The legislative history suggests this provision was intended to allow only small-scale water projects. Also on water, Section 1133(d)(6) provides that "nothing in this chapter shall constitute an express or implied claim or denial on the part of the Federal Government as to exemption from state water laws." Federal reserved water rights in wilderness is discussed in Chapter 6, *supra* p. 511.

Hunting and Fishing

Section 1133(d)(7) provides that "nothing in this Chapter shall be construed as affecting the jurisdiction or responsibilities of the several States with respect to wildlife and fish in the national forests;" thus hunting and fishing are generally allowed in most wilderness areas. In O'Brien v. State, 711 P.2d 1144 (Wyo.1986), the court relied on this section in holding that the Wilderness Act did not preempt a state law requiring non-resident hunters to employ guides when hunting in federal wilderness areas. But, the organic acts for the four principal federal land systems likely do provide preemptive authority if the agency chooses to use it.

Should managing agencies be under a legal obligation to reintroduce native species of flora and fauna that have been extirpated from wilderness areas, even those (like the wolf and the grizzly bear) that could pose a threat to persons or property inside or outside the wilderness? Should agencies have a duty to eliminate non-native species that have been introduced into such areas, even those (like certain species of sport fish) that attract substantial recreational use?

Buffer Zones

A number of statutes designating particular wilderness areas disclaim any intent on the part of Congress to create "protective perimeters or buffer zones around each wilderness area." *See, e.g.*, Arkansas Wilderness Act, § 7, 98 Stat. at 2352 (1984). In Newton County Wildlife Ass'n v. Rogers, 141 F.3d 803 (8th Cir.1998), the court relied on this language to reject a challenge to Forest Service timber sales outside of and upstream from designated wilderness areas, when the claim was that the logging would degrade the quality of water in streams flowing through the designated wilderness. If the Forest Service prohibited an activity outside a wilderness areas "solely because of its potential effect" on the area, it would violate the "no buffer zone" idea. The court went on, however, to conclude that the agency had "thoroughly considered the effect of logging and road construction on the water quality" of the streams in question, and concluded that it would be "insignificant," and the court found this not arbitrary or capricious. A similar interpretation was made in Northwest Motorcycle Association v. United States Department of Agriculture, 18 F.3d

1468, 1480 (9th Cir.1994), where the court upheld a Forest Service decision to eliminate ORV use in an area adjacent to a designated wilderness area, because it did so for numerous resource management reasons, including user conflicts, and not solely to create a buffer zone around the wilderness, even though the proximity to the wilderness was one factor in the agency's decision.

Air Quality

Congress recognized that preservation of the wilderness resource requires protection of the quality of its air as well as preservation of land and the living things on it. One part of the Clean Air Act, 42 U.S.C. §§ 7470–7492, restricts construction of major emitting facilities that will cause significant deterioration of air quality in areas zoned as "Class I," which includes designated wilderness areas over 5,000 acres (as well as national parks over 6,000 acres) in existence on August 7, 1977. Wilderness areas over 10,000 acres designated after that date may be re-designated as Class I.

3.   EXPANDING THE WILDERNESS SYSTEM

How many wilderness areas does the nation need? When asked this question long ago, Bob Marshall, one of the founders of the Wilderness Society, countered: "How many Brahms symphonies do we need?" But some oppose any wilderness at all, or say enough has already been designated.

Most of the wilderness areas designated in the Wilderness Act or shortly thereafter were so-called "rocks and ice" areas—high altitude, remote, relatively inaccessible and with few known resources of demand in the marketplace like timber and minerals. Since 1964, wilderness advocates have pushed for more designations, which have become more controversial over time.

Scrutiny of candidate areas for addition to the National Wilderness Preservation System has been conducted under several different processes, varying mostly by agency, with somewhat differing legal consequences. The Wilderness Act itself initiated the first of these wilderness study programs. In addition to creating "instant wilderness," it called for studies of three different categories of land for wilderness suitability, each to be completed within ten years: (a) Forest Service lands then administratively designated as primitive areas; (b) all roadless areas over 5000 acres and roadless islands of any size in the National Wildlife Refuge System; and (c) all National Park Service roadless areas of more than 5000 acres. 16 U.S.C. § 1133. In 1967 the Forest Service embarked on a voluntary study—beyond the requirements of the Wilderness Act itself—of all of its roadless lands (well over 50 million acres) for possible designation as wilderness. In 1976, FLPMA required a study of the wilderness potential of all roadless areas over 5000 acres on BLM lands, some 25 million acres. These last two major wilderness study efforts are treated in some detail further below.

One important question raised by many wilderness inventories is how to define a "road" because a key characteristic of wilderness is that it is "roadless." Many federal lands are traversed by jeep tracks or other ways created solely by use by vehicles, often 4x4s. Interestingly, the Wilderness Act itself does not define "road," even though it uses the term "roadless." Thus each agency has evolved its own definition of "road." *See, e.g.*, 43 C.F.R. § 19.2(e) (Fish and Wildlife Service and Park Service definition of "roadless area" to mean, among other things, where there is "no improved road that is suitable for public travel by means of four-wheeled, motorized vehicles intended primarily for highway use"). The BLM's definition comes from the House Committee Report on its governing statute, FLPMA, which defined "road" narrowly, to include only those vehicle tracks "which have been improved and maintained by mechanical means to insure relatively regular and continuous use. A way maintained solely by the passage of vehicles does not constitute a road." H.R.Rep.No. 94–1163, at 17 (1976).

The Forest Service's definition was discussed in Smith v. U.S. Forest Service, 33 F.3d 1072 (9th Cir.1994), as follows:

> [T]he agency has defined "roadless area" as an area "within which there are no improved roads maintained for travel by means of motorized vehicles intended for highway use." * * *
>
> The identification of "roads" in the National Forest System is a task legislatively delegated to the Department of Agriculture, and the agency is in far better position than we are to make these fact-specific determinations. In response to the district court's directive, Forest Service agents drove the length of Thompson Ridge Road in two four-wheel drive vehicles that were suitable for travel on U.S. interstates. The agency also conducted an historical evaluation and determined that Thompson Ridge Road had been created by bulldozer equipment in the early 1960s, and, periodically, had been maintained by the Forest Service. The agency concluded that the road was maintained for vehicles intended for highway use. After a careful review of the record, which includes photographs of Thompson Ridge Road, we find that the agency's conclusion, that the Conn Merkel Area is not a roadless area of more than 5,000 acres under the appropriate criteria, is not arbitrary and capricious. Accordingly, we are without jurisdiction to consider Smith's challenge to the agency's failure to consider the wilderness option in its NEPA documents. * * *

Another issue raised in many wilderness studies is how "purely natural" an area has to be to receive wilderness consideration. For quite some time, for example, the Forest Service was very reluctant to recommend wilderness designation for areas in the eastern United States. Many of these areas, almost all of which had been acquired under the Weeks Act, had been logged or otherwise developed decades earlier. Some critics argued that the agency was construing the definition of wilderness in the Act too narrowly. That definition seemed to offer something to each side of this "purity" debate, speaking as it did of areas "untrammeled by man" and "retaining * * * primeval character and influence," but also speaking of areas "generally *appear[ing]* to have been affected *primarily* by the forces of nature, with the imprint of man's work *substantially unnoticeable*." 16 U.S.C. § 1131(c) (emphasis added). Eventually the Forest Service adopted a more liberal view of wilderness for study purposes, and Congress has itself not hesitated to embrace wilderness that was less than pristine. For example, in its report on the Endangered American Wilderness Act of 1978, 92 Stat. 40, the House Interior Committee disapproved of the view that an area could be disqualified where "any trace of man's activity" was present, and where the "sights and sounds" of cities (often many miles away) could be perceived from anywhere in candidate areas. H.R.Rep. No. 95–540 at 4–6 (1977)). Two years earlier, finding that areas in "the more populous eastern half of the United States are increasingly threatened by the pressures of a growing and more mobile population, [and] large-scale industrial and economic growth," Congress designated as wilderness 15 national forest areas totaling 206,988 acres in Alabama, Arkansas, Florida, Georgia, Kentucky, North Carolina, New Hampshire, South Carolina, Tennessee, Virginia, Vermont, West Virginia, and Wisconsin. Pub.L. No. 93–622, 88 Stat. 2096. Many more eastern areas have been designated since then.

Congress has enacted dozens of statutes designating new wilderness areas. Each added area is governed generally by the provisions in the 1964 Act, although the legislation designating specific areas may vary these generic requirements in local settings. Often (though nothing requires this) Congress has found it easier to consider wilderness bills on a statewide basis, by individual federal managing agency. The Alaska National Interest Lands Conservation Act of 1980, 16 U.S.C. § 3101–3233, was easily the largest wilderness legislation; it designated 56.4 million Alaskan acres as wilderness, more than half of the entire system. All wilderness areas are listed in the Historical Note after 16 U.S.C. § 1132. The following charts show the size of the National Wilderness Preservation System as of 2007:

Agency	Units	Acres (in millions)	% of Total Area
Forest Service	418	35.4	32.9%
National Park Service	56	43.5	40.5%
U.S. Fish & Wildlife Service	71	20.7	19.3%
BLM	189	7.8	7.3%
	734	107.4	

Wilderness advocates have not, in general, focused all that much attention on securing legislation to designate Park and Refuge wilderness areas, and Congress has generally moved at a leisurely pace in making such designations. In both agencies, the acreage designated is heavily skewed toward Alaska. Eight Park Service wilderness areas in that state comprise more than 80% of the total park system wilderness acreage; just three of them—Gates of the Arctic Wilderness (over 7 million acres); Noatak Wilderness (5.8 million acres); and Wrangell–Saint Elias Wilderness (8.7 million acres)—together comprise almost one-half of all National Park wilderness acres. Twenty-one of the Fish & Wildlife Service's 71 designated wilderness areas are in Alaska, and they contain more than 90% of the total acreage in the refuge system. General Interior Department wilderness management regulations are found at 43 C.F.R. Pt. 19. De facto wilderness study and management in the U.S. Forest Service and the BLM have commanded the most attention and raised the most controversy. These are examined in turn.

a. THE NATIONAL FOREST SYSTEM

As noted above, the Wilderness Act itself required the Secretary of Agriculture to study all Forest Service lands administratively designated as "primitive areas" and recommend to the President, and the President to recommend to the Congress, whether such areas should be designated as wilderness. This gave rise to the first major court decision to address wilderness study issues. In Parker v. United States, 448 F.2d 793 (10th Cir.1971), the question was whether the Forest Service could sell timber in a national forest area that was adjacent to, but not within, such a "primitive area." The section of the Wilderness Act that called for a study and report to Congress on whether such "primitive areas" were suitable for designation as wilderness also provided that it should not "limit the President in * * * recommending the addition of any contiguous area of national forest lands predominantly of wilderness value." 16 U.S.C. § 1132(b). This seemed to leave it up to the executive branch to decide what to do with these adjacent areas, but the court didn't see it that way. The court began by describing the general purpose of the wilderness study provision this way:

> It is simply a congressional acknowledgment of the necessity of preserving one factor of our natural environment from the progressive, destructive and hasty inroads of man, usually commercial in nature, and the enactment of a "proceed slowly" order until it can be determined wherein the balance between proper multiple uses of the wilderness lies and the most desirable and highest use established for the present and future. A concerned Congress, reflecting the wishes of a concerned public, did by statutory definition choose terminology that would seem to indicate its ultimate mandate.

The court then held that the Forest Service and the timber company to whom it had sold timber in the area adjacent to the "primitive area" could not proceed to harvest the timber:

> Should we, in the case at bar, concede to federal appellants the discretionary right to destroy the wilderness value of the subject area, one contiguous to a designated wilderness, we would render meaningless the clear intent of Congress expressed in 16 U.S.C. § 1132(b) that both the President and the Congress shall have a meaningful opportunity to add contiguous areas predominantly of wilderness value to existing primitive areas for final wilderness designation. This statutory limitation on agency discretion is, of course, a narrow one dictated by necessity as contained in the definition of wilderness and by the specifics of the statutory words creating the limitation.

The court also ordered the Forest Service to include its study of the adjacent area in its report to the President and Congress, although it conceded that this did not limit the Secretary or the President in decided what to recommend to Congress about the future of the area.

Parker may have taken some liberties with the narrow statutory language, but its general thrust of limiting the discretion of federal land managing agencies to take wilderness-destroying actions in advance of congressional decision has generally been followed by the lower federal courts. The Supreme Court took a different path in the only decision it has rendered that deals with wilderness issues. Norton v. SUWA, *supra*, p. 224.

The Wilderness Act made no mention of the largest category of roadless areas in the national land estate—those wild lands in the National Forest System not already classified as wilderness or primitive areas or adjacent thereto. In a momentous step, the Forest Service voluntarily undertook a comprehensive wilderness study process of its roadless lands. This first Roadless Area Review and Evaluation (RARE I) evaluated all such areas for their wilderness potential, as a complement to the congressionally mandated study of primitive areas. The RARE I inventory, released in 1972, included 1449 areas totaling 56 million acres. Because this massive wilderness study was not mandated by the Wilderness Act, that statute provided no basis for judicial review. By this time, however, NEPA had been enacted, and it did give wilderness advocates a tool they have used frequently since.

When the Forest Service offered timber for sale in some of these inventoried roadless areas, the Sierra Club promptly filed suit under NEPA, and a district court in San Francisco preliminarily enjoined any new timber sales on RARE lands across the country until NEPA compliance was achieved. Sierra Club v. Butz, 3 ELR 20071 (N.D.Cal.1972). Soon thereafter the Tenth Circuit dropped a second shoe, by enjoining timber harvesting under some *existing* contracts in roadless areas because the Service failed to comply with NEPA. Wyoming Outdoor Coordinating Council v. Butz, 484 F.2d 1244 (10th Cir.1973). The court, echoing its earlier decision in *Parker*, found "there is an overriding public interest in preservation of the undeveloped character of the area."

The Service released a final national EIS on RARE I lands in October 1973. With the advent of a new Administration in 1977, the Forest Service essentially started over by developing a new roadless area inventory and a new study process, which naturally became known as RARE II. The new inventory included 2918 units (more than twice as many as RARE I) comprising slightly more than 62 million acres—six million more acres than RARE I and one-third of all land within the national forest system. The 1979 Final RARE II EIS recommended Congress designate fifteen million acres of RARE II lands as wilderness, called for further assessment of 10.8 million acres, and allocated the remaining thirty-six million acres to non-wilderness.

Once again wilderness advocates returned to court, challenging the adequacy of the agency's NEPA compliance. In the following case, the court sent the agency back to the drawing boards. The court described the "fundamental issue" as whether the Forest Service had made a critical decision with respect to lands it designated for nonwilderness uses.

California v. Block

United States Court of Appeals, Ninth Circuit, 1982.
690 F.2d 753.

■ JUDGE TANG

* * *

The Forest Service argues that the district court erred in concluding that Nonwilderness designation is tantamount to a decision to permit development. It emphasizes that the RARE II process is only the first step in a multi-stage planning process to allocate roadless areas to competing social uses. At this step, the Service contends, a RARE II Nonwilderness designation means only that the areas will not be considered for inclusion in the NWPS during the first generation of forest management plans under the NFMA, a period lasting between ten to fifteen years. In the meantime the Forest Service will entertain specific development proposals concerning these areas, but will prepare separate EIS's if federal action is contemplated and will consider wilderness values in devising forest plans for these areas. Given the limited impact of the Nonwilderness designation, the Forest Service urges that it is permissible to limit the scope of the EIS to a generalized discussion of the designations' overall impact.

California argues, and the district court agreed, that the Forest Service unfairly minimizes the consequences of the Nonwilderness designation. California and the district court decision focus upon the following Forest Service regulation pertaining to Nonwilderness designated areas:

> Lands reviewed for Wilderness designation under the review and evaluation of roadless areas conducted by the Secretary of Agriculture but not designated as wilderness or designated for further planning * * * will be managed for uses other than wilderness in accordance with this subpart. No such area will be considered for designation as wilderness until a revision of the forest plan....

36 C.F.R. § 219.12(e) (1981).

California and the district court decision interpret this regulation to mean that the Forest Service will not consider a Nonwilderness area's *wilderness features* for *any* purpose during the area's forest plan life. Thus, while an EIS on specific development proposals will consider substantial pollution effects, California argues that the Forest Service will be precluded from considering the desirability of utilizing the proposed site as a wilderness area, and will not consider wilderness features (e.g., solitude, primitive character and wilderness recreation) in assessing the environmental consequences. They conclude that if the wilderness features and values of each Nonwilderness area are ever to be individually evaluated, they must be evaluated now.

On balance, we conclude that California's description of the effect of Nonwilderness designation is more accurate and therefore affirm the district court. We agree with the Forest Service that the *last* sentence in the above quoted regulation only restricts the Forest Service from considering Nonwilderness areas for Wilderness designation, and does not explicitly forbid the Forest Service from considering Nonwilderness areas' wilderness features or values in devising forest plans. The sentence that *precedes* this clause, however, explicitly mandates that Nonwilderness areas "will be managed for uses other than wilderness." This command is not subject to any ambiguity. At least during the first generation of forest plans, Nonwilderness designated areas will be managed for purposes other than wilderness preservation. This command is repeated in the text of the Final EIS itself, which indicates that "[a]reas allocated to nonwilderness *will* become available on April 15, 1979, for multiple resource use activities *other than wilderness.*"

Future decisions concerning these areas will be constrained by this choice. While the regulations technically permit consideration of wilderness values and features in forest planning, such consideration is pointless in the absence of the discretion to manage a Nonwilderness area in a manner consistent with wilderness preservation. Similarly, the promise of site-specific EIS's in the future is meaningless if later analysis cannot consider wilderness preservation as an alternative to development. The "critical decision" to commit these areas for nonwilderness uses, at least for the next ten to fifteen years, is "irreversible and irretrievable." The site-specific impact of this decisive allocative decision must therefore be carefully scrutinized now and not when specific development proposals are made.

* * *

[The court went on to conclude that the final RARE II EIS was woefully lacking in site-specific consideration of the areas it recommended for nonwilderness uses.]

* * * Under Forest Service regulations, Nonwilderness areas may be reconsidered for Wilderness System inclusion in devising the second generation of forest plans ten to fifteen years hence. In the interim, however, these areas will be managed for uses other than wilderness. The foreclosing of the wilderness management option requires a careful assessment of how this new management strategy will affect each area's benchmark characteristics as identified in the Wilderness Act.

* * * While the EIS carefully identifies the economic benefit attributable to development in each area, no effort is made to weigh this benefit against the wilderness loss each area will suffer from development. This evaluation need not be in the form of a formal cost benefit analysis, but it should reflect that the Forest Service has compared for each area the potential benefits of Nonwilderness management against the potential adverse environmental consequences.

* * *

We concede that conducting a detailed site-specific analysis of the RARE II decision will be no simple task and will be laden with empirical uncertainty. The scope of the undertaking here, however, was the Forest Service's choice and not the courts'. NEPA contains no exemptions for projects of national scope. Having decided to allocate simultaneously millions of acres of land to nonwilderness use, the Forest Service may not rely upon forecasting difficulties or the task's magnitude to excuse the absence of a reasonably thorough site-specific analysis of the decision's environmental consequences.

* * *

NOTES AND QUESTIONS

1. On the EIS's lack of specificity in commenting upon individual roadless areas, the district court opinion noted (483 F.Supp. at 486 n. 22):

> The comments are of a brief, and very general nature. For example, one comment under the "opportunity for solitude" attribute merely stated "good topographical variation." The type of land features or vegetation present in this area is undisclosed. Major features of an area are reduced to highly generalized description such as "mountain" or "river." One can hypothesize how the Grand Canyon might be rated: "Canyon with river, little vegetation."

2. Does the decision in this case suggest that the RARE process—representing a systematic, nation-wide, comprehensive single process to evaluate wilderness suitability—was a mistake? If the agency had not embarked on the RARE II process, it would still have had to consider impacts on possible wilderness designation each time it undertook to sell timber or build roads or otherwise take actions in de facto wilderness that threatened the area's potential for designation as wilderness. But it would have been easier and less controversial to take such action individually and locally, rather than in a comprehensive, high visibility effort. Did the Clinton Administration's "roadless area initiative" recounted in Chapter 8C(6), make the same mistake?

3. The injunction entered in *California v. Block* covered only roadless areas recommended for non-wilderness in California, but it was still a major blow to the Forest Service wilderness review program because it effectively called into question the entire RARE II process. Shortly thereafter the Reagan Administration announced plans to scrap RARE II and start over with a new program dubbed (surprise) "RARE III," but soon Congress itself stepped into the breach, substantially short-circuiting the RARE III process in many states by passing nineteen separate wilderness bills in 1984 alone, adding nearly nine million acres (nearly all of it national forest land studied in the RARE II process) to the NWPS. This burst of legislation included about twenty individual state bills covering territory from New Hampshire to Georgia to California.

4. As explained in the following discussion of "release," the courts continue to hold agencies to a standard of strict accountability under NEPA when they propose to take actions on roadless lands that have the effect of removing an area from consideration for designation as wilderness.

NOTE: FUTURE WILDERNESS CONSIDERATION AND THE "RELEASE" ISSUE

For a long time a major point of contention in Forest Service (and BLM) wilderness legislation was the extent to which a congressional decision *not* to designate particular roadless tracts as statutory wilderness "released" them from further wilderness consideration in individual forest (or BLM) land use plans and NEPA decisionmaking. The timber and minerals industries and other wilderness opponents generally advocated what came to be known as "hard" release; namely, that once Congress had not included a particular area as wilderness in a piece of wilderness legislation covering that state or locality, it should be fully and permanently made available for non-wilderness uses without the need for further restrictions or evaluation. Wilderness advocates, on the other hand, argued for no release; that is, they wanted the agency to continue to consider the wilderness option in plans and EISs on development proposals as long as the area remained roadless.

The chasm between "hard" and no release stymied legislative action on wilderness for some time. In 1984 Congress adopted a compromise formula that came to be known as "soft" release, and thereafter included it in individual bills. "Soft" release means that roadless areas not designated by Congress as wilderness in a bill are "released" from further consideration until the agency prepares next generation of land use plans. The 1984 Washington State Wilderness Act (WSWA) contained typical "soft release" language, which came in two parts: One part provided that, with respect to lands reviewed in the RARE II process, and roadless tracts under 5000 acres in size, "the Department of Agriculture shall not be required to review the wilderness option prior to the revisions of the [NFMA] plans, but shall review the wilderness option when the plans are revised." In the meantime, such areas "shall be managed for multiple use: in accordance with applicable plans." 98 Stat. 299, 303–304. The other part aimed at preventing further environmental challenges to its decision to release roadless lands in the Washington national forests. The Act directed that RARE II be deemed adequate consideration of the suitability of inventoried land for classification as wilderness. 98 Stat. at 302–03.

The net effect was that the WSWA provided temporary general immunity for the Forest Service from wilderness-based judicial review with one exception: The agency had to consider the wilderness option prior to authorizing development in a roadless area if (1) the area had not been inventoried pursuant to RARE II; *and* (2) the area is larger than 5,000 acres in size. Smith v. United States Forest Service, 33 F.3d 1072 (9th Cir.1994), explores the implications of this "soft release" language. Wilderness advocates claimed that the Forest Service had failed in NEPA documents to address the impact of a timber sale on a roadless area of more than 6000 acres. The tract in question consisted of 4200 acres of uninventoried land and 2000 acres of inventoried land. The court concluded that it could "not review the adequacy of the agency's consideration of the wilderness option for this land because a portion of the land was inventoried pursuant to RARE II and the remainder is smaller than 5,000 acres." The wilderness advocates then argued that the agency still had a legal duty to consider the effect on the area's *roadless character* before deciding to sell timber in the area, and the court should enforce that duty. The Forest Service countered that the sole significance of the fact that a parcel of land is roadless is that the parcel is potentially eligible for wilderness designation. Because Congress has, in the WSWA, precluded judicial review of the suitability of inventoried lands for inclusion into the wilderness system, the appellees argue, the fact that a parcel of released land is roadless is, in itself, immaterial and need not be addressed in NEPA documents.

The court rejected the Forest Service's argument. It relied on an earlier decision, National Audubon Society v. U.S. Forest Service, 4 F.3d 832 (9th Cir.1993), which construed identical language in the 1984 Oregon Wilderness Act to allow judicial review of the agency's decision not to consider the effect of the proposed sale on roadless parcels of inventoried land. The language prohibiting judicial review, the court said in *National Audubon*, "applies not to *roadless or roaded* determinations, but to the Act's *wilderness or non-wilderness* designations. * * * Further, the Act provides that review of the *wilderness* option, and not of the *roadless* option," is not required prior to plan revision. 4 F.3d at 837 (emphasis in original). The court in *Smith* continued:

> The distinction we drew in *National Audubon* between wilderness designations and roadless determinations would be meaningless if, as the appellees suggest, an area's roadless character has no environmental significance. As we stated in that case, "the decision to harvest timber on a previously undeveloped tract of land is 'an irreversible and irretrievable decision' which could have 'serious environmental consequences.'" That the land has been released by Congress for nonwilderness use does not excuse the agency from complying with its NEPA obligations when implementing a land-use program.

> There is, moreover, an additional significance, beyond the effect on "roadlessness," to the agency's decision to approve a logging sale on a 5,000 acre roadless area. Judicial review of the wilderness option is not foreclosed forever by the WSWA. Under that Act, the wilderness option for inventoried lands may be revisited in second-generation Forest Plans. Accordingly, when the agency is considering the development of a 5,000 acre roadless area, selection of a no-action alternative, which the agency is required to consider [under NEPA], would preserve the possibility that the area might some day be designated as wilderness. Clearly, under the WSWA, the agency is not required to preserve any released roadless area for wilderness consideration in second-generation Forest Plans. But the possibility of future wilderness classification triggers, at the very least, an obligation on the part of the agency to disclose the fact that development will affect a 5,000 acre roadless area.

> The Forest Service argues that even if the fact that an area is roadless is environmentally significant, the documents it prepared in this case—the Colville Forest Plan EIS and the Gatorson EA—are adequate under NEPA. "Roadless character," the Forest Service asserts, is merely a synonym for specific environmental resources, including soil quality, water quality, vegetation, wildlife and fishery resources, recreational value, and scenic quality. All of these resources were addressed explicitly in the Gatorson EA, and the Forest Supervisor's finding that the

Gatorson Sale will have no significant impact on these resources has not, itself, been challenged by Smith. In addition, the Gatorson EA specifically discussed the effect of the sale on "unroaded solitude."

Nevertheless, we must conclude that the agency's NEPA documents are inadequate. * * * The agency has never, in its NEPA documents, taken into account the fact that the sale will affect a 5,000 acre roadless area. In both the Colville Forest EIS and the Gatorson EA, the agency recognized that a portion of the Twin Sisters RARE II Area contains no roads, but dismissed the fact as irrelevant for wilderness consideration purposes because that portion would not stand alone as a 5,000 acre roadless area. Similarly, in both documents, the agency concluded that the Conn Merkel Area cannot stand alone as a 5,000 acre roadless area because of Thompson Ridge Road. But nowhere has the agency disclosed that the inventoried and uninventoried lands together comprise one 5,000 acre roadless area. * * * [T]he decision to harvest timber in a 5,000 acre roadless area is environmentally significant. We held in *National Audubon* that the agency must, under NEPA, consider the effect of a logging project on such a resource. We now therefore must hold that the agency's obligation to take a "hard look" at the environmental consequences of the proposed sale and consider a no-action alternative require it, at the very least, to acknowledge the existence of the 5,000 acre roadless area.

The courts have construed the "release" immunity from judicial review narrowly in other contexts as well. *See, e.g.*, City of Tenakee Springs v. Block, 778 F.2d 1402 (9th Cir.1985).

A number of the statewide acts also direct that some specific roadless areas be put in a "further planning" category. The Forest Service employed this category for more than ten million acres in RARE II. The category is a form of limbo. Such lands are not wilderness per se but must be managed to preserve their wilderness characteristics until Congress revisits the question of whether to include them in the NWPS at some future time. Congress has, in other words, forbidden the agency from "releasing" these lands to nonwilderness uses.

The upshot of all this activity and controversy is a decidedly mixed legal picture for wilderness evaluation and planning on the national forests, varying from place to place, depending upon whether Congress has enacted a wilderness bill following on the RARE II process, and the specific terms of that bill. Where Congress has not acted, Forest Service proposals to develop areas that it has recommended against wilderness will presumably be subject to NEPA obligations (such as those spelled out in *California v. Block*), as well as possible challenge under other statutes such as the NFMA or the ESA. And, as we have seen, the lower courts have historically held the Forest Service strictly accountable for full compliance with NEPA on any decision to develop roadless lands in a way that takes the wilderness designation option off the table. Even where Congress has acted, areas not designated as wilderness that are subject to "soft release," and that have retained their wilderness characteristics, will be subject to further consideration for wilderness designation in the next generation of NFMA land use plans.

b.   BUREAU OF LAND MANAGEMENT LANDS

Considered strictly from a legal standpoint, Congress happily avoided many of the knotty problems involved in wilderness review on national forest lands when it came to create a wilderness review process for the BLM lands in 1976. Specifically, FLPMA established an unambiguous directive that within fifteen years the Secretary of the Interior "review those roadless areas [of the public lands] of five thousand acres or more * * * identified * * * as having wilderness characteristics described in the Wilderness Act." 43 U.S.C. § 1782(a). FLPMA directed the Secretary to recommend the suitability of the areas for wilderness preservation to the President. The President in turn was to forward his own recommendations to the Congress within two years of receiving those of the Secretary. As with other agencies, the executive's recommendations for wilderness "shall become effective only if so provided by an Act of Congress." 43 U.S.C. § 1782(b).

From a practical standpoint, however, the BLM wilderness review process has not been free from difficulty. BLM manages considerably more land than the Forest Service, with considerably fewer employees. In addition, BLM roadless areas tend to be more arid, at lower elevation, and tend to attract more competing uses in the form of hardrock mining, mineral leasing, and off-road vehicle recreation. Congress provided specific guidance on how the BLM lands identified as candidates for wilderness designation were to be managed during the study process, until Congress made final decisions. This so-called "interim management policy" generally requires that these lands must be managed "so as not to impair the[ir] suitability * * * for preservation as wilderness, subject, however, to the continuation of existing mining and grazing uses and mineral leasing in the manner and degree in which the same was being conducted on October 21, 1976." 43 U.S.C. § 1782(c), FLPMA § 603(c).

The key questions that have emerged in the BLM wilderness review may be subdivided into two categories: First, questions about the inventory process, of identifying public lands that are "roadless * * * with wilderness characteristics" for intensive study of their suitability for wilderness designation; and second, questions about "interim management" under Section 603(c)—how these identified lands are to be managed pending final decisions by Congress on whether to add them to the NWPS. These will be addressed in turn.

i.   THE INVENTORY PROCESS

The process by which the Secretary of the Interior was to identify BLM lands that were "roadless * * * with wilderness characteristics" was, according to FLPMA, to be the "inventory" of the "values and resources" of the public lands that Section 201(a) of FLPMA required to be maintained on a continuous basis. 43 U.S.C. § 1711(a). Partly for speed, administrative convenience, and efficiency, and partly to avoid disabling litigation over

proposals to develop roadless areas that had not yet been formally inventoried, the Secretary decided to conduct a generic, one-time review of all BLM
lands to identify these so-called "wilderness study areas," or WSAs. The
review was conducted pursuant to a "Wilderness Inventory Handbook"
("Handbook"), which identified the criteria for selecting wilderness study
areas (emphasis in original):

1.   Size. At least 5,000 contiguous roadless acres of public land.

2.   Naturalness. The imprint of man's work must be substantially
unnoticeable.

3.   Either:

   a.   An *outstanding* opportunity for solitude, or

   b.   An *outstanding* opportunity for a primitive and unconfined
   type of recreation.

Only areas meeting both factors 2 and 3 would be considered for wilderness
study. The Handbook also directed that areas with fewer than 5,000 acres
but which met factors 2 and 3 should also be identified as WSAs if they
were contiguous with land managed by another agency which either had
been formally determined to have potential wilderness values (for example,
Forest Service RARE II lands) or when combined with adjacent lands
managed by another agency totaled 5000 acres or more. Finally, the
Handbook also called for BLM voluntarily (that is, outside the scope of the
section 603 inventory, which applied only to tracts of 5,000 acres or more)
to identify tracts fewer than 5,000 acres which had "strong public support"
for wilderness study status, and which were "clearly and obviously of
sufficient size as to make practicable [their] preservation and use in an
unimpaired condition, and of a size suitable for wilderness management."

The initial inventory, completed in November 1980, reviewed nearly
174 million acres, and identified 919 WSAs totaling nearly twenty-four
million acres. The balance of land was found to be without the requisite
wilderness characteristics. 45 Fed.Reg. 77,574 (1980). In 1982 Secretary of
the Interior James Watt ordered that three categories of land be deleted
from WSA status: (1) lands in which the United States does not own the
subsurface mineral rights (split-estate lands); (2) lands that had been found
to have wilderness characteristics only in conjunction with lands administered by another agency; and (3) lands with fewer than 5,000 total acres.
All told, Watt's order stripped about 1.5 million acres of WSA status.

The Sierra Club promptly challenged these exclusions, and the court
rejected Watt's order in Sierra Club v. Watt, 608 F.Supp. 305 (E.D.Cal.
1985). On the exclusion of "split-estate" lands, the court noted that
FLPMA required wilderness review of "public lands," and that FLPMA
defined public lands as including "any land and interest in land owned by
the United States" with certain exceptions. 43 U.S.C. § 1702(e). It also
noted:

   A final basis for the IBLA's decision was that placement of the split-
   estate lands into the wilderness study under section 603 would be a
   futile exercise as the lands could never be placed in permanent wilder-

ness status. * * * It appears to the court that the IBLA simply misconstrues the statutory scheme and the nature of the wilderness review process. * * * The statutory scheme contemplated executive study but congressional disposition of wilderness issues. Clearly, if Congress elects to include within the wilderness preservation system split-estate lands, it may authorize the purchase or condemnation of the reserved mineral rights in the subsurface estate, or the exchange of reserved mineral rights for other federal lands or mineral interests.

608 F. Supp. at 335–6. The court went on to hold that the other parts of Secretary Watt's order were likewise invalid on the ground that it rested on the mistaken determination that Secretary Watt had no legal authority to classify tracts of BLM-managed land smaller than 5,000 acres as wilderness study lands. The court acknowledged that the Secretary had concluded, correctly, that sub–5,000 acre areas were exempt from the § 603 wilderness review process. But the Secretary overlooked the fact that he retained authority to classify these smaller tracts as wilderness study areas under FLPMA's general land use planning authority in § 202. Because of that, until the Secretary decided to overrule his predecessor and exclude the areas from wilderness consideration (a decision to which NEPA attaches), the court directed that the lands be managed to preserve their suitability for possible preservation as wilderness.

Given the long tradition of many BLM lands being open to mining, mineral leasing, grazing, and many other laws allowing exploitation and disposition, it was perhaps not entirely surprising that BLM's initial inventory of "wilderness study areas" yielded only about 24 million acres, or only about 13 percent of the roughly 180 million acres it manages in the lower 48 states (compared with somewhere between 30 and 40 percent of the national forest system being roadless). The rest were "released" from further study. Wilderness advocates and their allies in Congress did, however, produce considerable evidence that BLM inventory decisions in some regions, especially in the canyonlands of southern Utah, had wrongfully excluded roadless areas because of their potential for mineral or other uses. As the court pointed out in *Sierra Club v. Watt*, under FLPMA such a balancing of competing uses was to be made by BLM only at the second stage of the process—the determination whether to WSA was "suitable" for preservation as wilderness. And even then BLM's decision was only a recommendation, for Congress carefully reserved for itself, rather than the executive, the final decision on wilderness suitability.

The Interior Department chose not to appeal the *Sierra Club v. Watt* decision. A considerable portion of the split-estate lands in WSAs were then consolidated in U.S. ownership through land exchanges. Congress in 1990 enacted the first major BLM wilderness bill, which included as wilderness a number of these formerly split-estate areas (as well as several other tracts of BLM land in Arizona). 104 Stat. 4469 (1990).

A number of the BLM inventory decisions were appealed to the IBLA, where wilderness advocates met with mixed success. In the most important such case, covering nearly one million acres of Utah lands that BLM had not designated as WSAs, the IBLA reversed and remanded many of the individual areas to the BLM in a lengthy decision. Utah Wilderness Coalition, 72 IBLA 125 (1983). BLM ultimately reclassified about half this land as WSAs. In 1984 and 1985, the House Public Lands Subcommittee under Congressman John Seiberling held a series of oversight hearings to investigate problems with the BLM inventory, and requested the Secretary of the Interior to reexamine a number of specific areas in Utah, but the request was rebuffed. For a long time wilderness advocates adopted a rallying cry that BLM lands in Utah contained 5.2, then 5.4, then 5.9, and eventually something like nine million acres of wilderness, even though BLM's official inventory includes only about 3.25 million acres.

In the late 1990s, Secretary Bruce Babbitt ordered BLM to undertake another review of BLM lands in Utah to try to settle the question of how much roadless land existed under BLM's management there. The BLM's survey, begun in 1996, was interrupted when the State of Utah and other wilderness opponents obtained an injunction. After the appellate court threw out all but one of the State's claims on standing grounds, Utah v. Babbitt, 137 F.3d 1193 (10th Cir. 1998), BLM completed its survey in 1999, concluding that nearly six million acres could be classified as roadless with wilderness characteristics.

The story did not end there, however. The sole claim remanded by appellate court challenged BLM for illegally managing the inventoried areas as "de facto wilderness." Utah v. Babbitt, 137 F.3d at 1210–11. On remand, the claim languished until early 2003, when Utah filed an amended complaint and promptly reached what critics labeled a "sweetheart deal" settlement with the Interior Department, then headed by Secretary Gale Norton. In the settlement, the Interior Department repudiated prior agency legal positions and agreed that BLM was without authority to manage lands to protect their wilderness character if those lands had not been identified in BLM's initial inventories completed by 1991. (FLPMA called for the BLM lands to be reviewed and recommendations made to Congress regarding their wilderness suitability within fifteen years of enactment, or by October 1991.) A district court upheld the "no more wilderness" settlement against a challenge by conservation groups. Utah v. Norton, 2006 WL 2711798 (D.Utah 2006). As of this writing, that decision is on appeal.

Despite the settlement, the 1999 inventory may yet be relevant to land management in Utah. One court has held that BLM must at least consider impacts on wilderness character lands identified in the 1999 survey before permitting activities—such as leasing for oil development—that could destroy that character. Southern Utah Wilderness Alliance v. Norton, 457 F.Supp.2d 1253 (D.Utah 2006). As of this writing, that decision, too, is on appeal. These appeals may provide the appellate courts with an opportunity to address whether the Supreme Court's decision in Norton v. SUWA requires a retreat from the heightened scrutiny that the lower federal courts have generally brought to federal land management agency actions that would disqualify roadless areas from further consideration of wilderness.

ii.   INTERIM MANAGEMENT: FLPMA § 603(c)

Overall, about fourteen million acres of BLM land are in 610 wilderness study areas. Utah (3.3 million acres), Nevada (2.8), and Oregon (2.3) account for more than half of the WSA acreage. Although Section 603 originally applied to BLM lands in Alaska, ANILCA exempted Alaskan BLM lands from further mandatory wilderness study, although it allowed the Secretary to identify areas in Alaska "suitable as wilderness" and to recommend that Congress designate them. 94 Stat. 2487 (1980); adding 43 U.S.C. § 1784. Secretary Watt promptly ordered BLM not to consider wilderness any further in Alaska; Secretary Babbitt reversed that order, and Secretary Norton reinstated the Watt approach for the most part, ordering BLM to consider wilderness in planning only where it had broad support among elected Alaska officials. Her order did, however, allow BLM to continue to manage 800,000 acres in the Central Arctic Management Area primarily as wilderness.

The issues posed in the following case illuminate the interim management standards for WSAs under FLPMA. They also provide a useful lens for examining a host of issues already addressed, including statutory interpretation and deference to agencies; states' rights in common school grants; rights of access to inholdings and regulation of those rights; property rights/takings issues; regulation of mining claims; and preservation versus development.

State of Utah v. Andrus

United States District Court, District of Utah, 1979.
486 F.Supp. 995.

■ CHIEF JUDGE ANDERSON

[Cotter Corporation (Cotter), a uranium mining subsidiary of Commonwealth Edison, an electrical utility in northern Illinois, acquired mining claims on federal land and a mineral lease on a state school section in an area of Utah, and began exploration for uranium deposits. Cotter constructed some access roads across BLM land without notifying the agency. BLM was in the meantime engaged in its wilderness inventory under FLPMA, and preliminarily identified land in the vicinity of the Cotter exploration as a wilderness study area. When BLM became aware of Cotter's road construction, it requested that it be halted. Cotter agreed for a period of time, but then decided to resume construction, and BLM brought suit. The state of Utah intervened as a defendant.]

* * *

At stake here are three very important and conflicting interests. The state of Utah has a clear interest in protecting its rights under the grant of school trust lands and in being able to use those lands so as to maximize the funds available for the public schools. Cotter, of course, has an interest in developing its claims in the most economical way possible. Finally, the United States has an interest in preserving for future generations the opportunity to experience the solitude and peace that only an undisturbed natural setting can provide. As noted herein, these public interests conflict. This is reflected in the more narrow questions of statutory interpretation and reconciliation posed for decision. In order to resolve the issues and effect a balance of interests, it is important to examine each interest and its statutory base.

I. State School Trust Land

* * * [T]he state school land grants were not unilateral gifts made by the United States Congress. Rather, they were in the nature of a bilateral compact entered into between two sovereigns. In return for receiving the federal lands Utah disclaimed all interest in the remainder of the public domain, agreed to forever hold federal lands immune from taxation, and agreed to hold the granted lands, or the proceeds therefrom, in trust as a common school fund. Thus, the land grants involved here were in the nature of a contract, with a bargained-for consideration exchanged between the two governments.

Recognition of the special nature of the school land grants is important both in determining the Congressional intent behind the grant and in understanding judicial treatment of similar grants. Generally, land grants by the federal government are construed strictly, and nothing is held to pass to the grantee except that which is specifically delineated in the instrument of conveyance. E.g., United States v. Union Pacific Railroad Co., 353 U.S. 112, 116 (1957). But the legislation dealing with school trust land has always been liberally construed. * * *

Given the rule of liberal construction and the Congressional intent of enabling the state to use the school lands as a means of generating revenue, the court must conclude that Congress intended that Utah (or its lessees) have access to the school lands. Unless a right of access is inferred, the very purpose of the school trust lands would fail. Without access the state could not develop the trust lands in any fashion and they would become economically worthless. This Congress did not intend.

Further, traditional property law concepts support Utah's claimed right of access. Under the common law it was assumed that a grantor intended to include in the conveyance whatever was necessary for the use and enjoyment of the land in question. * * * When a grantor conveys only a portion of his land, and the land received by the grantee is surrounded by what the grantor has retained, it is generally held that the grantee has an easement of access, either by implication or necessity, across the grantor's land. * * * Although this common law presumption might not ordinarily apply in the context of a federal land grant, the liberal rules of construction applied to school trust land allow for the consideration of this common law principle and justify its application here.[2]

Therefore, the court holds that the state of Utah and Cotter Corporation, as Utah's lessee, do have the right to cross federal land to reach

---

2. The case of Leo Sheep Co. v. United States, 440 U.S. 668 (1979) is not apposite. In that case the United States Supreme Court held that the government had not reserved an access easement in a particular land grant because the government had the power to condemn the land in question. The defendants in this case have no such power.

section 36, which is a portion of the school trust lands. The extent and nature of that right, however, remain to be determined. In order to reach that decision the court must examine the character and extent of BLM's authority under the Federal Land Policy and Management Act.

II. Federal Land Policy and Management Act

* * *

A. BLM's Authority under FLPMA

Under section 603(c) [43 U.S.C. § 1782(c)], BLM is required, during the period of wilderness review, to manage the public land

> in a manner so as *not to impair the suitability of such areas for preservation as wilderness, subject,* however, to the continuation of *existing mining* * * * *uses* * * * *in the manner and degree* in which the same *was being conducted* on October 21, 1976: *Provided,* That, in managing the public lands [BLM] shall by regulation or otherwise *take any action required to prevent unnecessary or undue degradation* of the lands and their resources or to afford environmental protection.

(Emphasis added in part.)

Cotter argues that this language authorizes only one management standard: preventing undue or unnecessary degradation of the environment. It is Cotter's position that the use of the word "impair" "merely gives direction to the existing authority of [BLM] to manage with a view toward environmental protection."

The United States, on the other hand, argues that under section 603(c) there are two management standards: one that applies to uses of the land existing on October 21, 1976, and one that applies to uses coming into existence after that date. Under this interpretation, existing uses are to be regulated only to the degree required to prevent unnecessary and undue degradation. New uses, however, may be (indeed, must be) regulated to the extent necessary to prevent impairment of wilderness characteristics. Obviously, the latter standard is more strict.

The Solicitor of the Department of Interior has issued an opinion dated September 5, 1978, (hereinafter referred to as "Solicitor's Opinion") which interprets the effect of section 603(c). Under this interpretation, section 603(c) does indeed mandate two standards, the first of which governs regulation of uses not in existence on October 21, 1976, and the second of which governs uses existing on that date. Generally, the interpretation of a statute by those charged with its execution is entitled to great deference. E.g., Udall v. Tallman, 380 U.S. 1, 16 (1965). The court can find no reason not to give such deference in this case.

Further, the Solicitor's interpretation finds support in the Act's legislative history. In the Report accompanying the House version of what was to become FLPMA, the language of section 603(c) was described as follows:

> While tracts are under review, they are to be managed in a manner to preserve their wilderness character, *subject to continuation of existing grazing and mineral uses and appropriation under the mining laws.*

The Secretary *will continue* to have authority to prevent unnecessary and undue degradation of the lands, including installation of minimum improvements, such as wildlife habitat and livestock control improvements, where needed for the protection or maintenance of the lands and their resources * * *. (Emphasis added.)

It appears to the court that the above passage indicates that the authority to manage lands so as to prevent impairment of wilderness characteristics was meant to be a new addition to the Secretary's continuing authority to regulate all uses so as to prevent undue degradation. Other parts of the legislative history confirm this view. * * *

* * * It appears that the Senate and the House were concerned about devising a way to protect both existing uses and wilderness values present on tracts not subject to existing uses. As interpreted by the Solicitor, section 603(c) reflects that concern. The Secretary's authority to preserve wilderness is subject to existing uses which may not be arbitrarily terminated, nor regulated solely with a view to preserving wilderness characteristics. But the Secretary may continue to regulate such uses in order to prevent unnecessary or undue degradation. On the other hand, activity on lands with potential wilderness value which are not subject to existing uses may be regulated more stringently so as to preserve wilderness characteristics. The Solicitor's interpretation is consistent with the Act's legislative history and reflects the full measure of Congressional intent in the adoption of 603(c). Cotter's interpretation reflects only one of Congress' concerns, i.e., protection of existing uses.

Finally, the Solicitor's interpretation is supported by the language and structure of the statute itself. The word "impair" would prevent many activities that would not be prevented by the language of "unnecessary or undue degradation." For example, commercial timber harvesting, if conducted carefully, would not result in unnecessary or undue degradation of the environment. But the same activity might well impair wilderness characteristics as those are defined in 16 U.S.C. § 1131. * * * Further, if Congress had not intended to mandate two standards, it would merely have indicated that the Secretary was to continue to manage all lands so as to prevent unnecessary degradation. If one takes the position that this is what Congress intended, then the language of impairment must be mere surplusage. Statutory rules of construction are against such a finding.

* * *

Therefore, the court holds that under the terms of FLPMA the BLM has the authority to manage public lands so as to prevent impairment of wilderness characteristics, unless those lands are subject to an existing use. In the latter case BLM may regulate so as to prevent unnecessary or undue degradation of the environment.

B. Cotter's Rights under FLPMA

Given that there are two standards by which BLM can manage the public lands, it remains to be determined what standards apply to Cotter's activity. Cotter argues that its activity falls within the existing use provision of 603(c). The main thrust of Cotter's argument is as follows:

(1) under the Mining Law of 1872, Cotter has a right of access to its unpatented claims;

(2) Cotter, as Utah's lessee, also has a right of access to state school land;

(3) these rights, even though not exercised prior to October, 1976, constitute existing uses under FLPMA.

Section 603(c) mandates that existing uses may continue in the "same manner and degree" as being conducted on October 21, 1976. Unless the statute is referring to activity that was actually taking place on that date, there is no way to give meaningful context to the "manner and degree" language. In order to determine whether or not a given operation is being conducted in the same manner and degree as it was formerly being conducted, there must be *some* former activity against which the extent of the present operation can be measured. Presumably, when the statute refers to existing uses being carried out in the same manner and degree it is referring to *actual* uses, not merely a statutory right to use.

Cotter next points to section 302(b) as an indication that its rights of access cannot be denied under FLPMA. Cotter's emphasis in quoting 302(b) is, however, selective. Section 302(b) provides in pertinent part:

Except as provided in 1744, 1781(f) and *1782 [section 603]* of this title and in the last sentence of this paragraph no provision of this section or any other section of this Act shall in any way amend the Mining Law of 1872 or impair the rights of any locators of claims under that Act, including, but not limited to, rights of ingress and egress. (Emphasis added.)

Cotter emphasizes only the latter portion of this section and from this argues that no provision of FLPMA can be taken to amend the Mining Law of 1872. On its face, however, this section makes clear that section 603 *does* amend the Mining Law of 1872. Rights under that law, including rights of ingress and egress, can be impaired by virtue of section 603. Moreover, the Mining Law itself makes clear that rights of access to mining claims are not absolute. Such rights are subject to regulation under 30 U.S.C. § 22.

* * *

It is clear that the Congress intended to provide a balanced solution to the problem of land management during the inventory process. While Congress did not intend the use of public lands to be frozen pending the outcome of the inventory process, neither did it want future uses to be foreclosed by the impact of present activity. Further, the Congress recognized that it might not be possible to both allow present uses and prevent foreclosure of certain other future uses.

This is consistent with the decision in Parker v. United States, supra. In that case, involving the Wilderness Act, the court held that the Department of Agriculture could not take any action that would foreclose Congressional consideration of an area's potential for wilderness designation. In this case, if BLM could not prevent activity that would permanently impair wilderness characteristics, then those characteristics could be destroyed before either BLM or the Congress had the chance to evaluate an area's potential uses. This Congress did not intend.

* * *

BLM's authority is, however, limited to preventing *permanent* impairment of potential wilderness values. Although it is not explicitly provided for in FLPMA, it is consistent with Congress' attempt to balance competing interests and with the Wilderness Act which provides the legislative backdrop for section 603 to find that if a given activity will have only a temporary effect on wilderness characteristics and will not foreclose potential wilderness designation then that activity should be allowed to proceed.

The definition of wilderness provided for in the Wilderness Act (16 U.S.C. § 1131[c]) and incorporated by reference into FLPMA in section 603(a) contemplates that some human activity can take place in wilderness areas as long as the area "*generally* appears to have been affected *primarily* by the forces of nature, with the imprint of man's work *substantially* unnoticeable * * *."

Further, the draft statement of BLM's Interim Management Policy and Guidelines for Wilderness Study Areas recognizes that temporary activities, the negative impacts of which could be substantially reversed through appropriate reclamation procedures, would not impair wilderness characteristics under the terms of 603(c).

There has been a great deal of argument in this case over whether or not the effects of Cotter's proposed road and drilling operations can be successfully reclaimed. Unfortunately the factual matters inherent in such an argument have not been sufficiently addressed. At the July 12 hearing on the motion for permanent injunction, Cotter proffered, for the first time, its reclamation plan. BLM has not had the opportunity to review the plan nor to make a comparison of the costs and feasibility of reclamation of a land access route over the cost and effect of other forms of access.

In view of the court's findings and conclusions of law, the BLM must be given the opportunity to review and respond to Cotter's reclamation plan. * * * The court is ill-equipped at this stage of the litigation to make a factual determination on the complex question of the comparative costs and feasibility of reclamation efforts over other forms of access. Thus, the court orders that BLM must be given the opportunity to expeditiously review Cotter's reclamation plan with a view to determining whether or not the impact of the proposed road will be temporary or permanent and with a view toward comparing the cost and feasibility of reclamation with the cost and feasibility of alternative forms of access.

If BLM should decide that the effects of the road will, indeed, be permanent, then the parties (and probably this court) may be required to confront this and other disputed issues. * * * [I]n light of the possibility that further litigation will be necessary, and in light of the fact that throughout the litigation BLM has assumed that the effects of the road would be permanent and thus has put the questions of regulation of access to federal and state land at issue, the court will address the questions remaining in the lawsuit.

III.   FLPMA and the State School Lands

The state must be allowed access to the state school trust lands so that those lands can be developed in a manner that will provide funds for the common schools. Further, because it was the intent of Congress to provide these lands to the state so that the state could use them to raise revenue, the access rights of the state cannot be so restricted as to destroy the lands' economic value. That is, the state must be allowed access which is not so narrowly restrictive as to render the lands incapable of their full economic development.

* * *

Thus, the court finds that (1) BLM can regulate the method and route of access to state school trust lands; (2) this regulation may be done with a view toward preventing impairment of wilderness characteristics (assuming no existing use); (3) the regulation may not, however, prevent the state or its lessee from gaining access to its land, nor may it be so prohibitively restrictive as to render the land incapable of full economic development.

IV.   FLPMA and Access Rights Over Federal Land

Section 701(h) [codified at 43 U.S.C. § 1701 note] of FLPMA provides:

"All actions by the Secretary concerned under this Act shall be subject to valid existing rights."

The Solicitor has interpreted this section to mean that valid existing rights cannot be taken pursuant to section 603. The court agrees with this interpretation. The court has also found, however, that Cotter's right of access to both its federal and state claims can be regulated.

The parties have stipulated that "Cotter's proposed road appears to be the only feasible and least environmentally disruptive *land access* for Cotter to its targeted drilling sites *and* for entry into state section 36 * * *." Thus, in this case, regulation to prevent wilderness impairment could result in total prohibition of land access. BLM has contended that helicopter access is available, feasible and acceptable to the agency. Cotter contends that such access would be prohibitively expensive and would not result in any substantial saving of the environment. This issue was not, however, the subject of live testimony with full cross-examination. The court is not, therefore, provided with sufficient information on which to base a ruling. To further complicate the case, it is not clear that the entire proposed road is necessary for Cotter to gain access to section 36. This is important because different criteria may be applied to judge the propriety of regulation of state, as opposed to federal, access rights. It may be that requiring helicopter access to section 36 would be sufficiently expensive so as to render minerals on that section incapable of economic development. Therefore, requiring such access and denying land access would violate the intent of the school trust grant. It may be, however, that requiring such access to federal claims would not be so expensive as to constitute a taking under 701(h). If the entire road is not necessary to gain access to section 36, then it could be that substantial parts of it could be prohibited, while other parts could not. Unfortunately, on the record as it now stands, this matter is far from clear.

* * *

In sum, the court holds that Utah does have a right of access to state school trust lands. That right is subject to federal regulation when its exercise requires the crossing of federal property. Such regulation cannot, however, prohibit access or be so restrictive as to make economic development competitively unprofitable. Further, the court holds that BLM may regulate federal public land so as to prevent impairment of wilderness characteristics. Such authority is, however, subject to uses which were existing on October 21, 1976. These uses must have been actually existing on that date. Cotter's right to gain access was not an existing use on October 21, 1976. Therefore, Cotter's activity may be regulated so as to prevent wilderness impairment. But such regulation cannot be so restrictive as to constitute a taking. * * *

* * *

NOTES AND QUESTIONS

1.   On these facts, does Cotter Corp. have valid rights against the federal government under the Mining Law? Do its claims give it the right to build a road across federal lands to its claims? Might, instead, the BLM require Cotter to use helicopter or pack mule access to its claims? Is Cotter protected by the "grandfather" clause of Section 603 of FLPMA?

2.   What right of access does the state of Utah have to cross federal land to reach the isolated common school grant sections of land it owns? Notice that this case was decided before Congress added a general access provision in the Alaska National Interest Lands Conservation Act in 1980. If this case arose today, would the BLM access section of that legislation apply? Would it change the outcome? Assuming the state has some right of access to its inholding, to what extent can the access rights be regulated by the United States? Is the state protected by the "grandfather" clause of Section 603?

3.   Is the state's right of access to its inholding stronger, weaker, or the same as Cotter Corp.'s right of access to its federal mining claims?

4.   Section 302(b) of FLPMA directs the Secretary to prevent "unnecessary or undue degradation" of public lands everywhere. 43 U.S.C. § 1732(b). What is the difference, if any, between regulating against a standard of "non-impairment" of suitability for preservation as wilderness, and regulating against a standard of preventing "unnecessary or undue degradation of the lands"? Section 603(c) of FLPMA repeats this language as a standard for regulating grandfathered "existing mining and grazing uses and mineral leasing" in WSAs, and then adds the directive that the Secretary shall "afford environmental protection." What do those last three words add, if anything, to the Secretary's authority to regulate the State or Cotter here?

5. Another part of Section 603(c) provides that the Secretary shall not withdraw BLM wilderness study areas from operation of the Mining Law *except* "for reasons other than preservation of their wilderness character." Could the Secretary withdraw the area involved in *Utah v. Andrus* from the Mining Law in order to protect its wildlife values or its scenery? Assuming the Secretary did so, and the withdrawal was valid, what effect, if any, would it have on Cotter Corp.'s rights to develop its uranium claims?

6. Is the court realistic in its expectation that access can be regulated to prevent impairment of wilderness values without rendering "the land incapable of full economic development"? Should the court have removed the word "full"? The Wilderness Act and FLPMA, like most statutes, are products of compromise. Is the court's interpretation of this particular compromise realistic? Should the court have chosen to privilege either the wilderness or the mining use? Or did it?

The district court's opinion in Utah v. Andrus was not appealed. Instead, the BLM determined that the specific area in question did not have "wilderness characteristics" and it was not classified as a wilderness study area under Section 603. Years later, however, the Tenth Circuit in effect affirmed much of the district court's view of Section 603 in Sierra Club v. Hodel, 848 F.2d 1068 (10th Cir.1988). There, having determined that the county in that case had a valid existing right of way under R.S. 2477, the court proceeded to mesh that right with the interim management scheme of § 603(c).

In the meantime, shortly after the Reagan Administration had taken office, its new Solicitor issued an opinion modifying the 1978 opinion discussed in Utah v. Andrus, 88 I.D. 909 (1981). The new opinion focused on the "savings clause" in FLPMA that made "[a]ll actions by the Secretary * * * under this Act * * * subject to valid existing rights." § 701(h); 43 U.S.C. § 1701 note. In conformity with this opinion, BLM modified its Interim Management Policy to provide, in pertinent part (quoted at 848 F.2d at 1086):

> Valid existing rights limit the nonimpairment standard. Although the nonimpairment standard remains the norm, valid existing rights that include the right to develop may not be restricted to the point where the restriction unreasonably interferes with the enjoyment of the benefit of the right. Resolution of specific cases will depend upon the nature of the rights conveyed and the site-specific conditions involved. When it is determined that the rights conveyed can be exercised only through activities that will impair wilderness suitability, the activities will be regulated to prevent unnecessary or undue degradation. Nevertheless, even if such activities impair the area's wilderness suitability, they will be allowed to proceed.

The Tenth Circuit approved this approach:

> The conflict between FLPMA's savings provisions [protecting "valid existing rights"] and the nonimpairment standard of § 603(c) constitutes a latent ambiguity in the statute. * * * BLM * * * [has] reconciled FLPMA's express protection of valid existing rights with the conservation duties under § 603(c) by analogizing the valid existing rights to the grandfathered uses and affording them the same protections. We uphold this interpretation as a reasonable one.

848 F.2d at 1087–88. The Tenth Circuit went on to affirm the district court order that the county apply for a right-of-way permit under FLPMA in order to move the road in question from an area known as The Gulch to another location on an adjacent bench. The lower court had made this order based on its finding that, while the county had a "valid existing right" to the existing road in the Gulch area, a significant upgrading of that road in that location would "unreasonably or unduly degrade the adjacent WSA * * *." The Tenth Circuit approved the trial judge's fine-tuned accommodation of "valid existing rights" with protection of wilderness values:

> Although the district court ordered the County to apply to BLM for a permit to move the road, we do not construe that order to mean that BLM may deny the permit, or impose conditions it might [impose] on ordinary right-of-way requests under FLPMA which would keep the County from improving the road. Rather, the effect of the order is to require BLM to specify where on the bench the road should be located in order that it make the least degrading impact on the WSA, the court having already determined that location on the bench would be less degrading than in the Gulch. * * * [W]e are satisfied that BLM * * * must allow the road improvement in one place or the other. So construed, we have no problems with the [lower] court's order. This did not end the matter, however, because the court then addressed whether NEPA applied to the BLM's regulatory decision in applying the "unnecessary or undue degradation" standard to the county's valid existing right. Here it agreed with the Sierra Club that the BLM's duty to regulate injects an element of federal control for required action that elevates this situation to one of major federal action [subject to NEPA]. * * * [A]s to improvement on rights-of-way affecting WSAs, while BLM may not deny improvements because they impair WSAs, it retains a duty to see that they do not unduly degrade. * * * Thus, when a proposed road improvement will impact a WSA the agency has a duty under FLPMA § 603(c) * * * to determine whether there are less degrading alternatives, and it has the responsibility to impose an alternative it deems less degrading upon the nonfederal actor. While this obligation is limited by BLM's inability to deny the improvement altogether, it is sufficient, we hold, to invoke NEPA requirements.

848 F.2d at 1090–91.

Shortly after the district court opinion in Utah v. Andrus, and with guidance from the Solicitor, BLM promulgated its so-called IMP, or "Interim Management Policy and Guidelines for Lands Under Wilderness Review." Among other things, the IMP said that activities may be deemed nonimpairing if they are "temporary." It defined "temporary" as where the impacts are "capable of being reclaimed to a condition of being substantially unnoticeable in the wilderness study area * * * as a whole by the time the Secretary is scheduled to send his recommendations on that area to the President." The objective was, according to the IMP, to avoid "significantly constrain[ing] the Secretary's recommendation with respect to the area's suitability or nonsuitability for preservation as wilderness."

In Sierra Club v. Clark, 774 F.2d 1406 (9th Cir.1985), challenging the Barstow to Las Vegas motorcycle race, the plaintiffs attacked the BLM's decision to allow the race despite its adverse impacts on a WSA. The court conceded the adverse impacts, but upheld BLM's determination that they were not "sufficiently egregious" to violate the IMP standard. It permitted the race to proceed because its impacts would be substantially unnoticeable "in the context of the WSA as a whole—not on a parcel-by-parcel basis." Does the BLM's interpretation, which the Court allowed to stand, mean that the larger the wilderness study area, the greater the impact allowed on any one part of it?

Numerous questions remain regarding the IMP. For example, may the BLM open up a previously ungrazed WSA to livestock grazing, arguing that this does not impair its suitability for preservation as wilderness because livestock grazing is itself allowed in designated wilderness? *See* Committee for Idaho's High Desert, 108 IBLA 277 (1989).

In enacting wilderness bills in California, Arizona and Nevada, Congress has generally included "soft release" language providing that all the WSAs in the area covered by the bill not designated as wilderness by that bill "are no longer subject to" the non-impairment standard of § 603(c), with some exceptions. See, e.g., 108 Stat. 4482–83 (1994). While this approach releases BLM from any mandatory obligation to protect the wilderness qualities of these areas, it does not prevent BLM from managing these areas as *de facto* wilderness or reconsidering whether to recommend that any of them be designated as wilderness in future BLM land use planning. But the "no more wilderness" settlement between the Bush Administration and the State of Utah (described above) effectively converts this "soft release" language into "hard" release, because the settlement embodies the position that Interior no longer has authority to protect wilderness qualities per se in its roadless areas.

c.   MINERAL LEASING IN WILDERNESS STUDY AREAS

Because the Forest Service roadless area review was not driven by statute (other than respecting so-called "primitive areas"), mineral leasing was still possible in national forest roadless areas for many years (assuming NEPA would have been complied with). When Congress directed a wilderness review for BLM lands in FLPMA (discussed further below), it did address mineral leasing. Specifically, § 603(c) provided generally that wilderness study areas should be managed to preserve their suitability for designation as wilderness until Congress decides upon their future, and then provided, somewhat awkwardly, for "the continuation [in wilderness study areas] of * * * mineral leasing in the manner and degree in which the same was being conducted on October 21, 1976." In a 1978 opinion, the Interior Solicitor concluded that the reference to "existing * * * mineral leasing" in the grandfather clause referred to actual, on-the-ground activities being conducted under mineral leases in force on that date. BLM could continue to issue mineral leases in WSAs, but only if it included in the leases themselves a standard "wilderness protection stipulation" that put lessees on notice that any activity they might wish to undertake on the lease was subject to the "non-impairment" standard.

The oil and gas industry promptly challenged the Solicitor's interpretation of the grandfather clause, but the Tenth Circuit upheld the Solicitor. Rocky Mountain Oil & Gas Ass'n (RMOGA) v. Watt, 696 F.2d 734 (10th Cir. 1982). Closely analyzing the statute and its legislative history, the court concluded:

> One of the prime concerns of Congress in enacting the FLPMA was that BLM lands suitable for wilderness preservation at the date of the Act's passage be given a chance for consideration as wilderness. Under Interior's policy, the wilderness review period will result in only a brief hiatus from potential mineral development for most of the lands concerned. Lands containing oil and gas, and of no wilderness value, will be released from the review unharmed and fully suitable for mineral development. Under RMOGA's interpretation, however, lands suitable for wilderness could be irrevocably altered by development and their wilderness values destroyed. It would be [inconsistent with the statute to] give disruptive mineral leasing activities carte blanche.

> In light of the language of section 603(c) and its legislative history, we hold that Interior's interpretation of the section's effect on mineral leasing activities, as expressed in the Solicitor's Opinion of September 5, 1978, is reasonable and entitled to deference. Indeed, under our analysis it is compelling. We hold that mineral leasing is subject to the nonimpairment standard of section 603(c), and that the grandfather clause affords protection only to activities on mineral leases in the manner and degree actually occurring on October 21, 1976. * * *

Eventually, in the wake of strenuous efforts by Secretary of the Interior James Watt to open both designated wilderness and wilderness study areas to mineral leasing, Congress confirmed and expanded upon the result in the *RMOGA* case by calling a nearly complete halt to mineral leasing in wilderness study areas on both BLM and national forest land. A moratorium on mineral leasing (including geothermal leasing) was first adopted annually as an appropriations rider and was made permanent in the Federal Onshore Oil & Gas Leasing Reform Act in 1987; *see* 30 U.S.C. § 226–3. The only exception is "where oil and gas leasing is specifically allowed to continue by the statute designating the study area." Congress left intact the Secretary's authority to issue permits for mineral exploration under the mineral leasing laws "by means not requiring construction of roads or improvement of existing roads if such activity is conducted in a manner compatible with the preservation of the wilderness environment." *Id.* § 226–3(b).

While there generally can be no new mineral leasing in such areas until Congress acts, some of these study areas on both Forest Service and BLM lands are encumbered with mineral leases issued prior to the moratorium. On BLM land, *RMOGA* affirmed the conclusion in the 1978 Solicitor's Opinion that the FLPMA grandfather clause protects only actual physical activities being conducted on those leases from the non-impairment standard. Mineral lessees who were not conducting any such activities when FLPMA was enacted might have had a takings or a rescission argument if they were prevented from developing their leases by the non-impairment standard. But this risk has diminished over time as leases in wilderness study areas have expired. On Forest Service land, where no statute addresses the handling of existing mineral leases, the matter is less clear.

B. EXTERNAL THREATS

Previous chapters considered a variety of what might be called "internal" threats to the "naturalness" of federal land areas; *e.g.*, off-road vehicles in Chapter 11. The federal land management agencies generally have adequate legal authority to deal with such internal threats, if they can muster the political will to do so and valid existing rights do not interfere. Sometimes, however, activities conducted outside a land unit's boundaries pose equally serious threats to the preservation resource. External threats arise with respect to all federal land management agencies. But, the problem has received the most attention at national parks. The materials that follow in this section consider two different kinds of "external" threats: First, those emanating from non-federal lands; and second, those emanating from federal lands or projects under the jurisdiction of other federal agencies.

1. EXTERNAL THREATS FROM NON-FEDERAL LANDS

No generic legislation deals with such external threats, but Congress, the Park Service, and the courts have occasionally addressed such issues in specific contexts. The Redwood National Park litigation that follows raises a variety of interesting questions on this dilemma.

Sierra Club v. Department of Interior I

United States District Court, Northern District of California, 1974.
376 F.Supp. 90.

■ JUDGE SWEIGERT

This is an action by plaintiff, Sierra Club, against the Department of the Interior, and officials of the Department, to obtain judgment of this court directing defendants to use certain of their powers to protect Redwood National Park from damage allegedly caused or threatened by certain logging operations on peripheral privately-owned lands.

* * *

[Congress created the Redwood National Park by statute in 1968. Little of the 58,000 acres Congress included in the Park was then in federal ownership; most of it was acquired by exchange and purchase. At an initial authorized cost of $92 million, the Park was the most expensive (in terms of federal outlay of funds) in history. The coastal redwoods, *Sequoia Sempervirens* (to be distinguished from the *Sequoia Gigantea* in the Sierra Nevada foothills) are the tallest living things in the world, some reaching more than 350' in height. They are also old—some were alive at the time of Christ. The wood is a highly prized building material—straight, clear-grained, light, strong, and rot-resistant. Much of the land in the area of the Park was being logged, providing jobs for the chronically depressed economy along California's north coast.

Because of the expense and other political considerations, the boundaries of the Park drawn by Congress were quite gerrymandered. As the Park bill was making its way through Congress, a grove of redwoods outside the boundaries as then drawn was discovered to contain what were then thought to be the very tallest of these tall trees. (Other even taller trees were discovered on nearby lands, outside the 1968 boundaries.) The bill was then changed to include a narrow eight-mile strip of land along Redwood Creek to ensure that this "tall trees grove" was included within the Park. The upland part of the Redwood Creek watershed outside this "worm" area remained in private hands, and logging of it continued after establishment of the Park. Indeed, it was said that the crowd assembled to hear First Lady Bird Johnson dedicate the Park could not hear her remarks because of the noise of chainsaws operating just outside the nearby Park boundary.

The court was ruling on the government's motion to dismiss or, in the alternative, for summary judgment. The plaintiff's complaint contained the following allegations:]

That subsequent to the establishment of the Redwood National Park in 1968 plaintiff learned that logging operations on slopes surrounding and upstream from the park were seriously endangering the park's resources, and that these dangers were reported to defendants and were offered in testimony at United States Senate hearings in Washington, D.C., on May 10, 1971;

That on September 24, 1971, plaintiff formally petitioned the Secretary of the Interior to take immediate action pursuant to his authority under the Redwood National Park Act to prevent further harm to the park's resources, and that a task force was then created by the Department of the Interior to make intensive field investigations of the threatened and actual damage to the Redwood National Park and to prepare a report of its findings;

That defendants have taken no action to prevent damage to the park from the consequences of logging on lands surrounding or upstream from the park, except to request the voluntary cooperation of timber companies to reform their operations on minor portions upstream and upslope from the park; that the timber companies have not effectively cooperated with this request and that defendants manifest no intent to protect the park from further damage to the park's trees, soil, scenery and streams;

That past and present logging operations on privately-owned steep slopes on the periphery of the park leave the park vulnerable to high winds, landslides, mudslides and siltation in the streams which endangers tree roots and aquatic life.

Plaintiff, citing 16 U.S.C. § 1 (hereinafter referred to as the National Park System Act) and 16 U.S.C. § 79a et seq., particularly § 79b(a), 79c(c), 79c(d) (hereinafter referred to as the Redwood National Park Act) contends that defendants have a judicially-enforceable duty to exercise certain powers granted by these provisions to prevent or to mitigate such actual or potential damage to the park and its redwoods as is alleged in the complaint. * * *

* * *

The National Park System Act, 16 U.S.C. Sec. 1, provides [that] the National Park Service * * * shall:

> promote and regulate the use of Federal areas known as national parks, monuments, and reservations * * * by such means and measures as conform to the fundamental purpose of said parks, monuments, and reservations, which purpose is to conserve the scenery and the natural and historic objects and the wild life therein and to provide for the enjoyment of the same in such manner and by such means as will leave them unimpaired for the enjoyment of future generations.

The responsibilities of the Secretary of the Interior concerning public lands have been stated in Knight v. United Land Association * * * as follows:

> The secretary [of the Department of the Interior] is the guardian of the people of United States over the public lands. The obligations of his oath of office oblige him to see that the law is carried out, and that none of the public domain is wasted or is disposed of to a party not entitled to it. 142 U.S. 161 at 181 (1891). * * *

In addition to these general fiduciary obligations of the Secretary of the Interior, the Secretary has been invested with certain specific powers and obligations in connection with the unique situation of the Redwood National Park.

The Redwood National Park was created on October 2, 1968 by the Redwood National Park Act, 16 U.S.C. Secs. 79a–79j,

> to preserve significant examples of the primeval coastal redwood (Sequoia sempervirens) forests and the streams and seashores with which they are associated for purposes of public inspiration, enjoyment, and scientific study * * *.

Congress limited the park to an area of 58,000 acres; appropriated 92 million dollars to implement the Act, of which, according to the Second Claim of the Amended Complaint, 20 million dollars remain unspent; and conferred upon the Secretary specific powers expressly designed to prevent damage to the park by logging on peripheral areas.

Title 16 U.S.C. Sec. 79c(e) provides:

In order to afford as full protection as is reasonably possible to the timber, soil, and streams within the boundaries of the park, the Secretary is authorized, by any of the means set out in subsection (a) and (c) of this section, to acquire interests in land from, and to enter into contracts and cooperative agreements with, the owners of land on the periphery of the park and on watershed tributary to streams within the park designed to assure that the consequences of forestry management, timbering, land use, and soil conservation practices conducted thereon, or of the lack of such practices, will not adversely affect the timber, soil, and streams within the park as aforesaid.

The question presented is whether on the allegations of the amended complaint, considered in the light of these statutory provisions, this court can direct the Secretary to exercise the powers granted under 16 U.S.C. Secs. 79c(e), 79b(a), 79c(d).

Under the Administrative Procedure Act agency action becomes non-reviewable only upon a clear and convincing showing that Congress intended to preclude judicial review. Abbott Laboratories v. Gardner, 387 U.S. 136 at 141 (1967).

The mere fact that the statute is couched in terms of a grant of discretion to the agency does not necessarily indicate an intent to preclude judicial review of the exercise of such discretion; judicial non-reviewability must be determined by an analysis of the entire statutory scheme.

Good sense suggests that the existence, nature and extent of potentially damaging conditions on neighboring lands and the effect thereof on the park, and the need for action to prevent such damage are matters that rest, primarily at least, within the judgment of the Secretary. However, neither the terms nor the legislative history of the Redwood National Park Act are such as to preclude judicial review of the Secretary's action or inaction.

In Rockbridge v. Lincoln, 449 F.2d 567 (9th Cir.1971) our Circuit * * * held that, in view of the trust relationship of the Secretary toward the Indians * * * such discretion as was vested in the Secretary was not an unbridled discretion * * * and, therefore, a cause for judicial relief under the Administrative Procedure Act was stated * * *.

* * *

In view of the analogous trust responsibility of the Secretary of the Interior with respect to public lands as stated in Knight v. United Land, supra, and the analogous legislative history indicating a specific set of objectives which the provisions of the Redwood National Park Act were designed to accomplish, we consider Rockbridge, supra, to be strongly persuasive to the point that a case for judicial relief has been made out by plaintiff.

* * *

We are of the opinion that the terms of the statute, especially § 79c(e), authorizing the Secretary "in order to afford as full protection as is reasonably possible to the timber, soil, and streams within the boundaries of the park"—"to acquire interests in land from, and to enter into contracts and cooperative agreements with, the owners of land on the periphery of the park and on the watersheds tributary to streams within the park"—impose a legal duty on the Secretary to utilize the specific powers given to him whenever reasonably necessary for the protection of the park and that any discretion vested in the Secretary concerning time, place and specifics of the exercise of such powers is subordinate to his paramount legal duty imposed, not only under his trust obligation but by the statute itself, to protect the park.

* * *

* * * Although the inquiry into the facts is to be searching and careful, the ultimate standard of review is a narrow one that stops short of substitution of the court's judgment for that of the Secretary.

* * *

Accordingly, defendants' motion to dismiss and defendants' motion for summary judgment should be, and hereby are, denied.

Sierra Club v. Department of Interior II

United States District Court, Northern District of California, 1975.
398 F.Supp. 284.

■ JUDGE SWEIGERT

* * *

* * * [T]he issue for decision is whether the Secretary, since the establishment of the Park, has taken reasonable steps to protect the resources of the Park and, if not, whether his failure to do so has been under the circumstances arbitrary, capricious, or an abuse of discretion. * * *

In the pending case the conduct of the Secretary must be considered in the light of a very [sic] unique statute—a statute which did more than establish a national park; it also expressly vested the Secretary with authority to take certain specifically stated steps designed to protect the Park from damage caused by logging operations on the surrounding privately owned lands.

As the legislative history shows, these specific provisions were put into the statute because the Park boundaries authorized by Congress represented a compromise and did not include certain lands within the Redwood Creek Watershed upslope and upstream from the southernmost portion of the Park. Out of its concern that continued logging operations on those privately owned lands could cause damage within the Park, the Congress expressly invested the Secretary with these specific powers to take administrative action designed to protect it.

These specific powers include:

(1) power to modify the boundaries of the Park with particular attention to minimizing siltation of the streams, damage to the timber and preservation of the scenery, 16 U.S.C. § 79b(a).[*]

(2) power to acquire interests in land from and to enter into contracts and cooperative agreements with the owners of land on the periphery of the Park and on watersheds tributary to streams within the Park designed to assure that the consequences of forestry management, timbering, land use and soil conservation practices conducted thereon, or the lack of such practices, would not adversely affect the timber, soil and streams within the Park, 16 U.S.C. § 79c(e).

(3) power to acquire lands and interests in land bordering both sides of the highway near the town of Orick to a depth sufficient to maintain a corridor—a screen of trees between the highway and the land behind the screen and the activities conducted thereon, 16 U.S.C. § 79c(d).

As pointed out in this court's previous decision, there is, in addition to these specific powers, a general trust duty imposed upon the National Park Service, Department of the Interior, by the National Park System Act, 16 U.S.C. § 1 et seq., to conserve scenery and natural and historic objects and wildlife [in the National Parks, Monuments and reservations] and to provide for the enjoyment of the same in such manner and by such means as will leave them unimpaired for the enjoyment of future generations * * *.

The evidence in the pending case shows that, beginning in April of 1969, the Secretary has conducted a series of five consecutive studies of damage and threats of damage to the Park caused by the logging operations of certain timber companies on adjacent lands. These studies have resulted in many specific recommendations for steps to be taken by the Secretary, pursuant to his various powers set forth in the statute, to prevent or minimize such damage.

[The opinion discusses each of the five reports at length. The reports analyzed the factual setting; emphasized the destructive effects of nearby logging on the Park; and urged that the Park Service develop a master plan and otherwise take action to protect the Park from the logging. The following excerpt from one of the reports is illustrative.]

* * *

---

* [Eds. The authority given to the Secretary in this section to modify the boundaries of the Park did not on its face authorize the Secretary to acquire nonfederal lands in order to expand the boundaries and the protection of the Park resources, and it did not make any appropriations of funds for this purpose.]

The Curry Task Force Report—1973

In February, 1973, the defendants released a document prepared by Dr. Richard Curry, an official within the Department of the Interior. The Curry Task Force Report * * * set forth in detail the damage and threats of damage to the Park resources posed by logging practices on the lands adjacent to the Park. * * * The Curry Task Force Report found, as did the earlier reports, that, while landslides, erosion, and consequent high sediment loads in Redwood Creek are naturally occurring phenomena within the Redwood Creek watershed, man's timber harvesting activities within the watershed accelerate and aggravate these natural processes. In this regard, the Curry Task Force Report specifically identified such timber harvesting practices as clearcutting, the use of bulldozers within unstable areas to yard logs, and the construction of layouts and road systems over steep and unstable terrain.

The Curry Task Force Report made five specific recommendations for actions to be taken by the Secretary:

"1. Since the greatest threat to the Park emanates from man-induced acceleration of natural erosion processes, it is imperative that present land use practices be revised. The Secretary must secure the cooperation of the companies * * * to use harvesting techniques that minimize the degree of ground surface and vegetation disruption and to perform maintenance management on the harvested land in an effort to reduce the rate of erosion in these areas.

"These actions might include but are not limited to:

"a. Cable logging or such other system that minimizes ground disruption.

"b. More sensitive placement of the road net so as to minimize land slippage.

"c. A high performance road maintenance system which would include an effective erosion control program. * * *

"d. Application of stabilization procedures in active slide areas.

"e. Minimize the burning of slash.

"f. Planting of areas where regeneration from seeding and/or sprouting may be difficult.

"2. The Secretary should seek by cooperative agreement with the companies at least a two-year cutting moratorium extending at least 75 feet from the bank of all second order and higher tributary streams that are upslope from the Corridor. The purpose is to permit the accumulation of baseline data for these streams. At the end of the period, the companies would be permitted to continue with their operations as long as the integrity of the stream is maintained.

"3. The acquisition in fee of a management zone around the 'worm' portion of the Redwood Creek unit that would be contoured to deal with specific impact and terrain conditions. The buffer would average 800 feet in width or encompass approximately 1,650 acres. * * *"

* * *

The evidence shows, and the court finds, that to date the Secretary has not implemented any of the recommendations made by or on behalf of his own agency in the above mentioned studies except (1) to enter into so-called "cooperative agreements" with the timber companies who own and operate on the lands surrounding the Park and (2) to conduct further studies.

The Secretary contends that these cooperative agreements amount to reasonable compliance with the intent of the statute and with his trust duties, pointing out that the timber companies voluntarily abstained from logging operations within an 800–foot zone of the Park until 1973 when they resumed logging under the so-called cooperative agreements; that their operations since 1973 have conformed to these agreements and that the agreements have restrained the harvesting practices of the timber companies and have thus mitigated damage to the Park.

The Secretary further points out that he is presently conducting another study through the U.S. Geological Survey of the Redwood Creek watershed and that this study, headed by a Dr. Richard Janda, is expected to be completed by the fall of 1975, at which time the Secretary will be in a position to further consider the Park situation.

The Secretary also contends that his failure to thus far implement other recommendations made by his own agency has been reasonable because of lack of sufficient scientific data to justify some of the recommendations already received and because of lack of the funds that would be required for the adoption of others.

* * *

On the other hand, plaintiff Sierra Club contends that the Secretary has complied with neither the intent of the statute nor with his general fiduciary duty to protect the Park * * *.

Plaintiff contends and the Court finds that the so-called cooperative agreements with the three timber companies are in fact not contracts or cooperative agreements within the meaning of Section 79c(e) because only one has been signed by one of the timber companies, and none of them has been signed by the Secretary; that they are, therefore, not legally binding contracts enforceable against the timber operators; also that, even if the so-called cooperative agreements were enforceable, their language is so general and so full of qualifications as to render them practically meaningless and unenforceable for that reason as well; also, that in any event the so-called cooperative agreements do not purport to carry out any of the recommendations of the defendants' studies with the arguable exception of Recommendation Number One of the Curry Task Force Report and, indeed, are contrary to other specific recommendations.

* * *

The Court further finds that the cooperative agreements do not fully implement even Curry Task Force Recommendation Number One in that the agreements set up an arbitrary 800 foot area surrounding the corridor portion of the Park while the recommendations do not so limit the harvesting restrictions.

The Court also finds that, even assuming none of the above deficiencies existed, the restraints placed upon the companies by the so-called cooperative agreements are unreasonably inadequate to prevent or reasonably minimize damage to the resources of the Park resulting from timber harvesting operations; that there is substantial on-going damage presently occurring to the timber, soil, streams, and aesthetics within the Park downslope from and as a result of clearcutting within the so-called buffer zone, even as such clearcutting is done in conformity with the so-called cooperative agreements.

With respect to the defendants' contentions concerning unavailability of funds, the Court further finds that it is the Congress which must make the ultimate determination whether additional sums should be authorized or appropriated and also the ultimate determinations concerning the items to which such funds should be applied; that the Secretary has never yet gone to the Congress * * * either to request the appropriation of the balance of money authorized by the statute, or to obtain whatever additional sums of money may be necessary to implement the specific powers of the statute designed for the protection of the Park.

Finally, the Court finds that in light of the emphasis in each of the Secretary's own studies that time is of the essence, the Secretary has taken (to the detriment of the Park) an unreasonably long period of time to negotiate the proposed cooperative agreements. * * *

* * *

The foregoing findings must be considered in the light of what might be called an implied recognition by the defendants of some degree of fault on their part. This recognition is evidenced by the fact that, prior to the time the Curry Report was released to the public (which was not until after and as a result of legal steps taken in this action by the Sierra Club under the Freedom of Information Act), the Department of Interior had intentionally removed from the Report the last two pages which contained the five recommendations for action to be taken by the Secretary of the Interior. The existence of these last two pages was thereafter discovered only in the course of subsequent discovery proceedings which were initiated by the Sierra Club in the instant action.

With all due respect for the narrow limits of judicial intervention in matters entrusted primarily to executive agencies, the Court concludes that, in light of the foregoing findings, the defendants unreasonably, arbitrarily and in abuse of discretion have failed, refused and neglected to take steps to exercise and perform duties imposed upon them by the National Park System Act, 16 U.S.C. § 1, and the Redwood National Park Act, 16 U.S.C. § 79a, and duties otherwise imposed upon them by law; and/or that defendants have unreasonably and unlawfully delayed taking such steps.

Therefore * * * it is hereby ordered:

That defendants Secretary of the Interior and Assistant Secretary for Fish, Wildlife and Parks, take reasonable steps within a reasonable time to exercise the powers vested in them by law (particularly 16 U.S.C. § 79c(e), 79c(d) and 79b(a)), and to perform the duties imposed upon them by law (particularly 16 U.S.C. § 1), in order to afford as full protection as is reasonably possible to the timber, soil and streams within the boundaries of the Redwood National Park from adverse consequences of timbering and land use practices on lands located in the periphery of the Park and on watershed tributaries to streams which flow into the Park; that such action shall include, if reasonably necessary, acquisition of interests in land and/or execution of contracts or cooperative agreements with the owners of land on the periphery or watershed, as authorized in 16 U.S.C. § 79c(e); that such action shall include, if reasonably necessary, modification of the boundaries of the Park, as authorized in 16 U.S.C. § 79b(a); and that such action shall include, if reasonably necessary, resort to the Congress for a determination whether further authorization and/or appropriation of funds will be made for the taking of the foregoing steps, and whether the powers and duties of defendants, as herein found, are to remain or should be modified.

Defendants are further ordered to file herein, and serve upon plaintiff [within a specified time] * * * a progress report upon their compliance with the foregoing order, or, in lieu of compliance, a report, showing cause why compliance has not been made, is not being or will not be made with the foregoing order.

* * *

NOTES AND QUESTIONS

1.   Notice the court in *Sierra Club I* analogized the Secretary's fiduciary duty toward parks with the duty toward Indians. Along that line, what role did the public trust doctrine play in this case? How does the court's approach compare to Sierra Club v. Andrus, 487 F.Supp. 443 (D.D.C.1980), *aff'd on other grounds*, 659 F.2d 203 (D.C.Cir.1981), *supra* p. 88.

2.   Examine closely the court's order at the end of the second opinion. The court here professes to apply a "narrow" standard of review. Is the order broad or narrow? Does it have any teeth? What *must* the Secretary do to comply with it? Does anything in the order give the timber companies an incentive to negotiate and execute cooperative agreements with the Secretary that meaningfully restrict their actions?

3.   Is there any doubt about the constitutional power of Congress to authorize the Secretary to regulate logging on private lands around the Park? The National Park Service for a long time expressed doubt about the constitutional power of the federal government to regulate lands near and within the parks, but the general issue would seem to have been laid to rest by decisions like Kleppe v. New Mexico and Minnesota v. Block; *see* Chapter 3C. The more vexing questions are usually whether, in any particular instance, Congress has delegated authority to the federal land

managing agency to abate the threats from non-federal development—and if so, whether the agency has the will to exercise it.

4. Look closely at what Congress has authorized the National Park Service to do. For example, note that the National Park Organic Act, 16 U.S.C. § 1, directs the Secretary to "regulate the use of *Federal areas* known as national parks." (emphasis added). Does the italicized language allow an inference against regulating *non-federal* areas? Does it allow an inference that the Park Service can regulate activities on non-federal inholdings (entirely surrounded by federal Park land), but not activities on adjacent land outside park boundaries?

5. To what extent has Congress authorized the Secretary to address logging on adjacent private lands in the specific statute creating Redwood National Park, 16 U.S.C. § 79c(e)? Does the statutory reference to "cooperative agreements" (presumably referring to agreements reached by mutual consent) negate any argument that Congress intended to authorize the Secretary to regulate logging around the Park *without* the companies' consent?

6. On the reviewability in court of the Secretary's inaction, one part of the Administrative Procedure Act authorizes courts to "compel agency action unlawfully withheld or unreasonably delayed." 5 U.S.C. § 706(1). Does that apply here? If this case were brought after the Supreme Court's decision in Norton v. SUWA, *supra* p. 224, would the outcome be the same?

7. Could the Secretary take actions other than those listed in Section 79c(e)? For example, could the United States bring a common law public nuisance action against the timber companies, arguing that their logging practices unreasonably interfered with the Park? Under federal or state common law? In 1979 the Secretary of the Interior was unsuccessful in attempting to stop construction of four office towers and a hotel that allegedly interfered with visual enjoyment of the Washington D.C. national capital park units. United States v. County Bd. of Arlington County, 487 F.Supp. 137 (E.D.Va.1979). The court ruled the Attorney General could bring suit on federal public nuisance grounds without express statutory authority in order to protect the federal property but held, on the merits, that the United States had not made a case that the construction was a nuisance. Another court granted a request by the Park Service to enjoin pesticide spraying by the State of West Virginia on federal and private land within the boundaries of New River Gorge National River without permission from the Park Service, citing general grants of authority from the Congress to the Secretary to make necessary and proper regulation of National Park System units. United States v. Moore, 640 F.Supp. 164 (S.D.W.Va.1986).

8. Unsuccessful efforts have been made by third parties to protect national parks from private developments, using state law. *See, e.g.,* Commonwealth v. National Gettysburg Battlefield Tower, Inc., 311 A.2d 588 (Pa.1973). There the Commonwealth of Pennsylvania sought, on public nuisance grounds, to stop construction of a large, Seattle-space-needle type observation tower on an inholding in Gettysburg National Battlefield Park. The National Park Service stood on the sidelines in the litigation because it

had, reluctantly, negotiated an agreement with the tower developer to relocate the tower on a site a little more removed from the heart of the battlefield. The litigation failed, the tower was built and loomed as an eyesore over one of America's most historic places for a quarter of a century before the Clinton Administration worked with Congress to find several million dollars to condemn, demolish, and remove it.

9. Sometimes the best way for a federal land manager to preserve a resource from development outside of the federal boundary is to get involved in local permitting. In 2004 FWS officials helped stop a 19,250–seat concert amphitheater on a tract of land adjacent to the Minnesota Valley National Wildlife Refuge by testifying before the local county commissioners in opposition to a permit application. The action by local and regional FWS officials was supported by the national refuge management policy, which calls for land managers to seek redress before local planning and zoning boards, and state administrative and regulatory agencies, if voluntary or collaborative attempts to forge solutions do not work. FWS Manual 601 § 3.20. Likewise, the 2006 NPS Management Policies (§ 1.6) provides encouragement for assertive engagement:

> Superintendents will monitor land use proposals, changes to adjacent lands, and external activities for their potential impacts on park resources and values. * * * Superintendents will encourage compatible adjacent land uses and seek to avoid and mitigate potential adverse impacts on park resources and values by actively participating in the planning and regulatory processes of other federal agencies and tribal, state, and local governments having jurisdiction over property affecting, or affected by, the park. If a decision is made or is imminent that will result in unacceptable impacts on park resources, superintendents must take appropriate action, to the extent possible within the Service's authorities and available resources, to manage or constrain the use to minimize impacts.

Does the 2006 policy implicitly endorse the concept of buffer zones around parks to protect park resources?

––––––––––

Pursuant to the District Court's order, the Department of the Interior undertook a series of efforts without beneficial results: (A) Interior requested permission from the Office of Management and Budget (OMB) in the White House (which must approve agency requests to Congress for funding and legislation), to seek additional statutory authority for the regulation of off-park timber operations; the OMB disapproved the request. (B) Interior requested the timber companies to comply voluntarily with timber harvesting guidelines; the companies declined. (C) Interior asked the Governor of California to review an earlier rejection by the State Board of Forestry of the same proposed guidelines; the Governor did not respond. (D) Interior asked the Justice Department to commence litigation against the timber companies to restrain timber practices imminently endangering the Park; the Justice Department did not act. In addition to these rebuffs, the

Department determined that it lacked sufficient appropriations to embark on acquisitions beyond those already made.

In the third Redwood decision, Sierra Club v. Department of the Interior, 424 F.Supp. 172 (N.D.Cal.1976), the district court found that the Department had made a good faith attempt to perform its statutory duties as ordered, that it was therefore "purged" of its previously-found failure to do so, and that "in order adequately to exercise its powers and perform its duties in a manner adequately to protect the Park, Interior * * * stands in need of new Congressional legislation and/or new Congressional appropriations." *Id.* at 175.

Congress did respond with the Redwood Park Expansion Act of 1978, 92 Stat. 163 (1978), which authorized the purchase of an additional 48,000 acres for the Park (including much of the upland in Redwood Creek, a substantial amount of it already logged). The total cost of the expansion was about $350 million, making the Park the most expensive acquisition in the System. Among other things, the 1978 Act provided economic benefits to certain forest industry workers who lost their jobs due to the decrease in timber harvesting.

NOTES AND QUESTIONS

1.   Could the court have ordered Congress to appropriate funds to enlarge the Park? Could it have ordered the President's Office of Management & Budget to send Interior's request for more money to the Congress? Consider U.S. Constitution, Art. I, § 9, cl. 7, "No Money shall be drawn from the Treasury, but in Consequence of Appropriations made by Law." In its third opinion in this case, the Court refused the Club's request to add OMB as a party and hold it in contempt for blocking Interior's request, explaining (424 F.Supp. at 175):

> Such decisions of the Congress and/or the Executive concerning further, future, additional legislation, funds or litigation, involve new policy-making which is the exclusive function of the Congress and the Executive under the doctrine of separation of powers.

> It is beyond the province of this court to say whether and, if so, to what extent the Congress or Executive should act—much less to order such action. All that this court can do, and now has done, is to make sure that Interior has taken all reasonable steps toward the exercise of its statutory powers and performance of its duties within the limits of existing law and available funds.

> Any further orders of this court, designed to mandate the Congress or the Executive to act to provide new legislation, new funds or new litigation, no matter how well intended by the court or how desirable for the protection of the Park, would be an extra-judicial and, therefore, futile injection of this court into the prerogatives of the Congress and the Executive.

2.   On a few occasions Congress has directly authorized the regulation of a class of activities that threaten a number of Parks. In 1987, for

example, in response to numerous complaints about noise and safety in connection with the growing popularity of commercial sightseeing flights over such parks as the Grand Canyon, Congress enacted legislation directing the Secretary of the Interior to conduct a study of the problem, and in the meantime ordered the Federal Aviation Administration to take specific action to control flights over the Grand Canyon, on the basis of a congressional finding that the noise associated with such flights "is causing a significant adverse effect on the natural quiet and experience of the park." 101 Stat. 674. In Grand Canyon Air Tour Coalition v. FAA, 154 F.3d 455 (D.C.Cir.1998), the court upheld the FAA's plan to reduce aircraft noise against attack by a variety of interests claiming the rule was too lenient or too strict. The court deferred to the agency's reasonable exercise of its judgment and technical expertise but noted that many of the challenges failed on ripeness grounds because the FAA's proposed solution was to be implemented in phases. In the National Parks Air Tour Management Act of 2000 (Pub.L. No. 106–181), Congress required the FAA and NPS to work together to create management plans for air tours at most park units throughout the system. The plans could put route and altitude limitations on such tours or prohibit them altogether. The Act also required the FAA to do more to regulate at the Grand Canyon. The D.C. Circuit shortly thereafter required the FAA to use NPS "natural quiet" standards in developing air tour overflight regulations and rejected several air tour industry challenges. Grand Canyon Trust v. FAA, 290 F. 3d 339 (D.C.Cir. 2002).

3. The Clean Air Act contains some mechanisms for protecting air quality over national park system and national wilderness preservation system lands from external sources. See 42 U.S.C. §§ 7470–7492. Conservationists and electrical utilities reached landmark agreements in 1991 and 1999 to install scrubbers on large coal-fired power plants in the southwest to protect visibility over the Grand Canyon. The Clean Water Act and the Endangered Species Act have been used as levers to obtain agreement on a multi-billion dollar plan to restore a semblance of natural flows to protect Everglades National Park while still providing water and flood protection for the several million residents of southeast Florida. Projected to cost at least $8 billion (shared by the federal government and the State of Florida), it is one of the most ambitious environmental restoration initiatives ever undertaken.

4. As of this writing, an "external threat" is unfolding at the Newberry Volcanic National Monument, a 55,000 acre preserve established by Congress in 1990. Geothermal energy developers propose to build a geothermal power plant on private land on the west flank of the crater. Some estimates put the geothermal potential of the area as between 13,000 and 16,000 megawatts, or the equivalent of a couple of dozen nuclear plants. In addition, a private developer proposes to construct a large pumice mine and 100 homes on private land inside the boundaries of the monument.

2. EXTERNAL THREATS FROM OTHER FEDERAL LANDS

Some external threats originate on nearby federal land, or from federal projects authorized by other agencies. And some external threats stem from

both federal and non-federal sources. For example, the geothermal resources that originally inspired the creation of the world's first national
park at Yellowstone might be impaired by geothermal development on both
nearby private and Forest Service lands. A proposal to lease coal for a
surface mine on BLM land near the boundary of Bryce Canyon periodically
revives (most recently in 2007).

Sometimes Congress provides site-specific guidance. For example, in
Friends of the Earth v. Armstrong, 485 F.2d 1 (10th Cir.1973), the
plaintiffs sought to require the Secretary of the Interior to prevent the
water being impounded behind Glen Canyon Dam on the Colorado River
from spreading into Rainbow Bridge National Monument. Rainbow Bridge,
reserved by President Taft under the Antiquities Act in 1910, is a huge
natural sandstone arch extending across a creek tributary to the Colorado
River upstream from the dam. The dam was authorized in 1956 in the
Colorado River Storage Project Act and completed in 1963; when filled to
capacity its reservoir, Lake Powell, backs water up the creek to a depth of
about 48 feet below Rainbow Bridge (with the water surface reaching
within 25 feet of the base of the arch itself). The 1956 Act declared the
"intention of Congress that no dam or reservoir constructed under * * *
this Act shall be within any national park or monument." 43 U.S.C.
§ 620b.

Despite the seeming clarity of this phrase, the Tenth Circuit, sitting en
banc, reversed a lower court ruling, held that subsequent acts of Congress
appropriating funds for construction of the dam had implicitly repealed this
section, and denied relief. These subsequent appropriations acts specifically
prohibited federal funds from being spent "for construction or operation of
facilities to prevent waters of Lake Powell from entering any National
Monument." This "specific prohibition," said the court, "has overridden
the expression of intent in [the 1956 dam authorization]." Two judges
dissented. On this issue of "legislation by appropriation," compare the snail
darter case, TVA v. Hill, *supra* p. 272.

Remarkably, after reaching this conclusion, the Tenth Circuit nevertheless went on to direct the trial court to retain jurisdiction for ten years
to permit the plaintiffs to apply for further relief if "some unexpected
structural damage to the Arch might become evident." 485 F.2d at 12. This
order seems wholly inconsistent with the holding that Congress had decided not to prevent the reservoir from entering the national monument. If
Congress acted on the assumption that the reservoir would not damage the
Arch, can the courts supply a remedy if that assumption proved false?
Perhaps the Tenth Circuit's order is explainable, if at all, by an unarticu-
lated notion that the Secretary remains some sort of "trustee" for Rainbow
Bridge despite Congress's determination to permit Lake Powell to invade it.

The Park Service was not a separate party to this case; the defendants
were the Secretary of the Interior and the Commissioner of the Bureau of
Reclamation. If agencies within the Interior Department (here, the Bureau
and the Park Service) disagree, the Secretary of the Interior would normally resolve the matter. Where the disagreeing federal agencies are in
separate cabinet departments, the Executive Office of the President may

resolve the matter or, if it is in litigation, the Attorney General has statutory authority to set the federal government's litigation position. *See generally* 28 U.S.C. §§ 516–519. On rare occasions, the Department of Justice has advocated the position of one agency but advised the court of the views of the dissenting agency by means of a "split brief." See TVA v. Hill, *supra* p. 272.

The kinds of legal issues that can arise in coordinating management policies of different federal land agencies are illustrated by the following hypothetical, which also provides a useful review of material in some earlier chapters.

PROBLEM: GEOTHERMAL LEASING ADJACENT TO YELLOWSTONE NATIONAL PARK

The Secretary of the Interior has discretionary authority to lease geothermal resources on BLM and Forest Service land when he determines the "public interest" will be served. Suppose that geothermal resource developers apply for geothermal leases on national forest land adjacent to Yellowstone.

(1) May the Secretary consider the effect of leasing on the Park? *Must* she do so?

(2) Suppose the Secretary considers the effect, and the evidence is not clear whether Old Faithful and the other geothermal resources inside the Park will be harmed because of possible "plumbing" interconnections with the geothermal resources targeted for leasing outside the Park. May the Secretary issue the leases?

(3) What law applies to this secretarial decision, the Geothermal Leasing Act or the National Park Service Organic Act, or both?

(4) Does NEPA help address this kind of problem? How? What about the following provision of the National Parks Omnibus Management Act of 1998? "The Secretary shall undertake a program of inventory and monitoring of National Park System resources to establish baseline information and to provide information on the long-term trends in the condition of National Park System resources. The monitoring program shall be developed in cooperation with other Federal monitoring and information collection efforts to ensure a cost-effective approach." 16 U.S.C. § 5934.

(5) Would the analysis be any different if, instead of geothermal leases, the Forest Service proposes to sell timber on a national forest outside the Park, which might adversely affect the migration route of an elk herd that spends part of each year inside the Park, and is a prime tourist attraction? Does the National Forest Management Act or the Multiple–Use, Sustained Yield Act help answer these questions?

(6) Would the analysis be different if the proposal were to develop an open-pit gold mine under the Mining Law of 1872 on BLM land just outside the Park, which could cause noise, odors, water quality deterioration, and other impacts that could interfere with wildlife and visitor enjoyment in the Park? Would FLPMA come into play here? How?

In recent years pressure has grown on the federal land management agencies to pay more attention to what happens across jurisdictional boundaries. Some of this pressure has been exerted by a new kind of environmental advocacy organization that is to some extent positioned between national groups (like the Sierra Club and NRDC) and local groups. The Greater Yellowstone Coalition and the Grand Canyon Trust, for example, both seek to address a range of environmental management issues across a relatively distinct bioregion (the greater Yellowstone ecosystem and the Colorado Plateau, respectively) which contains mostly federal land, but divided among the federal agencies rather than in unitary management.

These larger areas often have economic and well as ecological unities, but coordinating the activities of these different agencies, with different legal mandates for management, has proved a challenge, especially given some of the traditional rivalries that exist among the agencies. The Forest Service and the Park Service worked for some years to prepare a common "vision" for management of the federal lands in the Greater Yellowstone region, but it raised concerns of some local residents and politicians that it was too preservationist in orientation.

As the questions listed above hint, existing laws contain some mechanisms that allow, and to some extent direct, federal land management agencies to consult with their brethren. The Forest Service and BLM planning mandates, for example, generally require consultation with interested federal and state and local agencies, as well as the general public. NEPA contains a similar consultation process. On their face, however, none of these *mandate* that the land manager follow the recommendations of another agency managing land nearby, and the courts have rarely been asked to intervene in this consultation process.

The hypothetical regarding geothermal development around Yellowstone National Park is based upon genuine proposals for such development. Congress responded in 1984 with an appropriations act rider flatly banning federal geothermal leasing on national forest land in the Island Park area west of the Park, 98 Stat. 1874. Then in 1988 it amended the geothermal leasing act to require that "all leases or drilling permits issued, extended, renewed or modified" contain stipulations "necessary to protect significant thermal features" within national park system units whenever the Secretary determines, "based on scientific evidence," that geothermal development is "reasonably likely to adversely affect [such a feature]." 30 U.S.C. § 1026. In 1994, the Interior Department and Montana agreed to monitor and control the use of groundwater in areas just north of the park. Proponents of water use must show that proposed geothermal development will not adversely affect park features.

The Interior Solicitor issued an opinion in 1998 addressing the Secretary's responsibility under the National Park Organic Act in making discretionary decisions on proposals outside units of the national park system that could have adverse effects on those units. *See* Options Regarding Applications for Hardrock Mineral Prospecting Permits on Acquired Lands Near a Unit of the National Park System, M #36993 (April 16, 1998) (known colloquially as the Doe Run opinion, after the mining company involved). At issue was whether to grant prospecting permits for mineral activity on the Mark Twain National Forest in Missouri, in the face of concern that mining could disrupt and degrade water flows in the nearby Ozark National Scenic Riverway. (Under the law applicable to this acquired federal land, the Secretary of the Interior issues such permits, with the Forest Service holding a veto.)

After reviewing the Organic Act (including the 1978 amendment), the legislative history, case law and commentary, the Solicitor concluded that the Secretary's discretionary decisions in such circumstances must be "infuse[d] . . . with a concern for park values and purposes, and [he must exercise] caution where [they] . . . could be threatened." The Opinion says that the 1978 amendment does not require the Secretary "to overhaul the Department's decisionmaking apparatus to make park protection the paramount concern," nor does it require the Secretary to "give credence to every imaginable threat that a proposed Secretarial action may have" on the parks. It does mean, however, that the Secretary has a duty to "ensure that potential impacts on park units have been thoroughly examined in the Department's decisionmaking process," which would ordinarily be done through the NEPA process.

In one of the more celebrated resolutions of an external threat in modern times, the Clinton Administration in 1996 engineered a buy-out of the site for the proposed New World Mine a couple of miles from the northeast border of Yellowstone National Park. A company had proposed to build a large underground gold mine in the area, which had been the scene of some mining many decades ago, leaving a legacy of acid mine drainage. The mine would have put a tailings pile in a wetland and created concern about eventual contamination of Soda Butte Creek, which flowed into the Park. Much of the mine site was private, having been patented under the Mining Law many decades ago, but the company needed Forest Service approval (because a piece of the mine was on a national forest), as well as a wetlands permit from the Corps of Engineers. The mining company was, ironically, subject to potential liability under the federal Superfund Law because it had bought the contaminated property. The deal struck by the Administration, and eventually funded by Congress, paid the company $65 million for the property; the company in turn devoted about half that to clean up the existing contamination.

What are the policy advantages and disadvantages of pursuing negotiated settlements of such controversies that involve compensation to the proponents of such developments, as opposed to trying to deal with them through regulatory means alone?

Professor Robert Keiter suggests a buffer category of public lands to protect national parks from adjacent uses:

> There also is another approach to the external threats problem that would substantially protect selected parks, and that might be adopted alone or in conjunction with one of the proposed statutory schemes. Under this approach Congress should create a national resource area land management program to administer federal lands located adjacent

to designated national parks and encompassed within the park's ecosystem boundaries. This would protect selected parks against incompatible activities traceable to these federal lands. Congress also should combine the national resource area approach with meaningful federal spending limitations keyed to insuring consistency in federal policy respecting the encompassed state and private lands. In particular, Congress should condition grants to the states under the Land and Water Conservation Fund Act upon a state's willingness to establish land-use policies protective of national park resources. Although this approach does not present a plausible systemwide solution for the parks' problems, it provides meaningful protection once Congress has been persuaded to act, and it does so without administrative restructuring or drastic displacement of state prerogatives.

On Protecting the National Parks from the External Threats Dilemma, 20 LAND & WATER L.REV. 355 (1985). Is this a desirable approach? Is it feasible?

In short, the wisdom of John Muir's *dictum* that everything "is hitched to everything else in the universe" (MY FIRST SUMMER IN THE SIERRA 157 (1917)) influences how Congress and the federal land managers operate, but no uniform policy response has emerged. A pair of articles by Professors Sax and Keiter traces the ad hoc developments in interagency coordination around Glacier. *Glacier National Park and Its Neighbors*, 14 ECOL. L.Q. 207 (1987); and *The Realities of Regional Resource Management: Glacier National Park and Its Neighbors Revisited*, 33 ECOL. L.Q. 233 (2006).

C. RIVER PRESERVATION

Over time Congress has changed its perception of the primary value of rivers. For many decades the touchstone was navigability; from the beginning, the federal government has asserted a strong interest in maintaining the navigable capacity of waterways in order to assist the commerce of the Nation. Gibbons v. Ogden, 22 U.S. (9 Wheat.) 1 (1824). Flood control was another early (and continual) impetus for river development by means of dams, diversions, dredging, and channelization. 33 U.S.C. § 701 *et seq.* As advancing settlement crossed the one-hundredth meridian and encountered the arid and semiarid areas of the west, the focus shifted to using rivers for irrigation, culminating in the Reclamation Act of 1902. 43 U.S.C. §§ 371–376. Within a few years, the potential of rivers for hydroelectric power generation led to the Federal Power Act of 1920. 16 U.S.C. § 791 *et seq. See* Chapter 6B.

All this emphasis on controlling and manipulating river systems led to a vast network of dams and other works which dwarfs the Interstate Highway System as an engineering marvel. A 1982 survey by the National Park Service counted some 300,000 dams in the United States and found only about two percent of the river mileage in the country was in relatively natural, undeveloped condition. Another estimate identifies 75,000 dams more than six feet tall in the U.S., one built for every day since Thomas Jefferson was President.

These water resource developments have costs as well as benefits, and many costs were not reflected in the traditional cost/benefit calculations used to justify the dams and storage projects. One of the first major political conservation battles was fought over whether a river in Yosemite National Park should be dammed to provide a water supply for San Francisco. The 1916 NPS organic act came as a consolation prize for the loss of the dammed Hetch Hetchy Valley, which remains within the park boundary. Later, many came to believe that the sacrifice of the natural values of the Nation's dwindling supply of free-flowing rivers was ultimately counterproductive. Bureau of Reclamation's proposal to build the Echo Park Dam in Dinosaur National Monument on the Colorado River in the early 1950's sparked the first major conservation fight in the modern era. Dam opponents won the battle, but at a significant cost—the tradeoff was to build another, even larger dam (Glen Canyon) that flooded the heart of southern Utah's canyon country with Lake Powell. It did not take long before battles over whether particular river segments should be preserved in free-flowing condition occurred in many areas of the United States.

Support began to grow to establish a system that would make informed judgments on which river segments were worthy of preservation before crises were reached. In 1960, the National Park Service recommended to the Senate Select Committee on National Water Resources that some remaining free-flowing streams be preserved. The need for such preservation was documented in a 1962 Outdoor Recreation Review Commission Report, later endorsed by President Johnson. The concept of a river-based, park-like reservation reached initial fruition in 1964 when Congress created the Ozark National Scenic Riverways, 16 U.S.C. § 460m to 460m–7, under which the Current and Jack's Fork Rivers in Missouri became "national rivers," ribbon-like units of the park system. (The Buffalo River in Arkansas became a national river in 1972, 16 U.S.C. § 460m–8 to 460m–14.)

The culmination of the rivers preservation movement was the 1968 enactment of the Wild and Scenic Rivers Act (WRSA), 16 U.S.C. §§ 1271–1287.

In passing a national WSRA, Congress was responding to three major concerns. The first was the apparent inadequacy of state systems for preserving and protecting rivers, especially in the West. More Western States have historically followed the water rights doctrine of prior appropriation which evolved to encourage private development of water. Traditionally, water left in place was not a "beneficial use" of water and, hence, was not protected under state law. Even though several state legislatures have moved to include instream uses within their appropriation systems, states still have the reputation of being poor guardians of these uses. A major goal of WSRA was to enhance both state and federal attention to protection of instream values.

Congress' second concern was to control federal water development. * * * The federal presence in developing water, spread among numerous agencies, was piecemeal and poorly integrated, yet powerful. As the country's "environmental consciousness" evolved, it became highly controversial. In passing WSRA, Congress sought balance in the federal program.

A third congressional goal behind WSRA was to increase congressional control over the federal land management agencies. In the 1960's and 1970's, "Congress took unprecedented steps in giving the land managing agencies specific directions for managing designated areas of the public lands" for environmental purposes. The WSRA was part of this trend toward specialized, environmentally protective legislation.

Sally K. Fairfax et al., *Federalism and the Wild and Scenic Rivers Act: Now You See It, Now You Don't*, 59 WASH. L.REV. 417 (1984).

Like the Wilderness Act, the WSRA established a framework for a system of protected river segments. Designation does not alter the identity of the agencies and owners managing the lands within the unit. Wild and Scenic Rivers ("WSRs") are therefore represented in all four federal public land systems. On the other hand, management problems along WSRs are usually more complex than management problems in wilderness areas. Areas designated as wilderness are usually entirely or almost entirely federal land. By contrast (primarily because settlers tended to concentrate along rivers), much of the land along many of the designated WSRs is privately owned. The Act contains a number of features that seek to deal with this situation, including provisions for land acquisition (16 U.S.C. § 1277) and cooperative agreements with state and local governments (*id.* § 1281(e)). But the extent to which the Act authorizes federal regulation of non-federal lands in these river corridors, and preempts state and local land use regulation, is nowhere plainly answered. We first take up issues relating to designation of units in the wild and scenic river system, and then management limitations.

1.   DESIGNATING WILD & SCENIC RIVERS

The national wild and scenic river system comprises 164 units along over 11,000 river miles. Waters and lands undergo a variety of procedures before entering the system.

a.   *By Congress.* Usually Congress designates individual river segments as WSRs by statute. The political process in Congress tends to dictate, with rare exceptions, that any such designation have the support of the entire (or at least most) of the state's congressional delegation before it will be enacted.

b.   *By the Secretary.* The Act contains a mechanism to bypass Congress. The Secretary of the Interior may, upon request of a state's governor, include rivers in the federal system that have been designated as wild, scenic or recreational rivers by an "act of the [state] legislature." 16 U.S.C. § 1273(a)(ii). If the Secretary agrees and the rivers are designated for inclusion in the federal system, they are basically managed the same as other rivers designated by Congress, although they are administered by the state or its political subdivision. The federal lands in the included segment, however, remain under federal control.

In June 1980, Governor Jerry Brown of California requested Interior Secretary Cecil Andrus to designate five river segments in northern California, which had been protected under state law, as part of the national system. An expedited EIS process ensued, during which counties in California and Oregon obtained preliminary orders enjoining the Secretary from acting. On the last day of the Carter Administration, however, the Ninth Circuit vacated the injunctions. Secretary Andrus had been optimistic enough to anticipate the decision: When President Carter had sent a routine memo to all cabinet officers requesting their resignations as of 5:00 p.m. on January 19th, Andrus asked permission to delay his resignation. A devotee of wild rivers, Carter, who had been one of the first persons to raft the Chatooga River in his native Georgia and who, while President, spent several days rafting the Middle Fork of the Salmon River with Secretary Andrus, agreed. The Secretary was attending a reception at the White House on the evening of January 19th when an aide phoned to say that the injunction had been lifted. Andrus returned to his office to sign the North Coast river proclamations, his last official act in office. In Del Norte County v. United States, 732 F.2d 1462 (9th Cir.1984), the court upheld the Department's accelerated NEPA compliance.

c. *Study Rivers*. Congress has also from time to time passed legislation requiring federal agencies to study particular river segments for possible inclusion in the system and to report their findings to Congress for possible action. In the meantime, federal land in a quarter-mile corridor on each side is withdrawn from "entry, sale, or other disposition" and from the Mining Law (but not the Mineral Leasing Act). 16 U.S.C. §§ 1279(b), 1280(b). Furthermore, the Federal Energy Regulatory Commission (FERC, formerly the Federal Power Commission, or FPC) may not license hydro-electric dams on any "study" river for a period of time to allow for the study and congressional consideration. *Id.* § 1278(a). But such protection against the FERC apparently does not extend to rivers that a state has studied and applied to the Secretary for inclusion. *See* North Carolina v. FPC, 533 F.2d 702 (D.C.Cir.1976), remanded, 429 U.S. 891 (1976). Thus the FERC could license a dam on the river anytime before the Secretary designated it for inclusion.

d. *Determining the Boundaries of Designated River Segments.* The Act contemplates that the Congress, in designated a river segment for inclusion in the system, will not specify how much land along the river should be included. Instead, it directs the administering Secretary to select detailed boundaries within one year of designation, which "shall include an average of not more than 320 acres of land per mile measured from the ordinary high water mark on both sides of the river." 16 U.S.C. § 1274(b).

In Sokol v. Kennedy, 210 F.3d 876 (8th Cir.2000), an adjacent land-owner challenged the boundaries of the Niobrara WSR. The court rejected the Park Service's argument that it had complete discretion (other than the acreage limitation) regarding its selection of land for inclusion in the unit. Instead, the court opined, the selection process should be governed by a determination that the land has "outstandingly remarkable scenic, recreational, geologic, fish and wildlife, historic, cultural, or other similar values," because Congress used that phrase in the Act's introductory statement of policy, 16 U.S.C. § 1271, which was incorporated into the general management standard of 16 U.S.C. § 1281(a). This meant, according to the court, that the agency was not prohibited from including

> unremarkable land; indeed, the Act could require such inclusion where necessary to protect outstandingly remarkable resources, e.g., because of the need for buffer zones around resources or because of discontinuities in a resource's locations. Equally, the Act does not require that the boundaries encompass all the outstandingly remarkable resources; this might be impossible given the acreage limitation. * * * The Act allows the administering agency discretion to decide which boundaries would best protect and enhance the outstandingly remarkable values in the river area, but it must identify and seek to protect those values, and not some broader category.

The court therefore struck down the agency's boundary-setting, which had used the standard of including "significant" or "important" resources rather than "outstandingly remarkable."

In Friends of Yosemite Valley v. Norton, 348 F. 3d 789 (9th Cir. 2003), the court held that the Park Service violated the Act by drawing the boundaries of the Merced WSR at Yosemite too narrowly. The NPS set the river boundaries through the El Portal administrative site to include the river floodplain plus adjacent wetlands and meadows, whereas along the rest of the designated segment the boundary was set at one-quarter mile above the highwater mark on either side of the river. The court followed the Eighth Circuit's analysis in *Sokol* that the boundaries should be set on the basis of the river's "outstandingly remarkable values." *Sokol* involved alleged over-inclusiveness, while Friends of Yosemite Valley involved under-inclusiveness, because the record showed that some of the "outstandingly remarkable values" identified by the Park Service were not protected by the narrower boundaries. The court said the Park Service did not have to designate the maximum number of acres allowed, but that the boundaries "must be drawn so as to protect and enhance the [outstandingly remarkable values] causing that area to be included" in the Wild & Scenic River System. *Id*. at 799.

2. MANAGING WILD & SCENIC RIVERS

The Act directs that, upon designation, every river "shall be classified, designated, and administered" as either

> (1) *wild*; that is, "generally inaccessible except by trail, with watershed or shorelines essentially primitive and waters unpolluted * * * represent[ing] vestiges of primitive America;"

> (2) *scenic*; whose shorelines and watershed are "still largely primitive and * * * undeveloped, but accessible in places by roads;" or

(3) *recreational*; that is, "readily accessible by road or railroad," with some development along their shorelines, and that "may have undergone some impoundment or diversion in the past."

16 U.S.C. § 1272(b)(1–3). These definitions have been further refined by "guidelines" adopted by the agencies; 41 Fed.Reg. 39,454 (1982). Almost half of all river miles in the system are classified "wild."

"One might suppose that the degree of protection afforded a river would be based on the river's classification. However, one would be wrong: the Act specifies protections based on river classification *only* with regard to mining." Fairfax et al. at 429 (emphasis in original). While it is true that the Act expressly differentiates among the categories of rivers only with respect to mining, the commentators' conclusion may be overstated. As shown in the next principal case, the controlling management directive is to protect rivers "in accordance with the purposes of" the Act. Because the Act itself creates these different categories, presumably Congress intended them to serve somewhat different purposes, so their management should be affected accordingly.

Mining. 16 U.S.C. § 1280 covers mining. Generally speaking, it provides that designation permanently withdraws federally owned minerals within one-quarter mile of the bank of a designated river that is classified as *wild* from development under the Mining Law or the leasing acts. All mining activity in all designated river corridors, regardless of how they are classified, is to be regulated "to effectuate the purposes of" the Act, including to provide "safeguards against pollution of the river involved and unnecessary impairment of the scenery within the component in question." Mining patents shall convey the right to the minerals only. All these restrictions are "subject to valid existing rights."

Dams. The WSR designation forbids dams and other interferences with the free-flowing condition of the designated river segment, regardless of whether it is classified as wild, scenic, or recreational. The pertinent statutory section, 16 U.S.C. § 1278(a), is not a paragon of clarity. It begins by prohibiting FERC from licensing any project "on or directly affecting" a designated river. The same sentence goes on to prohibit *all* federal agencies (including FERC) from assisting any water project that would have a "direct and adverse effect on the values for which such river was established, as determined by the Secretary charged with its administration." The next sentence says that these limitations shall "not preclude licensing of, or assistance to, developments below or above [the designated reach] or on any stream tributary thereto which will not invade the area or unreasonably diminish the scenic, recreational, and fish and wildlife values present in the area" when it was designated. It is not clear whether the second sentence establishes an independent standard or is merely an elaboration of the "direct and adverse effect" standard in the first sentence. For discussion of these provisions, see High Country Resources and Glacier Energy Co. v. FERC, 255 F.3d 741 (9th Cir.2001). This section does not, however, apply to a congressionally authorized dam. Oregon Natural Resources Council v. Harrell, 52 F.3d 1499 (9th Cir.1995).

Planning and Resource Management.

Each component of the national wild and scenic rivers system shall be administered in such manner as to protect and enhance the values which caused it to be included in said system without, insofar as is consistent therewith, limiting other uses that do not substantially interfere with public use and enjoyment of these values. In such administration primary emphasis shall be given to protecting its esthetic, scenic, historic, archeologic and scientific features. Management plans for any such component may establish varying degrees of intensity for its protection and development, based on the special attributes of the area.

16 U.S.C. § 1281(a).

For rivers designated before January 1, 1986, the agency charged with the administration of each component of the WSR System is directed to review "all boundaries, classifications and plans * * * for conformity within the requirements of this subsection within ten years through regular agency planning processes." 16 U.S.C. § 1274(d)(2).

For rivers designated on or after January 1, 1986, the agency shall, within three years of designation, prepare a comprehensive management plan to provide for the protection of the river values. "The plan shall address resource protection, development of lands and facilities, user capacities, and other management practices necessary or desirable to achieve the purposes of this chapter. The plan shall be coordinated with and may be incorporated into resource management planning for affected adjacent Federal lands." 16 U.S.C. § 1274(d)(1).

In Friends of Yosemite Valley v. Norton, 348 F. 3d 789 (9th Cir. 2003), the Court held that the Park Service's plan for the Merced River violated this section by not sufficiently "address[ing] * * * user capacities." The court said the plan must "provide actual limits" on public use in its plan; that is, some "concrete measure of use" necessary to avoid adversely impacting the river's "outstandingly remarkable values." The court said this did not necessarily require specifying numeric caps on the number of visitors, but did require "adoption of quantitative measures * * * of user capacities."

Newton County Wildlife Ass'n v. U.S. Forest Service

United States Court of Appeals for the Eighth Circuit, 1997.
113 F.3d 110.

■ JUDGE LOKEN

Newton County Wildlife Association, the Sierra Club, and certain individuals (collectively "the Wildlife Association") sued the United States Forest Service and four of its employees (collectively the "Forest Service") seeking judicial review of four timber sales in the Ozark National Forest. Parties favoring timber harvesting intervened to support the Forest Service. The Wildlife Association filed sequential motions to preliminarily

enjoin the sales as violative of the Wild and Scenic Rivers Act ("WSRA").[*]
* * *

* * *

In 1992, Congress designated segments of six rivers within the Ozark National Forest. The Forest Service's three-year deadline for completing comprehensive management plans for these segments (the "Plans") was September 30, 1995. It is undisputed that the Plans were not completed on time. Therefore, the Wildlife Association argues that logging under the four timber sales must be preliminarily enjoined until the agency complies with this statutory mandate.

The Forest Service issued final agency actions approving the four timber sales between August 23, 1994, and September 12, 1995, before the agency's WSRA planning deadline. The Wildlife Association fails to relate this subsequent planning delinquency to judicial review of the timber sales. It relies upon cases in which plans or studies were a statutory precondition to the agency actions under review. But WSRA does not mandate completion of § 1274(d)(1) plans before timber sales may be approved. Therefore, the Forest Service did not violate WSRA by approving timber sales during the planning process. That being so, the agency was not required to suspend on-going implementation of the timber sales when it later failed to complete the Plans on time. Absent specific statutory direction, an agency's failure to meet a mandatory time limit does not void subsequent agency action.

Moreover, because the preparation of WSRA Plans was not a precondition to approving the timber sales, a reviewing court may not enjoin or set aside the sales based upon the failure to prepare the Plans. Although the Forest Service may well have WSRA compliance obligations in approving timber sales (an issue not before us), the agency has substantial discretion in deciding procedurally how it will meet those obligations. The Forest Service maintains land and resource management plans for each national forest. Those plans "provide for multiple use and sustained yield of [forest] products and services . . . [and] coordination of outdoor recreation, range, timber, watershed, wildlife and fish, and wilderness." 16 U.S.C. § 1604(e)(1). In 1994, the Forest Service amended its management plan for the Ozark National Forest to take into account the 1992 WSRA designations. In addition, the agency prepared an environmental assessment before approving each of the timber sales in question. Had the Forest Service relied on WSRA Plans as evidencing its compliance with WSRA in approving the timber sales, then we would carefully examine that rationale. But absent a specific statutory directive, we would usurp the agency's procedural autonomy if we compelled it to channel its compliance efforts into a particular planning format.[3]

---

* [Eds. The plaintiff also alleged violation of the Migratory Bird Treaty Act; that issue is discussed in Chapter 10.]

3. Of course, a party aggrieved by an agency's failure to meet a statutory planning deadline may seek a court order compelling the agency to complete the required plan. However, the Wildlife Association has not separately challenged the Forest Service's failure to prepare WSRA Plans.

Finally, a preliminary injunction would be inappropriate in this case because the Forest Service contends that the four timber sales lie outside the boundaries of the WSRA-designated river segments, and the Wildlife Association has not refuted that contention. The district court avoided this issue by ruling that WSRA plans must encompass federally controlled areas that lie outside but *may affect* a designated river segment. On appeal, the Forest Service argues that WSRA plans need only encompass lands lying within a designated segment and therefore its failure to timely prepare the Plans cannot affect the timber sales in question. We agree.

Under WSRA, each designated river segment becomes a "component" of the national system. § 1274(a). Following designation, the responsible agency defines the boundaries of "each component," determining how much land adjacent to the river is included in the designation. § 1274(b). At that point, the agency "charged with the administration of each component ... shall prepare a comprehensive management plan for such river segment to provide for the protection of the river values." § 1274(d)(1). In our view, the plain meaning of that provision limits the planning requirement to the boundaries of the designated river segment, because it is the designated "segment" that becomes a "component" of the national system. This reading is confirmed by § 1281(a) of the Act, which links agency planning and administration to the designated component.[4] Because the Forest Service may limit WSRA plans to lands lying within designated river segments, failure to timely prepare the Plans cannot be a basis for enjoining timber sales on lands lying outside any designated area.

* * *

NOTES AND QUESTIONS

1. Other courts have agreed that the requirement to prepare a management plan under 16 U.S.C. § 1274(d) is independent of whatever duties § 1283(a) places on federal land management agencies, and that a failure to prepare a management plan within the statutory deadline is not in itself grounds for enjoining timber sales or other activities being conducted within the designated river corridor. In Sierra Club v. United States, 23 F.Supp.2d 1132 (N.D.Cal.1998), the court held that the Act "provides no indication that a court may enjoin an agency's land management activities with respect to a wild and scenic river area merely because the agency has failed to timely adopt a comprehensive management plan." But Sierra Club v. Babbitt, 69 F.Supp.2d 1202, 1251 (E.D.Cal.1999), cautioned that the agency's failure to develop the required plan may be "highly material in the analysis of the agency's compliance with the substantive requirements of the WSRA." The latter court went on to find

4. WSRA § 1283(a) imposes a general obligation on agencies having jurisdiction over lands "which include, border upon, or are adjacent to" a designated river segment to protect the river in accordance with WSRA. But in our view, § 1283(a) does not require agencies managing adjacent federal land to prepare or join in a WSRA plan. It merely instructs their managers to take actions that protect designated rivers. Whether that standard has been met in a particular case is a question of fact.

the Park Service's program to reconstruct one of the major access roads in Yosemite National Park violated the substantive requirements of the Act in part because it was planned and executed "without reference to the required comprehensive management plan or any other pre-existing plan that would have adequately informed the decision whether the construction activities * * * were an allowable degradation of the values for which the Merced River was included in the [NWRS] System."

2.   What kind of evidence would have been persuasive in showing that the proposed timber sales conflicted with the WSRA? What governing standard does that Act contain? Consider the following provisions from the WSRA, 16 U.S.C. § 1283:

(a) The Secretary of the Interior, the Secretary of Agriculture, and the head of any other Federal department or agency having jurisdiction over any lands which include, border upon, or are adjacent to, any river included within the National Wild and Scenic Rivers System or under consideration for such inclusion * * * shall take such action respecting management policies, regulations, contracts, plans, affecting such lands * * * as may be necessary to protect such rivers in accordance with the purposes of this chapter. * * * Particular attention shall be given to scheduled timber harvesting, road construction, and similar activities which might be contrary to the purposes of this chapter.

(b) Nothing in this section shall be construed to abrogate any existing rights, privileges, or contracts affecting Federal lands held by any private party without the consent of said party.

(c) The head of any agency administering a component of the [WSR System] shall cooperate with the Administrator, Environmental Protection Agency and with the appropriate State water pollution control agencies for the purpose of eliminating or diminishing the pollution of waters of the river.

Does the NEPA analysis for the timber sale have to demonstrate that logging will not "substantially interfere with public use and enjoyment" of the values which caused this river to be designated a WSR? (§ 1281.) Does the Forest Service here have the burden of showing that the proposed timber sale is consistent with the WSRA, or do the opponents have the burden of showing the opposite? Does section 1281's reference to giving "primary emphasis" to "esthetic, scenic, historic, archeologic, and scientific features" create a "compatibility" principle similar to the one applied on national wildlife refuges? What kind of standard is created for a reviewing court in Section 1283(a)'s direction to federal administering agencies to "take such action * * * as may be necessary to protect such rivers in accordance with the purposes of this chapter"? In Sierra Club v. United States, 23 F.Supp.2d 1132 (N.D.Cal.1998), the court characterized the substantive management requirements of the WSRA as "very broad and vest[ing] the relevant agency with substantial discretion in its management of protected river areas." Do you agree?

3.   In the original version of the Act, Section 1283(a) required federal agencies simply to "review" their activities in or near river segments being

studied for possible inclusion in the system "in order to determine what actions shall be taken to protect such rivers" while they were being considered for inclusion. In 1978 Congress amended the section to its current form, quoted in paragraph #2 above. The amendment thus both strengthens the agencies' duty to protect, and extends it to designated rivers as well as study rivers. Is this legislative background relevant to the questions in the preceding paragraph?

4.   What does the Forest Service need to show to demonstrate that it has "cooperated" with federal and state water quality authorities regarding water pollution control as required by Section 1283(c)? If responsible federal and state authorities object to the proposed sale on water quality grounds, can the Forest Service override their objections? Upon what kind of showing? Should a reviewing court defer to the expertise of the Forest Service, or the expertise of the water quality agencies, when there is a conflict between the two? Can this section be interpreted to give state water quality authorities a veto over federal land management where necessary to protect water quality? In Friends of Yosemite Valley v. Norton, 348 F. 3d 789 (9th Cir. 2003), the court held that the Park Service had adequately "cooperated" with federal and state water quality authorities even though NPS facilities had several times illegally spilled sewage into the river, leading the regional water quality authority to bring enforcement action against NPS. The court upheld the lower court's conclusion that, while the NPS record was "clearly not stellar[,] * * * it is not at such an abysmal level to constitute actual failure to cooperate with the Board."

5.   On remand of the principal case, the district court upheld the Forest Service's determination that the timber sales would not adversely effect WSR values, and in Newton County Wildlife Ass'n v. Rogers, 141 F.3d 803 (8th Cir.1998), the Court of Appeals affirmed in a terse opinion. After noting that the Act "requires federal agencies responsible for land adjacent to designated river components to protect designated rivers", with "[p]articular attention" paid to "scheduled timber harvesting, road construction, and similar activities which might be contrary to the purposes of this chapter," 16 U.S.C. § 1283(a), it said:

> [P]laintiff points to nothing in the administrative record establishing that the Forest Service acted arbitrarily and capriciously in finding that logging and road work will have an insignificant effect on WSRA-designated river components. The EAs [prepared on the sales] thoroughly discuss the impact of the sales on water quality of the Buffalo River and Richland Creek and call for mitigation measures designed to protect affected waters. We reject the Wildlife Association's contention that the Forest Service failed to cooperate with state water pollution control agencies simply because the Arkansas Department of Pollution Control and Ecology and the Arkansas Natural and Scenic Rivers Commission opposed the sales. The record reflects that the Forest Service considered the State's objections even though they were not expressed until after the comment period ended.

6.   In Wilderness Watch v. U.S. Forest Service, 143 F.Supp.2d 1186 (D.Mont.2000), the court held that the Forest Service's issuance of special

use permits to construct permanent resort lodges in a "wild" river corridor violated the provision in the WSRA that such corridors should be have "watersheds or shorelines essentially primitive." 16 U.S.C. § 1273(b)(1).

Oregon Natural Desert Association v. Green

United States District Court, District of Oregon, 1997.
953 F.Supp. 1133.

■ HAGGERTY, DISTRICT JUDGE:

Plaintiffs, various named environmental groups (collectively referred to as "ONDA"), filed this action * * * [alleging, among other things, that] the river management plan BLM prepared for the Donner und Blitzen Wild and Scenic River [designated by Congress in 1988] violates the Wild and Scenic Rivers Act, 16 U.S.C. §§ 1271–1287 * * * [and seeking] to enjoin BLM from any further implementation of the activities authorized in the river management plan.

* * *

The river area includes outstandingly remarkable vegetation, fisheries, wildlife, scenery, recreation, geology and cultural values. Of the 74.8 miles of streambed, 63 miles are publicly-owned and 11.8 miles are privately-owned. The river area is comprised of a total of 22,265 acres of land; 19,353 acres are publicly-owned and 3,312 acres are privately-owned.

In 1991, BLM hired five scientists from the Nature Conservancy to survey and report on sensitive native plants and unique natural areas in the river area. The scientists reported that the river area possesses an extraordinary number and diversity of native plant species. They also reported that the river area possesses plant communities that are rare in the Great Basin region. According to ONDA, the scientists determined that cattle grazing has had a broad scale adverse effect on native plants and plant communities. BLM and intervenors dispute this assertion and submit that the scientists actually stated that "[g]razing has had a broad scale effect upon the riparian and upland vegetation in the Blitzen River system." Harney County submits that the report also noted the "overall high quality condition of the natural communities found within the river corridor." The scientists expressed specific concern about the lack of reproduction in woody plant species in riparian areas.

The scientists unanimously recommended that BLM remove grazing from the entire river corridor and prevent any trespass cattle. BLM points out, however, that the Nature Conservancy biologist who authored the sensitive plants report subsequently advised BLM in comments on the River Plan that, while grazing should be banned "in the canyons of the river," grazing in the South Fork of the Blitzen was "recognized as not being as easily controlled as the river does not flow through steep canyons," and that a "well crafted" allotment management plan should be adopted to protect that part of the river.

[BLM issued its river plan, accompanied by an environmental assessment, in 1993, and] * * * has issued at least two other site-specific decisions that tier to and implement the River Plan.

ONDA maintains that cattle grazing has degraded and continues to degrade native plants and plant communities in part of the river area. BLM and intervenors agree that, in the past, cattle grazing has degraded native plants and plant communities in part of the river area. They dispute, however, ONDA's statement that the cattle grazing continues to degrade the native plants and communities. Rather, BLM insists that the trend in condition of riparian habitat, which includes vegetation, is stable or upward in all publicly-owned parts of the river area. According to BLM, changes in grazing management that it is implementing this year, including reduced stocking levels, changes in season of use and pasture rotation and periodic rest, will produce an upward trend in areas that are currently stable and will accelerate the improvement in areas that already show an upward trend.

* * *

The River Plan does not require the exclusion of cattle from any new part of the river area. ONDA contends that removal of cattle from parts of the river area and the prevention of any trespassing cattle is necessary so that certain native plants and plant communities may be restored to a natural function and may thereafter be protected and enhanced. BLM agrees that cattle should be removed from the high-elevation gorges of the river corridor; namely, Little Indian Gorge, Big Indian Gorge and Little Blitzen Gorge, where a number of sensitive plant communities are located. In fact, BLM represents that is has already excluded livestock from the Little Blitzen and Big Indian Gorges. Further, steep terrain allows only few livestock to reach Little Indian Gorge. BLM disagrees that livestock should be removed from other parts of the river because research has shown that, if livestock are carefully managed, riparian plant communities can be restored without completely eliminating grazing.

* * *

To address the impact of cattle on river values, the River Plan states as a management "objective" improving "trend in riparian condition." ONDA states that the trend standard fails to restore, protect or enhance certain native plants and plant communities in the river area. BLM and intervenors take exception to this assessment because the affidavit cited in support of this assertion is stated in general, hypothetical terms and does not identify any particular plant species or plant community that is native to the Donner und Blitzen River area that is located in parts of the river where livestock normally graze and that would not be likely to improve under a "trend" standard.

BLM defines "trend in range condition" as meaning a movement toward or away from the "climax or potential natural community." BLM considers the indicators of trend in riparian condition to include: 1) increase in ground cover; 2) composition changes in herbaceous species; 3) establishment or increase in woody species; 4) changes in streambank stability; and 5) changes in stream depth and width. BLM classifies riparian condition as "poor," "fair," "good," or "excellent," depending on several criteria, including: 1) percent of the stream that is shaded; 2) vegetation species composition, vigor and abundance; and stability of streambanks.

* * *

In 1988, the Donner und Blitzen was designated by Congress as a component of the System [in the Omnibus Oregon Wild and Scenic Rivers Act of 1988 ("OOWSRA") 16 U.S.C.] § 1274(a)(74). Significantly, when Congress designated the Donner und Blitzen it classified the river, including its major tributaries, as a "wild" river. *Id.* Under the WSRA, a "wild" river is defined as "[t]hose rivers free of impoundments and generally inaccessible except by trail, with watersheds or shorelines essentially primitive and waters unpolluted. These represent vestiges or primitive America." *Id.* at § 1273(b)(1). The classification "wild" is the most restrictive of the three possible classifications.

ONDA argues that BLM violated the WSRA by adopting, without any rational basis, a management plan for the river that fails to protect and enhance native plants, plant communities and fisheries. Specifically, ONDA insists there are four aspects of the River Plan that violate the WSRA. Namely, the River Plan improperly authorizes the: 1) continued grazing of cattle, 2) construction of new parking lots, 3) the improvement of a secondary access road, and 4) implementation of a water resource project to divert water to irrigate hay fields.

ONDA submits that BLM had an affirmative duty under the WSRA and NEPA to fully consider, disclose and analyze whether excluding cattle grazing from all or part of the public lands in the river area was necessary to restore, protect and enhance the values of the Donner und Blitzen River. According to ONDA, BLM failed to meet this duty in preparing the River Plan and the EA because it: 1) erroneously concluded that it did not have authority under the WSRA to exclude cattle from public lands in the river area, and 2) erroneously concluded that the River Plan could not affect activities allowed under pre-existing programmatic plans for the river area.

BLM does not dispute that it had authority to exclude cattle grazing from the river area. Further, it insists that the River Plan does not presume that BLM lacked authority to exclude livestock from the river area. In fact, BLM refers the court to the following portion of the River Plan: "Grazing management changes will be implemented to protect and enhance the outstandingly remarkable values of the Wild and Scenic River System. This will require fencing, development and protection of alternative water sources, or elimination of livestock grazing." The River Plan also describes the segments of the river totaling 40 miles of the 74.8 mile river corridor that already have been excluded from grazing.

[The intervening local county and affected ranchers] * * * maintain, however, that Congress intended existing livestock grazing, as well as other commercial uses, to continue in designated wild and scenic river areas. Specifically, they argue that the OOWSRA was designed to "maintain the status quo and specifically recognized that existing uses and facilities were 'grandfathered' under the [OOWSRA] and were not required to be extracted from the river corridor." Harney County relies extensively on the legislative history of both the WSRA and the OOWSRA to argue that those statutes are intended to preserve and protect the outstandingly remarkable features of the designated rivers by maintaining the existing character and status quo of the rivers at the time of designation.

The court agrees with ONDA and the BLM that the BLM had authority to exclude cattle grazing from the river area. The plain language of the statute mandates that the federal agency administer the river in such a manner as "to protect and enhance the values which caused it to be included in said system without, insofar as is consistent therewith, limiting other uses that do not substantially interfere with public use and enjoyment of these values." 16 U.S.C. § 1281(a). Absent ambiguity or an absurd result, the plain meaning of the statute must control. In addition, the court is able to discern from other federal statutes that Congress is cognizant of its ability to grandfather specific commercial uses of a wild and scenic river that might otherwise be prohibited by the WSRA.

Moreover, the legislative history relied on by the intervenors is unpersuasive. The legislative history consists primarily of statements made by individual legislators during the hearings on the OOWSRA. The OOWSRA simply designated the Donner und Blitzen, classified it as "wild" and established its length by river mile. The OOWSRA did not alter any substantive provision of the WSRA. This does not mean, however, that cattle grazing must be excluded from the river area. Rather, cattle grazing may continue, but only in accordance within the strictures of the WSRA to protect and enhance.

Here, BLM contends that it was required to restrict grazing only where grazing would "substantially interfere" with the public's enjoyment of river values. According to BLM, because the WSRA does not define "substantially interfere," it is left to its judgment to determine whether grazing is compatible with protection and enhancement of river values. BLM determined that livestock should be excluded from some parts of the river, but that grazing in other parts of the river would not "substantially interfere" with the public's enjoyment of river values. BLM determined that it is possible to protect and enhance river values and allow grazing to continue in some areas on a managed schedule. As such, BLM insists that the court must defer to its judgment.

The court disagrees with BLM's assertion that the River Plan strikes the appropriate balance between continued grazing and protecting and enhancing the river values. The River Plan identifies seven outstandingly remarkable values: scenic, geologic, recreational, fish and wildlife, vegetation, cultural—traditional practices/prehistoric, cultural—historic. The record in this case establishes that several of these values are being degraded by continued cattle grazing in the river area.

The *Final Report* prepared by the five botanists in cooperation with BLM, included the following Management Recommendation for grazing in the river area:

Grazing has had a broad scale affect upon the riparian and upland vegetation in the Blitzen River System. Nearly every reach of every river segment had been grazed this year, some of which was obvious trespass. The South Fork Blitzen River was so heavily grazed that the riparian [area] had been essentially destroyed over a significant part of the segment. In contrast, in most of the upper reaches of the glacial canyons of the Blitzen River system * * * [it] was essentially intact and in good condition. The detrimental effects of grazing in riparian systems is well documented and the Blitzen River system exhibits the usual effects. Of greatest concern to the surveyors was the general lack of reproduction in black cottonwood and willow stands. *Our unanimous recommendation is to remove grazing from the entire river corridor and to effectively prevent trespass from nearby allotments.*

Final Report Donner Und Blitzen Wild & Scenic River Sensitive Plants And Unique Natural Areas Inventory (emphasis added).

In addition, nearly half of the surveyed aquatic habitat remains in a "poor" or "fair" condition due to poor water quality and riparian vegetation. It is undisputed that the health of the coldwater fish in the river area is linked to the vitality of water and vegetation. Further evidence of the declining water quality was delivered on June 26, 1996. The Environmental Protection Agency issued a final decision approving the State of Oregon's finding that two of the major streams in the river area are "water quality limited" under the federal Clean Water Act, on the ground that the water temperature exceeds the allowable maximum standard established for the protection of the native fish. The BLM does not challenge ONDA's assertion that the primary cause of the overheated water and siltation in the river is "denuded and collapsed streambanks due to grazing."

* * *

It also appears from the record that at the time BLM prepared the River Plan it did not believe it had authority to exclude cattle grazing entirely from the river area. Further, it appears from the record that BLM relied on the Andrews Management Framework Plan, written well before the Donner und Blitzen was designated a part of the System as a "wild" river, to determine the impact of cattle grazing in the river area for purposes of the River Plan. While BLM was permitted to coordinate and incorporate the River Plan into other resource management plans for affected adjacent Federal lands, 16 U.S.C. § 1274(d)(1), those existing plans do not simply excuse the agency's duties under the WSRA.

* * *

ONDA also challenges the River Plan on the ground it illegally allows motorized vehicles to operate in more than seven miles inside the river area. In addition, BLM plans to build two "high standard gravel roads" along "primitive secondary access roads not usually frequented by the general public." BLM also plans to build two new parking lots in the river area. ONDA insists that these BLM decisions that improve and increase vehicle access within the river area violates the WSRA and NEPA.

As stated above, Congress defined "wild" rivers as "free of impoundments and generally inaccessible except by trail." 16 U.S.C. § 1273(b)(1). Section 1283(a) directs that the agency charged with managing the river pay "particular attention ... to ... road construction." In fact, federal regulations authorize BLM to close roads, if necessary, to comply with the WSRA. *See* 43 C.F.R. § 8351.2–1(a).

In spite of its express duties under the WSRA, BLM authorized the construction of new parking lots and the improvement of primitive roads within the river area [and] * * * it appears BLM failed to consider, much less analyze, whether such new development would violate the WSRA. * * *

* * *

NOTES AND QUESTIONS

1.   In Oregon Natural Desert Ass'n v. Singleton, 75 F.Supp.2d 1139 (D.Or.1999), the same judge ordered livestock grazing to be eliminated permanently from specific areas of the Owyhee WSR, 120 miles of which Congress designated as "wild" in 1984, adding 66 miles of tributaries in 1988. Livestock had been grazing the river corridor for many years. In its 1993 management plan, BLM found that eighteen river miles (mostly places where livestock come to the river to drink) constituted "areas of livestock concern," *i.e.,* showed noticeable negative effects created by grazing. The court was rather harsh in its assessment of the BLM's failure to control livestock grazing.

> The court might be more inclined to maintain the status quo if it were persuaded that continuation of the BLM's current grazing management practices could lead to restoration of the areas of concern. However, the BLM has not demonstrated that its current practices have led to any significant improvement in the areas of concern over the past seven years, and the court concludes that the continued degradation of the areas of concern can be remedied only by closing these areas entirely to cattle grazing.

> The BLM has previously closed certain areas to grazing but then allowed the affected permittees to add their herds to those grazing in other areas. The court therefore concludes that only the complete elimination of permits for a certain number of animal unit months ("AUMs") will prevent the possibility that cattle will be removed from one degraded area only to increase grazing pressure elsewhere.

> The court now permanently enjoins cattle grazing in the "areas of concern" identified by the BLM, including the Deary Pasture area, which is currently closed. The permits for those AUMs are to be eliminated, rather than shifted to more lightly grazed areas.

* * *

Although the BLM asserts that its grazing management practices have generated improvements in the areas of concern first identified in

1993, the court concludes that the assertion is unsubstantiated by objective evidence except for the closure of Deary Pasture. Perhaps the most troubling evidence is Mr. Taylor's testimony that the numbers of animals and the seasons of use have remained completely unchanged since implementation of the Plan, except when grazing permits have been increased to exploit good water years.

* * *

The Plan provided that restrictions on levels and seasons of use would be implemented where necessary to ensure that utilization standards were met, riparian vegetation was in a properly functioning condition, and livestock impacts on vegetation and soils within the river corridor, at water gaps and trail crossings were minimized so that vegetative cover would not decrease and, if possible, would increase. None of this has been done. Mr. Taylor testified that the BLM has neither made changes to seasons of use nor reduced the number of AUMs permitted for any of the allotments since the Plan was implemented. In fact, Mr. Taylor admitted that the BLM has actually *increased* the number of AUMs in some allotments, because greater than anticipated rainfall had yielded more vegetation. The court is troubled by this indication that the BLM regards beneficial natural events as justifications for increased grazing, rather than as opportunities for recovery and enhancement of natural resources.

* * *

It has been almost seven years since the BLM recognized that cattle grazing was creating noticeable negative effects on the rivers' values in some parts of the corridor. The BLM found that grazing conflicted with recreational values where livestock congregated, grazed and defecated around campsites; that the visual impact of livestock trailing and grazing affected scenic and recreation values; and that the ecological condition of upland and riparian areas was being degraded by livestock grazing, trampling and defecation. The BLM designated specific areas of concern in 1993, and stated its goal of managing those areas so as to maintain or improve the vegetative cover of key species and the visual aspect of native perennial plants, ensure proper utilization of key species, minimize livestock impact on vegetation and soils, and reduce livestock/recreation conflicts.

75 F.Supp.2d 1141–51. The court also considered the economic impact, noting that closing the areas of concern would represent a loss of 26,976 AUMs, or about twenty-six percent of the total in the river corridor. The court found that eliminating these AUMs would cause a maximum loss of personal income in the county of approximately $700,000, against a total personal income in the county of $491 million. The court concluded that while the "reduction in subsidized grazing privileges will have an adverse economic effect on some of the individual permit holders, its overall effect on the county's economy is negligible." What if anything in the WSR Act allows consideration of this economic issue?

2.   In National Wildlife Federation v. Cosgriffe, 21 F.Supp.2d 1211 (D.Or.1998), a different judge ruled that the BLM had violated the WSR Act by failing to produce a management plan for the John Day River components of the WSR System, which included 194.5 miles of the main stem and a tributary, designated by Congress in the 1988 OOWSR Act as a "recreational" river. BLM managed only about forty-two percent of the lands on the main stem and about twenty-nine percent of the tributary. BLM had categorized some of the lands in the corridor that were subject to livestock grazing as in poor or fair condition. The court did, however, reject plaintiffs' request to halt grazing on lands so identified. It distinguished ONDA v. Green on the ground that here there was no expert scientific report recommending a halt to grazing; here many of the facts relied on by plaintiffs here "fail to link the BLM's *current* grazing practices to the health of the John Day WSRs." Also, "BLM only manages a relatively small amount of public land within the John Day WSRs interim river areas, making it likely that management practices on private land may have more affect on the overall health of the rivers." Further, "[b]ecause private land makes up the majority of the John Day WSRs, the shifting of grazing onto unregulated private land could well cause the overall health of the John Day WSRs to suffer as an unintended and unfortunate effect of plaintiffs' requested injunction."

3.   The private lands that predominated along the John Day River represent a common challenge in WSR management. The Act allows the United States to acquire "scenic easements," defined as the "right to control the use of land (including the air space above such land) within the authorized boundaries of [a designated river segment] for the purpose of protecting the natural qualities of a designated * * * river area," but it goes on to caution that "such control shall not affect, without the owner's consent, any regular use exercised prior to the acquisition of the easement." 16 U.S.C. § 1286(c). In condemnation proceedings, a district court held that the Interior Department was entitled to obtain an easement prohibiting logging, since one previous harvest, in 1958, was not a "regular" use. The defendants did, however, establish the regular use of a "salmon board"—a temporary fishing platform—and the court ruled that the defendant was entitled to continue the use. United States v. Hanten, 500 F.Supp. 188 (D.Or.1980).

4.   WSR corridor management can be complicated in other ways too. For one thing, there is always the delicate matter of state-federal relations in water rights. The federal reserved water rights doctrine applies to WSRs, *see* Chapter 6, *supra* p. 512. For another, the state may have an ownership interest in the bed of the designated river if the river was "navigable" at statehood. The Act provides that it shall not "affect existing rights of any State, including the right of access, with respect to the beds of navigable streams" in the designated area. 16 U.S.C. § 1284(f). Could a state authorize, over federal objection, oil drilling in the bed of a federally designated "wild" river that was navigable at statehood? Could it allow private parties to travel by off-road vehicle below the highwater mark of a federally-designated "wild" river, over the managing federal agency's objection that this would interfere with the wild character of the river?

5. The BLM has faced an interesting management dilemma on the Fortymile Wild & Scenic River in Alaska, the scene of the first gold rush in the State around the turn of the twentieth century. On a portion of the river that is conceded to be navigable, the state of Alaska issued permits for suction drudges to take gold from the river bottom. Initially, BLM refused to issue permits to these miners to camp on BLM land, above the highwater mark. The miners then camped on gravel bars below the highwater mark, on state land. This posed some danger to the miners because of the potential of floods, created eyesores for recreational users of the river, and threatened pollution from gasoline caches. Should BLM issue permits for miners to camp on the uplands away from the river? In the "wild" as well as the "scenic" portions of the River? Note that the Act withdraws a quarter mile on each side of the "wild" portion from the Mining Law. Does the Act give BLM the authority to prohibit mining altogether; i.e., by preempting state permitting authority below the highwater mark?

D. Preservation of Archaeological, Cultural and Historical Resources

Some of the most valued and scarce federal resources derive directly from human activities. This final subchapter examines the three most important categories, archaeological, cultural, and historical resources. The conflicts that erupt from efforts to preserve these resources bear important similarities to, but also some striking differences from, the other programs considered in this chapter.

1. Archaeological Resources

America's historical and archaeological sites, many found on federal lands, constitute a resource that Congress has deemed important for over a century. In 1906, Congress enacted the Antiquities Act, 34 Stat. 225, (*codified as amended at* 16 U.S.C. §§ 431–433). The first section authorized the President to withdraw and reserve lands containing objects or values of historic, scientific, or scenic significance as national monuments. *See* Chapter 5C(3). The second section was intended to halt commercial exploitation of cultural and historic objects on the public lands.

> Since the 1890's there had been great public interest in the art and history of the Indians of the southwestern United States, and this interest had created a great demand for authentic prehistoric artifacts. As a result, ruins and cliff dwellings, such as Casa Grande, Mesa Verde, and Chaco Canyon, were indiscriminately excavated and vandalized. There were no state and federal laws that provided for the protection of prehistoric sites, and there were few professional archaeologists. Thus, the need for protective legislation was particularly acute when the Antiquities Act was passed in 1906.
>
> The act * * * prohibited the appropriating, excavating, injuring, or destroying of any "historic or prehistoric ruin or monument" or "object of antiquity" found on government-owned or-controlled land,

without the permission of the secretary of the department of the government having jurisdiction over the land.

Robert Bruce Collins & Dee F. Green, *A Proposal to Modernize the American Antiquities Act*, 202 SCIENCE 1055 (1978). A variety of problems hobbled the effectiveness of the Antiquities Act. The maximum fine of $500 was not a sufficient deterrent, and the Act imposed penalties only on appropriators, not on dealers or other purchasers. Worse yet, one federal appellate court struck down the Act's definition of "object of antiquity" as unconstitutionally vague. United States v. Diaz, 499 F.2d 113 (9th Cir. 1974); *contra*, United States v. Smyer, 596 F.2d 939 (10th Cir.1979).

These difficulties were each overcome by passage of the Archaeological Resources Protection Act of 1979 (ARPA), 16 U.S.C. §§ 470aa–470*ll*. It prohibits excavation, removal, or damaging archaeological resources on federal or Indian lands without a permit and also prohibits trafficking in illegally acquired artifacts. The Act contains a broad definition of the resources subject to its preservation regime:

> The term "archaeological resource" means any material remains of past human life or activities which are of archaeological interest, as determined under uniform regulations promulgated pursuant to this chapter. Such regulations containing such determinations shall include, but not be limited to: pottery, basketry, bottles, weapons, weapon projectiles, tools, structures or portions of structures, pit houses, rock paintings, rock carvings, intaglios, graves, human skeletal materials, or any portion or piece of any of the foregoing items. Nonfossilized and fossilized paleontological specimens, or any portion or piece thereof, shall not be considered archaeological resources, under the regulations under this paragraph, unless found in an archaeological context. No item shall be treated as an archaeological resource under regulations under this paragraph unless such item is at least 100 years of age.

16 U.S.C. § 470bb(1). Note that the category of "archaeological resource" is expandable. Materials containing traces of DNA may now be intensively mined for useful data, even though techniques for doing so were unknown when Congress enacted ARPA. Is it advisable for Congress to define a resource in terms of the practices of a scientific profession? Is this comparable to the National Wildlife Refuge System Improvement Act's definition of conservation, which limits management to "methods and procedures associated with modern scientific resource programs"? 16 U.S.C. § 668ee.

The key prohibition of ARPA is that "[n]o person may excavate, remove, damage, or otherwise alter or deface, or attempt to excavate, remove, damage, or otherwise alter or deface any archaeological resource located on public lands or Indian lands unless such activity is pursuant to a permit ... [or] exemption. 16 U.S.C. § 470ee(a). One commentator noted that

> ARPA gives the federal land managers considerable discretion to deny permits if development is inconsistent with land management plans or if conservation is more appropriate. ARPA leaves the resolution of

conflicts with natural resource development to other federal laws; implicitly, ARPA says that the public interest in such cases requires preservation only of "archaeologically significant" resources. ARPA also contains the first statutory recognition of Indian religious and cultural interests in archaeological resources and offers them a greater role in archaeological resource management, particularly on Indian lands.

Lorrie D. Northey, *The Archaeological Resources Protection Act of 1979: Protecting Prehistory for the Future*, 6 HARV. ENVTL. L.REV. 61, 113 (1982).

The Act defines "public lands" to include all four federal systems, and all other lands where the United States owns fee title, other than lands on the Outer Continental Shelf and lands under the jurisdiction of the Smithsonian Institution. *Id.*, § 470bb(3). It does not "affect the lawful recovery, collection, or sale of archaeological resources from land other than public land or Indian land," 16 U.S.C. § 470kk(c).

United States v. Shivers

United States Court of Appeals, Fifth Circuit, 1996.
96 F.3d 120.

■ JUDGE JONES

Billy Ray Shivers found buried treasure at the site of an abandoned lumber mill company town. Unfortunately for Shivers, the site is located in the Angelina National Forest, and the federal government claimed ownership of and seized from Shivers some 50–70 metal tokens he uncovered with a metal detector. The district court denied his Fed. Rule Crim. Proc. 41(e) motion seeking return of the tokens, as it concluded Shivers did not own them pursuant to either the Archeological Resources Protection Act ("ARPA"), 16 U.S.C. § 470ee, or the common law of finds. This court approves the district court's conclusion and therefore affirms.

The tokens that Shivers excavated from the Aldridge Lumber Company mill site were used by the saw mill as payment for workers 50–100 years ago. The tokens and other items were seized pursuant to a search warrant from Shivers's home when the government came to believe he had obtained them in violation of ARPA, which forbids the un-permitted excavation of archeological resources from federal lands.

When the government chose not to pursue criminal charges against Shivers, it eventually gave back the rest of the seized property, but refused to return the tokens to him. * * *

* * *

Shivers argues that the plain language of ARPA § 470kk vests him with ownership of the Aldridge tokens because he is a private collector of coins and other artifacts not defined by the ARPA as archaeological resources.

ARPA was enacted by Congress to protect "archaeological resources" found on public lands and to promote study and evaluation of these resources. *See* 16 U.S.C. § 470aa(b). An "archaeological resource" is statutorily defined as

> any material remains of past human life or activities which are of archeological interest, as determined under uniform regulations promulgated pursuant to this chapter.... No item shall be treated as an archaeological resource under regulations under this paragraph *unless such item is at least 100 years of age.*

16 U.S.C. § 470bb(1) (emphasis added). "Archaeological resources" so defined remain property of the United States if removed from public lands. Since the Aldridge tokens are between 50 and 100 years old, however, they are not "archaeological resources" for purposes of the ARPA.

Shivers's principal argument rests on a facile premise: because the tokens are not "archaeological resources," § 470kk of the ARPA conveys an ownership interest to him as a private collector of coins. Section 470kk provides that

> [n]othing in this chapter applies to, or requires a permit for, the collection for private purposes of any rock, coin, bullet, or mineral which is not an archaeological resource, as determined under uniform regulations promulgated under section 470bb(1) of this title.

16 U.S.C. § 470kk(b). From this provision, Shivers infers that private individuals are authorized by ARPA to remove coins less than 100 years old from public land and to retain ownership.

* * *

But the premise on which Shivers's argument rests is a faulty one, belied by the very passage on which he relies. * * * Because the ARPA does not apply to artifacts less than 100 years old, it does not regulate the private collection of such non-"archaeological resources". This statute cannot vest Shivers with an ownership interest in the tokens because it neither divests ownership interest from the United States or, indeed, says anything at all about "archaeological resources" it does not cover.

Even assuming arguendo that the ARPA regulates private collection of non-"archaeological resources," however, Section 470kk(b) does not transfer to or vest ownership of the Aldridge tokens in Shivers. The statute merely provides that private collectors need not obtain a permit for the collection of certain artifacts. Shivers implies a transfer of property rights from this provision, arguing that since the statute allows for the private collection of non-"archaeological resources," it necessarily entitles the collector to retain or own what he has collected. This conclusion, however, is neither supported by the text of the statute nor is it a necessary implication of the right to collect non-"archaeological resources." Admittedly, the express statutory authorization to collect non-"archaeological resources" without a permit is much less valuable to a private collector if he may not retain what he collects; unless the collector enjoys collection for its own sake, ARPA furnishes little incentive to discover and gather non-"archaeological resources." But it would not be absurd to conclude that Congress dispensed with the cumbersome process of requiring permits for gathering non-"archaeological resources," even though it refused to transfer ownership of these less ancient artifacts.

Further, the ARPA is concerned with protecting the integrity of archaeological sites, presumably even more so if they are located in national forests. *See, e.g.,* 16 U.S.C. § 470cc(b)(1)-(b)(2) (requiring that those who apply for a permit to excavate archaeological resources be "qualified to carry out the permitted activity"). The record suggests that several hundred shovel holes found at the Aldridge site were attributed to Shivers's excavation activities. Considering the resulting landscape alteration, Congress's intent to regulate digging or excavating on public archaeological sites is easy to understand, while Shivers's contrary position in favor of encouraging unregulated amateur collection is virtually incomprehensible.

Finally, the "arrowhead exception" to the ARPA discussed by Shivers is inapposite and irrelevant. This exception is not intended to encourage removal of arrowheads from public lands, but rather to exempt such removal from the civil and criminal penalty provisions of the ARPA. Unlike the tokens excavated by Shivers, the arrowhead exception is limited to those found on the surface of public lands. *See* 16 U.S.C. § 470ff(a)(3) ("[n]o penalty shall be assessed . . . for the removal of arrowheads located on the surface of the ground."). Also, the ARPA expressly provides that the removal of arrowheads can be penalized under other regulations or statutes. *See, e.g.,* 49 Fed.Reg. 1016, 1018 ("regulations under other authority which penalize [the removal of surface arrowheads] remain effective.") No inferences or implications helpful to Shivers are found in these provisions.

Because the ARPA does not vest Shivers with an ownership interest in the tokens, we need not discuss the Forest Service regulations, relied upon by the government, which go beyond ARPA and attempt to define as "archaeological resources," prohibited from excavation, artifacts that are at least 50 years old. *See* 36 C.F.R. §§ 261.2, 261.9(g). The asserted conflict between the Forest Service regulations and the ARPA does not need to be resolved in this case.

The district court concluded not only that the ARPA did not convey to Shivers an ownership interest in the Aldridge tokens, but also that in the absence of express or statutory title transfer, the federal common law of finds dictates that the United States, not Shivers, owns the tokens.

The federal common law of finds, including certain critical exceptions, is pertinent to this case. As the Eleventh Circuit explained,

> [t]he common law of finds generally assigns ownership of the abandoned property without regard to where the property is found. Two exceptions to the rule are recognized: *First, when the abandoned property is embedded in the soil, it belongs to the owner of the soil;* Second, when the owner of the land where the property is found (whether on or embedded in the soil) has constructive possession of the property such that the property is not "lost," it belongs to the owner of the land.

Klein v. Unidentified Wrecked & Abandoned Sailing Vessel, 758 F.2d 1511, 1514 (11th Cir.1985) (emphasis added). In Klein, a vessel submerged beneath the waters of Biscayne National Park, Florida, had been rediscovered and salvaged by a private diver. Holding that the wreck was property of the government, not the diver, the court emphasized that the "ship is *buried in the soil*. The soil belongs to the United States as part of its national park system. . . . When the United States acquired title to the land from Florida in 1973, it also acquired title to the shipwrecks embedded in that soil. . . . Thus the United States has never legally lost the subject shipwreck and, as the owner of the land on and/or water in which the shipwreck is located, it owns the shipwreck." Id. at 1514 (emphasis added). Similarly, the Aldridge tokens excavated by Shivers were buried in the soil of the Angelina National Forest. As in Klein, this soil belongs to the United States, and with it the embedded tokens under the first exception to the federal common law of finds discussed in Klein.

Shivers does not challenge this interpretation of the federal common law of finds. Indeed, his only retort is that the common law of finds is inapplicable because Congress expressly provided in § 470kk(b) of the ARPA that private collectors enjoy ownership of the non-archaeological resources that they discover on public lands. As already discussed, this contention is indefensible. The district court correctly held that the United States owns the tokens that Shivers discovered.

For the foregoing reasons, the judgment of the district court denying Shivers's 41(e) motion for the return of the Aldridge tokens is AFFIRMED.

NOTES AND QUESTIONS

1. As the *Shivers* opinion points out, the metal tokens he found on federal land were not covered by ARPA because they were not 100 years old. Could a criminal prosecution be brought against a person for removing, say, pottery shards from federal lands without an ARPA permit when their age could not be determined without sophisticated testing? What kind of scienter does the Act required?

2. Besides detection, proof that artifacts in someone's possession came from federal or Indian land may be difficult. Particularly in the southwest, where federal lands extend over vast areas, and estimates of undiscovered archeological resource sites run into the millions, enforcement remains a huge problem. ARPA was amended in 1988 to (a) criminalize attempts to take as well as actual takings; (b) strengthen the penalties for violation; and (c) require federal agencies to establish programs to "increase public awareness" of the significance of and need to protect archaeological resources; and (d) to undertake surveys and formulate plans to protect these resources.

3. Does ARPA fully cure the problems of vagueness the Ninth Circuit found in its predecessor? In United States v. Austin, 902 F.2d 743 (9th Cir.1990), the government indicted Austin on eight counts of violating ARPA and five counts of theft of government property after seizing 2,800 Native American artifacts, excavation implements, photographs, and documents on his property. The parties eventually stipulated to a bench trial on one count, charging him with violating ARPA by excavating "archaeological

resources in an archaeological site, including obsidian weapon projectile points and tools such a scrapers." In upholding his conviction, the court tersely rejected his argument that ARPA was unconstitutionally vague, finding "no doubt nor lack of fair notice that the scrapers and arrow points for which he was convicted are indeed weapons and tools. The statute provided fair notice that it prohibited the activities for which Austin was convicted." The court also rejected his "creative" argument that, "because curiosity motivated him, his activity was academic," noting that he "has not demonstrated that he is affiliated with any academic institution, nor has he posited how his own curiosity is otherwise academic." How does this square with the court's discussion in *Shivers* of the "arrowhead" exemption from liability found in 6 U.S.C. § 470ff(a)(3)? Why should arrowheads found on the ground be treated differently from other valuable archaeological resources, such as shell mounds?

4. In Attakai v. United States, 746 F.Supp. 1395 (D.Ariz.1990), Navajo tribal members resisting relocation from land belonging to the Hopi tribe claimed that the construction of fences and livestock water facilities violated ARPA. The court rejected the argument on a variety of grounds: (a) the statute exempts excavations by an Indian Tribe on its land, 16 U.S.C. § 470cc(g)(1); (b) its implementing regulations exempt activities carried out under the direction of the federal land manager and general earth moving excavations pursuant to other authorization (43 C.F.R. § 7.5); and (c) the statute "is clearly intended to apply specifically to purposeful excavation and removal of archeological resources, not excavations which may, or in fact inadvertently do, uncover such resources." 746 F.Supp. at 1410–11. Could the Interior Secretary modify 43 C.F.R. § 7.5 to prohibit even incidental disturbance of archaeological resources by otherwise lawful activities? Does ARPA authorize an "incidental take" permit program like the ESA? *Cf.* 16 U.S.C. 1539(a).

5. Would non-Indian mining create ARPA liability for incidental destruction of archaeological resources? The Act provides that it shall not be "construed to repeal, modify, or impose additional restrictions on the activities permitted under existing laws and authorities relating to mining, mineral leasing, reclamation, and other multiple uses of the public lands." 16 U.S.C. § 470kk(a). Could the Secretary of the Interior include in a mineral lease (or in an approval of a plan of operations for a mining claim), a specific stipulation or condition requiring protection of archaeological resources encountered in mining? Where would the Secretary find legal authority to include such a provision—in ARPA or somewhere else? Is such a condition forbidden by § 470kk(a)? *See* generally 43 C.F.R. § 7.5(b)(1).

6. A number of states have adopted regulations similar to ARPA, although the extent to which they apply to private lands varies. Controversies have flared in some areas over "pot hunting" and "grave plundering" on private land. Interesting preemption questions might be raised if states adopt more protective laws than ARPA and try to apply them to federal lands. Suppose a state outlawed collecting archaeological resources older than 50 years of age (as compared to the 100–year age limit in ARPA) anywhere in the state. Could that expanded prohibition be applied to

federal lands? ARPA speaks in several places of "uniform regulations" (16 U.S.C. § 470bb(1)) and outlaws trafficking in interstate commerce of any archaeological resource held in violation of State or local law (§ 470ee(c)). In United States v. Gerber, 999 F.2d 1112 (7th Cir.1993), the court upheld an ARPA conviction for transporting in interstate commerce Indian artifacts taken from private lands without the consent of the owner (which the court determined to be criminal trespass and conversion in violation of state law, even though the state's theft statute was not specifically directed at archaeological resources). Judge Posner's opinion found federal law sufficient to cover situations where the violated state law "related to the protection of archaeological sites or objects" even if the law is not "limited to that protection."

7.   Fossils, too, have generated litigation in recent years. Ownership of a well-preserved Tyrannosaurus Rex skeleton (named "Sue") discovered on Indian allotted land in South Dakota, held in trust by the United States for an individual Indian, generated several judicial opinions. *See* Black Hills Inst. v. South Dakota School of Mines, 12 F.3d 737 (8th Cir. 1993) (holding that the fossil was governed by Indian statutes concerning land—not personal property—and therefore title was held by the United States in trust for the Indian owner).

2.   CULTURAL AND RELIGIOUS RESOURCES

Lyng v. Northwest Indian Cemetery Protective Association

Supreme Court of the United States, 1988.
485 U.S. 439.

■ JUSTICE O'CONNOR DELIVERED THE OPINION OF THE COURT.

This case requires us to consider whether the First Amendment's Free Exercise Clause prohibits the Government from permitting timber harvesting in, or constructing a road through, a portion of a National Forest that has traditionally been used for religious purposes by members of three American Indian tribes in northwestern California. We conclude that it does not.

As part of a project to create a paved 75–mile road linking two California towns, Gasquet and Orleans, the United States Forest Service has upgraded 49 miles of previously unpaved roads on federal land. In order to complete this project (the G–O road), the Forest Service must build a 6–mile paved segment through the Chimney Rock section of the Six Rivers National Forest. That section of the forest is situated between two other portions of the road that are already complete.

In 1977, the Forest Service issued a draft environmental impact statement that discussed proposals for upgrading an existing unpaved road that runs through the Chimney Rock area. In response to comments on the draft statement, the Forest Service commissioned a study of American Indian cultural and religious sites in the area. The Hoopa Valley Indian

Reservation adjoins the Six Rivers National Forest, and the Chimney Rock area has historically been used for religious purposes by Yurok, Karok, and Tolowa Indians. The commissioned study, which was completed in 1979, found that the entire area "is significant as an integral and indispensible part of Indian religious conceptualization and practice." Specific sites are used for certain rituals, and "successful use of the [area] is dependent upon and facilitated by certain qualities of the physical environment, the most important of which are privacy, silence, and an undisturbed natural setting." The study concluded that constructing a road along any of the available routes "would cause serious and irreparable damage to the sacred areas which are an integral and necessary part of the belief systems and lifeway of Northwest California Indian peoples." Accordingly, the report recommended that the G–O road not be completed.

In 1982, the Forest Service decided not to adopt this recommendation, and it prepared a final environmental impact statement for construction of the road. The Regional Forester selected a route that avoided archeological sites and was removed as far as possible from the sites used by contemporary Indians for specific spiritual activities. Alternative routes that would have avoided the Chimney Rock area altogether were rejected because they would have required the acquisition of private land, had serious soil stability problems, and would in any event have traversed areas having ritualistic value to American Indians. At about the same time, the Forest Service adopted a management plan allowing for the harvesting of significant amounts of timber in this area of the forest. The management plan provided for one-half mile protective zones around all the religious sites identified in the report that had been commissioned in connection with the G–O road.

* * *

The Free Exercise Clause of the First Amendment provides that "Congress shall make no law . . . prohibiting the free exercise [of religion]." It is undisputed that the Indian respondents' beliefs are sincere and that the Government's proposed actions will have severe adverse effects on the practice of their religion. Those respondents contend that the burden on their religious practices is heavy enough to violate the Free Exercise Clause unless the Government can demonstrate a compelling need to complete the G–O road or to engage in timber harvesting in the Chimney Rock area. We disagree.

In *Bowen v. Roy,* 476 U.S. 693 (1986), [the Court rejected a challenge to a federal requirement that applicants to certain welfare programs use their Social Security numbers, the challengers arguing that it violated their religious beliefs.] * * * Similarly, in this case, it is said that disruption of the natural environment caused by the G–O road will diminish the sacredness of the area in question and create distractions that will interfere with "training and ongoing religious experience of individuals using [sites within] the area for personal medicine and growth . . . and as integrated parts of a system of religious belief and practice which correlates ascending degrees of personal power with a geographic hierarchy of power." ("Scarred hills and mountains, and disturbed rocks destroy the purity of the sacred areas, and [Indian] consultants repeatedly stressed the need of a training doctor to be undistracted by such disturbance"). The Court rejected this kind of challenge in *Roy:*

> "The Free Exercise Clause simply cannot be understood to require the Government to conduct its own internal affairs in ways that comport with the religious beliefs of particular citizens. Just as the Government may not insist that [the Roys] engage in any set form of religious observance, so [they] may not demand that the Government join in their chosen religious practices by refraining from using a number to identify their daughter. . . .
>
> . . . The Free Exercise Clause affords an individual protection from certain forms of governmental compulsion; it does not afford an individual a right to dictate the conduct of the Government's internal procedures." 476 U.S., at 699–700.

The building of a road or the harvesting of timber on publicly owned land cannot meaningfully be distinguished from the use of a Social Security number in *Roy.* In both cases, the challenged Government action would interfere significantly with private persons' ability to pursue spiritual fulfillment according to their own religious beliefs. In neither case, however, would the affected individuals be coerced by the Government's action into violating their religious beliefs; nor would either governmental action penalize religious activity by denying any person an equal share of the rights, benefits, and privileges enjoyed by other citizens.

We are asked to distinguish this case from *Roy* on the ground that the infringement on religious liberty here is "significantly greater," or on the ground that the Government practice in *Roy* was "purely mechanical" whereas this case involves "a case-by-case substantive determination as to how a particular unit of land will be managed." Similarly, we are told that this case can be distinguished from *Roy* because "the government action is not at some physically removed location where it places no restriction on what a practitioner may do." * * * In this case, * * * it is said that the proposed road will "physically destro[y] the environmental conditions and the privacy without which the [religious] practices cannot be conducted."

These efforts to distinguish *Roy* are unavailing. This Court cannot determine the truth of the underlying beliefs that led to the religious objections here or in *Roy* * * * and accordingly cannot weigh the adverse effects on the appellees in *Roy* and compare them with the adverse effects on the Indian respondents. Without the ability to make such comparisons, we cannot say that the one form of incidental interference with an individual's spiritual activities should be subjected to a different constitutional analysis than the other.

* * *

Whatever may be the exact line between unconstitutional prohibitions on the free exercise of religion and the legitimate conduct by government of its own affairs, the location of the line cannot depend on measuring the effects of a governmental action on a religious objector's spiritual development. The Government does not dispute, and we have no reason to doubt, that the logging and road-building projects at issue in this case could have devastating effects on traditional Indian religious practices. Those practices are intimately and inextricably bound up with the unique features of the Chimney Rock area, which is known to the Indians as the "high country." Individual practitioners use this area for personal spiritual development; some of their activities are believed to be critically important in advancing the welfare of the Tribe, and indeed, of mankind itself. The Indians use this area, as they have used it for a very long time, to conduct a wide variety of specific rituals that aim to accomplish their religious goals. According to their beliefs, the rituals would not be efficacious if conducted at other sites than the ones traditionally used, and too much disturbance of the area's natural state would clearly render any meaningful continuation of traditional practices impossible. To be sure, the Indians themselves were far from unanimous in opposing the G–O road, and it seems less than certain that construction of the road will be so disruptive that it will doom their religion. Nevertheless, we can assume that the threat to the efficacy of at least some religious practices is extremely grave.

Even if we assume that we should accept the Ninth Circuit's prediction, according to which the G–O road will "virtually destroy the . . . Indians' ability to practice their religion," the Constitution simply does not provide a principle that could justify upholding respondents' legal claims. However much we might wish that it were otherwise, government simply could not operate if it were required to satisfy every citizen's religious needs and desires. A broad range of government activities—from social welfare programs to foreign aid to conservation projects—will always be considered essential to the spiritual well-being of some citizens, often on the basis of sincerely held religious beliefs. Others will find the very same activities deeply offensive, and perhaps incompatible with their own search for spiritual fulfillment and with the tenets of their religion. The First Amendment must apply to all citizens alike, and it can give to none of them a veto over public programs that do not prohibit the free exercise of religion. The Constitution does not, and courts cannot, offer to reconcile the various competing demands on government, many of them rooted in sincere religious belief, that inevitably arise in so diverse a society as ours. That task, to the extent that it is feasible, is for the legislatures and other institutions. Cf. The Federalist No. 10 (suggesting that the effects of religious factionalism are best restrained through competition among a multiplicity of religious sects).

* * * Respondents attempt to stress the limits of the religious servitude that they are now seeking to impose on the Chimney Rock area of the Six Rivers National Forest. While defending an injunction against logging operations and the construction of a road, they apparently do not *at present* object to the area's being used by recreational visitors, other Indians, or forest rangers. Nothing in the principle for which they contend, however, would distinguish this case from another lawsuit in which they (or similarly situated religious objectors) might seek to exclude all human activity but their own from sacred areas of the public lands. The Indian respondents insist that "[p]rivacy during the power quests is required for the practitioners to maintain the purity needed for a successful journey." Similarly: "The

practices conducted in the high country entail intense meditation and require the practitioner to achieve a profound awareness of the natural environment. Prayer seats are oriented so there is an unobstructed view, and the practitioner must be surrounded by *undisturbed* naturalness." No disrespect for these practices is implied when one notes that such beliefs could easily require *de facto* beneficial ownership of some rather spacious tracts of public property. Even without anticipating future cases, the diminution of the Government's property rights, and the concomitant subsidy of the Indian religion, would in this case be far from trivial: the District Court's order permanently forbade commercial timber harvesting, or the construction of a two-lane road, anywhere within an area covering a full 27 sections (*i.e.* more than 17,000 acres) of public land.

The Constitution does not permit government to discriminate against religions that treat particular physical sites as sacred, and a law prohibiting the Indian respondents from visiting the Chimney Rock area would raise a different set of constitutional questions. Whatever rights the Indians may have to the use of the area, however, those rights do not divest the Government of its right to use what is, after all, *its* land.

Nothing in our opinion should be read to encourage governmental insensitivity to the religious needs of any citizen. The Government's rights to the use of its own land, for example, need not and should not discourage it from accommodating religious practices like those engaged in by the Indian respondents. It is worth emphasizing, therefore, that the Government has taken numerous steps in this very case to minimize the impact that construction of the G–O road will have on the Indians' religious activities. * * *

* * * In fact, a major factor in choosing among alternative routes for the road was the relation of the various routes to religious sites: the route selected by the Regional Forester is, he noted, "the farthest removed from contemporary spiritual sites; thus, the adverse audible intrusions associated with the road would be less than all other alternatives." * * *

Except for abandoning its project entirely, and thereby leaving the two existing segments of road to dead-end in the middle of a National Forest, it is difficult to see how the Government could have been more solicitous. * * *

* * *

The dissent proposes an approach to the First Amendment that is fundamentally inconsistent with the principles on which our decision rests. Notwithstanding the sympathy that we all must feel for the plight of the Indian respondents, it is plain that the approach taken by the dissent cannot withstand analysis. On the contrary, the path towards which it points us is incompatible with the text of the Constitution, with the precedents of this Court, and with a responsible sense of our own institutional role.

* * *

■ JUSTICE KENNEDY took no part in the consideration or decision of this case.

■ Justice Brennan, with whom Justice Marshall and Justice Blackmun join, dissenting.

* * * [The majority] concludes that even where the Government uses federal land in a manner that threatens the very existence of a Native American religion, the Government is simply not *"doing"* anything to the practitioners of that faith. Instead, the Court believes that Native Americans who request that the Government refrain from destroying their religion effectively seek to exact from the Government *de facto* beneficial ownership of federal property. * * * The constitutional guarantee we interpret today, however, * * * is directed against any form of governmental action that frustrates or inhibits religious practice. * * *

* * *

* * * [F]or Native Americans religion is not a discrete sphere of activity separate from all others, and any attempt to isolate the religious aspects of Indian life "is in reality an exercise which forces Indian concepts into non-Indian categories." * * * A pervasive feature of this lifestyle is the individual's relationship with the natural world; this relationship, which can accurately though somewhat incompletely be characterized as one of stewardship, forms the core of what might be called, for want of a better nomenclature, the Indian religious experience. While traditional Western religions view creation as the work of a deity "who institutes natural laws which then govern the operation of physical nature," tribal religions regard creation as an on-going process in which they are morally and religiously obligated to participate. Native Americans fulfill this duty through ceremonies and rituals designed to preserve and stabilize the earth and to protect humankind from disease and other catastrophes. Failure to conduct these ceremonies in the manner and place specified, adherents believe, will result in great harm to the earth and to the people whose welfare depends upon it.

* * *

* * * [T]oday's ruling sacrifices a religion at least as old as the Nation itself, along with the spiritual well-being of its approximately 5,000 adherents, so that the Forest Service can build a 6–mile segment of road that two lower courts found had only the most marginal and speculative utility, both to the Government itself and to the private lumber interests that might conceivably use it.

Similarly, the Court's concern that the claims of Native Americans will place "religious servitudes" upon vast tracts of federal property cannot justify its refusal to recognize the constitutional injury respondents will suffer here. It is true, as the Court notes, that respondents' religious use of the high country requires privacy and solitude. The fact remains, however, that respondents have never asked the Forest Service to exclude others from the area. Should respondents or any other group seek to force the Government to protect their religious practices from the interference of private parties, such a demand would implicate not only the concerns of the Free Exercise Clause, but also those of the Establishment Clause as well. That case, however, is most assuredly not before us today * * *.

Today, the Court holds that a federal land-use decision that promises to destroy an entire religion does not burden the practice of that faith in a manner recognized by the Free Exercise Clause. Having thus stripped respondents and all other Native Americans of any constitutional protection against perhaps the most serious threat to their age-old religious practices, and indeed to their entire way of life, the Court assures us that nothing in its decision "should be read to encourage governmental insensitivity to the religious needs of any citizen." I find it difficult, however, to imagine conduct more insensitive to religious needs than the Government's determination to build a marginally useful road in the face of uncontradicted evidence that the road will render the practice of respondents' religion impossible. Nor do I believe that respondents will derive any solace from the knowledge that although the practice of their religion will become "more difficult" as a result of the Government's actions, they remain free to maintain their religious beliefs. Given today's ruling, that freedom amounts to nothing more than the right to believe that their religion will be destroyed. The safeguarding of such a hollow freedom * * * fails utterly to accord with the dictates of the First Amendment.

NOTES AND QUESTIONS

1. Does the majority deny that the U.S. has any constitutional obligation to use its vast tracts of federal land in any way that accommodates religious practices? Should Indians have some special access or consideration regarding federal land use, given their history and the character of their beliefs, as discussed in Brennan's dissent? Is it relevant that the Constitution acknowledges Indian Tribes (*e.g.*, U.S. Const., Art. I, § 8, cl. 3 authorizes Congress to "regulate commerce * * * with the Indian tribes")? On the specific terrain at stake in *Lyng*, two years later Congress designated part of the national forest area considered sacred by the Indians as wilderness, and the road was not built. 104 Stat. 3209 (1990).

2. Could Congress reverse this decision by statute and adopt a general policy requiring the federal land managing agencies to give priority to protection of Native American cultural and religious interests? The Religious Freedom Restoration Act of 1993 ("RFRA"), Pub.L.No. 103–141, *codified at* 42 U.S.C. § 2000bb et seq., allows federal agencies to "substantially burden" a person's exercise of religion only where they demonstrate that the burden "(1) is in furtherance of a compelling governmental interest; and (2) is the least restrictive means of furthering that compelling governmental interest." In City of Boerne v. Flores, 521 U.S. 507 (1997), the Court overturned the RFRA provisions as applied to state governments, but left standing the federal prohibition. If *Lyng* were decided today under the RFRA, rather than as a purely constitutional case, would the federal government win?

3. In Navajo Nation v. U.S. Forest Service, 479 F.3d 1024 (9th Cir. 2007), Indian tribes successfully challenged federal approval of a proposed expansion to the Arizona Snowbowl ski area in the San Francisco Peaks, part of the Coconino National Forest just outside of Flagstaff, Arizona. The

court found that the Forest Service's authorization of artificial snowmaking from recycled sewage effluent violated the RFRA.

The burdens on the tribal religions, especially those of the nearby Navajo and Hopi tribes, fell into two categories:

(1) the inability to perform a particular religious ceremony, because the ceremony requires collecting natural resources from the Peaks that would be too contaminated—physically, spiritually, or both—for sacramental use; and (2) the inability to maintain daily and annual religious practices comprising an entire way of life, because the practices require belief in the mountain's purity or a spiritual connection to the mountain that would be undermined by the contamination.

The court found these burdens to be "substantial" under the RFRA. Moreover, the Forest Service failed to demonstrate that they were "in furtherance of a compelling governmental interest" and constituted "the least restrictive means of furthering that compelling governmental interest." 42 U.S.C. § 2000bb–1(b). The court explained as follows:

The Supreme Court has recently emphasized that, even with respect to governmental interests of the highest order, a "categorical" or general assertion of a compelling interest is not sufficient. In Gonzales v. O Centro Espirita Beneficente, 546 U.S. 418 (2006), the Court held under RFRA that the government's general interest in enforcing the Controlled Substances Act was insufficient to justify the substantial burden on religious exercise imposed on a small religious group by a ban on a South American hallucinogenic plant. * * * "[S]trict scrutiny 'at least requires a case-by-case determination of the question, sensitive to the facts of each particular claim.' " Id. at 1221.

* * *

* * * [The] Forest Service's interests in managing the forest for multiple uses, including recreational skiing, are, in the words of the Court in O Centro Espirita, "broadly formulated interests justifying the general applicability of government mandates" and are therefore insufficient on their own to meet RFRA's compelling interest test. Appellants argue that approving the proposed action serves the more particularized compelling interest in providing skiing at the Snowbowl, because the use of artificial snow will allow a more "reliable and consistent operating season" at one of the only two major ski areas in Arizona, where public demand for skiing and snowplay is strong. We are unwilling to hold that authorizing the use of artificial snow at an already functioning commercial ski area in order to expand and improve its facilities, as well as to extend its ski season in dry years, is a governmental interest "of the highest order."

* * *

Even if there is a substantial threat that the Snowbowl will close entirely as a commercial ski area, we are not convinced that there is a compelling governmental interest in allowing the Snowbowl to make artificial snow from treated sewage effluent to avoid that result. We are struck by the obvious fact that the Peaks are located in a desert. It is (and always has been) predictable that some winters will be dry. The then-owners of the Snowbowl knew this when they expanded the Snowbowl in 1979, and the current owners knew this when they purchased it in 1992. The current owners now propose to change these natural conditions by adding treated sewage effluent. Under some circumstances, such a proposal might be permissible or even desirable. But in this case, we cannot conclude that authorizing the proposed use of treated sewage effluent is justified by a compelling governmental interest in providing public recreation. Even without the proposed expansion of the Snowbowl, members of the public will continue to enjoy many recreational activities on the Peaks. Such activities include the downhill skiing that is now available at the Snowbowl. Even if the Snowbowl were to close (which we think is highly unlikely), continuing recreational activities on the Peaks would include "motorcross, mountain biking, horseback riding, hiking and camping," as well as other snow-related activities such as cross-country skiing, snowshoeing, and snowplay.

The *Navajo Nation* court distinguished *Lyng* on two grounds. First, the RFRA legislative standard for a federal action burdening religion is "is significantly more demanding than the standard under the Free Exercise Clause."

Second, the facts in *Lyng* were materially different from those in this case. In *Lyng*, the Court was unable to distinguish the plaintiffs' claim from one that would have required the wholesale exclusion of non-Indians from the land in question. Further, the government had made significant efforts to reduce the burden, locating the planned road so as to reduce as much as possible its auditory and visual impacts. The Court wrote, "Except for abandoning its project entirely, and thereby leaving the two existing segments of road to dead-end in the middle of a National Forest, it is difficult to see how the Government could have been more solicitous." Finally, the failure to build the six-mile segment of road would have left the unconnected portions of the road virtually useless.

By contrast, Appellants in this case do not seek to prevent use of the [San Francisco] Peaks by others. A developed commercial ski area already exists, and Appellants do not seek to interfere with its current operation. There are many other recreational uses of the Peaks, with which Appellants also do not seek to interfere. Far from "seek[ing] to exclude all human activity but their own from sacred areas of the public lands," Appellants in this case are not seeking to exclude any of the extensive human activity that now takes place on the Peaks. The currently proposed expansion of the Snowbowl may reasonably be seen as part of a continuing course of development begun in 1938 and continued in 1979. The equivalent in this case to "abandoning the project entirely" in *Lyng* would be abandoning the ski area altogether. The equivalent of the Forest Service's minimizing the adverse impact of the road in *Lyng* by carefully choosing its location would be minimizing the adverse impact of the Snowbowl by restricting its operation to that which can be sustained by natural snowfall.

4. In 1996 President Clinton signed an Executive Order on Indian sacred sites that directed every federal land managing agency (including the military) to "(1) accommodate access to and ceremonial use of Indian sacred sites by Indian religious practitioners and (2) avoid adversely affecting the physical integrity of such sacred sites." E.O. No. 13007, § 1. The directive was qualified: "to the extent practicable, permitted by law, and not clearly inconsistent with essential agency functions." A sacred site was defined as "any specific, discrete, narrowly delineated location on Federal land that is identified ... as sacred by virtue of its established religious significance to, or ceremonial use by, an Indian religion." § 1(b)(iii). The Order also included boilerplate that it was for internal housekeeping purposes only and did not create any right of action against the U.S.

Armed with this Order, on the facts of *Lyng v. Northwest Indian Cemetery Protective Ass'n*, could the Forest Service have decided not to authorize road construction and timber harvesting in the area sacred to the Indians?

5. Justice Brennan's dissent notes that, should the government act to protect religious practices from interference by others, it "would implicate not only the concerns of the Free Exercise Clause, but also those of the Establishment Clause as well." If the government were to fence off federal lands to protect Indian religious practices or concerns, would it violate the Establishment Clause? So far, courts have not squarely answered that question.

The Park Service, in the two highest profile cases, adopted plans encouraging, but not requiring, visitors to respect Indian sacred sites. In one case challenging the plans under the Establishment Clause, the court reached the merits. Natural Arch and Bridge Soc'y v. Alston, 209 F.Supp.2d 1207, *aff'd* 98 Fed.Appx. 711 (10th Cir. 2004). At Rainbow Bridge, the park plan resulted in a wayside sign and brochure explaining "the spiritual significance to the Native Americans and the Park Service's request that the public respect cultural differences by voluntarily not walking underneath Rainbow Bridge." 209 F.Supp.2d at 1214. The court held that the policy of discouragement did not violate the Supreme Court's Establishment Clause teachings and noted that Native American Tribes are "religious in nature, [but] they are also social and cultural institutions, which tends to negate plaintiff's suggestion that because Native American tribes are primarily religious, the [management plan] necessarily entangles church and state." Does this suggest that Establishment Clause challenges to such governmental policies involving Indians and federal lands may be deflected by characterizing the Indian interests as based in culture rather than simply religious?

The other case involved Devils Tower, the nation's first national monument, designated by Theodore Roosevelt weeks after the he signed the 1906 Antiquities Act. Bear Lodge Multiple Use Ass'n v. Babbitt, 175 F.3d 814 (10th Cir.1999). The park plan provided that "in respect for the reverence many American Indians hold for Devils Tower as a sacred site, rock climbers will be asked to voluntarily refrain from climbing . . . during the culturally significant month of June." 175 F.3d at 819. The monument, an ancient volcanic plug, is a world-renown climbing site:

> Activities performed by the numerous climbers on the tower during the spring through fall climbing season have affected nesting raptors, soil, vegetation, the integrity of the rock, the area's natural quiet, and the rock's physical appearance. Some American Indians have complained that the presence of climbers on the sacred butte and the placement of bolts in the rock has adversely impacted their traditional activities and seriously impaired the spiritual quality of the site.

> In addition to placing permanent and temporary metal "protection" in the rock, climbing requires climbers to yell certain commands to their partners. Climbers have also taken pictures of Native Americans in ceremonies, removed sacred prayer bundles, and intruded on solitude.

175 F.3d at 818. The court held that plaintiffs had no standing to bring the Establishment Clause challenge because the government policy did not injure them, as they could still climb during June. Suppose the NPS decided to prohibit climbers' use of bolts in order to preserve the integrity of the rock. Would that cross the line prohibiting establishment of religion?

6. Buono v. Norton, 371 F.3d 543 (9th Cir. 2004), involved an Establishment Clause challenge to the maintenance of a Latin cross on federal land in the Mojave National Preserve in California, managed by the National Park Service. The Court, per Judge Kozinski, first held that plaintiff Frank Buono, a retired former Assistant Superintendent of the Preserve, had standing to challenge the cross. Buono alleged he limited his visits to the area because he is deeply offended by the cross, and the court found that "inability to unreservedly use public land suffices as injury-in-fact." The Court then held that the cross, as a patently Christian symbol, violated the Establishment Clause. It noted that Easter Sunrise services had been held there for nearly seventy years, and the Park Service had denied a request to erect a Buddhist stupa near the cross. It rejected the government's argument that its remote location cured the constitutional problem: "National parklands and preserves embody the notion of government ownership as much as urban parkland, and the remote location [of the cross] does nothing to detract from that notion." As the challenge to the cross was unfolding, Congress got in the act but only made constitutional matters worse. It first enacted a rider in 2002 on a Defense Department appropriations bill to designate the cross as a war memorial. Then a year later it put another rider on another Defense appropriation bill that required the Secretary of the Interior to exchange the land where the cross was found for other privately-owned acreage elsewhere, but it also provided that if the property were no longer maintained as a war memorial it would revert to the United States. The Ninth Circuit held neither enactment mooted the case because the transfer had not been completed, and the reversionary clause also operated to keep the dispute alive.

7. In the Timbisha Shoshone Homeland Act, Pub.L.No. 106–423, 114 Stat. 1875 (2000), Congress approved an agreement negotiated between the Tribe and the National Park Service that gave the Tribe certain rights in

land and other resources of Death Valley National Park and nearby BLM land, which embraced its ancestral homeland. Among other things, the legislation established the Timbisha Shoshone Natural and Cultural Preservation Area on federal land, and provided that, "on request of the Tribe, the National Park Service and the Bureau of Land Management shall temporarily close to the general public, one or more specific portions of the area in order to protect the privacy of tribal members engaging in traditional cultural and religious activities in those portions [provided] such closure shall be made in a manner that affects the smallest practicable area for the minimum period necessary for the purposes described." Section 5(e)(5)(E)(i) and (ii). Is this constitutional?

8.   In 1990, Congress adopted the Native American Graves Protection and Repatriation Act (NAGPRA), codified at 25 U.S.C. §§ 3001–3013. It establishes, among other things, a protocol for the protection and return to Native Americans of cultural items (broadly defined to include not only human remains and associated funerary objects, but also sacred objects and objects of cultural patrimony) found on federal land (broadly defined to include all land "controlled or owned by" the United States). Its most controversial application so far has to do with the so-called "Kennewick Man," a 9,000–year-old skeleton discovered on land managed by the Corps of Engineers along the Columbia River in 1996. *See* Bonnichsen v. United States, 367 F. 3d 864 (9th Cir. 2004); see also United States v. Corrow, 119 F.3d 796 (10th Cir.1997) (discussing the statutory definition of "objects of cultural patrimony" and rejecting arguments that it is void for vagueness).

9.   Another controversy involving religion and the public lands erupted in the early part of the twenty-first century, when it was disclosed that Bush Administration officials had intervened to permit the sale of a book at Grand Canyon National Park bookstores which took the position that the Canyon had developed on a biblical rather than an evolutionary time scale and had also discouraged the Park Service rangers from providing estimates of the geologic age of the Canyon to park visitors. National Park Service policy on interpretation and education generally provides that the "history of the Earth must be based on the best scientific evidence available, as found in scholarly sources that have stood the test of scientific peer review" and cautions that "[i]nterpretive and educational programs must refrain from appearing to endorse religious beliefs explaining natural processes." An internal review of the Grand Canyon issues, promised in 2003, has not been completed as of this writing.

NOTE: THE CONSTITUTION AND FREE SPEECH ON FEDERAL LANDS

The other first amendment issue relevant to federal lands is the prohibition on laws abridging free speech. Here the leading case is Clark v. Community for Creative Non–Violence, 468 U.S. 288 (1984), upholding Park Service regulations prohibiting demonstrators (seeking to call attention to the plight of the homeless) from sleeping in District of Columbia national park system units. The majority concluded that the Court's First

Amendment decisions do not "assign to the judiciary the authority to replace the Park Service as the manager of the Nation's parks or endow the judiciary with the competence to judge how much protection of Park lands is wise and how that level of conservation is to be attained." Since then a variety of cases have sustained federal agency regulation of recreational activities against first amendment challenges. *See, e.g.*, Craft v. Hodel, 683 F.Supp. 289 (D.Mass.1988) (no constitutional right to nude sunbathing on federal lands). The National Mall in Washington D.C., sometimes called the "nation's front yard" and managed by the National Park Service, is the scene of frequent public demonstrations and litigation over first amendment issues.

Perhaps the most extensive consideration of the collision between free expression and use and occupancy of federal lands can be found in United States v. Rainbow Family, 695 F.Supp. 294 (E.D.Tex.1988). There the United States sought to enjoin a gathering of several thousand "Rainbow Family" members on a national forest in Texas, on the ground that they had failed to apply for and obtain a "special use" permit from the Forest Service. The "Family" is, according to the district court, a "loosely-knit but identifiable group of persons" who use their annual gatherings to exchange views on many subjects, including political topics (such as peace and ecological concerns), as well as educational seminars and various forms of worship. In the first decision, the court found that the applicable regulations embodied a decision by the agency to treat "expressive" activity differently from other forms of group activity on the forests, and thus implicated the First Amendment. Like public streets and parks, the public lands are, said the court, "the type of forum in which expressive activity has historically occurred, and in which public expression of views must be tolerated to a maximal extent." Regulation of such activity "must therefore be narrowly tailored as to time, place and manner, and serve substantial governmental interests, as well as leave open ample alternative channels of communication. Any prior restraint on expressive activity in such a context is particularly suspect." The regulations were struck down because they left "virtually unfettered discretion" to the agency, with no requirement to "justify or explain any denial of a permit."

Shortly after this decision, the court issued another opinion acknowledging that where there is some "genuine interest to protect or defend, such as preserving public health and safety, the federal government may justifiably seek equitable intervention of the courts to forestall irreparable damage or some other public nuisance." 695 F.Supp. 314 at 326. Acting on the agency's evidence that a previous Family gathering had caused outbreaks of bacterial infections due to unsanitary conditions and also that a prior gathering had left garbage, the court issued an order limiting the number of persons on any one site to 5,000, imposed basic sanitary standards and required the Family to comply with "reasonable requirements for cleaning and rehabilitating any gathering site." 695 F.Supp. at 327–32.

Litigation between the Rainbow Family and the Forest Service has become practically an annual event, with the Rainbow Family usually losing. *See, e.g.*, United States v. Kalb, 234 F.3d 827 (3d Cir.2000) (upholding convictions of organizers of Rainbow Family gathering for using Forest Service land without permission, rejecting various challenges). *Cf.* United States v. Beam, 686 F.2d 252 (5th Cir.1982), where the court reversed the conviction of the Grand Dragon of the Texas Ku Klux Klan for conducting military maneuvers on national forest land without a permit. The court found the agency regulation requiring a written permit for "public meetings, assemblies and special events" not applicable because the KKK activities were decidedly not open to the public.

In United States v. Griefen, 200 F.3d 1256 (9th Cir.2000), the court rejected a First Amendment defense in upholding the convictions of protestors against logging on federal lands who violated a Forest Service "closure order" that prohibited persons from entering the area of the logging operation without permission. The court found the closure order embodied reasonable time, place, and manner restrictions, served a significant governmental interest, and was narrowly tailored to protect health, safety and property. The court also sustained a conviction for violating a Forest Service regulation that required a permit for maintaining structures on national forest land.

3.   HISTORICAL RESOURCES

The Historic Sites Act of 1935, 16 U.S.C. §§ 461–470t, gave the Secretary of the Interior responsibility to "preserve for public use historic sites, buildings, and objects of national significance for the inspiration and benefit of the people of the United States." Id. § 461. The Act calls for protective activities when any federally-licensed activity or program threatens a qualifying resource, but imposes few substantive constraints.

In 1966, Congress extended federal protection to historic resources of other than "national significance" in the National Historic Preservation Act (NHPA), 16 U.S.C. §§ 470–470w–6. The NHPA requires the Secretary to maintain the National Register of Historic Places, and section 106 creates a NEPA-like process requiring federal agencies to "take into account the effect of" any action they take (including funding or approving projects) on historic properties eligible for or actually listed in the National Register. 16 U.S.C. § 470f. Like NEPA, the NHPA demands only consideration, not substantive protection, but it also requires a rather formal consultation process. *See* Davis v. Latschar, 202 F.3d 359 (D.C.Cir. 2000) ("section 106 only requires that the Park Service consult the SHPO [State Historic Preservation Officer, pronounced "ship-O"] and the ACHP [the federal Advisory Council on Historic Preservation, created by the Act, no pronunciation available] and consider the impacts of its undertaking"). The ACHP has promulgated binding regulations that require federal agencies during this consultation process to examine potential adverse effects of federal undertakings on historic and other resources protected by the Act, and to seek methods to avoid, minimize, or mitigate such effects. *See* 36 C.F.R. §§ 800.1–800.16. Section 110 of the NHPA also gives federal agencies a stewardship mandate, requiring them to "assume responsibility for the preservation of historic properties" they own or control, including

establishing a program to identify, evaluate, and nominate suitable properties for inclusion on the National Register. 16 U.S.C. § 470h–2(a). Often
NHPA and NEPA counts are married in complaints and judicial opinions.
Court decisions finding a failure to adequately consult under the NHPA are
rare, but remain a risk for an agency inattentive to historical preservation.

In 1992, Congress expanded the NHPA to embrace properties of
"traditional religious and cultural importance" to Indian tribes (and Native
Hawaiian organizations) as historic resources eligible for the National
Register. 16 U.S.C. § 470a(d)(6)(A). This inclusion of what are called
"traditional cultural properties" (TCPs) made federal agencies responsible
to consult with pertinent tribes in the section 106 process. *See, e.g.,*
Montana Wilderness Ass'n v. Fry, 310 F. Supp. 2d 1127, 1153 (D. Mont.
2004) (BLM failed to consult sufficiently with tribe in connection with
federal oil and gas lease sales).

In National Mining Ass'n v. Slater, 167 F. Supp. 2d 265 (D.D.C. 2001),
industry challenged several parts of revised section 106 regulations adopted
in 2000. The court rejected most challenges but upheld two, striking down
one regulation that required a federal agency to continue the section 106
process if the ACHP disagreed with the agency's determinations, and
another that granted the ACHP authority to review an agency finding of no
adverse effect if other interested parties disagreed with the finding. The
court held these beyond ACHP's authority because "they require the
agency to proceed with the § 106 process in the face of that agency's own
determination to the contrary." On appeal, the D.C. Circuit upheld an
additional challenge to the ACHP regulations that the district court had
rejected: The circuit court found that projects licensed by state and local
agencies pursuant to delegations approved by federal agencies are not
"undertakings" covered by the NHPA. National Mining Ass'n v. Fowler,
324 F.3d 752 (D.C.Cir. 2003). The ACHP then revised its regulations to
conform with the decisions. 69 Fed.Reg. 40,544 (2004).

Historic preservation concerns can also lead to special legislation. Just
such a statute preserved Bodie, California—by most accounts the largest,
best-preserved ghost town in the western United States—from a modern
gold mining operation proposed to be conducted on patented and unpatented mining claims adjacent to the town. In its heyday Bodie—listed on the
National Register and made a State Park in 1962—was, ironically, a mining
town. In 1994, Congress ended the controversy by enacting the Bodie
Protection Act, which withdrew the federal lands in and around the town
from the Mining Law, subject to valid existing rights. 108 Stat. 4509 (1994).

INDEX

References are to pages.

†